W9-CDO-308

PROFILES IN BELIEF

Profiles in Belief

THE RELIGIOUS BODIES
OF THE UNITED STATES AND CANADA

VOLUME II

PROTESTANT
DENOMINATIONS

By ARTHUR CARL PIEPKORN

Published in San Francisco by
HARPER & ROW, PUBLISHERS, INC.

NEW YORK, HAGERSTOWN

SAN FRANCISCO, LONDON

1817

FIRST EDITION

Designed by Sidney Feinberg

Library of Congress Cataloging in Publication Data (Revised)

Piepkorn, Arthur Carl, 1907–1973.
   Profiles in belief.

   Includes bibliographies and index.
   CONTENTS: v. 1. Roman Catholic, Old Catholic,
Eastern Orthodox.   v. 2. Protestant denominations.
   1. Sects—United States   2. Sects—Canada.
I. Title.
BL2530.U6P53   1977   200'.973   76-9971
ISBN 0-06-066582-3

78 79 80 81 82 10 9 8 7 6 5 4 3 2 1

Contents

PART II
EPISCOPAL CHURCHES

PART IV
CHURCHES WITH ORIGINS IN THE
RADICAL REFORMATION

PART V
METHODIST CHURCHES

PART VI
OTHER PROTESTANT CHURCHES
FORMED SINCE THE REFORMATION

Foreword

"One book is about one thing—at least the good ones are." Eugen Rosenstock-Huessey's famous dictum may seem inappropriate in the eyes of readers who might casually come across the present work. That it is a "good book" will be immediately apparent, even to the casual user. But that it is "about one thing" may seem less obvious at first.

Arthur Carl Piepkorn's good and even great work seems to be about many things. It concerns itself with profiles of the many beliefs of millions of Americans who are separated into hundreds of religious bodies. Many of them, it may safely be presumed, will not even have been known by name to most readers before they acquaint themselves with the table of contents. Never before within the covers of several volumes in a single series will the student of American religion have been able to find convenient and reliable access to so many different religious groups. How can one in the midst of such variety think of Piepkorn's book as being "about one thing"?

The answer to that question, on second thought and longer acquaintance, could well be, "Easily!" For here is a single-minded attention to the one thing that is supposed to be at the heart of almost all of these religious groups, their beliefs. The telephone book includes many names, but it is "about one thing," and no one will mistake its purposes or its plot. So with Piepkorn's presentation of *The Religious Bodies of the United States and Canada*. It is precisely what its precise author's title claims it to be: *Profiles in Belief*.

Profile: it is a side view, an outline, a concise description. This book offers such an angle of vision. No individual can speak from within all these denominations and movements. To invite a separate speaker from each tradition would be to convoke a new Babel of tongues. Here we have something coherent and believable, the voice of a single informed observer. He establishes the "side view" and then invites criticism and approval by a member of each group to check on the accuracy of the portraits. This process assures evenness in tone and consistency in proportion without sacrificing either fairness or immediacy. While the description inevitably has had to grow long because of the number of groups presented, even its several volumes will be seen to be but an outline, something concise.

Beliefs: these by themselves do not constitute or exhaust all that a religion is or is experienced to be. For a full description the student will want to learn about social contexts and environments, about behavior patterns and practices of individuals and groups. But since these external marks purportedly grow out of the group's shared set of formal meanings and values and since these, in turn, derive from root beliefs, somewhere and somehow it is important to gain access to such beliefs. Had we all world enough and time it is possible that the knowledgeable could establish for themselves the profile of a large number of these religious bodies. But with the industry and intelligence for which he was noted, Dr. Piepkorn devoted years to the task of assembling the data for others. His profiles can be ends in themselves or instruments for further research. Of one thing we can be sure: they will force all thoughtful readers to take the beliefs more seriously than before.

Arthur Carl Piepkorn was a confessional Lutheran, but he does not use the confessional stance as a means of ranking the value of beliefs. Instead, that stance turned out to be the means of assuring readers that the author knew the importance of beliefs, knew what it was to confess a faith, was aware of the intellectual power that can reside in a religious tradition. If, as a book title of some years ago asserts, "beliefs have consequences," the opposite was also true for Piepkorn. He could look at behavior and practice and step back, in effect saying, "consequences also have beliefs."

This is not the place to read the narrative of American religion, be enthralled by anecdote, or ramble with a sage author dispensing practical advice. This is a very formal guide to belief systems. As an ecumenist of note, Dr. Piepkorn came to be empathic about others' beliefs. As a military chaplain he had practical experience encountering people of faiths remote from his own in the American and Canadian contexts. As a teacher he knew how to get ideas across. As a confessor he valued faith. His book is certain to be a classic.

A classic is, among other things, a book behind which or around which one cannot easily go. Once it has appeared and come into common use it is a measure or benchmark for others. While the official title of this series is likely to endure, it is probably destined to be referred to in shorthand as "Piepkorn." If so, as the standard reference in the field, the designation will be a fitting tribute to the person who prepared himself well and spared himself not at all for the writing of this life work.

MARTIN E. MARTY
The University of Chicago

Editor's Preface

Soon after Arthur Carl Piepkorn died in December 1973, his widow, Miriam Södergren Piepkorn, asked me to assume responsibility for the publication of his almost-completed magnum opus on the religious bodies of the United States and Canada. I undertook the task gladly as a way to pay tribute to a respected colleague, a valued counselor, and a good friend. Because of the sheer mass of manuscript material it was decided to issue the publication in seven volumes under the title *Profiles in Belief: The Religious Bodies of the United States and Canada.* Volume I on Roman Catholic, Eastern Orthodox, and related churches has already appeared and has been welcomed in reviews as the first installment of a major new reference work.

The title chosen for this second volume, "Protestant Denominations," poses a problem. Adherents of some of the churches described in these pages may not appreciate the label. For example, some Lutherans and Anglicans bristle when described as Protestants. Then, too, a large number of churches usually numbered among Protestant denominations are not described in this volume but will be treated in two subsequent volumes dealing with Holiness, Pentecostal, Evangelical, and Fundamentalist churches. The churches described in Volume II are those which in a direct way have been shaped and influenced by the sixteenth-century movement of Reformation in the church and in popular parlance are referred to as Protestant.

In contrast to the material in Volume I, which was ready for publication at the time of Arthur Carl Piepkorn's death and needed only updating, the material in the present volume had a number of gaps which had to be filled. Regrettably for those who appreciate Arthur Carl Piepkorn's contribution to Lutheran self-identity, he did not provide us with manuscript material on his own church family, the Church of the Augsburg Confession, as he would undoubtedly have called it. Writing "the Lutheran chapter" was to be his next task when death put an end to his work. Nor had he written up a number of mainline denominations, such as the Episcopal Church in the United States, the United Presbyterian Church in the U.S.A., the United

Methodist Church, the Southern Baptist Convention, and a few others, though he did provide descriptions of the numerous other churches in the Episcopal, Presbyterian, Methodist, and Baptist families. Presumably he was leaving the "easy" ones to the last.

Several of my colleagues have assisted me in filling the gaps. The material in Part I on Lutheran doctrine and practice was written by a former doctoral student of Arthur Carl Piepkorn, the Reverend Dr. David G. Truemper, Assistant Professor in the Department of Theology at Valparaiso University. He wrote the material on the basis of Piepkorn's own published articles and unpublished essays, wherever possible using Piepkorn's own words and phrases from the Piepkorn papers assembled in the Seminex library and attempting to say what Piepkorn might have said had he lived to write the material. Truemper is responsible for chapters 2 and 3. The historical material in Chapter 1 was provided by a colleague of mine at Seminex, the Reverend Dr. Kurt Hendel, Assistant Professor of Historical Theology. Except for the description of several of the smaller churches, I wrote the material in Chapter 4 on the Lutheran churches in the United States and Canada.

Another colleague of mine at Seminex, the Reverend Dr. John Groh, Associate Professor of Historical Theology, helped fill the gaps in other sections. He is responsible for the material on the Anglican Communion in North America (Chapter 6); the United Presbyterian Church in the U.S.A., the Presbyterian Church in the U.S., and the Presbyterian Church of America (in Chapter 9); the Southern Baptist Convention (in Chapter 12); and the United Methodist Church (Chapter 15). In addition, in order to provide material comparable to that on the Roman Catholic and Eastern Orthodox churches in Volume I and on the Lutheran Church in Volume II, he wrote the material on the history and beliefs of the Anglican Communion (Chapter 5), the Reformed and Presbyterian Churches (Chapter 8), and the Methodist churches (Chapter 14).

I made some revisions of the material written by Arthur Carl Piepkorn to assure that it was up-to-date and that it included major developments that have taken place within the church bodies since his death. I am grateful to the many church-body officers who responded to my requests for information.

I express gratitude to another Seminex colleague, the Reverend Thomas Rick, Director of Technical Services in our library, for providing the index, and to my secretary, Miss Rosemary Lipka, for her valued assistance in contacting the church bodies and in preparing the manuscript for publication.

This volume, like the first one, is dedicated to Miriam Södergren Piepkorn, whose patient understanding of her husband's relentless scholarship contributed so much to his work.

JOHN H. TIETJEN
St. Louis, Missouri

Introduction

The study of religion in America is at the point where Arthur Carl Piepkorn's seven-volume work, *Profiles in Belief,* is much needed—something he foresaw many years ago when he began his wide-ranging researches. The significant achievement of several successful narrative histories of religion in the United States, such as Sydney E. Ahlstrom's *A Religious History of the American People* and Winthrop S. Hudson's *Religion in America,* have helped to show the need for further studies in depth of the various religious traditions. This encyclopedic study of the many denominations in the United States and Canada therefore comes at a good time. Previous similar studies, such as F. E. Mayer's *The Religious Bodies of America* and J. Paul Williams' *What Americans Believe and How They Worship,* both written in the early 1950s (though helpfully expanded and kept up to date through later revisions), have been useful, but now something longer, more detailed, and deeply informed by the last several decades of historiographical and ecumenical development is needed. It is fortunate that a man of Piepkorn's scholarly ability, theological acumen, and ecumenical perspective saw the need years ago and addressed it.

It has also been fortunate that former students and colleagues of his, headed by John H. Tietjen, determined that the vast amount of research and writing done by Piepkorn before his untimely death would not be lost. In the case of this second volume of *Profiles in Belief,* on *Protestant Denominations,* they have had to work with an unfinished text, filling in sections (by drawing on Piepkorn's other writings when possible) and bringing the whole up to date. They have kept to the style and intent of the originator of this massive study, so that one can fairly refer to the author as "Piepkorn." The final judgment as to how well he has done with the vast range of denominations that go under the generic heading "Protestant" cannot be given until Volume III, *Holiness, Pentecostal, Evangelical and Fundamental Bodies,* is published. But it is clear from this volume alone that an important and clarifying work is now available to us. For each major tradition with its various institutional embodiments in denominations, Piepkorn provides an historical introduction, a profile of major beliefs, and a description of each body's present strength, spread, and organizational patterns. As John H. Leith noted in his 1977 review in *The Christian Century* of Volume I, *Roman Catholic, Old Catholic, Eastern Orthodox,* the work is ". . . characterized by depth, breadth, objectivity, a compact style, and a wealth of factual data." This is also true for the present volume; indeed, one can expect it for the entire series.

How to classify the vast spectrum of bodies called Protestant (not all of which want to be so labelled) is always problematic, and not all will be satisfied with what Piepkorn has done in every case. Some of the parts of this work are superbly conceived, especially the chapters on Piepkorn's own tradition, "The Church of the Augsburg Confession." But his scholarly and ecumenical gifts are also brilliantly displayed in such historical chapters as those on "The Anglican Communion" and "Methodism and the Methodist Church." The treatment of John Wesley is particularly perceptive. Though the work does focus on the American scene, Piepkorn explores the European roots of American Protestantism. His treatments often begin with analysis of the origins and formative period of a given tradition, and then move quickly through the centuries to the present to focus on current situations and emphases.

Less successful than his handling of Lutheranism, Anglicanism, and Methodism, in my judgment, is his treatment of the backgrounds of "The Reformed and the Presbyterians" and "The Radical Reformation." The treatment of the Calvinist Reformation is very good as far as it goes, but it neglects to deal with Puritan Calvinism—so important for understanding not only the Presbyterians but also the Congregationalists and Baptists in England and America. The historical chapter on "The Radical Reformation" seems much too brief; it does include a few paragraphs on Puritanism—wrongly placed, I believe. As such scholars as Champlin Burrage, Perry Miller, Winthrop S. Hudson and Robert G. Torbet have shown, the Congregationalists and Baptists have grown more out of the left wing of Calvinism than out of the left wing of the Reformation, despite some similarities with and borrowings from the latter. A separate part of the book for the congregationally-ordered bodies that grew out of Puritanism in England would have been justified, or Piepkorn could have followed the example of his late colleague, F. E. Meyer, who placed the Congregationalists and the Baptists under "The Reformed Bodies." The chapter on the Baptist Churches is thorough, however; that on "Churches Perpetuating the Congregationalist Tradition" would have been stronger if the main line of historic American Congregationalism had been treated there and not left entirely for the last chapter on "Uniting Churches," where it also belongs.

Though the classifications may not be just right in every case, the treatment of the many denominations is fair and balanced; the informative notes show how widely historical and theological works have been explored, and how industriously efforts were undertaken to get up-to-date information from contemporary leaders of the denominations. *Profiles in Belief* will become a series frequently consulted in my own courses and writings. The emphasis on doctrines is especially helpful; comparative treatments of Protestant bodies too often miss what is so important to a confessional Lutheran like Piepkorn, and so well done by him. The attention given to beliefs is not a narrow one, however. To quote John Leith again, for it is true for this volume as for the first, "Beliefs are at the center of his attention. Yet he also includes in his descriptions a great deal of historical data and information about the life and practices of the religious bodies."

A feature of this series is its inclusion of Canadians—a matter long over-due, for many American denominations are related historically and ecumeni-cally to Canadian churches, and a number continue to have organic ties. Happily, scholars are beginning to pay closer attention to the inter relation-ships of the religious histories of the two nations. In 1973, what had been the *Yearbook of the American Churches* became the *Yearbook of the American and Canadian Churches*, edited by Constant H. Jacquet, Jr. Now that useful annual handbook will serve as a companion to this new series, to help us to keep up with statistics and major organizational changes. The new *Oxford History of the Christian Church* includes a volume entitled *A History of the Churches in the United States and Canada*. Perhaps in time works will appear which will include serious treatment of *all* the religious traditions of the North American continent, south as well as north of the borders of the United States; meanwhile the inclusion of Canada in this series is most welcome.

This volume of *Profiles in Belief* does help us to perceive anew both the unities and the diversities of North American Protestantism. The tracing of the historical lineages and contemporary beliefs and practices of the major communions show in a fresh way how much Protestants share in common, not only within but between denominational families. The tracing also shows how the accidents of history have caused divisions that stubbornly persist, long after the occasions for the original schisms have passed. The volume also mercilessly reports on many, many small denominations, some of them of very limited geographical spread and made up of a tiny handful of con-gregations; later volumes will continue to spell out the details of the more than seven hundred religious bodies on the North American scene. It is good to have all this information in one place; it does make us aware of one of the inevitable corollaries of religious freedom: a diversity that in some respects contributes to the trivialization of organized religion. Probably most of us feel that this price of freedom is worth paying, but the litany of diversity does grow long and monotonous. The book implicitly raises again, as all serious studies of religion in America do, important questions about the real sources of religious authority—in the Bible, tradition, and reason; or in social, eco-nomic, and cultural realities?

Each major part of this scholarly volume concludes with a selected bibliography, showing once again the wide range of interest and competence of Piepkorn and his colleagues. Sometimes a rather poor book may have a good bibliography; in this case the text shows that the books and articles cited have been studied and utilized—a further tribute to the breadth and ability of the author. The bibliographies alone justify securing this volume, one worth reading through and then keeping near at hand for continual reference.

ROBERT T. HANDY
Union Theological Seminary
New York City

PART I

LUTHERAN CHURCHES

1. The Church of the Augsburg Confession

Martin Luther and the Wittenberg Reformation

The Lutheran Church is not Martin Luther's church. He himself did not intend it to be that and objected to the use of his name for the purpose of identifying the evangelical movement. Those significantly influenced by Luther have throughout history designated their church as the Church of the Augsburg Confession. Yet Luther's contemporaries were willing to be known as Lutherans, as have generations of others since the sixteenth century. Indeed, the Church of the Augsburg Confession and Martin Luther are intricately related. Any examination of Lutheranism must consider Luther. He was clearly the dominant figure of the Lutheran movement during its formative period. He gave the movement its message and character. His personality and authority were dominant, his theological insights shaped the theology of Lutheranism and his writings were normative in matters of faith and practice. While his dominance abated after his death, he has continued to be the most respected and authoritative church father for Lutherans. It is not the purpose of this section to examine his work or theology in detail. Numerous excellent sources for such study are available.[1] Some reflective comments are necessary, however, because of his impact on the Church of the Augsburg Confession.

In order to understand and evaluate the person and work of Martin Luther it is essential to identify the basic motivation of the man. What was it that not only led him to an ecclesiastical career but inspired him to become a reformer of the church and a leader of a powerful confessing movement?

Luther's destiny was not at all clear during his early life. He was the eldest son of a pious peasant-burgher family of Thuringia. Both his home and his educational contexts were informed by the piety of the late Middle Ages, and he participated regularly in the religious observances and practices of his day. However, none of these experiences was in any way unusual. Indeed, unlike so many bright young men, Luther was not even destined for an ecclesiastical career. His father, Hans, a relatively prosperous miner, sent his eldest son to the University of Erfurt to study law. Although such study also served to prepare an individual for service in the church, Luther's father clearly expected his son to remain a layman and to pursue a profitable legal career.

In most ways Luther was a typical sixteenth-century man, except for one very important characteristic. He possessed an unusually sensitive conscience and experienced profound concerns over his personal spiritual welfare. He was plagued by what he called *Anfechtungen,* intense spiritual struggles, which revolved around the basic question: How can I be saved? Luther was keenly aware of his own sinfulness, which resulted in disobedience and even rejection of God. Because he pictured God essentially as a holy and just Judge who cannot and will not overlook and disregard such shortcomings, he was filled with anguish and spiritual turmoil. He wanted to please God, yet he was convinced that he displeased Him. He wanted to be saved, but he was deathly afraid that he would be damned. Therefore, he searched for an acceptable answer to his basic question. It was this search which led him to Wittenberg, to Worms, to the Reformation. It was his discovery of the answer which inspired him to continue his work of reform and renewal.

Not surprisingly, Luther first sought an answer to his spiritual inquiry through the means provided by the church. Monasticism had long been promoted as the ideal expression of the Christian life. Those who wished to dedicate themselves completely to God were advised to pursue the monastic life. Although Luther was deeply concerned about his father's displeasure over his decision, he nevertheless entered the Augustinian monastery at Erfurt on July 17, 1505. The fear for his soul was greater than his concern not to displease his father. He had come to this momentous decision when a sudden bolt of lightning threw him to the ground as he returned to Erfurt from a visit with his parents. This episode reminded him of the transitoriness of life and reawakened his spiritual anguish. He was determined to dedicate himself to the way of life which could bring assurance of salvation.

Luther pursued the monastic discipline with characteristic vigor. He fasted; he prayed; he disciplined his body; and for a time he appears to have found relative peace. Later in life he remarked that the devil remains quiet during the first year in the monastery. Uneasiness and uncertainty persisted, however. Even the taking of the vows, the "monastic baptism," which supposedly resulted in the remission of both the guilt and the punishment of sin, brought only temporary respite. The celebration of his first Mass after his ordination in 1507 reminded him of his utter unworthiness to perform such a sacred act. Neither monasticism nor the priesthood answered his haunting question. No matter how diligently he pursued the monastic life, a sense of failure and the awareness of sin persisted. All of his efforts, however diligent, could not bring peace to his soul.

But the church assured the faithful that they did not have to depend solely, or even primarily, on their own efforts. Through the sacraments the church could provide succor and strength. Specifically through the sacrament of penance, a person could be assured of forgiveness. For sins to be forgiven, however, they had to be confessed. Luther made every effort to fulfill this requirement and to avail himself of the sacramental grace. He racked his memory in order not to forget a sin. He confessed often and sometimes as long as six hours. John Staupitz, the vicar of the Augustinians and Luther's close friend and confessor, attempted to assure the young monk that his confessions were acceptable and that God was a gracious God. But Luther was not consoled. He panicked when he remembered failures that he had not confessed. He was aware that sins are sometimes not recognized for what they are. If absolution depended on full confession, then Luther knew that he would never be absolved completely. He also realized that sin does not consist merely of specific offenses but that human nature itself has been corrupted. That very nature must be transformed. Thus the sacrament of penance, too, was not the answer to Luther's spiritual question.

Indeed, none of the answers proposed by the church or by the popular piety of the day was acceptable to Luther. He visited the relics of the saints. He went on a pilgrimage to Rome. While in Rome he climbed Pilate's twenty-eight steps, repeating the "Our Father" at each step in the hope of releasing his grandfather's soul from purgatory. But when he had finished he wondered: "Who knows whether it is so?"[2] He read the mystics and listened to Staupitz, who encouraged him to trust only in God and his love. But Luther only shuddered, for how could he love a God who is a righteous and frightening Judge?

When Staupitz recognized that the conventional answers which brought comfort to so many could not quiet Luther's troubled and searching conscience, he determined that his talented young monk should study for the doctorate, teach philosophy and theology, and begin to preach regularly. Staupitz's goal was to direct Luther to the Scriptures, and it was there that Luther found the answer he sought.

Although he objected at first, claiming that he could never fulfill so many responsibilities, Luther soon pursued his duties with vigor and dedication. His lectures on the Psalms, on Romans, on Galatians, Hebrews, and Titus prepared him for his evangelical insight, and they serve as primary sources for his theological development. His final insight, the so-called "tower experience," came quite suddenly as he was preparing lectures in his study in the tower of the Augustinian monastery. While he did not date the experience specifically, he himself described it in the preface to the complete edition of his Latin writings.[3] The insight which literally opened the Scriptures for Luther was the proper understanding of the biblical phrase "the righteousness of God" (Romans 1:17). He had interpreted the phrase in the active sense as that righteousness which characterizes God and which causes him to deal justly by punishing the sinner. Such an understanding inspired only fear in Luther. After years of study, however, it suddenly occurred to him that "the righteousness of God" should be interpreted in the passive sense as that righteousness which God freely imputes to the individual. Justification, then, is an instantaneous act whereby God imputes Christ's righteousness to the sinner and declares him to be righteous. The individual appropriates this gift solely through faith.

Luther now realized that his justification depended only on God, not on his own efforts. He perceived that he could stand before a just and righteous God because that God was ultimately a loving God who had clothed him with Christ's own righteousness. Luther had appropriated the Pauline doctrine of justification, and it was this doctrine which constituted the heart of his theology.

This insight crystallized Luther's theological thinking. It enabled him to delineate the proper relationship between law and Gospel, between faith and good works, between justification and sanctification. Although his theology matured, it was always shaped and influenced by the "tower experience." He had found the answer to his question. The Gospel announced that Jesus Christ was the answer. He now wanted to share that answer with others. This motivated him to do the work for which he has been acclaimed as a major reformer of the church.

Luther really had no carefully planned, fully delineated program of reform. He did, however, function with a guiding principle in his work of reformation: that which affirms the Gospel and facilitates its proclamation must be promoted and that which is a corruption of the Gospel and which hinders its proclamation must be corrected or rejected. It was with this general principle in mind that Luther reformed the theology, the practices, and the piety of his contemporary church. His reformation was neither superficial nor revolutionary. He had no desire to extricate himself from or to reject his tradition. He merely wanted to bring it into conformity with the Gospel. As Jaroslav Pelikan has pointed out, the genius of Luther's reformation was his balance of Catholic substance and Protestant principle.[4] Luther saw himself and his message as standing firmly within the Catholic tradition. He therefore asserted that the papal church had corrupted or forgotten much of this tradition, that he had rediscovered it, and that he was its rightful and true representative.

Luther's legacy to the Church of the Augsburg Confession is varied and profound. Quite obviously, he must be given credit for initiating the Lutheran movement and for providing it with dynamic and creative, though at times oppressive, leadership. He served as the cohesive force of Lutheranism in its early stages. Individuals, cities, territories, and even whole kingdoms rallied not only around his ideas and theological insights but also around the man himself. Luther has been the dominant theological force within Lutheranism. He identified and articulated the biblical and theological themes which have characterized Lutheran theology ever since: justification by faith, the priesthood of all believers, the doctrine of the church, law and Gospel, the centrality of the cross, the ultimate authority of Scripture. His theological acuity and his rare ability to articulate profound theological insights in clear and comprehensible language enabled him to make his message understandable and attractive not only to the theologians and the educated but also to the common people.

The means that Luther employed to share his insights and to spread his ideas were the written and printed word. Luther's writings, most of which have been preserved, constitute a voluminous corpus. They are one of his most important and certainly long-lasting contributions not only to Lutheranism but to the whole Christian community. The value of some of his writings, particularly the correspondence, is primarily historical. Many others, however, continue to be positive expressions of Luther's theological creativity, useful sources for the scholarly study of his thought and popular devotional resources for numerous Lutherans and other Christians throughout the world. The Weimar edition[5] remains the most extensive and authoritative collection of Luther's writings. Although not as complete, the American edition[6] in English is a fine scholarly production.

Finally, it was ultimately Luther who imbued Lutheranism with its catholic identity. As has been indicated, Luther saw himself as a defender and faithful son of the church and of the catholic faith. He had no intention of rejecting that faith or of breaking away from the church. The ecclesiastical divisions that occurred during the sixteenth century did not please him, for he was no sectarian and he confessed the unity of the church. This self-understanding is affirmed by the Lutheran community when it describes itself as a confessing movement within the church catholic.

Luther was clearly the dominant figure of the Lutheran movement during its formative years. However, he soon attracted a capable supporting cast who gathered at the University of Wittenberg.[7] It was at this center of reform activity that the ideas, methodologies, and general spiirt of the Reformation were developed and from which they reached much of Europe. The two most illustrious co-workers of Luther were Philipp Melanchthon and Johannes Bugenhagen.

Philipp Melanchthon (1497–1560), the grandnephew of the courageous humanist and Hebraist Johannes Reuchlin (1455–1522), was a brilliant humanist in his own right who came to the University of Wittenberg in 1518 to teach Greek and Latin. He continued to be an able linguist and respected humanist scholar, but through the influence of Luther he concentrated on the study of Scripture and theology. Although Luther and Melanchthon were two different personalities, they became close friends who worked well together. While Luther was concerned about Melanchthon's irenicism and his willingness to compromise, he never lost respect for his friend and defended him in the face of criticism. The two men complemented each other well, and Luther was keenly aware of Melanchthon's contributions to the Reformation.

Those contributions were extensive and may be summarized under two categories. Melanchthon has been called *praeceptor Germaniae,* the teacher of Germany, and deservedly so.[8] He was the leading educator among the Lutherans during the sixteenth century and became one of the most famous teachers in Germany during his lifetime. His humanist convictions and Lutheran theological insights convinced Melanchthon of the necessity and efficacy of education, and he devoted much energy to the revival and reform of education. But he did not only labor for education in the classroom. His "Instruction of the Visitors" (1528) articulates specific guidelines for the establishment of Latin schools, the major institutions during the sixteenth century for secondary, classical education and the forerunners of the German gymnasia. His advice was sought often as cities and territories established schools, and under his guidance numerous monasteries became territorial schools. He gave advice on such matters as curriculum, teaching methodology, and educational theory. The University of Wittenberg profited from his presence, and under his guidance it was reformed on the basis of humanistic and evangelical principles. The new universities of Magdeburg, Tübingen and Königsberg benefited from Melanchthon's advice and guidance. Finally, Melanchthon also provided the universities and Latin schools with new education materials. His textbooks on grammar, rhetoric, logic, psychology, physics, ethics, and theology indicate the diversity of his genius. The gamut of curricular experiences was influenced by Melanchthon. He did much to facilitate the revival of education during the sixteenth century and to make an effective educational program a lasting ideal within Lutheranism.

Melanchthon's other major area of contribution lies in the theological realm, and he effectively complemented Luther in this area. Melanchthon's *Loci communes* serve as the first systematization of Luther's theological ideas. He also functioned as the theological diplomat of Lutheranism, especially in its dealings with the Roman Church. His irenic personality, his ability to express himself in temperate language, and his willingness to discuss and compromise in theological matters enabled him to provide leadership in an area where Luther could not. Melanchthon was as significant as Luther in the writing of the Lutheran confessions. The Augsburg Confession (1530), the Apology (1531), and the Treatise on the Power and Primacy of the Pope (1537) emanated from his pen. The Lutheran movement, therefore, owes a lasting debt to this co-worker of Luther.

The same is true of the third member of the triumvirate of major Lutheran reformers, Johannes Bugenhagen (1485–1558). Bugenhagen was attracted to the Lutheran movement after reading Luther's revolutionary pamphlet of 1520, "The Babylonian Capitivity of the Church." After coming to Wittenberg in 1521 in order to study with Luther, he soon taught at the university, became the close friend and spiritual adviser of Luther, was chosen the pastor of the city church, and emerged as a leader of the Reformation.

Although he participated in the major theological decisions made by the Lutheran reformers, Bugenhagen's unique contribution lay in the practical area of church organization and administration. Between the years 1528 and 1543 he spent much time away from Wittenberg traveling throughout northern Germany and in Denmark, organizing the new Lutheran ecclesiastical communities and giving guidance and direction to the Reformation. Wherever he went he provided the churches with constitutions, called church orders, on the basis of which the ecclesiastical life in specific areas was constituted.

Bugenhagen addressed particularly three concerns in his church orders. First, he carefully described and explained an evangelical liturgy for the Lutheran congregations. Second, he formulated an extensive educational system, for he was convinced that the welfare of both church and society required effective education. That system included not only the Latin schools and universities but also vernacular boys' and girls' schools. Bugenhagen may be given much credit for the revival of education in northern Germany. Third, he also addressed the social needs of his society and included a precise description of the common chest, the institution through which the Lutherans cared for the poor and needy in their midst. Through his church orders Bugenhagen provided the legal and constitutional basis for the Lutheran Church in northern Germany and parts of Scandinavia. Such institutional and administrative contributions became necessary as the permanency of the break between Wittenberg and Rome became apparent and the Lutheran movement matured into the Lutheran Church.

Wittenberg continued to be the center of the Lutheran movement throughout Luther's lifetime. During that period the University of Wittenberg became one of the most popular and well-attended educational institutions in Germany. Individuals from all parts of Europe came to study with Luther and the other reformers. Often these individuals became leaders of the Reformation in their own homelands. For three decades Luther and his colleagues at Wittenberg shaped the Luthern Reformation theologically, liturgically, and administratively. The impact of these early years is still evident today.

From the Augsburg Confession to the Book of Concord

In order to commemorate the presentation of the Augsburg Confession to Emperor Charles V on June 25, 1530, the leaders of the Lutheran territories determined to issue a collection of those doctrinal writings which had received general recognition as correct explications of the evangelical doctrines. The Book of Concord was, therefore, published in Dresden on June 25, 1580, in the German language. A Latin edition was produced in Leipzig later in the same year. Although it was not the first *corpus doctrinae,* or collection of doctrinal writings, the Book of Concord replaced all others as the official corpus of Lutheran confessional writings.[9] It contains the three ecumenical creeds, the Augsburg Confession, the Apology of the Augsburg Confession, the Smalcald Articles, the Treatise on the Power and Primacy of the Pope, the Small Catechism, the Large Catechism, and the Formula of Concord.

Not all of these writings have received universal Lutheran acceptance. The creeds, the Augsburg Confession, and Luther's Small Catechism have clearly enjoyed preeminence. Nevertheless, a large number of Lutherans, including the major Lutheran bodies in the United States and Canada, have professed their acceptance of all the confessional writings contained in the

Book of Concord as correct expositions of the Word of God. While the meaning of confessional subscription has been debated and discussed, for a large portion of the Lutheran community throughout the world the confessions continue to be creative and living articulations of their faith. Their value and significance, therefore, is not limited to the past. They embody the heart of the theological tradition of Lutheranism, but that tradition is not merely a historical entity. It is a living tradition with significance in the present and for the future.

The three ecumenical creeds were incorporated into the confessional corpus of Lutheranism consciously and with a purpose. The creeds had long been accepted as corrected summaries of the apostolic tradition, the true faith of the church. Their acceptance and confession was a sign of orthodoxy. By consciously affirming the creeds, the Lutherans were asserting their own orthodoxy. Furthermore, they gave expression to their catholicity by asserting that they accepted and believed the ancient doctrines of the church. The creeds, therefore, constitute an integral and essential part of the Lutheran confessional corpus.

The Augsburg Confession has served as the most widely accepted statement of the evangelical understanding of the catholic faith. Although it affirms the catholic heritage, it clearly interprets that heritage from an evangelical perspective. The doctrine of justification by grace through faith stands at the center, and all other doctrines are explicated with that center in mind.

The Augsburg Confession was formulated as a summary statement and apology of the faith confessed by the Lutherans. It was prepared for presentation to Emperor Charles and the estates of the German nation who gathered at Augsburg in 1530. Charles had summoned the Diet in order to deal particularly with the Turkish threat and with the Lutheran problem. Although he had not been able to silence Luther at Worms, he was determined to restore unity and to eradicate heresy. In order to be prepared for the proceedings at Augsburg, Elector John of Saxony (1468–1532) commissioned Martin Luther, Justus Jonas (1493–1555), Johannes Bugenhagen, and Philipp Melanchthon to produce a document that would clearly articulate and defend the Lutheran position and at the same time identify the major reforms they desired. Since the Schwabach Articles (1529) had already summarized the major Lutheran doctrines, the theologians concentrated on a description and defense of the reforms they had initiated. Their formulations were accepted at a meeting in Torgau, hence they are generally known as the Torgau Articles. Armed with these documents, the Saxon representatives proceeded to Augsburg.

When they arrived on May 2, 1530, the Lutherans were confronted by a concerted effort on the part of their opponents to brand them as heretics. In order to present a common front, to answer the accusations, and to defend their orthodoxy a new document was required. Melanchthon, therefore, produced the Augsburg Confession, using the Schwabach Articles, the Torgau Articles, and the Marburg Articles, which Luther had produced at the end of his discussions with Zwingli, as resources. He also consulted with Luther, who was impatiently languishing at Coburg and who approved a preliminary draft of the Augsburg Confession.

Melanchthon was concerned to articulate the faith of the Lutherans clearly and effectively, to do so in conciliatory language, and yet to defend the orthodoxy and catholicity of the Lutheran position. Although he was confronted with a difficult task, he met the challenge. He proceeded carefully and did not address a number of volatile and divisive issues, such as indulgences, purgatory, transubstantiation, and the papacy's claims of power. Yet he did not compromise the central affirmations of the Lutheran theological position but articulated them concisely and affirmatively. He was able to demonstrate the conservative nature of Lutheran theology and its continuity with the tradition of the church and at the same time to clarify its evangelical and catholic confession of faith. That confession has become the most important of the Lutheran confessional writings. The Lutheran Church has, therefore, justifiably identified itself as the Church of the Augsburg Confession.

At the insistence of the Lutherans, their confession was read in German before the Diet on June 25, 1530. They expected that the Roman Catholic estates would present a similar document and that the two sides would then discuss their differences. However, the Roman Catholic theologians did not intend to defend their faith or to discuss the possibility of mutual compromise. Charles was also neither prepared nor willing to accept the Lutheran position. A committee of theologians was, therefore, given the task to refute the Augsburg Confession. After several drafts, the Confutation was read on August 3. The emperor accepted it as his own response and demanded that the Lutherans agree that they had been proven wrong.

Although some negotiations followed, it was clear that neither side would compromise. The Lutherans, therefore, decided to answer the Confutation with a defense of their own position and their own confession. Melanchthon again was the obvious candidate for this task, although he was assisted by a number of other theologians. The first draft of the Apology was completed in three weeks. When an attempt to present it to the emperor on September 22 was rejected, the Lutherans began to leave the Diet soon thereafter.

Melanchthon revised the Apology throughout the winter months that followed and finally published it in the spring of 1531. The Apology serves as a scholarly defense, as well as a lengthy explanation, of the Augsburg Confession. Melanchthon was still determined to defend the orthodoxy and catholicity of Lutheran theology. He therefore cited substantial support from Scripture and the church fathers. However, he was far less concerned about alienating the Catholics. Not surprisingly, his hopes for reunion had been severely dampened by the Diet. The Apology is, therefore, far less irenic than the Augsburg Confession.

It is not surprising that the Apology gained recognition and acceptance as an official confession of faith quite readily. Its intimate relationship with the Augsburg Confession, both in content and also in its historical context, fostered this acceptance. Already in 1532 Lutheran representatives who were meeting at Schweinfurt pointed to both the Augsburg Confession and the Apology as their confession of faith. They described the latter as "the defense and explanation of the Confession."[10] It also received the approval of the clergy who met at Smalcald in 1537 and was mentioned in the Recess signed by the princes. Thereby it was proclaimed an official confessional writing together with the Augsburg Confession. During subsequent decades it was included in various *corpora doctrinae,* was recognized as official by the Peace of Augsburg in 1555, and was cited among the confessional writings of the Lutheran Church by the Formula of Concord. The authors of the Formula affirm:

> We therefore unanimously pledge our adherence to this Apology also, because in it the cited Augsburg Confession is clearly expounded and defended against errors and also because it is supported with clear and irrefutable testimonies from the Holy Scriptures.[11]

The call for a general council was heard repeatedly during the first two decades of the Reformation. Luther voiced it and so did the Lutheran estates. They had even repeated it in the preface of the Augsburg Confession. It is important to note, however, that the Lutherans expected a free council, that is, free from papal control. The emperor, too, had encouraged the papacy to convene a council, for he hoped that the religious questions which troubled the church and his own rule could be settled at such an assembly. Although he rejected the Lutheran position at Worms, he nevertheless repeated his intention to work for the calling of a general council.

The papacy was reluctant to heed these demands, primarily because it feared that it might not be able to control the decisions of a council. Nevertheless, primarily because of outside pressure, Paul III finally summoned a general council, which was to meet at Mantua in May 1537. That summons was issued in June of the previous year. For a variety of reasons, the council did not meet until 1545 and then at Trent. However, in order to be prepared for possible attendance, Elector John Frederick of Saxony (1503–1554) asked Luther to prepare a statement of faith. It seemed appropriate to the elector and other Lutheran leaders that a more direct and less compromising document than the Augsburg Confession, or even the Apology, be formulated. Luther was the man for this task.

He began to write immediately, for he welcomed the opportunity to state his faith publicly once more. Although he became severely ill on December 18, 1536, he completed his articles, thinking that they might be his last theological testament. He writes in the preface to the Smalcald Articles:

> . . . I have decided to publish these articles so that, if I should die before the council meets . . . , those who live after me may have my testimony and confession . . . to show where I have stood until now and where, by God's grace, I will continue to stand.[12]

After he completed the first draft, Luther called together a number of theologians who discussed, amended, and then signed the document.

The Articles were to be discussed and, it was hoped, accepted when the Smalcaldic League met on February 8, 1537. Luther, however, was unable to attend, and Melanchthon, still imbued with an irenic spirit, argued that they might cause divisions in the Lutheran camp if officially endorsed. The princes were influenced by his concerns, but a large number of the theologians present signed what came to be known as the Smalcald Articles.

The Articles clearly reflect both Luther's theology and his temperament. He summarizes major theological concerns, including the trinitarian faith, the doctrine of justification, the sacraments, and penitence. His treatments are concise, and they confront the basic issues which divided Catholics and Protestants. Luther was concerned to articulate his faith boldly, and he had no intention of avoiding divisive issues.

Even though they failed to be officially adopted as a confessional writing in 1537, the Smalcald Articles gained influence as a powerful statement of orthodox Lutheranism. They were included in various *corpora doctrinae* and eventually in the Book of Concord.

While the representatives of the Lutheran estates who had gathered at Smalcald did not accept the Articles written by Luther (though it appears that the vast majority were in agreement with them), they did wish to articulate their attitude toward the papacy. Melanchthon, therefore, quickly produced his Treatise on the Power and Primacy of the Pope, and it was officially endorsed at Smalcald. Historically, it came to be identified as a companion of the Smalcald Articles. Actually, it was intended to supplement the Augsburg Confession by dealing with an issue which the Augsburg Confession had ignored for diplomatic reasons.

Melanchthon had subscribed to the Smalcald Articles only by including a reservation concerning Luther's opinion about the papacy. Melanchthon believed that if the papacy supports the Gospel it may be granted that the pope is superior to other bishops by human right. In his Treatise, however, he articulated a position which was similar to Luther's. Both men rejected the papacy's claim to be the temporal head of Christendom by divine right, and both repudiated the assertion that obedience to the pope is necessary for salvation. Even the blunt language of the Treatise emulates Luther.

Because of its acceptance at Smalcald and its close relationship to the Smalcald Articles, the Treatise received official recognition from its inception. It, too, was included in the *corpora doctrinae* of various Lutheran areas and was ultimately incorporated into the Book of Concord. The Formula of Concord cites it among the generally accepted confessional writings and refers to it as an "appendix to the Smalcald Articles."[13] However, it was clearly considered to be authoritative.

Luther's theology was existential and experiential. He did not view his theological insights merely as intellectual formulations. Rather, he considered them to be matters of faith, because they addressed and answered his faith questions. For this reason, he was convinced that all people were in need of the spiritual insights God had granted him and that the Word must be taught to people in its evangelical clarity. In addition to the German Bible, the two catechisms became the main textbooks for Luther and for the Lutheran churches in the pursuit of this goal. They also became part of the Lutheran confessional corpus.

The necessity and efficacy of education in general and of catechetical instruction specifically were affirmed quite early by the leaders of the Lutheran Reformation. Since most of them were teachers, this is not surprising. Such instruction, however, was not confined to the classroom. It also took place in the pulpit. A regular schedule of catechetical preaching had been instituted in Wittenberg by 1523, and Luther's catechetical sermons of 1523 serve as the primary source for his catechisms.

The immediate impetus to the production of the catechisms was the ecclesiastical visitation of Electoral Saxony in 1528. Luther himself indicates this in the preface to the Small Catechism:

> The deplorable conditions which I recently encountered when I was a visitor constrained me to prepare this brief and simple catechism or statement of Christian teaching. Good God, what wretchedness I beheld! The common people, especially those who live in the country, have no knowledge whatever of Christian teaching, and unfortunately many pastors are quite incompetent and unfitted for teaching.[14]

While he was working on what came to be known as the Large Catechism in the early months of 1529, he also produced summary statements of the five parts of the catechism (Ten Commandments, Creed, Lord's Prayer, Baptism, and Lord's Supper) in the form of wall charts and posters. He intended these to be used particularly in the instruction of children.

The German Catechism (Large Catechism) was completed in March and published in April 1529. Because of the length and nature of this work, Luther also decided to publish in book form the concise charts he had prepared. The first edition of the Small Catechism was available by May of the same year.[15]

The catechisms were intended to be didactic tools, and they have served this purpose well since the sixteenth century. Because of its clarity and conciseness Luther envisioned the Small Catechism especially for the laity. He hoped, however, that the material in the Large Catechism, which was intended primarily for the clergy, might also be used for more advanced instruction of the laity. Luther clearly expected theological instruction to be a continuing process for both laity and clergy, and he maintained that the catechisms could facilitate such ongoing study of God's Word. Therefore he argued in the preface to the Large Catechism:

> Many regard the Catechism as a simple, silly teaching which they can absorb and master at one reading. . . . As for myself, let me say that I, too, am a

doctor and a preacher—yes, and as learned and experienced as any of those who act so high and mighty. Yet I do as a child who is being taught the Catechism. Every morning, and whenever else I have time, I read and recite word for word the Lord's Prayer, the Ten Commandments, the Creed, the Psalms, etc. I must still read and study the Catechism daily, yet I cannot master it as I wish, but must remain a child and pupil of the Catechism, and I do it gladly.[16]

Luther could make such assertions because he did not see the catechisms solely as didactic tools. He had explicated the meaning and implications of central affirmations of the Christian faith from the evangelical perspective. The Ten Commandments are defined as responses of love to God and to the neighbor. The creed emerges as a record and reminder of God's creative, redemptive, and sanctifying action. The Lord's Prayer is a means of communicating with God about the essentials of daily life. Baptism is a divine, grace-dispensing gift, which has meaning and efficacy throughout the Christian's life. Confession is an opportunity to unburden the conscience, and absolution is the concrete expression of God's forgiveness. Finally, in his discussion of the Lord's Supper, Luther emphasizes the real presence of Christ and assures the individual that forgiveness of sins, life, and salvation are the gifts dispensed in the sacrament.

Although they were readily employed in the religious instruction of both laity and clergy, the catechisms were accepted as confessional writings only gradually. That process was facilitated and encouraged by their inclusion in church orders and by their use as doctrinal norms. They were promoted as such norms especially when bitter theological disagreements emerged within Lutheranism after Luther's death and when Lutherans confronted the challenge of Calvinism. By the 1560s the catechisms appeared in a number of *corpora doctrinae* and their status as symbols was assured with their inclusion in the Book of Concord. By that time they were popularly known as the "Bible of the laity," a description which Luther himself had promoted and which is used in the Epitome of the Formula of Concord.[17]

The Formula of Concord stands last, both chronologically and also in the arrangement of the Book of Concord, among the official symbols of the Lutheran Church. As its name indicates, it was drafted in order to restore unity, especially theological unity, within a feuding and divided Lutheran community. Controversies and differences of opinion had already arisen during Luther's lifetime, but the authority and respect enjoyed by Luther were powerful cohesive forces. After his death, however, German Lutheranism experienced a series of volatile and divisive theological battles. The theologians debated such issues as the place of the Old Testament law in the New Testament era (Antinomian Controversy); whether liturgical ceremonies and ecclesiastical structures could be considered as adiaphora (Adiaphoristic Controversy); the doctrine of justification (Osiandrian Controversy); the relationship of good works to salvation (Majoristic Controversy); the eucharistic doctrine of the real presence (Crypto-Calvinist Controversy); and original sin, its effects on human nature, and the individual's role in the justificatory process (Synergistic Controversy).

The debates centered on central issues of the evangelical faith, and they engendered a great deal of bitterness and division. Two major theological camps emerged. The Gnesio-Lutherans, led by Matthias Flacius Illyricus (1520–1575), claimed to be the authentic (Greek *gnesios*) representatives of Luther's theological position. Magdeburg and the University of Jena were centers of their activity. Their inflexibility and extreme militancy toward Melanchthon and his supporters counterbalanced their eagerness to preserve the purity of Lutheran theology. The Philippists, so named because their leading spirit was Philipp Melanchthon, also pledged their loyalty to Luther and asserted that they correctly interpreted his thought. Nevertheless, they were characterized by a willingness to compromise and to allow a degree of theological ambiguity. The Philippists dominated the universities of Wittenberg and Leipzig.

The theological divisions also had political implications. Although the Lutheran territories had been officially recognized in the Peace of Augsburg (1555), there were those who feared that this victory might easily be lost if the Lutherans continued to argue and remained divided. Some of the princes, especially Duke Christopher of Württemberg and Elector Frederick III of the Palatinate, who eventually became a Calvinist, urged the solution of the theological debates. A group of orthodox, though more moderate, theologians also devoted themselves to the resolution of the doctrinal differences and the reunification of German Lutheranism. The centers of their activity were the universities of Rostock, Marburg, and Tübingen. Jakob Andreae (1528–1590) and Martin Chemnitz (1522–1586) emerged as their leaders. Their work was facilitated by the death of Melanchthon in 1560, the expulsion of Flacius from Jena in 1561, and the concerns of the princes for peace and unity.

Although a number of efforts at restoring unity failed, Andreae and Chemnitz continued their work. In 1573 Andreae published "Six Sermons on the Controversies within the Lutheran Church from 1548–73" and offered them as a basis for union among the Lutherans. Chemnitz and the duke of Braunschweig responded favorably but suggested that the sermons be recast as a series of tneses. Andreae agreed and produced the Swabian Concord of 1573. The Concord was carefully examined and revised by theologians in northern Germany, particularly by David Chytraeus (1531–1600) of the University of Rostock. This revision is known as the Swabian-Saxon Formula. Serious and progressive discussions among the Lutherans had begun.

Meanwhile Elector August of Saxony heeded the repeated warnings that his theologians at Wittenberg were not thoroughly Lutheran. After a careful examination, most of the Wittenbergers were dismissed. The elector then proposed further discussion of the issues on the basis of the Swabian-Saxon Formula. The meetings of theologians at Torgau revised the Formula and produced the Torgau Book.

This document was widely circulated and reactions were gathered. Finally, in 1577 the theologians were called together once again at Bergen Abbey. They submitted the Torgau Book to another careful examination, considered the various reactions to the document, and revised it once more. Because the statement had become quite lengthy, a summary was also produced by Andreae. That summary is known as the Epitome and the large document as the Solid Declaration. Together they constitute the Formula of Concord.

The lengthy discussions had facilitated a thorough examination of the issues and a general meeting of minds among the Lutherans. Fifty-one princes, thirty-eight imperial cities, and over eight thousand theologians had signed the Formula by 1580. The Lutherans had indeed produced a document on which they could agree. The Formula reflects the theological maturity and the scholastic tendencies of its framers. It addresses the theological issues which had divided the Lutherans and articulates positions which were accepted as correct and official. The framers of the Formula also recognized and affirmed the stature of the Augsburg Confession and consciously attempted to clarify and explain more fully certain of its articles whose meaning had been debated. Thus the authors and Lutherans ever since have seen the Formula as an interpretation and explication of the Augsburg Confession. The Formula also affirms Luther's understanding of the evangelical faith rather than Melanchthon's. Although the authors did not capture the freshness and existential vitality of Luther's theology, they did affirm and summarize his theological position.

The Formula of Concord quickly attained confessional status. It also cited the other writings which had been accepted as symbols by the Lutheran Church. Those symbols were gathered together in the Book of Concord as an acceptable summary of the Lutheran understanding of the Word of God. No other theological statements have gained the stature of the ecumenical creeds and these sixteenth-century theological works. They remain the symbols of the Church of the Augsburg Confession.

The Development of the Church of the Augsburg Confession

The Church of the Augsburg Confession did not expend all its energies during the sixteenth century in theological and political battles. Much energy was also devoted to the witness of its beliefs and to the extension of its influence. The growth and spread of Lutheranism is a striking, but in many ways unexpected, development in the sixteenth-century context.

That the Lutheran movement was able to grow and consolidate at all is a surprising reality. The two leading representatives of the ecclesiastical and secular contexts, the pope and the emperor, had rejected Luther and his theological position and had publicly taken their stand against the reformer and his supporters. Luther himself was excommunicated by the pope and outlawed by the emperor. Although its beginnings were relatively inauspicious and the obstacles in its way appeared to be formidable, the Church of the Augsburg Confession emerged as a powerful challenge to the Church of Rome and continues to be a significant segment of the church catholic.

The context helps to explain these developments. Charles V's decision to outlaw Luther reflects his determination to defend the orthodox faith and the church, a pledge he had made in his coronation oath. Although he attempted to resolve the Lutheran problem a number of times and encouraged the various Diets to do the same, he could not devote extensive attention to the Lutherans.

Political exigencies repeatedly distracted him. Charles ruled a diverse and extensive empire which included Spain, the Netherlands, Austria, and the territory of the Holy Roman empire. The difficulties and challenges of governing and controlling such vast holdings were immense, and they required a great deal of attention.

Even more problematic was the Hapsburg–Valois rivalry which resulted in periodic wars and was not fully resolved until 1559 after both of the major antagonists had died. Francis I (1515–1547), the ambitious and capable monarch of France, was eager to extend the power of the Valois dynasty in Europe. He was particularly concerned about the encirclement of France by the Hapsburg empire. He therefore challenged Charles's control of areas bordering France and his territorial claims in Italy. Although Francis was unable to achieve his goal of diminishing the power and territorial holdings of Charles, his repeated attempts served to keep Charles out of Germany and to divert his attention from the Lutheran problem.

The Turks were perceived as a major threat to Europe during the sixteenth century. Under the able leadership of Suleiman they mounted several attacks on the Hapsburg territories and even reached Vienna. Although they probably did not have sufficient military or economic strength to proceed much further, contemporary Europe did not know this. As the emperor and as claimant to the territories of Hungary and Austria, Charles had to accept the major responsibility for halting the Turkish advances. The struggle with the Turks, like the Hapsburg–Valois conflicts, also diverted Charles's attention and resulted in the postponement of his efforts to deal with the Lutherans. Because the emperor also depended on the support of German princes in his struggles with the Turks, he had to consider their religious convictions. Some of those princes either had become Lutheran or favored the Reformation. Quite obviously, Charles could not press them on the religious question and expect their military and monetary support. When Charles was finally able to turn his full attention to Lutheranism in the 1540s, it was too late. Although he defeated the Lutheran forces at Mühlberg in April 1547 this military defeat did not result in the demise of Lutheranism. It had had ample time to grow, to mature, and to organize. The Peace of Augsburg (1955) marks the official recognition of the Church of the Augsburg Confession by the political authorities. Political exigencies, therefore, resulted in a relatively favorable milieu for the spread of the Reformation.[18]

The papacy also did not devote its major energies to the resolution of the challenge presented by Luther and those who joined him. Although Leo X (1513–1521) excommunicated Luther in 1521, he had initially dismissed the spiritual and intellectual unrest that focused around Luther as a squabble among the monks. Leo was essentialy a Renaissance man with intellectual and artistic interests, but with limited spiritual concerns. He did not identify with questions of theology or faith. His successor, Adrian VI (1522–1523), was a dedicated individual, but his papacy was too short to affect the religious scene. Clement VII's, 1523–1534) major goal was the defense of the papal states. He therefore devoted most of his attention to Italian political affairs and did not present a significant challenge to the Lutheran movement. It was not until Paul III (1534–1549) ascended the chair of St. Peter that the papacy affirmed its spiritual responsibility and recognized the necessity of papal leadership in the reformation of the Church of Rome. With some trepidation Paul III agreed to call a council in order to address the religious controversies which had divided Western Christendom for almost two decades. Although it was originally called to meet at Mantua in 1537, the council finally assembled at Trent (1545–1563). While it stands as one of the signs of the reformation and renewal of the Church of Rome, it was not able to resolve the religious problem. Rather, its adamant refutation of the Lutheran doctrinal position and its unwillingness to heal the schism mark the tacit acceptance of Lutheranism by the Roman Church.

The favorable milieu was important for the spread of the Lutheran movement. However, that movement also had to be able to take advantage of the milieu. Internal strengths were, therefore, absolutely essential for growth and development. Such central evangelical doctrines as justification by grace through faith, *sola Scriptura,* and the priesthood of all believers quite obviously addressed the spiritual needs of a large portion of European Christendom during the sixteenth century. The diligent and dynamic leadership provided by Luther, Melanchthon, Bugenhagen, Jonas, and many others was a crucial asset. The effective articulation and promulgation of the evangelical message through the preached and printed word, through extensive educational programs, through various art forms, and through powerful confessional statements were highly significant. The catholic and conservative nature of the Lutheran Reformation also contributed to its attractiveness. Finally, the sincere spiritual commitment of numerous leaders, including many rulers and city councils, was crucial for the success and growth of the Church of the Augsburg Confession.

That growth, of course, occurred initially in Germany. Northern Germany was particularly amenable to the Lutheran message. Students and merchants carried evangelical ideas from place to place. The theological treatises of the day, particularly Luther's, were sold and read, at times even in Low

German translations. The University of Wittenberg became an important center for not only the study but also the expansion of Lutheranism.[19] Bugenhagen's organizational travels facilitated the maturation and organization of the Lutheran movement, particularly in the cities. Saxony and Thuringia were the heartland of the Reformation, but from there it quickly expanded into the surrounding areas. Braunschweig, Hamburg, Lübeck, Schleswig-Holstein, Hannover, Bremen, and Pomerania were largely Lutheran by 1535. In the south, the Catholic resistance was more significant, and Lutheranism also competed with Zwinglianism and later Calvinism. Nevertheless, Nürnberg, Augsburg, and Württemberg became centers of the Lutheran movement. Johannes Brenz (1499–1570) emerged as a leading proponent of the Augsburg Confession in the south. This Confession and the other symbols became normative in the various Lutheran territories, as the large number of signatures on the Formula of Concord indicates.

Scandinavia was the next major area of triumph for the Lutheran Church. Rather than a movement of the masses, however, it was generally imposed from above by the rulers. Political goals and concerns were, therefore, integrally related to the protestantization of Scandinavia. The work of diligent and capable reformers, however, was essential and cannot be ignored.

The Reformation in Denmark was promoted by the tolerant policies of Frederick I (1523–1533), who had come under the influence of Lutheranism. He encouraged the work of evangelical preachers, especially Hans Tausen (1494–1561), who had studied at Wittenberg. Although significant gains were made and the New Testament was translated into Danish during the 1520s, the ultimate victory of the Reformation did not occur until Christian III's (1536–1559) reign.

Shortly after his accession Christian called a national assembly in Copenhagen, which officially accepted Lutheranism as the state religion. Bugenhagen was then called to Denmark to assist in the establishment of the Lutheran Church. During his stay he reorganized the University of Copenhagen, supervised the production of a church order, and crowned the king and queen. He also ordained seven superintendents who later assumed the traditional title of bishop. In 1561 the Church in Denmark accepted the Augsburg Confession as its symbol. The Book of Concord, however, was rejected because King Frederick II (1559–1588) was convinced that it contained Melanchthonian notions. In 1683 the acceptance of specific confessional statements was required by law:

> In the king's realms and lands only that religion is to be allowed which is in agreement with the Holy Scriptures, with the apostolic, Nicene, and Athanasian symbols, as also with the unaltered Augsburg Confession, submitted in 1530, and with Luther's Small Catechism.[20]

This confessional tradition has characterized the Church of the Augsburg Confession in Denmark to the present time.

The history of Lutheranism in Norway is closely allied with that of Denmark, for the country was ruled by the Danish monarchs. The Reformation was imposed from above when Christian III declared the Lutheran Church to be the state church in 1537. Lutheran ideas had made only limited inroads in Norway, however, and there was significant opposition to the new church, partly because of political opposition to the crown. A number of evangelical preachers did emerge, especially Jörgen Erikssön (1535–1604), who has been called "Norway's Luther." Although the protestantization of Norway was a slow process, it did proceed. During the sixteenth century the Augsburg Confession clearly gained preeminence as the important symbol, and in 1687 a law was promulgated which articulated the same confessional basis as in Denmark.

Lutheran ideas were introduced in Iceland particularly by Oddur Gottskalkson (c. 1500–1556), who had studied in Germany and returned to preach the evangelical faith in 1533. He attracted significant followers and in 1540 Gissur Einarsson (c. 1508–1548), a Lutheran, was elected bishop of Skalholt. Although the Lutheran Church was officially established in 1554 by royal decree, Catholic opposition was strong throughout the sixteenth century. Under the able leadership of Gudbrandur Thorlaksson (c. 1541–1627), who was bishop from 1571 to 1627 and translated the Bible into Icelandic, opposition was gradually overcome and the evangelical faith was accepted by the people. The confessional stance of the Church in Iceland was the same as in Denmark and Norway.

Sweden had rejected Danish rule under the leadership of Gustavus Vasa (1523–1560). Vasa supported the Reformation because of his own religious leanings and also because the Roman Church had cooperated with the Danes and because the crown was in dire financial difficulties and needed at least some of the wealth controlled by the church. He, therefore, encouraged the work of such evangelical reformers as the brothers Olavus (1493–1552) and Laurentius (1499–1573) Petri and Laurentius Andreae (1482–1552). The Swedish people supported their king in his conflict with the church, and they also readily accepted the Lutheran teachings. The Diet of Vesterås, which met in 1527, marks the victory both of the crown and of the evangelical faith. The king was given the right to appropriate as much ecclesiastical property as he needed and only the "pure Word of God" was to be preached.[21] The Swedish Church, therefore, became the first Protestant national church.

The New Testament was translated into Swedish by 1526 largely through the efforts of Olavus Petri and Laurentius Andreae, and the complete Bible was published in 1541. Olavus Petri emerged as the leading theologian and literary figure of the Swedish Reformation. Among his numerous writings are theological treatises, sermons, a Swedish Mass, and a manual of liturgies for worship and pastoral acts. His brother, Laurentius, became the first Lutheran archbishop of Uppsala in 1531.

Although the immediate successors of Gustavus Vasa were either Catholic sympathizers or professing Roman Catholics, Catholicism was not restored in Sweden. A synod, which met at Uppsala in 1593, promulgated the three ecumenical creeds and the Augsburg Confession, although it was slightly revised and adapted to the Swedish context, as the confessional basis for the Church in Sweden. In 1686 a royal law also incorporated into the church's confessional corpus the other symbols contained in the Book of Concord. The creeds and the Augsburg Confession have retained their preeminence, however, and the other symbols are considered basically as explications and interpretations of the former.

Finland's religious developments are closely related to those in Sweden, for Finland was a province of Sweden until 1809. Michael Agricola (1508–1557), who had studied at Wittenberg and received Luther's strong recommendation, was the leading spirit of the Finnish Reformation. His contributions were extensive and included the translation of the New Testament (1548) and portions of the Old Testament (1551), the publication of a prayer book, the formulation of an order of worship, and the collection of Finnish hymns. During the last years of his life he also served as one of the two bishops in Finland. Because of its close relationship to Sweden, the Finnish Lutheran Church affirmed the same confessional position as the Church in Sweden. During the nineteenth century, after Finland had become a possession of Russia, the confessional commitment of the church became even stronger. The creeds and the Augsburg Confession retained their centrality, but the intrinsic authority of the other symbols was also affirmed.

The Church of the Augsburg Confession emerged as the dominant religious force in much of Germany and in the Scandinavian countries. Other parts of Europe were also touched by the evangelical movement, although its successes were not as striking and its influence not as extensive. Furthermore, the Catholic counteroffensive was much more successful in the rest of Europe.

Because there were no strong national rulers in eastern Europe who could impose the Reformation from above, evangelical ideas were promoted primarily by preachers and theologians who had studied at Lutheran universities and by merchants who transported ideas as well as commercial products. Powerful nobles also facilitated the spread of the Reformation in their territories.

A variety of circumstances had prepared the way for the Reformation in Poland. The Renaissance had made significant inroads, particularly at the University of Cracow, and there was significant interest in humanism and in education. Interest in Luther was evident especially among the university students. Groups of Bohemian Brethren had emigrated to Poland, and they fostered the tradition of reform within the church. Loyalty to Rome was not particularly strong because of the geographic distance and also because the original impetus toward the Christianization of Poland had come from the Teutonic knights and not from Rome. A significant portion of the urban population was German, and these burghers were attracted by evangelical ideas. The nobility, some of whom accepted Lutheranism, were powerful and able to support a variety of religious ideas in their territories. Although the church was influential and wealthy, a tradition of relative religious and ideological toleration had developed in Poland, largely because of a lack of central authority and because of the diversity of the population.

Lutheranism attracted significant support among students who studied at Wittenberg and other German universities, among the German burghers, and among the nobility. Other Protestant movements, especially Calvinism under the leadership of Jan Laski (1499–1560), also gained supporters. Laski attempted to unite the various Protestant groups, but his efforts were in vain. The competition among the Protestants and a strong Catholic offensive during the last part of the sixteenth century and thereafter assured the resurgence and dominance of the Church of Rome in Poland.

Bohemia had been a center of reform activity since the beginning of the fifteenth century. It is not surprising, therefore, that Protestant ideas found a ready audience, both among the Utraquists and the more radical Bohemian Brethren. Luther himself corresponded with both groups and dedicated writings to them. Johannes Mathesius (1504–1565) and Gallus Cahera were leading Lutheran preachers, and they were able to attract some of the Hussites, as well as a number of the German nobility and burghers. Efforts at uniting the various evangelical parties failed, although they did cooperate in their resistance to Rome and to their rulers. Lutheranism never became dominant in Bohemia, however, and when the Bohemians were asked to articulate a statement of faith in 1575 the *Confessio Bohemica* was produced, for the Utraquists and Bohemian Brethren could not accept the Augsburg Confession. Lutheran elements, however, have continued to persist in the area of modern Czechoslovakia.

The success of the Reformation in Hungary was substantial. It found ready adherents not only among the Germans and Slavs but also with the Magyar nobles, many of whom had studied in German universities. The spirit of religious toleration under the Turks, who ruled most of Hungary after the Battle of Mohács in 1526, facilitated the spread of Lutheran ideas. The Magyars eventually came under Calvinist influence, but the Germans and Slavs continued their adherence to Lutheranism. The Heidelberg Catechism of 1563 became normative among the Calvinists, while the Lutherans accepted the Augsburg Confession. Although he was forced into exile in Württemberg, Primus Truber (1508–1586) contributed much to the Reformation among the Slavs through his literary activity. The Bible, a catechism, a collection of sermons, a church order, and the Formula of Concord were all translated into the Slovene language by him or under his guidance. Máyás Dévay (c. 1500–1545) and Silvester Erdösy (c. 1504–c. 1552) were the leading Lutheran reformers among the Magyars and have also been recognized as the fathers of Hungarian literature. Johannes Honter

(1498–1549) may be given much credit for the successes of the Reformation in Transylvania among both the Germans and the Magyars. Early in the seventeenth century the whole Book of Concord was accepted as the symbolic basis of the Lutheran Church in Hungary and it has remained such.

Lutheranism also attracted numerous adherents in Austria. Through the preaching of such individuals as Paul Speratus (1484–1551), Lutheranism spread rapidly and by 1550 most of Austria had accepted the evangelical faith. Although the government of Ferdinand I (1503–1564) remained staunchly Catholic and did not authorize evangelical preaching, the threat of the Turks prevented it from halting the Lutheran expansion. In spite of its initial strength, however, Lutheranism could not withstand the power of the Counter-Reformation. Numerous leaders and large segments of the population were persecuted and exiled. A significant number died in defense of their religious convictions. Others continued to practice their faith secretly. Although Lutheranism was not eradicated, it was severely weakened and became a distinct minority in an area that it had conquered rapidly and almost completely during the first half of the sixteenth century. Today the Lutherans and a smaller number of Reformed are united in the Austrian Evangelical Church of the Augsburg and Helvetic Confessions. Although there is organizational unity, each group is free to articulate the faith according to its own confession. The Lutherans affirm "the confessional writings which have been gathered together in the Book of Concord of the Lutheran Church,"[22] while the Reformed profess their allegiance to the Second Helvetic Confession and the Heidelberg Catechism.

Lutheran ideas were carried into almost all parts of Europe, including England, France, Spain, and even Italy, and pockets of Lutherans existed in all of these countries. Yet northern Germany, Scandinavia, and parts of eastern Europe were the regions where the Church of the Augsburg Confession flourished most. The development, spread, and organization of Lutheranism is a diverse and complex story which must take into consideration not only the magnetism of new ideas and the dedicated work of individual reformers, but also poliitcal, economic, and social factors. Wherever evangelical ideas were accepted during the sixteenth century, the centrality of Scripture was affirmed and the Lutheran symbols, particularly the Augsburg Confession, became authoritative expressions and articulations of the faith that was taught and confessed.

Formative Movements within Lutheranism

There have been a number of formative movements since the sixteenth century which have had significant effects on the Church of the Augsburg Confession. Although they did not necessarily develop within the Lutheran context, or were not limited to it, they helped shape the theological affirmations, the piety, and the priorities of Lutheranism.

The production of the Formula of Concord and the publication of the

Book of Concord mark the beginnings of what has been called the Age of Lutheran Orthodoxy.[23] The period lasted about a century, although vestiges continued to be evident into the eighteenth century.

In response to attempts to bring about union between Lutherans and Calvinists an uncompromising confessionalism developed. Although the orthodox theologians, whose leading spirit was Johann Gerhard (1582–1637), were careful to avoid the Melanchthonian tendency to compromise, they did build on Melanchthon's work of systematizing Luther's theological thought. Aristotelianism was reintroduced into German universities and Latin schools, and the theological formulations of the orthodox period are characterized by scholastic methodology and terminology. Logic and rationalism became integral to the Lutheran theological task. The period is, therefore, also known as that of Lutheran Scholasticism.

A tremendous emphasis on careful dogmatic definition characterized the era of orthodoxy. Lutheran theology was articulated in precise and comprehensive fashion, and the ultimate goal was to produce a thorough system of orthodox thought. The truths of Christianity were identified with Lutheran dogma, and faith was thus intellectualized. Although the ultimate authority and centrality of Scripture were professed, practical authority was assigned to the orthodox interpretations of Scripture. Too often the Bible became little more than a source for prooftexts.

The orthodox fathers were deeply concerned about articulating their faith. They were committed and serious individuals who were devoted to their tradition and were convinced of its validity. However, their methodology and intricate dogmatic formulations resulted in a diminution of certain principles within that tradition. Furthermore, theological formalism and rationalism replaced the creative, existential vitality of Luther's theological insights and of the early confessional writings.

It is important to note, however, that the age of orthodox scholasticism was not only a period of vast, logical, dogmatic masterpieces. Johann Gerhard, for example, produced not only his nine-volume *Loci theologici* (1609–1622) but also his *Meditationes sacrae* (1606), a popular devotional work with mystical tendencies. The most popular devotional writer of the period was Johann Arndt (1555–1621), who represented the mystical tradition that can be traced back through Johannes von Staupitz and Luther to Johannes Tauler, Bernard of Clairvaux and, ultimately, to St. Augustine. His *Books on True Christianity* and particularly his *Little Garden* were and have continued to be valued devotional treasures. Paul Gerhardt (1607–1676), the illustrious poet and hymn writer of the period, combined a concern for pure doctrine with an emotional spirituality. Such hymns as "O Sacred Head Now Wounded" are not only worthy theological statements but also powerful devotional pieces. Gerhardt illustrates that concern for doctrinal definition and purity did not necessarily imply a rationalistic, formalistic faith. Thus a deep, mystical piety was also evident during the age of orthodoxy both among the leading theologians and among the laity.

Pietism, which developed into the most important religious movement within Protestantism during the seventeenth and eighteenth centuries, was able to build on these foundations within Lutheranism as it challenged orthodox scholasticism. The advent of Pietism and its success is explained partially by the context in which it developed. Luther's thought, especially such emphases as the priesthood of all believers and the importance of a living, existential faith, served as essential background to Pietism. To a degree, Pietism was also a response to the tremendous emphasis on doctrinal purity which characterized the age of orthodoxy. Probably more important was the devastation and secularity which accompanied the Thirty Years' War. The physical destruction and brutality of the time deeply affected the psyche and the soul of people. Moral laxity was prevalent. Education was limited, even among the clergy, and a shortage of clergy presented difficulties. Pietism addressed this essentially negative context and attempted to initiate reform and renewal, both within the church and also within society in general. Finally, the concern of English Puritanism for a complete reformation and its emphasis on conversion also influenced and encouraged the Pietist movement.[24]

Although the devotional literature and mystical spirituality of Johann Arndt provided an essential impetus,[25] Philipp Jacob Spener (1635–1705) is generally identified as the "father of Pietism." Spener was influenced by Arndt and also by the devotional literature of English Puritanism, especially the works of Richard Baxter (1615–1691). Spener believed that the Lutheran Reformation had not achieved its full potential or the full expectations of Luther. Although it accomplished a theological renewal, its ethical impact was limited, for it had not brought about a reformation of life. Spener dedicated himself to the pursuit of the latter goal, and he was convinced that he was a good Lutheran and a faithful disciple of Luther in doing so.

Spener articulated his clarion call in 1675 when he published his *Pia desideria* (Pious Desires). In this important work he not only criticized the corruptions of the church but also articulated a program of reform which revolved around the study of Scripture, effective education, and personal piety. The basic themes of Pietism had been articulated.

In order to implement those ideas, Spener adopted the *collegia pietatis* which had been advocated by Martin Bucer (1491–1551).[26] They consisted of small groups of Christians who gathered together to study the Scriptures and devotional literature and to discuss and foster the spiritual life. Although Spener did not use the word, he and his followers were soon referred to as "Pietists" because of these conventicles and also because of their emphasis on and practice of the pious life.

While Pietism experienced significant opposition from both ecclesiastical and secular authorities, it also attracted numerous adherents. The nature of its message, the support it enjoyed among the nobility, and the diligent labors of Spener's pupils are major reasons. The most illustrious disciple of Spener was August Hermann Francke (1663–1727), who made Halle, both the university and the city, the center of Pietism in Germany. As a theologian he articulated and promoted pietistic themes through sermons, lectures, and literary productions. As an effective organizer he established his world-famous orphanage, which became the center of education, of charitable work, and of missionary outreach.

The impact of Pietism on the Church of the Augsburg Confession was profound. Because of its emphasis on rebirth it centered its attention on the doctrine of sanctification rather than justification. Although it placed great significance on education, the ultimate goal of the educational process was not the intellectual comprehension of carefully articulated doctrines but, rather, the inculcation of ethical ideals and of a vibrant spirituality. The manner of life was finally more important to Pietism than correct doctrine. This emphasis on the Christian life rather than on doctrine fostered an ecumenical consciousness within Pietism that resulted in contacts with Christians of other denominations. The ecumenical spark was thus ignited among Lutherans through the influence of Pietism. Mission outreach also received a tremendous impetus from Pietism, and Lutheran missionaries were sent to such diverse places as India and the American colonies. Although it affirmed the authority of Scripture, orthodox theology focused its attention on the Lutheran confessions and their systematic explication. In a sense, Pietism marks the restoration of the centrality of Scripture and the revival of biblical exegesis within Lutheranism. Pietism, of course, searched Scripture primarily for its inspirational value and its ethical counsels. Finally, with its emphasis on sanctification and moral purity, Pietism tended toward a rejection of everything which was considered to be tainted by worldliness. In spite of its social consciousness, it withdrew from the world. The political quietism and the reluctance to become involved in secular affairs that has generally characterized Lutherans, particularly in the American context, may be ascribed partially to the influence of Pietism.

Rationalism, the philosophy of the Enlightenment, focused on reason rather than revelation as the ultimate source of knowledge, even in the religious sphere. Christian von Wolff (1679–1754), who was influenced by the philosophy of Wilhelm von Leibniz (1646–1716), formulated a system of natural theology based on deductive logic. He is generally known as the "father of German rationalism." Through the influence of such scholars as Johann S. Semler (1725–1791) rationalistic principles were applied to the study of Scripture. Although he affirmed the doctrine of revelation, Semler asserted that the Holy Spirit accommodated itself to the limited capacities of the human authors. A revolution in biblical exegesis was initiated which culminated in the development of the historical-critical method. In addition to affecting biblical studies, rationalism also had a radical effect on theology. Many of the essential doctrines of Christianity, including original sin, grace, the atonement, inspiration, and miracles, were eventually rejected by such proponents of rationalism as Gotthold Ephraim Lessing (1729–1781), who denied the uniqueness of the Christian revelation and promoted deism. The

Enlightenment made its impact throughout Europe and deeply disturbed the Church of the Augsburg Confession out of whose context many of the proponents of rationalism had come.

However, defenders of orthodox Christianity opposed the principles and assertions of rationalism. Such biblical scholars as Gottlob Storr (1746–1805) and Franz Reinhard (1753–1812) defended the doctrine of revelation and the uniqueness of Scripture. In addition, Immanuel Kant (1724–1804), an heir of rationalism, dealt rationalism an incisive blow when he pointed out the clear limitations of reason in his works, and Friedrich Schleiermacher (1768–1834) attacked the Enlightenment by arguing that feeling or emotion, not reason, is the essential factor in the religious experience. Although the effects of rationalism were not completely eradicated, such challenges effectively stemmed or redirected its tide.

A creative response to the challenges of both Pietism and rationalism was the confessional revival within Lutheranism during the nineteenth century. Its impact is still very much evident in the Church of the Augsburg Confession today, especially in the North American context. Primary motivating factors toward a renewed confessionalism were: (1) the desire to counteract what were considered to be negative effects of Pietism and rationalism; (2) deep opposition to the Prussian Union; and (3) renewed interest in Luther and the Lutheran confessions as the tricentennial of the Reformation approached.

Claus Harms (1778–1855), who had turned to Scripture and the Lutheran confessions when he could find no satisfaction in the rationalistic theology of his day, published *Ninety-Five Theses* in 1817. In his *Theses* he not only deplored the proposed union of all Protestants and the rationalism and other abuses which he saw extant within the Lutheran community, but he also appealed for a return to orthodox Lutheranism. Harms's *Theses* constituted a clarion call for a confessional revival.

Neo-Lutheranism, as that revival is general referred to, may be divided into two basic segments: repristinationism and the Erlangen school. The former, among whose leading representatives were Ernst Wilhelm Hengstenberg (1802–1869), Wilhelm Löhe (1808–1872), and August Vilmar (1800–1868), attempted to recover historic Lutheranism by emphasizing the authority of Scripture, the historic Lutheran confessions, and the seventeenth-century orthodox fathers. The proponents of repristination theology identified truth with orthodox Lutheran dogma and therefore adamantly defended that tradition. Löhe, for example, argued that the confessional position of the Church of the Augsburg Confession is identical with that of the New Testament church. He could, therefore, also affirm the catholicity and ecumenicity of the Lutheran confessions.

The Erlangen school, whose leading spirit and initiator was Adolf von Harless (1806–1879), also affirmed the necessity of a confessional revival, but it interpreted confessionalism in a dynamic rather than static sense. Confessions were not seen as static summaries of the faith but, rather, as statements and affirmations of the church's continuing experience of that faith.[27]

For the Erlangen theologians confessionalism did not mean merely a return to the confessions of the sixteenth century. These confessional writings and their seventeenth-century systematizations and explications were held in high esteem, but they were not identified with the confession of the church. Gottfried Thomasius (1802–1875), another member of the Erlangen school, distinguished between confession and theology. The theological expressions of the church change as situations and times change, though that development is based on solid confessional foundations. He maintained, therefore:

> We too desire progress in all branches of theology, but not the kind that first breaks down the old foundations, not the kind that hangs in the air, but progress on the old solid foundation, organic progress.[28]

Although there were obvious differences among them, the proponents of confessionalism agreed on their ultimate goal, and their influence was profound. They achieved their goal and brought about a confessional revival within the Church of the Augsburg Confession. The confessional consciousness and commitment which characterizes Lutheranism today is a clear reflection of the impact and the continuing significance of the nineteenth-century confessional revival.

The ecumenical movement reflects the desire of the Christian church to live out the unity which God has given to his people. Although that unity has always been affirmed by the church, institutional, organizational, and theological divisions have also been a reality from the very beginning. Efforts to resolve the causes of disunity have, of course, persisted throughout the history of the church. The modern ecumenical movement, however, is a twentieth-century phenomenon which received its impetus and strength from the missionary impulse of the church.

Its beginnings are generally traced to the World Missionary Conference that met at Edinburgh in June 1910. John Raleigh Mott (1865–1955), a major figure in the early ecumenical movement, chaired the conference. Experiences in the various mission fields, especially the recognition that a united witness by the Christian church is essential, precipitated the meeting.

A number of movements resulted from the Edinburgh Conference. The International Missionary Council developed into the major coordinating agency for Protestant missionary work and served as a continuing impetus toward ecumenical cooperation within the Christian church. In 1961 the Council was incorporated into the World Council of Churches as the Commission of World Mission and Evangelism. The Faith and Order and the Life and Work movements were also inspired by Edinburgh. Faith and Order conferences addressed major theological issues which divided Christendom, while the Life and Work movement attempted to apply the Gospel and Christian ethics to social concerns. The recognized desirability for closer cooperation led to the amalgamation of the two movements and the establishment of the World Council of Churches (WCC) in 1948. The Council's major activities continue to revolve around the concerns which were identified at

Edinburgh: missions, theological discussion, and social action. The WCC remains the most concrete organizational expression of the ecumenical movement.

During the first half of the twentieth century the Roman Catholic Church refused to participate in ecumenical activities. However, a radical change of attitude was initiated by Pope John XXIII (1958–1963) and the Second Vatican Council. Since the early 1960s Roman Catholicism has actively engaged in ecumenical discussions, although it has not joined any ecumenical organization. Quite obviously, the input and cooperation of the Roman community is crucial for the future of ecumenism.

The ecumenical spirit has also touched the Church of the Augsburg Confession. Because it sees itself as a confessing movement in the church catholic, it has sought closer cooperation not only among its constituent bodies but also with other Christian communities. Attempts at organic union have resulted in the creation of the American Lutheran Church (1960) and the Lutheran Church in America (1962). Inter-Lutheran cooperation has effected such organizaions as the Lutheran Council in the United States of America (LCUSA) and the Lutheran Council in Canada (LCIC), which enable the participating bodies to coordinate their efforts in such areas as missions, education, public relations, and military chaplaincy. The Lutheran World Federation, which facilitates a united witness by worldwide Lutheranism, will be discussed in the next section. Theological discussions have been carried out with Reformed bodies, with the Roman Catholic Church, with Eastern Orthodoxy, as well as with the Jewish community. Although clear theological differences persist, much understanding has been fostered by these dialogues. Individual Lutherans, such as the influential archbishop of Sweden, Nathan Söderblom (1866–1931), the leading spirit behind the Life and Work movement, have contributed significantly to the ecumenical movement. Finally, a large number of Lutheran bodies, including the American Lutheran Church and the Lutheran Church in America, have joined the World Council of Churches and are active participants in its work.

Contemporary Lutheranism is serious about both its confessional and its ecumenical commitment. It asserts the catholic and ecumenical character of its confessional writings and is eager to share the evangelical insights it affirms. Therefore, it is a willing participant in theological discussions and cooperative Christian witness. As it confesses the God-given unity of the church, it also commits itself to the concrete expression of this unity. The m'ssion of the church requires such commitment.

Lutheranism throughout the World

The expansion of Lutheranism beyond the borders of Europe is a diverse and complex story with numerous individual chapters. It is only possible to present some highlights in this discussion. Europe and North

America have remained the areas with the largest concentrations of Lutherans. Nevertheless, missionary outreach from both contexts has resulted in the establishment of Lutheran communities throughout the world. Although these communities were initially dominated by missionaries, both theologically and administratively, significant native leadership has emerged, especially during the past two decades. A spirit of independence and autonomy has both accompanied and inspired such developments. As it has addressed and has been accepted by people of various cultures, the Church of the Augsburg Confession has been strengthened and diversified.

Although there were apparently missionary attempts by Lutherans during the century after the Reformation,[29] these were not effective. Lutheranism was, therefore, brought to the African continent by European traders who settled on the coasts, especially of South Africa, from the seventeenth century on. For some time Europeans remained the sole adherents of the Church of the Augsburg Confession in Africa. The membership of the first Lutheran congregation, organized in Capetown in 1779, was totally European. There is no evidence to determine whether these early Lutherans attempted to evangelize the native population.

The Moravian Brethren initiated the first extensive European missionary efforts on the African continent. Although they were not specifically Lutheran, they had been influenced by and had affirmed Lutheran theological insights. Through them at least some Lutheran ideas were brought to native Africans.

Substantial Lutheran missionary outreach did not occur until the nineteenth century, however, with the advent of numerous Lutheran mission societies. The societies, which dominated European missions, initiated a variety of endeavors, often without the support of specific church bodies. Lutheran communities in North America also developed a mission consciousness, but the churches themselves, rather than mission societies, carried out the work.

South Africa continued to be the major context for Lutheran missionary efforts during the first half of the nineteenth century. With the great exploratory ventures during the latter half of the century, however, Lutheran missions expanded as the influence of the white man become dominant in much of Africa. That mission work was related to and often shaped by the colonizing interests of the European powers. Thus nationalistic concerns at times displaced the Gospel as primary motivating factors. Nevertheless, Lutheran communities were established throughout Africa. Through the preaching and teaching of individual missionaries, through Bible translations, and through education the evangelical perspective was promulgated. Europeans continued to constitute a portion of the Lutheran Church's constituency, but native converts also increased.

During the twentieth century not only Christianity in general but also Lutheranism has grown significantly in the African context. Lutherans cooperated not only with one another but also with other Protestant groups. Established missions were continued or revitalized and new endeavors were initiated. With the departure or removal of the European powers the churches have changed dramatically, both in their constituency and also in their self-consciousness and leadership. Some missions have matured into church bodies, native pastors are being trained, and the future of Lutheranism in Africa no longer depends on foreign missionary work. South Africa, the Malagasy Republic, Tanzania, Ethiopia, Liberia, and Nigeria have been the areas where Lutheran work has been most extensive and most successful. Africa remains a promising challenge for the Church of the Augsburg Confession. Its significance in the present and for the future was symbolically and, at the same time, concretely affirmed when the Lutheran World Federation held its Sixth Assembly (1977) at Dar-es-Salaam.

Of all the areas in the world, Asia has been touched the least by Lutheranism. This is due partly to the diversity and strength of Hinduism, Buddhism, Islam, and other religious and philosophical systems and partly to the fact that, with a few exceptions, Lutherans did not really reach out to this vast and populous region until the twentieth century. Furthermore, the rise of nationalism has resulted in negative reactions to the Christian message. Social, political, and religious factors have been powerful obstacles to the Gospel in Asia.

Although Christians constitute a distinct minority in India and although Lutherans are only a small portion of the total Indian population, the Church of the Augsburg Confession has expended significant energy and has enjoyed significant success in this country. The first mission was undertaken by two men from Halle, Heinrich Plütschau (c. 1678–c. 1747) and Bartholomaeus Ziegenbalg (1683–1719), under the auspices of King Frederick IV (1671–1730) of Denmark. They landed in Tranquebar on July 9, 1706, and initiated a challenging though successful mission in southern India. A community of several thousand Christians with their own Bible, catechism, hymnal, and parochial school system developed during the eighteenth century. Although there was a period of decline in the early years of the nineteenth century, the work was revived by the Leipzig Mission in the 1840s. The Church of Sweden Mission also became involved and provided significant leadership, particularly during the two world wars. In January 1919 the Tamil Evangelical Lutheran Church was established, and in 1956 Dr. Rajah B. Manikam was consecrated as the first Indian bishop of the church, a clear sign of the emerging autonomy of this community.

While the Tamil Evangelical Lutheran Church is the heir of the first missionary efforts in India, it is not the largest Lutheran body. The distinction belongs to the Andhra Evangelical Lutheran Church, whose beginnings can be traced to the work of the American missionary, J. C. F. Heyer (1793–1873), who began his activity in July 1842, under the auspices of the Pennsylvania Ministerium. The church was organized in 1927, has an extensive parochial school system and its own seminary, and is involved in a broad social ministry.

The Gossner Evangelical Lutheran Church constitutes the third large community of Lutherans in India. It is active in the regions west of Calcutta among the agricultural Kolarian tribes. The work in this area was begun by four men sent by the Gossner Mission Society in 1844. After slow beginnings, significant progress was made in the second half of the nineteenth century. By 1900 about 100,000 people had been converted. When the German missionaries were expelled in 1914, the native leaders determined to organize an autonomous church in order to preserve their Lutheran character. The Gossner Lutheran Church was, therefore, founded in July 1919. It has retained a spirit of independence and self-support, although it has received some financial aid from German and American sources and from the Lutheran World Federation.

A number of smaller Lutheran churches are also pursuing their mission in the Indian context. There has been much cooperation among the groups, and already in 1926 the Federation of Evangelical Lutheran Churches in India was formed to facilitate collaboration. Although the obstacles of language, polity, and geographical separation stand in the way, unification of the various Lutheran bodies in India is a real possibility. Some type of direct relationship between the Church of South India and the Lutheran churches in southern India may very well precede such pan-Lutheran union. Porgress toward regional unification has also been facilitated by the existence of the Federation of Evangelical Lutheran Churches in India. A common liturgy, a theological college in Madras, and confessional discussions with the Church of South India are examples of cooperative efforts among Indian Lutherans.

The Rhenish missionaries, led by Ludwig Nommensen (1834–1918), who initiated the Batak mission in Indonesia, represented the union church of Germany and therefore were not strictly Lutheran. Yet Lutheran influences are strong in the Batak Protestant Christian Church (Huria Kristen Batak Protestant), and it has identified most closely with Lutheranism. Although it did not adopt the Augsburg Confession, its confession reflects the Lutheran heritage. Furthermore, Luther's Small Catechism, one of the historic symbols of the Lutheran Church, has been traditionally used for Christian instruction. Therefore, the Batak Church, which was formally established in 1930, was admitted into membership by the Lutheran World Federation in 1952. It constitutes the largest community of Christians with a Lutheran heritage in Asia.

Lutheran missionaries did not reach Japan until 1892. Their work centered on the island of Kyushu; however, converts were attracted only slowly. Although the Japan Evangelical Lutheran Church was established in 1920, it only numbered 7,400 baptized members in 1940. During World War II the church experienced numerous hardships, and by 1945 less than 2,500 Lutherans could be identified.

After World War II concerted mission efforts were initiated by various Lutheran bodies. Missionaries came from Europe and the United States, and numerous new mission fields were opened, particularly on the island of

Honshu. Although the growth of the Lutheran Church has not been phenomenal, there has been promising progress. Through the Lutheran Literature Society, Christian writings are published and distributed. The Japan Lutheran Hour, under the auspices of the Lutheran Church–Missouri Synod, has been an effective means for reaching people. Lay and clerical education has been pursued with significant success. While foreign missionaries are still active in Japan, the indigenous church has become largely responsible for its witness and ministry in the Japanese context.

The Lutheran Church of China, which was organized in 1920, numbered about 100,000 baptized members when communist rule effectively separated it from the Church of the Augsburg Confession in the rest of the world. By 1951 the large number of missionaries who had been working in China had left the country. Information about Chinese Lutheranism has been sparse since. Although its membership has dwindled and its functions have been severely curtailed, the Lutheran Church of China continues to exist and to worship.

As mainland China was closed to them, Lutherans turned their attention to Hongkong and to Taiwan. The Evangelical Lutheran Church of Hongkong has been a vibrant and growing community since the 1950s. A number of independent bodies, especially the Missouri Synod Mission, have also enjoyed significant success. In addition to evangelism, Lutherans have been involved particularly in education and in social ministry. Hongkong has emerged as an important center of Lutheranism in Asia.

Lutheran work in Taiwan did not begin until the 1950s, and it accompanied the Chinese refugees who settled there after the communist victory on mainland China. A diverse group of missionary endeavors was united under the Taiwan Lutheran Mission in 1953, although a number of independent projects, especially that of the Lutheran Church–Missouri Synod, continue. The Taiwan Lutheran Church was organized in 1954.

Because the majority of the population is already Christian, the Philippines present a context which is quite different from the rest of Asia. Lutheran work did not begin until 1946 when the Missouri Synod established a mission in Manila. The witness in the Philippines has been facilitated by the effective use of the Lutheran Hour on the radio and by the training of Filipino pastors at a Lutheran seminary.

The impact of the Church of the Augsburg Confession in Papua New Guinea has been extensive. Indeed, the Lutheran Mission New Guinea, founded in 1953, developed into the largest single mission in the world.[30] In addition the Missouri Synod's independent work has resulted in the establishment of the Wabag Lutheran Church. Thus the Church of the Augsburg Confession has emerged as the leading Christian denomination on the island. Through an effective system of native lay evangelists the diverse, linguistically separated, primitive tribes of New Guinea have been gradually reached. The foreign missionaries, though also involved in this outreach, have provided necessary leadership and have served as teachers and resource persons. As the church has confronted the various tribes it has preached the good news of the Gospel. But it has also been largely responsible for the education, the technical training, and the medical care of the people. The Lutheran Church has, therefore, played an integral role in shaping not only the religious but also the social and economic life of present-day Papua New Guinea.

Barton Justinian von Welz, an Austrian Lutheran, had come to Dutch Guiana in 1665 with the intention of promoting his evangelical faith. However, he died within a year. With the exception of this isolated attempt and efforts by the Dutch to evangelize African slaves and Indians in the Virgin Islands, Lutheran missionary work in Latin America did not begin in earnest until the turn of this century.

Not only did the work begin rather late but it has also focused primarily on Lutheran European immigrants. When various Lutheran bodies from North America turned their attention to Latin America, their basic concern was to gather and serve fellow Lutherans. Much of the work was done in the languages of the immigrants, especially German, and Lutherans only slowly became involved in Spanish work. Even then a major impetus was the desire to reach the descendants of Europeans who no longer spoke their mother tongue. It is not surprising, therefore, that the Lutheran Church has to a large degree remained a community of immigrants and their descendants. The dominance of the Roman Catholic Church among the older, generally Spanish-speaking segments of the population also has contributed to this reality.

The largest concentrations of Lutherans in Latin America are to be found in Argentina and Brazil, but Lutheran missions and Lutheran communities have been established in every country of South America. After a half century of activity the total number of Lutherans on the continent was about 750,000.[31] The second half of the twentieth century is producing greater expansion, partly because of internal growth and partly because of an awakened home mission consciousness by the existing Lutheran churches. In addition to people of European heritage, Latin Americans and Indians have gradually been brought inot the Lutheran communities, although they remain minorities. The Iglesia Evangelica Luterana, for example, has focused its attention on the large Indian population of Bolivia.

A significant beginning has been made by the Church of the Augsburg Confession in Latin America. Tremendous challenges remain. Among them are the establishment of positive relationships with other Christian communities, continued outreach to non-Europeans, creative response to political, social, and economic discontent and turmoil, the training of a sufficient number of pastors, and the achievement of financial stability.

Since the Reformation the Church of the Augsburg Confession has developed into a diverse and complex community which, nevertheless, shares a common theological heritage and a particular understanding of the Gospel and its implications for faith and life. The Lutheran World Federation (LWF) affords the various communities of the Church of the Augsburg Confession an opportunity to share their unity, to discuss their differences, to relate to the broader Christian community, and to make a common witness to the church and to the world.

The LWF is in a very real sense the result of the awakened ecumenical spirit, especially within American Lutheranism, since World War I. The concern to assist fellow Lutherans after the ravages of the war also served as an impetus toward a federation of Lutheran bodies. The desirability and appropriateness of closer relationships, more direct cooperation, and a united witness of the Gospel seemed obvious to many Lutherans. Through the coordinated efforts of the National Lutheran Council in the United States and the General Evangelical Lutheran Conference in Europe a meeting of world-wide Lutheranism was scheduled at Eisenach in August 1923. One hundred fifty-one delegates constituted the first Lutheran World Convention. Succeeding meetings were held at Copenhagen in 1929 and at Paris in 1935. The fourth assembly was to meet at Philadelphia in 1940, but World War II intervened. When Lutheran delegates gathered once again at Lund, in 1947, a constitution was adopted, and the name of the organization was changed to the Lutheran World Federation.

Its constitution makes it clear that the Lutheran World Federation does not envision itself as a church body. Rather, it is a "free association of Lutheran Churches."[32] Members retain their autonomy, and they determine the programs and specific tasks of the Federation. They also have the right to reject policies and decisions made by the Federation. While such guidelines have been articulated, a certain degree of ambiguity remains, and the exact nature of the LWF continues to be debated.

The major functions of the LWF are delineated in Article III of the constitution. The Federation intends to:

1. Further a united witness before the world to the Gospel of Jesus Christ as the power of God for salvation.

2. Cultivate unity of faith and confession among the Lutheran Churches of the world.

3. Develop fellowship and cooperation in study among Lutherans.

4. Foster Lutheran interest in, concern for, and participation in ecumenical movements.

5. Support Lutheran Churches and groups as they endeavor to meet the spiritual needs of other Lutherans and to extend the Gospel.

6. Provide a channel for Lutheran Churches and groups to help meet physical needs.[33]

The LWF has attempted to address all of these areas through its various programs.

While the LWF is not a church body, it has articulated a doctrinal basis. Article II of the constitution reads:

> The Lutheran World Federation acknowledges the Holy Scriptures of the Old and New Testaments as the only source and the infallible norm of all church doctrine and practice, and sees in the three Ecumenical Creeds and in the Confessions of the Lutheran Church, especially in the Unaltered Augsburg Confession and Luther's Small Catechism, a pure exposition of the Word of God.[34]

This doctrinal statement serves both as a description of the confessional position of the Lutheran churches that belong to the LWF and also as a norm for the Federation itself. Although the confessional heritage of the Church of the Augsburg Confession is clearly affirmed, the acceptability of new confessional statements, as long as they agree with the historic Lutheran symbols, is not discounted. This position has facilitated the acceptance of the Batak Church into the LWF. It will also enable other church bodies of the Lutheran tradition, especially from the third world, to join the LWF even though they may find it necessary to formulate their own confessions rather than adopt the historic Lutheran confessions.

Since its inception three decades ago, the LWF has been particularly active in missions, in relief work (especially after World War II), in ecumenical endeavors, and in theological discussions. It has served as an effective arena for inter-Lutheran cooperation and has facilitated the Lutheran contribution and response to the church and to the secular context.

NOTES

1. In addition to those cited in subsequent notes, other useful biographies of Luther are: Jan Willem Kooiman, *By Faith Alone* (New York: Philosophical Library, 1955); Franz Lau, *Luther* (Philadelphia: Westminster Press, 1963); James Mackinnon, *Luther* and the *Reformation*; 4 vols. (London: Longmans, Green, and Co., 1925–1930); and Gerhard Ritter, *Luther: His Life and Work* (New York: Harper & Row, 1963). Among the numerous discussions of Luther's theological thought are: Paul Althaus, *The Theology of Martin Luther* (Philadelphia: Fortress Press, 1966); Heinrich Bornkamm, *Luther's World of Thought* (St. Louis: Concordia Publishing House, 1958); Gerhard Ebeling, *Luther* (Philadelphia: Fortress Press, 1970); George Forell, *Faith Active in Love* (Minneapolis: Augsburg Publishing House,

1964); Anders Nygren, *Eros and Agape*, 2 vols. (London: S.P.C.K., 1932–1939); Regin Prenter, *Spiritus Creatur* (Philadelphia: Muhlenberg Press, 1953); E. G. Rupp, *Luther's Progress to the Diet of Worms* (New York: Harper & Row, 1964); and P. S. Watson, *Let God Be God* (Philadelphia: Muhlenberg Press, 1947).

2. Roland Bainton, *Here I Stand* (Nashville: Abingdon Press, 1950), p. 51.

3. Martin Luther, *Career of the Reformer IV*, ed. Lewis W. Spitz, in *Luther's Works*, ed. Jaroslav Pelikan and Helmut T. Lehmann, XXXIV (Philadelphia: Muhlenberg Press, 1960): 337.

4. Jaroslav Pelikan, "Luther and the Liturgy," in *More about Luther*, Martin Luther Lectures, II (Decorah, Iowa: Luther College Press, 1968): 1-62.

5. Martin Luther, *D. Martin Luthers Werke* (Weimar: Hermann Böhlaus

Nachfolger, 1883–   ).

6. Martin Luther, *Luther's Works*, ed. Jaroslav Pelikan and Helmut T. Lehmann; 55 vols. (St. Louis: Concordia Publishing House; Philadelphia: Fortress Press, 1955–   ).

7. Cf. Ernest G. Schwiebert, *Luther and His Times* (St. Louis: Concordia Publishing House, 1950). Schwiebert has identified the essential role played by the University of Wittenberg in the sixteenth-century Reformation.

8. For a detailed discussion of Melanchthon's educational work, cf. Karl Hartfelder, *Philip Melanchthon als Praeceptor Germaniae*, Monumenta Germaniae Paedagogica, vol. VII (Berlin: A. Hofmann & Comp., 1889).

9. The two standard editions of the Book of Concord are: *Die Bekenntnisschriften der evangelisch-lutherischen Kirche* (Göttingen: Vandenhoeck and Ruprecht, 1930) and *The Book of Concord*, ed. Theodore G. Tappert (Philadelphia: Fortress Press, 1959).

10. F. Bente, *Historical Introduction to the Book of Concord* (St. Louis: Concordia Publishing House, 1965), p. 46.

11. *The Book of Concord*, ed. Theodore G. Tappert (Philadelphia: Fortress Press, 1959), pp. 504-505. Hereafter referred to as *The Book of Concord*.

12. Ibid., p. 289.

13. Ibid., p. 614.

14. Ibid., p. 338.

15. The most extensive discussion of the significance and history of Luther's catechisms is Johann Michael Reu, *Quellen zur Geschichte des Katechismusunterrichts Dritter Teil: Ost-, Nord- und West-deutsche Katechismen*, vol. III, part 1b of *Quellen zur Geschichte des kirchlichen Unterrichts in der evangelischen Kirche Deutschlands zwischen 1530 und 1600* (Gütersloh: C. Bertelsmann, 1932).

16. *The Book of Concord*, p. 359.

17. Ibid., p. 465.

18. For helpful discussions of the political milieu, cf. Harold J. Grimm, *The Reformation Era* (2nd edn.; New York: The Macmillan Company, 1973) and Hajo Holborn, *A History of Modern Germany: The Reformation* (New York: Alfred A. Knopf, 1959).

19. Cf. Ernest G. Schwiebert, *Luther and His Times*.

20. Vilmos Vajta and Hans Weissgerber, eds., *The Church and the Confessions* (Philadelphia: Fortress Press, 1963), p. 9. The confessional attitudes of the Lutheran churches in various areas of the world are discussed in this volume. Hereafter referred to as Vajta and Weissgerber.

21. Harold J. Grimm, *The Reformation Era*, p. 243.

22. Vajta and Weissgerber, p. 70.

23. An extensive and sympathetic study of the orthodox theologians is offered in Robert Preus, *The Theology of Post-Reformation Lutheranism*; 2 vols. (St. Louis: Concordia Publishing House, 1970–1972).

24. Cf. Martin Schmidt, *Pietismus* (Stuttgart: Verlag W. Kohlhammer, 1972), pp. 9-28.

25. F. Ernest Stoeffler, *The Rise of Evangelical Pietism* (Leiden: E. J. Brill, 1971). Stoeffler provides an excellent discussion of the nature of Pietism and its impact on the Church of the Augsburg Confession. He argues that Arndt deserves to be called the "father of Lutheran Pietism" (p. 202).

26. Julius Bodensieck, ed., *The Encyclopedia of the Lutheran Church* III (Minneapolis: Augsburg Publishing House, 1965): 1902.

27. E. Clifford Nelson, ed., *The Lutherans in North America* (Philadelphia: Fortress Press, 1975), p. 151.

28. Quoted in Julius Bodensieck, ed. *The Encyclopedia of the Lutheran Church* II (Minneapolis: Augsburg Publishing House, 1965): 911.

29. Fridtjov Birkeli, "Lutheranism in Africa," in *Lutheran Churches of the World* (Minneapolis: Augsburg Publishing House, 1957), p. 230. Birkeli cites two apparent attempts by Lutherans to bring their evangelical insights to Africa. As early as 1585 Duke Ludwig of Württemberg sent an embassy to Africa, one of whose major goals was missionary work. In 1634 Peter Heiling traveled to Ethiopia at the instigation of Duke Ernest I of Saxe-Gotha-Altenburg, but his early assassination precluded significant accomplishments.

30. Julius Bodensieck, ed., *The Encyclopedia of the Lutheran Church* I (Minneapolis: Augsburg Publishing House, 1965): 152.

31. Stewart Herman, "Lutherans in Latin

America," in *Lutheran Churches of the World* (Minneapolis: Augsburg Publishing House, 1957), p. 306.
32. Julius Bodensieck, ed. *The Encyclo-* *pedia of the Lutheran Church* II: 1430.
33. Ibid.
34. Ibid.

BIBLIOGRAPHY

Allbeck, Willard D. *Studies in the Lutheran Confessions*. Philadelphia: Fortress Press, 1968.

Bainton, Roland. *Here I Stand*. Nashville: Abingdon Press, 1950.

Bente, F. *Historical Introduction to the Book of Concord*. St. Louis: Concordia Publishing House, 1965.

Bergendoff, Conrad. *The Church of the Lutheran Reformation*. St. Louis: Concordia Publishing House, 1967.

———. *Olavus Petri and the Ecclesiastical Transformation in Sweden, 1521–1552*. Philadelphia: Fortress Press, 1965.

Bodensieck, Julius, ed. *The Encyclopedia of the Lutheran Church*. 3 vols. Minneapolis: Augsburg Publishing House, 1965.

Dunkley, E. H. *The Reformation in Denmark*. London: S.P.C.K., 1948.

Ebeling, Gerhard. *Luther*. Philadelphia: Fortress Press, 1970.

Elert, Werner. *The Structure of Lutheranism*. St. Louis: Concordia Publishing House, 1962.

Grimm, Harold J. *The Reformation Era*. 2nd edn. New York: The Macmillan Co., 1973.

Gritsch, Eric W., and Jenson, Robert W. *Lutheranism*. Philadelphia: Fortress Press, 1976.

Holborn, Hajo. *A History of Modern Germany: The Reformation*. New York: Alfred A. Knopf, 1959.

Huddle, B. F. *History of the Lutheran Church in Japan*. New York: United Lutheran Church in America, Board of Missions, 1958.

Lueker, Erwin, ed. *Lutheran Cyclopedia*. Rev. edn. St. Louis: Concordia Publishing House, 1975.

Lutheran Churches of the World. Minneapolis: Augsburg Publishing House, 1975.

Manschreck, Clyde. *Melanchthon. The Quiet Reformer*. Nashville: Abingdon Press.

Nelson, E. Clifford, ed. *The Lutherans in North America*. Philadelphia: Fortress Press, 1975.

Neve, J. L. *Introduction to the Symbolical Books of the Lutheran Church*. Columbus, Ohio: The Wartburg Press, 1956.

Preus, Robert. *The Theology of Post-Reformation Lutheranism*. 2 vols. St. Louis: Concordia Publishing House, 1970–1972.

Reu, Johann M. *The Augsburg Confession. A Collection of Sources*. St. Louis: Concordia Seminary Press, 1966.

Rupp, E. G. *Luther's Progress to the Diet of Worms*. New York: Harper & Row, 1964.

Scherer, James A. *Mission and Unity in Lutheranism*. Philadelphia: Fortress Press, 1969.

Schlink, Edmund. *The Theology of the Lutheran Confessions*. Philadelphia: Fortress Press, 1961.

Schwiebert, E. G. *Luther and His Times*. St. Louis: Concordia Publishing House, 1950.

Stoeffler, F. Ernest. *The Rise of Evangelical Pietism*. Leiden: E. J. Brill, 1971.

Swavely, C. *Mission to Church in Andhra Pradesh, India: The Andhra Evangelical Lutheran Church, 1942–1962*. New York: Board of Foreign Missions of the United Lutheran Church in America, 1962.

Swihart, Altman K. *Luther and the Lutheran Church, 1483–1960*. New York: Philosophical Library, 1960.

Swihart, Altman K., ed. *One Hundred Years in the Andhra Country*. Madras, India: The Diocesan Press, 1942.

Tappert, Theodore G., ed. *The Book of Concord*. Philadelphia: Fortress Press, 1959.

Vajta, Vilmos, and Weissgerber, Hans, eds. *The Church and the Confessions*. Philadelphia: Fortress Press, 1963.

Waddams, Herbert M. *The Swedish Church*. London: S.P.C.K., 1946.

Wentz, Abdel Ross, ed. *The Lutheran Churches of the World, 1952*. Geneva: The Lutheran World Federation, 1952.

Willson, T. B. *History of Church and State in Norway from the Tenth to the Sixteenth Century*. Westminster: A. Constable & Co., 1903.

2. Doctrine and Theology

Nature of Lutheranism

The churches which designate themselves as Lutheran are more correctly called churches of the Augsburg Confession. For to be Lutheran does not mean to accept as authoritative or binding the teachings—much less the casual and informal utterances—of Martin Luther.[1] It means, rather, to accept as binding and authoritative what Luther himself acknowledged, namely, the Word of God as received in the prophetic and apostolic Scriptures and that affirmation of the Word of God confessed in the declaration of faith made before the emperor and estates of the Holy Roman empire of the German nation at Augsburg on June 25, 1530, by seven electors and princes and by the city councils of the free imperial cities of Nürnberg and Reutlingen.

The authors of the Augsburg Confession and of the related Symbolical Books of the Lutheran Church, contained in the Book of Concord of 1580[2] (the three ecumenical creeds, the Apology of the Augsburg Confession, the Smalcald Articles, the Treatise on the Authority and Primacy of the Pope, the Small and the Large Catechisms of Martin Luther, and the Formula of Concord [Preface, Epitome, and Solid Declaration]), regarded themselves as the heirs of the Catholic Church of every century. And that fact governs the way in which those churches that bear the reformer's name look to the Reformation that likewise bears his name.

Those responsible for the Reformation that began in Wittenberg with Luther and his colleagues at the university understood themselves as consciously and conscientiously conforming to the doctrine of the church catholic, drawn from the Sacred Scriptures. At Augsburg, the princes and cities that had experienced that Reformation declared, "In doctrine and ceremonies nothing has been received on our part against Scripture or the Catholic Church. For it is manifest that we have taken most diligent care lest some new and impious dogmas creep into our Churches" (*Augsburg Confession*, Latin text, Conclusion, par. 5). And the very existence of a *Catalog of Testimonies* as a portion of the Symbolical Books, with its citations from the fathers of the church, has no other point than to prove "that we have taught and spoken . . . just as first of all the Holy Scriptures and afterwards the ancient pure Church have done."

There are characteristic emphases in Lutheran teaching. The doctrines of redemption, of God, and of Christ received particular stress in the heat of the controversies in the sixteenth century. But that does not mean that there is a diminution of emphasis on the doctrines of creation, of man, of the church, of the sacraments, and of the Christian life. Thus "Lutheran" does not mean "anti-Catholic" or "non-Catholic." The Lutheran reformers and those since then who have committed themselves to the Augsburg Confession are keenly aware of the fact that they are explicitly catholic and that their churches are a part of the one, holy, catholic, and apostolic church—Catholic in the full historic sense of the term as implying both extensive universality and creedal orthodoxy. Lutherans recognize no breach in the continuity that links them with the medieval Western church, with the Great Church prior to the schism between Rome and Constantinople, and with the "ancient pure Church" of the era of the first four ecumenical councils.[3]

Still, "Lutheran" must be defined over against two quite different antitheses. Over against those Christian traditions that have consciously broken with the past—and that are commonly designated "Protestant" in our vernacular—"Lutheran" implies Catholicity. But there are also Christian traditions that, with the Lutherans, have maintained continuity with the Catholic past—or, as in the case of Anglo-Catholicism, have deliberately recovered a measure of Catholicity. In this antithesis "Lutheran" implies certain insights which were long in the process of development before the conservative Evangelical Reformation of the sixteenth century crystallized them. These insights are opposed to ideas that developed chiefly in the waning Middle Ages and that found a creedal fixation in the canons and decrees of the Council of Trent and an organizational embodiment in the Roman Catholic Church.

This means that, on the one hand, the genetic history of the Lutheran Church included all the concerns, all the reflections, and all the achieved resolutions of the theological and ecclesiastical problems from the first to the sixteenth centuries which it has in common with all of Catholic Christendom and with all of Western Catholicity. On the other hand, it retains in even sharpened polarity the insights in the religious realm that brought about the schism of the sixteenth century, to the extent that it was a religious and not a cultural or political schism.

The Lutheran Church does not represent an effort to turn the clock of history back three or five or ten or fifteen or twenty centuries in a biblicistic or traditionalistic kind of repristination, as if it fondly hoped to reproduce the apostolic church of Jerusalem or Corinth or Rome. For all its professed loyalty to the written revelation of God, Lutheranism has not been blind to the historical nature of Christianity, the fact that God is working out the destiny of the church in history, that the Holy Spirit who spoke through the prophets has illuminated teachers of the church in every generation to understand and to apply that speaking to the church's situation in each century, and that the cultic and disciplinary and institutional traditions of the past possess a real (even though relative) value that is not lightly to be cast aside. Others might make the apostolic age their ideal pattern for restoration; Lutherans were content to retain such historical developments as private confession, altars, crucifixes, the church year, chanted services, the traditional vestments, the historic creeds, the hymns and prayers hallowed by centuries of use, the ordinary and the propers of the Mass, and substantially the whole inherited panoply of rite and ceremonial.

It is possible, indeed necessary, to say that the Lutheran Church refuses to absolutize any formula as the whole of the Christian faith. Lutheran theology canot be comprehended in any oversimplification or any shibboleth —not even in the Reformation slogans of *sola gratia, sola fide,* and *sola Scriptura,* or in justification through faith.[4] To classify the Lutheran faith in terms of a formal and a material principle,[5] to be set in opposition to the formal and material principles of other Christian communities, may be an initially useful technique for the academic discipline of comparative denominational theology, but it does little justice to the necessary complexities of the theology of a church that uses roughly a quarter of a million words to set forth its mind in its Symbolical Books, and that senses an indispensable obligation to be loyal to the total counsel of God as an integrated body of teaching and belief. On the contrary, the Lutheran Church has sought to affirm the very opposite by redistributing the articles of the creed in such a way that the first looks back via creation beyond creation and the third looks forward through the process of hallowing to the point where the faithful shall finally be made consummately holy when the Holy Spirit "will raise me and all the dead and will grant eternal life to me and to all who believe in Christ."[6] In this span of vision, of central importance is the altar-cross of Christ the Priest and Christ the Victim, for in Christ, God was reconciling the world of human beings to himself, not counting their trespasses against them. But at the same time the Incarnation and the Atonement and the Exaltation of the Redeemer are precisely only the center, not the whole, of the Christian faith. But they are that center, and the theology of the Lutheran Church seeks to show just how the center and the circumference are connected.

The authors of the Lutheran Symbolical Books, together with their followers, have recognized that the Reformation holds a significance for the whole church, one which lies in its doctrinal emphases. Against the optimistic view of man's capacities which the Renaissance and some of the late medieval theologians had affirmed, the Lutheran Reformation asserted a native and radical sinfulness in human beings. It recognized that they can perceive, learn, know, reason, decide, will, and create; but it limited the level of these operations to the transient world and to human society. Thus it took no dim and pessimistic view of the human being's social responsibilities, but it saw clearly the mortal organic defect in humanity's moral construction. Therein it furnished a realistic basis for understanding the perennial inability of people to achieve in practice that standard of virtue which they correctly sense exists objectively and which they approve even while the violate it.

The Reformation also makes clear that between sinful humanity and the holy God there exists a chasm which people cannot bridge. Humanity's un-aided search for God can lead only into an endless labyrinth of blind alleys. The Reformation affirmed that God pardons the penitent sinner wholly on the basis of the Incarnation and the Atonement of Jesus Christ, on whose holiness the individual lays hold by God-given faith.

Over against the subjective experiences of sectarian enthusiasts, the visions of ecstatics, the decrees of prelates, the canons of councils, the creeds of the church, the traditions of the fathers, and the systems of philosophers, the Lutheran Reformation asserted unqualified dependence upon the prophetic and apostolic Scriptures as the sole rule and standard by which all teachers and all teachings of the church are to be judged and evaluated.[7]

And, in an approach that largely gives the Church of the Augsburg Confession her specific and distinctive character, the Reformation described the sacraments as "signs and testimonies of God's will toward us for the purpose of awakening and strengthening our faith."[8] Thus the sacraments become the individual application of the universal promise in the fellowship of the church, the conveyance to each person in all his singularity and per-sonal aloneness of the grace that is God's gift-in-common to the whole Mystical Body of Christ.

The Augsburg Confession

When on June 25, 1530, Chancellor Christian Beyer read before the Im-perial Assembly the "Confession or Profession of Faith of Some Princes and Cities,"[9] neither the reader nor the principal author (lay theologian Philipp Melanchthon) nor the signatories understood their action as the founding of a new church, much less as an act of schism; rather, they were appealing for recognition that they were fully Christian in their teaching and preaching, and that their correction of abuses were steps in the direction of authentic reform, not revolt. But for that very reason, they were decidedly in earnest about that solemn profession of faith for which they were staking virtually everything.

In the first twenty-one articles the Lutheran reformers presented their confession of the ancient faith of the catholic church; condemned the heresies, ancient and modern, which the Catholic Church condemned; and were at pains to prove that on no doctrinal point did they vary from the teaching of the sacred Scriptures, the catholic church, or, as far as its approved literary representatives are concerned, the historic church of the West. Subsequently

Lutherans, by the very act of subscribing their signatures to the Augsburg Confession or by invoking its authority in synodical or congregational constitutions, have affirmed that these articles are the Lutheran witness to an evangelical catholicity and thus are a call to the church to be what she had been for the first eleven centuries and to reaffirm her intention of being what she was then (and always is) in peril of ceasing to be.

Rather than engage in a running commentary on the twenty-eight articles of the Augsburg Confession, it is perhaps advisable to summarize its emphases in a series of six theses, affirmations which are central to the theology and practice of Lutherans.

First, and primary, is the assertion that central in the faith and life of the church is the Gospel of God's love manifested through the atoning, sacrificial, victorious work of Jesus Christ. This point is made in Article IV against the background of the preceding witness to the biblical faith about God, human beings and sin, and Jesus Christ:

> It is also taught among us that we cannot obtain forgiveness of sin and righteousness before God by our own merits, works, or satisfactions, but that we receive forgiveness of sin and become righteous before God by grace, for Christ's sake, through faith, when we believe that Christ suffered for us and that for his sake our sin is forgiven and righteousness and eternal life are given to us. For God will regard and reckon this faith as righteousness, as Paul says in Romans 3:21-26 and 4:5."[11]

And the same emphasis is repeated throughout the confession.

> We do not become good in God's sight by our works, but it is only through faith in Christ that we obtain grace for Christ's sake. . . . The Gospel demands that the teaching about faith should and must be emphasized in the Church, but this teaching cannot be understood if it is supposed that grace is earned through self-chosen works.[12]

Similarly, Article XXVIII relates the power of bishops—or the authority of the keys—directly and exclusively to the Gospel and its propagation. The power of the bishops is a power and command of God to preach the Gospel of his grace, to forgive sins, in the case of the impenitent to retain sins, and to administer and distribute the holy sacraments by which his grace is communicated. This power of the keys, or power of bishops, is used and exercised only by teaching and preaching the Word of God and by administering the sacraments, by which God imparts the eternal gifts of righteousness, the Holy Spirit, and everlasting life. It is necessary—and to this necessary task the Augsburg Confession was dedicated—to preserve the doctrine of Christian liberty in Christendom, namely, that bondage to the law is not necessary for the forgiveness of sins. The chief article of the Gospel must be maintained.

The second affirmation in the theology of the Augsburg Confession deals with authority in the church. The authority of Christ in his church—as he exercises it through his Word and the sacred ministry of his Word—is supreme; nothing else dare rival it. This principle governs the biblical citations of the Augsburg Confession, which are adduced as the primitive record of Christ's will for his church. Article XXII asserts with unmistakable intransigence, "Among us both kinds [that is both the host consecrated to be Christ's true body and the wine consecrated to be Christ's true blood] are given to laymen in the Sacrament. The reason is that there is a clear command and order of Christ, 'Drink of it, all of you.' "[13] It is thereby simply affirming Christ's authority as solely decisive in his church. This point underlies the description of the nature of the church and her ministry in Articles VII and VIII as well. And the comments on the authority of the bishop and of the priest among Lutherans, presented in Article XXVIII, similarly insist that such authority as these human lieutenants have is a reflection of and is restricted by the authority of Christ. He and his Word, and in that order, rule the church.

The third thesis which runs through the Augsburg Confession affirms that the church in the process of Reformation must remain the church catholic. In faith and in practice, the confessors at Augsburg sought no innovations. Thus the ancient fathers were cited as support for the confessors' affirmations, and they were at pains to condemn the ancient heresies. In support of Communion under both kinds they cite St. Cyprian, St. Jerome, and St. Gelasius.[14] In defense of the Lutheran practice of administering Holy Communion to the congregation at every Mass, Article XXIV quotes St. John Chrysostom and the Council of Nicaea.[15] What was true of the Holy Eucharist was equally true of all points: "Our manner of holding mass ought not in fairness be condemned as heretical or unchristian precisely since we have introduced no novelty which did not exist in the Church from ancient times and since no conspicuous change has been made in the public ceremonies of our masses."[16] Article XXV quotes St. John Chrysostom. and even canon law to prove that the Lutheran position on confession is catholic;[17] confession as distinguished from holy absolution is not commanded by the Scriptures but was instituted by the church, but private absolution is to be retained, because absolution, which has God's command, is the chief and most important part of the sacrament of penance and because private absolution affords needed consolation to terrified consciences.

The fourth thesis which guides the Lutheran confessors affirms that the concern of the church and its pastors must be for the consciences of the people. It is not proper to burden the consciences of those who desire to observe the sacrament according to Christ's institution or to compel them to act contrary to the ordinance of our Lord Jesus Christ, says Article XXII. Article XV calls for instruction of the faithful "so that consciences may not be burdened by the notion that such things [usages and ceremonies] are necessary for salvation."[18] For this reason, says Article XXIV, almost all the customary ceremonies at worship are in fact retained, save only that here and there vernacular hymns are interspersed among the parts sung in Latin as a kind of commentary on the action, for ceremonies are needed especially for the instruction of the less learned.[19] This pastoral concern contemplates particularly the priests and the religious—especially the nuns—who took final vows when they were too young to understand the nature of their commitment or the limitations of their own constitution, with consequent scandals for the faithful and burdened consciences for the victims of the ill-directed insistence upon holding them to their promises.[20]

Fifth, the Augsburg Confession commits Lutherans to the principle that the sacraments which Christ instituted as channels of divine grace must be restored—or maintained—in their primitive place. The Eucharist was not instituted to provide a sacrifice which would expiate sins; that sacrifice has already taken place in Christ's once-and-for-all atoning action.[21] Nor is it a sign by which people might be identified as Christians, but a sign and testimony of God's gracious will toward people, for the purpose of awakening and strengthening their faith.[22] Baptism is regarded as necessary, and it is held that grace is offered through it, and it is insisted that children, too, should be baptized so that they "become acceptable to him."[23] Holy absolution needs always to be rescued from the legalism which puts the stress on the quality of the penitent's confession, on the completeness of his confession, or on the meticulous execution of satisfaction. Rather, the stress must be on the word of absolution, so that people may esteem that absolution as the pronouncement of the God who forgives sin, for it is spoken in God's stead and by God's command.[24]

The sixth thesis that finds expression in the Augsburg Confession affirms that against a false spiritualism which disparages God's material creation, the church needs to stress a Christian secularity. The confessors recognized the fact that the God of sanctification is the God of creation as well, and that the Christ who commanded people to pray "Thy Kingdom come" also bade them seek the grace to do God's will on earth, and to solicit from the Father in heaven daily bread for the needs of life in the world that now is. Marriage and life in secular vocations are authentically Christian; the hope of sainthood and spiritual perfection is not forfeited by the wife, the husband, the parent, the government official, the prince, the property owner, the business man, or by any other person who chose, as the phrase went, "to remain in the world." It is God's design that a husband labor to support a wife, that a father bring up his children in the fear of God, that a mother bear and care for children, that princes and officials govern land and people, that commerce and trade go on. The monk and nun did not have an exclusive claim on holiness.[25] Similarly, civil and ecclesiastical authority alike needed to be reminded that their respective spheres were both divinely authorized and divinely limited, that civil government had its task in protecting bodies and goods from manifest harm through the use of the sword and temporal sanctions, while the ministry of the Gospel in the Christian community was there to protect people from heresies, from the devil, and from eternal death. Thus both authorities deserve honor because of God's command.[26] To summarize:

First, central in the faith and life of the church is the Gospel of God's love, manifested through the atoning, sacrificial, victorious work of Christ Jesus. It must be central in the faith and the life of Christians.

Second, the authority of Christ in his church as he exercises it through his Word and the sacred ministry of his Word is supreme. One can acknowledge no other Lord.

Third, the church in the process of any reformation or change must remain the catholic church. Above any denominational commitment is the obligation to the church catholic.

Fourth, the concern of the church's leaders must be for the conscience of the people. This imposes the obligation of careful instruction with word and sacraments.

Fifth, the sacraments which Christ instituted as channels of grace must retain always their primitive primacy. This would involve an appreciation of baptism, at least the weekly availability and the frequent use of the sacrament of the altar, and the restoration of holy absolution to its ancient place.

Sixth, the church needs to repeat not only verbally but also practically the complete creed, and thus to stress a Christian secularity against the false spirituality that disparages God's material creation and the legitimate natural purposes and activities of human life and human society.

Sacred Scriptures and the Symbolical Books

For those committed to the Lutheran symbols, the Sacred Scriptures are an abolute norm of, and the only agency for establishing, doctrine or articles of faith. At the same time, by their subscription of the Symbolical Books of the Evangelical Lutheran Church, these same Lutherans ascribe a unique status to those Symbolical Books—that is, the three catholic creeds, the Augsburg Confession (1530) and its Apology (1531), the Smalcald Articles and the Treatise on the Authority and Primacy of the Pope (1537), the two catechisms of Martin Luther (1528–1529), and the Formula of Concord (Preface, Epitome, and Solid Declaration, 1577–1580); these documents are understood to participate in the normative authority of the Sacred Scriptures. And these affirmations and assertions are made over against the claims of all or any other documents to similar authority.[27]

The Symbolical Books stand as their signatories' once-and-for-all attempt to demonstrate the essential catholicity of the Lutheran Church, and they are regarded as the one necessary standard of doctrine and practice for those who profess to be Lutheran. Any other doctrinal statement, corporate or private, ancient or sixteenth century or modern, is regarded only as a witness to the conviction of its authors or signatories.

The catholicity which the Symbolical Books seek to demonstrate is understood, by those confessional writings, as a catholicity under the Scriptures of the church catholic. Those writings are understood to be nothing more than exposition of the Scriptures, and thus in accordance with the faith of the universal Christian church.

In the absence, then, of a specific article on the Scriptures in the Symbolical Books,[28] it is necessary to inquire into the implicit and explicit teaching about the Scriptures which is contained in the Lutheran Symbolical Books.

Primarily, the Sacred Scriptures, the prophetic and apostolic writings of the Old and New Testaments, are held to be the Word of God. As such, they are the standard according to which all teachers and teachings are to be judged. But the symbols do not expand upon or define such an assertion in a refined, reasoned, philosophical way. Instead, the symbols deal existentially and functionally with the doctrines which traditionally are used to amplify and support the assertion that the Scriptures are the Word of God: namely, the doctrines of inspiration, authority, and infallibility or inerrancy. Thus they do not make use of technical terms, such as verbal inspiration, perspecuity, and sufficiency, and they likewise do not make a two-way equation between the Scriptures and the Word of God. But they do offer some amplification of the fundamental assertion that the Scriptures are the written Word of God.

The Apology of the Augsburg Confession (Preface 9) describes the Bible as "the Scriptures of the Holy Ghost." Yet the classical prooftexts for a doctrine of inspiration are significantly neglected. II Timothy 3:16 is quoted twice (FC SD VI, 14; XI, 12), in neither instance to prove the inspiration of the Scriptures, but rather, to show the sanctification of the apostolic witnesses by the "eternal Word" of God. In this connection it is useful to add that, at its best, the later doctrine of verbal inspiration among Lutherans in America has little in common with the similarly labeled doctrine of some Baptists, fundamentalists, or such groups as the Jehovah's Witnesses—whose doctrines of verbal inspiration share a tendency to speak of the authority of the Sacred Scriptures in their own right, apart from the authority of their Divine Author, and to identify some literalistic interpretations with the very truth of the divine revelation. Lutherans in America, however, have assimilated a good deal of this view of inspiration.

The Symbolical Books make a practical, if not explicit, affirmation of the perspicuity of Scriptures when, for example, the Apology (IV, 107) expresses its astonishment that the adversaries are not moved by those many Bible passages which clearly attribute justification to faith.

Similarly, Lutherans affirm the veracity of the Scriptures when, as in the Large Catechism (Sacrament of the Altar, 75) they advise that, if one cannot perceive the sinfulness of his flesh, he ought to believe the Scriptures, which will not lie, inasmuch as they know man's flesh better than he does.

Further, the Lutheran Confessors regard the Scriptures, if not explicitly as the source of doctrine, then at least as the foundation or establishing force for doctrine in the church. The invariable rule according to the Smalcald Articles (II II, 15) is, "The Word of God shall establish articles of faith and no one else, not even an angel." And when those who framed the Formula of Concord sought to express their orientation to the Scriptures, they spoke of the Scriptures as the World of God from which the "summary and generally accepted concept and form" of what is to be agreed on in the church is drawn; and in the same context they refer to the prophetic and apostolic Scriptures as the "pure, limpid fountain of Israel" (FC SD Summ. 1, 3).

Likewise, the Scriptures are regarded as the only certain rule according to which all teachers and teaching are to be evaluated. The Scriptures are called the unique standard, judge, rule, and touchstone for doctrine. All postapostolic writings, by contrast, are seen merely as witnesses to the way in which the apostolic doctrine was preserved (FC Ep Summ. 2).

Finally, the Symbolical Books commit Lutherans to the view that the ability to understand the Scriptures comes only from the Holy Spirit, that human beings do not natively possess such ability (FC SD II, 25-28). That assertion is followed by a string of twenty-five Bible passages as support (plus a quotation from St. Augustine), after which the Formula concludes, "This doctrine [concerning human will] is founded upon the Word of God." This point similarly underlies the assertion of Justus Jonas in his German translation and paraphrase of the Apology of the Augsburg Confession that the doctrine of justification serves preeminently to clarify the right understanding of the whole of the Sacred Scriptures (Apology IV, 2 German).

Thus, without using the term "verbal inspiration," the Lutheran symbols appeal to a Bible, taken to be composed of the prophetic and apostolic Scriptures of both Testaments, a Bible which in all its parts and as a whole is taken to be inspired by the Lordly and Life-giving Spirit who spoke by the prophets; which is the rule and norm of all doctrine; which is truthful and clear on all matters of revelation; and for the proper understanding of which baptism and the gift of the Holy Spirit are necessary.

Since, however, the authors of the Formula of Concord ascribe such authority also to the earlier Symbolical Books, foremost among them the Augsburg Confession, one confronts the question of the relation of the Symbolical Books to the Sacred Scriptures. Some of the theologians of Lutheran scholasticism (apparently after John William Baier's *Compendium,* which was first published in 1686) distinguished between the Scriptures as the *norma normans* (norming norm) and the symbols as a *norma normata* (normed norm). But the symbols do not make use of that distinction; the authors of the Formula of Concord regard the earlier symbols also simply as *norma,* by whcih the doctors of the past are to be judged and the doctors of the future are to be guided.

In contrast to the theologians of Lutheran scholasticism, who often contented themselves with reflections about the symbols and who argued themselves into positions where they circumvented the symbols and proposed to rest their case directly on the Scriptures, the fathers of one branch of American Lutheranism (The Lutheran Church–Missouri Synod), anticipating the confessional revival in the rest of the Lutheran Church by from one to three generations, sought to rescue the status of the symbols. They correctly recognized that if Symbolical Books are to mean something for the contemporary church, then pastors and public teachers must interpret the Sacred Scriptures in accordance with the exposition of them in the Symbolical Books, and not vice versa.[29] Though that insistence was not always consistently followed in the dogmatic work of those Lutherans, it does not bely the principle: In the Scriptures, in the symbols, in the concrete expressions of the church's continuing ministry of Word and sacrament, the Word of God in the Scriptures is the perpetual and supreme norm; the symbols are uniquely effective witnesses to the proper understanding of that Word, by which other efforts at interpreting the Scriptures are to be judged. They are norms which the church has subjected to the judgment of the Sacred Scriptures and by which the day-to-day expressions of the mind of God in the public ministry of the church must be evaluated, in order that the latter will as completely and correctly as possible exhibit the form of the Sacred Scriptures properly understood. Thus the value of the Symbols in this connection is seen to lie in their being regarded as the correct interpretation of the sense of the Scriptures, and as the norm that gives shape to the contemporary ministry of the church.

Creation

Put simply, the doctrine of creation for Lutherans means that God is the maker of the Universe and its all-ruler (*pantokrator*). Of course, that faith is shared with all Christendom, for whom the opening statements of the Apostolic and Nicene creeds need little amplification. But the doctrine of creation seems most often to come into conflict, not with alternative theological systems, but with the nontheological systems of the natural sciences and evolutionary thought. It is true that many Lutherans have been as agitated about "creation versus evolution" as adherents of more fundamentalistic groups. And it is also true that Lutherans figure prominently among the leadership of that group of theologians and scientists known as the "Creation Research Society," whose principal published aim is to find scientifically valid proof for the special creation of the universe by God.[30]

There is nothing, however, in the Symbolical Books of the Lutheran Church to impel one toward such agitation or research. The theological stake of Lutherans is not with the protagonists of the Scopes trial half a century ago. It is, rather, in simply affirming God's responsibility for the world that is.

God made what is. That is meant exclusively and inclusively. What exists is either God or a creature of God; there is no third possibility. That affirmation receives at least two decisive accents among Lutherans. First, with the explanation to the first article of the Apostolic Creed in the Small Catechism, Lutherans confess that the word of creation is a word about "me," the present-day confessor of the creed: "I believe that God has made me, together with all that exists, and that he has given me and still sustains my body and soul." Second, Lutherans recognize that the acknowledgment of God as creator obligates the confessor of such faith to thankful and serving obedience: "For all of this I am bound to thank, praise, serve, and obey him."[31]

In both instances, the stress is on the contemporary. God made me together with all that exists; and God's creating obligates me and all human beings to thankful obedience and service. As a theological exposition of a confession of faith, a Lutheran understanding of God's creative work stresses these facets of the relationship between God and creation and leaves the questions of cosmology and worldview and of the manner or time of the origin of the universe relatively open. The stress is not on the mode of creation but on the fact that God created the universe—and me.

This point of departure, and the direction of the argument just sketched, involve the Lutheran in a polemic against several antitheses. The confession that God is the creator of all that exists is made over against a false spirituality which, with gnostics of all times, would despise matter, the body, and things earthly as if they were inferior or inherently evil and unworthy of the attention of God or of human beings. Rather, the Lutheran recognizes that, in dealing with the body as well as the soul, with the earth as well as the eternal, one is dealing with a product of God's creative work. Similarly, since the doctrine of creation speaks about the world that now is, and not merely about the origins of that world years or aeons ago, Lutherans recognize that culture and the arts, government and social structures are not to be despised, but valued also as God's creation. Although Lutherans have frequently acted in the realm of politics and social concerns in ways that deserved the label "quietism,"[32] such behavior is not the product of the theology of creation with which the Symbolical Books equip them.

The affirmation that God has made the universe involves Lutherans in a polemic against any attempt so to stress the redemption of human beings in Jesus Christ that creation would be relegated to a position of no real importance. Nor would Lutherans have the creation eliminated from the Christian hope regarding the end (*eschaton*). Instead, they recognize that just as people are created together with all creatures, so they are sinners fallen together with all creatures who are involved in the sympathetic "groaning of all creation" in anticipation of the liberation of the children of God. The division of the creed into three articles, on creation, on redemption, and on sanctification, is for Lutherans a constant reminder of the need to avoid collapsing the Christian confession into a few words about Jesus Christ and redemption.

This does not mean, however, that the centrality of Jesus Christ in the Christian's faith is minimized or sacrificed. The evangelical point of departure which characterizes the Augsburg Confession is not abandoned in the understanding of creation. For the Creator God is precisely that One whom Jesus Christ made known as the Father, giving to his followers the right and privilege to address him as "Abba," dear Father. Thus the article of creation, affirming that the Father of the Lord Jesus Christ is the maker of "me together with all that exists," is as much a confession of faith as the article about redemption through Jesus Christ.

To acknowledge God as creator of all things and therefore also as the kindly giver of "all that I need to support this body and life,"[33] is to acknowledge also the Christian's debt of gratitude and service—in this sense the Small Catechism simply echoes St. Paul in the opening chapter of the Epistle to the Romans. "This article would humble and terrify us all if we believed it" (LC II, 22). Who can afford to confess God as creator? Only that one who has in Jesus Christ the assurance of divine forgiveness for his sin. Without that, the word of creation would be a word of condemnation, and the world of creation a world of threat and accusation, where even the rustling of a leaf in a darkening forest can frighten one almost to death.[34]

The Christian, on the other hand, is able to risk the admission that God has made him and obligated him, for he has heard the word of forgiveness and adoption and life. Instead of jumping at the rustle of the leaf, he can delight in his Father's world. The faith that acknowledges God as the all-ruling Father and Maker of me and of all that has being is already the change from dread and fear to pleasure and delight.[35]

Since for the Christian it is "my Father's world," to see only the evil and the nongodly or contragodly elements in that world would be seen as a relapse to atheism. By the same token, it would be rankest unfaith to suppose and to act as if the God who is quite content to make use of mediate and secondary causes in the creating and sustaining of his world, would not employ the mediate and secondary causes of his redeemed people in asserting his kingly rule in Christ over the redeemed world. In other words, Lutherans see God's redeemed people as standing under the indispensable obligation to oppose evil and the demonic powers in every legitimate way according to their vocation, their means, their opportunity, and their ability. Far from quietism, the faith that confesses God the creator should find itself at work in the Father's world, once more showing how this faith is a "living, busy, active, mighty thing."[36]

Human Beings and Sin

The doctrine of sin, and therefore of original sin as the root of sin in human beings, as it is taught in the Church of the Augsburg Confession, reflects both the essential catholicity of that confession and the distinctive evangelical concern of the Lutheran Reformation. The Augsburg Confession (Latin version) sets that tone in its second article:

Our churches also teach that since the fall of Adam all men who are propagated according to nature are born in sin. That is to say, they are without fear of God, are without trust in God, and are concupiscent. And this disease or vice of origin is truly sin, which even now damns and brings eternal death on those who are not born again through Baptism and the Holy Spirit.

Rejected in this connection are the Pelagians and others who deny that original sin is sin, for they hold that natural man is made righteous by his own powers, thus disparaging the sufferings and merit of Christ.

Thereby the confessors at Augsburg sought to identify with the ancient church's condemnation of Pelagius and his followers[37] who had taught that human beings are not sinful by nature and that they can be saved by an act of their own will aided by the grace of God. At the same time, the distinctive emphasis is set. The vice of origin is described as truly sin, and as the grounds for the condemnation of human beings under the wrath of God. The confessors strike a further characteristic note when they point to the reason for their assertion; the Pelagians' error is that they "obscure the glory of Christ's merits and benefits" (German version), or "disparage the sufferings and merit of Christ" (Latin version).

In the Latin version of the Augsburg Confession the troublesome word "concupiscent," which is often given a merely sexual connotation, is explained in other words in the German version: all human beings "are full of evil lust and inclinations from their mother's wombs and are unable by nature to have true fear of God and true faith in God." The intent of this is to affirm that there is no human being without sin; that there is no neutral position between sinnerhood and righteousness before God; that, since there is no sin which is not in fact enmity against God, all human beings are in hopeless opposition against their creator.

Far from reducing an individual's guilt before God or his responsibility for his sinnerhood, the teaching of the Augsburg Confession about original sin serves in fact to underscore that personal responsibility. At the same time, this teaching raises most painfully the problem of mankind's relationship with a righteous God. It affirms on the one hand that there is no possibility of our not being in active opposition against God, for, with Romans 8:7 and Ephesians 20:16, Lutherans understand sin as enmity against God. And it affirms on the other hand that, although a person cannot help himself out of that enmity, he is absolutely responsible for his enmity against God. One can only hate a God who produces such a situation. One can only recoil in horror before a God who in the very process of calling us into life puts a weapon into our hands so that we must fight against him, who then destroys us because we fight against him, and who tops that off by holding us utterly responsible for that state of affairs. The teaching on original sin presents the mystery of the hidden God.[38]

What is an unsatisfying logical dilemma is nevertheless held to be a piece of God's truth. "The law brings wrath," St. Paul had written.[39] The very diagnosis which God's law performs upon the human being and his inescapable sinner-situation, inevitably produces the enmity it condemns. God's law produces wrath—both God's and that of human beings. "You have not fulfilled it, nor can you, yet you must."[40] With those words Luther had described the dilemma.

The Lutheran teaching about original sin is therefore not only about the native situation of human beings but also about God. It reminds that God cannot be reduced to a mere principle, a neuter being (*ens*) stripped of all personal attributes. It recognizes that the enmity is mutual, that God's wrath is a reality to be dealt with and that in his law God condemns human beings locked in sinner-opposition to him.

The Lutheran teaching recognizes that the term "original sin" is neither a biblical term nor a catholic term used in the same sense in all times and places by all Christians. In the West the term seems to have arisen at the time of St. Augustine of Hippo (d. 430) or shortly before, and in the East the term has never really been adopted. As it is used in the Symbolical Books, it refers to the native sinfulness that characterizes every human being, and to the retroactive persistence of this native sinfulness as far back as human history goes. This native sinfulness is not merely the absence of the kind of trust, love, and obedience that God as the creator of human beings has a right to demand but the native inability of human beings born in this world to give God that kind of trust, love, and obedience. And, while baptism takes away the guilt of this native sinfulness, it nonetheless continues to affect people as long as they live; while the Holy Spirit assists people in restraining its vicious effects in their lives, this process is always imperfect, and Lutherans accordingly underscore the necessity for daily repentance.

By thus once more setting the polarity of law and Gospel, of repentance and faith, of human sin and Christ's cross, the Lutheran teaching aims to avoid a superficial understanding of sin as only a series of infractions against divine directives, of law as merely divine legislation, of God as merely the author of moral codes of a high order, of human beings as merely imperfect in moral conduct. Being a sinner is not understood as the cumulative result of a series of individual errors. Rather, wrong deeds and thoughts are sins because they are the deeds and thoughts of one who is hopelessly locked in enmity against God; they are the deeds and thoughts of a sinner. Accordingly, original sin is regarded not merely as one kind of sin among many but as *the* sin, that of which all others are only the fruits. "Whatever does not proceed from faith is sin."[41] Original sin is seen as native unbelief, persistent and incorrigible. That native unbelief is the essential character of sin and the quality imparted by the sinner to all his deeds. It is inseparably connected with the beginning and entire course of human existence, something without which one cannot exist, whether knowing it or not, whether wishing it or not.

That situation is dealt with, according to Lutherans, not by minimizing its seriousness, not by trivializing its dilemma, not by shunting off human responsibility. It is dealt with by magnifying "the sufferings and merit of Christ."[42]

Jesus Christ

The intention of the Lutheran reformers to preserve the doctrine of the one holy catholic and apostolic church, a struggle which inevitably involved the effort to conserve venerable terminology and ancient definitions while at the same time maintaining the distinctive focus on the clear promises of the Gospel, is perhaps nowhere so apparent as in the understanding of the person and work of Jesus Christ.

In the Book of Concord the Church of the Augsburg Confession places in first position the three so-called ecumenical creeds, reaffirms their content repeatedly in its particular symbols, and (at least in some early editions) closes, in the appended Catalog of Testimonies, with extensive citations from the councils and fathers of the earliest church. The development of the orthodox teaching about the person and the natures of Christ which began at Nicaea (325) and was concluded at Chalcedon (451) is vigorously and explicitly affirmed.[43] Basic is the formulation of the Augsburg Confession (Article III), laced as it is with the phrases of the ancient creeds:

> It is also taught among us that God the Son became man, born of the virgin Mary, and that the two natures, divine and human, are so inseparably united in one person that there is one Christ, true God and true man, who was truly born, suffered, was crucified, died, and was buried in order to be a sacrifice not only for original sin but also for all other sins and to propitiate God's wrath. The same Christ also descended into hell, truly rose from the dead on the third day, ascended into heaven, and sits on the right hand of God, that he may eternally rule and have dominion over all creatures, that through the Holy Spirit he may sanctify, purify, strengthen, and comfort all who believe in him, that he may bestow on them life and every grace and blessing, and that he may protect and defend them against the devil and against sin. The same Lord Christ will return openly to judge the living and the dead, as stated in the Apostles' Creed.

In that confession it is also made clear that the interest in the orthodox understanding of the person of Christ is not a merely formal one. The four "that" clauses underscore the evangelical thrust of Reformation theology. In this way the Symbolical Books preserve and pass on distinctive contributions of Martin Luther in this area.

The paradox of the Incarnation is affirmed. God has become man. The creator has become a creature. The action is God's; the direction is from God toward his creation, and not the other way round. It is the Incarnation of the Son of God, not the divinization of a son of man. Yet not "by changing the Godhead into flesh, but by taking on the humanity into God."[44]

The oneness of the person of Jesus Christ is similarly affirmed. Not two Christs, but one Christ, was the affirmation of the ancient symbol, *Quicunque vult*.[45] Not half man and half God. Not all man and as much God as finite man was capable of containing. God, wholly. Man, wholly. And yet one Christ, one person, in whom divine and human are united (as the formula from Chalcedon has it) "in an unmixed fashion, immutably, indivisibly, inseparably."[46]

Here the insistence on right teaching for the sake of believing becomes clear. God and man are one Christ—with the result that Christ's works are in fact God's works, Christ's words are in fact God's words, and Christ's offer of forgiveness is in fact God's offer of forgiveness, and all in such a way that the words and the works and the suffering and the dying are not magic or pretense or play-acting but the action and passion of a human being. In Jesus Christ God shows himself kindly disposed toward sinners. Outside of Jesus Christ the sinner encounters only a wrathful God.[47]

This concern for the comfort of sinners is at the core of the response of the framers of the Formula of Concord to those, both inside and outside Lutheranism, who would either limit the divine nature by asserting that the finite human nature is not capable of bearing the infinite divine nature or who would remove the humanity of Jesus from any genuine presence in our world by insisting on confining him to a fixed place in the heavens.[48]

Such concern had in fact been behind Luther's use of the idea of the omnipresence of the human nature of Christ—more so than as a guarantee for the real presence of Christ's body and blood in the sacrament of the altar. For, he reckoned, if one abandons the humanity of Christ to the heavens, then one in fact abandons the God graciously present and incarnate in Christ in favor of that remote *Deus nudus* before whose wrath one withers and dies. God has bound his gracious presence to the man Jesus Christ, and if the sinner is to have forgiveness and life, then he must find it in that *Deus incarnatus,* in the presence of the man Christ, in Jesus our brother, who is flesh of our flesh and bone of our bone, who is God himself present to deal with us in love and grace. By contrast, if only the deity is present, we perish.[49]

The Formula of Concord incorporates that concern into the confessional basis of Lutheranism when it refers to Luther's *Great Confession concerning the Holy Supper* and when it is careful to include among the properties of the divine nature which belong to Christ not only power and authority, but also "to cleanse from sin."[50]

The same concern must be seen behind the way in which the Formula of Concord seeks to settle the dispute about the *communicatio idiomatum*, the exchange of properties between the divine and the human natures in Christ. Two emphases must be mentioned, short of a detailed analysis of both the controversy and the Formula's attempt at a solution. First, it is affirmed that the unity or communion or sharing or exchange between the two natures in Christ is a real exchange, not a rhetorical one or one that is true only after a manner of speaking. This is affirmed for the sake of the redemptive validity of the suffering and death of Jesus Christ. If it was only a man who died, then that is of no benefit to sinners. But if, as the creeds assert, the Son of God has suffered and died—really, and not only after a manner of speaking—then there can be good news for sinners.

Second, the framers of the Formula of Concord (including Martin Chemnitz, the first edition of whose book *On the Two Natures in Christ* had appeared in 1570[51]) affirmed that the real exchange of properties between the two natures in Christ takes place in such a way that it is proper to ascribe divine majesty to Christ according to his human nature. Put most simply, this is seen only as a formal way of preserving the truth of such biblical statements as "The blood of Jesus his Son cleanses us from all sin" (I John 1:7). Given the complicated antitheses of the day, the assertions needed to be framed with many qualifications lest, for example, one mistakenly suppose that the Lutherans meant that the Godness of God was diminished because a part of it was in the man Jesus, or that God made only temporary use of the human nature of Christ. God and man in one Christ—that is the subject of all the affirmations in the creed, not just of those about conception, birth, suffering, death, and burial. "Apart from this man there is no God," the Formula quotes from Luther's *Great Confession* and concludes,

> . . . to deprive Christ according to his humanity of this majesty [exaltation, divine attributes, presence, and so on] . . . robs Christians of their highest comfort, afforded them in the cited promises of the presence and indwelling of their head, king, and high priest, who has promised that not only his un-veiled deity, which to us poor sinners is like a consuming fire on dry stubble, will be with them, but that he, he, the man who has spoken with them, who has tasted every tribulation in his assumed human nature, and who can there-fore sympathize with us as with men and his brethren, he wills to be with us in all our troubles also according to that nature by which he is our brother and we are flesh of his flesh.[52]

One way of understanding the ebb and flow of Christology through recent centuries would be to see it as the continued wrestling with the tensions or frictions created when the traditional orthodox affirmations together with the concern of the Symbolical Books for "comfort for troubled consciences," are rubbed against the picture of Jesus in the synoptic Gospels and against the insights and fashions in the thought world of these eras.

Within limits, the Symbolical Books leave Lutherans room to develop a Christology in several directions. They also set the parameter for determining when and to how great an extent such a Christology will still be entitled to the label "Lutheran."

Justification

When at Augsburg in 1530 the Lutheran princes and theologians placed the doctrine of the justification of the believing sinner into the center of their confession of faith, they were not consciously making any innovation in the interrelationship of doctrines. They understood what they were doing and saying to be necessary if what they saw as the fundamental truth of the Christian faith was to come to expression with full clarity, namely, that troubled consciences be comforted with the certainty of forgiveness and that the glory of Christ be magnified. They asserted:

> It is also taught among us that we cannot obtain forgiveness of sin and right-eousness before God by our own merits, works, or satisfactions, but that we receive forgiveness of sin and become righteous before God by grace, for Christ's sake, through faith, when we believe that Christ suffered for us and that for his sake our sin is forgiven and righteousness and eternal life are given to us. For God will regard and reckon this faith as righteousness, as Paul says in Romans 3:21-26 and 4:5.[53]

Although the repudiation of "our own merits, works, or satisfactions" must be seen as a consciously critical judgment on what the confessors under-stood the teaching of the opponents to be, it must nevertheless be recognized that the confessors expected their almost matter-of-fact statement to be received and acknowledged as the faith of the primitive church. As in the preceding articles, so also in Article IV there is no argumentative tone. There is no condemnation of opposing erroneous opinions—as if the con-fessors' intention was simply to be saying the obvious truth, as self-evident in its sphere as the paraphrase and expansion of the Apostles' Creed in the third article of the Confession. Finally, one observes that in Article IV there appears for the first time a reference to the Sacred Scriptures, to Romans 3 and 4 as illustration of reckoning or imputing of faith as righteousness for the believing sinner.

The burden of the present sketch of the theological profile of Lutheran-ism must be to see the grounds for placing the doctrine of justification into the center of the confessional structure, to portray the effect or result of that movement on the overall understanding of the faith, and in the process to il-luminate that very operation of center-making, a process which will of course necessitate an exposition of the Lutheran understanding of justification.

The Lutheran symbols do not commit Lutherans to any particular theory of the Atonement, Anselmian or otherwise.[54] When they speak of Christ and of his work, the Symbolical Books are concerned to affirm that Christ's saving work effects the comfort of troubled consciences and that Christ's work alone be celebrated as the grounds for the justification of believing sinners. A Lutheran is therefore free to make use of various biblical and traditional metaphors for the Atonement, so long as he does so in a way that magnifies Christ and provides real comfort for the faithful.[55] For God grants what is impossible for human beings to produce, namely, an end to the enmity between God and human beings, release from bondage to sin, forgiveness, new life.

The concern behind the triad "by grace, for Christ's sake, through faith" as the necessary qualifying phrases for the justification of believing sinners is not to produce a new theory for the application of Christ's saving work, but is an attempt to preserve that very work as the essentially saving thing—against a host of potential alternatives, only some of which are named in the Augsburg Confession. That triad, however, is not so much an accumulation of three separate ideas as an interrelation of three facets of the same idea, that the justification of the believer in fact be a reality. Those terms aim to safeguard the Lutheran concern about justification in three areas: the divine motivation and initiative, the saving ground and basis, and the means of its reception by the penitent sinner. "We receive forgiveness of sin and become righteous before God by grace, for Christ's sake, through faith, when we believe that Christ suffered for us and that for his sake our sin is forgiven and righteousness and eternal life are given to us." Each prepositional phrase serves the same basic concern, albeit in different areas or directions.

The Augsburg Confession itself spells out what antithesis the definition "by grace" aims to rule out. "We cannot obtain forgiveness of sin and righteousness before God by our own merits, works, or satisfactions." Thereby Lutherans mean to make of justification solely and completely God's work and God's initiative and to remove from that work all grounds or preconditions on the human side. The Apology adds the clarification that, if human merits, works, or satisfactions replace sheer divine grace as the cause of justification, then any and all certainty of forgiveness and comfort is destroyed.[56] For the sinner could never be confident that he had done enough, deserved enough, rendered sufficient satisfaction.

In the second place, justification, frequently identified also as the forgiveness of sins,[57] occurs "for Christ's sake." Here the antithesis is not spelled out, that is, not until the Apology's lengthy defense of the Augsburg Confession. There one repeatedly finds Melanchthon writing such phrases as "Christ was not promised, revealed, born, crucified, and risen in vain."[58] "The Gospel compels us to make use of Christ in justification."[59] Further, if the Lutherans' confession is condemned, "Of what use, then, is Christ?" he asks repeatedly.[60] Works must be commended, he insists, but not at the expense of Christ.[61] When the opponents imply that forgiveness is to be grounded in Christ *and* human merit, they "bury Christ."[62] The Scriptures, indeed the church catholic, Melanchthon affirms, compel one to credit Christ's work alone with providing the basis for the forgiveness of sins. For that reason, justification is confessed to be "for Christ's sake."

Decisive in terms of the controversy of the sixteenth century, if not also subsequently, is the third prepositional phrase, "through faith." Although the Lutheran position is frequently labeled "justification by faith," accuracy is best served by preserving the "through" (*per, durch*) as the crucial preposition for linking justification and faith. It is of course also possible, as Melanchthon repeatedly does in the Apology, to omit the preposition entirely and to speak of faith with the Latin ablative case, *iustificatio fide,* or, following the lead of the New Testament, to make faith the subject of the verb, and to say, "Faith justifies,"[63] just as the Evangelists report Jesus as saying, "Your faith has saved you." But neither the instrumental nor the direct, subject-of-the-verb, sense is self-evident. Nor can they be, without recalling the understanding of the biblical message which both underlies and emerges explicitly in the Lutheran symbols, namely, that "all Scripture should be divided into these two chief doctrines, the law and the promises."[64] The "promises" are then defined as the promises in the Old Testament "that the Messiah will come," and that there will be "forgiveness of sins, justification, and eternal life for his sake," and in the New Testament as those promises of Christ himself of "forgiveness of sins, justification, and eternal life."[65] Now, the only way to respond positively to a promise is to believe it, to trust it. This point is made explicitly and repeatedly by Melanchthon.[66] Since God offers the forgiveness of sins as a "promise," it follows that justification must occur "through faith." "The promise of Christ is necessary. But this can be accepted only by faith."[67] That is what is behind the earlier statement, that "at every mention of faith we are also thinking of its object, the promised mercy."[68]

For the Symbolical Books, faith is not a commodity picked up in the religious bazaar, but rather, a precise and well-defined reality—defined, in fact, by its object, the promise of forgiveness "for Christ's sake," which it trusts. Likewise, "faith does not simply mean historical knowledge but is a firm acceptance of the promise. . . . For . . . only faith can accept the promise."[69] On that basis, then, the Lutheran symbols predicate justification of faith. After citing Romans 1:16 and 10:17 Melanchthon continues, "faith justifies. For if justification takes place only through the Word, and the Word is received only by faith, then it follows that faith justifies."[70] Faith is the receiving of the divine promise, and that is justification. "Why not say something about faith?"[71] That question stands near the conclusion of the fourth article of the Apology as a rhetorical reminder of the article's center.

When the Apology and other symbols say that "faith justifies," they are not contradicting what they otherwise maintain about the divine initiative and the purely passive role of the believing sinner. Melanchthon devotes several paragraphs of the Apology to an explication of the assertion that "faith justifies."[72] And the Formula of Concord speaks quite succinctly when it says, "For faith does not justify because it is so good a work and so God-pleasing a virtue, but because it lays hold on and accepts the merit of Christ in the promise of the holy Gospel."[73] Of course, faith is a very good work, and of course, faith is a very God-pleasing virtue. But faith does not justify because it is good and God-pleasing, or because it rightly gives God the honor of being just, or because it is the proper attitude to adopt toward God. Such a conception of faith sees faith in terms of the believing subject, and it suggests that believing is the grounds, in one way or another, for justification. Rather, the decisive factor in faith is what is believed, or, better,

Who is believed. For Lutherans, faith arises only from the hearing of the Gospel. And faith consists fundamentally in the confidence that its content, the person and the work of Christ, actually applies to the believer. Faith justifies, then, by virtue of its content, Jesus Chrst. He is what is so righteous about faith. Thus "through faith" is a corollary, not a rival, to "for Christ's sake."

The triad of prepositional phrases "by grace, for Christ's sake, through faith" is thus aimed at the center of Christian believing, at the "main doctrine of Christianity." For, says the Apology, "when it is properly understood, it illumines and magnifies the honor of Christ and brings to pious consciences the abundant consolation that they need."[74] Yet the crucial place is occupied by "through faith." For faith alone justifies, because faith alone receives the promised forgiveness of sins.

We must now ask about that which is received "by grace, for Christ's sake, through faith." The previous paragraphs have already shown that the Lutheran Symbolical Books frequently equate "justification" with "forgiveness of sins," and they frequently also add "eternal life" to the chain of parallel phrases. Parallel terms generally illuminate, but they do not always define the meaning of a term. The Apology offers one definition: " 'To be justified' means to make unrighteous men righteous or to regenerate them, as well as to be pronounced or accounted righteous."[75] In the immediately following paragraphs, that double definition is once more linked with the forgiveness of sins: "faith alone makes a righteous man out of an unrighteous one, that is, . . . receives the forgiveness of sins."[76] "Therefore we are justified by faith alone, justification being understood as making an unrighteous man righteous or effecting his regeneration."[77] Faith itself is pulled into the definition when the Apology says that "faith is the very righteousness by which we are accounted righteous before God."[78] As Lutherans see it, justification therefore includes being declared righteous, being made righteous, receiving the forgiveness of sins, as well as the very believing of the promise through which God chooses to act propitiously toward sinners when they believe his promise.

Since the sixteenth century, theologians have debated occasionally quite fiercely over the propriety or the continued usefulness of such language as justification and the imputation of faith as righteousness. Was the forensic, juridical model really so necessary or useful or even understandable?[79] Was there not an important difference between being accounted righteous and being made righteous? Was there not something just a little bit suspect about sinners being exonerated or pardoned?

The use of juridical or forensic terminology is not a special fascination of Lutherans. The terminology is in the Scriptures, which speak of human beings standing accused before the divine law, that ineluctable demand for righteousness, and that as sinners they confront the righteous wrath of God as the deadly truth about their existence.[80] There can therefore be no honest and useful talk about justification, according to the Lutheran symbols, that does not come to terms with the law of God and the wrath of God against sin.

The appeal to or the rejection of "purely forensic" terminology in the doctrine of justification must be made carefully. On the one hand, the biblical language of law and accusation and wrath and judgment seems to make the use of juridical terminology unavoidable. On the other hand, the mere continued use of forensic terminology will not guarantee that one is reproducing the substance of the New Testament teaching on justification. For one could, purely forensically, speak of God as simply declaring a sinner to be innocent and in that process to "bury Christ completely and do away with the whole teaching of faith," as the Apology puts it.[81] The Lutheran understanding of justification is not safeguarded by an insistence on purely forensic terminology, important and probably unavoidable as such terminoloy is.

It is helpful to call to mind the associations the word "justification" had when the doctrine bearing that name became confessed as the "main doctrine" of Christianity. For if the problem of justification is whether and in how far man's need to justify himself before the law of God is actually met by the Atonement or reconciliation accomplished by Christ's death, then it already makes a difference if, in the doctrine of justification, one keeps in mind that justification is something God does, not the sinner. The sinner, though summoned by the law to justify himself, cannot. The judge does the justifying. Again, the sinner is summoned to exonerate himself, but he cannot. Still, the process does not end with his exoneration by God, for a sentence is passed when the law's verdict is rendered. That is to say, God justifies the sinner by executing the just sentence. In the usage of the sixteenth century, justification did not mean to exonerate oneself, or to prove one's innocence, but referred, rather, to the criminal proceeding itself or more frequently to the execution of the sentence on the culprit. Saxon law could speak, for example, of the "body of the person justified by the sword," meaning thereby corpse minus sword-severed head.[82]

The situation envisioned by this use of the term "justification," then, is that of a human being standing accused before a just judge who will mete out justice to him—an exceedingly perilous situation, for the just verdict is "guilty" and the sentence is "death." If the sinner gets justified, that means that he has that sentence executed. If the sinner nevertheless lives, then that does not mean a simple exoneration, nor even an instance of justice tempered with mercy. Rather, it produces the happy surprise reflected in St. Paul's exclamation, "Dying, and behold we live.!"[83]

In the moment of that awareness, justification "by grace, for Christ's sake, through faith" can only mean that the wrath of God has had its righteous way. Christ has died, sentenced by the authorities, and has done so, according to the apostolic witness, for humankind. The believing sinner finds that Christ has died the death that was due for him. The death sentence on the guilty sinner has been executed on the righteous Son. With the apostle, the believer knows that he has been "buried with Christ by Baptism into death,"[84] and that he is a new person.

That God should act thus is "by grace." The justification thus achieved is "for Christ's sake." And it is received by the sinner "through faith" in the promise.

Justification, or its real content the forgiveness of sins, is thus seen as no mere exoneration or suspended sentence. It is God's gracious initiative, based on the mediating and propitiatory work of Christ, received by a repentance-emptied believing sinner. As a sentence, it is the execution of what St. Paul calls the old self. It is his death, his end. But it is, by happy exchange,[85] the resurrection of the "new self," the believer.

It is no accident then that the Lutheran Symbolical Books link justification and repentance by calling them cognate doctrines.[86] For repentance is the sinner's admission of guilt, his acceptance of the verdict due him as culprit, his assent to the righteous death sentence. Such repentance is possible only for the believer who, hearing the promise of forgiveness and new life in Christ, and trusting that promise, lets the death sentence be executed and finds that God keeps his promises: dying, and behold we live!

The doctrine of justification "by grace, for Christ's sake, through faith" is the main or chief doctrine of Christianity, according to the Lutheran symbols.[87] To say so is still not the same as to make it in fact the central and determining point in a theological or confessional system. It is no accident, therefore, that the fourth article of the Apology spends so much time and so many words in discussing the interpretation of the Sacred Scriptures from the standpoint of the distinction between the law and the Gospel. And it is likewise no surprise that the frequent refrain appears, "Whoever fails to teach about this faith we are discussing completely destroys the Gospel."[88]

For Lutherans, the touchstone of any theological discussion that wishes to lay claim to faithfulness to the Lutheran Symbolical Books remains to make the righteousness of faith the obviously main and central and critically determinative point. And that means, as the Apology puts it, that one "illumines and magnifies the honor of Christ and brings to pious consciences the abundant consolation that they need."[89]

NOTES

1. Luther himself urged that his name not be used as a label for the churches of the Reformation: "I ask that men make no reference to my name; let them call themselves Christians, not Lutherans. What is Luther? After all, the teaching is not mine. Neither was I crucified for anyone. St. Paul, in I Corinthians 3, would not allow the Christians to call themselves Pauline or Petrine, but Christian. How then should I—poor stinking maggot-fodder that I am—come to have men call the children of Christ by my wretched name? Not so, my dear friends; let us abolish all party names and call ourselves Christians, after him whose teaching we hold." *Luther's Works* (American ed.), Jaroslav J. Pelikan and Helmut T. Lehmann, general eds. (St. Louis: Concordia Publishing House, and Philadelphia: Fortress

Press, 1957 ff.), vol. XLV, pp. 70-71. Hereafter, this edition will be cited as LW, followed by volume and page numbers.

2. The standard critical edition of the Book of Concord is *Die Bekenntnisschriften der evangelisch-lutherischen Kirche*, Herausgegeben im Gedenkjahr der Augsburgischen Konfession (6th edn.; Göttingen: Vandenhoeck & Rupprecht, 1967); ET: *The Book of Concord*, trans. and ed. Theodore G. Tappert, in association with Robert H. Fischer, Jaroslav J. Pelikan, and Arthur Carl Piepkorn (Philadelphia: Fortress Press, 1959). Citations from the Lutheran confessional writings are normally taken from this volume. References will be made according to the following series of abbreviations facilitating reference to a number of different editions: AC—Augsburg Confession; Apol—Apology of the Augsburg Confession; SA—Smalcald Articles; Tr—Treatise on the Power and Primacy of the Pope; SC—Small Catechism; LC—Large Catechism; FC Ep—Epitome of the Formula of Concord; FC SD—Solid Declaration of the Formula of Concord. These abbreviations will be followed by the article number in roman numerals and the section number in arabic numerals.

3. Thus they include the three creeds from the ancient church among their symbols, and they are at pains in the Augsburg Confession to identify their confession as one in accord with the ancient faith; see especially AC I-III.

4. Though useful summaries, such terms inevitably reproduce less than the catholicity intended in the Lutheran confessional writings.

5. These terms, dating from the dogmatic theology of Lutheran scholasticism in the seventeenth century, have received some prominence in recent comparative symbolics thanks to their use by Frederick E. Mayer, *Religious Bodies of America*, 4th edn. by Arthur Carl Piepkorn (St. Louis: Concordia Publishing House, 1961), esp. pp. 144-147.

6. SC II, 6.

7. FC SD Rule and Norm, 1, 7.

8. AC XIII, 1.

9. Only the German version of the Augsburg Confession was read, but both the German and the Latin versions were submitted and thus carry equal authority. Neither version is a translation of the other; each was composed in its own right, though the composition of both versions proceeded simultaneously.

10. AC Preface.

11. AC IV.

12. AC XXVI, 5, 20.

13. AC XXII, 1.

14. AC XXII, 4-7.

15. AC XXIV, 36-38.

16. AC XXIV, 40.

17. AC XXV, 10.

18. AC XV, 2.

19. AC XXIV, 2-3.

20. See AC XXVII.

21. AC XXIV, 26.

22. AC XIII, 1.

23. AC IX.

24. AC XI, XXV.

25. AC XXVII.

26. AC XVI.

27. See the extended discussions of this question in Edmund Schlink, *The Theology of the Lutheran Confessions* (Philadelphia: Fortress Press, 1961), pp. 1-36; in Holsten Fagenberg, *A New Look at the Lutheran Confessions* (St. Louis: Concordia Publishing House, 1972), pp. 15-58; and in Eric W. Gritsch and Robert W. Jenson, *Lutheranism: The Theological Movement and its Confessional Writings* (Philadelphia: Fortress Press, 1976), pp. 2-16.

28. Although there is no article in the Book of Concord on the doctrine of the Sacred Scriptures, the nature of scriptural authority for the church is touched on in the Formula of Concord, Summary Rule and Norm; see both Epitome and Solid Declaration. These paragraphs seem to envision a kind of hierarchy of authority: Scripture, the creeds, the Augsburg Confession, the other confessional writings, and, in some sense, the body of Luther's writings as further explication. In this connection, see Warren A. Quanbeck, "The Formula of Concord and Authority in the Church," *Sixteenth Century Journal* VIII, 4 (1977). See also Arthur Carl Piepkorn, "Suggested Principles for a Hermeneutics of the Lutheran Symbols," *Concordia Theological Monthly*

XXIX, no. 1 (January 1958): 1-24.
29. See especially Carl Ferdinand Wilhelm Walther, "Why Should Our Pastors, Teachers, and Professors Subscribe Unconditionally to the Symbolical Writings of Our Church," trans. and abridged Alex Wm. C. Guebert, CTM XVIII (April 1947): 241 ff.
30. Walter E. Lammerts, past president of the Creation Research Society and a former editor of the society's Journal and other publications, states as the conclusion of the society's members "that the remarkable features of life and the various living creatures could result only from the creative design of a supreme being whom we Christians know as our Lord and Savior Jesus Christ." Walter E. Lammerts, ed., *Scientific Studies in Special Creation* (n.p.: Presbyterian and Reformed Publishing Co., 1971), p. viii. Members of the Society come from several denominations, including also Lutherans.
31. Both citations are from Luther's explanation to the first article of the Apostolic Creed, SC II, 1.
32. The charge of quietism, or of non-involvement in secular or political affairs, was raised frequently in criticism of the failure of many Lutherans to become involved in the resistance movement against the Hitler regime, or to have worked to combat his rise to power in the first place.
33. The phrase is from SC II, 1.
34. The imagery, which Luther employed frequently, was a common one of the times.
35. The motif of delight in God's creation is central to many of the hymns of the renowned Lutheran hymn writer, Paul Gerhardt (1607–1676).
36. LW 35, 370.
37. See vol. I, this series, pp. 120-121, for the work of St. Augustine.
38. Luther's distinction between "hidden God" and "revealed God" has passed into regular use in much of Lutheran theology. By "hidden God" is meant the God of speculative theology, God "as he is in himself," God understood or described in any terms other than as he is revealed in the suffering and crucified Jesus. As we shall see below, this has profound effects on Lutheran Christology. For the use of the terms

in Luther, see Gerhard Ebeling, "God Hidden and Revealed," in *Luther: An Introduction to His Thought* (Philadelphia: Fortress Press, 1970). See also Werner Elert, *The Structure of Lutheranism* I (St. Louis: Concordia Publishing House, 1962): 71-73, 108, 118, *et passim*.
39. Romans 4:15.
40. WA XL, 1; 256.15.
41. Romans 14:23.
42. Apol IV, 9, 44, 48, 154, 299, *et passim*.
43. See vol. I, this series, pp. 3-4, 13.
44. The reference is to the symbol *Quicunque vult*, the "Athanasian" Creed.
45. The text is printed in vol. I, this series, 149-151.
46. On Chalcedon, see Jaroslav J. Pelikan, *The Emergence of the Catholic Tradition* (Chicago: University of Chicago Press, 1971), pp. 263-266.
47. This motif recurs frequently and in varied form in Luther's Christology; see, e.g., LW 24, 61, 141; see also FC SD VIII, 81-84.
48. This concern is expressed particularly in FC SD VIII, 78, 87.
49. FC SD VIII, 87.
50. FC SD VII, 55.
51. English translation by Jacob A. O. Preus, *Two Natures in Christ* (St. Louis: Concordia Publishing House, 1971). See the extensive review of this edition by Arthur Carl Piepkorn, *Concordia Theological Monthly* XLIV (May 1973): 218-226.
52. FC SD VIII, 87.
53. AC IV.
54. See vol. I, this series, pp. 121-122.
55. These two criteria are the recurring standards to which Melanchthon appeals in Apology IV.
56. Apol IV, 20-21, 60.
57. The German version of the Augsburg Confession speaks of "forgiveness of sins" and "becoming righteous"; the Latin of "justification" and "being justified."
58. Apol IV, 291, 297.
59. Apol IV, 291.
60. Apol IV, 12.
61. Apol IV, 69-70.
62. Apol IV, 18, 81.
63. See, e.g., Apol IV, 68.
64. Apol IV, 5.
65. Apol IV, 5, 291.
66. Apol IV, 43-70.

67. Apol IV, 70. See also Apol XIII, 20: "A promise is useless unless faith accepts it."
68. Apol IV, 55.
69. Apol IV, 50.
70. Apol IV, 68.
71. Apol IV, 382.
72. Apol IV, 69-72.
73. FC SD III, 13.
74. Apol IV, 2.
75. Apol IV, 72.
76. Apol IV, 72.
77. Apol IV, 78.
78. Apol IV, 86.
79. In the twentieth century, one thinks of the virtual inability even of the 1963 Helsinki Assembly of the Lutheran World Rederation to adopt a common statement on "justification today." See *Messages of the Helsinki Assembly: "Christ Today"* (Minneapolis: Augsburg Publishing House, n.d.), esp. the Foreword, p. v.
80. E.g., Romans 1 and 2.
81. Apol IV, 81.
82. See, e.g., Robert C. Schultz, "Baptism and Justification," *Una Sancta*, XVII (Easter 1960), esp. pp. 11-14.
83. II Corinthians 6:9.
84. Romans 6:4.
85. This motif, according to which human sin is realistically predicated of Christ, so that Christ's righteousness may realistically be predicated of the believer, plays a sizable role in Luther's *Lectures on Galatians*; cf. LW 26, 159-160, 164, 280-282, *et passim* .
86. Apol XII, 59.
87. AC XX, 8; Apol IV, 2; SA II, I, 1.5; FC SD III, 6.
88. Apol IV, 120.
89. Apol IV, 2.

BIBLIOGRAPHY

GENERAL

The Encyclopedia of the Lutheran Church. Ed. Julius Bodensieck for the Lutheran World Federation. Minneapolis: Augsburg Publishing House, 1965.

Mayer, Frederick E. *The Religious Bodies of America.* 4th ed., revised by Arthur Carl Piepkorn. St. Louis: Concordia Publishing House, 1961. Part III: The Lutheran Church, pp. 127-196; see especially the extensive bibliography, pp. 192-196.

LUTHERAN REFORMATION AND SYMBOLICAL BOOKS

PRIMARY SOURCES

The Book of Concord. Trans. and ed. Theodore G. Tappert, in association with Robert H. Fischer, Jaroslav J. Pelikan, and Arthur Carl Piepkorn. Philadelphia: Fortress Press, 1959.

Luther's Works. American Edition. Ed. Jaroslav J. Pelikan and Helmut T. Lehmann. 56 vols. St. Louis: Concordia Publishing House, and Philadelphia: Fortress Press, 1957 ff.

ADDITIONAL SOURCES

Althaus, Paul. *The Ethics of Martin Luther.* Trans. Robert C. Schultz. Philadelphia: Fortress Press, 1972.

————. *The Theology of Martin Luther.* Trans. Robert C. Schultz. Philadelphia: Fortress Press, 1966.

Bente, F. *Historical Introductions to the Book of Concord.* St. Louis: Concordia Publishing House, [1921].

Bohlmann, Ralph W. *Principles of Biblical Interpretation in the Lutheran Confessions.* St. Louis: Concordia Publishing House, 1968.

Ebeling, Gerhard. *Luther: An Introduction to His Thought.* Trans. R. A. Wilson. Philadelphia: Fortress Press, 1970.

Elert, Werner. *The Structure of Lutheranism.* Trans. Walter A. Hansen. St. Louis:

Concordia Publishing House, 1962.

Fagerberg, Holsten. *A New Look at the Lutheran Confessions.* Trans. Gene Lund. St. Louis: Concordia Publishing House, 1972.

Gritsch, Eric W., and Jenson, Robert W. *Lutheranism: The Theological Movement and Its Confessional Writings.* Philadelphia: Fortress Press, 1976.

Krauth, Charles Porterfield. *The Conservative Reformation and Its Theology.* Original ed. 1871; reprinted Minneapo-

lis: Augsburg Publishing House, [1963].

Reu, Johann Michael. *The Augsburg Confession: A Collection of Sources with an Historical Introduction.* Chicago: Wartburg Publishing House, 1930.

Schlink, Edmund. *Theology of the Lutheran Confessions.* Trans. Paul F. Koehneke and Herbert J. A. Bouman. Philadelphia: Fortress Press, 1961.

Schwiebert, Ernest G. *Luther and His Times.* St. Louis: Concordia Publishing House, 1950.

SELECTED TOPICS

Chemnitz, Martin. *The Two Natures in Christ* [1578]. Trans. J. A. O. Preus. St. Louis: Concordia Publishing House, 1971.

Piepkorn, Arthur Carl. "Do the Lutheran Symbolical Books Speak Where the Sacred Scriptures Are Silent?" *Concordia Theological Monthly,* XLIII (January 1972): 29-35.

————. "Suggested Principles for a Hermeneutics of the Lutheran Symbols," *Concordia Theological Monthly* XXIX (January 1958); 1-24.

Walther, Carl Ferdinand Wilhelm. *The Proper Distinction between Law and Gospel.* Trans. W. H. T. Dau. St. Louis: Concordia Publishing House, [1928].

3. Nature and Function of the Church

The Church

Lutheranism's self-conscious determination to have its contemporary witness to the Gospel shaped and normed by the concerns and the language of the Symbolical Books is seldom as sorely tested as in its theology of the church. Many of the familiar terms and categories for contemporary language about the church simply do not appear in the Symbolical Books, and the terms which do appear serve for Lutherans both to call much of present talk about the church into question, and to provide the basis for serious discussion about the nature and mission of the church in an increasingly secular and pluralistic age.

The present discussion can hardly claim to be exhaustive. It will summarize those elements in the theology of the church which emerge from a study of the Symbolical Books, only occasionally drawing on critical and contemporary comments.

Because the doctrine of the church was one of the main controverted points in the time of the Wittenberg Reformation, the contribution of the Symbolical Books to Lutheranism's understanding of the church is complicated by controversy. Also, because the documents contained in the Symbolical Books arose in distinct periods, it will be necessary especially in this point to proceed with care—in order always to read the documents in the sense that their words conveyed to the people by and for whom they were originally written. Accordingly, we shall first discuss the ancient ecumenical creeds, then those symbols which come from Luther's pen, then those from the pen of Philipp Melanchthon, and finally the Formula of Concord.

The present-day baptismal (Apostles') and eucharistic (Nicene) creeds[1] stress a combination of "spiritual" and "empirical" aspects of the church's existence which receive further development in the particular Lutheran symbols of the sixteenth century. The reference to the church as holy entered the creedal formulae at a very early date, linked with a reference to the Holy (that is both sacred and sanctifying) Spirit or to the forgiveness of sins, or to both, as to cause and effect. The church is also called "catholic," the first such reference apparently being St. Ignatius' Letter to the Smyrnaeans

(8:2). Accordingly, *the* church exists wherever *a* church exists. But *the* church is also orthodox, not heretical or sectarian.

In this connection the phrase *sanctorum communio* (usually translated "communion of saints") in the baptismal creed requires special mention. From pre-Reformation times until the end of the nineteenth century, Western Christendom (including the authors of the particular Lutheran symbols) held that the baptismal creed described the church as a *sanctorum communio*—consistently taking the *sanctorum* as a masculine and giving *communio* a predominantly corporative interpretation. Evidence accumulated since the beginning of this century seems, however, to urge the possibility that: (1) *sanctorum communio* was not originally an apposition to *sancta ecclesia catholica* (the holy catholic church), but a separate article of the creed; (2) *sanctorum* is not masculine, but neuter, and hence to be translated not "saints" but "holy things," that is, either the Holy Eucharist or the sacraments in general; (3) *communio* does not mean "communion with the saints," nor does it designate a society or community, but it refers to the benefits that God confers upon those who participate in the Holy Eucharist (or the sacraments in general). But however the term is explained, *communio* must be taken in a dynamic rather than a static sense. It is a sharing, a taking part with other Christians, in the holy things that make them one, rather than a mere abstract being-in-association with other individuals. Being in the church is to live as part of a process in which there is constant forgiveness of the sins constantly committed by people who are simultaneously sinners and holy people. Those who are being constantly *declared* holy by God's grace for Christ's sake through faith are constantly *becoming* holy by God's grace for Christ's sake through faith.[2]

The unity which the creeds confess about the church is seen, not as an administrative or organizational unity, which the church of that time did not know except on a regional basis, but as a unity of the sacraments, of worship, of confession. Such unity was not of human creation; it was something given by God.

Similarly, the apostolicity of the church was an affirmation of the church's historic character. It was a commitment to the apostolic ministry, a traceable linkage of ministry of word and sacrament to a church founded by one of the apostles. Apostolicity was thus an empirical characteristic of the church.

Thus the baptismal and the eucharistic creeds agree in their conception of a dynamic church which is simultaneously, on the one hand, empirical and phenomenal and perceptible with the bodily senses and, on the other hand, spiritual and perceptible only in its effects and only to faith. It is significant that at this early period the church sensed no contradiction in the assertion of these paradoxical ideas about itself.

The paradox of empiricality and spirituality in the church's self-understanding receives similar stress in the particular Lutheran symbols. When Luther's Small Catechism puts the baptismal creed into German, it follows the precedent of fifteenth-century vernacular versions, rendering *ein heilige christliche Kirche, die Gemeine der Heiligen* (one holy Christian church, the community of holy people). No deliberate alteration of meaning should here be supposed. The "holy Christian church" is no less empirical than the "holy catholic church," and it is no less catholic than other Christians confess it to be. The church is not only one and holy, but also catholic and therefore empirical. And when Luther uses the words *Gemeine* and *Christenheit* he is also referring simply to the holy community by which the Holy Spirit brings people to faith and which it uses to put the Gospel into effect by which it creates and increases holiness.[3]

The title of Article XII of Part Three of the Smalcald Articles reads "Of the Church." And in that article occurs the famous manifesto, "We do not concede that [the papalist opponents] are the church, for they are not." Here the antithesis must be kept in mind. The adversaries profess to be *the* church and condemn as heretics all those not in communion with the pope. That insistence is here rejected categorically. Thereupon follows, "A child of seven years [the canonical age of reason] knows what the church is, namely, holy believers and sheep who hear the Shepherd's voice."[4] This is clearly no exhaustive definition of the church; the sense is that the church is characterized by adherence not to the See of Rome but to Christ.

Luther also links the church with the Kingdom of God or of Christ, though he doesn't identify the church with the Kingdom. The Kingdom of God is more inclusive than the church, because while the church exists in time, the Kingdom of God is eternal. The church is at best the Kingdom of God in its temporal aspect, but the line that divides the Kingdom of God from the Kingdom of Satan cuts across the church and also through the individual believer. It is to Christians that the Large Catechism says, "You are daily under the dominion of the devil, who neither day nor night relaxes his efforts to steal upon you unawares and to kindle in your heart unbelief and wicked thoughts against all these commandments [of the Decalogue]."[5]

If one examines all the direct and indirect references to the church in the symbols that come from Luther's pen, one finds ascribed to the church such a variety of attributes and activities that we cannot define the church either wholly in empirical terms or wholly in spiritual terms; each description is to be affirmed in such a way that it includes the other. For Luther it is, finally, the hearing and speaking of the Word of God that locates the church.

In the symbols that come from the pen of lay theologian Philipp Melanchthon, the vocabulary is markedly different from Luther's, but the emphases are consistently similar. We find references to the catholic church, the universal church, sometimes the whole church both in contrast to the territorial churches and also in distinction from the sectaries which hold a doctrine of God different from the Scriptures and Nicene orthodoxy. The stress on the empirical is unmistakable. Decisive is the sort of language used in the Apology of the Augsburg Confession: "[The church] is made up of people scattered throughout the world who agree on the Gospel and have the same Christ, the same Holy Spirit, and the same sacraments, whether they have the same human traditions or not."[6] That simply repeats the basic confession at Augsburg: "It is also taught among us that one holy Christian church will be and remain for all time. This is the assembly of all believers, among whom the Gospel is preached in its purity and the holy sacraments are administered according to the Gospel."[7]

Still, the Lutheran symbols recognize that until the end of time false Christians and hypocrites will remain among the pious as members of the church. Thus statements about the church are regularly bipolar. The church is not only a body politic of good and evil people or an association of external matters and rites like other governments but in principle it is an association of faith and of the Holy Spirit in the hearts, yet identifiable by external notes or marks. Lutherans explicitly reject the idea that sees the church as a Platonic, ideal state. The church is oppressed and threatened with destruction by endless perils; suffers from damnably false teaching that Satan has sown in its midst; is disturbed by impious dogmas; is divided by the bishops; is plagued by canon law; has Antichrist reigning within her; institutes traditions; baptizes; condemns heresies; engages in corporate, public prayer; sings sequence hymns; prays collects; teaches; administers sacraments; calls and ordains priests; absolves; exercises discipline.

This variety of uses for the term "church" underscores the fact that a simple pattern of analysis cannot be coaxed out of the Symbolical Books. Concrete and empirical, yet spiritual and characterized by faithful teaching and hearing of the Gospel and celebration of the sacraments, the church exists in time, scattered, yet one and holy, catholic and apostolic.

The church is surely one, according to the Lutheran symbols. And that remains a scandalous assertion from the century of splits in the church. Yet the church's unity is always distinguished from organizational integrity or harmony. For true unity, the Augusburg Confession avers, it is enough to agree in teaching the Gospel and administering the sacraments.[8] It is not necessary that human traditions, including matters of polity and organization, be everywhere alike. This "true unity" is crucial; without it faith cannot come into existence and people cannot become righteous before God.[9] The objective of human institutions and ordinances is organizational integrity and external union or at least intercommunion—an important and ongoing agenda. "True unity" is God-given; organizational integrity must be worked on by Christians.

The ecclesiology of the Formula of Concord is significant not because it adds anything substantially new to the views of the older symbols—it does not—but because it comes out of a period in which the ecclesiological problem had been intensified by the course of events. The schism between the Lutheran and the papalist parties had hardened. Much of the theology against which the reformers had protested had achieved organizational embodiment at the Council of Trent in the Roman Catholic Church. The Lutheran movement felt itself quite barely to have been rescued from disintegration through valiant efforts by princes and theologians. And in areas affected by the more radical reformations the fragmentation of Western Christianity was proceeding apace. In the face of it all, the Formula adds nothing new to the tension of the earlier symbols between the empirical and the spiritual, or to the dynamic idea of a community gathered around the sanctifying Word of the Gospel and the celebration of the sacraments.

Thus the Formula speaks of a church in which there are lay and clergy;[10] the latter as ministers of the Word preside over the community of God.[11] This community exists in space and time,[12] but it cannot be narrowly equated with a parish or a voluntary local congregation. And the Formula specifically commits itself to the ecclesiology of the earlier Symbolical Books by citing their explanations of the doctrine of the church with approval.[13]

In all, what emerges is a view according to which in this world one can know the church only in her present aspect, worshiping and serving, suffering and struggling.

Divine Election

The doctrine of divine election, often indiscriminately called predestination, was a focus of debate and controversy among adherents of the Augsburg Confession both in Germany in the sixteenth century and in America in the late nineteenth and early twentieth centuries.[14] As a result, the theology of American Lutherans concerning the election of grace has been rather carefully and distinctively nuanced, a fact which the relative lack of dogmatic interest in the topic in recent years would seem to belie.

The point of departure in the Symbolical Books for their summary of the biblical teaching on the election of grace is found in this statement of the Formula of Concord: "The Christian is to concern himself with the doctrine of the eternal election of God only insofar as it is revealed in the Word of God, which shows us Christ as the 'book of life.' "[15] To the extent that any discussion of election is judged distinctively Lutheran, it will have this assertion at its core. From this assertion grow the decisive emphases of a theology of election based on and informed by the Symbolical Books.

Against the antithesis of Calvin's theology of predestination in the sixteenth century, the Lutheran confessors felt constrained both to stress the universality of the love of God and of his gracious will, as well as decisively to reject any hint of a predestination to damnation. Those affirmations are held in admitted tension by Lutherans—a tension they sense as unavoidable if they are to maintain the first assertion about the need to consider the matter of election only in Christ and not outside him. One could, of course, speculate about the hidden will of God. But Lutherans hold that Christian theology deals with what God has revealed in his living and spoken and written Word in Christ and the Gospel and the Sacred Scriptures. Therefore the "terrible decree" of Calvin's theology is dismissed as groundless speculation, while at the same time grounds are found for asserting the sole activity of God's grace in bringing human beings to salvation. In fact, the idea of "decree" is studiously avoided; in its place one reads of "choice" and "gracious giving."[16]

Lutherans understand divine election as embracing the whole scope of God's saving work. "We must always take as one unit the entire doctrine of God's purpose, counsel, will and ordinance concerning our redemption, call, justification, and salvation,"[17] says the Formula of Concord in a rather densely piled collection of nouns. To unpack the contents of that affirmation, the Formula goes on to list eight points by which it intends to summarize its understanding of what it is that God has chosen and willed to accomplish. Accordingly, for Lutherans election includes God's counsel and purpose (1) to redeem humankind and to reconcile all human beings with God through Christ's innocent obedience, suffering, and death; (2) to communicate these merits and benefits of Christ to us through his Word and the sacraments; (3) to be present with his Holy Spirit through the Word preached, heard, and meditated on, and to be active in us to convert us to true repentance and to enlighten our hearts with genuine faith; (4) to justify all those who accept Christ in true repentance through genuine faith and to receive them into grace as sons and daughters and heirs of eternal life; (5) to hallow in love those whom he thus justifies; (6) to protect them in their great weakness against the devil, the world, and their own flesh, direct them in his ways, raise them up when they stumble, and comfort and preserve them in cross and afflictions; (7) to confirm and increase the good work that he began in them and preserve it in them until their life's end, provided that they adhere to God's Word, pray diligently, remain in God's goodness, and make faithful use of the gifts they have received; and finally (8) to make those whom he has chosen, called, and justified eternally blessed and glorious in the life everlasting.

The proviso called for in the seventh item deserves special attention. This condition, if one may call it that, appears several times in the Formula of Concord's discussion of election: "if we ourselves do not turn away," and "if they will return to him in true repentance and through a right faith."[18] This proviso is to be brought together with the insight of an earlier article (II) of the Formula, that baptized Christians have a freed will (*liberatum arbitrium*), and that as soon as the Holy Spirit has begun his work of rebirth and renewal in a person, that person can and must cooperate with him through the powers that he confers.[19] Far from any kind of synergism,[20] this proviso simply takes realistically the promise that God does in fact mean it when he offers forgiveness of sins and new life to those who repent and believe the Gospel.

There is repeated emphasis on the place of Word and sacrament in this understanding of divine election. Both the proviso just mentioned and the third item listed above make this point, along with numerous other references to the Gospel and the means of grace. Lutherans hold that Christ does not arrange to have the promise of the Gospel offered to people merely in general, but has appended the sacraments as seals of the promise, and thereby confirms the election of every single believer individually. On this account, the Formula observes, we retain individual absolution for our individual comfort; this comfort we should not have if we could not argue from the call that we encounter through the Word and through the sacraments to the will of God toward us. God has sworn our election with an oath and has sealed it with the sacraments. In this light, the proviso of the seventh point means that, in terms of the practice of the life of faith, we are in effect elected to a faithful and effective use of the means of grace.

It is significant, too, that the Lutheran understanding of election stresses in particular the use that is to be made of the doctrine for the comfort of troubled consciences. Against the sense of one's own unworthiness, and against the temptation of the devil, the world, and one's own flesh, the doctrine of the eternal election of God underscores the deepness of God's concern and the utter seriousness of his good intentions. "In his counsel before the foundation of the world God has determined and decreed that he will assist us in all our necessities, grant us patience, give us comfort, create hope, and bring everything to such an issue that we shall be saved."[21] To say that God's choice occurred "before the foundation of the world" is then not a lapse into a deterministic worldview, but a reminder that God acts consequently also according to his gracious will, a reminder that "in Christ" he carries out what he wishes and promises to accomplish. Lutherans see it, therefore, as purely a confession of faith to join St. Paul in saying that one is chosen "in Christ before the foundation of the world,"[22] for such a statement fastens solely to God as he is revealed in Christ. What God determined to do in Christ includes each "me" who trusts the Gospel. And that means that for Lutherans the certainty of election, as the high point of the certainty of salvation, is especially comforting.

Another side of the Lutheran understanding of election must be mentioned. In their struggle to use the election of grace for comfort and assurance and against despair, the Lutheran confessors do not fail also to use it against complacency. Embodied in the very idea of election (Greek *ekloge,* a choosing-out-of) is the ugly antithesis of the prior condition. Salvation is *from* something. The Christian has an unavoidable sense of having been rescued from what is evil and perishing. "I chose you out of the world"[23] was Christ's statement to the disciples. Thus the conditional clause in the seventh point above, along with its parallels, has as its obverse the awful possibility of eternal loss—in the spirit of a St. Paul who, conscious that he is a "chosen vessel,"[24] is still aware of the possibility that he who preached the Gospel to others might himself become unworthy,[25] and who warns his readers, "Let anyone who thinks that he stands take heed lest he fall."[26] True, God's call and purpose, which cannot fail or be overthrown, protects the faithful even against the weakness and malice of their own flesh,[27] so that no one can tear them out of the Good Shepherd's hand and no creature can separate them from the love of Christ. Yet Lutherans can see Judas Iscariot as a reminder of the fact that even one upon whom the choice of God's own Son has fallen possesses the awful power to say a final No to God. Both aspects are affirmed in II Timothy 2:19: "God's firm foundation stands, having this seal, 'The Lord knows those who are his.'" And, "Let every one who names the Name of the Lord depart from iniquity."[28]

Finally, the Lutheran understanding of election recognizes that God's choice of an individual does not leave him an isolated individual, but embeds him into the social and corporate context of the church, and there obligates and enables him to responsibility and service, not to position and privilege. This frequently recurring biblical theme, surfacing for example in the label "light for the nations,"[29] for God's chosen Israel, counters all tendencies toward privatism and individualism which might otherwise so easily infect a theology of divine election.

The controversy which raged among Lutherans in North America between 1872 and 1925[30] was particularly virulent and served mainly to underscore but one facet of divine election, namely, that it is solely God's gracious action, without consideration of anything meritorious in the chosen person. In fact, that controversy was more about synergism, human cooperation in the work of salvation, than directly about divine election. As a result, the literature of some strains of American Lutheranism seems to content itself with the affirmation of this one point, omitting the evangelical, Christocentric thrust of the Formula of Concord and underplaying both the comfort which the doctrine intends to offer and the impulse it gives toward faithful and effective use of the Gospel and the sacraments within the context of the church. Similarly, some catechetical literature which makes use of the biblical image of the "Book of Life" in this connection, fails to make the identification of that Book of Life with Christ and his Gospel,[31] in whom and from which people learn of God's gracious election.

Sacraments

Lutherans understand themselves, as they do the earliest church, to be a sacramental church. They assert that the ancient creeds are thoroughly sacramental, the Apostolic Creed being originally a baptismal symbol whose phrase *communio sanctorum* can also be taken as a neuter "communion of holy things," that is, a sacramentally established fellowship, and the Nicene Creed relating the forgiveness of sins to sacramental experience in its declaration, "I acknowledge one Baptism for the remission of sins." Thus Lutherans do not want to be construed merely as a church of the word, as if the pairing "word and sacrament" could be dissolved without great loss to the faith and life of the church.

The sacramental thought of the Church of the Augsburg Confession is necessarily affected by the fact that "sacrament" in the sense in which theology uses it is not a scriptural term. Although the Greek *mysterion* is employed some thirty times in the New Testament, *mysterion* as the equivalent of "sacrament" as used in Western Christianity is not employed by the sacred writers. In discussing the nature and number of the sacraments, therefore, there are no inspired definitions, only ecclesiastical distinctions. St. Thomas Aquinas and the Council of Lyons in 1274 fixed the number at seven.[32] When the question was reopened at the time of the Reformation, the Apology of the Augsburg Confession declared in favor of three primary sacraments—baptism, Eucharist, and absolution—and it was willing to grant the name in a secondary sense to marriage, ordination, confirmation, and unction, provided these were understood evangelically and distinguished from the three chief sacraments.[33]

Lutherans affirm the necessity of the sacraments, and, in doing so, also stress their primary dynamic significance as actions rather than things—actions of God. In this connection, Lutheran theology emphasizes the coordination of word and sacrament in its willingness to speak of the sacraments as *verbum visibile* (visible word) and of the word as *sacramentum audible* (audible sacrament). In both, the decisive element is the divine mandate to *do* the sacrament, and the divine promise of grace *through* the sacrament. The Apology of the Augsburg Confession names that element when it calls baptism, Eucharist, and absolution the three chief sacraments; "for these rites have the commandment of God and the promise of grace, which is the heart of the New Testament."[34] Or again, they are "rites which have the command of God and to which the promise of grace has been added."[35] Institution by God and evangelical purpose are decisive.

This means that Lutherans stress the need for faith if the sacraments are to be used properly. The idea that the sacraments convey grace *ex opere operato,* by the mere performance of the deed, is rejected. "Thus we teach that in using the sacraments there must be a faith which believes these promises and accepts that which is promised and offered in the sacrament. The reason for this is clear and well founded. A promise is useless unless faith accepts it. The sacraments are signs of the promises. When they are used, therefore, there must be faith."[36] For Lutherans, faith in the sacrament, and not the sacrament alone, justifies. Thus the proper human bearing in relation to the sacraments is receptivity, trust in the promises. Any sense of magic or any focus on the mere performance of the rite would seem to change the human being from a recipient of God's grace to a coercer of God's grace—in other words, would be blasphemy and not faith. The correlatives, once more, are promise and faith—for the comfort of the sinner's conscience.

Holy Baptism

Lutheranism's mind on the sacrament of holy baptism is spoken most concisely in the Augsburg Confession, "It is taught among us that Baptism is necessary and that grace is offered through it. Children, too, should be baptized, for in Baptism they are committed to God and become acceptable to him."[37] Because of that affirmation, it was the practice in the churches of the Augsburg Confession for a long time after the Reformation to baptize a child on the day of his birth. And that practice reflects the seriousness with which Lutherans view the sacrament.

The baptized person receives God's grace through the sacrament and becomes acceptable to God thereby. The visible word does what the spoken word does: it reconciles the sinner to God and makes the believer acceptable to God. Like the Gospel in any other form, it is able to accomplish the divine purpose. It receives the candidate into the Christian community, the fellowship of all those who faithfully receive the grace of God. The human being is the receiver, the one acted upon; God is the giver, the donor, the actor in the sacrament.

Lutheran sacramental realism insists that holy baptism is not merely a symbolic enactment of God's acceptance of the candidate but the very action of that acceptance. For Lutherans, baptism is not a rite that signifies the candidate's coming to faith, his joining of the fellowship, his self-dedication or confession of loyalty. It is, rather, the sign and the reality of God's gracious will, of the godly promise of "forgiveness of sins and eternal salvation."[38] And the baptized person thereby receives what the promise offers. He is incorporated, accepted into the body of Christ. Less a rite of entrance, baptism is more a rite of incorporation and acceptance.

Baptism is water, to be sure. Lutherans have historically insisted on at least the trine affusion of water in such quantity that it runs. (Sprinkling, as that is usually understood among Protestants, is discountenanced.) However, baptism is not "simply water," but water in connection with God's Word offering forgiveness of sins, life, and salvation. God's Word makes the water a baptism: "God himself stakes his honor, his power, and his might on it."[39]

The effect of baptism is to save, to deliver from sin and death and the devil, to bring one into the rule of Christ. This is no compromise of the role of faith, of justification "by grace, for Christ's sake, through faith."[40] Faith trusts the God who commands baptism and promises deliverance. The stress on faith is simply the obverse of the stress on God's gracious action in the sacrament.

As the sacrament of acceptance into the church, Lutherans affirm that baptism should be administered in the church before the congregation of the faithful. Lutherans therefore admit the importance of ceremony in connection with such administration of baptism. The use of an initial exorcism is appropriate: "Depart thou unclean spirit and make room for the Holy Spirit."[41] The use of the white baptismal mantle has survived or been restored in numerous parishes, as has the giving of the candle to the candidate or chief sponsor with words such as "Receive the Light of Christ and see that you keep unspotted your baptismal purity."[42]

Baptism is meant to be used, Lutherans hold, in daily contrition and repentance; that is the way to make faithful use of baptismal grace. The

Small Catechism directs the head of the family to instruct the members of his household to bless themselves morning and evening in this fashion: "In the morning when you get up, and in the evening when you retire, you shall bless yourself with the Sign of the Holy Cross and say, 'In the Name of the Father and of the Son and of the Holy Ghost. Amen.' Then, kneeling or standing, repeat the Creed and the Lord's Prayer; if you wish, you may also say the little prayer, *I Thank Thee*."[43] This brief office is closely related to the sacrament of holy baptism, and is, in effect, the ritual carrying out of the Small Catechism's affirmation about the significance of baptism, "that the old Adam in us, together with all sins and evil lusts, should be drowned by daily sorrow and repentance and be put to death, and that the new man should come forth daily and rise up, cleansed and righteous, to live forever in God's presence."[44] Thereupon Romans 6:4 is quoted. In the morning and evening blessing, the Sign of the Holy Cross corresponds to the Signing with the Holy Cross at baptism with the formula, "Receive the Sign of the Holy Cross both upon the forehead and upon the breast, in token that you have been redeemed by Christ the Crucified."[45] The trinitarian invocation reminds that one was baptized "In the Name of the Father and of the Son and of the Holy Ghost." The Apostles' Creed has from its inception been the baptismal symbol, and its use is to remind one of baptism's divine gift of faith. The "Our Father" recalls that in order to implore the blessing of Almighty God upon the baptized person, the minister laid his hands on the candidate's head and bade the congregation pray with him the "Our Father" with special intention for the candidate's eternal salvation. Such daily consecration and daily pleading of the merits of Christ become the way for living in the grace of holy baptism.

Already in the sixteenth century the idea of baptismal regeneration became a bone of contention among the various movements for reform. Here Lutherans have with unanimity affirmed the apostolic words: it is a "washing of regeneration and renewal in the Holy Spirit."[46] Similarly. Lutherans have in mind the statement of Jesus to Nicodemus: "Unless one is born of water and the Spirit, he cannot enter the kingdom of God."[47] For Lutherans, the essence of baptismal faith is the trust that what God here promises, that he here fulfills.

The Sacrament of the Altar

The theology of the sacrament of the altar among Lutherans has been strongly affected by the numerous and vigorous struggles and controversies over that doctrine in the sixteenth century. As such, the nuances in theological statements about the Holy Communion are frequently more technical, more fine, more carefully worked-out than in many other doctrines. The present discussion will therefore first seek to discuss the sacrament in positive terms, then with reference to the polemics with the Swiss and South German reformers, and then in its polemical formulation in opposition to post-Tridentine Roman Catholic developments. Then there will be attention to some especially problematic areas.

The Lutheran understanding of the Holy Eucharist can be summarized in a series of positive affirmations.

1. Jesus Christ himself instituted the sacrament of the altar as a ceremony and a sign which the church was to continue.[48] This and subsequent affirmations are based on a straightforward reading of the four biblical accounts of the words of institution.[49]

2. The sacrament of the altar is the body and blood of Jesus Christ.[50] When, regularly, the Symbolical Books prefix the words "true" or "truly," they follow medieval usage to distinguish the body of Christ in the sacrament from the mystical body the church, and they affirm (especially with the adverb "truly") the reality of the presence of the body and blood of Christ in contrast to a merely symbolical element. Thus the Augsburg Confession states, "The true Body and Blood of Christ are really present in the Supper of our Lord under the form of bread and wine and are there distributed and received."[51] And the Small Catechism of Luther says, "It is the true Body and Blood of our Lord Jesus Christ, for us Christians to eat and to drink."[52] Most explicit is the statement (also from Luther's pen) in the Smalcald Articles: "The bread and wine in the Supper are the true Body and Blood of Christ, and . . . these are given and received not only by godly but also by wicked Christians."[53]

3. In all this the Lutheran symbols are concerned to be preserving catholic doctrine. Accordingly, the symbols stress participation in Holy Communion. They affirm the indispensable importance of the sacrament of the altar as a means of communicating salvation and redemption. They stress the essentially corporate nature of the Holy Eucharist, as well as the value of reception in both kinds. The Lutheran symbols claim to be affirming the position of the primitive church of the East and of the West: "Whoever eats this bread eats the Body of Christ. This has also been the unanimous teaching of the leading church fathers, such as Ss. John of the Golden Mouth, Cyprian, Leo the Great, Ambrose, and Augustine."[54]

4. The Lutheran symbols are concerned that the sacraments be received. Against the long trend toward decreasing Communions, the Lutheran reformers insisted that every Mass had to be a community Mass and that at every celebration there ought to be communicants who received from the elements there consecrated. The net effect of this radical departure from conventional practice was twofold. It increased the opportunities for Holy Communion to every Sunday and major holy day, and other occasions when the people wished;[55] and it radically decreased the number of ferial Masses, while still clearly contemplating the possibility of daily celebrations.[56] In this connection pastors are urged to preach winsomely on the benefits of frequent Communion, and the faithful are warned to regard lack of desire for

the sacrament of the altar as a serious symptom of moribund spirituality.[57] Since a communicant's fitness to receive the sacrament consists wholly in one's contrition and faith in the promise of Christ, the Large Catechism can quote St. Hilary of Poitiers in favor of a reception of the Holy Communion by every qualified communicant at every celebration.[58]

5. The Lutheran Reformation, taking its cue from Christ's command "This do," and from St. Paul's "As often as you eat this bread and drink this cup,"[59] stressed the dynamic rather than the static element in the sacrament. Reception is preferred to veneration: "Nothing has the character of a sacrament apart from the use of it which Christ instituted."[60]

6. The essentially social and corporate, not individualistic, character of the sacrament of the altar is extensively stressed. Therefore, a priest's right to celebrate the Holy Eucharist privately even for the laudible purpose of receiving Holy Communion is rejected.[61]

7. The benefit of a fruitful reception of the sacrament of the altar is understood by Lutherans as the "forgiveness of sins, life, and salvation."[62] A great variety of other terms appear in the Symbolical Books to describe this benefit. One may cite the following: through Holy Communion strained consciences find comfort, faith is strengthened, Christ's benefits are recalled and received by faith, we are assured of being joined with Christ and washed with his blood; the sacrament of the altar is a remedy against sin, flesh, devil, world, death, danger, and hell; it is a safeguard against death and all misfortune, and a pure and soothing medicine which aids and quickens the recipient in soul and body; it bestows grace, life, Christ, God, and everything good.[63]

One of the focal points for the polemical development of the Lutheran doctrine of the sacrament of the altar was the debate with the Swiss and South German reformers. In contrast to the sacramental realism of Luther and the Wittenberg reformers such opponents as the Münzerite "Heavenly Prophets" of Zwickau, Andrew Bodenstein von Carlstadt, Huldreich Zwingli, John Oecolampadius, and other Swiss and South German reformers (in spite of significant differences in eucharistic doctrine among them) shared the common ground of saying that the body and blood of Christ are not present on earth but only in heaven, and that neither godly nor wicked communicants receive Christ's body and blood with their mouths. At most, only believing communicants can be said to eat Christ's flesh and drink his blood—but only in a spiritual sense and by faith.

Lutherans have, to the contrary, insisted upon the union of bread and the body of Christ, of wine and the blood of Christ, as well as upon the *manducatio oralis* (eating of Christ's body with the mouth of the body in the Holy Communion) and the *manducatio indignorum* (reception of the body of Christ also by unfit and wicked communicants). All efforts at an accommodation between Lutheran and Reformed doctrine on this point have failed.[64]

The attack on the Lutheran position resulted in a partly vehement, partly quietly reasoned defense and clarification of the Lutheran position. Luther himself contributed four brochures to which the Symbolical Books make explicit appeal, in which he insists that "the words of the testament of Christ are to be understood in no other way than in their literal sense, and not as though the bread symbolized the absent Body and the wine the absent Blood of Christ."[65] Because of political considerations in the sixteenth century it was necessary for Reformed Christians to subscribe the Augsburg Confession, while still maintaining their central affirmations about the Lord's Supper. Since they were able to penetrate some Lutheran churches and theological faculties under the (politically necessary) pretense of loyalty to the Augsburg Confession, the Formula of Concord took pains to reject their reformulations specifically and sharply, as well as to defend the Lutheran position against a series of charges. Thus the Formula rejects the charges that the Lutherans taught eucharistic cannibalism, that they taught a local extension of the body of Christ throughout the created universe, and that they based their eucharistic doctrine upon a Eutychian Christology.[66] In turn, they insisted that a perversion of the meaning of the words of institution by "enemies of the Sacrament" made the "enemies'" use of those words incapable of bringing about a valid sacrament.[67]

The vehemence and acrimony with which both sides waged this theological battle seems scandalous to our century. The Lutheran side believed that the other had based its eucharistic doctrine upon a faulty Christology which, if taken seriously, would "have Christ's deity denied," and "we should lose Christ altogether along with our salvation."[68]

In contrast to certain late medieval and post-Tridentine elements in Roman Catholic eucharistic doctrine, Lutherans developed their own position in four areas.

1. The Lutherans from the first insisted on Holy Communion under the species of the consecrated wine as well as under the species of the consecrated host. Christ's command, they affirmed, supported this practice, as did the practice of the primitive church. Though reception under only one kind does not invalidate the sacrament, they nevertheless argued that "administration in one form is not the whole order and institution as it was established and commanded by Christ."[69]

2. The Lutheran position with reference to the idea of transubstantiation underwent a change, at first not polemicizing against the idea at all and even regarding it as preferable to the symbolist position of the Swiss reformers and the Enthusiasts. Later, in the heat of polemics in several directions, the Smalcald Articles could declare the idea of a change in the substance of the bread and wine to be a "subtle sophistry" for which "we have no regard";[70] and, after Trent, the Formula of Concord asserts, "We unanimously reject and condemn . . . transubstantiation, when it is taught . . . that the bread and the wine in the Holy Supper lose their substance and natural essence and

are thus annihilated in such a way that they are transmuted into the Body of Christ and that only the exterior appearance remains."[71] In this connection it must, however, be noted that the rejection is of a specific metaphysical concept and not primarily of the term.

3. The formula "in, with, and under the bread and the wine," which (borrowed from scholastic terminology) affirms an unspecifiable relationship between Christ's body and blood on the one hand, and the elements on the other hand, is explicitly a polemical formula: "We at times . . . use the formulas 'under the bread, with the bread, in the bread' . . . to reject . . . transubstantiation and to indicate the sacramental union between the transformed substance of the bread and the Body of Christ."[72] Thus the formula "in, with, and under" has meaning only in terms of its antithesis; it is not regarded as a new metaphysical theory or a distinctive position in its own right.

4. With reference to the cult of the reserved sacrament, Lutherans tended to appeal to the dynamic character of the Holy Eucharist, and to voice the conviction that Christ instituted the sacrament of the altar "for us Christians to eat and to drink," and thus to oppose any cult of the reserved sacrament. Still, "only an Arian heretic" would deny that Christ as God and man "should be adored in spirit and in truth in the valid celebration" of the Holy Eucharist.[73]

Two principles combined to determine the Lutheran position on private and solitary Masses without communicants other than the celebrant. The first is the essentially corporate, not individual, nature of the Eucharist, which is violated when there are no communicants other than the celebrant. The second is the reaction against the "traffic in Masses," born of the medieval conviction that the Mass is in itself a meritorious and expiatory sacrifice which avails before God for the benefit of the living and especially of the dead *ex opere operato sine bono motu utentis.*[74] The Lutherans affirm that a Mass celebrated not for the people but only to obtain favor from God is at least invalid, if not a blasphemous perversion of Christ's intention.[75]

It remains to discuss some problems posed by Lutheran sacramental theology, especially as these surface in an ecumenical context. There are the questions of the omnipresence of the human nature of Christ, the role of the celebrant at the Holy Eucharist, and the idea of the sacrifice of the Mass.

The first problem, that of the omnipresence of the human nature of Christ, was the focus of heated discussions among Lutherans in the sixteenth century and between Lutherans and Roman Catholics in the sixteenth and seventeenth centuries. Based on the idea of a real exchange of properties (*communicatio idiomatum*) between the divine and human natures in Christ, Lutherans intended nothing more by this assertion than what the ancient fathers taught, namely, that what Christ received in time he received according to the human nature he had assumed. And, though the idea of the omnipresence of Christ's human nature was used by Lutherans in connection with the doctrine of the sacrament of the altar, Lutherans neither taught a local extension of the body of Christ throughout the universe, nor based their eucharistic doctrine on the idea of the communicated omnipresence of Christ's human nature. That basis is always the words of institution. Further, the idea played only a minor role as a subsidiary theological support for the rational credibility of the sacramental union; Luther made use of the idea only between 1526 and 1529, and, though later polemicists revived the issue, the authors of the Formula of Concord were also ready to make use of alternate explanations. In essence, Lutherans intended to affirm that Christ as God is present everywhere. Because of the hypostatic union of the two natures, his human nature participates in the presence which he promises when he says, "I am with you always." Accordingly, they say, we must not suppose that it is difficult for him to give us his body and his blood when the Holy Eucharist is celebrated.

The second problem area, the role of the celebrant, is occasioned largely by Roman Catholic polemics, especially since the beginning of the seventeenth century, which have regularly charged that Lutherans do not have a valid Eucharist on the ground that their clergy do not have valid orders. Lutherans have responded by insisting that the celebrant is a clergyman who functions before the altar by virtue of his authority of order (*potestas ordinis*), which he received when he was ordained by another clergyman. As such, he acts both as Christ's agent and as the president of the celebrating congregation (to use St. Justin the Martyr's designation). And the sacrament he confects is held to be objectively valid, apart from the sanctity or wickedness of either the celebrant or the communicant.[76] The argument hinges, obviously, on the validity of Lutheran orders—a subject of continuing discussion between Lutherans and Roman Catholics, in which promising results have recently been achieved.[77]

The final problem area, the sacrifice of the Mass, calls for careful distinction-making. The Lutheran symbols reject the idea that the Mass is a meritorious and in itself expiatory sacrifice which can be applied on behalf of the living and the dead in such a way that by the mere performance of the rite it confers grace and merits the remission of venial and mortal sins, of guilt and punishment. But they do affirm that sacrifice is one of the ends and purposes of eucharistic worship. When the term "unbloody sacrifice" is correlated with "reasonable" or "intellectual" in the sense of Romans 12:1 and I Peter 2:5, the Lutheran symbols approve that designation. More positively, they grant that the whole ceremony of the Mass—with the preaching of the Gospel, the response of the worshipers' faith, invocation, thanksgiving, and the reception of the Lord's body and blood—is a sacrifice of praise and thanksgiving, a Eucharist in the etymological sense of that word.[78] And theologians of the era of classic Lutheran orthodoxy, such as Johann Gerhard and David Hollaz, spoke of the eucharistic sacrifice in related terms. Commenting on the canon prayer *Supplices,* Gerhard wrote, "It is clear that the sacrifice takes place in heaven, not on earth, inasmuch as the death and passion of God's beloved Son is offered to God the Father by way of commemoration. . . . In the Christian sacrifice there is no victim except the real and substantial Body of Christ himself. Hence this sacrifice once offered on the cross takes place continually in an unseen fashion in heaven by way of commemoration, when Christ offers to his Father on our behalf his sufferings of the past, especially when we are applying ourselves to the sacred mysteries, and this is the 'unbloody sacrifice' which is carried out in heaven."[79] And David Hollaz declares, "For on the cross an offering was made by means of the passion and death of an immolated living thing, without which there can be no sacrifice in the narrow sense, but in the Eucharist the oblation takes place through the prayers and through the commemoration of the death or sacrifice offered on the cross."[80]

Holy Absolution

For Lutherans whose orientation is toward the Symbolical Books the sacramental life without sacramental confession and absolution is unthinkable. The third major sacrament of Lutheranism, what the Apology of the Augsburg Confession calls *sacramentum poenitentiae,* is holy absolution. The Augsburg Confession asserts, "It is taught among us that private absolution should be retained and not allowed to fall into disuse. However, in confession it is not necessary to enumerate all trespasses and sins, for this is impossible."[81] Lutheranism thus reflects Luther's enthusiastic endorsement of private confession and absolution: "I will not allow anyone to deprive me of private confession, nor would I exchange it for all the treasures of the whole world, for I know what strength and consolation it has given me. No one knows the power of private confession, except he be compelled frequently to fight and wrestle with the devil. I had long since been conquered by Satan and liquidated, had I not been preserved by confession."[82] If it is true that the practice of American Lutherans only occasionally reflects that endorsement, it is also true that Lutherans are giving increasing energies to recovering that sort of piety once more.

Apart from the decided advantages which a regular discipline of private confession and absolution affords for the life and piety of Christians, Lutherans understand the individual pronouncement of holy absolution to be a most important utterance of the promise of the Gospel. In response to the penitent Christian's confession, his pastor speaks directly to him the assurance of forgiveness. Such a pointed statement of the divine verdict of forgiveness must be cherished greatly.

In the Lutheran view of confession and absolution no one is forced to enumerate his sins; confession is contingent only upon the individual's willingness and desire except in cases of public scandal; absolution is offered without condition and without penance—yet it is personal, individual, and operative (not merely a wishful pronouncement, but a declaration).

It must be said that, on this point, Lutheranism's theology far outstrips its practice. The number of parishes in which the sacrament of holy absolution is administered in a way that reflects this understanding of it is extremely small. But that number is also growing.

The Sacred Ministry

The basic statement of Lutheranism on the ministry of the church is from the Augsburg Confession:

> To obtain such faith God instituted the office of the ministry, that is, provided the Gospel and the sacraments. Through these, as through means, he gives the Holy Spirit, who works faith, when and where he pleases, in those who hear the Gospel. And the Gospel teaches that we have a gracious God, not by our own merits but by the merit of Christ, when we believe this.[83]

In the course of the confessional revival in the Church of the Augsburg Confession during the nineteenth and twentieth centuries, Lutheran theologians have interpreted this and other statements of the Symbolical Books about the sacred ministry in three typical ways.

1. Some have held that the sacred ministry is only the activity of the universal royal priesthood of belivers, the public exercise of which the Christian community has committed to certain persons for the sake of efficiency and good order.

2. An opposite pole sees the sacred ministry as the contemporary form of the primitive apostolate and the incumbent as the personal representative of Christ.

3. Occupying middle ground and combining elements of both positions, a third view sees the sacred ministry as a divine institution, essential to the church's existence. This view regards the responsible public proclamation of the Gospel and the administration of the sacraments as the primary content of the sacred ministry, and it looks upon ordination as the indispensable act of admission to the sacred ministry.

There are, of course, modifications and variations of these views. And those who hold these varying views regard their positions as the correct exposition of the Lutheran symbols. The present exposition falls into the third of the categories mentioned above.

Without carefully delineating kinds and classes of people in the Christian church, the Lutheran Symbolical Books follow the New Testament traditional usage in speaking of preachers and Christians, of pastors and people, of rectors and parishioners, of laymen and those who preside over the community.

The symbols are careful to speak of the sacred ministry as a divine institution. God instituted the sacred ministry, they affirm—the ministry of teaching the Gospel and of administering the sacraments. And his purpose in doing so is that he might forgive them "by grace for Christ's sake through faith." The Word of God and the sacraments are means by which God gives the Holy Spirit that works faith when and where God wills it in those who hear the Word and receive the sacraments. And they reject the position that the Holy Spirit is received by purely interior preparation, meditation, and activity without the external Word of God personally communicated through the sacred ministry.[84] Thus the content of the sacred ministry is the responsible public proclamation of the Gospel and the administration of the sacraments.

Although the Symbolical Books see the sacred ministry cheifly (but not exclusively) in dynamic and functional terms, they are nevertheless also conscious of the fact that apart from its incumbents the sacred ministry is an abstraction. Thus the church has the divinely imposed responsibility not merely of proclaiming the Gospel and of administering the sacraments, but also of choosing, calling, and ordaining fit persons to carry out these functions.[85] Accordingly, the incumbents of the office of the sacred ministry are the human instruments through whom the Holy Spirit governs and sanctifies the church.[86]

The sacred ministry is understood as just that, a service or ministry, not as a source of prestige or privilege or power. Nevertheless, the Symbolical Books see that ministry not merely as a function but also as an order in the church, yet without narrowly clerical or hierarchical implications.[87]

For the clergyman is understood as no more and no less than the representative of God and of Christ. In his preaching and application of the Gospel and his administration of the sacraments, the officiant or celebrant acts in the stead of Christ, not in his own person. Christ binds his promise and his activity in the sacrament of the altar to the speaking of the celebrant who consecrates the elements. In the words of Luke 10:16, "He who hears you hears me." Yet the force of those words is not in the direction of priestly privilege but in the direction of obligating the clergy to teaching according to Christ's Word and not according to human traditions.[88]

The authority of the clergyman is primarily the responsible public proclamation of the Gospel and administration of the sacraments. Accepting the medieval distinction between the authority of the clerical order (*potestas ordinis*) and the authority of jurisdiction (*potestas jurisdictionis*), the Symbolical Books affirm the competence of the pastor/bishop to do all that he needs to do in order to proclaim and apply the Gospel and administer the sacraments, as well as his competence (to be exercised according to the instructions contained in the Word of God) to excommunicate notorious evil-doers and to reconcile them to the church again when they repent.[89]

Since the activity just named is the core of the life of the church, it is no surprise that the symbols consider the sacred ministry as one of the signs (*signa*) or marks (*nota*) of the church. The church is noted when the Gospel is preached and the sacraments are administered at specific times and in concrete places. Since this activity is the task of the sacred ministry, this ministry itself becomes a "mark" or characteristic of the church.[90]

The Symbolical Books nowhere attempt to derive the sacred ministry from the universal priesthood of the faithful. In fact, the doctrine of the universal priesthood of believers had receded into minor importance—also for Luther himself—by the time the Symbolical Books were being framed. The classical prooftext for this teaching, I Peter 2:9, is cited only once,[91] and there it is likely that the term is best taken as a designation for the people of God—certainly not merely a local congregation that might delegate authority to one of its number.

The sacred ministry in the Lutheran symbols is unitary, not hierarchical. There is basically only one holy order, the presbyterate-episcopate. The symbols never call into question the existence of the sacred ministry by divine right (*jure divino*). Rather, they call into question the postapostolic differentiation of grades within that ministry. The separation of the presbyterate and the episcopate, along with the introduction of the initially lay office of deacon into the major orders of the sacred ministry they hold to be developments by human right (*jure humano*). Regardless of their title, all ordained clergymen have the same basic authority to discharge the duties of their office.[92]

Regarding church organization and polity, the Symbolical Books affirm that, as long as the divinely ordained necessity of the sacred ministry is recognized and provided for, polity is an *adiaphoron* (indifferent matter). Nevertheless, the Symbolical Books affirm a preference for episcopal polity.[93] The ideal is a universal episcopalism in which all bishops are equal in office, united in doctrine, belief, prayer, sacraments, and works of love.[94]

Bishops have the right to establish regulations for the government of the church and for worship in the interest of good order, and the congregations and subordinate clergy are bound in charity to obey such canons. But the bishops have no authority to make the salvation of the faithful dependent upon obedience to such regulations, nor may they institute any regulation and declare that observance of it earns forgiveness of sins.[95] The authority of the bishops dare never conflict with the Gospel. And they have no right to arrogate to themselves authority in temporal matters.

Without discussing the necessity of a succession of ministers, the Symbolical Books operate explicitly with the concept of a de facto succession of ordained ministers.[96] The pastor/bishop is thus regarded as the successor of the apostles in the government of the church—even though the sixteenth century made it impossible for the adherents of the Augsburg Confession to perpetuate the historic episcopate with apostolic succession.

Regarding the papacy, in the sense of the claim of the bishop of Rome to universal primacy of jurisdiction, the Symbolical Books assert that it is a historical phenomenon that exists by human right only, not by divine right. The bishop of Rome is by divine right the bishop and pastor only of the Church of Rome, as well as of those who of their own will or by political arrangement have attached themselves to him. While not denying it, the Smalcald Articles are nevertheless dubious about the value of the papacy even as a humanly instituted symbol of Christian unity. And as long as the pope insists on the last seventeen words of *Unam sanctam* ("Further, we declare, state and define that for every human being it is absolutely necessary for salvation to be under the bishop of Rome"), he is the Antichrist of II Thessalonians 2:4.[97]

Ordination to holy orders, that is, to the sacred ministry, is granted the label "sacrament,"[98] and is affirmed as effective by divine right. Because the authority to minister the Gospel exists wherever the church is, the church necessarily possesses the authority to choose, call, and ordain ministers; in fact, the church is compelled to exercise this authority.[99] Ordination is the indispensable rite of committing the sacred ministry of Gospel and sacraments to qualified candidates. Only persons who are duly chosen, called, and ordained are competent publicly and responsibly to proclaim the Gospel and to administer the sacraments.[100] The verbs in Article XIV of the Augsburg Confession (*debeat/soll*) allow no option; they are the same verbs which describe the indispensable relation of good works to faith in Article VI. They have the force of the modern English "must" rather than "should." Ordination need not be an elaborate ceremony; originally it was a simple rite in which a bishop laid hands on the candidate. Still, the Apology sees the imposition of hands in ordination as an integral part of what it is ready to call the "sacrament of orders."[101] And, since the differentiation of grade between bishop and presbyter is not by divine right, it is therefore by divine right that presbyters have the authority to ordain.[102] An ordination that a pastor performs in his own church upon a qualified candidate is valid by divine right.[103] In the emergency and irregular situation of northern Europe in the sixteenth century, the adherents of the Augsburg Confession enunciated the principle that when bishops become heretics or refuse to ordain fit persons, "the churches are compelled by divine right to ordain pastors and ministers, using their own pastors for this purpose."[104] They regarded ordination by the existing bishops as permissible and even desirable, but not as necessary. Therefore, under the circumstances, the reformers propose to ordain fit persons to the sacred ministry.

Accordingly, the churches of the Augsburg Confession hold that the ordinary minister of baptism, absolution, and the Eucharist is a clergyman. They concede, following a medieval tradition of canon law, that a layman be the extraordinary minister of baptism and absolution in a life-and-death emergency.[105] Since, however, the Eucharist is not as indispensably necessary as baptism or reconciliation with the church (absolution), they do not accord a layman the authority to consecrate the eucharistic elements.

Political, Social, and Cultural Matters

Lutherans have a characteristic, if seldom understood, approach to the understanding of, and a stance toward, the whole range of reality outside of Christ and the Gospel and the holy catholic church. The label "secular" is all too frequently and all too hastily applied in this connection, but it really ought to be avoided, both because it is imprecise and because it is often taken to mean a realm separate from the realm where human beings are supposed to confront God. For reasons which will become clear below, the latter supposition is in fact diametrically opposed to the position of the Lutheran Symbolical Books. Besides, such a view would, in the end, prove to have said either too much or too little.

The question at hand is simply this: What resources are available to adherents of the Augsburg Confession and related symbols for a theological understanding of the great, buzzing, attractive and repulsive, beautiful and ugly, ennobling and debasing world around them—that world of governmental and social institutions, of art and music, of education and recreation?

In one sense, the answer to this question is little more than a corollary to the doctrine of creation. But clarity in our present secularized age requires a special discussion, for the problems Christians confront when they deal, as they must, with social and political and cultural forces are massive and extremely difficult of resolution, especially for those committed to the kind of understanding of the Christian Gospel to which the Lutheran symbols make their witness.

A complete discussion of this topic would require a careful look at a number of passages in the symbols—notably the discussions of creation and the explanations of the fourth petition of the "Our Father" in the two catechisms, and the articles on free will and original sin in the Augsburg Confession, the Apology, and the Formula of Concord. But for the present discussion, the most explicit sections of the symbols are Article XVI of the Augsburg Confession and the related portion of the Apology. Though the focus there is mainly on the political sphere, one finds there the basis for the Lutheran view also of the whole of culture as well.

Article XVI of the Augustana teaches that all authority in the world and all orderly government and statutes are good ordinances which God has created and instituted, that Christians can be government officials or judges or princes without committing sin thereby, that they can hand down verdicts and render decisions according to customary law-codes, that they can be members of armed forces, buy and sell, swear oaths as required, own property, marry and be married, and the like. These affirmations are made against the antitheses of Anabaptist rejection of all these matters as unchristian, and of monastic perfectionism which taught that a better holiness lay in deserting these areas and avoiding such activities. Genuine perfection under the Gospel, said the Lutheran confessors, consists in genuine reverence for, and faith in, God. The Gospel does not teach an external and temporal, but an internal and eternal (that is, eschatological), existence and a corresponding righteousness of the heart. Prior to the Parousia, one is not to overthrow temporal administrations and political institutions; as authentically divine ordinances, all these things are to be kept. In these different orders one is to exhibit authentically good works, each according to his station in life. The proviso is then added that one is to be obedient to such authority as long as such obedience does not cause sin, for then one must obey God rather than men.

Despite the rather enthusiastic endorsement of this article by the Papal Confutation,[106] Melanchthon nevertheless chose to expand and amplify this line of argument in the Apology, apparently with a view to defending the Lutheran movement in the court of international opinion against the charge of responsibility for the Peasants' Uprisings.[107]

The new note which the Apology introduces is the difference between the *regnum Christi* and the *regnum civile,* the realm or regime of Christ and the civil realm or regime. The rule of Christ is the "knowledge of God in the heart, the fear of God and faith." It initiates an eschatological righteousness and an eschatological life. In the meantime, it permits us to "make use of medicine or architecture, food or drink or air." The Gospel does not furnish new laws for the state, but it requires that we obey existing laws, whether they were formulated by pagans or by anybody else. And in this obedience it requires Christians to exercise love. Christians are thus to accept political institutions in the same way as the changing of the seasons, namely, as divine ordinances. The Apology concludes with the observation, "Endless discussions about contracts will never satisfy good consciences unless they keep the rule in mind, that a Christian may legitimately make use of civil ordinances and laws. This rule safeguards consciences, for it teaches that if contracts have the approval of magistrates or of laws, they are legitimate in the sight of God as well."[108]

Although, as in the Augsburg Confession, the weight in Apology XVI is on the political sphere, in the final analysis the significance of this article transcends the merely political and involves the total cultural sphere. The world of culture is for Lutheran theology a unified world with an authentic meaning and significance in its own right. It does not receive its significance or its norms from the eschatological world, nor from that eschatological world's beachhead in this aeon, the church. Thus not heteronomous, it is also not autonomous. It may seem so at times, but it has not evolved from itself, and it neither creates its own materials nor determines its own ultimate purposes. And it surely does not render the ultimate verdict on its achievements. The world of culture is, rather, theonomous. It is God who creates its materials, directs its course, determines its ends, and finally and infallibly judges its effectiveness and its achievements.

Crucial for Lutherans at this point, as catholic Christians, is the insight that the God at work in the world of culture and politics is the same God at work in the redemption of the world through Jesus Christ and in the sanctifying of an eschatological community that will survive the cataclysmic end of the present aeon. Put in other terms, the Symbolical Books invite Lutherans to hold that the universe of culture "consists" (as the Authorized Version reads), that is, hangs together, in the same Word through whom

God made the cosmos, who hung on the cross, and who, raised from the dead, is present in his body and blood in the Holy Eucharist. That universe of culture owes every positive achievement to the same Creator Spirit who brooded on the face of the primeval deep in the creation epic, was poured out on the waiting disciples at Pentecost, and is communicated in the church through the Word and the sacraments. The divine work of culture is, like the work of redemption and the work of sanctification, the work of the Holy Trinity—a different work, to be sure, but a divine work and therefore to be respected and appreciated and lauded as a work of God.

In this understanding, the sphere of the political and the cultural is the law of God. Here one deals with God acting through his law, making possible the perpetuation of humankind until God's design accomplishes the "making new" of all things in Christ. That assertion has two important consequences. The work of culture thus broadly conceived is nothing less than a divine work and is to be treated as such. But it is by no means God's ultimate work, just as the Word of God operative there, the divine law, is not his ultimate Word, but must give place to the Gospel. And that sense of a proper, but penultimate, significance for the world of culture is reflected also in the sacramental theology of Lutherans, with its focus on God's use of people and matter in the sacraments as the evidence of God's own willingness to acknowledge and employ his world of creation and culture for the sanctification of his creatures.

That does not mean, of course, that Lutherans idealize the situation. What the Lutheran symbols say of human nature is applicable to the larger totality of nature as well.[109] Although it is essentially and substantially good, it is existentially and accidentally corrupted in an abominable and horrible fashion. The world of culture is thus a world of ambiguities and of conflict and of struggle. God is in control, but his control does not go unchallenged for a moment. The material world is the mask of the Creator, but the fact that the Creator chooses to be thus masked is sometimes perverted by the satanic enemy to his own deceptive purpose. There is no culture, no society, no government, no technology that is consummately evil, but there is no aspect of any culture or society or government or technology that is perfectly good.

Lutheran theology seeks to avoid the delusion that it is possible to build Jerusalem in the green and grassy land of any country. Cultural development is not the highway over which the Kingdom of the Heavens enters the world, and it is not by the redemption of culture or the sanctification of politics that the Parousia will be hastened. But this does not justify the opposite extreme of magnifying only the taint from which the world of culture suffers. Lutherans would agree that only a Manichaean heretic would give the devil more than his due, for Satan only corrupts, but cannot create. The world of culture and politics is still the Father's world, for sin can only corrupt and deface but cannot destroy the handiwork of the Pantocrator.

At this point some of the post-Enlightenment distinctions, such as that between Creation (before the Fall) and Preservation (after the Fall of the first parents), obscure an important facet of the theology of the Symbolical Books. The authentic Lutheran position is a doctrine of contemporary and continuous creation. "I believe that God has made me and all creatures," the Lutheran confesses with the Small Catechism's explanation of the first article of the creed. And it is this doctrine which the Formula of Concord applies when it affirms that even after the Fall God continues to create human nature.[110] This means that the continuing existence of any and every culture is seen as a sign across the face of history reading, "God at work!"

A Lutheran will therefore avoid drawing unduly sharp lines between the "secular" and the eschatological, for he would then be open to the charge of dualism. Similarly, most of the criticism of the Lutheran doctrine of the distinction between the "two kingdoms" which implies that that doctrine involves a dualism or a separation, has simply failed to understand what the Symbolical Books affirm. True, the two "regimes" are discrete, as distinct from one another as the law and the Gospel, as different as works and faith. But they are one at the ultimately decisive point that one and the same Truine God is working in both, and one and the same Christian person is functioning and being acted upon in both. The divine work has already been discussed. The human activity need only be described as the Chrsitian's obligation to practice charity in the cultural, the political, the economic, the social relationships in which he finds himself—so long as that charity is understood purely as the *agape* of which the New Testament speaks, that *agape*-love which the Christian learns from his experience in the eschatological world and practices in the present world of culture. For the Christian is obligated both to see the world of culture, in the light of the Christ-event, as a work that exhibits God's "fatherly, divine benevolence and mercy without any merit or worthiness in us";[111] and henceforth, without a self-regarding appraisal of the value to him of the persons with whom he is confronted in his cultural relations, he is to exercise such *agape*-love.

That obligation to "charity" is the first of two really revolutionary forces which, according to Lutherans, the Christian turns loose in the world of culture. Though (with but one important qualification to which we must yet turn) the Christian does not call into question the cultural categories he finds in the society in which, by birth or by choice or by circumstance, he lives, he nevertheless tries to reflect within those categories the love with which God has loved him in Christ. To the extent that they do so, Christians (albeit quite incidentally) do transform culture, for against the infiltration of such "charity" no cultural defenses have proved adequate. "The gates of hell," Christ promised, "will not prevail against it."[112]

In this connection, and in the light of some of the history of Lutheranism, it will be useful to remember that the idea of a "Christian culture" is a highly imprecise one. Since, as Lutherans understand it, the church is not exclusively an eschatological community of faith and of the Holy Spirit, but also an empirical one, a body social and a body politic, expressed in local institutions with local membership and local histories, the culture of any land in which the church has been planted will bear, to a greater or lesser degree, the marks of the church's presence. But that does not mean that church and culture can be identified—no matter how pervasively the church may have influenced its cultural environment.

The one exception to the Christian's readiness to accept cultural patterns and political or domestic or social institutions is at the same time the second really revolutionary force which the Christian unleashes in a culture. That exception to the principle of acceptance of the authority of the "powers that be"[113] is the apostolic injunction that one must obey God rather than men. For here is carried out the contemporary contest of Christ with Satan. Here, where Satan is perverting the works of God, here obedience to God necessarily embroils the Christian in a conflict with the accepted patterns of behavior.

The application of this exception in explicitly political matters has reguarly been recognized—even if in practice the number of Lutherans sentenced for such "civil disobedience" may be disproportionately low. Lutherans have tended, moreover, to apply that principle rather narrowly. Yet "the powers that be" is a much more inclusive concept than city or state or federal government. Particularly in a democratic political state, the "powers that be" are any element in the existing power structures that control, by restraint or inducement, the behavior of people. Their authority affects people in every aspect of their involvement with power, not just the state. It expresses itself in labor unions, in boards of directors, in professional societies, in academic committees, in political parties, in media of mass information—in all the associations of which people are members, whether by choice or against or without their will. At these levels, and especially at these levels, Christian confessors who are unafraid to stand for what is morally right are a really revolutionary force—for they take that stand because of their inevitable compulsion to obey God rather than any creaturely might that resists his will for his creation.

Far from the political quietism for which Lutherans have frequently been blamed, such an understanding of the Christian's responsibility in and for the world of culture would actively involve him in the ministry of charity, the love that does not regard the value of the object to the lover, even when that service is as varied as the tasks that are his immediate responsibility for the time being. At the level of the cultural, the political, the economic, the social aspects of life, the Christian is called upon to do what he has to do as well as he can do it. There, his specifically Christian competence—his knowledge of God, his insight into the divine will, his familiarity with the Sacred Scriptures, his devotion to worship in Word and sacrament—is no substitute for professional competence or plain ordinary craftsmanship.

To summarize the Lutheran view of the world of culture: for the Christian, but only for the Christian, there are two aeons, two worlds, two realms, two kingdoms, existing contemporaneously. The one is the world of the new creation, the eschatological reality of the Kingdom of Christ that finds its contemporary expression in the one, holy, catholic, and apostolic church (without being precisely identified with it). The other is the world of the present creation, the world of God's making for the use of human beings, the world of water and earth and air and fire and natural resources and light and processes of growth, the world of government and social forces and education and the arts and the family and the means of communication. It is the world where God sends his rain upon the just and the unjust and makes his sun to shine on the evil and on the good, where he gives "daily bread indeed without our prayer, also to all the wicked."[114]

Lutherans nevertheless regard this latter world as one of God's making for man's remaking. It is that, they understand, by God's own design: a world where mankind builds houses and shrines and warehouses and stock exchanges, where he heals and fortifies, where he organizes and mobilizes, where he regulates and punishes, where he employs the resources of society to accomplish tasks beyond the powers of individuals and groups, where he paints and sculpts and composes and performs and dances and listens and smiles and plays and communicates.

Because this world is a world of reason, that reason which human beings share ever so remotely with God, and because the other, the eschatological, world is the world of the Spirit of God, both can and do coexist for the Christian, the latter superimposing itself increasingly on the former. Both worlds, Lutherans understand, are God's, and there is no intrinsic contradiction between them. And they would have the Christian note with a smile the cracks in the surface of the old, and work his love there in those cracks for the sake of the new.

Worship and Piety

That the Lutheran Reformation was a conservative Reformation is perhaps most obvious when one considers the theology and practice of worship which takes it bearings from the Lutheran Symbolical Books. In general, the norm for Lutheran worship and piety is essentially medieval piety modified by the doctrinal reforms of the Lutheran movement. The Augsburg Confession was speaking of practice no less than of doctrine when it affirmed that the churches of the confessors departed in no way from the catholic tradition.[115] In this sense, at least, Lutherans understand their worship and piety to be both catholic and evangelical.

The effort to sketch the profile of Lutheranism at the point of worship and piety is complicated (as is the discussion of the actual practice of any religious group) both by the wide variations among various groups of Lutherans, variations often reflecting their countries of origin as well as the degrees of contact with eastern or middle-western or "frontier" American culture, and also by the deviations from the norm of the symbols, which occurred already before the various groups emigrated from their European homelands to the New World. It will therefore be necessary mainly to describe what that symbolical norm is, while admitting that in actual practice the worship and piety of Lutherans in North America is as often as not a chameleonlike adaptation to the forms that are prevalent in American Protestantism.

Theoretically, the norm of Lutheran worship and piety is the combination of the directives found in the Symbolical Books (which are never so detailed as to include even a single "order of service"), along with what we can discover to have been the practices and usages that one finds in those places and at those periods in which Lutheranism was permitted to express its character and peculiar genius free of external influences and interference. In what follows, we shall attempt to describe those directives and those practices.

The Lutheran theology of worship has its center in the recognition that the purest worship is simply faith in the promised forgiveness of sins for Christ's sake. Particular forms and ceremonies are normally incidental, indifferent matters, and it is specifically affirmed that ceremonies and other matters of human institution can vary from place to place and from time to time.[116] What is insisted upon is that the Gospel be preached according to a pure understanding of it and that the sacraments be administered according to Christ's institution.[117] Word and sacrament for the sake of faith in the promises of the Gospel—that is the central concern. Those twin foci, sermon and sacrament, had their place in the liturgies of the early decades of the Lutheran Reformation, and they have their place in the Common Service which is the basic liturgy in use among Lutherans in America in the twentieth century. Accordingly, to the charge of the Confutation that the churches of the confessors at Augsburg were "desolate" because of the cessation of canonical hours and daily Masses, Melanchthon reiterated in the Apology that "we keep both the proclamation of the Gospel and the proper use of the sacraments," and that the "real adornment of the churches is godly, practical, and clear teaching, the godly use of the sacraments, ardent prayer, and the like."[118] This concern underlies and informs that which is authentically Lutheran in a theology of worship and piety, for it connects with and develops from the concern of articles IV and V of the Augsburg Confession, where justification is credited to God's action "by grace, for Christ's sake, through faith," and where the obtaining of such justifying faith is affirmed to be the reason for God's provision of the office of the ministry, the preaching of the Gospel, and the administration of the sacraments.[119]

What in addition can and should be said about Lutheran attitudes toward worship can be summarized quite briefly.

Lutheran theology of worship and liturgy is explicitly trinitarian. Against a popular and sentimental "Jesus-theology,' against moralisms which teach the ascent from earth to heaven on the ladder of moral virtue at the expense of wasting the redemption offered in the Gospel, the Lutheran liturgy is explicitly trinitarian at virtually every stage of its progress.

The Lutheran attitude toward worship seeks adequately to comprehend the whole human being. Against an exclusive stress on the "spiritual," against a view of the church's sphere of interest as restricted to "souls," against preaching which allegorizes Chirst's miracles to produce moral lessons, against a narrow focus on purely "religious" matters, Lutheran liturgical theology stresses the involvement of the human being as a physical and spiritual totality in worship by retaining elements which appeal to and involve all the senses, by insisting on prayers and intercessions for church and state, for deliverance from disease, for liberation of prisoners and slaves, for safe journeys for travelers, for due enjoyment of the fruits of the earth.

Related to that emphasis is the sacramental orientation of Lutheran worship, both in the strict sense as referring to holy baptism, holy absolution, and Holy Communion, and also in a looser sense as embracing the whole realm of sign and symbol. The specifically sacramental emphasis is primary. The sacraments just named are regarded not only as outward and visible signs of invisible, inward, and spiritual graces, but also as the very channels of grace itself, marks of the presence of the church, and the individualization to each of the faithful of that salvation which in the Gospel is offered to all. Further, symbols in thing and in action are affirmed: standing for the Gospel after sitting for the Epistle in order to offer the greater honor to the Gospel narrative of the words and deeds of Christ, kneeling for acts of penitence and for the reception of the eucharistic Christ in the sacrament of the altar, bowing the head at the name of Jesus and at other points in the service, using the sign of the cross by both the priest in blessing the people and the people in blessing themselves, using candles and incense and vestments and paraments and everything else that could be retained with a good conscience from the heritage of preceding generations in the church.

Lutheran liturgical theology is a seriously social-corporate theology. Against the individualism that would shrink the faith to what transpires "between my God and me," Lutherans understand their worship to be that of people who are part of a living, identifiable, and empirical fellowship, the body of Christ that lives by and for the preaching of the Gospel and the administration of the sacraments by which God incorporates the individual into the redeemed community. The presence of the sacramental element alluded to above is a guarantee of objectivity and of corporateness, for the sacraments remain channels of God's grace for the whole community that hears and receives, unaffected in their validity by the faith either of the minister or of the recipient.

Further, a Lutheran view of worship reflects an ecclesiology that sees the church as an outpost in the present aeon of the new and eschatological world promised and initiated by the Gospel. Accordingly, the sacraments are not regarded merely as signs of the ecclesial allegiance of the recipient, but as means for God's action of creating and preserving his new and holy community for his own new age.

Finally, Lutherans see in worship a mixture of sacramental and sacrificial elements, that is, of the conveying of divine grace to people and of the offering of the sacrifice of the people's praise and thanksgiving to God. The rejection of the "sacrifice of the Mass" by the reformers is all too often understood as a rejection of the very idea of sacrifice in connection with worship or especially the Mass. Even a casual reading of Article XXIV of the Apology would dispel that notion. It is not the idea of sacrifice that is rejected but the idea that the Mass is a *propitiatory sacrifice* which benefits the worshiper by the mere performance of the deed. It is, rather, affirmed that the Mass is a eucharistic sacrifice, a sacrifice of praise and thanksgiving, to which category belong faith, prayer, thanksgiving, confession, and proclamation of the Gospel, and suffering because of the Gospel.[120] And when some objected that the Holy Communion must be understood either as sacrament or as sacrifice but surely not as both, Melanchthon replied with two paragraphs, the opening sentences of which are these: "This use of the sacrament, when faith gives life to terrified hearts, is the worship of the New Testament." And, "There is also sacrifice, since one action can have several purposes. Once faith has strengthened a conscience to see its liberation from terror, then it really gives thanks for the blessing of Christ's suffering. It uses the ceremony itself as praise to God. . . . Thus the ceremony becomes a sacrifice of praise."[121]

On these principles, the norm of Lutheran piety would include the following:

As the principal service, Holy Communion with sermon, those worshipers communicating who have previously been absolved, on every Sunday and major holy day and as often in addition as there are desiring communicants.

The retention of the chief daily choir offices, matins and vespers, with Saturday vespers often appointed as a preparation for confession and absolution.

The maintenance of the church year with its appointed readings, days, and observances.

Prayer upon retiring in the evening and upon rising in the morning, comprising the sign of the cross with trinitarian invocation, the Apostles' Creed, and the "Our Father," along with other optional prayers.

The blessing of the table and the saying of grace at meals.

Private absolution before receiving Holy Communion.

Personal and corporate intercession for church, state, and all sorts and conditions of people.

All prayer in the name of Jesus, directed (according to the ancient canon of the Synod of Hippo in A.D. 397) always to the Father.

The norm of Lutheran piety is honored among American Lutherans perhaps more in the breach than in the keeping. But it is a norm, and Lutherans find themselves giving now less, now more, attention to the realization of that norm.

Biblical Studies

While it is true that the Reformation can be understood, at least in part, as a "hermeneutical revolution," a revolution which had at its heart a new way of understanding the Sacred Scriptures, it is also true that Lutherans, especially in America, have not really practiced a distinctive way of reading and understanding the Scriptures. Instead, under the influence of their environment, they have participated in, reflected, and absorbed the various currents and forces found in other branches of American Christianity. In one sense, then, to describe what Lutherans in fact do when they read the Bible would be to describe both fundamentalist literalism and historical criticism, and all the alternatives between.

This is not to say, however, that the basis for a distinctive approach to the Scriptures is lacking in the Symbolical Books of the Lutheran Church. It is, rather, to admit that that approach has not been fully developed and put into practice, and that, in its stead, Lutherans have tended to do their biblical studies at second hand, working more with the systematized statements of and about the faith which were produced principally in the seventeenth and eighteenth centuries in Europe by the dogmaticians of Lutheran orthodoxy, or with the products of biblical study growing largely out of the circles of American fundamentalism in the early twentieth century. Thus, instead of furthering the hermeneutical revolution that was their birthright, they have most often simply joined forces with prevailing approaches to biblical studies (when those approaches seemed to be promising), or recoiled in horror from them (when they seemed to be destructive). And the judgments about whether an approach to blibical studies was promising or destructive were themselves not always made on the basis of the Lutheran symbols, but on the grounds of recent tradition or a hardened dogmaticism.

As a result, the middle decades of the twentieth century have been ones of not a little turmoil among American Lutherans. For more and more Lutheran theologians and exegetes worked to acquaint themselves with European biblical scholarship, and increasing numbers of them went to Europe to study with the leaders of the resurgent biblical movement there. And those who were not professional exegetes more often than not sought to refresh their dogmatic language and their homiletical efforts and their pastoral care with biblical insights once more. But what was fresh air for some was a damp and chilling wind for others, who found in the resurgence of biblical studies a threat to the faith as they understood it and to the comfortable terminology in which they expressed it.

Lutherans acknowledge no fixed rules for the interpretation of the

Scriptures. It is a truism that the Lutheran symbols insist upon no a priori assertions about the Bible, but only the a posteriori confession that the prophetic and apostolic Scriptures are the Word of God and the rule and norm for faith and life.[122] Truism or not, a Lutheran approach to the study of the Scriptures, that is, an approach reflected in and called for by the Lutheran confessions, is not tied to any approved school of biblical interpretation, nor to any authorized hermeneutical method.

It is, of course, a matter of historical fact that Luther's reformatory insights came in connection with a progressive abandonment of the medieval fourfold sense of the Scriptures and a progressive adoption of what some have called a "grammatical-historical" method of interpretation, a method which focuses on the meaning of the words in their historical context, without searching for allegorical or anagogical or tropological significances.

Nevertheless, Lutheranism has remained open to other ways of approaching the sacred text, notably those of pietism and of the new historical criticism. This is so because the decisive element in the approach to the Scriptures taken by the authors of the Lutheran Symbolical Books is their focus and stress on the proclamation of the good news of forgiveness "by grace, for Christ's sake, through faith."[123] Biblical students in the churches of the Augsburg Confession are thus quite free to adopt any of a variety of hermeneutical methods, judging and criticizing all of them on the basis of whether the results of such interpretation and proclamation "magnify Christ" and enable the preaching of the Gospel or "bury Christ" and "waste the merits of Christ."[124]

Such freedom and openness, coupled with the insistence that the study of Scripture must produce an evangelical message, means that the Lutheran exegete, insofar as he is being distinctively Lutheran about his exegetical work, works with a stress on frankly theological criteria as decisive, not on any single approved school of interpretation. The recent history of American Lutheranism bears abundant testimony to the tensions which result when the guarantees for proper biblical study are sought elsewhere than in the recognition that the prophetic and apostolic Scriptures are the Word of God and that, because they urge Christ and his good news, they are the only rule and norm for the faith and life of Christian people.

There is for Lutherans no single "key" to the meaning of the Sacred Scriptures. The Lutheran exegete has, rather, a ring of keys available to him. Some are quite general, even surprisingly secular, in their origin or manner of application. But others are necessarily and decisively Christian-theological—as, for example, the recognition of the law-Gospel polarity of the Word of God, about which Luther, in a document not a part of the Symbolical Books, commented, "Whoever has mastered this ability to distinguish the Law from the Gospel, place him at the head and call him a doctor of the Holy Scripture. For without the Holy Spirit it is impossible to make this distinction."[125] The Formula of Concord speaks authoritatively for Lutherans: "The distinction between law and Gospel is an especially brilliant light which serves the purpose that the Word of God may be rightly divided and the writings of the holy prophets and apostles may be explained and understood correctly. We must therefore observe this distinction with particular diligence lest we confuse the two doctrines and change the Gospel into law. This would darken the merit of Christ and rob disturbed consciences of the comfort which they would otherwise have in the holy Gospel when it is preached purely and without admixture, for by it Christians can support themselves in their greatest temptations against the terrors of the law."[126]

In summary, it should be said that, for Lutherans, the interpretation of the Sacred Scriptures is both like and quite unlike the interpretation of any other written document. The Scriptures themselves give us no list of principles for their interpretation. The frequently cited principles of the oneness of the literal sense, and of the internal consistency of the Scriptures, are rational and not biblical principles, which find their application in the interpretation of secular texts as well. The ability to see the Scriptures as the written Word of God is a gift that the Holy Spirit must grant. There are no criteria that can be devised that will prove such a thesis. Lutherans regard the ability to see in the Scriptures what the Holy Spirit designed them to disclose as an ability dependent upon the illumination of the Holy Spirit that presided over their production. And they find in their experience that in these areas the Scriptures are unlike any other documents and their interpretation requires more than linguistic and historical competence.

Lutherans also recognize, on the other hand, that God chose to use a variety of human authors, who wrote in human words over a long period of time and in at least three different languages, in quite varied historical circumstances, in a variety of literary forms (not all of which are immediately obvious to us in our culture), and who were as limited in their scientific and historical knowledge as their contemporaries were. The way in which the individual documents came to be, the manner in which their component parts were compiled and edited, the mode by which they were transmitted from generation to generation—all these processes are amply illustrated by what we know about other but similar documents that came from the same period and the same cultural matrix. From these aspects, the interpretation of the Sacred Scriptures does not differ significantly from the interpretation of other contemporary documents. One must proceed to establish the text as well as possible. One needs to know as much as possible about the historical circumstances that attended the production of the document. One needs to know about the language, the grammar, the syntax, the vocabulary, the literary forms, and the underlying world-pictures that he encounters. One needs to take due cognizance of the theological emphases of the author, as well as of the broader and immediate contexts of the passage under study. Today, by God's providence, it is possible to know much more about these things than any previous generation and many passages of the Sacred Scriptures have gained in clarity as a result; at the same time, some commonly accepted past interpretations, based upon inadequate information, have had to be abandoned.

Since God's saving action in Christ—or speaking more generally so as to include the Old Covenant—since God's merciful, gracious, and compassionate disposition toward human beings is the one decisive religious datum which human beings can know only through divine revelation, the specific contribution that the Sacred Scriptures make to religious knowledge as the written Word of God is to document God's saving action in Christ. In this way God's saving action in Christ is the core, center, heart, and chief part of the Scriptures. Other areas of religious data in the Scriptures are ultimately significant only as they relate to this central datum. Some are so very intimately related to this central datum that they are substantially an integral part of the central datum—the biblical teaching about God, about the church, about the ministry and what theology calls the sacraments, and about the relation of the present age and the age to come, to cite a few examples. Others are less directly, although importantly, related to the central datum—the biblical teaching about creation, about secular government, about personal and social ethics, and about the Sacred Scriptures themselves, to cite examples. These less directly related data are important, but they are not autonomously so; they derive their Christian significance from their relation to the central datum which they subserve. In the hierarchy of verities that the church has always taught, Lutherans hold that the Gospel is the crucial, decisive, and unique item; all the other items derive their ultimate significance from their relationship to it.

NOTES

1. See vol. I, this series, pp. 3-4, 151-153, and the literature cited there.
2. See Arthur Carl Piepkorn, "What the Symbols Have to Say about the Church," *Concordia Theological Monthly* XXVI (October 1955), esp. pp. 726-727, and the literature cited in note 11. The present discussion reproduces that essay in large part.
3. See LC II, 53. For an explanation of the abbreviations and citations of the Lutheran symbols and of Luther's writings used in the notes in this chapter, see chap. 2, above, notes 1 and 2.
4. SA III, XII, 2.
5. LC I, 100.
6. Apol VII, 10.
7. AC VII, 1.
8. AC VII, 2.
9. Apol VII, 31.
10. FC Ep Rule and Norm, 5; SD Rule and Norm, 8.
11. FC SD X, 10, 25, 27.
12. FC Ep X, 4; SD X, 9.
13. FC SD V, 15; VII, 11; X, 19-22.
14. For the discussion on election in the sixteenth century, see F. Bente, *Historical Introductions to the Lutheran Confessions* (St. Louis: Concordia Publishing House, 1921, 1965), pp. 195-208, and Eric W. Gritsch and Robert W. Jenson, *Lutheranism* Philadelphia: Fortress Press, 1976), pp. 153-163. For the controversy among American Lutherans, see the relevant articles in the *Encyclopedia of the Lutheran Church*, ed. Julius Bodensieck for the Lutheran World Federation (Minneapolis: Augsburg Publishing House, 1965).
15. FC Ep XI, 13. See also SD XI, 65:

"We should accordingly consider God's eternal election in Christ, and not outside of or apart from Christ."

16. See the discussion of Calvin's predestination theology in chap 8, below.
17. FC SD XI, 14.
18. FC SD XI, 32, 75.
19. FC SD II, 65.
20. Synergism refers to the assertion that the human subject can, unaided by grace, cooperate with the Holy Spirit in conversion.
21. FC SD XI, 48.
22. Ephesians 1:4.
23. John 15:19; see also 17:6.
24. Acts 9:15.
25. I Corinthians 9:27.
26. I Corinthians 10:12.
27. FC SD XI, 45, 90.
28. Quoted in FC SD XI, 49.
29. Isaiah 42:6.
30. On the controversy, see the summary provided by Eugene L. Fevold in *The Lutherans in North America*, ed. E. Clifford Nelson (Philadelphia: Fortress Press, 1975), pp. 313-325, and the literature cited there.
31. This identification is clearly made in FC SD XI, 70, 89.
32. See vol. I, this series, pp. 126, 131-132.
33. The data are summarized by Arthur Carl Piepkorn, *What the Symbolical Books of the Lutheran Church Have to Say about Worship and the Sacraments* (St. Louis: Concordia Publishing House, 1952), pp. 16-18.
34. Apol XIII, 4.
35. Apol XIII, 3.
36. Apol XIII, 19-20.
37. AC IX, 1 & 2.
38. SC IV, 6.
39. LC IV, 17.
40. AC IV, 2.
41. See the two baptismal liturgies of Martin Luther, LW 53, 95-103 and 106-109.
42. The *Lutheran Book of Worship*, due to be published late in 1978, reflects several of these emphases in its baptismal rite.
43. SC VII (Morning and Evening Prayers). See also Arthur Carl Piepkorn, "As You Get Out of Bed—As You Go to Bed," *Response* V (Pentecost 1963): 35-39.
44. SC IV (Baptism), 12.
45. See the rites referred to in notes 11

and 12, as well as most Lutheran service books.
46. Titus 3:5.
47. John 3:5.
48. FC SD VII, 44; LC V, 47.
49. FC Ep VII, 21, 25.
50. For example, AC X, 1; Apol X, 54, 57; SC VI, 2; LC V, 28; FC Ep VII, 6; FC SD VII, 14.
51. AC X, 1.
52. SC VI, 2.
53. SA III, VI, 1.
54. FC Ep VII, 15.
55. AC XXIV, 34; Apol XV, 40; Apol XXIV, 1.
56. LC V, 39; FC SD VII, 77.
57. SC Preface 21-25; cf. AC XXIV, 7 and LC V, 44.
58. LC V, 59.
59. I Corinthians 11:26.
60. FC SD VII, 85.
61. SA II, II, 8, 9; cf. AC XXIV, 34 and Apol XXIV, 6.
62. SC VI, 6.
63. For example, AC XXIV, 7; Apol III, 89; Apol XXIV, 72; FC SD VII, 16; Apol XXII, 10; SC Preface, 23; LC V, 22-24, 27, 66, 70.
64. Consider, for example, the conversations among Lutheran and Reformed theologians in America in the early 1960s. Papers and common statements were published as *Marburg Revisited: A Reexamination of Lutheran and Reformed Traditions*, ed. Paul C. Empie and James I. McCord (Minneapolis: Augsburg Publishing House, 1966). There only an unspecified reference to Christ's "presence" is spoken of without reference to the bread and the wine (p. 103).
65. FC Ep VII, 7.
66. FC Ep VII, 11-15.
67. FC SD VII, 32.
68. FC Ep VIII, 39.
69. SA III, VI, 2-4.
70. SA III, 5.
71. FC Ep VII, 22; SD VII, 108.
72. FC SD VII, 35.
73. FC SD VII, 126.
74. Apol XXIV, 12, *et passim*.
75. SA II, II, 9.
76. LC V, 5; FC SD VII, 32.
77. See *Eucharist and Ministry*, vol. IV of *Lutherans and Catholics in Dialogue*, ed. Paul C. Empie and T. Austin Murphy (New York and Washington: U.S.A. National Committee of the

Lutheran World Federation and the Bishops' Committee for Ecumenical and Interreligious Affairs, 1970).

78. Apol XXIV, 35-36, 74, 87, 88, 93; cf. FC SD VII, 83-84.

79. Johann Gerhard, *Confessio catholica* (Frankfurt-am-Main: Christianus Genschius, 1679), vol. II, par. II, art. siv, cap. 1, ekthesis 6, col. 1204.

80. Daniel Hollaz, *Examen theologicum acroamaticum*, 4th edn. by John Henry Hollaz (Stockholm: Johannes Heinricus Russwormius, 1725) II: 620.

81. AC XI, 1.

82. LW 51, 98.

83. AC V, 1-3.

84. AC V, 4.

85. Tr 67, 69, 72.

86. Tr. 60-61; cf. Apol XIII, 11-12 (German).

87. Apol XIII, 11-12; XXII, 13; XXVIII, 13; SA III, XI, 1; cf. Table of Duties, 1.

88. Apol VII, 28 and 47; XIII, 12; XXVIII, 19.

89. Apol XXVIII, 13-14.

90. Apol VII, 3.

91. Tr 69.

92. AC XXVIII, 8 and 21; Tr 60-61, 74.

93. Apol XIV, 1 and 5.

94. SA II, IV, 9.

95. AC XXVIII, 30-64.

96. SA III, X; Tr 72, *adhibitis suis pastoribus*, using their own pastors for this purpose. These words have unfortunately been omitted in the Tappert edition.

97. SA II, IV, 10-13.

98. Apol XIII, 9-13.

99. Tr 67, 72.

100. AC XIV.

101. Apol XIII, 12.

102. Apol XIV, 1.

103. Tr 65.

104. Tr 72.

105. Tr 67.

106. The Papal Confutation was submitted by the Roman party at the Augsburg Diet of 1530 and was publicly read on August 3 in the same room in which the Augsburg Confession had been read six weeks earlier. The text is available in English translation in Johann Michael Reu, *The Augsburg Confession: A Collection of Sources with an Historical Introduction* (Chicago: Wartburg Publishing House, 1930), pp. 348-383.

107. The Peasants' Uprisings, or Peasants' War, embraced a series of battles in southwestern and central Germany, mainly in 1525. Some of the peasant leaders understood themselves to be bearing arms for the Gospel and in support of Luther's reforms. The peasant armies were badly beaten by the armies of the princes.

108. Apol XVI, 12.

109. Apol XIX.

110. FC SD I, 2.

111. SC II, 2.

112. Matthew 16:18.

113. Romans 13:1, AV.

114. SC III, 4.

115. AC, Summary after XXI, 1.

116. FC SD X, 9; AC VII, 3.

117. AC VII, 1-2.

118. Apol XXIV, 49, 51.

119. See above, chap. 2, section on "Justification" and chap. 3, section on "The Sacred Ministry."

120. Apol XXIV, 30.

121. Apol XXIV, 71, 74.

122. FC SD Rule and Norm, 3.

123. AC IV, 1.

124. Apol IV, *passim*.

125. This oft-cited statement from a sermon may be found, slightly amplified, in Ewald Plass, *What Luther Says* (St. Louis: Concordia Publishing House, 1959), II, 732.

126. FC SD V, 1.

BIBLIOGRAPHY

rtram, Robert W., ed. *Theology in the Life of the Church*. Philadelphia: Fortress Press, 1963.

unner, Peter. *Worship in the Name of Jesus*. Trans. Martin H. Bertram. St. Louis: Concordia Publishing House, 1968.

entz, Edgar M. *Biblical Studies Today: A Guide to Current Issues and Trends*. St. Louis: Concordia Publishing House, 1966.

———. *The Historical-Critical Method*. Philadelphia: Fortress Press, 1975.

Maier, Gerhard. *The End of the Historical-Critical Method*. Trans. Edwin W. Leverenz and Rudolph F. Norden. St.

Louis: Concordia Publishing House, 1977.

Nelson, E. Clifford, ed. *The Lutherans in North America*. Philadelphia: Fortress Press, 1975.

Piepkorn, Arthur Carl. "Christ and Culture: A Lutheran Approach," *Response* II (Pentecost 1960): 3-16.

———. "Inspiration: The Position of the Church and Her Symbols," *Concordia Theological Monthly* XXV (October 1954): 738-742.

———. "The Life of God in the Life of the Parish," *Response* IV (Pentecost 1962): 38-48.

———. "The Lutheran Church a Sacramental Church," *Augustana Quarterly* XVII (January 1938): 45-58.

———. "The Lutheran Doctrine of the Sacrament of the Altar, Ecumenically Considered," *National Liturgical Week* XXV (1964): 135-154.

———. "The One Eucharist for the One World," *Concordia Theological Monthly* XLI (February 1972): 94-108.

———. "The Sacred Ministry and Holy Ordination in the Symbolical Books of the Lutheran Church," *Concordia The-* *ological Monthly* XL (September 1969) 553-573.

———. "What Does Inerrancy Mean?" *Concordia Theological Monthly* XXXV (September 1965): 577-593.

———. *What the Symbolical Books of the Lutheran Church Have to Say about Worship and the Sacraments*. St. Louis Concordia Publishing House, 1952.

———. "What the Symbols Say about the Church," *Concordia Theological Monthly* XXVI (October 1955): 721-763.

Schlink, Edmund. *The Doctrine of Baptism*. Trans. Herbert J. A. Bouman St. Louis: Concordia Publishing House 1972.

Schroeder, Edward H. "Is There a Lutheran Hermeneutics?" in *The Lively Function of the Gospel*, essays in honor of Richard R. Caemmerer, Sr. Ed Robert W. Bertram. St. Louis: Concordia Publishing House, 1966. Pp. 81-97

Schultz, Robert C. "Baptism and Justification," *Una Sancta* XVII (Easter 1960) 8-21.

Tietjen, John H. *Which Way to Lutheran Unity?* St. Louis: Clayton Publishing House, 1976.

4. Lutheranism in the United States and Canada

Lutheran Council in the United States of America

Organized at Cleveland, Ohio, in November 1966, the Lutheran Council in the United States of America is the cooperative agency for the three major Lutheran church bodies in the United States: the Lutheran Church in America, The American Lutheran Church, and The Lutheran Church–Missouri Synod. Its threefold purpose is "to further the witness, the work and the interests" of the participating church bodies, "to seek to achieve consensus in a systematic and continuing way," and "to provide an instrumentality" through which its church bodies "may work together in fulfilling their responsibility of Christian service."[1]

In some ways the Lutheran Council in the U.S.A. is a successor organization to the National Lutheran Council, the cooperative agency for nearly all Lutherans except those in the Lutheran Synodical Conference from 1918 to 1966. When mergers were about to reduce the number of church bodies in the National Lutheran Council from eight to two, the National Lutheran Council extended an invitation in 1958 to the other Lutheran church bodies to consider whether it might be possible to work together in a new cooperative agency. The Lutheran Church–Missouri Synod and the Synod of Evaneglical Churches[2] accepted the invitation and joined with the Lutheran Church in America and The American Lutheran Church to form the Lutheran Council in the United States of America. Incorporated within the new agency were some of the cooperative activities previously conducted by the National Lutheran Council, such as its News Bureau and Washington public affairs office. The Lutheran Council also embraced the work of several independent agencies of cooperation which had been working in fields of immigration services, films, scouting, and Spanish publications. In addition it took on the responsibility of coordinating the work of the participating church bodies in the field of American missions and social ministry services.

The Lutheran Council is an agency of its participating church bodies without authority of its own. Each of its participating church bodies determines the extent of its involvement in cooperative activities except that all participants are required to be part of the program of theological study. The governance of the Lutheran Council is an annual meeting of representatives of the church bodies. Its headquarters are at 360 Park Avenue South, New York, New York 10010. The Association of Evangelical Lutheran Churches, the church body emerging from controversy in The Lutheran Church–Missouri Synod, was received as a member in 1978.

Lutheran Council in Canada

The cooperative agency for the Lutheran groups in Canada is the Lutheran Council in Canada. It began operations on January 1, 1967, and serves the Evangelical Lutheran Church of Canada (formerly a district of The American Lutheran Church), the Lutheran Church–Canada (the agency for Missouri Synod Lutherans in Canada), and the Lutheran Church in America–Canada Section.

Like its counterpart in the United States, the Lutheran Council in Canada continues some of the work of a predecessor organization, the Canadian Lutheran Council, whose members were reduced to two as a result of the mergers producing The American Lutheran Church in 1960 and the Lutheran Church in America in 1962. As The Lutheran Church–Missouri Synod was able to enter into a cooperative, agency in the United States, so its Canadian members helped to form a new cooperative organization in Canada. In many ways the constitution of the Lutheran Council in Canada parallels that of the Lutheran Council in the United States of America.

Headquarters are at 500–365 Hargrave Street, Winnipeg, Manitoba R3B 2K3.

Lutheran Church in America

The largest of the churches of the Augsburg Confession in the United States and Canada is also the one with major roots reaching back to the colonial period in North American history. Organized in 1962, the Lutheran Church in America united four church bodies: the Augustana Lutheran Church; the American Evangelical Lutheran Church; the Finnish Evangelical Lutheran Church, known also as the Suomi Synod; and the United Lutheran Church in America, the group which traced its heritage to the immigrations in the colonial period.

Lutherans were among the early settlers of the New World, coming as Swedes to Delaware and among the Dutch to New Amsterdam. At the time of the American Revolution, Lutherans were scattered throughout the colonies with major concentrations in New York, Pennsylvania, North Carolina, and Georgia. By 1790 their number was estimated to be about 122,000.[3] Henry Melchior Muhlenberg (1711–1787), known as the patriarch of American Lutheranism, helped to gather the Lutherans into congregations, provided them with pastors, and in 1748 established the first general organization of Lutherans, ambitiously designated as the Evangelical Lutheran Ministerium in North America and later more appropriately named the Pennsylvania Ministerium.

After congregations in New York and North Carolina had each established similar organizations, the Pennsylvania Ministerium, sparked by secessionist movements among its congregations in Ohio and Maryland, led the way in establishing a general synod, composed of the regional synods. The General Synod of the Evangelical Lutheran Church in the United States of America was established in 1820. Though almost destroyed by the withdrawal of the Pennsylvania Ministerium three years later, the General Synod survived and prospered under the capable leadership of Samuel Simon Schmucker (1799–1873), who helped establish a theological seminary for General Synod Lutherans at Gettysburg, Pennsylvania.

By 1860 the General Synod had succeeded in embracing 864 of 1,313 ministers and 164,000 of the 245,000 members of Lutheran congregations, about two-thirds of the Lutheran Church in the United States.[4] But the civil strife which divided the nation cost the General Synod its southern synods, which at the conclusion of the war in 1865 chose to continue the separate organization established in 1863. In 1886, with the addition of several independent synods, the southern organization was reconstituted as the United Synod of the Evangelical Lutheran Church in the South.

In addition to the loss of its southern synods the General Synod underwent the strain of tension between those who advocated an "American Lutheranism" in harmony with the Protestant evangelicalism of the period, and those who, influenced by the confessional revival in Europe and by a new wave of immigration beginning in 1840, argued for a return to strict Lutheran standards in theology and church life. Tension turned to conflict, and in 1867 a number of synods under the leadership of Charles Porterfield Krauth (1823–1883), having withdrawn from the General Synod and joining forces with a number of midwestern synods newly established by the immigrants, established the General Council of the Evangelical Lutheran Church in North America. The alliance with the foreign-language-speaking midwestern synods did not last however. With the exception of the continued membership of the Augustana Synod, most of the newer bodies withdrew to join with the rapidly growing Missouri Synod to form still another general organization, the Evangelical Lutheran Synodical Conference, established in 1872.

Through several decades of cooperation the three eastern general organizations with strands reaching back to Muhlenberg overcame the difficulties that had led to separate organizations. Sparked by the quadricentennial anniversary of the Reformation in 1917, the General Synod, the General Council, and the United Synod of the South formed the United Lutheran Church in America in 1918. The Augustana Synod chose not to take part in the merger, giving as reason its commitment to continue work in the Swedish language. At its founding the United Lutheran Church in America numbered almost 800,000 confirmed members, with about 2,800 ministers and nearly 4,000 churches, totaling approximately one-third of the Lutherans in America.[5]

The Reformation anniversary coupled with the necessity of cooperating in ministry to military personnel during World War I led to the formation in 1918 of the National Lutheran Council (NLC), an agency of cooperation for all the Lutheran church bodies except those in the Evangelical Lutheran Synodical Conference.

After several decades of cooperation within the council, a movement began following World War II to effect organic union among the NLC participants. In another decade the decision had been made to reduce the eight participating churches by merger into two. Failing in its efforts to effect the union of all NLC participants, the United Lutheran Church in America joined with the Augustana Lutheran Church, the United Evangelical Lutheran Church, and the Finnish Evangelical Lutheran Church to establish the Lutheran Church in America in 1962. The new church body took over from The Lutheran Church–Missouri Synod the distinction of being the largest church body in the United States and Canada with an inclusive membership of 3.2 million.

The three smaller church bodies that helped form the Lutheran Church in America were the result of major immigrations to the United States from northern Europe in the second half of the nineteenth century. The Augustana Lutheran Church, established in 1860 for Scandinavians, very quickly became an organization for Swedish Lutherans. Associated with the General Council from 1860 to 1918, it was natural enough for the Augustana Lutheran Church to join in a new church body with the United Lutheran Church in America, even though it had strong ties with those churches in the National Lutheran Council that were to form The American Lutheran Church in 1960. The second largest church in the merger that produced the Lutheran Church in America, the Augustana Lutheran Church contributed 630,000 members to the new organization. The American Evangelical Lutheran Church was one of two Danish groups produced by the nineteenth-century immigrations. Established in 1872, it embraced those with strong ties to the state church of Denmark. It brought 24,000 members into the new Lutheran Church in America in 1962. The Finnish Evangelical Lutheran Church, or the Suomi (that is, Finnish) Synod, was formed in 1890 to bring together the Finns who had settled in the midwestern United States. Its membership stood at 36,000 when it joined in forming the Lutheran Church in America.[6]

Of all the Lutheran church bodies in the United States and Canada, the Lutheran Church in America is the most acculturated. It has adapted from its ethnic past to American and Canadian life and therefore appears to the outside observer to be more "liberal" than other members of the Lutheran family. It is by far the most ecumenical of the Lutheran churches in America with membership in the Lutheran World Federation, the World Council of Churches, and the National Council of Churches of Christ in America (the only Lutheran body in the NCCCA). For many years its late president, Franklin Clark Fry (1900–1968), was an acknowledged leader in the ecumenical movement. The Lutheran Church in America is also the most advanced of the Lutheran churches in America in relating the church to social issues and in utilizing the knowledge and skills of American business management in the church structure.

As Article II of its constitution, the Lutheran Church in America makes the following "Confession of Faith":

Section 1. This church confesses Jesus Christ as Lord of the Church. The Holy Spirit creates and sustains the Church through the Gospel and thereby unites believers with their Lord and with one another in the fellowship of faith.

Section 2. This church holds that the Gospel is the revelation of God's sovereign will and saving grace in Jesus Christ. In Him, the Word Incarnate, God imparts Himself to men.

Section 3. This church acknowledges the Holy Scriptures as the norm for the faith and life of the Church. The Holy Scriptures are the divinely inspired record of God's redemptive act in Christ, for which the Old Testament prepared the way and which the New Testament proclaims. In the continuation of this proclamation in the Church, God still speaks through the Holy Scriptures and realizes His redemptive purpose generation after generation.

Section 4. This church accepts the Apostles', the Nicene, and the Athanasian creeds as true declarations of the faith of the Church.

Section 5. This church accepts the Unaltered Augsburg Confession, and Luther's Small Catechism as true witnesses to the Gospel, and acknowledges as one with it in faith and doctrine all churches that likewise accept the teachings of these symbols.

Section 6. This church accepts the other symbolical books of the evangelical Lutheran church, the Apology of the Augsburg Confession, the Smalcald Articles, Luther's Large Catechism, and the Formula of Concord as further valid interpretations of the confession of the church.

Section 7. This church affirms that the Gospel transmitted by the Holy Scriptures, to which the creeds and confessions bear witness, is the true treasure of the Church, the substance of its proclamation, and the basis of its unity and continuity. The Holy Spirit uses the proclamation of the Gospel and the administration of the Sacraments to create and sustain Christian faith and fellowship. As this occurs, the Church fulfills its divine mission and purpose.[7]

The Lutheran Church in America is organized into thirty-three synods, one of which, the Slovak Zion Synod, is nongeographical. Its Canadian members, present in all nine provinces of Canada, deal with their concerns through an organization of their own, the Lutheran Church in America– Canada Section. Representatives of the church body meet in national convention biennially. Headquarters of the church body are at 231 Madison Avenue, New York, New York 10006. There are 5,771 congregations and an inclusive membership of 2,974,749.[8]

The American Lutheran Church

Among the churches of the Augsburg Confession in the United States and Canada, The American Lutheran Church is a blending of several church bodies established by immigrants from northern Europe who settled in the Middle West during the latter half of the nineteenth century. Formed in 1960, The American Lutheran Church brought together four church bodies: the American Lutheran Church,[9] the Evangelical Lutheran Church, the United Evangelical Lutheran Church, and the Lutheran Free Church, the latter group entering in 1963.

The four merging church bodies, along with the four church organizations which in 1962 formed the Lutheran Church in America, had cooperated in the National Lutheran Council for several decades. More significant for the merger was the association of the four merging groups, along with the Augustana Lutheran Church, in the American Lutheran Conference, a confederation established in 1930 as both a buffer and a bridge between the large United Lutheran Church in America and the equally large Lutheran Church–Missouri Synod.[10] The American Lutheran Conference was the practical consequence of doctrinal agreement reached by the participating church bodies in 1925 and formulated in a statement known as "The Minneapolis Theses,"[11] by which the church bodies recognized one another as orthodox in Lutheran teaching and entered into fellowship with one another. The proposal that ultimately led to the establishment of The American Lutheran Church was made at a meeting of the American Lutheran Conference by one of its smaller members, the United Evangelical Lutheran Church. The proposal met with the approval of all participants except the Augustana Lutheran Church, which argued for a more inclusive merger of all eight groups in the National Lutheran Council and ultimately helped to establish the Lutheran Church in America.

Three of the church bodies which formed The American Lutheran Church were themselves the results of mergers. One of them, the American Lutheran Church, provided the new church with a constituency that was Germanic in background.

Formed in 1930, the former American Lutheran Church brought three organizations together. One was the Evangelical Lutheran Joint Synod of Ohio and Other States, organized in 1818 by Ohio members of the Pennsylvania Ministerium. The German immigrants who settled in Ohio from 1840 on gave the Ohio church body both an increasingly German and a more fervent Lutheran character. The Joint Synod of Ohio refused to become a member of the General Council of the Evangelical Lutheran Church in America when it was founded in 1867 because of the latter group's failure to give acceptable statements on four issues: pulpit fellowship, altar fellowship, chiliasm, and membership in secret societies.[12] The Joint Synod of Ohio instead joined with the Missouri Synod in creating the Evangelical Lutheran

Synodical Conference in 1872, leaving in 1881 because of disagreement with the Missouri Synod over the doctrine of election.

The departure of the Joint Synod of Ohio from the Synodical Conference led it to explore relations with the Iowa Synod, the second church body involved in establishing the American Lutheran Church of 1930. The Iowa Synod was established in 1854 by Lutherans under the leadership of the Bavarian churchman Wilhelm Löhe (1808–1872) after he and they had had a major disagreement with the leaders of the Missouri Synod over the nature of the church's ministry and the relation of the Lutheran confessional writings to the Scriptures. Leaders of the Ohio and Iowa church bodies entered into doctrinal discussions and after several decades formulated their agreement in a statement known as "The Toledo Theses"[13] and entered into fellowship with one another.

As the Ohio and Iowa synods began to give consideration to organic union of their groups, the Buffalo Synod, the third group to help form the 1930 American Lutheran Church, entered the discussion. Established in 1845 by Lutherans from Prussia, the Buffalo Synod remained small, losing a major portion of its constituency in 1866 to the Missouri Synod after discussions of differences between the two groups over the nature of the ministry.

The 1930 merger was almost disrupted by last-minute disagreement between the two groups over the inspiration and inerrancy of the Scriptures, but the issues were satisfactorily resolved. At its founding in 1930 the American Lutheran Church consisted of more than 2,000 congregations and a half million members.[14] Thirty years later the American Lutheran Church contributed to the larger organization by the same name approximately the same number of congregations but a doubled membership of somewhat more than one million.[15]

The Evangelical Lutheran Church was the second church body, itself the result of a merger which helped to form The American Lutheran Church in 1960. Established in 1917, the Evangelical Lutheran Church sought to be the rallying point for Norwegian Lutheranism and succeeded in uniting three organizations.

One group which shared in the 1917 merger was known as Hauge's Synod, established in 1846 by those who were influenced by Hans Nielsen Hauge (1771–1824), Norway's evangelist-reformer, and who like him emphasized conversion and lay leadership. A second group in the 1917 merger was known as the Norwegian Synod, established in 1853 by those in close association with the state church of Norway. The Norwegian Synod developed close relations with the Missouri Synod and for a time was a member of the Synodical Conference until internal tensions in its own midst over the doctrine of election caused it to withdraw. The third group to share in the 1917 merger was the United Norwegian Lutheran Church of America, formed in 1890 as a merger of three groups and the catalyst for the effort to unite the Norwegians at the turn of the twentieth century.

Uniting the Norwegian Lutherans in America was not a simple task. They disagreed sharply over issues which had their origin in their Norwegian homeland, among them differences in understanding of the ministry, conversion, and sanctification. The chief obstacle to union lay in differences over the doctrine of election, the issue that had split the Synodical Conference several decades earlier. A breakthrough was achieved in 1912 in the Madison Agreement (*Opgjoer*), in which it was decided that the two contending views on election were "two forms" of the same doctrine and that both were in harmony with the Scriptures as taught in the Lutheran symbols.[16] Convinced that the agreement had compromised the truth, a small group within the Norwegian Synod refused to enter the new church and organized what they claimed to be the continuation of the Norwegian Synod (later renamed the Evangelical Lutheran Synod).

At its founding in 1917 the Evangelical Lutheran Church[17] numbered a little over 1,000 congregations and almost half a million members, incorporating in its organization 92 percent of Norwegian Lutherans.[18] It acculturated to American life following World War I and by the time of the 1960 merger had close to 2,700 congregations with almost 1.2 million members.[19]

The remaining church which helped form The American Lutheran Church in 1960 was the United Evangelical Lutheran Church, one of two church bodies in the United States with Danish heritage. The United Evangelical Lutheran Church[20] was formed in 1896 as a result of a merger of two Danish groups opposed to the already established Danish Evangelical Lutheran Church in America because of its alleged false doctrine, a reference to characteristics of teaching espoused as a result of the influence of the noted Danish pastor, Nicolai F. S. Grundtvig (1783–1872). At its founding the United Evangelical Lutheran Church numbered 127 congregations and nearly 14,000 members.[21] Acculturated by 1960, the church body brought 181 congregations and more than 70,000 members into The American Lutheran Church.

The fourth church body which helped to shape the constituency of The American Lutheran Church was the Lutheran Free Church. It joined only in 1963, since it did not receive the required ratification by its congregations before that time. The Lutheran Free Church was formed in 1897 by a minority within the United Norwegian Lutheran Church of America who were concerned about the future of a seminary of one of the groups which helped form the United Church and who argued for congregational freedom. At the time of its formation the Lutheran Free Church included 125 congregations and 6,250 members.[22] When the required majority of its congregations ratified the decision to be part of The American Lutheran Church, a minority reorganized and is now known as the Association of Free Lutheran Congregations. At the time it decided for merger the Lutheran Free Church consisted of 288 congregations and 88,500 members.[23]

In its constitution The American Lutheran Church makes the following "Confession of Faith":

Section 1. The American Lutheran Church accepts all the canonical books of the Old and New Testaments as a whole and in all their parts as the divinely inspired, revealed, and inerrant Word of God, and submits to this as the only infallible authority in all matters of faith and life.

Section 2. As brief and true statements of the doctrine of the Word of God, the Church accepts and confesses the following Symbols, subscription to which shall be required of all its members, both congregations and individuals:

(1) The ancient ecumenical Creeds: the Apostolic, the Nicene, and the Athanasian;

(2) The Unaltered Augsburg Confession and Luther's Small Catechism.

Section 3. As further elaboration of and in accord with these Lutheran Symbols, the Church also receives the other documents in the Book of Concord of 1580: the Apology, Luther's Large Catechism, the Smalcald Articles, and the Formula of Concord; and recognizes them as normative for its theology.

Section 4. The American Lutheran Church accepts without reservation the symbolical books of the evangelical Lutheran Church, not insofar as but because they are the presentation and explanation of the pure doctrine of the Word of God and a summary of the faith of the evangelical Lutheran Church.[24]

Predominantly midwestern in its location, The American Lutheran Church also has strength on the Pacific coast and in Texas. Its membership is concentrated most heavily in Minnesota with major strength also in Ohio, Michigan, and the Dakotas. Its character is still more rural than urban. Since its founding it has succeeded well in its efforts to blend diverse groups with a variety of cultural heritages.

In its structure The American Lutheran Church is more centralized than the other two major Lutheran church bodies in the United States. Its eighteen districts are slowly gaining responsibility and becoming more comparable to the synods of the Lutheran Church in America. In 1966 The American Lutheran Church's Canada District became an autonomous church body; its 334 congregations and more than 77,000 members were organized as the Evangelical Lutheran Church of Canada.

The American Lutheran Church is a member of the Lutheran World Federation and of the World Council of Churches of Christ in America. It participates in the Lutheran Council in the United States of America, the agency of cooperation for Lutherans in the United States.

Headquarters of The American Lutheran Church are at 422 South Fifth Street, Minneapolis, Minnesota 55415. It has 4,814 congregations and 2,402,261 members.[25]

The Association of Free Lutheran Congregations

With the Lutheran Free Church scheduled to become part of the American Lutheran Church on February 1, 1963, a group of congregations belonging to the Lutheran Free Church withdrew from it late in 1962 and formed the Lutheran Free Church (Not Merged). When a court order restrained the organizers from using this name, they called themselves the Association of Free Lutheran Congregations. The Association affirms its belief in Christian unity as a unity of the Spirit with an emphasis on the fellowship of all believers in Christ, rather than on a man-made unity that neglects fundamental doctrines and may lead to a world church. It accepts the Bible as the Word of God, to which human understanding, reasoning, and theories must bow, and the Lutheran Symbolical Books as a correct statement of biblical truth. It insists that the local congregation is the right form of the Kingdom of God on earth and that there is no higher human authority. It regards the preaching of the gospel of redemption and not of the social gospel as the central duty of a Christian congregation. "Liturgies, ceremonies, and forms must not be overemphasized in the church services and life" of the Christian community. It calls for Christians to lead lives "free from compromise and worldliness."[26]

Since its organization the Association has established a number of new missions and has attracted some congregations that before 1961 had belonged to the Evangelical Lutheran Church, the American Lutheran Church, and the Suomi Synod. It has 127 congregations and missions with a total membership of 14,000. It conducts foreign missions in Brazil and Mexico. Its headquarters are at 3110 East Medicine Lake Boulevard, Minneapolis, Minnesota 55441.[27]

Evangelical Lutheran Church of Canada

When The American Lutheran Church was formed in 1960, the congregations of its merging church bodies were brought together in the Canada District. After receiving a charter from the Canadian parliament as the Evangelical Lutheran Church of Canada, the district functioned as an autonomous body beginning in January 1967.

The heritage of the Evangelical Lutheran Church of Canada reaches back to German and Norwegian pioneers who settled in the prairie provinces in the latter nineteenth and early twentieth centuries. There are 318 congregations with an inclusive membership of 82,000. Headquarters are at 247 First Avenue North, Saskatoon, Saskatchewan S7K 4H5.

The Lutheran Church–Missouri Synod

The Lutheran Church–Missouri Synod owes its origin and development to nineteenth-century immigrations from Germany. Established by German immigrants who championed the Lutheran confessional revival, it developed a reputation for its uncompromising and combative defense of Lutheran orthodoxy. It is the only major Lutheran church body in the United States and Canada which has not experienced a merger.[28] In recent years it has been racked by internal controversy which has resulted in division.

Two separate groups of immigrants joined together to form The Lutheran

Church–Missouri Synod at Chicago, Illinois, in 1847. One group consisted of Lutherans from Saxony who had settled in Missouri in 1839 and, through the theological leadership of C. F. W. Walther (1811–1887), professor at its theological seminary, had survived the trauma of deposing its leader, Martin Stephan (1777–1846). The second group was composed primarily of Bavarian (Franconian) immigrants who had settled in Michigan and Indiana under the sponsorship of the influential German theologian Wilhelm Löhe (1808–1872), pastor of the church in Neuendettelsau, Bavaria. Twelve congregations and twenty-two pastors of the two groups united because of their conviction that they could not join existing Lutheran synods without compromise of the truth.

The German Evangelical Lutheran Synod of Missouri, Ohio, and Other States was the name chosen for the new organization.[29] The inclusion of "German" in the name was not only descriptive of the language of the founders but a clear statement of the new group's intention. The church body vigorously strove to be German in its American environment. It sponsored an active program to meet the newly arriving German immigrants at United States port cities and to guide them into the congregations of the church body, growing rapidly to a size of 1,500 congregations and 1,000 pastors over four decades. Its congregations established parochial schools to provide the children of its members with instruction in the true doctrine by means of the German language.

"The Missouri Synod" is the name by which the church body has been known throughout its history. Though "Missouri" originally designated location, it quickly became a synonym for theological stance and organizational character. Leaders of the church body carried on the polemic over the nature of Lutheranism, in which they had participated in their homeland, against their fellow Lutheran immigrants in America and against the Lutheran church bodies already established in the United States. Opposed to the "unionism" by which Lutherans and Reformed were being regarded as one in their homeland, they insisted on complete unity in doctrine and practice as the requirement for organizational unity.[30] Together with other Lutheran church bodies which shared their view of the requirement for unity, the Missouri Synod helped to establish the Evangelical Lutheran Synodical Conference of North America in 1872. After two key members, the Joint Synod of Ohio and the Norwegian Synod, withdrew from the Synodical Conference in the 1880s because of disagreement over the doctrine of election, the Missouri Synod continued as the dominant member until the Synodical Conference was dissolved a century after its founding.

While the rest of Lutheranism gradually drew together through the merger of many separate church bodies, the Missouri Synod remained apart, except for its relations with three small synods in the Synodical Conference.[31] It did not participate in the formation of the National Lutheran Council in 1918 or in the conferences which produced the Lutheran World Federation in 1947. Nor did it ever join the World Council of Churches or the National Council of the Churches of Christ in America. However, it continued to grow in numbers, from nearly 350,000 members in 1884 to almost 1,300,000 by 1935,[32] and in the late 1950s became the largest Lutheran church body in America until the Lutheran Church in America took over that position when it was formed in 1962.

Of the major Lutheran church bodies in the United States and Canada, The Lutheran Church–Missouri Synod retained its ethnic character the longest and is still in the process of acculturating. The shift from German to English signaled other changes. In 1967 the Missouri Synod found its way clear to join with the Lutheran Church in America, The Ameircan Lutheran Church, and the Synod of Evangelical Lutheran Churches[33] in establishing the Lutheran Council in the United States of America as an agency of co-operation. In 1969 the Missouri Synod declared itself in fellowship with The American Lutheran Church. The Missouri Synod's increasing relations with other Lutherans was the major reason for the decision by the Wisconsin Evangelical Lutheran Synod and the Evangelical Lutheran Synod to sever relations with the Missouri Synod, actions which led to the dissolution of the Evangelical Lutheran Synodical Conference of North America in 1967.

In the 1960s and 1970s serious controversy led to division within the church body. The primary theological issue was the nature of biblical authority with concentration also on the nature of the church's mission and unity, though some argued that theological issues were misused in behalf of a political effort to reverse the tide of change within the synod.[34] The controversy led to a mass exodus of faculty and students from Concordia Seminary in February 1974 and to the formation of a new seminary, known as Seminex. Disciplinary action against several presidents of the synod's regional districts precipitated the formation of the Association of Evangelical Lutheran Churches in December 1976 by those presidents' supporters. At its 1977 convention the Missouri Synod announced its intention of severing fellowship with The American Lutheran Church in two years unless that church body conforms to Missouri Synod views against the ordination of women and ecumenical relationships. In recent years the Missouri Synod has reduced the amount of its participation in the cooperative work of the Lutheran Council in the United States of America.

The doctrinal basis of The Lutheran Church–Missouri Synod is set forth in Article II of its constitution:

The Synod, and every member of the Synod, accepts without reservation:

1. The Scriptures of the Old and the New Testament as the written Word of God and the only rule and norm of faith and of practice;

2. All the Symbolical Books of the Evangelical Lutheran Church as a true and unadulterated statement and exposition of the Word of God, to wit: the three Ecumenical Creeds (the Apostles' Creed, the Nicene Creed, the Athana-

sian Creed), the Unaltered Augsburg Confession, the Smalcald Articles, the Large Catechism of Luther, the Small Catechism of Luther, and the Formula of Concord.[35]

However, there is more to the Missouri Synod's doctrinal standards than the doctrinal basis in its constitution. The place of synodically adopted doctrinal statements has been an issue under debate in the recent controversy within the synod. In 1973 a synod convention decided that the synod had an obligation to adopt doctrinal statements from time to time and to declare them binding on synod members insofar as they were in accord with the Scripture. The same convention then adopted such a doctrinal statement, "A Statement of Scriptural and Confessional Principles," and declared it to be binding on the synod's members because it was in all of its parts in accord with the Scriptures.[36] The primary concern of the adopted doctrinal statement is with the inspiration and authority of the Bible and with listing the views and practices concerning the Bible which are to be disallowed within the synod, among them the use of historical criticism.

In its organization The Lutheran Church–Missouri Synod has been the most congregational of the major Lutheran bodies in the United States. Its congregationalism is rooted in the early experience of the Missouri Saxons who were disillusioned by the autocratic rule of the leader they deposed. From the beginning in 1847 the constitution has assured the member congregations that no action of the synod is binding on the congregations if they consider it to be contrary to the Word of God or inexpedient for their local situation.[37] The question of congregational autonomy versus synodical authority has been at issue in the recent controversy. The forty districts of the synod, including two in South America, three in Canada, and two that are nongeographical (English and SELC), function as the synod for the congregations in their jurisdiction; but the movement toward centralization, which began twenty years ago, is continuing and is shifting the responsibility from districts to national organization. A major study of reorganization of the synod is in process. The Canadian congregations of the Missouri Synod have been united since 1958 in a federation as Lutheran Church–Canada. A biennial church convention is the synod's legislative authority.

With its membership strength in the Midwest, the Missouri Synod changed rapidly from a rural to an urban church following World War II. It has 5,796 congregations and missions and 2,757,271 members.[38] In addition, it claims 1,361 parochial schools.[39] Headquarters of the church body are at 500 North Broadway, St. Louis, Missouri 63102.

The Concordia Lutheran Conference

In 1951 the founders of the Orthodox Lutheran Conference withdrew from The Lutheran Church–Missouri Synod because of that body's "progressive deterioration in doctrine and practice during the two preceding decades, in spite of much patient admonition to the contrary on the part of many pastors and congregations in its midst," and, more specifically, because of its "unionistic character" and its "tyrannical procedures against its own protesting pastors and congregations." In January 1956 a break in the fellowship of the Orthodox Lutheran Conference took place. Both parties continued to call themselves the Orthodox Lutheran Conference.[40] In 1957 the members of one group, while insisting that they were "bonafide orthodox Lutherans," resolved for practical reasons to reorganize as the Concordia Lutheran Conference.[41]

The Concordia Lutheran Conference accepts without reservation the canonical Scriptures as the verbally inspired Word of God and the only rule and norm of faith and life, the symbolical writings that comprise the Book of Concord of 1580 "as a true statement and exposition of God's Word," and *A Brief Statement*, drawn up by The Lutheran Church–Missouri Synod in 1932, "as a further correct exposition of God's Word and as an uncompromising basis in our time for God-pleasing union" with other Lutherans.[42]

In its relation to the member congregations, the conference does not regard itself as a church or church government with legislative or coercive powers, but only as an advisory or service body.[43]

The conference has five congregations, with a total baptized membership of 343. There are no central headquarters.

Lutheran Churches of the Reformation

As "an attempt in a day of utter confusion to witness to the overwhelming truth of the infallible Scriptures" the Lutheran Churches of the Reformation held their organizational meeting in Chicago, Illinois, on April 28-29, 1964. Authorizing the meeting were four complete congregations that had withdrawn from The Lutheran Church–Missouri Synod and six other congregations whose charter members were laymen who had left either The Lutheran Church–Missouri Synod or the Wisconsin Evangelical Lutheran Synod.

The Lutheran Churches of the Reformation hold that the Bible is "the very Word of God, His infallible revelation given by inspiration of the Holy Spirit, in all parts and words recorded without error in the original manuscripts by the prophets, apostles, and evangelists." They accept as "true and correct exposition of the doctrines taught in the Scriptures" the confessions of the Book of Concord and *A Brief Statement of the Doctrinal Position of the Missouri Synod* (1932).

The Lutheran Churches of the Reformation regard themselves structurally not as a synod but as a federation of independent churches and as "a service organization to assist pastors, teachers, congregations in developing a sense of fellowship, consistence in purity of doctrine and practice." They maintain fellowship relations with the "Evangelical Lutheran Congregations of the

Reformation," organized in 1966 by a group of five congregations in Queensland, Australia, that had withdrawn from the Evangelical Lutheran Church of Australia, and with the Bible Lutheran Church of Nigeria, a group of fifteen indigenous congregations, some of whose pastors were formerly members of the Evangelical Lutheran Church of Nigeria.[44]

The federation consists of 29 congregations and missions in seven states and the provinces of Ontario, with a total membership of 6,273. The headquarters are at 440 St. James Street, Detroit, Michigan 48210.

Association of Evangelical Lutheran Churches

A church body still in the process of formation, the Association of Evangelical Lutheran Churches was established in December 1976 by members of The Lutheran Church–Missouri Synod for whom continuing membership in that church body had become intolerable. The new church body is one of the consequences of the controversy which is continuing within The Lutheran Church–Missouri Synod.

Precipitating the formation of the Association of Evangelical Lutheran Churches was the ouster in April 1976 by Missouri Synod president Jacob A. O. Preus of four of eight district presidents who had refused to state their compliance with a resolution of the synod's 1975 convention forbidding district presidents to ordain graduates of Seminex, the seminary established in 1974 by all but a few of the faculty and students of Concordia Seminary over the suspension of the seminary's president, John H. Tietjen. The four presidents and their district supporters ignored the ouster action and the appointment of acting presidents as successors. Three of them, joined by three more of the eight presidents, led the way in forming the Association of Evangelical Lutheran Churches by establishing five constituent synods which in turn joined together in the national church body.

At its constituting convention in December 1976 the Association of Evangelical Lutheran Churches adopted a constitution with a doctrinal article whose substance is identical with the doctrinal article of The Lutheran Church–Missouri Synod. The Missouri Synod's doctrinal basis has been one of the issues in the controversy in that church body. The debate has been over the right of synod conventions to make binding on members of the synod doctrinal statements adopted by majority vote. Those who formed the Association of Evangelical Lutheran Churches argued that no other document besides those enumerated in the Missouri Synod's doctrinal basis could serve as a standard for teaching or a criterion for ministry within the church body. Thus in establishing the new church body they committed themselves to the "old" doctrinal basis of the Missouri Synod to express their conviction that they and not the advocates of binding doctrinal statements were the true representatives of the Missouri Synod's historic position. The doctrinal article declares:

We joyfully acknowledge and confess without reservation the Scriptures of the Old and New Testament as the written Word of God and the only rule and norm of faith and of practice; and all the Symbolical Books of the Evangelical Lutheran Church as a true and unadulterated statement and exposition of the Word of God, to wit: the three Ecumenical Creeds (the Apostolic Creed, the Nicene Creed, the Athanasian Creed), the Unaltered Augsburg Confession, the Apology of the Augsburg Confession, the Smalcald Articles, the Treatise on the Power and Primacy of the Pope, Luther's Large and Small Catechisms, and the Formula of Concord.[45]

At its constituting convention the new church body declared itself on another issue in controversy within the Missouri Synod: Lutheran unity and ecumenism. The Association of Evangelical Lutheran Churches extended the hand of fellowship specifically to the Lutheran Church in America and to The American Lutheran Church, expressed the hope that its members could continue in fellowship with The Lutheran Church–Missouri Synod, and stated its desire to be in fellowship with Lutheran churches around the world. The Lutheran Church in America and The American Lutheran Church accepted the proferred fellowship, but The Lutheran Church–Missouri Synod decided not to act before giving the matter careful study.

In addition, the Association of Evangelical Lutheran Churches resolved to join the Lutheran Council in the United States of America and the Lutheran World Federation. The Lutheran Council responded positively to the request at its 1978 meeting, and the Lutheran World Federation received the new church body as a member at its convention at Dar es Salaam in 1977. Expressing its desire to cooperate in the church's mission with all Christian churches, the Association of Evangelical Lutheran Churches resolved to consider membership in the World Council of Churches and in the National Council of the Churches of Christ in America at a subsequent convention.

The Association of Evangelical Lutheran Churches has entered into working relationships with Seminex, the seminary produced by the Missouri Synod controversy, and Partners in Mission, an agency established by former mission staff members of the Missouri Synod to provide alternatives to the synod's program for mission. It declared itself in favor of ordaining women to the pastoral ministry, one of the issues over which the Missouri Synod is threatening to break fellowship with The American Lutheran Church, and ordained the first woman pastor in October 1977.

Organization within the Association of Evangelical Lutheran Churches is decentralized and congregational. Its members are concerned to perpetuate the principle of congregational autonomy, which they feel has been subverted within the Missouri Synod. The congregations comprise five synods, four of which are regional and one, the English Synod, is nongeographical. The national organization meets biennially and is limited to purposes and functions assigned by the synods.

Headquarters of the organization are presently at 12015 Manchester, St. Louis, Missouri 63131, but a move to Chicago is anticipated. Membership statistics are constantly changing as more Missouri Synod congregations decide whether or not to join. As this is written there are 250 congregations with more than 100,000 members.

Evangelical Lutheran Church in America (Eielsen Synod)

The first Norwegian Lutheran Synod to be organized in North America was the Evangelical Lutheran Church in America, which came into being at Jefferson Prairie, Wisconsin, in 1846. Its constitution was written by its founder and first preisdent, Elling Eielsen (1803–1883), who after his conversion had become an itinerant lay preacher in the Hauge movement in Norway, had later served as a missionary among the Norwegian Lapps, and had come to America in 1839. The church body makes proof of conversion a condition of membership and places the Apostles' Creed and the Augsburg Confession on the same confessional plane as the Bible. Through its history the body had little use for liturgy, but stressed strongly positive and courageous evangelism, the priesthood of believers, and the development of spiritual gifts among the laity. A majority of the membership withdrew in 1848 under Paul Anderson, and the seceders later organized the Northern Illinois Synod in 1851 and the Scandinavian Augustana Synod in 1860. Another schism took place in 1858 when P. A. Rasmussen led a group out of the church and, in 1860, into the Norwegian Synod. A third schism took place in 1876, when the majority voted to reorganize the church as Hauge's Norwegian Evangelical Lutheran Synod in America; a minority held to the original constitution and perpetuated the parent body as The Evangelical Lutheran Church of America (Eielsen Synod). In addition to missions among the North American Indians of Wisconsin and Michigan, it supported a foreign mission in India. With the loss of its young people in the twentieth century as a result of its slow acculturation, it has all but died out. Three churches with a total membership of 125 remain.

The Wisconsin Evangelical Lutheran Synod

The Wisconsin Evangelical Lutheran Synod—known until 1959 as the Joint Synod of Wisconsin and Other States—came into being in its present form in 1917. In that year three synods that since 1892 had been associated in a "general" synod but that had retained their individual identities merged. All three—the Synod of Minnesota, the Synod of Wisconsin, and the Synod of Michigan—were of German immigrant origin and initially drew their clergy from the German Evangelical missionary schools and societies.

In 1840 three pastors—among them Friedrich Schmid (d. 1883), who came to Ann Arbor, Michigan, in 1833—organized a "missionary synod" in Michigan, but it broke up over the issue of loyalty to the Lutheran Symbolical Books. In 1860 nine pastors, Schmid among them, organized a second "missionary synod," more staunchly Lutheran in its composition, which survived but remained small. It joined the General Council in 1867, withdrew in 1888, and ultimately entered into union with the synods of Wisconsin and Minnesota and joined the Synodical Conference.

John Mühlhäuser (1804–1868), a graduate of the Barmen Mission House, came to Wisconsin as a missionary of the Langenberg Society for North America in 1848. A warmhearted Lutheran who "was more interested in combating unbelief than in arguing doctrinal differences," he organized the Synod of Wisconsin at Granville, near Milwaukee, in 1850. Its constitution, the work of Mühlhäuser, hopefully specified that "everything must agree with the pure biblical word and with the symbolical books of our Evangelical Lutheran Church," but the general attitude of the new synod reflected the tolerant views prevalent in the Lutheran synods of the eastern states and in the broadly Evangelical German missionary societies that provided the missionaries with much of their support. The arrival of a number of confessional pastors—among them Philip Köhler (1828–1896), John Bading (1824–1913), William Streissguth (1827–1915), and Gottlieb Reim—in the mid-1850s contributed to the development of a stricter Lutheranism. Bading succeeded Mühlhäuser as president in 1860, and served in that office until 1889 (except for the period 1864–1867). Under the spiritual leadership of Bading and of Halle-trained Adolf Hönecke (1835–1908), who became the synod's leading theologian, the synod severed its connection with the eastern Lutherans and suffered the loss of its German financial support. In 1869 it approved a doctrinal accord with The Lutheran Church–Missouri Synod.

Johann Christian Friedrich Heyer (1793–1873), a member of the Pennsylvania Ministerium, while in America between his second and third periods of activity in India as the first foreign missionary to be sent out by American Lutherans, began to provide ministrations to scattered Germans in Minnesota, and in 1860, together with a number of other clergymen, he organized the Synod of Minnesota. Under the presidencies of Georg Fachtmann, through whom the Synod of Minnesota became a member of the General Synod in 1864 and a charter member of the General Council in 1867, and of Johann Heinrich Sieker (1838–1904), the Synod of Minnesota was drawn into the orbit of the Synod of Wisconsin, left the General Council, and established doctrinal agreement with the Synod of Wisconsin in 1869.

In 1872 the synods of Wisconsin and Minnesota became charter members of the Synodical Conference. Two decades later they joined together with the Synod of Michigan in a "general synod," in order to engage in common missionary activity among the Apaches and in common educational work. The first president of the "general synod" was Augustus Friedrich Ernst (1841–

1924), a creative educator who had reorganized the major secondary school of the Synod of Wisconsin, Northwestern College, Watertown, Wisconsin (founded 1865), and through it had profoundly shaped the synod itself. A major schism in the Synod of Michigan that began in 1896 ended with a reunion in 1909.

Under a series of influential theologians that included Hönecke, John Philipp Köhler (1859–1951), who was relieved of his theological professorship in connection with the Protéstant Conference controversy, August Pieper (1850–1950), Johannes Schaller (1859–1920), and John Meyer (1873–1964), the synod developed a characteristic theology that has laid great stress on the analytical study of the church's history and upon the study of the Sacred Scriptures in their original languages as the inspired record of God's gracious dealings with humankind. Its teaching about the church denies that "the local congregation is specifically instituted by God in contrast to other groups of believers in Jesus' name, or that the ministry of the keys has been given exclusively to the local congregation."

In 1926 the Protéstant Conference separated from the synod on the issue of "officialdom." Some doctrinal differences between the Wisconsin Synod and The Lutheran Church–Missouri Synod had always existed. An increasingly vehement controversy between the two bodies, complicated by a number of nontheological factors, developed in the 1930s about the propriety of membership in Boy Scout troops, military chaplains, participation in prayers and devotions with other Christians with whom pulpit and altar fellowship had not been established, and the inerrancy and inspiration of the Holy Scriptures. In the course of the controversy a group of clergy and laity, dissatisfied because the Wisconsin Synod had not broken off fellowship relations with The Lutheran Church–Missouri Synod, withdrew in 1961 to form the Church of the Lutheran Confession. The formal break of the Wisconsin Evangelical Lutheran Synod with The Lutheran Church–Missouri Synod later in 1961 failed to mollify the seceding party. In 1963 the Wisconsin Synod withdrew from the Synodical Conference. Reduced to two members, the Synodical Conference dissolved in 1967.

In 1967 the Lutheran Confessional Forum came into existence. This commission consists of twelve official delegates from the Wisconsin Evangelical Lutheran Synod and the Evangelical Lutheran Synod. Its purpose is to "preserve [the] unity [of the participating synods] in scriptural doctrine and practice and to confirm their confessional fellowship and, God willing, to extend it." Each delegation is divided into three groups representing respectively administration, the standing doctrinal committees, and the departments of missions and of education. In 1970 the Lutheran Confessional Forum charged the presidents of the two participating synods to seek "to arrange for an exploratory meeting with leaders of other confessionally-minded Lutheran churches to discuss a doctrinal basis for the possible establishment of a federation similar to the former Synodical Conference."[46]

Its 1,082 congregations in the United States and Canada, with 399,114 baptized members, make the Wisconsin Evangelical Lutheran Synod the fourth largest Lutheran body in North America. It maintains its own system of Christian elementary schools and high schools. It carries on foreign missions in Japan, Hong Kong, Malawi, Zambia, and Germany. The headquarters are at 3512 West North Avenue, Milwaukee, Wisconsin 53208..

The Protestant Conference

During the first quarter of the present century an approach to theology developed at the Wisconsin Evangelical Lutheran Synod's theological seminary, then located at Wauwatosa, Wisconsin, that called for the interpretation of the Sacred Scriptures without the systematic preconceptions imposed by the dogmatics which Lutheran theology had inherited from the era of orthodoxy (about 1580 to 1713). The leader of the "Wauwatosa Theology" was the church historian John Philipp Köhler (1859–1951). Another feature of this theological approach was the teaching of church history within the matrix of the total history of culture in order to transcend the sacred–secular dichotomy. A third feature was a call for rigorous self-analysis and self-criticism.

The "Wauwatosa Theology" met with considerable resistance within the synod. Indications of an impending rupture appeared in the mid 1920s. In 1924 a conflict between the board of control and the faculty of Northwestern College, Watertown, Wisconsin, over the expulsion of a number of students led to the resignation of Karl Köhler (1885–1948), son of the Wauwatosa theologian. In the autumn of 1926 the Reverend William F. Beitz (1888–1965) read before the Wisconsin River–Chippewa Valley Pastoral Conference of the Wisconsin Synod at Schofield, Wisconsin, a paper entitled "God's Message to Us in Galatians: The Just Shall Live by Faith."[47] A concrete application of many of the emphases in the "Wauwatosa Theology," it excoriated what the author called the "dogmatical stress at our seminaries," the Lutheran Church's "spiritless Christianity," its failure "to live by faith," and its emphasis on "forms, works, rituals, ceremonies, institutions, [and] constitutions."

The paper precipitated a vehement controversy. Within the Wisconsin Evangelical Lutheran Synod the reaction to it was largely negative. Ultimately the synod expelled or suspended nearly forty of its pastors, teachers, and professors on charges of false doctrine, for alleged insubordination, or merely for protesting the synod's action. Among those ousted was the elder Köhler, in spite of the criticisms that he had voiced of the Beitz paper and subsequently of some of the actions of its proponents. In 1927 the suspended clergymen organized the Protestant Conference, a loose organization that has made no attempt either to become a synod or to expand.[48]

Each issue of the conference's periodical, *Faith-Life* (originally a monthly, but since January 1965 a bimonthly), carries on its first page the statement of policy and purpose that Karl Köhler drafted when he became its editor. The statement concedes that its editors' "procedure arouses much hostile attention and is condemned by friend and foe as uncharitable because it conflicts with pet but mistaken dogmas current in the church." It asserts the periodical's purpose "to break down the influence of the misleaders of the church and free their followers from their thraldom," to shatter "the spirit of self-righteousness and self-sufficiency which breeds uncharitableness and unwarranted judgment of others, and thus leads to controversy," and to "call men from a comfortable gospel that acts as a soporific and permits unrighteousness to run riot in the church to the Gospel that is in truth comforting to stricken sinners . . . the Gospel of forgiveness of sins through our blessed Saviour, coupled with the warning of the hardening of hearts and of the judgment upon those who reject this message and its implications."

Three major ruptures within the Protestant Conference—in 1930, in 1952, and in 1964—have reduced the size of the conference to 10 churches with a total membership of 1,440.

The Church of the Lutheran Confession

The Church of the Lutheran Confession came into being at Sleepy Eye, Minnesota, in January 1961. The bulk of its initial membership comprised congregations and clergymen that had withdrawn from the Wisconsin Evangelical Lutheran Synod because of dissatisfaction with what they regarded as a lack of doctrinal discipline in the Evangelical Lutheran Synodical Conference of North America and because of what it regarded as the Wisconsin Synod's unscriptural fellowship principles. But among the charter members there were also congregations and clergymen that had belonged to the Evangelical Lutheran Synod and to the Orthodox Lutheran Conference (subsequently absorbed into the Wisconsin Synod).

The Church of the Lutheran Confession holds uncompromisingly to the Holy Scriptures as the verbally inspired Word of God and subscribes without reservation to the Book of Concord as a clear and correct exposition of biblical doctrine. It regards *A Brief Statement of the Doctrinal Platform of the Doctrinal Position of the Missouri Synod* (adopted in 1932) as "a confessional statement."

The Church of the Lutheran Confession has authorized initial discussions with the Wisconsin Synod looking toward doctrinal agreement and mutual recognition.

There are 74 churches and missions in eighteen states with a total baptized membership of approximately 9,817. The president of the church body resides at 213 East Spring Street, Mankato, Minnesota 56001. The Church of the Lutheran Confession maintains a foreign mission in Japan.[49]

Evangelical Lutheran Synod

When Norwegian Lutherans ended decades of separation and controversy by uniting to form the Norwegian Lutheran Church of America in 1917, a minority within one of the uniting groups, the Norwegian Synod, refused to be part of the new body on the grounds that it was the result of a compromise on doctrine. In 1918 thirteen pastors, together with a group of like-minded laity, organized the Norwegian Synod of the American Evangelical Lutheran Church in Lime Creek Church near Lake Mills, Iowa, claiming that it was the continuation of the Norwegian Synod established in 1853. Shortly afterward it became a member of the Evangelical Lutheran Synodical Conference of North America.

In 1958, reflecting the acculturation process under way, the church body changed its name to Evangelical Lutheran Synod. Three years earlier more than a decade of controversy with The Lutheran Church–Missouri Synod came to a head when the church body resolved to break fellowship with the Missouri Synod.[50] In 1961 the Evangelical Lutheran Synod took the position that the Synodical Conference was "no longer functioning according to the prime purposes stated in its constitution." When it and the Wisconsin Evangelical Lutheran Synod were unsuccessful in dissolving the Synodical Conference, both church bodies withdrew from it in 1963. Since 1967 the Evangelical Lutheran Synod and the Wisconsin Evangelical Lutheran Synod have worked through a twenty-four-member joint commission known as the Lutheran Confessional Forum to coordinate common concerns.

Headquarters are at 5530 Englewood Drive, Madison, Wisconsin 53705. There are 106 congregations and missions with a total membership of 19,571.

The Apostolic Lutheran Church of America, Apostolic Lutheran Congregations, and other Laestadians

Lars Levi Laestadius (1800–1861) became rector of the northernmost parish of the Church of Sweden, Karesuando, in Lapland, after his ordination in 1825. Here his observations established for him an international reputation as a botanist. In 1843 the church authorities named him provost of the Lapland deanery and in 1849 they transferred him to the parish of Pajala, farther south, but still above the Arctic Circle. Both Karesuando and Pajala were composed almost entirely of Lapps and Finns. After a severe illness of his own and the death of his three-year-old son, Laestadius came into contact with Maria, a Lapp girl who was a disciple of Pehr Brandell, one of the most eminent clerical supporters of the *Gammalläseri* ("Old Readers'" movement). As a result Laestadius underwent a profound spiritual experience in the winter of 1844/1845. He began to attack the vices of his people with prophetic vehemence and to preach the Gospel with warmhearted power to those distressed over their past sins. A revival resulted that spread throughout Lapland but that found its greatest following in northern Finland.

Laestadius had as his most notable co-worker in the revival a schoolteacher, Juhani Raattama (1811–1899). After the death of Laestadius, Raattama became the leader of the movement. Indeed, his influence on the doctrinal position of the movement has been even greater than that of Laestadius. The spiritual needs of converts led Raattama in 1853, with the approval of Laestadius, to introduce personal confession and absolution, administered publicly at first, but after some years generally administered in private, with public confession reserved for public offenses.

Economic distress in Finland, Sweden, and Norway led many Finns in the northern parts of all three countries, among them many Laestadians, to emigrate to America. The first wave settled in Minnesota, but afterward they gravitated toward the copper country of Upper Michigan in the vicinity of Hancock. Here they joined the pan-Scandinavian congregation at Quincy. In 1870 a revival began among the Laestadians of this area; this, together with an increasing flow of immigrants, added to their numbers. They became dissatisfied with the congregation's new Finnish-speaking Norwegian pastor and tried to correct him; he responded by excommunicating them. Under the leadership of Salomon Korteniemi, a lay preacher, the Laestadians organized a congregation of their own in Calumet in the winter of 1872/1873. In 1879 it took the name The Finnish Apostolic Lutheran Congregation of Calumet. Since then the North American Laestadians have been known as Apostolic Lutherans, a designation that has never been in vogue in Scandinavia.[51]

The Calumet congregation received its first (and until 1916 its only) professionally trained and ordained clergyman in the person of the late Arthur Leopold Heideman (d. 1928) in 1890. Most of the work of expansion was done by lay preachers, many of whom received ordination later.

Since the 1890s there had been latent divisions among the Apostolic Lutherans which reflected parallel divisions among the European Laestadians. Thus a split had developed in Scandinavia between the "Old Laestadians," represented in North America by the followers of Heideman, and the "Firstborn," who looked to Gellivaara in northern Sweden for leadership. The "New Awakenist" movement also began about the same time. In 1908 some of the members of the Apostolic Lutheran congregations in Upper Michigan arranged a "Big Meeting" in Calumet after they had heard of similar assemblies among the European Laestadians. Heideman himself refused to approve this step because in his opinion the wrong men were leading it. The "Big Meeting" crystallized the latent divisions among North American Laestadians into an open split between the supporters of Heideman and the "Big Meeting" party. The latter group included the relatively few "New Awakenists" in North America; this contributed to the internal tensions within the "Big Meeting" group.

A strongly evangelical trend manifested itself among some of the followers of Heideman shortly after the 1908 assembly. In the 1920s a separation took place between the supporters of Heideman and the Evangelicals. The latter party was first known as "Pollarites" (after Juhani Pollari, their leading preacher), but it has subsequently divided into at least three subgroups.

After more than a decade of discussion and consideration, the "Big Meeting" group organized itself as the [Finnish] Apostolic Lutheran Church of America in an assembly at Calumet in 1928; in 1929 the newly formed body met at Pendleton, Oregon, and adopted a constitution and bylaws.[52] Its headquarters are at Route 3, Kimball, Minnesota 55353. It numbers 9,384 supporting members in 64 congregations in the United States and Canada and maintains a mission in Nigeria. Its journal is the *Christian Monthly*. It continues to include in its membership the North American representatives of the "New Awakenist" and "Small Firstborn" movements in Europe.

The followers of Heideman, who officially call themselves Apostolic Lutheran Congregations, continue as a group of independent churches united by a common spiritual bond. There are 60 or so congregations in the United States and Canada with between 6,000 and 7,000 members. Their journal is the monthly *Greetings of Peace*.

The remaining Apostolic Lutheran groups have no national organization and no formal headquarters. The various streams of the Evangelical movement have less than 3,000 baptized members altogether. The Firstborn, who acculturated most rapidly to the American scene, have a similar number of members.

Doctrinal differences among these groups are relatively minor. All of them require total abstinence from alcoholic beverages; all use "God's peace" in greeting one another; all stress the universal priesthood of believers and practice it in confession and absolution as well as otherwise; all interpret literally the apostolic affirmation that "faith comes by what is heard"; all emphasize the absolute authority of the Bible and call for simple adherence to its teachings. In all groups only confessing believers can enjoy the privileges of full church membership in the local congregation, such as the right to vote and to hold office; those who accept the church's teaching without personal faith can only become "supporting members." All have very simple services of worship, limited to hymns, biblical lessons, prayers, and a sermon, with the addition of the Apostles' Creed and the words of institution at celebrations of the Holy Communion.

The Firstborn lay greater stress than the others on plainness of dress (no jewelry), manners, and mode of life. While the churches of the Apostolic Lutheran Church and of the Heidemanians remain severely simple, the use of organs and pianos in their services has become increasingly common, and radio and television sets are also seen in growing numbers in the homes of their people. A tendency to depreciate formal ministerial training, born partly of the movement's necessary dependence in North America on lay readers, is still present to a great extent, but many, particularly in the Apostolic Lutheran Church, have come to see the desirability of such training. The ecstatic loud thanking and praising of Jesus that was common at Laestadian church services in the past has become somewhat rarer, but there are considerable differences among the various groups in this respect.[53]

Church of the Lutheran Brethren

After the revival that had swept through the North American Norwegian Lutheran settlements in the 1890s, eight pastors and the lay representatives of five congregations of the United Norwegian Lutheran Church of America came to the conclusion that there was no Lutheran synod in North America with sufficiently strict rules on the reception and disciplining of church members. Accordingly they gathered at Milwaukee, Wisconsin, in 1900 and organized a new body, the Church of the Lutheran Brethren.

The Church of the Lutheran Brethren has always stood committed to the Lutheran doctrinal position, but it differs from other Lutheran bodies in a number of ways. It accepts as members only persons who profess a personal experience of salvation; it stresses nonliturgical worship; and it emphasizes lay participation. Its clergy wear no vestments and its churches have no altars; the communicants receive the sacrament of Christ's body and blood in the pews. The Lutheran Brethren do not believe in receiving absolution from the pastor. They encourage free prayer and personal testimony. Children receive instruction for two years, after which they take part in a ceremony called confirmation. The ceremony is in the nature of a public examination; there is no repetition of baptismal promises, and the confirmands do not automatically become communicants. If the candidate has experienced awakening and conversion he becomes a communicant at this time; many do. But if not, he postpones becoming a communcant until he has had this experience.

To put a stop to glossolalia and other Pentecostal-type practices in which some pastors were engaging, the 1967 synod resolved to drop clergymen who "cease to reflect the position of the Church [of the Lutheran Brethren] in doctrine, ethical standards, or spiritual emphasis."

The annual synod is an advisory body; the local congregations are autonomous. The headquarters are at 704 Vernon Avenue West, Fergus Falls, Minnesota 56537. There are 90 churches in the Middle West and on both coasts, with an inclusive membership of 8,656, of which about one-fifth maintain only a loose affiliation with the Church of the Lutheran Brethren but have members of the ministerium of the Church of the Lutheran Brethren as pastors. The Church of the Lutheran Brethren carries on foreign missions in Africa, Japan, and Taiwan (Republic of China), these missions have a larger membership than the parent church.[54]

NOTES

1. Article IV of the constitution sets forth the purposes and objectives of the agency; for the constitution, see Richard C. Wolf, *Documents of Lutheran Unity in America* (Philadelphia: Fortress Press, 1966), pp. 630-637.
2. The Synod of Evangelical Lutheran Churches became the SELC District of The Lutheran Church–Missouri Synod in 1971 and therefore is no longer a participant on its own in the Lutheran Council.
3. E. Clifford Nelson, ed., *The Lutherans in North America* (Philadelphia: Fortress Press, 1975), p. 37.
4. Abdel Ross Wentz, *A Basic History of Lutheranism in America* (rev. edn.; Philadelphia: Fortress Press, 1965), p. 140.
5. Ibid., p. 273.
6. The membership statistics in this paragraph are from Robert C. Wiederaenders and Walter G. Tillmans, *The Synods of American Lutheranism* (Lutheran Historical Conference Publication No. 1, 1968), p. 62.
7. Cited in Richard C. Wolf, *Documents of Lutheran Unity* (Philadelphia: Fortress Press, 1966), pp. 566-567.
8. Statistics for 1976 presented in a compilation of the Lutheran church bodies in the United States and Canada, published by the Lutheran Council in the U.S.A.
9. The new organization was distinguished from a merging group of the same name by use of a capital letter in the definite article (The), although the new ALC rejected the acronym TALC in favor of the acronym for one of its founders, ALC.
10. See the description of the American Lutheran Conference in E. Clifford Nelson, *Lutheranism in North America 1914–1970* (Minneapolis: Augsburg Publishing House, 1972), pp. 29-32.
11. For "The Minneapolis Theses," see Richard C. Wolf, *Documents of Lutheran Unity in America* (Philadelphia: Fortress Press, 1966), pp. 340-342.
12. A statement of the issues, known as "The Four Points," and the General Council's response are included in Wolf, *op. cit.*, pp. 155-158.
13. "The Toledo Theses" are presented in Wolf, *op. cit.*, pp. 216-219.
14. Abdel Ross Wentz, *A Basic History of Lutheranism in America* (rev. edn.; Philadelphia: Fortress Press, 1964), p. 288.
15. Robert C. Wiederaenders and Walter G. Tillmanns, *The Synods of American Lutheranism* (Lutheran Historical Conference Publication No. 1, 1968), p. 4.
16. The text of the agreement is included in Wolf, *op. cit.*, pp. 228-235.
17. It replaced "Norwegian" with "Evangelical" in its corporate name in 1946.
18. E. Clifford Nelson, ed., *The Lutherans in North America*, p. 372.
19. Wiederaenders and Tillmanns, *The Synods of American Lutheranism*, p. 4.
20. It substituted "United" for "Danish" in 1946.
21. Nelson, ed., *The Lutherans in North America*, p. 271.
22. Ibid., p. 343.
23. Wiederaenders and Tillmanns, *The Synods of North American Lutheranism*, p. 5.
24. Wolf, *Documents*, pp. 532-533.
25. Statistics for 1976 in a compilation of the Lutheran church bodies in the United States and Canada, published by the Lutheran Council in the U.S.A.
26. *This We Believe* (Minneapolis: The Association of Free Lutheran Congregations, 1966) (4-page pamphlet), p. [2].
27. Letters from the Reverend John P. Strand, president, The Association of Free Lutheran Congregations. See also Rolf E. Aaseng, "Association of Free Lutheran Congregations: Pietism and Participation," *Lutheran Forum* III, no. 3 (March 1969): 10-11.
28. It did absorb small independent synods into its membership at various times in its history, e.g., the English Synod in 1911 and the Synod of Evangelical Lutheran Churches in 1971.
29. The church body's present name was adopted in 1947.
30. For a description of the requirement for unity, see John H. Tietjen, *Which*

Way to Lutheran Unity (St. Louis: Clayton Publishing House, 1975), pp. 59-85.

31. The three synods were the Wisconsin Evangelical Lutheran Synod, the Evangelical Lutheran Synod, and the Slovak Evangelical Lutheran Church.

32. Erwin L. Lueker, ed., *Lutheran Cyclopedia* (St. Louis: Concordia Publishing House, 1975), p. 491.

33. Formerly the Slovak Evangelical Lutheran Church.

34. For a contrasting description of the issues, see "Integrity, Schism, Neither, Both," an interview with Jacob A. O. Preus, president of The Lutheran Church–Missouri Synod, in *Christianity Today*, October 25, 1974, pp. 2 ff.; and John H. Tietjen (former president of Concordia Seminary, St. Louis), "Piercing the Smokescreen," ibid., April 11, 1975, pp. 8-10.

35. *Handbook of The Lutheran Church–Missouri Synod*, 1975 edn., p. 15.

36. The pertinent resolutions (2-12 and 3-01) are in *Proceedings of the Fiftieth Regular Convention of The Lutheran Church–Missouri Synod*. New Orleans, Louisiana, July 6-13, 1973, pp. 111-115, 127-128.

37. Cf. Article VII of the constitution in the *Handbook*, pp. 17-18.

38. Statistics for 1976 in a compilation of Lutheran church bodies in the United States and Canada, compiled by the Lutheran Council in the U.S.A.

39. *1976 Statistical Yearbook*, The Lutheran Church–Missouri Synod, p. 224.

40. After another division within itself, the unreorganized group continued as the Orthodox Lutheran Conference until 1962, when the remaining clergymen and congregations dissolved the organization and joined the Wisconsin Evangelical Lutheran Synod.

41. Preamble, *Constitution of the Concordia Lutheran Conference* (approved 1958) (undated pamphlet), p. 1.

42. Article II, ibid., p. 2.

43. Article VI, ibid., p. 4.

44. *What is L. C. R.?* (Detroit: Lutheran Churches of the Reformation, 1966) (pamphlet), pp. 3-5; *The Faithful Word* III, no. 3 (1966): 11, 13-15, 20, 32-34, 36-38, 41; letter from the Reverend Roy B. Faulstick, pastor of Trinity Church, Wayland, Michigan.

45. Article II of the constitution of the Association of Evangelical Lutheran Churches; mimeographed document.

46. Carl Lawrenz, "Confessional Forum Meets," *The Northwestern Lutheran* LXVIII (1971): 37.

47. Reproduced in *Faith-Life* XXXIII, no. 5 (May 1960): 1.4-12.

48. For a summary survey of the history of the Protestant Conference, see Leigh Jordahl, "Protestant Conference," in Julius Bodensieck,, ed., *The Encyclopedia of the Lutheran Church* (Minneapolis: Augsburg Publishing House, 1965), 3, 1978–1979, as well as the letter of the Reverend Philemon Hensel of April 18, 1968, reproduced in *Faith-Life* XII, no. 3 (May–June 1968): 19.

49. See Anne Jorheim, "The Church of the Lutheran Confession: Fossil or Fortress?" *Lutheran Forum* I, no. 9 (September 1967): 10-11.

50. The convention resolution was made and seconded by Jacob A. O. Preus and his brother, Robert, two pastors who shortly thereafter entered the Missouri Synod and rose to prominence as synodical president and seminary president, respectively.

51. While North American Laestadians are sometimes referred to (and on occasion refer to themselves) as "Holy Rollers," there is no historical connection between the Laestadian movement and Pentecostalism.

52. *Finnish Apostolic Lutheran Church of America: Constitution and By-Laws* (undated [after 1951] 32-page pamphlet), pp. 5-7.

53. The present writer gratefully acknowledges the counsel and assistance of the Reverend Uuras Saarnivaara, Ph.D., Th.D., in the preparation of this section.

54. Letter from the Reverend Omar Gjerness, secretary, Church of the Lutheran Brethren, Fergus Falls, Minnesota.

BIBLIOGRAPHY

Bachmann, E. Theodore. "Lutheran Churches in the World: A Handbook," *Lutheran World* XXIV (1977), nos. 2 and 3.

Lueker, Erwin L., ed. *Lutheran Cyclopedia*. St. Louis: Concordia Publishing House, 1975. A valuable resource of information on Lutheranism.

Nelson, E. Clifford. *Lutheranism in North America 1914–1970*. Minneapolis: Augsburg Publishing House, 1972. An account of twentieth-century Lutheranism in America by an excellent historian.

————, ed. *The Lutherans in North America*. Philadelphia: Fortress Press, 1975. An up-to-date history of Lutheranism in North America by six Lutheran historians.

Tietjen, John H. *Which Way to Lutheran Unity?* Saint Louis, Mo.: Clayton Publishing House, 1975. A history of the efforts to unite the Lutherans of America.

Wentz, Abdel Ross. *A Basic History of Lutheranism in America*. Rev. edn. Philadelphia: Fortress Press, 1964. The standard text on the history of Lutheranism in America.

Wiederaenders, Robert C. and Tillmanns, Walter G. *The Synods of American Lutheranism*. Lutheran Historical Conference Publication No. 1, 1968. A listing of present Lutheran church bodies and a detailed presentation of their predecessors and present components.

Wolf, Richard C. *Documents of Lutheran Unity in America*. Philadelphia: Fortress Press, 1966. A compilation of 250 documents related to Lutheran unity and union from 1730 to 1965.

PART II

EPISCOPAL CHURCHES

5. The Anglican Communion

The Church of England in the Reformation and Early Modern Periods

The exact origin of the church in England is difficult to determine, but the presence of an English bishop at the Council of Arles in 314 gives evidence of an early organization. The invasion of Britain by the Anglo-Saxons and their subsequent conversion to Christianity by Augustine and other monks helped reestablish Christianity on the island after it was almost completely eradicated. By the late seventh century it was once again populated by many Christians.

During the Reformation period the church in England became the Church of England. A review of this church's history during the Reformation and the early modern period shows how the adjectives "Catholic" and "Reformed" are both applicable to this church. Since Anglicanism in North America was an extension of the Church of England until the American Revolution, the history of this church in the early modern period provides the background of the Episcopal Church in the United States and the Anglican Church of Canada. In addition, the pivotal role of the Church of England in the expansion of Anglicanism around the globe makes its history an important one.

At the time of the Reformation through an act of state the Church of England declared its independence from the church in Rome. The theological and organizational repercussions of this act of state must be understood in the light of this people's religious life early in the sixteenth century. While the Renaissance brought enlightenment to England which endangered many of the superstitious beliefs of the monks and lower clergy, anticlericalism and loss of repect for priests made the English church ready for reform. Dissatisfaction with financial and judicial matters was heightened by subterranean currents of discontent and criticism of doctrinal subjects.[1] In late medieval times, early stirrings for reform by John Wyclif (1329–1384) and his followers, the Lollards, led to persecution but also laid the groundwork for later successes in reform.

The English Reformation occurred in the context of political relations that involved the English monarchy and the European power structure. Henry

VII restored peace after he ascended the throne in 1485 and strengthened England's position with Spain through marriage. Henry VIII became king in 1509. A gifted man, he befriended learned men and admired the internationally known scholar Erasmus. Loyal to the church, he attacked Luther's *Babylonian Captivity of the Church* in a document that defended the Roman Catholic Church's sacramental system.

His chief adviser in foreign and domestic relations was the papal legate in England, Cardinal Wolsey, who helped solidify the Spanish alliance and elevated England's importance in relations with the papacy and other nations. Through his influence the pope bestowed the title "Defender of the Faith" upon the king. Henry seemed even more important after Charles V, his wife's nephew, became the Holy Roman emperor.

But the stirrings of the continental Reformation were at the same time influencing people in England. Reformation literature from Germany flowed into the country, and scholars at both Oxford and Cambridge examined the new religious publications. At Cambridge a group met at White Horse Inn under the leadership of an Augustinian named Robert Barnes. Other scholars set out to translate the Bible into English. Chief among them was William Tyndale (c. 1494–1536), who was unable to secure the assistance of the bishop of London. Tyndale fled to Wittenberg and Antwerp to continue his work of translating, and later (1526) published an English Bible. Barnes too fled to Wittenberg. The reason for their flight was that Henry VIII and Cardinal Wolsey were growing increasingly concerned about heretical activity in England, and the chancellor, Sir Thomas More, put some of the alleged heretics to death.

Things improved for the reformers when Henry VIII resolved to end his eighteen-year marriage to Catherine of Aragon. His wife had borne him one daughter and several stillborn sons. Interested in having a male heir, Henry asked Wolsey to secure the pope's annulment of his marriage. Wolsey failed and fell from the king's good grace, but died before the sentence of execution could be carried out. Henry set about to cut off all relations between the English church and the papacy. Using the resourceful leadership of his chief minister of state, Thomas Cromwell, and summoning Parliament in 1529, he accomplished his goal. In sum, the episode of his divorce from Catherine was "the occasion of the Reformation, not its cause."[2]

Between 1529 and 1536 Parliament passed legislation that gave national independence to the Church of England under the king's headship. Thomas Cranmer (1489–1556), appointed archbishop of Canterbury by the king, officially set aside Henry's marriage. Henry had convinced himself that his marriage to his elder brother's sister had violated biblical law. The Act of Supremacy required the king to "be taken, accepted, and reputed the only supreme head in earth of the Church of England, called *Anglicana Ecclesia*." But at the same time, the acts of Parliament affirmed that the king's subjects were "as devout, obedient, catholic, and humble children of God and Holy

Church as any people be within any realm christened," nor did the Church of England have plans "to decline or vary from the congregation of Christ's Church in any things concerning the very articles of the Catholic Faith of Christendom, or in any other things declared by Holy Scripture and the Word of God, necessary for your and their salvation." While ordinarily Parliament was more compliant, Convocation, the church's legislative assembly, was sometimes a more willing instrument (as in antipapal matters) than in others (such as giving Henry the title "Supreme Head").[3]

Increasingly isolated from Europe because of conflict with the pope and Charles V, England now turned to the Lutheran princes of the Schmalkaldic League for allies. During the 1530s there were political and theological discussions with Lutherans in Germany, while the new archbishop encouraged reform of the English church. Barnes was recalled from Germany and the publication of an English Bible was authorized. But while things looked promising for some sort of Lutheranization of England, there seemed to be little promise of rapid or thoroughgoing reformation. This was evident in the first attempt of the English bishops to state their position, the Ten Articles of 1536. The object of the articles was "to establish Christian quietness and unity among us and to avoid contentious opinions." While the king participated in their formation, Convocation acted on the final draft. The first five articles on Christian doctrine listed three sacraments (recognizing the Real Presence) and defined justification in Melanchthonian terms while insisting that it is attained by "inward contrition, perfect faith and charity, certain hope and confidence." The second set of five concerned "the laudable ceremonies used in the Church." Among other things, these articles commended prayers for the dead and invocation of saints.[4]

While setting aside papal authority in England in the Act of Supremacy, Henry VIII did not give up the Catholic faith. When political events at the end of the thirties made an alliance with German Lutherans unnecessary, he repudiated the Protestant policy advocated by Cromwell, whom he executed along with Barnes. He secured parliamentary legislation intended to maintain Roman Catholic theology in England while also suppressing the monasteries of his country.

While Henry's royal injunctions to the clergy showed his desire for Catholic theology, the most influential of the injunctions was the one requiring that the Great Bible should be set up in every church. "The importance of the vernacular Bible," wrote the influential scholar Norman Sykes, "was as great in England as in Germany, perhaps even greater, for the English Reformation gave birth to no such outburst of hymnody as the Lutheran movement." He added that "the" popularization of the English Bible led to that silent religious revolution which produced a new pattern of individual and family piety and found public expression throughout the history of seventeenth-century England." But by the end of the 1530s it was clear that Reformation in England was in a state of suspended development. The Six

Articles of 1539, imposed on all Englishmen, virtually reaffirmed trans-substantiation, forbade the marriage of priests (Cranmer had to put his wife away for a time), permitted private Masses, and declared auricular confession to be necessary. The *King's Book* (1543), a popular name for *The Necessary Doctrine and Erudition for any Christian Man,* contained a preface by the king and included many of his comments. Reactionary in character, it was issued on authority of Convocation, Parliament, and the king, and was probably intended to be the final statement on England's theological position.[5] English subjects who rejected the principal teachings of the Roman Catholic faith were severely penalized, although the death penalty was seldom imposed.

Edward VI, a mere nine years old when Henry died in 1547, ruled through a council of regents during his short reign of seven years. In general, the cause of reformation advanced during this period. Two bishops were imprisoned, a *Book of Homilies* was issued (1547), royal injunctions ordered the removal of images that led to superstition, and Parliament repealed the Six Articles and ordered that the laity should receive the bread as well as the wine in Communion.[6]

Meanwhile Archbishop Cranmer supported the publication of an English Bible, worked on a service book designed to provide a liturgy for a reformed Church of England, and published a summary of theology that clearly identified England as Protestant. Cranmer's Book of Common Prayer (1549) was the result of a genius's use and adaptation of the Roman liturgy, a re-formed Breviary, Lutheran experiments in liturgical reform, and the Greek liturgies of St. Basil and St. John Chrysostom, among others. Cranmer and his associates intended to simplify the liturgical offices by eliminating many variable elements and translating them into English, providing the whole corpus needed for worship in one book; in addition, the doctrine of the Prayer Book was to be revised on the basis of the Holy Scriptures so as to conform with biblical teaching. The resulting vernacular liturgy was conservative, using the form and structure of the old rites, ceremonies, and ornaments. The eight canonical hours were reduced to two, while all saints' days were eliminated except those recognizing figures from the New Testament. After men of strongly Protestant sympathies gained power in the later years of Edward's reign, a second edition of the Book of Common Prayer was issued in 1552. It eliminated all mention of the offertory of bread and wine, broke the consecration prayer into parts that preceded and followed Communion, and inserted the formula "Take and eat this in remembrance," etc., at the Communion for the earlier "The Body of our Lord Jesus Christ," etc. Immediately before printing, over Cranmer's protest, the famous Black Rubric was inserted which declared that kneeling to receive the sacrament did not imply

> that any adoration is done, or ought to be done, either unto the Sacramental bread or wine there bodily received, or unto any real and essential presence there being of Christ's natural flesh and blood.[7]

The Book of Common Prayer was a complete manual of worship that used the rich forms of the medieval church and adapted them, as did Luther, to contemporary use. With minor revisions, the Prayer Book is still widely used in Anglican churches.

Cranmer's second major contribution was the so-called Forty-Two Articles, which drew heavily on the Augsburg Confession and joint doctrinal declarations of German and English theologians who met in Wittenberg in 1536 and London in 1538. During the reign of Queen Elizabeth I these articles were adopted and issued as the Thirty-Nine Articles, and they have played a prominent role among some members of the Church of England and among some Anglicans to the present.

After several revisions, the official edition of the original Forty-Two Articles appeared in 1553 when a royal mandate commanded that all clergy, schoolmasters, and members of a university taking a degree should subscribe. Whether or not Convocation officially acted on these articles is debated, but they were not acted on by Parliament at this time. The articles were intended to attack medieval teaching and abuses as well as Anabaptist tenets, but the articles aimed at concord rather than exclusive definition. They made no pretension to be setting forth a complete system of belief. In the article on the Holy Communion both transubstantiation and the doctrine of the Real Presence were denied.[8] The articles showed that Cranmer was increasingly being influenced by Reformed rather than Lutheran figures.

These articles had little immediate impact because Mary, the Roman Catholic daughter of Henry VIII and Catherine, ascended the throne. Determined to restore Roman Catholicism to England during her reign (1553–1558), Mary married Philip II, the new king of Spain. Protestants were persecuted unmercifully, and more than 300 Protestants accused as heretics were burned, including Cranmer and two other bishops. These deaths helped alienate people from the church that the action was designed to protect. More than 800 English Protestants, the so-called Marian exiles, fled to the Continent where they accepted help in Reformed centers such as Geneva, Strassburg, Frankfort, and Zurich. Upon their return they brought a distinctively Reformed as opposed to Lutheran influence into the English church.

Elizabeth I succeeded her half-sister as queen of England in 1558 and ruled for forty-five years. Her major task was to resolve the religious ferment of the three previous rules. Without question she was a *politique,* committed foremost to the business of government and only secondarily concerned with a partisan religious viewpoint. This was a necessity, since many of her loyal subjects—possibly even a majority—still held to the old religion when she came to the throne.

She accepted the advice of her counselors and practiced moderation in making religious innovations. Preferring religious ceremonialism and a doctrinal statement that would unite rather than divide her subjects, she was well served both by Cranmer's Book of Common Prayer and by his Forty-Two

Articles. She showed that she had little desire to reconcile with Rome when she declined to marry Philip II of Spain, but she also evidenced a disinclination toward presbyterian ecclesiastical polity when she selected Matthew Parker as archbishop of Canterbury and had him consecrated in the tradition of apostolic succession.

She set the course for religious settlement in acts of Parliament adopted in 1559, shortly after she ascended the throne. The Act of Supremacy reaffirmed the rejection of papal authority and papal representatives and invalidated Mary's Roman Catholic legislation. The act gave her the title "supreme governor of this realm as well in all spiritual or ecclesiastical things or causes, as temporal," rather than the formula preferred by Henry, "supreme head of the church."

The Act of Uniformity (1559) provided a revised edition of the Book of Common Prayer, which was made the compulsory form or worship for the Church of England, now formally and officially established. Clergy were obligated to use this book in public worship, and all English citizens were compelled to attend church. The revised Prayer Book combined the Words of Administration for Holy Communion found in both the 1549 and 1552 books and eliminated the Black Rubric. This liturgy has remained the basic liturgy of the Church of England to the present, though some additions were made in 1604 and a general revision of the book occurred in 1661 when the monarchy was restored. The Prayer Book editions of 1549, 1552, 1559, and 1604 were authorized by act of Parliament without consulting the clergy in their Convocations, the assumption being that the Crown in parliament represented the laity of the entire Church of England.[9]

In 1563 Cranmer's Forty-Two Articles, now the Thirty-Nine Articles, received royal assent. It is interesting to note that Elizabeth first set out to formalize the church's ceremonial worship before taking up the delicate task of providing a statement of doctrine and belief. In the interim, it must be assumed, the Book of Common Prayer served as the primary official standard of doctrine; many Anglicans and people in the Church of England continue to insist that the articles are to be interpreted in the light of the Prayer Book.

The revision of Cranmer's Forty-Two Articles (1553) was carried through essentially by the Convocation of 1563. Lutheran influence once more played a role in the revision, in part because the archbishop used the Confession of Württemberg in his editing process. Convocation added four new articles, removed four old articles, and struck out three articles, forwarding thirty-nine to the queen. She removed Article 29 in order not to offend the Romanist party and added a preface to Article 20, which asserted the church's authority to decree rites and ceremonies. The thirty-eight articles remained until Convocation carried out a final revision in 1571, altering several minor points. Since a papal bull eliminated all possibility for reconciliation with Rome, Article 29 was restored. The Thirty-Nine Articles were passed by Convocation in that year, and Parliament made subscription mandatory for all candidates for ordination and for those who were to receive benefices. Assent was required to those articles "which only concern the confession of the true Christian faith and the doctrine of the Sacraments" in a move designed to remove the scruples of Puritans on matters of church order. Meanwhile Convocation on its own authority stipulated that the requirement of subscription to all thirty-nine articles (including the Ordinal in Article 36) should be enforced.[10]

The Thirty-Nine Articles stated the main doctrines in such matters as justification and the sacraments but did not attempt too detailed or narrow a definition. In this regard they approximated contemporary Reformed confessions more than the decrees of Trent or the later Westminster Confession. A recent study by the archbishop of Canterbury's commission in Britain concludes that the doctrine of the articles "was demonstrably Protestant as opposed to Roman Catholic and Anabaptist, and within the Protestant spectrum Reformed as opposed to Lutheran; hence the inclusion of the Articles in the volume *A Harmony of the Confessions of Faith of the Orthodox and Reformed Churches,* published in Geneva in 1581."[11]

Articles 1 to 5 restated and amplified the faith professed in the creeds in the Trinity, Incarnation, and the true atoning death and bodily resurrection of Jesus Christ. Six to 8 established the Bible as the sufficient rule of faith for salvation. Nine to 18 concerned man's inability to please God or merit his favor, and the grace that justifies and saves persons through Christ "by faith only." Articles 19 through 39 determined questions about the church in regard to its nature, authority, ministers, sacraments, worship, ritual, discipline, relations with the state, and domestic organization. The articles were not meant to be a complete and systematic statement of Christian truth, but rather, to set the boundaries by answering specific and important questions disturbing the church.[12]

The Thirty-Nine Articles were designed in part to create a common front against Rome. Various plots against Elizabeth made her and her subjects even more determined to resist the growth of Roman Catholicism in England. When the pope excommunicated and deposed Elizabeth in 1570—without effect—160 Roman Catholic priests and sixty laypersons were executed under the charge of treason. The infiltration of Jesuits into England in 1579–1580 led Parliament to make it treason for anyone to attempt to convert another to Roman Catholicism with the intent to "withdraw any of the Queen Majesty's subjects from their natural obedience to her Majesty."[13] The final overt attack on Protestant England came in 1588 when the Spanish Armada attempted to reimpose Roman Catholicism by force. "The winds of God and the skill of the English seaman," one pious English writer noted, destroyed the great Armada.

Elizabeth's other major concern was the Puritans. Puritanism is difficult to define, since it was at the same time a state of mind, a program, and a movement within the English church with roots in the early Reformation period. There were numerous varieties of Puritans, many of whom were

Marian exiles or familiar with this phase of the church's history. During Elizabeth's reign Convocation entertained a proposal in 1563 to abolish the practices that tended toward "superstition," including the priest's praying with his face turned from the people, his use of the sign of the cross in baptism, and the kneeling of communicants. In addition, the document suggested that the surplice was to be the adequate clerical vestment. After the proposal lost by a single vote, a long debate over vestments ensued. A number of other items were also debated, and after 1570 Puritan propaganda became more effective. The Puritan witness became more powerful in Parliament, and attacks on prelates became more violent. The Act of Uniformity was invoked to repress the movement's "prophesyings" and attacks on bishops. But little was accomplished, and in the 1580s Puritan propaganda became more violent than ever. A number of *Homilies* were published for mandatory use by parsons who were not licensed to preach.[14]

A thriving, prosperous middle class provided most of the adherents of the growing Puritan movement, and when Elizabeth died they were a formidable element in the country. During her reign the Church of England had been engaged in a triangular struggle. While some bishops fought a losing battle for Roman Catholicism, the Puritans tried to work through the established church from the inside in their efforts to make it one of the "best reformed." The queen tried to keep Roman Catholic opposition in check while restraining the Puritans as well.[15]

Early in Elizabeth's reign a former Marian exile, Bishop John Jewel, defended the Church of England against Roman Catholic detractors in his *Apology for the Church of England* (1562), in which he pledged to submit to Rome if it were demonstrated that Roman doctrine agreed with the consensus of the church's first centuries. Near the end of Elizabeth's reign Richard Hooker wrote *Laws of Ecclesiastical Polity* (1593–1597), defending the church against Puritan writers. In Hooker's work "for the first time in any systematic way Anglicanism presents itself as a *via media* between two systems accused of betraying traditional Catholicity. Both Puritans and Romans sin, by default or excess. Anglicanism stands in the middle, preserving the Catholic faith from all corruptions. This at least is the picture that Hooker conveys."[16]

Relative quiet prevailed while Elizabeth lived. Many individuals worshiped privately as they wished, and at the end of her reign as many as 200 identifiable dissenting sects existed in England. But Elizabeth skillfully circumvented efforts of Parliament to institute a thoroughgoing Puritan regime. The Elizabethan Settlement was the queen's settlement. Her successors found the Puritans gaining control of Parliament and establishing a political unity that threatened England's governmental system. Meanwhile, Puritan attacks on the Prayer Book led Anglicans to give far more scholarly scrutiny to its meaning, structure, and method than it might otherwise have received; no less ironically, since the Prayer Book was proscribed during the Puritan Commonwealth, it entered deeply into underground use in private and family life.[17]

Church government was probably the most important issue in the Puritan protest. James I, Elizabeth's successor, responded to Puritan urgings to abolish the episcopal system with the maxim, "No bishop, no king." Already in the previous century the Anglican church had been divided over two views of the episcopacy. Gardiner stressed that the episcopate was established by the apostles to preside authoritatively over the church until the Lord's return, while Cranmer argued that, in view of Roman errors, the tyrannic authority of the bishops was no longer apostolic, and the king had the obligation to appoint bishops. The English Ordinal of 1550 provided for three major orders of bishop, priest, and deacon, demonstrating historic continuity with the Christian tradition in England. The bishop alone laid hands on the deacon, he and attendant presbyters on ordered priests, and three bishops at the consecration of a bishop. The Marprelate tracts issued secretly in 1588–1589 were part of the Puritan propaganda against the hierarchy of the established church. Earlier a pamphlet entitled *A Brief and Plain Declaration* (also known as the *Learned Discourse,* 1584) attacked Anglican bishops and argued for presbyterian governance of the church.[18]

James I, who ruled from 1603 until 1625, did not bring the kind of relief that Puritans expected in the realm of church government, although one positive result of the Hampton Court Conference (1604) was the Authorized (King James) Version of the Bible published in 1611. William Laud (1573–1645) became the archbishop of Canterbury in 1633, named to the post by Charles I (1600–1649). The king's marriage to a Roman Catholic and his dissolving of Parliament for eleven years after the body's refusal to grant money for foreign military expeditions brought great unpopularity. Relying on the theory of the divine right of kings, Charles enforced his will and found in Laud an able proponent of High Church reforms and a headstrong opponent of Puritan opposition. After Scotland was invaded, he was forced to call Parliament in 1640 to secure funds. The long Parliament of 1640 curtailed the monarch's independent power, but continuing conflict brought civil war and the king's execution.

Parliament abolished the episcopacy in 1643, and two years later Laud was executed for treason. At the Westminster Assembly in 1643 the gathered divines drew up a confession and shaped a presbyterian discipline for the church's governance that was implemented only in London and the area of Manchester. As the governmental and church crisis escalated, the Independents took control from the presbyterian elements. They conceived of the national church as being composed of an aggregate of mutually independent churches or congregations. Clergymen who were in sympathy with the Puritans were given the more lucrative livings, and it was forbidden to read the service from the Prayer Book, although some clerics recited the services from memory.[19]

The rebellion ended with the return of the Stuart king Charles II in 1661 and the restoration of the old character of the national church, complete with the episcopacy and the Prayer Book. The Act of Uniformity (1662) compelled all ministers to give their "unfeigned consent and assent" to the Prayer Book and to obtain episcopal ordination if they were not so ordained. These provisions led to the "Great Ejection" of about 2,000 Presbyterian, Independent, and Baptist ministers, the final parting between Anglicans and Puritans, and the birth of English Nonconformity. One scholar remarks that "the outstanding innovation of the Anglican restoration settlement was the unvarying requirement of episcopal ordination for ministry in whatever capacity in the church."[20] The parochial clergy had to deal with two immediate effects of the interregnum. Private baptisms had increased considerably, and one of the goals of the restored clergy was to stress the duty of public baptism in church except for grave energency. No less important was the need to offer greater opportunity for participation in the Lord's Supper.[21]

One of the most important theological results of the upheavals of the seventeenth century was the eclipse of Calvinism in the Church of England. By 1660, according to Gordon Gragg, Calvinism had passed the peak of its power in England, though few contemporaries seemed to recognize the fact. The change became more apparent in the succeeding generation. "At the beginning of the century, [Calvinism] had dominated the religious life of England; by the end its power had been completely overthrown." Charles II's return was simultaneously a defeat of Puritan theology as well as the overthrow of the Puritan party.[22]

During the seventeenth century the Cambridge Platonists showed that zeal and charity could dwell together, a difficult feat at the time. While they defy classification—belonging fully neither to the world of the Commonwealth nor to the society that replaced it—they were most at home in the Restoration, since their teaching basically attacked the foundations of the prevailing theology of Calvinism. They conceived of salvation, says Cragg, "in a form and spirit entirely different from the vivid pictorial imagery of the Calvinists," who stressed the teaching of Christ's sacrifice for sin. In opposition to the Calvinists they stressed that reason should not be fettered, but against those committed to Laud's ideals they argued that conduct and morality were more important than church polity.[23] Their mystical apprehension of God, influenced by Plato's idealism and Neoplatonism, rescued them from the arid rationalism of the deists.

"Latitudinarianism" was a name first coined to designate the Cambridge Platonists, but in the latter part of the seventeenth century it was applied to those who demonstrated a liberal theological spirit. Many of the leading Latitudinarians were taught by Cambridge Platonists, but they seemed to lose some of the earlier mysticism and relied more heavily on reason, partly in reaction to the excesses of certain Puritan sects and the "enthusiasts." They were less inclined to praise reason than define it, using the word to signify ather generally the exercise of all mental faculties. They stressed the practical and speculative importance of immortality, argued that the true corrective to dogmatism was the recognition of the limitations of human knowledge, and insisted that superstitious beliefs and practices were indefensible.[24]

The short reign of James II (1685–1688) was due in great part to his Roman Catholicism and his alienation of Parliament and influential Anglicans, as well as his appointment of co-religionists to high offices. The "Revolution" of 1688 brought a return to normalcy with the crowning of William and Mary as joint monarchs in 1689. This short and final controversy with Romanism was matched on the other side with toleration for the dissenting Protestant groups. A significant change in political theory occurred with the erosion of the theory and theology of the divine right of kings and the end of a purely passive view of the citizen's responsibilities. After the Restoration the theory of divine right was expounded by both political theorists and theologians, but the fall of James II overthrew the doctrine once and for all. This theory had proved to be an effective defense against the pretensions of papists in the sixteenth century as well as the Puritans' onslaught in the seventeenth, and after the Restoration churchmen expressed appreciation for the theory in sermons, treatises and devotional tracts. But James II showed that many had misplaced their confidence in this theory. The subsequent crisis and combined action of church and state brought his downfall and the scuttling of the theory, as well as the doctrine of passive obedience. Soon after the new monarchs were crowned in 1689, the question of appropriate oaths led many anxious clergymen to search for some satisfactory formula. That only a few clergymen did not make the appropriate oath showed that the doctrine of divine right of kings had outlived its usefulness. If was clear that popery and the claims of divine right were no longer counterbalancing forces, and both were repudiated while the Puritan threat was no longer considered to be as serious as it once had been. Meanwhile, increasing dependence on reason made people sensitive to extravagant claims.[25]

Religious toleration became the law of the land in 1689 with the Act of Toleration. The thrust of events convinced the people of England that persecution did not pay. This bill, "exempting their Majesties' Protestant Subjects dissenting from the Church of England from the penalties of certain Laws," passed easily. It granted freedom of public worship and legal protection to trinitarian Protestant dissenters who met in registered meeting places, with doors open, and whose ministers subscribed to the doctrinal articles of the Thirty-Nine Articles, took the oath of allegiance, and made declaration against transubstantiation. Norman Sykes suggests that "this revolution in the position of Protestant dissenters after 1689 was perhaps the most influential single circumstance affecting also the situation of the established church," since the power of the Church of England was restrained as a result. Convocation was subsequently silenced, certain ecclesiastical reforms were denied, and no bishops were sent to the American colonies.[26]

Deism was the subsequent examination of creedal presuppositions in the light of the defeat of the two internal foes, Romanism and Puritanism. While it was not an entirely new phenomenon, its proponents openly attacked revelation and freely discussed the significance of faith for daily living. The movement signaled the growing importance of John Locke.

In the century between 1550 and 1650 the episcopate was under intense pressure, but Anglican divines developed

> a positive, constructive, and consistent apologetic for episcopacy as retained in the church of England. It was held to be not of dominical but of apostolic appointment, and as *divino jure* only in that sense; as necessary where it could be had, but its absence where historical necessity compelled did not deprive a church of valid ministry and sacraments.[27]

The divines fiercely rebutted Roman efforts to deprive the English church of its catholicity by discovering flaws in the consecration of Elizabethan bishops, holding that

> the spiritual function of the priesthood was proved by experience to depend for its higher and purer efficacy on the Apostolic Succession of the bishops. And from this pragmatic argument they could go on to infer that episcopacy, even though devised by man rather than commanded by revelation, was sanctioned by Providence to be the means of preserving the Church as the channel of Grace.[28]

In 1691 England experienced the only High Church schism in the history of the Church of England when Archbishop Sancroft and about ten bishops and some 400 clergy suffered deprivation rather than take the oath of allegiance to the new monarchs. They saw such an obligation as inconsistent with their duty to James, the previous king. The shadow episcopate died out in 1805. A tract that appeared early in the eighteenth century, entitled *Essay toward a Proposal for a Catholic Communion* (1704), called for union with the old Church of Rome, but drew its sharpest rejoinder from the ranks of the Non-Jurors who feared that troubles would increase for them if public opinion associated them with a Romanizing view. In 1717 the government suspended Convocation for more than a century for its opposition to certain Protestant ideas and because of High churchmen's efforts to gain control of the lower house.[29]

While High churchmen suffered near collapse in the eighteenth century, by the end of the century some of them found ways to coalesce around the divine commission of bishops, the catholicity of each episcopal church, and the authority of the church fathers in interpreting the Scriptures. The Oxford Movement of the mid-nineteenth century (c. 1833–c. 1845) asserted the doctrine of apostolic succession as the cornerstone of catholic doctrine. This group, which included John Henry Newman until his conversion to Roman Catholicism, John Keble, and Edward Pusey, had its center in Oxford. It opposed the growth of liberalism and began as an attack on the government's intention to reduce the number of bishoprics in Ireland. The Tractarians' *Tracts for the Times* began appearing in 1833; central concerns were a revival of a high doctrine of the church and its ministry. The Tractarians' deep interest in the church as the body of Christ collided with the views of others when they seemed to decry the Reformation of the Church of England, and their proposals were seen as innovations by the majority in the church.

Worship and Order in the Anglican Communion

Anglican worship traditionally has sought to blend and express devotion to the Holy Scripture and the inculcation of the habit of private prayer in corporate spirituality. Liturgy, says one Anglican scholar, is

> the fulness of both devout biblicism and interior prayer, and it presupposes a devout biblicism and a profound life of prayer outside and yet continuous with the life that is lived in the liturgy. And this is because our liturgical life will necessarily be a rather thin and tenuous reality unless it is the liturgical life of the man who is, even outside his liturgical life in the narrower sense of the word, both a man of the Bible and a man of prayer. The liturgy is the central element of the three precisely because it is the element which unifies the other two and in which they reach the fulness of their self-expression.

For this reason the Anglican liturgy is essentially a vernacular, conservative, scriptural, and patristic liturgy.[30] Liturgy is the center of life and service in the Anglican communion.

The Book of Common Prayer in its various editions and vernacular languages stands in a firm historical succession, organically continuous with the church's rites in the centuries before the Reformation era. The primary source is the Latin Rite of the medieval English church; the liturgy's framework is the calendar of seasons and holy days of the Western medieval church. The structure and content of the daily offices of Morning and Evening Prayer more closely approximate the canonical hours of the Latin Breviary than the Puritans' supposedly apostolic "prayer meetings." Anglicans have retained the distinction between the rites of baptism and confirmation that was observed in the West, and in some later revisions the Book of Common Prayer has reinserted the offertory of the bread and wine that was eliminated in the revision of 1552.[31]

Except for a few cathedrals and large parishes, after the Reformation the customary Sunday service included Morning Prayer, Litany, Ante-Communion, and Sermon, while the celebration of Holy Communion was observed four times a year or in some places monthly. By the end of the nineteenth century most parishes celebrated Holy Communion every Sunday and holy day, but the Sunday celebration did not in many places come to be the "principal" parish service more than once a month. The liturgy of the service prior to Communion generally followed this outline, with optional parts indicated in brackets:

[Introit—a psalm, hymn, or anthem, or the Litany]
[Lord's Prayer—a survival of the priest's preparation, usually said quietly by the celebrant alone]
The Collect for Purity
The Commandments (either the Ten Commandments or our Lord's Summary of the Law, or both) with the response:
Kyrie eleison ("Lord, have mercy upon us")
[The Prayer, "O Almighty Lord," after the Commandments]
The Salutation and Collect of the Day
The Epistle
[Gradual—a psalm, hymn, or anthem]
The Gospel with its responses . . .
The Creed (usually the Nicene Creed, sometimes the Apostles' Creed)
[Prayers]
The Sermon

The introduction of the Commandments was the distinctively Anglican feature of this liturgy.[32]

Basically there are two eucharistic liturgies in the Anglican Communion, which stem respectively from the first two Prayer Books. The most apparent difference between them is the relative position of the Prayer of Oblation. In the first Prayer Book this prayer preceded the act of Communion and formed a part of the Prayer of Consecration, but in the second, since the act of Communion followed immediately after the Words of Institution, the Prayer of Oblation was shifted to a position after Communion. The Elizabethan Settlement established the second Prayer Book as the norm, and this liturgy is still official in the Church of England (with some minor revisions) as well as the Anglican churches in Wales, Ireland, Canada, Australia, and New Zealand. The Scottish Book (1637) returned to the pattern of the first Prayer Book and, though not widely used, it became an important contributor to the Scottish liturgy of 1764. Since the first American bishop was consecrated by Scottish bishops, this form was adopted in the American Prayer Book, as well as by churches in South Africa, India, Pakistan, Burma, Ceylon, and Japan. A good deal of discussion and debate has centered on this issue, which involves the fundamental question of the nature and character of the Eucharist as a sacrifice.[33] One author makes the assertion that "wherever the churches of the Anglican Communion have been freed from parliamentary interference and control there has been a reversion to the type of liturgy exemplified in the First English Prayer Book of 1549," adding that a recent expression of this spirit is the "liturgy of the Canadian Church

in 1959 and that of the Province of the West Indies of the same year."[34]
There is presently a movement in the Church of England to emphasize the
offering of praise and thanksgiving of the bread and wine as representing
man's life and labor.[35]

The centrality of the Holy Communion in worship is not an object of
debate. For decades and centuries the Church of England welcomed Lutherans and Reformed to communicate with the Anglican church. In 1968 the
Lambeth Conference of bishops of the Anglican communion resolved to
recommend that "to meet special pastoral needs of God's people, under the
direction of the bishop Christians duly baptized in the name of the Holy
Trinity and qualified to receive Holy Communion in their own Churches may
be welcomed at the Lord's table in the Anglican Communion." The conference further recommended that "while it is the general practice of the
Church that Anglican communicants receive the Holy Communion at the
hands of ordained ministers of their own Church or of Churches in communion therewith," to meet special pastoral needs such communicants are
"free to attend the Eucharist in other Churches holding the apostolic faith as
contained in the Scriptures and summarized in the Apostles' and Nicene
Creeds, and as conscience dictates to receive the sacrament, when they know
they are welcome to do so." Three hundred and fifty-one bishops voted for
and seventy-five against this second provision which, while not binding on
the churches of the Anglican communion, has the force of the bishops'
opinion.[36]

The importance of Holy Communion in Anglican worship is signaled by
the growing number of pages in editions of the Book of Common Prayer that
concern the Eucharist. The English Prayer Book of 1663 dedicated 222 pages
to this area of a total of 670 that included the Communion Service, the
Collects, Epistles, Gospels, and the Ordinal. The English Prayer Book of
1928 had 300 (of 760) devoted to eucharistic forms. The 1928 American
Prayer Book and the recent South African Book dedicated well over half
their pages to eucharistic material.[37]

Traditional vestments are now widely used in Anglican churches, many
of them making a reappearance in the nineteenth century. In addition, most
priests appear to use at the altar some actions—for example, the sign of
the cross when blessing—that are not prescribed in the Prayer Book.

The Prayer Book indicates that baptism is always to be administered
publicly in the church except for "urgent cause." God's people are present
to receive the new member and support the baptized individual by their
prayers and faith.

In its title the Prayer Book traditionally distinguishes between "Common
Prayer" and the "Sacraments and Other Rites and Ceremonies of the Church"
whose essential elements are fixed. The "Common Prayer" stems from the
devotions of Christian people. They are, says the Anglican liturgiologist
Massey H. Shepherd, "essentially liturgies of the laity" which "do not

require the ministry of ordained clergy." The daily offices of Morning and Evening Prayer and the Great Litany compose this "common prayer."[38]

Anglican worship is ordered, historically rooted, and anchored in the Christian Scriptures. Various churches in the communion have modified and revised the Book of Common Prayer, as we shall see below, but its core remains much the same from one national church to another.

All Anglican churches have three orders: episcopate, priesthood, and diaconate. Many of these churches have archbishops who are primates, equal among equals, of the respective national church, such as is the case in New Zealand and Australia. Others select a presiding bishop, such as the Episcopal Church in the United States. England has two archbishops, the archbishop of Canterbury and the archbishop of York. The archbishop of Canterbury serves as titular and honorific head of the Anglican communion of churches although he exercises no canonical control over the various national churches. Since the latter part of the nineteenth century he traditionally calls the bishops of the church together every decade for the Lambeth Conference of bishops.

Archbishop Cranmer issued an English *Ordinal* in 1550, which contained simplified vernacular liturgies for the ordination of bishops, priests and deacons. While the *Ordinal* has been revised slightly, it remains substantially the same throughout the Anglican communion The chief emphasis of these liturgies is the laying on of hands with prayer. Both the examination of the candidates for all three orders and the exhortations expressed to them strongly insist on the Holy Scriptures as the norm for their teaching and life. The three rites are embodied in the eucharistic celebration, and each requires a sermon regarding the order's duties, its necessity in the church, and the people's esteem for it.[39] The *Ordinal* in the United States also provides two rites generally conducted by the bishop, consecration of a church or chapel and the induction of ministers into parishes or churches. Upon ordination the new deacon, priest, and bishop receive a copy of the Bible. The process of selecting archbishops and bishops has some variation from church to church within the communion.

Traditional theory identified three elements in the succession of bishops. *Successio personalis* meant consecration by three bishops, *successio localis* required consecration in the government of a diocese of the church, and *successio doctrinalis* the maintenance of purity of faith. At the time of declaring independence from Rome, the Church of England understood all three elements to be preserved. But in the sixteenth and later centuries there "was no condemnation of ministries without bishops outside the Church of England, and always the more representative theologians have preserved the old tradition of a generous charity or silence at this point."[40] In the eighteenth century a good deal of correspondence between Anglican church-men and others, based on serious patristic study and scholarship, resulted in only one official act of recognition when by act of Parliament the *Unitas Fratrum* was recognized in 1749 as "an ancient Protestant Episcopal Church." But an impressive apology for episcopacy was constructed, and foreign Reformed churches came to recognize how valuable was the Anglican *via media* with its firm grasp upon the historic episcopate.[41]

John Wesley concluded that there was no distinction between the episcopate and the presbyterate, and eventually his Methodist revival in England and the American colonies resulted in separations from the Church of England. In the nineteenth century the Oxford Movement proposed to use the episcopate to define the boundaries of ordination exclusively. Newman's first tract contended that the function of the bishop in ordination was that "he but *transmits*; and that the Christian ministry is a succession." He concluded that "we must necessarily consider none to be *really* ordained who have not *thus* been ordained."[42] Newman and others were outraged by what seemed to be unwarranted state control of the church. After 1832 supreme ecclesiastical jurisdiction was vested in the Privy Council or a subordinate council rather than a spiritual court; the next year a number of Irish sees were combined while agitation mounted against certain church abuses. The Oxford Movement reinforced the episcopate as a proper form of church order, but in the meantime evangelical bishops such as Bishop Blomfield and Bishop Wilberforce helped transform the image of the bishop into a recognizably ecclesiastical and spiritual office through the idea of the "busy bishop."[43]

Today the Anglican bishop is expected to give clergy and laity a vision of the church with its unchanging call to holiness and self-sacrifice in love of humanity. Where necessary he may discipline, but normally his message is imparted through his own life and words of admiration and affection. He approves the nominations of local churches or other authorities as worthy to minister as priest or deacon, provides for their training, and presides at their ordination. He may also help at the ordination of another bishop. Through confirmation he admits candidates to full church membership and participation in the Holy Communion.[44]

In a preparatory essay for the 1968 Lambeth Conference, the Anglican scholar R. P. C. Hanson offered three propositions that are perceived as justifying the episcopacy as it is preserved within the Anglican communion:

1. The Anglican Churches inherited an episcopal form of government from the late medieval Church.

2. They regarded this form of ministry as agreeable to the Word of God as it is found in the Scriptures, and the actual holders of episcopal office during the reigns of Henry VIII, Edward VI, and Elizabeth I either encouraged a Reformation according to the Word of God or did not render such a Reformation impossible.

3. The Anglican Churches therefore believed that they had no authority to alter the episcopal form of government.

Hanson wrote that the theological justification for the Anglican episcopacy is "tradition found to be agreeable to the Scriptures," adding that while the Anglican divines made it clear that "they do not regard episcopacy as an *articulum stantis aut cadentis ecclesiae*" (article by which the church stands or falls), they recognized as well that "where episcopal government can be preserved and had, there not only *might* it be adopted but there it *should* be adopted." He insisted that the bishop's authority should be regarded as basically moral inasmuch as "the constant use of ecclesiastical coercion, whether exercised through the bishops or not, is not an Anglican characteristic." The peculiarly episcopal function of an Anglican bishop is that he "wields central representative authority in the Church," according to Hanson. "Each bishop is a representative of the Church, within the Church, expressing its life and thought and actions. The bishop's position should be thought of as central rather than hierarchical," he added.[45]

By episcopacy, said one important speaker at the Anglican Congress in 1954,

> we mean episcopacy in what we believe to be its primitive and essential form, bishops who are superintendent ministers with the right of conferring orders of the ministry and of handing on their own ministry in due succession from generation to generation. We claim on the one hand not to have broken that succession, and on the other hand not to have exalted any one of our bishops to have exclusive powers over his brethren and over the Church at large. . . . However, we are not peculiar in our view of episcopacy, for it is roughly the same as that taken by the Orthodox Churches of the East, by the Old Catholics, and by some sections of the Lutherans.

He went on to discuss with the delegates the question "whether episcopacy is of the *esse* or the *bene esse* of the Church, whether, that is to say, it is necessary or merely advisable to have bishops. Recently there has arisen a new school of thought which ignores the alternatives of *esse* and *bene esse* but affirms that episcopacy is of the *plene esse,* the fulness of the Church. That means, as I understand it, that you can have a Church in embryo without a duly constituted order of bishops, but that you cannot have a complete or perfect Church without them."[46] The Lambeth Quadrilateral issued by the third Lambeth Conference in 1888 required acceptance of the historic episcopate for "Home Reunion" in these words:

> The Historic Episcopate, locally adapted in the methods of its administration to the varying needs of the nations and peoples called of God into the unity of His Church.

But the Lambeth Appeal of about thirty years later showed that the bishops were desirous of offering a provisional explanation of this, the fourth of four articles. "May we not reasonably claim," asked the bishops,

> that the Episcopate is the one means of providing such a ministry [namely, recognized by the whole Church]? It is not that we call in question for a moment the spiritual reality of the ministries of those Communions which do not possess the Episcopate. On the contrary, we thankfully acknowledge that

these ministries have been manifestly blessed and owned by the Holy Spirit as effective means of grace.[47]

This discussion will be resumed below in the section dealing with the Anglican communion and its involvement in the Ecumenical movement.

The Anglican priest performs the typical priestly duties upon ordination by a bishop. The majority of priests are engaged in their work full time, but in 1958 and again in 1968 the Lambeth Conference resolved that "there is no theological principle which forbids a suitable man from being ordained priest while continuing in his lay occupation."[48]

A serious debate about whether or not women should be ordained to the order of priest has raged through the various Anglican churches in the last several decades. In 1948 the Lambeth Conference of bishops reaffirmed a resolution of 1930 that "the Order of Deaconess is for women the one and only Order of the Ministry which we can recommend our branch of the Catholic Church to recognize and use." It also approved the resolution adopted in 1939–1941 in the Convocations of Canterbury and York, "that the order of Deaconesses is the one existing ordained ministry for women in the sense of being the only Order of Ministry in the Anglican Communion to which women are admitted by episcopal imposition of hands." Another resolution added that

> the Conference is aware that in some quarters there is a desire that the question of ordination of women to the priesthood should be reconsidered. The Conference, recalling that the question was examined in England by the Archbishop's Commission on the Ministry of Women whose Report was published in 1935, is of opinion that the time has not come for its further formal consideration.

The immediate occasion of these resolutions was a request from the diocese of South China that "for an experimental period of twenty years a deaconess might (subject to certain conditions) be ordained to the priesthood"; the General Synod of the Church in China had asked the conference "whether or not such liberty to experiment within the framework of the Anglican Communion would be in accordance with Anglican tradition and order."[49]

The item continued to generate discussion and debate. In the mid-sixties a Commission of the Church of England issued a report entitled *Women and Holy Orders* (London, 1966) which showed that irreconcilable views were held within this church on the subject. In 1968 the committee of the Lambeth Conference charged with examining the issue concluded that "we find no conclusive theological reasons for withholding ordination to the priesthood from women as such." It noted that appeal to Scripture and tradition deserved to be taken with utter seriousness, but "the data of *Scripture* appear divided on this issue" while "the *tradition* flowing from the early Fathers and the medieval Church that a woman is incapable of receiving

Holy Orders reflects biological assumptions about the nature of woman and her relation to man which are considered unacceptable in the light of modern knowledge and biblical study and have been generally discarded today." The bishops resolved, on the basis of the committee's report, that "the Conference affirms its opinion that the theological arguments as at present presented for and against the ordination of women to the priesthood are inconclusive." It asked national and regional churches and provinces to study the question and report findings to the Anglican Consultative Council, and in turn requested this council to distribute the information received and "to initiate consultations with other Churches which have women in their ordained ministry and with those which have not." The conference also recommended that

> before any national or regional Church or province makes a final decision to ordain women to the priesthood, the advice of the Anglican Consultative Council (or Lambeth Consultative Body) be sought and carefully considered.

"In the meantime," according to the conference, "national and regional Churches or provinces should be encouraged to make canonical provision, where this does not exist, for duly qualified women to share in the conduct of liturgical worship, to preach, to baptize, to read the epistle and gospel at the Holy Communion, and to help in the distribution of the elements."[50]

The movement to ordain women as priests commenced in 1971 when the bishop of the small diocese of Hong Kong ordained two women. In the same year the Anglican Consultative Council voted by a narrow majority to favor the ordination of women to the priesthood; the archbishop of Canterbury voted in opposition to the recommendation. The previous year the General Convention of the Episcopal Church in the United States approved the ordination of women as deacons. The church in Wales followed in 1973 with approval in principle of the ordination of women to the priesthood. In 1975 the General Synod of the Church of England voted by a majority of two to one that in principle there was no objection to the ordination of women, but such ordinations would be inexpedient as long as a sizable minority was opposed. In 1975 the Canadian Anglicans' General Synod authorized the ordination of women, and five months later the bishops ratified the decision. The Anglican Church of Canada saw its first female priest ordained in November 1976. In the same year the General Synod of the New Zealand church approved by the necessary two-thirds vote the constitutional amendment that allowed women to become priests. The General Synod of the Church of Ireland experienced a heavy majority vote favoring the acceptance of ordaining women in principle. And the General Convention of the Episcopal Church in the United States acted positively on the matter as well in 1976, and in 1977 the first female priests were regularly ordained following the convention's action. In 1977 the national Commission on Doctrine of the Anglican Church in Australia advised the church to adopt legislation allowing the ordination of women as priests "where practicable." The General

Synod was expected to approve the ordination of women when it met later that year.

The order of deacon has been discussed above. The office is often held by a person for a year immediately after graduation from theological training and prior to ordination to the priesthood. The deaconess traditionally has been considered an ordained order, although the bishop consecrates women to this work of education, charity, and prayer. In 1968 the Lambeth Conference recommended an upgrading of the order of deacon while at the same time narrowly recommending by a vote of 221 to 183 "that those made deaconesses by laying on of hands with appropriate prayers be declared to be within the diaconate."[51]

Creed and Doctrine

As we have seen, the great breadth and catholicity of Anglican teaching and doctrine is due in part to the historical circumstances surrounding the Church of England's declaration of independence from Rome and subsequent encounters with Romanism and Puritanism. Anglicanism has no one distinguishing doctrine; rather, it is the peculiar balance of doctrines and beliefs that gives to the Anglican communion its distinctiveness as a body of believers.

The words of the great Anglican scholar J. W. C. Wand provide an apt introduction to Anglican theology. "It is sometimes said, even by its friends," he wrote,

> that the trouble with Anglicanism is that it has no theology. That surely must be wrong. Did Hooker and Jewell, Pearson and Bicknell live in vain? If it is meant that we have no comprehensive and articulated system like the *Institutes* of Calvin or even the *Decrees* of the Council of Trent, it is true enough. But it is already something of a theology to deny the necessity of binding such burdens, grievous to be borne, on men's shoulders. If it is meant that we have no special and peculiar doctrines of our own, that too may be taken as part of our glory. We claim to believe what is in the Creeds and in the Bible, that is to say, what is common to all Christendom. We have our Catechism and our Articles, although we regard them as on a lower level of authority than the creed. The Lambeth Conference of 1888 declared that missionary churches "should not necessarily be bound to accept in their entirety the Thirty Nine Articles of Religion." It is propably just this refusal to be wise above what is written or to regard every doctrinal issue as closed that makes the critics regard Anglicans as lacking a theology.[52]

Wand further suggested that an overview of the breadth of Anglican doctrine is provided in the volume entitled *Doctrine in the Chucrh of England* (London, 1938), edited by William Temple. Sixteen years before this work was published the bishops of the provinces of Canterbury and York appointed a commission to document the agreement of doctrine in the Church of England,

and the volume summarized its findings. The book indicates that a tolerant attitude and freedom of thought were evident at the time.

With some hesitation, several generalizations might be offered about the creed and doctrine of the Anglican communion. In one important sense the Anglican church is the "Church of Christmas" inasmuch as the theology of the Incarnation played an important role in such modern Anglican theologians as Maurice, Westcott, Gore, Thornton, and Temple. According to Wand, this stress on the Incarnation, the taking of the manhood into God, "has led to the recognition of a diffusive aspect of the grace and power of God, and this in turn has prevented Anglican claims from becoming exclusive." In Wand's words, this is one reason why Anglicanism "manages to be authoritative without claiming infallibility, liberal without lapsing into mere vaguenes."[53]

Comprehensiveness is a trait that provides a certain hue or color to Anglican doctrine. Denounced by some uninformed critics, in general it is a characteristic that is praised by Anglicans around the world. Generalities always need to be qualified, but despite this caveat it is generally true to say that the Anglican churches have a Catholic liturgy and a Calvinist set of articles of belief. Some critcs allege that Anglicanism seeks to hold together two opposing theological and religious tendencies, one Evangelical and the other Catholic. Some Anglicans also decry the comprehensiveness of Anglican belief that prevents dogmatic precision and encourages the view that articles of faith should be few and as simple as possible. But comprehensiveness is an essential trait of Anglicanism; according to Wand, "if we did not possess it, there would scarcely be justification for our separate existence." The Church of England reacted in various ways against Puritanism and Romanism, but both left their imprint on the wider Anglican communion. These two complementary ways of thought make their greatest impact in different emphases within the communion's worship.[54]

No less important is the trait of continuity, which also provides a hermeneutic for understanding Anglican doctrine and belief. While the stress on continuity of ministry has been an important one, no less important is the stress on continuity of doctrine. In fact, for many the second is considered to be more important than the first; apostolic ministry is considered to offer the greatest assistance in the preservation of the apostolic tradition. This argument rests on the assertion that the outward form is itself the best guarantee of the preservation of the inward life, just as the shell preserves the kernel from the elements of weather. "This is in conformity," says Wand, "with the general sacramental principle by which the existence of the Church is governed. The physical continuity is the outward and visible sign of the inward and spiritual grace," just as is the case in the sacraments of Eucharist and baptism. This helps one understand the significance that Anglicans attribute to the episcopacy and their insistence that Christianity is a sacramental religion in which the sacraments belong to the very essence of the church and are not merely "picturesque excrescences upon the worship of the Church."

Jeremy Taylor described the Anglican trait of continuity well in 1661 when he wrote:

> What can be supposed wanting [in the Church of England] in order to salvation? We have the Word of God, the Faith of the Apostles, the Creeds of the Primitive Church, the Articles of the four first General Councils, a holy liturgy, excellent prayers, perfect Sacraments, faith and repentance, the Ten Commandments, and the sermons of Christ, and all the precepts and counsels of the Gospel. We teach the necessity of good works, and require and strictly exact the severity of a holy life. We live in obedience to God, and are ready to die for Him. . . . We worship Him at the mention of His Name. . . . We love all Christians, even our most erring brethren. We confess our sins to God and to our brethren whom we have offended, and to God's ministers in cases of scandal or of a troubled conscience. We communicate often. We are enjoined to receive the Holy Sacrament thrice every year at least. Our priests absolve the penitent. Our Bishops ordain priests, and confirm baptized persons, and bless their people and intercede for them.[55]

The comprehensiveness and continuity generally stressed by Anglicans were aptly summarized by a commission report at the Lambeth Conference of 1930, which reported that

> the Anglican Communion includes not merely those who are racially connected with England, but many others whose faith is grounded in the doctrines and ideals for which the Church of England has always stood.

> What are these doctrines? We hold the Catholic Faith in its entirety; that is to say, the truth of Christ, contained in Holy Scriptures; stated in the Apostles' and Nicene Creeds; expressed in the Sacraments of the Gospel and the rites of the Primitive Church as set forth in the Book of Common Prayer with its various local adaptations; and safeguarded by the historic threefold Order of Ministry.

> And what are these ideals? They are the ideals of the Church of Christ. Prominent among them are an open Bible, a pastoral Priesthood, a common worship, a standard of conduct consistent with that worship, and a fearless love of truth. Without comparing ourselves with others, we acknowledge thankfully as the fruits of these ideals within our Communion, the sanctity of mystics, the learning of scholars, the courage of missionaries, the uprightness of civil administration, and the devotion of many servants of God in Church and State.

> While, however, we hold the Catholic Faith, we hold it in freedom. Every Church in our Communion is free to build up its life and development upon the provisions of its own constitution. Local Churches . . . have no power to change the Creeds of the Universal Church or its early organization. But they have the right to determine the best methods of setting forth to their

people the contents of the Christian faith. They may regulate rites, ceremonies, usages, observances and discipline for that purpose, according to their own wisdom and experience and the needs of the people.[56]

As traditionally described for Anglicans, authority in matters of faith rests in the Scriptures, the creeds, the first four General Councils, and reason. The Bible is considered to be the charter, trust deed, and foundation document of the church. Article 6 of the Thirty-Nine Articles states that

Holy Scripture containeth all things necessary to salvation; so that whatsoever is not read therein, nor may be proved thereby, is not to be regarded of any man, that it should be believed as an article of Faith, or be thought requisite or necessary to salvation.

Characteristically Anglican, the article does not claim that nothing can be legitimately thought or done that is not in the Bible, but it insists that no doctrine can be forced as an article of necessary faith if it is not directly contained in the Bible or clearly demonstrable from it. The sixty-six canonical books of the Old and New Testaments make up the Bible; in regard to the Old Testament Apocrypha, the article states that these books "the Church doth read for example of life and instruction of manners; but yet doth it not apply them to establish any doctrine." In its worship the Anglican communion uses the Bible more, in all probability, than any other group of Christians. Old and New Testament lessons are prescribed for each Matins and Evensong, and the Psalter is recited completely each month in this daily office. The Old Testament is read through once each year and the New Testament twice.[57] About 80 percent of the traditional Book of Common Prayer is taken directly from the Bible.

In the Lambeth Conference of 1958 the Anglican bishops affirmed in resolution that "the Bible discloses the truths about the relation of God and Man which are the key to the world's predicament and is therefore deeply relevant to the modern world." They affirmed that "our Lord Jesus Christ is God's final Word to man, and that in his light all Holy Scriptures must be seen and interpreted, the Old Testament in terms of Promise and the New Testament in terms of Fulfilment." While asserting that the church is "both guardian and interpreter of Holy Scriptures," the bishops also warned that "the Church may teach nothing as 'necessary for eternal salvation but what may be concluded and proved by the Scripture.' "[58]

Some churches in the Anglican communion continue to follow the Thirty-Nine Articles of 1571 and 1662 in designating the Nicene Creed, the Apostles' Creed, and the Athanasian Creed as warranting reception and belief. Others, including the Episcopal Church in the United States, have modified the articles to remove the Athanasian Creed from this listing, although the revised Book of Common Prayer of this church incorporates this creed, also called the *Quicunque Vult,* along with the Thirty-Nine Articles in the section headed "Historical Documents of the Church."[59]

In the Anglican communion the Book of Common Prayer is generally regarded as a bond of unity in doctrine and worship. But as indicated above, the two basic patterns of approach to the question of eucharistic sacrifice in various Prayer Books have in some instances produced stress and confrontation.[60]

The Thirty-Nine Articles have varying importance in the different churches of the Anglican communion. In 1968 the Lambeth Conference of bishops voted (with 37 negatives) to accept

> the main conclusion of the report of the Archbishops' Commission on Christian Doctrine entitled Subscription and Assent to the Thirty-Nine Articles (1968) and in furtherance of its recommendation
>
> (a) suggests that each Church of our communion consider whether the Articles need be bound up with its Prayer Book;
>
> (b) suggests to the Churches of the Anglican Communion that assent to the Thirty-Nine Articles be no longer required of ordinands;
>
> (c) suggests that, when subscription is required to the Articles or other elements in the Anglican tradition, it should be required, and given, only in the context of a statement which gives the full range of our inheritance of faith and sets the Articles in their historical context.

The bishops acted on the recommendation of their conference committee's report, which said that the "full range of the Anglican inheritance" in which the articles should be set included three strands: the unique demonstration of the inheritance of faith shown forth "in the holy Scriptures and proclaimed in the Catholic Creeds set in their context of baptismal profession, patrisic reasoning, and conciliar decision"; the "historic formularies" of the Church of England of the sixteenth century, including the Thirty-Nine Articles, Book of Common Prayer, *Ordinal,* and *Homilies*; and the succeeding "responsible witness to Christian truth" of the Anglican communion through preaching and worship, writings of scholars and teachers, "the lives of its saints and confessors, and the utterances of its councils," all of which show "the authority given within the Anglican tradition to reason" and "an acknowledgement of the claims of pastoral care."[61] Earlier the Archbishops' Commission reported on the status of the articles throughout the Anglican communion. It noted among other things that the articles were nowhere mentioned in the constitution of the Church of India, Pakistan, Burma, and Ceylon, and that revisions of the articles, restricted to a few small points of political rather than theological significance, have been undertaken in the Church of the Province of New Zealand and the Episcopal Church in the United States. The commission also reported that only two churches outside England required lay members on certain occasions to subscribe to the articles, namely the Church of the Province of New Zealand and the diocese of Sydney in Australia. The report concluded that "most Churches of the Anglican Communion retain the Articles in their Constitution and of these, all require some form of ministerial assent or subscription, either explicitly or, as in the

Protestant Episcopal Church in the U.S.A., implicitly; though there is wide variety within the Anglican Communion both in the place given to the Thirty-Nine Articles and in the practice of subscribing to Anglican formularies."[62]

While according to the Archbishops' Commission "the majority of Anglicans appear unconcerned about the Articles and subscription to them," two tendencies were evident. One was the growing dissatisfaction with present requirements, and the other regarded "attacks on the Articles and subscription as part of a general erosion of doctrine within the Church of England which endangers the *locus standi* of certain groups within the Church."[63] The second tendency has recently been discussed in a critical essay on the purpose and function of the articles. "The current neglect or evasion or even defiance of the Articles," according to the author,

> is one of the greatest tragedies of modern Anglicanism. As they were conceived in the first instance, they gave hope of promoting both the unity in truth and the freedom under authority which are so necessary to the well-being of the Church. In spite of every obstacle, they have not wholly failed in their purpose. But quite obviously they cannot to-day exercise their functions in the fruitful way which could mean so much not only for doctrinal but for spiritual and disciplinary health.[64]

A brief description of the articles has been provided above.

The two sacraments of the Eucharist and baptism play a prominent role in Anglican belief. But the communion's emphasis on comprehensiveness makes it difficult to say precisely what is the Anglican belief about the Lord's Supper. The form of Christ's presence in the Supper is variously described as mystical, representational, symbolic, and real. Generally it is stressed that the sacrament is a mystery that is not open to full rational and hence verbal comprehension. In the Supper Christ is said to teach, forgive, and heal while imparting his life and nourishing the life already imparted. Some Anglicans believe that somehow the bread and wine become the body and blood of Christ; others believe that Christ's body and blood are truly present in the hearts of the recipients, but not in the elements themselves (thus the term "receptionalism"); and others believe that the elements receive a "spiritual virtue" in the consecration and can be called "sacramental body and blood."

Baptism is believed to be the entrance into the fellowship of Christ's church, the means of cleansing from sin, and the impartation of new life. Baptism is the sacrament of initiation through which a person is grafted into the visible church.

Five other rites are called sacraments by some Anglicans but simply rites by others. They are Confirmation, Ordination, Marriage, Absolution, and Anointing of the Sick. Confirmation by the bishop imparts a special gift of God's Spirit to meet temptation and to live the Christian life. It is the prerequisite for the Lord's Supper, following baptism. Ordination imparts

God's Spirit to persons chosen for a specific ministry, namely that of deacon, priest, and bishop Marriage is a Christian rite inasmuch as Jesus elevated it and gave it a Christian character; he imparts his blessing through the church on those united according to law. While not the only channel for pardon, absolution is God's freeing of people from sin's guilt. Anointing the sick is the church's act of bringing healing and fuller life rather than preparation for death as such.[65]

Some Anglicans observe regular fasting and strict observance of marriage laws. There is much latitude in the understanding of the doctrines of God, the Trinity, the person and work of Christ, and the nature of man, as well as the sacraments and rites. American Episcopalians have an "Outline of the Faith, Commonly Called the Catechism" in their proposed Prayer Book which "is not meant to be a complete statement of belief and practice," but rather, "a point of departure for the teacher, and it is cast in the traditional question and answer form for ease of reference." Nevertheless, the Catechism "is to provide a brief summary of the Church's teaching for an inquiring stranger who picks up a Prayer Book," according to the preface. The Catechism defines the sacraments as "outward and visible signs of inward and spiritual grace, given by Christ as sure and certain means by which we receive that grace." Replying to the question "How do [sacramental rites] differ from the two sacraments of the Gospel?" the Catechism answers: "Although they are means of grace, they are not necessary for all persons in the same way that Baptism and the Eucharist are."[66]

The Anglican communion never adopted the complex machinery used in the Roman Catholic Church for formally "canonizing" a saint. Local and provincial churches exercise liberty in drawing up lists of saints whose lives have special meaning. A recent liturgical conference in Britain considered the addition of new figures to the list of commemorated persons, including the dissenters John and Charles Wesley, George Fox, John Bunyan, John Keble, David Livingstone, the Jesuit missionary St. Francis Xavier, and St. Francis de Sales.[67] Churches in the Anglican communion do not accept the Roman Catholic doctrine of the immaculate conception of the Virgin Mary or the doctrine of her assumption, but she is highly honored as the Mother of God and among some Anglicans considered to have had perpetual virginity.

Especially since 1912, prayers for the dead have been included in many permanent or experimental revisions of the burial service, the Communion service, and the Occasional Prayers and Thanksgivings in churches of the Anglican communion. One collect provided in *The Draft Proposed Book of Common Prayer of the Episcopal Church in the U.S.A.* is the following:

> Father of all, we pray to you for those we love, but see no longer: Grant them your peace; let light perpetual shine upon them; and, in your loving wisdom and almighty power, work in them the good purpose of your perfect will; through Jesus Christ, our Lord. *Amen.*[68]

High, Broad, and Low Church

Three distinguishable church parties or groups continued to exert influence in the Church of England and throughout the Anglican communion during the twentieth century: the Anglo-Catholics, the Liberal or Broad Church movement, and the Evangelicals. Some observers insist that most parishioners and clergy are more likely to locate clergy and parish in the first or the last of the named groups. In one effort to explain the simultaneous commonality and difference between Anglo-Catholics and Evangelicals, a speaker at the Anglican Congress in 1954 said that "we have the Evangelicals representing the psychological relation to God through faith, and we have the Catholics representing the ontological union with Christ through the sacraments." He added that while the Evangelical "cannot altogether neglect the sacraments" or "altogether belittle their meaning," neither can the Anglo-Catholic "rid himself of the doctrine of faith, because if he does so, he destroys the very efficacy of the sacraments he is trying to defend."[69] These comments must of course be circumscribed by the decades that have intervened.

It is tempting to see the beginning of High churchmanship in Queen Elizabeth I, but at least there is little doubt that Hooker gave immense theological authority to the effort to synthesize Evangelical, Catholic, and rationalist strains. His claim that the Bible is to be interpreted by reason, and that where the Bible is silent the church must speak, provided a foundation for the High Church party, although this attitude ran the risk of deteriorating into a mere antiquarianism. Laud and his school pushed this movement to a fatal extreme in the seventeenth century, but with the Restoration, High churchmanship came into its own with the monarchy. The Revolution of 1688 checked High-churchly progress while the Non-Juring schism drained off major High churchmen from the national church. The High Church party ceased to wield influence during most of the eighteenth century. The party was marshaled anew and given new instruction in the Oxford Movement discussed above. This "Catholic Revival" showed that custom rather than official regulation had led to the abandonment of historical ajuncts of worship. Bitter opposition to this revival led to widespread use of the expression "Anglo-Catholic" as a term of abuse. "To be an Anglo-Catholic," wrote J. W. C. Wand,

> meant not only to wear vestments, to reserve the Blessed Sacrament, and to emphasize the corporate reality of the Church as the Body of Christ, but to teach openly the virtues of private confession, to sing Mass in place of Matins at the most popular hour for service on a Sunday morning, and to cultivate such extra-liturgical devotions as Benediction and Stations of the Cross.

The Public Worship Regulation Act of 1874 failed to solve the problem of ritualist priests who allegedly deviated from the liturgical norms of the

Prayer Book. Their imprisonment merely added fuel to the fire of the "ritualist" controversy.[70]

One important phase of the Anglo-Catholic revival of the nineteenth century which continued to exert major influence in the twentieth was the revival of religious communities in the English church. The first religious community that was founded in the Anglican communion after the Reformation and that achieved settled existence was the Sisterhood of the Holy Cross in 1845. Pusey was the moving spirit. The first religious community for men was the Society of St. John the Evangelist, founded in Cowley, Oxford, in 1865. The monastic movement developed despite the general opposition of the bishops, and for a long time the communities had little to do with the episcopate. But apparently now there is little conflict between the religious and the bishops. The exact number of existing communities is not easily determined, although there may be as many as a hundred communities (or whole societies, in contrast with the houses, cells, or branches of a community). It has been said that today there are twice as many Anglican nuns as there were nuns in England at the beginning of the Reformation. A number of communities collapsed soon after they were founded, and some have become Roman Catholic. There are about three times as many communities of women as men.[71]

A number of factors contributed to the growing influence of the Anglo-Catholic movement in the Church of England between the two world wars. The revival of churchly ideas spread with extraordinary speed as a series of interlocking influences led to emphasis on the doctrine of the church. Biblical scholarship stressed that the Bible was a church book, while biblical criticism and the loss of the theory of biblical infallibility helped people find authority and security in the church. Lights, vestments, incense, and ceremonial splendor were used with increasing regularity apart from violent opposition or persecution. A series of congresses in Albert Hall in London between 1920 and 1933 was a forum for papers by Frank Weston, the theologian-bishop from Zanzibar, and others on various topics of Anglo-Catholic interest.[72]

The Catholic Revival influenced the Church of England and other Anglican churches immensely. Wand insists that "when due allowance is made for such qualifications [as are necessary] it is possible to say that there is scarcely a church in the whole length and breadth of the Anglican Communion today that has not been to some extent affected by the Catholic Revival." The cathedrals were slower to seize the opportunity than most parish churches, although they too came to be used for "the spiritualization of the tourist traffic." Church music was given greater emphasis and hymn singing became an almost universal practice (it was largely an inheritance from the Evangelicals), but the greatest shift of a liturgical nature created by the Anglo-Catholic movement was the substitution in many churches of the chanted Eucharist in place of Matins during the most popular Sunday morning worship hour.[73]

The second of the three major groups or parties in the Church of England, which also has parallels in most of the Anglican churches of the world, is the Broad Church movement, a term less widely used today than the Liberal movement. The group ordinarily wishes to avoid expressions of doctrine that are too narrow, desiring to leave room for broad views. While the period of the Reformation permitted little opportunity for this quality to be displayed, it might be argued that the Church of England was itself a manifestation of this spirit. In the latter half of the sixteenth century, liberal views emerged more clearly in the Latitudinarians (and perhaps also in the Cambridge Platonists). This title went out of fashion in the nineteenth century, and the term "Broad churchman" was coined for a new type of liberal figure who had more intellectual and fewer political interests than his precursors. The great manifesto of this school was the book *Essays and Reviews* published in 1860. Frederick Denison Maurice and Charles Kingsley are considered by some to have been in this camp. In the twentieth century the Modernist movement of W. R. Inge, Hastings Rashdall, H .D. A. Major, and others demanded a modern creed for modern people. While as a movement Liberalism seems to have declined somewhat in the twentieth century, it might be argued that insofar as "liberal" signifies opposition to fanaticism, bigotry, and intransigence, the whole of the Church of England has moved in this direction. The relative ease with which biblical criticism is accepted and used is another signal of the movement's success. The Liberal movement's chief organ is *The Church of England Newspaper*.[74]

As a title for an Anglican party or group, the term "Evangelicals" is of rather recent origin. By the end of the seventeenth century the term "Low Church" was used to refer to those who repudiated the sacramental and sacerdotal ideas of the High churchmen; the term was also regularly used for the Latitudinarians before the term "Broad Church" came into popular usage. It was used once again in the mid-nineteenth century and applied to Evangelicals, but they preferred the term "Evangelicals" to signal the renewed spiritual vitality of their movement, just as the Anglo-Catholic movement eventually preferred its title to "High Church." But probably the Evangelicals' origin lay not so much in the eighteenth century as with Cranmer, Edward VI, and Puritan supporters of continental Protestantism. Some left the Church of England when Elizabeth provided a settlement and again after the failure of the Puritan revolt, but others stayed on to form the nucleus of what today is the Evangelical party. A general dislike of Rome and avoidance of form and ceremony, together with identification with the Whig party in the eighteenth century, helped to give a sense of solidarity. New zeal was infused by the Evangelical Revival of the eighteenth century when George Whitefield preached conversion and tended more toward Calvinist theology than Wesley, another important revivalist within the church. In the late eighteenth and early nineteenth centuries the Evangelicals gained control of many of the bishoprics, organized and funded substantial missionary endeavors throughout the world, mounted an assault on slave traffic, organized Sunday schools to teach reading and the Bible, and inculcated a moral system that, among other things, discouraged theater, dancing, and other alleged abuses. When Queen Victoria came to the throne they enjoyed the monarch's sympathy, and by the twentieth century they made up an important part of the tapestry called the Church of England. A major division has occurred between so-called Liberal and Conservative Evangelicals over the question of the manner of the inspiration of the Scriptures.[75]

The significance of the identifiable groups in the Church of England is that "wherever Anglicanism is planted, there the same differences begin to appear," as J. W. C. Wand explained.[76] It is the genius of Anglicanism in Britain and throughout the world to unite these various tendencies in religious belief, tradition, and liturgical practice.

Anglican Churches throughout the World

In the twentieth century the Church of England continued to exert a major influence in the Anglican communion to which it had given birth in the preceding centuries, especially the nineteenth. While Anglican churches in the United States and Canada were formed before the major colonial thrust of the British Empire in the nineteenth century, most of the other Anglican churches took root during the missionary thrust that accompanied British commercial, military, and cultural expansion in that century. Together with earlier historical developments, this expansion has led to an Anglican communion of more than twenty national and autonomous churches that accord special honor to the archbishop of Canterbury and whose dioceses are in communion with the See of Canterbury. These churches include the Church of England; the Episcopal Church in the United States of America; the Church of England in Australia and Tasmania; the Anglican Church of Canada; the Church of the Province of New Zealand; the Church of the Province of West Africa; the Church of the Province of South Africa; the Church of the Province of Central Africa; the Church of the Province of East Africa; the Church of Uganda. Rwanda, and Burundi; the Church of the Province of the West Indies; the Church in Wales; the Church of Ireland; the Church of India, Pakistan, and Ceylon; the Episcopal Church in Scotland; the Chung Hua Sheng King Hi (The Holy Catholic Church in China); Nippon Sei Ko Kai (The Holy Catholic Church in Japan); the Igreja Episcopal do Brasil (Episcopal Church of Brazil); Iglesia Episcopal de Cuba (Episcopal Church of Cuba); the Council of the Church of South-East Asia; the Jerusalem Archbishopric; and the missionary dioceses not attached to member churches or to the South-East Asian Council, namely, the Extra-Provincial Dioceses to the See of Canterbury. More recently, independent Anglican churches have also been established in Burma, Tanzania, and Kenya. Only one of the churches explicitly calls itself "Anglican."

The territorial expansion of the nineteenth century increased the number of Anglican dioceses from 75 in 1800 to 320 in 1939. Only 12 of the 75 were outside the British Isles in 1800, ten in the United States and two in the rest of the world. In 1939 this number had increased to 251, with 105 in the United States and 146 in the remainder of the world exclusive of the British Isles. Nineteen of the 79 bishops who attended the first Lambeth Conference in 1867 came from the United States, and 24 from colonial and missionary dioceses; of the 329 bishops attending the Lambeth Conference in 1948, 133 were from the British Isles.[77] By 1973, for the first time in history, just over half of the reported 65 million Anglicans in the world lived outside England, while there were 360 Anglican dioceses around the world. Anglicans worship in about 100 countries and nearly 200 languages.

That the Church of England remains a "national," established church is well known. The historical developments that led to this situation have been described above. Here it remains to discuss the twentieth century, the impact of establishment, and Parliament's control of the church.

The mother church of Anglicanism is the only member of the Anglican communion that is established by law as the official religion of the land and that enjoys the nominal majority membership (around 60 percent) of the national population. That there are a number of "nominal" Anglicans is no secret; only about 2 million of the more than 27 million baptized members regularly make their Easter Communions. Only about 10 million are confirmed, and only about 4.3 percent of England's population (fewer than 2 million) are currently registered on the national church's parish electoral rolls. But there are more than 100 bishops at work in 43 dioceses, and nearly 18,000 active clergy in the nearly 14,500 parishes. Bishops are allotted 26 seats in the House of Lords, and the church plays an important role in the nation's ceremonial life. The principal church governing body is the General Synod. The Church Commissioners control the considerable investments and land holdings of the Church of England.[78]

A major shift occurred in 1974 when the English General Synod approved the decision of the church to order its own worship and doctrine without reference to Parliament, as had previously been the case. In December Parliament passed the Worship and Doctrine Measure as requested. The General Synod also said that the church would appoint bishops without reference to the prime minister, as had been customary.

This was an important step in seeking some larger degree of self-governance in the church. The suspension of Convocations from 1717/1741 until 1855, through which the church had exercised some measure of self-governance, may have been part of the reason why the church formulated no coherent policy toward emerging Methodism and failed to respond effectively to the social problems related to the industrial revolution. In any case, the beneficiary of Convocation's demise was Parliament, which took over the function of an ecclesiastical legislature.[79]

In the early twentieth century Parliament was involved in disestablishing

he Church in Wales in an act in 1914 that took effect six years later and in
establishing the Church Assembly (1919) which, instituting an electoral roll
or each parish, seemed to give the Church of England a more denominational
character. The Church Assembly enabled the church to initiate legislative
action subject only to Parliamentary veto and brought the laity into the
church's conciliar government for the first time. But doctrinal decisions were
reserved for the Convocations of York and Canterbury.[80] In 1970 the church
inaugurated a General Synod consisting of bishops and elected clergy and
laity. It assumed the power of the purely clerical Convocations and absorbed
the fifty-year-old Church Assembly as well.

Parliament played a major role in the attempted revision of the Prayer
Book earlier in the twentieth century. After a preparatory period of twenty
years and passage of a proposed draft both by Convocations and by the
Church Assembly, the House of Lords in 1927 approved the revised Book
of Common Prayer but the House of Commons rejected it. The next year the
revision was once again introduced to the House of Commons but once more
defeated. The revision had not been tried out in parishes over a long period.
Rebuffed in this matter of its own worship, for a moment it seemed as if the
church might demand disestablishment, but nothing happened. The bishops,
recognizing the vociferous opposition of extremists in both the Evangelical
and the Anglo-Catholic wings, decided that "the Bishop, in the exercise of
that legal or administrative discretion, which belongs to each Bishop in his
own diocese, will be guided by the proposals set forth in the Book of 1928."
Parliament overlooked the bishops' declaration, and the bishops regarded the
1928 book as marking boundaries within which variations from the 1662
book were, though not legal, permissible. The first major revision in the
Prayer Book in three hundred years is underway in Britain today.[81]

As the "national" church the Church of England faced enormous challenges in the mid-twentieth century. World War II dealt another blow to the
habit of going to church through the damage it brought to the churches, lack
of fuel, and the results of evacuation. Earlier the practice of going to church
had been interrupted by the first war and the rapid industrialization and
urbanization of the nineteenth century. Meanwhile the clergy's average age
was rising while a shortage in manpower developed: the number of men
ordained as deacons dropped from 620 in 1910 to 419 in 1950 and 479 in
1957. And while the percentage of children born between 1956 and 1960
who were subsequently baptized in the Church of England dropped nearly 10
percent, the rate of confirmation among persons aged twelve to twenty also
dropped in the years between 1957 and 1962. The marriages solemnized in
the Church of England dropped steadily from 907 per 1,000 marriages in
1844 to 496 in 1957. Other statistics indicated similar patterns. In 1851
there was 1 Anglican clergyman for every 1,043 persons in the nation,
but population growth changed the ratio to 1 for 1,295 in 1901 and 1 to
2,271 in 1951, while at the same time the total number of clergy increased

slightly while the average age rose appreciably to fifty-five years of age in 1961. In the early 1960s a major trend was reversed and the number of entrants into the clergy exceeded the number lost through death, retirement, and in other ways.[82]

The vigorous growth of the Evangelicals was one response to these events, and there were contributions by others as well, including a growing number (about 6,000) of "lay readers" who are licensed by the bishop to conduct and preach at Matins and Evensong.

Few members of the Church of England seek the church's disestablishment. In the early 1960s the historian Alec R. Vidler wrote that the national church "is a constant reminder to its members and to the nation that it is inescapably involved with the whole of the society in which it is set." At least theoretically, the latitude of its customs and formularies enables it to serve the whole people. It is a standing witness, Vidler wrote, "to the fact that man, every man, is a twofold creature with a twofold allegiance" as a political creature and a spiritual being.[83]

In most instances the bishops of the national church exercise their office in dioceses that have at least 300 clergy. Some critics suggest that the number is too large for effective pastoral oversight. The two archbishops of Canterbury and York are appointed by the Crown after the prime minister makes a choice. The archbishop of Canterbury is officially designated the "principal focus of unity" in the Anglican communion throughout the world, and also "Primate of all England." In 1974 the archbishop of York, Donald Coggan, was selected as the 101st archbishop of Canterbury to succeed the retiring Michael Ramsey. He came to office at a time when the church was disturbed by the new modern services, discussion over the marriage of divorced persons, and the ordination of women to the priesthood.

Theological tendencies in the Church of England have changed markedly during the twentieth century. Under the impulse of World War I the stress on relations between religion and science and on historical foundations of Christianity gave way to consideration of the ethical, social, and political elements of the Christian faith; between the wars there was a growing sense of moral catastrophe. This served as the background for demands for usable biblical study and a coherent view of biblical revelation, as well as concentration on the study of the church's nature and the tendency to set the church in opposition to the world. Archbishop William Temple may well have been the most influential figure in this period.[84]

In the decades following the attempt to revise the Prayer Book in 1927 and 1928 there has been a remarkable advance in the appreciation of the importance of worship in the public life of the Church of England. According to the American scholar Horton Davies, this was evident in three ways. First, English liturgical work exerted considerable influence in the revision of Prayer Books in several other provinces of the Anglican communion so that "the fruits of twenty years of liturgical research and revision in England were not lost." Second, several important treatises demonstrated that there was "a deeper theological understanding of the place of the Liturgy, and especially of the Eucharist, in the life of the Church." And third, the Liturgical movement of the continent, the revival of vigorous biblical theology and the Ecumenical movement helped stimulate "an unprecedented desire to make unofficial, and largely local, liturgical experiments of great fertility and relevance, as well as originality."[85] Clearly the party exclusiveness that characterized internal relationships at the beginning of the century has given way to a sense of common loyalty to the church, a unity manifested most clearly in the conjoined emphasis on word and sacrament. Among the most important treatises on Anglican worship in this period were the works of A. G. Hebert (*Liturgy and Society,* 1935), and Dom Gregory Dix (*The Shape of the Liturgy,* 1948).[86]

The Church of England has engaged in a wide variety of ecumenical discussions in the twentieth century. In 1946 Archbishop Fisher preached a sermon at Cambridge suggesting that intercommunion might be achieved if means could be found for other churches to "take episcopacy into their systems." Earlier, the Lambeth Appeal of 1920 had resulted in discussions between the Church of England and the Free Churches, and the subsequent publication of the *Outline of a Reunion Scheme* (1938). After the war a joint body of Anglicans and Free churchmen discussed the problem and issued a report entitled "Church Relations in England" (1950), which indicated that six conditions had to be fulfilled for advance and that each Free Church needed to make its own approach to the Church of England, since different problems were involved in each case. Two years later the English Convocations recommended opening discussions with the Church of Scotland, also involving the Episcopal Church in Scotland and the Presbyterian Church in England. The report of these conversations in 1957 commended the historic episcopate. Meanwhile, Anglican-Methodist unity conversations were inaugurated in 1955 on the basis of the church-relations report issued in 1950; the Methodists responded to the invitation to enter into conversation with a view toward establishing closer relations. The resulting discussions and meetings produced a report in 1963 that warned of the need to "see that the united Church is not bound too strictly by doctrinal and other such formulations which may quickly be out of date," but others declared that this insistence had to be balanced by a further warning against doctrinal laxity. Both churches adopted plans in 1965 aiming at reconciliation and eventual organic union. The Anglican-Methodist Unity Commission issued its Final Report in 1968, and in the same year the Lambeth Conference heard a report from its Unity Section which drew attention "to the vital significance of the proposed coming together of these two churches in Great Britain," since "the healing of this breach in Great Britain is likely to be influential for the relations of Anglicans and Methodists in many other parts of the world."[87]

In 1969, after more than thirteen years of unity discussions, the Convocations of Canterbury and York voted on the proposition that "this Convocation gives final approval to the inauguration of Stage One of the Anglican-Methodist proposals and desires necessary legislation to be prepared in co-operation with the Methodist Church." The resolution required a two-thirds majority in each Anglican House of Convocation and a 75 percent overall majority from both Convocations; it secured the necessary two-thirds majority in each of the four houses, but the aggregate vote was only 69 percent. The bishops approved the resolution by more than the necessary percentage, but the Canterbury clergy (67 percent) and York clergy (69 percent) fell short of the necessary percentage average. At the same time the Methodist clergy and laymen voted in favor of the plan by 524 to 153, a majority of more than 77 percent. This action resulted in the failure of the first stage of the reunion plan, which would have required the Methodist acceptance of the "historic episcopacy" and a "service of reconciliation" recognizing the validity of each church's ministerial orders. This in turn would have brought the two churches into "full intercommunion." While Methodists appeared able to accept the broadly nonspecific definition of "historic episcopacy," many Anglicans found unacceptable the proposed "service of reconciliation" in which the archbishop of Canterbury and the president of the Methodist Conference were to exchange a mutual "laying on of hands," and the Methodist president would also accept episcopacy. The ambiguous ceremony, during which God would be asked to bestow "upon both the gifts which he has given each in our separation," was constructed to allow conservative Anglicans to feel that Methodists were receiving holy orders and to permit Methodists to believe that they were not.[88] Further efforts to consummate the elaborate scheme for reunion between Anglicans and Methodists in England collapsed in 1972 when the General Synod approved the plan by a 65 percent majority while 75 percent was required.

The first bishop consecrated for service outside the British Isles was Samuel Seabury, consecrated in 1784 by bishops of the Episcopal Church in Scotland for service in the United States. Canada received a bishop for Nova Scotia in 1787, and in 1824 the West Indies received a bishop for Jamaica and Barbados. A bishop was consecrated for Australia in 1836, for New Zealand in 1841, for South Africa in 1847, for West Africa in 1852, for Eastern Equatorial Africa in 1884 (in 1854 and 1874, respectively, Mauritius and Madagascar received bishops), for Hong Kong in 1849, and for Japan in 1883. In the mid-twentieth century the number of dioceses grew from 330 in 1960 to 360 in 1973.

The Church of Wales was founded by Roman missionaries of the fourth century. Agitation for disestablishment became strong around 1885, and the act of Parliament separating the four Welsh dioceses from the state became effective in 1920. The church has an archbishop and six dioceses, together with about 1,000 clergy and about 1⅓ million baptized members (roughly half the population). A revision of the Prayer Book was undertaken in 1957, and union discussions have been held with the Methodist Church. The Church of Ireland emerged as a body set on demonstrating distinction from both Canterbury and Rome. Pressed between Presbyterianism in the north and Roman Catholicism in the south, it has evolved a unique combination of Low Church ceremonial and High Church teaching. It has two archbishops and a membership of about 475,000, about 10 percent of the population. The church has existed since the time of St. Patrick in the fifth century. The parliamentary procedure for reducing the number of Irish bishoprics was the spark that kindled the Oxford Movement in England; the church was disestablished from the state in 1869 when the statuatory union between the churches of England and Ireland was dissolved.[89]

The Episcopal Church in Scotland, in great part because of its Non-Juring and Jacobite sympathies, displays a "Catholic" color. It is a small communion of about 100,000 members and 55,000 communicants in a country where Presbyterianism replaced it as the established church more than two centuries ago. Three of its bishops passed on the episcopacy to the American church in 1784. Seven bishops currently have oversight over about 300 priests. John Howe, one of the Scottish bishops, later became the executive officer of the Anglican communion. The church has seven dioceses but no archbishop, although a primus is elected for life. The liturgical tradition is somewhat distinct from that of England; since this tradition was introduced to the United States, the American liturgy is nearer to that of the 1637 Scottish Prayer Book than the 1552 English Prayer Book.[90]

The Church of England in Australia manifests a variety of theological and ecclesiological tendencies. High Church practices predominate in West Australia and Queensland, while in the diocese of Sydney it is reported that churchmanship is rigidly Low. This is the largest Anglican body outside England, with a membership of over 4 million, about a third of the continent's population. The initial synod was convened in 1872; the church now has about thirty dioceses, and a majority of its bishops are Australian-born. Several native orders assist in the evangelization of Australia, as well as Tasmania to the south and New Guinea to the north. There are four archbishops, one of whom is primate. Most of the Anglicans are concentrated in major cities. While the church is not officially established, it has the character of being a "national" church, since nearly 50 percent of the population is Anglican in declaration. While for a long time the church had no constitution of its own, one was finally adopted in 1959, although the General Synod had been established in 1872.[91]

The Church of the Province of New Zealand retains some of the Low churchmanship of the Victorian era during which major colonization occurred, but subsequent developments have made the church representative of the "central" type of churchmanship in the Anglican communion. The church became the empire's first autonomous body in communion with the See of Canterbury in the mid-nineteenth century. It now has 9 dioceses and a membership of about 1 million, composing a third of the population. Its primate is also an archbishop. Gothic architecture has had a major impact on the church edifices.[92]

The Church in the Province of South Africa was founded in 1853. It is the largest and oldest of the Anglican churches in Africa with more than 1½ million members and 14 dioceses. Opposition to *apartheid* has been a major issue for many of the Anglican leaders in recent years. The church has a metropolitan whose archiepiscopal see is that of Cape Town. The province has remained since its inception a High Church. Religious communities give the province the distinction of having more Anglican monks and nuns in proportion to the size of the church membership than any other church in the Anglican communion. The church was the scene of the most famous ecclesiastical trial in the Anglican world in the nineteenth century when Bishop Robert Gray took Bishop J. W. Colenso to trial for heresy. Colenso was convicted in the church court but was then reinstated by the British Privy Council, which made no pronouncement on the spiritual aspects of the case. The church has steadfastly insisted on the equality of all persons in the sight of God.[93]

The Church of the Province of West Africa was founded in 1951. It now has nearly twenty bishops. The area was one of the oldest mission fields in the Anglican communion, incorporating the work of the Episcopal Church of the U.S.A. in Liberia. The Church of the Province of Central Africa was formed in 1955. It is among the smallest of the African churches, covering the territories of Rhodesia, Zambia, and Malawi, among others. The quarter of a million Anglicans compose about 2 percent of the population. The church has an archbishop and about a half dozen other bishops. The Church of the Province of East Africa was formed in 1960. It now has over a dozen dioceses and about a half million members. A special provision in its constitution describes the doctrine of man as related to the life of new Africa:

> In conformity with Christian doctrine, the Church of this Province proclaims that all men are of equal value and dignity in the sight of God and, while careful to provide for the special needs of different peoples committed to its charge, allows no discrimination in the membership and government of the Church based solely on grounds of racial differences.

Native bishops outnumber British bishops. The church has an archbishop. The Church of Uganda, Rwanda, and Burundi was the fourth of five African churches inaugurated by Geoffrey Fisher while serving as archbishop of Canterbury. The event occurred in 1961. The church has about 1½ million members in nearly a dozen dioceses. The government of Uganda has recently engaged in terrorist activities against several high Anglican officials.[94]

The Church in India, Pakistan, and Ceylon began in 1814 with the founding of the diocese of Calcutta, but an independent Anglican body was established in 1835. There are about 1 million Anglicans in the church, which shortly after World War II reluctantly gave permission to the dioceses of

Madras, Travancore, Tinnevelly, and Dornakal to become part of the newly formed Church of South India. There are nearly two dozen bishops. The bishop of Calcutta is a metropolitan. Anglicanism was first introduced in India in 1614, although actual missionary work began in 1789. In the main the church has been a village church. Connection with the state persisted until as late as 1930 when the church became an independent province.[95]

The Holy Catholic Church in Japan held its first General Synod in 1887. In the late 1960s the church had about 350 priests and only about 50,000 members. The first work by Anglicans in Japan were missions by American missionaries begun in 1859. Largely a city church, the church has nearly a dozen dioceses and a presiding bishop. The Holy Catholic Church in China was begun by missionaries of the American church in 1844 and later strengthened by missionaries from other lands. The first Chinese bishop was consecrated in 1918. The church has 15 dioceses. The two in Hong Kong and Macao have a membership of about 20,000, while the other dioceses have faced great difficulty during the war period and the subsequent Communist Revolution. Formed in 1954, the Council of the Church of South-East Asia is composed of representatives of the dioceses of Hong Kong and Macao, Seoul, Taejon, Singapore and Malaya, Kuching, Sabah, Rangoon, the Philippine Episcopal Church, and the Missionary District of Taiwan.[96]

The Episcopal Church of Brazil became a small independent province in 1965, but has only about 25,000 members. The Episcopal Church of Cuba was for more than sixty years a missionary district of the American church before a bishop was consecrated in 1967. The single diocese has about 75,000 members and is the only body in the Anglican communion governed by a metropolitan council which includes, as an ex officio member, the metropolitan of Canada. The Archbishopric in Jerusalem was created by the archbishop of Canterbury in 1957. There are about 200,000 Anglicans in Jerusalem and the four other dioceses of the Middle East.[97]

"Anglicanism"

In view of the earlier history of the Church of England and this discussion of the expansion of the Anglican communion, it is appropriate to venture into the difficult task of defining "Anglicanism." J. V. Langmead Casserley, an Anglican scholar, described the essence of Anglicanism, "whether considered as a historical or contemporary phenomenon," as "the proposal to contain the validities of the Reformation protest within the context of Catholic institutions." He insisted that the Reformation protest is only properly understood "when we interpret it as a prophetic purgation of our Catholicism, necessitated not so much by the historical corruption of Catholics as by the richness of the Catholic achievement."[98] During the Middle Ages the term *ecclesia anglicana* was the regular title of the section of the church found in the provinces of York and Canterbury. After the Reformation and especially in the nineteenth century, the term "Anglican" was used in the wider sense to modify the churches that were in full organizational fellowship with the See of Canterbury. In 1930 the Lambeth Conference defined Anglicanism as

> a fellowship within the one Holy Catholic and Apostolic Church of those duly constituted Dioceses, Provinces or Regional Churches in communion with the See of Canterbury which have the following characteristics in common—
>
> a. They uphold and propagate the Catholic and Apostolic Faith and Order as they are generally set forth in the Book of Common Prayer as authorized in their several Churches.
> b. They are particular or national Churches, and as such promote within each of their territories a national expression of Christian faith, life and worship.
> c. They are bound together not by a central legislative and executive authority, but by mutual loyalty sustained through common council of the Bishops in conference.

Using this definition and his wide knowledge of Anglicanism, J. W. C. Wand, the bishop of London, described organizational Anglicanism as "a fellowship of free and independent churches whose Bishops meet in conference at Lambeth and recognize the Archbishop of Canterbury as their senior." On another occasion, addressing the Anglican Congress in 1954, he said that the Anglican communion "strives to give expression to the full teaching of the Bible as reflected in the age-long history of the Christian Church."[99] Another writer concluded that "there is, on analysis, no such thing as Anglicanism; there are simply Catholic and Reformed, orthodox and modern safeguards of Christian belief, held together by people living together."[100]

The Anglican communion of churches, which in their separate national lives and their communal life offer the best living definition of Anglicanism, is not a church but a closely knit fellowship of churches. No central executive or legislative authority exists for the communion, no one archbishop or bishop is supreme, and no national church has jurisdiction over another. While the Anglican communion lacks a written constitution, its various churches possess constitutional documents, giving them more visible unity than the communion itself. The approximately 5 percent of Christians in the world who belong to this communion were described by a committee report of the 1948 Lambeth Conference as

> a river that is made up of streams, each of which passes through a different country, each with a colour drawn from the soil through which it passes, each giving its best to the full strength of the river, flowing toward that ocean symbolic of a larger comity when the Anglican Communion itself will once again become part of a reunited Christendom. No one stream is superior to another. The glory of each is its contribution to this river which, while being enriched by all, enriches all the countries of the world wheresoever it flows.[101]

A special place of honor in the communion is reserved for the archbishop of Canterbury as head of the primatial see of the mother Church of England, and the test of membership in the communion is whether or not a diocese is in communion with the See of Canterbury. The archbishop is president of the Lambeth Conference of bishops and is consulted on a great number of questions from throughout the world. But he does not posses jurisdiction over the whole communion. "His position of preeminence," said one speaker at the 1954 Anglican Congress, "would appear to rest on long-continued historic tradition, which has steadily increased in dignity with the expansion of the Anglican Communion."[102]

The great symbol of Anglican unity ever since 1867 has ben the Lambeth Conference of bishops. While neither a council nor a synod, and although its resolutions and recommendations have no force in any province unless they are formally adopted by the synod or general council of that province, the conference's deliberations and resolutions carry great weight. The conference supplies a forum for the exchange of information, discussion of emerging problems, and the expression of the mind of the bishops who have assembled. The conference normally meets once each decade. The years in which the conference assembled and the number of bishops who attended are as follows: 1867 (76), 1878 (100), 1888 (145), 1897 (194), 1908 (242), 1920 (252), 1930 (308), 1948 (326), 1958 (310), 1968 (462).

The case of Bishop Colenson in the mid-nineteenth century awakened strong feelings and some anxiety among Anglicans, both because of the doctrinal questions involved and especially the question of the relation of the colonial churches to England. A proposal arose in a rather inauspicious way at the provincial synod of the United Church of England and Ireland in Canada, meeting in 1865, which requested the Convocation of Canterbury if means could be adopted "by which the members of our Anglican Communion in all quarters of the world should have a share in the deliberations for her welfare, and be permitted to have a representation in one General Council of her members gathered from every land." The Canadians were proposing a General Council or Synod, but the archbishop of Canterbury insisted that he would not convene any assembly that pretended to enact any canons or make binding decisions. Nevertheless, Archbishop Longley sent a letter under his signature notifying bishops of a meeting of bishops at Lambeth in 1867. Surprisingly the archbishop of York and five other English bishops refused to attend the conference, which appeared to lack canonical precedent. But the first Lambeth Conference met with seventy-six bishops attending.[103]

The Lambeth Conference in 1888 adopted an expression of unity in Christ as both gift and calling. Earlier, in 1870, a member of the Protestant Episcopal Church in the U.S.A., William Reed Huntington, proposed four principles upon which Christian churches might agree in order to bring about unity. In 1886 the American bishops adopted these principles in a meeting in Chicago. The formulation was known as the Chicago Quadrilateral. In 1888 the Lambeth Conference adopted a revised form of the articles, subsequently known as the Lambeth Quadrilateral. The formulation read:

> That, in the opinion of this Conference, the following Articles supply a basis on which approach may be by God's blessing made towards Home Reunion:—
>
> (A) The Holy Scriptures of the Old and New Testaments, as "containing all things necessary to salvation," and as being the rule and ultimate standard of faith.
>
> (B) The Apostles' Creed, as the Baptismal Symbol; and the Nicene Creed, as the sufficient statement of the Christian faith.
>
> (C) The two Sacraments ordained by Christ Himself—Baptism and the Supper of the Lord—ministered with unfailing use of Christ's words of Institution, and of the elements ordained by Him.
>
> (D) The Historic Episcopate, locally adapted in the methods of its administration to the varying needs of the nations and peoples called of God into the unity of His Church.

This expression has passed through a number of formulations, including the conference's modification of the fourth point with the following words in the Appeal of 1920: "a ministry acknowledged by every part of the Church as possessing not only the inward call of the Spirit, but also the commission of Christ and the authority of the whole body."[104]

The conference in 1958 was the first to which only the diocesan bishops were invited, and it was the last to issue an encyclical letter after the usual five weeks of deliberation. At the 1968 Conference Archbishop Ramsey said in his introductory press briefing that the conferences "are not legislative—a resolution passed is not binding unless adopted by the churches, though resolutions of the Lambeth Conferences have been found subsequently to have effect." He noted that diocesan bishops were invited, as well as suffragan bishops and assistant bishops who were working in dioceses. A new feature at this conference was the presence of official observers from the Armenian Church, Assemblies of God, Baptist World Alliance, Church of South India, Coptic Church, Evangelical Church in Germany, International Congregational Council, Lusitanian Church, Lutheran World Federation, Mar Thoma Church, Orthodox Church, Philippine Independent Catholic Church, Religious Society of Friends, Roman Catholic Church, Salvation Army, Spanish Reformed Episcopal Church, Syrian Orthodox Church, World Convention of Churches of Christ, World Council of Churches, World Methodist Council, and World Presbyterian Alliance. A total of nearly eighty observers participated in sessions and committees. With the addition of a footnote which included the original formulation of the Quadrilateral in 1888, the bishops adopted a new statement of the Quadrilateral which in the fourth part referred to "common acknowledgement of a ministry through which the grace of God is given to his people." In addition, the conference "[took] note of the papal encyclical letter *Humanae vitae* recently issued by His Holiness Pope Paul VI," expressed its appreciation of "the Pope's deep concern for the institution of marriage and the integrity of married life," but found itself "unable to agree with the Pope's conclusion that all methods of conception control other than abstinence from sexual intercourse or its confinement to periods of infecundity are contrary to the 'order established by God.' " The conference also invited the archbishop of Canterbury on its behalf to

> consult with the Pope and the Ecumenical Patriarch and the Praesidium of the World Council of Churches on the possibility of approaching leaders of the other world religions with a view to convening a conference at which in concert they would speak in the interests of humanity on behalf of world peace.

The conference also adopted a number of other resolutions, none of which "is binding upon any part of the Anglican Communion unless and until it has been adopted by the appropriate canonical authority," as a note preceding the resolutions indicated. All main sessions were open to the press. The general theme of the conference was renewal of the church in faith, in ministry, and in unity.[105] The 1978 conference was scheduled once again to meet in Canterbury. The estimated cost of $1 million for the worldwide conference brought some debate in the Anglican Consultative Council, but the majority in 1976 favored the meeting, for which Archbishop Coggan issued the official conference call.[106]

Another unifying factor in the Anglican communion was for some time the Anglican Congress, a less official gathering of bishops, clergy, and laity. The first met in London in 1908, the second in Minneapolis, Minnesota in 1954, and the third and last in Toronto, Canada in 1963. The congress had no legislative power, but was a gathering for discussion of problems and programs of the member churches. The 1954 congress included 657 representatives, 201 of whom were bishops. The presiding officer was not the archbishop of Canterbury but the presiding bishop of the American church, Bishop Henry Knox Sherrill. Its theme was "The Call of God and the Mission of the Anglican Communion."[107] At the Lambeth Conference in 1968 it was decided no longer to hold Anglican congresses but instead a joint meeting, at the time of the Assembly of the World Council of Churches, of the Anglican Consultative Council and of Anglican participants in the assembly, as well as regional meetings of representatives of Anglican churches.[108] The Anglican Regional Council for North America, which included the churches of Canada, the United States, and the West Indies, met for the first time in 1969.

Another unifying element in the Anglican communion is the Anglican Consultative Council, a body which originated in 1897 as the Consultative Body of the Lambeth Conference. It has the nature of serving as a continuation committee of the Lambeth Conference. The new organization of the council created in 1968 provided for two or three delegates from each church to function collectively as a permanent channel of communication and cohesion, to offer counsel on inter-Anglican, provincial, and diocesan relationships, to stress the importance of Anglican collaboration with other Christian churches, and various other facets. Meeting every other year, the council first convened in Kenya in 1971 and two years later in Dublin. Among those holding the post of Anglican Executive Officer have been three bishops, Stephen Bayne, Jr., Ralph Dean, and John Howe.

The central college of the Anglican communion, established at St. Augustine's College, Canterbury, after the Lambeth Conference of 1948, has become a striking symbol of the communion's fellowship. The college has priest-students from nearly every church in the communion. In addition, Anglicans express unity through a manual of prayer and intercession for the Anglican fellowship around the world, the journal *Pan-Anglican*, personal contacts among bishops and clergy, and a host of other formal and informal means. One central feature of Anglican fellowship continues to be high regard for and use of the Book of Common Prayer.

Ecumenical Relations

In a sermon to the Lambeth Conference in 1888, Bishop Whipple of Minnesota in the United States referred to the "Church of the Reconciliation." This phrase has become a classic, but Whipple was referring not to the Anglican communion in present reality as much as the Anglican communion in its future fulfillment. "The Church of the Reconciliation will be," he said, "an historical and Catholic Church in its Ministry, its Faith and its Sacraments." He continued:

> It will inherit the promises of its Divine Lord. It will preserve all which is Catholic and Divine. It will adopt and use all instrumentalities of any existing organization which will aid it in doing the Lord's work. It will put away all which is individual, narrow and sectarian. It will concede to all who hold the Faith all the liberty wherewith Christ has made His children free.[109]

In the twentieth century the Anglican communion seems to have moved in the directions which Whipple suggested.

On an international level, the Ecumenical movement owes much to this "Church of the Reconciliation." American and American-born Episcopalians, notably Bishop C. H. Brent, contributed much to the early "Faith and Order" discussions. Archbishop William Temple and Bishop G. K. A. Bell contributed much to the development of the World Council of Churches, declared duly constituted in 1948 by the archbishop of Canterbury, Geoffrey Francis Fisher. Archbishop Ramsey moved vigorously to open channels of communications with the Roman Catholic pontiff and Patriarch Athenagoras, as well as other major figures of the church throughout the world. Anglicans around the globe have assumed important posts in the Ecumenical movement.

Ecumenical relations between the Anglican communion and Eastern churches have intensified in the twentieth century. After earlier contacts, the Eastern Church Association, founded in 1863 to study the Eastern churches and reactivated thirty years later, was a precursor of the Anglican and Eastern Orthodox Churches Union (1906), which was more directly concerned with ecumenical relations. These organizations merged in 1914 to form the Anglican and Eastern Association. As a result of a resolution of the Lambeth Conference in 1908, the archbishop of Canterbury appointed a permanent Eastern Churches Commission that was charged with taking cognizance of "all that concerns our relations with the Churches of the Orthodox East." The same Lambeth Conference recommended that members of the Orthodox Eastern communion in good standing be admitted to communicate in Anglican churches. The tragic circumstances of the Russian Revolution complicated efforts to create a better climate between the two communions, although a delegation of the ecumenical patriarch of Constantinople attended the Lambeth Conference in 1920. Upon its return this delegation gave an account of its experiences to the Holy Synod of the Greek Church. In 1922 the archbishop of Canterbury received a letter from the ecumenical patriarch informing him that the Holy Synod had studied the question of Anglican ordinations carefully and had concluded that, in the view of the Orthodox Church, Anglican ordinations of bishops, priests, and deacons had the same validity as the Roman, Old Catholic, and Armenian churches. The letter added that the whole Orthodox Church would have to concur with this view of holy orders for it to be the basis for complete sacramental communion between the churches. In 1923 the patriarch of Jerusalem and the archbishop of Cyprus spoke favorably of the validity of Anglican ordinations, and by 1935 the churches of Alexandria and Romania had expressed their agreement with Constantinople as well.[110]

After World War II a pall fell over Anglican-Orthodox relations for some time. At the Moscow Conference of the heads of autocephalous Orthodox churches in communion with the patriarch of Moscow in 1948 a lengthy resolution declared among other things that the official doctrine of the Anglican church differed from accepted dogma, doctrine, and tradition of the Orthodox Church, and essential agreement on the fundamental principles that govern the sacraments was the legitimate basis for the recognition of the validity of Anglican ordinations.[111]

In 1956 a conference in Moscow between representatives of the Church of England and the Russian Orthodox Church discussed among other things the Thirty-Nine Articles. Professor A. I. Ivanov of the Moscow Theological Academy, speaking from the Orthodox point of view, found that two of the articles (5 and 22) were totally unacceptable, eleven were vague and allowed various interpretations, six were not substantially in discord with Orthodox teaching, and twelve were wholly in agreement with it, while the other articles were not of a doctrinal nature. Two years later the Orthodox churches sent delegates to the opening ceremonies of the Lambeth Conference to conduct unofficial exchanges of views with Anglicans. Despite goodwill on both sides and the efforts of the ecumenical patriarch and the archbishop of Canterbury to resume the meetings of the Joint Anglo-Orthodox Doctrinal Commission before the conference began so that a report could be issued to the bishops, the effort was delayed. In 1960 Archbishop Fisher journeyed to Jerusalem where he met the patriarch of the Holy City and the ecumenical patriarch, Athenagoras. While the Lambeth Conference in 1958 endorsed the "desire of the Patriarch for a continuation of Joint Anglican-Orthodox doctrinal discussions," for its part the Orthodox community soon conducted three Pan-Orthodox conferences on the island of Rhodes in 1961, 1963, and 1964. The third conference decided unanimously to resume the joint doctrinal discussions, which were subsequently convened.[112]

In 1968 the Lambeth Conference welcomed the proposed Pan-Orthodox and Pan-Anglican discussions, which originally began in 1931. In 1976 during a meeting of the Anglican-Orthodox commission in Moscow, Anglican theologians declared that they were prepared to see the *filioque* clause in the Nicene Creed removed, while Orthodox delegates expressed satisfaction. After the archbishop of Canterbury visited Moscow in May 1977, the Anglican-Orthodox commission announced in October that the centuries-old dispute had been settled inasmuch as the Anglicans agreed that the original form of the creed was authentic, and that the phrase "and the Son" (*filioque*) was inserted without permission from the church universal. The ordination of women to the priesthood in some of the Anglican churches has been met with strong resistance by a number of Orthodox spokesmen, but efforts to establish deeper ecumenical relations continue through visits and doctrinal discussions.

A great measure of success attended the discussions between the Anglican communion and the Old Catholics and closely associated Polish National Catholics, with whom intercommunion has been effected. Bishops on both sides share in consecrations, and the faithful are freely admitted to the sacraments through the Agreement of Bonn (1931), which was subsequently accepted by the majority of Anglican churches. In 1946 the Protestant Episcopal Church in the United States established relations of intercommunion with the Polish National Catholic Church of America. Since 1958 this intercommunion between Anglicans and Old Catholics has been "full" in every sense.[113]

Ecumenical relations with the Roman Catholic Church developed rather slowly. Queen Victoria's congratulatory letter to Pope Leo XIII on his sacerdotal jubilee in 1887 might well have been the first letter of a British soverign to a pope since Queen Elizabeth I was excommunicated in 1570. In any case, the papal bull *Apostolicae curae* of September 13, 1896, soured relations for some time with its condemnation of Anglican orders. The bull concluded with these words: "We pronounce and declare that Ordinations carried out according to the Anglican rite have been and are absolutely null and utterly void." The bull argued that the forms of ordination used in the Church of England between 1550 and 1662 were incapable of conveying holy orders in the Catholic sense, since the English reformers deliberately fashioned them to express their denial of eucharistic sacrifice.[114]

Between 1921 and 1926 the so-called Malines conferences explored the profound differences that seemed to separate the Roman and Anglican communions. Under the leadership of the earl of Halifax and Bishop Gore, Anglo-Catholics conversed with Archbishop Mercier at his palace in Malines. Archbishop Davidson of Canterbury insisted that those who participated in the conversations should not regard themselves as delegates of the Church of England, nor were the conversations to be seen as "negotiations." The conversations ended with Mercier's death in 1926. The previous year the Anglican group made a statement indicating that

> the Church is a living body under the authority of the bishops as successors of the Apostles: and from the beginnings of Church history a primacy and leadership among all the bishops has been recognized as belonging to the Bishop of Rome. Nor can we imagine that any reunion of Christendom could be affected except on the recognition of the primacy of the Pope.[115]

Vatican II signaled a new day in relations between the two communions. In 1970, for the first time since the Reformation, a Roman Mass was celebrated in an Anglican cathedral, namely at Coventry. In 1966 Archbishop Ramsey and Pope Paul VI engaged in conversations in Rome and signed a "Common Declaration" that thanked God for the new atmosphere of Christian fellowship and declared their intention of inaugurating "a serious dialogue which, founded on the Gospels and on the ancient common traditions, may lead to that unity in truth, for which Christ prayed." Dialogue was to include "not only theological matters such as Scripture, Tradition and Liturgy, but also matters of practical difficulty felt on either side." As a result a Joint Preparatory Commission was created, followed later by the Joint Anglican-Roman Catholic International Commission. In 1971 this commission reported a considerable measure of essential agreement on the doctrine of the Eucharist. In 1973 an encouraging report appeared on the course of the discussions of the ministry, but many feared that the question of authority in the church would be a major stumbling block. Early in 1977 the commission released a statement on authority which revealed a substantial degree of agreement, as had the earlier documents. The report indicated that "a primate exercises his ministry not in isolation but in collegial association with his brother bishops," and asserted as well that "the Roman Catholic Church is today seeking to replace the juridical outlook of the nineteenth century by a more pastoral understanding of the authority of the church."[116]

A few days after the commission's third report was issued, the Vatican's Sacred Congregation for the Doctrine of the Faith issued a document on women's ordination. The document's negative answer to the question of women's ordination confirmed an exchange of four letters between the pope and Archbishop Coggan between July 1975 and March 1976 that were published in the official Vatican newspaper in August 1976. One of the pope's letters (November 30, 1975) said that "we recognize with regret that the new course taken by the Anglican community in admitting women to the priesthood cannot but introduce in this dialogue (on Christian unity) an element of serious difficulty." When Archbishop Coggan met with the pope in the spring of 1977 it was clear that the question of eucharistic intercommunion was far from settled, while other points of difference included the Anglicans' refusal to recognize papal primacy and infallibility, the problem of mixed marriages, and the ordination of women as priests in some branches of the Anglican communion. Despite these differences, the pope acknowledged that the pace of collaboration "has quickened marvelously in recent years."[117]

The Anglican communion continues to engage in fruitful ecumenical relations with a variety of other churches as well, including in some cases joint conversations on a worldwide basis (such as with Lutherans) as well as national or regional ecumenical conversations and activities. One significant and creative effort among many was the 1968 Lambeth Conference proposal for a General Episcopal Consultation on a worldwide scale to which would be invited those churches with bishops that were in full or partial communion. Regional Episcopal consultations on a wider basis of representation were also proposed. An earlier conference at Canterbury in 1964 brought together bishops of the Anglican churches, the Church of Finland, Spanish Reformed Episcopal Church, Lusitanian Church of Portugal, Mar Thoma Syrian Church, Old Catholic Churches, Philippine Independent Catholic Church, Polish National Catholic Church of America, Church of South India, and the Church of Sweden.[118]

NOTES

1. Norman Sykes, *The Crisis of the Reformation* (London: Geoffrey Bles, 1950), pp. 77-78.
2. Ibid., p. 79.
3. Ibid., p. 81; Craig R. Thompson, *The English Church in the Sixteenth Century* (Washington: The Folger Shakespeare Library, 1958), p. 6.
4. Sykes, p. 83; E. J. Bicknell, *A Theological Introduction to the Thirty-Nine Articles of the Church of England* (3rd edn., rev.; London: Longmans, Green and Co., 1935), pp. 8-10.
5. Sykes, pp. 84-85; Bicknell, pp. 9-10; Thompson, p. 6.
6. Thompson, p. 7.
7. Massey H. Shepherd, Jr., *The Worship of the Church* (Greenwich, Conn.: Seabury Press, 1952), pp. 88-90.
8. Bicknell, pp. 10-13.
9. Shepherd, pp. 89-90; D. L. Edwards, *Not Angels but Anglicans* (Naperville, Ill.: SCM Book Club, 1958), p. 43.
10. Bicknell, p. 14; *Report of the Archbishop's Commission on Christian Doctrine, Subscription and Assent to the 39 Articles* (London: S.P.C.K., 1968), p. 9.
11. *Churchmen Speak, Thirteen Essays* England: Marcham Manor Press, 1966), p. 84; *Report of the Archbishop's Commission,* p. 9.
12. See Bicknell, pp. 15-17, for a discussion of the revision of the Forty-Two Articles and the response offered to claims that the articles are Calvinist.
13. Thompson, p. 12.
14. Ibid., pp. 13-15.
15. George H. Tavard, *The Quest for*

Catholicity, a Study in Anglicanism (New York: Herder and Herder, 1964), p. 23.

16. Ibid., p. 41.
17. Martin Thornton, *English Spirituality, An Outline of Ascetical Theology According to the English Pastoral Tradition* (London: S.P.C.K., 1963), pp. 261-262.
18. Tavard, pp. 9-12; Sykes, pp. 87-88; Thompson, p. 54.
19. Edward William Watson, *The Church of England* (London: Oxford University Press, 1961), pp. 103, 113-116.
20. Norman Sykes, *Old Priest and New Presbyter* (Cambridge: University Press, 1956), pp. 116-118.
21. Norman Sykes, *From Sheldon to Secker; Aspects of English Church History, 1660–1768* (Cambridge: University Press, 1959), pp. 25-26.
22. G. R. Cragg, *From Puritanism to the Age of Reason; a Study of Changes in Religious Thought within the Church of England, 1660 to 1700* (Cambridge: University Press, 1966), p. 13.
23. Ibid., pp. 37-41.
24. Ibid., pp. 61-86.
25. Ibid., pp. 156-187.
26. Sykes, *From Sheldon to Secker*, pp. 89-90, 216 (quotation).
27. Sykes, *Old Priest*, p. 81.
28. Paul Elmer More and Frank Leslie Cross, eds., *Anglicanism; the Thought and Practice of the Church of England, Illustrated from the Religious Literature of the Seventeenth Century* (London: S.P.C.K., 1962), p. xxxv.
29. Cragg, p. 182; Watson, p. 124; Stephen Neill, *Anglicanism* (Baltimore: Penguin Books, 1958), pp. 173-175; Tavard, pp. 96-98.
30. J. V. Langmead Casserley, *Christian Community* (London: Longmans, 1960), pp. 150-153; quotation from p. 153.
31. Powel Mills Dawley, ed., *Report of the Anglican Congress, 1954* (Greenwich, Conn.: Seabury Press, 1954), p. 72.
32. Shepherd, pp. 149-151. The 1928 American Prayer Book required that the Ten Commandments be read "at least one Sunday each month."
33. Dawley, ed., *Report*, pp. 77-78.
34. Percy Dearmer, *The Parson's Handbook, Practical Directions for Parsons and Others . . .* , revised and rewritten by Cyril E. Pocknee (13th edn.; London: Oxford University Press, 1965), p. xviii.
35. Edwards, p. 97.
36. *The Lambeth Conference, 1968, Resolutions and Reports* (London: S.P.C.K., 1968), p. 42.
37. Dawley, ed., *Report*, p. 88.
38. Shepherd, pp. 123, 134.
39. Shepherd, pp. 202-203. In the United States the *Ordinal* also provided two rites generally conducted by the bishop, consecration of a church or chapel and the induction of ministers into parishes or churches.
40. Edwards, pp. 22, 24.
41. Sykes, *From Sheldon to Secker*, pp. 138-139.
42. Quoted in Sykes, *Old Priest*, p. 209.
43. Watson, p. 146; Edwards, p. 24. See also C. K. Francis Brown, *A History of the English Clergy, 1800–1900* (London: The Faith Press, 1953), pp. 15, 28, 40, 43.
44. Edwards, p. 41.
45. R. P. C. Hanson, "The Nature of the Anglican Episcopate," in *Lambeth Conference, 1968, Preparatory Essays* (London: S.P.C.K., 1968), pp. 209-300, 305.
46. Dawley, ed., *Report*, pp. 32-33.
47. See Sykes, *Old Priest*, p. 219; and William H. van de Pol, *Anglicanism in Ecumenical Perspective*, Duquesne Studies, Theological Series, 4 (Pittsburgh: Duquesne University Press, 1965), p. 132.
48. *The Lambeth Conference, 1968, Resolutions and Reports*, p. 39.
49. *The Lambeth Conference, 1948* (London: S.P.C.K., 1948), p. 52.
50. *The Lambeth Conference, 1968, Resolutions and Reports*, pp. 39-40, 106-107.
51. Ibid., p. 39.
52. J. W. C. Wand, *Anglicanism in History and Today* (London: Weidenfeld and Nicolson, 1961), p. 227.
53. Ibid., p. 230.
54. Ibid., pp. 46-50.
55. Ibid., pp. 51-55.
56. Quoted in de Pol, p. 117.
57. Wand, pp. 56-61.
58. *The Lambeth Conference, 1958* (London: S.P.C.K., 1958), p. 133.
59. *The Draft Proposed Book of Common Prayer and Administration of the Sacraments and Other Rites and*

Ceremonies of the Church (New York: The Church Hymnal Corporation, 1976), pp. 864-865, 869.

60. See the discussion in R. T. Beckwith, *Prayer Book Revision and Anglican Unity* (London: Church Book Press, 1967), pp. 7-12, 19, 21, *passim*.

61. *Report of the Archbishop's Commission*, p. 82.

62. Ibid., pp. 19-22.

63. Ibid., p. 29.

64. *Churchmen Speak, Thirteen Essays*, p. 87. For a discussion of English Evangelicals of the eighteenth and nineteenth centuries, and how Calvanism virtually disappeared in Evangelical circles, see Neill, pp. 181-182, 191-192, and 232-243, and Watson, pp. 132-137.

65. See *The Church and the Sacraments* [pamphlet] (Cincinnati: Forward Movement Publication, n.d.).

66. *The Draft Proposed Book*, pp. 844, 857, 860; see pp. 845-862 for the catechism.

67. Shepherd, p. 114; *Time*, February 14, 1969.

68. *Draft Proposed Book of Common Prayer*, p. 504 (quotation); Beckwith, p. 12.

69. Dawley, ed., *Report*, p. 42.

70. Wand, pp. 96-102 (quotation from p. 102). See Horton Davies, *Worship and Theology in England* (Princeton: Princeton University Press, 1962), IV: 114-130, for the Catholic trend of Anglican worship and the "ritualist" controversy of the last decades of the century.

71. Davies, IV: 135 (see pp. 131-138 for a discussion of religious communities as houses of spiritual devotion and major contributors to remarkable liturgical leadership); Wand, pp. 185-187.

72. Wand, pp. 140-144.

73. Ibid., pp. 144-146.

74. Ibid., pp. 103-108; Edwards, pp. 15-16.

75. Wand, pp. 109-115; Edwards, p. 13. See also G. R. Balleine, *A History of the Evangelical Party* (London: Longmans, Green and Co., 1908), and the recent study of Ian C. Bradley, *The Call to Seriousness; the Evangelical Impact on the Victorians* (New York: Macmillan Publishing Co., 1976). In 1967 the Evangelicals held a major conference at Keele called the National Evangelical Anglican Congress. It is regarded by Evangelicals in the Church of England as a milestone where they admitted the failure of many old ways, declared that something in traditional evangelism was "less than biblical," and pledged themselves to face the challenges of injustice in society. At that time there were perhaps three or four Evangelicals in the House of Bishops, but it is reported that by 1977 nearly a dozen bishops, in addition to the two archbishops of Canterbury and York, were part of Anglican Evangelicalism. The second National Evangelical Anglican Congress met in 1977 in Britain. It issued a 20,000-word document which, among other things, recommended tithing, cautiously approved the charismatic movement, upheld the episcopal system (though regarded as nonessential to the church's existence), seemingly approved women ministers but not female bishops, and rejected indiscriminate baptism, abortion on demand, and disestablishment of the church. See *Christianity Today*, July 8, 1977, pp. 30-41, 44.

76. Wand, p. 115

77. *The Lambeth Conference, 1948*, pp. 87-88.

78. James B. Simpson and Edward M. Story, *The Long Shadow of Lambeth X* [1968] (New York: McGraw-Hill Book Company, 1969), p. 292.

79. Neill, p. 180; Sykes, *From Sheldon to Secker*, pp. 67, 22.

80. Watson, pp. 173, 176-177; Kenneth Slack, *The British Churches Today* (London: SCM Press, 1961), pp. 44-45. Slack notes that in 1956 £12.5 million of the Parochial Church Councils' income of £17.25 million came from ordinary contributions; the remainder came from specific appeals, legacies, and endowments.

81. Neill, pp. 395-398; Edwards, pp. 79-80; Watson, pp. 179-180; Wand, pp. 135-136.

82. Edwards, p. 68; Wand, p. 149; Leslie Paul, *The Deployment and Payment of the Clergy* (Westminster: Church Information Office, 1964), pp. 17-23.

83. A. R. Vidler, ed., *Soundings; Essays Concerning Christian Understanding*

(Cambridge: University Press, 1962), pp. 256-263.

84. Watson, pp. 180-185. See also John Kenneth Mozley, *Some Tendencies in British Theology from the Publication of Lux Mundi to the Present Day* (London: S.P.C.K., 1952).

85. Horton Davies, *Worship and Theology in England* (Princeton: Princeton University Press, 1965), V: 307; see also pp. 307-37. Davies indicates that among the liturgical experiments the most important were "parish communion," namely the Communion as the parish's chief service of the day; the "House Church," which attempted to combine the celebration of Communion with evangelism by taking the church to the homes of people; the "Clare College Liturgy," which provided a manual of instruction for the Order of Holy Communion; the "Experimental Liturgy" of 1958, a new liturgy constructed within a broad ecumenical context; and the official report of the Church of England Liturgical Commission published in 1959, *Baptism and Confirmation*, which demonstrated the radical rethinking of baptism among Anglican theologians.

86. Ibid., V: 344-45; see pp. 38-47 for an appraisal of the influence of the Liturgical movement in England. During the same period cathedrals were described as the "visible counterparts of the episcopal system" and "the natural centre for ordinations and some other episcopal functions" in a report issued in 1961. In addition, the cathedral is seen as a "living centre of worship" and the locus of such important ancillary activities as theological study, the improvement of Christian education, and glorification of God through music, drama, and the plastic arts. Among the new edifices constructed during this period were the colossal Liverpool Anglican Cathedral and Guildford Cathedral in Surrey. An exciting edifice is Coventry Cathedral, constructed on the gaunt ruins of the old cathedral destroyed in bombing attacks of World War II. Other efforts are underway to restore all historic churches and cathedrals, and a special fund was inaugurated in 1976 to save Canterbury Cathedral from neglect and the ravages of air pollution. See Davies, V: 51-60.

87. Simpson and Story, p. 221; Neill, pp. 376-377; *Unity Trends*, 2, 19 (September 1, 1969), pp. 1-2.

88. See *Unity Trends*, pp. 3-4, 6-9; *Time*, July 18, 1969.

89. Wand, pp. 36, 116; Simpson and Story, pp. 291-292; Neill, pp. 292-297.

90. Neill, pp. 279-282.

91. Simpson and Story, pp. 294-295; Neill, pp. 308-313; Wand, p. 116.

92. Wand, pp. 38-39, 116; Simpson and Story, p. 295; Neill, pp. 288-292.

93. Simpson and Story, pp. 295-296; Neill, pp. 303-308; Wand, pp. 39-41, 116.

94. Neill, pp. 339-388; Simpson and Story, pp. 296-298; Wand, p. 45. The quotation from the constitution is from Simpson and Story, p. 297.

95. Simpson and Story, pp. 298-299; Neill, pp. 323-330; Wand, pp. 41-43.

96. Simpson and Story, pp. 299-300, 302; Neill, pp. 330-338.

97. Simpson and Story, pp. 301-302.

98. Casserley, pp. 114-115.

99. Wand, pp. xiii-xiv; Dawley, ed., *Report*, p. 25.

100. Edwards, p. 106; see pp. 106-111 for a description of the adjectives "Catholic and Reformed, orthodox and modern."

101. *The Lambeth Conference, 1948*, p. 83.

102. Dawley, ed., *Report*, pp. 1-2, 45.

103. Neill, pp. 358-365.

104. *The Lambeth Conference, 1968, Resolutions and Reports*, pp. 123-124; Neill, pp. 366-369.

105. *The Lambeth Conference, 1968, Resolutions and Reports*, pp. 29, 31, 36, 123-124, 151-154; Simpson and Story, pp. 210-211.

106. *Christian Century*, September 1-8, 1976, p. 727.

107. Dawley, ed., *Report*, pp. 8, 221 and passim; *The Lambeth Conference, 1948*, pp. 92-93.

108. *The Lambeth Conference, 1968, Resolutions and Reports*, p. 145.

109. Quoted in Edwards, pp. 121-122.

110. De Pol, pp. 141-142, 164; Neill p. 371.

111. De Pol, pp. 166-167; Neill, p. 371.

112. *Report of the Archbishop's Commission*, p. 24; V. T. Istavridis, *Ortho-*

doxy and Anglicanism, trans. Colin Davey (London: S.P.C.K., 1966), pp. vii, 69-70.
113. Wand, p. 159; De Pol, p. 168; Neill, pp. 372–373.
114. Neill, p. 369. John Jay Hughes, *Absolutely Null and Utterly Void; the Papal Condemnation of Anglican Orders, 1896* (Washington: Corpus Books, 1968), pp. 198, 287 and *passim.*
115. *The Lambeth Conference, 1968, Resolutions and Reports,* p. 334 (quotation); Neill, pp. 369-370; Wand, p. 158; see also De Pol, pp. 38-77.
116. *The Lambeth Conference, 1968, Reso-*

lutions and Reports, pp. 134-135; *Christian Century,* March 9, 1977, p. 211; *The Lamp, a Christian Unity Magazine,* June 1972, pp. 6-9. See also the volume edited by Herbert J. Ryan, S.J., and J. Robert Wright, *Episcopalians and Roman Catholics: Can They Ever Get Along?* (Denville, N. J.: Dimension Books, 1972).
117. *Christian Century,* May 25, 1977, p. 503; *St. Louis Post Dispatch,* August 22, 1976.
118. See *The Lambeth Conference, 1968, Resolutions and Reports,* pp. 147-148, and *The Lambeth Conference, 1968, Preparatory Essays,* pp. 397-400.

BIBLIOGRAPHY

THE CHURCH OF ENGLAND IN REFORMATION AND EARLY MODERN PERIODS

Bromiley, G. W. *Thomas Cranmer, Theologian.* New York: Oxford University Press, 1956.

Church, Richard William. *The Oxford Movement; Twelve Years, 1833–1845.* Ed. and with an introduction by Geoffrey Best. Chicago: University of Chicago Press, 1970.

Cragg, G. R. *From Puritanism to the Age of Reason; a Study of Changes in Religious Thought within the Church of England, 1660 to 1700.* Cambridge: University Press, 1966.

Elton, G. R. *England under the Tudors.* London: Methuen, 1955.

Fairweather, E. R., ed. *The Oxford Movement.* New York: Oxford University Press, 1964.

Haller, William. *Liberty and Reformation in the Puritan Revolution.* New York: Columbia University Press, 1955.

———. *The Rise of Puritanism.* New York: Columbia University Press, 1938.

Haugaard, William P. *Elizabeth and the English Reformation: The Struggle for a Stable Settlement of Religion.* Cambridge: University Press, 1968.

Hughes, Philip. *The Reformation in England.* 3 vols. London: Hollis and Carter, 1950–1954.

Knappen, M. M. *Tudor Puritanism.* Chicago: University of Chicago Press, 1965.

Meyer, Carl S. *Elizabeth I and the Religious Settlement of 1559.* St. Louis:

Concordia Publishing House, 1960.

More, Paul Elmer, and Cross, Frank Leslie, eds. *Anglicanism; the Thought and Practice of the Church of England, Illustrated from the Religious Literature of the Seventeenth Century.* London: S.P.C.K., 1962.

New, John F. H. *Anglican and Puritan; the Basis of their Opposition, 1558–1640.* Stanford: Stanford University Press, 1964.

Packer, John W. *The Transformation of Anglicanism, 1643–1660.* Manchester: University Press, 1969.

Parker, T. H. L., ed. *English Reformers.* Vol. XXVI in Library of Christian Classics. Philadelphia: Westminster Press, 1966.

Powicke, Maurice. *The Reformation in England.* London: Oxford University Press, 1961.

Rupp, Gordon. *Six Makers of English Religion, 1500–1700.* London: Hodder and Stoughton, 1964.

Sykes, Norman. *The Crisis of the Reformation.* London: Geoffrey Bles, 1950.

———. *From Sheldon to Secker; Aspects of English Church History 1660–1768.* Cambridge: University Press, 1959.

Thompson, Craig R. *The English Church in the Sixteenth Century.* Washington: The Folger Shakespeare Library, 1958.

Watson, Edward William. *The Church of England.* London: Oxford University Press, 1961.

Wilson, John T. *Pulpit in Parliament; Puritanism during the English Civil Wars, 1640–1648*. Princeton: Princeton University Press, 1969.

Woodhouse, H. F. *The Doctrine of the Church in Anglican Theology, 1547–1603*. New York: The Macmillan Company, 1954.

WORSHIP AND ORDER

Beckwith, R. T. *Prayer Book Revision and Anglican Unity*. Prayer Book Reform Series. London: Church Book Room Press, 1967.

Brandreth, Henry R. T. *Episcopi Vagantes and the Anglican Church*. London: Society for Promoting Christian Knowledge, 1947.

Carey, K. M., ed. *The Historic Episcopate*. London: Black, 1955.

Clark, Francis, S.J. *Anglican Orders and Defect of Intention*. London: Longmans, Green and Co., 1956.

Clarke, W. K. Lowther, and Harris, Charles. *Liturgy and Worship, a Companion to the Prayer Books of the Anglican Communion*. London: S.P.C.K., 1932.

Cuming, G. J. *A History of Anglican Liturgy*. London: Macmillan, 1969.

Davies, Horton. *Worship and Theology in England*. 5 vols. Princeton: Princeton University Press, 1961–1975.

Dearmer, Percy. *The Parson's Handbook. Practical Directions for Parsons and Others According to the Anglican Use, as Set Forth in the Book of Common Prayer*. Revised and rewritten by Cyril E. Pocknee. 13th ed. London: Oxford University Press, 1965.

———. *The Story of the Prayer Book in the Old and New World and throughout the Anglican Church*. New York: Oxford University Press, 1933.

Echlin, Edward P. *The Anglican Eucharist in Ecumenical Perspective. Doctrine and Rite from Cranmer to Seabury*. New York: Seabury Press, 1968.

Fairweather, E. R., and Hettlinger, R. F. *Episcopacy and Reunion*. Toronto: General Board of Religious Education of the Church of England in Canada, 1952.

Grisbrooke, W. J. *Anglican Liturgies of the Seventeenth and Eighteenth Centuries*. London: S.P.C.K., 1958.

Harford, George, and Stevenson, Morley, eds. *The Prayer Book Dictionary*. New York: Longmans, Green and Co., 1912. Revised 1925.

Harrison, D. E. W. *The Book of Common Prayer, the Anglican Heritage of Public Worship*. London: Canterbury Press, 1946.

Hughes, John Jay. *Absolutely Null and Utterly Void; the Papal Condemnation of Anglican Orders, 1896*. Washington: Corpus Books, 1968.

———. *Stewards of the Lord; a Reappraisal of Anglican Orders*. London: Sheed and Ward, 1970.

Kemp, E. W. *Introduction to Canon Law in the Church of England*. London: Hodder and Stoughton, 1956.

Muss-Arnolt, William. *The Book of Common Prayer among the Nations of the World*. London: S.P.C.K., 1914.

Peck, A. L. *Anglicanism and Episcopacy*. London: The Faith Press, 1958.

Ratcliff, Edward C. *The Book of Common Prayer of the Church of England: Its Making and Revisions 1549–1661*. London: S.P.C.K., 1949.

Shepherd, Massey H. *The Worship of the Church*. Greenwich, Conn.: Seabury Press, 1952.

Stranks, Charles. *Anglican Devotion. Studies in the Spiritual Life of the Church of England between the Reformation and the Oxford Movement*. London: SCM Press, 1961.

Sykes, Norman. *Old Priest and New Presbyter*. Cambridge: University Press, 1956.

Wigan, B., ed. *The Liturgy in English*. 2nd rev. edn. London: Oxford University Press, 1964.

CREED AND DOCTRINE

Bicknell, E. J. *A Theological Introduction to the Thirty-Nine Articles of the Church of England*. 3rd edn., revised by H. J.

Carperter. London: Longmans, Green and Co., 1955.

De Satgé, J. C., Packer, J. I., et al. *The*

Articles of the Church of England. London: Mowbray, 1964.

Doctrine in the Church of England; Official Report of the Commission on Christian Doctrine Appointed by the Archbishops of Canterbury and York in 1922. London: S.P.C.K., 1938.

Echlin, Edward P. *The Anglican Eucharist in Ecumenical Perspective: Doctrine and Rite from Cranmer to Seabury.* New York: Seabury Press, 1968.

Knox, David Broughton. *Thirty-Nine Articles: The Historic Basis of Anglican Faith.* London: Hodder and Stoughton, 1967.

Matthews, W. R. *The Thirty-Nine Articles:*

A Plea for a New Statement of the Christian Faith as Understood by the Church of England. London: Hodder and Stoughton, 1961.

Paton, David M., ed. *Essays in Anglican Self-Criticism.* London: SCM Press, 1958.

Stibbs, Alan M. *Sacrament, Sacrifice and Eucharist; the Meaning, Function and Use of the Lord's Supper.* London: The Tyndale Press, 1961.

Subscription and Assent to the Thirty-Nine Articles; a Report of the Archbishops' Commission on Christian Doctrine. London: S.C.P.K., 1968.

HIGH, BROAD AND LOW CHURCH

Bradley, Ian. *The Call to Seriousness; the Evangelical Impact on the Victorians.* New York: Macmillan, 1974.

Brilioth, Yngve. *The Anglican Revival.* London: Longmans, Green and Co., 1925.

Brown, C. K. Francis. *A History of the English Clergy, 1800–1900.* London: The Faith Press, 1953.

Chadwick, Owen. *The Victorian Church.* 2 vols. New York: Oxford University Press, 1966–1970.

Churchmen Speak; Thirteen Essays. Foreword by P. E. Hughes. Appleford: Marcham Manor Press, 1966.

Elliott-Binns, L. E. *English Thought, 1860–1900.* Greenwich, Conn.: Seabury Press, 1956.

Every, G. *The High Church Party, 1688–1718.* London: S.P.C.K., 1956.

Mozley, John Kenneth. *Some Tendencies in British Theology from the Publication of Lux Mundi to the Present Day.* London: S.P.C.K., 1952.

Stewart, H. L. *A Century of Anglo Catholicism.* London: J. M. Dent and Sons, 1929.

Tavard, George H. *The Quest for Catholicity; a Study in Anglicanism.* New York: Herder and Herder, 1964.

Thornton, Martin. *English Spirituality; an Outline of Ascetical Theology according to the English Pastoral Tradition.* London: S.P.C.K., 1963.

Wand, J. W. C. *The High Church Schism.* London: The Faith Press, 1951.

ANGLICAN CHURCHES THROUGHOUT THE WORLD

Casserley, J. V. Langmead. *Christian Community.* London: Longmans, Green and Co., 1960.

Edwards, D. L. *Not Angels but Anglicans.* Naperville, Ill.: SCM Book Club, 1958.

Gray, G. F. S. *The Anglican Communion; a Brief Sketch.* London: S.P.C.K., 1958.

Morgan, Edmund R., and Lloyd, Roger. *The Mission of the Anglican Communion.* London: S.P.C.K., 1948.

Paul, Leslie. *The Deployment and Payment of the Clergy.* Westminster: Church Information Office, 1964.

Rawlinson, A. E. J. *The Anglican Communion in Christendom.* London: S.P.C.K., 1960.

———. *Current Problems of the Church.* London: S.P.C.K., 1956.

Slack, Kenneth. *The British Churches Today.* London: SCM Press, 1961.

Vidler, A. R., ed. *Soundings; Essays Concerning Christian Understanding.* Cambridge: University Press, 1962.

Wand, J. W. C. *The Anglican Communion.* New York: Oxford University Press, 1948.

ANGLICANISM

Dawley, Powel Mills, ed. *Report of the Anglican Congress, 1954.* Greenwich, Conn.: Seabury Press, 1954.

De Pol, William H. *Anglicanism in Ecumenical Perspective.* Duquesne Studies, Theological Series, 4. Pittsburgh: Duquesne University Press, 1965.

Jefferson, P. C., ed. *The Church in the Sixties; the Anglican Congress, 1963.* Greenwich, Conn.: Seabury Press, 1962.

The Lambeth Conference, 1948. London: S.P.C.K., 1948.

The Lambeth Conference, 1958. London: S.P.C.K., 1958.

Lambeth Conference, 1968; Preparatory Essays. London: S.P.C.K., 1968.

The Lambeth Conference, 1968; Resolutions and Reports. London: S.P.C.K., 1968.

The Lambeth Conferences, 1867–1948. London: S.P.C.K., 1949.

Neill, Stephen. *Anglicanism.* Baltimore: Penguin Books, 1958.

Ramsey, Arthur Michael. *The Gospel and the Church.* 2nd edn. London: Longmans, Green and Co., 1956.

Simpson, James B., Story, Edward M. *The Long Shadows of Lambeth X [1968].* New York: McGraw-Hill Book Company, 1969.

The Six Lambeth Conferences. London: S.P.C.K., 1920.

Wand, J. W. C. *Anglicanism in History and Today.* London: Weidenfeld and Nicolson, 1961.

ECUMENICAL RELATIONS

Bayne, Stephen F., Jr., ed. *Mutual Responsibility and Interdependence in the Body of Christ.* New York: Seabury Press, 1963.

Beckwith, R. T. *Priesthood and Sacraments; a Study in the Anglican-Methodist Report.* Latimer Monographs, 1. Appleford: Marcham Manor Press, 1964.

Bell, G. K. A. *Christian Unity; the Anglican Position.* London: Hodder and Stoughton, 1948.

Bill, E. G. W. *Anglican Initiatives in Christian Unity.* London: S.P.C.K., 1967.

The Church of England and the Churches of Norway, Denmark and Iceland. Report of the Committee Appointed by the Archbishop of Canterbury in 1951. London: S.P.C.K., 1952.

Deanesly, Margaret, and Willis, Geoffrey G. *Anglican-Methodist Unity; Some Considerations Historical and Liturgical.* London: The Faith Press, 1968.

Good, James. *The Church of England and the Ecumenical Movement.* London: Cork University Press, 1961.

Hodges, Herbert A. *Anglicanism and Orthodoxy, a Study in Dialectical Churchmanship.* London: SCM Press, 1955.

Istavridis, V. T. *Orthodoxy and Anglicanism.* Trans. Colin Davey. London: S.P.C.K., 1966.

Packer, J. I., ed. *All in Each Place; Towards Reunion in England. Ten Anglican Essays.* Appleford: Marcham Manor Press, 1965.

Ramsey, A. M. *Constantinople and Canterbury.* London: S.P.C.K., 1962.

Ryan, Herbert J., and Wright, J. Robert, eds. *Episcopalians and Roman Catholics: Can They Ever Get Together?* Denville, N. J.: Dimension Books, 1972.

Waddams, H. M., ed. *Anglo-Russian Theological Conference, Moscow, July 1956.* London: The Faith Press, 1958.

6. The Anglican Communion in North America: The Episcopal Church and the Anglican Church of Canada

The Anglican communion in the United States has two alternate official names: the Episcopal Church, and the Protestant Episcopal Church in the United States of America. The first of these, officially adopted in the 1960s, appears to be preferred by the majority of the members. But the alternate aptly signals the church's historical connections with the Church of England, since the adjective "Protestant" was traditionally construed as the opposite of Roman Catholic and "Episcopal" the antithesis of a Free Church system. The counterpart church in Canada is aptly named the Anglican Church of Canada. The history of these two churches reaches back through Anglicanism in the American colonies to the long history of the Church of England. To gain a comprehensive understanding of these churches, it is important to review the story of colonial Anglicanism, the formation of the Episcopal Church after the American Revolution together with its growth, expansion, worship, order, and creed within the Anglican communion, and the growth and development of the Anglican Church of Canada.

The Church of England in the American Colonies

The first Anglican service of worship on North American shores occurred during the Hudson's Bay expedition of Martin Frobisher in 1578. The next year a similar service of worship was offered near San Francisco while Sir Francis Drake voyaged along the West coast. But various efforts to establish colonies on North American territory during these years proved unsucessful.

During the seventeenth century the influence of the Church of England in North America was limited almost exclusively to the colonies of Virginia and Maryland. As late as 1700 only four Anglican parishes were located north of Maryland. During the eighteenth century the church appeared in all the colonies and was assisted in its work by missionaries of the Society for the Propagation of the Gospel in Foreign Parts (S.P.G.), but the shattering experiences of the American Revolution and separation from the mother country brought severe testing to the Anglicans living in the colonies. Throughout these two centuries, developments in the Church of England, including the Puritan Revolution, toleration, the resistance to providing bishops for the colonies, and other factors, were formative for church life on the colonial frontier. In addition, the church had the disadvantage of being generally unpopular among many colonists, since conditions in seventeenth-century England generally favored the emigration of persons who were unfriendly to bishops. Most of the colonies were founded during a period when authorities looked down on the Puritans, and the dispossessed and silenced Puritan clergy and their followers often migrated to the new colonies to escape oppression.[1]

When Anglicanism took permanent root on North American shores in Virginia, Queen Elizabeth I had just died and the Church of England was emerging from a critical period of the Reformation. Scholars were hard at work translating the King James Version of the Bible when a small company landed and settled what was called Jamestown in 1607. Robert Hunt was their chaplain. According to Captain John Smith, the hastily constructed lean-to church provided a place for "daily Common Prayer morning and evening, every Sunday two sermons, and every three months the Holy Communion, till our minister died; but our prayers daily, with a homily on Sundays, we continued two or three years after, till more preachers came." The Virginia Company guided religious affairs in the colony during the difficult years between 1607 and 1619. One chartered purpose of the colony was to spread the Gospel to infidel and native. More than two thirds of those who arrived during the early months died within the first year. A relatively strong Puritan element prevailed in the colony until a royal government was appointed in 1624. Five years earlier a House of Burgesses was created that included ecclesiastical representatives. After the colony became a royal colony Anglicanism was "established," although the establishment was only partial, since there were no bishops and Nonconformists were present. The third stage in church settlement occurred in 1643 when vestries were elected as trustee groups with rather extensive local control of church affairs.[2]

The first commissary appointed by the bishop of London to serve as his representative and to exercise as much discipline as possible under the circumstances was James Blair (1656–1743). Appointed for Virginia, he helped establish the College of William and Mary (1693). The colony had about seventy places of worship, half with ordained ministers and the other half with lay readers. Extensive glebe lands and parsonages for the ministers helped give the church a sense of stability. By 1720 there were forty-four parishes in Virginia's twenty-nine counties, but still about seventy places of worship. Tobacco and slavery were woven into the social and economic fabric of the colony. In 1667 Virginia lawmakers declared that "baptism doth not alter the condition of the person as to his bondage or freedom."[3]

The neighboring colony of Maryland had a large degree of religious liberty, and Anglican parishes were established side by side with Roman Catholic parishes and other churches. In 1691 King William III made Maryland a royal colony, and in 1702 the establishment of the Church of Englind became a legal fact. Provinces were divided into parishes, vestries were established, and the clergy supported by a tobacco tithe. The English Parliament rejected the colonial legislator's move to make Prayer Book worship compulsory for all. The historian Powel Mills Dawley wrote that church establishment in Maryland was "never popular" and "was more of a hindrance than a help to the spread of Anglicanism." During the eighteenth century the formation of congregations was slow, but church life flowed together with the establishments in Virginia, the Carolinas, and Georgia to create, according to Sidney Ahlstrom, "a unique tradition of southern Anglicanism."[4]

The man established as commissary for Maryland, Thomas Bray (1656–1730), performed a singular service for the Church of England in the colonies when he founded the Society for the Propagation of the Gospel in Foreign Parts (S.P.G.) in 1701. In 1699 he had been instrumental in founding the Society for the Promoting of Christian Knowledge (S.P.C.K.) before he left England for the colonies. This voluntary society of individuals provided libraries to train clergy and elevate the religious and cultural knowledge of the colonists, published and circulated books and Bibles, and founded schools. The S.P.G. provided the resources and men for extending the Church of England to the middle and northern colonies during the eighteenth century. Bray established the society during a trip back to England in 1701, and it soon won tremendous royal, political, and episcopal support. The S.P.G. provided over three hundred missionaries to the colonies up to the Revolution, though very few were sent to Maryland and Virginia. All S.P.G. support was withdrawn after the Revolution. The "Venerable Society," as it was also called, sent converted Quaker George Keith and John Talbot as the first missionaries. They visited many of the colonies and found fifty clergymen of England at work, seventeen in Maryland, twenty-five in Virginia, and, among others, two in Pennsylvania, two in New England, and one in New York. There were only four church buildings outside of Maryland and Virginia: St. Philip's in Charleston (1682), King's Chapel in Boston (1689), Christ Church in Philadelphia (1695), and Trinity Church in New York (1697). The S.P.G. missionaries sustained the religious life of many of the Anglicans in areas where they were a minority and worked zealously in areas where no colonial establishment provided support for the church. In 1725 the S.P.G. circulated its missionaries to take proper care "to instruct in the Christian religion and baptize the Negroes in the plantations in America."[5] Most of the Anglican clergy in the colonies opposed the Great Awakening as a movement of dissenters, and the church did not experience the revival and expansion that other groups did. Without the S.P.G.'s work it is difficult to imagine that the church would have entered the difficult period of the Revolution with as much strength as it did.

In the Carolinas the church was established in both the south and the north, but despite technical establishment in the north, no organized parishes with a settled ministry existed until well into the eighteenth century. In South

Carolina Anglicans fared better, though Anglicanism never dominated the colony as it did Virginia. The first church was built in Charleston toward the end of the seventeenth century, and by 1723 there were thirteen parishes. In 1704 the assembly required conformity to the Church of England and passed an act of establishment that created parishes, provided for vestries and ecclesiastical taxes, and authorized a lay commission to supervise the clergy. The act was repealed in 1706 after the House of Lords and the queen condemned it, largely because of the last provision. Georgia provided a parallel to North Carolina. John and Charles Wesley served there early in the eighteenth century as missionaries, but the colonists went for long periods without Anglican clergy. After the colony became a crown colony an act of establishment was passed in 1758, but as late as 1769 there were only two Anglican churches, in Savannah and Augusta.[6]

In his important book *Mitre and Sceptre* (1962), the historian Carl Bridenbaugh argued that "aggression by the Anglicans touched off a series of long and bitter ecclesiastical wars in the Northern colonies." England's Toleration Act forced a profound readjustment in religious life across the Atlantic. The S.P.G. moved to strengthen the position of episcopacy where it had already taken root and to plant it in areas north of Maryland. "Henceforth," Bridenbaugh continued, "Anglicanism, with all the appurtenances and traditional associations symbolized by mitre and sceptre, ceased to be a regional ecclesiastical activity; it became an intercolonial and transatlantic institution." Established Congregational or Presbyterian churches in Massachusetts (including Maine) and Connecticut, as well as those that faced little opposition in New Hampshire and enjoyed the benefit of religious liberty in Rhode Island, were composed of people who did not think of themselves as "dissenters." Rather, the Anglicans were viewed as the exception, and in truth they were; in 1690 the Church of England had only one congregation in all of New England, namely, in Boston. The formation of the S.P.G. raised anxieties in part because its charter made no mention of Indians or Negro slaves. And despite a decision in 1710 to concentrate on converting the heathen and infidels, and the allocation of more than half of the income for work among Mohawk Indians in New York, it was feared that proselytizing was the society's true goal. By 1718 only Connecticut lacked an Episcopal church.[7]

The Anglicans faced great difficulty in the Puritan stronghold of Massachusetts, but some progress occurred after the royal government enforced a degree of toleration. Puritan preachers labeled the King's Chapel in Boston a "High Place" with its "Priests of Baal," but some advance was made early in the eighteenth century. Anglican parishes were located in the chief centers of the colony, though the church never attained the significance it held in Virginia. Christ Church was built in Boston in 1723, and Trinity Church in 1735.[8]

The Anglicans had a difficult time as well in New Hampshire and Maine, but circumstances in Rhode Island allowed them to form parishes in the eighteenth century and to enjoy rapid growth with the creation of flourishing churches in Newport, Bristol, Providence, and other towns. In Connecticut the church advanced in one of the most dramatic events in the ecclesiastical history of the American colonies. At the Yale College commencement in 1722 the rector, the Reverend Timothy Cutler, stunned the audience by the closing words of his prayer, "and let all the people say, amen." This phraseology was considered to be Episcopalian if not popish, but certainly not Congregational. The next day Cutler confirmed the fears of the college's trustees when he announced that he, several tutors, and some prominent pastors of Connecticut could not accept Presbyterian ordination and had decided to rectify their uneasiness at not being in "visible communion with an Episcopal Church." Several of the converts, including Cutler, soon left for England to seek episcopal ordination. News also spread that an Episcopal church was soon to be built in Stratford, and it was completed in 1724. Congregational leaders and many of the colonists were stunned at the news and these developments, and their fears and anger aroused great agitation. Meanwhile the church increased in strength. The fourteen parishes of 1742 grew to forty churches and twenty resident clergymen at the time the Revolution broke out. Samuel Johnson, later president of King's College (now Columbia University) in New York, helped secure an act that enabled the Anglicans to pay taxes to their own ministers instead of the local Congregational pastor. In sum, during the second decade of the eighteenth century

> the Episcopalians in the S.P.G. had launched their drive for ecclesiastical power in New England. At New Haven in 1722 they brilliantly ambushed the Congregationalists, forcing them into a rear-guard action as they retreated. During the next ten years the Anglicans gained in numbers, and by 1735, with the able and indefatigable Bishop of London back of them, they had broken down the exclusive Massachusetts establishment and severely fractured that of Connecticut. It is no wonder that these victories seemed portentous to the Churchmen.

The stream of letters to London pleading for more missionaries and the formation of new churches substantiated the claims that the Episcopalians were harvesting a bumper crop. The S.P.G. resumed efforts to send bishops to the colonies, but was unsuccessful.[9] Nevertheless, the success in Connecticut was of such a magnitude that Anglicans in this state played a leading role in the organization of the independent Protestant Episcopal Church in the United States of America after the Revolution.

The middle colonies were not forgotten. Characterized from the beginning by their religious heterogeneity, the four middle colonies did not develop the religious tension and bitterness that characterized much of New England until the mid-eighteenth century. Toleration was vital for the continuing existence of Pennsylvania, Delaware, New York, and New Jersey with their Dutch, Swedes, English, Finns, French, and Germans. But in 1690 the Anglicans conducted weekly services in only one location in the middle colonies—in the small town of New York where they were outnumbered by others forty to one. Christ Church was founded in Philadelphia in 1695, and it soon became the leading parish in the area. Anglicans formed an influential group in the larger towns of Pennsylvania and Delaware as time passed, but they were never present in large numbers.[10]

Colonial New York was conquered from the Dutch in 1664, recaptured by the Dutch in 1673, and captured again by the English in 1674. Its population was overwhelmingly Dutch, Huguenot, and Quaker, but in 1693 the colonial assembly created a limited establishment of the Church of England. The governors interpreted the phrase "sufficient Protestant ministers" to refer to Anglican clergymen, who were to be supported in the counties of New York, Richmond, Westchester, and Queens, while no establishment was erected in Kings and four other counties that were primarily composed of Dutch or English dissenters. Varying interpretations of this Ministry Act brought eight decades of ecclesiastical strife. Nevertheless, the first Anglican parish was chartered in New York City in 1697 when the governor granted "king's farm" on lower Manhattan to Trinity parish, an act that eventually made this the wealthiest parish in the land. The S.P.G. sent numerous missionaries into the middle colonies, including New York, and in the early years of the eighteenth century the Anglican church grew in New York. King's College (1754) remained under Anglican control until after the Revolution.[11] The Church of England appeared rather late in New Jersey where beginnings were made in the first quarter of the eighteenth century. St. Mary's Church in Burlington (1703) was discussed as a good seat for an American bishop. Once again, S.P.G. missionaries contributed to the increasing strength of Anglicanism up to the Revolution.

Anglican church life in the colonies included rather restrained and simple worship with monotonous metrical psalms and an hourglass appropriately placed on the pulpit. Holy Communion was celebrated quarterly or in some cases monthly; most congregants came from the upper classes of colonial society. A few of the earliest church structures remain standing; the more impressive "great churches" of colonial Anglicanism had triple decks and spacious proportions and showed the influence of the baroque and Wren architectural design of the age. What colonial Anglicanism lacked was the familiar episcopal organization. Each church was virtually independent and parishes were not even grouped into dioceses. While the S.P.G. exercised some supervision, the real seat of ecclesiastical authority was thousands of miles away in the office of the bishop of London.[12]

While Anglicans in the colonies had no bishop until after the Revolution, the problem was much discussed for decades. When some American Anglicans appealed for a bishop in the seventeenth century, they were met largely with English indifference; when English churchmen wanted to send a bishop to America in the eighteenth century, they were met with American hostility. Influenced by a number of political and ecclesiastical factors, the deadlock produced no bishop.[13]

While as early as 1638 there were discussions about the need for a bishop in the colonies and efforts to secure one, the pace quickened with the creation of the S.P.G. early in the eighteenth century as missionaries pleaded for one or more resident bishops. Queen Anne was memorialized about an American bishop by the S.P.G. in 1712; the plan called for two bishops for the mainland and one for each of the islands of Barbados and Jamaica. A bill was ready for submission to Parliament when her death ended the project. As was the case earlier with Charles II, the ministers of state seemed to be the ones least inclined to pursue this course. The project received new impetus when Gibson became bishop of London in 1723. His plan for two bishops, one for the mainland and one for the islands, provided full details for funding the project and pointed up some of the advantages, including an indigenous clergy consecrated on colonial soil by a bishop. Men who made the treacherous voyage to secure ordination did not always return to the colonies; it was reported to a clergy meeting in New York in 1760 that ten of fifty-one who set out on the trip had perished in the effort. In addition, a resident bishop would be able to administer the rite of confirmation regularly, since the commissaries were unable to perform this rite. Gibson's plan went nowhere, but his successor, Sherlock, took up the issue once again with the Privy Council in 1749. He was met with the argument that dissenters at home would surely raise substantial opposition, and there were other problems as well. Would the bishop assume the powers of an officer of state and exercise certain powers of coercive jurisdiction? How could a royal mandate be framed to permit the consecration to occur, especially since there were no precedents?[14]

The major opposition came from the colonists themselves, and that not merely from dissenters. For example, it was not certain that Anglican vestries in Virginia would readily yield the appreciable power they held. Among the dissenters a powerfully persuasive case against episcopacy was developed before 1760; the basis of this grand argument was a special interpretation of colonial history. A certain Reverend Nathaniel Appleton typically declared that year that "it is grievous to think that when *our Pious Ancestors* came over into this land, then an *howling wilderness*, to *enjoy the Gospel* in the *purity and simplicity of it*, that the Church of England should thrust itself in among us." In New England Episcopalians had grown from a mere handful in 1690, according to the calculations of Ezra Stiles, to 12,600 souls worshiping in nearly fifty churches under the care of twenty-seven missionaries seventy years later. Even more frightening were the yearly conventions of Anglican clergy that began in New Jersey in 1758, followed by clergy meetings in Pennsylvania (1760), Connecticut (1765), and northern New England (1766). Public notices of these conventions aroused curiosity and alarm. "There is no reasonable doubt," the historian Bridenbaugh concludes,

> that in 1765–66 the colonies verged on armed rebellion, nor that religious fears quite as much as political sentiments and economic distress during the five

years immediately preceding the crisis contributed to the excited state of public opinion.

The Stamp Act of the spring of 1765 was repealed a year later, but the political and economic stresses of this year did not totally divert public attention in the northern colonies from the ecclesiastical question of bishops. Adding fuel to the fire was the fact that almost to a man the Anglican clergy opposed any resistance to the Stamp Act; in the main they counseled passive obedience and called any other conduct disloyal. The uproar created by the Stamp Act made it virtually impossible in the years that followed to distinguish religion and politics, and between 1767 and 1770 the great fear of episcopacy reached a fever pitch as Anglican missionaries persisted in attempts to secure bishops for America. From 1770 to 1774 agitation over ecclesiastical matters dropped off appreciably, but while political affairs occupied more space in the public press, especially after 1772, ecclesiastical news continued to remind dissenters that religious as well as civil liberties were being threatened.[15]

The Revolution left the Anglican church in shambles. In his recent history of North American churches, Robert Handy summarized the tensions that were experienced by Anglicans. "In the south the majority, both laymen and clergy, supported the struggle for independence," he wrote, adding that

> probably two-thirds of those who signed the Declaration of Independence were affiliated with the Church of England. In the northern colonies the influence of the high church S.P.G. missionaries was strong, and there the majority opposed the Revolution—many to join the Loyalist migration to Canada. Both because of the tides of feeling against the Church of England as the church of the enemy, and because of the way the destructiveness of war hit some areas heavily, the Anglican churches emerged from the struggle seriously weakened and isolated, so much so that some feared for their recovery.[16]

For some of the S.P.G. missionaries, one third of whom worked in New England in 1750, the ordination oath of allegiance to the Crown was an insuperable obstacle to their supporting the cause of independence. Some Anglicans openly opposed the First Continental Congress when it assembled in September of 1774, while others ardently supported it. A special ecclesiastical issue was raised when Congress declared that July 20, 1775 was to be observed in the churches as a day of fasting and prayer. Samuel Seabury of Connecticut, later the first bishop in the United States, refused to open his church for this purpose and four months later was imprisoned as unfriendly to the American cause. Once the Declaration of Independence was signed in 1776, Anglicans faced the problem of whether to pray the mandatory prayers for the king and royal family provided in the church's liturgy. Loyalist clergy claimed they had no choice but to offer the prayers, and some closed their churches rather than omit them. Meanwhile the patriot clergymen who supported the cause of independence omitted the royal prayers, in some cases substituting prayers for the new states. Loyalists such as Seabury, who for a time served as a chaplain to British forces, had their counterparts in such patriots as William White of Philadelphia, who served as chaplain to the American congress.[17]

The war brought severe hardship to many Anglicans, and it is estimated that as many as 70,000 left the country during or shortly after the war, many of them traveling to the Canadian maritime provinces or the West Indies. During the war two thirds of the parish rectors left Virginia, and for a time there was only one Anglican priest in Pennsylvania. In two centuries the church made some progress in the colonies, but the future looked grim around 1780. In 1701 the S.P.G. estimated that there were 43,000 Anglicans in the colonies of whom 20,000 lived in Virginia and another 20,000 in Maryland, with 1,000 in New York; of the 50 clergy, 25 were in Virginia and 17 in Maryland. The number of Anglican churches grew from 41 in 1660 (35 in Virginia) to 111 in 1700, 246 in 1740, and 406 in 1780 (when the congregationalists had 749, the Baptists 457, and the Presbyterians 495).[18]

Formation of the Protestant Episcopal Church in the U.S.A.

It was no easy task to provide a structure for a church so hard hit by the Revolution, but by 1789 the constitutional framework was completed. In the course of the Revolution church and state were separated in every state where the Church of England had been established, a process fully accomplished in Virginia in 1799. This brought a loss of public support and land for the church, while Latitudinarianism made inroads into a number of parishes. The Episcopalians in 1780 had nearly as many churches as the Baptists and Presbyterians—though half as many as the Congregationalists—but by 1820 they trailed Baptists, Lutherans, Presbyterians, and Methodists, as well as Congregationalists, in number of churches. The church's difficulty in the period after the Revolution is signaled by church-membership statistics in 1830 when there were 30,000 Episcopalians, but six times that many Presbyterians, ten times that many Baptists, and eighteen times that many Methodists, who were now independent of their parent body. Immediately after the Revolution there was a dearth of clergy and a decrease in the number of church members. Meanwhile, the S.P.G. gradually withdrew all resources while the bishop of London no longer sent missionaries. Important figures such as Jefferson, Franklin, Washington, Jay, Marshall, Henry, James Madison, Lee, and others were in some sense children of the Anglican tradition, but this meant little for the church at the time. Nevertheless, the laity continued to play a dominant role in the development of church structure, just as it had during colonial times. In fact, Dr. Stephen Bayne, at one time executive director of the Anglican communion, insisted that "the most characteristic contribution of the American Church to Anglicanism is doubtless in the part that the laity play in in the life and government of the church," a contribution with roots in the colonial history of this church.[19]

Since the Anglican churches had no resident bishop and no duly authorized governing body or widely recognized leadership, it was necessary to work out a form of government. The first effort to organize an independent Episcopal Church in the United States came in Maryland in 1780. Dr. William Smith called a meeting for the purpose of organizing the Anglican churches in Maryland as an official body which, it was hoped, with other churches would secure state tax support. The conference was attended by twenty-four prominent laymen and three clergy, and it was here for the first time that the name "Protestant Episcopal" was formally used. Low Church and lay emphases were strong, and a state organization was formed to hold property and serve the church's needs. After securing permission from the assembly, a clergy convention met in 1783 and stressed that the Maryland church was independent from England while at the same time in continuity with the Church of England on the basis of orders. The clergy elected Smith to go to Europe "*to be ordained an antistes*, President of the Clergy or Bishop (if that name does not hurt your feelings)." The chief problem in Maryland had been to establish the legal status of the Episcopal Church as heir to the Church of England, under the legislature's authority. A democratic polity based on parish vestries pointed the way toward a church government.[20]

Plans were moving in a different direction in Connecticut where the leader was Samuel Seabury (1729–1796), a High churchman who had been an S.P.G. missionary. Here the goal was to secure a duly consecrated bishop to head the church in that state. The clergy insisted that only a bishop could have authority to govern in an Episcopal church. Ten of the state's fourteen clergy met in 1783 and elected a bishop, Seabury, to obtain consecration in England or, if that failed, to apply to the Non-Juring bishops of Scotland. Existing ecclesiastical laws prevented the archbishop of Canterbury from consecrating a man who was no longer able to take the oaths of allegiance and supremacy, so Seabury was consecrated by three bishops of the Scottish Episcopal Church (Kilgour, Petrie, and Skinner) on November 14, 1784. He acceded to their request to try to persuade the church to adopt the Communion Office of the Non-Jurors, a liturgy that returned in some measure to the Prayer Book of 1549. Seabury was the first Anglican bishop appointed to minister outside the British Isles.[21]

A mediating position was struck in Pennsylvania under the leadership of William White (1748–1836). His pamphlet *The Case of the Episcopal Churches in the United States Considered* (1782) argued that under the circumstances it would be proper for clergy and laity together to elect a titular bishop without waiting for succession, but he withdrew the proposal when relations with Britain improved. But at bottom he was proposing a federal polity in which the authority to govern the church derived from elected representatives of all the churches in the United States, united by their voluntary acceptance of a constitution or a body of canon law. White joined with others to call a meeting of representatives of all states in October 1784, while Seabury was still abroad. In preparation, White held a meeting in Pennsylvania at which parishes were formally represented by laymen as well as clergy, an arrangement that had no precedent in England. The October conference scheduled a General Convention to meet in Philadelphia on September 27, 1785.

When the convention met, it was composed largely of deputies from Virginia and Maryland, though seven states were represented. No one was present from New England, since no provision had been made for a bishop to preside. Meeting again the next year, the convention heard that the archbishops of Canterbury and York had consented for arrangements to be made for bishops to be consecrated in England. Meanwhile Seabury refused to cooperate. In 1787 White and Samuel Provost (1742–1815) were consecrated at Lambeth chapel. In 1790 a third bishop was added to these two, James Madison of Virginia.

The organizational work was finished in 1789 when the General Convention met again to act on the final draft of the constitution and to unite the churches of the different states into a single Episcopal Church. The constitution now provided for a House of Bishops as well as a House of Deputies (laity and clergy), and a unanimous resolution affirmed the validity of Seabury's consecration. The convention adjourned at one point until Seabury attended. Also adopted were a constitution, a body of canons, and an American Book of Common Prayer.

Several innovations distinguished the new denomination from the Church of England. The church was entirely free of state control, its bishops had exclusively ecclesiastical authority, and the principle of lay representation was inaugurated at every level of church government, from vestry through the national level. The church was called the "Protestant Episcopal Church in the United States of America" as well as "Protestant Episcopal Church" in the constitution of 1789, following the precedent established in naming the state churches of Maryland, Pennsylvania, and Virginia.[22]

Initial efforts to get Bishop Seabury to cooperate with the two other bishops who had been consecrated at Lambeth were unsuccessful for a variety of reasons. Seabury and Provost had taken directly opposite positions during the Revolution, and Provost continued to insist for some time that Seabury's orders were invalid. Finally, in 1792, the four American bishops cooperated in the first consecration of an Episcopal bishop on national soil when Thomas John Claggett of Maryland became a bishop. At this General Convention and in succeeding conventions the question of adopting the Thirty-Nine Articles was debated until finally in 1801 it was decided to adopt them without any changes except those required by the American form of government. Final action on the Prayer Book was taken in 1792.[23]

The Episcopal Church and Nineteenth-Century Expansion and Controversy

While neither the Great Awakening of the eighteenth century nor the Second Great Awakening of the early nineteenth century found much of a following among Anglicans and Episcopalians, the church experienced a season of revival soon after the nineteenth century began. It was preceded by a slump that persisted after the Revolution, despite the creation of a national body. In 1811 Alexander Viets Griswold (1776–1843) was consecrated bishop of the "Eastern District," which covered all of New England except Connecticut. He worked valiantly in the cause of the Evangelical party and was an exponent of experiential Christianity. Evangelical renewal also occurred in Virginia and the area beyond the Appalachians. In the same year the High Church party received leadership with the consecration of John Henry Hobart (1775–1830) as bishop of New York. Another arm of this party was found in North and South Carolina as well as New Jersey and Pennsylvania. Hobart was instrumental in the development of General Theological Seminary in New York City. Despite the new bishops, the Episcopalians moved westward rather slowly, penetrating Ohio in 1817; Kentucky, Tennessee, Alabama, and Michigan by 1830; and Illinois, Indiana, Missouri, Wisconsin, Louisiana, and Iowa by 1840. In the meantime the bishop of Vermont, John Henry Hopkins, published an *Essay on Gothic Architecture* (1836) which helped stimulate the vogue for Gothic revival in Episcopal churches. Also influential was the model of Trinity Church in New York City, built in this style between 1839 and 1846. Despite their successes, Episcopalians counted only about 30,000 communicants in their midst in 1829.[24] Bishop Hobart started a program of evangelism among the Oneida Indians in New York state, and the church followed the Oneida when they were deported to Wisconsin in 1823. Episcopalians have had a long history of mission among native Americans.[25]

Hobart and Griswold, as well as Richard C. Moore in Virginia, Philander Chase in the Midwest, Theodore Dehon in South Carolina, and others, were part of the new generation of episcopal leadership which inaugurated a revival in Episcopal Church life after 1811. Their deep evangelical earnestness brought wide response despite the rather slow westward pace of the Episcopal witness. In addition, such new efforts as Sunday schools, Bible classes, academies, and colleges helped stir the revival. General Theological Seminary (1817) became the nursery of the ecclesiastical or High Church movement in the United States, while Virginia Theological Seminary, founded in Alexandria in 1823 primarily by Bishop Moore, became the nursery of the Evangelical movement. Tension and antagonism flared between these two groups, but the expansion movement helped prevent a major upheaval for the moment. In fact, a deeper sense of misionary responsibility was one of the results of the revival of the church. Already in 1821 the convention formed the Domestic and Foreign Missionary Society, but it lacked widespread support until 1835 when the denomination established a Board of Missions and when it was determined that the ground of membership in the society was membership in the church itself. Soon the society's income doubled and work increased. In the same year the convention created the "missionary bishop," enabling bishops to be consecrated to serve outside diocesan limits in the vast areas of the West. In an act that marked an era of expansion and growth, Jackson Kemper was consecrated as a missionary bishop for the Northwest. He was one of a score of bishops and priests who worked zealously to cover the wide expanse of the land, though seldom did the Episcopalians move with the speed of the Methodists, Baptists, Presbyterians, and others. Nevertheless, the extent of their expansion up to the Civil War was nothing short of amazing. More than eighteen dioceses appeared west of the Alleghenies while communicant membership increased from 30,000 to nearly 150,000 by 1860. There were 600 Episcopal churches in 1820 and 2,145 in 1860; the number of communicants tripled between 1833 and 1853, then doubled again between 1860 and 1870. Between 1835 and 1850 the number of clergy doubled from 700 to 1,500.[26]

In 1853, on behalf of a number of notable signers, William A. Muhlenberg presented a memorial to the House of Bishops asking whether

> the Protestant Episcopal Church, with her present canonical means and appliances, her fixed and invariable modes of public worship, her traditional customs and usages, is competent to the work of preaching and dispensing the Gospel to all sorts and conditions of men, and so adequate to do the work of the Lord in this land and in this age. . . .

The memorial requested that clergy in various denominations be ordained without requiring them to surrender "*all* the liberty in public worship to which they have been accustomed." The memorialists wanted the church to breathe American air and respond to American opportunities. Addressed to the bishops rather than the House of Deputies, the memorial found little acceptance, but in the course of time many of its elements have become reality. The memorial helped pave the way for the Lambeth Quadrilateral of 1888 and the revisions of the American Prayer Book in 1892, 1928, and in the present.[27] The growth of such need-filling mission services as the Seamen's Church Institute of New York, founded in 1834 as the Protestant Episcopal Church Missionary Society for Seamen, is a witness to the vitality of the memorialists' concerns.

Foreign missions were expanding at the same time that the church worked to meet domestic challenges. The greatest expansion in foreign missions came in the two decades after the Civil War, but already in 1830 a mission was opened in Greece, and in 1844 a bishop was consecrated for "the Dominions and Dependencies of the Sultan of Turkey" in a short-lived experiment. Two missionaries, one High Church and the other Evangelical, sailed for China in 1835, and soon the first Episcopal missionary entered Japan as well. Liberia was opened to mission work in the same year, and a bishop was consecrated for the area in 1850. Work in China and Japan multiplied after the Civil War, when the church also moved into Alaska. As the twentieth century began, independent Episcopal churches in Brazil, Haiti, and Mexico became missionary districts, congregations of the Church of England in the Hawaiian Islands were taken under Episcopal jurisdiction, and missionary districts were formed in Cuba, Puerto Rico, and the Philippine Islands.[28] Meanwhile in the States Daniel S. Tuttle (1837–1923) was appointed bishop of the newly designated Rocky Mountain jurisdiction, composed of 340,000 square miles. Working in an area that initially had no priests, he pursued his mission zealously, then returned to the Mildwest to become bishop of Missouri and for twenty years presiding bishop of the national body, the last to serve in this capacity by right of seniority among bishops.

The Civil War brought strife to the church although it did not result in a permanent separation as was the case in several other major denominations. After signing the call to organize a separate Protestant Episcopal Church of the South as war erupted, Leonidas Polk, the bishop of Louisiana, joined the Confederate forces as a major-general. Led by Polk and Bishop Stephen Elliott of Georgia, southern Episcopalians organized the Protestant Episcopal Church in the Confederate States of America in 1861. Composed of dioceses in the states that withdrew from the Union, the body adopted a slightly modified constitution, body of canons, and Prayer Book. But the next year the General Convention's roll call included the names of the dioceses that were not represented. Before the convention in 1865 the presiding bishop invited the southern bishops to attend the next meeting, and six months after Lee's surrender two bishops and a few deputies attended the General Convention in Philadelphia. A month later the General Council of the southern church voted that, in view of the fact that the circumstances that brought it into existence no longer existed, the dioceses could renew their previous affiliation. This brought the temporary division to an end and the Church of the Confederacy ceased to exist.[29]

The controversy over slavery was one of the many that disturbed the church's life during the second half of the nineteenth century. The three parties in the Church of England (High, Broad, Evangelical) found their counterparts in the American church, and relations were not always amicable. The Oxford Movement began to make its influence felt in the forties, and soon it created sharp antagonism between High and Evangelical churchmen. Evangelicals were suspicious of "Romanizing" tendencies and aghast at the small number of persons who converted to the Roman Catholic Church. Approximately fifty priests or seminary graduates took this step after Newman's conversion at midcentury, including in 1852 the bishop of North Carolina, Levi S. Ives, who was formally deposed—after resigning—by the House of Bishops for not conforming with canon law. Partisan strife escalated as ritual and ceremonial practices were debated with great zeal in the decade of the seventies. A canon adverse to the ritualists in 1874 did not settle much of anything, since ritual liberty had been so firmly established as a working principle. Meanwhile the Evangelicals attacked the idea of baptismal regeneration, which had been given a rather new popular meaning

in the country's awakenings. Dissension over this issue resulted in the formation of the Reformed Episcopal Church (q.v.) in 1873. Another disturbance
was created by advances in the physical sciences and the new biblical criticism
that was entering the country by way of the English church. As so-called
Broad churchmen such as Phillips Brooks of Boston and others tried to come
to terms with these aspects of modern thought, some saw a greater need to
defend orthodox, traditional Christianity than to restate fundamental truths
in new ways. After the so-called Second Ritualistic War, the issue of the
name "Protestant Episcopal" finally came up for consideration in the General
Convention of 1877, and thereafter (except for 1880, 1922, and 1928) each
convention debated the issue until "The Episcopal Church" was ratified as
an alternate name in 1967.[30]

Private preparatory schools were important adjunct institutions of the
Episcopal Church in these years of strife, but even more significant were the
new seminaries that sprang up, including Berkely in Middletown, Connecticut
(1850), the Philadelphia Divinity School (1862), the Episcopal Theological
School at Cambridge, Massachusetts (1867), and the Western Theological
Seminary at Chicago (1885). Despite a rash of controversies, the body continued to grow rapidly with the clergy numbering 5,000 by 1907 and communicant membership reaching 800,000.

The Episcopal Church in the Twentieth Century

The early decades of the twentieth century were years of vigorous missionary expansion for the Episcopal Church. After the missionary diocese of
Mexico was established in 1904, Panama and the Canal Zone also became a
missionary diocese, and separate dioceses were formed for Costa Rica, El
Salvador, Guatemala, Nicaragua, Honduras, Columbia, and other states in
Central and South America. After prolonged negotiations, in 1948 the House
of Bishops granted the request of certain Filipinos for orders within the
historic apostolic succession. Three prelates of the Philippine Independent
Church were consecrated as bishops in the apostolic succession.

While the Fundamentalist movement was not successful in gaining much
of a following in the church early in the century, a Broad churchman named
Algernon Sidney Craspey (1847–1927) was charged with heresy. A priest in
Rochester, New York, who lectured widely on social and economic reforms,
Craspey was brought to trial in the diocese of Western New York for casting
doubt on the divinity of Christ, his conception by the Holy Ghost, his virgin
birth, and his resurrection from the dead. Craspey claimed to hold "spiritual"
allegiance to the creeds of the church. Convicted of heresy, he lost his appeals and was deposed in 1906, but his case had no ramifications in the
various Episcopal seminaries of the land.[31]

In general, Broad churchmen played an important role in the Social
Gospel movement. The Episcopal Church was a channel for British Christian

Socialism to reach the United States, and this English influence was partly responsible for transforming the socially conservative Episcopal Church into one of the leading exponents of the Social Gospel. An Episcopal priest named W. D. P. Bliss formed an American branch of the Society of Christian Socialists in Boston in 1889 and also edited *The Encyclopedia of Social Reform*. Bishop Henry Codman Potter and Bishop Frederic Dan Huntington gave leadership to the Church Association for the Advancement of the Interests of Labor, which was established in New York City in 1887. This association urged the use of prayer, sermons, the press, lectures, and the ballot box to acquaint clergy and laity with the social question. It soon spread across the country and helped inaugurate in Episcopalian churches the first observance of Labor Sunday in 1890. Active for forty years with its sister organization, the Church Social Union, the Church Association was instrumental in getting the General Convention to adopt various social service measures. Bliss became the traveling secretary of the Church Social Union after 1897. Together with the Northern Presbyterians, the Episcopalians were the first denomination early in the twentieth century to add an official commission to its national organization to keep abreast of social problems. The commission was staffed by a paid secretary.[32]

Based on statistics from 1946–1947, interviews of Episcopalians in 1952, U.S. census data in 1957, and a Gallup poll of 16,000 persons in 1970, it is possible to provide a demographic profile of Episcopalians in the United States. In a public opinion poll in 1946–1947, 599 representative persons who described themselves as Episcopalians were placed in the following social class rankings after careful appraisal of the data: 24.1 percent, "upper"; 33.7 percent, "middle"; 42.2 percent, "lower." In 1952 a major study of the Episcopal Church commissioned by the church determined that according to annual income Episcopalian parishioners were distributed in the following way:

$4,000 or less	40.0 percent
4,001-6,000	26.8 percent
6,001-7,500	9.9 percent
7,501-10,000	9.6 percent
10,000 or more	12.0 percent

The study concluded that socially and economically "the Episcopalian parishioners in our sample closely resemble those described in the poll." It added that the two bodies of data "document the fact that the average Episcopalian is far from being wealthy and confirm the general pattern by which Episcopalians are distributed across the class structure."[33] Data derived largely from a 1957 U.S. census sample provided additional information on the social and economic status of Episcopalians, as the following table[34] indicates:

Percent	Catholic	Baptist	Methodist	Lutheran	Presbyterian	Episcopalian	Jewish
Percent of population	25	21	14	7	6	3	3
Percent of college-educated	17	10	20	20	34	45	44
Percent white	95	76	91	99	98	94	99
Percent professional and business	23	15	24	24	31	37	51
Percent living East and Midwest	78	33	53	76	56	50	90
Percent earning more than $7,000	47	26	42	49	60	64	69
Percent living in cities over 500,000	51	19	21	28	30	41	80
Percent weekly church attendance	68	37	34	43	36	31	22
Percent Democratic	56	55	40	34	28	27	64

A Gallup poll of 16,000 persons in 1970 revealed that, according to this representative sampling, 47 percent of Episcopalians were college graduates (versus 42 percent of Jews, 21 percent of Roman Catholics, and 22 percent of Protestants). They headed the list of Protestant groups in total income; 32 percent had incomes of $15,000 or more, a percentage followed by the Presbyterians (21 percent) and Lutherans (15 percent). Among Protestants they had the lowest weekly church attendance (29 percent) as contrasted with Lutherans (43 percent) and Roman Catholics (60 percent). In a Gallup poll in 1971, 3 percent of those interviewed indicated that they were Episcopalians, while in 1970 Episcopalians composed approximately 2.3 percent of the total inclusive church and synagogue membership in the United States of 130 million persons.[35]

The more than 1½ million Episcopalian communicants of 1952 were distributed in parishes of varying sizes. While 56 percent of the parishes (3,777 of 6,674) were composed of 1 to 150 members, this accounted for only 14 percent (221,063) of the total communicant membership of 1,619,703. The other parish sizes and their relative percentages were as follows:[36]

Size of Parish	Number of Local Units	Percentage of Churches	Percentage of Total Communicants
151-305	1,452	21	21
351-500	497	7	13
501-750	474	7	18
751-1,000	210	3	11
1,001-1,500	193	3	14
1,500+	71	1	9

In sum, in 1952 more than half of the Episcopalian churches had no more than 150 communicant members, but this group of churches served only 14 percent of the total communicant membership of the national body.

This 1952 questionnaire also secured other data that provide insight into the Episcopal Church at midcentury in terms of both views on worship and the linkage between religion and social action. Most Episcopalians disagreed (bishops, 1 percent; priests, 3 percent; parishioners, 10 percent) that "aside from preaching, there is little the church can do about social and economic problems," but fewer parishioners (46 percent) than bishops (72 percent) or priests (70 percent) said that "it is proper for the church to state its position on political issues to the local, state, and national government." It was deemed more appropriate for the clergy to speak out on some issues than on others. For example, "prayers in schools" (91 percent, bishops; 95 percent, priests; 88 percent, parishioners) was a more appropriate discussion topic than labor relations (62, 63 and 35 percent, respectively), and political corruption (96, 96, and 75 percent) more appropriate than anti-Semitism (87, 95, and 69 percent) or birth control (78, 80, and 64 percent) for the clergyy to discuss publicly. In 1943 the General Convention of the church created a joint committee on conscientious objectors, among other things to "assure the members of the Church who by reason of religious training and belief are conscientiously opposed to participation in war of the continuing fellowship of the Church with them and care for them." While over 90 percent of both bishops and priests agreed in 1952 that "Episcopalians should recognize the right of conscientious objectors to refuse to bear arms," 53 percent of the parishioners also concurred, while a substantial minority of 34 percent did not. It was also reported that the clergy were more likely than parishioners to believe that prayers were efficiacious in preventing war. Reflecting the position of the convention in 1949, which resolutely opposed the use of state or federal funds for supporting private or parochial schools, 96 percent of the bishops, 85 percent of the priests, and 79 percent of the parishioners rejected the proposal that "government funds should be used for support of parochial or religious schools." The clergy (both bishops and priests) were more likely than parishioners to rule out joint worship services with Protestant churches which would include Holy Communion, and parishioners were more likely to accept a visiting Protestant preacher in the local church than bishops and priests, according to the study. Fifty-five percent of the bishops disagreed with the statement that "Protestants and Roman Catholics should be allowed to intermarry freely," as did 51 percent of the priests but only 29 percent of the parishioners.[37]

Sociological studies of various beliefs of persons in the early 1960s provide information on certain beliefs held by the Episcopalians sampled at that time. The following tables[38] illustrate the way the sampled Episcopalians responded to questions about belief in God and in Jesus Christ. (See next pages.)

The traditional Anglican parties continue to function within the Episcopal Church in the United States. Special concern has arisen among some High

Belief in God

"Which of the following statements comes closest to what you believe about God?"	Congregationalists	Methodists	Episcopalians	Disciples of Christ	Presbyterians	American Lutherans§	American Baptists	Missouri Lutherans	Southern Baptists	Sects ||	Total Protestants	Catholics
"I know God really exists and I have no doubts about it."	41%	60%	63%	76%	75%	73%	78%	81%	99%	96%	71%	81%
"While I have doubts, I feel that I do believe in God."	34	22	19	20	16	19	18	17	1	2	17	13
"I find myself believing in God some of the time, but not at other times."	4	4	2	0	1	2	0	0	0	0	2	1

"I don't believe in a personal God, but I do believe in a higher power of some kind."	16	11	12	0	7	6	2	1	0	1	7	3
"I don't know whether there is a God and I don't believe there is any way to find out."	2	2	2	0	1	*	0	1	0	0	1	1
"I don't believe in God."	1	*	*	0	0	0	0	0	0	0	*	0
No answer	2	*	1	4	*	*	2	0	0	1	1	1
Per cent† =	100	99	99	100	100	100	100	100	100	100	99	100
Number of respondents‡ =	(151)	(415)	(416)	(50)	(495)	(208)	(141)	(116)	(79)	(225)	(2326)	(545)

* Less than ½ of 1 percent.
† Some columns fail to sum to 100 percent due to rounding error.
‡ The number of respondents shown for each denomination in this table is the same for all other tables in this chapter.
§A combination of members of The Lutheran Church in America and the American Lutheran Church.
‖Included are: The Assemblies of God, The Church of God, The Church of the Nazarene, The Foursquare Gospel Church, and one independent Tabernacle.

209

Belief in the Divinity of Jesus

"Which of the following statements comes closest to what you believe about Jesus?"	Congregationalists	Methodists	Episcopalians	Disciples of Christ	Presbyterians	American Lutherans	American Baptists	Missouri Lutherans	Southern Baptists	Sects	Total Protestants	Catholics
"Jesus is the Divine Son of God and I have no doubts about it."	40%	54%	59%	74%	72%	74%	76%	93%	99%	97%	69%	86%
"While I have some doubts, I feel basically that Jesus is Divine."	28	22	25	14	19	18	16	5	0	2	17	8
"I feel that Jesus was a great man and very holy, but I don't feel Him to be the Son of God any more than all of us are children of God."	19	14	8	6	5	5	4	0	0	*	7	3
"I think Jesus was only a man, although an extraordinary one."	9	6	5	2	2	3	2	1	1	*	4	1
"Frankly, I'm not entirely sure there was such a person as Jesus."	1	1	1	0	1	*	0	0	0	0	1	0
Other and no answer	3	3	2	4	1	0	2	1	0	1	2	2

* Less than ½ of 1 percent.

Additional Beliefs about Jesus

	Congregationalists	Methodists	Episcopalians	Disciples of Christ	Presbyterians	American Lutherans	American Baptists	Missouri Lutherans	Southern Baptists	Sects	Total Protestants	Catholics
"Jesus was born of a virgin." Percentage who said, "Completely true."	21%	34%	39%	62%	57%	66%	69%	92%	99%	96%	57%	81%
"Jesus walked on water." Percentage who said, "Completely true."	19	26	30	62	51	58	62	83	99	94	50	71
"Do you believe Jesus will actually return to the earth some day?" Percentage who answered:												
"Definitely."	13	21	24	36	43	54	57	75	94	89	44	47
"Probably."	8	12	13	10	11	12	11	8	4	2	10	10
"Possibly."	28	25	29	26	23	18	17	6	0	1	20	16
"Probably not."	23	22	17	12	12	6	6	4	1	2	13	11
"Definitely not."	25	17	11	6	8	7	5	1	1	3	10	12
No answer.	3	3	6	10	3	3	4	6	0	3	4	4

Church Episcopalians about proposed revision of the Prayer Book and the ordination of women, although opposition is not limited to this grouping. In addition, the "Bishop Pike Affair" in the 1960s showed that Episcopalians sometimes held widely divergent views on any number of subjects.

No full summary of the affair can be provided here, but it is widely acknowledged that Bishop James Albert Pike of California was, in the mid-sixties, a visible and public questioner of most of the dogmas and doctrines of orthodox Christianity. Proposing that Christianity needed "more belief, fewer beliefs," he seemed willing to dispose of much of traditional doctrine in order to preserve the central and irreducible message, namely God as the loving personal ground of existence, and Jesus as the one in whom God "broke through" and whose self-giving life is the prime example for Christians who would follow him to gain eternal life. Four times after his ordination as priest in 1946 Pike was denounced as a heretic and a trial was demanded, the last time in 1966, soon after he resigned as bishop of California to join the Center for the Study of Democratic Institutions. The House of Bishops subsequently denounced Pike's theologizing as "offensive" and "irresponsible," but fore-stalled a heresy trial. The vote was 103 to 36. In 1967 Pike called for a modern creed to replace the Apostles' and Nicene creeds.[39]

A rising conservative tide made its influence felt in the Episcopal Church in the mid-twentieth century. In 1970 the Foundation for Christian Theology, a Texas-based organization of conservatives, attempted to secure the resigna-tion of Presiding Bishop John E. Hines. The foundation, which claimed a membership of 200,000 members, showed deep disappointment over the church's support of black militants; reportedly the church raised $200,000 for its National Committee of Black Churchmen, which channeled most of the money through the Black Economic Development Committee founded by James Forman. Also criticized was a $40,000 grant to a militant Mexican-American organization in New Mexico, the Alianza Federal de Mercedes. Two small splinter groups were formed in the sixties, the Anglican Orthodox Church of North America (q.v.) and the American Episcopal Church (Spar-tanburg, South Carolina; q.v.). In February, 1973, more than three hundred Episcopal clergymen from all over the nation formed the Episcopal Charis-matic Fellowship, the first formal neo-Pentecostal group in that denomination. The fellowship insisted that it was not a pressure or separatist group in the denomination.[40] The issue of ordaining women to the priesthood also aroused a great deal of conservative resistance, as indicated below.

The issue of racial prejudice has been an item of concern in the church for some years. In the mid-fifties approximately 80,000 Episcopalians were black, and the largest parish in the denomination, St Philip's Church in New York City, was almost totally black in membership. The Anglican Congress, which met in 1954 in Minneapolis, Minnesota, asserted that "in the work of the Church we should welcome people of any race at any service conducted by a priest or layman of any ethnic origin, and bring them into the full fellowship of the congregation and its organization." In 1964 the General

Convention amended Canon 16 and banned the exclusion of any member from worship in any parish on racial grounds. St. John's Episcopal Church of Savannah, Georgia, founded in 1840, had been a steadfastly segregated church. In 1965 it voted 785 to 75 to secede, becoming the only Episcopal church that refused to obey Canon 16. Under the leadership of its priest, Ernest Risley, it became an independent Protestant congregation.[41] In 1969 at a special General Convention the Episcopal Church created a $200,000 fund for black economic development as well as a $100,000 fund for self-development work with American Indians. In the intervening year before the regular General Convention in 1970 the church gathered the full $200,000 for black development and subscribed the fund for Indian self-development.

At the regular General Assembly in 1967 the church had made several important institutional decisions. Acting on the recommendation of the Special Committee on Episcopal Theological Education headed by Harvard president Nathan M. Pusey, the convention established a Board for Theological Education designed to work on a broad scale for renewal of the seminaries and the training for ministry. The committee's study, published as *Ministry for Tomorrow* (1967), criticized much contemporary theological education, charging that it failed to prepare young ministers to cope with the modern age. Written by the Reverend Charles L. Taylor, former executive director of the American Association of Theological Schools, the study found that more than a third of the clergy in the Episcopal Church lacked the prescribed seminary education. Referring to the eleven accredited seminaries of the church, the study recommended higher scholastic standards, cooperation with universities and other seminaries, and provision for financial support to students and seminaries. Unlike many other bodies, the Episcopal Church had assumed no official responsibility for the support or standards of its theological training schools. Only the General Theological Seminary in New York City had a very limited relationship to the General Convention, which elected a certain number of board members and received a report from the seminary. Other seminaries were related to dioceses or in some cases a Provincial Synod. Final responsibility for determining the adequacy of preparation of a candidate for ministry rests with the diocesan bishop and the board of examining chaplains.[42]

The General Convention in 1967 also defined the role of the presiding bishop as "chief pastor," giving him the right to speak for the church, visit dioceses at his own intiative, and develop plans for the church's work and mission. It authorized laymen to administer the chalice and set in motion a process for revising the entire Book of Common Prayer. The convention ratified the constitutional change first proposed in 1964 which made "The Episcopal Church" fully acceptable as an alternate to the name "The Protestant Episcopal Church in the United States of America." It also adopted the first reading of a constitutional change, subsequently ratified in 1970, that allowed women to serve in the House of Deputies.

One means of support for Episcopal seminaries is the regular Theological

Education Sunday Offering received on the Sunday nearest January 25, the Feast of the Conversion of St. Paul. Established in 1940, this offering gathered nearly $400,000 in 1954. Other special campaigns for funds have included the collection for the creation of the Church Pension Fund (1917), the Reconstruction and Advance Fund (1947) for world relief and the rebuilding of missions, and the Builders for Christ (1954–1955) campaign to provide building assistance for seminaries as well as schools and missions overseas. These campaigns were supported by the many weekly or fortnightly magazines published independently for Episcopalians, including *The Living Church, The Episcopal Churchnews, The Witness, The Churchman,* and others. For students and scholars the two most important quarterlies are the *Anglican Theological Review* and the *Historical Magazine of the Protestant Episcopal Church,* the latter published by the official Church Historical Society.

Never before incorporated in the American Book of Common Prayer, the "Reproaches" were included as an optional part of the Good Friday service in a newly revised draft of the Prayer Book distributed for experimental use in the 1970s. After resistance arose, the church's Standing Liturgical Commission voted to remove the "Reproaches" from the draft, and the General Convention finalized the deletion in 1976. The "Reproaches" were judged by many to be anti-Semitic. Earlier, in 1964, the House of Bishops adopted a statement entitled "Deicide and the Jews" which said, among other things, that "the charge of deicide against the Jews is a tragic misunderstanding of the inner significance of the crucifixion." Jesus' crucifixion, said the bishops, "cannot be construed as imputing corporate guilt to every Jew in Jesus' day, much less the Jewish people in subsequent generations."[43]

In the 1970s the church also acted on the nation's Bicentennial and the question of remarrying divorced persons. In 1973 the General Convention encouraged churches to participate in observances of the Bicentennial, suggesting among other things "that emphasis be placed in these observances not only on past history, but primarily upon the opportunities in the present to affirm and extend the promise of 'liberty and justice for all' . . . ." In the same year a new canon was adopted, to be effective in 1974, which enabled a priest with the bishop's consent to marry a divorced person without waiting a year after the legal decree of divorce, as was previously required.

The Episcopal Church was an active participant in the eumenical initiatives taken by Anglicans in the twentieth century, as described above. It contributed to the founding of the World Council of Churches inasmuch as the American Charles Henry Brent, a missionary in the Philippines and later bishop of New York, spearheaded the first meeting of the World Conference of Faith and Order which eventually entered the World Council. The church joined the Federal Council of Churches in 1940 and is a member of the National Council of Churches, as well as a participant in the Consultation on Church Union (COCU) after 1966. The Episcopal bishops' Chicago Quadrilateral (1886), also discussed above, laid the foundation for the Lambeth Quadrilateral two years later.

In the early twenties the Episcopal Church held unsuccessful union conversations with the Congregationalists. Prolonged and intensive negotiations with the Presbyterian Church in the U.S.A. from 1937 to 1946 ended when they were terminated by the General Convention in 1946. Preliminary discussions opened with the Methodist Church in 1949, but they have not led to organizational union. Ecumenical conversations have also been held with Lutherans and other groups. Intercommunion was established between the Episcopal Church and the Polish National Catholic Church in the United States in 1946 as part of a broader Anglican-Old Catholic agreement. The consecration of three Filipino bishops of the Philippine Independent Church by Episcopal bishops in 1948 further stabilized a longstanding relationship. Formal intercommunion has not been established between the Episcopal Church and any Eastern Orthodox church in the United States.

In 1976 the United States Anglican-Roman Catholic Consultation (ARC) agreed on the mission and purpose of the church "insofar as it faithfully preaches the gospel of salvation, celebrates the sacraments, and manifests the love of God in service." The ARC's statement also endorsed social action on behalf of human liberation as part of the church's mission, and noted that "Roman Catholics and Episcopalians believe that there is but one Church of Christ." Originated in 1965, the ARC previously issued statements on the Eucharist (1967) and organic unity (1969). These statements, like the one issued in 1976, carried only the authority of the nearly twenty theologians in the consultation, but were commended for "the study and response of the people of our churches."[44] The ordination of women has become a matter of grave concern to some Episcopalians and Roman Catholics interested in closer relations.

Episcopalians continued to increase in size in the twentieth century. When the century opened approximately one out of every 100 Americans was an Episcopal communicant. The ratio of communicants to the general population between 1830 and 1950 shifted appreciably:

Year	Communicants	Ratio to U.S. Population
1830	30,939	1 to 415
1840	55,477	1 to 307
1850	98,655	1 to 235
1860	150,591	1 to 208
1870	231,591	1 to 166
1880	341,155	1 to 147
1890	531,525	1 to 118
1900	742,569	1 to 102
1910	930,037	1 to 98.9
1920	1,073,832	1 to 98.4
1930	1,261,167	1 to 97
1940	1,437,820	1 to 91.6
1950	1,640,101	1 to 91.9

Meanwhile, the total membership of the church continued to grow at the vigorous pace of approximately 500,000 new members per decade in the twentieth century until about 1960, although between 1900 and 1930 the rate of growth was somewhat slower than between 1930 and 1960. In 1919 the denomination expanded the term "member" to include all baptized persons, not only communicants. By 1960 there were approximately 3.29 million members; peak membership was attained in 1966 with about 3.4 million members, but then, like several other mainline churches, the denomination experienced a period of leveling and decline attributed by some to many of the clergy's vigorous opposition to the Vietnam war. The *Yearbook of American and Canadian Churches, 1973* listed an inclusive membership of 3,217,365 with 7,116 churches and 11,108 ordained clergy. The national body's statistics, compiled from the previous year's diocesan figures, always show a time lag. In 1976 the Episcopal Church reported 3,039,519 baptized members, 2,128,857 communicant members, 7,383 parishes and missions, and 12,300 deacons, perpetual deacons, priests, and bishops.[45]

In 1950 the denomination's 6,467 churches were geographically concentrated in fourteen states, each of which had more than 175 churches. These states, with a total of over 4,000 churches, had within their boundaries about 80 percent of the total number of Episcopal churches in the nation. They were California (263), Connecticut (184), Florida (180), Illinois (198), Maine (217), Massachussets (255), Michigan (203), New Jersey (300), New York (804), North Carolina (256), Ohio (178), Pennsylvania (460), Texas (286), and Virginia (371). Episcopalians composed approximately 2.7 percent of the inclusive religious group membership of about 125 million persons in the United States in 1965. The church had about 80,000 black members in the mid-sixties.[46]

During the colonial period Episcopalians occupied an identifiable place on the religious map of the colonies. Their strength was concentrated in Virginia and Maryland. By 1970, however, they had virtually disappeared from a map of the United States that portrayed the territorial strength of various denominations on a county-by-county basis. But this absence of concentrated geographical strength does not prepare the interested observer to explain the fact that in 1974 sixteen United States senators were Episcopalians (compared with 17 Methodists and 15 Roman Catholics), while in the House of Representatives 50 individuals identified themselves as Episcopalians (compared with 108 Roman Catholics, the largest single religious group, 68 Methodists, 50 Presbyterians, and 48 Baptists). In 1967 *Christianity Today* discovered that 15 percent of the United States senators were Episcopalians (second in size only to the group of 24 percent who were Methodists); Episcopalians ranked fourth in size in the House of Representatives with 12 percent, compared with 22 percent of the representatives who were Roman Catholic, 17 percent who were Presbyterian, and 16 percent who classified themselves as Methodist. In the same year Episcopalians occupied 16 percent of the governors' chairs (versus 20 percent who were Methodists and 18 percent who were Roman Catholic). They composed approximately 2 percent of the nation's population.[47] In the twentieth century a great number of important political, military, and cultural figures of the nation were Episcopalians including, among others, President Franklin D. Roosevelt, General Douglas MacArthur, and such writers as Chad Walsh, Norman Pittenger, J. V. Langmead Casserley, and Bishop Pike.

Like many other mainline educational agencies, enrollment in Episcopal church schools plummeted in the sixties from 980,000 in 1959 to 730,000 in 1970. A variety of factors, including demographic slowdown, contributed to this phenomenon.

The church continues to have a surplus of trained clergy. Between 1970 and 1974 there was a 7.3 percent increase in the number of clergy despite a 6 percent drop in ordinations. Of the 12,837 clergy in 1974, about 7,700 were in parochial ministries, 1,800 in nonparochial ministries, 1,650 secularly employed, and 1,700 retired. The five-year period found a 70 percent increase in the number of clergy deriving the major portion of their income from nonecclesiastical sources. A moratorium on applications for the ministry was instituted in the dioceses of Atlanta, Bethlehem (Pa.), Missouri, and southern Ohio, and the denomination used an employment agency to assist clergy in seeking employment outside the church.[48]

Bishop John Naury Allin of Mississippi was elected in 1973 to a twelve-year term as presiding bishop of the church and was installed in June 1974. The issue of ordaining women, discussed below, has been a major one for him and the church during the seventies.

The headquarters of the Episcopal Church is 815 Second Avenue, New York, New York 10017. Its archives are located in Austin, Texas.

Order and Organization of the Episcopal Church

The Episcopal Church has the three traditional Anglican orders of deacon, priest, and bishop. These orders have been discussed at length in the preceding chapter.

The issue of ordaining women to the priesthood has caused great conflict in the Episcopal Church in recent years. The ramifications of this problem within the Anglican communion have also been discussed above.

While not directly related to the ordination of women, the question of seating women as lay delegates in the House of Deputies in a sense foreshadowed the issue of women's ordination. While the House of Deputies (which, together with the House of Bishops, composes the General Convention) for the first time permitted a woman to be seated as a deputy in 1946, the convention refused a request to interpret the word "layman" in church law to include women as well as men. In 1949 the House of Deputies declined to seat four women. In 1961 the house refused by an overwhelming vote to approve an amendment to the constitution that would have changed the word "layman" to "lay person."[49] In 1967 the General Convention accepted a constitutional amendment that permitted women delegates to serve in the House of Deputies; at the time most diocesan canons permitted women to serve on vestries in local parishes. In 1970 this constitutional change was ratified for the second time as required, and women served in the House of Deputies for the first time. At this convention it was also agreed to permit women to be ordained as deacons in the church.

Five years earlier, in 1965, members of the Church of the Holy Spirit in Salinas, California apparently became the first Episcopalian communicants in the United States to receive communion from a woman. The previous year the church changed canon law to say that women were "ordered" deaconesses by a bishop, instead of "appointed." The bishop of this diocese, James A. Pike, proposed to ordain an active deaconess, Mrs. Phyllis Edwards, to the diaconate. Before this step occurred Mrs. Edwards, a widow, distributed the bread and wine of Communion that the church's rector had consecrated at the previous service.[50]

In 1973 the General Convention of the Episcopal Church faced the issue of women's ordination head-on. While approving for three more years the use of *Services for Trial Use,* commonly called the Green Book, thereby moving ahead on revision of the Book of Common Prayer, the convention rejected a resolution authorizing the ordination of women as priests. At an open hearing female deacons were among the speakers favoring the move (the word "deaconess" had been dropped in 1970), while others warned that the ordination of women would damage ecumenical talks with both the Orthodox and Roman Catholic traditions. The complicated voting procedure in the House of Deputies may have contributed to the defeat of the measure in that body. Each diocese is authorized a deputation of four clergy and four lay delegates. Any deputation may request a division of the house on any vote, and then each diocese is polled by clergy and lay order. A tie vote of 2 to 2 in either the clergy or lay delegation automatically counts as a negative vote. On the roll call on the ordination measure, 50 clergy delegations voted Yes, 43 No, and 20 were divided, while 49 lay delegations voted in the affirmative, 37 negatively, and 26 were divided. Twenty of the twenty-four female deacons who would have been eligible for ordination in January of 1974 attended the convention. The proposal to ordain women also had been defeated in 1970 by the House of Deputies, while the bishops supported women's ordination in unofficial votes in 1972 and 1974. At the same General Convention in 1973 when the House of Deputies rejected the proposal for the second time, Bishop John Naury Allin of Mississippi was elected as presiding bishop for a twelve-year term by the House of Bishops, and the House of Deputies ratified the election by the required two-thirds vote. The post has been elective since 1926.[51]

Less than a year after the 1973 General Convention, three retired

Episcopal bishops and a bishop from Costa Rica ordained eleven women deacons as priests in a highly publicized ceremony in North Philadelphia. The ordinations occurred in July 1974. In an extraordinary meeting on August 14-15 the House of Bishops declared the ordinations invalid, since they were performed contrary to canon law, which required approval of the bishops and the standing committees of the candidates' dioceses. But the bishops endorsed in principle the admission of women to the priesthood.

On April 30, 1975, the Reverend William A. Wendt, rector of the Episcopal Church of St. Stephen and the Incarnation in Washington, D.C., was formally tried in a church court on the charge of having failed "to reverently obey his bishop and follow his godly admonitions." The bishop of Washington, William F. Creighton, had written to Wendt "inhibiting" Alison Cheek, one of the eleven women ordained in 1974, from presiding at a service of Holy Communion on November 10 in the church where Wendt was rector. Supported by his vestry and apparently a large majority of the congregation, Wendt went ahead with plans. Tried before a five-member court of three priests and two communicant lawyers, one male and one female, the court case featured lay theologian and lawyer William String-fellow as Wendt's lawyer and E. Tillman Stirling as church advocate. Wendt insisted that he had to follow his conscience and had not invited Alison Cheek flippantly. As a result of the trial, Wendt was formally admonished by Bishop Creighton for disobeying a "godly admonition" not to permit an uncanonically ordained person to celebrate Communion in the parish, and was warned not to repeat the action. In May 1975 Peter Beebe, the rector of Christ Church in Oberlin, Ohio was tried and convicted on a similar charge.[52] Meanwhile, late in 1975 the House of Bishops voted 115 to 17 to censure the three retired bishops, Robert L. DeWitt, Daniel Corrigan, and Edward R. Welles, who participated in the ordination of the eleven female priests the year before in Philadelphia. The house also censured Bishop George W. Barrett, who ordained four women to the priesthood in September 1975 in Washington D.C.[53]

In a joint statement on the ordination of women late in 1975, members of the U.S. Anglican-Roman Catholic Consultation (ARC) declared that a decision by either church to ordain women would not bring an end to their dialogue. But early in 1976 the U.S. Episcopal-Eastern Orthodox Consultation issued a joint statement indicating that no agreement had been reached on the issue of women's ordination. The Orthodox members warned that if the Anglican communion took the decisive action of admitting women to the priesthood and the episcopate, the issue would involve not only a point of church discipline but the basis of the Christian faith. The Episcopalian members suggested that the question of women's ordination necessitated "a willingness to be led into a new perception of the truth and fidelity to the basic tradition of the faith."[54]

As part of the pressure exerted on the General Convention preparing to meet in 1976, four unofficial Episcopal publications and six organizations issued an open letter to Episcopal bishops stating that they "will refuse to recognize the validity" of the convention to authorize the ordination of women as priests. Signers included the editor of *The Living Church,* Carroll Simcox, and the president of the American Church Union, Albert J. DuBois.[55]

Persons favoring the ordination of women were bouyed by the decision of the General Convention's leadership to submit the issue first to the House of Bishops in 1976 and then to the House of Deputies. At one point, sixty-seven bishops cosponsored enabling legislation favoring women's ordination.[56] The General Convention met in September in Minneapolis, Minnesota. The House of Bishops voted 95 to 61 (with 2 abstentions) favoring the ordination of women, while in the House of Deputies the vote was 64 to 49 among laymen and 60 to 54 among clergy delegations.

The beginning of the new year brought a rash of "regular" ordinations of females in 1977. On New Year's Day, Jacqueline Means became the first "regularly" ordained female priest, ordained by Bishop Donald J. Davis in Indianapolis at the request of Bishop John P. Craine, who was ill. Another female was ordained on January 2 in Washington, D.C., and a third on January 3 in the diocese of New York. One of the fifteen irregularly ordained women priests, Nancy Witting, had her orders recognized in Newark, New Jersey. A black female was ordained as well in Washington, D.C., and an Episcopal nun, Sister Mary Michael Simpson, was also ordained. The first self-acknowledged lesbian to become a priest, Ellen Marie Barrett, was ordained by Bishop Paul Moore of New York City. It was expected that about forty women would be ordained by the end of January, while a number of the previously ordained fifteen women would participate in services publicly recognizing their priestly orders.[57] In October 1977 the Reverend Alison Palmer administered Holy Communion in a public service in Manchester, England, becoming the first woman to administer Communion publicly in the Church of England. Reportedly a secret plan led to the occasion in Manchester, which was repeated in Newcastle where she was invited by the church council. Both of the British archbishops, who reportedly favored ordination for women, were said to be privately unhappy, but a number of Anglican clergy and officials immediately denounced the action.[58]

Response to the General Convention's approval of the ordination of women followed swiftly as 1976 ended. The council of the unofficial American Church Union called for a "Council of those clergymen and laymen who remain faithful to the Episcopal Church as historically constituted." On December 1-2, 1976, 250 persons including sixteen bishops met in Chicago, Illinois to work at setting up "a supportive ecclesial entity *within* the Episcopal Church" in view of the convention's decision. Twelve of the sixteen bishops were among the signers of two documents, entitled "Evangelical and Catholic Covenant" (which affirmed "the tradition of male priesthood ordained by the Father in his choice of his Son, The One High Priest") and "Statement of Action" (which pledged continued fellowship with Anglicans throughout the world and "increased fellowship with other churches of the Apostolic ministry"). Several weeks earlier the Fellowship of Concerned Churchmen, a coalition of sixteen groups and publications, met in Nashville, Tennessee, and issued a statement declaring that "it is impossible for Episcopalians who are determined to keep the faith whole and entire to remain in communion with the Protestant Episcopal Church." The fellowship scheduled a congress to convene in St. Louis, Missouri, on September 14-16, 1977, to delimit the "spiritual principles and ecclesial structure of the Continuing Episcopal Church."[59]

Breakaway groups and two "shadow dioceses" were formed before the September meeting in St. Louis. One diocese was called the Diocese of the Holy Trinity and the other the Diocese of San Francisco. Retired Bishop Albert A. Chambers of Springfield, Illinois, the president of Anglicans United, confirmed about twenty-five people in the Los Angeles area, including four priests suspended by the bishop of the Los Angeles diocese, as members of the new diocese of the North American Province of the Holy Catholic and Apostolic Church, the diocese of the Holy Trinity. Opposition focused on the ordination of women and the revision of the Prayer Book. The first congregation to secede was St. Mary's in Denver, Colorado; there were also four parishes in Los Angeles (of 150 in the diocese) as well as others in Boulder City, Nevada and Mountain Home, Arkansas. A number of priests felt impelled to leave their dioceses and in some cases also their parishes, and a few reportedly converted to Roman Catholicism and the Eastern Orthodox faith. Anglo-Catholics or "High Church" Episcopalians appeared to make up the majority of those interested in seceding. Among the groups dissenting especially on the issue of women's ordination, but pledged to remaining in the church and opposing the changes, were the hierarchically oriented Evangelical and Catholic Mission, and the Coalition for the Apostolic Ministry.[60]

About 1,750 registrants, including 350 clergymen, attended the Congress of Concerned Churchmen in St. Louis, Missouri on September 14-16, 1976. The meeting was called by a coalition of conservative groups, then fifteen in number. A planning session for the congress occurred in July in Estes Park, Colorado. One of the planners was the Reverend George Clendenin of Glendale, California, who indicated that the decision had been made to ban Presiding Bishop John M. Allin from attending the meeting. By mid-July approximately fifty Episcopal congregations, including about sixteen established parishes and thirty-five missionary congregations, had split from the parent denomination. The planners indicated in July that the primary focus of conservative discontent was official church acceptance of policies undermining the Christian family, including the ordination of women priests and the ordination of a self-avowed lesbian.[61]

Presiding Bishop Allin showed up uninvited at the congress, along with a number of other bishops who indicated that they were present not to speak but to observe and listen. Speeches during the three days of the un-official gathering provided insight into the kinds of grievances the conserva-tives, largely Anglo-Catholics, felt. One key issue seemed to have been a loss of confidence in the church's bishops. Also mentioned were the bishops' refusal to discipline Bishop James Pike and his heresies in 1967; the ordina-tion of an avowed lesbian; the alleged liberal brand of leadership of former Presiding Bishop John Hines and the General Convention's programs to secure money for "militant, radical, secular groups"; the supposed in-ability of Presiding Bishop Allin to provide leadership; the alleged un-orthodox theology of Bishop Jack Spong, and the church's ecumenical flirta-tions with churches that are not "catholic and apostolic," such as the Church of South India; and the church's positions on homosexuality, adultery, divorce, remarriage, and abortion. Seminars were conducted on how congrega-tions might seek to retain church property, on pension plans, and other organizational matters. Another item of great concern was the Episcopal Church's revision of the 1928 Prayer Book. Reportedly persons attended from nearly all the church's ninety-two dioceses as well as dioceses of the Anglican Churches of Canada, Puerto Rico and Hawaii. Presiding Bishop James P. Dees of the Anglican Orthodox Church advertised his availability for telephone conversations or meetings with any of the congress's par-ticipants. On the final day of the meeting the "Affirmation of St. Louis" was read by Perry Laukhuff, president of the Fellowship of Concerned Church-men. The six-page single-spaced statement outlined the theory and practice of a "continuing Anglican Church," tentatively named the "Anglican Church of North America." Drafted by leaders of the fellowship, the statement was not scheduled for formal debate or action by the congress participants. It declared that the Episcopal Church and the Anglican Church of Canada "have departed from Christ's One, Holy, Catholic and Apostolic Church" through their recent approval of women priests and other changes. According to the "Affirmation" these parent bodies were "lawless" and "schismatic," not the dissenters. "In this gathering witness of Anglicans and Episcopalians, we continue to be what we are. We do nothing new. We form no new body, but continue as Anglicans and Episcopalians." The "Affirmation" urged dissent-ing conservatives to work in months to follow to gather congregations, form dioceses, and elect nominees for bishops. Then conservative Episcopal bishops would step forward and convene the delegates to institute a new church body. There was some dispute as to whether the three bishops re-quired to consecrate a bishop were or would be available, although reportedly Bishop Albert A. Chambers, retired from the Springfield, Illinois diocese, and Bishop Clarence J. Haden, Jr., of the diocese of Northern California signified their willingness to conduct a consecration. At the congress members of the diocese of the Holy Trinity selected as a candidate for their bishop the Reverend James O. Mote of Denver, Colorado, whose parish was the first to break from the Episcopal Church after the General Convention in 1976. The "Affirmation" also indicated that the proposed new body would have a three-branch Holy Synod composed of episcopal, clerical, and lay members under the presidency of the church's primate; concurrence of all three branches would be required. It also pledged that the new body would not join the World Council of Churches or other such councils, nor would it participate in COCU. Doctrinally the "Affirmation" pledged dissenters to the Sacred Scriptures, the Nicene Creed, the Apostoles' Creed, the Creed of St. Athanasius, and seven sacraments. It was hoped that the convening convention of the new church would meet in 1978. One leader of the seceders indicated that as many as 250 of the 7,192 parishes in the Episcopal Church would join the group by the end of 1978, while another claimed that the movement represented a half million of the 2.8-million-member church. According to James E. Adams of the *St. Louis Post Dispatch,* "a key sociological factor in the conservative movement is that a significant number of the rank and file are not 'hereditary' Episcopalians, but came from mainline Protestant churches as adults 20 years ago when the Episcopal Church was more traditional in orientation." He added in an article in the paper on September 18, 1977, that "this intensifies their sense of betrayal at the current liberal regime."[62]

In October 1977 the House of Bishops met in session in Florida. Approximately sixty women had been ordained as priests since the General Convention approved women's ordination in 1976. Reportedly by October 3, eighteen parishes around the nation had voted to leave the body, in addition to a number of newly formed mission churches. In his opening speech to the bishops Presiding Bishop Allin offered to resign if his fellow bishops were unwilling to accept his outright opposition to the ordaining of women as priests. "To date I remain unconvinced that women can be priests," he asserted. "If it is determined by prayerful authority that this limitation prevents one from serving as the Presiding Bishop of this church, I am willing to resign the office." He indicated that "my mind holds no question or doubt as to the rights and abilities of women to be elders, rulers, executives, generals, presidents, judges or queens." But, he emphasized, "I remain unconvinced that women can become priests." After informal assurances were given that his resignation was not required, the bishops passed a resolution saying that he was entitled to hold office despite his dissent from the church's stand in favor of ordaining women. The bishops insisted that Bishop Allin's views not interfere with his duty to uphold "the law of the church and the action of the General Convention in his official actions." The bishops also chose to pass a resolution that "deplores and repudiates" the efforts of retired Bishop Albert A. Chambers to aid the cause of separatists, and appealed to Chambers to refrain from dissenting activities in the future. The body chose not to use the word "censure" in the resolution. It also approved the formation of a special group, the "Committee to Restore Relationships," that would offer "means of healing" with the "distressed and the separated members of this church." The bishops refused to respond to Presiding Bishop Allin's suggestion that the church might help legitimate a hierarchy for the dissenters. In other major action, the bishops gave nearly unanimous sanction to the right of bishops to refuse to ordain women and to bar female priests ordained in other dioceses from serving in their dioceses. They also declared that practicing homosexuals should not be ordained to the priesthood or joined in church marriage rites, but refused by a vote of 62 to 48 to censure Bishop Moore, Jr., of the New York diocese for ordaining an avowed lesbian. The "conscience" clause that affirmed the right of every Episcopalian to remain in good standing while opposing women's ordination opened the way for Bishop Allin's continued service as presiding bishop and provided a powerful argument to counter the claims of the dissenters who met two weeks earlier in St. Louis. The basic issue of women's ordination was not directly addressed; one bishop raised the possibility of reaffirming the General Convention's decision on women's ordination, but the proposal was not taken up.[63]

The basic structure of the Episcopal Church's organization is set forth in a set of brief constitutional articles adopted by the convention in 1789 and amended from time to time by other conventions. Most of these articles concern the government of the national church and its dioceses, regulating such matters as the composition and work of the General Convention, the erection of dioceses and missionary districts, the bishop's jurisdiction, and ecclesiastical courts. Constitutional provisions may be amended only when two successive conventions take action. The constitution leaves considerable freedom for amplification in the church's canon law and local diocesan regulations. Among the constitutional provisions is an article enjoining the use of the authorized and official Book of Common Prayer.[64]

The church's canon laws are the ecclesiastical law governing the life of the Episcopal Church. *General canons* are enacted by the General Convention to apply to all dioceses and missionary districts. *Diocesan canons* are passed by diocesan conventions to apply only within the pertinent diocese. Many of the general canons have their origin in the early church. Two groups of these canons govern the general ministry of the church, another regulates ecclesiastical organization and administration, and a fourth group concerns aspects of worship, supplementing rubrics of worship provided in the Book of Common Prayer.[65]

The church's national legislative synod is the *General Convention*. Meeting every three years or in special session, it amends the constitution, adopts budgets, prepares the church's national program, enacts, repeals or amends general canons, authorizes changes in the Prayer Book or hymnal, admits new dioceses, and receives reports from official commissions, among other things. Like the federal Congress, it is composed of two houses, the *House of Bishops* and the *House of Deputies*, the latter composed of eight elected representatives (four priests and four laypersons) from each diocese. The houses deliberate and vote separately, but all acts of the convention must pass both houses. Together the two houses may have nearly one thousand delegates. Upon specific request the House of Deputies may be called upon to "vote by orders," which is at the same time a "vote by dioceses." In this process each diocese has one vote among its clerical deputies and one among its laypersons; a measure must secure concurrence of both orders and a majority of all votes cast in each to pass. A vote divided equally is regarded as a negative vote. Some critics claim that this provision, as well as the fact that dioceses have equal representation without regard for communicant strength, unnecessarily restricts the democratic process, but others insist that it assures that serious matters will pass only if they command a large measure of support. At each meeting the House of Deputies elects a president. The presiding bishop presides in the House of Bishops, which usually also meets at least once in the interim between General Conventions.[66]

The *presiding bishop* is elected by the House of Bishops. His election for a twelve-year term must be ratified by at least a two-thirds vote in the House of Deputies.

The *National Council* administers the General Convention's program between meetings. It is an executive body selected by a number of elements in the church, including the General Convention. The presiding bishop is chief executive officer of the General Convention. His office is ordinarily the point of official contact with other Anglican churches or provinces, and he exercises jurisdiction possessed by the House of Bishops over the missionary districts of the church. Since 1943 he has been required upon election to resign his diocesan jurisdiction.[67]

The basic organizational unit in the Episcopal Church is the diocese. The diocesan convention chooses the bishop, whose election must be approved by a two-thirds majority of the standing committees of the other dioceses and a two-thirds majority of the bishops. Annual diocesan conventions, consisting of the bishop, the clergy, and lay representatives from each parish, regulate the affairs of the diocese and elect clergy and laypersons for the General Convention. They may also elect assistant bishops, called *suffragan bishops*. For the bishop to ordain a person to the priesthood, at various stages written approval must be received from a priest and the vestry of a parish, and the standing committee of the dioceses (including both clergy and laypersons) must give consent after evidence is received from examining chaplains and physicians. Bishops are not moved from one diocese to another, and serve until retirement.

Dioceses are collected into geographical units called *provinces*. Since these entities do not have archbishops, they apparently have little corporate consciousness.

The local parish church is not ordinarily conceived in geographical terms, although technically it is a geographical division. The parish is a community of people who worship together. It is legally and canonically in union with the diocese. The elected vestry handles the financial affairs of the local church, selects the rector, and performs other functions.

Episcopal canon law governs the ministry of men and women who carry out their vocation to the religious life in various religious communities. More than a dozen orders for women engage in a wide variety of activities including operation of homes for aged persons, retreat houses, hospitals, and convalescent centers. The religious orders also frequently engage in educational activities, as well as regular prayer and worship. Nearby an equal number of religious orders for men conduct religious retreats, preach parochial missions, carry on educational work, pray, and study. The best-known community of men is the Society of St. John the Evangelist, popularly known as the Cowley Fathers.[68]

Creed, Liturgy, Worship, and Doctrine of the Episcopal Church

The creed, liturgy, worship, and doctrine of the Episcopal Church must be understood in the broad context of the independence of the Church of England from Rome in the Reformation era and that church's subsequent developments and expansion, as well as its earlier history in the ancient and medieval Western church. Probably no better way is available for understanding the worship and doctrine of the Episcopal Church than to focus on the Prayer Book, which occupies the central place in organized worship life.

The first Standard Edition of the Prayer Book, printed "By Order of the General Convention," was issued in 1793, followed by Standard Editions of 1822, 1832, 1845, and 1871. The first Standard Book appeared in 1892, and the second Standard Book in 1928. The text of the book remained almost unchanged from the first Standard Edition until the first Standard Book of 1892. Despite the fact that the first Standard Edition appeared in 1793, the most important American editions of the Book of Common Prayer have been those of 1789, 1892, and 1928 inasmuch as the 1789 book was essentially the 1793 first Standard Edition.[69]

In 1973 the General Convention asked the Standing Liturgical Commission to present a draft of a proposed revision of the Book of Common Prayer for the next convention's consideration. In the interim the commission completed its review and revision and presented the General Convention in 1976 with *The Draft Proposed Book of Common Prayer and Other Rites and Ceremonies of the Church* (New York: The Church Hymnal Corporation, 1976). The convention adopted the *Draft Proposed Book* with amendments by impressive majorities. The vote in the House of Deputies was by more than 95 percent in the clerical order and 80 percent in the lay order, with near unanimity in the House of Bishops. In a separate resolution the convention authorized the alternative use of the *Proposed Book of Common Prayer* during the interim until 1979. If accepted without change by the General Convention in 1979, it will become the established Book of Common Prayer of the Episcopal Church.[70]

Because it is difficult to interpret liturgical texts, it is not possible to state *the* theology of any of the existing Anglican Prayer Books, including the *Proposed Book of Common Prayer*. But the Standing Liturgical Commission of the Episcopal Church provided assistance when it outlined the four criteria that had guided it with respect to the essential qualities of doctrine, discipline, and worship in the *Proposed Book*. The first norm for judgment was the 1928 American Prayer Book and the long tradition of Prayer Books behind it. Another was the effort to meet adequately the worshiping needs of contemporary Episcopalians in America. Another set of criteria was provided by the pre-Reformation liturgical tradition; this period of history offered worship resources that were incorporated into the *Proposed Book,* including the provision for applying ashes on Ash Wednesday, the procession with palms on Palm Sunday, and other features. The last stated criterion was that both relevance and tradition were brought under the demands of the Gospel as recorded in Scripture.[71]

Among other things, a brief survey of the contents of the *Proposed Book* indicates that two separate rites, one with traditional language and the other with contemporary language, are offered for Morning and Evening Prayer and the Holy Eucharist. The *Proposed Book* does not print the proper lessons in order that the new three-year common lectionary (Roman Catholic, Anglican, Lutheran, Methodist, and Reformed) could be used and so that no one of the nine authorized Bible translations would be given arbitrary preference. A new section of the *Proposed Book* contains special liturgies for Ash Wednesday, Palm Sunday, Maunday Thursday, Good Friday, Holy Saturday, and the Great Vigil of Easter. For the first time pastoral offices have been provided for Commitment to Christian Service, Blessing of a Civil Marriage, an Order for Marriage, Reconciliation of a Penitent, Ministration at the Time of Death, and an Order of Burial; the 1928 Prayer Book as well as the *Proposed Book* include pastoral offices of Confirmation, Celebration, and Blessing of a Marriage, Thanksgiving for the Birth or Adoption of a Child, Ministration to the Sick, and Burial of the Dead. The *Proposed Book* also contains a completely new catechism. While the 1929 Prayer Book included only the Thirty-Nine Articles, the *Proposed Book* contains a section entitled "Historical Documents of the Church (including the Articles of Religion)" that contains historical documents. They are the Chalcedonian Definition of the Union of the Divine and Human Natures in the Person of Christ, the Athanasian Creed, the Preface to the first Book of Common Prayer (1549), the Articles of Religion (the Thirty-Nine Articles), and the Chicago-Lambeth Quadrilateral.[72]

Among the general features of the *Proposed Book*, perhaps the most striking departure from the 1928 Prayer Book is the use of contemporary language in Rite II services and throughout the rest of the book. Old English forms have been revised, and in most cases sexist language eliminated, although each case was considered on its own merit. In addition, the *Proposed Book* provides more variety of worship for the Episcopal Church than earlier editions. Many of the rubrics are designed to provide essential information without requiring compliance. Rite I of Morning Prayer and the celebration of the Eucharist are nearly identical with the 1928 Prayer Book; simple orders are provided for celebrating Eucharist, marriage, and burial as well as more elaborate services. Another general feature is the book's emphasis on the maximum participation of worshipers in the various rites and services. In addition, the *Proposed Book* explicitly moves the Holy Communion to a more prominent place among the services of the church and incorporates most of the agreed versions of liturgical texts created by the International Consultation on English Texts.[73]

Among the prominent theological emphases in the *Proposed Book* are creation, redemption, sin and penitence, Christian hope, and Christian community. The *Proposed Book* brings the doctrine of creation to new expression in several ways, including new canticles in Morning Prayer and the recognition of God's work of re-creation in the new eucharistic prayers. The order for holy baptism also shows a more positive attitude toward creation. In reference to redemption, the prayer of consecration in the 1928 Prayer Book discredited Christ's death as a "sacrifice, oblation, and satisfaction," and his work as "our redemption." The new eucharistic prayers use a notably larger supply of images to tell of God's act in Christ, including "reconcile us to you," "Savior and Redeemer of the World," "deliver us from evil" (victory), "made us worthy to stand before you," "to open for us the way of freedom and peace," "we are healed," "and made a new people . . . ," "destroy death" (victory), "made the whole creation new," "sanctification," "redemption," and "salvation." The tone of unrelieved penitence and unworthiness found in early Prayer Books was mollified somewhat in the revisions of 1892 and 1928, and later even the requirement to use the Ten Commandments at least once a month with the Communion service was widely disregarded. The *Proposed Book* retains many of the expressions of penitence found in the 1928 edition and for the first time in any English or American Prayer Book includes as well a form for the reconciliation of a penitent. It also uses one of the striking recoveries of the liturgical movement, namely, giving greater prominence to an emphasis on Christian hope. In addition, the exchange of peace found in every Eucharist and the greater stress laid on the Eucharist are consonant with the liturgical movement's emphasis on Christian community. While the Standing Liturgical Commission recommended in 1967 that the words "and the son" (*filioque*) should be omitted from the Nicene Creed, the General Convention decided to retain the words in the *Proposed Book*.[74]

The church-year calendar of the *Proposed Book* emphasizes Sunday as the weekly remembrance of the Lord's resurrection, giving precedence to Sundays as feasts of Jesus Christ except for major saints' days. The Sundays "after Trinity" have become the Sundays "after Pentecost" to stress the Christian's life in the Spirit. Seven "red-letter" saints' days for saints of the

New Testament have been added, and for the first time in an American Prayer Book the calendar makes provision for a large number of "black-letter" days whose observance is optional. According to Charles Price, the distinction between these days is comparable "to the distinction between canonical scripture and other works in which believers sense the Spirit of God to be moving."[75]

Heightened emphasis on the seasons of the church year, one of the marked changes in the 1928 revision, has been retained and deepened in the *Proposed Book*'s Morning and Evening Prayer and elsewhere. The new offices, for Noonday and Compline, have been added. Human sinfulness is vividly acknowledged in a number of the prayers in the *Proposed Book*'s section of collects. One of the new prayers is the Collect for Independence Day. The collect's opening, "in whose Name the founders of this country won liberty for themselves and us, and lit the torch of freedom for nations then unborn," observes the worldwide significance of the American Revolution.[76]

In earlier drafts of the initiatory rite of holy baptism, the Standing Liturgical Commission's service of baptism with the laying on of hands, represented a sharp break with traditional Anglican practice, abandoning confirmation as a separate rite. The decision to drop confirmation as a separate rite proved impossible to sustain; it seemed necessary to provide a special rite through which an adult could make an individual, mature commitment by reaffirming baptismal vows. According to Price, "confirmation" as a term is now reserved "for the first time a person who grows to maturity under the discipline of the Episcopal Church makes commitment to Christ by a formal reaffirmation of baptismal vows in the presence of a bishop." On other occasions as well persons are given opportunity to receive the strengthening gifts of the Spirit through a special rite. Two provisions have been made: for a person joining the Episcopal Church, in the presence of a bishop; and when a person enters a new phase of life with Christ. The two rites have been titled "reception" and "reaffirmation." The Standing Liturgical Commission and the Theological and Prayer Book committees of the House of Bishops reached agreement on a number of points concerning baptism and postbaptismal affirmation of vows. Among them are the following regarding baptism:

1. There is one, and only one, unrepeatable act of Christian initiation, which makes a person a member of the Body of Christ.

2. The essential element of Christian initiation is baptism by water and Spirit, in the name of the Holy Trinity, in response to repentance and faith.

3. Christian initiation is normally administered in a liturgical rite that also includes the laying on of hands, consignation (with or without Chrism), prayer for the gift of the Holy Spirit, reception by the Christian community, joining the eucharistic fellowship, and commissioning for the Christian mission. When the bishop is present, it is expected that he will preside at the rite.

Regarding postbaptismal affirmation of vows, it was agreed, among other things, that

1. It is both appropriate and pastorally desirable that affirmation should be received by a bishop as representing the diocese and the world-wide church, and that the bishop should recall the applicants to their Christian mission, and, by a laying on of hands transmit his blessing, with a prayer for the strengthening graces.

2. The rite embodying such affirmations should in no sense be understood as being a "completion of Holy Baptism," nor as being a condition precedent to the Holy Communion, nor as conveying a special status of Church membership.

3. The occasion of the affirming of baptismal vows and obligations that were made by godparents on one's behalf in infancy is a significant and unrepeatable event. It is one's "Confirmation Day."

4. The rite itself, however, is suitable, and should be available for other occasions in the lives of Christian people. . . .

As a consequence of these agreements, the *Proposed Book* contains no rubric suggesting that a baptized person is not eligible to receive Holy Communion. However, it is a judgment of the House of Bishops that infants should not receive Communion until they have reached an "appropriate age." Omitted is a rubric from the Book of Common Prayer that "there shall be none admitted to the Holy Communion, until such time as he be confirmed or ready and desirous of being confirmed." In sum, the *Proposed Book* stresses the rite of baptism and the reunification of the two parts of the initiatory rite, namely, water baptism in the name of the Trinity, and the laying on of hands and consignation (with or without Chrism) with a prayer for the gift of the Spirit.[77]

The full title of the eucharistic service in the *Proposed Book*, "The Holy Eucharist: The Liturgy for the Proclamation of the Word of God and Celebration of the Holy Communion," formally recognized the two parts of the service. Disuse of the title "Lord's Supper" has led to its being dropped; more commonly used are Holy Communion and Eucharist. Old Testament lessons are incorporated in both Rite I and Rite II of the Eucharist; this was not true in the older American Prayer Books. The offering has been moved to a position just before the Prayer of Consecration, the Great Thanksgiving; and the Breaking of Bread moved from the Prayer of Consecration to a place just before Communion. Rite II provides four eucharistic prayers, one of which is the work of an unofficial committee of Roman Catholic, Episcopal, Presbyterian, Lutheran, and Methodist scholars. The Invocation, or *Epiklesis*, that part of the Great Thanksgiving in which the Holy Spirit is invoked, in American Prayer Books has traditionally followed the *anamnesis,* as in Orthodox liturgies. In this the American books followed the Scottish Prayer Book of 1637, and the *Proposed Book* continues the practice. While the 1928 Prayer

Book prohibited the reservation of the sacrament, the *Proposed Book* makes provision for this reservation in two situations: for the communion of parishioners who are sick or shut-in, and for the communion of a congregation when a priest's services cannot be obtained. Permission for a bishop to authorize a deacon to distribute Holy Communion from the reserved sacrament if a priest's services cannot be obtained was first granted by the House of Bishops in 1965.[78]

For the first time the purposes of marriage are stated in the pastoral office of marriage. The three stated purposes are: for the husband and wife's "mutual joy"; "for the help and comfort given one another in prosperity and adversity"; and "when it is God's will, for the procreation of children and their nurture in the knowledge and love of the Lord." In the Reconciliation of a Penitent, the two services offer liturgical forms for private confession. One form of absolution is a prayer that Christ will absolve the penitent of sins; the other states, "by the authority committed to me, I absolve you from all your sins." The services that provide ministry to the sick retain a penitential interpretation of illness where appropriate, but the leading accent is the power of God to restore health and Christ's healing work as a sign of God's Kingdom.[79]

In the catechism the *Proposed Book* answers the question "Who are the ministers of the Church?" with this sentence: "The ministers of the Church are lay persons, bishops, priests, and deacons." Thus ordained ministers are persons who express and enable the ministry of God's people. The *Proposed Book* speaks of the "ordination" of these three orders. It is required that lay persons and priests present a bishop for ordination, and that at least one lay person and one priest present a priest or deacon for ordination. Each of these ordination rites lacks the kind of imperative statement that is found in the 1928 Prayer Book; in each rite the consecration formula is a prayer accompanied by the laying on of hands, conforming to traditional Anglican teaching about ordination.[80]

The account of the office of the bishop is much fuller in the *Proposed Book* than the 1928 Prayer Book. He is to be "one with the apostles in proclaiming Christ's resurrection and interpreting the Gospel," and should "guard the faith, unity, and discipline of the Church." Celebrating and providing for the sacraments, ordaining, and being a "faithful pastor and wholesome example" to Christ's flock, he is exhorted to follow Christ. In addition, he is to be fervent in prayer and the study of the Scripture, to enlighten minds and stir consciences by proclaiming the Gospel, to encourage and enable others in their ministries, to participate in the government of the whole church, to be a pastor to clergy, and to have compassion on all. According to the Examination, the priest is to "work as a pastor, priest, and teacher, together with your bishop and fellow presbyters, and to take your share in the councils of the Church." Proclaiming the Gospel, fashioning life according to its precepts, loving and serving people, preaching, declaring forgiveness, sharing in the administration of the sacraments, the priest is to respect and be guided by the bishop's direction, study the Scriptures and other things that will make for a more able minister, and persevere in prayer. The priest is explicitly enjoined to function as a councilor with the bishop in the church's governance. Deacons are "called to a special ministry of servanthood directly under the bishop," according to the *Proposed Book*. They are to serve all, especially the poor, weak, sick and lonely, to study the Scriptures, to make Christ known in word and deed, to "interpret to the Church the needs, concerns, and hopes of the world," to be guided and led by the bishop, and to seek "not their own glory, but the glory of Christ." One new charge has been inserted, namely, "to interpret the world to the Church." Greater stress has also been laid on the deacon as a helping ministry. The *Proposed Book* requires that the bishop give authorization for deacons to baptize infants, and the new rite does not assume that all deacons will be admitted to the priesthood.[81]

The *Proposed Book* allows chapels or churches to be dedicated or consecrated to God even before all of a mortgage is retired, in contrast with the 1928 book. The Psalter has eliminated many masculine nouns where a generic meaning is intended. In the section on Prayers and Thanksgivings, the order of the prayers has been revised. Traditionally Anglican Prayer Books include intercessions for the state, the church, the social order, and finally personal life, in that order. The order in the *Proposed Book* is world, church, national life, social order, natural order, family and personal life. Among the new prayers are those for persons who suffer for the sake of conscience, a prayer for cities, one for towns and rural areas, one for those who are alone, and another for victims of addiction. A prayer for enemies is contained for the first time in an English or American Prayer Book.[82]

The catechism is a new compendium of 112 questions and answers that is much larger than the 1928 Prayer Book of 25. The Outline of Faith includes questions on human nature; God as Father, Son and Spirit; the Old and New Covenants; sin and redemption; the Scriptures; prayer; and Christian hope. Also included are sections on the creed, prayer and worship (with the Lord's Prayer), the Ten Commandments, and the sacraments. Baptism and the Eucharist are the "great sacraments" or "sacraments of the Gospel," while the five "other sacramental rites" are clearly distinguished from them. These sacramental rites include confirmation, ordination, holy matrimony, reconciliation of a penitent, and anointing of the sick. The catechism describes the basic teachings of the Episcopal Church. According to the accompanying rubric, it

is primarily intended for use by parish priests, deacons, and lay catechists, to give an outline for instruction. It is a commentary on the creeds, but is not meant to be a complete statement of belief and practice; rather, it is a point for departure for the teacher, and it is cast in the traditional question and answer form for easy reference.[83]

Included in the section titled "Historical Documents of the Church" are the Chalcedonian Definition of the Person of Christ, the Athanasian Creed (which has appeared in all English Prayer Books, but never before in an American Prayer Book), the preface to the first Book of Common Prayer (1549), the Thirty-Nine Articles of Religion, and the Chicago-Lambeth Quadrilateral (1886–1888). Only the Thirty-Nine Articles appeared in the 1928 Prayer Book.[84]

The ecumenical nature of the *Proposed Book* is clear both in the elements it shares with the Roman Catholic, other Anglican, and Protestant churches (liturgical texts, common lectionary, and one eucharistic prayer), and the elements that have been adopted from Orthodox liturgies. Among the latter are the reunification of the rites of initiation, the opening acclamations of the Eucharist, concluding anthems of the burial service, and other items.[85]

The Anglican Church of Canada

Until 1955 this church was known as "The Church of England in Canada." Its close relationship with the Church of England was due in part to the fact that at the time of the American Revolution many British loyalists fled from the American colonies to Canada. In addition, during the nineteenth century Britain dominated the area that became Canada.

The earliest permanent Anglican presence in Nova Scotia was a congregation founded in Halifax soon after the town was settled in 1749. Anglican chaplains had accompanied British expeditions in Nova Scotia since 1710. Missionaries of the Society for the Propagation of the Gospel in Foreign Parts (S.P.G.) worked zealously among the inhabitants of Halifax and the population that soon settled in Lunenburg and other areas. Some of the settlers were New Englanders, especially near the Bay of Fundy. The first provincial legislature established the Church of England in 1758 but still allowed Protestant dissenters to function. By 1775 the province (including New Brunswick) had nearly 18,000 people; many of the new settlers were Congregationalists, and Anglican privileges were curtailed.[86]

The Island of Saint John (later called Prince Edward Island) secured colonial status in 1769. Five years later an Anglican priest named Theophilus Des Brisay received a royal warrant to serve the parish in Charlottetown, which for a long time was the island's only parish. He was partially supported by public funds, but Roman Catholics and Protestant dissenters were tolerated.

During the American Revolution Nova Scotia was officially aligned with England, and soon as many as 30,000 Loyalists left the American colonies for these undeveloped lands; some continued their journey to England. In 1784 New Brunswick was separated from Nova Scotia. Known as the "Loyalist Province," New Brunswick was more homogeneous than Nova Scotia and made fewer concessions to dissenters. At its first session in 1786 the legislature established the Church of England, and by 1800 six Anglican parishes had been created in major communities.

Set on solving the problem that troubled colonial American Anglicans for so long, eighteen Loyalist clergy met in New York in 1783 to lay plans for a bishop for Nova Scotia. Four years later an Irishman who had been rector of Trinity Church in New York City, Charles Inglis (1734–1816), was consecrated in London as bishop of a diocese that included the Maritimes, Newfoundland, Quebec, and Bermuda. Inglis became the first overseas bishop of the Church of England; the Crown gave him all the authority and power exercised by bishops in England. He began at once to build a strong Episcopal Church as a defense against republicanism, but the serious shortage of clergy complicated matters. In his first visit to the Maritimes in 1788 he found that Anglican services were conducted in ten communities in Nova Scotia, six in New Brunswick, four in Newfoundland, and one on Prince Edward Island. The Anglicans, as well as the Methodists and the Baptists, carried on mission work among the slave and free blacks who had come north from the American colonies. Clearly, Anglicanism could not be established to the exclusion of other denominations already functioning in the area.

The Church of England followed as the British population moved westward. Loyalists who settled in Quebec were the nucleus for new congregations. The "Father of the Anglican Church in Upper Canada," John Stuart, had followed his scattered flock of Loyalists to Montreal in 1781 and continued to work among them there and in areas west of town. He also maintained his interest in Indian mission work. By the end of the eighteenth century churches stood in four centers along the St. Lawrence River, and Stuart was named commissary for the western districts. In 1791 Quebec was officially divided into Upper Canada (the future Ontario) and Lower Canada (the future Quebec). In 1841 Upper Canada became Canada West, and Lower Canada became Canada East. When the Dominion of Canada was formed in 1867, Canada West became the province of Ontario and Canada East the province of Quebec.

In 1793 the major ecclesiastical event for Anglicans in the whole area of Quebec was the consecrating of Jacob Mountain (1749–1825) as bishop of Quebec. Called "Lord Bishop," a title that Inglis had not received, he became a member of the legislative and executive councils of both Upper and Lower Canada. Upper Canada was largely wilderness with population along the upper St. Lawrence, while in Lower Canada the Church of England was a very small minority among the many Roman Catholics, despite official support. Mountain successfully obtained governmental and S.P.G. funds for clergy support; the number of clergy increased from nine to sixty during his long episcopate, which ended in 1825.

In 1867 the Dominion of Canada was formed out of the four provinces of Nova Scotia, New Brunswick, Quebec, and Ontario—soon to be joined by Manitoba, British Columbia, and Prince Edward Island (and much later, in 1949, by Newfoundland). But before the mid-nineteenth century an intense ecclesiastical and political struggle rocked the provinces. Those who wanted some sort of religious establishment found themselves opposed by those committed to freedom of religion and voluntary support of churches. In general the proponents of freedom, voluntaryism, and diversity won the day, although Canada's religious institutions were never so sharply distinguished from other major cultural institutions as in the United States, nor was the image of a "wall of separation" between church and state used as readily.

During the nineteenth century the Church of England enjoyed certain initial advantages in the Atlantic colonies of Nova Scotia, New Brunswick, Prince Edward Island, and Newfoundland. Inglis drew a government salary and after 1808 served in the appointive legislative council of Nova Scotia. The S.P.G. administered an annual parliamentary grant in the province (£13,000 in 1830), while other funds and land-grants also assisted the work. But dissenters reacted vigorously to an English commission's ruling that students at King's College in Windsor had to subscribe to the Thirty-Nine Articles and were to be taught by an all-Anglican faculty. Inglis's son John assumed resident leadership when his father died in 1816, and nine years later he became bishop in the diocese of more than 150 churches. He concentrated much of his effort on promoting Christian knowledge and building educational institutions.

By midcentury it was clear that the privileges of the Church of England in the Atlantic colonies were soon to end. This turn of events followed growth and the division of the huge diocese of Nova Scotia into new dioceses for Newfoundland and Bermuda (1839) and New Brunswick (1845). In the 1820s questions arose in England about the use of parliamentary grants for S.P.G. mission work, and the sums were reduced. In the colonies Anglican clergy had to yield their sole authority to marry. When the new bishop of Nova Scotia was refused a seat in the legislative council in 1851, it was clear that the preferred position of the Church of England was seriously in danger. Establishment ended in New Brunswick six years later. Meanwhile, a new college in Halifax gained strength at the expense of King's College.

Learning the lessons of voluntaryism was not easy for Anglicans in Canada, but between 1837 and 1843 "Church Societies" of laymen and clergy were formed under episcopal leadership in all the Atlantic Colonies. These societies supplemented the financial aid coming from English sources. In addition, the S.P.G. raised endowments in England for the Colonial Bishoprics Fund; the bishops supported by these new endowments were usually High churchmen.

During the first half of the nineteenth century the Church of England continued to grow in Upper and Lower Canada as well, but here too the conflict over establishment and public support reached a fever pitch. Bishop Mountain's hopes for full establishment received a setback when British officials also gave recognition to Roman Catholics. In Lower Canada (later Quebec) the Anglican church was not permitted to collect tithes, since it was expected that sufficient financial support would come from the Clergy Reserves, a tract of 675,000 acres in the area. At first the lands scarcely covered administrative expenses, and as resources grew the congregations of the Church of Scotland insisted on a major share of the revenues. This debate raged for several decades after Mountain died in 1825 and was succeeded by James Stewart, who was more attuned to the Canadian scene.

In Upper Canada (later Ontario), the church's growth came from the iron-willed leadership of John Strachan (1778–1867), a native Scot who in 1827 became archdeacon of York (later called Toronto). He secured a charter for King's College in York which made him president and required that all faculty members be Anglicans, although students had to pass no religious test. Strachan sometimes defended the church too ardently, presenting inaccurate information about Anglican strength as part of a plan to sell off some of the Clergy Reserves to be used as income only for the Church of England. In the 1830s the controversy over the Clergy Reserves intensified in Upper Canada, where nearly 2½ million acres were involved. The religious and secular press and governmental halls in Upper and Lower Canada, as well as in England, were filled with bitter debate. Tension flared when during the last hours of his administration in 1836 the lieutenant-governor, Sir John Colborne, endowed each of forty-four Anglican rectories with 400 acres. Economic and political factors were the primary causes of the rebellion that shook Upper Canada in 1837, but the issue of the Reserves and these rectories were also involved. The commissioner from London investigating the uprising criticized the Anglicans' virtual monopoly of the Reserves despite the fact that they were only about one fifth of the population. Law officers of the Crown disallowed legislation passed in Upper Canada in 1839 providing for the sale of the Reserves and the use of proceeds for religious purposes. After a number of other unsuccessful efforts to settle the problem, finally in 1853 Parliament passed an act allowing for the matter to be settled in Canada. A provincial act in 1854 indicated that it was desirable to remove "all semblance of connection between Church and State," and arranged for the sale of the Reserves to provide life income for those dependent on them, while the remainder of the proceeds would go to municipal public works. The life-income provision brought sizable sums to the Church of England and the Church of Scotland, but the act made all of the churches, including the Church of England, ultimately dependent on voluntary support.

Other organizational plans were laid for the development of an autonomous Anglican church. Strachan, the bishop in Toronto after 1839, invited laymen in 1851 to participate in church government in his diocese. The same year five of the seven bishops of British North America recommended that synods of bishops, clergy, and laymen be formed in each diocese. Strachan presided over the first official diocesan synod in 1856, and the next year the synod elected a bishop for the diocese of Huron, newly formed in the west. Other dioceses were also formed out of what was now Canada West. The church's self-government was finalized by the Crown's naming of Francis Fulford, bishop of Montreal, as metropolitan (or presiding bishop) for the Canadas. The name "The Church of England in Canada" was selected for the provincial synod that included all the dioceses of this province. In 1865 this synod proposed to Canterbury that a "Pan-Anglican Conference of Bishops" be held, a proposal that ultimately led to the first Lambeth Conference.

Mission work among Indians and Anglican settlers even farther west had early beginnings. Founded by Evangelical churchmen in England in 1799, the Church Mission Society helped evangelize Indians in the Hudson Bay and other areas. A diocese was formed in 1849 for the area west of the Great Lakes. The diocese of Rupert's Land, which remained under the jurisdiction of the archbishop of Canterbury and did not become part of the Church of England in Canada until 1893, at one point covered vast areas from the Labrador coast to the Rockies—an expanse about the size of the United States, nearly 3 million square miles. A Scot named Robert Machray (1831–1904) became bishop of Rupert's Land in 1865. Organizing scattered missions as parishes and helping them to become self-supporting, he was unquestionably the outstanding churchman of Canada during the last half of the nineteenth century. He also served as chancellor of the University of Manitoba from 1877 until his death. The Church Missionary Society and a number of other groups assisted him, and much of this part of Canada retains the evangelical Anglican flavor of this evangelical missionary bishop. Ten priests and eighteen lay delegates attended Machray's first diocesan conference; he worked rigorously to form new dioceses, and when he died, Rupert's Land was a province of nine fully constituted dioceses, of which he was archbishop or metropolitan.

Machray played a pivotal role in the development of an autonomous synod for the Anglican church in Canada in 1893. This synod was composed of a House of Bishops and a House of Delegates with clergy and lay representatives. The General Synod of the Church of England in Canada first met in 1893, and Machray was chosen as the first "Primate of All Canada" by unaminous vote.

Work in the far west had been underway for some time, but progress was slow. The first bishop of Columbia on the Pacific coast was appointed in 1859. The early beginnings made by the Church Missionary Society were given impetus when the Canadian Pacific Railway connected the two coasts in 1885. The province of British Columbia was created in 1914. In 1933 it was decided to gather the far-flung missions among the Indians and the Eskimos in Canada's far north into the diocese of the Arctic. The diocesan cathedral at Aklavik lies north of the Arctic Circle. Bishop A. L. Fleming, called "Archibald the Arctic," carried the Gospel to the far corners of this cold northern climate.

When the General Synod formed the Church of England in Canada in 1893, it created the office of "Primate of All Canada" and called the metropolitans of the various provinces "archbishops." While the primate has often been one of the four metropolitans, this is not a requirement. About the turn of the century a unified missionary society was formed, but in the interim foreign mission work was begun in Japan. Vigorous work among the Eskimos made 80 percent of them Anglicans by the mid-1960s.[87]

In the mid-twentieth century Anglican officials invited a journalist to offer his opinion of what was going on in the churches. Pierre Berton's *The Comfortable Pew* (1965) probed inconsistencies in modern church life and drew responses from the United Church of Canada (*Why the Sea Is Boiling Hot: A Symposium on the Church and the World*, 1965) and from Anglicans (*The Restless Church, A Response to the Comfortable Pew*, 1966, edited by William Kilbourn).

The census of 1842 listed 151,318 Anglicans in Canada as compared with 630,000 Roman Catholics, 130,000 Presbyterians, and 100,000 Methodists, among others. State censuses between 1871 and 1961 reported the following numbers of Anglicans in Canada, their relative percentage of the total population, and the percentage of increase over the last census:

1871	504,393	14.1	—
1881	589,599	13.6	16.9
1891	661,608	13.7	12.2
1901	689,540	12.8	4.2
1911	1,048,002	14.5	52.0
1921	1,410,632	16.1	34.6
1931	1,639,075	15.8	16.2
1941	1,754,368	15.2	7.0
1951	2,060,720	14.7	17.5
1961	2,409,068	13.2	16.9

According to the census, in 1961 the Anglicans had 12 percent of their members under fifteen years of age, 12.7 between fifteen and forty-four, 14.5 between forty-five and sixty-four, and 18.2 percent over age sixty-five. Eighty-four percent of the Anglicans were of British ethnic background, with a smattering of others from French (2.5 percent), German (2.8 percent), and other backgrounds. Twenty-five percent of the Anglicans lived in rural or small-town areas, nearly 50 percent in urban areas of over 100,000 people, and the rest in urban areas of varying sizes. Anglicans were scattered among the provinces, with a heavy concentration in Ontario (1,117,862) and in five other provinces where they had more than 100,000 adherents (Nova Scotia, Quebec, Manitoba, Alberta, and British Columbia, which had the second highest concentration with nearly 400,000). In 1971 the census indicated that 11.8 percent of the population was Anglican compared with 46.2 percent Roman Catholic and 17.5 percent United Church of Canada.

In 1970 the church reported 1,126,570 members, 1,736 churches, 2,658 clergy, and 1,690 pastors having charges. In 1976 the church reported 1,057,012 members, 1,720 churches, and 2,649 clergy.

In creed and doctrine, order and worship, the Anglican Church of Canada, as the church was renamed in 1955, follows principally the same forms and adheres to the historic confession as the other churches of the Anglican communion. Its clerics give assent to the Thirty-Nine Articles. The Prayer Book authorized by the General Synod in 1962 is *The Book of Common Prayer and Administration of the Sacraments and Other Rites and Ceremonies of the Church According to the Use of the Anglican Church of Canada.*

The church participates in all activities of the Anglican communion. In October 1968 the Canadian bishops met with other bishops of the Western hemisphere to form a regional council through which the Canadian church, the Episcopal Church of the United States, and the Church of the Province of the West Indies coordinate many activities. The Anglican Congress met in Toronto in 1963.

The basic unit of the church is the diocese, of which there are 28. Each of the four provinces has an archbishop. There is also an episcopal district. The General Synod met in 1977 and is scheduled to meet again in 1980.

Early efforts to incorporate the church into the United Church of Canada were unsuccessful, but in the 1960s plans were revitalized to unite the two churches organically. A draft proposal for union was issued in 1964.[88] In 1969 the Disciples of Christ were invited into the talks, and a "Plan of Union" was proposed that provided for the United Church and the Disciples to accept the episcopate and to agree on various theological points. Optimistic forecasts of union by 1973 proved to be unfounded; by late 1971 the Anglicans were stressing the need to enable churches to grow together rather than the need to prepare a plan of union. In 1975 the General Synod formally withdrew from union negotiations with these two churches. At the 1977 General Synod it was generally acknowledged that union plans were dead, at least for the decade of the seventies, although delegates affirmed that the church was committed to working with the United Church on the question of the mutual recognition of ministers. The synod requested the church's Doctrine and Worship Committee to devise a rite for mutual recognition that is "agreeable to the one, holy, catholic and apostolic faith." The church is involved in more than fifty shared ministries with the United Church, but members of the rather conservative and tradition-minded "Council for the Faith" continued to insist that "creeping unionism" was a major problem. That same General Synod commended the Anglican-Roman Catholic statement on authority in the church to its dioceses for study and comment before the next General Synod. The commission's two previous statements, on the Eucharist and on ministry, had been approved by the church. The body is a member of the Canadian Council of Churches and the World Council of Churches.

The question of ordaining women has aroused some controversy in this church, the first major Anglican body to ordain women. Several months after the 1968 Lambeth Conference called for canonical provision for "duly qualified women to share in the conduct of liturgical worship," the House of Bishops granted permission for "lay persons, either men or women," to administer consecrated bread and wine in Holy Communion.[89] In 1975 the General Synod approved the ordination of women to the priesthood but gave bishops opposed to the act the right to refuse to perform ordinations. Twenty-six of the 34 bishops voted in favor of ordination. Five months later by a 31-to-3 vote the bishops gave individual bishops the right to ordain qualified women to priestly orders as of November 1, 1976, but also set as a condition that there be no "overwhelming negative reaction" from other national or area churches in the Anglican communion before the decision was implemented. A coalition of High and Low Anglicans in Canada, the "Council for the Faith," urged Anglicans to boycott the ministrations of any women who might be ordained, and 350 male priests signed a manifesto saying that "it is an impossibility in the divine economy for a woman to be a priest." In the spring of 1976, Michael Ramsey, the former archbishop of Canterbury, declared in Toronto that the ordination of women as priests might impede moves toward unity with the Roman Catholic Church. But on November 30, 1976, the first women priests were ordained as six deacons received priestly orders in the Ontario and British Columbia dioceses. More ordinations followed in 1977.[90]

Conservatives have found another target in the church's 1973 decision to permit the remarriage of divorced persons. The meeting of traditionalists in St. Louis, Missouri, in September 1977, referred to above, apparently included some members of the Anglican Church of Canada.

The church's headquarters is Church House, 600 Jarvis Street, Toronto, Ontario, Canada M4Y 2J6. The primate is the Reverend E. W. Scott. Four metropolitans (archbishops) are provided for the ecclesiastical provinces of Canada, Rupert's Land, British Columbia, and Ontario. Each province has its own provincial synod and executive council, and diocesan synods usually meet annually in the twenty-eight dioceses.

NOTES

1. George Hodges, *A Short History of the Episcopal Church*, with introduction and conclusion by Powel M. Dawley (Cincinnati, Ohio: Forward Movement Publications, [1947]), pp. 31-32.
2. Ibid., pp. 15, 32; Sydney E. Ahlstrom, *A Religious History of the American People* (New Haven: Yale University Press, 1972), pp. 188-191; Powel Mills Dawley, *The Episcopal Church and Its Work* (Greenwich, Conn.: Seabury Press, 1955), pp. 25-25. Dawley

mentions that in addition to the services conducted in 1578 and 1579, Anglican chaplains also conducted services for the men in Humphrey Gilbert's expedition in Newfoundland in 1582. About the time of the settlement of Virginia, worship was held as well for the temporary settlement on Monhegan Island off the coast of Maine, and before that on the shores of Buzzards Bay and in the ill-fated Roanoke Colony.

3. Ahlstrom, pp. 188-191; Hodges, pp. 34-35.
4. Dawley, pp. 30–31; Ahlstrom, pp. 194-195.
5. Stephen Neill, *Anglicanism* (Baltimore: Penguin Books, 1958), pp. 197, 219-220; Dawley, pp. 33-34; Ahlstrom, pp. 219-221; Hodges, pp. 35-36; Edwin Scott Gaustad, *Historical Atlas of Religion in America* (Rev. ed. New York: Harper & Row, 1976), p. 8.
6. Dawley, p. 30; Ahlstrom, pp. 197-198, 226-229.
7. Carl Bridenbaugh, *Mitre and Sceptre; Transatlantic Faiths, Ideas, Personalities, and Politics, 1689–1775* (New York: Oxford University Press, 1962), pp. 54-58.
8. Dawley, pp. 28-29; Hodges, p. 40. See Bridenbaugh, pp. 44-45, for an example of a legal case involving the gift of land to "an orthodox minister" which was appealed to England after both a S.P.G. missionary and a Congregational minister claimed legal ownership. The Protestant Dissenting Deputies in England assisted their colonial friends in financing the appeal to the Privy Council.
9. Dawley, pp. 29-30; Bridenbaugh, pp. 68-69, 76-77 (quotation), 85-87; James McGinnis, "Anglicans in Connecticut, 1725–1750," *The England Quarterly* (March 1971), pp. 66-81.
10. Bridenbaugh, pp. 116-117; Dawley, p. 30.
11. Dawley, pp. 31-32; Ahlstrom, pp. 215-216; Bridenbaugh, pp. 117-119.
12. Dawley, pp. 34-38.
13. Hodges, p. 30.
14. Neill, pp. 223-224; Norman Sykes, *From Sheldon to Secker; Aspects of English Church History, 1660–1768* (Cambridge: University Press, 1959), pp. 205-210; Bridenbaugh, pp. 27-28.
15. Bridenbaugh, pp. 171-172, 178-181, 207 (quotation), 230-231, 255, 260, 288, 314.
16. Robert T. Handy, *A History of the Churches in the United States and Canada* (New York: Oxford University Press, 1977), p. 138.
17. Claro O. Loveland, *The Critical Years, the Reconstruction of the Anglican Church in the United States of America: 1780–1789* (Greenwich, Conn.: Seabury Press, 1956), pp. 10-18.
18. Ahlstrom, pp. 217, 368; Gaustad, pp. 3-4, 43, 54.
19. J. W. C. Wand, *Anglicanism in History and Today* (London: Weidenfeld and Nicolson, 1961), p. 33 (quotation); Loveland, pp. 6, 18-20; Gustad, pp. 68, 70.
20. Loveland, pp. 21-32.
21. Ibid., p. 48; Hodges, pp. 51-52.
22. See Robert W. Shoemaker, *The Origin and Meaning of the Name "Protestant Episcopal"* (New York: American Church Publications, 1959), pp. 101-121 and *passim*.
23. Loveland, pp. 276-279.
24. Gaustad, p. 70; Ahlstrom, pp. 624-626; Neill, p. 282.
25. See R. Pierce Beaver, *Church, State and the American Indians* (St. Louis: Concordia Publishing House, 1966).
26. Dawley, pp. 50-60; Hodges, pp. 64-65, 72-78; Gaustad, pp. 52, 69, 71 and *passim*.
27. Lewis Bliss Whittemore, *The Care of All the Churches; the Background, Work, and Opportunity of the American Episcopate* (Greenwich, Conn.: Seabury Press, 1955), pp. 25-28.
28. Dawley, pp. 61-62.
29. Ahlstrom, pp. 671, 696; Dawley, pp. 62-63; Winthrop S. Hudson, *Religion in America* (2nd edn.; New York: Charles Scribner's Sons, 1973), pp. 216-217.
30. Dawley, pp. 64-66; Shoemaker, pp. 212-213 and *passim*; Ahlstrom, p. 548; Hodges, pp. 84-86.
31. Henry Warner Bowden, *Dictionary of American Religious Biography* (Westport, Conn.: Greenwood Press, 1977), pp. 114-116.
32. Ronald C. White, Jr., and Hopkins, C. Howard, *The Social Gospel; Religion and Reform in Changing America* (Philadelphia: Temple University Press, 1976), pp. 26, 70-72, 149, 190.
33. Charles Glock; Ringer, Benjamin; and Babbie, Earl R., *To Comfort and to Challenge, a Dilemma of the Contemporary Church* (Berkeley: University of California Press, 1967), pp. 80-83.
34. From *The Denominational Society, a Sociological Approach to Religion in America* by Andrew M. Greeley. Copyright © 1972 by Scott, Foresman and Company. Reprinted by permission.
35. Gaustad, p. 170.
36. Glock et al., pp. 220-221.

37. Ibid., pp. 120-122, 149, 176-179, 188-191.
38. Greeley, pp. 98-101. Greeley reproduced these tables from Charles Y. Glock and Rodney Stark, *Religion and Society in Tension* (Chicago: Rand McNally & Company, 1965), pp. 191-192, 201, 116, 120.
39. *Time*, October 21, November 4, November 11, 1966; *New York Times*, March 7, 1967.
40. *St. Louis Post Dispatch*, October 9, 1970; February 23, 1973.
41. *Time*, May 7, 1965; letter of the Reverend Ernest Risley, St. John's Church, Madison Square, Savannah, Georgia.
42. See John McGill Krumm, *Why I Am an Episcopalian* (Boston: Beacon Press, 1957), pp. 174-175.
43. See Thomas A. Idinopulos, "Old Forms of Anti-Judaism in the New Book of Common Prayer," *Christian Century*, August 4-11, 1976, pp. 680-684.
44. *Christian Century*, February 4-11, 1976.
45. Dawley, p. 288; Gaustad, pp. 71-72; Constant H. Jacquet, Jr., ed., *Yearbook of American and Canadian Churches, 1973* (Nashville: Abingdon Press, 1973), p. 52.
46. Gaustad, p. 177; Edwin S. Gaustad, "America's Institutions of Faith," *The Religious Situation: 1968*, ed. Donald R. Cutler (Boston: Beacon Press, 1968), pp. 840, 845.
47. Gaustad, *Atlas*, pp. 167, 169; Gaustad, "America's Institutions of Faith," pp. 851-852.
48. *Christian Century*, February 4-11, 1976.
49. J. Paul Williams, *What Americans Believe and How They Worship* (Rev. edn.; New York: Harper & Row, 1962), p. 185.
50. *Time*, April 30, 1965.
51. *Christianity Today*, October 26, 1973, pp. 55-57.
52. *Christian Century*, May 21, 1975, pp. 517-519; January 28, 1976, p. 63; April 14, 1976, p. 352.
53. *Christian Century*, October 8, 1975, p. 871.
54. Ibid., December 10, 1975, p. 1129; February 25, 1976, p. 167.
55. Ibid., March 24, 1976, p. 279.
56. Ibid., July 7-14, 1976.
57. Ibid., January 26, 1977, p. 55.
58. *New York Times*, October 18, 1977.
59. *Christian Century*, December 22, 1976, p. 1143; November 24, 1976.
60. *New York Times*, August 24, 27, 1977; *Christian Century* XCIV (1977): 27.
61. *St. Louis Post Dispatch*, July 15, 1977; *Christian Century*, October 5, 1977, p. 867.
62. *Christian Century*, October 5, 1977, pp. 867-868; *St. Louis Post Dispatch*, September 14, 15, 16, 18, 1977; *New York Times*, September 15, 17, 19, 1977.
63. *New York Times*, October 1, 3, 6, 7, 1977; *St. Louis Post Dispatch*, October 2, 7, 14, 1977.
64. Dawley, pp. 74-77.
65. Ibid., pp. 85-86.
66. Ibid., pp. 98-102.
67. Ibid., pp. 99-108.
68. The current edition of the *Episcopal Church Annual* (Wilton, Conn.: Morehouse, 1977) provides a full listing of men's and women's orders and their work.
69. See John Wallace Suter and George Julius Cleaveland, *The American Book of Common Prayer, Its Origin and Development* (New York: Oxford University Press, 1949), pp. 56-59, and pp. 63-68, for a succinct description of the revisions of 1892 and 1928.
70. Charles P. Price, *Introducing the Proposed Book of Common Prayer* (New York: Seabury Press, 1977), p. 9. Price's study was prepared at the request of the church's Standing Liturgical Commission. On pages 9-15 he provides a description of the revision process which has, in a sense, gone on since 1928, culminating in the *Proposed Book of Common Prayer*. The Standing Liturgical Commission undertook a complete review of the Prayer Book between 1950 and 1963, which resulted in a series of Prayer Book studies that were not authorized for trial use. The *Liturgy of the Lord's Supper* (1967) was authorized for optional use, as were ten other studies released after 1968, including the revised *Authorized Services* (1973).
71. Price, *Introducing the Proposed Book of Common Prayer*, pp. 16-19.
72. Ibid., pp. 20-23.
73. Ibid., pp. 24-35.
74. Ibid., pp. 36-45.
75. Ibid., pp. 46-49.

76. Ibid., pp. 50-60.
77. Ibid., pp. 60-72.
78. Ibid., pp. 72-86.
79. Ibid., pp. 89-97.
80. Ibid., pp. 100-103.
81. Ibid., pp. 103-107.
82. Ibid., pp. 108-112.
83. Ibid., pp. 112-114.
84. Ibid., pp. 115-116.
85. Ibid., p. 121.
86. Unless otherwise indicated, this historical account of the Anglican Church of Canada is drawn from Robert T. Handy's excellent work, *A History of the Churches in the United States and Canada* (New York: Oxford University Press, 1977), pp. 124-126, 132-133, 228-230, 235-236, 240-249, 255, 348-350, 366, 376, 423-424.
87. Stephen Neill, *A History of Christian Missions* (Baltimore: Penguin Books, 1964), p. 393.
88. See *The Strattford Beacon-Herald*, November 14, 1964.
89. James B. Simpson, and Story, Edward M., *The Long Shadows of Lambeth X* [*1968*] (New York: McGraw-Hill Book Company, 1969), pp. 196-197.
90. *Christian Century*, July 9-16, 1975, p. 665; October 1, 1975, p. 841; November 19, 1975, p. 1048; May 19, 1976, p. 478; December 29, 1976, p. 1168.

BIBLIOGRAPHY

THE CHURCH OF ENGLAND IN THE AMERICAN COLONIES

Boscher, Robert S., compiler. "The Episcopal Church and American Christianity: A Bibliography." *Historical Magazine of the Protestant Episcopal Church* XIX (1950): 369-384.

Bridenbaugh, Carl. *Mitre and Sceptre: Transatlantic Faiths, Ideas, Personalities, and Politics, 1689–1775.* New York: Oxford University Press, 1962.

Brydon, George Maclaren. *Virginia's Mother Church and Political Conditions under which It Grew.* 2 vols. Richmond: Virginia Historical Society, 1947 (I, 1607–1727); Philadlephia: Church Historical Society, 1952 (II, 1727–1814).

Calam, John. *Parsons and Pedagogues; the S.P.G. Adventure in American Education.* New York: Columbia University Press, 1971.

Cross, Arthur L. *The Anglican Episcopate and the American Colonies.* Hamden, Conn.: Archon Books, 1964.

Dorsey, Stephen P. *Early English Churches in America, 1607–1807.* New York: Oxford University Press, 1952.

Hodges, George. *A Short History of the Episcopal Church.* Rev. edn. with introduction and conclusion by Powel M. Dawley. Cincinnati: Forward Movement Publications, [1974].

Humphreys, David. *An Historical Account of the Incorporated Society for the Propagation of the Gospel in Foreign Parts.* New York: Arno Press, 1969.

Manross, William Wilson. "Catalog of Articles in the 'Historical Magazine.'" *Historical Magazine of the Protestant Episcopal Church* XXIII (1954): 367-420.

————. *A History of the American Episcopal Church.* New York: Morehouse, 1935.

McConnell, S. D. *History of the American Episcopal Church.* 9th edn., rev. and enlarged. New York: Thomas Whittaker, 1904.

McCulloch, Samuel Clyde. "The Foundation and Early Work of the Society for Promoting Christian Knowledge." *Historical Magazine of the Protestant Episcopal Church*, XVIII (1949), 3-22.

Rightmyer, Nelson Waite. *Maryland's Established Church.* Baltimore: Church Historical Society for the Diocese of Maryland, 1956.

FORMATION OF THE PROTESTANT EPISCOPAL CHURCH IN THE U.S.A.

Loveland, Clara O. *The Critical Years; the Reconstruction of the Anglican Church in the United States of America, 1780–1789.* Greenwich, Conn.: Seabury Press, 1956.

Shoemaker, Robert W. *The Origin and*

Meaning of the Name "Protestant Episcopal." New York: American Church Publications, 1959.

Steiner, Bruce Edward. *Samuel Seabury,* 1729–1796; a Study in the High Church Tradition. New York: Garland Press, 1971.

THE EPISCOPAL CHURCH AND NINETEENTH-CENTURY EXPANSION AND CONTROVERSY

Addison, James Thayer. *The Episcopal Church in the United States, 1789–1931.* New York: Charles Scribner's Sons, 1951 (reissued 1969).

Albright, Raymond W. *A History of the Protestant Episcopal Church.* New York: Macmillan, 1964.

Cheshire, Joseph Blount. *The Church in the Confederate States: A History of the Protestant Episcopal Church in the Confederate States.* New York: Longmans, Green and Co., 1912.

Chorley, Edward Clowes. *Men and Movements in the American Episcopal Church.* New York: Charles Scribner's Sons, 1946.

DeMille, George Edmed. *The Catholic Movement in the American Episcopal Church.* 2nd edn. rev. and enlarged. Philadelphia: Church Historical Society, 1950.

Whittemore, Lewis Bliss. *The Care of All the Churches; the Background, Work, and Opportunity of the American Episcopate.* Greenwich, Conn.: Seabury Press, 1955.

THE EPISCOPAL CHURCH IN THE TWENTIETH CENTURY

Addison, James Thayer. *Our Expanding Church.* Rev. edn. New York: The National Council, 1944.

Brewer, Earl D. C., and Johnson, Douglas W. *An Inventory of the Harlan Paul Douglas Collection of Religious Research Reports.* New York: Department of Research, National Council of the Churches of Christ, 1970.

DeMille, George E. *The Episcopal Church since 1900.* New York: Morehouse-Gorham, 1967.

Documents on Anglican/Roman Catholic Relations. Washington, D.C.: United States Catholic Conference, 1972.

The Episcopal Church Annual. Wilton, Conn.: Morehouse, 1977.

Elgin, Kathleen. *The Episcopalians; the Protestant Episcopal Church.* New York: D. McKay Co., 1970.

Glock, Charles Y.; Ringer, Benjamin B.; and Babbie, Earl R. *To Comfort and to Challenge; a Dilemma of the Contemporary Church.* Berkeley: University of California Press, 1967.

Jansen, Hugh M., Jr. "Algernon Sidney Craspey: Heresy at Rochester." In *American Religious Heretics: Formal and Informal Trials.* Ed. George H. Shriver. Nashville: Abingdon Press, 1966. Pp. 188-224.

Krumm, John McGill. *Why I Am an Episcopalian.* Boston: Beacon Press, 1957.

Lutheran-Episcopal Dialogue; a Progress Report. Cincinnati: Forward Movement Publications, 1972.

Weston, M. Moran. "Social Policy of the Episcopal Church in the Twentieth Century." Unpublished Ph. D. dissertation, Columbia University, New York, N.Y., 1953.

ORDER AND ORGANIZATION OF THE EPISCOPAL CHURCH

Anson, Peter F. *The Call of the Cloister: Religious Communities and Kindred Bodies in the Anglican Communion.* London: S.P.C.K., 1955.

Barnes, C. Rankin. *The General Convention: Offices and Officers, 1785–1950.* Philadelphia: Church Historical Society, 1951.

Constitution and Canons for the Government of the Protestant Episcopal Church in the United States of America, Otherwise Known as the Episcopal Church Adopted in General Conventions, 1789–1967. [New York:] Printed for the Convention, 1967.

Dawley, Powel Mills. The Episcopal Church and Its Work. Vol. VI in The Church's Teaching. Greenwich, Conn.: Seabury Press, 1955.

Episcopal Clerical Directory. New York: Church Hymnal Corporation, 1977.

Ervin, Spencer. Some Deficiencies in the Canon Law of the American Episcopal Church and Related Matters. New York: American Church Publications, 1961.

Smith, Charles W. F. "Discovering the Episcopal Church" [brochure]. Cincinnati: Forward Movement Publications, n.d.

CREED, LITURGY, WORSHIP, AND DOCTRINE OF THE EPISCOPAL CHURCH

The Book of Common Prayer and Administration of the Sacraments and Other Rites and Ceremonies of the Church According to the Use of the Protestant Episcopal Church in the United States of America. Greenwich, Conn.: Seabury Press, 1952.

The Draft Proposed Book of Common Prayer and Other Rites and Ceremonies of the Church According to the Use of the Protestant Episcopal Church in the United States of America, Otherwise Known as The Episcopal Church. New York: The Church Hymnal Corporation, 1976.

Parsons, Edward Lambe, and Jones, Bayard Hale. The American Prayer Book, Its Origins and Principles. New York: Charles Scribner's Sons, 1937.

Pittenger, W. Norman. The Episcopal Way of Life. Englewood Cliffs, N.J.: Prentice-Hall, 1957.

Prayer Book Studies, XVII. The Liturgy of the Lord's Supper, a Revision of Prayer Book Studies IV. New York: The Church Pension Fund, 1966.

Prayer Book Studies, 18. On Baptism and Confirmation. New York; The Church Pension Fund, 1970.

Price, Charles P. Introducing the Proposed Book of Common Prayer. New York: Seabury Press, 1977.

Shepherd, Massey Hamilton, Jr. The Oxford American Prayer Book Commentary. New York: Oxford University Press, 1950.

————. The Worship of the Church. Vol. IV in The Church's Teaching. Greenwich, Conn.: Seabury Press, 1952.

Suter, John Wallace, and Cleaveland, George Julius. The American Book of Common Prayer, Its Origin and Development. New York: Oxford University Press, 1949.

THE ANGLICAN CHURCH OF CANADA

The Book of Common Prayer and Administration of the Sacraments and Other Rites and Ceremonies of the Church According to the Use of the Anglican Church of Canada. Toronto: Anglican Book Centre, 1962.

Carrington, Philip. The Anglican Church in Canada: A History. Toronto: Collins, 1963.

Clifford, N. K. "Religion in the Development of Canadian Society: An Historiographical Analysis." Church History XXXVIII (1969): 506-523.

Ervin, Spencer. The Political and Ecclesiastical History of the Anglican Church of Canada. Ambler, Pa.: Trinity Press, 1967.

Grant, John Webster, ed. A History of the Christian Church in Canada. 3 vols. Toronto: Ryerson Press and McGraw-Hill Ryerson, 1966–1972.

Masters, D. C. Protestant Church Colleges in Canada: A History. Toronto: University of Toronto Press, 1966.

Millman, Thomas R. Jacob Mountain, First Lord Bishop of Quebec: A Study in Church and State, 1793–1825. Toronto: University of Toronto Press, 1947.

Moir, John S. Church and State in Canada, 1627–1867: Basic Documents. Toronto: McClelland and Stewart, 1967.

————. Church and State in Canada West: Three Studies in the Relation of Denominationalism and Nationalism, 1841–

1867. Toronto: University of Toronto Press, 1959.

Shortt, Adam, and Doughty, Arthur G., eds., *Canada and Its Provinces.* Vol. XI. Edinburgh: T. and A. Constable, for the Publishers Association of Canada, 1914–1917.

Wilson, Alan. *The Clergy Reserves of Upper Canada: A Canadian Mortmain.* Toronto: University of Toronto Press, 1968.

7. Churches Deriving from the Anglican Communion in North America

The Reformed Episcopal Church in the United States of America

The organizers of the Protestant Episcopal Church in the United States of America succeeded initially in 1789 in harnessing together the divergent thrusts of High Church and Low Church theologies. But by the 1860s intervening developments seemed to many Low churchmen to have weighted the balance so much in favor of the High Church position that the very existence of the Protestant Episcopal Church as a Reformed denomination was threatened.

A number of developments led to a crisis. In 1868 a church court tried the Reverend Stephen S. Tyng, a New York rector, for having preached in a Methodist Church in New Jersey, found him guilty, and sentenced him to be "admonished." The same year an anonymous tract came out with the rhetorical question in its title, *Are There Romanizing Germs in the Prayer Book?*[1] In 1869 eleven Evangelical bishops urged the next General Convention to meet a major concern of the Low Church party by authorizing alternate phrases, or "some equivalent modification in the Office for the Ministration of Baptism to Infants," which would not seem to allow the idea of baptismal regeneration.[2] In the same year another church court began the trial of the Reverend Charles E. Cheney of Chicago for deliberately omitting "regeneration" and "regenerate" from the rite when he baptized infants; nineteen months later it found him guilty and sentenced him to suspension. A declaration by all but one of the bishops at the General Convention of 1871 that "the word "regenerate' in the Offices for the Ministration of Baptism to Infants . . . is not there so used as to determine that a moral change in the subject of baptism is wrought in the recipient"[3] was not sufficient to reassure the Low Church group.

In October 1873 George David Cummins, assistant bishop of Kentucky and one of the leaders at an informal meeting held in 1870 to discuss the feasibility of organizing a new Episcopal church, received the Holy Communion and administered the cup at an international and interdenominational communion service held in New York in connection with the Sixth General Convention of the Evangelical Alliance. The following month he submitted his resignation to the bishop of Kentucky, declaring that the ritualism and sacerdotalism of the Protestant Episcopal Church and the impossibility of meeting fellow Christians of other churches around the Lord's Table prevented him from continuing as a Protestant Episcopal bishop. On December 2, 1873, he presided at a meeting which organized the Reformed Episcopal Church with himself as presiding bishop. It was his hope and confidence that this body, with a primitive episcopacy, a scriptural liturgy, and "a fidelity to the doctrine of justification by faith only" would provide "a basis for the union of all Evangelical Christendom."[4]

The new denomination's Declaration of Principles—still adhered to—committed it to the Old and New Testaments as the Word of God and the sole rule of faith and practice, to the Apostoles' Creed, to the divine institutions of baptism and the Lord's Supper, and to "the doctrines of grace substantially as they are set forth in the Thirty-Nine Articles of Religion." It recognized episcopacy "not as of divine right, but as a very ancient and desirable form of church polity." As its thoroughly Reformed and Protestant liturgy it accepted a modified version of the 1785 draft American Book of Common Prayer,[5] but not as "imperative or repressive of freedom in prayer" and with the reservation of full liberty to alter it "provided that the substance of the faith be kept entire." It condemned five teachings as contrary to God's word: (1) That the church exists only in one order or form of church polity; (2) that ministers are "priests" in a sense other than that in which all believers are "a royal priesthood"; (3) that the Lord's Table is an altar on which the oblation of Christ's body and blood is offered anew to the Father; (4) that Christ's presence in the Lord's Supper is in the elements of bread and wine; and (5) that regeneration is inseparably connected with baptism.[6]

As a result of omissions, additions, and combinations the Reformed Episcopal Church has thirty-five Articles of Religion; it has extensively revised many of those that it has retained. It prescribes the use of its Book of Common Prayer on Sunday mornings and commends it for use at other times at the discretion of the minister. It prohibits the construction of any Communion table in the form of an altar and forbids retables, candles, candlesticks, and crosses as Communion table ornaments.[7]

The Reformed Episcopal Book of Common Prayer authorizes the substitution of the Anglican version of the Nicene Creed for the Apostles' Creed and explains "the holy catholic church" of the latter and the "one catholic and apostolic church" of the former as "the blessed company of all faithful people in Christ" and the "one baptism for the remission of sins" as "the baptism of the Holy Ghost."[8] It prints the text of the Apostles' Creed without "he descended into hell." It specifies that in the Holy Communion "the acts and prayer of consecration do not change the nature of the elements, but merely set them apart for a holy use; and the reception of them in a kneeling posture is not an act of adoration of the elements."[9] It affectionately invites to the Lord's Table "fellow Christians of other branches of Christ's church and all who love our divine Lord and Saviour Jesus Christ in sincerity."[10] It prescribes that members of other denominations who unite with the Reformed Episcopal Church "need not be confirmed, except at their own request," and restricts administration of confirmation to the bishops "not as of divine right," but as a "very ancient and desirable form of church usage."[11] No provision is made for the keeping of saints' days.

The word "priest" does not occur as a designation for the ministers. The absolution becomes a "declaration concerning the remission of sins," and the statement that God has given his ministers power to pronounce absolution and remission of sins to his people is omitted as untrue. The teaching about the sacraments is consciously Reformed. The body and the blood of Christ are not "present in the elements of bread and wine in the Lord's supper" and infant baptism is "a dedication of children to God by believing parents and the reception of them into the nurturing care of the church."[12]

The Reformed Episcopal Church "denies the fiction of Apostolic Succession."[13] A form prescribes the manner in which presbyters ordained in other denominations are received without ordination. The Reformed Episcopal Church has two orders in its ministry, the diactonate and the presbyterate. Although there is a form of consecrating a bishop, bishops are only "presbyters elected to office by the [General] Council, we holding that the bishopric is an office not an order."[14] Bishops are addressed as "reverend brother in Christ"; they do not meet in a separate house of the General Council and they vote in the clerical order.

The Reformed Episcopal Church normally administers the Lord's Supper on the first Sunday of the month. In 1897 the council prescribed the black academic gown as the official dress of the ministers when conducting services but provided that churches then using surplices and bishops then using episcopal robes might continue their use.[15]

The Reformed Episcopal Church has maintained close ties with Moody Bible Institute, to which it has given two presidents, James M. Gray, one of the editors of the Scofield Reference Bible, and Bishop William Culbertson. The orientation of the Reformed Episcopal Church is biblical and conservative, and it has strongly resisted the inroads of liberalism. In 1942 the Reformed Episcopal Church withdrew from the Federal Council of Churches; it does not participate in the organized Ecumenical movement.

Currently two synods and a missionary jurisdiction comprise 68 churches and 6,500 members. The church carries on foreign mission work in India and cooperates with nondenominational mission boards in missionary work in Africa and Europe. The secretary has his office at 560 Fountain Street, Havre de Grace, Maryland 21078.

The First Synod in the Dominion of Canada of the Reformed Episcopal Church

In 1844 the Free Church of England came into being in protest against the "ritualism" of the Oxford Movement. At the time of its registration in chancery by deed poll in 1863, its ministry was Presbyterian with recognition of and provision for episcopacy.[16] Upon the organization of the Reformed Episcopal Church in 1873, the Free Church established contact with the new American body; in 1876 it adopted the latter's Declaration of Principles and received the historic episcopate for two of its bishops from the Reformed Episcopal Church. In 1877 the American body established an English branch, which became independent in 1883 and after long negotiations united with the Free Church of England in 1927. The united body, which is in communion with the American church, is officially known as the "Free Church of England, Otherwise Called The Reformed Episcopal Church in the United Kingdom of Great Britain and Ireland."

The first Canadian congregation of the Reformed Episcopal Church was organized in 1874 at Monkton, New Brunswick. By 1879 the creation of a Canadian Synod, with its own bishop, became feasible. The First Synod in the Dominion of Canada was chartered in 1886. From 1930 to 1942 the Canadian Synod was part of the Free Church of England; in the latter year the Free Church of England felt that it could no longer administer the Canadian work and the latter became independent, although it remains in communion with both the British and the American bodies. Its polity, worship, and teaching are in agreement with those of its American counterpart. It has one synod with three churches, located in British Columbia. While membership has declined, new interest is reported.[17] The secretary resides at 626 Cumberland Street, New Westminster, British Columbia V3L 3G8.

The Free Protestant Episcopal Church

The Free Protestant Episcopal Church traces its origin back to 1897, when three small British episcopal bodies united. The first of these was the Ancient British Church, which Richard Williams Morgan (Mar Pelagius I, d. 1889), who stood in the "Ferrete Succession,"[18] reportedly had restored in 1876/1877; its primate in 1897 was Morgan's successor, Charles Isaac Stevens (d. 1916).

The second body was the Nazarene Episcopal Ecclesia, which James Martin (d. 1919) had founded in 1873. Martin had been consecrated both by the former Reformed Episcopal bishop A. S. Richardson (d. 1907) and by Leon Checkemian (or Chechemian) (d. 1920), reputedly a former Roman Catholic prelate of the Armenian Rite who had been conditionally reconsecrated by Stevens and Richardson.

The third body was the Free Protestant Church of England, which Checkemian had founded in 1889. The last-named became the first archbishop of the Free Protestant Church of England.

The published "line of archbishops and bishops" of the Free Protestant Episcopal Church indicates that Checkemian was succeeded in the primatial office in turn by Stevens in 1900, after Checkemian had withdrawn from the church that he founded; by Martin in 1916; by Andrew Charles Albert Mac-

Laglen (d. 1930) in 1919; by Herbert James Monzani Heard (d. 1947) in 1930; and by William Hall (d. 1959) in 1939, upon Heard's resignation of the office.[19]

Hall consecrated Charles Dennis Boltwood (b. 1889)[20] as primate in 1952. In 1958, under Hall's direction, Boltwood established the Free Protestant Episcopal Church (which as an international body now dropped "of England" from its name) in North America. In the course of a visit to the New World in that year he consecrated Emmet Neil Enochs of Los Angeles as archbishop of California and national primate for the United States of America; Charles Kennedy Stewart Moffatt of Brandon, Manitoba, as archbishop of western Canada and national primate of the dominion; and Emanuel Samuel Yekorogha of Monrovia as archbishop and national primate of Liberia and administrator of the churches in Nigeria. On the same trip he also consecrated John M. Stanley as the bishop of the state of Washington and Benjamin C. Eckardt as bishop of Ontario and Quebec.[21] Additional bishops have since been consecrated for the United States.[22]

The Free Protestant Episcopal Church sees it as its mission "to maintain the principles of the Reformation and ecumenical union and to work for the unity of Christendom." It describes itself as scriptural in its tenets and liturgical in its worship. "It holds the doctrines of grace substantially as they are set forth in the Anglican Thirty-Nine Articles or Religion." It condemns seven doctrines as strange, erroneous, and contrary to God's Word: (1) that the church exists in only one order or form of polity; (2) that ministers are "priests" in any other sense than that in which all believers are a "royal priesthood"; (3) that the Lord's Table is an altar on which the oblation of the body and blood of Christ is offered anew to the Father; (4) that Christ is present in the elements of bread and wine in the Lord's Supper; (5) that regeneration and baptism are inseparably connected; (6) that the law should punish Christians with death; and (7) that Christians may bear weapons and serve in war except in aiding the wounded or assisting in civil defense.[23]

The ministry of the Free Protestant Episcopal Church comprises four orders: bishops, priests (presbyters), deacons, and deaconesses. Membership in the Free Protestant Episcopal Church is not exclusive, and while dual or multiple memberships are exceptions rather than the rule, even prelates may hold memberships in the ministry of other denominations as well as in the ministry of the Free Protestant Episcopal Church.[24] In general, bishops and presbyters of the Free Protestant Episcopal Church earn their livelihood as professional people or as tradespeople.

The national primates have a primacy of honor and a right to the style Most Reverend, but each overseas diocese operates directly under the bishop primus and the church council. The international headquarters are at St. Andrew's Collegiate Church, Stonebridge Road, Tottenham, London, England.

In the United States the Free Protestant Episcopal Church reports 23 congregations and a larger number of affiliated missions in 21 states from coast to coast. In Canada there are 10 congregations and missions. Exact membership figures are not available; the most conservative estimates put the total in both countries in excess of 2,000.[25]

Philippine Independent Church (Iglesia Filipina Independiente)

Christianity came to the Philippine Islands in the 1560s along with the Conquistadores. Augustinian, Dominican, Franciscan, and Jesuit missionaries learned the native dialects, proclaimed the Gospel, identified themselves with their parishioners by their diligent pastoral labors, and protected them against the Spanish army. But what began as a friar mission ultimately degenerated into a corrupt friar rule, marked by a stubborn resistance to train a sufficient number of indigenous priests to assume responsibility for the Roman Catholic Church in the Philippines. The revolt against friar domination had its first martyr in Apolinario de la Cruz (1815–1841), founder of the Confraternity of St. Joseph. Others followed him, notably José Rizal (1861–1896).

Admiral Dewey's victory at Manila Bay in 1898 marked the end of Spanish domination, but the failure of the United States to grant immediate independence to the Philippines led to the revolt under Emilio Aguinaldo. As president of the revolutionary government of the country, Aguinaldo appointed Gregorio Aglipay (1860–1940) military vicar general and thereby, in effect, head of the Roman Catholic Church in the areas where the revolution established itself. When the ultimate triumph of the American forces over the revolutionaries became obviously certain in 1899, the archbishop of Manila excommunicated Aglipay and the Iglesia Filipina Independiente came into being.

Aglipay became a guerrilla general, but he finally surrendered in 1902 (the last of the guerrilla leaders to do so), and gave his entire attention to the organization of the Independent Church. He retained the traditional episcopal structure and cultus, but under the influence of the American governor, William Howard Taft, Aglipay began to steer the new church theologically into an extreme form of Unitarianism. By 1906 the number of adherents had grown to 2 million,[26] more than a quarter of the Filipino population. The right to local property was extensively litigated. The decision of the Supreme Court of the Philippines in 1906 in two crucial cases was in favor of the Roman Catholic Church; on appeal the Supreme Court of the United States upheld the decision in 1909. Thus the Independent Church lost most of its properties and some of its members. The theological movement toward Unitarianism continued—at least among the bishops, although it is doubtful that it ever penetrated the faith and practice of the actual membership of the Independent Church to any great extent. In 1939 the Independent Church named the president of the American Unitarian Association, Dr. Louis C. Cornish, its own honorary president.

In 1946, under the supreme pontificate of Aglipay's successor, a schism took place, with about 10,000 following the supreme bishop; the remainder of the church, with 38 bishops and over 1,500,000 members, rallied behind the new supreme bishop, Isabelo de los Reyes, Jr. (b. 1900). A consistent trinitarian even during Aglipay's lifetime, de los Reyes succeeded in leading the Independent Church to adopt a Declaration of the Faith in 1947 that affirms the Trinity (in terms taken from the Athanasian Creed), the deity of Christ and of the Holy Spirit, and the one holy catholic and apostolic church "founded by Christ for the redemption and sanctification of mankind." The appended Articles of Religion declare that salvation is obtained only through a vital faith in Christ that should manifest itself in good works; that the Holy Scriptures contain everything necessary for saving faith; that the faithful are to accept the so-called Apostles' and Nicene creeds; and that "the sacraments are outward and visible signs of our faith and a means whereby God manifests His good will toward us and confers His grace on us."[27] In the same year the Protestant Episcopal Church in the United States of America acted favorably on the petition of the Philippine Independent Church for the apostolic succession, which the supreme bishop and two diocesan bishops received in 1948. The two bodies formally established full intercommunion in 1961.

In 1959 the Episcopal bishop of Honolulu gave his patronage to a mission of the Philippine Independent Church among the 75,000 Filipinos who live in Hawaii. Currently three Philippine Independent priests minister in eleven missions, with an estimated total membership of 800. The Protestant Episcopal bishop of Honolulu represents the supreme bishop of the Philippine Independent Church in acting as the ordinary of these priests. They hold services—in Episcopal churches where these are available—in Ilocano and English.[28] Their Hawaiian headquarters are at St. Andrew's Episcopal Cathedral, Honolulu.

The Anglican Orthodox Church of North America

On November 15, 1963, James Parker Dees (b. 1915), former rector of the Protestant Episcopal Church of the Holy Trinity, Statesville, North Carolina, an active proponent of conservative causes such as "national sovereignty, freedom of enterprise, and the preservation of racial integrities," and the founder and president of the North Carolina Defenders of States' Rights, Incorporated, voluntarily submitted his renunciation of the ministry of his denomination. The diocesan bishop accepted this renunciation without prejudice to the Reverend Mr. Dees. The statement that the latter made at the time gave as his reasons the heretical views of many Protestant Episcopal clergymen, notably in such matters as the Trinity, Christ's virgin birth, and his resurrection; their sacerdotalism, their invocation of the Blessed Virgin Mary, and their idolatrous reservation of the bread and wine of the Holy Communion; the denomination's association with the National Council of the

Churches of Christ in the United States of America, its promotion "of the international Communist conspiracy," its exaggerated orientation toward a program of political and social action, and its efforts "to destroy race, peace, and American culture by advocating the use of force by the Federal government." In the statement he invited the support of others in setting up "a new Episcopal Church patterned after the historic Anglican faith and tradition."[29]

With other former members of the Protestant Episcopal Church he established the Anglican Orthodox Church of North America "as an independent episcopal church holding strictly to basically Anglican doctrine, discipline, and worship."[30] The Articles of Incorporation of the new denomination provide that "the Bible and the Book of Common Prayer shall be the standard of doctrine, discipline, and worship." The Book of Common Prayer is taken to include the Apostles' and Nicene creeds as well as the Thirty-Nine Articles of Religion, which the Anglican Orthodox Church considers "to contain basic elements of the historic Faith," specifically Christ's virgin birth, Incarnation, and vicarious sacrifice, and the Trinity. Parishes may own their own property. The theological position of the denomination is strongly conservative.[31] It describes its churchmanship as intermediate between the High Church and the Low Church positions.

On March 15, 1964, the founder and presiding bishop of the Anglican Orthodox Church was consecrated to the episcopate by the Most Reverend Wasyl Sawyna, primate of the Holy Ukrainian Autocephalic Orthodox Church, in the Cathedral of St. Basil the Great, Emmaus, Pennsylvania, with the Most Reverend Orlando Jacques Woodward as co-consecrator. The new prelate was consecrated "to serve as primate of the Anglican Orthodox Church, free of the jurisdictions of his consecrators."[32]

The Anglican Orthodox Church has about 35 congregations throughout the United States and branches in England, Rhodesia, Colombia, Fiji Islands, Pakistan, South India, Nigeria, and Madagascar, claiming an inclusive membership of 200,000.[33] Its headquarters are at 323 Walnut Street, Statesville, North Carolina 28677, where it has operated Cranmer Seminary since 1971.

American Episcopal Church (Spartanburg, South Carolina)

In May 1968 a group of former Protestant Episcopal presbyters and laypeople organized the American Episcopal Church at Mobile, Alabama. They had withdrawn from the Protestant Episcopal Church because they were concerned that the "management of the Protestant Episcopal Church has fallen into the hands of those who have permitted the faith and practice of Christianity to deteriorate in favor of forcing their own political and sociological concepts upon the church." The Right Reverend James H. George, Jr., previously the rector of a Protestant Episcopal parish in Charleston, South Carolina, whom the new denomination chose as executive secretary and presiding bishop, declared: "The faith of the apostles has been watered down."[34]

Bishop George's consecration took place in the chapel of the Masonic Temple in Cincinnati, Ohio, in December 1968. The consecrator was the Most Reverend Joseph Chengalvaroyan Pillai (Mar James) (d. 1970), metropolitan of the Indian Orthodox Church (Antiochean Succession) and director of the Department of Interdenominational Relations of the Orthodox Catholic Patriarchate of America.[35] The identity of the co-consecrators is not known.

The headquarters of the American Episcopal Church are at 121 Greengate Lane, Spartanburg, South Carolina 29302. No information is available on the number of parishes and missions or on the membership of the church body.

NOTES

1. The author was Franklin S. Rising. The substance of this tract is reproduced in Appendix III of *A History of the Free Church of England, Otherwise Called the Reformed Episcopal Church* (2nd edn.; Morecambe, Lancastershire, England: The Free Church of England Publications Committee, 1960), pp. 157-170.

2. Clowes Chorley, *Men and Movements in the American Episcopal Church* (New York: Charles Scribner's Sons, 1950), pp. 403-404.

3. Ibid., p. 409.

4. Ibid., p. 416.

5. The so-called "Proposed" or "Bishop White" Book of Common Prayer. The Reformed Episcopal Church holds that since the "Second" Book of Common Prayer of Edward VI, in use for a few months in 1552, no Book of Common Prayer has been wholly "in harmony with the clear teachings of the word of God as expressed in the doctrines of the Reformed faith" (*The Book of Common Prayer According to the Use of The Reformed Episcopal Church in the United States of America* [5th edn.; Philadelphia: The Reformed Episcopal Publication Society, 1932], p. vi). It sets great store by the revision that a commission of Evangelical bishops and theologians drafted in 1689 (unpublished until 1854, and then only as a matter of record). The "Proposed" or "Bishop White" American Prayer Book of 1785 preserved many features of the 1689 draft. The Reformed Episcopal Book of Common Prayer was first adopted in 1874.

6. Ibid., p. v.

7. Ibid., p. xxx.

8. Ibid., pp. 12, 69.

9. Ibid., p. 82.

10. Ibid., p. 71.

11. Ibid., p. 491.

12. Tract, *The Reformed Episcopal Church* (Philadelphia: Reformed Episcopal Publication Society, n. d.), p. 6.

13. Ibid., p. 7.

14. Annie Darling Price, *A History of the Formation and Growth of the Reformed Episcopal Church 1873–1902* (Philadelphia: James M. Armstrong, 1902), p. 150; *The Reformed Episcopal Church*, p. 7.

15. Price, pp. 195-196.

16. *A History of the Free Church of England, Otherwise Called the Reformed Episcopal Church* (Morecambe, Lancastershire, England: The Free Church of England Publications Committee, 1960), p. 35.

17. Communication from W. J. Calhoun, secretary.

18. See Arthur Carl Piepkorn, *Profiles in Belief: The Religious Bodies in the United States and Canada I* (New York: Harper & Row, 1977): 90-92.

19. During their respective tenure of the archepiscopal office of the Free Protestant Episcopal Church of England, some of these prelates held parallel offices in other jurisdictions for at least part of the time.

20. Bishop Primus Boltwood is also the president of the British Synod of the Ecumenical Church Foundation; the rector of both the International Free Protestant Episcopal University (founded by Checkemian in 1898) and of the Seminary of the Free Protestant

Episcopal Church (founded by Martin in 1890 as the Nazarene College); and head of St. Andrew's Correspondence College (Tottenham), Limited, and of the James Martin Bible College. The handbook of the Free Protestant Episcopal Church states that Bishop Primus Boltwood has been "honoured with nobility titles, knighthoods of many ancient and Knight Templar orders, and over one hundred academic awards, including gold and silver medals, etc., for his writings in theology, philosophy, literature, and in the arts and sciences in the field of culture and art" (*The Origins, Orders, Organisation, Etc., of the Free Protestant Episcopal Church* [London: St. Andrew's Collegiate Church, 1960] [16-page pamphlet], p. [iv]).

21. Ibid., pp. [v]-[vii], 1.
22. *The Intuitive Interpreter*, No. 244 (November–December 1967), p. 2.
23. *The Origins, Orders, Organisation, Etc., of the Free Protestant Episcopal Church*, pp. 7-8.
24. Thus Bishop Eckardt was also the pastor of the First Church of Christ (Disciples), London, Ontario, and president of Philathea College.
25. Letters from the Most Reverend Charles Dennis Boltwood, D.D., D.C.L., O.S.G., bishop primus, The Free Protestant Episcopal Church; the Right Reverend Benjamin C. Eckardt, LL.B., Ed.D., LL.D., D.D., bishop of Ontario and Quebec, The Free Protestant Episcopal Church 1033 Adelaide Street, London, Ontario; the Right Reverend Albert J. Fuge, Ph.D., LL.D., bishop of New York, The Free Protestant Episcopal Church, 80 Broad Street, New York, N.Y.; and the Right Reverend Harry Kenneth Means, D.D., missionary bishop of the Southeastern diocese and the Bahamas, 3770 Northeast 15th Avenue, North Pompano Beach, Florida. Repeated requests to the two North American national primates, Bishops Enochs and Moffatt, for information about their jurisdictions have gone unanswered.
26. The considered estimate of Lewis Bliss Whittemore, *Struggle for Freedom: History of the Philippine Independent Church* (Greenwich, Conn.: Seabury Press, 1961), p. 129.
27. Quoted ibid., pp. 176-178.
28. Letters from the Reverend Timoteo P. Quintero, vicar, St. Paul's Philippine Independent Mission, St. Andrew's Protestant Episcopal Cathedral, Queen Emma Square, Honolulu, Hawaii.
29. *Statement of the Most Reverend James P. Dees, Presiding Bishop of The Anglican Orthodox Church, Made When He Resigned as Priest from The Protestant Episcopal Church on November 15, 1963* (Statesville, N.C.: James P. Dees, 1964) (8-page pamphlet).
30. *The Anglican Orthodox Church of North America* (Statesville, N.C.: The Anglican Orthodox Church, 1964) (6-page pamphlet). The first Protestant Episcopal clergyman to join the new denomination affiliated with it in January 1966 ("Dees Is Joined by Littlewood," *Statesville* [N.C.] *Record and Landmark*, January 10, 1966, p. 2).
31. Bob Jones University, Greenville, S.C., conferred an honorary doctorate of divinity on Presiding Bishop Dees in 1965 ("Bishop Dees Given Honor," *Statesville* [N.C.] *Record and Landmark*, June 4, 1965, p. 1).
32. *The Most Reverend James Parker Dees, AB., B.D., D.D. . . . Some Biographical Data* (Statesville, N.C.: The Anglican Orthodox Church of North America, 1966) (single multilithed sheet). Sawyna's address is given as 304 South 16th Street, Allentown, Pennsylvania, Woodward's as Fort Oglethorpe, Georgia. The present writer has not been able to secure information about the jurisdictions of the consecrating prelates or about the sources of their own orders. Three letters to the former and two to the latter have gone unacknowledged. In the case of the former, the efforts of the Reverend John Daniel, M.A., D.D., pastor of St. John's Church, Allentown, to secure a personal interview were unavailing; but Dr. Daniel did establish that Sawyna is married, a canonical impediment to receiving bishop's orders according to the current canon law of the historic Eastern Orthodox jurisdictions. Sawyna was reportedly consecrated by Evhen Batchinskiy in Switzerland; Batchinskiy in turn was consecrated by Nikolai Urbanovich of the Aneed Succession and the Mariavite prelate Efrem Maria Mauro Fusi. Woodward is described as

a bishop of the Old Catholic Church; he was ordained by William Henry Francis of the Old Catholic Church in America and, according to James Edward Burns of the American Orthodox Catholic Church (Bronx, New York), Burns consecrated Woodward to the episcopate (telephone conversation with Bishop Burns).

33. Letter from Mrs. Betty Hoffman, secretary to the Most Reverend James Parker Dees, D.D., presiding bishop, the Anglican Orthodox Church of North America.

34. Both quotations from James L. Adams, "New Episcopal Splinter," *Christianity Today*, April 11, 1969, p. 49.

35. The Indian Orthodox Church (Antiochean Succession) has no parishes in the United States or Canada. Since 1947 Archbishop Pillai had been in the

United States "on a special mission." Under the name of James Charles Ryan, Pillai had been consecrated to the episcopate in 1944 by Charles Leslie Saul (Mar Leofric), head of the Evangelical Church of England; Saul's orders derived via Leon Chechemian (or Checkemian) (Mar Leon), archbishop of the Free Protestant Church of England. Hugh George de Willmott Newman (Mar Georgius I), archbishop and metropolitan of Glastonbury and Catholicos of the West, whose episcopal orders derived from Ferrete, reconsecrated Pillai in August 1945. (Henry R. T. Brandreth, *Episcopi Vagantes and the Anglican Church* [2nd edn.; London: S.P.C.K., 1961], pp. 70-85; Peter F. Anson, *Bishops at Large* [New York: October House, 1964], pp. 31-47, 216-251, 263-264).

BIBLIOGRAPHY

The Book of Common Prayer According to the Use of The Reformed Episcopal Church in the United States of America. 6th (rev. 5th) edn. Philadelphia: The Reformed Episcopal Publication Society, 1963.

Chorley, E. Clowes. *Men and Movements in the American Episcopal Church.* New York: Charles Scribner's Sons, 1950. Chap. 14, "The Passing of the Low Churchmen."

Clifford, (Sister) Mary Dorita. "Iglesia Filipina Independiente: The Revolutionary Church." In: Gerald H. Anderson, ed., *Studies in Philippine Church History*. Ithaca, N.Y.: Cornell University Press, 1969. Pp. 223-255.

Deats, Richard L. *Nationalism and Christianity in the Philippines.* Dallas, Texas: Southern Methodist University Press, 1967. See especially chap. 3, "The Philippine Independent Church as an Outgrowth of Nationalism" (pp. 63-87).

A History of the Free Church of England Otherwise Called The Reformed Episcopal Church. Second edition. Morecambe, Lancs., England: The Free Church of England Publications Committee, 1960.

History of the Reformed Episcopal Seminary. Philadelphia: Reformed Episcopal Church, 1965.

Mueller, Walter. *Foundations of Our Faith.* Philadelphia: Committee on Christian Education of the Reformed Episcopal Church, 1959. A 56-page manual for use in preparing adolescents for confirmation.

Peck, Robert L. "A Brief Study of the Reformed Episcopal Church." In: *American Church Quarterly* III (1963): 253-262. A critical analysis of the Reformed Episcopal Church from a Protestant Episcopal viewpoint.

Price, Annie Darling. *A History of the Formation and Growth of the Reformed Episcopal Church, 1873–1902.* Philadelphia: James M. Armstrong, 1902. For the early period Mrs. Price makes extensive use of the otherwise inaccessible work of Benjamin Aycrigg, *Memoirs of the Reformed Episcopal Church* (New York: Privately printed, 1880).

Whittemore, Lewis Bliss. *Struggle for Freedom: History of the Philippine Independent Church.* Greenwich, Conn.: Seabury Press, 1961. A carefully written account designed to inform members of the Protestant Episcopal Church about the Philippine Independent Church in connection with the concordat presented to the General Convention of the American body in 1961.

PART III

REFORMED AND
PRESBYTERIAN CHURCHES

8. The Reformed and the Presbyterians

The Calvinist Reformation

The eminent scholar Roland Bainton has noted that in the Reformation Wittenberg, Zurich, Geneva, and Canterbury were sisters rather than lineal descendants. The Reformed churches in Zurich and Geneva originated as two distinct but similar expressions of the Protestant spirit. The first movement was led by Zwingli, who died while Luther was in mid-career; it was confined almost exclusively to German Switzerland. John Calvin led the second movement in French Switzerland from 1536 to 1564, three decades of diminished energy in Lutheranism and growing strength in the Roman Catholic Reformation. Calvin's movement spread to a number of nations and cities, and it is clear that without him the survival of Protestantism on the Continent would have been greatly imperiled.[1]

Political circumstances played an important role in the emergence of Reformed churches in the Swiss cantons. The burghers and magistrates of Swiss cities were able and confident leaders who made important decisions that advanced the cause of the Reformation. Through skillful argument Calvin was sometimes able to persuade leaders in Geneva, but never could he bully them to get his way. The special target of reform was the priest of the pre-Reformation era who, it was claimed, was part of the hierarchy that subjected all of Christendom to tyranny. In the Holy Roman empire the Treaty of Westphalia in 1648 finally recognized "the Reformed" as a protected group, but progress came more quickly elsewhere.

Ulrich Zwingli (1484–1531), at one time a shepherd and a promising musician, was the leader of the Reformation in German Switzerland. Educated at Basel in a humanist environment, he was thoroughly trained in medieval theology with particular competence in the thought of Thomas Aquinas. But his lecturers also included men who called for the reform of the church. In 1506 Zwingli was appointed vicar at Glarus. He suffered spiritual anguish over his inability to keep the vow of chastity but relished the opportunity to study the New Testament and the early fathers. Zwingli was indebted to Erasmus for texts and methodology, but eventually he broke with the humanist.

In 1516 his opposition to the lucrative Swiss mercenary system forced his release from Glarus. The Benedictines in Einsiedeln used him as a chaplain for pilgrims to this famous Swiss shrine. Here Zwingli become an evangelical scholar with the help of Erasmus's Greek New Testament (1516) and much study.

In 1519 Zwingli, now a celebrated preacher, was inducted into an eminent post as preacher in the Great Minster of Zurich. He announced that he would preach a series of sermons on Matthew instead of the appointed lessons. Lutheran ideas were also in the air, and his correspondence in 1519 spoke highly of this "Elijah" whom he admired. But he refused to be called a Lutheran, preferring the term "Paulinian." The plague that killed one third of Zurich's 7,000 townsmen in 1519 brought him much anguish.

Arguing from the Bible, Zwingli said in 1520–1521 that certain types of conventional piety such as fasting should be curtailed. The magistrates intervened on his behalf late in 1520. Some Zurichers broke the Lenten fast in 1522, and in that same year Zwingli authored a petition on behalf of eleven priests who invoked their scriptural right to marry (he secretly married that year as well). Local friars challenged these events, but the Zurich Council supported Zwingli, resolving to follow Scripture in doctrine and worship. Zwingli's reliance on the Bible as guide and norm was clarified in the preface of his Sixty-Seven Articles: "If I do not correctly understand the Scripture, I undertake to allow myself to be better instructed, yet only from the aforementioned Scripture." These *Articles* were the basis of a public disputation in Zurich in 1523; they became the first confessional document of the Swiss Reformation. The bishop's representative offered no serious opposition in this Town Hall debate, and the magistrates mandated that the canton's clergy were to preach "nothing but that which can be proved by the Holy Gospel, and the pure Holy Scriptures." Zwingli continued to consolidate his gains by issuing several theological treatises and engaging in a second disputation (1523), with 500 priests present, which resolved that images were unscriptural and the Mass was not a sacrifice but a memorial of Christ's all-sufficient offering. These decisions were not implemented until 1524, when the parish churches were swept clean of images, whitewashed, and the organs nailed shut, and in 1525 when the rite of the Roman Mass was abolished.

Zwingli's doctrine was cast in a mold that had itself been shaped by his humanist training. He contended, for example, that Scripture describes God as "the being (*esse*) of all things," the "life and motion" of all that lives, the "source and fountain of all good," and that He is Love, most fully expressed in the delivery of his Son to the cross for man's sins. "That alone is God which is perfect, that is, absolute, and to which nothing is lacking, but everything is present that belongs to the highest good," he said while repudiating the service of philosophy. On the other hand, man always does everything from self-love, and unless a change occurs he will always do so, Zwingli taught. Man's fall was due to self-love that led him to think he had equal status with God.

Zwingli taught that religion originated when God called runaway man back and showed him what loyal devotion is. Christ satisfied divine judgment and offers remission of sins. He was born of Mary, who remained a virgin according to Zwingli, and took flesh without imperfection.

Zwingli's views on church order were based on his belief that in a Christian state, *corpus Christianum*, church and state would reciprocate with trust and freedom. Minister and magistrate both would hold "spiritual" offices. Zwingli founded a synod (1528), composed of ministers and lay delegates from each parish who met twice a year to consider intemperances and neglect of church ordinances. Governmental representatives also participated in the proceedings; the synod was in no sense a rival of the political authority. This system spread to other areas and was important in maintaining standards for the ministry.

Zwingli described the "Gospel" as "everything that is made known of God to men, which instructs them and assures them of his will." More precisely, "The sum of the Gospel is that Christ, the Son of the living God, made known to us the will of the Heavenly Father and by His innocence redeemed us from eternal death and reconciled us to God." Election is the expression of God's undivided justice and mercy, the "free disposition of the divine will in regard to those that are to be blessed." It precedes faith, and faith follows as a sign of election. Faith is the new relationship created by the Holy Spirit; it delivers one from anxiety and involves a spiritual union with Christ.

Zwingli's experiences in Zurich led him to minimize those structures of the visible church that were manifested in the period before the Reformation. Equally important as an influence in this area was his doctrine of election, since he held that God's free election chose children and even various pagans without regard for the church's structure. He defined "church" in two ways. The invisible church, the whole company of the elect, is known only to God. This is the spotless Bride of Jesus Christ governed by the Spirit of God. Not locally confined, it spreads throughout the world and receives members everywhere. "Church" is also the visible institution including all who were rated as Christians. Among the indications that God is actively working in the congregation are the facts, said Zwingli, that the people gather around God's Word, discipline is practiced, the sacraments are celebrated correctly, and Christ is confessed. He avoided describing the church as separated Christians, as was advocated by the Aabaptists.

Baptism was initiation into the Christian society, much like circumcision in Israel. The use of the font was maintained, and Zwingli's order of baptism featured a prayer for the kindling of the light of faith in the child's heart. Zwingli firmly supported the baptism of infants and held that the faith of parents makes them heirs of the covenant; as a covenantal sign, baptism established the covenantal promise for them.

Unleavened bread was retained in the Lord's Supper. According to Zwingli the Supper was not a channel of grace but a sign and memorial, the public testimony of one's adherence to a religious community. The sacrament was called a memorial and a thanskgiving; Christian people bear witness in this meal, he argued, to the death of Christ as the only source of their salvation. The sacrament was prized as a special means of appropriating grace; the group that commemorated Christ's passion and sacrifice nurtured one another's faith and appreciated its value. "Christ's true body is present by the contemplation of faith . . . and thus everything wrought by Christ becomes, as it were, present by the contemplation of faith." By 1531 Zwingli's Communion rite was being used in Bern, Basel, and other Protestant parts of Switzerland. It retained the *Gloria in excelsis* and the Apostles' Creed and was usually celebrated in Zurich quarterly. The Supper was an occasion of profound contemplation of Calvary, such powerful contemplation that the worshiper could, said Zwingli, "grasp the thing itself." Stillness and repose were required in the service; there was no music or speech except the Scripture and people did not leave their seats to commune. Luther and Zwingli agreed on fourteen of fifteen points in their conference at Marburg in 1529; the one point of vigorous disagreement was the mode of Christ's presence in the Lord's Supper.

Zurich's missionary spirit spread the Reformed faith to Bern and Basel in the north, both of which went Protestant. The same was true of Schaffhausen, St. Gall, and the free imperial city of Constance. The south cantons, however, held firm for the old faith. The failure of the Swiss Protestants to seal an alliance with the German Protestants in 1529 meant that they had to fight the Roman Catholic cantons alone. Zwingli died as a combatant, along with twenty-five of Zurich's pastors, in the second battle of Kappel in 1531. The treaty of peace that followed permitted the Reform in Switzerland to stand without spreading. Medieval unity of one faith in one land was gone inasmuch as Catholic minorities were permitted in Protestant cantons while the opposite was not true.[2]

The second major Reformed center was the independent city of Geneva where John Calvin (1509–1564) worked. The term "Calvinism" derives from his name. Historians have observed that the word "Calvinist" first appeared in printed English in 1579, but apparently they overlooked the earlier use of the equivalents "Calvinian" (1566) and "Calvinism" (1570).[3]

References to Calvin and Calvinism often accompany a reference to the "glory" or "sovereignty" of God as the controlling theme of Calvin's theology. This has been overworked. It can be argued that the predominant motif in his theology was "union with Christ," or "the work of the Spirit," or "appropriation of grace." For Calvin God's sovereignty was a sovereignty of love and holiness; the doctrine was a comforting and consoling one in disturbing times as we shall see.

Calvin was born in Noyon, France. His father directed him to study law in Orleans (1528) and Bourges, but he abandoned the field three years later when his father died. Returning to Paris, he started a literary career although the scholarly world did not seem interested in his work. In 1534 he penned the first theological tract, a preface for his cousin's French translation of the New Testament. He later told of a "sudden conversion," probably in 1533 and probably related in some way to his vocational enthusiasm for Protestant theology. Later (1539) Calvin described a spiritual struggle that was brought to a finish by the message of the Gospel; his testimony may have been auto-biographical. His *Preface to the Psalms* also indicated that his conversion to Protestantism entailed soul-searching. After conversion he still thought of himself primarily as a writer; by 1535 he had given the first edition of his *Institutes* to a printer in Basel, and the work was published the next year.

Traveling widely, he finally decided to use Strassburg as the base of his literary work, but he and his small party had to detour through Geneva on the way. In that free Swiss city William Farel tried to enlist him in the cause of reform but was unsuccessful until he warned Calvin that he was indulging himself and would feel God's curse unless he relented. Calvin acceded, though he did not think of himself as a reformer. His official appointment was as "reader in Holy Scriptures." His first efforts at reform ended in failure; in 1538 he and Farel were relieved of their appointments in a dispute over the spheres of authority of church and state. Calvin reluctantly joined Martin Bucer in Strassburg where he served as pastor of the French congregation and lecturer in the academy. During these happy and productive years he married the widow of an Anabaptist.

In 1541 the magistrates at Geneva asked Calvin to respond to a letter from Cardinal Sadoleto which invited them to turn from the Reformation and return to Rome. Since the party favoring Calvin had won the local elections, Calvin returned to Geneva that year despite grave misgivings and a desire to stay in Strassburg.

Calvin is often perceived to have been an inhuman or semihuman person. While he was a habitual insomniac and a man whose temper, he said, "is naturally inclined to be violent," and while he labored under such physical ailments as asthma, catarrh, migraine, indigestion, pluerisy, calculus, ulcerous hemorrhoids, quartan fever, and tuberculosis, he was not dour or dreary. He wrote and spoke about wine, color, and clothes with appreciation. Among the many assets of his mind were a memory stocked with thousands of passages of Scripture and a fluency in expression that made him an early master of French prose.

He wrote the first edition of the *Christianae Religionis Institutio* (1536) as a layman. This edition of six chapters was a confession of faith dedicated to the French king, Francis I; it was aimed at winning freedom from persecution for those who held Calvin's opinions, but it was also an instruction book for those interested in religion. Like Luther's catechisms, it contained sections on the law, creed, Lord's Prayer, and the two sacraments of baptism and the Lord's Supper. Chapter 5 discussed the five rites mistakenly called sacraments, and Chapter 6, "Christian Liberty," discussed church and state and the duties of the Christian life. A second edition appeared in 1539, nearly three times the original size. The French translation (1541) of this Latin version became a landmark in the history of French prose; Calvin's skill with French made him an important creator of the French literary tradition. A new expanded Latin revision was issued in 1543. There were other minor revisions and printings until 1559 when the final revision of the Latin *Institutes* appeared in Geneva. This definitive edition was nearly five times as long as the original version; its four books covered in a general way the themes of the Apostles' Creed, namely, the Father, Son, Spirit, and church. In a masterful way Calvin's *Institutes* show the vigorous rhetorical skill and communicative power of a theologian deeply committed to his religious faith. The *Institutes* breathe the Word of God; the work contains 2,474 quotations from the Old Testament and 4,330 from the New Testament.[4]

Calvin's other writings clustered around this great work. His works covered fifty-nine quarto volumes and included commentaries on twenty-three Old Testament books and all the New Testament books except the Apocalypse. His rigorous effort to utter biblical truths kept him from pressing the material into nicely formed molds. He tried to be simple and clear, but it is a "superficial judgment," says one important scholar, to regard him as a "resolute systematizer whose ideas are wholly unambiguous and consistent and set in a mold of flawless logic."[5]

No native son of Geneva, Calvin was an alien working in a strange and unfamiliar environment. But he was also a cosmopolitan figure who escaped narrow parochial bonds, and this enabled him to become a reformer for Europe rather than Geneva alone. Nevertheless, it was reform in Geneva that lay at the basis of much of his influence elsewhere.

When he returned in 1541 Calvin laid down the goals of reformation in Geneva. His celebrated *Ecclesiastical Ordinances* will be discussed below in the section on Reformed order, but it should be noted that the reform was slow in coming. His triumph was not complete until the Perrinist party was routed in 1555 after which, a chronicler reported, "everyone went to sermons regularly now, even the hypocrites."[6]

There were many reasons for Calvin's permanent triumph in Geneva in 1555. Geneva, Bern, and France had no local theologians of his stature. Calvin and his pastoral colleagues had a monopoly on the most important mass medium in Geneva, namely, the sermon, and they used this means of public communication effectively in each of the four churches where an average of twelve sermons were heard each week. Thorough religious indoctrination of Genevan children also reinforced Calvin's reform program; his Genevan catechism (1541) taught the fundamentals of his doctrine in fifty-five lessons spread over one year. The catechism insisted that the principal end of human life was to "know" God; this knowledge came by "honoring" God, and the proper way to honor him was "by putting all our trust in Him." The catechism contained nothing on election; the bulk of its material concentrated on the activities of the Savior and the nature of the true church.[7]

Calvin's powerful preaching reinforced the thrust of his reform. He is said to have preached about 2,400 sermons that were in some way recorded. The power of his message derived from the primacy of the Bible in his preaching. When he grew too sick with tuberculosis to walk to St. Pierre, he was carried there by friends to do his preaching. His influence in Geneva rested on his pastoral role, since he held no political authority. While he offered advice on a variety of subjects (suggesting for example that buildings should have balconies to protect children), he did not as a habit attend all sessions of the Small Council or give advice on every matter before the council. Even after 1555 his advice was not always accepted; the rulers of Geneva rejected his suggestion in 1560 that copper slugs should be given to all qualified laypersons to admit them to the next Communion.[8]

But he succeeded well enough in his reform of Geneva that by the time of his death he could invite the magistrates of the Small Council to visit him on his deathbed. Five years earlier, in 1559, he had been offered—and had accepted—citizenship in the free city. His final speech to the magistrates illustrated his positive attitude toward political order based on divine authority and natural law. He held that the best way to avoid tyranny was in a government that combined aristocracy and democracy. He thought that the combination of theocracy and elective government was the political order authorized by God inasmuch as it allowed for ordered freedom. He denounced the oppression and godless pride of some kings but acknowledged that they were vicegerents of God.

The spread of Calvin's reformation was due in great part to two factors: the fact that Geneva was a refugee center, and the educational academy opened in the city. Calvin was in a sense a refugee working among refugees in Geneva, and this fact gave added significance to his theological emphasis on "union with Christ," just as it helps to explain the comforting character of God's sovereignty in his thought. In 1557 it was discovered that the number of foreigners in Geneva was greater than the number of citizens. The city included a population of several thousand refugees from several different nationalities. Although one listing of immigrants is probably incomplete, it shows that 5,000 refugees entered the city between 1549 and 1560; this was a sizable number for a city with a total population of about 10,000 in Calvin's time. The overwhelming majority of these refugees came to Geneva after Calvin's decisive and permanent triumph in 1555, peaking in 1559.[9] Refugees fled from France, Holland, England, Scotland, Germany, Italy, Spain, Hungary, Poland, and many other countries in Europe. The influx of French refugees heightened the tense relations between Geneva and the French Crown and were a factor in the civil war between Huguenots and Catholics in France.

The centers of the refugee colonies were the national churches. The English, Italian, and Spanish refugees had their own churches; they also published material that was shipped back to their native land to further the cause of reform. French refugees centered their lives around the established church in

Geneva; most of the printers in Geneva were French refugees, and they played a powerful role in the spread of the reform.[10]

Geneva's academy was publicly dedicated in 1559. For quite some time Calvin had hoped to construct a free public school. The new school's rector was Theodore Beza, who later succeeded Calvin in his position of leadership in the Genevan church. The primary school's seven grades served all of the youth, but the advanced *schola* was primarily for advanced training in theology. By the time of Calvin's death it had 300 students; it served as a theological seminary for the Reformed church in France. Geneva's Company of Pastors (eight urban and ten rural ministers) performed a phenomenal missionary feat as they trained and sent pastors to a variety of places. Between 1555 and 1562 more than 100 different men were sent to almost 120 missions; most of them went to France, but some also went to the valleys of Piedmont, to Turin, Antwerp, London, and even a French colony in Brazil.[11]

Calvin grew to maturity after the early stressful days of the Reformation had passed. As a member of the movement's second generation, he had the special task of reconstructing, building, and organizing rather than rejecting and repudiating. For him "reformation" meant taking a stand on behalf of the Gospel and leaving the consequence to God. His treatise *On the Necessity for Reforming the Church* (1543) argued that the glory of Christ had been impaired; the reformers opposed this in the name of the catholic church, since the Gospel constitutes the church, and not the church the Gospel.[12]

Already in his introduction to Olivetan's New Testament (1535) Calvin offered his fundamental ideas about the Christian faith. After sketching a brief history of salvation, he wrote a long lyrical passage praising the Gospel and Jesus Christ. He expressed some of the ideas that were determinative for his theology: man is blessed in acknowledging God as the source of good; Jesus Christ is the heart of the Scripture; the Gospel, God's Word, confers faith.[13] The fact that in his *Institutes* he presented his material as the story of the human race, and not of an individual, enabled him to show that sin's removal was no mere negative act but a positive restoration of true piety in persons.

For Calvin piety was the total zeal of loving God as Father and revering him as Lord. This knowledge of God embraced the knower as well as the divine benefits that bring piety in the first place. True knowledge of God, said Calvin, takes root in the heart rather than flitting through the brain; it involves commitment and devotion. While both creation and Scripture reveal God as Creator, only the Scripture reveals him as Redeemer.

Calvin's doctrine of man rested on the assumption that people had been made for piety; had they not fractured themselves they would have been led by nature to true knowledge of God. But their conscious response of thanksgiving to God set them apart from the rest of creation; their souls could reflect God's glory and recognize God as the source of all good. Calvin's discussion of the fallen state of mankind is found in his section of the *Institutes* that concerns "Redemption in Christ" (Book II, chapters i-v). The fallen man has turned from God, he argued, and spurned God's bounty while opening himself to the sins of carnal self-indulgence. This does not prevent Calvin from recognizing man's abilities as a social being, pursuing science and virtue. But all stand under the blight of sin and the just judgment of God.

Calvin described the rescue of fallen man as the "end" of the Mosaic law; it resides in the cross and faith in Christ. Christ's sacrifice overcame the malignity of sin. Humble embrace of the cross is the way persons return to God their Father. Faith is no mere assent to information but an embracing of Christ so that he can dwell in the believer. Faith creates a hidden communion between the believer and Christ; it reconciles people to God and sanctifies them in Christ's Spirit. Redemption, in sum, is the "mystical union" of the believer with Christ; this union follows the communion the believer has with Christ in his Incarnation and precedes the communication of Christ's benefits.[14]

Calvin contended that the Christian life was structured by the imitation of Christ, or the two tables of the law which were fully embodied by Christ. Obedience to the law, which represented the good pleasure of the heavenly Father, was possible only by the Spirit. Humility was basic to all Christian behavior; Christians loved and served the neighbor. All that people have they possess as stewards of divine gifts, and one's vocation was the "post assigned" for faithful duty. Calvin inaugurated the *consistory*, composed of pastors and elders (laymen), to regiment the lives of citizens. One of the most critical issues in Geneva was not whether Calvin could force his will on the city council, but whether the church could regulate its own life without governmental interference. This meant in particular the power to excommunicate unworthy members, a point that Calvin finally won in 1561.[15]

The doctrine of election is the final consequence of Calvin's theology rather than its first principle. In the 1559 edition of the *Institutes* the doctrine was placed after the chapters on Christ's twofold gifts; it has the appearance of being an appendix to the affirmation of his central theme, namely "Christ alone." Since election precedes faith and causes faith in the order of reality, while faith precedes election in the order of knowing, election plays no role in Christian proclamation according to Calvin. Rather, it is a confession of those who believe; for them it is an explanation of why they have faith that is consistent with the content of their faith.[16] Calvin avoided the doctrine of double predestination in his catechism for children, and in his preaching apparently did not terrify or damage tender hearts with the doctrine. Inasmuch as he did not treat the doctrine in isolation from his soteriology, it is false to say that for him God is capricious will, or power without justice and love.[17]

The doctrine of the church was an extremely important one for Calvin. The book on this subject, the fourth, is the longest of the *Institutes*. Calvin had no place for solitary piety but, rather, stressed that the church was the mother and nurse of the Christian life in her children. According to Calvin the Gospel treasure is deposited in the church. The elect known only to God are the true universal church; it is invisible. The visible church also contains hypocrites, but according to Calvin schism is to be avoided as long as the marks (*notae*) of the church remain. They include the true preaching and reverent hearing of the Gospel, administration of sacraments according to Christ's institution, and discipline, the "nerves" or ligaments of the church. The church, in sum, is the communion of Christ, the community of believers who mutually share their spiritual benefits. Calvin warned his readers to avoid schism over false ideas of perfection, but he urged that in nonessential points persons in the church's fellowship should attempt to correct errors. He allowed for an episcopacy in the church if it is free from "dominion," "principality," and "tyranny," and in fact he did not suggest that Archbishop Cranmer of England should rid himself of primacy. For Poland he recommended the creation of an episcopally ordered reformed church.[18]

Both Word and Spirit work in the church, according to Calvin, to bring the gift of faith. It is their gift, since the two are indissolubly linked; the Word is the Spirit's instrument. In the deepest sense of the term, the church was a means of grace for Calvin. He held that revelation was progressive; God accommodated it to man's differing capacities to receive it. Thus the Scripture contains parts that are accommodating to the kind of language which people could grasp at the time (e.g., Genesis 1:16). The Scriptures put forth the promise of salvation with the Gospel as the special "word of faith."[19]

The sacraments were visible words that were without effect unless and until they worked faith. They offered grace to all according to Calvin, but it was not received by all. Baptism symbolized membership in the household of faith. While not effecting salvation, it was an initiation into the church's fellowship. It was not to be administered where there was no evidence of faith; for infants this faith was that of the parents. Calvin rejected the view that unbaptized infants were damned if they died, but at times he suggested that the rite conveyed regenerating grace to infants.[20] Baptism represents symbolically the cleansing through Christ which comes in communion with him.

In the Lord's Supper, the Supper signifies nourishment from Christ. In the Eucharist a real communion with Christ's body occurs. Calvin's stress on the spiritual presence of Christ's body put him closer to Luther than to Zwingli, but like Zwingli he rejected the idea of the "ubiquity" of Christ's body. In the sacrament the believer enjoys a vivid moment of communion with Christ; through the Spirit's mysterious intervention he partakes spiritually in Christ's glorified body. This "spiritual" miracle shows that the doctrine of the Eucharist is also a doctrine of the Holy Spirit. The Supper liturgically represents as well the whole life of the Christian as a sacrifice of thanksgiving to God. For Calvin the Supper also strikes the chords of thanksgiving, remembrance of Christ's death, and eschatological expectation, as well as spiritual and social communion among the people.[21] There is no question that for Calvin the presence of Christ in the Supper is his personal and spiritual presence.

Calvin's theology appealed to various people in sections of northern Europe. From Geneva Calvinism spread to his native country, France; to Switzerland, his adopted home; to the Dutch part of the Netherlands, which teetered on the threshold of commercial prosperity as it struggled for freedom; for a brief time in Poland, and later in Hungary; to Germans in areas as widely separated as Brandenburg and the Palatinate; in England as Puritanism; in Scotland, where as we shall see an act of Parliament established it in 1560; and still later in America and other parts of the globe. In fact, the first settlers in Canada were French Huguenots. In Scotland and New England the ideal was most nearly achieved, while in France, Holland, and old England Calvinism became a militant minority. The international spread of Calvinism was due in part to the blockage of Lutheranism, in the east by Slavic orthodoxy and to the south by the Counter-Reformation, with a resultant westward thrust of Reformed Protestantism. In addition, the Calvinist minorities in many lands had the choice of being aggressive or succumbing to the majority, and that gave impetus to the movement.[22]

France was an instance where Protestantism was nearly—but only nearly —successful. The king of France had been centralizing his power for some time, and his relation with the church was so much to his advantage that he had little reason to reject Roman Catholicism. Neither did he have a great point of tension with the church, such as did Henry VIII in England. The succession of kings in France was more concerned with the monarchy and with France than with deeply religious sentiment.

Early activity by Protestant reformers in France made the situation somewhat precarious by the time of Francis I's death in 1547. His policy of moderate suppression had enabled Protestants to flourish, but Henry II set out to reverse that trend. His "fire court" was the legal instrument of persecution, although he was unable to root out "the Protestant heresy." By the 1550s the French exiles in Geneva were exerting a major influence on French Protestantism, and this increased the tension. Unlike other lands, the issue was not decisively settled, and persecution of Protestants continued year after year.

When the question of succession broke out in 1559 French Protestants married their theological opinion with opposition to the government. Soon outright war ensued, first in 1562, as religion became a convenient pretext for the goals and objectives of two warring noble groups. The St. Bartholomew Day Massacre in 1572 was a notorious instance of wholesale murder of Protestants, but the Wars of Religion continued, since no strong ruler came on the scene after Henry II. In 1562 the Huguenots (Protestants) were permitted freedom of public worship outside of town and private assembly within the walls; this gave limited recognition to Calvinism in France.

The inconclusive situation prevailed in France until Henry IV, a Huguenot, became king in 1589. The Protestants thought they were successful at this point until Henry announced that he was a Roman Catholic. He feared for the well-being of France, especially since the Spanish king was laying claim to the French throne. Henry's Edict of Nantes (1598) brought full religious pluralism to France for eighty-seven years. The Huguenots received full civil rights and could worship privately anywhere; public worship was designated in certain places, including the estates of 3,000 nobles. The Huguenots were also given control of 200 fortified towns.[23]

The Reformation came late to Scotland despite the earlier efforts of Patrick Hamilton and George Wishart. John Knox (1513/15–1572) was a small child when Luther affixed his theses to the church door in Wittenberg. Before 1560 much had happened in Zurich, Geneva, France, and other parts of Europe. Scotland took advantage of the experience of others; it was able to adopt a ready-made system of doctrine, worship, and church government. The Reformation in Scotland was inextricably tied to efforts at breaking the old alliance with France and establishing new ties to England without being subjected to the Tudor dynasty.

Knox, the man most responsible for the Reformation in Scotland, publicly appeared on the scene in 1546 while protecting Wishart with a claymore. His support of Protestantism brought him a nineteen-month tour of duty as a prisoner on a French galley ship. Five years in England (1549–1554) found him preaching in London, ministering in Berwick, and conversing on occasion with Archbishop Cranmer. When Mary Tudor began her reign, he fled to Frankfurt and finally Geneva, where he became pastor of the English exiles. When he first reached Geneva he probably was in most respects a Zwinglian, but Geneva and Calvin soon made him a Calvinist.[24]

He returned to Scotland in 1559, and the next year a treaty secured the withdrawal of both French and English forces from Scotland. It was now necessary to reshape the Scottish church. A confession of faith, the Scots Confession of Faith (1560), was drawn up by the "six Johns"—Knox, Willock, Spottiswood, Winram, Douglas, and Row. Their joint product, also called the "First Scottish Confession," was passed without delay by Parliament on August 17, 1560. Since the queen was still in France and refused to ratify the decision, it did not become the official confession until 1567 when Parliament reenacted it after Mary's deposition. Parliament also acted to abolish the pope's jurisdiction and to oppose the celebrating of Mass. The *First Book of Discipline* (1561), though never ratified by the state, guided early practice in the reform of the church's order; it generally followed Calvin's scheme for the order of the church. The *Second Book of Discipline* was approved by the church in 1578 and at various times thereafter by the state.

Knox's famous five interviews with Queen Mary did not bring her to break with Roman Catholicism, but his religious certainty provided a basis for his insistence that he could speak on a matter of great public concern because he was born as a subject of the realm. He held that the subject was free to advise the ruler and also insisted on the church's corporate freedom to assemble and determine its own policies. The General Assembly met for the third time in 1561, and the next year provincial synods were created as well.

One distinctive feature of the Reformation in Scotland was "covenanting." Late in 1557 a few Protestant nobles formed the First Scottish Covenant, pledging that "before the majesty of God" they would commit their power, property, and lives to the cause of "the Word of God and his Congregation." The term "Congregation" referred to the Scottish followers of the Reformation. The covenants of 1581, 1638, and 1643 were important political and religious agreements on behalf of national interest and in opposition to the papacy and the episcopacy. "Scotch" and "Presbyterian" were two adjectives welded into one.

Reformed Churches Throughout the World

The generic term "Reformed" is often used to refer to the churches that trace their Reformation parentage to Zurich, Geneva, Scotland, or other areas where non-Lutheran, non-Anglican, or non-Anabaptist Protestant influences prevailed. The reformers in whose lineage the Reformed churches took their origin are Calvin, Zwingli, and others who stood in close relationship to these men. While in the United States the term "Reformed" is sometimes used as an adjective in the name of a denomination, in wider religious circles the term encompasses Presbyterian, Reformed, and other related bodies.

More than 55 million persons in the world belong to Reformed churches, but only in Switzerland, the Netherlands, and Scotland do they compose the majority of the population. The oldest Reformed church is the one in France; it celebrated its 400th anniversary in 1959.[25] In 1938 the Reformed Church of France came into existence with the merger of the Free Evangelical Churches, the Methodist Church, the Reformed Evangelical Church and the Reformed Church.

The Presbyterian Church in Canada is presently a denomination of about a quarter-million members. In 1925 about 40 percent of the nearly 400,000 Presbyterians remained outside when the United Church of Canada was formed (q.v.).

Reformed churches are found on every continent. In 1960 about 18 million members resided in Europe; 15 to 16 million in North America; 1 million in Latin America; 4 million in Africa (with the largest concentration in South Africa); 5 million in Asia (with about 2½ million in Indonesia and 1 million in Korea); and 1½ million in Oceania. The largest Reformed church in the world is the United Presbyterian Church in the U.S.A.

Reformed churches have been involved in ecumenical and union efforts throughout the twentieth century. In 1972 the Presbyterian Church of

England and the Congregational Church in England and Wales formed the United Reformed Church by merging. The combined membership was approximately a quarter million. This was the first union across confessional boundaries in England since the time of the Reformation.

In addition to the Reformed Church in France, a number of other church mergers in this century have involved Reformed and Presbyterian bodies, among others. This was the case in the formation of the United Free Church of Scotland in 1900 and the South India United Church in 1901. In 1924 the United Church of North India brought together the churches of Western India and the Presbyterian Church of India. In 1947 the Presbyterian Church became one component of the Church of South India. The nucleus and chief constituent of the Church of Christ in China (1927) was the Presbyterian Church in China; the majority of former Presbyterians are members of the Church of Christ in Japan (1941), a body formed largely as a result of political duress. Presbyterians constituted the majority of the membership at the time the Church of Christ in Thailand was formed in 1934. Presbyterians and Congregationalists joined the United Evangelical Church of the Philippines when it came into existence in 1929.

Among the major Reformed contributions to the ecumenical movement, those made by W. A. Visser 't Hooft of the Dutch Reformed Church were extremely important. At one time the general secretary and chairman of the World's Student Christian Federation, he was the first and long-time general secretary of the World Council of Churches. In 1966 Eugene Carson Blake, stated clerk of the United Presbyterian Church in the USA, assumed the post. Six years earlier he preached a sermon in San Francisco, California, entitled "A Proposal toward the Reunion of Christ's Church," which became the rallying cry for the formation of the Consultation on Church Union (COCU), a venture in reconciliation among nearly a dozen American communions.

In 1970 the World Alliance of Reformed Churches merged with the International Congregational Council to form the World Alliance of Reformed Churches (Presbyterian and Congregational). When the two ecumenical-confessional organizations merged at this meeting in Nairobi, Kenya, the World Alliance of Reformed Churches (Presbyterian and Congregational), abbreviated WARC, represented 130 churches in 75 countries, a total of 55 million people, 3 million of whom were in Congregational churches. An International Congregational Council first met in 1891 in London under the leadership of R. W. Dale. An ongoing organization was established at the meeting in Wellesley, Massachusetts in 1949. The World Alliance of Reformed Churches originated in London in 1875 as the Alliance of the Reformed Churches throughout the World Holding the Presbyterian System; it was said to be the first such world confessional organization. Its first General Council met in 1877. The alliance's role was primarily consultative and advisory; it had an executive committee and regional groupings. It also engaged in relief work, theological consultation, publishing efforts, and dialogue with Rome. In September 1971 the Lüneburg Concord was the result of nearly ten years of conversation between the WARC and Lutheran representatives in Europe; it opened the way to intercommunion between the groups involved. In 1974 the executive committee of the WARC unanimously agreed to enter into theological discussions with the Baptist World Alliance. WARC membership in 1976 stood at 143 churches, thirty-eight of which were engaged in union negotiations with other churches. The Reverend James McCord, president of Princeton Theological Seminary, was elected president of WARC in 1977. Its office is located at 150, Route de Ferney, 1211 Geneva 20, Switzerland.

John A. Mackay of the Presbyterian Church in the USA was speaking for many of the millions of Reformed people in the world when he said in 1953:

> There are Presbyterians today, and I would class myself among them, in whose spirit something paradoxical is taking place. On the one hand we can say, unequivocally and unashamedly, "We never felt ourselves to be *more* Presbyterian than we do today." But then we go on to add, "We never felt ourselves to be *less* Presbyterian than we do today." Both affirmations are true. We are less Presbyterian than ever before because we never, for a moment, allow ourselves to believe that Presbyterianism exhausts the Christian religion. . . . On the other hand, we were never more Presbyterian than today because we believe that there are insights in our Presbyterian heritage of faith, and attitudes in our Presbyterian tradition of life, which the Church Universal needs in this tremendous hour.[26]

Creed and Doctrine

For a variety of reasons—theological, political, and others—Reformed churches did not see it necessary or desirable to settle on a single compendium of creedal statements and confessions as the Lutherans did in the Book of Concord. Reformed churches in general have no conception of a corpus of doctrine that is hermetically sealed and permanently expressed for all time in a single document or set of documents. Their designation of the minister as a *teaching* elder and their firm reliance on the Scripture as Word of God point the way in which a written "confession" is to be understood.

For most people in Reformed churches, the primary function of a confession is to anchor the churchly proclamation in the Scripture and to regulate it by the Scripture. Each confessional document is seen as having emerged in a historical context as a confession of faith in that contemporary situation, as an instrument of union or collaborating among likeminded people, as a catechetical aid, and as an evaluation of conflicting points of doctrine. Several of the signers of the First Helvetic Confession (1536), including Bullinger, pointed the way from the very beginning. "We wish in no way to prescribe for all the churches," they wrote,

> through these articles a single rule of faith. For we acknowledge no other rule of faith than Holy Scripture. We agree with whoever agrees with this, although he uses different expressions from our Confession. For we should have regard for the fact itself and for the truth, not for the words. We grant to everyone the freedom to use his own expressions which are suitable for his church and will make use of this freedom ourselves, at the same time defending the true sense of this Confession against distortions.[27]

Despite this view of confession in the Reformed churches, efforts have been made to compile synopses and harmonies of the various Reformed confessions. Two attempts, in 1581 in Geneva and in the *Corpus et syntagma* (1612), showed the unwillingness or inability of the Reformed churches to draw up a general confession of faith. Collections of Reformed confessions illustrate the variety and diversity of the documents rather than their total uniformity. "A collection of Reformed Confessions," says a prominent scholar of the confessions, "will attest the freedom with which many particular Churches have confessed Jesus Christ quite independently of the others."[28]

Reformed Protestantism has produced an abundance of creedal statements or confessions. The exact number cannot be determined, since the boundaries distinguishing these creeds are unfixed, but it is estimated that "more than sixty creeds would qualify as Reformed." This abundance and variety is "the nemesis of all those who would write *the* theology of *the* Reformed confessions."[29]

Inasmuch as the Reformed churches took their origin in the sixteenth-century Reformation movement, the confessions of the sixteenth century have a very significant place in their doctrine and life. Among these confessions the Zwingli's Sixty-Seven Articles of Religion (1523); The Ten Theses of Berne (1528); The Confession to Charles VI (written by Zwingli in 1530); The Confession to Francis I (written by Zwingli in 1531); The Tetrapolitan Confession (1530); The First Confession of Basel (1534); The First Helvetic Confession of 1536 (The Second Confession of Basel); Calvin's Catechisms (1537 and 1541); The Lausanne Articles (1536); The Geneva Confession (1536); The Zurich Consensus (1549); The Confession of Faith of the English Congregation at Geneva (1566); The Gallican (French) Confession of Faith (1559); The Scots (or Scottish) Confession of Faith (1560); The Belgic Confession Faith (1561); The Heidelberg Catechism (1563); and The Second Helvetic Confession (1566).

The Second Helvetic Confession, the Gallican Confession and the Belgic Confession expressly approved the three ecumenical creeds as "agreeing with the written Word of God." The Genevan and Heidelberg catechisms expounded the Apostles' Creed as part of the catechetical process. Some Reformed theologians also include the Lutheran Augsburg Confession in any listing of Reformed confessions of the sixteenth century. One scholar stresses that "the Reformation Churches were born with the Confessions of the sixteenth century; those of the seventeenth and twentieth centuries are interpretive and explanatory supplements to the original documents." But not all Reformed theologians would agree with his statement that the Westminster standards of the seventeenth century "reflect a legalism, moralism, and rationalism that is foreign to the Confessions of a century earlier."[30]

The Second Helvetic Confession showed the growing ecumenical consciousness of the Protestants in the Swiss cantons as well as the expansion of their theological horizons. Reformed churches of Scotland, Poland, and Hungary promptly approved it, and it has retained a place of high esteem. The confession warned that certain specific persons were not to be regarded as reprobate, or nonelect. Generally speaking, this confession enjoys the highest authority among Reformed confessions. Written by Bullinger in 1562 as a legacy for the city in which he labored so long, it showed the influence of this Zuricher's wide acquaintance with Protestants in Europe. After slight alteration it was published for the first time in 1566. It had its greatest influence in Switzerland, and still serves as the living confession of Reformed churches in Hungary, Austria, Poland, and Czechoslovakia. In 1967 it was included in the *Book of Confessions* of the United Presbyterian Church in the USA. The confession expresses biblical and theological concepts simply and clearly and rejects all sectarian divisions.

The Scots Confession, composed in four days, remained the confession of the Church of Scotland until 1647 when it was superseded by the Westminster Confession in hopes that a united Reformed Church would cover the British Isles. The theology of the confession was Calvinist; the Gallican Confession also influenced the authors. Election out of "mere grace" was tied firmly to Christ's mediation; only in a subordinate clause were "the reprobate" mentioned incidentally. The three marks of the church followed Calvin's description; the article on the Eucharist affirmed Christ's mystical presence for believers.

The Heidelberg Catechism is probably, of all Reformed catechisms, "the most widely accepted doctrinal standard among Reformed Churches."[31] It was the first Protestant confession to arrive in the New World with European explorers in 1609. A new English translation in 1963 honored its 400th anniversary. Chiefly responsible for its authorship was the Heidelberg theologian Zacharias Ursinus. It has been widely used by Reformed churches in Hungary, the Netherlands, Germany, Scotland, and the United States.[32]

The Canons of Dort (1619) is a Reformed confession adopted at the Synod of Dort (1618–1619) in Holland to which representatives of the Reformed churches of England, Switzerland, the Palatinate, and Scotland were invited. The synod leveled judgment against James Arminius (1560–1609) and his followers, called Arminians. Arminius had come to the conclusion that God's grace was universal and man was in a position to exert his will. In 1610 the Arminians submitted their "Five Points" or "Remonstrance" to the estates of Holland in the hopes of obtaining religious toleration. In subsequent theological and political controversy, however, the contra-remonstrants got the upper hand and controlled the Synod of Dort, which issued the canons against the Arminians. Some scholars contend that the canons clearly evidenced a scholasticized form of Calvinism that Calvin would have had difficulty identifying with his own theology. The "Five Points" of Calvinism elucidated in the canons focused on election, atonement, total depravity, irresistible grace, and perseverance in grace.

The Westminster Confession (1647) was authored by a congress of Puritan clergymen of the Church of England meeting in 1643 by order of the Long Parliament. The broad assignment of the group was to create a Presbyterian church order for all the British Isles. Named to the congress were 121 ministers from England, most of them Puritan Calvinists but a few of them Puritan "Independents," and thirty members of Parliament; after the Solemn League and Covenant with Scotland was adopted in 1643, four Scottish ministers and two laymen participated in the debate without vote. The average attendance was said to have been "threescore" in view of the civil strife that was widespread. The Westminster Assembly was a pawn of sorts in the revolution sweeping England in the 1640s; both the king and the archbishop of Canterbury were beheaded before its 1,163 sessions ended in 1649. Cromwell's Independents took charge over the Presbyterian parliamentarians, and Presbyterian clergy were thrown out of the Church of England after the monarchy and bishops were restored in 1660. Presbyterians gained freedom with the Act of Toleration in 1689, but the church never again attained the popularity it held in the 1640s.

The Westminster Confession remained a creedal standard in Scotland. This most massive and intricate of Reformed confessions had tremendous influence in colonial and nineteenth-century America. The Confession broke no new ground but consolidated gains since the last confession had been written more than fifty years earlier. The document breathes the kind of orthodox or scholastic spirit that was prevalent in Europe in the early years of the Age of Reason. Religious wars and grave economic and political instability encouraged the search for stability in doctrine, worship, and order. In doctrinal matters the Westminster divines had few differences, but fierce fighting ensued over whether or not the Presbyterian order of church government was by "divine right" or "human right." The divine right won the day. The lasting achievement of the assembly was "to refine a predestinarian, two-covenant system of theology into confessional form."[33]

In 1729 the first Presbyterian synod in North America, the old Synod of Philadelphia, in its Adopting Act adopted the confession together with the Larger and Shorter catechisms as "the Confession of our Faith." Action was also taken by the first General Assembly in 1788. Through a series of revisions of the Westminster Confession in a process that reached from 1903 to 1942, the three major Presbyterian bodies in the United States at that time (Presbyterian Church in the USA, United Presbyterian Church of North America, and Presbyterian Church U.S.) had "officially omitted the causal foreordination, predestination, election features of Calvinism and [had] included the offer of Christ's atonement to all men, such changes bringing these denominations into accord with the Arminianism of the Remonstrants at the Synod Dort." The United Presbyterian Church of Scotland and the Free Church of Scotland had taken similar action in 1879 and 1892 respectively.[34]

The Shorter Catechism and Larger Catechism were also accepted by the English Parliament after having been written by the assembly. Together with the Westminster Confession, the Form of Church Government, and the Directory for Public Worship, they make up the Westminster Standards. The assembly's work, in sum, was not legally a church assembly's work but the result of a council summoned by Parliament to give counsel and advice to civil authorities to promote unity and uniformity in the work of reformation. In 1967 the Larger Catechism ceased to be part of the constitution of the United Presbyterian Church in the USA. The Shorter Catechism contained no sections on Christian liberty and the doctrine of the church.

Among twentieth-century Reformed confessions, two are of major importance. The Barmen Theological Declaration (1934) arose in response to the pro-Nazi "German Christian" party which gained control of the regional and national Protestant churches in Germany by mid-1933. The Pastors' Emergency League created in response to this crisis was an early effort to counter the curbs against so-called non-Aryans in the church. Various movements and groups opposing the "German Christians" gathered in the Confessional Synod of the German Evangelical Church which met at Barmen, May 29-31, 1934. Adoted were an "Appeal," a "Theological Declaration," and several other documents. The Theological Declaration enunciated the church's confession in the face of the Nazi ideology of "blood and soil." The Swiss Reformed theologian Karl Barth was the chief author of the document. In 1967 the United Presbyterian Church in the USA added the Barmen Theological Declaration to its *Book of Confessions*. The second important twentieth-century Reformed confession is the Confession of 1967, adopted by the United Presbyterian Church in the USA and discussed below under that body's heading.

A helpful summary of the points of doctrine covered in seven major Reformed confessions has been prepared by Professor Edward A. Dowey of Princeton Theological Seminary.[35]

Topic	Second Helvetic Confession Chapter	Scots Confession Chapter	Heidelberg Catechism Question	Westminster Confession Chapter	Shorter Catechism Question	Barmen Declaration Thesis	Confession of 1967 Paragraph
Scripture	I-II	XVIII-XX	21	I	2-3, 88-90	1	3, 27-30, 49
Trinity	III	I	25	II	6		5, 7
Creation	VII	II	26	IV	(1), 9-10		16-17
Providence	VI	I	1, 27-28	V	11-12		16-17
Covenant	XX	IV-V	19, 74	VII, XIX	20		18-19
Sin	VIII-IX	III	3-11	VI, IX	12-20, 82-85		12-14
Election	X	VII-VIII	26, 31, 52, 54	III, X	7-8, 20		(18-20)
Jesus Christ	XI	V-XI	29-52	VIII	21-28	1-2	3, 8-11, 15, 24, 32
Holy Spirit	III, etc.	XII	53-64	XXXIV			Part I, Section C
Law	XII	XIV-XV	3-4, 92-115	XIX, (VII, XIII)	39-81		
Gospel	XIII	IV-V	19, etc.	VII, XXXV			6, 7, 18, etc.
Repentance	XIV	(XII)		XV	87		21

Topic							
Justification	XV	(XV)	31-34, 60-64	XI	32-33		22
Faith	XVI	XII	1-2, 21, 32, 53, 60-61, 74	XIV	86, (30-38)	2	10, 21
Christian Life	XVI	XII-XIV	Part III	XIII, XVI, XIX-XX	35, 39-82	2-3	21-26, 41-47
Church	XVII-XVIII	V, XVI, XVIII, XX to XXII	54, 85	XXV-XXVI, XXX-XXXI		3-4	20, 22, 25, etc.
Mission				XXXV		6	31-33, 41-47
Sacraments	XIX	XXI-XXIII	65-68	XXVII	88, 91-93		51
Baptism	XX	XXI-XXIII	69-74	XXVIII	94-95		52
Lord's Supper	XXI	XXI-XXIII	75-85	XXIX	96-97		
Worship	IV-V, XX-XXVII			XXI-XX	45-62		36, 49-52
Marriage	XXIX			XXIV			17, 47
State	XXX	XXIV		XXIII		5	17, 25, 45
Consummation	(XI)	XVII, XXV	57-58	XXXII	37-38		11, 26, and Part III

Reformed doctrine, as indicated above, had among its first spokesmen Zwingli and Calvin, but a host of other reformers must also be recognized, including Bucer, Oecolampadius, Bullinger, Beza, and Knox. In the sixteenth century Arminius and the Arminians, as well as the contra-remonstrants of the Synod of Dort, claimed to speak truthfully of Reformed doctrine. Other summaries of theology were written by William Perkins (1600); William Ames (1623); John Owen (1674); Francois Turretin (1679–1686), who was especially influential in nineteenth-century America; Charles Hodge (1871–1872); Abraham Kuyper (1893–1894), leader of a Calvinist revival in the Netherlands; and Herman Bavinck (1895–1901). In eighteenth-century England the evangelical Calvinism of the revivalist George Whitefield had tremendous impact, just as it did as well in the new American colonies. Jonathan Edwards remains the greatest American theologian; he was an evangelical Calvinist of the first order. In nineteenth-century America the Mercersburg theology of John Williamson Nevin and Philip Schaff stressed the possibility of reunion with Rome and a High Church view of Reformed sacraments. B. B. Warfield played an important role in perpetuating the rather more rigid brand of Princetonian Calvinism supported earlier by Hodge.

Karl Barth wrote a declaration of theological warfare in his *Römerbrief* (1919); he firmly opposed the presuppositions of the old liberalism and every facet of natural theology. His multivolume *Church Dogmatics* has assumed an important place in Reformed dogmatics. Emil Brunner accompanied Barth part of the way and contributed to the rebirth and revival of Reformed theology on the Continent in the twentieth century. In the United States the Niebuhr brothers, Reinhold and Richard, combined searing realism about the human predicament with a searching proclamation of God's grace to launch neo-orthodoxy on this side of the Atlantic. In the whole Anglo-Saxon world the revival of Calvinism has occupied such thinkers and writers as Thomas M. Lindsay, Herbert Darling Foster, A. Mitchell Hunter, Quirinius Breen, Georgia Harkness, R. N. Carew Hunt, James Mackinnon, Arthur Dakin, Thomas F. Torrance, Edward A. Dowey, Jr., and T. H. L. Parker. Undeviating Calvinism appears in the pages of such periodicals as the *Evangelical Review* and the *Calvin Forum* while the *Reformed Theological Review, Scottish Theological Review,* and *Theology Today* are scholarly organs with a Calvinist orientation.[36]

While no abbreviated summary of Reformed doctrine and theology can do justice to the subject, it may be argued that certain themes appear with some regularity in Reformed theology. Reformed theology tends to stress the revelation of God in Christ who is the instrument of God's redemptive will for mankind, as recorded in Scripture, and his revelation in creation. Human blindness prevents the appropriate reception of this revelation; nevertheless, man's chief aim is to glorify God and enjoy him forever. The Bible is the final and ultimate authority in matters of theology, doctrine, and Christian living. God's supreme glory and freedom and his redemption of man in Jesus Christ is a major unifying and organizing principle. He controls history, and man is truly free when he is God's captive. The early reformers' insistence that *finitum non est capax infiniti* (the finite is incapable of the infinite) continues to play a major role in Christology and sacramental theology, just as it served as a major impetus for the development of the dialectical theology of Barth and others. Some Reformed theologians insist that God's law remains applicable for the justified sinner because of the continuing dialectic between justification and sanctification. It is the source of ethos and of the ordering of human life; this theme often leads to deep concern for the church's involvement in social action and its active criticism of political authority and ideology. The church is frequently viewed as a unity with Christ the head, and the body (ie., the church) serving him. It has a prophetic mission in human history and society. Its marks are the proper preaching of the Word of God, the appropriate administration of the two sacraments of baptism and the Lord's Supper as signs of the covenant between God and his people, and discipline. Confessions are often viewed as the expressions of faith of a functioning ecclesiastical community in a certain time and place.[37]

Recent conversations between representatives of Lutheran churches in the United States and representatives of the North American Area of the World Alliance of Reformed Churches holding the Presbyterian Order showed a surprising agreement in a number of significant doctrinal areas.[38]

The German sociologist Max Weber asserted in his volume *The Protestant Ethic and the Spirit of Capitalism* (English trans. 1930) that Calvin's doctrine of election brought a sense of "unprecedented inner loneliness," and as a result later Calvinists—rather than Calvin himself—were led by this sense to seek vocational success in efforts to ally anxiety about divine favor. This assertion has in many instances led to the popular misconception that Calvin held that the believer's prosperity was a proof of his election, a view that perverts both the thinking of Calvin and Weber's initial argument. Weber erred in carrying his argument through Baxter, who was an Arminian, and Franklin, who was an American deist. Calvin's commentaries repeatedly assert that for the believer success and prosperity are an occasion for anxiety rather than a cure. The eminent Calvin scholar John T. McNeill argued that "those who have been taught to think of Calvinism as important chiefly for some (usually misunderstood) connection with capitalism and middle-class society will have difficulty in discovering its real significance."[39] Subsequent research has shown that Weber's thesis had numerous faults and was susceptible to severe criticism. The same could be said for the arguments of R. H. Tawney and Ernst Troletsch, who followed him at many points.[40]

Order and Worship

It is said that the essence of Presbyterianism in the area of polity or order is union of interest, confederation, and solidarity. This is probably true, but the statement should not lead one to overlook the significant Reformed doctrine of the church that lies at the basis of Presbyterian church order. The church is not identified with the clerical order but with the body of professing Christians.

The reformer of Basel, Johannes Oecolampadius, seems to have been the first to attempt to institute an eldership, independent of civil authority, that would look after discipline in the church. Martin Bucer of Strassburg adopted his views, and from him they reached John Calvin in Geneva. But as we have seen, it took Calvin several decades before he accomplished what he, Bucer, and the founder had in mind.[41]

Calvin had a difficult time finding explicit scriptural warrant for the kind of eldership-for-discipline that he envisioned. Among the texts he cited were I Timothy 5:17, his favorite locus; Romans 12:8; and I Corinthians 12:28. The matter was open to some dispute. The Westminster Form of Presbyterial Church Government (1645) failed to quote the passage from I Timothy, offering instead II Chronicles 19:8-10 and the Jewish synagogue's practice of having elders as sufficient basis for divine authority. But for Calvin, as well as for the Scots Confession, the constitution of the church was a matter of faith and dogma, settled by biblical authority.[42] Influenced both by theological and practical considerations, Calvin sought to ensure that all sovereignty and authority should rest with Jesus Christ and that organizational structure should serve this function.

Calvin's *Ecclesiastical Ordinances* (1541) described in some detail the "right order" of the church as described in God's Word. Four types of ecclesiastical officers were listed. The pastor was to minister in word and sacrament, the doctor (teacher) to instruct the faithful with sound doctrine, the elder to assist the pastor in the church's discipline, and the deacon to manage the church's finances or care for the poor and the sick. Pastors were to meet weekly in open sessions (later called congregations) to exposit the Scripture, and once a quarter for fraternal admonition in the "venerable company." Discipline rested with the consistory, composed of pastors and elders, which was to meet weekly. Civil authorities did not fully accept the elements of Calvin's draft plan for nearly two decades, retaining the power of electing elders and deacons and supervising the selection of pastors and doctors.[43]

Calvin described the minister or preacher's duty "to announce the word of God, to indoctrinate, admonish, exhort, and encourage both in public and in private." He himself was ordained although it is questionable whether he ever received ordination by the laying on of hands. The *Ordinances,* unlike his *Institutes,* did not suggest that the imposition of hands was required, though desirable, for a genuine call to ministry of word and sacraments. Calvin stressed the approbation of the people, a secret call from God, and the need for the candidate to pass an examination on doctrine, piety, and gifts.[44]

The order of doctor or teacher was given full responsibility for teaching all branches of knowledge, but biblical subjects in particular. Doctors held the teaching responsibility for primary-school children and mature youth at the university level. In Geneva the candidates were examined by the pastors with two representatives of the city present. Doctrinal integrity and academic ability were paramount; the appointed doctor or teacher held no liturgical, homiletical, pastoral, sacramental, or disciplinary responsibilities. They worked —eventually in the academy—to prepare candidates for the ministry and laymen for productive citizenship as servants of God.[45]

The eldership continued to be a distinctive feature of Presbyterianism centuries after its inauguration. The office provided a way of turning the day's Renaissance individualism to the service of Christ and Christian witness.[46] It gave the laity a large voice in the administration and discipline of the church. Calvin envisioned elders whose authority in spiritual matters distinguished them from civil rulers, but he failed to achieve his goal. In Geneva the people did not choose the elders; that task was performd by the magistrates. What was to have been a court of the church was actually a court of the state.

The twelve selected elders in Geneva, together with the Company of Pastors, met weekly as the Consistory. Elders were supposed to "keep watch over everyman's life, to admonish amiably those whom they see leading a disorderly life, and where necessary to report to the assembly which will be deputized to make fraternal correction." The assembly, or Consistory, could admonish and censure, but the power to excommunicate was not definitively confirmed until 1561. This was a vital victory for Calvin even though the excommunicated Genevan was supposed to hear the sermon every Sunday except the four times when Communion was served.[47] The Genevan elders sometimes required humiliating acts of penance, such as kissing the ground for blasphemy, and penalties for missing church or misbehaving during the service were rather common. Other offenses included the acts of the goldsmith who made a Catholic chalice, and a person who said that the pope was a fine man.[48] Calvin thought of the Consistory's work as essentially remedial rather than oppressive.

In subsequent years the functions of the elder have changed appreciably. The elder now has less authority, in part because civil authorities have accepted more responsibility for public order while the rights of personal freedom have grown. With the passage of time the emphasis has shifted from cure to prevention, with emphasis on good habits and religious observance; the elder's primary concern remains the positive spiritual health of the people. While elders in Reformed and Presbyterian churches are not universally "ordained," the practice is widespread; other churches "install" elders to avoid usage of a word ordinarily reserved for the call to public ministry.[49].

In Geneva the deacons were divided into procurators, who administered funds, and hospitallers, who cared for the sick and unfortunate. The sale of church lands, alms boxes, annual collections, and direct grants from the council funded such charity administered by the deacons as the General Hospital and institutions for the rehabilitation of refugees.[50]

Calvin's first edition of the *Institutes* discussed deacons in a brief paragraph, and in 1543 and later editions he indicated that the office was created not only for the situation described in the book of Acts or for a town like Geneva, but as a permanent feature in Christian society. Deacons had no specific ecclesiastical functions except that, like the elders, they could give the cup to the people at Communion. The French Discipline of 1559 listed deacons as one of the scriptural offices; while not a perpetual office, men were encouraged to continue in this service. In Holland and in the Lower Rhine the tradition was also adopted, and in Scotland deacons were elected "by common consent and free election" according to the First Book of Discipline (1561).[51]

The presbytery came to be the central legislative and judicial body in Presbyterian church polity. Composed of equal numbers of ruling elders (elders) and ministers (teaching elders) from each congregation within its geographical boundaries, it exercises oversight over all congregations in the jurisdiction, ordains candidates for ministry, inducts ministers into congregational charges, serves as an appeals court for each congregation, and transmits overtures to the provincial or national general assembly. Most moderators or chairmen of presbyteries are elected, although in some instances efforts have been made to have bishops as permanent chairmen. The presbytery in Presbyterian churches corresponds with the *classis* in Reformed churches. Initially the word *classis* was used to describe such a group in England and Holland, while the French preferred *colloque*. In Scotland the body was called "presbytery." Discussion and debate in mid-seventeenth-century Britain over the "preaching presbyters" (ministers), and the Westminster Assembly's explicit description of its form of polity as "presbyterial," helped make the use of the term "Presbyterian" widespread. On the Continent the term "Reformed" was used and adopted to emphasize the thoroughness of the Calvinist reform, as compared with the supposed halfhearted reform of the Lutherans.[52]

The first hierarchy of councils governing the Reformed church appeared in France. They included the four ascending judicatories of *classis,* colloquy, provincial synod, and national synod. While the Consistory handled disciplinary problems in Geneva, a different form of unity was required for the Reformed congregations spread so widely in France. In 1559 a discipline was adopted that regulated the congregational consistories of ministers, elders, and deacons, as well as the provincial synods that ruled and advised these consistories. A national synod was to meet occasionally as supreme court and consultative body. Apparently the *colloque,* or *classis* (presbytery for English-speaking churches), was not adopted until 1572.[53] Progress in the realm of presbyterian polity came much slower in Britain, while in Scotland an act of Parliament in 1592 established the full governmental structure of Kirk Session (congregation), Presbytery, Provincial Synod, and General Assembly. Already in 1561, however, the third meeting of the General Assembly occurred as the church's central board of control functioned apart from civil authority.[54]

Today in presbyterian polity, each level of government is organizationally elated to the next higher level. The church's foundational structure is the *ession* of the local congregation. It is elected by all communicant members ind is composed of *ruling elders* and the *minister,* or *teaching elder,* whose primary responsibility is to teach the Word of God. The minister, also the session's *moderator,* is called by the congregation but ordained and inducted by the *presbytery,* the principal governing body in Presbyterian polity. In some Presbyterian churches, lay men and women can serve as preachers in local churches for limited periods of time, without ordination, after approval by the presbytery.

While the session has authority to receive, examine, admonish, and suspend members, the *presbytery* examines, licenses, and ordains ministerial candidates and supervises the various congregations of its district. It is composed of the minister and the "representative" elder of each congregation in its geographical boundaries (though not all presbyteries are geographic in nature); it unites representatives of perhaps twenty or thirty sessions and has extensive supervision over congregations in its jurisdiction.

The next higher level is the *synod,* which is usually composed of at least three presbyteries; its members are either appointed by the presbyteries or directly by the sessions involved. Modern communications have in some instances made the synod less important, especially since presbyteries deal directly with the *General Assembly* more frequently. The General Assembly is composed of equal numbers of ministers and elders who are presbyterial representatives. Like the synod, it usually meets annually; the highest court in any Presbyterian church, it has final authority in all judicial and legislative matters, but in most cases changes in doctrine, government, or worship must be referred back to the presbyteries for ratification by a majority of one half or two thirds. The General Assembly's *moderator* is its elected president or presiding officer; the *stated clerk* is the assembly's executive secretary. Each judicatory in the presbyterian system is also a court with appellate powers. Only the session has original jurisdiction over communicant members, and only the presbytery has original jurisdiction over ministerial members of the church.

This system of polity generally prevails in the United States and Canada, but historical conditioning has led to a number of variations in Reformed and Presbyterian churches around the world. In Hungarian-speaking churches, for example, the territorial bishop, who might be described as a superintendent, shares authority with a layman at a certain judicatory level, while the presbytery still has an important role. The history of churches in one or another area has led to modification of the system in a variety of ways, without altering its basic structure and intent.

This historical conditioning, as well as theological reflection, has produced a number of fundamental questions about the presbyterian form of polity. Some question whether the presbyterian structure is by "divine right" and whether explicit scriptural authority can be found to support it. Others ask whether theological changes in Calvinism require an updating in polity as well. A literal interpretation of parity in church polity would seemingly preclude the creation of the office of stated clerk. Others have broached the question of the episcopacy, pointing to approval of the function among some early Calvinists. But it should be added as well that the presbyterian system seems to have influenced both congregational and episcopal bodies with its stress on representation and the formation of a church government that effectively serves the head of the church, Jesus Christ.

Public worship in the Reformed churches is anchored in the liturgical reforms of Zwingli, Calvin, Knox, and others in the sixteenth century. Knox's English liturgy, revised in Geneva, became the basis of the Book of Common Order, which in 1564 came to be the authorized standard of worship in Scotland. Its form of public worship substantially followed Calvin's *Form of Prayers*. In Scotland and elsewhere in Reformed churches, psalm singing was an identifying mark of public worship. In 1644 the Westminster Assembly proposed a Directory for the Worship of God. This Westminster Directory played an important role in the development of worship in Reformed and Presbyterian bodies in the United States, especially in its stress on gravity and reverence in worship. The earliest information available on the order of worship followed by some Presbyterians in the American colonies is a reference in 1716 to the use of the Scottish Directory.[55]

In the 1750s a heated controversy erupted in New York City's only Presbyterian congregation. The issue was whether the traditional book of metrical psalms used in worship could be replaced by a book of hymns written by Isaac Watts. Hallowed Calvinistic and Puritan views held that only scripturally authorized elements such as the Psalms should be used in worship, but the congregation's majority found Watts's hymns on specifically Christian topics more satisfying than the ancient Hebrew psalms. The Great Awakening's emphasis on touching the affections of people's souls stirred this first great debate on worship, and the majority of the congregation came to favor this approach.[56]

Colonial worship in America often included the special "sacramental season" inherited from Scotland which placed infrequent celebrations of the Lord's Supper within a series of services. Some congregations also used tokens to admit worshipers to the Communion table.

In 1729 the colonies' original Presbyterian synod gave only qualified endorsement to the Westminster Directory for public worship, recommending to members that they use the directory "as near as circumstances will allow, and Christian prudence direct." In 1786 the Presbyterians merely "received" the directory "as in substance agreeable to the institutions of the New Testament."[57] The exact status of the directory in the colonial church is difficult to measure.

After the American revolution the Presbyterians' first General Assembly adopted a directory that blended practicality and the revivalist emphases of the Great Awakening. An early draft proposed this order of worship:

Prayer of adoration, invocation and preparation
Reading of Scripture
Singing of praise
Long prayer of adoration, confession, thanksgiving, supplication and interces-
    sion, followed by Lord's Prayer
Sermon
(Lord's Supper, when celebrated)
Prayer
Singing of a psalm
Offering
Blessing

But the directory was largely ignored throughout the nineteenth century while the actual practice of Presbyterian worship went through a number of changes. Presbyterians had scrupulously avoided binding the church to eighteenth-century practices, enabling worship to be shaped by and adapted to the changing culture of the early national period and the nineteenth century.[58] To make the Gospel known in the most effective way, some Presbyterians in the nineteenth century used revivalist preaching and "new measures" in public worship.

At midcentury Charles Baird's rediscovery of the pre-Puritan Reformed liturgical heritage sensitized many American Presbyterians to the question of liturgical worship. In the 1870s and 1880s many more Presbyterians became aware of this heritage. In 1882 the General Assembly in the North, when asked to publish an authorized, optional manual of worship, reminded its ministers of the liberty of each "to avail himself of the Calvinistic or other ancient devotional forms of the Reformed Churches, so far as may seem to him for edification." Private enterprise took up where the denomination left off. Already in 1877 Archibald Alexander Hodge introduced his *Manual of Forms,* which though it concentrated on occasional services and ordinances, was quite popular.[59]

The Northern General Assembly finally took action in 1906 to issue a Book of Common Worship carefully described on the title page as "prepared by the Committee of the General Assembly of the Presbyterian Church in the U.S.A. for voluntary use." The book was used primarily for special services, especially funerals, weddings, and installations. Some few churches used it for regular worship, but the others practiced the liberty to which they had grown accustomed in the ordering of their services.[60] Southern Presbyterians, on the other hand, received denominational assistance in standardized forms before those in the North. Efforts to revise the directory (1788) began in 1867 but did not end until 1893. This revision specified the offering as an act of worship, included missionary efforts in the list of intercessions, removed archaisms, inserted chapters on "Sabbath School" and "Prayer Meetings," and added the Holy Spirit to the list of items for thanksgiving. This directory included questions for use at baptisms and for admission to communicant status, while the appendix included a marriage ceremony and two funeral services. The homogeneity of the Southern church, as well as the fact that it was a relatively new body less than fifty years old, may have contributed to the greater openness to denominational direction for worship in the South.[61]

In the twentieth century the major Presbyterian groups in the United States produced four different editions of the Book of Common Worship. The edition in 1906 included a cautious espousal of the Christian liturgical year and sought corporate participation by the worshipers. The edition in 1932 added much new material and increased the emphasis on the Christian year; it also included a rudimentary lectionary. These two editions were issued by the General Assembly of the Presbyterian Church in the U.S.A. (traditionally called "Northern"); the Presbyterian Church in the U.S. (Southern) accepted the 1932 edition "for the optional and selective use of our ministers." In 1946 the Northern Presbyterians issued another edition with a thorough revision. It owed much to the excellent Book of Common Order of the Church of Scotland published six years earlier, and reproduced its lectionary. It included five complete Sunday services and services for children and young people, as well as an expanded collection of prayers.

The most recent revision of the Book of Common Worship was preceded by revision of the Directory of Worship of 1788 in the three major American Presbyterian bodies. The Northern and Southern assemblies agreed, together with the United Presbyterian Church of North America, to the work of revision which resulted in a draft in 1959. The Northern group and the United Presbyterian Church, merged in 1958 to form the United Presbyterian Church in the U.S.A., approved the draft directory in 1961; the Southern Presbyterians adopted the Directory for the Worship and Work of the Church in 1963. Two separate directories did not halt cooperation in the production of a common worship book; in fact, the Cumberland Presbyterian Church also joined the effort. The Joint Committee distributed an experimental "Service for the Lord's Day" in 1964. In 1972 these three bodies published *The Worship Book, Services and Hymns*.

The effects of the Liturgical movement are apparent within American Presbyterian and Reformed churches. They are evident in the newly revised directories and *Worship Book*; significant progress has been made in distilling the biblical and historical bases of the church's liturgy and in incorporating the results. The congregation more actively participates in a ritual that has been recast along more ecumenical lines. Congregational singing has also been revitalized through the new *Worship Book*, published in coordination with several Reformed bodies.

NOTES

1. John McNeill, *The History and Character of Calvinism* (New York: Oxford University Press, 1967), p. 4.
2. Helpful in compiling the information in this section were McNeill, pp. 3-4, 76-79, 82-87; G. D. Henderson, *Presbyterianism* (Aberdeen: The University Press, 1954), p. 42; Roland H. Bainton, *The Reformation of the Sixteenth Century* (Boston: Beacon Press, 1952), pp. 77, 80-94; and Bard Thompson, "Ulrich Zwingli," in *Reformers in Profile*, ed. B. A. Gerrish (Philadelphia: Fortress Press, 1967), pp. 115-140.
3. McNeill, p. 309.
4. Ibid., pp. 119-128, 213.
5. Ibid., pp. 201-202.
6. William Monter, *Calvin's Geneva* (New York: John Wiley and Sons, 1967), p. 99.
7. Ibid., pp. 99-107.
8. Ibid., pp. 107-108.
9. Ibid., pp. 109, 165-170.
10. Ibid., pp. 176-187.
11. Ibid., pp. 112-113, 134-135.
12. B. A. Gerrish, "Calvin," in *Reformers in Profile*, ed. B. A. Gerrish (Philadelphia: Fortress Press, 1967), pp. 161-162.
13. Ibid., pp. 152-153.
14. Ibid., pp. 157-158. For evidence of the centrality of God's love in Calvin's theology, see his *Institutes*, II, xvi, 1; II, xv, 3; III, i, 1; III, ii, 8.
15. See the section on "Order and Worship," below.
16. Gerrish, "Calvin," pp. 158-159.
17. McNeill, pp. 212-213.
18. Ibid., p. 217.
19. Ibid., pp. 214-215.
20. Ibid., p. 218.
21. Ibid., pp. 218-219.
22. Henderson, p. 27; Bainton, pp. 111, 121-122.
23. Bainton, pp. 160-172; Hans J. Hillerbrand, *Men and Ideas in the Sixteenth Century* (Chicago: Rand McNally & Company, 1969), pp. 50-54.
24. McNeill, p. 295.
25. *Die Religion in Geschichte und Gegenwart* (3rd edn.; 6 vols.; Tübingen: J. C. B. Mohr, 1957–1962), V: 890.
26. Gaius Jackson Slosser, ed., *They Seek a Country: the American Presbyterians, Some Aspects* (New York: The Macmillan Company, 1955), p. 291.
27. John H. Leith, ed., *Creeds of the Churches* (Richmond: John Knox Press, 1973), pp. 127-128.
28. Arthur C. Cochrane, ed., with historical introductions, *Reformed Confessions of the 16th Century* (Philadelphia: Westminster Press, 1966), p. 17.
29. Leith, p. 128.
30. Cochrane, p. 30.
31. Ibid., p. 8.
32. Edward A. Dowey, Jr., *A Commentary on the Confession of 1967 and an Introduction to "The Book of Confessions"* (Philadelphia: Westminster Press, 1968), p. 187.
33. Ibid., pp. 214-215.
34. Slosser, ed., p. 261.
35. Dowey, foldout at end of volume
36. McNeill, p. 432.
37. *Die Religion in Geschichte und Gegenwart* V: 887.
38. See *A Reexamination of Lutheran and Reformed Traditions*, published jointly by representatives of the North American Area of the World Alliance of Reformed Churches holding the Presbyterian Order and the U.S.A. National Committee of the Lutheran World Federation (4 vols.; New York: National Lutheran Council, 1964–1966).
39. McNeill, pp. 222-223, 437.
40. See Robert W. Green, *Protestantism, Capitalism, and Social Science: The Weber Thesis Controversy* (2nd edn.; Lexington, Mass.: D. C. Heath & Co., 1973): Kurt Samuelsson, *Religion and Economic Action*, trans. E. Geoffrey French (London: Basic Books, 1961); and W. I. Hudson, "The Weber Thesis Reexamined," *Church History* XXX (1961): 88-99.
41. Henderson, p. 56.
42. Ibid., pp. 62-63, 65.
43. Gerrish, "Calvin," p. 149; see also Allan L. Farris, "Calvin and the Laity," *Canadian Journal of Theology* XI (1965): 54-67.
44. Farris, pp. 56-57.
45. Ibid., pp. 58-59.
46. Henderson, p. 70.
47. Monter, p. 140.
48. Ibid., pp. 137-138.
49. Henderson, pp. 166-169.
50. Farris, pp. 60-61.

51. Henderson, pp. 77-82.
52. Ibid., pp. 93-98.
53. Ibid., p. 100.
54. Ibid., pp. 103-104.
55. Maurice W. Armstrong, Lefferts A. Loetscher, and Charles A. Anderson, *The Presbyterian Enterprise; Sources of American Presbyterian History* (Philadelphia: Westminster Press, 1956), p. 19.

56. Julius Melton, *Presbyterian Worship in America; Changing Patterns since 1787* (Richmond: John Knox Press, 1967), pp. 11-12.
57. Ibid., p. 17.
58. Ibid., pp. 21-27.
59. Ibid., pp. 79, 100-108.
60. Ibid., pp. 134-135.
61. Ibid., pp. 111-113.

BIBLIOGRAPHY

THE CALVINIST REFORMATION

Bainton, Roland H., and Gritsch, Eric W. *Bibliography of the Continental Reformation; Materials Available in English.* 2nd edn., rev. and enlarged. Hamden, Conn.: Shoestring Press, 1972.

Biéler, André. *La Pensée économique et sociale de Calvin.* Geneva: Georg, 1959.

———. *The Social Humanism of Calvin.* trans. Paul T. Fuhrmann. Richmond: John Knox Press, 1964.

Cadier, J. *The Man God Mastered.* London: Inter-Varsity Fellowship, 1960.

Calvin, John. *Commentaries.* Ed. Joseph Haroutunian. The Library of Christian Classics. Vol. XXIII. Philadelphia: Westminster Press, 1958.

———. *Institutes of the Christian Religion.* Trans. Ford Lewis Battles and ed. John T. McNeill. The Library of Christian Classics. Vols. XX and XXI. Philadelphia: Westminster Press, 1960.

———. *Theological Treatises.* Ed. J. K. S. Reid. The Library of Christian Classics. Vol. XXII. Philadelphia: Westminster Press, 1954.

Courvoisier, Jaques. *Zwingli, A Reformed Theologian.* Richmond: John Knox Press, 1963.

Cowan, Henry. *John Knox, the Hero of the Scottish Reformation.* New York: AMS Press, [1970].

Dowey, Edward A., Jr. *The Knowledge of God in Calvin's Theology.* New York: Columbia University Press, 1952 (rev. edn. 1966).

———. "Studies in Calvin and Calvinism since 1948." *Church History* XXIV (1955): 360-367.

———. "Studies in Calvin since 1955." *Church History* XXIX (1960): 196-204.

Drury, Clifford M. *Four Hundred Years of World Presbyterianism* (typescript and film; 914 pp.) San Anselmo: n.p., 1961.

Duffield, G. E., ed. *Courtenay Studies in Reformation Theology, I: John Calvin.* Grand Rapids: Eerdmans, 1966.

Farner, Oskar. *Huldrych Zwingli.* 4 vols. Zurich: Zwingli Verlag, 1945–1960.

———. *Zwingli the Reformer: His Life and Work.* Trans. D. G. Sear. New York: Philosophical History, 1952.

Farris, Allan L. "Calvin and the Laity." *Canadian Journal of Theology* XI (1965): 54-67.

Forstman, H. Jackson. *Word and Spirit: Calvin's Doctrine of Biblical Authority.* Stanford: Stanford University Press, 1962.

Fuhrmann, Paul T., ed. *[Calvin's] Instruction in Faith (1537).* Philadelphia: Westminster Press, 1949.

Garside, Charles, Jr. *Zwingli and the Arts.* New Haven: Yale University Press, 1966.

Gerrish, B. A. "John Calvin." In *Reformers in Profile.* Ed. B. A. Gerrish. Philadelphia: Fortress Press, 1967. Pp. 142-164.

Green, Robert W. *Protestantism, Capitalism, and Social Science: The Weber Thesis Controversy.* 2nd edn. Lexington, Mass.: D. C. Heath & Co., 1973.

Grimm, Harold J. *The Reformation Era, 1500–1650.* 2nd edn., with rev. and expanded bibliography. New York: Macmillan, 1965.

Henderson, G. D. *The Burning Bush: Essays in Scottish Church History.* Edinburgh: Saint Andrew Press, 1957.

———. *Presbyterianism.* Aberdeen: The University Press, 1954.

Hoogstra, Jacob T., ed. *John Calvin: Contemporary Prophet.* Grand Rapids: Eerdmans, 1959.

Hudson, W. I., "The Weber Thesis Reexamined." *Church History* XXX (1961): 88-99.

Hughes, Philip E. *The Register of the Company of Pastors of Geneva in the Time of Calvin.* Grand Rapids: Eerdmans, 1966.

Hansen, J. F. *Calvin's Doctrine of the Work of Christ.* London: J. Clark, 1956.

Kingdon, Robert. *Geneva and the Consolidation of the French Protestant Movement, 1564–1572.* Madison: University of Wisconsin Press, 1967.

Köhler, Walther. *Huldrych Zwingli.* Leipzig: Koehler und Amelang, 1943.

———. *Zwingli und Luther.* Gütersloh: C. Bertelsman Verlag, 1953.

Wolfhaus, W. *Christusgemeinschaft bei Johannes Calvin.* Neukirchen: Neukirchener Verlag, 1939.

Léonard, Émile G. *Histoire générale du protestantisme.* Vol. I: La Réformation. Paris: Presses Universitaires de France, 1961.

MacGregor, Geddes. *The Thundering Scott, a Portrait of John Knox.* Philadelphia: Westminster Press, 1957.

McDonnell, Killian. *John Calvin, the Church and the Eucharist.* Princeton: Princeton University Press, 1967.

McNeill, John. *The History and Character of Calvinism.* New York: Oxford University Press, 1967.

———. "Thirty Years of Calvin Study." *Church History* XVII (1948): 207-240.

Monter, William. *Calvin's Geneva.* New York: John Wiley and Sons, 1967.

Niesel, Wilhelm. *Calvin-Bibliographie 1901–1959.* Munich: Christ Kaiser Verlag, 1959.

———. *The Theology of Calvin.* Trans. Harold Knight. Philadelphia: Westminster Press, 1956.

Parker, T. H. L. *The Oracles of God: An Introduction to the Preaching of John Calvin.* London, 1947.

Preus, J. Samuel. "Zwingli, Calvin and the Origin of Religion." *Church History* 46, 2 (June 1977): 186-202.

Revesz, Imre. *History of the Hungarian Reformed Church.* Trans. George A. F. Knight. Washington: The Hungarian Reformed Federation of America, 1956. (From the Reformation to after World War II.)

Ridley, Jasper. *John Knox.* Oxford: Oxford University Press, 1968.

Rilliet, Jean. *Zwingli, Third Man of the Reformation.* Philadelphia: Westminster Press, 1964.

Samuelsson, Kurt. *Religion and Economic Action.* Trans. E. Geoffry French. London: Basic Books, 1961.

Stauffer, Richard. *The Humanness of John Calvin.* Trans. George H. Shriver. Nashville: Abingdon Press, 1971.

Thompson, Bard. "Ulrich Zwingli." In *Reformers in Profile.* Ed. B. A. Gerrish. Philadelphia: Fortress Press, 1967. Pp. 115-141.

———. "Zwingli Study since 1918." *Church History* XIX (1950): 116-128.

Torrance, T. F. *Calvin's Doctrine of Man.* Grand Rapids: Eerdmans, 1957.

Van Til, Henry R. *The Calvinist Concept of Culture.* Philadelphia: Presbyterian and Reformed Publishing Co., 1959.

Walker, Williston. *John Calvin, the Organizer of Reformed Protestantism, 1509–1564.* New York: Schocken Books, 1969.

Wallace, Ronald S. *Calvin's Doctrine of the Word and Sacrament.* Edinburgh: Oliver and Boyd, 1953.

Watt, H. *Recalling the Covenants.* London: Nelson, 1946.

Weber, Mat. *The Protestant Ethic and the Spirit of Capitalism.* Trans. Talcott Parsons. London: George Allen and Unwin, 1930.

Wencelius, Léon. *L'ésthétique de Calvin.* Paris: Société d'édition "Les Belles letres," 1937.

Wendel, Francois. *Calvin: The Origins and Development of His Religious Thought.* Trans. Philip Mairet. New York: Harper & Row, 1963.

———. *Calvin et l'humanisme.* Paris: Presses Universitaires de France, 1976.

Willis, Edward David. *Calvin's Catholic Christology.* Studies in Medieval and Reformation Thought, II. Leiden: E. J. Brill, 1966.

Wright, Ronald Selby. *Fathers of the Kirk: Some Leaders of the Church in Scotland from the Reformation to the Reunion.* London: Oxford University Press, 1960.

Zwingli and Bullinger. Ed. G. W. Bromiley. The Library of Christian Classics. Vol. XXIV. Philadelphia: Westminster Press, 1953.

REFORMED CHURCHES THROUGHOUT THE WORLD

Henderson, G. D. *Presbyterianism*. Aberdeen: The University Press, 1954.

Hunt, Georg Laird, ed. *Calvinism and the Political Order*. Philadelphia: Westminster Press, 1965.

Leith, John H. *Introduction to the Reformed Tradition*. Richmond: John Knox Press, 1977.

Mackay, John A. *The Presbyterian Way of Life*. Englewood Cliffs, N.J.: Prentice-Hall, 1960.

Nichols, James Hastings. *Democracy an, the Churches*. Philadelphia: Westminste Press, 1965.

Ogilvie, James Nicoll. *The Presbyteria. Churches of Christendom*. London: *A* & C. Black, 1925.

Peel, Albert, and Horton, Douglas. *Intel national Congregationalism*. London Independent Press, 1949.

Warr, C. L. *The Presbyterian Traditior* London: A. Maclehose, 1933.

CREED AND DOCTRINE

Bangs, Carl. *Arminius: A Study in the Dutch Reformation*. Nashville: Abingdon Press, 1971.

Berkhof, Louis. *Systematic Theology*. Grand Rapids: Eerdmans, 1953.

Bruggink, Donald, ed. *Guilt, Grace and Gratitude. A Commentary on the Heidelberg Catechism*. New York: Half Moon Press, 1963.

Cochrane, Arthur C., ed. *Reformed Confessions of the 16th Century*. Philadelphia: Westminster Press, 1966.

Hendry, George S. *The Westminster Confession Today*. Richmond: John Knox Press, 1960.

Heppe, Heinrich. *Die Dogmatik der evangelisch-reformierten Kirche dargestellt und aus den Quellen belegt*. Ed. Ernst Bizer. 2nd edn. Neukirchen: Neukirchen Verlag, 1958.

Jacobs, Paul. *Theologie reformierter Bekenntnisschriften in Grundzügen*. Neukirchen: Neukirchener Verlag, 1959.

Kuyper, A. E. *Voto Dordraceno*. 4 vols. Amsterdam, 1892–1894. (An exposition of the Heidelberg Catechism.)

Lamont, D. *The Church and the Creeds*. Edinburgh: James Clarke & Co., 1923.

MacGregor, Geddes. *Corpus Christi. The Nature of the Church according to the Reformed Tradition*. Philadelphia: Westminster Press, 1959.

Niesel, Wilhelm. *The Gospel and the Churches; a Comparison of Catholicism Orthodoxy, and Protestantism*. Trans David Lewis. Philadelphia: Westminste Press, 1962.

———. *Reformed Symbolics*. Edinburgh Oliver and Boyd, 1962.

Niesel, Wilhelm, ed. *Bekenntnisschrifte und Kirchenordnungen der nach Gotte Wort reformierten Kirche*. 3rd edi Zurich: EVZ-Verlag, 1958.

A Reexamination of Lutheran and R, formed Traditions. Published jointly b representatives of the North America Area of the World Alliance of Reforme Churches holding the Presbyteria Order and the U.S.A. National Con mittee of the Lutheran World Federatio I. Gospel, Confession and Scriptu (1964); II. Christology, The Lord Supper and Its Observances in th Church (1964); III. Justification ar Sanctification; Liturgy and Ethics; Cr, ation and Redemption; Law and Gosp, (1965); IV. Ethics and Ethos; Sun maries and Comment (1966). 4 vol New York: National Lutheran Counci 1964–1966.

Routley, Erik. *Creeds and Confessio, from the Reformation to the Mode, Church*. Philadelphia: Westminster Pres 1962.

Schilder, K. *Heidelbergische Catechismu, 4* vols. Goes, 1947–1951.

ORDER AND WORSHIP

Farris, Allan L. "Calvin and the Laity." *Canadian Journal of Theology* XI (1965): 54-67.

Hageman, Howard G. *Pulpit and Tabl* Richmond: John Knox Press, 1962.

Henderson, G. D. *Presbyterianism*. Abe

deen: The University Press, 1954.

Henderson, Robert W. *The Teaching Office in the Reformed Tradition; a History of the Doctrinal Ministry.* Philadelphia: Westminster Press, 1962.

Melton, Julius. *Presbyterian Worship in America; Changing Patterns since 1787.* Richmond: John Knox Press, 1967.

Nichols, James Hastings. *Corporate Worship in the Reformed Tradition.* Philadelphia: Westminster Press, 1968.

Smith, Elwin A. *The Presbyterian Ministry in American Culture; a Study in Changing Concepts, 1700–1800.* Philadelphia: Westminster Press, 1962.

9. Presbyterian and Reformed Churches in the United States and Canada

American Presbyterians: Colonial to Nineteenth Century

Apparently the first Calvinist ministers to enter the New World were two French Protestant pastors sent from Geneva to Rio de Janeiro in 1556 in an effort to establish a Huguenot colony, which ended in failure. The first "presbyterians"—Christian Protestants known by the name of their church polity—were groups of people in "Congregational–Presbyterian" churches established by emigrants from New England on Long Island in the 1640s. Earlier, in 1629, Samuel Skelton had established the first essentially Presbyterian church in Massachusetts Bay Colony. New England Puritanism was the environment of the first Presbyterian churches in the American colonies.

Frances Makemie (1658–1708) is regarded as the founder of American Presbyterianism. Educated in Glasgow, he arrived in America in 1683 and worked as an itinerant missionary in North Carolina, Maryland, New York, Virginia, and New England. Scottish, Scotch-Irish, and New England representatives formed the Presbytery of Philadelphia, established in 1706 by seven ministers, including Makemie. The presbytery had no official connection with the Church of Scotland, and the New England element soon gained prominence in the group. By 1716 a synod was formed with four constituent presbyteries that included 25 ministers, 3,000 members, and about 40 churches.

Colonial Presbyterianism was appreciably influenced by the Great Awakening, while immigrants from England and Scotland increased the church's size. For Presbyterians, important figures in the Awakening were George Whitefield, William Tennent, and his son Gilbert. Some division occurred along ethnic lines with the Scots and the Scotch-Irish taking a stricter doctrinal position than the New Englanders. Tension revolved around the value of emotionalism in revivals, the educational qualifications of minister, polity, and itinerant ministers. Theologically the struggle centered on the latitude with which the Westminister Confession could be interpreted.

The struggle between the "Old Side" and "New Side" early in the eighteenth century had as its formal issue the place of the presbytery in the Presbyterian system. The New Side, including the Tennents and other "Log College" and New England men, argued that the presbytery had, as one contemporary scholar notes, "unimpeachable authority in its own sphere and that the higher courts could not encroach legislatively upon it." The material issue was the place of revivalism in the Westminster tradition, or the relationship between doctrinal orthodoxy and experimental knowledge of Christ. The droves of Scotch-Irish immigrants who emigrated to the new land, especially to areas in and around Philadelphia, made up a ripe mission field for colonial Presbyterians; they did much to open Presbyterianism to experimental religion.[1]

The Adopting Act of 1729 took the middle road confessionally in order to avoid schism between the two sides. The synod adopted the Westminster confessional catechisms as "the confession of faith," compromising between those who wanted unqualified subscription to the creed (Old Side) and those who objected to the limitations of man-made formulae. This act officially tied the church to the Westminster Standards, but allowance was made for understandings and interpretations of a broadening character. The uncertain boundaries of the limits of orthodoxy made the act, generally speaking, a victory for the antisubscriptionist (New Side) party.[2]

Continuing dissension over revivalism and the licensing of untrained men brought a schism between the two sides in 1741 that lasted until 1758. The New Side found its strength in the Synod of New York while the Old Side clustered around the Synod of Philadelphia. When the breach was healed in 1758, the terms of reunion essentially represented the position of the New Side, which made nearly all the overtures for reunion. These revival-oriented Presbyterians had experienced phenomenal growth in the last two decades; the number of ministers tripled to seventy-three men, and lay people enthusiastically supported their work.[3]

By the time of the American Revolution the Presbyterians had grown from very small beginnings to overtake all other bodies in the number of churches, with the exception of the Congregationalists. In 1788 they had 177 ministers and 220 congregations in 16 presbyteries and 4 synods. From the start, English, Welsh, and New England influences directed them to deeper and broader theological currents than the Presbyterians in Scotland. Their strength was concentrated in the middle colonies.[4] But the South was not forgotten. In the mid-sixteenth century the New Side Presbyterians of the New Brunswick Presbytery sent William Robinson as a missionary to the southern regions of Carolinia and "western" Virginia. He drew a good response while preaching what apparently filled a void left by four Old Side ministers already working in the area. Other New Side men also made journeys through the area, but physical obstacles and the limited number of pastors prevented rapid success. Nonetheless, Presbyterianism was poised for the challenge of mission to the trans-Appalachian area after the Revolution. By 1784 the first Presbyterian minister was already working in Kentucky.[5]

A Hessian soldier fighting in the American Revolution, on the British side wrote that war was "an Irish-Scotch Presbyterian rebellion." The Presbyterians, concentrated in the middle colonies, were heavily involved in the Revolution. Their Calvinist tradition provided some important impulses for involvement: Calvinism was born in republican Swtzerland; it failed to make terms with monarchy in France; and it was first established in Scotland in the absence of the monarch, and was in constant tension with the Stuarts.

The favoritism shown to the Anglican church by royal governors in New York, Virginia, and South Carolina helped turn the majority of Presbyterians against the mother country. The tradition of "election-day" sermons helped mold public opinion, and the reunification of the Old and New sides in 1758 brought a sense of unity and purpose. In general Presbyterian pastors supported the war without any reference to the doctrine of the "spirituality of the church," later so important in the South. One permitted the hymn and psalm books of his church to be used as cannon wadding, saying as he carried the books to the colonial troops, "Give 'em Watts, boys, give 'em Watts." Various presbyteries and groups memorialized colonial legislatures and urged support for independence.[6] John Witherspoon (1723–1824), president of Princeton University after 1768, was the only cleric to sign the Declaration of Independence; he served as a member of the Continental Congress for six years. In October 1776 the Presbytery of Hanover in Virginia was the first judicatory to openly recognize the declaration; relying on Jeffersonian arguments rather than the Westminster divines, it also called for clear separation of church and state.

In 1786, while the federalists were drafting a constitution for the new nation, the synod created in 1717 found that an annual meeting of all ministers had become impractical. The synod in 1788 adopted a constitution that provided for an annual General Assembly of delegates, but in contrast with the Scottish system (where the assembly was supreme), it left ultimate power in the hands of presbyteries.[7] The General Assembly had four synods and sixteen presbyteries, with 420 congregations. Scottish forms predominated in the new Plan of Government and Discipline, but it melded the different traditions that made up Presbyterianism in America. The synod also amended the Westminster Confession and Larger Catechism to bring them into consonance with the American theory of separation of church and state. The synod also adopted a Directory of Public Worship. The next year Witherspoon presided over the formation of the General Assembly in Philadelphia.

After the Revolution America seemed to be on wheels as it rolled westward. State after state was admitted to the Union. On the frontier the Presbyterian Church and the Congregational Associations of New England agreed to a Plan of Union for the sweep westward. After 1801 this plan permitted a congregation of one denomination to call a pastor of the other. The "presbygational" arrangement of the plan permitted Congregational and Presbyterian settlers in a community to establish a single congregation with a minister from either denomination. Aimed chiefly at facilitating mission in the expanding areas of western New York and points west, in the long run the plan gave the advantage to the Presbyterians, whose inherent connectionalism tended to absorb the more independent Congregational churches. One Yankee wit said that "the Presbyterians milked Congregationalist cows, only to make Presbyterian cheese!" Between 1807 and 1834, Presbyterian communicant membership grew from 18,000 to 248,000; between 600 and 2,000 Congregational churches—but probably not more than 600—became Presbyterian. The money and personnel resources of Presbyterians in the middle colonies gave strong impetus to their mission program. Presbyterians and Congregationalists were for all intents a single denomination in New York, Ohio, Indiana, Illinois, Michigan, and Wisconsin.[8] The Home Mission Society was formed in 1812 as the chief instrument for furthering the Plan of Union, and the Presbyterians gave official support to the interdenominational American Board of Commissioners to Foreign Mission in 1812. The reinvigorated New England heritage in the Presbyterian Church brought cries of resistance from the conservative party, which forced abandonment of the Plan of Union by certain Presbyterians in 1838, although the Congregationalists did not reject the plan until 1852.

In the first three decades of the nineteenth century Presbyterian membership increased by 144 percent, to 173,000, while the population of the new nation increased only 33 percent. Larger growth was prevented by the Presbyterians' divided opinion over the administration of missionary funds, their refusal or inability to adapt polity and traditions to the needs of the frontier, and their insistence on an educated ministry.[9]

Presbyterians on the frontier were legatees of a dogmatic tradition that was not easily adapted to the simplifications of frontier preaching. The tradition demanded sustained preaching, an educated ministry, and a "teaching" church. Some Presbyterians modified their message, sometimes adopting plain forms of Arminianism. Others broke rather clearly with the doctrinal and educational restrictions of their past; in areas west of the southern colonies where this approach was taken, a rash of conflicts and schisms occurred.[10]

Meanwhile, in the northwestern sections of the new nation the influence of Congregationalism helped to create a "New School" within Presbyterianism after 1800. Rather unorganized at first, the group favored interdenominational mission societies and cooperated in the Plan of Union. Its members felt that frontier challenges took precedence over traditional forms of polity. They sought to present a message of simplicity to the untutored people of the frontier and were somewhat embarrassed with the intricacies of the Westminster Confession. In addition, strict Calvinism, especially its doctrine of double predestination, seemed somewhat out of step with the Enlightenment and its impact on the nation's democratic faith. Revivalism seemed to be an effective way of winning people to the Gospel, but it implied that theological revision was necessary. The only recourse seemed to be a form of Arminianism.[11]

While the New School despaired of the "letter-learned" and of "hiding the glorious Work of divine Grace," the "Old School" antirevivalists showed grave concern about "enthusiasm" and "censoriousness" and worked to keep the "new measures" of the revivalists out of the church. The Old School group held firm to the tenet that church polity matters were in the realm of divine law (*jus divinum*); the church's constitution was an article of faith, and the Plan of Union bordered on blasphemy for some of them. No less offensive were the voluntary and interdenominational organizations that lay outside the church. But they were most disturbed by what they viewed as heretical aberrations from the Westminster Standards.[12]

In 1837 the General Assembly, under Old School control, abrogated the Plan of Union and then in an unconstitutional act made the abrogation retroactive. This took off the church's rolls 553 churches, 509 ministers, and about 60,000 members in the four western synods that had grown up from the plan. This act sapped the New School of much of its organizational strength, and schism followed the next year. For nearly a generation (1838–1869), two distinct general assemblies claimed to speak for the nation's Presbyterians. Numerically the Old School held some edge with 125,000 members in 1840 and 258,000 by 1869, versus 102,000 for the New School in 1840 and 172,000 by 1869. The two sides reunited in Pittsburgh, Pennsylvania in 1869 to become the *Presbyterian Church in the United States of America* (also called the "Northern Presbyterians").[13]

Presbyterians were active in the field of education with the creation in 1768 of what was to become Princeton University. This new Presbyterian college devoured five presidents, including Jonathan Edwards, in two decades. By 1837 the Presbyterians had formed at least nine colleges. Archibald Alexander (1772–1851) of Philadelphia led a movement to create a theological seminary at Princeton. He succeeded in 1812 and was named the first professor. Much of the theological history of American Presbyterianism was determined by the appointment of this Scotch-Irishman to the chair of theology. He took his intellectual and doctrinal guidance not from the New England Edwardsean tradition, nor from the New Divinity of the later Puritans or the Scottish philosophical traditions of Witherspoon, but from the seventeenth-century Dutch scholastic theologian François Turretin (1623–1687). Turretin was a stalwart defender of a strict doctrine of predestination and of a literalistic view of scriptural interpretation. Sydney Ahlstrom contends that Turretin's *Institutio Theologiae Elencticae* "stood side by side with the Swiss Confessions and the Westminster formularies to provide both structure and content for the message which hundreds of the seminary's graduates carried across the land and into many foreign mission fields," until replaced in 1873 by the *Systematic Theology* of Alexander's protégé, Charles

Hodge (1797–1878).[14] Alexander set "Princeton theology" in motion, and Hodge perpetuated the tradition throughout the century. Presbyterians were also active supporters of the newly emerging public schools, and in 1824 their General Assembly officially recognized Sunday Schools as effective teaching instruments.

Slavery was a divisive issue for Presbyterians already in the schism between Old and New schools in 1837. In 1834 ninety students withdrew from Lane Theological Seminary in Cincinnati because the trustees had forbidden them to discuss the issue of slavery. In 1834–1867 the short-lived and small Presbyterian Free Church Synod, formed by antislavery men of both the Old and New schools, denied membership to slave owners.

The New School took a stand against slavery in 1850 that led some synods and presbyteries in the South (approximately 15,000 adults), to withdraw in 1857. This group organized the United Synod of the Presbyterian Church in 1858. After the Civil War began, the Old School Assembly adopted a resolution in May 1861 stating that the Assembly was obliged "to promote and perpetuate, so far as in us lies, the integrity of these United States . . . ." In December of that year commissioners from forty-seven Southern presbyteries organized the General Assembly of the Presbyterian Church in the Confederate States of America in Augusta, Georgia. Later in the decade after the war this group, together with the United Synod of the Presbyterian Churches and the Independent Presbyterian Church of South Carolina, united in the General Assembly of the *Presbyterian Church in the United States* (also known as "Southern Presbyterians").

As Presbyterians moved toward the twentieth century they looked back on a century in which their General Assembly issued a pastoral letter (1818) recommending total abstinence from liquor and condemning lotteries, theaters, and dancing. Many Presbyterians joined the last major effort of Protestants to affect directly the course of private morality, namely, the campaign for prohibition and temperance in the early twentieth century.

In the fifty years between 1870 and 1920 the nation's population increased by 300 percent, while membership in Presbyterian churches increased 400 percent, to 1,800,000. Between 1920 and 1950 the nation grew by nearly 50 percent, while growth in Presbyterianism slowed to 40 percent.[15] On the basis of interviewing 3,000 representative Protestants in 1952 a scholar determined that Presbyterians fell pretty much in the middle of all Protestants in terms of "measurable piety" such as church attendance, praying, and Bible reading. See the chart provided by John L. Thomas on the next page.[16] Presbyterianism continued to have a major impact on the wider society in the mid-1960s insofar as this impact can be measured by the religious affiliation of major politicians. In 1967, 12 percent of the U.S. Senate, 17 percent of the House of Representatives, and 10 percent of the nation's governors were Presbyterians.[17]

A more detailed description of the Presbyterian bodies follows, including

Religious Practices of Major Protestant Denominations

Denominations	Church-goers percent	Night Prayers	Grace before Meals	Morning Prayers	Twice a day or more	Bible Readers
Baptist	61	60	43	15	39	48
Methodist	50	58	33	14	35	34
Lutheran	52	67	39	16	37	29
Presbyterian	55	58	33	14	41	38
Episcopal	45	58	33	19	34	34
Congregational	38	57	22	13	20	19
Other	53	61	35	20	41	46

the story of the Presbyterian Church in the USA and the Presbyterian Church in the United States in the twentieth century.

United Presbyterian Church in the USA

The United Presbyterian Church in the USA was formed in 1958 when the Presbyterian Church in the USA ("Northern Presbyterians") merged with the United Presbyterian Church of North America. It is the largest Presbyterian denomination in the United States and the world. Membership in the Presbyterian Church in the USA rose from 450,000 in 1870 to 2,300,000 in 1950. Largely Scottish in background, the United Presbyterian Church of North America was formed in 1858; by 1865 it had 68,000 members, about 100,000 by the turn of the century, and 250,000 when the merger occurred in 1958.[18] The larger body grew through a number of earlier mergers in the twentieth century.

The doctrine, worship, and early history of this body are described above, while its Confession of 1967 is discussed below. During the twentieth century the body became more inclusive in doctrine and practice. Its story is that of a "broadening" church despite the fact that in the 1880s the General Assembly warned that the "national life, and the purpose of God in it, are threatened by the introduction of millions of people, whose sole education has been under conditions diametrically opposed to those which subsist here . . . ."[19]

For this church the century opened with official action in 1903 that revised the Westminister Confession of Faith. The result of nearly fifteen years of struggle and debate, this revision made several verbal alterations in the confession that even conservatives acknowledged did not alter basic Calvinism. Most important was the addition of two chapters to the confession, entitled

"Of the Holy Spirit" and "Of the Love of God and Mission," which stressed God's love for all persons, and a "Declaratory Statement." Referring to chapter 3 of the confession, this statement affirmed that "the doctrine of God's eternal decree is held in harmony with the doctrine of his love to all mankind . . . ." Referring to chapter 10 of the confession, the statement explained that the section "is not to be regarded as teaching that any who die in infancy are lost."[20] The United Presbyterian Church of North America and the Presbyterian Church in the United States took similar action at the same time.

The decade preceding this confessional revision was one during which theological conservatism prevailed. In 1892 the General Assembly declared that biblical inerrancy was the official doctrine of the church, a position that was tacitly abandoned in the twentieth century. Three great Presbyterian scholars were taken to task in the nineties for not beginning their biblical studies with the "doctrine" of inerrancy. In 1893 and 1894 Charles Briggs, an Old Testament scholar at Union Seminary, and Preserved Smith, professor of Old Testament at Lane Theological Seminary, were dismissed from the church's ministerium. In 1900 A. C. McGiffert, church historian at Union who also taught New Testament literature, resigned from the ministerium.[21]

Relative calm prevailed between 1904 and 1922. The teaching of Charles Hodge and Benjamin Warfield on biblical inerrancy, namely, that "the inspired Word, as it came from God, is without error," was reaffirmed in 1893, 1894, and 1899. In 1910 the General Assembly adopted a five-point doctrinal program that extended the battle line beyond biblical inerrancy to other theological areas under attack. Declaring that the Adopting Act of 1729 required the church judicatory to decide what articles of faith are "essential and necessary," the assembly named five as "essential": (1) the Holy Spirit so inspired the biblical writers "as to keep them from error"; (2) "our Lord Jesus Christ was born of the Virgin Mary": (3) Christ offered up himself as "a sacrifice to satisfy divine justice": (4) "he arose from the dead, with the same body in which he suffered"; (5) Christ "showed his power and love by working mighty miracles." The assembly declared these five articles of faith "essential and necessary," but avoided the charge of reductionism by adding that "others are equally so." The five points resembled the points of the Niagara Bible Conference of 1895 and showed the influence of fundamentalism within the denomination. The Northern Presbyterians had taken the Arminian position on free will to accommodate the Cumberland Presbyterians in the merger of 1906, a shocking development for many Old School thinkers and undoubtedly a precipitant for this action in 1910.[22] In 1916 the assembly required all ministerial candidates to subscribe to these five points.

A strongly mediating liberalism was espoused by the talented preacher and writer Henry Van Dyke (1852–1933), who declared one of the five points unessential and four of them unbiblical. A popular author and spokesman for revising the Westminster Confession, he called the orthodox position on "prenatal election" a "horrible" doctrine. The fact that he was professor of English at Princeton University (after 1899) rather than a seminary professor probably saved him from being tried as a heretic.[23]

Two decades of comparative calm, from 1904 to 1922, were followed by another period of controversy that extended to 1936. During this period it was decided that the body should be more inclusive in nature; heresy prosecutions were not attempted, and the church felt its way toward recognizing the full right of moderate liberals to be ministers and officials. More organic views of the church made theology a part of the church's larger common life, not its sole reason for existence. There was, as one commentator notes, a "recovery of the 'communion of saints,' the sense of a common participation in the Christian heritage, and a growing sense of spiritual solidarity." But these developments came slowly.[24]

Extreme conservatives failed to reverse the tide at two vital points during the meeting of the General Assembly in 1924. They were unable to secure the removal on strictly theological grounds of a liberal Baptist minister, Harry Emerson Fosdick, from his post in a Presbyterian church in New York City, and they were unable to require office holders to subscribe to the five points of 1910. In 1924 more than 1,200 ministers subscribed their signatures to the Auburn Affirmation, issued in response to the five points of 1910 and subsequent efforts of the strict constructionists on behalf of fundamentalist views, especially at the General Assembly of 1923. The affirmation contended that two thirds of the presbyteries were required to amend the church's confession, and argued that the five points were theories about certain Christian facts which could be affirmed apart from these specific theories.

A Special Commission was established in 1925 to take up these concerns. In 1926 and 1927 the General Assembly adopted the commission's reports, making official an important part of the Auburn Affirmation's theological argument and all of its constitutional argument. The commission signaled a turning point in the church body's theological history; its reports denied that the assembly could define authoritatively the "essentials" of the church's faith, in this way eliminating the five points of 1910 as a source of controversy.[25]

The election of Robert E. Speer (1867–1947) as moderator of the church in 1927—only the second layman to hold the office—was a sign of the times. Speer served nearly fifty years as the chairman of the Board of Foreign Missions; he supported theological decentralization and pluralism and insisted that the individual missionary's presbytery, rather than the mission board, should exercise theological jurisdiction.[26]

John G. Machen (1881–1937), professor at Princeton Seminary, was a leading apologist for fundamentalism who figured prominently in the church's struggles during these years. His *Christianity and Liberalism* (1923) continues to hold a place of prominence among many conservative Protestants. After leading in the formation of a new seminary, called Westminster Seminary, in 1929, and urging the support of a separatist mission board, Machen was removed from the ministry by the action of the General Assembly in 1936. He and his followers subsequently formed the Presbyterian Church of America in 1936, renamed the Orthodox Presbyterian Church in 1939.

After the mid-thirties a new dynamism, influenced by Christian existentialism, began to influence the body. A vigorous curriculm for schools was put into operation in 1948. A "New Life" movement in 1947–1949 provided four-day training schools for pastors and extensive distribution of literature. During the three-year period 650,000 new members entered the church compared with 155,000 in the preceding five years.[27]

In the twentieth century the Presbyterian Church in the USA had become an inclusive church both theologically and in terms of merging with other bodies. In 1906 the church moved in the direction of becoming a national body when much of the Cumberland Presbyterian Church rejoined the body from which separation had occurred in 1809–1813. The larger body's revision of doctrinal standards in 1903 facilitated the reunion, and in the process the Northern Presbyterian body effectively committed itself to Arminianism, although some individuals registered dissent. Only 72,000 of the 195,000 Cumberland Presbyterians of 1906 remained in the original church a decade later.

In 1920 the Welsh Calvinistic Methodist Church united with the Presbyterian Church in the USA. Reportedly, however, some congregations did not enter the union and continued the Welsh Calvinistic Methodist movement in North America. Repeated letters in 1970 to the Countess of Huntingdon's Connexion, 136a Pack Lane, Kempshott, Basingstoke, Hampshire, England, with whom the continuing Welsh Calvinistic Methodists were allegedly in fellowiship, brought no response.

In 1958 the Presbyterian Church in the USA merged with the United Presbyterian Church of North America to form the United Presbyterian Church in the USA. The smaller United Presbyterian Church was a largely Scottish body that traced its history back to the Covenanter and Secession movements in Scotland during the eighteenth century. In 1858 it gathered two groups of Scottish Secession and Covenanter movements, the Associate Reformed Synod (1782) and the Associate Synod of North America (1782). Union negotiations in 1858 centered on close Communion, public testimony, covenanting, the magistracy, Psalmody, Christ's purchase of common benefits, slaveholding, and secret societies. The union occurred in Pittsburgh, Pennsylvania, and subsequently the church was engaged in union negotiations with a variety of churches including the General Synod of the Reformed Church, the Associate Reformed Synod of the South, and the Holland Christian Reformed Church. On all occasions the body voted affirmatively for uniting but was rebuffed; it refused an earlier invitation from the Northern Presbyterians to unite in 1872.[28] A rather conservative body theologically, it did assert the unequivocal universal salvation of infants. Its Confessional Statement of 1925 abandoned its position on close Communion, lodge membership, and exclusive use of psalms in worship. The merger with the Presbyterian Church in the USA in 1958 brought a heavy Scots body into this larger denomination with its strong Scots and English origins.

In 1963 the moderators of the United Presbyterian Church in the USA, the Presbyterian Church in the United States (Southern Presbyterians), the Cumberland Presbyterian Church, and the Reformed Church in America began meeting annually to explore their common heritage in the Reformed tradition. Six years later, in 1969, the general assemblies of the Northern and Southern Presbyterians authorized the holding of formal reunion conversations between their two bodies. As many as fourteen previous efforts to reunite the two bodies, separated during the Civil War, had failed, including efforts more recently in 1931 and 1954. Progress was slow, and by 1977 no union had been effected. Two thirds of the Northern Presbyterian presbyteries and three fourths of the Southern Presbyterian presbyteries had to approve the merger. The Joint Committee proposed that individual churches not desiring to enter the union would legally be permitted to withdraw and take their property with them. In 1970 both general assemblies voted to receive representatives of six other bodies as full partners in the merger negotiations; included were the Reformed Church in America, the Cumberland Presbyterian Church, the Second Cumberland Presbyterian Church, the Associate Reformed Presbyterian Church, and the United Church of Christ. In the early seventies the Northern Presbyterians were represented in fifty states and the Southern Presbyterians in sixteen. In 1971 the two churches merged the sales organizations of the John Knox and Westminster presses and jointly published the magazine *Church and Society*. The general assemblies of the two bodies met concurrently in Louisville, Kentucky in 1974. In 1971 the United Presbyterian Church in the USA also authorized conversations on the possibility of organic union with four largely black denominations, the African Methodist Episcopal Church, the African Methodist Episcopal Zion Church, the Christian Methodist Episcopal Church, and the Second Cumberland Presbyterian Church.

The American Federation of Italian Evangelicals is a federation of Italian Presbyterian congregations in the United Presbyterian Church in the USA. Its periodical *Il Rinnovamento* originated in 1925; it once had a circulation of 1,000 but has decreased to 350 and is printed mostly in English. The federation was incorporated in the state of New Jersey in October of 1931.[29]

A Waldensian congregation in Monett, Missouri, is a member of the United Presbyterian Church in the USA, while allegedly another group of Waldenses in Utah have become affiliated with the Church of Jesus Christ of the Latter-Day Saints.[30]

In the 1850s Bohemians and Moravians from the vicinity of Bethlehem, Pennsylvania began settling in the vicinity of Ely, Iowa. In 1860 the First Bohemian and Moravian Brethren Church was organized under the leadership of the Reverend Francis Kun (1825–1894), who was responsible for the establishment of churches among Czech immigrants in Minnesota, Wisconsin, South Dakota, Nebraska, Kansas, and Iowa. From 1910 to 1948 the Central West Presbytery of the Evangelical Synod, which at its peak numbered twenty-one churches, provided an organizational link for many of these congregations. The Ely church, however, remained independent. From 1893 to 1936 an affiliated branch was located near Swisher, Iowa. Since 1895 another affiliated church at Rogers Grove has shared the pastor of the Ely congregation. In 1956 the Ely-Rogers Grove parish joined the Presbyterian Church in the USA, now part of the United Presbyterian Church in the USA.[31]

A major signal that the Northern Presbyterians had become an inclusive church in the twentieth century was their early support of the Consultation on Church Union (COCU). Eugene Carson Blake (1906–), general secretary of the World Council of Churches from 1966 to 1972 and stated clerk (executive secretary) of the church body's General Assembly from 1951 to 1966, preached a sermon in San Francisco, California in 1960 proposing the union of Methodist, Episcopal, Presbyterian, and United Church of Christ bodies. Presbyteries overtured the General Assembly in 1961 to invite the Protestant Episcopal Church to join with the Northern Presbyterians in an invitation to the Methodist Church and the United Church of Christ to explore the establishment of a united church. The first meeting was held in 1962, and the Disciples of Christ and Evangelical United Brethren joined the four for the second meeting in 1963.[32] In 1973 the Northern Presbyterians' General Assembly voted nearly 2 to 1 to reenter COCU, reversing the assembly's decision to withdraw in 1972. Since 1971 children and youth in Northern Presbyterian congregations and in the United Methodist Church have used the same church school materials.

In the twentieth century the Northern Presbyterians have been outspoken in their support of social justice and the church's mission in social action. Already in 1901 the church body added an official commission staff and a paid secretary to be concerned with social action; this was the first denomination to take this action, together with the Episcopalians who did the same that year.[33] In the 1950s John A. Mackay, moderator of the church, provided signal leadership in calling a halt to Senator Joseph McCarthy's witchhunt for communists in the federal government. Chiefly under Mackay's impetus the church's General Council unanimously adopted "A Letter to Presbyterians, Concerning the Present Situation in Our Country and in the World" late in 1953, and the next year the General Assembly declared that "under the plea that the structure of American society is in imminent peril of being shattered by a satanic conspiracy, dangerous developments are taking place in our national life."[34]

In the late fifties the General Assembly declared its opposition to capital punishment. In 1967 the assembly elected as moderator the Reverend Eugene Smathers, known for his pioneering social work in a poverty-ridden region deep in the Cumberland Mountains. In 1970 the assembly debated a study titled "Sexuality and the Human Community," produced over a three-year period under the direction of the Reverend John C. Wynn. In 1977 the newly elected moderator of the church, the Reverend John T. Conner, indicated that he favored continuation of a study by a church committee on the possible ordination of homosexuals. "I support full civil rights in employment for homosexuals," the Reverend Mr. Conner said. But the 1977 General Assembly reaffirmed its decision of 1976 that the ordination of homosexuals "would at the present time be injudicious, if not improper."[35]

The 1971 General Assembly vigorously debated the granting of $10,000 for the legal defense of the self-proclaimed black communist professor, Angela Davis, but the Fund for Legal Aid was again budgeted $100,000. The assembly also requested a halt to all United States military involvement in Indochina no later than the end of 1971, and called for general and complete disarmament, repeal of the Selective Service Act, environmental renewal, and far-reaching innovations in the nation's health-care system. In 1972 the General Assembly supported busing as a means of achieving integration, reaffirmed a liberal stand on abortion, and changed the rules to permit laymen to assist at Communion. It also acted to centralize the church's office in New York City. In 1973 the Assembly called for an immediate study of the Wounded Knee situation and left the door open for the denomination to grant legal aid funds to those arrested. It rejected a renewed attempt to involve the denomination officially in the Key 73 evangelistic program. In the sixties the church was heavily involved in the civil rights struggle despite some opposition in local churches, but conservative currents led the General Assembly in 1975 to turn down a $90,000 self-development grant for a social-change group in Colombia after funding the project since 1971.

In 1967 the General Assembly enacted an overture that provided for the constitution of the church to consist of two parts. The first, the Book of Order, included the Directory for Worship, the Form of Government, and the Book of Discipline. The second part, the Book of Confessions, included the following confessional statements: the Nicene Creed, the Apostles' Creed, the Scots Confession, the Heidelberg Catechism, the Second Helvetic Confession, the Westminster Confession of Faith, the Shorter Catechism, the Theological Declaration of Barmen, and the Confession of 1967.[36]

The new Book of Confessions did not include the Larger [Westminster] Catechism because it was never as widely used as the two other Westminister Standards.[37] With the exception of these two standards, the other confessional statements were new additions to the church's constitution. Discussion and controversy focused primarily on the Confession of 1967, a new confession of faith and the first written on American soil.

The Confession of 1967 was prepared by the Special Committee on a Brief Contemporary Statement of Faith, a committee of fifteen authorized by the 170th General Assembly (1958) which merged the United Presbyterian Church of North America and the Presbyterian Church in the USA. Appointed by the assembly's moderator, the committee reported to six subsequent general assemblies. Its chairman was Edward A. Dowey, Jr., a professor at Princeton Theological Seminary.

In 1965 this committee reported to the General Assembly. The report included a 4,200-word draft of the proposed Confession of 1967 as well as the proposal to create the Book of Confessions and questions that would be asked of candidates to be ordained as ministers, elders, and other officers. The assembly received the report and adopted its recommendations, setting in motion the constitutional procedures that would amend the confessional portion of the constitution of the church.[38] The procedure included approval by the next two general assemblies and by two thirds of the church's nearly two hundred presbyteries before acceptance.

Elected as moderator at the 1965 General Assembly was William Phelps Thompson, a Kansas lawyer. He immediately appointed a fifteen-man committee, the Special Committee of Fifteen chaired by the Reverend W. Sherman Skinner of St. Louis, Missouri, that studied proposals and received criticism and suggestions for amending the draft. In consultation with the original committee, the Special Committee of Fifteen prepared a somewhat revised draft that was presented to the General Assembly in 1966. The revised draft included a stronger statement on the divinity of Jesus Christ and described the Bible as "witness without parallel," in contrast with the earlier "normative witness." Retaining the emphasis on social morality, the revision added a statement on personal morality, deploring "anarchy" in sexual relationships and affirming the church's belief in the necessity of faithful and loving marriage. The assembly passed the draft by voice vote and forwarded it to the presbyteries for ratification. In the course of the next year more than the requisite two thirds ratified the Confession of 1967; by the end of 1966 only 2 of 25 presbyteries had turned it down, and by June 1967 only 19 of 184.

In 1967 the General Assembly gave final approval to the *Book of Confessions*, which included the Confessions of 1967. This action modified the church's constitution. Elected stated clerk in 1966, Thompson was reportedly the first layman to hold the chief administrative post of the church since 1883. The assembly "humbly commended" the confession to other Christians "for their prayerful consideration and study, that, if need be, this our confession may be corrected out of God's mouth, the Holy Scriptures."

Conservative resistance to the Confession of 1967, organized primarily in the Presbyterian Lay Committee, Inc., found much of the phrasing inadequate and contrary to the church's Westminster Confession. Some conservatives rejected the confession's description of the Bible as "the normative witness," and later "witness without parallel," to Jesus Christ rather than calling it God's infallible Word. Some also objected to the statement's stress on the church's need to serve as God's reconciling agent in such social issues as discrimination and poverty, to the absence of a reference to the virgin birth, to its allegedly discarding the Calvinist teaching on the predestination of God's elect, and to its allegedly providing theological justification for eliminating Presbyterian polity as a prelude to merger with other denominations. Another conservative pressure group was named the Presbyterians United for Biblical Confession.

In 1970 the General Assembly amended the Confession of 1967 in one sentence of Part II ("The Ministry of Reconciliation") to read, "This search [for cooperation and peace among nations] requires that the nations pursue fresh and responsible relations across every line of conflict, even at risk to national security, to reduce areas of strife and to broaden international understanding." According to the draft adopted in 1967, the sentence read that the search for "cooperation and peace . . . requires the pursuit of fresh and responsible relationships across every line of conflict, even at the risk of national security, to reduce areas of strife and to broaden international understanding." The phrase "at the risk of national security" evoked loud protest. Some critics equated it with treason, and reportedly some Presbyterians working in top-secret government jobs felt that subscription to the new creed might endanger their security clearance. Several pastors in Maryland and Kansas resigned because they reportedly scented inferences of disloyalty. The stated clerk, William P. Thompson, discussed the matter with Pentagon officials before the General Assembly in 1967, and Assistant Secretary of Defense Thomas D. Morris issued a memorandum stating that "from the plain meaning of the language in the confession we find nothing to suggest that disloyalty to the U.S. is encouraged."[39]

The Confession of 1967 opens with the assertion that "the church confesses its faith when it bears a present witness to God's grace in Jesus Christ." Arguing that "no one type of confession is exclusively valid, no one statement is irreformable," the confession states that its purpose is "to call the chuch to that unity in confession and mission which is required of disciples today." The preface concludes with the theme of the confession: "God's reconciling work in Jesus Christ and the mission of reconciliation to which he has called his church are the heart of the gospel in any age. Our generation stands in peculiar need of reconciliation in Christ. Accordingly this Confession of 1967 is built upon that theme."

Part I, "God's Word of Reconciliation," opens with the statement that "in Jesus of Nazareth true humanity was realized once for all." When God raised Jesus from the dead, he vindicated him "as Messiah and Lord," and "the victim of sin became victor, and won the victory over sin and death for all men." This risen Christ "is the savior for all men" even as he is "the judge of all men."

Man's sin is that "men claim mastery of their own lives, turn against God and their fellow men, and become exploiters and despoilers of the world." While it is true that "all men, good and bad alike, are wrong before God and helpless without his forgiveness," it is no less true that "God has created man in a personal relation with himself that man may respond to the love of the Creator." The Holy Spirit "fulfills the work of reconciliation in man" and "creates and renews the church as the community in which men are reconciled to God and to one another." The new life "takes shape in a community in which men know that God loves and accepts them in spite of what they are." It finds direction "in the life of Jesus, his deeds and words, his struggles against temptation, his compassion, his anger, and his willingness to suffer death." Jesus Christ, the Word of God incarnate, is the "one sufficient revelation of God"; to this Christ "the Holy Spirit bears unique and authoritative witness through the Holy Scriptures, which are received and obeyed as the word of God written. The Scriptures are not a witness among others, but the witness without parallel." The Bible is to be interpreted "in the light of its witness to God's work of reconciliation in Christ." The Scriptures "reflect the view of life, history and the cosmos" which were current in the "places and times at which they were written."

Part II, "The Ministry of Reconciliation," states that "to be reconciled to God is to be sent into the world as his reconciling community." This is the church's mission. In regard to forms and order, the confession indicates that "the institutions of the people of God change and vary as their mission requires in different times and places." As a reconciling community the church "calls, trains, and authorizes certain members for leadership and oversight." "A presbyterian polity," the confession states, "recognizes the responsibility of all members for ministry and maintains the organic relation of all congregations in the church. It seeks to protect the church from exploitation by ecclesiastical or secular power and ambition." The confession adds that "every church order must be open to such reformation as may be required to make it a more effective instrument of the mission of reconciliation." In terms of concrete reconciliation in society, the church "labors for the abolition of all racial discrimination and ministers to those injured by it" and commends to the nations "as practical politics the search for cooperation and peace." "Enslaving poverty in a world of abundance is an intolerable violation of God's good creation" in view of the reconciliation of man through Jesus Christ. In terms of personal morality the confession insists that "the relationship between man and woman exemplifies in a basic way God's ordering of the interpersonal life for which he created mankind. Anarchy in sexual relationships is a symptom of man's alienation from God, his neighbor, and himself." To fulfill its service of God among men, Jesus Christ has given the church "preaching and teaching, praise and prayer, and Baptism and the Lord's Supper." Baptism represents "not only cleansing from sin but dying with Christ and a joyful rising with him to new life. It commits all Christians to die each day to sin and to live for righteousness." The Lord's Supper celebrates "the reconciliation of men with God and with one another, in which they joyfully eat and drink together at the table of their Savior." In the Supper sinful men "have communion with him and with all who shall be gathered to him." They partake "in him as they eat the bread and drink the wine in accordance with Christ's appointment."

Part III, "The Fulfillment of Reconciliation," notes that God's reign is already "present as a ferment in the world, stirring hope in men and preparing the world to receive its ultimate judgment and redemption." In steadfast hope "the church looks beyond all partial achievement to the final triumph of God," the confession states, closing with the biblical doxology, "Now to him who by the power at work within us is able to do far more abundantly than all we ask or think, to him be glory in the church and in Christ Jesus to all generations, forever and ever. Amen."[40]

The church includes the following questions among those it asks ministers to answer affirmatively for ordination: "Do you trust in Jesus Christ, your Savior, acknowledge him Lord of the world and head of the Church, and through him believe in one God, Father, Son and Holy Spirit? Do you accept the Scriptures of the Old and New Testaments to be, by the Holy Spirit, the unique and authoritative witness to Jesus Christ in the Church Universal, and God's word to you? Will you be instructed by the Confessions of our Church, and led by them as you lead the people of God? Will you be a minister of the Word in obedience to Jesus Christ, under the authority of the Scripture, and continually guided by our Confessions?"[41]

After 1930 the Presbyterian Church in the USA (subsequently to become part of the United Presbyterian Church in the USA) ordained women as ruling elders. The body approved the ordination of women ministers in the 1956 General Assembly after the presbyteries had voted affirmatively. Between 1971 and 1976 the number of ordained women ministers grew from 103 to 248, composing 2 percent of the nearly 14,000 ordained ministers. A survey in 1976 indicated that 41 percent of the members and 43 percent of the elders thought that their congregations would accept a woman as their pastor. In 1974 Katie Cannon was ordained as the first black female minister in the church.[42]

In 1971 the General Assembly elected Lois H. Stair as the first woman moderator in Presbyterian history.[43] In 1976 the General Assembly elected a black laywoman, Thelma Davidson Adair, as its moderator, while William P. Thompson was reelected stated clerk for a third term of five years.

Neo-pentecostalism apparently first surfaced among Presbyterians in 1956 when a Presbyterian minister told his congregation that he had experienced the gift of tongues. In 1972 the National Charismatic Conference of Presbyterian Ministers included 284 ordained ministers, but the estimate in 1972 that 10,000 to 15,500 United Presbyterian laity had received the gift of tongues or related gifts of the Spirit may have been less reliable.[44]

In observance of the nation's Bicentennial the General Assembly adopted a policy statement in 1975 indicating that the Bicentennial was a "civic event" and not a "religious observance" or "Christian festival." The statement acknowledged the role of Presbyterians in the American Revolution and the nation's history, but added that "we are bound first of all to Jesus Christ. His rule, not that of a nation, is fundamental to us." The best way to honor the nation's founding was by "committing ourselves as Christians and as citizens to the continuing revolution toward the full realization of human well-being for all."

Membership in the denomination crested in 1965 with 3,300,000 members. Losses in subsequent years climbed as high as 104,000 in one year (1972), dropping nearly three quarters of a million members between 1966 and 1976, but by 1975 the losses had been cut to approximately 65,000, a decrease of 20,000 from the previous year and the lowest decrease since 1959.[45] In 1976 the church's membership was 877,664, with 5,156 ministers serving 4,036 churches.

The church moved its headquarters from Philadelphia, Pennsylvania to New York City under authorization of the General Assembly in 1972. Its headquarters are located at 475 Riverside Drive, New York, New York 10027. Its historical archives are located in the Presbyterian Historical Society, 425 Lombard Street, Philadelphia, Pennsylvania 19147. Currently some forty institutions of higher learning are connected with the denomination.

By 1970 Presbyterians of all bodies in the United States no longer appeared on a map that visually represented the comparative territorial strength of various denominations. The only exceptions were several small territorial areas in North Carolina, Illinois, Missouri, Colorado, and mission outposts in Alaska and the Northwest. And yet in 1970 Presbyterians of all kinds composed 3.1 percent of the approximately 130 million church and synagogue members in the nation. They continued to exert major influence in the political sphere; in late 1974 their approximately 4 million members had 15 U.S. Senators and 50 Representatives, demonstrating that their religious practices reached beyond the walls of their churches. In polls taken in 1957 and 1971, respectively, 5.6 and 6 percent of those polled listed Presbyterian as their religious preference. In a poll of 16,000 people taken in 1971, Presbyterians (21 percent) were second only to Episcopalians (32 percent) among those who were people polled who had incomes over $15,000, followed by Lutherans (15 percent), Methodists (13 percent) and Baptists (6 percent). Only 4 percent of the Presbyterians were farmers compared with 12 percent of those who were Lutherans.[46]

Presbyterian Church in the United States

The origins of this church, formed when Northern and Southern Presbyterians parted company at the time of the Civil War, are discussed above. The General Assembly of the Presbyterian Church in the Confederate States of America (1861) met in Macon, Georgia late in 1865 and picked one of the sixteen proffered names for its own: Presbyterian Church in the United States. The church deliberately rejected any name bearing a sectional connotation despite its southern character; it adopted as much of its earlier name as possible and kept open the door to union with the Northern Presbyterians.

The famed and aged theologian James Henley Thornwell (1812–1862) had presented the "Address by the General Assembly to the Churches of Jesus Christ Throughtout the Earth" at the General Assembly in 1862, justifying the new church's existence. "We are not conscious of any purpose to rend the body of Christ," he said. Separation had occurred because "we are persuaded that the interests of true religion will be more effectually subserved by two independent Churches, under the circumstances in which the two countries are placed, than by one united body." Then he discussed the proper relations of church and state, a concept earlier formulated by John Holt Rice (1777–1831) and championed by Thornwell for some years. For more than seventy years Southern Presbyterians would claim that this doctrine of the "Spirituality of the Church" was a distinctive mark of their church and justification for its existence. "The provinces of Church and State are perfectly distinct," said Thornwell, "and the one has no right to usurp the jurisdiction of the other." He added that "there can be no collision, unless one or the other blunders as to the things that are materially right." The church could not, under pretext of deciding a moral question, interpose a political issue as had occurred among Northern Presbyterians in 1861, he said.[47]

During the 1860s there were no official relations between the Northern and Southern Presbyterian churches. The Old School Northern Assembly conveyed its Christian salutations to the southern church's General Assembly in 1869. Various efforts at reunion were undertaken without success, and by 1895 the lines were drawn that governed relations between the two groups through much of the twentieth century. The two would cooperate and enjoy fraternal relations, but there would be no organic union.[48] In its early years the southern church's major theologians included Robert L. Danbey (1820–1902), William Swan Plumer, and John L. Girardeau.

When the nineteenth century closed, the church, says its major historian, "seemed solidly conservative, strongly Calvinistic, distinctly sectional, and remarkably homogeneous in outlook and belief." The moderator of its assembly in 1897 stressed three distinctive emphases in the church: a positive written creed based only on the Scriptures; total and everlasting separation of church and state; and its ruling and teaching elders, educated men divinely ordained and permanent in office. But the burning theological issue of the nineties was the inspiration of Scripture and the claim that its original autographs were inerrant. In the next few years the elect-infant clause in the Westminster Confession of Faith aroused a great deal of controversy. The dilemma was that while most Southern Presbyterians agreed that the confession could not be construed to teach that any of those who die in infancy are lost, they feared that amending the confession, even by attaching a footnote to this effect, would open the floodgates to doctrinal revision. Without amending the confession or adding an explanatory footnote, the general assemblies in 1900, 1901, and 1902 took action in a positive statement to this effect.[49]

In the early twentieth century theological battles were fought over evolution and several other subjects. For a number of years attempts to have the assembly issue a statement of fundamentals of faith were unsuccessful. Finally in 1938 the assembly indicated that "involved in the ordination vows to which we subscribe" were "acceptance of the infallible truth and divine authority of the Scriptures and of Christ as very and eternal God, who became man by being born of a virgin, who offered up himself a sacrifice to satisfy divine justice and reconcile us to God, who rose from the dead with the same body with which he suffered, and who will return again to judge the world."[50] But in 1941 the assembly refused to have a committee investigate the teachings of all faculties of its seminaries, insisting that all charges against any minister should be brought before the presbytery of which he was a member.[51] Late in the nineteenth century James Woodrow (1828–1907), professor at Columbia Theological Seminary, was dismissed from his post by the General Assembly for suggesting that evolutionary theory could be reconciled with a "not unreasonable interpretation of the Bible."

In the 1930s the church body experienced change, ferment, and a desire to move away from certain aspects of its past. But a more liberal spirit, desiring reunion with the Northern Presbyterians, continuing membership in the Federal Council of Churches, using the critical results of studying the Bible, demonstrating greater social concern, and seeking a more comprehensive theological viewpoint, was met by a movement of "fear, of protest against all such departures from the past."[52] Finally in 1939 the Westminster Confession was amended to delete the section that described the pope as Antichrist and to modify the section on the decree of election. Three years later two chapters were added, "Of the Holy Spirit" and "Of the Gospel," identical with changes made by the Northern Presbyterians a generation earlier. In 1959 the confession was amended, after over a decade of debate, to permit the remarriage of divorced persons.

In 1913 the assembly had approved a Brief Statement for general information and distribution as a tract. In 1931 and 1939 the assembly ordered it bound and published together with the Westminster Standards of the church. In 1962 the assembly adopted a Brief Statement of Belief that was "not [to] be considered a substitute for or an amendment to our Standards," but a statement prepared "to present in the language of our time the historic Christian doctrine set forth in Scripture and affirmed by the Presbyterian Church." Its six sections are titled "God and Revelation," "Man and Sin," "Christ and Salvation," "The Church and the Means of Grace," "Christian Life and Work" and "Judgment and the Life to Come." The statement makes no mention of predestination. "God has an eternal, inclusive purpose for his world," it says, "which embraces the free and responsible choices of man and everything which occurs in all creation. This purpose of God will surely be accomplished." The statement has aroused neither heavy opposition nor enthusiasm.[53]

The Westminster Confession of Faith, Larger Catechism, and Shorter

Catechism continue to be the church's Confession of Faith. In the early 1970s, as part of the unsuccessful process of merging with the United Presbyterian Church in the USA, the Southern Presbyterians examined the advisability of adopting a Book of Confessions. The proposed Book of Confessions was made up of ten confessions dating from the early church to the present, including a "Declaration of Faith" in modern language, which a committee under the Reverend Albert Currie Winn's leadership framed over a period of nearly seven years. Also included were the Scots Confession (1560), the Geneva Catechism (1541), the Westminster Standards, and the Barmen Declaration. Also proposed was a new ordination vow. Referring to the Westminster Standards, the old vow asked, "Do you sincerely receive and adopt the Confession of Faith and the Catechisms of this Church, as containing the system of doctrine taught in the Holy Scriptures?" The new vow proposed, "Do you sincerely receive and adopt the Confessions of this Church as, in their essentials, authentic and reliable expositions of what Scripture leads us to believe and do, and will you be instructed and led by them as you lead the people of God?" In 1973 the General Assembly defeated the attempt of conservatives to include the Ten Commandments in the proposed new confession of faith. In 1976 the General Assembly voted by a substantial majority to adopt the ten documents and the altered ordination vows, and passed the material to the presbyteries before it was to be returned to the assembly in 1977. Less than the required three fourths of the presbyteries approved the proposed Book of Confessions. In 1977 the General Assembly adopted the new ordination vows, against the standing committee's recommendation that their tie to the Book of Confessions made this impractical. A majority of the presbyteries had approved the new vows.[54]

The doctrine of the "spirituality of the church" continued to exercise extraordinary influence in the church in the early decades of the twentieth century, although challenges were arising. Silence over social needs and stress on the need for reconciliation with God—since social evils were the effects of sin as primary cause—was seen as the "distinctive" doctrine of the Southern Presbyterians. As early as 1890, however, some insisted that the doctrine was being carried too far when it was used to keep the church from condemning the abuses of child labor in southern mills. The first significant breach in the long-established tradition came with World War I and the desire of some churchmen to endorse the war being waged to make the world "safe for democracy." Others found it increasingly difficult to remain silent about the race problem, which was greatly intensified by the war. Finally, the Depression and its aftermath was a great stimulus toward social concern. In 1934, responding to presbyterial pressure, the assembly established a Committee on Social and Moral Questions in rather extraordinary action. Recent reorganization has delegated this responsibility to the Division of Church and Society. In 1966 the assembly adopted a paper entitled "Theological Basis for Christian Social Action," demonstrating that by this time the church's earlier doctrine of the "purely spiritual" nature of the church's mission had been completely transformed.[55]

The question of race was intertwined with this doctrine. In 1864 the church had resolved that "we hesitate not to affirm that it is the peculiar mission of the Southern Church to conserve the institution of slavery, and to make it a blessing both to master and slave."[56] Things changed quickly in the mid-twentieth century. In 1943 the General Assembly stressed that Christians who condemned Nazi persecution must "combat with all earnestness and power racial prejudice against Negroes in the South." Its Council of Christian Relations drew up a comprehensive report prior to the Supreme Court's desegregation ruling in 1954, which helped the church accept the integration of church and society. Meeting ten days after the Court's ruling, the assembly adopted the council's recommendations, including the affirmation that "enforced segregation of the races in discrimination which is out of harmony with Christian theology and ethics," and urging the sessions of local churches to admit persons to membership "without reference to race." The assembly indicated in 1958 that it opposed the use of any church-owned facilities for schools designed to evade desegregation rulings. In 1967 the assembly instructed all synods with black churches in their boundaries to report on how much longer it would take to incorporate these churches into geographical presbyteries. The final step in this integration process occurred in 1968. In the mid-sixties the Directory of Worship was amended with the sentence, "No one shall be excluded from participation in public worship in the Lord's house on bounds of race, color or class."[57] In 1970 the assembly opened with a memorial service for Dr. Martin Luther King, Jr., in a church in Memphis, Tennessee; in 1965 plans for the assembly to meet in this church had been canceled because the church was not integrated. In 1974 the assembly elected the Reverend Lawrence Bottoms of Decatur, Georgia as the first black moderator of the denomination.

Church polity in the denomination was formally structured by the revised Form of Government adopted in 1879, which included a clear statement of *jure divino* presbyterianism, said to be essential for the church's perfection rather than its being. It provided that all officers should be ordained through the laying on of hands, the session serving in the case of elders and deacons. A revision in 1925 dropped the statement that ruling elders do not labor in word and doctrine. In 1932 the assembly decided to permit elders and deacons to be elected to limited terms of office rather than for life; the proposal had been before the assembly nearly a quarter century. In 1962 the constitution was altered to permit women to serve in any office, including the teaching elder (minister). Dr. Rachel Henderlite was the first woman minister in the church, ordained in 1965.[58] Before the graduations in 1977, there were ninety-five female seminary graduates, seventy-five of whom were ordained. About forty more graduated from seminaries in 1977.

A major struggle about the use of wine or grape juice in the Lord's

Supper ensued between 1892 and 1916. It was decided that the final decision rested with the session. In 1950 the assembly positively endorsed the religious observance of Easter and Christmas, though the church had unofficially recognized these festivals for some time. In 1965 the assembly agreed to the addition of the four Sundays of Advent, Epiphany, and the beginning of Lent to the church calendar.[59]

The church's growing interest in unity and union movements first became evident after World War I when its Executive Committee of Foreign Missions formulated the idea of the Interchurch World Movement. This plan for evangelical cooperation in educational, missionary, and benevolent programs was not successful among Protestants, but it sounded a new ecumenical note in the Southern Presbyterian Church.[60] About the same time the church entered the Federal Council of Churches but withdrew in 1931 while it moved toward isolationism. After much vigorous debate about reentry, it again joined what was later called the National Council of Churches of Christ in the USA in 1941, but debate and conflict over membership in the National Council persisted. In the mid-sixties the council's civil rights activities caused added difficulty. But repeated efforts to withdraw failed; in 1970 the assembly voted 245 to 156 to remain in the council, and in 1971 (213 to 189) and 1973 similar votes occurred. Efforts to force withdrawal from the World Council of Churches were no more successful; in 1971 the assembly's vote was 216 to 185, and a similar margin prevailed in 1973. In a rather surprising move the assembly approved full participation in the Consultation on Church Union (COCU) in 1966, and in 1972 the assembly voted 261 to 164 to remain in COCU although the United Presbyterian Church in the USA had withdrawn that year.

Efforts to reunite with the Northern Presbyterians occurred at regular intervals after the schism of the Civil War. In 1914 the Southern church raised a sizable barrier to union when the assembly amended the Book of Church Order so that three fourths of the presbyteries had to approve a union or merger. For the first time in its history the church in 1917 appointed a committee to consider union with the larger body, but this and other efforts at organic or federal union were unsuccessful. The chief obstacle during the first decades of the twentieth century appeared to be the traditional view of the church's "spirituality," but in later years the Auburn Affirmation (1924) of more than 1,200 Northern churchmen was cited as evidence of major theological differences with the larger Presbyterian body in the north.[61] A major effort at union was defeated by the Southern branch in 1954 when 42 presbyteries voted for the merger while 43 opposed.

In 1961 major initiatives were taken to make the church more of a national body by merging with the Reformed Church in America, whose major strength lay in the New York-New Jersey and Michigan-Iowa areas of the country. The suggested name for the new denomination was "Presbyterian Reformed Church." In 1968 the General Assembly approved merger plans by the overwhelming vote of 406 to 36, and the General Synod of the Reformed Church gave similar approval that year in a vote of 183 to 103. Even though the requisite three fourths of the Southern church's presbyteries approved the plan, the promising effort collapsed in 1969 when it failed to receive approval of two thirds of the Reformed Church's regional classes.

A renewed effort to unite with the Northern Presbyterians was mounted in 1969 when a Joint Committee of Twenty-four was established. The name proposed for the body was "Presbyterian Church (USA)." But by late 1970 more than half the number of Southern presbyteries required to block the merger had already passed resolutions that disapproved of any denominational action, including merger, that would dilute or demean the church's confessional position.[62] In 1969 a constitutional change permitting the formation of union presbyteries (but not synods) between the Southern churches' presbyteries and other Reformed and Presbyterian presbyteries failed. Repeatedly the General Assembly voted positively to keep merger or union hopes alive, but the failure of the Southern presbyteries to approve the proposed Book of Confessions in 1977 (by a vote of 39 to 21, with three fourths required) was a damaging blow. In 1977 the general assemblies of the Northern and Southern Presbyterians urged extensive cooperation between agencies of the two largest Presbyterian bodies in the United States, and called for concurrent meetings of the general assemblies every second year beginning in 1979. Drafts of three documents, A Book of Government, a Book of Discipline, and Covenants of Agreement, were to be brought to the assemblies in 1978 for review by the presbyteries. National and international agencies of both bodies were urged to undertake cooperative and joint work "except in those cases where such would be constitutionally or legally impossible . . . ," and with the specification that the action "does not include or imply any organic merger of the boards and agencies of the respective assemblies." The formation of union presbyteries was encouraged, synods in overlapping areas were encouraged to schedule joint meetings, and presbyteries in overlapping areas were encouraged to schedule a joint meeting annually beginning in 1978. The Joint Committee's recommendation set no date for formal binding vote on reunion by the assemblies or presbyteries. It did recommend review of the Southern church's rules with a view toward possible approval of union synods by that denomination.[63]

The church's General Assembly decided in 1977 to invite eight to twelve denominations to send one "ecumenical participant" each to its annual meetings. Each would have a vote in standing committees and a voice on the floor. It also approved for study a 10,000-word paper on homosexuality and asserted that "[Christians] should advocate and defend for homosexual persons . . . the civil liberties, equal rights, and protection under the law from social and economic discrimination which are due all other citizens." Despite the difficulties it encountered in failing to muster three fourths of the presbyteries' votes, the new Declaration of Faith was adopted as "a contemporary statement of faith, a reliable aid for Christian study, liturgy, and inspiration," though the Westminster Standards alone remain constitutional. The assembly also forwarded a number of recommendations to Congress and the President on a morally responsible food policy, stressed human rights, condemned violence on TV and grand-jury abuse, and designated the Sunday nearest St. Valentine's Day as the time for special concern for prisoners and criminal justice.[64] Elected moderator of the assembly was Harvard A. Anderson. In 1970 the General Assembly adopted a statement on abortion indicating that "willful termination of pregnancy by medical means on the considered decision of a pregnant woman may on occasion be morally justifiable." It was reaffirmed in 1971.[65]

Twenty-two colleges were associated with the body in 1960. Its four seminaries are Union Theological Seminary in Virginia, Richmond, Virginia, which published the important journal *Interpretation: A Theological and Biblical Quarterly*; Columbia Theological Seminary in Columbia, South Carolina; Austin Presbyterian Theological Seminary in Austin, Texas; and Louisville Presbyterian Theological Seminary in Louisville, Kentucky. The John Knox Press was established as the body's publishing house in 1955. The denomination's official monthly magazine is the *Presbyterian Survey*; three independent magazines, the *Christian Observer*, the *Presbyterian Outlook* and the *Presbyterian Journal*, have played important roles in the church's history.

At the time of the Civil War the Southern Presbyterians made up about one third of the Old School branch. By 1870 the denomination had 82,000 members. The depression years brought retrenchment in both home and foreign missions, but the national revival in religious interest of the 1940s and 1950s made an impact. Membership more than doubled between 1900 and 1925, from 225,000 to 457,000; the increase between 1925 and 1950 was smaller, from 457,000 to 675,000. Between 1954 and 1959, growth in black churches was 40 percent, nearly three times the church as a whole. The church's membership is found in the sixteen southern and border states of Florida, Georgia, Alabama, Mississippi, Louisiana, Texas, Oklahoma, Missouri, Arkansas, Tennessee, Kentucky, Virginia, West Virginia, Maryland, North Carolina, and South Carolina.[66] In 1976 the church had 2,615,662 members, with 13,846 ministers serving 8,675 churches. Its central office is located at 341 Ponce de Leon Avenue, N.E., Atlanta, Georgia 30308, and its archives are the Presbyterian Foundation, Box 847A, Montreat, North Carolina 28757.

A group of Waldenses from the Waldensian Valleys of Italy, with headquarters in Torre Pellice, emigrated to Valdese, North Carolina in 1893. Successive groups joined them through the years, making this the largest settlement of Waldenses in the United States. Since they were so distant from the Waldensian Church of Italy and could not have ready contact, they petitioned Concord Presbytery of the Presbyterian Church in the United States for membership and were promptly received in that church. Since that time the Waldensian Presbyterian Church of Valdese has been a member of the denomination. The congregation gathers an offering each year for the

Waldensian Church of Italy and is visited by the moderator of that church or his representative.[67]

In 1976 the General Assembly ruled that its congregations cannot leave the denomination by voting to take this action. This decision upheld a preliminary judgment of the assembly's Permanent Judicial Commission relative to cases of congregational defections to the Presbyterian Church in America (q.v.), organized in 1973 by people whose roots were in the Southern Presbyterian church. The East Alabama Presbytery had allowed about half of its congregations and ministers to transfer to the Presbyterian Church in America. The assembly's action suggested the possibility of civil court action to reclaim church property.[68]

Presbyterian Church in America

This church was organized late in 1973 in Birmingham, Alabama by Presbyterians who were dissatisfied with events in their parent body, the Presbyterian Church in the United States (Southern Presbyterians). Four hundred and fifteen delegates from fourteen states established the body on December 4, 1973. Among the issues that led to the new body's formation were alleged differences over the authority of the Bible, the ordination of women, the church's involvement in social issues, moves toward union with the United Presbyterian Church in the USA,, the claim that church leaders were deviating from historic Presbyterian doctrine, resistance to centralization, and other issues of faith and order.

As early as 1964 a group had organized itself as "Concerned Presbyterians, Inc." within the parent body. A successor of the old Continuing Church Committee of the 1940s, the group opposed membership in the National Council of Churches, World Council of Churches, and Consultation on Church Union, as well as the Southern Presbyterians' growing concern with social issues. Its editorial voice was the *Presybterian Journal* (1942–   ). The group helped organize an independent seminary in Jackson, Mississippi in 1964, which eventually described itself as committed to the "plenary, verbal inspiration" of the Bible and "its absolute inerrancy as the divinely revealed and authoritative Word of God," to "the sovereignty of God as a central tenet of Biblical faith, along with the related doctrines of absolute predestination and unconditional election," and to "strict creedal subscription to the whole Reformed faith."[69] In 1970 Kenneth S. Keyes, president of the group, a businessman and elder in a Southern Presbyterian church in Miami, Florida gave speeches on the subject "The Crisis in Our Church." An advertisement for his speech in St. Louis, Missouri, on April 5, 1970, indicated that "the time has come for all loyal Presbyterians to join hands" with 600 miinsters who, it was claimed, "oppose the liquidation of our Church and its historic evangelical testimony." Two points of special concerns were the merger talks with the Northern Presbyterians and efforts to adopt a Declaration of Faith in the Southern church.[70] In 1976 C. Gregg Singer, president of the group and professor at Catawba College in Salisbury, North Carolina, was charged with disturbing the peace in the Concord Presbytery of the Southern Presbyterian Church by distributing unrequested literature, "demoralizing" the minister of his home church, encouraging two congregations to separate from the denomination, and appealing to others as editor of the *Concerned Presbyterian* to leave the denomination.[71] While Concerned Presbyterians, Inc. was primarily a lay operation, the Presbyterian Churchmen United was formed in 1969 by about 600 pastors in the parent body along parallel lines.[72]

The Covenant Fellowship was founded early in 1970 by moderates in the parent body who hoped to reconcile the differences in the emerging conflict. The fellowship's statement at that time indicated that "honest dissent can be healthy if it is the working of the leaven of the Spirit. But when dissent creates . . . polarization, the church has become unconvincing to the world and unfaithful to her Lord." Another "Statement of Position" released in November by Dr. William M. Elliott of Dallas, Texas, its president, called on all Southern Presbyterians to maintain unity and deplored "any efforts or movements" toward fragmentation of the denomination. Apparently the group once met with the more conservative groups but then voted unanimously not to attend subsequent meetings.[73]

A decisive event appears to have been the Southern assembly's decision in 1971, by a narrow vote of 217 to 207, to restructure its synods along new boundaries. Some conservatives interpreted the move as an effort to shift the balance of power in certain synods, which in turn could adjust presbyteries; others claimed that the reduction of synods from fifteen to seven was an effort to improve efficiency.[74] On August 11, 1971, at Weaverville, North Carolina, leaders of conservative organizations announced plans for a new church. Concerned Presbyterians, Presbyterian Churchmen United, and the Presbyterian Evangelistic Fellowship gathered almost 550 supporters for the meeting. It was indicated that the escape clause in the proposed Plan of Union with the Northern Presbyterians deserved support, since congregations could remain out of the union and retain their property. One opposing voice at the meeting was the influential director and associate editor of the *Presbyterian Journal*, Dr. L. Nelson Bell. He insisted on witnessing within the parent body and resigned his editorial post in short order.[75]

In 1972 several conservative congregations in the parent body reportedly joined with five independent Presbyterian churches to form a group called "Vanguard Presbytery, a Provisional Presbytery for Southern Presbyterians and Reformed Churches Uniting." In May 1973 a "convention of sessions," claiming that the positions of the Southern church were out of step with its doctrinal and constitutional requirements, voted 349 to 16 to begin a new Presbyterian church in 1973. In August 1973 representatives of about 200 churches met in an "advisory convention" to prepare for the denomination's formation. The convention decided that only churches firmly committed to the new denomination could send delegates to its first General Assembly. Proposed for adoption as doctrinal standards were certain versions of the

Westminster Confession of Faith with the Larger and Shorter Catechisms, and the Southern Presbyterians' 1933 Book of Church Order. Earlier that summer the Southern Presbyterian's assembly had for the most part ignored those threatening to form the new body.[76]

Complications arose as congregations separated. In 1973 Trinity Presbyterian Church of Montgomery, Alabama voted 848 to 112 to withdraw from the parent body and join the new denomination. The area's presbytery approved the action, but the synod judicial commission ruled that the minority's property rights were not adequately protected. Then the presbytery ruled that the loyal minority was the true church; without the presbytery's approval there would be no civil litigation.[77]

The new body was initially called the National Presbyterian Church when organized in December 1973. The name was subsequently changed to Presbyterian Church in America. Its initial strength was estimated to be between 200 and congregations and 50,000 to 75,000 members. In 1976 the church had 61,100 communicant members (60,926 the previous year), 405 churches, 457 ministers, 2,629 elders, and 21 presbyteries. Its members contributed $20,143,308 for local causes and $1,704,675 for assembly causes.

In its 1975 General Assembly the church called for a "Day of Prayer and Fasting for revival in the United States," directing that all congregations observe the day of July 4, 1975. The assembly failed to adopt a report indicating that there is no biblical basis for a major distinction between ruling elders (laypersons) and teaching elders (clergy), and that "all elders rule together and are together responsible for the teaching of the church."[78]

The body is a member of the North American Presbyterian and Reformed Council and has scheduled its General Assembly to meet concurrently with other members of the council in Grand Rapids, Michigan in 1978. The church cooperates in a publishing venture with the Orthodox Presbyterian Church. The Reformed Presbyterian Church–Evangelical Synod recently elected a member of the Presbyterian Church in America to serve on the board of its seminary, Covenant Seminary, in St. Louis, Missouri. The recently retired president of the seminary, the Reverend Robert G. Rayburn, and two faculty members attended the founding convention of the Presbyterian Church in America as fraternal delegates.[79]

In 1977 the stated clerk of the denomination was Morton H. Smith. The headquarters address is P.O. Box 1473, Jackson, Mississippi 39205. The archives is the Office of Stated Clerk, P.O. Box 256, Clinton, Mississippi 39056.

Cumberland Presbyterian Church

As an outgrowth of the great revival of 1800, three Presbyterian ministers in Dickson County, Tennessee—Finis Ewing, Samuel King, and Samuel MacAdow—in 1810 reconstituted as an independent organization the Cumberland Presbytery that the Synod of Kentucky had dissolved in 1806. Among the factors that led to the organization of the new presbytery were the founders' conviction that the exceptional circumstances on the American frontier demanded a relaxation of the rigid educational requirements for ordination that the Presbyterian church had traditionally imposed, as well as their rejection of what they saw as a fatalistic strain in the predestinarianism of the Westminster Confession of Faith. In the late 1860s the white and black constituencies of the Cumberland Presbyterian Church separated amicably by mutual consent.

In 1901 the Arkansas Synod ordered the consolidation of the Porter Presbytery with the Fort Smith Presbytery. The former refused to accept the synod's decision and late in 1902 a council of members of the Porter Presbytery resolved to organize as an independent body. In July 1903 they carried out this resolution by organizing the Reformed Cumberland Presbyterian Church at the Pilot Prairie Church near Waldron, Arkansas. In 1905 the new body changed its name to This Cumberland Presbyterian Church. In 1906, with a membership of about 1,200 communicants it successfully petitioned for reentry into the Arkansas Synod.[80]

In 1906 a considerable segment of the Cumberland Presbyterian Church reunited with the then Presbyterian Church in the United States of America and gave that body its base in the American South. But a significantly large part of the Cumberland Presbyterian Church's membership regarded the terms of union as unsatisfactory and continued the latter body as a separate denomination. An effort to unite the Second Cumberland Presbyterian Church in the United States (as the black body is now known) with the continuing white Cumberland Presbyterian Church was approved by the latter body in 1966, but failed to secure the required proportion of favorable votes in the presbyteries of the black group.

In 1955 the division that led to the formation of the Upper Cumberland Presbyterian Church took place.

The Cumberland Presbyterian Center, 1978 Union Avenue, Memphis, Tennessee 38104, serves as the national headquarters. The General Assembly meets annually. The churchbody carries on foreign missions in Colombia, Japan, and Hong Kong. There are 860 churches and missions in the United States with a total membership of 87,970.

Second Cumberland Presbyterian Church in the United States

In 1869 the black membership of the Cumberland Presbyterian Church withdrew from the white body with the latter's approval to form the Colored Cumberland Presbyterian Church. The association of a presbytery in Liberia with the black body in 1940 was short-lived. More recently the church took the name Second Cumberland Presbyterian Church in the United States. Its commitment to the Westminster Confession is qualified; it prides itself on a mediating theology "which is neither Calvinistic or Armenian." It holds that the responsibility for an individual's salvation is "not wholly upon God and not wholly upon man, but there is a sensible balance of these two forces which makes salvation not an arbitrary matter on the part of God and not a question of man's work alone.[81] In 1966 the general assemblies of both Cumberland Presbyterian bodies approved a plan that looked toward the reunification of the two in 1967. The requisite two-thirds majority of the Second Cumberland Presbyterian Church did not concur in the proposal. There are no central headquarters. The Second Cumberland Presbyterian Church has about 20,000 members in 100 churches.[82]

The Orthodox Presbyterian Church

In 1929 John Gresham Machen (1881–1937), Robert Dick Wilson (1856–1930), and other proponents of the historic confessional standards in the Presbyterian Church in the United States of America, alarmed at what they regarded as an irreversible drift toward liberalism, established Westminster Theological Seminary at Philadelphia. This was to be an independent conservative counterpart to Princeton Theological Seminary. In 1933 Machen failed to secure passage of an overture which he had drafted and which a number of presbyteries had proposed to that year's assembly; it called for care on the part of the Board of Foreign Missions to keep modernists from the board and from the roll of missionaries and to avoid doctrinally compromising union enterprises. Thereupon he, J. Oliver Buswell (then president of Wheaton College), Carl McIntire (pastor of the Collingswood [New Jersey] Presbyterian Church), and other likeminded leaders brought into being the Independent Board for Presbyterian Foreign Missions and urged the laity of the denomination to support the new board rather than the official board. The 1934 General Assembly demanded the dissolution of the Independent Board and support of the official board. When Machen and his associates refused, the church tried them, found them guilty of insubordination, and suspended them from the ministry. Thereupon they organized the Presbyterian Church of America on June 11, 1936.

Machen died on January 1, 1937. Within six months the new denomination had split, with McIntire and his followers forming the Bible Presbyterian Church. The Presbyterian Church in the United States of America won its suit to enjoin the continuing segment of the Presbyterian Church of America from using that name, and in 1939 it adopted the designation Orthodox Presbyterian Church.

At its organization the denomination solemnly declared "(1) that the Scriptures of the Old and New Testament are the Word of God, the only infallible rule of faith and practice, (2) that the Westminster Confession of Faith and Catechisms contain the system of doctrine taught in the Holy Scriptures, and (3) that we subscribe to and maintain the principles of Presbyterian church government as being founded upon and agreeable to the Word of God."

At the second General Assembly of 1936 the changes that the Presbyterian Church in the United States of America had made in the Westminster Confession in 1903 were eliminated, except for two small changes in chapter XXII concerning oaths and in chapter XXV, section 6, which designates the pope as the Antichrist.

The theological posture of the Orthodox Presbyterian Church is that of Reformed Orthodoxy.

The Orthodox Presbyterian Church has 131 churches with 15,300 members. The form of government is presbyterian; the General Assembly meets annually. Its headquarters are at 7401 Old York Road, Philadelphia, Pennsylvania 19126. It carries on foreign missions in the Republic of China (Taiwan), Egypt, Ethiopia, Japan, Korea, and Lebanon.

Bible Presbyterian Church

In 1937 a segment of the Presbyterian Church of America (now the Orthodox Presbyterian Church) withdrew from that body and established the Bible Presbyterian Church. The following year the Synod of the Bible Presbyterian Church altered articles 32 and 33 of the Westminster Confession and questions 84 through 90 of the Larger Catechism to affirm Christ's premillennial return, the resurrection of the departed believers, the rapture of the church, and a literal millennial reign of Christ, followed by the resurrection and judgment of the wicked.[83]

In the 1940s the Bible Presbyterian Church helped to establish the American Council of Churches and the International Council of Churches. In the mid-1950s, a division of opinion developed in the body on the desirability of the continued support of these councils. Simultaneously a group in the Bible Presbyterian Church felt rising within the synod "a movement for tighter ecclesiastical control."[84] In 1956 a large segment of the membership under the leadership of one of the founders of both the Presbyterian Church of America and the Bible Presbyterian Church, Dr. Carl McIntire of Collingswood, New Jersey, formed a separate Bible Presbyterian Association to maintain membership in the American Council of Christian Churches. The association became known as the Collingswood Synod of Bible Presbyterian Church, to differentiate it from what it called the Columbus Synod of the Bible Presbyterian Church, which is now a part of the Reformed Presbyterian Church, Evangelical Synod.

The doctrinal standard of the Bible Presbyterian Church are the Larger and Shorter Westminster catechisms, the Westminster Confession of Faith, the Form of Government of the Bible Presbyterian Church, and the Book of Discipline. The sermon is the central feature of its worship. Each local congregation owns its church property without reservation, elects its minister and elders, and possesses the power to leave the synod for any reason that seems sufficient to itself. The church operates through independent agencies such as the Independent Board for Presbyterian Home Missions, the Indepen ent Board for Presbyterian Foreign Missions, Faith Theological Seminary, and other institutions and agencies, all of which the church promotes.

Theologically very conservative, it belongs to and supports both the American Christian Action Council and the International Council of Christian Churches.

Faith Theological Seminary, Elkins Park (Philadelphia), Pennsylvania, serves as the headquarters of the stated clerk. There are 72 churches in 23 states with 5,490 communicant members and 2 churches in Canada with just under 200 communicants. Through the Independent Board for Presbyterian Foreign Missions the church supports missions in Africa, the Middle East, Latin America, England, India, Japan, the Republic of China (Taiwan), Korea, and Singapore.[85]

Reformed Church in America

The Reformed Church in America goes back to the early seventeenth century. In 1621 the States-General chartered the Dutch West India Company to develop the colony of the New Netherlands along the Hudson River. Two Kranken-Besoeckers ("visitors of the ill") or Zieken-Troosters ("comforters of the sick") came with Governor Peter Minuit's traders in 1626. The first minister, Jonas Michaelius (b. 1584), arrived in 1628, and organized a congregation of fifty Dutch and Walloon communicants.

Official establishment of the Dutch Church took place soon afterward. The church exerted limited influence during the generation before the British takeover, although the first entry in the city records of New Amsterdam is the prayer that Pastor Johannes Megapolensis (1601–1670) said at the opening of the court in 1653.

For the first century and a half the Classis (Presbytery) of Amsterdam supervised the church in America. This arrangement was not always satisfactory to the entire colonial church, which was divided between those who wanted to keep the church Dutch and those who sought accommodation to the American environment. In 1747 the Classis of Amsterdam gave reluctant approval to the colonists' request for the establishment of an American *Coetus*, one of whose leaders was the fervent and forceful Westphalia-born Theodorus Jacobus Frelinghuizen.[86] The ultra-Dutch dominies countered by organizing a *Conferentie*. A major problem was the provision of adequately trained young men for the American congregations. To return to the Netherlands for training and ordination involved arduous and dangerous travel, and many of the colonial churchmen called for a means of training and ordaining candidates on the American continent. Some wanted the ministerial candidates to receive their training at King's College in New York (now Columbia University). Others urged that theological training be made available at Queen's College, New Brunswick, New Jersey, founded in 1766 (now Rutgers University). The *Conferentie* group wanted candidates to return to the motherland for their education. A happy end to the controversy came with the return to America

of Utrecht-trained John Henry Livingston, who had worked out a Plan o
Union with the Classis of Amsterdam that proved acceptable to all parties
While the Revolutionary War prevented immediate implementation of th
plan, in 1784 the American church resolved the ministerial training probler
by establishing the first separate divinity school in the United States, locate
initially in New York, and after 1810 at New Brunswick.

The extensive retention of the Dutch language into the first quarter of th
nineteenth century retarded the growth of the church and alienated many o
its young people. Even as late as its first incorporation in 1819 the church too
as its name the Reformed Protestant Dutch Church; it legally became the Re
formed Church in America only in 1869.

This tactic was repeated in the Middle West, where from 1847 on larg
numbers of Hollanders migrated to Michigan and Iowa—in some cases entir
congregations with their pastors. Many of these immigrants, especially thos
who came under the leadership of Albertus Christianus Van Raalte (1811
1876) and Hendrick Pieter Scholte, fled their homeland to escape persecutior
The church also absorbed a large number of German Reformed immigran
to the Middle West.

In 1882 about twenty churches seceded to form the True Dutch Reforme
Church. The remnants of this schism were able to recruit large numbers o
adherents among the Dutch immigrants to the Middle West in the latter ha
of the century; ultimately this group became the Christian Reformed Churcl

Early efforts to unite the Dutch and German Reformed communities in th
East were unsuccessful. Nontheological factors, notably linguistic and cultur:
difficulties, were largely responsible; but in part the failure stemmed from th
Dutch demand that the united body subscribe to the Dutch confession:
standards as well as to the Heidelberg Catechism. Efforts made in 1920 t
effect a union of the Reformed Church in America with the Presbyteria
Church in the United States of America found little response. After Worl
War II a proposal for union with the United Presbyterian Church engaged th
attention of both denominations for four years following 1945, but the Pla
of Union did not elicit the necessary two-thirds majority from the classe
More recently, negotiations for union with the Presbyterian Church in th
United States seemed promising for a time, but in 1969 determined oppositio
of some midwestern congregations of the Reformed Church in America cause
the failure of the effort.

The Reformed Church in America requires its ministers and the professo
at its two theological seminaries (at New Brunswick, New Jersey, and Wester
Theological Seminary, Holland, Michigan) to subscribe to the three Formul:
of Unity, the Belgic Confession, the Canons of the Synod of Dort, and th
Heidelberg Catechism.

Liturgically there has always been considerable freedom within the pr
scription of dignity and order in worship. The older churches in the East ten
to be more open to the worship revival than the churches in the Middle Wes

In 1966 the General Synod adopted a new liturgy which now is mandatory for all congregations.

In recent years the Reformed Church in America has interested itself extensively in social issues and in matters of national policy. On occasion it has reached its decisions only after long and vigorous debate and by narrow margins.

The governing body of the local congregation is called a consistory. The classis is the Reformed counterpart of the presbytery. Particular synods are organized on a regional basis. The General Synod meets annually.

Headquarters are in the Interchurch Center, 475 Riverside Drive, New York, New York 10027. There are 902 churches in more than half of the states of the Union and in the province of Ontario, with an inclusive membership of 354,004. The denomination conducts missions in Mexico, Japan, Taiwan, Hong Kong, India, and Saudi Arabia.

Synod of the Reformed Presbyterian Church of North America

In 1969 the Reformed Presbyterian Church of North America absorbed the Associate Presbyterian Church of North America.

The Reformed Presbyterian Church of North America traces its lineage back to 1752, when the first minister from the Reformed Presbytery of Scotland came to the American continent. The first Reformed Presbytery in North America came into being at Paxtang, Pennsylvania in 1774.

In the meantime missionaries of the slightly older "Seceder" Associate Presbytery of Scotland had come to North America, and they too established a presbytery.

In 1782 the two presbyteries united to form the Associate Reformed Church of America. But some of the members of the Reformed Presbytery and some of the members of the Associate Presbytery remained outside the union. The continuing Reformed group reorganized formally as the Reformed Presbytery in 1798 at Philadelphia. It grew large enough to constitute a synod in 1809.

The members of this church refused to vote, hold office, or take part in the government until the Constitution of the United States should be changed to recognize the kingship of Christ. In 1833 the synod split over this issue. The "Old Light" Synod of the Reformed Presbyterian Church (Old School) continued to follow the traditional practice. The "New Light" Reformed Presbyterian Church, General Synod, held that the national constitution was defective but not immoral and that exercise of the franchise violated no oath or covenant. The latter body united in 1965 with the Evangelical Presbyterian Church to form the Reformed Presbyterian Church, Evangelical Synod.

The two ministers and three ruling elders of the Associate Presbytery that had stayed out of the union of 1782 continued the Associate Presbytery. It grew and in 1801 called itself the Associate Presbyterian Synod of North

America. In 1858, when the synod entered the United Presbyterian Church of North America, eleven ministers once more elected to continue the Associate Synod under the name of the Associate Presbyterian Church of North America. By the time of the merger of 1969 the continuing group had declined to four churches in Iowa and Kansas with an inclusive membership of about 350.

The "Old School" church's position on the issues that had divided it from the "New Light" Reformed Presbyterian Church is in a state of flux. In 1966 the Reformed Presbyterian Church of North America revised the crucial articles 29 and 30 of its "Declaration and Testimony." It now affirms that every nation ought to recognize in its organic law the sovereignty of God exercised by Christ, and its duty to rule civil affairs in accordance with God's will. Failure to do this is sinful and exposes the nation to God's wrath. All Christians should labor and pray for their nation's explicit recognition of the authority and law of Christ and for the conduct of all governmental affairs in harmony with the written Word of God. They should use every civil right available to them to accomplish both ends, as long as their use of such a civil right does not compromise their loyalty to Christ. If an oath of allegiance does this, they may not take it, nor may they participate in the selection of officials or civil servants who must take an oath that the Christian could not take. In qualifying for a civil position by appointment, election, or employment, Christians may take the oath of allegiance to civil authority only if the church's courts have determined that they are not promising more than due submission in the Lord, nor accepting an unchristian principle of civil government. When they participate in elections, they should support and vote only for candidates publicly committed to scriptural principles of civil government. When they seek office they must openly inform those who support they seek of their adherence to Christian principles.

The two chief past covenants that the Reformed Presbyterian Church of North America has signed are dated 1871 and 1954.[87] The church body accepts the Westminster Confession as its doctrinal standard. It observes close Communion and uses only psalms, without instrumental accompaniment, in its worship. It forbids its members to join secret societies. It exchanges fraternal delegates and cooperates with the Reformed Presbyterian Church, Evangelical Synod, and with other Presbyterian and Reformed churches.

Its organization is presbyterian; the synod meets annually. There are no central headquarters. The church body's weekly, *The Covenanter Witness*, is published from Pittsburgh, Pennsylvania. It reports 69 churches with an inclusive membership of 5,445. It carries on foreign missions in Cyprus and Japan.

General Synod of the Associate Reformed Presbyterian Church

Despite their historic differences, both Scottish Covenanters and Scottish Seceders among the North American colonists fought side by side in the

Revolutionary War. Heartened by this experience, they united in 1782 into a single church body, the Associate Reformed Church of America. In 1822 the distance that separated the congregations in the Carolinas from their co-religionists in the North led to the withdrawal of the Synod of the Carolinas, which took the name Associate Reformed Synod of the South. This body did not participate in the 1855/1856 union which brought into being the General Synod of the Associate Reformed Presbyterian Church of that period or in the 1858 union which created the United Presbyterian Church of North America. In 1912 the Synod of the South took the name, the Associate Reformed Synod. In 1935 it changed its name to the General Synod of the Associate Reformed Presbyterian Church.

Its doctrinal standards are the Bible and the Westminster Standards, the Westminster Confession of Faith and the Westminster Larger and Shorter Catechisms.[88] In 1946 it relaxed its strict position on the singing of psalms exclusively in its services by allowing the use of other selected hymns. The headquarters of the organization are at 300 University Ridge, Greenville, South Carolina 29601. It has 153 churches with 31,154 members. Its foreign mission fields are in Mexico and Pakistan.

Reformed Presbyterian Church, Evangelical Synod

The Reformed Presbyterian Church, Evangelical Synod, came into being through the union in 1965 of the Reformed Presbyterian Church in North America, General Synod, and the Evangelical Presbyterian Church.

From 1774 to 1833 the Reformed Presbyterian Church in North America, General Synod, and the Synod of the Reformed Presbyterian Church of North America had a common history. The General Synod, which did not demand that its members refrain from voting and holding public office, suffered a variety of disappointments in its subsequent history. Population shifts, heated debates about the exclusive use of its psalms in worship and about the prohibition of instrumental accompaniment for congregational singing, and the fundamentalist-modernist controversy all led to membership losses. By 1950 the Church reached its nadir in size, with only 9 congregations. Then it began to grow again, and by 1965 it had 23 churches.

The Evangelical Presbyterian Church had a shorter history. From the very beginning of the Presbyterian Church of America (later called the Orthodox Presbyterian Church) in 1936 there had been differences among its founders about dispensationalism of the Scofield Reference Bible type, the temperate use of alcoholic beverages, and the continuing support of the Independent Board for Presbyterian Foreign Missions after a majority of the board members had elected an ecclesiastically independent member as president. A minority in the Presbyterian Church of America insisted that attacks on dispensationalism were in reality an attack on premillennialism, called for a resolution advocating total abstinence, and urged continuing support of the Independent Board. When the 1937 General Assembly denied these pleas, fourteen ministers and three elders withdrew and formed the Bible Presbyterian Synod (or Church). A major leader was Dr. Carl McIntire of Collingswood, New Jersey. In 1938 the Synod altered the Westminster Confession of Faith and the Larger Catechism to affirm premilliennialism. In the 1940s the Bible Presbyterian Church played an important role in the formation and support of the American Council of Christian Churches and the International Council of Christian Churches. With the passage of time, the enthusiasm of the majority for these agencies waned. In 1956 the Bible Presbyterian Church withdrew from them and set up its own board for foreign missions. Thereupon McIntire led a large segment of the membership out of the Bible Presbyterian Church to form the Bible Presbyterian Association, commonly called the Collingswood (New Jersey) Synod of the Bible Presbyterian Church. To obviate the confusion that resulted from the existence of two Bible Presbyterian churches the majority body took the name Evangelical Presbyterian Church in 1961.

The united church stands committed to the Westminster Confession of Faith and the Larger and Shorter catechisms, without the modifications of 1938. The dominant view affirms premillennialism but disavows dispensationalism of the Scofield Reference Bible type. While the church continues to oppose the traffic in alcoholic beverages, it does not hold that total abstinence is the only way to give an effective Christian witness against intemperance. It exchanges fraternal delegates and cooperates with the Synod of the Reformed Presbyterian Church of North America, the Orthodox Presbyterian Church, and the Christian Reformed Church. Its organization is presbyterian. The General Synod meets annually. The stated clerk resides at 1818 Missouri Avenue, Las Cruces, New Mexico. There are 140 churches with 22,452 members. The church carries on foreign missions in India, Australia, Korea, Japan, the Republic of China (Taiwan), Saudi Arabia, Jordan, Grand Cayman Island, Chile, Peru, and Kenya.

The Presbyterian Church in Canada

The earliest Presbyterians in Canada were French Huguenots. The Presbyterian Church in Canada regards itself as "in historical continuity with The Church of Scotland, reformed in 1560." The influx of United Empire Loyalists from the newly independent United States after the Revolutionary War swelled the ranks of the membership, but in the main the leadership came from Scotland. After the second decade of the nineteenth century the immigration of large numbers of Scottish and Irish families added to the British flavor of Canadian Presbyterianism. The specifics of the Canadian situation, notably its geographical isolation from the British Isles, had some modifying effects. It limited the degree of supervision that the British church authorities could give the colonial churches. In a variety of ways it tended to increase disproportionately the number of Secession clergymen in the

Canadian Presbyterian ministry. The inability of the Presbyterians to obtain state support heightened the Presbyterian competition with the Anglican church and the Presbyterian rivalry with other Nonconformists. Finally, the Canadian environment fostered in the Presbyterians of Canada a profounder sense of missionary obligation.

The various schisms in British Presbyterianism—at least thirteen secessions occurred in Scotland between 1690 and 1900—crossed the Atlantic to Canada. The most serious for Canada was the "Great Disruption" from 1844 to 1875 that followed on the organization of the Free Church of Scotland. During this period the earlier Secessionist stream joined with the Free Church stream. Through a merging of all three streams, Canadian Presbyterians succeeded in achieving a nationwide unity by 1875, less than a decade after Canada had achieved political unity.

Many of the factors that operated to bring this unity about also favored participation of the Presbyterians in the formation of the United Church of Canada in 1925. Yet about two fifths of the Presbyterian community refused to enter the United Church and elected to continue separate existence. "It was a painful time for all concerned. Congregations were divided; friendships broken; families alienated, and a flood of bitterness, rancour, and recrimination was let loose hitherto unknown in Canadian Church History."[89]

Among the Presbyterians who opposed the union were some—the Presbyterian Church Association, for example—who did so because they felt that in its polity, practice, and doctrine the Presbyterian Church was the most scriptural of all churches, and that the church courts which voted the union had been unfaithful to the biblical truths set forth in the Presbyterian confessional standards. Others opposed the union because they felt that a federal form of denominational association was a viable and more effective alternative to organic union. Federalism, they felt, would enable the denominations to meet the problems common to all of them without the destruction of their identity and structure. Those in a third group were affronted by what they regarded as a lack of fairness, equity, and Christian consideration in the pro-union party. There were also a good many Presbyterians who feared that the United Church would "move steadily to the left into a thinner and thinner liberalism" and who opposed the union for this reason. They saw in the Basis of Union an adulterated theology born of a desire to provide a compromise that would accommodate both Calvinistic Presbyterians and Arminian Methodists. At the other end of the continuum of theological opponents of the union were some who regarded the Basis of Union as not sufficiently contemporary. Still another group lamented what seemed to them a lack of theological concern on the part of the leaders of the uniting bodies.

In the years that have elapsed since 1925, much of the bitterness that the division evoked has evaporated, as both groups have devised mechanisms designed to reduce friction.

The Presbyterian Church in Canada accepts as its supreme standard the canonical Scriptures of the Old and New Testaments and as its subordinate standards the Westminster Confession of Faith and the Longer and Shorter Westminster catechisms. The 1962 General Assembly resolved "that our church recognize the Second Helvetic Confession, the Belgic Confession, the Gallican Confession (Confession of La Rochelle), and the Heidelberg Catechism as standards parallel to ours, and direct that, as we recognize these as parallel, ministers and ruling elders of these standards coming to us recognize our standards as parallel to theirs, and for the sake of uniformity of law within our church that these ministers and ruling elders in ordinations and inductions subscribe to our subordinate standards as we do, it being permitted to these men, where so desiring, to teach from these confessions (Second Helvetic, Belgic, and Gallican) and the Heidelberg Catechism."

The Basis of Union in 1875 explicitly stipulated that the Presbyterian Church in Canada did not recognize Article 23 of the Westminster Confession on the power of the civil magistrate. This left a hiatus that the Assembly of 1955 filled when it finally ratified a Declaration of Faith Concerning Church and Nation.[90] Thirteen years in preparation, it proposes to set forth the biblical teaching on the relationship of church and state under the lordship of Christ.

In 1966 the Presbyterian Church in Canada voted to admit women to ordination as ministers and elders.[91] In the same year the Board of Evangelism and Social Action published its *Manual on Christian Social Action*, which assembled the board's statements on a wide variety of contemporary social questions and the recommendations made by the general assemblies.[92]

There is a mutual recognition of ministries among the Presbyterian Church in Canada, the United Presbyterian Church in the United States of America, and the Presbyterian Church in the United States. A Committee on Articles of Faith of the Presbyterian Church in Canada and the Committee on Faith and Order of the United Church of Canada have engaged in doctrinal conversations. Committees appointed by General Assemblies of the Presbyterian Church in Canada and by the Anglican Church in Canada have engaged in conversations mainly on the issues of order and of the ministry.

The Presbyterian Church in Canada counts 1,069 churches and missions with an inclusive membership of 174,555. The denominational headquarters are at 50 Wynford Drive, Don Mills, Ontario M3C 1J7. Foreign missions are conducted in the Republic of China (Taiwan), India, Japan, Guyana, and Nigeria.[93]

Christian Reformed Church

In 1834 the established Reformed (Hervormde) Church of the Netherlands sustained a serious secession, the members of which proceeded to form the Christian Reformed Church of the Netherlands. Some of these seceders moved to western Michigan in 1847. In 1849 they joined the Reformed Church in America. By 1857 there were eleven congregations in the area. In that year the Reverend Koene van den Bosch and parts of four congregations withdrew in a dispute over certain matters of doctrine and discipline and formed the True Dutch Church. In 1859 the new body changed its name to Holland Reformed Church and in 1861 to the True Dutch Reformed Church.

The decision that the Reformed Church in America reached in 1880 not to forbid its members to belong to secret societies had a twofold effect. The first was that five more churches in western Michigan left the Reformed Church in America in 1882 and joined the True Dutch Reformed Church, which in the same year once more changed its name, this time to the Holland Christian Reformed Church in America. The second result was the action of the Synod of the Christian Reformed Church in the Netherlands in 1882 (repeated in 1885). Before 1850 it had regarded the Reformed Church in America as its North American counterpart; now it advised all its consistories to transfer their members emigrating to North America not to the Reformed Church in America but to the Holland Christian Reformed Church in America. Since this was a period of massive Dutch emigration to the United States, the decision of the Christian Reformed Church in the Netherlands contributed to a marked increase in the membership of the Holland Christian Reformed Church.

In 1890 the church body adopted its present name. In the same year the remnants of another True Dutch Reformed Church, founded in 1822 by Dr. Solomon Froeligh at Schraalenburg, New Jersey, after he had withdrawn from the Reformed Church in America, united with the Christian Reformed Church as the Hackensack (New Jersey) Classis; but in 1908 seven of the ten churches in this classis again withdrew. Ultimately they disbanded or were absorbed into existing denominations.

Doctrinal controversies in the Christian Reformed Church led in 1924 to the withdrawal of the group that founded the Protestant Reformed Church of America. In 1944 a small group withdrew to become an element of the Free and Old Christian Reformed Churches. In recent years the Christian Reformed Church has grown rapidly in Canada as a result of expanded immigration to the dominion.

The Christian Reformed Church accepts the Belgic Confession, the Heidelberg Catechism, and the Canons of Dort. It holds a number of distinctive theological positions. Included among these is its conviction that the Bible is the inspired Word of God which has no fallible human element; that it must be believed on its own authority; and that the origin and history of the Old Testament writings cannot as such and from the standpoint of faith be the subject of empirical-critical investigation. From the organic character of the Bible it concludes to the typical and symbolical significance of Old Testament persons, events, and institutions.

It sees the confessional standards as infralapsarian, but it does not exclude or condemn the supralapsarian position, although it holds that the latter cannot be represented as *the* doctrine of the church. It also teaches that there is an objective (or eternal) justification sealed by Christ's resurrection that precedes subjective justification in time, and it warns against any view that would do violence either to Christ's eternal suretyship for the elect or to the requirements of a sincere faith in order to be justified before God.

It teaches that it is contrary to Reformed doctrine to deny that God is glorified by the perdition of the ungodly. It likewise teaches a "common grace" apart from saving grace and holds that God manifests this common grace toward his creatures in general. Unregenerate human beings are capable of doing acts that are civilly good, even though they are incapable of performing acts that are good in a saving sense.

It teaches that there is no essential difference between Israel of the Old Covenant and the church.

It regards the "seed of the covenant," that is, the children born to Christian parents, as regenerated, but it does so with a "judgment of charity" which is not at all intended to imply that each child is actually born again; at the same time it holds that neither the Scriptures nor the Reformed confessions prove that every elect child is, because of its election, regenerated in fact even before baptism, since God fulfills his promise in sovereign fashion before, during, or after baptism in his own time.

In opposition to what it describes as the Lutheran and Roman Catholic doctrine, it holds that regeneration is not effected through the Word of God or the sacraments as such but only through the almighty and regenerating operation of the Holy Spirit (although it does not conceive of the regenerating operation of the Holy Spirit as normally divorced or separate from the preaching of the Word of God). For that reason it describes the operation of the Holy Spirit as "immediate regeneration."

It sees the moral element in the observance of the Sabbath (and, in the postapostolic period, of Sunday) as involved in the fact that a certain day is set aside for worship and for as much rest as worship and hallowed meditation require; for that reason Christians must rest on Sunday from all servile work, except for the requirements of charity and present necessity, and from all recreations that interfere with worship.

A revived recognition that mission belongs to the church's essence has sparked a still unresolved controversy in the Christian Reformed Church, with a minority group affirming the inherent universality of God's redemptive love and of Christ's atonement, while the majority group continues to affirm the traditionally held view of a limited saving will of God and a limited atonement.

Members of the Christian and Reformed Church are united in the National Union of Christian Schools with members of the Reformed Church in America and of the Protestant Reformed Churches in the operation of a significant network of Christian elementary and high schools. Other members of the

Christian Reformed Church support the National Association of Christian Schools, a quite separate and considerably smaller organization with the same purpose but with a broader interdenominational base.

The headquarters of the Christian Reformed Church are at 2850 Kalamazoo Avenue Southeast, Grand Rapids, Michigan 49508. The General Synod meets annually. The church has 527 churches and missions in the United States and Canada, with a total membership of 206,000. It carries on foreign missions in Nigeria, Brazil, Japan, and the Republic of China (Taiwan).

Protestant Reformed Churches in America

In 1924 and 1925 the Christian Reformed Classis of Grand Rapids (Michigan) East and West deposed the Reverend Herman Hoeksema (1886–1965), the Reverend Henry Danhof, and the Reverend George M. Ophoff (1891–1962) as ministers of the denomination, along with three congregational consistories that shared the opposition of the three clergymen to the doctrine of common grace as the Christian Reformed Synod of Kalamazoo had enunciated it in 1924. In March 1925 three of the consistories formed a temporary organization called the Protesting Christian Reformed Churches. In 1926 the breach with the parent body became permanent and the protesting group reorganized under the name Protestant Reformed Churches in America.[94]

The strongly confessional denomination accepts as standards the Belgic Confession, the Heidelberg Catechism, the Canons of Dordrecht, and the Church Order of the Reformed Churches. It is emphatic in its affirmation of total depravity, unconditional election, limited atonement, irresistible grace, and the preservation and perseverance of the saints.[95] With reference to the issues that provoked the break with the Christian Reformed Church, the Protestant Reformed Churches "maintain that God is never gracious in time or eternity to the reprobate wicked."[96] They further affirm that the theory of general grace, which they hold that the Synod of Kalamazoo taught, "is a denial of the sovereign election and reprobation and of particular atonement, and teaches that Christ died for all, but that [the] application of His atoning death depends upon the choice of the will of the sinner."[97] They also hold that "the preaching of the Gospel is, both in God's intention and in actual application, grace to the elect only, while it is a savor of death unto death for the reprobate."[98] They deny that "there is an inwardly restraining operation of the Holy Spirit upon the heart of the natural man, which is not regenerating, whereby the progress of the corruption of sin in the human nature is being checked and restrained in such a way that a remnant of the original goodness in the state of righteousness is constantly preserved in it and also brought to bear fruit in many good works in this present life."[99] They also deny that "by virtue of a positive influence of God upon him for good the unregenerate is able to do good works in the sphere of things natural and civil."[100]

The denominational headquarters are at 16515 South Park Avenue, South

Holland, Illinois 60473. There are 21 churches and missions with 3,871 members. They carry on foreign and domestic missions.[101]

Netherlands Reformed Congregations

Dutch immigrants who in 1841 had seceded in their homeland from the established Reformed Church of the Netherlands laid the foundation for the Netherlands Reformed Congregations when they established two churches in South Holland, Illinois in 1865. The present organization dates from 1907. The Netherlands Reformed Congregations adhere firmly to the Bible as the inspired and inerrant Word of God and make Christ's requirement of rebirth a cornerstone of their teaching. Their doctrinal standards comprise the Confession of Faith of the Reformed Church Revised in the National Synod of Dort (commonly called the Belgic Confession of Faith), the Heidelberg Catechism, and the Canons of the Synod of Dort.[102] Twenty-three churches in the United States and Canada have a total baptized membership of 7,447. The Synod of the Netherlands Reformed Congregations meets every two years. There are no central headquarters.

Free Reformed Churches of North America

In 1944 the Free Reformed Church (founded in 1926 and since 1949 known as the Old Christian Reformed Church of Grand Rapids, Michigan) united with the Rehoboth Reformed Church (founded in 1942) of the same city. In 1947 it entered into a corresponding relationship with the Christian Reformed Churches in the Netherlands, a group of congregations that did not enter the 1892 union of the *Afscheiding* and the *Doleantie* into the Gereformeerde Kerken van Nederland, with whom the Christian Reformed Church on the American continent is in communion. In 1950 the Free and Old Christian Reformed Churches in Canada (where the first congregation had come into being in 1949) united with the two congregations in the United States—the other was the congregation in Clifton, New Jersey, founded in 1921—in a continentwide fellowship, now known as Free Reformed Churches of North America.

The Free Reformed Churches of North America accept the Bible as the Word of God, with the Apostolic, Nicene, and Athanasian creeds, the Belgic Confession, the Heidelberg Catechism, and the Canons of the Synod of Dort (1618–1619) as subordinate standards.[103]

One of the main differences between the Free Reformed Churches of North America and the Christian Reformed Church on the North American continent is in the doctrine of "presumptive regeneration," as the former calls the position taken by the Christian Reformed Church in 1908. This is the doctrine that "the seed of the covenant [that is, the children of believers] by virtue of the promise of God is to be regarded as regenerated and as sanctified in Christ, until the contrary is shown in their confession and conduct when they are reaching years of discretion; but that it is less correct to say that baptism is administered to children of believers on the ground of supposed regeneration, since the ground of baptism is the command and promise of God."[104] In contrast to this view the Free Reformed Churches of North America teach that all human beings, including those who by birth belong to the covenant of grace, are by nature dead in trespasses and sins. While the promise of the covenant of grace is for the children of believers, this does not mean that for that reason they are to be thought of as being born again.

The Free Reformed Churches of North America concede that the Christian Reformed Church does not deny this and emphasizes the necessity of the new birth. But the former see a very great danger in considering all young children of believers as already born again; the danger is that the necessity of rebirth and of repentance even within the circle of God's covenant will be less keenly felt and less forcefully preached, that the call to conversion will be absent or less frequently heard, and that people will be lost while they imagine that they are enjoying God's favor. The Free Reformed Churches of North America see their conception of the covenant as more realistic, that of the Christian Reformed Church as more idealisitc.

The Synod of the Free Reformed Churches of North America meets annually. There are 2 congregations in the United States (Michigan and New Jersey) with 575 members. There are 10 congregations in Canada (8 in Ontario and 2 in British Columbia) with a total membership of 2,524. The denomination's central address is 950 Ball Avenue, Northeast, Grand Rapids, Michigan 49503. It has a missionary and another worker in South Africa.[105]

Reformed Church in the United States

The Eureka Classis of the Synod of the Northwest of the Reformed Church in the United States was founded in 1911. When the Reformed Church in the United States united with the Evangelical Synod of North America in 1934, the Eureka Classis refused to join the union. Together with a number of individual congregations it determined to perpetuate the name, witness, ministry, and constitution of the Reformed Church in the United States.

The church body accepts the Heidelberg Catechism. Specifically, its strongly conservative theology affirms the absolute sovereignty of the Triune God; the unique inspiration and infallible communication of the Bible as originally written, "the special self-revelation of God whereby His will for man respecting salvation is exclusively made known"; the universe as "not the product of chance or an alleged evolution but the special creation of Almighty God"; the sinful condition of mankind ("all human beings are totally corrupted spiritually"); God's election of a definite number of human beings whom the perfect substitutionary sacrifice of Christ on the cross redeemed; the application of salvation to the elect by the Holy Spirit's "calling" and the imputation of Christ's righteousness by grace through faith alone; the irresistible and progressive (but in this life always incomplete) sanctification of the believer by the Holy Spirit; the "Covenant" nature of salvation; the invisible church as consisting of all of the elect of God; a divinely ordained government for the earthly form of the church consisting of a governing council of elders and deacons, with congregations bound together in classes (or presbyteries) and these again into synods; the perpetuation of the covenant primarily through the children of believers; the sacraments of baptism (given as a sign of church-membership also to infant children of believers) and the Lord's Supper, "which signifies conscious fellowship with the Christ of the covenant and seals the benefits of His death to the participants"; the entrance of the Christian soul into heaven at death; and the physical resurrection and judgment of all men at Christ's return, but no future millennial kingdom on earth ruled over by Christ and a revived Jewish nation.[106]

The Reformed Church in the United States maintains close relations with the Orthodox Presbyterian Church and the Christian Reformed Church. There are no central headquarters. *The Reformed Herald*, the church body's periodical, is published from Sutton, Nebraska 68979. There are 24 churches in the midwestern states and in California, with a total inclusive membership of 3,940.

Hungarian Reformed Church in America

Until after the mid-nineteenth century, Hungarian immigration to the United States was sporadic and limited, and even after it reached high tide as many as 70 percent of the immigrants from Hungary ultimately returned to their native land prior to World War I. The first organized Hungarian Reformed congregations came into being under the aegis of the (German) Reformed Church in the United States in 1890 at Pittsburgh and Cleveland. This set a pattern for a decade. Around the turn of the century other Hungarian immigrant congregations began to affiliate with the Presbyterian Church in the USA.

During the first years of the twentieth century a number of Hungarian congregations withdrew from the Reformed Church in the United States. Together with some newly formed churches they organized themselves into a classis and placed themselves under the supervision of the Reformed Church in Hungary in 1904. With the heavy immigration from Hungary prior to World War I this group grew rapidly; by 1910 it had to divide into two classes. Unable to maintain contact with the motherland when the war came, the American classes tried to negotiate an affiliation with some American denomination, but they were not successful. After the war the Hungarian mother church commended them to the Presbyterian Church in the USA, but the latter body was unwilling to let them continue as ethnic classes. Finally they reached a satisfactory agreement with the Reformed Church in the

United States, which was willing to leave them intact. In 1921, under the Tiffin (Ohio) Agreement, they and the churches that had not withdrawn in 1904 were combined in four classes. The merger of the Reformed Church in the United States with the Evangelical Synod in 1934 posed no insuperable problems, and the Hungarian classes eventually formed the Magyar Synod in the new denomination (called the Calvin Synod since 1964). The Magyar Synod opposed the entrance of the Evangelical and Reformed Church into the United Church of Christ, because the latter union recognized only geographical conferences and would have meant the end of the Magyar (Calvin) Synod.

Some of the Hungarian congregations in the Reformed Church in the United States were dissatisfied with the Tiffin Agreement and withdrew in 1921. Until 1924 they continued in complete independence, but in that year seven of them formed a new denomination at Duquesne, Pennsylvania—the Free[107] Magyar Reformed Church in America. By 1928 they had grown enough to organize two classes within an overarching diocese.[108] In 1958 they adopted the name Hungarian Reformed Church in America and gave the title of bishop to their administrative head, who is elected for three years and may serve only two successive terms.[109] While emphasizing its distinctive European heritage, this church body has assimilated itself to the American scene.

The Hungarian Reformed Church in America subscribes to the Heidelberg Catechism and the Second Helvetic Confession. In its Magyar services it uses the worship manual of the Reformed Church of Hungary; pending publication of an English Book of Common Worship, it employs verbatim translations of the Magyar texts in its English services. It has 28 congregations with an inclusive membership of 11,679. There are no central headquarters. *Magyar Egyhás(Magyar Church)*, the church body's monthly, is edited from 1657 Centerview Drive, Akron, Ohio 44321.

Ukrainian Evangelical Reformed Church in Exile

During the first two decades of the twentieth century many of the Ukrainian immigrants to North America joined congregations of the Presbyterian, Reformed, Methodist, and related traditions in the United States and Canada without rejecting their Ukrainian cultural background and loyalties. In 1922 some of these Ukrainians united to organize the Ukrainian Evangelical Alliance of North America, which describes itself as "a representative, coordinating and missionary center." It unites Ukrainians chiefly of Reformed background for the more effective evangelization of Ukrainians in Western Europe, the Commonwealth, and the United States by means of preaching and the publication and distribution of Bibles and Christian literature. It also sends relief to the poor, the old, and the sick among Ukrainian refugees, especially in Western Europe. Its total present membership is about 2,000.[110]

In 1925 the Ukrainian Evangelical Alliance began a Reformed mission in the western Ukraine with the assistance of the United Church of Canada and of various Reformed and Presbyterian church bodies in North America and Europe. The mission became the Ukrainian Evangelical-Reformed Church. By 1939 it had grown to 30 congregations with over 5,000 members, but in the antireligious reaction that followed World War II the government of the Union of Soviet Socialist Republics attempted to liquidate the church body. The late Superintendent Wasyl Kusiw returned to North America in 1939 and in 1958 the Consistory of the Ukrainian Evangelical-Reformed Church in Exile was formally organized. It accepts the Heidelberg Catechism and the Second Helvetic Confession as its doctrinal standard. The secretary of the consistory and acting superintendent of the Ukrainian Evangelical-Reformed Church in Exile resides at 22146 Kelly Road, East Detroit, Michigan 48021. Several years ago there were two congregations, one in Detroit, the other in Toronto, Ontario, with a total membership of about 100. There has been no response to recent communications to the church body. Outside of these two communities, members of the Ukrainian Evangelical-Reformed Church in Exile are encouraged to seek "dual membership" in existing local Presbyterian or Reformed churches.

Waldensian Church

The beginnings of the Waldensian Church go back to the 1170s, when Peter Waldo (or Valdes) (1140?–1218?), a wealthy merchant converted to the ideal of apostolic poverty, began to preach publicly in Lyons, France. He had the Bible translated into the vernacular and organized his followers into a paramonastic fraternity, the Pauperes Christi (Christ's Poor People). Less because of their faith, which seems at the time to have been orthodox enough, than because of their violation of the prohibition of preaching without episcopal permission, Lucius III excommunicated them in 1184. The character of the movement varied more or less from country to country and from period to period as a result of environmental influences. For a long period the Waldensians, much like the Cathari, differentiated the "perfected" Waldensians, who had professed the vows of poverty, obedience, and celibacy, from the "believers" or "friends," who continued to participate in the worship and sacraments of the medieval church. Finally these also received the name "Waldensians."

In the fourteenth century the Waldensians based their particular form of Christianity on the Sermon on the Mount. They rejected oaths, every kind of bloodshed, purgatory, indulgences, intercessions for the departed, and the veneration of the Mother of God and of the saints. They regarded all lying as a mortal sin, observed the canonical hours, and had a special devotion to the "Our Father." Their highest authority was the Bible; they had the whole New Testament and some of the books of the Old Testament (including the so-called Apocrypha) in the vernacular. Of the seven sacraments they attached special importance to the sacrament of repentance; the formula of absolution began "May God absolve you." They normally celebrated the Eucharist on Maundy Thursday; at other times they gave the sick bread and wine that had been blessed in place of the sacrament.

Around 1400 the legend developed that traces the Waldensians back directly to the apostolic church. Although they used the title of bishop, they never possessed the apostolic succession. In the fifteenth century the Waldensians and the Hussites strongly influenced one another.

In spite of persistent and sometimes bloody persecution, the Waldensians survived into the sixteenth century in many parts of Europe. Those in Bohemia joined the Unity of the Brethren. Those in the French Dauphiné and in Piedmont accepted the Swiss Reformation in 1532 at the General Synod of Chanforan.[111]

In the process of becoming a Reformed denomination, the Waldensians gave up many of their formerly distictive features, such as private confession and their commitment to the absolute requirements of the Sermon on the Mount. They accepted predestination and election, affirmed only two sacraments, adopted the Reformed position on the Holy Communion, recognized the civil authorities, and replaced their intinerating clergy with settled pastors. The resistance of some of the more conservative Waldensians to these changes was ultimately fruitless. In the seventeenth century the Waldensian Church promulgated a revised version of the Gallican Confession.[112]

With the restoration of Piedmont to Italy, the Counter-Reformation was able to destroy the congregations in the plains and seriously to threaten the mountain villages. In France proper, after a period of limited toleration and official recognition, the second half of the seventeenth century saw a new wave of persecution that drove the Waldensians out of that country. The eighteenth century was one of toleration in Piedmont. A spiritual revival began in the nineteenth century. In the late 1850s many Waldensians emigrated to South America.

The constitution of the Waldensian Church recognizes as its only head Jesus Christ, the Son of God and the Savior of men. It affirms the doctrine contained in the Bible and formulated in its confession of faith,[113] and it professes itself in brotherly communion with all the evangelical, that is, Reformed, churches of the world.[114] In 1960 there were over 46,000 Waldensians (over 17,000 of them in Uruguay and Argentina, 400 in Switzerland, and almost all the rest in Italy), of whom nearly 29,000 were actually members of the Waldensian Church.[115] The international synod meets annually at Torre Pellice, Italy.

First Waldensian Church (Prima Chiesa Valdese) in New York is the only Waldensian church in North America. Although the Beckwith Memorial Italian Presbyterian Church in Montreal, Quebec, in the past has had Waldensian ministers from Italy it has been a Presbyterian Church since it was first founded in 1874. Presbyterian and Reformed churches have absorbed most of the Waldensian immigrants to North America as well as the other organized Waldensian churches that once existed, like those in Chicago, in Valdese,

North Carolina, and in Monett, Missouri.[116] The New York church, at 127 East 82nd Street, was founded in 1912. It has approximately 150 members.

Moravian Church in America (Unitas Fratrum)

John Huss (1369?–1415), Czech patriot and dean of the theological faculty of the University of Prague, was one of the most faithful and persuasive exponents of the teaching of the English Lollard leader John Wyclif (1320?–1384), with whose views Huss fused Bohemian reforming sentiments. The year after Huss became *rector magnificus* of the university, the anti-Wyclifite archbishop of Prague excommunicated Huss and secured his dismissal from his influential position as preacher in Bethlehem Chapel, in spite of the nearly unanimous support of the king, the nobility, and the people that Huss enjoyed. His contact with Waldensian refugees at this juncture gave him renewed courage to defend his convictions. Certain of the rightness of his position, he responded to the summons of the Council of Constance in October 1414. In spite of the safe-conduct that had accmpanied the summons, he was imprisoned soon after his arrival in Constance, tried for heresy, convicted,[117] and finally burned on his birthday, July 6, 1415. He died standing erect, praying for his persecutors, and calling on Christ and the Mother of God.

His followers in Bohemia split into the conservative Utraquists[118] or Calixtines[119] and the radical Old Testament-oriented communistic Taborites. The latter met a decisive defeat in 1434. By confirming the Compact of Prague, the Council of Basel recognized the Calixtines as sons of the church and conceded to them the use of the chalice at the distribution of the sacrament of the altar. The efforts of church leaders during the next two decades to abrogate the concessions that the compact had made disillusioned some of the Utraquists. One group, led by Brother Gregory, the nephew of the unconsecrated Prague archbishop, John Rokycana, and by Peter Chelčický (1390?–1460), withdrew and settled at Kunwald, an estate near Lititz that belonged to George Podiebrad (d. 1471), soon to be elected king of Bohemia.[120] First called Brethren of the Law of Christ, they shortened their name to Brethren and after a few years took the formal name of Jednota Bratrská, the "Unity of the Brethren." They rapidly attracted likeminded supporters from all over Bohemia. In 1467 they determined to establish their own ministry. A visiting Waldensian clergyman ordained the first three priests, who had been chosen by lot. Second thoughts led the Brethren to decide that they wanted bishops. To secure episcopal succession they sent the parish priest of Senftenberg, Michael, to receive consecration from the elder (or bishop) of the Waldensians, who believed—incorrectly, we now know—that their succession had come down from the primitive church independently of the See of Rome.[121] Since then only a senior or bishop has had the authority to ordain in the Unity.[122]

A profound ethical concern characterized the primitive Unity and found expression in a vigorous community discipline.[123] They built their union on four principles: (1) the Bible as the sole source of teaching; (2) public worship on the biblical-apostolic pattern; (3) reception of the Lord's Supper in faith, without trying to provide an authoritative human explanation of the biblical record on this point; (4) a holy life as the indispensable proof of saving faith. They subscribed to the three Catholic creeds, favored adult baptism but practiced infant baptism at least to some extent, generally rebaptized converts, and taught seven sacraments but regarded them as ancillary, whereas faith, hope, and love were to them essential. Until the Amosite schism in the 1490s, the six "least requirements" of the Sermon on the Mount —to refrain from anger, lustful desire, divorce, swearing oaths, and resisting evil and to do good to one's enemies—were normative. The renunciation of their strict pacifism came gradually in the late fifteenth century, along with the introduction of liturgical form into their starkly simple worship. The clergy were celibate and unsalaried until the middle of the sixteenth century. In 1501 they published their first hymnal.

From 1522 on they established friendly contact with the Wittenberg, South German, and Swiss reformers.[124] In the middle of the sixteenth century, persecution drove many Brethren into the Lutheran duchy of East Prussia; within a generation they had been absorbed into the Lutheran Church, or they had returned home, or they had settled in Poland. In Bohemia many of the Utraquists became Lutherans; in 1609 the surviving Utraquists merged with the Lutherans and the Unity to form the Church of the Bohemian Confession, which briefly enjoyed religious toleration on the basis of the Letter of Majesty of Emperor Rudolph II, until the Battle of the White Mountain in 1620; by 1628 the Counter-Reformation had destroyed the church as an organized religious community. In Poland and in Hungary the Unity survived for another generation. In 1570 Moravian immigrants to Poland had established intercommunion with the Lutherans and the Reformed communities through the Consensus of Sendomir. In 1628 the last remnants of the organized Brethren church in Bohemia, the educator-bishop John Amos Comenius (1592–1670) among them, fled to Poland and established themselves at Lissa. Here the Reformed community gradually assimilated them, although some of the Reformed congregations regarded themselves as continuations of the old Unity and some of the clergymen were chosen as seniors of the Unity.

Meanwhile the faith of the Unity had lived on underground in Moravia and Bohemia. Some of these clandestine Brethren became known during the 1710s to Christian David (1691–1751), a German Roman Catholic convert to the Lutheran Church whom the Halle type of Pietism had profoundly influenced. About this time Nicholas Louis Count von Zinzendorf und Pottendorf (1700–1760), a Saxon nobleman whose socially conscious family had frustrated his desire to become a clergyman and on whom Pietism had taken a strong hold, established himself and his newlywed bride at the Berthelsdorf in Lusatia. John Andrew Rothe (1688–1758), who had received David into the Lutheran Church and whom Count Nicholas had appointed pastor of the

Berthelsdorf parish church, put David and the count in contact with one another. The count promised to help some of David's Moravian friends, and David promptly arranged for them to emigrate to the count's Lusatian estate in 1722. Count Nicholas became more and more interested in and increasingly affected by the religion of the Moravian immigrants who moved in growing numbers into his domain. By 1727 there were enough of them that the formal revival of the Unity was feasible. In that year Count Nicholas, who had resigned his place at the Dresden court to devote himself to the new project, drafted for his tenants at Herrnhut, as they called their settlement, a legal contract that set forth the terms of their relationship with him and the *Brotherly Agreement of the Brethren from Bohemia and Moravia and Others, Binding Them to Walk According to the Apostolic Rule.* The exigencies of the situation required the revival of the Unity within the framework of the established Lutheran Church of Saxony, a "little church within the church" (*ecclesiola in ecclesia*). At Berlin in 1735 the aged Daniel Ernest Jablonski (1660–1741), a court preacher of the Reformed Church and a titular "elder, senior and episcopus of the Bohemian-Moravian Brethren in Great Poland," privately ordained David Nitschmann (1696–1772), to be "a senior of the aforementioned congregations" and endowed him with authority "to take upon himself all those functions which belong to a senior and antistes [president] of the church." Two years later Jablonski and Nitchmann ordained Count Nicholas, who had become a Lutheran clergyman in 1734, to the same office. In 1740 the Renewed Moravian Church reinstituted the threefold ministry of deacons, presbyters, and bishops.

During the decade following the pentecostal experience of August 1727 the Moravian community developed most of its characteristic features. These included the division of the community into small cell groups that foreshadowed the later division into "choirs," the establishment of separate houses for the single men and the single women, marriage as and when the church directed, the lovefeast (originally quite informal), the weekly "hour of song," the cup of covenant, the sunrise Easter service, biblical texts chosen by lot as daily watchwords, the hourly intercessions (destined to be carried on without interruption for a century), and the beginning of the evangelistic mission (Diaspora) that ultimately spread throughout Germany and into Switzerland, France, Scandinavia, Poland, the Baltic countries, Greenland, Africa, India, the Holy Land, the Caribbean, Holland, England, Ireland, Russia, and North and South America. At its peak the Diaspora outside of continental Europe outnumbered the church on the Continent 8 to 1.

The Renewed Moravian Church established itself permanently in North America in 1740, with the settlement of Nazareth, Pennsylvania, followed by the settlement of Bethlehem, for the formal organization of which in 1742 Count Nicholas was himself present. From January to June of 1742 its synods were deliberately interdenominational, but from then on they became more and more exclusively Moravian until by 1747 they no longer pretended to be union conferences. These became the core of the present Northern Province. Efforts to establish Moravian congregations in the southern colonies in the 1750s proved unsuccessful; the first permanent settlement, Salem, the center of the present Southern Province, goes back to 1766. The two provinces became autonomous in 1857. In the late 1890s the Northern Province penetrated Alberta.

Today the Moravian Church is not markedly different from other acculturated church bodies in terms of denominational consciousness. Its history has conditioned the Moravian Church to be strongly ecumenical, although it has not traditionally been greatly interested in organic church union. In the same way, the Moravian Church regards doctrine as important but it has never stressed creedal definitions. It has found very congenial the concern of the Reformed tradition with the creation of a Christian community and its correlative emphasis on church discipline, just as it has shared the concern of Pietism for experiental "heart religion" rather than for doctrinal correctness. In North America the general orientation of the Moravian Church has been toward the Presbyterian, Methodist, and United Church of Christ communities.

The current Book of Order commits the Moravian Church to the doctrines of the Apostles' Creed and to the recognition that "in the fundamental confession of the Reformed churches the chief articles of the Christian faith are clearly and simply set forth," although it further specifies that "the liberty of conscience of our members is in no wise bound thereby, for we acknowledge no other canon or rule of doctrine than the Holy Scripture alone."[125] The General Synod of 1957 adopted a doctrinal statement entitled "The Ground of the Unity." It specifically recognizes the Apostles' Creed, the Athanasian Creed, the Nicene Creed, the Confession of the Unity of the Bohemian Brethren of 1662, the twenty-one articles of the Unaltered Augsburg Confession, the Small Catechism of Martin Luther, the Synod of Berne of 1532, the Thirty-Nine Articles of the Church of England, and the Theological Declaration of Barmen of 1934 as having "gained special importance" in the various provinces of the renewed Unitas Fratrum.

In summarizing the essentials of Christian teaching, the Book of Order stresses as the chief doctrine of the Christian faith the firm conviction that Jesus Christ "is the expiation for our sins, and not for ours only but also for the sins of the whole world," and it makes the person of Christ and his redeeming love the center of its preaching. In the Bible, which Moravians regard as the source of all Christian doctrine and the only rule of faith and life, the Book of Order sees eight subjects that are essential to a human being's knowledge of salvation: (1) the universal depravity of human nature, so that human beings have no power to save themselves; (2) the love of God the Father to fallen humanity and His choice of us in Christ before the foundation of the world; (3) the real Godhead and the real humanity of Christ; (4) our reconciliation with God, our justification before him through the sacrifice of Christ, who was put to death for our trespasses and raised for our justification, and forgiveness of sin and peace with God exclusively through faith in Christ; (5) the Holy Spirit and the workings of his grace, by which we know Christ and the truth and our spirits have his witness that we are God's children; (6) good works as the fruit of the Holy Spirit, in which faith manifests itself as a living, acting power that impels us in willing love and gratitude to follow God's commands; (7) the fellowship of believers with one another that makes them all one in Christ Jesus; and (8) the second coming of Christ in glory and the resurrection of the dead to eternal life or to judgment.[126]

The catechism defines baptism as a sign and pledge of grace, a covenant between the Lord and the believer, in which the use of water in the name of the Trinity is the sign of the cleansing of the soul from sin through the blood of Christ. In infant baptism parents dedicate their child to God and place it within the Covenant of Grace under the church's care. In the case of adults, they profess their faith and the church receives them into communicant membership. The Lord's Supper, in which the elements signify Christ's body and blood, the perfect sacrifice for sins, is a pledge of the benefits of Chist's atonement, a memorial of the death of Christ, the renewal of the communicant's public profession of faith, and a spiritual communion of the believer with Christ and fellow Christians.[127]

Liturgical form and biblical simplicity characterize the worship of the Moravian Church.[128] It is gradually abandoning its assumption that transformed Christians will transform society and is overcoming its reluctance to participate in direct social action. The difference between the two North American provinces are gradually being erased. In the past the Southern Province, located in territory dominated by Methodists and Baptists, made more extensive use of revivalism to recruit new members and reported more adult baptisms than did the Northern Province, which relied more on catechetical instruction and confirmation.

The Moravian Church describes its government as "conferential." The bishops have no administrative power or responsibility. In the Northern Province, which extends from coast to coast and into Alberta,[129] there are three districts; the Southern Province, restricted to North Carolina and Florida, has no subdivisions. The inclusive membership of the 149 churches is 54,892. It carries on its foreign mission work in concert with the other provinces of the worldwide Unity. The headquarters of the two provinces are respectively at 69 West Church Street, Bethlehem, Pennsylvania 18018, and 459 South Church Street, Winston-Salem, North Carolina 27108.

Unity of the Brethren

The roots of the Unity of the Brethren go back to the founding of the original Unitas Fratrum (Jednota Bratrská) in 1457. While the Moravian Church traces its history chiefly by way of Germany, the Unity of the Brethren came to the New World directly from its Bohemian homeland. After the Battle of the White Mountain in 1620, the Counter-Reformation forced the Unitas to go underground in Bohemia. The Austro-Hungarian emperor, Joseph II, proclaimed the Edict of Tolerance in 1781 as part of his program for reducing the power of the Roman Catholic Church in his domains. This directive granted a measure of religious liberty to the emperor's Lutheran and Reformed subjects, but not to the Unitas. To obtain a degree of relief, the Brethren temporarily united with the tolerated churches. At the same time they retained the distinctive feature of the ancient Unitas. After 1850 descendants of the Unity in Bohemia and Moravia began to migrate to the Fayetteville area of Texas. Later they spread to other parts. In 1864 the Reverend Joseph Opocensky (1814–1870) organized the first congregation at Wesley, Texas. After the failure of an effort at union in 1893, this church and several others united in 1903 as the Evangelical Union of the Bohemian and Moravian Brethren in North America. In 1915 the Independent Unity of the Bohemian and Moravian Brethren came into being. The two bodies united in 1919 to form the Evangelical Unity of the Czech-Moravian Brethren in North America; in 1959 it adopted the present name.

The Unity of the Brethren emphasizes that the Bible is the inspired word of God and the only infallible rule of learning, of faith, and of life. It stresses salvation through faith in Jesus Christ as personal Savior, the priesthood of all believers, freedom of conscience, and the glorious return of Christ. It regards the church as a fellowship of those who share a saving faith in Christ. A Christian life, it holds, is the best evidence of a reborn heart and doctrinal perfection. The use of water in baptism is a "sign of the cleansing of the soul from sin through the blood of Christ." In the Lord's Supper the bread (leavened or unleavened, or both) and the wine (fermented or unfermented, and mixed with water) are visible signs "signifying Christ's body and His blood, the perfect sacrifice for our sins."[130] The Unity of the Brethren practices infant baptism and open Communion. Children must normally be at least fourteen years of age to receive confirmation. The Unity subscribes to the Apostles' Creed[131] and sets forth its beliefs in detail in its confession[132] and its catechism.[133] Its polity is congregational, its worship nonliturgical. Several years ago its 32 predominantly rural churches in Texas had an overall membership of 6,200. There has been no response to recent efforts to contact the church body. Several conferences were held in 1964 and 1965 with representatives of the two provinces of the Moravian Church in America looking toward closer relations, but the meetings have been discontinued. There are no central headquarters.

NOTES

1. Sydney E. Ahlstrom, *A Religious History of the American People* (New Haven: Yale University Press, 1972), p. 271.

2. Lefferts A. Loetscher, *The Broadening Church; a Study of Theological Issues in the Presbyterian Church since 1869* (Philadelphia: University of Pennsylvania Press, 1954), p. 2; Ahlstrom, p. 269.
3. Ahlstrom, pp. 273-274.
4. Edwin Scott Gaustad, *Historical Atlas of Religion in America* (rev. edn.; New York: Harper & Row, 1976), p. 19; Ahlstrom, pp. 276-278.
5. Ahlstrom, pp. 316, 431.
6. Gaius Jackson Slosser, ed., *They Seek a Country; the American Presbyterians, Some Aspects* (New York: The Macmillan Company, 1955), pp. 83, 150-164. See also "Presbyterians and the American Revolution: A Documentary Account," *Journal of Presbyterian History* LII (1974): 299-488 [with bibliography].
7. Maurice W. Armstrong, Lefferts A. Loetscher, and Charles A. Anderson, *The Presbyterian Enterprise; Sources of American Presbyterian History* (Philadelphia: Westminster Press, 1956), p. 95.
8. Ahlstrom, pp. 431, 456-458, 462; Winthrop S. Hudson, *Religion in America; an Historical Account of the Development of American Religious Life* (2nd edn.; New York: Charles Scribner's Sons, 1973), p. 119.
9. Slosser, ed., pp. 177-179.
10. Ahlstrom, p. 444.
11. Ibid., p. 466.
12. Ibid., pp. 464-465.
13. Ibid., pp. 467-468; Gaustad, p. 91.
14. Ahlstrom, pp. 462-463. Ahlstrom adds, "Especially as developed and defended by Charles Hodge, the Princeton Theology became the criterion of Reformed orthodoxy in America. . . . Yet despite its negative features, the Princeton Theology had a great positive force, affording theological substance wherever revivalism threatened to vaunt experience only, fostering education and the learned tradition, and striving desperately to provide a Christian message that was not simply an amalgam of folk religion and Americanism. In the West, however, it would ultimately precipitate an immense crisis" (p. 463).
15. Slosser, ed., p. 186.
16. John L. Thomas, S.J., *Religion and the American People* (Westminster, Md.: Newman Press, 1963), p. 121.
17. Edwin S. Gaustad, "America's Institutions of Faith," in *The Religious Situation: 1968*, ed. Donald R. Cutler (Boston: Beacon Press, 1968), pp. 851-852.
18. Gaustad, *Atlas*, p. 92.
19. Armstrong et al., p. 257.
20. Ibid., pp. 268-269; Loetscher, p. 88.
21. Ahlstrom, p. 814.
22. Ibid., Loetscher, p. 98.
23. Ahlstrom, p. 815.
24. Loetscher, pp. 94-95.
25. Ibid., p. 135.
26. Ibid., p. 106.
27. Armstrong et al., pp. 301-306.
28. Slosser, ed., pp. 91-98.
29. Letter of the Reverend Joseph S. DeRogatis, D.D., Pastor, Our Saviour Presbyterian Church, 194 St. Mary's Avenue, Rosebank, Staten Island, New York.
30. Letter of Paul H. Felker, Minister, Waldensian Presbyterian Church, P.O. Box 216, Valdese, North Carolina.
31. *Our First 100 Years Serving Our Lord* [Ely, Iowa: First Presbyterian Church, 1958; 22-page pamphlet].
32. *COCU, the Reports of Four Meetings* (Cincinnati: Forward Movement Publication, [1966], pp. 7-19.
33. Robert C. White, Jr. and C. Howard Hopkins, *The Social Gospel; Religion and Reform in Changing America* (Philadelphia: Temple University Press, 1976), p. 190.
34. H. Shelton Smith, Robert T. Handy, and Lefferts A. Loetscher, *American Christianity, An Historical Interpretation with Representative Documents*, Vol. II, 1820–1960 (New York: Charles Scribner's Sons, 1963), pp. 549-550.
35. *New York Times*, June 24, 1977; *Christian Century*, August 3–10, 1977, p. 695.
36. *The Constitution of the United Presbyterian Church in the USA, Part I, The Book of Confessions* (2nd edn.; Published by the Office of the General Assembly of the United Presbyterian Church in the USA, 1970), pp. vi-vii.
37. Edward A. Dowey, Jr., *A Commentary on the Confession of 1967 and an Introduction to "The Book of Confessions"* (Philadelphia: Westminster Press, 1968), p. 245.

38. *The Constitution of the United Presbyterian Church in the USA*, p. vi; Dowey, p. 11.
39. Albert P. Stauderman, "New Words for Old Beliefs," *The Lutheran*, July 5, 1967, p. 15. For the amendment to the Confession in 1970, see *The Constitution of the United Presbyterian Church in the USA*, para. 9.45.
40. Ibid., para. 9.01-9.56.
41. Letter of Eugene Carson Blake in *Christian Century*, June 1, 1977, p. 542.
42. Letter and enclosure [report prepared for 1977 General Assembly] of Frank H. Heinze, Managing Director, Communications Division, United Presbyterian Church in the USA, 475 Riverside Drive, New York, New York 10027.
43. *Christianity Today*, June 18, 1971, p. 897.
44. Hudson, pp. 429-430.
45. *Christian Century*, June 9–16, 1976, p. 556; August 3–10, 1977, p. 695.
46. Gaustad, *Atlas*, pp. 165, 170.
47. Ernest Trice Thompson, *Presbyterians in the South* (3 vols.; Richmond: John Knox Press, 1963–1973), II: 29-30.
48. Ibid., II: 264.
49. Ibid., III: 215-217, 220-221.
50. Ibid., III: 326, 338, 492; see also pp. 303-338.
51. Ibid., III: 338.
52. Ibid., III: 486.
53. *The Confession of Faith, The Presbyterian Church in the United States* (Richmond: Printed by the Board of Christian Education, 1965), pp. 329-336.
54. *Christian Century*, February 16, 1977, pp. 142-145; July 20–27, 1977, pp. 646-647.
55. Thompson, III: 504-506, 509, 511.
56. Ahlstrom, pp. 671-672.
57. Thompson, III: 531, 539, 542, 547, 549.
58. Ibid., II: 414-417; III: 477, 479.
59. Ibid., III: 348, 353, 483.
60. Ibid., III: 370.
61. Ibid., III: 290-292, 297, 301.
62. *Christianity Today*, November 20, 1970.
63. *Philadelphia Informer, 189th General Assembly, United Presbyterian Church in the U.S.A.*, Issue No. 3, June 29, 1977; *The General Assembly Daily News of the United Presbyterian Church in the U.S.A.*, June 1977, p. 8.
64. *Christian Century*, July 20–27, 1977, pp. 646-647.
65. *Christianity Today*, July 2, 1971.
66. Gaustad, *Atlas*, p. 92; Thompson, III: 410, 423.
67. Letter of the Reverend Paul H. Felker, Minister, Waldensian Presbyterian Church, P.O. Box 216, Valdese, North Carolina 28690.
68. *Christian Century*, July 7–14, 1976, p. 624.
69. Thompson, III: 503, 580.
70. *St. Louis Post Dispatch*, April 3, 1970.
71. *Christian Century*, January 21, 1976, p. 39.
72. *St. Louis Post Dispatch*, April 10, 1970.
73. Ibid., January 16, 1970, November 6, 1970; *Christianity Today*, September 24, 1971, pp. 42-43. The Covenant Fellowship was not represented at the formative meeting of the new church late in 1973.
74. *Christianity Today*, July 2, 1971, p. 31.
75. Ibid., September 24, 1971, pp. 42-43.
76. *St. Louis Post Dispatch*, August 10, 1973; *Washington Post*, August 10, 1973; *Christianity Today*, September 11, 1973.
77. *Christian Century*, August 6–13, 1975, p. 704.
78. Ibid., November 5, 1975, p. 992.
79. *Christianity Today*, July 8, 1977, p. 37; *St. Louis Post Dispatch*, December 7, 1973.
80. Letter from the Reverend Thomas H. Campbell, D.D., Dean, Memphis Theological Seminary of the Cumberland Presbyterian Church, Memphis, Tennessee.
81. *The Cumberland Flag* XXXVI, no. 9 (September 15, 1966): 8.
82. Communication from Roy L. Tinsley, former stated clerk.
83. *The Constitution of the Bible Presbyterian Church: The Confession of Faith, the Larger and Shorter Catechisms, the Form of Government, The Book of Discipline* (Collingswood, N.J.: Independent Board for Presbyterian Home Missions, 1959), pp. 40-41, 65-68.
84. Allan A. MacRae, *The Story of the Bible Presbyterian Church (Collings-*

wood Synod) (Collingswood, N.J.: Bible Presbyterian Church, n.d.) (14-page pamphlet), p. 11.

85. Letter from the Reverend A. Franklin Faucette, stated clerk.

86. On Frelinghuizen and his times, see James Tanis, *Dutch Calvinistic Pietism in the Middle Colonies: A Study in the Life and Theology of Theodorus Jacobus Frelinghuisen* (The Hague: Martinus Nijhoff, 1967).

87. *The Covenant of 1954*, a four-page tract, contains the declaration of faith, confession of sin, and covenant obligations adopted by the Synod of 1953 and sworn to and signed at the Covenanter Convention at Grinnell, Iowa in 1954. The text of the Covenant of 1871 is reproduced in *The Constitution of the Reformed Presbyterian Church of North America* (Pittsburgh, Pennsylvania: The Synod of the Reformed Presbyterian Church, 1949), pp. 215-224.

88. E. Gettys and William C. Alexander, *We Believe and Teach: Studies Based on the Standards of the Associate Reformed Presbyterian Church*, 2nd printing (Due West, S.C.: General Synod of the Associate Reformed Presbyterian Church, 1962) (42-page brochure), is a study course for communicants' classes. Although the General Synod ordered its preparation, it has "no official sanction of the church" (p. 4).

89. Allan L. Farris, "The Fathers of 1925," in *Enkindled by the Word: Essays on Presbyterianism in Canada* (Toronto: Presbyterian Publications, 1966), p. 59.

90. *Declaration of Faith Concerning Church and Nation* (Toronto: The Board of Evangelism and Social Action, 1955) (3-page pamphlet).

91. Playing a significant role in this decision was a widely used study guide on the place of women in the church, Robert P. Carter, ed., *Putting Woman in Her Place* (Toronto: The Committee on the Place of Women in the Church, The Presbyterian Church in Canada, 1955) (16-page brochure).

92. A. J. Gowland, ed., *Manual on Christian Social Action* (Don Mills, Ontario: The Board of Evangelism and Social Action of The Presbyterian Church in Canada, 1966).

93. This writer gratefully acknowledges the patient and generously given assistance of the Reverend E. A. Thomson, D.D.; the Reverend H. F. Davidson, D.D.; the Reverend A. J. Gowland, M.A.; and the Reverend Allan L. Farris, all of the Presbyterian Church in Canada.

94. Letter of the Reverend Professor Homer C. Hoeksema, Grand Rapids, Michigan. For a documentary history of the first years of this body, see Part I of Herman Hoeksema, *The Protestant Reformed Churches in America: Their Origin, Early History, and Doctrine*, 2nd edn. (Grand Rapids, Mich.: First Protestant Reformed Church, 1947). The same author's fifteen-page tract, *Why Protestant Reformed?* 3rd printing (Grand Rapids, Mich.: Sunday School of the First Protestant Reformed Church, 1956), presents a summary account of the denomination's origins. At the time of the reorganization in late 1926, the Reverend Mr. Danhof and some of the members of his congregation, which came to be known as the Protesting First Christian Reformed Church of Kalamazoo, withdrew. They later rejoined the Christian Reformed Church.

95. See, for example, Homer C. Hoeksema, *Our Reformed Heritage* (Grand Rapids, Mich.: Mission Board of the Protestant Reformed Churches in America, 1965) (15-page tract), pp. 8-9, and Robert C. Harbach, *Calvinism the Truth (Arminianism the Lie)*, 2nd printing (Grand Rapids, Mich.: Sunday School Mission Publishing Society, 1959) (20-page pamphlet).

96. Hoeksema, *The Protestant Reformed Churches*, p. 323.

97. Ibid., p. 330.

98. Ibid., pp. 330-331.

99. Ibid., p. 356.

100. Ibid., p. 378.

101. Communication from church-body headquarters.

102. *Doctrinal Standards of the Netherlands Reformed Congregations* (Grand Rapids, Mich.: Netherlands Reformed Congregations, 1963). Appended to the doctrinal standards are the three ecumenical creeds, "A Compendium of the Christian Religion" (an abbreviated catechism), and the

"Church Order, drawn up in the National Synod of Dordrecht (held in 1618 and 1619) and accepted as a concord of ecclesiastic community by the Netherlands Reformed Congregations in America" (ibid., pp. 60-84).

103. The Free Reformed Churches of North America use *The Psalter with Doctrinal Standards, Liturgy, Church Order, and Added Chorale Section,* rev. edn., 3rd printing (Grand Rapids, Mich.: Eerdmans, 1960) in their churches.

104. See John Louis Schaver, *The Polity of the Church,* 6th edn. II (Grand Rapids, Mich.: Kregel's International Publication, 1961): 34-37.

105. Letter from the Reverend Cornelis Pronk, Grand Rapids, Michigan.

106. Norman L. Jones, Jr., *What Is the Reformed Church in the U.S.?* (Green Bay, Wis.: Reliance Printing Co., 1964) (12-page pamphlet), pp. 5-11.

107. *Független* ("Independent") in Hungarian. The adjective was chosen to assert the founders' determination to be independent of the supervision and missionary assistance of American church bodies, particularly of the Reformed Church in the United States (now part of the United Church of Christ) and the Presbyterian Church in the United States of America.

108. Under Archdean (the title then used for the head of the denomination) Charles Vincze (d. 1954) the Free Magyar Reformed Church in America belonged to the International Council of Christian Churches. It withdrew from this body shortly after Vincze's death and subsequently joined both the National Council of the Churches of Christ in the United States of America and the World Council of Churches.

109. Para. 3, Art. I, P. I, *Constitution and By-Laws* (Pittsburgh, Penn.: Expert Printing Company for The Free Magyar Reformed Church in America, 1954), as amended in 1958, p. 5.

110. Letters from the Reverend Wladimir Borowsky, executive secretary of the Consistory of the Ukrainian Evangelical-Reformed Church in Exile and of the Ukrainian Evangelical Alliance of North America.

111. On Waldo and the early history of the movement, see Jean Jalla, *Valdo: His Name and Origins* (*Pierre Valdo* [Paris: Éditions "Je Sers," 1934]) trans. Yda Grill Janavel (N. p.: N. p., 1961) (56-page brochure), and Alfred Janavel, *The Waldenses and the Reformation* (Staten Island, N.Y.: Alfred Janavel, 1960) (79-page brochure). Useful resources are Giovanni Gonnet, *Enchiridion fontium Valdensium du IIIe Concile de Latran au Synode de Chanforan (1179–1532)* (Torre Pellice: Libreria editrice Claudiana, 1958) and Augusto Armand Hugon and Giovanni Gonnet, *Bibliografia valdese* (Torre Pellice: Tipografia Subalpina, 1953).

112. The French text of the 1655 *Briève Confession de Foy des Églises Reformées de Piémont* (Short Confession of Faith of the Reformed Churches of Piedmont), with an English translation, is printed out in Philip Schaff, *The Creeds of Christendom with a History and Critical Notes,* 4th edn., III (Grand Rapids, Mich.: Baker Book House, 1966): 757-770. In essence it is a condensation and slight rearrangement of the Gallican Confession of 1559. The official Italian version was published in 1662. The *Atto dichiarativo* of 1894 supplements the Confession of Faith at a number of points: Even after the fall there is a certain knowledge of God in corrupted human beings and the moral law impressed on them makes them responsible for the evil deeds that they commit; God wills the salvation of all human beings in Christ; in affirming that Jesus Christ is true God and true man, the church does not intend to insist so much on theological definitions of the mystery as on the biblical witness concerning the Godhead and the humanity of the Savior; it does not intend to sanction any doctrine of baptismal regeneration and desires that baptism be regarded, rather, as the external evidence and symbol of an action that is efficacious only through God's grace; nor does it intend to profess faith in any kind of material eating of the body of Christ in the Holy Supper, but only that the soul is nourished spiritually, rejoicing by faith in the benefits obtained by the sacrifice that Christ

offered once for all time. In the twentieth century Swiss dialectic theology has profoundly influenced the actual preaching and teaching of the Waldensian clergy.

113. *Testo Unico della Costituzione, della Statuto dell'Ente Morale "Tavola Valdese" a dei Regolamenti Organici,* rev. edn. (Torre Pellice: Linotipo Arti Grafiche, 1945), p. 5.

114. Article 33 of the *Briève Confession de Foy* asserts its agreement "in the sound doctrine with all the Reformed Churches of France, England, the Low Countries, Germany, Switzerland, Bohemia, Poland, Hungary, and others, as it (*ainsi qu'elle*) is set forth in their Augsburg Confession, according to the explanation of it given by the author." The reference is to the 1540 "Variata" edition of the Augsburg Confession, which John Calvin endorsed with the same qualification.

115. *Relazione al Venerabile Sinodo sedente in Torre Pellice dal 28 agosto al 2 settembre 1960* (Torre Pellice: Tipografia Subalpina, 1960), 11.113-114 and section VIII.

116. See Isabel Whittier, *The [American] Waldensians* (Brunswick, Maine: The Brunswick Publishing Company, 1957) (16-page brochure).

117. Peter d'Ailly (1350–1420) and John le Charlier de Gerson (1363–1429) were the chief prosecutors of Huss.

118. From the Latin *utraque species,* "both appearances," that is, the consecrated wine as well as the consecrated host or bread.

119. From the Latin *calix,* "chalice," because they insisted on Communion with the chalice as well as with the host or bread.

120. The date of this settlement is uncertain, but Moravian tradition has long assigned it to March 1, 1457 (John R. Weinlick, *The Moravian Church Through the Ages* [Bethlehem, Penn.: Comenius Press, 1966], p. 30).

121. The date and place of Michael's consecration and the identity of his consecrator cannot be established.

122. For an Anglo-Catholic evaluation of Moravian orders, see Enrico S. Molnar, "The Problem of Episcopal Succession in the Moravian Church," *Anglican Theological Review* XLV (1963): 270-284.

123. See, for instance, Marianka S. Fousek, "The Perfectionism of the Early Unitas Fratrum," *Church History* XXX (1961): 3-20.

124. The early 1520s marked the height of the original Unity's strength. Membership estimates range from 100,000 to 200,000.

125. Quoted in Weinlick, p. 119.

126. Based on the summary in Walser H. Allen, *Who Are the Moravians?—The Story of the Moravian Church, a World-Wide Fellowship* (Bethlehem, Penn.: Walser H. Allen, 1966), pp. 90-91. See also chap. 3 of John S. Groenfeldt, *Becoming a Member of the Moravian Church: A Manual for Church Members,* rev. edn., 2nd printing (Winston-Salem, N.C.: Comenius Press, 1964), pp. 21-29.

127. Questions 60 and 61, *Catechism of The Moravian Church in America* (Bethlehem, Penn.: The Moravian Book Shop, 1964).

128. See "The Liturgy," pp. 7-171 of *Hymnal and Liturgies of the Moravian Church (Unitas Fratrum),* 8th printing (Bethlehem, Penn.: The Board of Elders of the Northern Diocese of the Church of the United Brethren in the United States of America, 1956).

129. Labrador is the responsibility of the British Province.

130. *Catechism of the Unity of the Brethren* (Taylor, Texas: Synodical Committee of the Unity of the Brethren, 1966), p. 23.

131. It follows Martin Luther's German catechisms in reading "the holy Christian Church" (ibid., p. 31).

132. The *Konfessi Bratrská* (Confession of the Brethren) of 1575 was originally written in Czech. It has been revised from time to time. The revision of 1869 is the basic statement of official doctrine for the Unity of the Brethren.

133. The *Catechism of the Unity of the Brethren* draws in part on the *Catechism of the Moravian Church in America (Northern Province)* (*Catechism,* p. 32).

BIBLIOGRAPHY

AMERICAN PRESBYTERIANS: COLONIAL TO NINETEENTH CENTURY

Ahlstrom, Sydney E., *A Religious History of the American People*. New Haven: Yale University Press, 1972.

Armstrong, Maurice W.; Loetscher, Lefferts A.; and Anderson, Charles A. *The Presbyterian Enterprise; Sources of American Presbyterian History* Philadelphia: Westminster Press, 1956.

Hodge, Charles. *Systematic Theology*. 3 vols. New York, 1873.

Hoogstra, Jacob T. *American Calvinism, A Survey*. Grand Rapids, Mich.: Baker Book House, 1957.

Hutchinson, William R. *The Modernist Impulse in American Protestantism*, Cambridge, Mass.: Harvard University Press, 1976.

Klett, Guy Soulliard. *Presbyterians in Colonial Pennsylvania*. Philadelphia: University of Pennsylvania Press, 1937.

Loetscher, Lefferts A. *The Broadening Church; a Study of Theological Issues in the Presbyterian Church since 1869*. Philadelphia: University of Pennsylvania Press, 1954.

McKinney, William Wilson, ed. *The Presbyterian Valley*. Pittsburgh: Davis and Warde, 1958.

Nichols, Robert Hastings, and Nichols, James Hastings. *Presbyterianism in New York State*. Philadelphia: Westminster Press, 1963.

Presbyterian Church in the USA. Records of the Presbyterian Church, 1706–1788.
Philadelphia, 1904.

Slosser, Gaius Jackson, ed. *They Seek a Country; the American Presbyterians, Some Aspects*. New York: The Macmillan Company, 1955.

Smylie, James H., ed. "Presbyterians and the American Revolution: A Documentary Account." *Journal of Presbyterian History* LII (Winter 1974): 303-488.

———. "Presbyterians and the American Revolution: An Interpretive Account." *Journal of Presbyterian History* LIV (Spring 1976).

Spence, Thomas H., Jr., "A Brief Bibliography of Presbyterian History." *Religion in Life* XXV (1956): 603-612.

Thompson, Ernest Trice. *Presbyterians in the South*. 3 vols. Richmond: John Knox Press, 1963–1973.

Trinterud, Leonard J. *The Forming of an American Tradition: A Re-examination of Colonial Presbyterianism*. Philadelphia: Westminster Press, 1949.

———, compiler. *A Bibliography of American Presbyterianism during the Colonial Period*. Philadelphia: The Presbyterian Historical Society, 1968.

Warfield, Benjamin B. *Revelation and Inspiration*. New York: Oxford University Press, 1927.

Zenos, Andrew C. *Presbyterianism in America*. New York: Thomas Nelson and Sons, 1937.

UNITED PRESBYTERIAN CHURCH IN THE USA

Brewer, Earl D. C., and Johnson, Douglas W. *An Inventory of the Harlan Paul Douglas Collection of Religious Research Reports*. New York: Department of Research, National Council of the Churches of Christ, 1970.

Constitution of the United Presbyterian Church in the United States of America. Part I. Book of Confessions. 2nd edn. Philadelphia: Published by the Office of the General Assembly of the United Presbyterian Church in the United States of America, 1970.

Dowey, Edward A., Jr. *A Commentary on the Confession of 1967 and an Introduction to "The Book of Confessions."* Philadelphia: Westminster Press, 1968.

Fry, John R. *The Trivialization of the United Presbyterian Church*. New York: Harper & Row, 1976.

Jamison, Wallace N. *The United Presbyterian Story: A Centennial Study, 1858–1958*. Pittsburgh: The Geneva Press, 1958.

Loetscher, Lefferts A. *The Broadening Church: A Study of Theological Issues in the Presbyterian Church Since 1869*. Philadelphia: University of Pennsylvania Press, 1954.

Rogers, Max Gray. "Charles Augustus

Briggs: Heresy at Union." In *American Religious Heretics: Formal and Informal Trials*. Ed. George H. Shriver. Nashville: Abingdon Press, 1966. Pp. 89-147.

Russell, C. Allyn. *Voices of American Fundamentalism: Seven Biographical Studies*. Philadelphia: Westminster Press, 1976.

Williams, Daniel Jenkins. *One Hundred Years of Welsh Calvinistic Methodism in America*. Philadelphia: Westminster Press, 1937. A definitive work on the Welsh Calvinistic Methodist Church and its gradual gravitation into the Presbyterian fold.

PRESBYTERIAN CHURCH IN THE UNITED STATES

Armstrong, Maurice W.; Loetscher, Lefferts A.; and Anderson, Charles A. *The Presbyterian Enterprise: Sources of American Presbyterian History*. Philadelphia: Westminster Press, 1956.

Bailey, Kenneth K. *Southern White Protestantism in the 20th Century*, New York: Harper & Row, 1964.

Dornbusch, Sanford M., and Irle, Roger D. "The Failure of Presbyterian Union." *American Journal of Sociology*. Reprinted in *Presbyterian Outlook*, February 23, 1959, pp. 5-6.

Mackorell, Virginia L. "An Historical Survey of the Hymnbooks of the Presbyterian Church in the United States." Unpublished Th.M. thesis, Presbyterian School of Christian Education, Rich-

mond, Va. 1942.

Melton, Julius. *Presbyterian Worship in America*. Richmond: John Knox Press, 1967.

Presbyterian Church in the United States, The Confession of Faith. Richmond,Va.: The Board of Christian Education, 1965.

Street, T. Watson. *The Story of Southern Presbyterians*. Richmond, Va.: John Knox Press, 1960.

Thompson, Ernest Trice. *The Changing South and the Presbyterian Church in the United States*. Richmond: John Knox Press, 1950.

———. *Presbyterians in the South*. 3 vols. Richmond: John Knox Press, 1963–1973.

———. *The Spirituality of the Church*. Richmond: John Knox Press, 1961.

PRESBYTERIAN CHURCH IN AMERICA

Presbyterian Guardian.
Presbyterian Journal.

Smith, Morton H. *How Is the Gold Become Dim*. N.p.: n. p., n.d.

THE ORTHODOX PRESBYTERIAN CHURCH

Cummings, Calvin K. *Confessing Christ*. Philadelphia: Committee on Christian Education of the Orthodox Presyterian Church, 1965.

The First Ten Years. Philadelphia: Committee on Home Missions and Church Extension of the Orthodox Presbyterian Church, 1946.

Rian, Edwin Harold. *The Presbyterian

Conflict*. Grand Rapids, Mich.: Eerdmans, 1940.

The Standards of Government, Discipline, and Worship of the Orthodox Presbyterian Church. 2nd edn., 3rd printing. Philadelphia: Committee on Christian Education of the Orthodox Presbyterian Church, 1965.

REFORMED CHURCH IN AMERICA

Bruggink, Donald, ed. *Guilt, Grace and Gratitude*. Grand Rapids, Mich.: Eerdmans, 1963. A commentary on the Heidelberg Catechism by Reformed theologians.

Eenigenburg, Elton M. *A Brief History of the Reformed Church in America*. Grand Rapids, Mich.: Douma Publications, 1958.

Hageman, Howard G. *Lily among the

Thorns. New York: Board of Education, Reformed Church in America, 1961. A popular history of the Reformed Church in America and its European antecedents.

——. *Pulpit and Table: Some Chapters in the History of Worship in the Reformed Churches.* Richmond: John Knox Press, 1962. Valuable for an understanding of the Reformed worship tradition.

ermelink, Herman, III. *Ecumenism and the Reformed Church.* Grand Rapids, Mich.: Eerdmans, 1968.

Lucas, Henry S. *Netherlands in America.* Ann Arbor, Mich.: University of Michigan Press, 1955.

Vanden Berge, Peter N., ed. *Historical Directory of the Reformed Church in America, 1628–1965.* New Brunswick, N.J.: Commission on History, Reformed Church in America, 1966.

SYNOD OF THE REFORMED PRESBYTERIAN CHURCH OF NORTH AMERICA

arson, David M. *A History of the Reformed Presbyterian Church in America to 1871.* Philadelphia: Unpublished University of Pennsylvania Ph.D. dissertation, 1964.

he Constitution of the Reformed Presbyterian Church of North America, Being

Its Standard Subordinate to the Word of God. Pittsburgh, Penn.: The Synod of the Reformed Presbyterian Church, 1949.

Glasgow, William Melanchthon. *The History of the Reformed Presbyterian Church in America.* Baltimore: Hill and Harvey, 1888.

GENERAL SYNOD OF THE ASSOCIATE REFORMED PRESBYTERIAN CHURCH

ing, Ray A. *A History of the Associate Reformed Presbyterian Church.* Charlotte, N.C.: Board of Education of the

Associate Reformed Presbyterian Church, 1966.

THE PRESBYTERIAN CHURCH IN CANADA

regg, William. *A Short History of the Presbyterian Church in the Dominion of Canada from the Earliest to the Present Times.* 2nd edn. Toronto: William Gregg, 1893.

mith, Neil Gregor. "The Presbyterian Tradition in Canada." In John Webster Grant, ed., *The Churches and the Canadian Experience* (Toronto: The Ryerson Press, 1966), pp. 38-52.

——, ed. *A Short History of the Presbyterian Church in Canada.* Toronto: Presbyterian Publications, 1965.

Smith, Neil Gregor; Markell, Keith; and Farris, Allan L. *Enkindled by the Word: Essays on Presbyterianism in Canada.* Toronto: Presbyterian Publications, 1966. Professor Allan A. Farris's chapter, "The Fathers of 1925," pp. 59-82, is an important contribution to the understanding of the theological and other concerns that marked the opponents of the entry of the Presbyterian Church in Canada into the United Church of Canada.

CHRISTIAN REFORMED CHURCH

erkhof, Louis. *Systematic Theology.* Rev. edn. Grand Rapids, Mich.: Eerdmans, 1953.

The Doctrinal Standards, Liturgy, and Church Order." In *The Psalter, with*

Doctrinal Standards, Liturgy, Church Order, and Added Chorale Section. Rev. edn., 3rd printing. Grand Rapids, Mich.: Eerdmans, 1960.

Komminga, Diedrich Hinrich. *The Chris-*

tian Reformed Tradition from the Reformation till the Present. Grand Rapids, Mich.: Eerdmans, 1943.
Schaver, J. L. *The Polity of the Churches.* Vol. II: *Concerns Reformed Churches,*

More Particularly, One Denomination 6th edn. Grand Rapids, Mich.: Kregel' Grand Rapids International Publications 1961.

HUNGARIAN REFORMED CHURCH IN AMERICA

Komjáthy, Aladar. *The Hungarian Reformed Church in America: An Effort to Preserve a Denomination Heritage.*

Princeton, N.J.: Princeton Theologica Seminary, unpublished Th.D. dissertation, 1962.

UKRAINIAN EVANGELICAL-REFORMED CHURCH IN EXILE

Bykovsky, Leo. *Basil Kusiw—A Biographical Study.* Toronto: Ukrainian

Evangelical Alliance of North America 1966.

MORAVIAN CHURCH IN AMERICA (UNITAS FRATRUM)

Allen, Walser H. *Who Are the Moravians? —The Story of the Moravian Church, a World-Wide Fellowship.* 2nd printing. Bethlehem, Penn.: Walser H. Allen, 1966.
Catechism of The Moravian Church in America for the Instruction of Candidates for Confirmation and Church Membership. Bethlehem, Penn.: The Moravian Book Shop, 1964. This 46-page brochure was ordered by the 1956 Synod of the Northern Province.
Groenfeldt, John S. *Becoming a Member of the Moravian Church: A Manual for Church Members.* Rev. edn., 2nd printing. Winston-Salem, N.C.: Comenius Press, 1964.
Hamilton, J. Taylor, and Hamilton, Kenneth G. *A History of the Moravian*

Church—The Renewed Unitas Fratrum 1722–1957. Bethlehem, Penn.: Interprovincial Board of Christian Education Moravian Church in America, 1967.
Hymnal and Liturgies of the Moravian Church (Unitas Fratrum). 8th printing Bethlehem, Penn.: The Board of Elder of the Northern Diocese of the Church of the United Brethren in the United States of America, 1956.
Strupl, Milos. "Confessional Theology of the Unitas Fratrum." In *Church History* XXXIII (1964): 279-293.
Weinlick, John R. *Count Zinzendorf* Nashville: Abingdon Press, 1956.
———. *The Moravian Church Through the Ages.* Bethlehem, Penn.: Comenius Press, 1966.

UNITY OF THE BRETHREN

Catechism of the Unity of the Brethren. Taylor, Texas: Synodical Committee of the Unity of the Brethren, 1966. A 32-page brochure designed for use in the instruction of candidates for confirmation and church membership.
Constitution and By-Laws of the Unity of

the Brethren. [Taylor, Texas:] Synodica Committee of the Unity of the Brethren 1965.
The Unity of the Brethren: Origin, Beliefs and Practices. Place of publication, publisher, and date of publication not given A 5-page pamphlet.

PART IV

CHURCHES WITH ORIGINS

IN THE RADICAL REFORMATION

10. The Radical Reformation

The Radical Reformation is a complex and multifaceted movement which is difficult to describe concisely and precisely. Diverse personalities, a significant number of distinct, though related, groups, and a variety of concerns and ideals constitute the movement. Even the choice of a name for this sixteenth-century reformation has been and remains a problematic issue. Traditionally the various groups that were not part of the mainline Protestant bodies have been referred to as Anabaptists. Although rebaptism was practiced among them, their concern was not specifically anabaptism but, rather, adult baptism. Thus the name is somewhat misleading, and the groups themselves preferred to be called Baptists. Recent scholarship has tended to ascribe the names Left-wing Reformation[1] or radical Reformation[2] to the movement. Both terms are useful and descriptive, though certain difficulties of definition persist.

Historical Overview

The Radical Reformation is a polygenetic movement. Its beginnings are usually traced to Zurich in the early 1520s, although there is some justification to point to Andreas Carlstadt (c. 1480–1541), Thomas Müntzer (c. 1489–1525), and the Zwickau prophets in Saxony as its earliest manifestations. It was in Zurich that the first case of rebaptism occurred when Conrad Grebel (1498–1526) baptized Georg Blaurock (c. 1480–1529) in January 1525. Blaurock, in turn, baptized the initial group of Swiss Brethren, who numbered about fifteen. Although opposition was immediately forthcoming from the Swiss Reformer Ulrich Zwingli (1484–1531) and a policy of persecution was initiated by the secular authorities, Grebel and Blaurock were able to attract and baptize a substantial group of followers. The intolerance of the Swiss authorities, both ecclesiastical and secular, resulted in the expulsion or execution of leaders and the flight of Swiss Brethren into other areas of Europe. There they were generally incorporated into other radical groups. Nevertheless, pockets of Anabaptists continued to persist within the Swiss borders throughout the sixteenth century.

The Radical Reform movement also manifested itself in southern Germany, the Austrian lands, especially Moravia, along the Rhine, and in the Netherlands. Augsburg, Strassburg and Münster became early centers of Anabaptist activity. In addition to Grebel, Jakob Huter (d. 1536), the founder of the Hutterites; Balthasar Hubmaier (1485–1528), an able organizer; Melchior Hofmann (c. 1495–c. 1544), whose powerful eschatological accents and volatile personality inspired much opposition; Pilgram Marpeck (c. 1495–1556), a powerful figure among the Anabaptists of southern Germany; Kaspar Schwenkfeld (1489–1561), who articulated a spiritual interpretation of the Eucharist and whose followers eventually also reached the American shores, and particularly Menno Simons (1496–1561), who brought stability to the movement at a crucial time and who attracted a significant following, emerged as the leaders of the Left-wing Reformation during the sixteenth century.

George Williams[3] has divided the vast array of sixteenth-century radical groups into three major categories: the Spiritualists, the Evangelical Rationalists, and the Anabaptists. The Spiritualists were characterized by mystical tendencies, by the emphasis on personal rebirth and the inner experience of the Spirit, and by an affirmation of divine immediacy. Kaspar Schwenkfeld was an influential representative of this point of view. The strict biblicism and rationalism of the Evangelical Rationalists led them to challenge basic affirmations of the Christian faith, particularly in the areas of Christology and the doctrine of the Trinity. Specifically, they advocated unitarianism and a rejection of the divinity of Christ. They flourished particularly in northern Italy and eastern Europe, and the Polish Socinians are the most distinguished representative group. Michael Servetus (1511–1553) and Lelio (1525–1562) and Fausto (1539–1604) Sozzini were effective articulators of the antitrinitarian position. Although the Socinians were expelled from their center of activity in Rakow after 1638, Socinian, antitrinitarian ideas continued to be expressed and professed throughout Europe, especially in Holland, Germany, and England.

For the specific context of this discussion the third of Williams's categories, the Anabaptists, is most significant. They include the Swiss Brethren, the Hutterites, and the Mennonites, three of the most important manifestations of the Radical Reformation. The Hutterites, heirs of Jakob Huter, were communistic communities that flourished particularly in Moravia. The individual congregations gathered in *Bruderhöfe*, where they lived, worked, and worshiped together. After a half century of peaceful existence in Moravia they were expelled in 1622. For a time they settled in Hungary, Transylvania, and the Ukraine, where they came under the influence of the Roman Catholic Church. In the late nineteenth century a significant number emigrated to the New World and settled particularly in South Dakota and Canada.[4]

Menno Simons provided competent and moderating leadership within the Radical Reformation after 1536. He joined the movement shortly after the unfortunate episode at Münster, where a group of militant and revolutionary Anabaptists, led by Jan Matthys and Jan Beuckelsz, established what they considered to be the "heavenly Jerusalem" on earth and then took up arms to defend their utopia against the combined forces of the Catholic bishop and the Lutheran landgrave Philip of Hesse. A large number of Anabaptists lost their lives during the struggle, including Menno Simons's brother. Menno determined to provide leadership to a persecuted and scattered Anabaptist community but to avoid excesses. Numerous groups throughout the Low Countries and northern Germany came under his influence. Although doctrinal disagreements resulted in divisions, the Mennonite movement has been a vibrant religious force since the sixteenth century.

Major Emphases

While there are profound differences within the Radical Reformation, in both theology and methodology, it is possible to identify recurring and characteristic themes, which shed much light on this diverse movement. Major affirmations of early evangelical Anabaptism are articulated in seven articles known as the Schleitheim Confession of 1527. The document was addressed specifically to fellow Anabaptists and attempted to correct excesses that had developed within the movement. It was widely circulated, however, and was also used as a source of Anabaptist teachings by the magisterial reformers.

Each article identifies a specific concern and articulates an acceptable position. Article I deals with baptism and notes that it is to be administered to "all those who have learned repentance and amendment of life, and who believe truly that their sins are taken away by Christ, and . . . who walk in the resurrection of Jesus Christ, and wish to be buried with him in death, so that they may be resurrected with him, . . ." This view clearly reserves the sacrament for adults and rejects infant baptism. Article II identifies the ban (excommunication) as the means of keeping the community pure. It is to be employed before the celebration of the Lord's Supper against those who have fallen "into error and sin. . . ." The procedure outlined in Matthew 18 is to be followed. Article III prescribes that only the baptized are to partake of the Lord's Supper, which is described as a memorial feast. Article IV stipulates that the baptized community must be separated from all that is evil and must avoid such things as Roman and Protestant worship services, drinking houses, and the use of force. The fifth article deals with the office of the pastor. The pastor must be an individual who has a good reputation even among those outside the community. His duties are "to read, to admonish and teach, to warn, to discipline, to ban in the Church, to lead out in prayer for the advancement of all the brethren and sisters, to lift up the bread when it is broken, and in all things to see to the care of the body of Christ in order that it may be built up and developed. . . ." Article VI addresses the crucial question of the relationship between church and state. The sword is viewed as "ordained of God outside the perfection of Christ. It punishes and puts to death the wicked, and guards and protects the good." Within the baptized community, however, "only the ban is used for a warning and for the excommunication of the one who has sinned, . . ." The warning is also given that baptized believers dare not participate in any functions of the government. The strict separation of church and state and the refusal to participate in affairs of the state are essential aspects of the Anabaptist position. Finally, oaths are forbidden in Article VII.[5] While the Schleitheim Confession is an occasional document and is certainly not a complete articulation of the Anabaptist position, it is a clear and widely accepted statement of essential doctrinal affirmations.

As such it also reflects some characteristic emphasis within the Radical movement. Certainly one of those emphases is the rejection of infant baptism. The nature of baptism, as defined by the Anabaptists, explains this rejection. The concept of a voluntary, pure, and separated church is also basic. That church consists of the faithful who have professed their faith in their baptism and who remain separated from the world. An emphasis on ethics and on moral transformation is, therefore, a dominant theme within the radical movement, for when the radical reformers speak of purity they do so in ethical rather than a doctrinal terms. The doctrine of the ban is important because it is the main instrument whereby the church is kept pure. According to some, its use is the basic sign of the true church. The separation of church and state is essential if the church is to remain pure and separated. Because the church rejects the use of force, it is a suffering community that offers no resistance when it is persecuted. It also advocates religious freedom, for the sword is a worldly instrument that has no place in the realm of the Spirit. Indeed, its use is rejected completely by the faithful. Therefore they are pacifists. A heightened eschatological consciousness accompanies and, to a degree, is responsible for these affirmations. A final characteristic which must be noted is described as "primitivism" by Bainton[6] and as a desire for restitution (restitutio) rather than reformation (reformatio) by Williams.[7] Indeed, they sought to restore the simplicity and purity of the primitive, apostolic church. In order to discover the features and ideals of that church, they, of course, turned to Scripture and vociferously defended the ultimate and central authority of the Word of God. While different emphases and priorities can be identified among the various radical groups, these concerns are typical of the movement as a whole and serve to characterize and describe it.

The Puritans

Puritanism constitutes a distinct, though important, chapter in the history of Radical Reform. There are, of course, clear differences between the Puritans and the various radical groups of the Continent, particularly the

Anglican and Calvinist ecclesiastical and theological heritage of the former. Similarities in outlook and emphasis, however, are also evident.

Puritans certainly constitute the most significant manifestation of radical reform within the English context. They emerged historically during the reign of Queen Elizabeth I (1558–1603) as vociferous opponents of the Elizabethan Settlement, which resulted in the establishment of the Church of England. During the reign of Mary (1553–1558) a substantial number of Protestants had fled to the Continent, where they had come under the influence of John Calvin (1509–1564) and of more radical reforming ideas. When they returned to England during Elizabeth's reign, they were imbued with a deep commitment to ecclesiastical renewal. Although some agreed to the Elizabethan Settlement, they expected it to be the initial step in that process of renewal. Their ultimate goal was to restore the church to its apostolic purity. They were, therefore, quickly called Puritans, an appropriate and descriptive epithet. Elizabeth, on the other hand, wanted a national church to which all of her subjects could belong. She had no intention of implementing the Puritan program. Conflict was, therefore, inevitable.

During the sixteenth century the struggle revolved around the issues of vestments and of church polity. Taking their cue from Calvin, the Puritans argued that vestments were Roman accretions which must be eliminated. More volatile and crucial was the controversy over the episcopacy. The Puritans, led by Thomas Cartwright (d. 1603), attacked the polity of the Anglican church and argued that it was contrary to the New Testament. The episcopacy must, therefore, be replaced by a presbyterian system of church government according to the guidelines of the New Testament and following the model of Geneva. While a significant amount of pamphleteering and argumentation was carried on over these issues, Elizabeth was able to keep the Puritan movement under control, primarily because of her political acumen. However, she was not able to silence its witness.

During the seventeenth century the Puritan witness became more vociferous. Puritanism emerged as a political as well as a religious force. Although the Stuart monarchs attempted to suppress the movement, especially through Archbishop Laud, Puritanism continued its offensive both within the church and within Parliament. That offensive ultimately led to the difficult step of rebellion against the Crown and the execution of Charles I (1625–1649). Under the leadership of Oliver Cromwell (1599–1658) the Puritan commonwealth was established, and, until the restoration of Charles II (1660–1685) in 1660, Puritanism reigned supreme in England, both religiously and politically. It was during the first decades of the seventeenth century, however, when they experienced much oppression, that Puritans began to emigrate from England, first to the Low Countries and finally to the New World. In the wilderness of New England they hoped to establish their city set on a hill where they could implement their ideals and be an example to the nations.

Much like the continental radicals, the Puritans are a diverse and complex movement. They may, however, be divided into two general groups. The Nonseparatists, sometimes also called dissenters or Nonconformists, considered themselves to be a confessing movement within the Church of England. Although they wanted to purify the church, they wished to do so from within. The dissenters may be subdivided further according to the church polity which they advocated. The majority were Presbyterians, but a substantial number were Congregationalists. The latter, of course, played a more significant role in the New England context, for the Massachusetts Bay Puritans were nonseparatist Congregationalists. The other major group of Puritans were the Separatists. They were the most radical segment of Puritanism, who argued that the Church of England was beyond reformation. Puritans must, therefore, separate from the Anglican communion and pursue their goal of perfection independently. The Separatists also advocated a strict congregational polity. Robert Browne (c. 1550–v.1633) was an early leader of separatism, and Cambridge University became its intellectual center. The Pilgrims who settled at Plymouth represented this tradition.

The Puritan Spirit

Like the continental Radical Reformation, Puritanism was characterized by an idealistic primitivism. It, too, focused its attention on Scripture and attempted to resurrect the theological, organizational, and ethical purity of the apostolic church. Of course, Puritanism did not only concern itself with corporate or institutional reform. Its ultimate focus was on the individual. Therefore, the conversion experience is the very essence of Puritanism, as Alan Simpson has pointed out.[8] Only after the individual has had such an experience is he assured of his election, and only after he has convinced the other saints of the validity of his experiences is he welcomed into the community of saints, the congregation.

The significance of the covenant in Puritan thought is related to this emphasis on the conversion experience. It is through the covenant of grace that God establishes an intimate relationship with his elect. The individual becomes experientially aware of this covenant relationship in the conversion experience. Therefore, in the life of the saint the establishment of the covenant and the conversion experience are intrically related. After God has covenanted with his saints, the saints, in turn, covenant with one another. Thus they establish not only their spiritual community, the congregation, but also their civic community. The Mayflower Compact, for example, is a covenant by means of which the Pilgrims established their body politic in the New World. It is not surprising, therefore, that the Puritans envisioned a close relationship between church and state, at least in the New England context where the saints ultimately constituted and dominated both.

The covenant idea resulted in a self-conception as God's chosen people with a specific mission. That mission was to be the purified church of Christ on earth and an example to all people. John Winthrop (1588–1649), the leader of the Massachusetts Bay Puritans, articulated that mission clearly in a lay sermon entitled "A Modell of Christian Charity," which he preached during their voyage to the New World. Winthrop reminded his fellow saints:

> . . . for wee must Consider that wee shall be as a Citty upon a Hill, the eies of all people are uppon us; soe that if wee shall deale falsely with our god in this worke wee have undertaken and soe cause him to withdrawe his present help from us, wee shall be made a story and a by-word through the world, . . . Therefore lett us choose life, that wee, and our Seede, may live; by obeyeing his voyce, and and cleaveing to him, for hee is our life, and our prosperity.[9]

The privilege of being God's people also brought with it lofty responsibilities. A tremendous ethical emphasis is, therefore, also characteristic of the Puritan spirit. The saints were expected to live morally pure and upright lives worthy of God's elect. Rebirth and conversion clearly implied moral reformation for the Puritans.

Finally, the Puritans affirmed an absolute concept of truth. They were convinced that God had revealed truth fully and clearly in his Word. The saints, using their enlightened reason properly, could perceive that truth through the study of Holy Scripture. Since there is only one truth, they will, of course, agree among themselves. While they soon discovered the difficulties of this position, the concept of absolute truth contributed significantly to the Puritan reluctance to compromise and their tendency toward intolerance.

The Puritans were a dedicated, serious, and highly motivated community of believers whose impact on the English and American contexts has been profound. They influenced not only the Congregational and Presbyterian but also the Baptist traditions. While the so-called General Baptists, whose early leaders in England were John Smith (c. 1570–1612) and Thomas Helwys (c. 1550–c. 1616), were deeply influenced by the Mennonites and manifested Arminian tendencies, the Particular or Calvinistic Baptists emerged from the Puritan context. During the early seventeenth century some of the Separatist Puritans accepted the doctrine of believer's or adult baptism and became Baptists. This was also the case with the radical Puritan Roger Williams (c. 1603–1683), whose creative individualism and religious intensity led him to theological conclusions and affirmations quite unlike those of most of his contemporaries. Although he remained a Baptist for only a short time, he did make Rhode Island a haven for Baptists, as well as for all other religious groups. The heritage of both Calvinistic Puritanism and Mennonite Arminianism continues to be evident among Baptists today. Such emphases as religious freedom, the separation of church and state, and the individual's responsibility in spiritual matters are obvious influences of the Mennonite tradition. On the other hand, the strong congregational heritage and such theological affirmations as unconditional election and the total depravity of human beings are clear reflections of the Calvinistic-Puritan influence. The significance and impact of the Radical Reformation is certainly not limited to the sixteenth century. Many of its tenets are readily identifiable within the religious context of the late twentieth century.

Persecution and the desire to find a favorable context in which to pursue their convictions and to implement their ideals were primary reasons for the emigration of the various radical groups to the New World. As they fled the animosity of Catholic and Protestant Churches and rulers, Mennonites, Schwenkfeldians, Hutterites, Baptists, Puritans, and others looked to America as a haven. Although their hopes were not always fully realized, they generally survived and in most cases flourished in the American context.

NOTES

1. See Roland Bainton, *Studies in the Reformation* (Boston: Beacon Press, 1963). Hereafter referred to as Bainton.
2. See George H. Williams, *The Radical Reformation* (Philadelphia: Westminster Press, 1962). Hereafter referred to as Williams.
3. Ibid., p. 846.
4. Owen Chadwick, *The Reformation* (Baltimore: Penguin Books, 1964), p. 194.
5. Hans J. Hillerbrand, *The Reformation* (New York: Harper & Row, 1964), pp. 235-238. For a helpful discussion of the Schleitheim Confession, see also Williams, pp. 182-185.
6. Bainton, p. 123.
7. Williams, pp. XXVI 857.
8. Alan Simpson, *Puritanism in Old and New England* (Chicago: University of Chicago Press, 1955), p. 2.
9. H. Shelton Smith, Robert T. Handy, and Lefferts A. Loetscher, *American Christianity,* 2 vols. (New York: Charles Scribner's Sons, 1960–1963), I (1960): 102.

BIBLIOGRAPHY

Ahlstrom, Sydney E. *A Religious History of the American People.* New Haven: Yale University Press, 1972.

Bainton, Roland. *Studies on the Reformation.* Boston: Beacon Press, 1963.

———. *The Travail of Religious Liberty.* Philadelphia: Westminster Press, 1951.

Chadwick, Owen. *The Reformation.* Baltimore: Penguin Books, 1964.

Haller, William. *Liberty and Reformation in the Puritan Revolution.* New York: Columbia University Press, 1955.

———. *The Rise of Puritanism.* New York: Harper & Row, 1957.

Hershberger, Guy F., ed. *The Recovery of the Anabaptist Vision.* Scottdale, Pa.: Herald Press, 1957.

Hillerbrand, Hans J. *The Reformation.* New York: Harper & Row, 1964.

Meyer, Carl S. *Elizabeth I and the Religious Settlement of 1559.* St. Louis: Concordia Publishing House, 1960.

Morgan, Edmund S. *Visible Saints. The History of a Puritan Idea.* New York: New York University Press, 1963.

Simpson, Alan. *Puritanism in Old and New England.* Chicago: University of Chicago Press, 1955.

Steinmetz, David C. *Reformers in the Wings.* Philadelphia: Fortress Press, 1971.

Torbet, Robert G. *A History of the Baptists.* 3rd edn. Valley Forge, Pa.: Judson Press, 1975.

Williams, George H. *The Radical Reformation.* Philadelphia: Westminster Press, 1962.

Zuck, Lowell, ed. *Christianity and Revolution: Radical Christian Testimonies, 1520–1650.* Philadelphia: Temple University Press, 1975.

11. Churches Perpetuating the Congregationalist Tradition

The congregationalist tradition has had a long and noble history in the United States, reaching back to the Pilgrims and to the Puritan settlers of New England. In the course of time most churches of the congregationalist tradition associated together in the Council of Congregational Christian Churches. In 1957 the Council of Congregational Christian Churches united with the Evangelical and Reformed Church to form the United Church of Christ (see chap. 21), thus bequeathing the congregationalist tradition to the new church body. A number of churches declined to participate in the formation of the new church and organized separately to perpetuate the congregationalist tradition.

Conservative Congregational Christian Conference

In the mid-1930s, some of the evangelicals in the General Council of Congregational Christian Churches began to associate informally in order to meet felt needs for fellowship and service. Out of this came the Conservative Congregational Christian Fellowship, established in 1945 to maintain a biblical witness within the council. When it became apparent that the General Council of Congregational Christian Churches would unite with the Evangelical and Reformed Church to form the United Church of Christ, the fellowship reorganized at Chicago in 1948 as the Conservative Congregational Christian Conference in order to provide a continuing fellowship for evangelical churches and ministers on a national level. Early growth was slow, but since the 1953 meeting at Wheaton, Illinois, progress has been healthy and stable. The conference has also attracted increasing numbers of Bible and community churches with other than Congregational-Christian backgrounds.[1]

The organization describes itself as a "fellowship of churches" and as in no outward sense a church. It isolates five identifying principles in Congregationalism and affirms its commitment to them: (1) the necessity of a regenerate church membership; (2) the authority of the Holy Scriptures; (3) the Lordship of Christ, exercised by the Holy Spirit and through the Scriptures; (4) the autonomy of the local church; and (5) the voluntary fellowship of believers. In the question of polity, it rejects the idea that the local congregation must decide on every issue, insists that each local church has the right to determine how it is to be governed, and sees nothing inappropriate in the delegation of certain authority and responsibility to a board of elders or deacons.[2]

Its seven-article Statement of Faith affirms that the Bible is "the only inspired, the inerrant, infallible, authoritative Word of God"; confesses the Trinity and Christ's deity, virgin birth, sinless life, miracles, vicarious and atoning death, bodily resurrection, ascension, and personal return in power; asserts the absolute essentiality of regeneration by the Holy Spirit for the salvation of lost and sinful human beings; teaches the present ministry of the Holy Spirit to enable Christians to live a godly life in this present evil world; declares its belief in the resurrection of the saved to life and of the lost to damnation; and asserts the spiritual unity of all believers in Christ.[3]

Membership in the conference may be held by churches, ministers, and individual laymen. Other affiliations do not necessarily bar churches as long as they adhere to the statements of faith and polity. Regional fellowships can be either in affiliation with the conference, in sympathy with it, or in recognition by it. A relation "in sympathy" makes communication and cooperation possible; in the case of regional fellowships "in recognition," the conference will not promote a competitive group in that region. The conference meets annually. It is a member of the World Alliance of Reformed Churches (Presbyterian and Congregational).

The address of the headquarters of the conference is Box 171, Hinsdale, Illinois 60521. There are 127 churches in the United States and Canada with a total membership of 21,975. Members of its ministry serve under varied sponsorship in the Western Caroline Islands, Japan, Malawi, Brazil, Kenya, Ethiopia, and Belgium.

The National Association of Congregational Christian Churches

By the end of 1955 it had become obvious to all that the General Council of Congregational Christian Churches would unite organically with the Evangelical and Reformed Church. For some local churches of the Congregational and Christian traditions, the union posed a mortal threat to the essence of Congregationalism as they understood it. So on November 9 and 10, 1955, elected delegates from a number of these churches met in Detroit and formed the National Association of Congregational Christian Churches. The following year the churches concerned formally covenanted "to walk together in the ways which God anciently revealed to our fathers, and in such further ways as He may yet reveal to us."[4] In 1961 the association declared itself the successor to the former General Council of the Congregational Christian Churches and asserted its readiness to serve all Congregational Christian churches that had not become a part of the United Church of Christ. In 1962 it formed a Committee on World Christian Relations for the purpose of maintaining fellowship among free churches in this country and abroad. It sponsors the National Congregational Fellowship for individual Congregationalists who wish to foster the congregational way, whether or not they are members of churches belonging to the association.

As "the custodian of the Pilgrim heritage," the association stresses as the chief truths to which it holds "the freedom of the Christian man maintained at all costs and all hazards; the right of the local church to self-government in all matters temporal and spiritual, because of Christ's word that where two or three are gathered together in His Name He is in their midst"; and "the fellowship of the churches in the spirit of love, without compulsions or restraint and free from the bondage of creed or ecclesiastical control."[5]

The association exercises no ecclesiastical authority and imposes no binding creed. Local churches are associations of "people of independent mind and heart who by their profession and life give evidence that they are disciples of our Lord and Master, Jesus Christ," and who accept "his requirements of equality and mutual responsibility among his disciples."[6] To prevent boards and officials from taking action contrary to the will of many of the local churches, the association has developed a protective mechanism called a "Referendum Council," which provides a way for the local churches to exercise their right and power to review and modify any action or proposal of any national bodies or officers.[7]

Each local church has its own covenant, which all members are required to "own," that is, acknowledge, assent to, and appropriate. Some local churches write wholly new covenants for themselves, while others adopt (or adapt) a historic covenant of some other church. A "typical" set of by-laws provided for the guidance of Congregational Christian churches in the process of organization suggests this article on "Faith":

"This church recognizes the right and duty of each member to determine his own beliefs according to the dictates of his conscience. It joins, however, with churches of like mind in testifying: We believe in the love of God, our Father, and in the revelations of that love in Jesus Christ, our Lord and Saviour. We confess our faith in Him, and will strive to live together in the fellowship and service of the spirit of God. We earnestly desire to know our duty as taught in the Holy Scriptures and to walk in the ways of the Lord, made known and to be made known to us through the guidance of the Holy Spirit. With loyalty to God and love for all men we will labor for that righteousness which is profitable for the life that now is and gives assurance for the life everlasting."[8]

The actual theological position of the churches and ministers in the association ranges from conservative to liberal.

Some Congregational Christian churches waive baptism whenever a new member prefers for reasons of conscience not to receive it. Most Congregational Christian churches have "open" communion services, where the invitation is given "to all who may wish to partake, whether they be members of this church, or of any other church, or of no church at all."[9] The association admits women to ordination on a parity with men.

The association reports 378 churches with an inclusive membership of about 90,000. In addition there are 12 associate member churches (abroad) and 28 affiliated churches, including the North Carolina State Conference, Incorporated, an association of black churches. In addition to Congregational-Christian clubs, councils, fellowships, and meetings across the country, there are 30 independent and autonomous regional associations of Congregational Christian churches and/or ministers and one conference of Congregational Christian churches (in Michigan) that voluntarily cooperate with the association. The address of the executive secretaries is Box 1620, Oak Creek, Wisconsin 53154.

Midwest Congregational Christian Fellowship

Among the Congregational Christian churches that did not enter the United Church of Christ was a group of largely rural congregations in Indiana, Ohio, and Illinois. They remained outside the union partly because they felt that the government of the new body would jeopardize their traditional freedom and partly because they felt that liberal pressures would be too strong in the United Chuch of Christ.[10] In 1958 these congregations banded together as the Midwest Congregational Christian Fellowship.

The Statement of Faith in their constitution is identical with the statement of faith of the National Association of Evangelicals, of which the fellowship is a member-body.[11]

The fellowship is not affiliated with the National Association of Congregational Christian Churches. Both men and women are admitted to the ministry. There are 31 churches and chapels with a total membership of 1,890.[12]

NOTES

1. *The Conservative Congregational Christian Conference: History—Principles —Ministry* (Scotia, N.Y.: Conservative Congregational Christian Conference, 1966) (6-page tract).
2. See *Are You Congregational?* (Scotia, N.Y.: Conservative Congregational Christian Conference, n.d.) (6-page tract); Article IV ("Statement of Polity"), Constitution and By-laws, in *Annual Report 1965–1966* (Scotia, N.Y.: Conservative Congregational Christian Conference, 1965), p. 31.
3. Article III ("Statement of Faith"), ibid.
4. "Articles of Association of the National Association of Congregational Christian Churches in the United States," in *The 1965–1966 Handbook* (Milwaukee: National Association of Congregational Christian Churches, 1966), p. 94.
5. "Preamble to the Articles of Association," *The 1965–1966 Handbook*, p. 94.
6. A. Vaughan Abercrombie, *How to Gather and Order a Congregational Christian Church* (Milwaukee: A. Vaughan Abercrombie, 1966), pp. 3-4.

7. Article VIII, Articles of Association, and Article VII, By-laws, *The 1965– 1966 Handbook,* pp. 97, 100-101). The "Referendum Council" is seen as "an adaptation of the Con'gregational custom of a vicinage council" (ibid., p. 101).

8. Abercrombie, p. 24.

9. Ibid., p. 17.

10. Communication from the Reverend Hubert K. Clevenger, Winchester, Indiana.

11. Article III, *Constitution and Manual of the Midwest Congregational Christian Fellowship* as amended September· 17, 1964 (17-page brochure), p. 3.

12. The largest church in the fellowship is the Winchester (Indiana) Congregational Christian Church. The fellowship as such does not have a headquarters.

12. Churches of the Mennonite Tradition

Mennonite Church

The first reference to Mennonites in the New World is a report in a French Jesuit's travel account of 1643 that on the island of Manhattan there were some Anabaptists, or "Menists," that is, followers of Menno Simons. The first permanent Mennonite settlement in North America comprised immigrants of Dutch extraction from Krefeld in the Ruhr district of Germany, who made their homes in Germantown, Pennsylvania, in 1683. In 1708 a group of Swiss Mennonites from the Palatinate who had come to Germantown the year before joined them. In 1710 a large number of Swiss Mennonites from the canton of Bern, which had been trying to deport them ever since 1672, settled in Lancaster County, Pennsylvania. They were a part of the first great wave of Mennonite immigration to the United States—involving from 3,000 to 5,000 persons—that lasted until the outbreak of the French and Indian Wars in 1754. The second wave brought three thousand Amish of Swiss antecedents from Alsace, Bavaria, and Hesse into the Northwest Territory and Ontario between 1815 and 1880. A third, smaller wave began in 1830 and, over thirty years, brought 500 Swiss Mennonites to Ohio and Indiana, followed by 300 Palatine Mennonites, who came into the same general territory in the era of the War between the States, and 400 Mennonites of Swiss origin who migrated from central Europe to Kansas and South Dakota in the late 1870s.

The major waves of Mennonite immigrants of Dutch ethnic origin began in 1873. In the following decade 18,000 settled on the prairies of the United States and Manitoba. In the 1920s, following World War I, 21,000 fled before Soviet communist persecution to Canada, along with 4,000 who took refuge in Latin America. During World War II the German National Socialists deported 35,000 Mennonites from their Russian homes to Germany, of whom 12,000 escaped repatriation; ultimately over 7,000 reached Canada and the remainder went to South America.

The Mennonite Church, frequently referred to as the "Old" Mennonite Church to distinguish it from the considerably smaller General Conference

Mennonite Church, comprises chiefly the descendants of the Palatine and Swiss Mennonites who emigrated to Pennsylvania before the Revolutionary War, the Swiss Amish who came into the Northwest Territory and Ontario in the nineteenth century, and individuals and groups that withdrew from the Old Order Amish during the last hundred years. Like the rest of their fellow Americans, Mennonites moved westward with the frontier and now span the continent.

In the course of time the Mennonite Church suffered some divisions— those resulting from the excommunication of Martin Boehm (1725–1812), one of the co-founders of the United Brethren in Christ, for his revivalistic beliefs and practices; the excommunication of Christian Funk (1731–1811) for his advocacy of the cause of the American colonies in a nonresistant church; the withdrawal of Jacob Engle (1753–1832), founder of the River Brethren and of the Brethren in Christ; the disfellowshiping of Francis Herr (d. 1810) and his son John Herr (1782–1850), organizers of the Reformed Mennonite Church; the withdrawal of Jacob Stauffer (1811–1855), whose followers make up a number of small groups, chiefly in Pennsylvania; the withdrawal of John H. Oberholtzer (1809–1895), one of the organizers of the General Conference Mennonite Church; the secessions from the Ontario Mennonites of Daniel Hoch (1806–1878) in 1848, of Solomon Eby (1834– 1931) in 1872, and of Daniel Brenneman (1834–1919) in 1874 that played a part in the creation of the Mennonite Brethren Church, now the United Missionary Church and the Bible Fellowship Church; the withdrawal of John Holdeman (1832–1900), who founded the Church of God in Christ (Mennonite); the "Old Order" Mennonite schisms that took place from 1872 to 1901 over Sunday schools and other "innovations," and the transfer of several hundred members and a few ministers to the General Conference Mennonite fellowship in the 1920s.

The Mennonite Church has all but completed the transition from German to English. In the process the sociological factors that helped to give the denomination its strong ingroup feeling and its deep sense of common identity have extensively vanished—the Palatine German dialect, the typical garb, the rural-agricultural orientation. The leadership of the church is aware of the jeopardy in which this loss of accidental distinguishing marks has placed the authentic Mennonite distinctives—the tradition of nonresistance, the refusal to take oaths, believer's baptism, the permanence of marriage, the use of church discipline to maintain standards of faith and life, and the whole conception of Christianity as redeemed discipleship.[1]

Since 1725 the Dordrecht Confession of 1632 has been the official creed of the Mennonite Church. A supplement in the form of an eighteen article statement on the Fundamentals of the Christian Faith adopted in 1921 was superseded in 1963 by the Mennonite Confession of Faith,[2] epitomized in a Brief Statement of Mennonite Doctrine.[3] This confession affirms the Trinity; the revelation of God in the Scriptures and supremely in his Son; the free will, moral character, and spiritual nature of human beings; the self-centered and self-willed state of human beings after the fall, unwilling and unable to break with sin; Christ as the unique Mediator; salvation by grace through faith in Christ; conviction of sin, new birth, guidance in life, power for service, and perseverance in faith and holiness through the Holy Spirit; the church as the body of Christ, the brotherhood of the redeemed, a disciplined people obedient to the divine Word, and a fellowship of love; Christ's commission to evangelize and to minister to every human need; the divine sanction for the ministry; believer's baptism with water as a symbol of baptism with the Spirit; the Lord's Supper as a symbol of Christ's broken body and shed blood and of the fellowship of the church; washing of the saints' feet, the right hand of fellowship, and the holy kiss; the unique roles of men and women, symbolized by the former's bared and the latter's veiled head; Christian marriage as a lifelong union "only in the Lord"; conformity to Christ rather than to the world; nonuse of oaths; abstention from force and violence; love for all people; government as a divine ordinance and the obligation of Christians "to honor rulers, be subject to authorities, witness to the state, and pray for governments"; everlasting punishment for the unsaved and everlasting bliss for the saved after Christ returns to be the judge of all people and to bring in God's everlasting Kingdom.[4]

Structurally the Mennonite Church has evolved from strict congregationalism to a point where the district conference plays a significant organizational role in the life of the denomination at large while the congregation remains the key organization in the daily life and witness of the church. The officers of the churches are preachers, deacons, and elders or bishops. The Mennonite General Assembly meets biennially with delegates from 23 conferences and districts. The General Board, newly organized in 1971, has its headquarters at 528 East Madison Street, Lombard, Illinois 60148.

The Mennonite Church comprises 96,092 members in the United States and 9,682 in Canada for a total of 105,774. Missionary work is carried on in Europe, Latin America, Africa, and Asia. Overseas churches related to the Mennonite Church represent an additional 25,781 members.[5]

Reformed Mennonite Church

Around 1785 the Mennonite Church in West Lampeter Township, Lancaster County, Pennsylvania, expelled Francis Herr, partly at least because he criticized the departure of the church leaders from the principles of Menno Simons and for tolerating laxity in religious life and social practices. He and his fellow expellees and supporters met informally for divine services in one another's homes until his death in 1810. Two years later the group decided to organize and selected John Herr (1782–1850), the son of Francis, as pastor and bishop, even though he was as yet unbaptized. Like the original Zurich Anabaptists in 1525, Abraham Landis, who no longer regarded his Mennonite baptism as valid, baptized Herr, who thereupon rebaptized Landis. Originally called "New Mennonites" and "Herrites" by outsiders, the new organization finally adopted the name "Reformed Mennonites." After John Herr's death expansion practically ceased, and the church has managed to resist significant changes in doctrine and practice.

The Reformed Mennonites hold that Christ in our form and in our stead reconciled God's righteousness and mercy. The power of the Holy Spirit creates the church, and his presence and guidance alone assure its continuity and succession. They administer adult baptism, usually by pouring and after a year of probation of the candidate, on profession of faith and evidence of a consistent life. They practice close Communion. In applying Matthew 18:15–17 to erring fellow Christians they may regretfully have to apply the ban, both for the sake of the church's purity and in the hope of bringing the sinful person to repentance. The washing of one another's feet, in which all participate, exemplifies their concern for the spiritual welfare of fellow members, the original washing of regeneration, and the daily need of pardon. Both layfolk and ministers greet one another with the kiss of charity. They are entirely nonresistant and do not vote, hold government office, act as jurors, or sue at law, although they pay taxes. They try to live simply, abhor worldliness, counsel against too much reading of popular literature, and dress plainly in a uniform garb. The women wear a head covering at all times. Believers are not at liberty to marry unbelievers. They do not participate in the worship of those "who do not live in harmony with the doctrines of Christ." They hold that in any one place there can be only one true church of Christ. They believe "that there may be many individuals throughout the world who are united in spirit with them, but do not have knowledge of the [Reformed Mennonite] Church." They hold that such persons "would not be found joined in worship with those who obviously do not carry out all scriptural teachings, but would, of necessity, stand alone."[6] They reject a literal millennium, regard beneficiary organizations as worldly institutions, and do not engage in business partnerships with nonmembers. They have no Sunday schools and do not engage in missionary work. They select by vote the members of their threefold (and unpaid) ministry of deacons, ministers, and bishops.

The Reformed Mennonite Church has no official headquarters. The address of the Reverend Earl Basinger, one of five bishops, is 1036 Lincoln Heights, Ephrata, Pennsylvania 17522. He reports less than 500 members in the United States and 190 in Canada, gathered in approximately 20 churches, but warns against being "impressed with the statistics of men."[7]

The General Conference Mennonite Church

Mennonite historians use the word "lethargic" to describe the situation of the Mennonite community in North America around the 1840s. The ferment that had agitated other religious bodies in the eastern United States began to penetrate the Mennonite community as well. Issues like the legitimacy of

Sunday schools, the propriety of evangelistic services, the value of Bible study and prayer meetings, the desirability of evening services, and the necessity of better agencies of administration and of intercongregational and denominational boards of missions, charities, education, and publishing continued to recur.

In Pennsylvania the church authorities that represented the conservative past excommunicated John H. Oberholtzer (1809–1895), a young minister and schoolteacher who later became a locksmith and a publisher, and fifteen other ministers for demanding a written constitution. Thereupon they organized the East Pennsylvania Conference of Mennonites in 1847, which called for the keeping of minutes of meetings, putting out a catechism, free association with Christians of other denominations, mission work and Sunday schools, renewal of contact with the European Mennonite community, ministerial visitors to stimulate the congregations to spiritual growth and the abandonment of the traditional collarless ministerial coat.[8]

In 1849, two years after the Franconia Conference had excmmunicated Oberholtzer in Pennsylvania, the Ontario Conference expelled Daniel Hoch (1806–1878) and a number of other leaders. In 1855 three small congregations with Hoch (who ultimately defected to the Mennonite Brethren in Christ) of Ontario and Ephraim Hunsberger (1814–1904) of Ohio as leaders organized the Conference Council of the United Mennonite Community of Canada West and Ohio. This body also stressed both home and foreign missions.

Around 1850 several groups of relatively progressive Mennonites from the Palatinate and Bavaria settled in Illinois and Iowa. This group, led by Daniel Krehbiel (1812–1888), soon established contact with the Oberholtzer group and the Hoch-Hunsberger group. Representatives of the three groups met at West Point, Lee County, Iowa, in 1860, worked out a plan of union, and voted the General Conference of the Mennonite Church of North America into being. The new body grew rapidly and succeeded in attracting most of the late-nineteenth-century Swiss, Polish, Prussian, and Russian Mennonite immigrants. In 1953 it received the Central Conference Mennonites— a central Illinois group that had been organized in 1908 but traced its origins back to the 1870s—and changed its name to General Conference Mennonite Church.

Originally heterogeneous not only in national background, but also culturally in such matters as dress, food, world outlook, understanding of the Bible, and religious practice, the General Conference Mennonite Church has become more homogeneous as it has acculturated to the American scene.

Its basic faith, headed "Our Common Confession" in its constitution, affirms faith in the inspiration and infallibility of the Bible; salvation by grace through faith in Christ; baptism on confession of faith; avoidance of oaths; nonresistance; nonconformity to the world; and "the practice of Scriptural church discipline." It disavows oath-bound secret societies, military organizations, and other groups that "tend to compromise the loyalty of the Christian to the Lord and His Church."[9]

In 1902 and again in 1904 the General Conference Mennonite Church published as its recognized confession an English translation of *De Geloofsleere der waare Mennoniten of Doopsgesinden* ("The Teaching about the Faith of the True Mennonites or Baptists"), which Cornelis Ris (1717–1790) had published in Holland in the 1770s. This thirty-six-article confession has a mildly Reformed thrust and is generally regarded as more liberal than the Dordrecht Confession. The current constitution of the General Conference Mennonite Church appeals to it as a "fuller statement of the General Conference position."[10]

Likewise still in effect is the Statement of Doctrine that the General Conference Mennonite Church adopted in 1941. It accepts the "full Bible and the Apostolic Creed"; the Trinity; Christ's deity, humanity, virgin birth, atoning death, resurrection, and personal return; "the immortality of the soul, the resurrection of the dead, and a future state determined by divine judgment"; the inspiration and infallibility of the Bible; salvation by grace and the transformation of the Christian's life into the likeness of Christ; "nonresistance to evil by carnal means, the fullest exercise of love, and the resolute abandonment of the use of violence, including warfare," as well as nonconformity to the world in life and conduct, after the example of Christ; "prayer as fellowship with God, a desire to be in His will, and in its divine power"; the church as a company of penitent and reborn sinners endeavoring to live the Christian life; and "the brotherhood of the redeemed under the fatherhood of God in Christ."[11]

As far as other denominations are concerned, the orientation of the General Conference Mennonite Church is more toward the United Church of Christ, the American Baptist Convention, and the Methodist tradition. It practices open Communion, fellowships on a broad basis with other denominations, has traditionally had a strong ecumenical interest and a profound missionary concern, and has been hospitable to a wide variety of methods, practices, influences, and doctrines (including dispensationalism, millennialism, fundamentalism, liberalism, and various Reformed theological emphases). Past prohibitions of life insurance and the use of the political franchise have been abandoned. There has been a pronounced trend from a plural, untrained, and unsalaried ministry to a single, trained, and salaried minister, from an elder-bishop in charge of a number of congregations to an elder in each congregation, and from different levels of ordination (evangelist, preacher, elder) to one full ordination.

District conferences meet every year, the delegate general conference every three years. The local congregations are autonomous. The headquarters are at 722 Main Street, Newton, Kansas 67114. There are 188 churches in the United States with a total membership of 35,534, and 147 churches in Canada with a total membership of 23,000. The church body carries on foreign missions in the British West Indies, Latin America, Africa, India, Japan, and New Guinea.

The Conference of the Evangelical Mennonite Church

Henry Egli became the bishop of an Amish congregation near Berne, Indiana, in 1858. Around 1864 he declared that he had experienced a regeneration of the heart. He began to urge the necessity of a similar experience in the case of others and called for the rebaptism of those who had not yet experienced regeneration at the time of their first baptism. He upbraided his fellow Amish for their formalism, their lack of spiritual vitality and depth, and their disregard of the old customs, notably in the matter of dress. As a result a split developed in the congregation, with about half following Bishop Egli. With these supporters he organized his own church, the Defenseless Mennonite Church, popularly called the "Egli Amish," in 1866. It later took the name Conference of the Defenseless Mennonites of North America. The first inter-congregational conference convened in 1883; since 1895 the conference has met annually. The rigid conservatism of the denomination's early years gradually moderated, as the group accommodated itself to the customary standards of dress, accepted the introduction of Sunday schools, dropped the holy kiss among the laity, all but abandoned foot-washing, and admitted instrumental music into its worship services. In 1898 the church sustained a schism with the withdrawal of the founders of the Missionary Church Association. Efforts to reunite the two bodies in the 1940s proved unsuccessful. In 1948 the church adopted its present name. From 1953 to 1963 it participated with the Evangelical Mennonite Brethren in a quasi-union known as the Evangelical Mennonite Conference to carry on joint efforts in missions, education, promotion, and publication.

The Evangelical Mennonite Church has nine Articles of Faith. These discuss the Scriptures ("[the divinely chosen writers] were kept from error whether the truths were familiar or unknown"); the Trinity; Jesus Christ ("[He united] organically and indissolubly the divine and human natures in their completeness in one unique personality"); the Holy Spirit; man's creation, fall, and redemption ("as the gospel of redeeming love is proclaimed, nothing prevents the salvation of the greatest sinner on earth but his own stubborn will and the voluntary rejection of Jesus Christ as his sin-bearer"); salvation through repentance, faith ("it not only believes that the death of Christ is the sacrifice for sin, but is a trust in its efficacy"), justification, regeneration, sanctification ("made possible by a voluntary yielding to God resulting in a separation from sin"), divine healing ("God may work through human instrumentality or directly and independently of human means to alleviate human suffering"); the church; Christ's visible, premillennial, and imminent return in two stages, first to claim his waiting bride and the departed believers, and then, after tribulation, to establish his millennial reign on the earth, followed by the Great White Throne of unbelievers and two eternal conscious destinies for human beings, heaven for the righteous and hell for the unrighteous; and the ordinances ("not a means of salvation but . . . a source of spiritual inspiration and strength")—believer's baptism with the trinitarian formula, preferably by immersion ("water baptism . . . symbolizes the experience of regeneration and union with [Christ]; it does not save or cleanse from sin") and the Lord's Supper ("the emblems of bread and the fruit of the vine . . . symbolize the death of Christ"), open to all believers who feel themselves to be in a right relationship with God, irrespective of denomination, and to be celebrated two or more times annually.[12]

Nine Articles of Practice discuss the Lord's day; Christian stewardship ("tithing their income as a minimum expression of their stewardship"); dedication of infants; marriage ("our ministers may not officiate at the marriage of an unbeliever with a believer") and divorce; the home; Christian discipleship ("persons holding membership in secret societies shall not be eligible for [church] membership"); the Christian attitude toward civil government; the Christian attitude toward strife and military service ("the historic position of the Evangelical Mennonite Church is to oppose arms in warfare [but] the denomination . . . respects the right of individual conviction [and] our churches support our Christian youth who because of faith and conscience accept the exemptions or alternatives to combat service [but] give spiritual aid to all of our youth in service by encouraging them to exert a positive testimony for Christ"); and oaths (" 'Swear not at all' . . . includes the profane oath, the careless byword, and the judicial oath").[13]

The headquarters of the conference are at 7237 Leo Road, Fort Wayne, Indiana 46825. Currently it has 20 churches with 3,123 members. It maintains foreign missions in the Republic of Congo and in the Dominican Republic.

Church of God in Christ, Mennonite

John Holdeman (1832–1900), reared in the Old Mennonite Church by his parents, Amos Holdeman and Nancy, nee Yoder, had a conversion experience at the age of twelve. At the age of twenty-one he reconsecrated his life to God, accepted baptism in his native Wayne County, Ohio, at the hands of Bishop Abraham Rohrer, and sensed a call to the ministry. His own study of the Bible, of the writings of early Mennonites like Menno Simons and Dirk Philips, and of the *Martyrs' Mirror* convinced him that the Old Mennonite Church as he knew it had deviated greatly from its traditions. In 1859 he and a number of others began to hold separate meetings. In his exhortations Holdeman stressed the absolute necessity of the new birth and baptism with the Holy Spirit, of returning to the faith of the Mennonite founding fathers, of disciplining unfaithful church members, of practicing more spiritual rearing of children, and of avoiding apostates, world-minded churches and worldly associations. Early in the 1860s Holdeman and his associates organized the Church of God in Christ, Mennonite. After slow initial progress, the work began to spread. With the advent of Russian Mennonite immigrants to Kansas and Manitoba in 1874 considerable numbers of them in both regions joined the Church of God in Christ, Mennonite. Peter Toews and Wilhelm Giesbrecht led many members of the Kleine Gemeinde (now the Evangelical Mennonite Conference) of Canada into the Holdeman fellowship; Tobias Unruh, formerly of the General Conference Mennonite Church in Kansas, played a similar role.

The Church of God in Christ, Mennonite, accepts the Dordrecht Confession of 1632. In addition it professes twenty-six Articles of Faith of its own. These concern themselves with the Trinity; the fall of the angels; the fall of man; repentance in terms of a true conversion, justification, and new birth; believer's baptism ("we consider all baptisms which are not officiated by the true ministers of the Gospel upon faith in God and His church unevangelical"); the Lord's Supper ("when under certain conditions impure and irreconcilable members take too much time in becoming worthy of the Lord's supper, [this] should not hinder the church to observe [it]"); feet washing; the calling of ministers ("we do not believe that women are called to the office to preach the Gospel"); God's united church; the Scriptural guide ("the Church of God is the supreme judge which God has here on earth for gospel matters"); the relation of the Old and New Testaments; marriage ("when a member [brother or sister] of the Church of God marries outside of God's Church . . . he should be excommunicated"); divorce and remarriage ("the Lord prohibited divorcing excepting in case of adultery; yet we do not believe that a brother or sister should apply for a divorce"); oaths ("swearing of oaths for any purpose and for all circumstances is forbidden"); nonresistance ("the members of God's church cannot be permitted to serve in any office of the magistracy. . . . we shall not go to the polls and vote for men who are to bear the sword"); peace, war, and military service ("if we do noncombatant service . . . we thereby indirectly become responsible for the shedding of blood"); excommunication; avoidance ("we do not believe in a withdrawal which is limited to only withdraw from the Lord's supper, feet washing, kiss of peace, and brotherly counsel"); nonconformity to the world by avoiding theaters, amusement parks, public swimming pools, sports arenas, fairs, tobacco, intoxicating beverages, costly clothing, adorning and plaiting of the hair, wearing of gold and pearls, and the shaving or marring of the beard; method and general procedure of choosing and ordaining a minister; diving healing ("the anointing with oil, laying on of hands and prayer [are] to be administered by the ministry or by their approval"); devotional covering "sisters should wear a Christian devotional covering during worship as well as in praying and prophesying"); usury ("we believe it to be unscriptural to put our money into usury and gain in banks and investment stocks"); Christian nurture of children; high schools and colleges ("[members are to] have the approval of their home ministers"); and the esurrection of the dead ("we hold the amillennialist view of the Kingdom of Christ. . . . those looking for a personal reign of Christ in a liberal kingdom on earth for a thousand years are deceived").[14]

Baptism is by pouring a handful of water from a small vessel.[15] The Lord's Supper is "not the eating of Christ's real flesh nor the drinking of His real blood, but is a sign of the reality, a type and memorial that Jesus has redeemed us from eternal death by the offering of His flesh and blood."[16] The ministry consists of ministers (that is, elders or bishops) and deacons. The ministers are unpaid and depend for their livelihood upon other employment. The governing body of the church is the general conference, which meets on a two-thirds vote of all ministers, deacons, and delegates.

The United States headquarters are at 420 North Wedel Street, Moundridge, Kansas 67107. Including the North American Indian and Spanish-speaking missions, there are 60 churches in 21 states with 7,119 members and 23 churches in 5 Canadian provinces with 2,304 members. The Church of God in Christ, Mennonite, carries on foreign missions in Mexico, Haiti, Nigeria, Belize, India, the Philippines Republic, the Dominican Republic, and Guatemala.

Evangelical Mennonite Conference

The Kleine Gemeinde ("Little Community") came into being between 1812 and 1819 among the Mennonite settlers along the Molochnaya River in the Ukraine, largely through the work and witness of ordained Elder Klaas Reimer (1769?–1837?). The reason for the name is debated; it probably refers to the small size of the group's membership in contrast to the Grosse Gemeinde ("Large Community"). Reimer was an antimillenarian conservative who regarded drinking, smoking, cardplaying, and similar practices as unscriptural, who abominated worldliness in any form (including musical instruments), who insisted upon utmost simplicity in clothing, furniture, and housing, and who found intolerable the necessity of coercive punishment of fellow Mennonites that the existence of a Mennonite ecclesiastical-political community within the Russian state demanded. Once the Kleine Gemeinde had established itself, those within it recognized no true Christians outside their company, while the Grosse Gemeinde refused until 1838 to recognize the Kleine Gemeinde as a Mennonite body.

The fanaticism and extreme of asceticism that marked some of the more radical members of the Kleine Gemeinde helped to bring the whole body into disrepute and to limit its influence severly, although the community made economic progress. It received government recognition in 1843. The 1860s saw a schism in which the branch in the Crimea adopted immersion as the only acceptable mode of baptism and withdrew from the Kleine Gemeinde to form the Krimmer Mennonite Brethren (which merged with the Mennonite Brethren Church of North America in 1960).

In 1874 the Kleine Gemeinde—which then numbered about 100 families

—emigrated en masse to North America under Elder John Friesen to escape the newly imposed obligation of military service in Russia. About one third of the group settled in Nebraska; after suffering some losses, the survivors moved on in 1906–1908 to the vicinity of Meade in southwestern Kansas. The remainder of the emigrants established two colonies in the Red River valley in Manitoba. After 1896 each of the three colonies was autonomous. In the 1880s about one third of the Canadian group withdrew to become part of the Church of God in Christ that John Holdeman had founded. From 1897 on the Brudertal Conference (now the Evangelical Mennonite Brethren) attracted many of the Canadian Kleine Gemeinde members. A schism in the Kansas group in 1944 led to a break in fellowship between the Kansas majority group and the Canadian churches.

Limited modernization took place in the Kleine Gemeinde from 1920 on but the dominant conservatism remained. Following World War II about 15 percent of the Canadian Kleine Gemeinde members, concerned about the inroads of modern life into their privacy and fearful that they might in the future lose the privilege that the Canadian government had accorded them, emigrated to Mexico. In 1958 an Indian mission station was established in Paraguay. In 1952 the Kleine Gemeinde changed its name to Evangelical Mennonite Church; in 1959 the present name was adopted.[17]

The Statement of Faith of the Evangelical Mennonite Conference has sections on the Bible ("we believe in the plenary and verbal inspiration of the Bible . . . inerrant in the original writings"); the existence and nature of God; the creation ("the Genesis account of the creation is historic fact and therefore true"); the fall of man; Jesus Christ; salvation ("alone by grace through faith in Christ"); the Holy Spirit; assurance; the church ("composed of all those who through repentance toward God and faith in the Lord Jesus Christ have been born again and were baptized by one Spirit into one body") separation ("from all worldliness, carnal strifes and contentions in all areas and walks of life; from war, swearing of oaths, worldly amusements"); discipline; ordinances and practices (believer's baptism; the Lord's Supper; feet washing; a symbolic headcovering for women praying and prophesying; anointing of the sick with oil and special prayer in faith; marriage only with those of "like precious faith"); the resurrection of Christ and of all people, Christ's personal second coming; the intermediate state; and the final state.[18] It regards "as of great importance for us" the "Historic Articles of Faith of the Evangelical Mennonite Church of North America, 1954."[19]

There are 41 churches and missions in Canada with 14,146 members. Headquarters address is Box 1268, Steinbach, Manitoba, ROA 2AO.

Hutterian Brethren

The Hutterian Brethren in North America descend from the survivors of the Moravian branch of the sixteenth-century Anabaptist movement. The Anabaptist movement was first established in Moravia in 1528; it was reestablished on a firmer basis in 1533 with complete community of goods as Hutterian Brethren (*Hutterische Brüder*) by the Tyrolese Anabaptist Jacob Huter (burned at the stake in 1536). Hans Amon (d. 1542) succeeded Huter as head bishop of the brotherhood. Under his leadership the Hutterian Brethren began organized missionary activity (with 80 percent of the first missionaries dying martyrs' deaths). The "golden period" of the Moravian brotherhood under Emperor Maximilian II came to an end in 1599 with the advent of the Counter-Reformation. After sustaining serious losses of life and property prior to 1622, the Hutterian Brethren had to flee in that year to Slovakia and Transylvania, where they reestablished themselves under the influential leadership of Andrew Ehrenpreis (d. 1662). The Hutterian Brethren today preserve the Ehrenpreis tradition at least as much as any other, including that of Huter himself.

In Slovakia the exactions of the invading Turks, which the nonviolent Hutterians could not in conscience resist, were followed by forcible external conversion to Roman Catholicism in the latter eighteenth century, although the Hutterites maintained both their cooperative enterprises and, secretly, their religion and a skeleton organization. They have come to be known as Habaner. In Transylvania the accession of Lutheran transmigrants restored the moribund colony in the 1750s, but in 1767 they again felt forced to flee, first to Wallachia, then to the Ukraine. Here small Habaner reinforcements joined them; to escape military conscription under the tsarist regime, the colonists emigrated to South Dakota in the 1870s. Following the persecutions of the voluntary but almost dictatorial State Council for Defense, intense hostility at the local level, and the mistreatment of Hutterite conscientious objectors in federal prisons during World War I, all but one of the South Dakota colonies moved to Canada. The Hutterites have since expanded in both countries.[20]

There are three groups among the Hutterians, traceable to the three original colonies of the 1870s: "Darius people," who came over in 1874, led by Darius Walter; the "Schmiede ['Blacksmith'] People," who came over in 1877, led by Michael Waldner, a blacksmith; and the "Lehrer ['Teacher'] People," who came over in 1879, led by Jacob Wipf, a teacher. The last had not practiced community of goods in Russia, but began to do so in North America; those who preferred private ownership joined other Mennonite groups in the United States.

Hutterite Brethren affirm the Trinity, the deity of Christ, and the community of goods, described in Acts 2 and 4 as practiced by the early Jerusalem church, "as a perfect model of the Church of Christ on earth for all time."[21] They reject "worldly amusements," including "the dance, the theatre, the card-party, carousals, the pool-room, smoking, the circus, the motion-picture show. television and radios in the homes, the popular bathing resorts," and any social gathering where it is not possible to glorify God.[22] They see it as the mission of Christianity "to reform and convert the unregenerate world and to realize the Kingdom of God and Christ on earth by the lives we live."[23] They practice believer's baptism by sprinkling "in the name of the Father, the Son, and the Holy Ghost."[24]

The colonies maintain their own elementary schools (children usually cease their formal education at age fifteen) and pay property, corporation, and required income taxes. They do not exercise their right of franchise or accept old-age pensions or social security.[25]

The Hutterite Brethren's opposition to war is unqualified. They reject "service under the military arm of the government whether direct or indirect, combatant or noncombatant"; service "during war time under civil organizations temporarily allied with the military in the prosecution of war, such as the Y[oung] M[en's] C[hristian] A[ssociation and] the Red Cross"; any "part in the financing of war operations through the purchase of war bonds and war taxes in any form or through voluntary contributions" to civilian organizations allied with the military during war time, "unless such contributions are used for civilian relief or other purposes."[26]

Since the seventeenth century the Hutterite Brethren have not carried on mission work. At their services the sermons are read from the old sermon-books and the worship is largely traditional. They accept conveniences and farm machinery, but do not enter extensively into the life of the communities about them. They continue to copy their manuscript books by hand, and make only limited use of the printing press. The organization and genius of the Hutterian Brethren are reflected in their *Gemeindeordunugen* (ordinances and regulations for the brotherhood as a whole and for certain crafts and orders in the community), the most influential of which go back to Ehren-preis. These ordinances inculcate faithfulness and loyalty to the Hutterite tradition in every detail and are designed to meet and to reduce the temptations that members of the brotherhood encounter. Although the colonists learn English in their schools, their own German dialect is still in general use at home and in church.

There are 72 colonies in the United States, with 8,954 members, and 185 colonies in Canada with 17,358 members. There are no central head-quarters.

Mennonite Brethren Church of North America

In 1788 a company of Mennonites, mostly of Dutch antecedents, moved out of Prussia to Chortitza in the Russian province of Ekaterinoslav. By the mid-nineteenth century they had prospered materially but their spiritual life was of a low order. Then a revival began. Two elements combined to produce it. One was a new wave of immigrants from Prussia who had received spiritual stimulation from the Moravians and who had settled near the older colony in 1835. The other was the preaching of Edward Wüst (d. 1859), pastor of a nearby Lutheran community whose influence penetrated the Mennonite colony and who set up in various places groups that met for prayer and Bible study. The participants in these meetings called themselves "Brethren." The Brethren began to criticize the worldliness of some of their fellow Mennonites and called for more energetic church discipline. When their appeal failed, they requested a separate Communion service. The elders of the Mennonite community rejected this plea, so in December 1859 the Brethren of Gnadenfeld held their own Communion service. The following year eighteen of them organized the Mennonite Brethren Church as an independent religious body. They succeeded in obtaining legal recognition from the Tsar, other likeminded groups began to join them, and the new body grew rapidly. It drew up its own Confession of Faith in 1873 and formally adopted it in 1876.

When the Russian government instituted universal military service in 1870 and announced that the decree was to take effect in the Mennonite colonies in 1880, the Mennonite Brethren began to emigrate to North America in increasing numbers from 1874 on. They settled chiefly in Kansas, Nebraska, Minnesota, and the Dakota territory and began organizing congregations. In 1879 they organized the first annual conference. In 1888 the first church in Canada came into being. In 1902 the Mennonite Brethren Church of North America adopted as its own the Halbstadt Confession—a thorough revision of the 1873–1876 document—and later it had the Confession translated into English.[27]

In 1960 the Krimmer (that is, Crimean) Mennonite Brethren Conference joined the Mennonite Brethren Church. This group was the North American branch of a body organized in the Crimea in 1869. Colonists who had emigrated around 1860 from the same Mennonite community in which the Mennonite Brethren Church arose experienced a spontaneous revival. In 1874 they emigrated almost en masse to Kansas; the Krimmer Mennonite Brethren Conference came into being in 1880. A strain of Kleine Gemeinde influence out of their early years helped to reinforce for a long period of time their native conservatism and their resistance to both worldliness and acculturation.

The theological position of the Mennonite Brethren Church is typical of the Mennonite tradition. Participation in military service is forbidden. Conversion—in the sense of individual repentance and acceptance of Christ as Savior in faith—is essential to salvation and church membership. Baptism is exclusively by immersion. The church observes foot washing in connection with Holy Communion.

The congregations in the United States use English almost exclusively, while the Canadian churches have held more tenaciously to German.

There are 101 churches with 14,081 members in the United States, and 119 churches with 15,807 members in Canada. The denomination carries on missions in Austria, Germany, India, Japan, and Latin America, staffed by 224 missionaries. In 1966 it participated in the organization of the World Conference of Mennonite Brethren Churches with a total membership of about 85,000, one fourth of them in the Soviet Union, but decided not to pursue conversations looking toward organic union with other Mennonite bodies.[28]

Conservative Mennonite Conference

The Mennonite statistician M. S. Steiner coined the name "Conservative Amish Mennonite" around the turn of the century to differentiate this group of churches from the Old Order Amish churches, on the one hand, and from more progressive Amish Mennonite conferences, on the other. In 1910 Bishop S. J. Schwartzendruber and the Reverend M. S. Zehr, the ministers of the Conservative Amish Mennonite congregation on the Pigeon River near Pigeon, Michigan, invited the ministers of like-minded churches to attend a ministers' meeting in the Michigan church. At this meeting the ministers of three congregations formed the Conservative Amish Mennonite Conference. With the passage of time the policies and functions of the conference gradually clarified, although it was not until 1945 that it adopted a written constitution and by-laws. In 1954 it dropped the adjective "Amish" from its official name. It is sometimes referred to as the Conservative Mennonite Church.

The official statement of belief of the Conservative Mennonite Conference has always been the eighteen-article Dordrecht Confession of Faith. At the 1967 General Conference, the Conservative Mennonite Conference supplemented this statement of belief by espousing the Mennonite Confession of Faith adopted in 1963 by the Mennonite General Conference. The conference has stressed evangelism, benevolence, personal sanctification, and separation from the world. Specifically it has forbidden fashionable attire, the use of tobacco and intoxicating beverages, every kind of participation in war, worldly business associations, secret societies, life insurance, and the holding of political office.

The conference has approximately 90 congregations with 6,000 members. It carries on foreign work in Germany, Luxembourg, and Costa Rica. It is intimately associated with the Mennonite Church and reports its statistics through that body. Its address is Grantsville, Maryland 21536.

Evangelical Mennonite Brethren Church

The Brudertaler Mennonite Church at Mountain Lake, Minnesota, was the scene in 1889 of the organization meeting of the Conference of United Mennonite Brethren, popularly called the "Brudertaler Conference" and made up of Mennonite immigrants from Russia during the 1870s. Its leaders were Elders Isaac Peters and Aaron Wall. The new body demanded evidence of the new birth of a changed life as a requirement of baptism and church membership, called for a separated life as evidence of the new birth, and insisted on more rigid church discipline. Initially baptism was by pouring. The mode has since been made optional. In 1937 the group changed its name from

)efenseless Mennonite Brethren of Christ in North America to the Evangeli-
al Mennonite Brethren Church. From 1953 to 1963 it was loosely associated
'ith the Evangelical Mennonite Church in the Evangelical Mennonite Con-
:rence; the geographical distance between the congregations of the two groups
'as the chief reason for terminating the federation. The Evangelical Menno-
ite Brethren Church has 35 churches in the United States and Canada with
total membership of 4,150. It also has 300 members in Paraguay and carries
n foreign missions through a number of affiliated and nonaffiliated mission
rganizations. The headquarters are at 5800 South 15th Street, Omaha,
;ebraska 68107.

vangelical Mennonite Mission Conference

A schism in the conservative Sommerfeld (Manitoba) Mennonite congre-
ation as a result of the evangelistic activity of I. P. Friesen led in 1936–1937
) the organization of the Rudnerweide Mennonite Church. From the begin-
ing the new body exhibited a profound concern for both home and foreign
issions, as well as for discipleship, education, and Bible schools. While the
udnerweide Mennonites adhere to the same tenets as the parent body from
'hich they separated, and use the same catechism, they have laid greater stress
n an active and spiritual church life, on true conversion, on good fellowship
the church, and on cleanness of living. Unlike the mother church, they
llow their elected ministers to preach from a biblical text rather than require
em to read sermons handed down from the past. In 1959 they took the
ame of Evangelical Mennonite Mission Conference. There are 26 churches
nd missions in 4 Canadian provinces and 4 missions in Mexico, Bolivia, and
elize with a total membership of 2,400. Foreign missionaries are at work in
Aexico, Belize, Bolivia, Trinidad, Japan, West Germany, St. Lucia, Brazil,
ava, Philippines, and Ecuador. Headquarters address is Box 126, Winnipeg,
Aanitoba R3C 2G1, Canada.

onservative Mennonite Fellowship (Nonconference)

In the mid-1950s a number of Mennonites became greatly concerned
bout what they regarded as growing liberalism within the main branches
f the Mennonite movement in North America that had over wide areas
ermitted the conservative standards of nonconformity, nonresistance, and
:hristian separation from civil affairs to lapse. They were no less concerned
bout the invasion of many Mennonite institutions and publications by what
ey called neo-orthodoxy in theology. As a practical expression of this con-
ern they organized the Conservative Mennonite Fellowship (Nonconference)
n 1956. It accepts the Apostles' Creed, the Schleitheim Confession of 1527,
he Dordrecht confesssion of 1632, and the Christian Fundamentals of 1964.
The principle of separation from the world is a major emphasis.[29]
Once organized, the fellowship established effective contact with the

similarly minded Mennonite local fellowships. These cooperating group
sponsored a series of annual biblical discipleship and fellowship ministeria
meetings in 1962 at Shedd, Oregon, in 1963 at Sheldon, Wisconsin, and in
1964 at Hartville, Ohio. The last-named assembly published as a supplemen
to the Dordrecht Confession a statement of faith called "Christian Funda
mentals." It is designed as a supplement to the Dordrecht Confession and a
a restatement of the Articles of Faith accepted by the Mennonite Genera
Conference at Garden City, Missouri, in 1921. The eighteen articles concer
themselves with the Word of God ("we believe in the plenary and verbal in
spiration of the Bible . . . that it is . . . inerrant in the original writings. . . .
We reject Neo-orthodoxy, intellectualism, relativism, and other philosophie
where the authority of the word is rejected, questioned, or displaced b
human reason"); the Trinity; Jesus Christ ("born of a virgin, the perfect God
man; that He was without sin, the divinely appointed sacrifice, who by Hi
death on the cross made the only atonement for sin by the shedding of Hi
blood"); the Holy Spirit ("we warn against modern healing and tongue
movement, and the second work of grace emphasis"); creation ("the Genesi
account of creation is a historic fact and literally true"); the fall of man
salvation ("man is saved by the mercy and grace of God through faith in th
redemptive work of Christ, the power of the word of God, and the indwelling
renewing, and regenerating work of the Holy Spirit"); assurance ("the teach
ings of [absolute] predestination and unconditional eternal security of th
believer give false assurance of salvation"); the church as the body of Chris
("neither an ecclesiastical hierarchy . . . nor a democracy . . . but the churc
is a theocracy. . . . We consider intercongregational fellowship, counseling
and conferring both scriptural and necessary"); discipline ("the churc
must . . . maintain a pure and holy fellowship by exercising impartial, loving
scriptural discipline"); separation from the world, including the renunciatio
of "courtship and intermarriage with unbelievers, membership in secret order
and worldly business or labor associations," "of cooperation with religiou
organizations who do not hold to the whole Gospel," "luxury and ostentatiou
display," of immodest, flashy or superfluous clothing or makeup, weddin
rings, church weddings and funerals "which detract from the simplicity c
the Gospel," of instrumental music in worship, "sports, movies, television, an
radio," of participation in military service, "holding public office, voting, o
applying pressure on the government," and of life insurance; the ordinance
of water baptism of believers ("we reject the formal public dedication c
children"), of the Lord's Supper with close Communion and clean Com
munion, literal observance of the washing of the saints' feet as regularly a
the Lord's Supper, of the holy kiss practiced by brothers with brothers an
sisters with sisters whenever they meet, of the woman's veil worn at all time
of anointing of the sick with oil, and of marriage as indissoluble except b
death ("remarriage while the former companion is living is a state c
adultery"); the propagation of the faith; apostasy ("the emphasis on highe
education [colleges, universities, and seminaries] has resulted in the a

ceptance of ungodly philosophies and centralization of power that has under-
mined the faith of many"); the resurrection of Christ and of both the just
and the unjust; the personal, imminent coming of Christ; the intermediate
state ("the righteous will be with Christ in a state of conscious bliss and
comfort, but . . . the wicked will be in a place of torment, in a state of conscious suffering and despair"); and the final state.[30]

The Conservative Mennonite Fellowship (Nonconference) has 23 congregations with just over 980 members; it carries on a foreign mission in Guatemala. The cooperating local fellowships total about 50 congregations with a
membership estimated at over 2,400.[31]

Conservative Mennonite Church of Ontario

Around the mid-twentieth century some of the Old Mennonites in Ontario noted with increasing dismay what seemed to them a general disregard
for the historical Anabaptist landmarks and a toleration of liberal views on
the inspiration of the Bible and on morals. Under the leadership of Bishops
Moses H. Roth and Curtis C. Cressman a number of ministers and congregations organized to oppose this drift from traditional positions; the parent body
expelled the dissidents in 1959 and the latter thereupon organized the Conservative Mennonite Church of Ontario.

The Constitution and Faith and Practice, which they drew up in 1962,
affirms adherence to the Dordrecht Confession of 1632 and to the Christian
Fundamentals drawn up by the Mennonite General Conference in 1921. It
prohibits the use of strong drink and tobacco, attendance at movies, theaters,
dance halls, and similar carnal indulgences and amusements, including all
organized sports; the sale and use of television sets; listening to radio programs that are not conducive to holiness or that proclaim only a partial gospel;
wearing wedding rings, gold watch bands and other jewelry, as well as lace
and other ornamentation; membership in worldly organizations, secret orders,
and life insurance societies; the use of the coercive power of the law; carnal
warfare and military service of every kind; participation in politics, including
voting or jury service; divorce with subsequent remarriage; instrumental
accompaniment of church singing; church rehearsals and floral displays at
weddings; and extravagance at funerals. It calls for Christian women to wear
a veil and uncut hair and for sobriety and simplicity of dress for both men
and women.[32]

There are 8 congregations with 234 members.[33]

Mennonite Christian Brotherhood

The Mennonite Christian Brotherhood was organized in 1960 by congrega-
tions and ministers that withdrew from the Lancaster Mennonite Conference.
It has adopted the Articles of Faith drawn up by various nonconference
Mennonite groups at Hartville, Ohio, in 1964.[34] It holds that the New

Testament is the fuller revelation and as a higher standard is binding in such matters as marriage and returning good for evil. It administers believer's baptism by pouring; observes foot washing and Communion semiannually; practices close Communion and prohibits its members from receiving Communion in churches with a different faith and practice; sanctions marriage only when both parties are believers and live a nonconformed and nonresistant life; requires women members constantly to veil their heads with a covering; directs observance of the holy kiss when applicants are received into fellowship, in connection with foot washing, and often otherwise; encourages its members to call on the ministers for anointing with oil when sick; fixes rigid principles for attire; prohibits combatant and noncombatant military service under penalty of forfeiture of membership, as well as the assumption of governmental or civil offices, taking part in elections, or serving on juries; bans the sale and use of radio, television, tobacco, and intoxicating beverages; and forbids musical instruments in the home and the cultivation of secular music appreciation.[35] It sees these practices as the fruit of Christian experience, and as the works which accompany sound faith.

It has 4 congregations in Pennsylvania and 1 in Ohio, with a total membership of 160. The largest congregation is near Mount Pleasant Mills, Pennsylvania.

NOTES

1. J. C. Wenger, *The Mennonite Church in America* (Scottdale, Pa.: Herald Press, 1966), p. 15. See also *Declaration of Commitment in Respect to Christian Separation and Nonconformity ot the World: A Statement Adopted by Mennonite General Conference, August 27, 1959* (12-page pamphlet).
2. *Mennonite Confession of Faith*, 3rd printing (Scottdale, Pa.: Herald Press, 1964), pp. 7-25.
3. Ibid., pp. 27-29.
4. See also chap. 13, "Major Features of Anabaptist-Mennonite Theology," in Wenger and Bender, pp. 254-303; *The Theology of Christian Experience: A Statement Adopted by Mennonite General Conference, August 27, 1957* (3-page pamphlet); and *The Way of Christian Love in Race Relations: A Statement Adopted by Mennonite General Conference*, August 24, 1955 (10-page pamphlet).
5. Communication from Paul N. Kraybill, General Secretary.
6. *The Reformed Mennonites: Who They Are and What They Believe* (10-page pamphlet) (Lancaster, Pa.: Reformed Mennonite Church, 1968), p. 10.
7. Communication from the Reverend Earl Basinger, Bishop.
8. The new conference sustained some divisions in its turn. In 1851 a bishop and a minister whom the new conference had excommunicated organized the Trinity Christian Society (which eventually disappeared). In 1857 the new conference prohibited prayer meetings; when William Gehman (1827–1918) refused to accept the conference's decision, the conference excommunicated him and twenty-three others. They organized as the Evangelical Mennonites, a group which later merged with other groups to bring the Mennonite Brethren in Christ (now part of the Missionary Church) into being.
9. *Constitution of the General Conference Mennonite Church*, rev. edn. of 1956 3rd printing (Newton, Kansas: General Conference Mennonite Church, 1964), pp. 4-5.

10. Ibid., p. 5. In 1904 and in 1906 the General Conference Mennonite Church published a German translation of the same document.

11. Appendix 2, ibid., p. 31.

12. "Articles of Faith," *Evangelical Mennonite Manual*, rev. edn. (Fort Wayne, Indiana: Evangelical Mennonite Church, 1960) (72-page brochure), pp. 11-28.

13. "Articles of Practice," ibid., pp. 29-36.

14. *The Confession of Faith and Minister's Manual of the Church of God in Christ, Mennonite*, 3rd edn. (Lahoma, Okla: The Publication Board of the Church of God in Christ, Mennonite, 1962), pp. 31-58.

15. Ibid., p. 62.

16. Ibid., p. 67.

17. For the bulk of the historical information here offered, the present writer gratefully acknowledges his indebtedness to the Reverend Archie Penner, Kidron, Ohio, for making available to this writer the unpublished paper which the Reverend Mr. Penner had written in 1950, "A Brief History of the Kleine Gemeinde."

18. *The Constitution and By-Laws of the Evangelical Mennonite Conference* (Steinbach, Manitoba: Derksen Printers, 1960) (61-page pamphlet), pp. 13-17.

19. Text, ibid., pp. 37-61. The "brief introduction" to this document notes that "it has not been possible to trace the exact connections between it and the confessions which are much older. However, its content, as well as its spirit and approach, together with its direct historic connections, are in full accord with the historic confessions of the Mennonite church" (p. 36).

20. Eberhard Arnold took the name for his Society of Brothers from the Hutterian Brethren, as well as some details of organization and practice. But there is no direct connection between the two groups. The Hutterian Brethren gave a liberal grant to the Society of Brothers in its Paraguayan phase. See Paul K. Conkin, *Two Paths to Utopia: The Hutterites and the Llano Colony* (Lincoln, Neb.: University of Nebraska Press, 1964), pp. 95-98.

21. *The Hutterian Brethren of Montana* (Augusta, Mont.: Hutterian Brethren

of Montana, 1965) (41-page brochure), p. 4.

22. Ibid., p. 10.

23. Ibid., p. 12.

24. Ibid., p. 20.

25. Ibid., pp. 23-30.

26. "A Statement Submitted by Montana Hutterites, 1951," in Michael L. Yoder, ed., *Statements of Religious Bodies on the Conscientious Objector*, 4th edn. (Washington, D.C.: National Service Board for Religious Objectors, 1963), pp. 30-31.

27. *Confession of Faith of the Mennonite Brethren Church of North America: American Edition* (Hillsboro, Kan.: Mennonite Brethren Publishing House, 1965).

28. Communication from the Reverend Orlando Harms, 308 South Madison Street, Hillsboro, Kansas.

29. One of the missionaries of the fellowship, William R. McGrath, has adapted a religious song by Etta Gibson Hoffman, "Christ Makes the Difference" (sung to the tune of "I Thank the Lord My Maker" by George J. Webb). The McGrath version contains these stanzas:

1 God's standard for His people
  Has always been the same;
A call to separation
  Down through the ages came:
He wants us to be holy,
  His challenge still is hurled
That His peculiar people
  Be different from the world! . . .

4 He furthermore declares that
  All godly women dress
In modest, plain apparel
  And thus His Name confess.
No gold or pearls for Christians,
  Bobbed hair or painted face,
No knee-length skirts—
  We're different,
Redeemed by saving grace!

5 Men their holy hands, unstained
  By nicotine, should lift,
Rejecting neckties, pins, rings,
  And all such worldly drift.
True Christians take no part in
  Carnal warfare's murd'rous arts,
For Christ disarmed His soldiers
  And reigns within our hearts! . . .

7 Our interests are quite different—
No radio, TV!—
With those who walk in darkness
What concord can there be?
Business, marriage, social life—
Unequal yokes beware!—
"Come out and be ye separate!"
The word of God declares.

(William R. McGrath, *Separation Throughout Church History*, 3rd edn. [Mission Home, Va.: William R. McGrath, 1966], p. 53.)
30. For the full text see "Christian Fundamentals," in *Mennonite Confession of Faith*, 2nd printing (Crockett, Ky.: Rod and Staff Publishers, 1966), pp.

91-109.
31. Letters from Brother William R. McGrath, missionary, Conservative Mennonite Fellowship (Nonconference), Mission Home, Virginia.
32. *Constitution and Faith and Practice of the Conservative Mennonite Church of Ontario* (N.p.: N.p., 1962) (12-page pamphlet).
33. Letters from Bishop Curtis C. Cressman, Route 1, New Hamburg, Ontario, Canada.
34. *Mennonite Christian Brotherhood: Statement of Standards* (Crockett, Ky.: Rod and Staff Publishers, n.d.), pp. 1-17.
35. Ibid., pp. 23-30.

BIBLIOGRAPHY

Bennett, John W. *Hutterian Brethren: The Agricultural Economy and Social Organization of a Communal People.* Stanford, Calif.: Stanford University Press, 1967. A study of six Hutterian colonies in Saskatchewan made in 1964 and 1965. Chap. 2, "Hutterian History and Beliefs," pp. 23-52, is of special interest.

Conkin, Paul K. *Two Paths to Utopia: The Hutterites and Llano Colony.* Lincoln, Neb.: University of Nebraska Press, 1964.

Dyck, Cornelius J., ed. *Introduction to Mennonite History: A Popular History of the Anabaptists and the Mennonites.* Scottdale, Pa.: Herald Press, 1967. Chap. 14: "The General Conference Mennonite Church," pp. 192-208.

Friedmann, Robert. *Hutterite Studies.* Goshen, Ind.: Mennonite Historical Society, 1961.

Hofer, Peter. *The Hutterian Brethren and Their Beliefs.* Starbuck, Manitoba: Hutterian Brethren of Manitoba, 1955. Particularly important for its treatment of the baptismal vows.

Hostetler, John A., and Huntington, Gertrude Enders. *The Hutterites in North America.* New York: Holt, Rinehart, and Winston, 1967. A firsthand inquiry, which surveys the Hutterites of the United States and Canada in terms of cultural anthropology.

Lehman, Jacob S., and Lehman, Abraham, eds. *Christianity Defined: A Manual of New Testament Teaching on the Unity of the Church, Nonresistance of Evil, Nonconformity to the World in Deportment and Dress, the Proper Observance of the Ordinances, Separation from All Unfaithful Worship; Dissertation on Marriage, the Millennium, and Beneficiary Organizations.* Lancaster, Pa.: Reformed Mennonite Church, 1958. A 349-page survey of Reformed Mennonite doctrine and practice based chiefly on the works of Daniel Musser, John Kohr, Eli Herr, and Jacob S. Lehman.

Mennonite Confession of Faith, Adopted by Mennonite General Conference August 22, 1963. 3rd printing. Scottdale, Pa.: Herald Press, 1964.

Peters, Victor. *All Things Common: The Hutterian Way of Life.* Minneapolis: University of Minnesota Press, 1965.

Ridemann, Peter. *Confession of Faith.* Rifton, N.Y.: The Plough Publishing House, 1970. Peter Ridemann, or Riedemann (1506–1556), wrote his *Rechenschaft unserer Religion, Leer und Glaubens* ("Account of Our Religion, Teaching, and Belief") while in a Hessian prison in the 1540s. First published in 1565, it has become a major factor in forming the faith that underlies the communal life of the Hutterian communities all over the world, including those in North America.

Toews, John B. *Lost Fatherland: The Story of the Mennonite Emigration from Soviet Russia, 1921–1927.* Scottdale, Pa.: Herald Press, 1967.

Wenger, J. C. *The Mennonite Church in America, Sometimes Called Old Mennonites.* Scottdale, Pa.: Herald Press, 1966.

13. Baptist Churches

Baptist Beginnings in America

The Baptist tradition in the United States and Canada began with English Baptists who first came to the American colonies in the middle part of the seventeenth century. The first Baptist congregation was organized in Providence, Rhode Island, in 1639, through the assistance of Roger Williams (1603?–1683) and attracted refugees and rebels from the Massachusetts Bay Colony to the north. In 1641 John Clarke established a second Baptist congregation in Newport, Rhode Island. In spite of vigorous efforts by the Congregationalists in Massachusetts to keep them out, Baptists came to that colony, and in 1665 the first Baptist Church in Boston was formed.

The Providence congregation was Calvinist, or "Particular," in doctrinal orientation, asserting that Christ died for the elect. An Arminian, or "General," doctrinal position gained the ascendancy in the 1650s, as Baptists in Rhode Island affirmed that Christ died for all. They reorganized the Providence congregation and established additional churches in the colony. In 1670 four General Baptist churches in Rhode Island formed the first Baptist Association in North America. The Arminian Baptists in New England resisted the Great Awakening in the eighteenth century and experienced considerable growth after the revival had ebbed.

Philadelphia was destined to become the chief center of Baptist growth. Immigrants from Wales and Ireland established several Particular Baptist churches there in the late seventeenth century. In 1707 five congregations from three colonies formed the Philadelphia Baptist Association, which became a major stimulus for Baptist mission. Missionaries of the association journeyed through the colonies of the eastern seaboard, gathering converts into churches. By 1760 the association included churches from seven colonies, from Connecticut to Virginia, and became an organizational model for new associations in other colonies. The association adopted the Philadelphia Confession of Faith, a slightly emended version of a confession of English Baptists, which in turn was a form of the Presbyterian Westminster Confession, modified in accord with key Baptist convictions. In 1764 members of the association founded Rhode Island College (later Brown University).

In the southern colonies the first Baptist congregations were formed by English Baptists in South Carolina in 1696 and in Virginia in 1714. Two New Englanders, Shubal Stearns (b. 1706) and Daniel Marshall (b. 1706), who with others in New England had moved from a Separate Congregationalism to a Separate Baptist position, settled in Sandy Creek, North Carolina, and in 1755 started a Separate Baptist congregation there. By 1758 they had organized the Sandy Creek Association and extended their outreach into Virginia, South Carolina, and Georgia. There was tension between the Separate Baptists and the Calvinist Baptists who, under the Philadelphia Baptist Association, had begun work in North Carolina in 1729. They chose to call themselves Regular Baptists, forming the Ketockten (Virginia) Regular Baptist Association in 1765 and the Kehuckee (North Carolina) Regular Baptist Association in 1769. In 1787 the Regular and the Separate Baptists of Virginia merged.

Baptist beginnings in Canada were the result of transplantings of New England Baptists. In 1763 an entire Baptist congregation moved from Swansea in the Massachusetts Bay Colony to Sackville, New Brunswick. That same year other Baptists from Massachusetts who had resettled in Nova Scotia formed a congregation at Horton (now Wolfville). In 1800 nine churches including the New Brunswick congregation organized the Nova Scotia Baptist Association.

By the time of the American Revolution the Baptists were the third largest denomination in the colonies, superseded only by the Congregationalists and the Presbyterians. Their growth resulted especially from their ability to gather the poor and lower classes. The first black Baptist congregation was organized in Silver Bluff, South Carolina in 1775. In decades after the war the Baptists were successful in gaining members among the black population. As the eighteenth century began Baptists were involved in major missionary thrusts and could count nearly fifty Baptist associations.

American Baptist Churches in the U.S.A.

The American Baptist Churches in the U.S.A. (formerly the American Baptist Convention) was organized as the Northern Baptist Convention in 1907. In a sense, however, its organizational history goes back almost a century more.

In May 1814 the Baptists of America met in Philadelphia to bring into being the [Triennial] General Missionary Convention of the Baptist Denomination in the United States of America for Foreign Missions and its interim executive board, the Baptist Board for Foreign Missions for the United States. Preparing the way for this development were the creation of the Congregational and Presbyterian American Board of Commissioners for Foreign Missions (1810), the organization of many Baptist missionary societies at the local and regional level, and the conversion of missionaries Adoniram Judson (1788–1850) and Luther Rice (1783–1836) to the Baptist position on their way to Asia. Basically the convention was a missionary society, but in 1817 it took a step toward becoming a denominational convention when education, home missions, and journalism were added to its responsibilities. In 1826 the opponents of a national denominational convention—reflecting in part the influence of Baptists in England—succeeded in eliminating these other activities and reducing the convention's function to the carrying on of foreign missions.

Another problem was emerging: slavery. Prior to 1830 Baptist pronouncements against slavery came almost equally from the North and from the South. But from that year onward Baptists in the North began to urge emancipation more and more strongly, while those in the South increasingly defended slavery as an institution. The General Missionary Convention tried to maintain a neutral stance, but many northern leaders were impatient with this position. As a result the American Baptist Free Mission Society came into existence in 1843. In 1845 the Southern Baptist Convention was organized and absorbed the agencies and activities of the General Missionary Convention in the South. The next year the latter recognized the changed situation by changing its name to the American Baptist Missionary Union.

During the first half of the nineteenth century the Baptist community was pushing westward through the energetic efforts of its missionaries, of whom John Mason Peck is one of the outstanding examples.[1] Between 1820 and 1830 state conventions had begun to come into being in all the eastern and middle states, and twenty of the twenty-five that had come into existence by 1843 were related to the Home Mission Society.

This was the period when the Restoration movement associated with the name of Alexander Campbell (1788–1866) seriously depleted the ranks of the Baptists in the Midwest and the Southwest, when the Adventist teachings of Baptist layman William Miller (1782–1849) greatly disturbed the denomination's churches of the East, and when the antimission movement vigorously opposed the efforts in missions and evangelism that were winning the West and the Midwest. Theologically, the antimission movement was the result of an overemphasis on a Calvinistic predestinarianism that gave theological justification to an unwillingness to try to convert "aliens," of a biblicism that justified opposition to missionary organizations as unscriptural, and of a degree of envy of the theologically educated ministers on the part of the uneducated preachers.

The expansion and growth of the Baptist community in the North continued after the War between the States. New educational institutions opened at both the college and the divinity school levels. Existing theological schools included the theological faculties of Colgate University and the University of Rochester, and the Newton Theological Institution. To these were now added the Baptist Union Theological Seminary in Chicago (1865–1867)[2] and Crozer Seminary (1867).

During the generation prior to the creation of the Northern Baptist Convention, there was a palpable increase in ecumenical spirit among the bulk of the eventual constituency of this body, marked by comity arrangements, participation in interdenominational activities, and a broad acceptance of the principle of open Communion. The success of revivalism led to a divorce between evangelism and theology, which resulted in a certain aridity and superficiality of theology at the local church level. The theology that was generally professed was conservative and mildly Calvinistic. The New Hampshire Confession of Faith—with its deliberately taken position between the rigorously Calvinistic Philadelphia Confession and the Armnian Free Will Baptist Confession of Benjamin Randall—was in wide use. The *Systematic Theology* of Augustus Hopkins Strong, of the Rochester seminary, which went through four editions between 1886 and 1893, exerted great influence.

During this period the seminaries began to address themselves to the theological implications of the new biology, of geology, of sociology, and of the literary and historical criticism that European scholars were applying to the Bible. On the crucial biblical issue three views emerged: (1) the Bible is a fallible but useful record of the encounter and experiences of human beings with God; (2) the Bible is God's authoritative revelation, but there must be a reconciliation of the insights derived from it with the best elements and the assured results of scientific research; (3) the Bible is literally inerrant and no criticism that denies this is admissible.

One of the foci of controversy was the theological faculty at Colgate University, where William Newton Clarke (1841–1912) published *An Outline of Christian Theology* in 1894. Another was the University of Chicago Divinity School, which numbered on its staff Shailer Matthews (1863–1941), Shirley Jackson Case (1872–1947), and George Burman Foster (1858–1918). In 1906 the last-named published his *The Finality of the Christian Religion*, in which he denied both the inspiration of the Bible and Christ's deity.[3]

At this juncture 226 churches organized the Illinois Baptist State Association at Pinckneyville, Illinois, in 1907, as a protest against inclusivism.[4]

That same year the Northern Baptist Convention came into being at Washington, D.C., as "an organized expression of denominational unity." In the new body the America Baptist Missionary Union (known after 1910 as the American Baptist Foreign Mission Society), the American Baptist Home Mission Society, the two parallel women's organizations, and the American Baptist Publication Society became cooperating societies; the state conventions were the affiliating organizations; and the local churches were the basis of representation. The constitution affirmed its belief in the independence of the local church and the purely advisory nature of representative denominational organizations. The result was that the Northern Baptist Convention was to secure the money, to furnish the delegates, to supply inspiration and fellowship at the annual assemblies, to operate on a limited budget, and to possess a degree of authority incommensurate with its vast responsibilities. The difficulty of combining local church representation with the society method of organization proved to be formidable, and the rivalry of the independent cooperating organizations sometimes created considerable friction. With the passage of time the importance of state conventions and the influence of their executive officers, the state secretaries, have increased. Efforts to reorganize the convention along lines established by current requirements have been almost continuous. In 1961 a study by the American Institute of Management, with certain modifications and refinements, was implemented. Under the new plan the General Council and the general secretary received more power, while the cooperating societies and boards in effect became program agencies of the convention. The change in name to American Baptist Convention came in 1950.

In 1911, 1,586 Free Will Baptist churches with about 90,000 members merged with the Northern Baptist Convention. One concern from the beginning of the convention has been with what some have called the "Southern Baptist invasion" of territory that American Baptists regarded as theirs— especially Illinois, Indiana, Ohio, California, and Oregon. The "invasion" was occasionally justified on the ground that the American Baptist Convention practiced open Communion or "alien" immersion, held membership in the National Council of the Churches of Christ in the United States of America, or "did not preach the Gospel." There has been a limited kind of counter-invasion of the South by the American Baptist Convention since 1950.

Both the impassioned advocacy of the "social gospel" by men like Walter Rauschenbusch (1861–1918) in the period prior to World War I and the long-drawn-out fundamentalist-modernist controversy that was burgeoning when the Northern Baptist Convention was organized in 1907 took their toll in the convention. In 1922 a group of conservative leaders organized the Fundamentalist Fellowship in opposition to the theological liberalism in the denomination and its participation in the Interchurch World Movement of North America.[5] In 1922 a proposal to have the convention recommend the New Hampshire Confession of Faith to the local churches was defeated by a ratio of 2 to 1 with the passage of a substitute motion affirming the New Testament as the "all-sufficient ground of our faith and practice." This affirmation was repeated in 1946, when the fundamentalists in the convention proposed to require a creedal statement of all missionaries, and again in 1949.

In 1925 the convention defined a Baptist church in terms of New Testament loyalty, believer's baptism, and baptism by immersion; in 1926 it amended its constitution to require that all delegates to the convention be immersed church members. The failure to achieve a condemnation of open Communion and of "alien" immersion and to bring about the withdrawal of the convention from the Federal Council of the Churches of Christ in America led to the secession of an Arizona group in 1928. Liberalism in the leadership and centralization of authority in the convention was the reason given for the withdrawal in 1933 of the group that formed the General Association of Regular Baptists. The refusal of the convention's General Council in 1945 to recognize the Conservative Baptist Foreign Mission Society as a legitimate organization within the convention, in addition to the decision of the 1946 convention to adjust the number of local delegates in terms of the percentage of benevolent funds contributed by the sending church to convention causes, led to the organization of the Conservative Baptist Association of America in 1947.[6]

The union conversations between the American Baptists and the Disciples of Christ between 1947 and 1952 went as far as a joint Communion service in connection with simultaneous conventions in Chicago in the latter year, but instead of voting for the union, the American Baptists discharged the Baptist section of the Union Committee. It appears that institutional rather than theological factors accounted for this action.

While the (Swedish) Baptist General Conference withdrew in 1944 and set up its own program, in 1956 the Norwegian Baptist Conference of North America and in 1958 the Danish Baptist General Conference dissolved and turned their respective assets and programs over to the American Baptist Convention.[7]

In 1960 the convention responded to an influential church's proposal to delete all references to ecumenical organizations from the convention's literature by reaffirming its ecumenical relationships. Efforts from within the convention to have it participate formally in the Consultation on Church Union have been unsuccessful.

Lacking a confessional commitment, the spectrum of theological conviction within the American Baptist Churches is very broad. It ranges from proponents of thoroughly conservative traditional positions like Carl F. H. Henry through representatives of the theologies of Karl Barth, Reinhold Niebuhr, and Paul Tillich to Colgate-Rochester's William Hamilton, one of the most articulate spokesmen of the "God-is-dead" movement. With the secession of large numbers of fundamentalists the mean position of the American Baptist Convention theologically is probably the farthest left of the Baptist center among the major organizations in the Baptist family of churches. Social concerns continue to engage a great deal of the convention's attention.

In 1972 the name American Baptist Churches in the U.S.A. was adopted. Since 1962 the headquarters have been at Valley Forge, Pennsylvania 19481. There are 6,005 churches with 1,579,029 members, a figure that in spite of withdrawals and accessions has remained fairly stable since World War I. Membership in the American Baptist Churches in the U.S.A. is not exclusive and dual memberships in both the American and the Southern Baptist conventions are not uncommon for churches located in the border states. The foreign missions program of the American Baptist Churches in the U.S.A. (including American Baptist-related conventions overseas) reaches out to Burma, India, Thailand, Hong Kong, Japan, Okinawa, the Philippines Republic, and Europe.

Southern Baptist Convention

According to the Baptist World Alliance, world membership in Baptist churches has passed the 33 million mark. More than one third of the approximately 30 million Baptist members in the United States belong to churches affiliated with the Southern Baptist Convention, the largest Protestant body in the United States. In a remarkable way, the convention secures cooperation among Baptist churches for the purpose of mission and evangelism without destroying the autonomy of local churches to determine their own doctrine and practice.

Already in the seventeenth century Baptists began settling in the south, and their numbers expanded rapidly during the Great Awakening of the eighteenth century. Between 1814 and 1845 Baptists in the South cooperated with northern Baptists in the General Missionary Convention, the Baptist General Tract Society, and the American Baptist Home Mission Society. In 1840 there were about 320,000 Baptists in the states below the Mason-Dixon line and 250,000 in the states above it.[8]

In the two decades before the Southern Baptist Convention was organized in 1845, decentralization and abolitionism gathered impetus among Baptists in the North, while centralization and antiabolitionism prevailed among Baptists in the southern states. Social, political, and economic factors influenced religious life and eventually divided northern and southern Baptists even before the Civil War tested the national fabric. Northern and southern Baptist literature showed the growing importance of sectional interests, which found a focus in the cause of abolition in the north and the defense of slavery in the South. The cooperative ventures of the two groups of Baptists suffered. While slavery was not yet a divisive issue in 1832 when the American Baptist Home Mission Society was formed, the next year English Baptists addressed a lengthly treatise to American Baptists stressing the successes of the English emancipation movement. The document asked, "Is [slavery] not an awful breach of the Divine Law, a manifest infraction of that social compact which is always and everywhere binding?" The letter divided Baptists, though not until abolitionism gained increasing strength in American Baptist ranks was division fully along sectional lines. Slave uprisings in the South in the later 1830s brought fear to many. The General Convention in 1841 tried to maintain unity among Baptists, but in 1844 a major crisis arose when the Georgia Baptist Executive Committee nominated James E. Reeve to the Home Mission Society for appointment as a missionary. The committee volunteered the information that Reeve was a slaveholder. The society's executive Board refused to consider the case; it reasoned that the test case violated the purposes and letter of the constitution and circumvented the society's neutrality. In November 1844 the Alabama Baptist State Convention initiated the last step leading to the creation of a separate convention in the South. It insisted in a resolution that slaveholders were no less eligible than others to serve as agents and missionaries of the society. The Acting Board replied that if a person owning slaves should offer himself as a missionary "and should insist on retaining them as his property, we could not appoint him. One thing is certain; we can never be a party to any arrangement which would imply approbation of slavery."[9]

In 1845 the American Baptist Home Mission Society decided at a meeting that it would be more helpful if members would carry on their work in separate organizations for North and South. A convention was called to meet in May in Augusta, Georgia, to organize the Southern Baptist Convention. A leading figure in this organizational meeting was William B. Johnson of South Carolina, who had been one of the founders of the General Missionary Convention and for a time its president. Nearly three hundred accredited messengers attended the meeting; all but twenty were from the states of Georgia, South Carolina, and Virginia; but Alabama, the District of Columbia, Kentucky, Louisiana, Maryland, and North Carolina were also represented. Johnson was elected president after proposing the formation of "one Convention, embodying the whole Denomination, together with separate and distinct Boards, for each object of benevolent enterprise, located at different places, and all amenable to the Convention." While the convening messengers did not officially approve the Address to the Public that was issued, the document explained that the reason for the separation was basically constitutional, that separation had to occur for the sake of the missionary imperative, and that missionary societies had no right to judge the moral character and integrity of slaveholders, since this was the local church's responsibility. But the new convention's constitution incorporated what seemed to be opposing provisions. In a radical departure from previous Baptist societal patterns, the convention was structured as a single organization for all benevolences, including home and foreign missions. In contrast with this new type of convention structure, the constitution retained the old society pattern of financing and representation. Article III prescribed that the convention would consist of "members who contribute funds, or are delegated by religious bodies contributing funds." This method of financing the convention's work prevailed until 1925, but it meant that the convention had no funds of its own. Much criticism arose that the strictly financial plan of representation was not representative or equitable.[10]

By 1860 four new state organizations had been created in Texas, Arkansas, Louisiana, and Florida. Nine state organizations (South Carolina, Georgia, Alabama, Virginia, North Carolina, Missouri, Maryland, Mississippi, Kentucky) were already functioning in 1845 when the Southern Baptist Convention was organized. Forty-two of the 135 messengers at the 1846 convention were representatives of state bodies and local associations, while the others were from missionary societies, churches, and individuals making contributions to the convention. In 1861 this group sent only eight messengers, while state bodies and local associations sent 169 of the 177 delegates.[11]

The Landmark movement, or "Old Landmarkism," troubled the convention intermittently during the second half of the century and finally brought a minor schism early in the twentieth century. The principal antagonist in the conflict, J. R. Graves (b. 1820) of Memphis, Tennessee, was assisted by J. M. Pendleton of Kentucky and others. Landmarkism, which took its name from the "old landmarks" of New Testament Christianity that Graves sought to preserve, had three major emphases, each with ramifications in doctrine and polity. First, it stressed the authoritative character of the local and visible New Testament congregation, which was identified as Baptist. The result was antagonism toward any organization or doctrine detracting from the primacy of the local church. Second, Graves asserted that local congregations, the true churches of Christ, composed the Kingdom of Christ. Third, he insisted that to be part of this unbroken Kingdom of Christ, true churches had to possess all the doctrinal and churchly characteristics of the primitive churches. Landmarkers claimed that all pedobaptist bodies were unscriptural; they were not "churches" but "societies" that could not conduct the Lord's Supper or practice scriptural baptism. Their ordinations were not valid, and since their ministers were not New Testament ministers, they were not to be invited to share Baptist pulpits, as was sometimes the practice. Landmarkers claimed that only members of the local church should participate in the Lord's Supper ("close Communion"). They argued that the other ordinance of baptism also demanded close supervision; a church might readily accept a person baptized by another Baptist church without reimmersion, but an immersion based on confession of faith that was performed by a non-Baptist should not be recognized.

The Landmarkers' major target in the Southern Baptist Convention was its Foreign Mission Board, which they deemed unscriptural, unnecessary, and ineffective. Graves's newspaper, *The Tennessee Baptist*, reached over 10,000 subscribers with his message. In 1855 the convention felt the impact of his movement when the usual resolution to invite ministers of other denominations to join the proceedings was debated a full day before it was finally withdrawn. Four years later Graves again mounted a major assault on the convention, but the anti-Landmark states of Virginia, North Carolina, and South Carolina had more than a majority of the delegates and regularly defeated his proposals. Graves and his followers retained a good deal of power despite the fact that after 1859 there was less interest in abolishing the convention than in changing its character. Homer L. Grice, a historian of Landmarkism remarked that the Civil War "brought at least one great blessing to Southern Baptists: It ended the greatest controversy that ever afflicted them." The movement never again attained the strength it had before the war, but it did influence the convention appreciably. Among its long-term influences are the following: (1) an emerging ecclesiological emphasis that demanded modification of the strictly financial basis of representation to the convention to include some reference to church representation; (2) the practice of many Southern Baptist churches that restricts the Lord's Supper to Baptists alone, and in many cases to people who are members of the congregation observing the ordinance; (3) a general disinterest in cooperation with other denominations; (4) opposition to "alien immersion" and pulpit exchange. Landmarkism was part of a widespread "high church" movement in America in the mid-nineteenth century. Its central emphasis on the local church left an indelible imprint on the Southern Baptist Convention, especially in the Southwest where it was the strongest.[12]

During the Civil War the Southern Baptist Convention quite naturally gave full and unequivocal support to the Confederacy in public resolutions. One major result of the war was the exodus of perhaps as many as 400,000 black Baptists from the convention to organize their own bodies. Before the war some black Baptist preachers served churches in the convention; the membership of some churches was wholly black, but in other cases, separate pastors, deacons, and organizations for blacks and whites functioned within one church. During the Civil War the convention's foreign mission board funded its foreign workers by setting in motion a process through which cotton was run through the northern blockade and sold in England at a high price for cash that was channeled to Asia and Africa by secret commercial agents.[13]

During the Reconstruction era the northern Home Mission Society worked in and with the various southern states, since the Southern Baptist Convention refused organic union with the society. After long debate, the convention voted decisively in 1879 to continue functioning independent of the northern Baptists. The fact that the war seriously disrupted home missions in the South complicated matters. Dr. Patrick H. Mell was the convention's president during the troubled years 1861–1871 and again in 1879–1887.[14]

Toward the end of the century several comity conferences were held with representatives of the northern Home Mission Board, but they did not lead to any conclusive decisions that enabled the northern Baptists to work in the South. By 1917 it was clear that the Southern Convention had established a firm geographical base in the South while not ruling out the possibility of work in the North. In addition, in 1891 a permanent Sunday School Board undertook the publication work that the northern American Baptist Publication Society provided up to the Civil War, when an unsuccessful southern board had been created. By 1917 the constituency of the Southern Baptist Convention relied almost exclusively on the Sunday School Board for publications of all kinds. In addition to these two major successes, the Southern Baptists also weathered an ultimatum presented by about one hundred Landmark churches in 1905; the schism that followed was small. In many instances, the backbone of the new Southern Baptist church was a fervent "tentmaking" preacher who labored during the week at a secular job such as farming, but then exercised his license to preach or his ordination on

Sunday in the small congregation that heard him willingly. Reportedly in 1877 there were almost twice as many churches in the convention as there were ordained ministers. Unpaid preachers carried a good share of the load during this period of amazing growth in the rural areas of the South and the Southwest.[15]

The Foreign Mission Board had its headquarters in Richmond, Virginia. Work began first in South China, and Southern Baptists moved into North China in 1860. Before a third section of China was opened, the "Gospel Missionism" movement arose as a counterpart of the Landmarkers' opposition to the Home Mission Board's control of home missions rather than the local church's. But foreign work gathered momentum nonetheless. Africa was entered in 1856, and in 1870 a mission was opened in Italy followed by Brazil in 1880, Mexico the same year, and Japan about the same time. Nearly $3 million was contributed for foreign missions between 1845 and 1900. In the twentieth century the foreign mission program expanded rapidly into other South American countries (Argentina in 1900, Chile in 1917), Palestine, Syria, Yugoslavia, Hungary, Romania, the Ukraine, Spain, and other parts of Asia, Africa, and Europe. The constant goal was to develop self-sustaining churches, but the economic difficulties of the twenties caused a temporary retrenchment. After 1888 the development of the annual "Lottie Moon Christmas Offering for Foreign Missions," which recognized the work of a female missionary to the Chinese, was an important factor in the growth of foreign mission work. In 1977 the goal for this offering was $34 million. In 1976 the convention had 2,700 missionaries in 82 countries.[16]

The Home Mission Board was located in Marion, Alabama, until 1882 when it was moved to Atlanta, Georgia. Initially work was carried on among blacks and Indians, but there was also much interest in winning New Orleans for Protestantism. Vast areas of the South and the Southwest were evangelized by missionaries hired by the board. It employed only 22 missionaries in 1877, but this number leaped to 1,507 in 1917, due in great part to the aggressive leadership of Isaac T. Tichenor, its chief executive until 1899. Most of the work concentrated in rural areas, but Cuba and Panama were under the board's jurisdiction. The annual Annie T. Armstrong Easter Offering has played a major role in the board's work. In 1976 the board reported that 2,082 home missionaries were at work in the fifty states and Puerto Rico, while 1,208 "summer missionaries" worked in "bold Missions."[17]

Membership statistics show the rapid expansion of the Southern Baptist Convention in the nineteenth and twentieth centuries. Between 1846 and 1860 the average annual membership growth rate was 4.79 percent; membership increased from 367,017 to 649,518. The Civil War slowed the average annual membership growth rate to 2.25 percent up to 1877, when membership totaled 1,418,296. By 1917 the convention had 2,844,301 members; during the intervening period the average annual membership growth rate was 5.22 percent, while the population of the states served by the convention had an average annual increase of only 3.23 percent. During the same period Presbyterians increased at an average annual growth rate of 4.53 percent, Methodists at 3.77, and Roman Catholics (after 1891) at 3.91 percent. The number of Southern Baptist churches nearly doubled from 12,864 in 1877 to 24,883 in 1917. The average annual membership growth rate rose to 5.90 percent between 1917 and 1972, but the increase in total membership—from nearly 3 million in 1917 to over 12 million in 1972—made it difficult to sustain this rate, which was nearly three times the population's growth rate between 1920 and 1970. In 1940 there were slightly more than 5 million members, by 1950 slightly more than 7 million, 10,772,712 in 1965, 10,962,463 in 1966, and 12,067,284 in 1972. The convention's annual average membership increase of nearly 6 percent between 1918 and 1972 compared favorably with the growth of Episcopalians (3.57 average each year), the Lutheran Church—Missouri Synod (2.30), United Methodists (1.49), and United Presbyterians (1.29). In 1972, nearly 54 percent of all Southern Baptists lived in the eight south-central states of Kentucky, Tennessee, Alabama, Mississippi, Arkansas, Louisiana, Oklahoma, and Texas; these states made up 54 percent of the membership in 1917 as well. The convention's membership figures in 1973, 1974, and 1975 were 12,297,346; 12,515,842; and 12,735,663, respectively; a slower rate of growth was evident during the 1970s. In terms of new growth in membership, it required 28 years (1873) for the Convention to reach the 1 million mark, 34 more years (1907) for 2 million, 13 more years (1920) for 3 million, 12 more years (1932) for 4 million, 8 more years (1940) for 5 million, 6 more years (1946) for 6 million, 4 more years (1950) for 7 million, 4 more years (1954) for 8 million, 4 more years (1958) for 9 million, four more years (1962) for 10 million, five more years (1967) for 11 million, and 5 more years (1972) to reach the 12 million mark. In 1975 five state conventions had nearly half the total number of Southern Baptist members: Texas (2,073,284), North Carolina (1,082,175), Georgia (1,078,623), Tennessee (957,771), and Alabama (926,007), followed next by Florida (736,531). About 420,000 persons are baptized in one of the nearly 35,000 Southern Baptist churches each year. It is reported that about 90 percent of all Southern Baptist churches have fewer than 1,000 members, although at least 20 congregations have more than 6,000 members. The largest is First Baptist Church of Dallas, Texas, with 18,870 members; it is headed by the convention's former president, the Reverend Dr. W. A. Criswel. Ten of the 20 largest congregations are in Texas. Southern Baptists were said to have contributed $1.6 billion in 1976, up more than $300 million from the year before. In 1976, for the first time, indebtedness of Southern Baptist congregations exceeded the $1 billion mark. The value of all property reported in the convention in 1975 was $6.2 billion.[18]

The convention's geographical base remained fairly constant until World War II. Between 1845 and 1942 only six additional states—Arizona, California, Illinois, New Mexico, Oklahoma and Texas—were added to the original fourteen state conventions affiliated with the convention. But in less than thirty years this geographical base was extended to all fifty states in the Union. In 1951 the convention resolved that the Home Mission Board and all other agencies "be free to serve as a source of blessing to any community or people anywhere in the United States." In part this action was a response to the National Baptist Convention's change of name. Initially the Southern Baptist's northward expansion was largely due to the strong denominational consciousness of members who moved north. The first congregation was created in the New England region in 1960, New York in 1955, Pennsylvania in 1959, New Jersey in 1960, Delaware in 1951, Ohio sometime around 1940, Indiana and Michigan in 1914, Wisconsin in 1953, Minnesota in 1956, Iowa in 1954, North Dakota in 1953, South Dakota in 1953, Nebraska in 1955, Kansas in 1911, Wyoming in 1951, Montana in 1952, Colorado in 1954, Utah in 1944, Idaho in 1951, Nevada in 1951, and Oregon in 1946. By 1958 there were thirty-three Southern Baptist churches in West Virginia. The first church in Alaska was organized in 1943 and in Hawaii in the early 1940s. A Baptist church in Vancouver, British Columbia, was for the first time received into affiliation with the Oregon–Washington convention of the Southern Baptist Convention in 1953. The convention's rapid numerical and geographical growth has been attributed to a number of factors including "the simple biblical emphasis and democratic ecclesiology," the numerous instances of self-sustaining ministries, "identification with the culture-patterns of the environment," evangelical zeal, the role of leaders, the convention's structure and resulting denominational consciousness, the absence of significant schism, and the growing emphasis on an educated ministry. In the early 1970s, 62 percent of the denomination's 30,500 pastors had college education (14 percent) or more (48 percent), while only 8 percent had less than twelve years of education.[19]

In Puerto Rico the first Southern Baptist church was organized in 1965 at Aguadilla. Together with several others, this congregation maintained affiliation with the Tampa Bay Association of Florida until 1964, when the Home Mission Board appointed a superintendent of missions to coordinate the work in Puerto Rico. In 1965 the Puerto Rico Baptist Association was organized; it affiliated with the Southern Baptist Convention. By 1971 there were 11 churches, 15 missions, and about 20 preaching stations. In 1975 there were 10 missions in Puerto Rico.[20]

During the twentieth century the convention moved on several fronts to refine and solidify its organizational structure. The creation of the Sunday School Board in 1891 represented a significant step toward bridging the gap between the traditional program of supporting a few basic benevolences, such as home and foreign missions, and the convention's total denominational thrust. The profits of this new agency were a new source of income for the denomination that opened the way toward new undertakings. Between 1892

and 1951 the board provided nearly $11 million for causes within denomina-
tional channels. In 1975 the board provided nearly a $2 million subsidy to
the convention and state conventions. In 1917 the convention created an
Executive Committee to carry out limited responsibilities between conventions.
Despite much debate, the method of representation remained as it had been
in 1845: membership in the convention consisted of (a) messengers who
contributed funds or were elected by Baptist bodies that contributed funds
on the basis of one messenger for each $250 contributed to one of the boards,
and (b) one representative elected from each of the district associations
cooperating in the convention.[21]

After World War I the convention set a major goal of collecting $75
million in five years. Nearly a hundred million dollars were subscribed, but
financial conditions and other limitations resulted in a collection of only $59
million in 1920–1924. Two lasting results of the five-year campaign were
that Southern Baptists became more conscious of stewardship, while at the
same time it was recognized that a more systematic approach was necessary
for raising and disbursing finances within the convention. The Cooperative
Program of receipts and expenditures was soon designed by the Executive
Committee. However, since the major campaign fell short of its goal, the
boards faced a period of financial distress and debt. The Executive Committee was given increased power and responsibility in 1927, but it faced difficult
times; the radical drop in baptisms between 1925 and 1929 preceded the
serious drop in gifts between 1930 and 1933. In 1931 the constitution was
altered to provide a different basis for representation to the convention. As
subsequently revised and refined, the pertinent article provided that the convention would be composed of messengers who are members of missionary
Baptist churches cooperating with the convention; each church that contributes to the convention's work during the preceding fiscal year has one
messenger; one additional messenger may be elected from each church for
every 250 members, or for each $250 paid to the convention's work during
the preceding fiscal year; no church can send more than ten messengers, and
messengers must be members of the church by which they are appointed.
This provision for designated church representation was slightly different
from the Landmark proposal for delegated church representation. The new
provision gave larger churches more messengers and rewarded churches for
larger financial gifts, but it set a maximum of ten messengers. Subsequent
constitutional revisions in 1946 and 1958 have created a dual structure for
carrying out the convention's work. The principle of state representation on
the convention's boards, commissions, and standing committees was formally
adopted. This state-based form of representation is penultimate in authority,
aristocratic, widely representative, and powerful. The other form of representation is in the convention itself; this form is ultimate in authority, democratic,
and less representative. One observer of the polity structure wrote that "it is
likely that 95 percent of all deliberation is done by the penultimate dual

structure composed of over 1,000 leaders. Committees have not supplanted the authoritative Convention, but have evolved into technical and deliberative subsections of Convention life to bring recommendations to the whole body, thus supplementing the Convention."[22]

The Southern Baptist Convention has met annually since 1866. Thirty-four state conventions are presently affiliated with the convention. The constitution defines the convention's authority in Article IV: "While independent and sovereign in its own sphere, the Convention does not claim and will never attempt to exercise any authority over any other Baptist body, whether church, auxiliary organization, association, or convention." If each cooperating church sent only one messenger to the convention, attendance would be nearly 35,000. Since a greater number of messengers attend a convention held in their geographical area, the choice of a meeting place seems to have an effect on deliberations and voting. In 1963, for example, only about 20 percent of the 32,000 affiliating churches sent messengers; about 13,000 registered for the convention. The 1976 convention in Norfolk, Virginia, had 18,637 registered messengers; James L. Sullivan of Tennessee was elected president. The convention has four general boards, seven institutions (including six seminaries and the Southern Baptist Foundation, Nashville, Tennessee), seven commissions, and one auxiliary, the Woman's Missionary Union. The convention in 1976 approved a Cooperative Program budget of $55 million dollars for the next fiscal year. Women have been officially seated in the convention since 1918, although in 1877 and again in 1882 women were enrolled as members of the convention.[23]

A large pastor's conference is usually conducted immediately before the annual convention. Called "The Southern Baptist Pastors' Conference," it was started in 1935 by Pastor M. E. Dodd of Shreveport, La., who was president of the group until 1949. Dodd had also served as the convention's president in 1933–1935 and was a major figure in the formation of the Cooperative Program. The pastors' conference ordinarily includes inspirational music and preaching, some theological review, and practical advice on pastors' problems.[24]

The convention has demonstrated little interest in the ecumenical movement. The secretary of the Foreign Mission Board attended the annual meetings of the Foreign Missions Conference of North America between 1893 and 1919, then interest waned until 1938 when the board became a member of the Foreign Missions Conference. When this conference sought to merge with the National Council of Churches, the board voted unanimously in 1950 to withdraw from the conference. The convention declined an invitation to membership in the World Council of Churches on the grounds that such a "great over-all world ecclesiasticism would depend more on political pressure than upon spiritual power," among other reasons. In 1948 the president of the convention, Louis D. Newton, helped to found the Society of Protestants and Other Americans United for Separation of Church and State; the convention endorsed the new organization that same year. The convention has shown little interest in the National Association of Evangelicals and the Consultation on Church Union, but it regularly sends fraternal messengers to the annual sessions of the American Baptist Convention and the National Baptist Convention. The convention is the largest body affiliated with the Baptist World Alliance, a voluntary organization linking 106 Baptist conventions and unions with a combined membership of 29 million Baptists in 123 countries, 25.6 million of whom live in North America. The alliance was organized in London in 1905 and has met intermittently since then. Its most recent meeting was in Stockholm, Sweden, on July 8-13, 1975; the fourteenth meeting is scheduled for Toronto, Canada, in 1980. About four million Baptists in the world are not affiliated with the alliance, which according to its constitution serves "as an expression of the essential oneness of Baptist people in the Lord Jesus Christ, to impart inspiration to the brotherhood, and to promote the spirit of fellowship, service, and cooperation among its members." David Y. K. Wong of Hong Kong was elected president of the Baptist World Alliance in 1975. The alliance's General Secretary is Robert S. Denny, 1628 16th St., N.W., Washington. D.C. 20009.[25]

Religious education, Sunday schools, and music programs play an important role in Southern Baptist churches. Membership in Southern Baptist Sunday schools increased appreciably in the twentieth century, from an enrollment of 490,000 in 1891 to 3,400,000 in 1944, and another gain of a quarter million students by 1954. Forty-three senior colleges and universities were affiliated with the convention in 1976; they enrolled about 100,000 students, while ten junior colleges affiliated with the convention enrolled another 10,000 students. The convention operates six seminaries to train pastors and other church workers, including music and education ministers. They are Golden Gate Baptist Theological Seminary, Mill Valley, California; Midwestern Baptist Theological Seminary, Kansas City, Missouri; New Orleans Baptist Theological Seminary, New Orleans, Louisiana; Southeastern Baptist Theological Seminary, Wake Forest, North Carolina; Southern Baptist Theological Seminary, Louisville, Kentucky; and Southwestern Baptist Theological Seminary, Fort Worth, Texas. These schools had approximately 8,000 students in 1976. Southwestern Seminary is reportedly the world's largest seminary with an enrollment of 3,200 in the fall of 1976. At American Baptist Theological Seminary, Nashville, Tennessee, the convention cooperates in the training of black Baptist pastors through the American Baptist Seminary Commission, a commission sponsored jointly with the National Baptists.[26]

The Southern Baptist Convention's first step toward considering evils of the social order was prompted by the use of liquor traffic. With public sentiment growing and the temperance movement gathering influence, the convention of 1907 instructed its president to appoint a committee to arrange a mass gathering at its next meeting to consider social questions through mutual counsel. Since this time standing committees of the convention have reported on various aspects of the social scene. The Commission on Social Service created in 1913 soon absorbed the Committe on Temperance. This commission's first report insisted that "the Christian Church is directly responsible for the right solution of social problems" including "war, whether economic or political," "the traffic in alcohol and the habit-forming drugs," "vice," and "diseases which cut short the life otherwise spent in long service of the kingdom." It called on the church to "transform the individual life, infect it with the ideal of the kingdom, train it for the work on the kingdom." Most of the state conventions structured similar commissions, but in general the social views of Southern Baptists have been more conservative than most other major Protestant groups. A variety of explanations have been offered. Some suggest that Southern Baptist social attitudes have been shaped largely by a culture that resists urbanization and industrialization, but at the same time these Baptists were strongly committed to religious and political freedom. As a result, the sense of social responsibility traditionally followed in second place after the emphasis on individual salvation. John Lee Eighmy asserted that Baptist polity, on which ultimate authority rests in the autonomous congregations, tends to keep church leaders from supporting progressive social causes. He claimed that Southern Baptist churches usually reflect the attitudes of the surrounding culture rather than inspire social change. Revivalism encouraged greater concern for the spiritual and moral welfare of individuals than for the day's social problems. It should also be noted that the Social Gospel movement gave little attention to the chief social problem facing the South, namely, the race question, and in this sense it offered little in the way of an alternative for the Southern Baptist churches. The doctrinal liberalism of the movement had little appeal in the South.[27]

National and state conventions repeatedly took stands opposing intemperance, desecration of the Sabbath, gambling, and motion pictures, while encouraging high standards for family life. During World War II the convention recognized the right of a conscientious objector to stand by his conscience, but provided no financial support for his work in labor camps. In 1944 the convention appointed a Committee on World Peace to mobilize and register the feelings and opinions of its members in behalf of an enduring peace in a democratic world, as well as in behalf of Christian race relations, equal economic opportunity, and religious liberty. Southern Baptists contributed over $3 million in relief efforts after the war. The nagging problems of race relations and racial prejudice were taken up by the convention on a nmber of occasions. In 1954, 1959, and 1961 it urged churches to accept the Supreme Court decision on desegration, and its Christian Life Commission annually recommended ways to ease racial tensions, although progress was slow. In 1965 the 3,500 delegates of the North Carolina Baptist Convention condemned the Ku Klux Klan and its "perverted use of the Christian Cross." At the same time, Baptists in Virginia acknowledged "before God our partnership in guilt in the long, dark night of injustice and discrimination." At that summer's earlier Southern Baptist Convention, the Christian Life Commission, headed by Foy Valentine, brought to the floor a strong report against racial discrimination. This report was countered by a motion to delete the commission's proposed $18,500 budget increase, but the motion was defeated by a 2 to 1 vote. The convention's president, Wayne Dehoney, remarked that this convention signaled a shift from "reactionary, negative thinking and introspection to a fresh outlook and spirit." Three years later, in 1968, the Executive Committee presented a strong statement condemning racism, which received an affirmative vote of 73 percent.[28]

In 1972 the convention passed a resolution putting the convention "on record as opposed to any and all forms of anti-Semitism; that it declare anti-Semitism un-Christian; that we messengers to this Convention pledge ourselves to combat anti-Semitism in every honorable, Christian way." In a letter released by the White House in May 1977, a leading Southern Baptist layman, President Jimmy Carter, affirmed his personal gratification that there was a consensus among Christian churches rejecting "the charge that the Jewish people as a whole were then or are now responsible for the death of Christ."[29]

In 1976 the convention affirmed "our commitment to the biblical truth regarding the practice of homosexuality as sin," and urged "churches and agencies not to afford the practice of homosexuality any degree of approval through ordination, employment, or other designations of normal life-style." In a heated debate on abortion the convention affirmed the biblical view of the sanctity of human life, including fetal life, and urged Baptists not to use abortion as a means of birth control. The messengers also affirmed "our conviction about the limited role of government in dealing with matters relating to abortion, and support [of] the right of expectant mothers to the full range of medical services and personal counseling for the preservation of life and health." In 1977 the convention heavily applauded statements opposing gambling, immorality and violence on television, pornography, and profanity. Anita Bryant's antihomosexual campaign received a great ovation. Two resolutions opposed a governmental ruling that would permit both unmarried couples and homosexuals to live together in public housing, and opposed the hiring of homosexuals as teachers. Another resolution strongly opposed "abortion on demand and all governmental policies and actions which permit this." Other resolutions discussed senior citizens, hunger, the blind, energy, torture, and the security of South Korea.[30]

The 1977 convention also objected to the Internal Revenue Service's attempt to define "an integrated auxiliary of the church," contending that the IRS had no authority to make such a decision.[31] In doing so the convention reaffirmed long-standing Baptist convictions on the interrelation of religious liberty and the separation of church and state. The convention the previous year had declared that "the preservation of religious liberty and the right to religious diversity in the United States of America depends on keeping government—federal, state or local—out of the religious affairs of the churches" and urged all affiliated organizations to "be alert to detect and prompt to reject governmental threats to religious freedom."[32]

From Southern Baptist perspective, strict separation of church and state is the inevitbale consequence of concern for religious liberty. The voluntary character of faith requires religious liberty, which includes the right of the individual to be a Christian and of a group of Christians to be the church. Religious liberty implies "not only that the church is not to be arbitrarily subject to persecution and restriction by the state in fulfilling its mission, but even more important, is not to be dependent upon the sanction or support of the state in carrying out its mission in the world."[33] On the basis of this position Southern Baptists have consistently opposed the use of federal and state funds for children in nonpublic schools.

Concern for religious liberty and separation of church and state has led Southern Baptists to join with eight other national Baptist bodies in the United States and Canada to sponsor the Baptist Joint Committee on Public Affairs. The committee maintains four programs: government relations (communicating Baptist concerns to government agencies), denominational relations (correlating Baptist influence in public affairs), study and research (analyzing legislation, court decisions, government regulations), and information services (reporting trends and developments in public affairs).

At its organization in 1845 the Southern Baptist Convention declared, "We have constructed for our basis no new creed, acting in this matter upon a Baptist aversion for all creeds except the Bible."[34] Yet the concern to uphold specifically Baptist convictions has led the Southern Baptist Convention to adopt statements of faith from time to time, not as prescriptive norms of teaching but as affirmations of consensus.

The most widely used and influential statement of doctrine among American Baptists is the New Hampshire Confession, published in 1833 by the authority of the Board of the Baptist State Convention of New Hampshire and circulated in a revised and enlarged form by one of its authors, J. Newton Brown.[35] The New Hampshire Confession was the basis for a Statement of Faith authorized for publication by the Southern Baptist Convention in 1925 as its response to the fundamentalist-modernist controversy. The 1925 statement added on to the New Hampshire Confession ten additional sections concerning the resurrection, the return of the Lord, religious liberty, peace and war, education, social service, cooperation, evangelism and missions, stewardship, and the Kingdom of God. The confession was intended to serve not as a final or infallible statement of belief or as an authoritative creed or as an attempt to hamper freedom of thought, but as a consensus of opinion by this particular session to assist in the interpretation of the Scriptures.[36] Nevertheless, many Southern Baptists objected to the adoption of the confession on the grounds either that it would do little good or that it was not the prerogative of a convention to adopt such a confession.

The adoption of the confession of faith did not satisfy those who wanted a more clear statement against the theory of evolution. In 1926 the convention adopted as its own the statement of its chairman against evolution articulated in his opening address. Though a resolution requiring all of the convention's institutions, boards, and missionary representatives to acquiesce to the statement was adopted later in that convention, there was no way to enforce the resolution.

In 1962 dissatisfaction over teaching in the theological seminaries erupted in open controversy at the convention in San Francisco. Focus of the controversy was Midwestern Baptist Theological Seminary Professor Ralph H. Elliott's *The Message of Genesis*, which used some of the methods of historical criticism in interpreting Genesis. The 1962 convention affirmed faith in the entire Bible as the authoritative, authentic, infallible Word of God and rejected views which would undermine the historical accuracy and doctrinal integrity of the Bible, though the convention also declined to ban Elliott's book "in keeping with the historic Baptist principle of the freedom of the individual to interpret the Bible for himself."[37]

An outgrowth of the confrontation was the decision to prepare a new Statement of Faith as an interpretation of the statement adopted in 1925. Under the leadership of Convention Chairman Herschel H. Hobbs a committee presented a revised and updated version of the 1925 statement to the 1963 convention. In adopting the new statement the convention affirmed "that they are statements of religious convictions, drawn from the Scriptures, and are not to be used to hamper freedom of thought or investigation in other realms of life."[38]

The 1963 "Baptist Faith and Message" is comprised of seventeen separate articles on Scriptures, God, Man, Salvation, God's Purpose of Grace, the Church, Baptism and the Lord's Supper, the Lord's Day, the Kingdom, Last Things, Evangelism and Missions, Education, Stewardship, Cooperation, the Christian and the Social Order, Peace and War, and Religious Liberty. In each article there are doctrinal statements followed by a section of extensive Scripture references.

Even with the adoption of "The Baptist Faith and Message" Southern Baptists do not take a monolithic doctrinal stance. A basic principle is spiritual liberty.[39] Faith is voluntary and cannot be predetermined by baptizing children in infancy, nor assumed to be present when they reach maturity. Association with a religious body must also be voluntary, with the local congregation autonomous. Considerable diversity goes hand in hand with spiritual liberty. Some accept alien immersion and open Communion while others reject them. Some espouse Landmark views, others denounce them. Some engage in ecumenical relations, others take no part in them.[40]

According to one Southern Baptist spokesman, distinctive beliefs and practices include the following: (1) the authority and sufficiency of the Scriptures; (2) the responsibility and competency of the individual to deal directly with God; (3) salvation as God's gift of divine grace received by man through repentance and faith; (4) a regenerated church membership; (5) each church as an independent, self-governing body of immersed believers, the members possessing equal rights and privileges; (6) the ordinances as symbols and reminders; (7) baptism, by immersion of believers only; (8) absolute religious liberty for all; and (9) complete separation of church and state.[41]

The main features of Southern Baptist life include a major stress on evangelism and missions and a tradition of ministry to the common people. Southern Baptists claim a long tradition of eloquent evangelists, among whom the most well known is Billy Graham (1918–   ). Southern Baptists worship is simple, reflecting frontier traditions and focusing on the sermon. The *Baptist Hymnal*, published in 1975, includes 512 hymns and a series of Scriptures "for individual, union, responsive, or antiphonal reading."[42] The frequency of the observance of the Lord's Supper varies from church to church, though it is usually on a monthly basis. "The bread and the fruit of the vine are but symbols of the broken body and spilled blood of Jesus . . . a remembrance of what the Lord did for our salvation . . . until he comes again."[43] Baptism does not bring salvation; it pictures it. It is necessary not as a means of obtaining salvation but in order to obey the Lord's command. Immersion is the only proper form of baptism.[44]

Ordination of a pastor or an elder is on the basis of a congregation's request that the individual serve it as pastor and is performed by a group of ordained ministers. Ordination of women is not prohibited, but women ministers are rare.[45] The office of deacon is the only other office recognized by Southern Baptists as authorized in the New Testament.

Southern Baptist congregations are completely autonomous, "under no head except Christ."[46] Out of a desire to cooperate, congregations join together to form district associations, state conventions, and the national Southern Baptist Convention. Meetings of all organizations are on an annual basis. Yet the power of the congregation is never delegated. "There may be messengers of a church, but they cannot be delegates in the ordinary sense of the term."[47]

There are 34,880 churches in the Southern Baptist Convention with an inclusive membership of 12,733,124. Headquarters are at 460 James Robertson Parkway, Nashville, Tennessee 37219.

The National Baptist Convention of the United States of America, Incorporated

The oldest black Baptist Church on record in the United States seems to be the Silver Bluff (South Carolina) Baptist Church, whose beginnings go back beyond 1775 and possibly to 1750. The first organization of black Baptists above the local church level was the Providence Baptist Association, begun in Ohio in 1836. Nearly a half century more went by before the first black Baptist interstate body came into being.

W. W. Colley, a missionary to Africa under appointment of the Southern Baptist Convention, issued the call that resulted, in 1880, in the organization of the Foreign Mission Baptist Convention of the United States of America at Montgomery, Alabama, for the purpose of securing black Baptist support for black Baptist missions in Africa. Six years later, in 1886, the American National Baptist Convention came into being in St. Louis to coordinate generally black Baptist interests and activities within the United States. A third body, the Baptist National Education Convention, the primary concern of which was the development of an educated black Baptist ministry, was launched in 1893.

In the interest of economy and efficiency the three conventions merged as the National Baptist Convention of the United States of America in 1895, with the major concern of each of the uniting bodies represented in the new body by a board.

The following year the Home Mission Board of the united body inaugurated a publishing operation, which it incorporated in 1898 as a self-perpetuating activity under the name the National Baptist Publishing Board. The economic success of this operation seemed to vindicate its establishment, but unresolved questions surrounding its ownership and control led to a bitter quarrel. The controversy finally led to an effort on the part of one faction in the convention to secure control of the Publishing Board by incorporating the convention itself in 1915 and suing the board to compel it to submit to direction by the convention. The suit failed and a schism in the convention resulted, with each party claiming to be the continuation of the original convention.

By 1958, the latest year for which information is available about the incorporated convention, it had grown to an estimated 26,000 churches and 5.5 million members. It conducts foreign missions in Africa, South America, India, the Pacific Islands, and Japan. It supports the American Baptist Theological Seminary, Nashville, Tennessee, jointly with the Southern Baptist Convention. There are no national headquarters.

There are no significant differences between the two conventions except size. Both have their greatest numerical strength in the southeastern and southern states and both share the general theological position of other Baptists in this section of the country.[48] Both are members of the Baptist World Alliance, the National Council of the Churches of Christ in the United States of America, and the World Council of Churches.[49]

The National Baptist Convention of America

The supporters of the National Baptist Publication Board's secretary (see preceding section) reorganized as the National Baptist Convention of America, often referred to as the "unincorporated" convention. In 1956, the latest year for which information is available, it had grown to 11,398 churches with an inclusive membership of 2,668,799. It carries on foreign missions in Africa, Haiti, Jamaica, and Panama. There are no national headquarters.

The National Baptist Evangelical Life and Soul-Saving Assembly of the United States of America

Captain Arthur Allen Banks, Sr., organized the National Baptist Evangelical Life and Soul-Saving Assembly of the United States of America as an evangelistic, charitable, and educational fellowship within the National Baptist Convention of America in 1921. Paramilitary organizations like the Salvation Army and the Volunteers of America provided the inspiration for many aspects of the assembly's organization and activities. In 1937 the assembly severed its connection with the National Baptist Convention of America for internal political reasons rather than because of any serious theological difference. To unify the assembly the leadership proceeded to establish a correspondence school with courses in evangelism, missions, the pastoral ministry, the work of deacons, and lay activity; students who successfully completed 60, 90, and 120 days of this instruction received nonacademic degrees such as Doctor of Evangelism and Master Soul Winner. The correspondence school no longer functions and the assembly has largely suspended its publishing activities.

The assembly, now headed by the founder's namesake son, professes to hold no doctrine except "the Bible doctrine as announced by the Founder of the Church, Jesus Christ." Its emphases are those that Baptists generally hold. The headquarters of the assembly are at 441 Monroe Avenue, Detroit, Michigan 48226.

The assembly's membership has been relatively stable over the last three decades. To a large extent it has lost the character of a separate denomination, since most of the 264 congregations that comprise it are affiliated with the National Baptist Convention of America as well as with the assembly. The assembly reports a total membership of approximately 58,000. There has been no response to recent efforts to communicate with the assembly.

Progressive National Baptist Convention, Incorporated

At the Kansas City convention of the National Baptist Convention, Incorporated, in 1961, five years of growing discontent on the part of a considerable segment of ministers over a variety of administrative, organizational, and procedural matters reached a climax. Immediately after the convention, Dr. L. Venchael Booth of Cincinnati, Ohio, sent out a letter inviting "all ministers who were interested in peace, fellowship, and progress" to attend a meeting in his church on November 14 and 15. In the face of considerable opposition by some of the strongest pastors of the parent convention, thirty-three delegates from fourteen states across the country accepted the invitation and brought into being the Progressive National Baptist Convention of America, Incorporated. Two meetings in 1962 formally confirmed the creation of the new organization. Within five years the new body had enrolled 660 churches and 31 associations, conventions, and fellowships.[50]

The convention stands committed to "Baptist principles and procedure." It elects its officers, who are not eligible to succeed themselves, by majority vote for a specific term.

The convention has no stated headquarters; its executive secretary maintains an office at 907 Georgia Avenue N.W., Washington, D.C. 20011. Several years ago it had 487 churches with an inclusive membership of 516, 400. There has been no response to recent efforts to contact the group.

Fundamental Baptist Fellowship Association

In 1962 the Reverend Richard C. Mattox, pastor of the Community Baptist Church, Cleveland, Ohio, led a number of conservative Baptist ministers with predominantly black congregations into the organization of the Fundamental Baptist Fellowship Association. It proposes to offer its members identification with a biblically based philosophy of life and cooperation among conservative Baptist churches and individuals in the task of evangelizing the black community, in foreign missions, and in social action. While recognizing the independence of the local church, it undertakes to promote fellowship among all Baptists without regard to race or ethnic origin. A few white Baptists are active in the association's member churches and in the affairs of the association itself.

The Fundamental Baptist Fellowship Association meets annually. It has eleven churches in Wisconsin, Michigan, Illinois, Iowa, Indiana, Ohio, Pennsylvania, and New Jersey. No information is available on the number of active members that make up these churches.[51]

The American Baptist Association

The American Baptist Association is a fellowship of Missionary Baptist churches holding the Landmark Baptist principles.[52] Historically, these churches see themselves as standing in the tradition of the Donatists, the Waldensians, and the sixteenth-century Anabaptists.

In 1905 the General Association of Baptist Churches came into being in the American South to provide a means of cooperation for missionary Baptist churches who endorsed neither the convention system in general nor the politics and practices of the Southern Baptist Convention in particular. Around the same time some Texas Baptist churches formed the Baptist Missionary Association with the same purpose. In 1924 the two bodies merged, under the name of the American Baptist Association, "to encourage cooperation and Christian activity among the churches; to promote interest in and encourage missions on a New Testament basis among all peoples; to stimulate interest in Christian literature and general benevolence; and to provide a medium through which the churches may cooperate in these enterprises."[53] In 1950 the founders of the North American Baptist Association, now the Baptist Missionary Association of America, withdrew from the parent body.

The first nine articles of the association's doctrinal statement affirm belief in the infallible verbal inspiration of the whole Bible, the Trinity, the Genesis account of creation, Christ's virgin birth and deity, the vicarious and substitutionary character of his crucifixion and suffering, the bodily resurrection of his saints, his personal and bodily coming as the crowning event of the present Gentile age, and the eternal punishment of the finally impenitent.

The tenth article asserts that the "Great Commission" of Matthew 28:20 was given to the churches only, that in cooperative activities on behalf of the Kingdom of God the local church is the only unit that the churches have, that all churches should exercise equal authority in such activities, and that they should meet their common responsibility according to their several abilities. This insistence upon the complete sovereignty and equality of all local churches has secured for the members of the association the name "Church Equality Baptists."[54]

The eleventh article holds that all cooperative bodies, such as associations and conventions, together with their boards and committees, are and should properly be the servants of the churches.

The twelfth article concludes, from the Great Commission, that there has been a succession of missionary Baptist churches from Christ's time to the present.

The thirteenth and last article is that believer's baptism by immersion must be administered in a scriptural Baptist church in order to be valid.[55]

The American Baptist Association has a strong denominational sense. It firmly identifies itself "with the 50,000,000 who bled and died under the slaughter of Rome during the dark ages."[56] It stands in conscious and vigorous opposition both to the Roman Catholic Church and to the sixteenth-century reformers and the church bodies that descended from them. The reformers, according to the American Baptist Association, "brought with them many of the errors of doctrine and practice of the Roman church, such as sprinkling infants and attaching sacramental value to the Lord's supper" and "were not willing to return fully to New Testament Christianity in doctrine and practice,"[57] and "also turned upon us to persecute the Anabaptists even to the shores of America."[58] The churches descended from them are not New Testament churches and their ministers are not scripturally ordained.

The American Baptist Association sees the fundamental Baptists who are separated from the various conventions as moving back to ecclesiasticism, inclusive seminaries, and preoccupation with success and with numbers. Thy are menaced by the new evangelicalism and by the ecumenical evangelism represented by Billy Graham and the World Vision movement of Bob Pierce. In the eyes of the American Baptist Association, the fundamental Baptists stand in dire need of a new appreciation of Baptist history and theology.[59]

The association strongly opposes the ecumenical movement as a satanic system, corrupted by modernism and Roman Catholic heresy. In addition, the association holds, missionary Baptist principles make it impossible for Baptists to recognize as churches of Christ bodies that are not organized according to the pattern of the Jerusalem church and that have a different government, different officers, different classes of members, and different ordinances, doctrines, and practices. Baptists cannot call such bodies gospel churches, but churches only in the "religious" (or sociological) sense. Baptists cannot recognize the ministers of such irregular and unscriptural bodies as gospel ministers, either by inviting them into Baptist pulpits or by cooperating with them in any other act that would imply such recognition, nor can Baptists address as brethren those who do not hold to, but directly oppose, the doctrine of Christ.[60]

The American Baptist Association carries on an energetic publications program. Since 1947 it has published its own Sunday school and young people's work materials designed to take the student through the entire Bible.

The association's headquarters are at 4605 North State Line Avenue, Texarkana, Texas 75501. Although it is a continent-spanning body with 3,570 churches in the United States and Canada and a membership of 1,071,000, its strength is chiefly in the American South. It carries on foreign missions in Mexico, Nicaragua, Costa Rica, Jamaica, Peru, West Germany, Jordan, Africa, the Philippines Republic, and Japan.

Baptist Missionary Association of America

For years the American Baptist Association followed the practice of seating all "messengers," or elected representatives of member churches at its annual sessions, even when the messengers were not members of the churches that elected them. The 1949 session of the association referred back to the churches a resolution requiring messengers to be members of the electing churches. The sponsors of the resolution complained that the 1950 session provided no opportunity to vote on the issue. As a result 828 messengers from 463 protesting churches in sixteen states met in Little Rock, Arkansas, the same year and organized the North American Baptist Association. In the Statement of Principles of Cooperation that they adopted they specified that all messengers must be members of the churches electing them.[61] To avoid misunderstanding, the association renamed itself the Baptist Missionary Association of America in 1969.

The association's doctrinal statement commits the churches of the association to "the historic Missionary Baptist faith and practice." It specifies this faith and practice in terms of the Trinity; the infallible and plenary verbal inspiration of the Bible; the biblical account of creation; the personality of Satan; the hereditary and total depravity of man in his natural state; Christ's deity and virgin birth, his blood atonement for fallen human beings, and his bodily resurrection and ascension; the person and work of the Holy Spirit; justification by faith without the admixture of works; separation of God's children from the world; believer's baptism by immersion "by divine authority as given to Missionary Baptist churches"; the Lord's Supper as an ordinance of the church to be administered only to baptized believers "and in scriptural church capacity"; the eternal security of believers; Christ's personal establishment of a visible church; worldwide missions; the perpetuity of missionary Baptist churches from Christ's day until his second coming;[62] the equal rights and privileges of scriptural churches "in their associated capacities"; the subjection of all scriptural associational assemblies and their committees to the will of the churches that originated them; separation from all so-called churches and church alliances that advocate, practice, or uphold heresies and human innovations that are not in harmony with God's Word, such as "open communion, alien baptism, pulpit affiliation with heretical churches, modernism, and all kindred evils arising from these practices"; the exclusive validity of baptism "administered by the authority of a scriptural Missionary Baptist church";[63] Christ's personal, bodily, and imminent return to earth; the bodily resurrection of the dead; the reality of heaven and the "divine assurance of eternal happiness for the redeemed of God"; the reality and everlasting punishment of hell for the incorrigibly wicked; and the absolute separation of church and state.[64]

The preponderant opinion among the churches of the Baptist Missionary Association is that Christ's return will be premillennial, that he shall reign literally in peace for a thousand years, and that the Bible teaches two resurrections, that of the righteous at Christ's coming and that of the wicked dead at the end of the millennium. These points, however, are not "to be a test of fellowship between brethren of churches."[65]

The association meets annually. The functions of a headquarters are to some extent performed by the Baptist News Service Committee, Box 97, Jacksonville, Texas 75766. There are 1,457 churches with 211,000 members. The association's greatest strength is in Texas and Arkansas. It carries on missionary activity in twelve foreign countries.

General Association of Regular Baptist Churches

After the Northern Baptist Convention (now the American Baptist Churches in the U.S.A.) had refused in 1922 to affirm its adherence to the nineteenth-century New Hampshire Confession of Faith, a group of individuals concerned about "sound doctrine" within the convention gathered at Kansas City, Missouri, in May 1923 and organized the Baptist Bible Union.

The union proceeded to adopt the New Hampshire Confession with certain revisions and additions and heard its first president, T. T. Shields (1873–1955), pastor of the Jarvis Street Baptist Church in Toronto, Canada, describe the purpose of the union as the "purging out" from Baptist denominational life "of those elements which . . . must inevitably effect disintegration."[66]

At the 1932 meeting the union dissolved itself and in its place thirty-four delegates from twenty-two congregations of the Northern Baptist Convention in eight states organized a new Baptist fellowship, the General Association of Regular Baptist Churches. The name "Regular" was chosen to differentiate those who hold the "regular, historic Baptist position" from "the irregular Baptists who are tainted with Modernism." The new fellowship likewise represented a protest against what it saw as the Northern Baptist Convention's denial of the principle of the independence and autonomy of the local congregation, the inequality of representation in the convention's assemblies (which allowed larger churches to send more voting "messengers" than smaller congregations), the control of missionary work by convention assessment and budget, and the very convention principle itself.

Local churches that desire to enter into fellowship with the association and all voting "messengers" to the annual meetings of the association must subscribe to the Articles of Faith that became effective in 1934, a modern expansion of the New Hampshire Confession of Faith in a premillennial direction. These articles affirm the verbal inspiration and infallibility of the Bible; the Trinity; the activity of the Holy Spirit in creation, in the world, and in the believers; the personality of Satan ("the author of all the powers of darkness"); the Genesis account of creation ("man came by direct creation of God and not by evolution"); the fall of man; Christ's virgin birth and deity; the vicarious atonement; the necessity of rebirth ("instantaneous and not a process"); justification, understood as the pardon of sin and the gift of eternal life, solely through faith in Christ's blood; faith in Christ as the only condition of salvation; the autonomy of the local congregation of immersed believers; believer's baptism by immersion ("it is prerequisite to the privileges of a church relation") and the Lord's Supper; the security of the saints ("all who are truly born again are kept by God the Father for Jesus Christ"); the radical and essential difference between the righteous ("such only as through faith are justified in the name of the Lord Jesus Christ and sanctified by the Spirit") and the wicked and their respective everlasting destinies; the divine appointment of civil government; Christ's bodily resurrection, ascension, high priesthood, and second coming, and the resurrection of the righteous dead and the change of the living at Christ's return, the establishment of the throne of David, and Christ's millennial reign.[67]

The association is consciously separatist. It does not permit dual membership or fellowship and it rejects as unscriptural any participation in evangelistic campaigns, religious services, and ministerial associations with "modernists."

provides the churches in fellowship with it a list of independent Baptist mis-
onary agencies that the association's missionary committee (the Council of
ourteen, see below) examines and approves annually "to be sure that there
no deflection from approved standards of faith and practice." It follows the
ame policy with reference to the Bible colleges and theological seminaries
aat it endorses to ensure that they are "thoroughly Baptistic in teaching
nd training."[68]

The polity of the association is strictly congregational. The association
eets annually; each fellowshiping congregation, regardless of size, is repre-
ented by six voting "messengers." A Council of Fourteen, whose members
re elected for two-year terms, implements the decisions of the association.
here are also state and regional associations.

The headquarters are at 1800 Oakton Boulevard, Des Plaines, Illinois
0018. There are 1,503 churches in the United States, with an inclusive
embership of 250,000. The association lays great stress on missions and
ne churches in fellowship with it support 800 foreign missionaries around
he world.[69]

The Conservative Baptist Association of America

In the course of the fundamentalist-modernist controversy in the Northern
Baptist Convention (now the American Baptist Churches in the U.S.A.), the
onservatives in 1920 formed the National Federation of the Fundamentalist
Fellowship. Their purpose was to stop the convention's "drift toward division
nd estrangement by stopping the drift toward rationalism and materialism"
nd to counteract the increasing involvement of the convention in what
eemed to the conservatives specious social concerns. At a preconvention
onference in 1921 it adopted almost unanimously a short eight-paragraph
Statement of Faith drafted by Frank M. Goodchild, but it failed to secure
onvention approval of the document.[70] The conservatives made a parallel
effort in 1922 to pledge the convention to the New Hampshire Confession,
ut the convention substituted for this proposal another resolution, that "the
New Testament is the all-sufficient ground of our faith and practice and we
eed no other statement," and passed it 1,264 to 637.

As a rival to the Fundamentalist Fellowship, some less moderate conserva-
ives in the convention launched the Baptist Bible Union. When the Bible
Union gave birth to the General Association of Regular Baptist Churches
n 1932–1933, some of the members of the Fundamentalist Fellowship joined
he new body.

In 1943 the Fundamentalist Fellowship sponsored the Conservative Bap-
ist Foreign Missionary Society and required all officers, regular employees,
nd missionaries to subscribe to the Goodchild Confession of 1921. In 1946
he Fundamentalist Fellowship became the Conservative Baptist Fellowship of
Northern Baptists. By the next year it despaired of achieving its purposes

within the Northern Baptist Convention. Unable to negotiate a satisfactory affiliation with either the Swedish Baptist General Conference (now the Baptist General Conference) or the General Association of Regular Baptist Churches, its members helped form the Conservative Baptist Association of America at Atlantic City, New Jersey, in 1947. During the next five years a gradual separation from the American (formerly Northern) Baptist Convention took place.

The new association was a confessional body, a fellowship of independent churches, and an association without organic relationship to the organizations that its churches support (that is, the Conservative Baptist Home Mission Society, the Conservative Baptist Foreign Mission Society, and the theological seminaries). Contributions were not made a prerequisite for membership, and the monies that the association gave to young congregations were outright grants without strings attached.[71]

In facing the stresses of the early years of its existence, the association retained its somewhat sprawling decentralized polity. During this same period it moved from a "not inclusive" toward a more strongly separationist position, although it continued to leave the matter of affiliation with other conventions, fellowships, and associations to the decision of the local congregation ("separation by process"). Currently the established churches that join the association normally do so after a period of independency.

The doctrinal statement of the new body was substantially the Goodchild Confession of 1921, with an added explicit commitment to premillennialism. On the historic issues of Calvinist over against Arminian doctrine it did not pronounce. Its thrust is chiefly that of an affirmation of supernaturalism against theological liberalism. It affirms belief in the unique inspiration, absolute trustworthiness, and supreme infallible authority of the Bible; in God the Father; in Christ's Sonship, virgin birth, sinlessness, atoning death, bodily resurrection, ascension, and personal, visible, and premillennial return; in the Holy Spirit; in the sinfulness of men, in everlasting life for those who accept Christ as their Lord and eternal separation from God for those who reject Christ; in the church as the living spiritual body of which Christ is the Head and all regenerated people are members and in visible churches as companies of baptized believers who observe baptism and the Lord's Supper and who are to persuade a lost world to accept Christ as Savior and to enthrone him as Lord and Master; in the responsibility of every human being to God alone in all matters of faith; in the independence and autonomy of each church and in the separation of church and state.[72]

The address of the headquarters of the Conservative Baptist Association of America is Geneva Road, Box 66, Wheaton, Illinois 60187. It has 1,120 churches with a membership of 300,000. The related Conservative Baptist Foreign Missionary carries on mission operations in Latin America, Africa, Hong Kong, India, Indonesia, Japan, Jordan, Pakistan, the Republic of China (Taiwan), the Philippines, and Europe.[73]

The New Testament Association of Independent Baptist Churches

In the early 1960s a number of ministers and congregations of the Conservative Baptist Association of America felt that the association was drifting away from biblical separatism in the direction of ecclesiastical inclusivism, ecumenical evangelism, and the new evangelicalism. In 1964 they called a meeting at the Marquette Manor Baptist Church, Chicago, Illinois, to lay the groundwork for a new association that would hold unwaveringly to the biblical separatist position. As a result the New Testament Association of Independent Baptist Churches came into being at the Beth Eden Baptist Church, Denver, Colorado, in 1965. By the time it held its first annual meeting in the Eagledale Baptist Church, Indianapolis, Indiana, in 1966, twenty-seven churches had joined the new association.

The member churches of the association interpret the Bible literally, reject figurative explanations of the Genesis account of creation, and hold that the six days of creation were twenty-four-hour solar days. Its theological position is fundamentalist, conservative, dispensational, premillennial, and pretribulational in its understanding of the rapture. It disavows interdenominationalism, liberalism, the new evangelicalism, Covenant and Reformed theology, nonmillennialism and postmillennialism, and posttribulational or midtribulational interpretations of the rapture. It stresses the distinctively Baptist belief in the Bible as the only rule for faith and practice, in a regenerated church membership, in believer's baptism by immersion, in a church separated for Christ from false doctrine and from the world and its standards, in the priesthood of the believer, in the independence of the local church, and in the separation of church and state. In their church relationships the association and its member churches are autonomous, not ecumenical.

Several years ago the fellowship had 44 churches with about 7,000 members in all parts of the United States.[74]

Fundamental Baptist Fellowship

The Fundamental Baptist Fellowship traces its history gack to 1920, when the National Federation of Fundamentalists of Northern Baptists (the Fundamentalist Fellowship) was formed within the Northern Baptist Convention in protest against "theological modernism, a centralized ecclesiasticism, and an unbiblical ecumenism." In 1947 the members of the fellowship helped form the Conservative Baptist Association of America. Conflict within the movement developed in 1952. The initial center of division was the Conservative Baptist Theological Seminary at Denver, Colorado. During the next decade, the group that describes itself as "fundamentalist separatists" felt that the "soft-policy" forces were capturing the Conservative Baptist Association. The soft-policy forces, as the more rigorous group describes them, are individuals who deny the verbal and plenary inspiration of the Bible by tolerating amillennialism, who teach a posttribulation rapture of the church, who reject the "Baptistic distinctives," who disavow the dispensational divison of the Bible, and who are soft toward "Kierkegaardian neoorthodoxy," the Revised Standard Version of the Bible, the "new evangelicalism" represented by schools like Fuller Theological Seminary, "fellowship in service with apostates" in ecumenical evangelistic efforts, and the communist infiltration of the churches. The more rigorous group saw the victory of the soft-policy forces within the Conservative Baptist Association as having been completed by 1963.

In the meantime a gradual separation of the Conservative Baptist Fellowship as the standard-bearer of the "hard core" of the Conservative Baptist movement from the Conservative Baptist Association of America had been taking place.[75] In 1968 the fellowship adopted the name Fundamental Baptist Fellowship and moved its offices from Chicago to Denver.

The fellowship's doctrinal statement varies only slightly at most points from the declaration of faith of the Conservative Baptist Association of America. It omits "infallible" in describing the supreme authority of the Bible in matters of faith and conduct and describes Christ's birth as "miraculous" instead of specifying that he was conceived of the Holy Spirit and born of a virgin. It affirms Christ's perpetual intercession for his people and, in a paragraph added in 1955, declares its belief "in our Lord's return—a personal, visible, imminent, pretribulation rapture, and subsequent millennial enthronement, in fulfillment of His promise."[76]

The headquarters of the Fundamental Baptist Fellowship were at 3255 Lowell Boulevard, Denver, Colorado, but a recent letter to that address has been returned with the words "Not Here." The fellowship meets annually. It has in its membership about 800 ministers, almost all of them ordained, who represent about 650 churches. Some of these are independent churches, some belong to other organizations and fellowships. No estimate is available on the total active membership of these churches.[77] The fellowship sees its position shared by Central Baptist Seminary in Minneapolis and the San Francisco (California) Baptist Seminary, as well as by Pillsbury Baptist College, Owatonna, Minnesota, Maranatha Baptist Bible College, Watertown, Wisconsin, and the Denver (Colorado) Baptist Bible College. The fellowship itself does not carry on any foreign missionary activity.

Independent Bible Baptist Missions

In response to the call of the Reverend Harvey H. Springer, Englewood, Colorado, thirteen Baptist ministers attended a meeting in December 1949 at which they effected the temporary organization of the Missionary Fellowship of Baptist Churches. The fellowship held its first General Assembly in January 1950 and adopted the name Independent Bible Baptist Missions.[78]

The Doctrinal Statement of the fellowship explicitly forbids churches belonging to it to have any kind of affiliation with "any organization representing them before the Federal Council of Churches or its successors, the National Association of Evangelicals or its successors or any organization affiliated with [these] groups, or any church standing outside the stream of historical Christianity." The statement has sections on the Bible; God; the fall of man; the way of salvation ("wholly of grace through the mediatorial offices of the Son of God, [who] by His death made a full atonement for our sins"); justification ("not in consideration of any works of righteousness that we have done, but solely through faith in the Redeemer's blood"); the freeness of salvation to all; grace in regeneration; repentance and faith; election as God's purpose of grace, sanctification; the perseverance of saints ("such only are real believers as endure to the end"); the harmony of the law and the gospel; the visible gospel church and its biblical officers, bishop-pastors, and deacons; the necessity of believer's baptism by immersion ("a solemn and beautiful emblem [of] our faith") as a prerequisite to the privileges of a church relation and the Lord's Supper; the Lord's day; civil government, the personality of Satan; the imminent and personal return of Christ, appearing first for the church and later, with his church, for the millennium; Christ's personality and deity; and the Holy Ghost.[79]

An Executive Committee functions between sessions of the General Assembly. The headquarters address of the organization is Box 1991, Colorado Springs, Colorado 80901. It has twenty-five churches in Colorado, Kansas, Nebraska, Missouri, Texas, and Arizona, with a total membership of 3,000.[80] It carries on foreign missions in Brazil, Uruguay, and Mexico.

World Baptist Fellowship

In 1924 the General Baptist Convention of Texas, the state convention of the Southern Baptist Convention, expelled the well-known fundamentalist preacher, John Franklyn Norris (1877–1952), and his church. The action climaxed a long controversy in which Norris had denounced the denominational leadership for fostering evolution, winking at modernism, and abusing the democracy of the convention.[81] Other Baptist preachers and churches rallied around Norris.[82] Out of this group came the Pre-Millennial Baptist Missionary Fellowship, later called the World Fundamental Missionary Fellowship. In 1950 this organization divided into two denominations, the group that took the name World Baptist Fellowship in 1952 and the Baptist Bible Fellowship International. The World Baptist Fellowship claims the membership or support of over 850 churches and missions in 40 states with a total membership of 170,000. Missionaries of the fellowship are at work in 20 countries. The fellowship has doubled its foreign commitment in the last five years, including radio outreach to Spanish-speaking people of Central and South America.[83] Its headquarters are at 3001 West Division Street, Arlington, Texas 76010.

Theologically the World Baptist Fellowship stands close to the General

Association of Regular Baptists and the Baptist Bible Fellowship. It differs from them mainly in organizational structure and in the plan of its missions program. The World Baptist Fellowship teaches the unique verbal inspiration of the canonical books of the Bible; the Trinity; Satan as a fallen angel who is now the malignant prince of the power of the air and the unholy God of this world; literal acceptance of the Genesis creation account; the fall of man from a sinless and happy state in consequence of which all men are sinners not by constraint but by choice; the unique virgin birth of Christ; the vicarious atonement; the new birth as an instantaneous event and not a process; God's electing grace; justification through faith as including the pardon of sin and the gift of eternal life "on principles of righteousness"; repentance and faith as inseparable graces wrought in the soul by the quickening Spirit of God; the local church as a completely independent congregation of baptized believers associated by a covenant of faith and fellowship of the gospel, observing the ordinances of Christ, governed by Christ's laws, exercising the gifts, rights, and privileges invested in them by his Word, and cooperating with other true churches for the faith and furtherance of the Gospel in a measure and in a manner of which it is the sole and only judge, with pastors, elders, and deacons as its officers; believer's baptism by immersion as a solemn and beautiful emblem of faith in the crucified, buried and risen Savior, symbolic of death to sin and resurrection to a new life; the Lord's Supper as a commemoration of the dying love of Christ; the persevering attachment to Christ by real believers, whose welfare is watched over by a special providence and who are kept by the power of God through faith unto eternal salvation, in distinction from superficial professors; the everlasting felicity of the saved and the everlasting conscious suffering of the lost; civil government as a divine appointment to be prayed for, honored, and obeyed, except only in things opposed to the will of Christ; the premillennial return of Christ; the command to give the Gospel to the world as a clear and unmistakable commission to the churches; and tithing as one of the fundamentals of the faith.[84]

Baptist Bible Fellowship International

On May 23, 1950, fourteen minister-members of the World Fundamental Missionary Baptist Fellowship walked out of the organization. The next day at Denton, Texas, they signed a statement of the aims of a new organization, the Baptist Bible Fellowship. Other ministers and churches quickly followed their lead. The new body established its headquarters at 730 East Kearney, Springfield, Missouri, and built the three-year Baptist Bible College there to train its future workers.

The break did not come over doctrine but over what the withdrawing group regarded as "the dictatorial methods" of John Franklyn Norris. Apart from the added preamble, the Articles of Faith of the Baptist Bible Fellowship International are exactly identical with the Doctrinal Statement of the

World Baptist Fellowship. The preamble defines a Bible Baptist as one who believes in a supernatural Bible which tells of a Christ who is supernatural in his birth, words, miracles, life, death, resurrection splendor, priesthood, and glorious return and who will establish a supernatural Kingdom on the earth.[85] Churches and pastors must accept the Articles of Faith to belong to the fellowship. The premillennial emphasis is strong.

The fellowship derives its unity and cohesion from the missionary enterprise, which it sees as basic and central.[86] Since 1960 the number of fellowshiping churches has grown from 1,053 to 2,600. While membership in the fellowship is not in principle exclusive, the annual directory does not list churches known to be associated with other Baptist bodies. The fellowship has made no survey to try to determine the total membership of its churches. In addition to domestic missions (including work in Hawaii, Alaska, and Puerto Rico and among the Navajo Indians), foreign missionaries of the fellowship are at work in thirty-four countries of Latin America, Europe, Africa, the Middle East, and the Far East.[87]

South Carolina Baptist Fellowship

In October 1954 the Reverend John R. Waters of Laurens, South Carolina, and the Reverend Vendyl Jones, then a student at Bob Jones University, called together a meeting of independent Baptist pastors of South Carolina and the southern counties of North Carolina. At this meeting, held in Greenville, South Carolina, the Carolina Baptist Fellowship came into being.

In 1965 the Carolina Baptist Fellowship was incorporated as the South Carolina Baptist Fellowship. The Statement of Faith of the South Carolina Baptist Fellowship is identical with that of the Southwide Baptist Fellowship.[88] Although it is in a sense a state fellowship within the latter larger body, the South Carolina Baptist Fellowship holds independent membership in the American Council of Christian Churches and in the International Council of Christian Churches.

Normally the fellowship meets monthly, except during December when the Southwide Baptist Fellowship meets.

The headquarters of the South Carolina Baptist Fellowship are at 1605 Greenwood Road, Laurens, South Carolina 29360. There are 130 pastors and churches associated with it. The total active membership of these churches is estimated at 26,000.[89]

The Southwide Baptist Fellowship

Some of the participants in a tent meeting that the Carolina Baptist Fellowship sponsored at Aiken, South Carolina, in August 1955, urged the guest speaker, Dr. Lee Roberson of Chattanooga, Tennessee, to lead in the founding of a fundamental and premillennial fellowship of Baptist preachers and laymen throughout the South. The organization of the Southern Baptist Fellowship was effected in 1956 as a result. The name was subsequently changed to the Southwide Baptist Fellowship. It claims over 1,000 ministers, evangelists, and missionaries with an inclusive membership of over 500,000.[90] The headquarters are at 1605 Greenwood Road, Laurens, South Carolina 29360.

The constitution contemplates "the organization of regionals for states and areas" to meet monthly or quarterly. These "regionals" are "encouraged to assist in ordinations and the organization of Baptist Churches of like faith and order as the need arises." The American Council of Christian Churches represents the fellowship in radio and television matters.

The twelve-paragraph Statement of Faith affirms the fellowship's belief in "the verbal inspiration of the 66 books of the Bible in its original writings," the Trinity, the fall of mankind in Adam, the deity, incarnation, and vicarious sacrifice of Jesus Christ, the Holy Spirit, the salvation of a soul "when Christ is accepted as personal Savior and Lord and the Holy Spirit imparts eternal life," the "plan of God for each believer to walk after the Spirit," the eternal preservation and perseverance of the saints, the immersion of the believer in water, the independence of the local church from the authority of every other person, group, or body, and a premillennial doctrine of the last things. The Statement of Faith concludes: "We believe the Revised Standard Version of the Bible is a perverted translation of the original languages, and that collaboration or participation with all forms of modernism, whether in the National Council of Churches or otherwise is wrong, and demands separation on our part."[91]

Baptist Mid-Missions

In 1920 the intrepid Baptist missionary to Africa, the Reverend William Clarence Haas (1872–1924), organized the General Council of Cooperating Baptist Missions of North America, Incorporated. He returned to Africa the same year under the council's aegis to begin work in the Republic of Chad. Gradually the vision of the council changed from a program that limited itself to the evangelization of Central Africa to a program with a worldwide outreach. In 1924 the first missionaries went to Venezuela. Subsequently others began work in Brazil, Liberia, Ghana, the Republic of Congo, Mexico, Peru, Guyana, Honduras, Jamaica, Haiti, the Dominican Republic, the Bahamas, the Windward Islands, France, Germany, Italy, the Netherlands, Austria, Hong Kong, Indonesia, Korea, Japan, and India. In 1953 the council took its present name. In the United States (including Puerto Rico, Hawaii, and Alaska) and Canada, Baptist Mid-Missions carries on work among North American Indians, migrant workers, Jews, blacks, foreign-language groups, university students, and urban dwellers. It acts as the agency for some 3,000 individual fundamental Baptist churches, each of which authorizes and sends forth its own missionaries. It operates on the "faith principle" and does not guarantee a salary or allowance to any of its more than 750 missionaries.

The Articles of Faith affirm belief in the Bible ("verbally inspired of God and inerrant in the original writing"); the Trinity; the deity and manhood of Christ; the sinful nature of all human beings; Christ's representative and substitutionary sacrifice for each believer; the eternal security of those who are born into the family of God; Christ's resurrection, ascension, and session; his personal, premilliennial, pretribulational, and imminent return; the future regeneration and restoration of Israel as a nation; the rebirth of all who receive Christ by faith; the bodily resurrection of the just to everlasting blessedness and of the unjust to everlasting punishment; and the ordinances of believer's baptism by immersion ("as a symbol of their belief in the death, burial, and resurrection of our Lord and Savior") and the Lord's Supper.[92]

The headquarters of Baptist Mid-Missions are at 4205 Chester Avenue, Cleveland, Ohio 44103. The approximately 125 congregations and missions in the United States (including Hawaii, Puerto Rico, and Alaska) and Canada that Baptist Mid-Missions sponsors have an estimated total membership of 3,125.[93]

New England Evangelical Baptist Fellowship

In the early 1940s, when the union of the Congregational-Christian Churches with the Evangelical Reformed Church began to loom as an ultimate possibility, a number of churches in Maine, New Hampshire, Massachusetts, and Connecticut preferred association in a new organization, which they called the New England Evangelical Baptist Fellowship, to membership in the proposed United Church of Christ.[94] The fellowship joined the National Association of Evangelicals as a denomination in 1943; in 1959 its status was changed to that of an organizational member. Strongly evangelical and conservative, the fellowship holds quarterly conference meetings which attract from 100 to 200 participants. There are 10 active congregations, with a total membership of 1,022.[95]

General Six-Principle Baptists

In the early 1650s the Providence, Rhode Island, Baptist Church split. The main body of the congregation accepted the tenets of a movement that had begun among the General Baptists of England during the preceding decade. With reference to Hebrews 6:1-2 the adherents of this movement called themselves Six-Principle Baptists. Five of these principles—repentance, faith, baptism, the resurrection of the dead, and the final judgment—were not particularly crucial issues. But one was, "the laying on of hands," performed after baptism to symbolize a special imparting of the Holy Spirit. The fact

that its proponents made it a requirement of fellowship added to its importance. The Six-Principle movement grew quite rapidly in New England and
the first General Six-Principle Baptist association, the Rhode Island conference, dates back to 1670.

Although the General Six-Principle Baptists were a significant group during the colonial period, they gradually declined in strength and influence.

Currently one conference with three churches in Rhode Island, where
most of the members reside, and one church in Pennsylvania perpetuate the
Six-Principle tradition. There are a total of 180 members. There are no
general headquarters.

The General Association of General Baptists

The first organized Baptist church on British soil was a "General" or
Arminian, Baptist congregation. Thomas Helwys (1550?–1616?) and nine
or ten other seceders from the Amsterdam congregation of John Smyth
(1567?–1612) established it in Spitalfield, just outside the walls of London,
in 1611 or 1612. Spiritual descendants of these founders of the General Baptist tradition emigrated to the Atlantic seaboard of North America as early
as 1714, but by the end of the eighteenth century the organized General
Baptist movement in the New World was all but extinct. It has not been
possible to prove a direct link between these General Baptists of the Colonial
period and the revival of General Baptist principles in 1823, when Benoni
Stinson (1798–1869) founded in Evansville, Indiana, what is now the oldest
General Baptist church in America. One of the associations that carried on
the revived tradition was the Liberty Association of Indiana, organized the
following year. When the General Association of General Baptists came into
being on November 2, 1870, at Harmony Church, Gallatin County, Illinois,
it adopted the eleven Articles of Faith of the Liberty Association, with minor
changes, as its own Confession of Faith.[97]

General Baptists stand committed to the "five Baptist cardinal doctrines":
the inspiration and authority of the Scriptures, the priesthood of all believers,
believer's baptism by immersion, the autonomy of the local church, and the
separation of church and state.

At the same time, as their name implies, General Baptists hold that
Christ's blood atoned generally for all the sins of all men and not only for
those of the elect. The security of the Christian is a "conditioned security,"
that is, it is conditioned on a continued faith, and it is possible for a child
of God to turn away from God and finally to be lost.

On admission to the Lord's Supper, they are "open communionists." They
have long been divided on the issue whether or not foot washing is an ordinance; practically the decision has more and more fallen out in the negative
and the practice is disappearing. "Church" they understand, on the one hand,
as a local assembly of professing Christians and, on the other, as the sum

total of God's children. While the government of the denomination is congregational, General Baptists use a presbytery both for ordination and for control over the standing of ordained persons serving the churches.

Tolerant and relatively slow-growing, the General Association of General Baptists now comprises 58 regional associations, with a total of 837 churches in 16 states and an inclusive membership of 72,764. Its headquarters receives mail at Box 537, Poplar Bluff, Missouri 63901. The General Association conducts foreign missions in Jamaica, Guam, Saipan in the Marianas, and in the Philippines. In 1966 the association affiliated with the Baptist World Alliance.[98]

National Association of Free-Will Baptists

The first Free Will Baptists in North America were Welsh immigrants who settled on a grant of land in Pennsylvania, known as the Welsh Tract, in 1701. From here they spread rapidly through the colonies. In the South, Paul Palmer (flourished 1719–1739) organized a Free Will Baptist Church in Perquimans County, North Carolina, in 1727. His counterpart in the North was Benjamin Randall (d. 1808). He was first a Congregationalist and became a Baptist only in 1776. In 1779 he separated from his Calvinistic Baptist co-religionists and on June 30, 1780, he and a group of followers in New Durham, New Hampshire, signed a covenant and organized a Free Will Baptist congregation.

The Free Will Baptists rejected three of the cardinal tenets of classic Calvinism: (1) they denied a limited atonement and taught that the salvation Christ offered was available to all who freely believed in him; (2) they denied irresistible grace and taught that a human being might reject as well as accept God's grace in Christ; and (3) in the question that was the one overriding theological issue of the place and the period, they denied the perseverance of the saints and taught that a sinner once converted might fall again from grace. Less concerned about doctrine than daily Christian living, they allowed believers whose life gave evidence of Christian faith to take part in the Lord's Supper even if they had not been immersed.

The Free Will Baptists of North Carolina trace their history back to the last decade of the seventeenth century, when the first references occur to a Free Will or Six-Principle Baptist Church in North Carolina that Free Will Baptist ministers from England who subscribed to the Confession of 1660 had organized. By 1699 the number of churches in North Carolina was sufficiently large to warrant organization of an annual meeting.[99]

Their best-remembered leader of the eighteenth century besides Palmer was Joseph Parker (1705–1791). From the 1760s on many of their churches and members became Calvinistic Baptists. But a few Free Will Baptist churches survived. By 1802 they had begun meeting as the General Conference of the Free Will Baptists. In 1831 the General Conference dissolved itself and the churches that had made it up organized the Bethel Conference and the Shiloh Conference. By 1839 the followers of the Restoration leaders Thomas and Alexander Campbell in the Bethel Conference had gained effective control of the organization and in 1841 it dropped "Free Will Baptist" from its name and became simply the Bethel Conference of North Carolina. Although Restoration views penetrated the Shiloh Conference as well, it never abandoned its Free Will Baptist position. In 1842, with the Bethel Conference no longer professing to be a Free Will Baptist organization, the Shiloh Conference resolved to reconstitute out of its membership the Original Free Will Baptist General Conference of North Carolina. On the local level some churches for a long time had two congregations, one a Disciples of Christ congregation (generally a minority) represented at the Bethel Conference, the other a Free Will Baptist congregation represented at the General Conference.[100]

In 1853 the General Conference split into two parts on the question of excommunicating Masons and Odd Fellows. Each part claimed to be the original body. The part that stood for strict exclusion on principle finally dwindled away, while the part that ultimately survived resolved the problem by "giving each individual church its own key."

A strong bond of fellowship developed between the Randall group and the Palmer group, especially in the late 1820s and early 1830s, but no formal union took place, and in 1839 the northern General Conference dropped the two North Carolina conferences from its statistics. The Randall group expanded westward, organized itself into a General Conference, and in 1911 merged with the Northern Baptist Convention (now American Baptist Churches in the U.S.A.). But many individual churches refused to enter the union. Sensing the need for a central organization to replace the General Conference, a call went out for the union of "all Freewill Baptists" into one group in 1916. Messengers from Oklahoma, Texas, Missouri, Kansas, and North Carolina—representing both nonmerging churches of the Randall group and churches of the Palmer group—responded and formed the Cooperative General Association of Free-Will Baptists. A controversy about the Lord's Supper and foot washing (on which the Tennessee and North Carolina congregations insisted) broke out at the second triennial meeting. The Palmer group withdrew and, together with like-minded churches from Georgia and Alabama, organized the General Conference of the Original Free-Will Baptists of the United States at Nashville, Tennessee, in 1921.

By 1935 the issues that had divided the two bodies had been sufficiently ironed out for them to unite federally as the National Association of Free-Will Baptists; the federation became an organic union in 1938. The united group adopted "A Revision of the Treatise and the Faith and Practices of the Free Will Baptists," which called foot washing "a sacred ordinance which teaches humility" and which Christ instituted on the night of his betrayal as "an example."

In 1961–1962 a division among the Free Will Baptists of North Carolina led to the separate establishment of what is now the General Conference of Original Free Will Baptists.

The headquarters of the National Association of Free-Will Baptists are at 1134 Murfreesboro Road, Nashville, Tennessee 37217. The association meets annually. Government is strictly congregational. Quarterly conferences, combined into state associations that also meet annually, cover the entire church body. There are 2,350 churches with an inclusive membership of 215,000.

General Conference of Original Free Will Baptists

The General Conference of Original Free Will Baptists and the National Association of Free-Will Baptists share a common history down to 1961–1962. At this juncture dissension among the boards and departments of the association, the rise of what some saw as "excessive denominationalism," and the increasing authority of state and regional organizations led to the withdrawal of the North Carolina State Convention, and of smaller groups and individual churches elsewhere, from the National Association of Free-Will Baptists. Under the leadership of the North Carolina State Convention a five-state Fellowship for Original Free-Will Baptists came into being in 1963. The next year it took the name of International Convention of Original Free Will Baptists. In 1965 it redesignated itself the General Conference of Original Free Will Baptists; declared itself the "continuation and enlargement" of the former body of this name; and saw as its vocation the "reviving of the traditions and customs of the movement introduced in America by Paul Palmer."[101]

The General Conference's twenty-two-article Statement of Faith is identical with the one that the North Carolina State Convention of (Original) Free Will Baptists adopted in 1955. It affirms that the Bible is God's revealed Word to human beings and "a sufficient and infallible rule and guide to salvation and all Christian worship and service." It teaches the unity and uniqueness of God and affirms the divine government and providence, with "the power of free choice [as] the exact measure of man's responsibility"; but God's knowledge of events "does not in any sense cause them to occur, nor does he decree all events which he knows will occur." It teaches the creation of the world, of angels, and of human being by God: as a result of the fall, human beings "are not willing to obey God, but are inclined to evil: and cannot "by virtue of any natural goodness and mere work of their own" become God's children. It asserts Christ's deity, incarnation, vicarious atonement, and mediation, but declares that children dying in infancy "shall not suffer punishment in hell by the guilt of Adam's sin." It asserts the deity of the Holy Spirit and affirms the Trinity. "The call of the gospel is coextensive with the atonement to all men . . . so that salvation is rendered equally possible to all."

Repentance is essential; so are saving faith ("an assent of the mind to the fundamental truths of revelation, an acceptance of the Gospel through the influence of the Holy Spirit, and a firm confidence and trust in Christ") and regeneration ("an instantaneous renewal of the heart by the Holy Spirit"). Personal justification secures pardon from sin; sanctification is the Christian's continuous growth in grace and knowledge of Christ, which will finally be completed in heaven. "There are strong grounds to hope that the truly regenerate will persevere unto the end and be saved through the power of divine grace which is pledged for their support, but their future obedience and final salvation are neither determined nor certain"; through infirmity and temptations they are in danger of falling and they ought to watch and pray "lest they make shipwreck of their faith and be lost." The first day of the week is the Christian Sabbath. "A Christian church is an organized body of believers in Christ who stately assemble to worship God and who sustain the ordinances of the gospel"; the church of God is the "whole body of Christians throughout the whole world, and none but the regenerate are its members." Tithing is God's financial plan for the support of his work." Ministers must be qualified, especially called by God, and ordained by prayer and the laying on of hands. The ordinances of the gospel are the immersion of believers in water in the name of the Father, the Son, and the Holy Spirit; the Lord's Supper as a commemoration of Christ's death with the emblems symbolizing his broken body and shed blood; and the washing of the saints' feet. The soul does not die with the body, but goes immediately at death to a conscious state of happiness or misery. Christ's second coming to close the gospel dispensation is imminent; the bodies of all men will arise, "each in its own order"; and after the final judgment the final retribution will take place.[102]

The local churches are distinct and independent organizations. The general conference meets annually. Two regional organizations, the State Convention of Churches of the Original Free Baptists of North Carolina and the West Virginia Yearly Meeting of Free Will Baptist[s], organized in the mid-1880s, account for more than 90 percent of the churches. Several years ago the General Conference had 337 churches in 8 states, with a total active membership estimated at 40,000.[103] There has been no response to recent efforts to contact the denomination.

United American Free Will Baptist Church

The United American Free Will Baptist Church traces its beginnings to the initiative of a small number of black Free Will Baptists who in 1867 organized the Shady Grove Free Will Baptist Church under a bush shelter at Snow Hill, Greene County, North Carolina. Through the outreach of this church, a number of other bush shelter congregations were founded. Gradually, church buildings replaced the bush shelters. By 1870 the felt need for an annual conference led to the organization of the United American Free Will Baptist Church. The formal incorporation of the church body took place in 1887. With the passage of time, the number of annual conferences increased and a General Conference was created to coordinate the annual conference. The General Conference was incorporated in 1901.[104]

The United American Free Will Baptist Church has three statements of faith. One is entitled "Our Faith." The second is headed "Articles of Faith and Church Covenant." The third is an elaboration of the other two in twenty-one "chapters of doctrine." The Articles of Faith affirm the inspiration of the Bible; the Trinity; the incarnation and mediatorship of Christ; the Holy Spirit's possession of all personal divine attributes; the eternity and immutability of the divine purposes; the providence of God over all beings; the fallen nature of human beings, so that all who come to years of moral accountability sin; the atonement of Christ as free and open to all; salvation by grace only; repentance and faith as the only conditions of salvation; God's determination from the beginning to save all human beings who should comply with these conditions of salvation; the necessity of perseverance in holiness to the end of one's life in order to be saved; free salvation; the freedom and self-determination of the human will; believer's baptism by immersion, the Lord's Supper, and the washing of the saints' feet as gospel ordinances of universal obligation; the duty to observe the Christian Sabbath by abstaining from secular business and amusement and by consecrating Sunday to the worship of God and spiritual improvement; Christ's second appearance at the end of the world, the general resurrection, the final judgment, the eternal blessedness of the righteous, and the endless sufferings of the wicked.[105]

The General Conference, which normally meets once every three years, has the same relation to the annual conferences that the latter have to the individual churches. Since 1969 the presiding officer of the General Conference officially bears the title of senior bishop. The presiding officers of the annual conferences are called annual bishops.

The headquarters of the United American Free Will Baptist Church are at 1000 University Street, Kinston, North Carolina 28501. Several years ago there were 14 annual conferences, with about 300 churches, more than half of them in North Carolina, and a total active membership of about 35,000.[106] There has been no response to recent efforts to contact the organization.

Christian Unity Baptist Association

In 1909 a controversy about admitting Christians of other denominations to Communion divided the North Carolina Mount Union Association of Regular Baptists. The party that favored open Communion withdrew and organized the Macedonia Baptist Association in 1910. After six sessions it ceased to function as an association. Around 1930 the Mount Union Association once more divided over the right of women to preach. Those who took the negative view joined forces with the surviving remnants of the Macedonia Association and in 1935 they organized the Christian Unity Baptist association.

The articles of faith of the association affirm the Trinity ("these three are one in purpose"); the inspiration of the Bible; "the New Testament interpreted by the Holy Spirit" as the only rule of practice; the depravity of all human beings "who are accountable to God for sin"; Christ's death for every man; "the redemption of the bodies of saints, infants, and idiots" ("the latter two not being responsible for sin do not need regeneration of spirit"); the work of the Holy Spirit in calling, convicting, converting, regenerating, and sanctifying ("all who are thus born again by the Spirit of God and endure to the end shall be saved"); believer's baptism by immersion, the Lord's Supper, and foot washing as ordinances instituted by Christ; "the unity, liberty, and equality of all God's children"; the church as the company of "all who are born of the Spirit of God"; a God-called ministry ("preaching the word of God by inspiration of the Holy Spirit"); and the general resurrection of the just (to eternal joy) and of the unjust (to eternal punishment).[107]

The association, which meets annually, has only advisory authority. Several years ago there were 11 churches in North Carolina, Virginia, and Tennessee with an inclusive membership of 651. Recent efforts to contact the association have been unsuccessful.

General Association of Separate Baptists in Christ

In the course of George Whitefield's revivals in New England the assemblies of the "awakened" Congregationalists that withdrew under the impact of the revival were called Separate Congregational churchs, while the established churches from which they went out were referred to as Regular Congregational churches. By a somewhat imperfect analogy the two adjectives came to be applied to Baptists as well. The newly "awakened" Baptists were called Separate Baptists, while the existing churches that belonged to the Philadelphia Association and shared its Confession of Faith were called Regular Baptists.[108] As both schools moved south the names went along.

The Separate Baptists attracted considerable numbers of Separate Congregationalists in the course of the conflict between the Old Light and New Light groups. One of these was Shubal Stearns, who migrated to Sandy Creek, North Carolina, in 1755 and with his brother-in-law, Daniel Marshall, began the work that led to the organization of the Sandy Creek Separate Baptist Association in 1758. Theologically its leaders were "modified Calvinists."[109]

The movement spread rapidly through the southern conlonies from Virginia to Florida and westward into Kentucky and Tennessee.

In the course of the fusions and mergers of Separate and Regular Baptists that began in the late eighteenth century and that climaxed in a general coming together of Regular and Separate Baptists in Virginia under the name of United Baptists in 1787 and the union of the Salem and Elkhorn Regular Baptist Associations with the South Kentucky Separate Baptist Association in Kentucky in 1801, a number of Separate Baptist churches sturdily maintained their independence and identity as Separate Baptists. Thus, for instance, the South Kentucky Association of Separate Baptists was formed in 1803. Other isolated groups persisted in Tennessee, Indiana, and Illinois. In 1912 several district associations united to form the General Association of Separate Baptists in Christ.

Separate Baptists reject all statements of faith. They also refuse the designation "Protestant" on the ground that its adherents "have never protested against what we hold to be the faith once delivered to the saints." But in spite of their formally anticreedal stance, they have a motto: "The Bible is our Guide, God our Ruler, and Jesus Christ our Redeemer." In addition they publish in their annual general association minutes Articles of Doctrine that affirm the infallibility of the Scriptures; the Trinity; salvation, regeneration, sanctification, justification, and redemption through faith in Christ's life and work; man's natural inability to liberate himself from his fallen estate; the salvation of those who endure to the end; the eternity of the joys of the righteous and the punishment of the wicked; baptism by immersion, the Lord's Supper, and foot washing as ordinances of Christ, with only true believers as proper subjects; the sanctity of the Lord's day (Sunday), to be spent in public or private worship and abstention from worldly concerns except in case of necessity or mercy; a divine day of judgment; the obligation to be affectionate to one another, to study the happiness of God's people in general, and to spread the gospel; and Christ's tasting of death for every human being, but with participation in his benefits limited to penitent believers (infants and idiots, who are included in the covenant of God's grace, excepted).[110]

There are no general headquarters. Several years ago there were six corresponding associations comprising 88 churches with a total membership estimated at 7,900.[111] There has been no response to recent efforts to contact the organization.

Regular Baptists

In the latter nineteenth century the designation "Regular Baptist" was revived by a number of associations other than those calling themselves "Old Regular Baptists," especially in Virginia, North Carolina, West Virginia, and Kentucky. These professed to perpetuate the English Baptist tradition that antedated the division into General and Particular Baptists. As late as 1964 there were reportedly 22 such Regular Baptist associations, with no general organization.[112]

Some of these were associations with a moderately long history. Thus in 1766 the Philadelphia Association dismissed four churches, with 142 members, in Loudoun and three other Virginia counties to form the Ketocton

Baptist Association, named after the oldest of the four churches, where the organization of the new association was perfected.[113] The association grew to a point where it had around forty churches in Virginia and Maryland. Then some of the churches joined other associations and other churches became extinct for one reason or another, until by the end of the 1880s only eight churches, with under three hundred members, were left. These reorganized the association in 1890 as the Ketocton Association of Regular Baptists.[114] During the next eighty years it enjoyed a modest growth. Between 1920 and 1946 it and the Indian Creek Association of Regular Baptists (West Virginia), established in 1845, the Mount Tabor (originally Danville) Association of Regular Baptists (Indiana), established in 1889, and the Mount Pleasant and Richland (originally Richland) Association of Regular Baptist[s] (Indiana and Kentucky), established in 1867, entered into correspondence and fellowship with each other.[115]

The Ketocton Association itself stresses the complete independence of the local church in governing itself, so that there are variations in constitutions, by-laws, and articles of faith from church to church. Theologically the association's Articles of Faith tend in a "Calvinistic" direction. They affirm the Trinity; the Bible as the divinely inspired revelation of God, through which the Holy Spirit converts sinners; the fall in Adam of all human beings and their entire and universal native depravity; God's eternal choice of his people in Christ to salvation; the special (that is, limited) and complete redemption of the family of God through Christ's blood, vicarious suffering, and sacrificial death; the direct agency of the Holy Spirit in regeneration and sanctification, and simultaneously and coetaneously with these operations the bringing forth of the fruits of the Holy Spirit; justification of the ungodly by grace through the imputed righteousness of Christ to those who believe; the absolute necessity of a holy life as the result of faith and as the evidence of regeneration; the general resurrection and judgment of all human beings, after which the wicked will receive everlasting punishment and the righteous life eternal: the imperative obligation to preach the gospel in all the world; believer's baptism by immersion in the name of the Father and the Son and the Holy Ghost; the Lord's Supper for baptized believers only: the examination and ordination of elders (bishops) and deacons by the laying on of hands of a presbytery under the authority of the church; a gospel church as the highest earthly ecclesiastical tribunal, congregational polity, and the equal voice and authority of all members of the church; and the sanctity of the first day of the week.[116] The Articles of Faith of the Indian Creek association are identical. The similar but briefer Articles of Faith of the other two associations have emphases of their own. Thus the Mount Tabor association declares that "the gospel of Jesus Christ, coming not in word only, but in power and in the Holy Ghost and in much assurance, is a means through the Spirit of conversion and regeneration of sinners and the comfort of saints."[117] The Mount Pleasant and Richland Association lists foot washing as an ordinance and affirms the preservation to eternal salvation of the reborn.[118]

The four corresponding associations do not as such have individual or common headquarters. The Ketocton Association has 13 congregations with about 1,200 members; the Indian Creek Association 15 congregations with about 1,200 members; the Mount Tabor Association 8 congregations with about 800 members, and the Mount Pleasant and Richland Association 5 congregations with 185 members. In 1956 congregations of the four associations organized the Regular Baptist Missionary Fund, Incorporated, which carries on foreign missions in Morocco, Liberia, and Japan. But the bulk of the foreign-mission giving of the churches of the four associations is channeled through various independent boards.[119]

Old Regular Baptists

"Old Regular Baptist the Church of Jesus Christ"[120] is, with slight variations, the self-designation of a group of Baptist associations that finds its greatest concentration in a narrow band of the American mideast states from Indiana to Virginia, but that is represented as far afield as Florida, Michigan, Arizona, and Washington.

They represent a latter-nineteenth-century revival of the Regular Baptist tradition[121] after the unions of Regular and Separate Baptists in Virginia in 1786–1787 and in Kentucky in 1801. They undertake to trace their history back to the apostles, Christ, and John the Baptist by way of the Montanists ("Tertullianists"), the Novatians, the Donatists ("Numidians"), the Paulicians, the Albigenses, Waldensians, and Patarenes, the followers of Arnold of Brescia and Henry of Lausanne in the twelfth century, the Lollards, the Anabaptists, the English and Welsh Baptists, and the Philadelphia Baptist Association (1707).[122]

The Old Regular Baptists commit themselves to the "twelve marks" of the "apostolic church": (1) a church composed wholly of penitent believers; (2) baptism by immersion in water in the name of the Father, Son, and Holy Ghost; (3) frequent commemoration by the baptized believers of Christ's passion and death around the Lord's table "by partaking of the common bread to represent his broken body and the common wine to represent his shed blood"; (4) strict discipline; (5) the independent, or congregational, form of church government; (6) religious liberty, soul freedom, and complete separation of church and state; (7) a church membership consisting generally of the poor, obscure, unlearned, afflicted, despised, and persecuted; (8) the fraternal priesthood of all the members and the choice by the membership of the elders (or bishops) and deacons; (9) "a humble, God-called, and God-qualified ministry" that is (10) unsalaried and more or less self-supporting;[123] (11) the sending out of divinely called and qualified ministers at the Lord's direction; (12) the church[124] as "the only divinely recognized religious organization in the world."[125]

The Articles of Faith of the different associations vary in scope and detail. They commonly affirm the Trinity; original sin and the total inability of human beings to recover themselves; election by grace; the justification of sinners entirely by the imputation of Christ's righteousness;[126] the final perseverance of the saints; the church as a congregation of faithful believers; the resurrection of the just to happiness and of the unjust to eternal punishment; Christ as the Head and Governor of the church; believer's baptism by immersion in water ("back foremost, so as to cover all over," several of the associations say); the Lord's Supper and the washing of the saints' feet[127] as perpetual ordinances in the church; the rejection of every doctrine that encourages people in their sins or "cause[s] them to settle down on anything short of saving faith in Christ"; the disavowal of the doctrines of "particular election or reprobation so as to make God partial, directly or indirectly, so as to injure any of the children of men"; the necessity that ministers be regularly called and have the hands of a presbytery of the church laid on them before they may administer the ordinances;[128] and the obligation of all church members to contribute to the necessary expenses of the church and to remember the poor according to their ability.[129]

The Old Regular Baptists see themselves as having "practically" the same beliefs as the "old time" United Baptists, as represented by the Paint Union (1837), Tri-State Zion (1848), Mount Zion (1869), Bethlehem (1870), Blaine Union (1894), Iron Hill (1904), and New Hope (1920) associations.[130] But no Old Regular Baptist association corresponds with any of these United Baptist associations as far as this writer could determine.[131]

The churches regularly meet for divine service one Sunday or weekend each month,[132] and observe the Lord's Supper once a year.

Both the individual churches and the associations are strenuously independent and there is no central organization or headquarters. The 16 Old Regular Baptist associations that this writer knows from the examination of minutes published between 1962 and 1970 (all but one set published in 1966 or later) range in size from the Mud River Association with 4 churches and 120 members to the New Salem Association with 51 churches and 3,021 members and the Union Association with 64 churches and 3,518 members. The total number of churches is about 315, with 17,500 members.[133]

United Baptists

After two years of preliminary negotiations and meetings, the National Association of United Baptists of America held its first General Session at Huntington, West Virginia, in 1964. Four associations. with over 90 churches and an overall membership of more than 9,800, and 22 individual churches with over 2,500 members, associated with the national body. The churches of the association are located in West Virginia, Ohio, Kentucky, Missouri, and Arkansas. The basis of the association's faith and practice is the King James Version of the Bible, from which, the constitution prescribes, the association "shall never tolerate the departure." The final article of the constitution places it on record as "taking a stand against the National Council of Churches and the Ecumenical Council," that is, the World Council of Churches.[134]

The United Baptists take their name from a union of Regular Baptists and Separate Baptists initiated in 1772 and completed at Richmond, Virginia, in 1787, and from the "Terms of Union" that brought together the Salem and Elkhorn Regular Baptist Association and the South Kentucky Separate Baptist Association in 1801. Soon the adjective "United" was widely dropped, but it survived in Kentucky, West Virginia, and Missouri. In addition to the states already listed, there are United Baptists in Georgia, Alabama, North and South Carolina, Virginia, Tennessee, Indiana, and New England. A leader of the national association estimates that there may be as many as 40 regional associations.[135] Other estimates range from 11 to 32 associations, with from 8 to 18 in Kentucky.[136] Actual statistics are hard to come by. In 1955, 586 United Baptist churches reported an overall membership of 63,641.

There is a wide divergence in theology among United Baptists, with traces of both Arminianism and traditional Calvinism. United Baptists themselves frequently see their differences in terms of being progressive or conservative. "Progressive" associations practice open Communion, stress home and foreign missions and religious education, and welcome as ministers graduates of theological seminaries, while the "conservative" associations practice close Communion and are less hospitable to missions, religious education, and a professionally trained ministry. Polity is uniformly and ruggedly congregational and the regional associations exist only for fellowship and counsel. Communication between associations is optional and is still usually by way of "letters of correspondence" and fraternal delegates.

Typical of the "progressive" associations is the Bethlehem Association in West Virginia, with 52 churches and over 6,100 members. It prides itself on an extensive youth program and graded Sabbath (Sunday) schools with teacher-training classes. Some churches practice Communion every Sunday and foot washing as a third church ordinance. A twelve-article, biblically documented Synopsis of Faith teaches the infallibility of the Old and New Testaments and asserts that Christians must look to the New Testament as their only rule of practice. It affirms the necessity of regeneration "or begetting with the word of truth" and of the new birth "as a means of entering the kingdom of God." Repentance and conversion, accomplished by the faithful preaching of the gospel, are essential prerequisites to baptism, "the immersion of a penitent believer in water as a line of distinction between the world and the church." Finally, it affirms a universal resurrection and the eternal happiness of the just and the eternal punishment of the unjust.[137]

The General Association of Baptists (Duck River [and Kindred] Associations of Baptists)

In 1826 Arminian theology and the teachings of Alexander Campbell, one of the early leaders of the Restoration movement, split the strongly Calvinistic

Elk River Association of Primitive Baptists in Tennessee. More than a third of the churches withdrew to form the Duck River Baptist Association of Christ. In 1829 the group dropped "of Christ" from its name. During the next fourteen years the questions of joining the Baptist state convention that had been organized in 1833 to educate ministers and send out missionaries, of encouraging young people and ministers to attend the state's seminary at Murfreesboro, and of using the literature of the Philadelphia Baptist Publishing and Sunday School Society divided the Duck River Association. In 1843 the association split into almost equal parts. Since then each part has claimed to be the Duck River Association. The "Missionary" association ultimately affiliated with the Southern Baptist Convention. In 1953, in order to minimize the confusion attendant upon the identical names, it took the name Duck River Association of Missionary Baptists, even though "Duck River" is a geographical misnomer considering the territory its churches occupy. The two associations seem farther apart in teaching and practice than they were in 1842, although their mutual relations are friendly and in most cases they exchange letters of recommendation for transfer of membership.[138] The "Separate" Duck River Association—which is sometimes called the Baptist Church of Christ—in the meantime has entered into fellowship with the Mount Zion, Union, Original East Union, Ebenezer, New Liberty, and the two Mount Pleasant associations of Alabama, Tennessee, and Georgia. The Duck River, Mount Zion, Original East Union, New Liberty, and the two Mount Zion, Union, Original East Union, Ebenezer, New Liberty, and the two Mount Pleasant associations and the Pleasant Hill Church of Marion Kentucky, form the General Association of Baptists, which has 8,492 members in 81 churches.[139] In addition they are reportedly in "correspondence" with other associations in the states named and in Mississippi. They see themselves bound by close ties to Regular, United, and Separate Baptists.

The twelve Articles of Faith of the "Separate" Duck River Association combine both Calvinistic and Arminian tenets. "Jesus Christ by the grace of God tasted death for every man, and through his meritorious death the way of salvation is made possible for God to have mercy upon all who come unto him upon Gospel terms" (Article 4). "Sinners are justified in the sight of God only by the righteousness of God imputed unto them through faith in the Lord Jesus Christ" (Article 5). "The saints will persevere in grace and . . . not one of them will be finally lost" (Article 6). "The visible church of Christ is a congregation of faithful men and women, who have given themselves to the Lord, and have obtained fellowship with each other, and have agreed to keep a godly discipline according to the rules of the Gospel" (Article 8). Believer's baptism by immersion in water, the Lord's Supper and the washing of the saints' feet are perpetually binding "ordinances of the Gospel" (Article 10). "No person has the right to administer the ordinance of the Gospel, except that he is legally called and qualified" (Article 11). No work or worldly business—works of piety, mercy and necessity excepted—ought to be transacted on the Lord's day, which ought to be set apart for the worship of God (Article 12).[140] The other associations hold a similar position.

The associations take free-will offerings to cover the expenses of their unsalaried ministers, and while they object to the "antimissionary" label they have no missions, missionary societies, or benevolent organizations. Most churches now have Sunday schools and a few have some youth activities. The associations have no authority over the local churches.

Primitive Baptists of the Old School or Predestinarian Faith and Order

Primitive Baptist Elder Daniel Parker (1781–1844) was a redoubtable early nineteenth-century opponent of Methodist Arminianism, missions, Sunday schools, and an educated ministry. The son and grandson of Baptist ministers, Parker was baptized in his native Culpeper County, Virginia, in 1802. He was licensed as a Baptist preacher in 1803. The same year he moved with his parents and his wife to Dixon County, Tennessee. In 1806 he was ordained. Already strongly antimissionary himself, about 1810 he heard from the lips of an unnamed "older brother" in the Baptist ministry what became known as the "two-seed-in-the-spirit predestinarian" doctrine. After sixteen years of study and reflection—in the course of which he and his father and their families moved to Crawford County, Illinois, where he organized the Lamatte Baptist Church—he adopted the doctrine himself and began to propagate it energetically by mouth and in print.

In 1826, the year in which Parker was elected to a seat in the Illinois state senate, he published a thirty-seven-page pamphlet, *Views on Two Seeds*, in which he set forth his position, as follows:

Genesis 3:15 is the key to the understanding of the Word of God. God created man in his own image; thus Adam, the seed in him, and Eve are "the complete figure" of the Father, the Son, and the Holy Ghost. All that stood and fell in Adam were the elect of God, chosen in Christ before the foundation of the world. The nonelect, the serpent's seed, the extra production of Eve, were not created in Adam but were brought into the world as the product of sin. The two seeds, as well as the enmity between them, are exemplified in Cain and Abel, Ishmael and Isaac, Esau and Jacob. Conceding that God has made of one blood all the nations that dwell on the face of the earth, Parker argued that God did not create the serpent's seed, the nonelect, in Adam, but he gave to the male human being the power to beget and to the female human being the power to conceive. Satan by sin through the male begets his seed in the female, while God because of the woman's sin multiplies her conception. In this way the serpent's seed comes through the original stock, but God is not their creator in the original stock. The seed in Christ, chosen before the foundation of the world, becomes a seed that will endure forever and Christ becomes the covenant head in the plan of redemption. This seed, regenerated and born of the Spirit, washed and made clean in the blood of the Lamb, becomes the Lord's portion and the glory of God shines in the face of Jesus Christ.

The pamphlet evoked a considerable amount of debate, to which Parker contributed by a second pamphlet of thirteen pages, *A Supplement or Explanation of My Views*. In it he attempted to rebut the objections of his critics, but without further development of his original position.

A third pamphlet, eighty-three pages long, *The Second Dose of Doctrine*, develops the New Testament proof for Parker's radical predestinarianism. His key passage is Ephesians 1:19. The concluding summary emphasizes the cardinal point in his theology as "the seed is in the spirit, not the flesh." He affirms the resurrection of the body of Christ, the church, and the salvation of the elect by grace alone. The atonement, he asserts, applies only to those born of the good seed; those born of the evil seed are absolutely lost. From the premise that "Christ came to save sinners and He finished His work," Parker concludes that there should be no paid ministry. He affirms three ordinances: baptism, the Lord's Supper, and foot washing. He opposes all "human institutions," specifically missionary activity and schools of theology. Church government must be congregational; no person or body of persons should attempt to usurp the people's authority. Churches may legitimately form associations for fellowship only; benevolences are human works that the devil has inspired. Parker ends with a defiant "as God never intends to make peace with his enemies, neither does Daniel Parker intend to make peace with his enemies by compromising the truth of God's word."[141]

Late in 1832 Parker and three brothers made a trip to Texas. While a Mexican law of 1823 forbade organization of non-Roman-Catholic congregations in Texas, further study of the law persuaded Parker that it did not forbid the immigration of an organized Baptist congregation. So he returned to Illinois and in July 1833 he organized the Pilgrim Predestinarian Regular Baptist Church of Jesus Christ. The next month the congregation set out for Texas, where it arrived in 1834.

In spite of harassment by the authorities (even though the law against non-Roman-Catholic congregations was revoked in 1834), Indian raids, and war, the church survived.[142] The first "arm," or daughter church, came into being in 1837, and in 1840 the Union Association of Regular Predestinarian Baptists was organized. Its twelve Articles of Faith are identical—except for corrections in spelling and grammar—with the Articles of Faith that Parker drafted in 1833 for the Pilgrim Predestinarian Regular Baptist Church of Jesus Christ.[143] Significantly they do not explicitly affirm any "two-seed-in-the-spirit predestinarian" views.

They affirm belief in the Trinity and God's revelation of himself in the Scripture of truth; man's original goodness in creation and the depraved state into which he has fallen under the influence of the power of darkness; God's choice of the elect in Christ before the world began and Christ's life, death, resurrection, and ascension as the meritorious cause by which the church is ever reconciled to God; the ultimate effectual call, regeneration, and birth in the Spirit of the elect and their perseverance in grace to glory; good works as the effect of grace in the heart and an indispensable basis of the Christian union and relationship; washing one another's feet, baptism by immersion, and the Lord's Supper as standing ordinances; the restriction of the right to administer the ordinances to ministers ordained by laying on of hands of the presbytery and acting "under and by the authority of the Gospel church"; the obligation of the church to have no Christian fellowship with all false sects; the authority of the Bible, "keeping in view the expression of our understanding therein, as principles upon which we have agreed to unite"; the church as the invisible spiritual Kingdom of God set up in the world; resting from all temporal concerns on the Lord's day except in cases of necessity and mercy; and the resurrection of the just to eternal joy and of the unjust to endless punishment.[144]

The Union Primitive Baptist Association of Old School or Predestinarian Faith and Order, as the association is now known, has a membership of 110, with the Pilgrim Church, Palestine, Texas, reporting 16 members. In fellowship with the Union Association are the Primitive Baptist Association of the Regular Predestinarian Faith and Order, organized in 1884, with 2 active churches in Texas and 25 members, and the South Louisiana Primitive Association, organized in 1881, with 3 congregations and 28 members. The Articles of Faith of the Primitive Baptist Association of the Regular Predestinarian Faith and Order are identical with those of the Union Association.[145] The fourteen Articles of Faith of the South Louisiana Primitive Baptist Association are different in text and order but affirm essentially the same doctrinal position; the constituting churches identify themselves as "Absolute Predestinarian Primitive Baptist Churches."[146]

National Primitive Baptist Convention of the United States of America

The division of Baptists into "Missionary" and "Primitive" Baptists involved black Baptists as well as white Baptists. The Huntsville (Alabama) African Baptist Church (now the St. Bartley Primitive Baptist Church), organized in 1820, entered the white Flint River Baptist Association the following year. When the split came in the late 1820s, the Huntsville African Baptist Church sided with the Primitive party. In 1865, following the War between the States, the white membership forced the black churches out of the association; the latter formed the Indian Creek Primitive Baptist Association in 1869. The same process took place elsewhere in the American South. Around 1906 sentiment for a national convention of black Primitive Baptists reached the point where Elder Clarence Francis Sams of Key West, Florida, Elmer George S. Crawford of De Land, Florida, Elder James H. Carey of Charlotte, North Carolina, and others called on interested ministers to attend an organization meeting in Huntsville the following year. In July 1907 eighty-eight elders from seven southern states responded to the invitation and organized the National Primitive Baptist Convention.[147]

The convention reflects Primitive Baptist positions in its very loose organization, without centralization of authority. Again, the black Primitive Baptists have been less rigid theologically than their white counterparts. No common confession of faith binds the local congregations and associations together, so that there is some variation in doctrine within the convention, chiefly in the degree of stress on social action. A shift in thinking about missions has likewise been going on; the 1967 convention at least had before it a proposal to begin foreign mission work, even though it did not act favorably on the proposal.[148]

The convention's sixteen Articles of Faith affirm belief in the Trinity; the Bible; "the doctrine of eternal and particular election of a definite number of the human race . . . chosen in Christ before the foundation of the world"; a covenant [of] redemption between God the Father and God the Son"; and the fall of man and "the communication of Adam's sinful nature to his posterity by ordinary generation." They hold that all chosen in Christ shall hear his voice and "be effectually called, regenerated and born again." They teach justification "in the sight of God alone by the righteousness of Jesus Christ imputed to them by faith"; good works as the fruits of faith that "justify us in the sight of men and angels as evidences of our gracious state"; the final perseverance of the saints; the general judgment of both the just and the unjust followed by eternal joys and punishment respectively; the visible church as a complete and independent congregation of baptized believers adhering to a special covenant "which recognizes Christ as their only lawgiver and ruler"; pastors and deacons as biblical officers of the church; and believer's baptism by immersion in the name of the Father and of the Son and of the Holy Ghost. Only ministers who have been regularly baptized, called, and "come under the imposition of a presbytery by the majority of the Church of Christ" have the right to administer the ordinances of the gospel and only baptized and orderly church members have a right to Communion at the Lord's table. They affirm belief in "washing the saints' feet in a church capacity immediately after the Lord's Supper."[149]

The convention claims 2,196 churches with an inclusive membership of 1,465,000.[150] The mailing address for the headquarters of the convention is P. O. Box 2355, Tallahassee, Florida 32301. There has been no response to recent efforts to contact the convention.

The Baptist Federation of Canada

The Reverend Ebenezer Moulton (1709–1783) of Massachusetts Bay Colony came to Nova Scotia in 1760 and organized a Baptist congregation at Horton (now Wolfville) in 1763. That same year an entire Massachusetts

Bay Colony congregation, together with its minister, the Reverend Nathan Mason, moved from Swansea to Sackville, New Brunswick. Both congregations had very short lives, but Horton became the site of another Baptist congregation that Nicholas Pierson organized in 1778. It survives as the Wolfville Baptist Church.

It was the Baptists who capitalized on the brief itinerant ministry of fervent Henry Alline (1748–1784), the "New Light" Congregationalist mystic and evangelist of Falmouth, Nova Scotia, in the Maritime provinces. Important accessions were the American Loyalists who fled to the Maritimes after the Revolutionary War and the Anglican laymen of St. Paul's Church, Halifax, who renounced the domination of both bishop and Crown by forming the Granville Street Baptist Church in 1827.

Farther west, in what became the provinces of Quebec and Ontario, American Loyalists established themselves in the last two decades of the eighteenth century. Until 1820 (except during the War of 1812) they maintained ties with the United States associations that had sent them the first missionaries. More permanent was the tradition of "closed membership" that these missionaries planted, even though there were some early churches founded under American influence with Congregational cooperation that practiced open Communion. The controversy on the Communion question agitated the Canadian Baptists throughout the century.

The Canadian Baptist community took on a European cast from the first half of the nineteenth century on, with the coming of the Scottish Baptists, the English Baptists, and the French-speaking Swiss Baptists.

The "underground railroad" of the American Abolitionists in the period before the War between the States funneled considerable numbers of fugitive black slaves into Canada. Many of them were Baptists and the Baptist churches that they established have about 20,000 members today.

In the opening up of the Canadian west from the 1870s on, Baptists were in the van of homesteading farmers. In British Columbia in the 1890s, Canadian and American Baptists worked side by side in establishing Baptist churches. The twentieth century saw the big influx of Baptists from Scandinavia, Germany, Central Europe, Russia, and the Ukraine.

The major problem that faced Canadian Baptists—a problem heightened until recently by persisting difficulties of communication—was to combine the traditional Baptist free-churchmanship, concentrated on the spiritual freedom and purity of the gathered church, with the need for a wider fellowship that would enable the churches to accomplish together what they could not do singly.

The movement toward cooperation began with the formation of the Nova Scotia Baptist Association in 1800. In 1906 the Free Baptists and the Regular Baptists of Nova Scotia merged in a Maritime United Baptist Convention on a basis of union that recommended itself elsewhere.

In Upper Canada a series of associations came into being throughout the early nineteenth century, as far back as the Thurlow Baptist Association in 1802. The Baptist Convention of Ontario and Quebec (originally and somewhat ambitiously incorporated in 1880 as the Baptist Union of Canada) united the two major groupings in 1888. This group suffered the loss of about a fifth of its congregations in 1926 during the Canadian version of the fundamentalist-modernist controversy; the Fellowship of Evangelical Baptists ultimately grew out of this rupture.

In the western provinces the Baptist Union of Western Canada came into being in 1909; associated with it are seven European ethnic Baptist groups, two of which remain in affiliation with their fellows in the United States.

Despite promising but vain efforts in 1900 and again in 1905, the problem of a Dominion-wide organization eluded any kind of solution until the adoption of the federal principle in 1944, when the three regional conventions created the Baptist Federation of Canada. The federation is deliberately designed to be as loose as possible in order to allay fears that it would become a monolithic superchurch. It functions through a delegate assembly that meets every three years, a council that meets annually, and an executive committee that meets several times a year. Implementing of the federation's proposals rests with the three regional conventions and their boards. The federation has achieved the greatest success in the areas of Christian education, stewardship, missions, evangelism, relief for refugees and disaster victims, literature production, and ministerial training and retirement.

In terms of polity, the "carefully planned cooperative enterprises" that the situations confronting Canadian Baptists have demanded have shifted them "from a simple democracy of pure congregationalism over into a modified form of presbyterian polity." At the same time, Canadian Baptists still "stress the independence of the local church" and, in the words of one of their leaders, "occasionally suffer when [they] overdo it."[151]

The tradition of closed membership has persisted within the conventions of the federation and still remains the most common pattern. At the same time, an increasing number practice open Communion; it is all but universal in Ontario and Quebec churches, in spite of the close-Communion clause in their constitutions. Some churches have established associate memberships for non-Baptists, and there has even been some willingness to experiment with open membership.

Theologically there is the same continuum of opinion among Canadian Baptists that inclusive Baptist bodies exhibit elsewhere in the English-speaking world, modified in its expression by the characteristic Canadian temperament. The Regular or Calvinistic or Particular tradition is still stronger than the Free or Arminian tradition with its Anabaptist antecedents, but both emphases are apparent. The wounds struck by the bitter struggle between the fundamentalists and their opponents in the 1920s have not wholly healed. There is a certain uneasiness about the Ecumenical movement; the Convention of Ontario and Quebec is more ready to affiliate with the World Council of Churches than the other conventions.

The central stresses in Canadian Baptist theology continue to fall on the lordship of Christ, the sufficiency of the Bible (with a variety of understandings of the mode of biblical inspiration and the principles of biblical interpretation), the New Testament as the church's only creed, the competency of the individual soul in religion, a voluntary and regenerate church membership, believer's baptism by immersion, soul liberty, the autonomy of the local congregation as modified by participation in wider voluntary groupings of churches in response to existing needs, religious liberty, and the separation of church and state.[152]

Canadian Baptists have not been as ready as British and American Baptists to produce confessions of faith. They have, however, in recent years produced a number of serious efforts at theological statements that have exerted wide influence, even though the respective conventions have not formally adopted them as confessional documents. The Convention of Ontario and Quebec has been most productive in this area. As a result of the Canadian version of the fundamentalist-modernist controversy of the 1920s it put forth a statement that proposed to provide guidance at a time of great theological unrest. In 1947 the convention's Commission on Baptist Principles produced a document entitled *The Baptist Position*. A number of ministers in the same convention drafted a statement which, recast and rewritten by F. W. Waters, came out in 1958 under federation auspices as *Protestantism—A Baptist Interpretation*. Another commission of the same convention, under the chairmanship of Professor Russell Foster Aldwinckle, in 1965 produced a symposium of essays, *Things Most Surely Believed—A Baptist View*, on various aspects of Baptist belief and practice that the three conventions are currently studying.

The address of the Federation's headquarters: 91 Queen Street, Box 1298, Brantford, Ontario, N3T ST6. Its three regional conventions comprise a total of 1,117 churches with an inclusive membership of 119,329. They carry on foreign missions in India, Bolivia, and Angola. The federation belongs to the Baptist World Alliance and to the Canadian Council of Churches.

The Fellowship of Evangelical Baptist Churches in Canada

During World War I the fundamentalist-modernist controversy in the Baptist Convention of Ontario and Quebec lay dormant. In 1919 it revived, and McMaster University, then a Baptist institution located at Toronto, became the focus of the struggle. The leader of the fundamentalists was the Reverend T. T. Shields (1873–1975), pastor of the Jarvis Street Baptist Church in Toronto, which the convention excommunicated at its 1927 meeting as "not in harmony and cooperation with the work and objectives of the said Convention." Before this, Shields had already laid the groundwork for a new body and he proceeded to found the Union of Regular Baptist Churches with seventy churches that same year. Internal disagreements divided the new body; the Fellowship of Independent Baptist Churches split off in 1933, and in 1949 another group, including Shields and the Jarvis Street Church, withdrew. The Fellowship of Independent Baptist Churches and what remained of the Union of Regular Baptist Churches reunited in 1953 as the Fellowship of Evangelical Baptist Churches. In 1963 the Regular Baptist Missionary Fellowship of Alberta (organized in 1930), and in 1965 the Convention of Regular Baptists of British Columbia (founded in 1927), formally joined the fellowship.

The fellowship's Statement of Faith, adopted at the organizing convention of 1953, affirms the Bible "to be the complete Word of God," declares that its sixty-six books as originally written were verbally inspired and "entirely free from error," and that it is the final authority in all matters of faith and practice. It affirms the Trinity; the absolute and essential deity of Jesus Christ and of the Holy Spirit; the existence of Satan as an evil personality; the total depravity of man; salvation by the sovereign, electing grace of God; the vicarious expiatory and propitiatory nature of Christ's death; justification alone by faith in Christ's all-sufficient sacrifice and resurrection; the divine preservation and final perfecting of those whom God has effectually called; the personal return of Christ; the resurrection of the just and the unjust; the eternal blessedness of the redeemed, and the conscious, eternal punishment of the wicked; the sovereignty and independence of the local church of immersed believers under its pastors and deacons; believer's baptism by immersion and the Lord's Supper (in which the bread and wine symbolize Christ's body and shed blood) as the only two church ordinances; the entire separation of church and state; religious liberty; the Lord's day (Sunday) as the divinely appointed day for worship and spiritual exercise; the divine appointment of civil government; and the obligation of Christians to honor and obey the magistrates except in things opposed to Christ's will.[153]

The fellowship has 370 churches (including 19 French-speaking churches and missions with 44,00 members. It has more missionary members overseas —450—than it has pastors at home. These missionaries serve under different boards; 15 serve in India and Japan under the fellowship's board. The fellowship maintains relations with three Baptist bodies in the United States: the General Association of Regular Baptist Churches, the Conservative Baptist Association of America, and the Baptist Bible Fellowship. Its headquarters are at 74 Sheppard Avenue West, Willowdale, Ontario M2N 1M3.

Association of Regular Baptist Churches (Canada)

In the course of the fundamentalist-modernist controversy in the Baptist Convention of Ontario and Quebec, the 1927 meeting of the convention excommunicated the Jarvis Street Baptist Church, Toronto, Ontario, of which Dr. T. T. Shields (1873–1955), the militant leader of the fundamentalist party since 1919, was the pastor. Sympathetic churches followed the Jarvis Street Church out of the convention and in 1928 Shields and his supporters organized a new Union of Regular Baptist Churches in Hamilton, Ontario.

jurisdictional issues split the new body, and in the 1930s a group seceded to organize the Independent Fellowship of Baptist Churches. In 1949 another controversy moved Shields and the Jarvis Street Church to withdraw from the Union (which ultimately became a part of the Fellowship of Evangelical Baptist Churches).[154] In 1958 the Jarvis Street Baptist Church became the center of a new organization, the Association of Regular Baptist Churches (Canada). Its doctrinal statement commits the member congregations to the being and unity of God; the Trinity; the divine inspiration of the Bible ("absolutely free from error, as no other writings have ever been or ever will be inerrant"); the direct creation of man by "divine fiat, and not by evolution"; the fall of man in Adam; election according to the foreknowledge of God; "the virgin birth and its corollary, the essential Deity of Christ"; Christ's expiatory, vicarious atonement; justification by faith alone; the work of the Holy Spirit in regeneration and sanctification; the eternal security of all believers; the perseverance of the saints; the answerability of all men for accepting or rejecting Christ; Christ's bodily resurrection; his second personal and visible coming; the judgment and eternal punishment of the wicked and the everlasting blessedness of the righteous; immersion of believers in the name of the Father, Son, and Holy Spirit; the Lord's Supper; the church as "a company of immersed believers voluntarily associated and meeting on the first day of the week"; and churches whose doctrinal position may be generally defined by the Baptist Confession of Faith set forth at London in 1689, or the New Hampshire Confession of Faith, or the Philadelphia Confession of Faith, or any other statement of faith that enunciates the same truths. Churches permitting "the repeated denial of the supernaturalism of Christianity" or acquiesce in the omission of the teaching of the supernaturalism of Christianity as it affects the "character of the Scriptures, the person of Christ, His expiatory, redemptive work, the New Birth, or other principles of Christian supernaturalism" are barred from membership.[155]

The headquarters of the Association are at 337 Jarvis Street, Toronto, Ontario M5B 2C7. There are 10 churches in 2 provinces with an estimated total membership of under 1,500. Missions are supported in Jamaica, Martinique, St. Lucia, France, Belgium, Switzerland, and Spain.[156]

Fellowship of Fundamental Baptist Churches

The Fellowship of Fundamental Baptist Churches came into being in 1960 after a previous similar fellowship had begun to function only intermittently and finally had ceased to exist. This defunct fellowship consisted for the most part of pastors and congregations that had withdrawn from the Maritime United Baptist Convention as a protest against what they regarded as modernism.

The fellowship professes to adhere to "the historic Baptist position in polity and doctrine" and shares to a large extent the position of the General Association of Regular Baptist Churches in the United States. It rejects organized conventions on the ground that they jeopardize and restrict the freedom of the local churches. The Seventeen Articles of Faith appended to the fellowship's constitution have sections on the Scriptures ("the Holy Bible as originally written was verbally inspired and . . . has truth without any admixture of error for its matter"); the Trinity; the Holy Spirit; the devil, or Satan; creation ("we accept the Genesis account of creation and believe that man came by direct creation of God and not by evolution"); the fall of man; the virgin birth; the atonement for sin ("a voluntary substitution of [Christ] in the sinner's place"); grace in the new creation ("the new birth is . . . instantaneous and not a process, [and] its proper evidence appears in the holy fruits of repentance and faith and newness of life"); justification ("solely through faith"); faith as the only condition of salvation; the local church ("[it] has the absolute right of self-government free from the interference of any hierarchy of individuals or organizations [and] on all matters of membership, of polity, of government, of discipline, of benevolence, the will of the local church is final"); the ordinances of believer's baptism by immersion ("a solemn and beautiful emblem of our faith") and the Lord's Supper; the security of the saints; the radical and essential difference between the righteous ("such only as through faith are justified") and the wicked; civil government; and Christ, his resurrection, his imminent, personal, physical and premillennial return, and related events (completion of the church age by the rapture of all living believers; the great tribulation; Christ's return with his saints; the judgment of the nations; the millennial kingdom, "with regathered Israel central"; the great white throne judgment; the eternal peace of the righteous and the eternal damnation of the wicked).[157]

Thirteen congregations (7 in New Brunswick, 4 in Nova Scotia, and 2 in Maine) have an estimated 600 members.[158]

Primitive Baptist Conference of New Brunswick, Maine, and Nova Scotia

A number of Free Will Baptist groups in New Brunswick united to form the Christian Conference Church in 1832. In 1847 they changed their name to Free Christian Baptists.[159] Around 1875 George W. Orser, an able pioneer preacher of Carleton County, found himself in disagreement with the other Free Christian Baptists on the question of unsalaried ministers. As an eloquent champion of the "free Gospel," he opposed set stipends for ministers. Another tenet of his called for a "primitive" or "apostolic" form of church government. He also repudiated for the most part the idea of an educated ministry.

Orser withdrew from the Free Christian Baptists and with his supporters organized what became the Primitive Baptist Conference of New Brunswick, Maine, and Nova Scotia.

The conference's "treatise of the faith," which Orser sanctioned, has twenty-one chapters, covering the Holy Scriptures; the being and attributes of God; the divine government and providence; creation, the primitive state of man, and his fall ("[human beings] are not naturally willing to obey God, but they are inclined to evil. . . . none by virtue of any natural goodness and mere work of their own can become the children of God"); Christ; the Holy Spirit; the atonement and mediation of Christ ("sacrifice for the sins of the world, [that] made salvation possible for all men"); the Gospel call ("co-extensive with the atonement to all men . . . so that salvation is rendered equally possible to all"); repentance; faith; regeneration; justification and sanctification; rejection of an absolute perseverance of the saints ("there are strong grounds to hope that the truly regenerate will persevere . . . but their future obedience and final salvation are neither determined nor certain"); the Sabbath; the church; the Gospel ministry; believer's baptism by immersion and the Lord's Supper ("the bread . . . the emblem of His broken body, and the cup the emblem of His shed blood"); death and the intermediate state; Christ's second coming; the resurrection of the dead; the general judgment and future retribution.[160]

The conference is strongly evangelical, opposes modernism and compromise in any form, and belongs to no ecumenical organizations. Worship and church government are very free.

There are 20 churches (chiefly rural) in New Brunswick, 4 in Nova Scotia, 1 in Maine, the estimated total membership of these churches is 1,500.[161] The missionary program of the conference takes the form of support of faith missions. The headquarters are at the Saint John Valley Bible Camp, Hartland, New Brunswick.

The Covenanted Baptist Church of Canada

The Covenanted Baptist Church of Canada represents the Primitive Baptist tradition in the Dominion of Canada. The members chose the name because they "believe in a covenant of grace ordered in all things and sure." The church is concentrated in the vicinity of Dutton, Ontario, and is composed of descendants of emigrants from Scotland and from Caledonia, New York. The first elder, Dougald Campbell of North Knapdale, Scotland, came to Canada in 1818 and settled at Aldborough, near Dutton. The Covenanted Baptist Church of Canada teaches the absolute predestination of all things and is in fellowship with the Baptist churches of the United States that stand by the doctrine adopted at the Black Rock gathering in 1832. Services are conducted in six communities in the area.[162] The total active membership is estimated at about 30.[163]

The North American Baptist General Conference

The decade from 1841 to 1851 saw German Baptist immigrants establishing churches in various parts of the eastern and midwestern United States and in the province of Ontario. Among them were "The German Church of the Lord That Meets on Poplar Street" in Philadelphia (1843), now called the

Fleischmann Memorial Baptist Church after its founder, Konrad Anton Fleischmann (1812–1867); the churches that Alexander von Puttkamer founded in Buffalo and Albany; the Manitowoc (Wisconsin) congregation of East Prussian immigrants; and the Pin Oak Baptist Church at Mount Sterling, Missouri, founded by August Rauschenbusch, the father of Walter Rauschenbusch, the last two both organized in 1850. These and others joined together in the first meeting of the German Baptist Conference at Philadelphia in 1851. By 1859 it had 61 churches and over 2,600 members. Considerations of convenience dictated a division into independent eastern and western conferences. Since the rivalry that developed proved almost disastrous, representatives of all the German Baptist churches in the United States and Canada met at Wilmot, Ontario, in 1865 to organize the General Conference of German Baptist Churches in North America. The eastern and western conferences continued to meet annually and the General Conference convened every three years. The shift from German to English came rapidly after World War I, and in 1940 the organization officially changed its name to North American Baptist General Conference.

In 1946 the conference adopted the following tenets as the preamble to its constitution: "We, as New Testament Baptists, affirm our faith in the Lord Jesus Christ for our salvation and believe in those great distinctive principles for which Baptists have lived and died, such as (1) soul liberty; (2) the inspired authority of the Scriptures in matters of faith and conduct; (3) the separation of church and state; (4) the revelation of God through Jesus Christ as only Saviour and Lord; (5) regenerated church membership; (6) believer's baptism by immersion; (7) the congregational form of church government; and (8) the proclamation of the Gospel throughout all the world."[164]

The conference numbers 245 churches in the United States and Canada, with an inclusive membership of 41,437. It carries on foreign mission work in Africa, Japan, Brazil, and Austria. The headquarters are at 7308 Madison Street, Forest Park, Illinois 60130.

Baptist General Conference

The Baptist General Conference traces its history back to mid-1852. In that year Gustaf Palmquist, an immigrant schoolteacher and preacher who had been baptized and ordained earlier the same year, together with two other immigrants from Sweden, organized a Swedish Baptist congregation in Rock Island, Illinois. Other congregations were organized subsequently. At first they were a "missionary fellowship" serving Swedish immigrants especially and supported for several decades by English-speaking American Baptist agencies. A national conference, the Swedish Baptist General Conference, came into being in 1879. During the period following World War I it went through a bilingual transitional period, but since the 1940s it has come to use English exclusively. Fewer than half the clergy are of Swedish descent, and the membership is becoming increasingly diverse in terms of national backgrounds.

The organization achieved complete independence in 1944, when it discontinued its association with the American Baptist Foreign Mission Society and set up its own Board for Foreign Missions. The next year it dropped "Swedish" from its official name.

Wholly Baptist in its tenets and strongly conservative in its theology, the conference stresses the supremacy of the Bible as an authority in matters of faith and conduct; the Trinity; the sinfulness of human beings by nature and by choice; regeneration by the Holy Spirit for those who repent and trust in Christ as their Savior; the universal church as a spiritual body of which Christ is the head and all regenerated persons are members; local churches of believers baptized on a credible profession of faith and associated for worship, fellowship, and evangelism; Christian conduct; religious liberty; voluntary cooperation for promoting the cause of Christ; his personal and visible return; the resurrection of the body; and the final judgment of all men.[165] On minor points of theology the conference allows room for variant opinions among its membership.

The headquarters are at 1233 Central Street, Evanston, Illinois 60201. There are 632 churches in the United States and Canada with an inclusive membership of 111,093. In addition to a mission among North American Indians, the conference carries on work in India, Japan, Ethiopia, the Philippines Republic, Argentina, Brazil, Mexico, and the West Indies.

Independent Baptist Church of America

Swedish Free Baptist immigrants organized the Swedish Independent Baptist Church at Dassel, Minnesota, in 1893. Later the body changed its name to the Scandinavian Independent Baptist Denomination of America. A schism in 1912 resulted in the incorporation of one element as the Scandinavian Independent Baptist Denomination of the United States of America and of the other as the Scandinavian Free Baptist Society of the United States of America. In 1927 the two bodies reunited and took the present name. Intimately tied to the Swedish language and to Swedish culture, the church failed increasingly with the passage of time to hold its young people. By 1963 it had declined in the course of a generation from 11 to 2 churches (in Minneapolis, Minnesota, and Alma Center, Wisconsin) and from a total membership of 200 to 30. More recently the church has succeeded in reversing the trend; two churches report a membership of 70.

Theologically the church combines elements of both Calvinism and Arminianism. The typically evangelical Pietism of its members has always supported a strong missionary concern. It currently maintains missions in Natal, Zambia, and Hong Kong. The body is historically pacifist, but it urges members who are drafted to engage in noncombatant service. Laying on of hands accompanies admission to church membership. Recent efforts to contact the denomination have been unsuccessful.

The Russian-Ukrainian Evangelical Baptist Union of the United States of America, Incorporated

Organized Baptist work in the Ukraine dates back to the mid-nineteenth century. It built to a considerable extent upon a foundation provided initially by the Molokans.[166] and after 1867 by the Shtundists.[167] To a lesser degree the Baptists recruited converts among other Russian dissenters, like the Evangelical Christians, and among the non-Russian Mennonites and Lutherans. When the Baptists began to make inroads among the Eastern Orthodox, government persecution began. The movement grew in spite of it. At the time of the collapse of the tsarist government in 1917, the registered membership of the All-Ukrainian Baptist Conference exceeded 100,000. Since 1920, the attitude of the Soviet government toward the Baptists of the Soviet Union has varied.

Pioneer immigrants from the Russian Ukraine organized the first Russo-Ukrainian Baptist church in the United States in 1901, at Kiev, North Dakota. In the midwestern plains states the immigrant Baptist communities attracted and absorbed not only co-religionists but also other Russian and Ukrainian nonconformists, notably Shtundists[168] and Evangelical Christians. The year 1919 saw the organization of the Russian-Ukrainian Evangelical Baptist Union of the United States of America at Philadelphia, Pennsylvania. It has 35 churches and missions with about 2,000 members. Russian and Ukrainian are still extensively used. The union carries on a missionary ministry among Russians and Ukrainians in Australia, South America, and Europe.[169] The headquarters are at Roosevelt Boulevard and Seventh Street, Philadelphia, Pennsylvania 19120.

Ukrainian Evangelical Baptist Convention

The Ukrainian Evangelical Baptist Convention, organized in 1946, describes itself as a group of "fundamental Bible-believing Baptists who oppose and fight worldliness, socialism, and communism."[170] The convention is closely associated with the General Association of Regular Baptist Churches.

The oldest Ukrainian Baptist church in the convention came into being in Chicago in 1915. Subsequently a network of churches, most of them in metropolitan centers, arose across the United States. The Ukrainian Evangelical Baptist Convention has 20 churches, chiefly in the eastern and middle western states, with 3,000 members. The churches still use the Ukrainian language extensively. The convention maintains links with evangelistic diaspora churches in South America—notably in Argentina—and in western

Europe, as well as with its Canadian counterpart, the Ukrainian Evangelical Baptist Convention of Canada. While no organizational links exist with the Baptists in the Ukraine, the American churches maintain contact with their co-religionists in the homeland through personal correspondence and a radio ministry beamed at the Soviet Union. The headquarters are at 690 Berkeley Avenue, Elmhurst, Illinois 60125.

The Ukrainian Evangelical Baptist Convention of Canada

In the closing years of the nineteenth century the English-speaking Baptists of Manitoba sent a colporteur-missionary to the Ukrainians who were beginning to settle in western Canada in great numbers. This led to the organization of a Ukrainian Baptist Church in Overstone, Manitoba, in 1904. Meanwhile, Ukrainian Baptist immigrants, working independently of their English-speaking co-religionists, launched the first Ukrainian Baptist Church in Winnipeg in 1903. The third early Ukrainian Baptist center in Canada was Toronto, where English Baptists initiated the work in 1907; a Ukrainian Baptist missionary, the Reverend John Kolesnikoff, arrived the same year to carry it on. Work was begun in Saskatchewan about the same time, and the first annual intercongregational conference was held at Canora, Saskatchewan, in 1908. As in the United States, the Ukrainian Baptist churches attracted not only their immigrant co-religionists but also Mennonites and nonconformists from the Russian empire—notably Ukrainian Shtundists—and some converts from Eastern Orthodoxy. The Federation of Ukrainian Baptist Churches in Canada, reorganized in 1950 and incorporated under the name of the Ukrainian Evangelical Baptist Convention of Canada in 1961, numbers 25 churches from Ontario to British Columbia with 3,200 members.[171] They are in fellowship with the Ukrainian Evangelical Baptist Convention in the United States. Recent efforts to contact the church body have been unsuccessful.

The Union of Slavic Churches of Evangelical Christians and Slavic Baptists of Canada, Incorporated

Around 1940 the Ukrainian and Russian Baptists who had immigrated into eastern Canada in the late 1920s organized the theologically very conservative Russian-Ukrainian Evangelical Baptist Union of Eastern Canada. About the same time they established spiritual ties with some of the churches of the Union of Slavic Evangelical Christians, particularly those in Saskatchewan. In 1958 a number of churches belonging to the latter body joined with the Russian-Ukrainian Evangelical Baptist Union of Eastern Canada to form the Union of Slavic Churches of Evangelical Christians and Slavic Baptists of Canada.

In 1963 the union was federally incorporated. Theologically the union holds an evangelical and conservative position. It believes in the full inspiration of the Bible as the only authority and norm of faith and as the only source of divine revelation; in the Trinity; in Christ's deity and virgin birth in his redemptive work as the sole basis of salvation; in his premillennial second coming; and in eternal loss for sinners who do not accept Christ and eternal salvation for those who believe in him.

The secretary of the Union of Slavic Churches of Evangelical Christians and Slavic Baptists of Canada has his office at 20 Goswell Road, Islington, Ontario. There are 11 congregations across Canada, with a total active membership estimated at 500, not counting children and "unconverted adherents." The union supports missionary and charitable activities in Europe, Australia, and Argentina. It functions as the Canadian cooperative counterpart of the Russian-Ukrainian Evangelical Baptist Union in the United States of America, Incorporated.[172]

NOTES

1. On Peck, see Rufus Babcock, ed., *Forty Years of Pioneer Life: Memoir of John Mason Peck, D.D., Edited from His Journals and Correspondence* (Carbondale, Ill.: Southern Illinois University Press, 1965).

2. In 1892 it became the Divinity School of the University of Chicago.

3. A majority of the Chicago Baptist Ministers' Conference voted to censure the book but did not withdraw fellowship from the author until much later, when he became a Unitarian minister.

4. The association later joined the Southern Baptist Convention.

5. This movement—the sociological emphasis of which outweighed its theological concern—grew out of a meeting of home and foreign mission board representatives from various denominations in 1918. The movement was to undertake extensive fact-finding surveys at home and abroad that would analyze the church's efficiency in various areas and to coordinate the united raising of funds and the rendering of services. The movement collapsed in less than two years, the victim of postwar weariness and disillusionment, of the persisting disunity in the denominations at the grass roots, of the failure of friendly unchurched Americans to give its program the anticipated support, and of the movement's pro-labor position in its 1920 *Report on the Steel Strike of 1919*, which alienated many wealthy supporters within the cooperating denominations.

6. The liberal-conservative rivalry led to the founding of two conservative theological seminaries within the convention during this period, Eastern Baptist in 1925 and California Baptist in 1944.

7. The American Baptist General Conference of North America, of German origin, has its own program but cooperates in some areas with the American Baptist Convention. Many of its churches hold membership in both organizations.

8. Robert G. Torbet, *A History of the Baptists*, 3d edn. (Valley Forge, Pa.: Judson Press, 1975), p. 292. For a full account of Baptists in the South in the colonial period, see Robert A. Baker, *The Southern Baptist Convention and Its People, 1607–1972* (Nashville: Broadman Press, 1974), pp. 1-160.

9. Baker, pp. 153-159; William Wright Barnes, *The Southern Baptist Convention, 1845–1953* (Nashville: Broadman Press, 1954), p. 11.

10. Baker, pp. 161-162, 168-171, 174-176; Barnes, pp. 33-34. See also Torbet, pp. 286-297.

11. Baker, pp. 180-181, 204.

12. Barnes, pp. 105–113; Baker, pp. 208–219, 248; Torbet, pp. 281-282, 442-443.
13. Baker, pp. 222–223; Sydney Ahlstrom, *A Religious History of the American People* (New Haven: Yale University Press, 1972), p. 220.
14. Barnes, pp. 59, 63-70, 90; Baker, p. 224.
15. Baker, pp. 259, 268-269, 273, 276, 283, 334-345, 356.
16. Torbet, pp. 345-353, 402-410; Barnes, pp. 113-117, 157-158; *Annual of the Southern Baptist Convention, Nineteen Hundred and Seventy-Six* (Nashville: Executive Committee, Southern Baptist Convention, [1976]), p. 69.
17. Torbet, pp. 366-375, 419-423; Baker, p. 293; *Annual*, p. 69.
18. Barnes, pp. 306–307; Torbet, pp. 459, 492-493; Baker, pp. 322, 331, 338, 384-385, 398-399, 446; *Annual*, pp. 91, 93, 156; *St. Louis Post-Dispatch*, June 17, 1977.
19. Baker, pp. 355-383, 414, 447-448 (quotations regarding rapid numerical growth); Barnes, p. 291.
20. *Asociacion Bautista de Puerto Rico* [pamphlet] (Wolfe City, Texas: Southern Baptist Press, n.d.); letter of Milton S. Leach, Jr., Superintendent of Missions, Baptist Home Mission Board, Reparto Metropolitano Shoping Center, 303 San Juan, Puerto Rico 00921.
21. Barnes, p. 97; Baker, pp. 311–316.
22. Barnes, pp. 223-224, 231; Baker, pp. 345, 400-403, 405-406, 408-409, 424-427. The quotation is from Baker.
23. Baker, pp. 297, 450; Barnes, pp. 148-149; *Annual*, pp. 9, 29, 40, 65.
24. See Gerald Martin, *"Sir, We Would See Jesus"; The Story of the Southern Baptist Pastors Conference* (Memphis, Tenn.: Wimmer Bros., 1968).
25. Barnes, pp. 267–277; Torbet, p. 445; Baker, p. 411; John A. Hardon, *The Protestant Churches of America* (Garden City, N.Y.: Doubleday and Co., 1969), p. 50; *Annual*, pp. 20-21, 239-240, 245, 440.
26. Torbet, p. 449; *Annual*, pp. 204-206; *Christian Century*, February 2-9, 1977, p. 80; October 19, 1977, pp. 933-934.
27. Barnes, pp. 245–148; Torbet, pp. 496–497; Baker, pp. 306-308.
28. Torbet, pp. 467-468, 491-492; Baker, p. 415; *Time*, November 26, 1965, p. 68.
29. Carter's letter was quoted in the *New York Times*, May 14, 1977.
30. *Annual*, p. 58; *Christian Century*, July 6-13, 1977, p. 616.
31. *Christian Century*, July 6-13, 1977, p. 616.
32. *1976 Southern Baptist Convention Annual*, p. 38.
33. Ibid., p. 230; cf. the sections, "Separation of Church and State" and "Religious Liberty" in Herschel H. Hobbs, *What Baptists Believe* (Nashville: Broadman Press, 1964), pp. 122-125
34. Quoted in Barnes, p. 118.
35. The confession is included in the 34th printing of a pamphlet originally published in 1853: J. Newton Brown, *A Baptist Church Manual* (Valley Forge, Pa.: Judson Press, 1976), pp. 5-22.
36. Torbet, pp. 430-431; Baker, pp. 397-398.
37. Baker, pp. 416-417; Torbet, pp. 489-490 with the quotation from p. 490.
38. *The Baptist Faith and Message* (Nashville: The Sunday School Board of the Southern Baptist Convention, 1963), pp. 4-5.
39. Cf. the description of spiritual liberty in Hardon, pp. 52-53.
40. Baker, pp. 448-449.
41. Lynn E. May, Jr., *Baptists* (Nashville: The Historical Commission of the Southern Baptist Convention, n.d.), 16-page pamphlet.
42. *Baptist Hymnal* (Nashville: Convention Press, 1975), p. 510.
43. Hobbs, pp. 84, 85.
44. W. E. Davidson, *A Catechism of Bible Doctrine* (Nashville: Broadman Press, n.d.), pp. 22-23.
45. Less than 30 of 35,000 convention churches have ordained women, according to the *St. Louis Post-Dispatch*, November 18, 1977, p. 4B.
46. Joe T. Odle, *Church Member's Handbook*, rev. edn. (Nashville: Broadman Press, 1962), p. 31.
47. J. M. Pendleton, *Baptist Church Manual* (Nashville: Convention Press, 1955), p. 102.
48. In the case of the National Baptist Convention of the United States of America, Incorporated, Appendix C,

"What the National Baptist Convention Stands For," in Owen D. Pelt and Ralph Lee Smith, *The Story of the National Baptists* (New York: Vantage Press, 1960), pp. 209-212, undertakes to provide a summary "which will give the reader a bird's-eye view of what holds Negro Baptists together." (1) The New Testament in its entirety, and not the Old Testament, is humanity's whole rule and guide. (2) No one should add to or subtract from what Christ as Lawgiver practiced and commanded; hence Baptists do not circumcise, sprinkle, or administer baptism to infants. (3) Religion is a matter between God and the individual soul. (4) Christ sanctioned baptism for believers only; infants are not in this category. (5) Baptist churches of today are the same democratic organizations that the New Testament shows the churches to have been originally. (6) They know from the New Testament that immersion is baptism. (7) Baptism by immersion symbolizes Christ's death, the regeneration of the soul, and the final resurrection of the body. (8) The bread and wine in the Lord's Supper "are only as symbols of the body and blood of Christ, . . . it simply represents his flesh and blood." (9) Unbaptized persons must not be invited to the Lord's Supper and Baptists must not partake of the sacrament when unbapitzed persons administer it. (10) Baptists believe that they should "give the whole gospel to the whole world." (11) The National Baptist Convention stands for all the Bible sanctions. (12) The National Baptist Convention is against the union of church and state and for the constitution of the United States. (13) The National Baptist Convention stands for the Christianization of the nation. (14) The National Baptist Convention stands for the evangelization of all lands, and particularly Africa, the West Indies, and Latin America. (15) The National Baptist Convention stands for the ownership and absolute control of all boards and agencies created or authorized to function in its name.

49. This writer's repeated efforts to obtain information directly from the respective headquarters of the two National Baptist conventions were wholly unsuccessful. The information presented is based chiefly on Davis Collier Wooley, "The National Baptist Convention, U.S.A., Inc.," in Davis Collier Wooley, ed., *Baptist Advance: The Achievements of the Baptists of America for a Century and a Half* (Nashville: Broadman Press, 1964), pp. 186-189 and 190-226 respectively, and, in the case of the National Baptist Convention of the United States of America, Incorporated, the history by Pelt and Smith cited in the previous note. All three provide brief bibliographies.

50. W. H. R. Powell, *Towards the Creation of a New Convention, Being a Declaration of the Organization, Principles, and Aims of the Progressive Baptist Convention of America, Incorporated, Resolved and Authorized at Richmond, Virginia, Thursday Morning, May 10, 1962* (Philadelphia: Continental Press, 1962) (4-page pamphlet), p. 1; letter from Dr. L. Venchael Booth, executive secretary, Progressive National Baptist Convention, Incorporated.

51. Repeated efforts by the present writer to obtain information about the Fundamental Baptist Fellowship Association from its leadership were unsuccessful.

52. James A. Kirkland, *Missionary Baptists and the Ecumenical Movement* (Texarkana, Texas: Baptist Sunday School Committee of the American Baptist Association, 1964) (pamphlet), p. 2. The term "Landmarkism"—which reflects the injunction of Proverbs 23: 10 (KJV): "Remove not the old landmark"—goes back to the title of a tract which J. M. Pendelton published in 1856, *An Old Landmark Reset.* J .R. Graves popularized the term in his book of 1880, *Old Landmarkism, What Is It*? Both were members of the Southern Baptist Convention, but the American Baptist Association has purchased the plates for this and other books by Graves and republished them. While members of the American Baptist Association accept the name "Landmark Baptists" re-

luctantly, the association energetically affirms the principles which the term identifies. These are four in number: (1) the principle that in the New Testament the church is essentially the organized, visible, local congregation; (2) the doctrine of church perpetuity, understood as requiring a church succession in New Testament church history and the doctrinal and historical identity of present-day congregations with the churches of the past that kept the beliefs and followed the practices of the first church, even though a given local church is not required to trace its individual history link by link back to Christ and the apostles; (3) the authority of the corporate local church; and (4) baptism as an ordinance of the church validly administered only under church authority. "Landmarkism" has acquired renewed currency inside and outside the American Baptist Association in recent years. At least one church, the Landmark Baptist Temple at Lockland, Ohio, a suburb of Cincinnati, affiliated with the Bible Baptist Fellowship, uses the term as part of its official name; the pastor, John Rawlings, publishes *The Landmark Baptist Journal* and calls his radio program "The Landmark Baptist Hour." See I. K. Cross, *Spotlight on Landmarkism* (Texarkana, Texas: Baptist Sunday School Committee of the American Baptist Association, 1966) (pamphlet).

53. Quoted in I. K. Cross, *What Is the American Baptist Association?* (Texarkana, Texas: Baptist Sunday School Committee of the American Baptist Association, 1965) (pamphlet), p. 4.

54. See in this connection I. K. Cross, *The Church: Local or Universal, Visible or Invisible—It Cannot Be Both!* (Texarkana, Texas: Baptist Sunday School Committee of the American Baptist Association, n.d.) (pamphlet).

55. Cross, *What Is the American Baptist Association?* pp. 11-13. Persons who desire to join a church of the association after receiving "Protestant and other immersions without regard to doctrinal standards" must be rebaptized.

56. Cross, *The Church: Local or Universal*, p. 23.

57. Kirkland, p. 5.

58. Cross, *The Church: Local or Universal*, p. 23.

59. Chester E. Tulga, *Needed—A New Baptist Fundamentalism* (Texarkana, Texas: Baptist Sunday School Committee of the American Baptist Association, 1964) (pamphlet), pp. 12-20.

60. Kirkland, pp. 24-25. The American Baptist Association is not a member of the Baptist World Alliance.

61. Penrose St. Amant, "Other Baptist Bodies," in Davis Collier Woolley, ed., *Baptist Advance: The Achievements of the Baptists of North America for a Century and a Half* (Nashville: Broadman Press, 1964), p. 179.

62. This does not necessarily require a succession of associations (Leon Gaylor and James C. Blaylock, eds., *1969–70 Directory and Handbook: Vital Information on the Work and Workers of the Churches of the Baptist Missionary Association of America* [Jacksonville, Texas: Baptist News Service Committtee, 1969], p. 13). Nevertheless, the association rejects the term "Landmark" as applied to itself (communication from Dr. D. N. Jackson, director, Baptist News Service).

63. "Any so-called Baptist church which knowingly receives alien baptism, habitually practices this [evil or open Communion, pulpit affiliation with heretical churches, modernism, and all kindred evils arising from these practices] cannot be a scriptural Baptist church, nor can its ordinances remain valid" (Gaylor and Blaylock, eds., *1969–70 Directory and Handbook*, p. 25).

64. Ibid., pp. 25-26.

65. Ibid., p. 26.

66. Penrose St. Amant, "Other Baptist Bodies," in David Collier Woolley, ed., *Baptist Advance: The Achievements of the Baptists of North America for a Century and a Half* (Nashville: Broadman Press, 1964), p. 375.

67. "Articles of Faith," *1967–1968 Annual* (Des Plaines, Ill.: General Association of Regular Baptist Churches, 1967), pp. 9-11.

68. *The Missionary and Educational Policy of the General Association of Regular Baptist Churches* (Des Plaines, Ill.: General Association of Regular Baptist Churches, 1967) (6-page pamphlet), pp. 2-5.
69. Ibid., p. 4.
70. For the text, see Appendix IX ("Doctrinal Statement"), in Bruce Leon Shelley, *Conservative Baptists: A Story of Twentieth-Century Dissent,* 2nd edn. (Denver, Col.: Conservative Baptist Theological Seminary, 1962), p. 155.
71. See Shelley, pp. 68-69, for the exposition of these principles.
72. Article III ("Character"), *Constitution and Declaration of Faith of the Conservative Baptist Association of America* (undated 5-page document). William F. Kerr, *Conservative Baptist Distinctives* (Arlington Heights, Ill.: The Conservative Baptist Association of America, 1965) is a typical and quasi-official exposition of the Conservative Baptist position.
73. *Conservative Baptist Impact,* vol. 24, no. 3 (March 1967), p. 2.
74. Letters from the Reverend Wayne C. Musson, president, New Testament Association of Independent Baptist Churches, 3290 Harvester Avenue, Lake Elmo, Minnesota.
75. G. Archer Weniger, *A Brief History of the Conservative Baptist Fellowship* (Chicago: The Conservative Baptist Fellowship, n.d. [not earlier than 1965] (8-page pamphlet); Virgil Arrowood and others, "Conservative Baptist Cross Currents in Colorado," *Baptist Missionary-Evangelist,* vol. 17, no. 5 (May 1962), pp. 1-11.
76. *Fundamental Baptist Fellowship Information Bulletin,* vol. 14, no. 4 (July-August 1969), p. 14.
77. Letter from the Reverend Chester J. McCullough, D.D., treasurer, Fundamental Baptist Fellowship.
78. *Independent Bible Baptist Missions: Organization, Constitution, Articles of Faith,* rev. edn. (Englewood, Colo. Independent Bible Baptist Missions, 1952), pp. 1-11.
79. Article II ("Doctrinal Statement"), Constitution, ibid., pp. 12-20.
80. Letter from the Reverend Glen Smith, Independent Bible Baptist Missions.
81. E. Ray Tatum, *Conquest or Failure? —A Biography of J. Frank Norris* (Dallas: Baptist Historical Foundation, 1966), pp. 202-203.
82. Louis Entzminger, *The J. Frank Norris I Have Known for 34 Years,* 2nd printing (N.p.: N.p., 1950), pp. 55-56.
83. Letter from Robert O. Schmidt, director, World Baptist Fellowship.
84. "Doctrinal Statement [of the World Baptist Fellowship] (1952)," reprinted in Bruce D. Cummons, *Church Member's Handbook* (Massillon, Ohio: Massillon Baptist Temple, [1963]), pp. 17-23.
85. *Articles of Faith* (Springfield, Mo.: Baptist Bible Fellowship International, n.d.) (pamphlet), p. 1.
86. *Constitution and By-laws* (Springfield, Mo.: Baptist Bible Fellowship International, 1967) (pamphlet), pp. 6-7.
87. Communication from Don W. Brown, church body headquarters.
88. Article III ("Statement of Faith"), *Constitution and By-Laws of the South Carolina Baptist Fellowship* (Laurens, S.C.: The South Carolina Baptist Fellowship, 1965) (4-page pamphlet). p. [1]).
89. Communication from the Reverend John R. Waters, business manager and treasurer, South Carolina Baptist Fellowship.
90. Communication from Dr. Lindsay Terry, Southwide Baptist Fellowship.
91. *The Southwide Baptist Fellowship 1966,* unpaginated pamphlet (Laurens, S.C.: The Southwide Baptist Fellowship, 1966), pp. [4]-[5].
92. *Your Questions Answered* (8-page undated folder), p. 8.
93. Communication from Allan E. Lewis of the church body headquarters.
94. This shift from Congregationalism to the Baptist community had an eighteenth-century parallel in the New England Congregationalists who, upon moving to the South, became Baptists.
95. Letters from the Reverend Jerell B. Crum, dean, Barrington College, Barrington, Rhode Island; the Reverend William Nigel Kerr, Gordon Divinity School, Wenham, Massachusetts; Miss Mary Lou Balfour, secretary to the executive director, National Association of Evangelicals; and Dr. John

Viall, president, New England Baptist Fellowship, 40 Bridge Street, Newton, Massachusetts 02158.

96. Communication from Raymond L. Josephson, president.

97. Ollie Latch, *History of the General Baptists* (Poplar Bluff, Mo.: The General Baptist Press, 1954), reprints the original Articles of Faith of the Liberty Association on pp. 129-139. By 1870 they had undergone minor —largely stylistic—revisions; Latch prints the revised form on p. 200. The most significant change is the addition to Article 11 of a statement that infants and idiots are included in the covenant of God's grace and consequently do not need repentance and faith to partake of the benefits of Christ's death for every man. The "General Baptist Articles of Faith" of 1870 (printed by Latch on pp. 204-205) took over the revised Liberty Association articles almost word for word.

98. Letter from Glen O. Spruce, executive secretary, The General Association of General Baptists.

99. J. M. Barfield and Thad Harrison, *History of the Free Will Baptists of North Carolina*, rev. edn. by J. O. Fort (Ayden: N.C.: Free Will Baptist Press, 1960), pp. 38-39.

100. The account of events in this paragraph differs considerably from the history as usually presented. This account is based on the diligent research of Mr. George W. Stevenson, Free Will Baptist Historical Collection, Mount Olive College, Mount Olive, North Carolina, as he reported it in an article, "Some Light on a Confused Period of Free Will Baptist History," *The Free Will Baptist*, vol. 76, no. 38 (September 27, 1961), pp. 3-4. The present writer gratefully acknowledges Mr. Stevenson's helpful counsel in the preparation of this section.

101. *Minutes of the 1968 Annual Session of the General Conference of Original Free Will Baptists*, pp. 29-32. A measure of the difference between the General Conference of Original Free Will Baptists and the National Association of Free Will Baptists is that the General Conference uses the General Commission on Chaplains and Armed Forces Personnel as its military chaplain endorsing agency, while the National Association endorses its candidates for the military chaplaincy through the National Association of Evangelicals.

102. "Statement," ibid., pp. 32-48.

103. Letter from the Reverend Bobby G. Bazen, Route 5, Dunn, North Carolina, secretary, General Conference of Original Free Will Baptists. The present writer gratefully acknowledges the assistance of the Reverend Monte E. Frohm, Mobile, Alabama, then seminarian-assistant of the Church of the Ascension, Charlotte, North Carolina, who made initial contact with the North Carolina Original Free Will Baptists on behalf of this writer through Mr. C. H. Overman, Free Will Baptist Press, Ayden, North Carolina 28513.

104. "History of the United Free Will Baptist Church," in *The United American Free Will Baptist Church 1967* (Kinston, N.C.: United American F. W. B. Headquarters, 1967), p. [3]; Penrose St. Amant, "Other Baptist Bodies," in Davis Collier Woolley, ed., *Baptist Advance: The Achievements of the Baptists of North America for a Century and a Half* (Nashville: Broadman Press, 1964), p. 384; G. D. McNeil, Jr., ed., *The First Discipline of the United American Free Will Baptists*, 4th edn. (N.p.: N.p., 1959), p. 3.

105. *The First Discipline*, pp. 9-10. "Our Faith" supplements this by asserting that all human beings at one time or another are found in such a capacity that through the grace of God they may be eternally saved; that the Holy Spirit offers divine aid to all human beings, so that those who do not receive the Spirit's "divine impressions" must finally acknowledge the justice of their condemnation; that children dying in infancy are saved; and that God's ordinances also include the laying on of hands, anointing the sick with oil, fasting, prayer, singing praises to God, the public ministry of the Word of God and every institution of the Lord in the New Testament (ibid., pp. 5-7). The doctrinal chapters discuss the Bible;

the being and attributes of God; the divine government and providence; creation, the primitive state of the first human being, and his fall; Christ and his incarnation; the Holy Spirit; Christ's atonement for the sins of the whole world and his mediation; the Gospel call ("coextensive with the atonement"); repentance; faith; regeneration; justification and sanctification; the perseverance of the truly regenerate; the Sabbath; the church; the Gospel ministry; the two Gospel ordinances of believer's baptism by immersion "in the name of the Father, the Son, and the Holy Spirit" and the Lord's Supper (with the principle of open Communion affirmed in the words, "and no man has a right to forbid these tokens to the least of [Christ's] disciples"); death and the intermediate state; Christ's second coming; the resurrection of all human beings; and the general judgment and future retributions (ibid., pp. 21-38). These chapters reproduce the 1834 Confession of the Free-Will Baptists as revised in 1868 (see Philip Schaff, *The Creeds of Christendom, with a History and Criitcal Notes* 3 [Grand Rapids, Mich.: Baker Book House, 1966]: 749-756), expanded by the addition of footnotes providing biblical documentation. The section on Christ's incarnation, originally part of chap. 6, has been dislocated, so that it appears as a part of chap. 7. The liturgical portion of *The First Discipline* provides a rite for the Lord's Supper (observed with unleavened bread and the "unfermented fruit of the vine") under the title "Memorial Service" (ibid., pp. 39-40). The words of institution are set forth as formulas at the beginning of the distribution. The pastor must use the bread formula in presenting the plates with the bread to the deacons; he may use the "remark" about the cup when he passes the latter. There is also a form for the dedication of infants (ibid., pp. 48-49). It may be used "at any regular church service." In this service the officiant gives a symbolic red rose or carnation to the father and a symbolic white rose or carnation to the mother. As he gives a white sweet pea to the

child "as a token of your innocency and purity of soul in the sight of God," he prays "that when you lose your innocency and your eyes of understanding are opened, you will see Jesus, whom to see is life eternal."

106. This represents a considerable statistical decline from 1952, when the United American Free Will Baptist Church claimed 836 churches with about 100,000 members (St. Amant, loc. cit.).

The present writer gratefully acknowledges the indispensable help of the Reverend Robert Duddleston, pastor, Faith Church, Kinston, North Carolina, who established effective contact on this writer's behalf through Senior Bishop R. D. Pridgen with the headquarters of the United American Free Will Baptist Church.

107. "Articles of Faith," *The Christian Unity Baptist Association: Proceedings of the Thirty-Third Annual Session, 1967* (22-page pamphlet), pp. 1-2.

108. William Lantane Lumpkin, *Baptist Foundations in the South, Tracing through the Separates the Influence of the Great Awakening 1754–1787* (Nashville: Broadman Press, 1961), p. 68, has another explanation. He states that the Particular Baptists seem in the 1760s to have begun to call themselves "Regular" Baptists, apparently to underline the "irregularity" of the Separate Baptists. The self-given designation stuck as the popular designation for the Particular party.

109. Ibid., pp. 62-63. On the background and progress of the Separate Baptists, see also Morgan Scott, *History of the Separate Baptist Church, with a Narrative of Other Denominations* (Indianapolis: Hollenbeck Press, 1901).

110. *93d Annual Session of the General Association of Separate Baptists in Christ 1965*, p. 26.

111. Ibid., pp. 14, 16, 17, 19, 20, 22. Independent of the General Association of Separate Baptists in Christ, but cooperating with some Separate Baptist churches as an agency for their foreign missionary outreach is Christ for the World, Incorporated, Box 66, Tice, Florida, the founder of which, the Reverend Glenn Naphew, was formerly a Separate Baptist preacher.

His agency's doctrinal statement slightly condenses the statement of faith of the National Association of Evangelicals (*Christ for the World,* vol. 23, no. 2 [February 1969], p. 2).

112. C. Penrose St. Amant, "Other Baptist Bodies," in David Collier Woolley, ed., *Baptist Advance: The Achievements of the Baptists of North America for a Century and a Half* (Nashville: Broadman Press, 1964), p. 381. In Canada the antithesis to Regular Baptist was Free, Free Will, or Free Christian Baptist.

113. William Fristoe, "History of the Ketocton Baptist Association," *The Regular Baptist,* vol. 93, no. 2 (March–April 1968), pp. 1, 12.

114. Tom Marshall, "Editorials," *The Regular Baptist,* vol. 93, no. 6 (August 1968), p. 2. *The Regular Baptist* began publication in Missouri in 1870. In 1909 it absorbed *The Old Paths* (begun 1891) and moved its publication office to Nashville, Tennessee. After further moves, the publication office was located at Boyce, Virginia, in 1964. The Mount Tabor Association has been publishing the *Regular Baptist Messenger* since the latter 1920s; the publication office is at Whitestown, Indiana.

115. Since the mid-1930s the Indian Creek Association has ranged from 11 or 12 churches (1936–1950) to 17 (1958) churches and from 371 (1936) to 1,391 (1963) members (*Indian Creek Association of Regular Baptists 1968: Minutes of the One Hundred and Twenty-Third Annual Session,* inside back cover). The size of the Mount Tabor Association has fluctuated between 7 (1951–1958) and 21 (1894) churches and between 649 (1948) and 1,308 (1897) members (*Minutes of the Seventy-Eighth Annual Session of Mt. Tabor Association of Regular Baptists . . . 1968,* pp. 6-7). In 1908 the Richland Association, then at its peak membership of 10 churches and 605 members, split over a disagreement into the Mount Pleasant Association (5 churches, 205 members) and the Richland Association (5 churches, 400 members). Negotiations begun in 1917 led to a reunion in 1920 as the United Mount Pleasant and Richland

Association (15 churches, 428 members). One reason for the decline of this association is the location of the Crane United States Naval Ammunition Depot, consisting of approximately 60,000 acres, in the area where a large part of the association's constituency had lived. (Letter from Mr. Lyman F. Wagoner, 2024 16th Street, Bedford, Indiana.

116. *Minutes of the 201st Anniversary of the Ketocton Association of Regular Baptists . . . 1967,* pp. 17-18. The Ketocton Association regards the "present day ecumenical" movement as partaking of the nature of Antichrist (ibid., p. 8). Similarly, the Indian Creek Association in 1968 declared its intention never "to permit or endure the use of the R[evised] S[tandard] V[ersion] Bible" in its pulpits or "to have any teaching material from the same" (*Indian Creek Association . . . 1968: Minutes,* p. 3).

117. *Minutes of the Seventy-Eighth Annual Session of Mt. Tabor Association . . . 1968,* p. 11.

118. *Minutes of the Forty-Ninth Annual Meeting of the Mount Pleasant-Richland Association [of] Regular Baptists . . . 1968,* p. 13.

119. Letter from Mr. Tom Marshall, editor, *The Regular Baptist.*

120. So the Sardis Association of Old Regular Baptist (sic) the Church of Jesus Christ (established in 1893) (West Virginia, Kentucky, Virginia, and Florida); the Indian Bottom Association (1896) (Kentucky, Indiana, and Ohio); the Friendship Association (1917) (West Virginia, Virginia, and Pennsylvania); the Philadelphia Association (1925) (Kentucky, West Virginia, and Arizona); and the Northern New Salem Association (1957) (Ohio, Michigan, Indiana, Kentucky, and Virginia). Besides these there are the New Salem Association of Old Regular Baptist (sic) of Jesus Christ (1825) (Kentucky, Ohio, Indiana, West Virginia, Virginia, Illinois, and Washington), the Union Association of Old Regular Baptists of Jesus Christ (1859) (Kentucky, Virginia, Tennessee, Ohio, and Florida) and its offshoot, the Thornton Union Association (1945) (Kentucky); and

the Mud River Association of Regular Baptists of Jesus Christ (1889) (West Virginia). Rufus Perrigan, *History of Regular Baptist and Their Ancestors and Accessors* (Haysi, Va.: Rufus Perrigan, 1961), p. 2, gives 1876 as the year in which the Indian Bottom Association was organized; 1876 is the year of organization of the Sand Lick Association, from which the founders of the Indian Bottom Association seceded over what they regarded as the "erroneous and unorthodox doctrine" of absolute predestination (ibid., p. 332); see also *The Indian Bottom Association of Old Regular Baptist of Jesus Christ 1899–1968* [N.p.: N.p., 1968], p. 7.

The Kyova Association (now confined to West Virginia) began in 1924 with eight churches as an "arm" of the New Salem Association (see Perrigan, pp. 2, 93, 137, 271). Its Articles of Faith affirm the association's belief in the creator; in Christ the head and king of the church; in the Holy Ghost, the "sealer and applier of [Christ's] redemption"; in the Trinity; in the Scriptures as the infallible Word of God and the New Testament as the only rule of faith and practice; "in the free atonement of Jesus Christ, that he tasted death for every man, and that salvation is offered to all men and women on the terms of the gospel"; in repentance, faith, and regeneration as prerequisites of baptism, which must be by immersion; in "a legally ordained elder of our faith and order" as the only rightful minister of baptism; in one true Gospel church that will finally persevere through grace to glory; in the communion of the Lord's Supper, to which only "legal[ly] baptized members of our faith and order may be admitted"; in foot washing as an ordinance; in Christ as the first resurrection from the dead; "in the resurrection of the just and unjust"; and in the eternal happiness of the righteous and the final punishment of the wicked (*Minutes of the Kyova Association of Old Regular Baptist the Church of Jesus Christ . . . 1967*, pp. 17–19). In the 1950s it broke off correspondence with the other Old

Regular Baptist associations on the question whether or not labor unions are secret organizations. Since then it corresponds with no other association. (It also lost a number of its own churches on this issue.) It forbids its members to belong to secret societies and "recommends" the exclusive use of the King James Version of the Bible. (Letters from Mr. Sterling Cole, 1832 Washington Avenue, Huntington, West Virginia. Mr. Cole's father, Elder C. Cole [1862–1949], was a founder and for twenty-two years the moderator of the Kyova association.)

Other Old Regular Baptist associations known to the present writer through the kindness of Mr. Harless E. Potter, Route 3, Box 70, Clintwood, Virginia, who shared minutes in his possession with the present writer, include: (1) the Mountain Association of the Old Regular Baptist of Jesus Christ (1837) (Kentucky and Indiana); (2) the Mountain Union Baptist Association (1867) (Virginia, North Carolina, and Maryland); (3) the Little River Regular Baptist Association (1895) (Virginia and North Carolina); a second Indian Bottom Association of Old Regular Baptist of Jesus Christ (1896) (Kentucky and Indiana), resulting from a schism in the parent association in the 1960s; and (6) the Bethel Association of Old Regular Baptist of Jesus Christ (Virginia and Kentucky), organized in 1962 after a schism in the Union Association resulting from disorder in one of its churches (arising in part from the teaching "that a repentant sinner is a child of God prior to the new birth and that the Gospel is to be preached only to the church and is of no profit to the world" [*Minutes of the Union Association, Old Regular Baptists of Jesus Christ . . . 1962*, pp. 9–10; *Minutes of the Bethel Association of Old Regular Baptist of Jesus Christ . . . 1962*, pp. 3–9, 26–30].) The Little River, Little Valley, and Mountain Union associations correspond with one another.

121. According to Frank M. Masters, *History of Baptists in Kentucky,* cited in Perrigan, p. 127, the New Salem Association substituted "Regular" for

"United" in its name in 1854, apparently the first association to do so, and in 1870 it prefixed "Old" to "Regular." Another account has the New Salem association substitute "Regular" for "United" in its name in 1873 (ibid., p. 136).

122. So, for instance, Phillip K. Epling, *The Baptist Triumph* (N.p.: N.p., 1953) (74-page brochure); Perrigan, pp. 19-37. A traditional (and badly garbled) line of succession runs: the apostle John baptized Polycarp of Smyrna (69?–155) in 95; Polycarp organized the "Partus [Portus?] Church at the foot of the Tiber" in 150; "Tortullon" (Tertullian? [160?–220?]), a member of the Partus church organized the "Turan Church" at "Turan" (Turin?), Italy, in 237(!); Telesman, a member of the Turan church, organized the "Pontifossi Church" at the foot of the Alps in France in 393; "Andromicus" (Andronicus?), a member of the Pontifossi church, organized the "Dareth[e]a Church" in Asia Minor in 671; Archer Flavin (Flavian?), a member of the Dareth[e]a church, organized the "Timto Church" in Asia Minor in 738; Balcola, a member of the Timto church, organized the "Lima Church" in the Piedmont in 812; Aaron Arlington was ordained by the Lima church in 940 and organized the Hillcliff church in Wales, England, in 987; John Clark, a member of the church in Wales, organized a church at Rhode Island, Connecticut [actually Newport, Rhode Island], in 1638; the Rhode Island church helped to form the Philadelphia Association in 1707 (Perrigan, p. 31; Epling, pp. 17-18).

123. Old Regular Baptist elders still inveigh against "the learned clergy, who has received their call to the ministry from theological seminaries or other institutions of learning created by man" and who justify "studying in some accredited ministerial training institution" on the ground that this makes them "better able to understand the theory of interpeting [sic] the sacred scriptures," thus leaving "the impression that a scientific approach to gospel wisdom is to be prefered [sic] over a devine [sic] revealed approach as recommended by Jesus Christ and his apostles" (Roy B. Akers, "Facts and Truth from History and the Bible," in Perrigan, p. 317). A flood of books "has publicized the modern approach to repentance, and the paid clergy who know not the truth anyway has fell victim to their teachings" (ibid., p. 319). "Much time is consumed in the writing and preparation of their sermon[s]" (ibid., p. 320). "The paid clergy in colaberation [sic] with seminaries and other institutions, preacher factories, etc., have seized upon [the terms bigotry, heresy, and intolerance] in an effort to frighten people into accepting their form of godliness" (ibid., p. 327). "Since their learning came from men, they cannot know God. They teach private scripture interpretation as opposed to devine inspirational interpetation" (ibid., p. 328).

124. In contrast to Bible societies, missionary societies, associations and conventions of churches, educational institutions, and other "auxiliary agencies."

125. Perrigan, p. 37; Epling, pp. 6-7. Apropos especially of the seventh mark, Mr. Potter writes with reference to the Old Regular Baptists in the twentieth century: "We have many wealthy people among our membership; we have doctors, lawyers, jurists, educators, teachers, superintendents of schools, congressmen, and many other prominent, wealthy members. We are obscure, despised, and persecuted only by those who do not realize our sincerity and devotion to the Great I Am."

126. The Friendship and Kyova associations are exceptional in their explicit assertion of an "Arminian" position: "We believe in the free atonement of Jesus Christ; that he tasted death for every man; and that salvation is offered to all on the equal terms of the Gospel" (*Minutes of the Fifty-Second Annual Session of Friendship Association of Old Regular Baptist the Church of Jesus Christ . . . 1968*, p. 12; see also n. 120, above).

127. One Old Regular Baptist elder writes: "I am glad that I belong to a peculiar

family of God that still practices and teaches that feetwashing is essential to the common salvation of men and women that have been truly born again" (Akers, "Facts and Truth," in Perrigan, p. 329).

128. One implication of this "Landmark" tradition is that persons baptized by unordained or irregularly ordained ministers must be baptized again or forfeit church membership.

129. Individual associations include other items, for example, the duty of the churches of the association "collectively and indivdually to demonstrate against doctrine or opinion of men that does not comply with the principles of this constitution" (*Minutes of the 81st Annual Session of the Mud River Association of Regular Baptists of Jesus Christ . . . 1968*, p. 24), or, "the duty of all church members to attend church meetings" (*Minutes of the Seventy-Third Annual Session of the Indian Bottom Association of Old Regular Baptist the Church of Jesus Christ . . . 1968*, p. 25). The Little Valley and the Little River associations define a "Baptist church" as one that "holds the essential deity of Jesus Christ, the full inspiration and authority of the Bible as the written word of God, the absolute necessity of regeneration; salvation by grace through Christ's atoning blood; scriptural baptism and membership in a Baptist church as orderly and essential prerequisites to communion at the Lord's supper as observed among Baptists" (*Minutes of the Eighth Annual Session of the Little Valley Regular Baptist Association . . . 1967*, p. 1; *Minutes of the Seventy-Second Annual Session of the Little River Regular Baptist Association . . . 1966*, p. 11). Various controverted issues continue to come before the annual meetings of the associations in the hope of settlement, such as the wearing of short hair and the use of makeup by the sisters, allowing a sister to open or close a church service with prayer, stopping "men with two living women from taking any part in the ministry," songbooks with notes, membership in secret orders, publication of a periodical, and the demand of one church that the association "cite them the page, chapter and verse in the Bible that would condemn the installation of a sound system in their church" (the voŧe on the last item was 38 against the sound system, 13 for it) (*Minutes of the One Hundred and Forty-Third Annual Session of the New Salem Association of Old Regular Baptist of Jesus Christ . . . 1968*, pp. 6-7; *Minutes of the Seventy-Sixth Annual Session of the Sardis Association of Old Regular Baptist the Church of Jesus Christ . . . 1969*, pp. 14-15). The extracts from past minutes contained in *The Indian Bottom Association of Old Regular Baptist of Jesus Christ 1899–1968* (N.p.: n.p., 1968) indicate that many of these issues have been perennial ones.

130. Perrigan, p. 36.

131. An effort put forth in 1937 by the New Salem, Union, Sardis, and Kyova Old Regular Baptist associations and the Paint Union, Blaine Union, Zion, Bethlehem, New Hope, Iron Hill, and Olive United Baptist associations to reestablish fellowship failed. The representatives of the two groups jointly disavowed open Communion, Sunday schools taught or conducted through what they regarded as sectarian literature, "all so-called auxiliaries of the churches" apart from the ministry of "God-sent men preaching under the demonstration of the Holy Ghost," mourner's benches, "erected altars," membership in secret societies or orders, and the doctrine of some United Baptists that believers can "know beyond a doubt personally that they are saved" (Perrigan, pp. 271-272).

132. This pattern was occasionally justified by appealing to Revelation 22:2.

133. It is not possible to say how many, if any, of these associations are included in the 22 associations with about 7,000 members that William Lantane Lumpkin reported in Norman Wade Cox, ed., *Encyclopedia of Southern Baptists*, vol. 2 (Nashville: Broadman Press, 1958): 1138.

134. *Minutes of the Second Annual Session (Fourth Meeting) of the National Association of United Baptists held at . . . Roselle, Missouri, July 23, 24,*

and 25, 1965, pp. 1, 6-7, 12-13.

135. Letter from Elder Egbert E. Frye, Huntington, West Virginia. He estimates that the total membership might approach 500,000, but this seems impossible.

136. Penrose St. Amant, "Other Baptist Bodies," in Davis Collier Woolley and others, eds. *Baptist Advance* (Nashville: Broadman Press, 1964), p. 383; *Yearbook of American Churches for 1970,* pp. 77-78. Several churches of the Cumberland River Association of United Baptists belong to the American Baptist Association (St. Amant, ibid.).

137. *Minutes of the Bethlehem Association of United Baptist Churches of Jesus Christ Held at Pleasant View, West Virginia, at Their 94th Annual Session, 1965,* pp. 10-11.

138. Eleanor Templin, *History of the Duck River Association of Missionary Baptists* (Paragould, Ark.: White Printing Company, 1963), pp. 3-12; letters from the Reverend H. D. Standifer, superintendent of missions, Duck River Association of Missionary Baptists, Tullahoma, Tennessee.

139. *Minutes of the Twenty-Eighth Annual Session of the General Association of Baptist*[sic] *. . . 1966,* p. 4. Elder W. B. Kerby, Henegar, Alabama, then moderator of the General Association, kindly supplied these minutes to the present writer.

140. *Minutes of the One Hundred Fortieth Session of the Duck River Association of Baptists . . . 1966,* p. 4. The present writer acknowledges gratefully the efforts of the Reverend Thomas H. Carlson, Grace Church, Murfreesboro, Tennessee, to secure information for him about the Duck River Association of Baptists.

141. In addition to the pamphlets themselves, see also John Spencer, *A History of Kentucky Baptists from 1769 to 1885,* ed. Burrilla B. Spencer (Cincinnati, Ohio: J. R. Baumes, 1885), 1:576-578. Although the Parker movement ultimately allied itself with the Primitive Baptists, a spokesman for the latter, the Reverend Lasserre Bradley, Jr., Cincinnati, Ohio, director, Baptist Bible Hour, wrote in a letter: "Most of our people feel that Daniel Parker was never a sound Primitive Baptist."

142. A lively account of this period is contained in Ben J. Parker, "Early Times in Texas and History of the Parker Family," *Palestine* [Texas] *Daily Herald,* February 12, 1935.

143. Text in Guy W. Small, *The Life of Daniel Parker* (Marshall, Texas: Unpublished M.A. thesis, East Texas Baptist College, 1954), pp. 75-79.

144. *Minutes of the One Hundred Twenty-Seventh Annual Session of the Union Primitive Baptist Association of the Old School or Predestinarian Faith and Order . . . 1966* (Elon College, N.C.: Primitive Publications, 1966), pp. 4-5.

145. *Minutes of the Eighty-Third Annual Session of the Primitive Baptist Association of the Regular Predestinarian Faith and Order . . . 1966* (Elon College, N.C.: Primitive Publications, 1966), pp. 4-5.

146. *Minutes of the Eighty-Sixth Annual Session of the South Louisiana Primitive Baptist Association . . . 1966* (N.p.: N.p., 1966), pp. 5, 7-8. The present writer gratefully acknowledges the kindness of the Reverend Lenhart E. Etzel, then pastor of Bethlehem Church, Palestine, Texas, who interviewed Mr. Joe Bailey Parker, Elkhart, Texas, the great-great-grandson of Daniel Parker, Elder P. E. Weisinger, Grapeland, Texas, moderator, Union Primitive Baptist Association of the Old School or Predestinarian Faith and Order, and Mrs. Marjorie Whitescarver, clerk, Pilgrim Predestinarian Baptist Church, Palestine, Texas, on this writer's behalf.

147. C. P. Allen and Terry M. Batts, "Brief History of the National Primitive Baptist Convention of the United States of America," in Terry M. Batts, ed., *Souvenir Program, Golden Jubilee Session (1907–1957), Primitive Baptist National Convention, U. S. A. . . . August 21-25, 1957* (Huntsville, Ala.: National Primitive Baptist Convention of the United States of America, 1957), pp. [5]-[6].

148. Letters from the Reverend Terry M. Batts, 506 Summerville Street, Mobile, Alabama.

149. *Discipline of the Primitive Baptist*

Church, 4th rev. ed., 3rd printing (Huntsville, Ala.: National Primitive Baptist Publishing Board, 1966), pp. 3-5.

150. *Yearbook of American Churches for 1970,* p. 54. This would average out at 667 members per church. (The average membership of Primitive Baptist churches generally is slightly under 40.) The number of ordained clergy is given as 623. For 1957 the convention reported 1,100 churches, 80,983 members, and 500 ordained clergy having charges (*Yearbook of American Churches for 1961,* p. 22). The *Yearbook of American Churches for 1964,* p. 22, records 1,125 churches, 85,983 members, and 700 clergy having charges. The figures reported in the *Yearbook of American Churches for 1970* would imply an increase of 95.2 percent in the number of churches, an increase of 1,605 percent in the number of members, and a decline of 11 percent in the number of ordained clergy over a six-year period.

151. Watson Kirkconnell, *The Baptists of Canada: A "Pocket-Book" History* (Brantford, Ontario: The Historical Committee of the Baptist Federation of Canada, n.d.) (19-page pamphlet), p. 15.

152. Gordon C. Warren, *Basic Baptist Beliefs,* 4th printing (Brantford, Ontario: The Baptist Federation of Canada, 1965) (16-page pamphlet); Russell Foster Aldwinckle, *Of Water and the Spirit: A Baptist View of Church Membership* (Brantford, Ontario: The Baptist Federation of Canada, 1964) (28-page brochure), pp. 5-6.

153. Charles A. Tipp, id., *1964 Year Book* (Toronto: Trans-Canada Fellowship of Evangelical Baptist Churches, 1964), inside front cover and p. 92.

154. William C. Smalley, "The Baptist Convention of Ontario and Quebec," in Davis Collier Woolley, ed., *Baptist Advance: The Achievements of the Baptist of North America for a Century and a Half* (Nashville: Broadman Press, 1964), pp. 170-173.

155. Doctrinal statement, "Tentative Constitution of the Association of Regular Baptist Churches (Canada)," *The*

Gospel Witness and Protestant Advocate 37 (1958): 122-123. This constitution, adopted for the first time in 1958, is adopted in a tentative form by each annual convention to permit adaptation of the rules of order in the light of experience. The doctrinal statement can be changed only by a unanimous vote of the convention.

156. Letter from the church body headquarters.

157. "Articles of Faith," in *Constitution and Articles of Faith of the Fellowship of Fundamental Baptist Churches in the Maritime Provinces* (undated 5-page mimeographed document), pp. 2-5.

158. Letters from the Reverend Max V. Bolser, pastor, Calvary Baptist Church, Fredericton, New Brunswick, and from the Reverend Paul Brewer, Route, 2, Lepreau, New Brunswick.

159. In 1898 they changed their name once more, to the Free Will Baptist General Conference, and in 1905/1906 they helped to form the Baptist Convention of the Maritimes.

160. "Treatise of the Faith," *Constitution and By-Laws of the Primitive Baptist Conference of New Brunswick, Maine, and Nova Scotia* (N.p.: N.p., 1945) (41-page pamphlet), pp. 16-26. It is obvious that there is no connection between the Primitive Baptists of the United States and the Primitive Baptist Conference of New Brunswick, Maine, and Nova Scotia.

161. Letters of the Reverend Philip A. Giberson, Bath, New Brunswick EOJ INO.

162. Letter from Elder George Ruston, senior elder, Covenanted Baptist Church of Canada, Dutton, Ontario.

163. Letter from Mr. W. J. Berry, Primitive Baptist Publishing House and Library, Elon College, North Carolina.

164. Quoted in Martin L. Leuschner, "North American Baptist General Conference," in Davis Collier Woolley and others, *Baptist Advance* (Nashville: Broadman Press, 1964), p. 242.

165. "What We Believe," in *The Baptist General Conference and Its United Mission for Christ at a Glance* (Chicago: Baptist General Conference, n.d. (8-page pamphlet), p. [2].

An Affirmation of Our Faith (Chicago: Harvest Publications, n.d.) (1-page pamphlet). adopted in 1951, has sections on the Word of God ("fully inspired and without error in the original manuscripts"); the Trinity; the Father; Jesus Christ; the Holy Spirit; regeneration; the church; Christian conduct; the ordinances of immersions of believers in water into the name of the Triune God and the Lord's Supper as a commemoration of Christ's death; religious liberty; church cooperation; and the last things.

166. Nikita Isayevich Voronin, baptized at Tiflis on August 20, 1867, and regarded as the founder of the indigenous Baptist Church in Russia (as distinguished from Baptists converted among the colonies of western Europeans in Russia by Baptists from western Europe), was originally a Molokan, and so were most of the other charter members of the Baptist congregation in Tiflis.

167. Many of the early Ukrainian "Baptists" were actually Shtundists, adherents of a movement begun in Russia by a German Reformed minister of Pietistic orientation, Johann Bonekämper, and his son Karl around the beginning of the second half of the nineteenth century. Their Bible classes (*Bibelstunden*) were the inspiration for a lay-led Bible-study (*Shtunda*) movement among the indigenous Russian Orthodox peasants. It is documented as early as 1862 in the vicinity of Osnova. Under Mennonite Brethren, Molokan, and Baptist influence the Shtundists broke with the established church in the late 1860s, adopted believer's baptism by immersion (usually in a flowing stream), and began to establish autonomous congregations with their own presbyters and deacons. A biblicistic Pietism, an emphasis on personal conversion, a rigorous morality, a subordination of the possession of the Spirit to the Word of God, and a rejection of the worship and hierarchy of the established church marked these communities. The organization of the League of Russian Baptists in 1884 brought about an intensification of persecution by the government of Alexander III and the established church, but the Shtundist movement survived. In the United States and in Canada the first generation of Shtundists managed to maintain themselves but as the younger generation abandoned the Ukrainian Lanuage, it began to turn more and more to English-speaking churches in the vicinity, chiefly to the Baptists and to the Seventh-day Adventists (letter from Mrs. Andrew Duboviy, Minot, North Dakota). On the Shtundists in Russia, see Frederick Cornwallis Conybeare, *Russian Dissenters* (New York: Russell and Russell, 1962), pp. 331-335, and Serge Bolshakoff, *Russian Nonconformity: The Story of "Unofficial" Religion in Russia* (Philadelphia: Westminster Press, 1950), pp. 113-129. On the Shtundists in North Dakota, see the 80-page brochure in Ukrainian by Andrew Duboviy, *Na batkivshchini i na chuzhini* (Winnipeg: The Christian Press, 1957), and the article by Wasyl Halich, "Ukrainians in North Dakota," *North Dakota History* 18 (1951): 219-232. (This writer owes his knowledge of the Halich article to the late Reverend Professor Erich H. Heintzen, Ph.D., Concordia Theological Seminary, Springfield, Illinois.)

168. According to a letter from Mr. Pete Maloff, Sr., Thrums, British Columbia, the historian of the Russian immigration to North America, the state of North Dakota had about 10,000 nonconformist immigrants from the Ukraine during the last decade of the nineteenth century. About nine-tenths were Shtundists, the balance Russo-Ukrainian Mennonites, Evangelical Baptists, and Seventh-day Adventists.

169. Communication from the Reverend Peter Kowalchuk at the church body headquarters.

170. Letters from the Reverend O. R. Harbuziuk of the Ukrainian Evangelical Baptist Convention.

171. Letters from Mr. Michael Podworniak, editor of *Khristianskiy Visnik (Christian Herald),* 531 Newton Avenue, Winnipeg, Manitoba, and from the Reverend Nicholas Brych and the Reverend Peter Kindrath, Ukrainian Evangelical Baptist Convention of Canada. See also Ivan A. Kmeta,

With Christ in America: A Story of the Russian-Ukrainian Baptists (Winnipeg, Manitoba: The Christian Press, 1948), pp. 48-53, 95-108, and passim.

172. The present writer gratefully acknowledges the assistance of the Reverend Bohuslav D. Tuhy, pastor, Church of the Ascension, Montreal, Quebec, who kindly interviewed the Reverend Peter Kolibaiev, 3567 St. Urbain Street, Montreal, the president of the Union of Slavic Churches of Evangelical Christians and Slavic Baptists of Canada, on this writer's behalf.

BIBLIOGRAPHY

AMERICAN BAPTIST CHURCHES IN THE U.S.A.

Armstrong, O. K., and Armstrong, Marjorie M. *The Indomitable Baptists: A Narrative of Their Role in Shaping American History.* Garden City, N.Y.: Doubleday and Company, 1967.

Harrison, Paul M. *Authority and Power in the Free Church Tradition: A Social Case Study of the American Baptist Convention.* Princeton, N.J.: Princeton University Press, 1959.

Moody, Howard. "American Baptists: To Break the Bonds of Captivity." In Kyle Haselden and Martin E. Marty, eds., *What's Ahead for the Churches?* (New York: Sheed and Ward, 1967), pp. 61-68.

Starr, Edward C., ed. "American Baptist Convention." In Davis Collier Woolley, ed., *Baptist Advance: The Achievements of the Baptists of North America for a Century and a Half* (Nashville: Broadman Press, 1964), pp. 29-130.

SOUTHERN BAPTIST CONVENTION

Baker, Robert A. *A Baptist Source Book, with Particular Reference to Southern Baptists.* Nashville: Broadman Press, 1966.

———. *Relations between Northern and Southern Baptists.* 2nd edn. Fort Worth: Marvin D. Evans Printing Company, 1954.

———. *The Southern Baptist Convention and Its People 1607–1972.* Nashville: Broadman Press, 1974.

The Baptist Faith and Message. Nashville: The Sunday School Board of the Southern Baptist Convention, 1963.

Baptist History and Heritage, 1966–. [Historical Journal of the Historical Commission of the Southern Baptist Convention].

Baptist Hymnal (1975). Nashville: Convention Press, 1975.

Barnes, William Wright. *The Southern Baptist Convention 1845–1953.* Nashville: Broadman Press, 1954.

Brown, J. Newton. *A Baptist Church Manual.* Valley Forge, Pa.: Judson Press, 1976.

Cauthen, Baker James. *Advance: A History of Southern Baptist Foreign Missions.* Nashville: Broadman Press, 1970.

Cox, Norman W., and Woolley, Davis C. eds. *Encyclopedia of Southern Baptists.* 3 vols. Nashville: Broadman Press, 1958–1971.

Criswell, W. A. *Why I Preach That the Bible is Literally True.* Nashville: Broadman Press, 1969.

Davidson, W. E. *A Catechism of Bible Doctrine.* Nashville: Broadman Press, n.d.

Eighmy, John Lee. *Churches in Cultural Captivity. A History of the Social Attitudes of Southern Baptists.* Knoxville: University of Tennessee Press, 1972.

Estep, W. R. *Baptists and Christian Unity.* Nashville: Broadman Press, 1966.

Hastey, Stan L. "History of the Baptist Joint Committee of Public Affairs." Unpublished Th.D. dissertation, Southern Baptist Seminary, Louisville, Kentucky, 1973.

Hester, Hubert Inman. *Southern Baptists and Their History.* Nashville: Historical Commission, Southern Baptist Commission, 1971.

Hobbs, Herschel H. *What Baptists Believe.* Nashville: Broadman Press, 1964.

Lindsell, Harold. "Whither Southern Baptists?" *Christianity Today,* vol. XIV, no. 15 (April 24, 1970), pp. 667–669.

Martin, Gerald. *"Sir, We Would See Jesus";*

The Story of the Southern Baptist Pastors Conference. Memphis Tenn.: Wimmer Bros., 1968.

May, Lynn E., Jr. *Baptists.* Nashville: The Historical Commission of the Southern Baptist Convention, n.d.

McDonald, Erwin Lawrence. *Across the Editor's Desk: The Story of the State Baptist Papers.* Nashville: Broadman Press, 1966.

Neely, H. K., Jr. "The Territorial Expansion of the Southern Baptist Convention 1894–1959." Unpublished Th.D. dissertation, Southwestern Baptist Theological Seminary, Fort Worth, Texas, 1963.

Nordenhaug Josef, et al. *Baptists of the World, 1905–1970: Recollections and Reflections.* Fort Worth, Texas: Printed by the Southern Baptist Radio and Television Commission, 1970.

Odle, Joe T. *Church Member's Handbook.* rev. edn. Nashville: Broadman Press, 1962.

Shurden, Walter B. *Not a Silent People: Controversies That Have Shaped Southern Baptists.* Nashville: Broadman Press, 1972.

Steely, John E. "The Landmark Movement in the Southern Baptist Convention." In Duke K. McCall, ed., *What Is the Church? A Symposium of Baptist Thought.* Nashville: Broadman Press, 1958. Pp. 134-147.

Torbet, Robert G. *A History of the Baptists.* 3rd edn. Valley Forge, Pa.: Judson Press, 1975.

Tull, James E. "A Study of Southern Baptist Landmarkism in the Light of Historical Baptist Ecclesiology." Unpublished Ph.D. dissertation, Columbia University, New York, New York, 1960.

Wamble, H. "Landmarkism: Doctrinaire Ecclesiology among Baptists." *Church History* 33 (December 1964): 429-47.

GENERAL ASSOCIATION OF REGULAR BAPTIST CHURCHES

Hopewell, William J., Jr. *The Missionary Emphasis of the General Association of Regular Baptist Churches.* Des Plaines, Ill.: Regular Baptist Press, 1963.

Jackson, Paul R. *The Doctrine of the Local Church.* Des Plaines, Ill.: Regular Baptist Press, 1960.

Stowell, Joseph M. *Background and History of the General Association of Regular Baptist Churches.* 4th edn. Hayward, Calif.: Gospel Tracts Unlimited, [1955]. An updated and enlarged version of the author's M.A. thesis.

THE CONSERVATIVE BAPTIST ASSOCIATION OF AMERICA

Shelley, Bruce Leon. *Conservative Baptists: A Story of Twentieth-Century Dissent.* 2nd edn. Denver, Colo.: Conservative Baptist Theological Seminary, 1962. The story of the association from its prehistory to 1958.

WORLD BAPTIST FELLOWSHIP

Entzminger, Louis. *The J. Frank Norris I Have Known for 34 Years.* 2nd printing. N.p.: N.p., 1950. Available from the Bible Baptist Seminary Book Store, Arlington, Texas.

Tatum, E. Ray. *Conquest or Failure?—A Biography of J. Frank Norris.* Dallas: Baptist Historical Foundation, 1966. An objective study of John Franklyn Norris as preacher by one of Norris's assistants.

GENERAL SIX-PRINCIPLE BAPTISTS

Elliott, Nelson Robert. *A History of the General Six-Principle Baptists in America.* Unpublished Th.D. dissertation, South-western Baptist Theological Seminary, Fort Worth, Texas, 1958. Six-Principle Baptists regard this history, by an ordained minister of the American Baptist Convention, as definitive.

Lewis, William. "The General Six-Principle Baptists." In Ollie Latch, *History of the General Baptists*. Poplar Bluff, Mo.: The General Baptist Press, 1954. Pp. 105-111.

A brief account by a minister of the denomination.

McLoughlin, William G. "The First Calvinistic Baptist Association in New England, 1754?–1767." *Church History* 36 (1967): 410-418.

THE GENERAL ASSOCIATION OF GENERAL BAPTISTS

Latch, Ollie. *History of the General Baptists*. Poplar Bluff, Mo.: The General Baptist Press, 1954.

Runyon, Edwin. *This We Believe*. 3rd printing. Poplar Bluff, Mo.: The General Baptist Press, 1963.

THE BAPTIST FEDERATION OF CANADA

Ivison, Stuart. "Is There a Canadian Baptist Tradition?" In John Webster Grant, ed., *The Churches and the Canadian Experience: A Faith and Order Study of The Christian Tradition*. 2nd printing. Toronto, Ontario: The Ryerson Press, 1966, pp. 53-68. A moderately critical essay by a Canadian Baptist church historian, military chaplain, and pastor.

Jones, J. Gordon. *Greatness Passing By!* Brantford, Ontario: The Baptist Federation of Canada, 1967. Biographical sketches of 19 Canadian Baptists emphasize their contribution to the life of the Dominion from 1867 to 1967.

Kirkconnell, Watson, and others. "The Baptist Federation of Canada." In Davis Collier Woolley, ed., *Baptist Advance: The Achievements of the Baptists of North America for a Century and a Half*. Nashville: Broadman Press, 1964. Pp. 131-185.

Waters, F. W., ed. *Protestantism—A Baptist Interpretation*. Brantford, Ontario: The Baptist Federation of Canada, 1958. A 67-page brochure.

THE NORTH AMERICAN BAPTIST GENERAL CONFERENCE

Leuschner, Martin L. "North American Baptist General Conference." In Davis Collier Woolley and others, eds., *Baptist Advance: The Achievements of the Baptists of North America for a Century and a Half*. Nashville: Broadman Press, 1964. Pp. 227-250.

OLD REGULAR BAPTISTS

Perrigan, Rufus. *History of Regular Baptist and Their Ancestors and Accessors*. Haysi, Va.: Rufus Perrigan, 1961. This uncritical compilation of materials, a labor of love on the part of the now deceased author, does not pretend to be a scholarly history; nevertheless it contains a great many items of great historical and theological interest not accessible between two covers anywhere else. Perrigan was one of the founders and the clerk of the Bethel Association that split in 1962 from the Union Association.

PRIMITIVE BAPTISTS OF THE OLD SCHOOL OR PREDESTINARIAN FAITH AND ORDER

Parker, Daniel. *The Second Dose of Doctrine on the Two Seeds, Dealt Out in Broken Doses Designed to Purge the Armenian* [sic] *Stuff and Dross Out of the Church of Christ and Hearts and Heads of Saints*. Vincennes, Ind.: Elihu

Stout, 1826. Copy in the Library of Southern Baptist Theological Seminary, Louisville, Kentucky.

————. *A Supplement or Explanation of My Views on the Two Seeds*. Vandalia, Ill.: Robert Blackwell, 1826. Copy in the Library of Southern Baptist Theological Seminary, Louisville, Kentucky.

————. *View on the Two Seeds Taken from Genesis 3d Chapter and Part of the 15th Verse: "And I Will Put Enmity Between Thee and the Woman, and Between Thy Seed and Her Seed."* Vandalia, Ill.: Robert Blackwell, 1826. Copy in the Library of Southern Baptist Theological Seminary, Louisville, Kentucky.

Small, Guy W. *The Life of Daniel Parker*. Marshall, Texas: Unpublished M.A. thesis, East Texas Baptist College, 1954.

14. Churches That Perpetuate Continental Free Church Traditions

A considerable number of church bodies in the United States and Canada directly or indirectly perpetuate European Free Church traditions that have their origins in movements on the European continent since the sixteenth century. This chapter concerns itself with church bodies that continue traditions going back to Germany, Scandinavia, and the tsarist Russian empire.

The Schwenkfelder Church

Casper Schwenkfeld von Ossig (1489–1561), Lower Silesian Nobleman, was a learned, influential, and prolific lay thinker of the Reformation era. A mystic and a "spiritualist" only in a broad sense, he was at first a staunch supporter of the Wittenberg reformers, but by 1525 he had definitely broken with them (as he subsequently broke with the Swiss reformers and the Anabaptists). His chief reason was his belief that the Lutheran Reformation stressed saving faith too much and did not adequately emphasize holiness of life. Among the many important themes of his experimental theology were his teaching on the sacrament of the altar and on the "celestial flesh" of Christ. The flesh and blood of Christ in the sacrament, he held, are a true food and drink, "but not a corporal, corruptible food and drink, not an earthly and visible bread and wine, neither with, under, or in, but intrinsically a heavenly, divine bread, a spiritual, everlasting food and drink unto eternal life for all souls believing in Christ and all children of God." This food and drink "are truly eaten out of the living word of God by the mouth of faith and partaken of in the Lord's supper . . . for the satiation of the soul and increase in the accessions of grace in the new, inner man."[1] Of the "celestial flesh" he taught, as many of the Radical reformers did, that Christ's humanity was in no sense creaturely but that he had brought it with him from heaven. "I recognize nothing of creation or creatureliness in Christ," he wrote, "but rather a new divine birth and natural Sonship of God. Wherefore I cannot consider the man Christ with His body and blood to be a creation or a creature. Rather, I believe and confess with Scripture that he is wholly God's only begotten Son."[2]

Schwenkfeld founded no denomination. For the last thirty-two years of his life he lived as an exile, often in great danger. His followers after him were for generations subjected to bitter persecution. Finally 180 of them, exiled from Silesia, fled to Pennsylvania, where they arrived in 1734. In 1782 the immigrant colony formed the Society of Schwenkfelders. The Schwenkfelder Church was incorporated in 1909. The General Conference of the Schwenkfelder Church is a voluntary association of five local churches in Philadelphia, Norristown, Lansdale, Palm, and Worcester, Pennsylvania. Their total membership is about 2,520. All but one of the churches are associate members of the United Church of Christ. Their Mission Board has always worked closely with what is now the United Church Board for World Ministries, and they conduct an inner-city mission in Philadelphia. Education has always been high on their list of priorities; for over nine decades they have sponsored the Perkiomen College Preparatory School for Boys at Perkiomen. Their interest in the problems of the aging finds expression in a nursing home and retirement low-rent housing complex in the Lansdale area.

Schwenkfelders practice adult baptism, dedication of children, and open Communion. Since 1895 they no longer object to bearing arms, joining secret societies, and swearing oaths, but they still stress experiential religion and the right, privilege, and obligation of the individual conscience.

Schwenkfelders hold that the church is the company of those regenerated souls in all lands who worship the Father in spirit and in truth. The Bible correctly speaking, is not the Word of God but the record of the voice of God. The Word of God can be written only on the tables of the human heart. The Bible belongs to the order of earthly things and its function is to admonish and teach the external man. The Gospel is Christ himself, found not in the Scriptures or the written Gospel, but in the spirit. The Gospel manifests itself in good works and in a godly, righteous life. Faith, the gift of the Holy Spirit, is consciousness of God; since it belongs to the heavenly spiritual order, it cannot depend upon any external, physical thing. In the Lord's Supper the invisible, spiritual bread nourishes the believing soul as the physical bread nourishes the physical body; Christ would not unite himself with the earthly elements. Grace and forgiveness are not imparted by the external water of baptism, but by the washing of regeneration; there is no scriptural foundation for infant baptism. Christ Jesus, who gave himself a ransom for all, is the one mediator between God and man; God uses means, such as the spoken word, the ministers, the Holy Scriptures, and the sacraments, for the instruction of the outer man that he may walk uprightly and not hinder the inner man in his growth. Christian liberty is the liberty of the spirit of Christ, the spirit of love, obedience, kindness, and goodness. Christian brotherly love consists in unity of hearts that are of one mind, one will, and one soul in Christ. Obedience is due to constituted civil authority, but in the realm of the soul and conscience, obedience is due to God and his word only.[3]

The headquarters of the Schwenkfelder Church are at Pennsburg, Pennsylvania 18073.

Church of the Brethren

Dissatisfied with what they regarded as the low level of spirituality in the established churches of Germany, and influenced by contact with both Anabaptist and Pietist teaching, Alexander Mack, (1679–1735) and seven others formed a new denomination at Schwarzenau, then a part of Hesse, in 1708. They called themselves the *Brüder-Gemeinde* ("Community of Brothers"); popularly they were known as *Neu-Täufer* ("Neo-Baptists"). Persecution drove the rapidly expanding community out of Germany. In 1719 a group under the leadership of Peter Becker emigrated to Pennsylvania and settled at Germantown. The next year another group, led by Alexander Mack, went to Surhuisterveen, Holland, where they lived until 1729, when they too came to Germantown. (In 1933 another contingent came to America, leaving only a few members of the Church of the Brethren behind in Germany.)

The westward and southward movement of the Brethren on the American continent began soon afterward. By the late eighteen century they had established themselves in what is now eastern Missouri; by the mid-nineteenth century they were to be found on the West Coast as well as on the Great Plains. More recently they have moved north into Canada and southeastward into Florida. In the last few years they have been making a rapid transition from rural to urban life.

A number of secessions from the Church of the Brethren have taken place. Conrad Beissel and his followers withdrew in 1728 to form the German Seventh-day Baptists. In 1848 Peter Oyman (hence the nickname Oymanites) and George Patten left the Church of the Brethren to found the Church of God (New Dunkards); this movement survived until 1962, when the remnants of it disbanded. The extremely conservative founders of the Old German Baptist Church (Old Order Brethren) withdrew in 1881, followed by their more liberal opposite numbers, the organizers of the Brethren Church (Progressive), the next year. Other seceders established the Dunkard Brethren Church in 1926; a small secession in the early 1950s led to the formation of the Association of Fundamental Gospel Churches; and in 1962 another small group separated to form the Fundamental Brethren Church.

The Church of the Brethren is historically trinitarian and affirms "the Fatherhood of God, the Lordship of Christ and his cleansing and forgiving grace as shown on the cross, the empowering action of the Holy Spirit, the inspiration of the Scriptures, and the immortality of the soul." At the same time it concedes to its members considerable flexibility in the understanding of these doctrines. Noncreedal in principle, it views the New Testament, interpreted under the Holy Spirit's creative guidance, as a sufficient formulation of the truth. It administers believer's baptism by threefold immersion in the name of the Father and of the Son and of the Holy Spirit, although it acknowledges the validity of other modes when it receives new members baptized in other communions. The Communion is observed in the setting of (*a*) the love feast (the foot-washing service as a symbol of cleansing and humility), (*b*) the Lord's Supper in the form of a full meal as a symbol of Christian fellowship and an anticipation of the fellowship in the coming Kingdom, and (*c*) the bread and cup symbolizing the communion of the believer with Christ. Anointing of the sick and the dying with oil has the healing and encouragement of the former and the comfort of the latter in view. The laying on of hands takes place in baptism, the ordination of ministers, the consecration of missionaries, and the anointing of the sick.

The Church of the Brethren emphasizes the service of the Kingdom of God as the single purpose of the Christian life. This, it holds, implies— ideally, if not altogether successfully in practice—simplicity in dress, appearance, and living arrangements and the deliberate avoidance of extravagance and ostentation. It stresses the integrity of the individual's word and rejects oaths; sets up high standards of personal and social morality; fosters a high quality of family life; calls for abstinence from anything injurious to physical health; and urges the use of love and reason rather than force as a means of settling differences.

Its emphasis on reconciliation and peace underlies its official position that war is contrary to both the teachings and the spirit of Christ; at the same time it manages to maintain warm fellowship with those of its members who hold different convictions.[4]

Always concerned for the relief of human suffering in the wake of persecution, war, and disaster, the Church of the Brethren, through its Brethren Service Commission, since World War II has mounted an imaginative attack on a great veriety of human needs and on the prevention of social ills both in North America and in other lands.

Conversations among the Church of the Brethren, the Evangelical United Brethren, and the Churches of God in North America have looked more toward greater mutual understanding and cooperation than toward proposals for organic union.

The headquarters of the Church of the Brethren are at 1451 Dundee Avenue, Elgin, Illinois 60120. The highest policy-making body is the annual conference; a 25-member Brotherhood Board implements its decisions. There are 1,038 churches in the United States (including Puerto Rico) and Canada. with a total membership of 179,387. The church carries on foreign operations in India, Nigeria, Ecuador, and Indonesia.

Old German Baptist Brethren

While the Old German Baptist Brethren withdrew from the German Baptist Brethren, or Conservative Dunkards—now the Church of the Brethren— in 1881, the division must be considered in the context of the second break that followed the very next year, with withdrawal of the Brethren Church, or Progressive Dunkards. In this context the Old German Baptists emerge as the proponents of the inherited ways without change, the Progressive Dunkards are ones who call for relatively radical changes, while the German Baptist Brethren attempt to preserve a middle course between the two.

The schism was thirty years in the making. In 1851 the *Monthly Gospel Visitor* became the first periodical in Brethren circles. Other innovations that came during the next years were Sunday schools, revival meetings, and high school and college education. A hotly debated issue was whether or not the elements of the Lord's Supper (an actual meal among the Dunkards, consisting of bread, mutton or beef, and meat-broth soup) and the bread and wine of the Communion were to be placed on the tables at the beginning of the foot-washing service; the opponents of change said No, "because in the Old Testament dispensation it was not permitted to have two sacrifices before the Lord at the same time," while the center group affirmed the practice on the ground that John 13:2–5 required it.[5]

Another passionately argued issue was if two members at a time should perform the office of foot-washing, one washing and the other wiping (the "double mode," the inherited practice), or if the same person should do both (the "single mode"). Still other issues involved the solicitation of funds for the work of the church, a salaried ministry, a moderator and a standing committee at the annual meeting, missionary plans and mission boards, musical instruments, and the taking of interest. The proponents of the old order were strongest in southern Ohio.

While the schism was developing, the annual meeting of the denomination tried to steer a middle course. As late as 1880 it resolved: "While we are conservative, we are also progressive."[6] But the difference had become too great. When the annual meeting of 1881 refused to consider the petition of the Miami Valley (Ohio) elders and the Dry Creek (Iowa) church for a permanent return to the old order, the opponents of change withdrew and organized the Old German Baptist Brethren.

The denomination has succeeded in maintaining its traditional position. Its interpretation of the Scripture is literal. Baptism is by threefold forward immersion. The Communion rite consists of foot-washing according to the "double mode," followed by the Lord's Supper (an actual meal, which typifies the "marriage supper of the Lamb") and the Communion in unleavened bread and fermented wine, "emblematical of the broken body and shed blood of our Lord." The Old German Baptist Brethren practice close Communion. In worship they use no musical instruments; normally they kneel for prayer. They give one another the "holy kiss," brother kissing brother and sister kissing sister, publicly on special occasions and generally in private greeting, the sexes greeting one another with a handclasp. The Old German Baptist Brethren refuse to support war in any way and to join secret societies or support any organization, such as labor unions, that uses violent means to achieve its ends. At the request of a sick person, they anoint him with oil for forgiveness of sins and the restoration of health. They do not swear oaths, but merely affirm or deny. They permit marital separation only on the grounds of fornication and reject divorce absolutely. They keep Sunday, refuse to sue at law, reject the modern missionary movement as a presumptuous arrogation of a commission given to the apostles, disapprove of Sunday schools, do not serve in public office, refrain from voting, and engage in "occupations consistent with their holy calling." A reduction in their aversion to higher education and the general trend of the national economy have resulted in a larger number of their young people entering commerce, industry, and the professions. They continue to reject a trained and salaried ministry, oppose most forms of popular entertainment (including television), and maintain the traditional "bonnets, black hats and beards" both as a fulfillment of the biblical demand of modest apparel and simplicity and as a symbol of their determination to retain their inherited faith unchanged.[7]

There are 52 Old German Baptist Brethren churches, with a total membership of 4,900. The Annual Conference at Pentecost determines matters of general importance on which the Scriptures do not speak, and its decisions are binding.

Brethren Church (Ashland, Ohio)
(The General Conference of Brethren Churches)

In the face of considerable opposition, the conservative leadership of the Church of the Brethren succeeded in inducing the 1882 Annual Conference at Arnold's Grove, near Milford, Indiana, to expel Henry Ritz Holsinger, editor of *The Progressive Christian*. Holsinger had persistently criticized what he regarded as an overemphasis on the traditions of plain dress and worship. He had advocated the autonomy of the local congregation over against the Annual Conference. He had appealed for missions, Sunday schools, and a professionally trained and salaried ministry. One result of the Annual Conference's action was the exodus from the church body of a great many like-minded ministers and churches. At Ashland, Ohio, the same year, they convened the Progressive Convention of the Tunker Church; at Dayton, Ohio, in 1883 it organized itself as the Brethren Church. The name "Progressive Dunkers" has never been part of the official name of the church; originally it merely designated the "progressive" party in the old German Baptist Church (now the Church of the Brethren), in opposition to the "conservatives."

The Message of the Brethren Ministry, accepted by the General Conference in 1921, takes as its motto "the Bible, the whole Bible, and nothing but the Bible." It asserts the authority and integrity of the Bible ("as originally given, [they] are the infallible record of the perfect, fiinal, and authoritative revelation of God's will"); the preexistence and incarnation by virgin birth of the Son of God; man's fall and need of rebirth; Christ's vicarious atonement, resurrection, and subsequent glorification; justification by personal faith in Christ, resulting in obedience to God's will and works of righteousness; the resurrection of the dead, the judgment of the world, and life everlasting for the just; the personality and deity of the indwelling Holy Spirit; Christ's personal and visible return from heaven; the Christian's obligation not to conform to this world, not to engage in carnal strife, and not to swear at all; believer's baptism by threefold immersion; confirmation; the Lord's Supper (as a complete meal); the Communion of the bread and wine; the washing of the saints' feet; and the anointing of the sick with oil.[8]

Disagreement within the body over issues having to do with faith (primarily the question of the eternal security of the believer), polity, and secondary and theological education led to a division in 1939. The "Ashland Group" (The General Conference of Brethren Churches continued to maintain its headquarters at Ashland, Ohio 44805 (524 College Avenue).

The theology of the "Ashland Brethren" tends to be Arminian rather than Calvinist. It has 119 churches in the United States, with a total membership of 16,279. It carries on foreign missions in Argentina and Nigeria.

The National Fellowship of Brethren Churches

Out of the 1939 division of the "Progressive Dunkers" came the National Fellowship of Brethren Churches. In contrast to their "Ashland Brethren" the theological stance of the "Grace Brethren" inclines toward Calvinism, especially in the doctrine of eternal security. It has over 250 churches in the United States, with a total membership of 37,000.[9]

Dunkard Brethren Church

The Dunkard Brethren Church withdrew from the Church of the Brethren in 1926.

The church body's creed is the New Testament. Its doctrinal emphases cover nine areas: the Trinity, man by nature; the law of pardon; church rites; the Christian Sabbath and graces; nonconformity; powers and functions; and general principles.

"Man's disposition and nature are shaped by the law of heredity and his own volition in choosing right and wrong." The atonement is free, unlimited and unconditional to all the unaccountable part of humanity and free and unlimited, but conditional, to all accountable persons. "By the atonement, mankind was redeemed from the 'original' or 'Adamic' sin and is now accountable for individual sin only." Believer's baptism is by threefold forward immersion in a flowing stream in the name of the Father and of the Son and of the Holy Spirit; "kneeling or bowing is the scriptural posture." Former members of the Church of the Brethren and Old German Baptist Brethren are received into the Dunkard Brethren Church on the basis of their original baptism. Love-feast services consist of an examination service, the love-feast service proper, foot-washing, the salutation of the holy kiss, the Lord's Supper (full meal, with the soup eaten from a common dish), the Communion of the bread and cup (brought forward after the tables of the Lord's Supper have been covered), and closing devotions. Usually the Dunkard Brethren hold a love-feast service once in the spring and once in the fall. Christian women are to wear the veil or head covering at all times; it is to take the form of a plain white cap with strings. Two elders or bishops, if at all available, are to anoint the sick.

Christians are to obey civil government as far as its laws do not conflict with Christ's will. The brotherhood advises all its "members not to take part in politics or political matters." Dunkard Brethren believe in nonresistance. "Learning the art of warfare and participating in carnal warfare in any branch of military establishment, at any time, is forbidden by the Scripture; and the boy and girl scout movements and any other movement requiring a uniform, or having any military features, fall under the same condemnation." Dunkard Brethren must avoid games, plays, performances and unions that are manifestly evil. They may not affiliate with secret societies or lodges. "Members are forbidden to own or have television in their homes." They reject the rules and hurtful fashions of the world, "such as wearing of hats by Christian women and [of] neckties, gold, rings, bracelets and such like by either sex." They should not wear wristwatches.

The *Dunkard Brethren Church Polity* reaffirms the "dress decision of 1911," which calls for, among other things, plain clothing, coats with standing collar for the men, hair parted in the middle or combed straight back, and plain bonnets and hoods and hair "worn in a becoming Christian manner" for women. Men are urged but not required to wear beards; they may not wear mustaches alone. Dunkard Brethren are to avoid narcotics, including tobacco. They are not to use instruments of music in the house of God. They must not go to law with a brother without the church's permission, enter the legal profession, take or subscribe to an oath, divorce a spouse except for fornication, remarry after divorce during the lifetime of the divorced partner, or take out life insurance policies (except when civil or industrial conditions make it compulsory).

The church is a theocratic democracy. A salaried ministry does not have the warrant of Scripture and is contrary to the custom of the church. Women may not be church officials or engage in a preaching ministry.

The Bible, given by verbal, plenary inspiration, is God's only revelation to man. The New Testament contains the principles of the church and the plan of salvation. Election is God's sovereign mercy in calling those who of their own volition choose a life of righteousness. Those who reject the overtures in mercy in this life will be forever lost. The millennium will come at the end of this age. After the judgment the righteous and wicked will go to their respective coeternal abodes.[10]

The church does not permit special programs of worship, such as Thanksgiving and Christmas. Officials or members of other denominations are not to teach or preach at Dunkard Brethren Church services.[11]

The officials of the Dunkard Brethren Church consists of deacons, ministers, and elders [or bishops]. At the various levels, local conferences, four district conferences across the United States, and an annual General Conference govern the brotherhood. There are approximately 30 churches with an estimated total membership of 2,000. The brotherhood has no formal headquarters.

Association of Fundamental Gospel Churches

The Association of Fundamental Gospel Churches came into being at Hartville, Ohio, in 1954, under the leadership of G. Henry Besse (d. 1962), a Reformed minister who later entered the Church of the Brethren. The member churches withdrew in the early 1950s from the Church of the Brethren in protest against the parent body's affiliation with the National Council of the Churches of Christ in the United States of America.

The association accepts the New Testament as its creed. It believes in the Trinity; in Christ's virgin birth, crucifixion, death, resurrection, and ascension; in his blood poured out for the forgiveness of sins; in the resurrection of the dead; in Christ's return for his bride, the church; in a literal heaven and a literal hell; in the responsibility of every individual to work out his own salvation; and in the church, Christ's body, as the believers in every age whom God has accepted. It enjoins faith in Christ, repentance, and the new birth to a life dedicated and consecrated to God. It practices baptism by immersion as a means of applying Christ's blood for the forgiveness of sins; the laying on of hands for the gift of the Holy Ghost; foot-washing; the Lord's Supper as a complete meal; the Holy Communion in bread and wine; the kiss of charity; and the anointing of the sick with oil. Its women cover, its men uncover their heads during services of worship. It rejects as unbiblical going to war, taking an oath, obtaining a divorce, suing at law, and wearing ornamental adornment.[12] It accepts the Bible in its entirety as the Word of God. It believes "in the God-called rather than the man-made ministry"; the local congregations choose their ministers from their own midst and do not require them to have college or seminary education. The association, which meets annually, has no authority or power over the local congregations.

The largest and oldest congregation is located at Greencastle, Pennsylvania. There are three other congregations, in Meyersdale, Maryland, Hartville, Ohio, and Webster Mills Pennsylvania. The total membership is approximately 240.[13]

Fundamental Brethren Church

In 1964 four congregations in the mountainous region of Mitchell County, North Carolina, under the leadership of the Reverend Calvin Barnett withdrew from the Church of the Brethren and incorporated as the Fundamental

Brethren Church. The reasons given for the withdrawal were the membership of the Church of the Brethren in the National Council of the Churches of Christ in the United States of America and the parent church's use of the Revised Standard Version of the Bible.

The Fundamental Brethren Church regards itself as perpetuating the authentic Brethren tradition from which, in its view, the Church of the Brethren has departed. The Statement of Faith of the Fundamental Brethren Church reproduces with minor variations and abbreviations the Message of the Brethren Ministry adopted by the General Conference of the ["Progressive"] Brethren Church in 1921. It differs from the latter document in that it explicitly affirms that "the Scriptures of the Old and New Testaments of the King James Version" are divinely inspired and are the final and authoritative revelation of God's will for man. It also explicitly asserts "the bodily resurrection of the just and later of the unjust" and Christ's personal and imminent appearance "for the saints and later His coming with the saints." It defines the baptismal formula as "in the name of the Father and of the Son and of the Holy Ghost" and describes the Lord's Supper as "a light meal." An appended final sentence forbids preaching or teaching the Revised Standard Version of the Bible.[14]

The four congregations of the church have a total of about 200 members.[15]

The Church of the Brotherhood

The Church of the Brotherhood, the community in the world of which the Religious Order of Humanitas is the strictly disciplined core, sees itself as standing in the tradition established with the foundation of the first Anabaptist community in Zurich in 1525. Beyond the Zurich congregation it traces its origins back to the fourteenth and fifteenth-century Brotherhood of the Common Life in Holland and the Brothers of the Free Spirit in Eastern Europe. It established itself as an independent community in the United States in the early 1960s, under the leadership of the Reverend George von Hilsheimer, a Brethren minister.

Within the Anabaptist tradition it finds itself in closer affinity to the Hutterian Brothers, with their reputation for high-quality education and technology and their willingness to avail themselves of the labor-saving devices of science, rather than to the Amish and the Mennonites. But there are no longer any formal or ethnic ties with the Hutterians, although friendly and cordial relationships exist between the Church of the Brotherhood and the Hutterian colonies.

The Church of the Brotherhood proposes to continue in the Anabaptist channel by insisting on adult confession and baptism, relying on the Bible rather than on theology and doctrine, practicing nonresistance, and accepting literally the strict community of goods that the primitive church of Jerusalem practiced.

Its members believe that all human beings "are capable of facing the ultimate for themselves." Persuaded that all believers are priests, they do not elevate their ministers to priestly status, and they require them to earn their livelihood at pursuits other than their ministerial functions. They do not erect "church buildings, organize Sunday schools, separate worship from the ordinary course of life, or speculate on the nature of God or the ultimate." They recognize no sacraments, but they hold the love feast, the washing of feet, and believer's baptism by immersion as ordinances. Fundamentally, they say, "we are . . . trying to build our own faith and redemption." Their Anabaptist noncreedal inclusiveness enables them explicitly to welcome into their fellowship anyone—Christian, Jew, Hindu, Buddhist, Muslim, Humanist, or an adherent of any other religion or ethical system—as long as he is willing to accept their discipline.

Although the members of the Church of the Brotherhood live in communities they must also live in the world. Here they must maintain their "apartness" while dealing with nonbelievers in business, in service, and in reconciling witness-giving to the gospel. The Church of the Brotherhood forbids its communities to adopt any practice that it describes as "idolatrous," that is, they are to speak contemporary language, to wear clothing appropriate to their respective stations and work, and to express their witness and their identity not through symbols but through their lives. "Confessional" members must devote at least a tenth of their goods and wealth and a full day of work a week to service projects. "Full" members—who comprise the Order of Humanitas—must live in complete discipline and must dedicate all their wealth and work to the service of the community.

The Church of the Brotherhood uses austerity as a tactic for its own growth and good, and lives in community for its obvious advantages over life in individual isolation. It feels that it has "a research mandate in social engineering," to restructure society into communities that respect individual differences and support the freest individual expression.

It requires its research and service teams to make their projects self-directing in an absolute maximum of thirty-six months; to be regarded as successful the institution must survive for three years thereafter. The church further requires that when the techniques employed are committed to writing, film, or tape, they must prove to be 80 percent as effective as direct consultation. The institution may hire staff, but it must rely heavily on volunteers and laymen. The cost of operation is limited to one-third of common experience for comparable operations, while the program goals must be reached at a level substantially superior to common practice. Strongly stressed is the desirability of rotation in positions of leadership to the maximum extent.

The Church of the Brotherhood opposes the use of tobacco, intoxicants, and drugs. The brothers agree not to question each other about faith, and affirm together that no one should talk about God or pray publicly, memorize parts of the Bible, or make a child memorize Bible verses. It requires that covenants and contracts be reduced to writing, and that brothers settle disagreements within the community and that they do so before breaking the evening bread together.

The headquarters of the Church of the Brotherhood is at Green Valley School, Orange City, Florida 32763. It operates four centers for emotionally disturbed children and nearly fifty centers for slum families, migrants, and others, which after the original organizational period have become autonomous congregations or services. The Church of the Brotherhood reports approximately 30,000 "confessional" members, many of whom are not associated with a congregation but render their service through the national body. The Order of Humanitas has 200 disciplined members living in community.[16]

United Zion Church

In 1853 the Dauphin County, Pennsylvania, congregation of Matthias Brinser (1795–1889), a bishop of the River Brethren and an eloquent speaker, began the erection of a permanent 25- by 40-foot church building. Twenty-six Lancaster County Brethren agreed in council to request Brinser to desist from the project. When he and his people did not do so, the Lancaster County group expelled him and his followers from their fellowship in 1855. Thereupon the Dauphin County group, together with three other River Brethren ministers, organized as the United Zion's Children; the body, popularly known as Brinsers, adopted the name United Zion Church in 1954. Its churches are located wholly in three Pennsylvania counties: Lancaster, Lebanon, and Dauphin.

Opposition to church buildings began to wane among the Brethren in Christ in the 1860s. Today the United Zion Church stands in a close relation with the Brethren in Christ. It interchanges ministers with the latter, supports missionaries working under Brethren in Christ auspices, and participates in an Inter-Church Fellowship Committee of the two denominations. Like the Brethren in Christ, the United Zion Church has dropped many of the old River Brethren customs and traditions, without relaxing its emphasis on the virgin birth, regeneration, sanctification, holiness, the second coming, and other tenets that it regards as fundamental. It baptizes by threefold immersion and observes foot-washing in connection with the Lord's Supper. When new members who have not received threefold immersion transfer from other denominations, a second baptism is required.[17] The church has bishops, ministers, and deacons. An annual General Conference, at which the district conferences are represented, is the highest administrative authority. There are 13 churches and a camp-meeting site with an auditorium and youth tabernacle. The overall membership is 952.

Brethren in Christ Fellowship

In 1834 George W. Shoemaker, the son of a German Dunkard immigrant and himself apparently a former Dunkard preacher, organized an independent congregation under the name "Brethren in Christ" at Mount Pleasant, Westmoreland County, in western Pennsylvania. Later he organized at least one additional Brethren in Christ congregation, and possibly more, in the same general area.

About this same time, John Wenger, Sr., a River Brethren preacher who had broken with his denomination, was organizing Brethren in Christ congregations of his own in Montgomery and Medina counties in Ohio. One of his converts was John Swank, a former member of the United Brethren. John Wenger, Jr., succeeded his father, and in 1861 the younger Wenger and Swank broke with each other. In 1924, after a checkered history of nearly a century, the surviving Wengerites, by then called Pentecostal Brethren in Christ, joined the Pilgrim Holiness Church, now part of the Wesleyan Church. Swank's followers and Shoemaker's followers joined forces and organized the Church of the Brethren in Christ (with a written constitution) that same year.

Upon the deaths of Shoemaker in 1867 and of Swank in 1873, many of the Brethren in Christ were absorbed into other denominations. Those in Pennsylvania were attracted to the Free-Will Baptists. Those in Ohio ultimately joined with the Evangelical United Mennonites to form the Mennonite Brethren in Christ (now the United Missionary Church) in 1883. Only one Swank-Shoemaker Brethren in Christ minister, Samuel McDonald, remained in western Pennsylvania. But the denomination survived, and references in extant records indicate that a conference existed as far back as 1893. It incorporated itself as the Church of the Brethren in Christ in 1914.

Once again the denomination declined. Beginning in the late 1910s and the 1920s, because of the similarity of the Church of the Brethren in Christ and the General Eldership of the Churches of God in North America,[18] the Brethren in Christ came increasingly to be absorbed by the Churches of God. Once again, the number of Brethren in Christ ministers declined to one, Elmer Tantlinger (d. 1946); even in the case of the church of which he was pastor, the Limestone Church in the Adrian Valley, Armstrong County, the Churches of God came to regard the building as belonging to them.

In 1942 Tantlinger ordained to the ministry a young evangelist, Herman W. Mohney. Although at first there was no opening for him in the Church of the Brethren in Christ, he founded a Brethren in Christ mission in the late 1940s near Kittanning. Mohney provided leadership to the Brethren in Christ community in the Adrian Valley and assisted them in incorporating under the old name of Church of the Brethren in Christ in 1951.

In that year the minister of the local Churches of God congregation—

which purchased the Brethren in Christ share in the structure when the court suit was decided in the latter's favor—placed the local Brethren in Christ group in contact with the national Brethren in Christ. With the exception of the Adrian Valley congregation, which had secured another minister, the Armstrong County churches, calling themselves the Brethren in Christ, (Independent), placed themselves under the supervision of the General Executive Board of the national body in 1952.[19]

The Church of the Brethren in Christ (Independent) withdrew from its relation with the national body in 1963 and took the name Brethren in Christ Fellowship. In 1966 it reincorporated itself under the new designation. It has affiliated with the Associated Gospel Churches and its letterhead stresses that it is "not affiliated with the National Council of [the] Churches of Christ [in the United States of America] or the World Council of Churches," which it describes as "Anti-Christ movements."[20]

As "the essential and constituent elements" of its message the fellowship lists: the fearless declaration of the whole counsel of God; the authority and integrity of the Bible; Christ's preexistence, deity, and incarnation by virgin birth; the fall of man and his consequent spiritual death and utter sinfulness; Christ's vicarious atonement; his resurrection and glorification; justification by personal faith, the resurrection of the dead, the judgment of the world, and the life everlasting of the just; the personality of the Holy Spirit and the privilege of every reborn believer to be filled with the Holy Spirit for power, service, and witnessing; Christ's personal and visible return; the Christian's abstention from carnal strife and his separation from the present apostate world; and the ordinances of believer's baptism by threefold immersion, the Lord's Supper (as a complete meal), the Communion of the bread and wine, [the holy kiss,] the washing of the saints' feet, and the anointing of the sick with oil.[21]

The constitution specifies threefold forward immersion, because Christians are baptized into the likeness of Christ's death and Christ bowed his head forward on the cross when he died, not backward. It also specifies that the Communion be a triune service—foot-washing as a sacrament symbolizing a spiritual cleansing; believer's Communion together in the love feast (wherever the practice can be revived); and the Communion in the consecrated bread, which symbolizes the bread from heaven, and in the consecrated unfermented grape juice, which symbolizes the blood atonement. It directs that the holy kiss is not to be exchanged so often that it becomes a formality, but it should always be observed when members are about to separate or when they meet again after a separation for some time. It prohibits all immodest dress, membership in secret oathbound orders, the use and sale of alcoholic beverages, and attendance at shows and theaters.[22]

The Brethren in Christ Fellowship offers fellowship to "all Bible-believing Christians" who have been born again by Christ's atoning blood.

There are six churches in the fellowship, four in western Pennsylvania, and one each in Chicago, Illinois, and Nashville, Tennessee. The fellowship claims a membership of approximately 10,000. Its senior officer is called bishop. The headquarters are at Edmon, Pennsylvania 15630, where the conference of the fellowship meets annually.[23]

Calvary Holiness Church

The Brethren in Christ established a congregation in Philadelphia in 1897. Increasingly from the 1940s on the members of this congregation became dissatisfied with what they regarded as changes in their denomination's position on separation and on practical holiness and in its relation to other religious bodies. In 1963 the congregation withdrew from the Brethren in Christ to become the nucleus of a new denomination, the Calvary Holiness Church. It incorporated itself in 1964.

The seventeen Tenets of Faith and Doctrine of the Calvary Holiness Church affirm God's unity and creatorhood; "a plurality of Persons who reveals Himself through the God-head, namely Father, Son and Holy Ghost, but not separately subsisting"; the "untampered" Bible as the inspired Word of God; the historic factuality and literal truth of the Genesis creation account; the creation of man without sin "yet free to stand or fall"; the transmission of the corruption of fallen man to all generations; the love of God in the incarnation and reconciling death of Christ; Christ's triumphant resurrection and ascension; the sending of the Holy Ghost in Christ's stead; the blood atonement as the only means of salvation for human beings; justification, an instantaneous pardoning act of God's infinite mercy, through faith in Christ; the experience of entire sanctification in this life, likewise as an instantaneous act of God's mercy; the free moral agency of man, so that if the believer persists in obedience he will enjoy the state of the glorified in heaven and if he persists in a state of disobedience he will experience eternal damnation; the imminent coming of Christ; the general resurrection of the dead; the general judgment; believer's baptism in the name of the Trinity; the Lord's Supper observed by those of like faith; the literal observance by all believers of the washing of the saints' feet; the wearing of a veil by women for the purpose of prayer and prophesying; the dutiful and appropriate observance of the salutation of the holy kiss; anointing with oil of the sick who call for it in faith; marriage dissoluble only with death and in the case of a Christian only "in the Lord"; a life of separation from the follies, sinful practices, and methods of the world; and the demonstration by the believer of "the spirit of nonresistance in all matters according to Christ's sermon on the mount."[24]

The basic unit of local government is in the congregation. At the level of the general church an executive council of five elders has terminal authority and control in policy, doctrine, and standards.[25]

In application of "unchanging scriptural principles" a distinctive garb is prescribed for members. Men are to wear suits of plain material, black or dark brown shoes, and conservative hats. A "small collar inserted under the shirt collar . . . to give a religious appearance" is recommended. They may not wear jewelry or neckties for adornment. Women must wear conservative dresses with capes, full skirts, hemlines halfway between the knee and ankle, loose-fitting blouses, full-length sleeves, black or dark brown shoes, hose of good body, with seams and other than flesh-colored, and naturally long hair. They may not wear shorts, slacks, socks, jewelry, lace, bows, or artificial means to bedeck the face or hair." During all waking hours they are to wear the "prayer and prophecy veil" in the shape of a bonnet of at least white-parchment-organdy weight, covered with a black bonnet for outdoor use. Little girls are to wear their hair long and not curled.

Friends of the denomination who feel that they cannot unite with it but who enjoy its fellowship, attend its services, lead godly lives, and support the church with tithes and offerings may receive the rites of baptism, Communion, washing of the saints' feet, the visitation, counsel and comfort of the pastor, and a voice (but no vote) in the business meetings of the local church.[26]

Members covenant among other things to abstain from the handling and use of intoxicating liquors, tobacco, and all forms of drugs (except those prescribed by competent doctors or nurses for medical purposes); worldly amusements such as mixed bathing, theaters, shows, public competitive games and places where gambling is indulged in, circuses, carnivals, card playing, skating rinks, bowling alleys, and television; membership in secret lodges and organizations; and unnecessary secular business and all occupations and traveling that do not glorify God on the Lord's Day.[27]

The headquarters of the denomination are at 3423 North Second Street, Philadelphia, Pennsylvania 19140. There are two congregations with a total membership of 38.[28]

Old Order River Brethren (Yorkers)

From the late eighteenth century, when the River Brethren came into existence in Pennsylvania,[29] down to the mid-nineteenth century, when the group that formed the nucleus of the Old Order River Brethren and the group that later became known as the Brethren in Christ Church separated from each other, the two bodies have a common history. The break between them came when Bishop Jacob Strickler, Jr., along with his York County following and a few supporters in Lancaster County, withdrew from the other River Brethren "for orthodoxy." (Tradition puts this event in the year 1843, but there is no objective documentary evidence to support the date.) In 1860 the Jacob Strickler, Jr., group voted Jacob S. Hostetter (1832–1920) in as bishop.

In the meantime Bishop John I. Gisch's congregation in Conoy and

Donegal, Pennsylvania, dismissed twenty-seven families in the Waynesboro and Chambersburg areas in Franklin County under Bishop Christian Hoover for being "too orthodox." (In the absence of concrete evidence, the commonly accepted date for this expulsion is 1854.) The York County and Franklin County groups soon united as the Old Order River Brethren, although in York and Lancaster counties they are still commonly called "Yorkers."

As late as 1868 efforts were still being made to reunite them with the other River Brethren, but the well-meant attempts failed.

With the passage of time, some of the Old Order families moved westward and established colonies in Ohio and Iowa.

After Bishop Hostetter's death the Old Order River Brethren sustained at least four schisms. These schisms do not at bottom reflect doctrinal differences. In part they have resulted from personal and family quarrels, in part from group traditions that arose out of differing applications of the commonly accepted principle of separation from the world to concrete cases of twentieth-century technology.

Until the third decade of the twentieth century, the Old Order River Brethren functioned without an articulated system of doctrine and without a commonly accepted written confession of faith.[30] The positions that the Old Order River Brethren took tacitly conformed in general to the Dordrecht Confession of 1632, but the fellowship asserted that "the 18th chapter of St. Matthew is our discipline; we have no other, and we want no other."

Although the Old Order River Brethren hold in high esteem the memory of Jacob Engle (1753–1832), whom they regard as their prime founder, they feel themselves bound chiefly by what they understand as the biblical prescription in any issue. Where they believe that they have found such a prescription in the Bible, obedience is not subject to congregational decision.

Theologically the Old Order River Brethren stand solidly in the Anabaptist tradition. They share the conventional fundamental-evangelical view of the Bible, the Trinity, and Christ's person and work, especially his "sin-pardoning atonement." At Christ's resurrection, they hold, his flesh-body vanished and Jesus occupied a celestial body of the same shape and form as his material flesh-body.[31] They affirm the existence of angels and of Satan; they see the latter as a servant rather than as a free foe of God, but as a servant and foe of mankind.[32] They reject the theory of evolution. They hold that human beings become accountable after infancy, although the instinct to disobey is inherited from Adam and Eve.[33] To be saved, a person must undergo rebirth (understood as a fundamental change of heart) through repentance, an ordeal in which the weariness and anguish of one's soul-mind is removed by developing a love for God and all human beings.[34] The dead faith that God can and will forgive sins if a person sincerely asks him to do so must be transformed into living faith by deeds of true repentance; then God acknowledges the cry of the penitent person and forgives his sins. Total sanctification is an instantaneous work of the Holy Spirit, but this does not preclude a growth in holiness by the inward man.[35]

The church militant is the whole body of individuals that confess their faith in the Trinity; the Old Order River Brethren constitute one of many groups within it. Membership in the Old Order River Brethren is by confession of sin and appropriate restitution and reparation to the degree that this is possible, followed by baptism by a bishop "for the remission of sins in the likeness of Christ's death" through a threefold forward immersion in a stream in the name of the Father and of the Son and of the Holy Spirit.[36] The Communion is celebrated with unleavened bread and fermented wine. After the kiss of unity has been exchanged, the members of the congregation sit, and the elements are passed from hand to hand with the formula, "This bread that we break [this cup that we drink] is the communion of the body [blood] of our Lord and Saviour Jesus Christ," while the communicants recall Christ's passion and death and rejoice that his shed blood provides a way of escape from sinfulness.[37] The Old Order River Brethren practice what they call "closed Communion" and separate the Lord's Supper from fellowship meals. A third ordinance is foot-washing, observed before the Communion, men washing the men's feet, women the women's feet.[38]

On the basis of Ezekiel 18:25,29 (King James Version: "Is not my way equal?") male members of the Old Order River Brethren are to cut their hair at the base of the head, half its total growth, and on the basis of 2 Timothy 2:15 (KJV: "rightly dividing"), they are to part their hair to signify the dividing of good and evil.[39] Out of love for God the men are also to wear full beards, unmarred and unshaven at the "corners," since God made men like this in his own image.[40] Women are not to cut their hair; their dress is to be modest, their skirts ankle-length.[41]

The ministers anoint the sick with oil in the name of the Father and of the Son and of the Holy Ghost. Marriage may take place only within the denomination and before a minister of the same faith; remarriage after divorce is forbidden.

The Old Order River Brethren practice "separation from the world,"[42] as well as nonresistance; the members may not take up arms. The congregation has the responsibility of excommunicating impenitent offenders. Members of the Old Order River Brethren greet one another, but not an excommunicated person, with the holy kiss (kiss of unity). Daily devotions for the individual and family devotions for the household are part of the style of life. The ministry consists of bishops, ministers, and deacons, elected from and by the congregation.

The Old Order River Brethren doctrine of the last things sees the rapture of the church and the resurrection of the departed believers taking place at Christ's second advent, followed by the millennium,[43] the resurrection of the wicked, and their final consignment to everlasting punishment in hell.[44]

Typical of the Old Order River Brethren is their refusal to have church buildings. Services are held in the homes of the members on a rotating basis, with the benches transported from one home to another. Men and women sit on opposite sides of the bishop's table. The Sunday service begins with an hour-long "experience meeting," in which members confess their difficulties and shortcomings and affirm—sometimes very emotionally—their desire to be better Christians. Then follows the regular service, consisting of hymns, prayers, and sermons by the bishop and the ministers. This service in turn is followed by a fellowship meal provided by the host of the Sunday.[45]

The retirement and death of Bishop Hostetter in 1920 was followed by the first in a series of schisms. In that year a council of bishops was held near Rohrerstown, Pennsylvania, with a view to reconciling a bishop and a minister in Iowa who had fallen out with one another the year before. The action of this council went unheeded in Iowa and the minister returned to Lancaster County, Pennsylvania. With one exception the bishops who took part in the council were subsequently prevailed upon to rescind their decision. The exception was Bishop Simon H. Musser (b. 1878) of Centerville (near Rohrerstown), who declared that the original decision was right and refused to concur in its rescission. As a result Bishop Musser and his supporters and the remainder of the Old River Brethren separated from one another in 1921. The Silver Spring District, as the fellowship under Bishop Musser became known, numbers 32 members.[46]

In 1919 the "Jacob Keller group" of Greencastle, Pennsylvania, Bradford (Drake County), Ohio, and Dallas Center (Dallas County) Ohio, wanted freedom to own automobiles, and another breach in the larger fellowship ensued. The "Jacob Keller group" counts approximately 60 members.

In 1948 the Reverend John M. Strickler, Columbia, Pennsylvania, a minister for twenty-seven years, led a group consisting predominantly of farm families out of Bishop Musser's fellowship and became its bishop.[47] This congregation has 47 members. Late in 1968 it entered into fellowship with the "Jacob Keller group."

In 1959 the larger fellowship shunned Bishop Jacob L. Horst, Elizabethtown, Lancaster County, Pennsylvania, and his congregation for beginning to accept automobiles. A number of members of the larger fellowship, under Bishop Seth Myers, withdrew in sympathy with the expelled congregation, organized a congregation of their own, and allied themselves with Bishop Horst's group.[48] These two congregations have a total of 85 members.

The remaining four Old River Brethren congregations, with a total membership of 80, are located in York, Montgomery, and Franklin counties, Pennsylvania.[49]

Apostolic Christian Churches of America

Samuel Heinrich Fröhlich (1803–1857), descendant of a French Huguenot family by the name of de Joyeaux, was converted as a university student in 1825. In 1828 he entered the ministry of the Reformed Church in his native Switzerland. When he refused to use what he regarded as a rationalistic catechism that the church introduced in 1830, the ecclesiastical authorities dismissed him. Rebaptized by sprinkling in 1832, he organized a group of Reformed and Mennonite dissidents at Langnau in the Emmenthal into the Gemeinschaft Evangelischer Taufgesinnter (Community of Evangelical Baptists). The Mennonite influence on Fröhlich's theology was considerable, and included the rejection of combatant military service. The movement spread in Switzerland and beyond its borders. The adherents' refusal to bear arms caused them difficulties that moved many of them to emigrate to America in the 1850s.

The first Apostolic Christian Church in the United States came into being at Croghan, Lewis County, New York. Some of the Amish Mennonites of the community asked Fröhlich to send them an elder. He complied in 1847 by sending them Benedict Weyeneth. The latter began services, organized a congregation, ordained Joseph Virkler as minister, and returned to Europe.[50] He came back later to Woodford County, Illinois, where he established another congregation among dissident Amish Mennonites. Among his converts was Joseph Greybill, the first Apostolic Christian minister in Illinois. The initial progress of the church was slow, but the increasingly heavy emigration from Europe created new opportunities for growth, notably in Ohio, Indiana, Illinois, and Iowa.

The Apostolic Christian Churches of America have sustained two schisms. In 1906/1907 a division took place over a number of points of doctrine and practice in which the majority of Apostolic Christians in North America differed from their European co-religionists and from the more recent immigrants from Europe. The segment of the Apostolic Christian Churches of America that withdrew from the North American majority and continued in fellowship with the recent immigrants and the European communities became known as the Apostolic Christian Church (Nazarean). A second schism took place in the 1930s when Martin Steidinger of Fairbury, Illinois, led a group of the Apostolic Christian Churches of America to form the German Apostolic Christian Church.

The Apostolic Christian Churches teach the inherited sinfulness of human beings, and stress the need for rebirth, for the crucifixion of the body of sin in repentance, for burying it in the death of Christ through believer's baptism by immersion, and for rising with Christ to a new life of holiness. After the individual's baptism, prayer and the imposition of the elders' hands seal the Holy Spirit in his cleansed heart and lead him on the pathway of truth and righteousness. Apostolic Christians take church discipline seriously and expel the willfully disobedient and degenerate from membership. If by God's grace the offenders manifest amendment the assembly restores them, unless they have committed sin judged to be mortal. Apostolic Christians are willing to perform "any reasonable service for the Government aside from using weapons of combatant warfare." Draftees choose noncombatant service. The Apostolic Christian churches have no paid ministry, and their ministers depend on the inspiration and revelation of the Holy Spirit in their preaching.[51]

The use of English in worship has become universal. The organization of the denomination in the United States is very informal. There are 72 assemblies with 8,700 members and an "assembly attendance" of 10,000. There are also three assemblies in Japan.[52]

Apostolic Christian Church of America (Nazarean)

In 1906/1907 some of the members of the Apostolic Christian Churches of America, particularly in Ohio and Illinois, withdrew from the parent fellowship because of differences of opinion on some points of belief and practice. To distinguish the new association from the old, they came to be called by a name widely used for Apostolic Christians in central Europe, "Nazareans." The doctrinal differences between the two groups are minor. There is some fellowship between them, and, particularly since some of the issues that led to the division are no longer live questions, periodic efforts at reunion have originated on both sides.

The twelve-point Statement of Faith of the "Nazarean" Apostolic Christians affirms belief in the inspiration, completeness, and infallibility of the Bible; the divine Unity and Trinity; Christ's incarnation, virgin birth, sinlessness, and substitutionary atonement; his resurrection, ascension, and personal return; the sinfulness and lostness of all men and God's will that none be lost; salvation by repentance toward God and faith in Christ; the necessity of saving faith for rebirth by the Holy Spirit and salvation; the baptism of the Holy Spirit, "by whose indwelling the believer is empowered to live a godly life in a spiritual unity with Christ"; the resurrection of all men, the saved to eternal life, the lost to eternal damnation; the obligation of truthfulness and the impropriety of oaths; and civil government as a divine ordinance that Christians must support and obey ("the call to service in the military forces is respected and obeyed with the biblical limitation to noncombatant service").[53] Elders in each congregation have authority to baptize, lay on hands, and administer the Lord's Supper.

The Apostolic Church Foundation, Incorporated, Akron, Ohio, functions as a service organization and provides a headquarters for the denomination. The Apostolic Christian Church has 39 churches in the United States and 10 in Canada, with a total membership of 4,720.

German Apostolic Christian Church

In the 1930s the question of the language that was to be used in worship seems to have vexed a part of the Apostolic Christian Churches of America. The fear that worldliness would accompany the transition to English apparently played a role also. Reportedly in response to the direction of elders in Germany and Switzerland, Elder Martin Steidinger of Fairbury, Illinois, led a group estimated at about 500 members out of the parent church to form what ultimately became known as the German Apostolic Christian Church, with congregations in Fairbury, Morton, Cissna Park, and Tremont, Illinois; Silverton and Portland, Oregon; and Sabetha, Kansas. No information is available as to the present size of this fellowship.[54]

Unrest in the withdrawing group over a number of years led to a further division, when Elder Peter Schaffer, Sr., of Forrest, Illinois, and his followers in Illinois and Oregon broke with the others and formed the Christian Apostolic Church (Forrest, Illinois) in 1955.

Continuing interference by the European leadership reportedly also led in 1955 to the withdrawal from the German Apostolic Christian Church of the Christian Apostolic Church (Sabetha, Kansas).[55]

Christian Apostolic Church (Forrest, Illinois)

By 1952 some of the members of what is now known as the German Apostolic Christian Church had become restive under the transatlantic direction of the affairs of the church by the German and Swiss elders. Under the leadership of Elder Peter Schaffer, Sr., of Fairbury, Illinois, one of the founders of the German Apostolic Christian Church, some of the members in Illinois and Oregon withdrew in 1955, from the German Apostolic Christian Church and organized the Christian Apostolic Church (Forrest, Illinois). In addition to the church at the southeast edge of Forrest there is another in Silverton, Oregon. About 55 persons compose the actual membership of the two congregations; there are in addition about 150 sympathizers who worship with them.[56]

Christian Apostolic Church (Sabetha, Kansas)

In 1960 a division in the German Apostolic Christian Church over a difference in interpretation of the statutes and customs of the church body led to the organization of the Christian Apostolic Church under the late William Edelman. The headquarters of the latter body are at Sabetha, Kansas. Three churches in Kansas and Illinois have an estimated total of 100 members.[57]

Amana Church Society (Community of True Inspiration)

To escape the systematic and bloody suppression of the Camisards in France during the first decade of the eighteenth century, some of the leaders fled from France first to England, then to the Lowlands, and finally to Germany. In the Hessian Wetterau especially they found a cordial welcome among the Enthusiastic and Separatistic Pietists. Under the newcomers' influence ten "communities of inspiration" came into being in Hesse, led by John Frederick Rock (1678–1749), a saddler, Eberhard Louis Gruber

(1665–1728), a former clergyman of the Lutheran Church of Württemberg, and six other "instruments." The members of the new communities not only rejected the existing churches, but they believed that God could and would inspire men to speak and declare his word and his will and thus to act as messengers of divine teaching to the world.

In 1716 the leaders devised "Twenty-Four Rules for True Piety and Holy Living" and sent their disciples out to establish new societies elsewhere. They were especially successful in Württemberg, the Palatinate, Alsace, and Switzerland. Some of the members of these communities emigrated to Germantown, Pennsylvania, in 1725 and the years that followed. Many of those who stayed in Germany joined the Moravian Church. Rock died in 1749, and with him the gift of inspiration, and by 1799 the movement seemed to have disintegrated completely. But the atmosphere of revival that marked early nineteenth-century Germany proved to be favorable for a new upsurge of the "New Community" under the leadership of Michael Krausert, a Strasbourg tailor, Barbara Heinemann, an Alsatian peasant-girl, and Christian Metz of Ronneburg, all three of whom were persuaded that they had received the charism of inspiration. Krausert soon defected, but the "Society of True Inspiration," as it now called itself, continued to grow. The refusal of the members to swear oaths and to render military service created constant difficulties for them with the various territorial governments, notably those of Prussia and Hesse. In 1842 the community decided to emigrate to the New World. Between 1843 and 1846 eight hundred immigrants came over from Germany. For the next eight years the colonists, incorporated as the Eben-Ezer Society, occupied part of the former Seneca Indian reservation near Buffalo, New York, and two tracts not far off in Canada. In 1854 they determined to move west, and during the next decade they colonized their present location (which comprises about 20,000 acres) twenty miles west of Iowa City. In 1859 they incorporated themselves as the Amana Society ("Amana" means "remain true.") In order to be able to perform their duties as Christians better and more ably they made community of property obligatory. The gift of inspiration once more ceased with Metz's death in 1867 and that of Barbara Heinemann Landmann in 1883. The society reached its maximum membership of over 1,700 early in the present century; present membership is reported to be 1,500. Improved communications increasingly destroyed the isolation that the fathers of the movement had sought and the life of the communities could no longer be as fully protected against secularization. The group abolished the obligatory common ownership of property in 1932; the church continued as the Amana Church Society and a new corporation, the Amana Society, took over the community's business enterprises.

The confession of faith of the Community reads:

> We believe in God the Father, the almighty Creator of the heavens, and of earth, and of all that is visible and invisible, and in His only-begotten Son,

the Lord Jesus Christ, the Mediator and Savior of the world, the Word, who was in the beginning with God, the light of the world, who was made flesh, God of God and Son of man, sent unto the world, that whosoever believeth in Him should not perish; who suffered great agony, was crucified, died and shed His blood for the remission of sin. And also in God the Holy Ghost, who proceeds from the Father and Son, who is equally adored and honored, who has spoken and operated through the prophets of old, and who even now speaks and operates audibly through the instruments of true inspiration, and hidden inwardly, through the heart and conscience towards repentance and renewal of heart, teaching denial of ungodliness, and worldly lusts, and to live soberly, righteously and godly in the present world. We acknowledge and avow a holy, universal Christian Church, and a communion of saints, and all people of every nation who fear God and work righteousness are acceped with Him. We believe in the remission of sin, the ressurection of the body, and in life blessed and everlasting.

There is a church in each of the seven Amana villages. The worship services by long-time custom consist of a brief invocation, the singing of a hymn from the Amana Psalter, a reading from the *Book of Testimony* (the revelations given to the inspired members of the community, especially Metz and Barbara Landmann, in the past), a general prayer, a lesson from the Bible, a short sermon, a closing hymn, and a blessing. The Community of True Inspiration does not practice water baptism, because it sees this as only the unnecessary outward form of the true baptism of the spirit. Catechisms Numbers 1 and 2—still in the original German—provide the basis for the religious instruction of the children. Confirmation, or reception into the covenant of grace through a solemn vow made in the public service, takes place at fifteen; at twenty-one applicants may achieve full membership by signing the constitution. The congregations observe the Lord's Supper once every two years, but foot-washing no longer precedes the rite. Oaths are forbidden. The prohibition against participation in war is no longer enforced. Efforts to perpetuate the old traditions in dress, especially among the women, have met with declining success.

The Amana Church Society has no ordained ministry. Thirteen trustees, all of whom are elders of the church, are elected annually; they in turn designate the elders who are to conduct the services in the various communities. The Community of True Inspiration does not engage in missionary activity. Its address is Amana, Iowa 52203.

Evangelical Fellowship Chapels (Evangelical Fellowship Deaconry of the Fellowship Deaconry, Incorporated)

One of the byproducts of the late nineteenth-century spiritual revival called the "fellowship movement" (*Gemeinschaftsbewegung*) as it affected the Evangelical United Church of Prussia was the deaconess order that the

Reverend Ferdinand Blazejewski (1862–1900) founded in Borken, East Prussia, in October 1899. Upon his death half a year later, the talented Reverend Theophil Krawielitzki (1866–1942) took over the project; before the end of the year 1900 he transferred it to Vandsburg, West Prussia, from which it took the name by which it became widely known, the "Vandsburger Werk." Within five years of its first founding the number of deaconesses had grown in the face of both governmental and ecclesiastical pressures from the original four to 120. In 1908 the headquarters moved to Marburg-an-der-Lahn in Hesse, and the following year the organization opened its first house for deacons. A period of tension during which strong efforts were put forth to divert the movement into Pentecostal channels ended with Krawielitzki's definitive rejection of Pentecostalism. In 1922 the association took the name Deutscher Gemeinschafts-Diakonieverband (literally, German Association for the Fellowship Diaconate).

The dislocations that followed World War I and the inflation of the early 1920s caused many East Germans to emigrate to the United States. In response to the plea of these immigrants for the kind of diaconic service with which they had been familiar in their native land, Krawielitzki visited the United States in 1928 and upon his return to Germany dispatched two deaconess sisters to North America. After a few years of service in Philadelphia and Orange, and the accession of a number of American postulants, a motherhouse was established at Liberty Corner, New Jersey, in 1933.

The deaconess sisters in the United States continued the tradition of personal evangelistic witness and of tract distribution that had been an integral aspect of the movement in Germany from the beginning. Out of this activity grew small assemblies originally called "tract mission stations"; as these became full-fledged congregations they took the name Evangelical Fellowship Chapels.

The "doctrinal position" of the Evangelical Fellowship Chapels affirms belief in the Bible as the inspired Word of God; in the Trinity; in Christ's virgin birth and his true deity and true manhood; in the separation of human beings from God as the result of the primal sin of the first human beings; in Christ's death for the sins of human beings and in justification through faith in his blood; in his resurrection, ascension, continuing intercession, and imminent personal return; in the new birth of the Holy Spirit and adoption as God's children for all who receive Christ by faith; in the bodily resurrection of the just and the unjust; and in one baptism by the one Spirit into one body.

The headquarters of the Evangelical Fellowship Chapels are at the Fellowship Deaconry Motherhouse, Liberty Corner, New Jersey 07938. There are 10 chapels in five states and 6 chapels in Canada; the total active membership of the congregations of these chapels is estimated at 1,500.[58] The deaconess sisters of the North American motherhouse engage in foreign missionary activities in Japan and in the Republic of China (Taiwan). There has been no response to recent efforts to communicate with the group.

The Evangelical Covenant Church of America

Among the factors that made for religious revival in nineteenth-century Sweden both inside and outside the Lutheran folk church, some were native in origin, others foreign. One of the foreign agencies was a tract and Bible colportage association called Evangelisk Sällskapet (The Evangelical Society). It began in 1809 under the direction of John Paterson (1776–1855) and Ebenezer Henderson (1784–1858)—both of them former associates of the Haldane brothers—working in cooperation with German Moravians. Another element of foreign origin was the revival initated by the English Methodist George Scott (1804–1874), founder of the influential journal *Pietisten,* edited after Scott's expulsion from Sweden in 1842 by the Swedish lay churchman Carl Olof Rosenius (1816–1868) and, after Rosenius's death, by Paul Peter Waldenström (1838–1917), initially a Swedish Lutheran priest.

In 1856 Rosenius—who remained a lifelong member of the Lutheran folk church in spite of the support that he received from English Methodists—and others organized Evangeliska Fosterlandstiftelsen (The Evangelical Fatherland Foundation). Inclusive enough at first to be friendly to revival efforts outside as well as within the folk church, the foundation became more and more exclusively Lutheran. Events moved toward an open break between the Lutherans and the Free Church elements in the foundation.

The Free Church elements rallied around Waldenström, whose sermon on the atonement in 1875,[59] whose derogation of the creeds of the church, and whose activities in founding societies of "Mission Friends" (*Missionsvänner*) had already evoked strong reactions in Lutheran circles. The break came after the folk church refused to make Uppsala Cathedral available on Whitsunday 1876 to the free missionary societies for a celebration of the sacrament of the altar at which Waldenström was to have been the celebrant. As a result of the controversy arising from this refusal, Waldenström withdrew from the priesthood of the folk church of Sweden. In 1878 he and his supporters organized the first General Conference of Free Churches and Mission Societies. Later in that year the same group, but in Waldenström's absence, organized the Swedish Mission Covenant[60] Church.

Parallel developments were taking place among the Swedish immigrants in North America. While the influence of Rosenius was strong in the Swedish Augustana Synod, the latter body did not make the conscious experience of the new birth a condition of church membership. In some cases those who felt that they had had such an experience formed mission societies within the Augustana Synod congregations of which they were members. In other cases they withdrew and founded independent churches of "Mission Friends." In 1873 many of these groups formed what they called the Mission Synod. The year 1874 saw the organization of a second, smaller body, the Swedish Evangelical Lutheran Ansgar Synod. Both synods adhered to the three catholic creeds and to the Augsburg Confession. The controversy in Sweden about Waldenström's views on the atonement and on the creeds during these years and the organization of the Swedish Mission Covenant in 1878 helped to bring about a break between the committed Lutherans and the Free Church group in the two American synods. A series of conferences in 1883 and 1884 led in the latter year to the organization of the fellowship that became the Swedish Evangelical Free Church and in 1885 to the organization of the Swedish Evangelical Mission Covenant of America. Among the leaders of the latter were Erik August Skogsbergh (1850–1939), who had come to North America in 1876 and had been greatly impressed by the person and methods of Dwight L. Moody, Carl August Bjork (1837–1916), and Fredric Malkolm Johnson (1857–1930).

The Swedish Evangelical Mission Covenant adopted a very brief doctrinal statement, which described the Bible "as the only perfect rule for faith, doctrine, and conduct." Congregations, not individuals, comprised the membership. The organization encouraged, but did not insist upon, ordination of the ministers by the denomination. The aggressive interest of American Congregationalism in the new denomination led to the training of its ministers in the Chicago Theological Seminary from 1885 to 1891, when the covenant established its own school.

Rivalries within the church body and the decline in Swedish immigration to North America after 1910 adversely affected the later rate of growth of the denomination. Until 1920 acculturation to the North American scene was slow. In 1929 the designation "Swedish" was dropped from the name. The church took its present name in 1957.

The preamble to the 1957 revision of the constitution sees the church rooted in the sixteenth-century Reformation, in the "biblical instruction of the Lutheran State Church of Sweden, and in the great spiritual awakenings of the nineteenth century." It regards the Bible "as the word of God and the only perfect rule for faith, doctrine, and conduct. It has traditionally valued the historic confessions of the Christian Church, particularly the Apostles' Creed," but it has also "emphasized the sovereignty of the word [of God] over all creedal interpretations. It has especially cherished the pietistic restatement of the doctrine of justification by faith," the "New Testament emphasis upon personal faith in Jesus Christ as Savior and Lord, the reality of a fellowship of believers which recognizes but transcends theological differences, and the belief in baptism and the Lord's supper as divinely ordained sacraments of the church." It traditionally baptized infants but has given room to divergent views. It values the principle of personal freedom, but disavows the "individualism that disregards the centrality of the word of God and the mutual responsibilities and disciplines of the spiritual community."[61] Membership in a local congregation implies that the candidate has been born again to a living hope through faith in Christ. In the management of their local affairs the member congregations enjoy freedom.

The acculturation of the Evangelical Covenant Church of America has exposed the church to all the doctrinal and cultural variations of the North American scene. The church during the last generation has sought to define historic freedoms in a way to assure growth without anarchy or creedalism. It refuses to identify itself as either fundamentalist or liberal. Theological diversity characterizes its membership, but no single interest is strong enough to dominate. The faculty of its theological school, North Park Seminary, Chicago, exhibits some variation of view in its faculty, but the traditional covenant biblical orientation in combination with a broadly Lutheran theology and Rosenian piety is fundamental.[62] While the American Covenant has affiliated with no organized ecumenical organization, it has authorized its administrators to enter into discussions looking toward closer cooperation and possible union with other denominations that have a similar theological orientation and a similar view of the nature and mission of the church.

The Evangelical Covenant Church of Canada has a dual status: It is a conference of the Evangelical Covenant Church of America, but it also is an incorporated Canadian denomination and as such it is a member of the International Federation of Free Evangelical Churches in its own right. Its oldest congregation, the First Scandinavian Christian Church in Winnipeg, was organized by Swedish immigrants in 1885. The Scandinavian Mission Covenant of Canada was organized with five churches as a conference of the American Covenant in 1904. It looks forward to the ultimate integration under its leadership of the work that the American Covenant still carries on in Ontario and British Columbia. The transition to English began in earnest in 1940, and in 1945 the organization dropped "Scandinavian" from its name. Theologically it shares the position of the American Covenant.

A serious theological controversy about the doctrine of the atonement shook the Canadian body in 1945 and resulted in the withdrawal of seven churches and sixteen ordained and unordained ministers the following year. The ministers in the seceding group, largely trained at non-covenant institutions, held very strongly to a substitutionary doctrine of the atonement, with special stress upon its penal aspects, and insisted that the Canadian Covenant adopt their view as the exclusively right one.[63] A majority of the ministers and three of the churches joined the Fellowship of Gospel Churches, which merged with the Evangelical Free Church of America in 1957. Two other churches ultimately joined the Associated Gospel Churches and three returned to the Evangelical Covenant Church.[64]

The headquarters of the Evangelical Covenant Church of America are at 5101 North Francisco Avenue, Chicago, Illinois 60625. The general conference—called the Annual Meeting—meets once a year. The membership of the 508 churches in the United States (including Alaska) is 69,960. The headquarters of the Evangelical Covenant Church of Canada are at 8501 82nd Avenue, Edmonton, Alberta T6C OY7. The Canadian conference has 24 churches with 1,101 members in Alberta, Saskatchewan, and Manitoba.

The Evangelical Covenant Church of America carries on foreign missions of its own in the Congo, Ecuador, Hong Kong, the Republic of China (Taiwan), Indonesia, Japan, and Korea.

Evangelical Free Church of America

Like the Evangelical Covenant Church of America, the Evangelical Free Church of America is rooted in the Free Evangelical movement that began in Europe in the early nineteenth century. This movement received much of its initial impetus from the revival sparked by two Scotsmen, Robert Haldane (1764–1842) and James Alexander Haldane (1768–1851). The movement was reinforced, especially in Scandinavia, by the convictions which returning emigrants to North America brought with them as a result of their contact in the New World with the great American revivals of the nineteenth century.

As an organization the Evangelical Free Church of America resulted from the union in 1950 of the Swedish Evangelical Free Church and the Evangelical Free Church Association.

The organization of the Swedish Free Church followed a number of memorable conferences of Scandinavian immigrant churchmen. The first was at Bush Hall in Chicago in 1883; it brought together the early leaders of the movement that was to eventuate in the Evangelical Covenant Church of America and the early leaders of what was to become the Swedish Free Church. Among the latter John G. Princell was the most eminent; a former Lutheran clergyman whom the Swedish Augustana Synod had deposed from its ministry for his advocacy of Paul Peter Waldenström's theory of the atonement, he became the chief theological teacher of the Swedish Evangelical Free Church during its first generation. The second and third conferences were held in 1884 at Moline, Illinois, and at Boone, Iowa, respectively; at both, the nature and mission of the church figured prominently in the discussions. Out of the Boone meeting there grew an informal fellowship that evolved into the Swedish Evangelical Free Church; it was distrustful of organization and laid great stress on the autonomy of the local congregation. While it grew rapidly during the next quarter of a century, the need for at least minimal denominational organization became increasingly evident with the passage of time, and in 1908 the Swedish Evangelical Free Church was formally incorporated.

In its aversion to any creedal commitment, the Swedish Evangelical Free Church adopted a doctrinal statement that consisted of a single sentence: "This organization accepts the Bible, both the Old and New Testaments, as the word of God, containing the gospel of salvation for all men and the only rule for teaching, faith, and life."[65] During the next four decades the church veered away from the Waldenström theory of the atonement that most of its pioneer preachers taught in the direction of a strong advocacy of the vicarious atonement. In its teaching and practice on baptism it moved from a modified

Lutheran position toward believer's baptism by immersion, without, however, ordinarily requiring baptism as a condition for membership in the church. Its basic stance was summarized in the statement of Princell: "I want to have fellowship with all who love Jesus, whether they baptize in water or not, whether they baptize children or adults, whether they believe in a universal or limited salvation of mankind."[66]

Perennial efforts from the 1880s to 1920 to unite the Evangelical Covenant and the Swedish Evangelical Free movements were unsuccessful. By 1950 the Swedish Free Church had achieved a membership of over 14,000 in 190 congregations.

The Norwegian-Danish Evangelical Free Church Association traced its history back to 1884, when the Norwegian Free Church leader Severin K. Didriksen organized the first congregation in Boston. Other immigrant congregations developed in widely separated areas; some called themselves Scandinavian Congregational and others Norwegian Lutheran Evangelical Free, although most contented themselves with Evangelical Free. For a decade before and after the turn of the century the American Congregational Home Missionary Society assisted in the establishment of new churches and its Chicago Theological Seminary trained clergymen for them. The congregations tended to be strongly nationalistic, and the newly founded Norwegian-American periodical *Evangelisten* helped to forge ties among the scattered churches. The Western Missionary Association came into being in 1891, the Eastern Missionary Association in 1898. Although the two associations began to publish their reports in a single volume in 1900, they did not discuss union seriously until 1909. In 1912 they merged and incorporated as the Norwegian-Danish Evangelical Free Church Association. In 1910 the merging associations founded a Bible institute of their own in protest against the liberalism that had penetrated the Chicago Theological Seminary. In 1917 the association began work in Canada. By 1950 it had a total of just under 5,400 members in 78 congregations.

The Swedish Evangelical Free Church and the Norwegian-Danish Evangelical Free Church Association gradually grew together. An attempt to unite them in 1939 turned out to be abortive. Union negotiations were resumed in the late 1940s, and in 1950 both bodies voted unanimously to merge as the Evangelical Free Church of America. In 1957 the Fellowship of Gospel Churches, a Canadian association organized in 1941, affiliated with the Evangelical Free Church.

To supersede the one-sentence doctrinal statement of the Swedish body and the twelve-point declaration of the Norwegian-Danish group, the united church adopted an official twelve-point doctrinal statement. It affirms belief in the Bible ("the inspired word of God, without error in the original writings"); the Trinity; Christ's deity, incarnation, vicarious atonement, resurrection, and exaltation; the ministry of the Holy Spirit; man's creation in God's image, his loss of that image, and his need for rebirth; justification and salvation through the shed blood of Christ for all who believe and who by receiving Jesus Christ are born of the Holy Spirit and become children of God; water baptism and the Lord's Supper as ordinances to be observed during the present age but not as a means of salvation; the true church as "composed of all such persons as have been regenerated by the Holy Spirit and are united together in the body of Christ"; the restriction of eligibility for membership in the local church to members of the true church; the right of each local church under Christ to decide and govern its own affairs; the bodily resurrection of believers to everlasting blessedness and of unbelievers to judgment and everlasting conscious punishment.[67]

Because of this doctrinal statement, the Evangelical Free Church of America sees itself as allowing less latitude in doctrine than the Evangelical Covenant Church of America. At the same time, the Evangelical Free Church leaves to the conscience of the individuals involved the mode of baptism and the age of the candidate, and it bases church membership not on baptism but on a personal confession of faith. Similarly, it takes no official position for or against either the Calvinistic or the Arminian resolution of the points in dispute between these two systems of Reformed theology. It consciously upholds the view of Huldreich Zwingli that the Lord's Supper is a memorial feast in which the elements represent the body and blood of Christ. It takes no official stand on divorce and on the remarriage of divorced persons (although its ministers are reluctant to officiate at marriages in which either party is divorced) or on birth control. Some of its congregations prohibit, and all frown upon, the use of tobacco and alcoholic bevereages. Its position on the Bible has helped to make it hospitable to dispensationalism.[68] It affirms its intention to be fundamental without being fanatical, to be evangelistic without being stereotyped, to be congregational in polity without allowing its congregations to become isolated, to hold high standards of piety without becoming pharisaic and prudish, to capture spiritual fervor without succumbing to carnal fever, and to be ecumenical (in the sense that it strives "to bring together those who wish to separate themselves from the liberalism that has overtaken some churches")[69] without compromising. Evangelical Free Church people founded both the Christian Business Men's Crusade and Youth for Christ. The Evangelical Free Church of America has continued the Swedish Evangelical Free Church's membership in the National Association of Evangelicals.

The headquarters of the Evangelical Free Church of America are at 1515 East 66th Street, Minneapolis, Minnesota 55423. The church body has 660 churches in the United States and 77 in Canada. Its membership is about 80,000; but since attendance is generally higher than membership, the total constituency approaches 100,000. Foreign mission work is conducted in Zaire, the Philippines Republic, Malaysia, Hong Kong, Japan, Peru, Venezuela, and Germany. There are 204 missionaries sponsored in these fields. The church body in the United States is divided into 14 districts, with each district having a superintendent and in many cases an associate superintendent. The General Conference meets annually.[70]

Doukhobors

The Doukhobors ("Spirit-wrestlers") are descendants of a peasant religious movement that appeared in southern Russia after Peter the Great opened his domains to Western influences. The adherents of the movement suffered periodic persecution in the last three decades of the eighteenth century. In 1801 Alexander I gave the Doukhobors a general amnesty and settled the majority of them on the Molokhnaya River near the Sea of Azov. Under Nicholas I the era of toleration ended and in 1839 the Doukhobors were compelled to choose between returning to Eastern Orthodoxy and deportation to Transcaucasia. The Doukhobors opted overwhelmingly for the latter and the forced migration took place between 1840 and 1845. For four decades they enjoyed prosperity and peace in their new home, particularly under the leadership of Peter Kalmykov (d. 1864) and of his widow Lukeriya Hubanovna ("Lushechka") (d. 1887).

Peter Vasiliyevich Verigin ("the Lordly") (1859–1924) succeeded Lukeriya as leader of the "Larger Party," so called in contrast to the "Smaller Party" that followed Lukeriya's brother, Mikhail Hubanov. The authorities arrested Verigin almost immediately and shortly afterward banished him, first to Archangel and then to Siberia. He maintained contact with his followers by letter and inspired many of them to return to the communal life that they had abandoned, to forsake the use of tobacco and intoxicating beverages, and to adopt vegetarianism and strict pacifism.

On June 29—St. Peter's Day and Peter Verigin's birthday—in 1895, a solemn burning of arms and weapons by the "Larger Party" as a defiant symbol of their refusal to accept military service led to new persecution and deportations. In 1896, on Verigin's urging, the "Larger Party" took the name "Christian Community of Universal Brotherhood." In the same year Leo Tolstoy, whose writings had been exerting considerable influence on Verigin's thinking, began his campaign to persuade the tsar to allow the emigration of the persecuted Doukhobors. With royalties from Tolstoy's novel *Resurrection* and with the help of funds collected by English and American Quakers, 7,500 Doukhobors were transported to the Northwest Territories of Canada in 1899 and 1900, with a small group of amnestied recruits following in 1905.[71]

The Canadian government granted the immigrants land on easy terms and exemption from conscription. In 1902 a group of overzealous colonists, still dazed by the hardships that they had suffered in Russia and in the course of their emigration, began a series of marches in search of the "Promised Land" that divided the community. The Russian authorities released Verigin from his banishment in 1902 and he arrived in Canada at the end of that year to restore order among the colonists. While the Independent Doukhobors (see below) began to separate from the Verigin group from 1907 on, the communal settlements that Verigin headed prospered. He died in a mysterious bomb explosion aboard a railroad train.

His son, Peter Petrovich (Chistiakov) Verigin ("Peter II") (1881–1939), called the "Cleanser," who redesignated the communal movement "the Union of the Spiritual Communities of Christ," arrived in Canada from the Soviet Union in 1927. During the period of his controversial and somewhat idealistic leadership, the depression of the 1930s combined with great external pressures and internal difficulties to bring the communal enterprises to an end.

Upon the death of Peter II, Peter Petrovich Verigin ("Peter III") (1904–1942), was proclaimed leader, but he never succeeded in leaving the Soviet Union. The de facto leadership in Canada fell to John J. (Ivan Ivanovich) Verigin (b. 1921), the grandson of Peter II. He served as secretary of the Executive Committee of the Union of Spiritual Communities of Christ until his formal proclamation as leader in 1960, after the International Red Cross Society had established all the pertinent facts about the death of Peter III. Under John J. Verigin's leadership a measure of prosperity returned to the colonies as a result of the improved economic conditions that followed World War II.[72]

Canadian Doukhobors currently fall into five groups: (1) Orthodox (or Community) Doukhobors, the Union of Spiritual Communities of Christ; (2) the Independent Doukhobors; (3) the small Spiritual Community of Christ; (4) the Sons of Freedom ("Svobodniki") Doukhobors; and (5) the Reformed Sons of Freedom.

The Orthodox Doukhobors have about 7,200 members. For the most part they live in British Columbia; their headquarters are at Grand Forks. They regard their leader as having within him the Spirit of Christ in a greater measure than other people do. The spirit of this group is still expressed in a widely used hymn written by Saveli Kapustin, a late eighteenth-century Doukhobor leader:

What Is a Doukhobor?

Lord, give us Thy blessing! A Doukhobor is one whose body Christ has chosen for the continued manifestation of God's Spirit that was within Him. The Spirit of God dwells on earth within a physical body and it is the source of eternal wisdom. It was necessary for Jesus Christ to have a body and be a physical being, for it is through the lips of man that God speaks. The apostolic church and the Mount of Zion are embodied in the Doukhobor commune. Within this mount there dwells God's Spirit. Wisdom and the power of God are exemplified in man. Present within this mount is a source of living water that brings forth the glad tidings of life eternal. The commune's virtues, its exemplary life, shall overcome the world, the kingdom of this world whose end is nearing. Then the Doukhobors shall become known to all mankind, and Christ Himself shall be the worthy King. Around Him shall gather all nations.

Only this honor to the Doukhobors shall come after a time of great sufferings and tribulations. There shall be a great struggle in the world, but truth shall conquer all, and the Kingdom of God shall be brought into being on earth. Glory to God![73]

In 1961 this group began to abandon communal living, to buy land of their own, and to build modern homes. They give their children an education according to their individual outlook and means, and the percentage of young people with a higher education in this group is rising rapidly.

The Independent Doukhobors, whose numbers are estimated at from 3,500 to 10,000, live chiefly in the prairie provinces of Canada. Saskatoon, Saskatchewan, is a major center. They began to assimilate to their Canadian environment from 1907 on and generally have acculturated well. Many of them are leaders in their communities and their children are often university graduates and professional people.

The Sons of Freedom ("Svobodniki") are a generally semiliterate group whose numbers are estimated at from 700 to 2,500. They have clashed from time to time with the Dominion government over their refusal to comply with land, tax, and education laws. An extremist element has gained international notoriety through hunger strikes, bombings, arson, and nudist parades and courtroom displays. The principal targets of this destructive activity have been the communal property of the Orthodox Doukhobors, as well as schools, public utilities, and railway structures, but they have also burned and bombed privately owned buildings of their Orthodox neighbors and, to "cleanse themselves of worldly goods," their own buildings. Asserting that "the letter kills" and that "schools teach war," they try to prevent the formal education of their children. Their headquarters are at Krestova, British Columbia, in the Kootenay Mountains.

All Doukhobors are dedicated pacifists. Many refuse to take oaths. They stress the "inner light" that spiritual Christians possess and believe in direct individual revelation, supplemented by a growing body of oral tradition, the "Living Book." To the extent that they use the Bible at all, they tend to interpret it symbolically. Some are strict vegetarians and many regard the killing of animals as sinful. They have no ministry and no sacraments. Their sole corporate rite is the *sobraniva*, a kind of prayer meeting; in it they recite and sing hymns before a table upon which they have placed the Doukhobor symbols of "toil and the peaceful life"—bread, salt, and water. They hold that Spirit-led members are free from temptations to sin.

Russian Molokan Spiritual Christians

The founder of the Molokan movement is the Tambov tailor Semyon Matveyich Uklein (b. 1733). Initially a disciple of the Doukhobor leader and "Christ," Ilarion Pobirokhin,[74] also of Tambov, Uklein broke with Pobirokhin around 1780. Supported by the future martyr of the movement, Matvey Semyonovich Dalmatov,[75] by Peter Zhuravtsov, Maxim Losev, Matvey Motylev, and Gregoriy Nikitich Bulgakov,[76] Uklein mounted an energetic and effective campaign against the established church and many of its practices From his followers' practice of drinking milk (in Russian, *moloko*)—"food blessed by God"—on the Wednesday and Friday fasts when milk was forbidden, they received as early as 1765 the nickname *Molokanye*, "milk-drinkers." They refer to themselves as "True Spiritual Christians," or, more elaborately, as "the New Israel—the sons and daughters of the blessed Jacob who is the Christ [and] to us the eternal life"[77] or "members of the Woman Clothed with the Sun."[78]

In 1783, "an earnest search for the true path of Christ" on the part of the common people of Russia led to a revival, associated with the names of Sidor Andreyev, Isaiya Ivanov Krylov, Peter Dementev, and Moses the Dalmatian, and to a renewal of persecution. Under the mystically oriented Tsar Alexander I, the Molokans received official freedom to worship in 1805, but with his death in 1825 the period of toleration ended.

The year 1833 was marked by a new "powerful pouring out of the Holy Spirit activating in a marvelous manner many people given to the will of God." The leaders of the group during the 1830s included Nikita Ivanov and Terentiy Byelozorov, both of Melitopel, and Luk'yan Petrovich Sokolov (Anikey Ignatiyevich) of Moldavia.

Sokolov founded a Molokan center at Dilizhan in the Caucasus, to which he attracted the two leaders who most influenced American Molokanism, David Yesseyi[vi]ch (Feodor Ossipovich) (1809–1876) and Maxim Gavrilovich Rudametkin (1823?–1877).

The former by his own testimony was a participant in the revival of 1833 and may have been one of its leaders. He was twice sentenced to prison and spent a total of over four years in confinement. After his first imprisonment he was sentenced to be conscripted into the tsarist army out of turn, only to be discharged because the army leadership regarded the manifestations of the Holy Spirit in him as subversive of military discipline.

Rudametkin, born at Algasova near Morshansk, was less fortunate than Yesseyich. He spent nineteen years in prison, half of it in the infamous Solovky monastery prison on Solovetskij Island in the White Sea near the Arctic Circle, and almost as long a time in the Spasso-Effimovsky monastery prison in Suzdal'.

During its history differences in doctrine and administration have divided the Molokan movement into various groups. Two of these are represented in the western United States by immigrants who came to America chiefly between 1904 and 1912. They are the "Jumpers" (*Pryguny*), a minority group that separated from the mainstream as a result of the revival in the 1830s, in which Yesseyich and Rudametkin played prominent roles,[79] and the "Constant Ones" (*Postoyannaye*), descendants of the more conservative majority.

In North America the Jumpers are the larger group. They make extensive use of *The Book of Spirit and Life,* composed of writings of Sokolov, Effeem Gerasimov Klubnikin, Yesseyich, and Rudametkin.

Molokans confess the "indivisible God in the three persons," namely "that the Father, the Word, and the Holy Spirit are one in the Godhead, but are not of equal power and authority," the Word and the Spirit being subordinate to the Father.[81]

Chapter 9 of Book 5 of Rudametkin's doctrinal explanations in *The Book of Spirit and Life* contains this Molokan confession of faith:

> We believe that Jesus Christ is the Son of God born of the virgin Mary, begotten of the Holy Spirit by the word and kiss of the angel Gabriel. We believe that when at the age of thirty he was publicly baptized in the River Jordan and the Holy Spirit descended on him in the form of a dove, he was exalted by the voice of his Father which said unto him: "Thou are my beloved Son, in thee I am well pleased." This he said unto him upon the mountain [of the Transfiguration] also. Amen.

> We believe that he is the eternal Redeemer and Saviour of all who believe in him according to the true new commandment of the Gospel and the law of love of one for the other in the holiness of the Spirit of the inviolate apostolic union.

> We recognize him as the one sent from God for the purpose of taking away the sins of the world, and to give eternal life and the law of freedom in the true Spirit.

> We trust in him that he is now and ever the eternal Mediator of all who confess his name in truth. And in this same truth his light makes us free, eternally without sin, consciously alive in heaven and earth.

> Our hope is in him, that he alone could bring those who are like him unto his Father straight to Abraham in Paradise, eternally alive, quick in the flesh because he himself is the God of the living and not of the dead; and to him are given the keys of hell and death. Amen.

> Wherefore we always prostrate ourselves before him—the only eternal living one—as true Spiritual worshipers, and pray to him alone as our only Mediator,[82] forever standing between us and God his Father, for they abide together in their heavenly bosoms.

> We always stretch our innocent hands and pure hearts directly to him in heaven single-mindedly, like children unto their father, and pray unto him for the descent to us of the gift of the Holy Spirit in signs of the new tongues of fire and in measure as it pleases him according to the diverse secrets of the will of his Father, with whom we ever converse personally as the 144,000 do always converse with the Lamb on Mount Zion.

> In this his Holy Spirit we do not ask that anyone should teach us at second or third hand, but we learn from the one and only active Spirit of our God and his Lamb who always instructs us, the little ones as well as the great ones of both sexes together, in the various truths, at home or in the fields.

> We have no need now of any teacher or preacher who himself is not

baptized from on high with the Holy Spirit and fire, as we ourselves are always baptized in the manner of the holy apostles and of all of those who are like them, who in their time all spoke in the new tongues of fire of the mysteries of our God and his Lamb in various activities of the ten gifts. Amen.[83]

As their authority in faith, the Molokans appeal exclusively to the Sacred Scriptures, which they generally interpret in a strongly literal fashion. The Revelation of St. John the Divine enjoys particular favor.[84]

The church that Christ founded has always existed, they say, but from the beginning of the Constantinian era the established church has been a false church, and persecuted Spirit-led groups have perpetuated the true faith.[85]

The Molokans reject most of the sacramental structure of Russian Orthodoxy. Baptism is not to be administered to "the young infants in the cradle and not by dunking them nose-first in a barrel of water." Instead, God himself by his own invisible living water and blood baptizes and cleanses without hindrance all who come to him with full faith. Those of the New Israel "do not now need a bodily washing or a visible burial in the waters."[86]

There is no room for the sacrament of the altar. "Communion is not bread and wine, but the holy Spirit that cometh from the heavens is. He will give unto all who accept him eternal life and resurrection from the dead on the last day. For the Lord is the Spirit but his flesh profiteth nothing."[87]

Chrismation disappeared with water baptism. The institution of presbyters and elders[88] and the solemnization of marriage are not sacraments. Prayer and the blessing of a sick person with the laying on of hands by the presbyter and by the sufferer's parents replace the anointing of the seriously ill.[89]

The rite that comes closest to the parallel sacrament of the established church is the confession of sin before the presbyter. *The Book of Spirit and Life* insists strongly on the necessity of a careful mental examination and of a precise confession of sins, and calls it a sacrament established by Christ in which "the court of the Lord for a clean confession and repentance forgives and rewards with everlasting life." It warns against false shame at acknowledging one's sins before the presbyter, who is a guilty, sinful man like the offender himself.[90]

The weekly holiday of the Molokans is Sunday. This marks a departure from Rudametkin's prescription. He enjoined his followers to keep both "the Lord's day," that is, Saturday, "the holy Sabbath," and Sunday, "resurrection day." On the former the Molokans were not to do work of any kind. The latter day they were to observe solemnly, and on it they were to "eat and drink, get married and become espoused with joy."[91]

Molokans oppose military service,[92] participation in war, oaths, the use of alcohol and tobacco, theater-going, luxury in clothes, gambling, and social dancing. Molokan men habitually wear beards.

Beginning with Abraham, the Molokan understanding of history divides it into six epochs: (1) from Abraham to Moses, during which fathers transmitted the commandments to their children by oral tradition; (2) from Moses to Christ, when the written law supplemented the Abrahamic code; (3) from Christ to the destruction of Jerusalem, during which circumcision and the Abrahamic-Mosaic law continued, but during which there was Christ's added law of love of one for the other, to carry each other's burdens and forgive all of one another's offenses; (4) from the destruction of Jerusalem to the coming from heaven of the Revelation of St. John the Divine, when the true Hebrews kept all the laws of the previous epochs plus the law to be Christ's disciples until his glorious appearance on earth; (5) the present era from the advent of the Revelation of St. John to the first resurrection, in which the people of God consist only of "the community of the Woman Clothed in the Sun whom the blessed John saw in the heavens being pursued by the scarlet serpent from the very time of the coming of the Holy Apocalypse from heaven to them"; and (6) the peaceful millennial reign of Christ on earth, when the chosen ones shall gather together triumphantly to praise the name of God.[93]

The Book of Prayers and Songs (*Molitvennik*)[94] contains liturgical materials—largely drawn from or based on texts from the Revelation of St. John the Divine—for church services, the marriage rite, a form for the blessing of a newborn infant and the churching of its mother, and a variety of funeral services[95] for different circumstances.

A prominent elder of one of the American churches gives this description of a Molokan worship service:

> Our church interiors are entirely bare. The only furniture is a table covered by a white table cloth on which are placed [four opened books, namely,] an open Bible, the New Testament, our prayer book, and a book of spiritual writings of our founders called *The Book of Spirit and Life.*
>
> The table is surrounded on four sides by plain benches. Those benches on the three sides that are immediately next to the table are occupied by leading elders. Towards one side of the table the first three or four benches are occupied by the male chorus, while on the opposite side on the first bench sit the prophets. The benches back of these are occupied by the younger members and children.
>
> The fourth side facing the end of the table and completing the quadrangle are occupied by the women, with the most respected elderly women sitting on the front benches.
>
> Our regular church service begins with everyone sitting, and while the congregation is assembling we sing psalms and other passages from the Scriptures and from *The Book of Spirit and Life.* In between the songs our elders read and preach from the scriptures and deliver homilies.
>
> After about an hour of this, at a signal from the presbyter, the benches are removed and the prayer service begins. This consists in singing an appropriate song while everyone approaches by turns and places an offering on the table. Following this the presbyter leads in prayers while the congregation is all kneeling.
>
> About four prayers are recited when everyone rises. At this point we per-

form the ceremony of the holy kiss which we call the communion. Everyone, beginning with the assistant presbyter, kisses the presbyter and stands alongside of him, followed by others who kiss the presbyter and others standing in the line. This is followed by everyone, until the whole congregation, old and young, male and female, participates in the holy kiss. While this is done, the chorus is singing an appropriate song, such as the last five verses of Romans 8, "Who shall separate us from the love and Christ?" and so on.[96]

After this ceremony another prayer is recited with all kneeling, following which the chorus sings several joyful spiritual songs. But we consider that the service has not reached its fullness unless there is a manifestation of the Holy Spirit which activates and moves at least some of the members in joyful spiritual jumping.

The service is concluded with another prayer by the presbyter, this time all standing.[97]

For the church service the men have on a distinctive long shirt resembling a smock. This is worn outside the trousers and is girdled with a thin tasseled cord. The women also wear a distinctive dress and cover their head with a shawl.

The number of Molokan Jumpers in the United States is estimated at between 12,000 and 15,000. The bulk of these live in Los Angeles and its vicinity. San Diego County has about 50 families. A large number live in farming communities in the San Joaquin valley. Between 30 and 40 families live near Salem, Oregon, and a similar number near Phoenix, Arizona. About 50 families live in the area around Gervais and Woodburn, Oregon. The total number of churches presided over by a presbyter is 14.

The community of Molokan Spiritual Christian Jumpers has grown since World War II, but the increase has been almost exclusively by births. Leaders lament a degree of lukewarmness that is the consequence of the affluence of contemporary North American society. The Spiritual Christian Jumpers have sustained some losses to Jehovah's Witnesses and to the Pentecostal movement. A small number of Molokan Jumpers have emigrated to Australia in recent years; they are divided between the Perth and the Adelaide areas.

During the revival of the 1830s in Russia, many of the worshipers began to prophesy, to speak in tongues, and to jump for joy during the religious services. The conservative majority discountenanced these manifestations. The minority seceded and added "Jumpers" (*Pryguny*) to their denominational designation; the conservative majority identified itself with the adjective "Constant" (*Postoyannaye*). Initially both groups retained the same form of worship, the same prayers, and the same psalms and biblical chants. In the course of time the Jumpers began to use spiritual songs—which the "Constant" majority disavowed as not of divine inspiration—to supplement the psalms and other chants of biblical origin. The minority also began to use livelier tunes.

Both groups reject the cultus of the Virgin Mary and the saints, the veneration of icons, and the sign of the cross. Both interpret baptism spiritually, both observe the Mosaic dietary laws as far as feasible, and both honor the same founders of the movement—Semyon Uklein, Matvey Dalmatov, Peter Zhuravtsov, Maxim Losev, Matvey Motylev, and Gregoriy Nikitich Bulgakov—although the Jumpers added to this list their own leaders of the separation, like Yesseyitch and especially Rudametkin,[98] whom the Postoyannaye disavow and whom some of the Postoyannaye suspect the Jumpers of putting ahead of Christ.

An additional noteworthy difference is in the calendars of the two groups. Originally both observed Christmas, the Epiphany, the Purification and the Annunciation of the B.V.M., Lent, Easter, Ascension Day, Pentecost, and the Transfiguration.[99] But in the 1860s Rudametkin, writing from prison, persuaded the Pryguny to give up these "inventions of the ecumenical councils" and to substitute for them the Israelite commemorations of the Passover, the Feast of Weeks, the Day of Trumpets (New Year's Day), the Day of Atonement, and the Feast of Tabernacles. These received a Christian interpretation. The Pryguny break bread together to commemorate Christ's Last Supper on the night of the Passover and feast for the following seven days in honor of his resurrection. They keep Pentecost in commemoration of the outpouring of the Holy Spirit and the Day of Trumpets in anticipation of the call to the Last Judgment. They fast for twenty-four hours on the Day of Atonement in anticipation of the Day of Judgment itself and feast during the eight days of Tabernacles in anticipation of the millennium, whose early advent they expect.[100]

The service of the Postoyannaye is substantially that described above.[101] Occasionally the American members of this group will admit spiritual songs borrowed from the Pryguny.

There is considerable commingling between the two groups in California. Visitors from one group are welcome in the services of the other and the occasional cases of intermarriage are not interfered with.

The major concentration of Postoyannaye is in San Francisco. There are also small groups in Los Angeles, in Sheridan, California, and in Oregon. The total number of Postoyannaye in the United States is estimated at 700.[102]

The All-Canadian Union Slavic Evangelical Christians

The Evangelical Christian movement that developed in Russia in the second half of the nineteenth century had a number of sources.

Oldest in point of time was the Shtundist movement. In the 1860s two Reformed clergymen, Johann Bonekämper[103] and his son Karl, began to conduct *Bibelstunden* ("Bible hours") for the German colonists of Rohrbach, near Kherson in the Ukraine, with a view to raising the level of spiritual life among their parishioners. Laymen who mastered the technique of devotional

Bible study began to conduct similar meetings. By 1862 the movement had spread to the Russian Orthodox population of the area, where this type of meeting received the name *shtunda*. Mennonite and Molokan ideas soon penterated the movement. This led to a break between its adherents and the Orthodox established church. The persecuted "Shtundists," as their foes referred to them, formed autonomous congregations with their own presbyters and deacons. They professed to accept the Bible as the only source of faith rejected the Orthodox hierarchy and worship, forbade prayers for the dead condemned the veneration of the Blessed Virgin Mary and of the saints, and prescribed abstinence from intoxicating beverages, tobacco, and dancing for their adherents.

Almost simultaneously another German colonist from Lithuania, Martin Kalweit, an ex-Lutheran who in 1858 had become a Baptist during a visit to Germany, began to propagate Baptist doctrine in the Georgian capital of Tiflis. He baptized his first convert, a Molokan by the name of Nikita Voronin in 1867. The Baptist movement spread rapidly and soon had adherents throughout Russia.

In the 1870s Granville Augustus William Waldegrave Baron Radstock (1833–1913), an aristocratic English Wesleyan revivalist, came to St. Petersburg (Leningrad) and converted an impressive number of courtiers and members of the nobility, among them Colonel Vasili Petrovich Pashkov of the Imperial Life Guards. Down to the time of his banishment in 1884, Pashkov gave unstintingly of himself and of his considerable wealth to propagate his new-found conviction and to unite his own followers with the Shtundists the Baptists, and the Molokans into a single centralized and dynamic movement. The latter effort failed because of differences in the teachings of the various groups on baptism. One of Pashkov's disciples, Ivan Prokhanov (1869–1935), a Caucasian of Molokan parentage, founded the All-Russian Union Evangelical Christians in 1909; the following year the union adopted the "Confession of Faith of Evangelical Christians," which Prokhanov drafted for it.[104]

Evangelical Christians emigrated from Russia to Canada and the northern Plains States in considerable numbers during the first fifteen years of the present century. A second increment came after World War II in the form of displaced persons whom the National Socialists had transported from the western part of the Union of Soviet Socialist Republics into Germany to work on the land and in the factories and who successfully escaped repatriation The Evangelical Christians in both Russia and North America have held that they have no distinctive beliefs and practices and that they aim merely to restore primitive Christianity and the beliefs and practices of the New Testament Christian community. Evangelical Christians practice believer's baptism by immersion in the name of the Father and of the Son and of the Holy Spirit to which the words "for the forgiveness of sins" are sometimes added. Evangelical Christians have for the most part moved from their original Tolstoyan pacifism to the position where they are ready to engage in military service as part of the "taxes" that Romans 13:7 obligates Christians to pay to the governing authorities.

Many out of both waves of Evangelical Christian immigration to North America were promptly absorbed by Russian and Ukrainian Baptist congregations. The remainder tended to resist acculturation, and because of their refusal to introduce English into their services they have lost almost all of their children to English-speaking churches of various denominations.

The All-Canadian Union of Slavic Evangelical Christians was organized in 1930 with headquarters in Toronto, Ontario. In 1958 it sustained the loss of a number of churches that joined with the Russian-Ukrainian Evangelical Baptist Union to form the Union of Slavic Churches of Evangelical Christians and Baptists. Further reduction in membership has occurred as a result of the anglicization of the second generation. At present the union comprises 8 churches in 5 provinces from Ontario to British Columbia, with an estimated active membership of 225. It carries on missions among the Doukhobors of western Canada. Evangelical outreach in Poland and Argentina takes place partially through funds supplied by the union.[105]

Union of Russian Evangelical Christians

The Union of Russian Evangelical Christians was organized in the 1920s as a national branch of the All-Russian Evangelical Christian Union, with headquarters in Leningrad, Union of Soviet Socialist Republics. Later it became an independent association under its present name.

Its theological position is identical with that of the All-Canadian Union of Slavic Evangelical Christians, with which it stands in a relation of fellowship and cooperation.

The headquarters of the Union of Russian Evangelical Christians are at 261 East Sixth Street, Erie, Pennsylvania. It has eight churches in New Jersey, New York, Pennsylvania, Illinois, and California, with an active membership estimated at 300.[106]

NOTES

1. "An Answer to Luther's Malediction by Caspar Schwenckfeld," trans. Selina Gerhard Schultz, in George Huntston Williams and Angel M. Mergal, eds., *Spiritual and Anabaptist Writers: Documents Illustrative of the Radical Reformation* (Philadelphia: Westminster Press, 1957), p. 166.
2. Ibid., p. 180.
3. *Beliefs and Practices of the Schwenkfelder Church* (Norristown, Penn.: Board of Publication of the Schwenkfelder Church, 1962) (12-page tract).
4. Ora W. Garber, *The Church of the Brethren* (Elgin, Ill.: General Brotherhood Board—Church of the Brethren, 1964) (24-page brochure).
5. Harold Ritz Holsinger, *Holsinger's History of the Tunkers and the Brethren Church* (Oakland, Calif.: Pacific Press Publishing Co., 1901 [North Manchester, Ind.: L. W. Shultz, 1962]), p. 417.
6. Ibid., p. 442.

7. Fred W. Benedict, *A Concise Presentation of the History, Belief and Practice of the Dunkers (The Old German Baptist Brethren)* (Covington, Ohio: 1960); H. M. Fisher and others, *Doctrinal Treatise* (2nd edn. Covington, Ohio: The Little Printing Company, 1954), pp. 7-90. On the attitude to war and conscientious nonresistance, see Marcus Miller, *Nonresistance* (Covington, Ohio: "The Vindicator," n.d.).

8. Text in *The Ashland Theological Seminary: Catalogue 1967–1968* (Ashland, Ohio: Ashland College Theological Seminary, 1967), p. 17. The Reverend Albert T. Ronk, Ashland Theological Seminary, states in a letter: "At best the Message is only a partial statement of the Brethren theology. It was a compromise statement of differences in theology between elements of liberal and fundamental Brethren."

9. Communication from David R. Grant, statistician.

10. See *Dunkard Brethren Church Polity* (rev. edn. N.p.: n.p., 1957) (33-page pamphlet), pp. 1-18, 25-26.

11. Ibid., p. 29.

12. *Constitution and Statement of Practice of the Association of Fundamental Gospel Churches* (Hartville, Ohio: Association of Fundamental Gospel Churches, 1954) (3-page tract), p. [3].

13. Letters from the Reverend Maurice E. Brandt, superintendent, Association of Fundamental Gospel Churches, Greencastle, Pennsylvania, and the Reverend Lynn Besse, 9189 Grubb Court, North Canton, Ohio, pastor of Calvary Chapel, Hartville, Ohio. This writer acknowledges gratefully the assistance of the Reverend George W. E. Nickelsburg, Jr., then pastor of the Church of the Good Shepherd, Akron, Ohio, in securing information about the Association of Fundamental Gospel Churches.

14. *Minutes, 6th Annual Conference of the Fundamental Brethren Church, June 23-24, 1967, at Pigeon Roost Fundamental Brethren Church, Relief, North Carolina* (7-page pamphlet), pp. [5]-[6].

15. Letter from the Reverend Calvin Barnett, moderator, Fundamental Brethren Church, Relief, North Carolina.

16. Letter from the Reverend George von Hilsheimer, general superintendent, Church of the Brotherhood, Box 606, Orange City, Florida; *Humanitas* (Orange City, Fla.: Humanitas Curriculum, 1967) (15-page pamphlet).

17. *Minutes of the General Conference of the United Zion Church Held at Elizabethtown, Pa., April 24th, 1965*, item XV, p. 22. The same General Conference also dropped the question of the United Zion Church's becoming an associate member of the Mennonite Central Committe (ibid., item XIV).

18. The only obvious difference seems to have been that the Church of the Brethren in Christ washed feet after the Communion, while the Churches of God washed feet before the Communion.

19. The history of the Armstrong County Brethren in Christ is here summarized from an account written in 1953 by J. Carl Wolgemuth, "The Story of the Brethren in Christ in Western Pennsylvania," and submitted as a term paper in a course in church history at Messiah College, Grantham, Pennsylvania, under Professor C. O. Wittlinger. The Reverend Herman W. Mohney has kindly made his copy of the paper available to the present writer. See also *Brethren in Christ Fellowship Manual* (N.p.: n.p., 1963), pp. 1-2, 11-13.

20. Herman W. Mohney, "Foreword," ibid., p. 2.

21. Kenneth C. Mock, "The Message of the Brethren in Christ Ministry," ibid., pp. 5-9.

22. Articles V-X, ibid., pp. 33-49.

23. Letter from the Reverend Herman W. Mohney, bishop, Brethren in Christ Fellowship, Rural Route No. 6, Kittanning, Pennsylvania 16201.

24. Article 4, ("Tenets of Faith and Doctrine"), Constitution, *Manual of the Calvary Holiness Church* (Philadelphia: Calvary Holiness Church, 1963) (51-page mimeographed brochure), pp. 2-4.

25. Article 5 ("Government"), ibid., pp. 4-5.

26. Articles 3 ("Standard for Members") and 4 ("Friends of Church Unable to

Accept the Status of Church Membership"), Part II, Division Three, By-Laws, ibid., pp. 15-21.

27. Section 3 ("Church Covenant"), article 5, ibid., pp. 23-25.

28. Letter of the Reverend William L. Rosenberry, pastor, Calvary Holiness Church, Philadelphia. The denomination's monthly, *The Gospel Witness,* has a circulation of approximately 7,000.

29. The actual year is uncertain, but it falls between 1770 and 1788.

30. For the text of the long-forgotten "Articles of Faith of the Old Order River Brethren," drawn up around 1799 according to the common belief and rediscovered in 1921, when they were translated into English by their possessor, Charles Baker, see Asa W. Climenhaga, *History of the Brethren in Christ Church* (Nappanee, Ind.: E. V. Publishing House, 1942), pp. 99-103, reprinted in Laban T. Brechbill, *Doctrine: Old Order River Brethren* (Lancaster, Penn.: Laban T. Brechbill, 1967), pp. 200-210.

31. Brechbill, p. 85.

32. Ibid., pp. 42, 49.

33. Ibid., pp. 54, 113-114.

34. Ibid., p. 56. The case histories available to the present writer suggest that this experience frequently takes place in early maturity, between eighteen and twenty-five. The crucial aspect is seen as less acceptance of Christ than acceptance by Christ.

35. Ibid., pp. 91-93.

36. Ibid., pp. 128-133. "The militant church [is] to baptize the convert with material water, and God will baptize with the Holy Spirit" (ibid., p. 133). The Old Order River Brethren reject infant baptism.

37. Ibid., pp. 142-147.

38. Pp. 148-152. "In this exercise, the one wishing to wash, after girding himself with a towel, remarks to the one to be washed [that] he has a desire to wash his feet. He answers, 'I will try and hold still.' When the duty of washing is accomplished, [the one who washes will] then kiss and thank the brother for his favor, submission, and patience until he had the task completed. This [also applies] to the brother that does the drying. The

phrase used in this exercise [may] vary. . . . If a brother would admonish another brother and he would remonstrate in an unbecoming way, he would not be holding still and suffer his brother to end his admonishment" (ibid., p. 152).

39. Ibid., pp. 154-155.

40. Ibid., pp. 156-157.

41. While the garb of male members of the Old Order River Brethren is similar to that of Amish men, the clothing of the former is less likely to be homemade. The women of the Old Order River Brethren wear a bonnet that is longer and narrower than the Amish bonnet, with a long curtain falling to the shoulders.

42. For most members of the Old Order River Brethren separation from the world implies, in addition to wearing plain garb, desisting from the use (or at least ownership) of automobiles, radios, and television sets. Possession of these items is not regarded as intrinsically sinful, but they are regarded as temptations to compromise the standards. Prohibition of the use of automobiles dates back to a pastoral decree of 1919; it was a factor in the schisms of 1929 and 1959. Where automobiles are sanctioned, they are usually "all black," that is, without "worldly" chrome ornament. The principle of separation from the world is not extended to education. Children attend the same schools—through college, when the child's ability and the family's finances permit it—as other children.

43. Some members of the Old Order River Brethren put the battle of Armageddon after the millennium (ibid., p. 199).

44. This summary is based chiefly on Brechbill, pp. 7-199, supplemented with letters from Bishop Joseph H. Brechbill, Route No. 3, Chambersburg, Pennsylvania; Bishop Jacob K. Etter, Route No. 1, Bradford, Ohio; and Bishop Seth Meyers, Route No. 2, Mercersburg, Pennsylvania.

45. For a detailed description, see Wilmer J. Eshleman, "The River Brethren Denominations," *Papers of the Lancaster County Historical Society* 52 (1948): 198-201.

46. Eshleman, pp. 197-198; letter from Bishop Simon H. Musser, Route No. 1, Columbia, Pennsylvania. Bishop Musser emphatically denies that the question of the use of automobiles came up in connection with the 1920 council's discussion of the Iowa case.

47. Letter from Bishop John M. Strickler, Mountville, Lancaster County, Pennsylvania. Ira D. Landis, "The Old Order River Brethren (Yorkers)," in Charles D. Spotts, ed., *Denominations Originating in Lancaster County, Pennsylvania* (Lancaster, Penn.: Franklin and Marshall College Library, 1963), p. 19.

48. Cited letter from Bishop Brechbill.

49. Letters from Mr. Laban T. Brechbill, 945 East King Street, Lancaster, Pennsylvania. In 1966 an Old Order River Brethren family in Franklin County and a minister of the Brethren in Christ Church withdrew from their respective denominations, only to be absorbed in 1967 by the Beachy Amish Mennonites (William R. McGrath, *Separation throughout Church History* [3rd edn.; Mission Home, Virginia: William R. McGrath, 1966], chart following p. 66; letters from Brother William R. McGrath, Star Route, Mission Home, Virginia.

50. Some of these New York assemblies still call themselves Evangelical Baptists. Other names for Apostolic Christians are New Amish (especially in New York), New Baptists (in Switzerland), and "Nazareans" (in Hungary and Yugoslavia). On the early history of the Apostolic Christian movement in Europe and North America, see Henry Michel, *A Historical Sketch of the Apostolic Christian Church* (Lake Bloomington, Ill.: Apostolic Christian Camp, 1947) (32-page pamphlet). For the life of Samuel Heinrich Fröhlich, see "A Condensed Outline of the Life of S. H. Fröhlich" prefixed to *Meditations on the Epistles of John: Meditations of S. H. Fröhlich Delivered in Zuerich in the Years 1840–1842, Translated from the German* 1 (Syracuse, N. Y.: Apostolic Christian Publishing Company, 1958): i-xxii; and *Letters and Reflections Left by Samuel Heinrich Fröhlich* (Grabill, Ind.: The Gospel Press, n.d.), p. 1-23.

51. *History and Doctrine of the Apostolic Christian Church of America* (N.p.: n.p., n.d.) (4-page pamphlet). An effective unifying factor among Apostolic Christians has been their hymnal, *Zion's Harp,* which has been translated into eight languages. It consists of 253 hymns, plus an addendum—known as the *Heft*—which contains 78 more hymns.

52. Letter of Elder Ray L. Sander, bishop.

53. *We Believe: A Brief Statement of Faith [of the] Apostolic Christian Church of America* (Akron: Apostolic Christian Church Foundation, n.d.) (4-page pamphlet).

54. Elder Hari and Elder George Ifft, Rural Route 3, Fairbury, Illinois, both informed this writer by letter that the information which he requested about the history, teachings, and size of the German Apostolic Christian Church was not available for publication.

55. The information contained in this section is based in part on letters from Mr. James H. Roberts, publisher, The Blade Publishing Company, Fairbury, Illinois, and Elder Noah Schrock, 2925 Sunnyside Avenue, Burlington, Iowa.

56. Letters from Elder Sam Hoffman, senior elder, Christian Apostolic Church of Forrest, Route 2, Fairbury, Illinois.

57. Letters from Elder Ben Edelman, Sabetha, Kansas.

58. Communication from the Reverend Ludwig B. Amerding, president, Fellowship Deaconry, Incorporated, Box 204, Liberty Corner, New Jersey.

59. In essence, Waldenström held that the fall of man caused no change in God's heart and will; that there was never any anger in God that hindered the salvation of human beings; that the only change that the fall caused was in human beings themselves, in that, as sinners, they turned away from God and from life in him; that this change in man required an atonement for his salvation, but that this was not an atonement that had to conciliate God and make him gracious again, but an atonement that took away the sin of human beings and made them righteous; and that Christ by his suf-

fering and death on the cross accomplished this divine work of atonement. (See David Nyvall, *The Evangelical Covenant Church* [Chicago: Covenant Church Press, 1954], p. 32.)

60. The term "Covenant" refers to the solemn pledge of the members of the church to work together to advance the cause of Christ.

61. "Preamble (Historical Statement) to the Constitution," in Gerard Johnson, ed., *Covenant Yearbook for 1965* (Chicago: The Evangelical Covenant Church of America, 1965), p. 363. An officially approved 12-page tract, *Covenant Principles* (rev. edn.; Chicago: The Evangelical Covenant Church of Amercia, 1962) lists seven "principles of faith": in the Bible, the life in Christ, the dedicated life, the unity of all Christians ("differences in minor points of doctrine, in the modes of baptism, and interpretation of prophecy do not require different churches and must not divide us"), the principles of freedom within the disciplines of the spirtual fellowship, the evangelical witness, and the eternal kingdom of Christ.

62. See Karl A. Olsson, "The Evangelical Covenant Church of America," in Augustinus Keijer, ed., *Evangelicals: American and European* (Stockholm, Sweden: The International Federation of Free Evangelical Churches, 1966) (88-page mimeographed brochure, 1966), p. 78.

63. For a statement of the two positions see the 4-page supplement to *Timely Tidings*, vol. 3, no. 18 (May 11, 1946). See also Glen M. Enos, "Canadian Controversy," and Leonard M. Peterson, "The Doctrinal Issue in the Canadian Covenant Controversy," two unpublished research papers written in 1953–1954 by students in North Park Theological Seminary on the basis of archival material provided by the Reverend Leonard A. Quarnstrom; copies are on file in the Library of Concordia Seminary, St. Louis, Missouri.

64. Letter from the Reverend Leonard A. Quarnstrom, president, The Evangelical Covenant Church of Canada.

65. Arnold Theodore Olson, *Believers Only: An Outline of the History and Principles of the Free Evangelical Movement in Europe and America Affiliated with the International Federation of Free Evangelical Churches* (Minneapolis, Minn.: Free Church Publications, 1964), p. 295.

66. Quoted ibid., p. 296.

67. Ibid., pp. 304-305. See Arnold Theodore Olson, *This We Believe: The Background and Exposition of the Doctrinal Statement of the Evangelical Free Church of America* (Minneapolis, Minn.: Free Church Publications, 1961), for a detailed analysis and commentary.

68. Thus the Bethesda Mission, now an "approved" agency of the Grace Fellowship, had its beginning in an Evangelical Free Church congregation in Minneapolis.

69. Arnold Theodore Olsen, *This We Believe*, p. [3]. On the relationship of the Free Evangelical movement to the organized Ecumenical movement, see Olson, *Believers Only*, chap. 18.

70. Communication from the Reverend Thomas A. McDill, who has recently succeeded the Reverend Arnold Theodore Olson as president.

71. On the Doukhobors in Russia, see Frederick Cornwallis Conybeare, *Russian Dissenters* (New York: Russell and Russell, 1962), pt. II, chap. 1, "The Dukhobortsy," pp. 266-287, and Serge Bolshakoff, *Russian Nonconformity: The Story of "Unofficial" Religion in Russia* (Philadelphia: Westminster Press, 1950), pp. 97-105, in addition to the titles in the bibliography.

72. See Sally Clubb, "Toil and the Peaceful Life," *Arbos: Journal of the Saskatchewan Teachers' Federation*, vol. 2, no. 5 (May-June 1966), pp. 15-23, 35.

73. Translation from Eli A. Popoff, *An Historical Exposition on the Origin and Evolvement of the Basic Tenets of the Doukhobor Life-Conception* (Grand Forks, British Columbia: Iskra, n.d. [after August 1964]), (58-page mimeographed brochure), pp. 39-40.

74. According to some authorities, Uklein became Pobirokhin's son-in-law. (See Frederick Cornwallis Conybeare, *Russian Dissenters* [New York: Russell and Russell, 1962], pp. 305 and 318,

and Serge Bolshakoff, *Russian Nonconformity* [Philadelphia: Westminster Press, 1950], p. 105). Traditionally Molokans have regarded the Doukhobors as the seceders. In the early stages of both groups little differentiation seems to have taken place either among the ordinary membership or among outsiders (Conybeare, pp. 304-305).

75. The mid-nineteenth-century manual *The Confession of Faith of the Spiritual Christians Called Molokanye,* written in 1862 and published at Geneva, Switzerland, in 1865, confuses Dalmatov with a quasi-legendary dissenting martyr of the sixteenth century who died on the rack in the reign of Ivan the Terrible (quoted in Conybeare, p. 290). Bolshakoff describes Dalmatov as a convert minister of one of the Judaizing dissenting movements of the period who allegedly persuaded Uklein to institute more feasible Old Testament dietary practices (Bolshakoff, p. 107).

76. David Yesseyich, "Concerning the Pillars of the Church," in Maxim Gavrilovitch Rudametkin (co-author), *Selections from the Book of Spirit and Life,* ed. and trans. John K. Berokoff (Whittier, Calif.: Stockton Trade Press, 1966), pp. 32-33.

77. Ibid., p. 66.

78. Ibid., p. 106. The allusion is, of course, to Rev. 12. The prescribed Molokan greeting is "God lives; blessed be the Lord," to which the response is "And we are their people in the Holy Spirit" (ibid., p. 170).

79. The Pryguny hold Rudametkin in especially high esteem, while Rudametkin in Song 24 hails "the Jumpers and the Leapers" in the Spirit as "forever the ornaments of the Lamb and of myself [Rudametkin]" (ibid., p. 190).

80. The book contains passages of great spiritual ardor and devotion. The writings of Yesseyich tend to be more placid, the contributions of Rudametkin more vehement, apocalyptic, and bitterly polemical.

81. Ibid., p. 77. The Geneva Confession of 1862–1865 asserted: "*Father, Son, and Holy Spirit* are no more than titles of God which mark the different angles or aspects from or under which we contemplate him, without losing sight of his unity as Creator of ourselves and of the earth, as Life and Spirit of the universe, as the True Spirit by which he reveals himself to us" (quoted in Conybeare, pp. 295-296). As in other denominations with similar histories and constituencies, a considerable degree of variation in doctrinal detail exists among the Molokans.

82. This is directed against the Orthodox veneration of ikons.

83. Rudametkin, pp. 66-67. Words in the "new tongues of fire" are scattered through Rudametkin's writings in *The Book of Spirit and Life.* Although this "Pentecostal" feature is probably the result of Khlysty influence on the Pryguny, the words that Rudametkin uses have little in common with the "inharmonious specimen" of Khlysty glossolalia that Conybeare cites from Karl Konrad Grass (Conybeare, p. 350).

84. In Song 24, Rudametkin sings: "I always preach and confess only the one heavenly book, the Apocalypse, and the Spirit of revelation in the new tongues of fire" (Rudametkin, p. 198). He warns his Molokans with reference to the established church: "Do not accept a single line of their tenets except the Bible and the Holy Apocalypse" (ibid., p. 160).

85. On the Molokan teaching about the church, see Conybeare, pp. 299-300. *The Book of Spirit and Life* frequently attacks the established churches. More or less typical is the passage: "Defeat the seven-headed beast, that is, the doctrines of the ecumenical seven-headed councils, all of their rituals and holidays which are written in their book of the church fathers and their other books—beastly cuds. . . . Drop their holidays that were established by them at the above mentioned councils, where they acted in the spirit of the bottomless pit. . . . Mark the number of [the Antichrist's] name which contains 666 beastly numbers, that is ritualistic religions of the striped beast that emerged from the sea by the cunning spirit of the seven-headed ecumenical council by which the people separated in 666 heresies" (Rudametkin, pp. 71-72). Among those

"through whom the spirit of the bottomless pit of the ancient serpent and beast and their false prophet are acting" are first "the Greco-Russian faith," but also "the Armenian, [Roman] Catholic, Lutheran, Protestant, Reformist, Calvinist [faiths] and [the faith] of Simion Rudakoff" (ibid., p. 72). (Rudakov was a leader of the Postoyannaye.) Special targets of criticism are "to worship their ikons," to name children from the church calendar after the saints rather than from the Bible, and "to observe their demonic holidays which were established by them at their ecumenical beastliness by the invention of their seven-headed council" (ibid., p. 72). Particularly vehement is the Molokan rejection of Russian monasticism. The Molokan Jumpers also disavow any connection with the Old Believers, the Skopcy, the Doukhobors, those who practice visible water baptism, Communalists, and Sabbatarians (Yesseyitch, ibid., p. 32). The last three are Molokan sectarian movements. "Those who practice visible water baptism" are the so-called "Evangelical Christians" founded by a Don Cossack, Andrey Salamatin; they are the most churchly of the groups to come out of the Molokan tradition. The "Communalists" were founded by a Voskresnik ("Sunday-observing") Molokan peasant of Samara, Maxim Popov. The "Sabbatarians" are a theologically radical group founded by a Molokan peasant of the province of Saratov called Sundukov, who finally joined with the old Judaistic sect of Subbotniks (see Bolshakoff, pp. 108-111).

86. Rudametkin, p. 75.
87. Ibid., p. 78.
88. Molokans have neither bishops, thought of as an order superior to presbyters, nor deacons.
89. Ibid., p. 188.
90. Yesseyich, in Rudametkin, p. 57.
91. Ibid., p. 82.
92. In Russia a particularly praiseworthy act was the harboring of deserters from the army.
93. Ibid., pp. 69-70.
94. *Molitvennik ili Obriad Bogosluzheniya Khristnai Molokan Dukhovikh Prygunov* (Los Angeles: Paul Ivano-vich Samarin, 1959). Berokoff's English translation is reprinted in Rudametkin, pp. 169-197.
95. Following the interment, Molokans are asked "to fast and pray for the deceased all of the three days." The injunction continues: "And in the evenings you must offer a worthy feast, one according to your means, as much as you can afford from the fruit of your labor. . . . God himself does show mercy for the dead through such fasts and prayers with offerings, and likewise there will be salvation for this unto the living" (ibid., p. 196). Prayer 20—identified as "not by M. G. Rudametkin"—provides an appropriate form of intercession for one who has "died in the Spirit of truth" (ibid., p. 204).
96. In the nineteenth century a love feast usually followed the service but could be dispensed with (Conybeare, p. 303).
97. Letter of Mr. John K. Berokoff, 337 South State Street, Los Angeles, California, to this writer. The service here described is the one that both the Pryguny and the Postoyannaye commonly use on Sunday morning. On special solemn occasions and usually at Sunday evening services the Pryguny use the form contained in *The Book of Prayers and Songs* and called "The New Ritual" or "Maxim's Ritual" (after Maxim Rudametkin).
98. In one of his songs Rudametkin sings, seeing Revelation 3:12 fulfilled in himself: "I, Maxim, am now called by his new name, 'the king of the Spirits and God of the faithful of the whole earth for the new kingdom of peace of Christ for a thousand years.' " In the same song he also sees fulfilled in himself a prophecy of a young Molokan, Effeem Gerasimo v Klubnikin, at an earlier date: "Glory to God, the third person has appeared." The Molokan "Song for Our Final Principal Hero" hails Rudametkin as "king of the whole universe" and "the eternal heir of the throne of the earthly kingdom of Christ for a thousand years" (Rudametkin, p. 143).
99. So the Geneva Confession of 1862–1865 (Conybeare, p. 297).
100. When the Postoyannaye insisted on

retaining their old calendar, Rudamet-kin had some sharp things to say about "our strayed Molokans who are of the number of the striped beast" (Rudametkin, p. 160).

101. The Postoyannaye, of course, reject Rudametkin's "New Ritual" out of hand.

102. For the information here given about the Postoyannaye and the differences between them and the Pryguny, the writer is indebted in large part to a letter from Mr. Berokoff and to a letter from the Reverend James Zimmermann, pastor of St. John's Church, San Francisco, whose kindness in establishing contact with the Postoyannaye community on this writer's behalf the latter gratefully acknowledges. Pauline V. Young, *The Pilgrims of Russian-Town* (Chicago, Ill.: The University of Chicago Press, 1932), p. 65 and note 4, summarized the situation as it was forty years ago: "The *Postoyannaye*, or *Steady*, . . . do not jump, denying any religious validity of the ecstasy which sweeps over the individuals when under the influence of the Holy Ghost," but they are so close to the Molokan Jumpers "that they attend the same *sobranie* and even intermarry."

103. Other spellings of the name include Bohnekämper and Bonnenkemper.

104. Ivan S. Prokhanov, "Izlozheniye Yevangyelskoi Very (Phil. 1:27), ili Vye-rouchyeniye Yevangyelskikh Khristian (Faithful Exposition of the Gospel, or Evangelical Christian Doctrine), in his *Vyerouchyeniye Yevangyelskikh Khristian* (Chicago: World Fellowship of Slavic Evangelical Christians, 1961) (64-page brochure in Russian), pp. 3-32. Prokhanov has written a lively account of his own life under the title *In the Cauldron of Russia, 1869–1933: Autobiography of I. S. Prokhanoff, Founder and Honorary President of the All-Russian Evangelical Christian Union* (New York: All-Russian Evangelical Christian Union [John Felsberg], 1933). On the antecedents of the Evangelical Christians in Russia, see also N. I. Saloff-Astakhoff, *Christianity in Russia* (New York: Loizeaux Brothers, 1941), pp. 83-95; and Serge Bolshakoff, *Russian Nonconformity* (Philadelphia: Westminster Press, 1950), pp. 113-118.

105. Communication from the Reverend D. Koleba, pastor, Scarborough, Ontario.

106. Letters from the Reverend John Kalenikovich Huk, Toronto Christian Mission, 5 Lavington Drive, Weston, Ontario. The present writer's repeated efforts to obtain information directly from the headquarters of the Union of Russian Evangelical Christians were unavailing.

BIBLIOGRAPHY

THE SCHWENKFELDER CHURCH

Brecht, Samuel Kriebel, ed. *The Genealogical Record of the Schwenkfelder Families . . . Who Fled . . . to Pennsylvania in the Years 1731–1737.* New York: Rand, McNally and Co., 1923.

Corpus Schwenckfeldianorum. 19 vols. Pennsburg, Penn.: Board of Publication of the Schwenkfelder Church, 1909–1961. A critical edition of the writings of Caspar Schwenkfeld von Ossig.

Furcha, E. J. "Key Concepts in Caspar von Schwenckfeld's Thought: Regeneration and the New Life." In *Church History* 37 (1968): 160-173. An excerpt from a 1966 thesis written by the author for the Hartford Seminary Foundation, *Schwenckfeld's Concept of the New Man.*

Maier, Paul L. *Caspar Schwenckfeld on the Person and Work of Christ.* St Louis: School for Graduate Studies of Concordia Seminary, 1959.

Schultz, Selina Gerhard. *Caspar Schwenckfeld von Ossig (1489–1561).* Norristown, Penn.: The Board of Publication of the Schwenkfelder Church, 1946.

———. *A Course of Study in the Life and Teachings of Caspar Schwenckfeld von Ossig and the History of the Schwenckfelder Religious Movement.* Norristown, Penn.: The Board of Publication of the Schwenkfelder Church, 1964.

The Schwenkfeldian, a quarterly magazine

edited by J. R. Rothenberger, and published by the Board of Publication of the Schwenkfelder Church.

Seyppel, Joachim H. *Schwenckfeld, Knight of Faith: A Study in the History of Religion.* Pennsburg, Penn.: The Schwenkfelder Library, 1961.

Wach, Joachim. *Types of Religious Experience Christian and Non-Christian.* Chicago: University of Chicago Press, 1951. Chap. 7, "Caspar Schwenkfeld, a Pupil and a Teacher in the School of Christ." A comprehensive theological analysis of Schwenkfeld's basic ideas.

CHURCH OF THE BRETHREN

Brumbaugh, Martin Grove. *A History of the German Baptist Brethren in Europe and America.* North Manchester, Ind.: L. W. Shultz, 1961. An unaltered reprint of the 1899 edition.

Durnbaugh, Donald F. *The Brethren in Colonial America.* Elgin, Ill.: The Brethren Press, 1967. This source book on the history of the Church of the Brethren covers the period from 1719 through the Revolutionary War.

————, ed. *European Origins of the Brethren: A Source Book on the Beginnings of the Church of the Brethren in the Early Eighteenth Century.* Elgin, Ill.: The Brethren Press, 1958.

Eby, Kermit. *For Brethren Only.* Elgin, Ill.: The Brethren Press, 1958.

Holsinger, Howard Ritz. *History of the Tunkers and Brethren Church.* North Manchester, Ind.: L. W. Shultz, 1962. An unaltered reprint of the 1901 edition.

OLD GERMAN BAPTIST BRETHREN

Benedict, Fred W. *A Concise Presentation of the History, Belief and Practice of the Dunkers (The Old German Baptist Brethren).* Covington, Ohio: "The Vindicator," 1960. A 12-page pamphlet based on the *Doctrinal Treatise.*

Fisher, H. M., and others. *Doctrinal Treatise.* 2nd edn. Covington, Ohio: The Little Printing Company, 1954. The seven-man "Vindicator Committee" prepared this 90-page brochure, which sets "forth the nature and the purpose of the doctrine and ordinances as taught in the New Testament and practiced by the Old German Baptist Brethren," in response to the demand of the annual meet-

ing of 1952. It is "not intended to outline or establish a creed" (p. [3]).

Holsinger, Harold Ritz. *Holsinger's History of the Tunkers and the Brethren Church, Embracing the Church of the Brethren, the Tunkers, the Seventh-Day German Baptist Church, the German Baptist Church, the Old German Baptists, and the Brethren Church, Including Their Origin, Doctrine, Biography, and Literature.* Oakland, Calif.: Pacific Press Publishing Co., 1901. This comprehensive study of the Tunker movement in North America through the nineteenth century was reprinted by L. W. Shultz, North Manchester, Indiana, in 1962.

BRETHREN CHURCH (ASHLAND, OHIO)

Holsinger, Harold Ritz. *History of the Tunkers and the Brethren Church . . . Including Their Origin, Doctrine, Biography, and Literature.* North Manchester, Ind.: L. W. Schultz, 1962. An unaltered reprint of the 1901 edition. Its value lies in the fact that it provides a documentary history of the events leading up to the break of 1882 as Holsinger saw them.

A Manual of Procedure for the Brethren Church. Rev. 1966–1967 ed. Ashland,

Ohio: The Brethren Publishing Company, 1966. An 18-page pamphlet designed to "secure a uniform method of procedure in the organization of new churches and the administration of churches already established."

Ronk, Albert T. *History of the Brethren Church.* Ashland, Ohio: The Brethren Publishing Company, 1968.

Ronk, Albert T., and others. *Our Faith: A Manual of Brethren History, Bible Doctrine, and Christian Commitment.* Ashland, Ohio: The A. L. Garber Company, 1960. This work was prepared in response to a felt need for "a program of indoctrination for new church members."

Shultz, Joseph R. *The Soul of the Symbols: A Theological Study of Holy Communion.* Grand Rapids, Mich.: Wm. B. Eerdmans Publishing Company, 1966.

THE NATIONAL FELLOWSHIP OF BRETHREN CHURCHES

The Brethren Minister's Handbook. Winona Lake, Ind.: National Fellowship of Brethren Churches, 1945.

Kenut, Homer A., Sr. *250 Years . . . Conquering Frontiers.* Winona Lake, Ind.: The Brethren Missionary Herald Company, 1958. Chaps. 11 through 14 (pp. 125-168) deal at length with the issues that resulted in the division between the "Ashland Group" and the "Grace Group" of Brethren churches.

UNITED ZION CHURCH

Eshleman, Wilmer J. "The River Brethren Denominations." In *Papers of the Lancaster County Historical Society* 52 (1948): 190-192.

Spotts, Charles D., ed. *Denominations Originating in Lancaster County, Pennsylvania.* Lancaster, Penn.: Franklin and Marshall College Library, 1963, p. 20.

OLD ORDER RIVER BRETHREN (YORKERS)

Brechbill, Laban T. *Doctrine: Old Order River Brethren.* Lancaster, Penn.: Laban T. Brechbill, 1967. This comprehensive discussion of the teaching of the Old Order River Brethren was compiled over several years by a lay theologian of the denomination in consultation with a number of bishops and ministers.

Eshleman, Wilmer J. "The River Brethren Denominations." In *Papers of the Lancaster County Historical Society* 52 (1948): 197-201.

Landis, Ira D. "The Origin of the Brethren in Christ Church and Its Later Division." In *The Mennonite Quarterly Review* 34 (1960): 304-305. The cited section of the article is reprinted, without footnotes, in Charles D. Spotts, ed., *Denominations Originating in Lancaster County, Pennsylvania* (Lancaster, Penn.: Franklin and Marshall College Library, 1963), p. 19.

AMANA CHURCH SOCIETY (COMMUNITY OF TRUE INSPIRATION)

Holloway, Mark. *Heavens on Earth: Utopian Communities in America 1680–1880.* 2nd edn., New York: Dover Publications, 1966.

[Noe, Charles.] *A Brief History of the Amana Society or Community of True Inspiration 1714–1930.* 4th edn. Amana, Iowa: Amana Society, 1930. A 31-page summary. The confession of faith quoted above appears on pp. 28-29.

Shambaugh, Bertha Maud Horack. *Amana That Was and Amana That Is.* Iowa City, Iowa: State Historical Society of Iowa, 1932.

THE EVANGELICAL COVENANT CHURCH OF AMERICA

Frisk, Donald C. *What Christians Believe.* Chicago: Covenant Press, 1951.

Frisk, Donald C., Fryhling, Paul P.; and

Palmquist, Herbert E. *The Christian Fellowship: An Introduction to the Church.* 4th printing. Chicago: Covenant

Press, 1965. This is a 47-page manual for inquirers' classes.

Jacobson, E. Camilla. *Days of Our Years: Golden Jubilee of The Evangelical Mission Covenant of Canada, a History in Commemoration of Fifty Years 1904–1954.* Prince Albert, Saskatchewan: The Evangelical Mission Covenant of Can-ada, 1954.

Olsson, Karl A. *By One Spirit.* Chicago: Covenant Press, 1962. The author of this definitive history of the Evangelical Covenant Church of America was president of North Park College and Theological Seminary.

EVANGELICAL FREE CHURCH OF AMERICA

Olson, Arnold Theodore. *Believers Only: An Outline of the History and Principles of the Free Evangelical Movement in Europe and North America Affiliated with the International Federation of Free Evangelical Churches.* Minneapolis, Minn.: Free Church Publications, 1964. Chap.

16. The author is president of the Evangelical Free Church of America.

————. *This We Believe: The Background and Exposition of the Doctrinal Statement of the Evangelical Free Church of America.* Minneapolis, Minn.: Free Church Publications, 1961.

DOUKHOBORS

Bach, Marcus. *Strange Sects and Curious Cults.* New York: Dodd, Mead and Company, 1961. Chap. 14, "The Doukhobors," pp. 182-201.

Dawson, Carl Addington. *Group Settlement Ethnic Communities in Western Canada.* Toronto: Macmillan Company of Canada, 1936. Pp. 1-91.

Elkinton, Joseph. *The Doukhobors: Their History in Russia—Their Migration to Canada.* Philadelphia: Ferris and Leach, 1903.

Hawthorn, Harry B., ed. *The Doukhobors of British Columbia.* Toronto: J. M. Dent and Sons, 1955. A fair and objective presentation, with authentic documentation.

Holt, Simma. *Terror in the Name of God: The Story of the Sons of Freedom Doukhobors.* New York: Crown Publishers, 1965. A controversial account of the Svobodniki group by a Vancouver journalist.

Maude, Aylmer. *A Peculiar People: The Doukhobors.* London: Grant Richard, 1904. Maude was one of the leaders among those who helped the emigrant Doukhobors find sanctuary in Canada.

Popoff, Eli A. *An Historical Exposition on the Origin and Evolvement of the Basic Tenets of the Doukhobor Life-Conception.* Grand Forks, British Columbia: Iskra, n.d. [after August 1964]. A 58-page mimeographed brochure prepared for the National Museum of Canada by a leading member of the Grand Forks Orthodox Doukhobor community.

Woodcock, George, and Avakumovic, Ivan. *The Doukhobors.* New York: Oxford University Press, 1968. A substantial account of the Doukhobor movement by two professional historians. It should be read in conjunction with the careful and detailed review-article by Ethel Dunn, "Canadian and Soviet Doukhobors: An Examination of the Mechanisms of Social Change," *Canadian Slavic Studies* 4 (1970): 300-326.

Wright, J. F. C. *Slava Bohu: The Story of the Doukhobors.* New York: Farrar and Rinehart, 1940. This work presents the history of the Doukhobors in great detail, but some Doukhobors feel that it tends to overemphasize the shortcomings of the movement.

RUSSIAN MOLOKAN SPIRITUAL CHRISTIANS

Berokoff, John K. *Molokans in America.* Los Angeles, Calif.: John K. Berokoff (Whittier, Calif.: Stockton-Doty Trade

Press), 1969. A participant's account of the Molokan emigration from Russia to the New World between 1904 and 1912 and the subsequent experiences of the Molokans in America.

Bolshakoff, Serge. *Russian Nonconformity: The Story of "Unofficial" Religion in Russia.* Philadelphia: Westminster Press, 1950. Pp. 105-112. An account of Molokanism in Russia by a distinguished Russian Orthodox scholar.

Conybeare, Frederick Cornwallis. *Russian Dissenters.* New York: Russell and Russell, 1962. Pp. 289-326, "The Molokanye." This is an unaltered reprint of the orignial edition of 1921. Conybeare describes the Molokans of Russia on the basis of their own Confession of Faith of 1862 (printed at Geneva in 1865), the objective accounts of I. Yuzov (Uzov), Stollov, and Nikolai I. Kostomarov, and the admittedly hostile account of N. Ivanovskiy. He does not describe the dominant type of American Molokanism.

Rudametkin Maxim Gavrilovich (co-author). *Selections from the Book of Spirit and Life [Dukh i Zhizn], including the Book of Prayers and Songs.* John K. Berokoff, ed. and trans. Whittier, Calif.: Stockton Trade Press, 1966. This is the most comprehensive document available in English about the early history, the faith, and the worship of the Molokans. Included are a 12-page introduction by the editor-translator, a 37-page selection from the works of David Yesseyi[vi]ch (Feodor Ossipovich), 31 pages of doctrinal explanations by Rudametkin, 25 pages of his prophecies, 34 pages of his prayers and songs, 11 pages of excerpts from his letters, and a reissue of the now out-of-print 1944 English translation by Berokoff of *Russian Molokan Book of Prayers and Songs by Maxim G. Rudametkin, Written in 1858–1877 While Confined in the Monasteries of Salovetsk and Suzdal* (Los Angeles: Paul Ivanovich Samarin, 1944). Some of the Rudametkin material is taken from manuscripts in the translator's possession hitherto unpublished either in Russian or English. The remainder is abridged from the 773-page 1928 Russian edition of *Dukh i Zhizn* printed in Los Angeles.

Young, Pauline V. *The Pilgrims of Russian-Town (Obshchestvo Dukhovnykh Khristian Prygunov v Amerike): The Community of Spiritual Christian Jumpers in America, The Struggle of a Primitive Religious Society to Maintain Itself in an Urban Enviroment.* Chicago: University of Chicago Press, 1932. A very thorough sociological investigation into the Molokan community in Los Angeles four decades ago.

PART V

METHODIST CHURCHES

15. Methodism and the Methodist Church

Wesley and "the People Called Methodists"

John Wesley (1703–1791) and his younger brother Charles (1707–1788), both clergymen in the Church of England, stand in the forefront of the more than 20 million Methodist church members or 50 million Methodists in the world, including the nearly 15 million Methodist church members in the United States. Their revival movement in the eighteenth-century Church of England appreciably influenced the history of modern Christianity, especially in America. Charles Wesley remains one of Christendom's most influential hymn writers. His hundreds of hymns put into verse and music the theology his brother preached both in the open air and in humble chapels during England's early stages of industrialization. John Wesley (hereafter referred to as Wesley) traveled more than 200,000 miles during his life, most of them on horseback. Methodist ecumenical activity shows that the spirit of the Wesleys is still on pilgrimage.

Wesley wrote, translated, edited, or published more than four hundred books, brochures, pamphlets, and treatises during his long life. This mass of material has until recently been available to researchers only in woefully incomplete, poorly edited, and largely unannotated sources. Recently a breakthrough has occurred in deciphering his Oxford diaries, and enough new letters have been found to fill a large volume, while more than one hundred "unstandard" sermons, previously overlooked and unprinted, are being edited and soon will be published. The appearance of the first in a series of thirty-four volumes in a critical edition of his works brightens the future of Wesleyan research.[1]

In England "the People Called Methodists," as Wesley preferred to call them, were a religious society within the Church of England until after Wesley's death. In both England and the United States, Methodism was a religious society that eventually became a church body without the total loss of its character as a religious society. This fact predisposed Methodists toward ecumenism while at the same time often complicating efforts to arrive at a satisfactory self-definition in terms of theology.

The Methodist movement arose in a period of Western history which the eminent historian R. R. Palmer called "the age of democratic revolution."[2] Wesley was not alone in creating religious societies in the Church of England, but undoubtedly his revival efforts were part of the surge of interest in local control, democratic leveling, and the moderation of royal power. Commenting in 1760 on the refusal of a bishop to ordain one of his preachers, Wesley wrote in his *Journal*:

> . . . our church requires that clergymen should be men of learning, and to this end have a university education. But how many have a university education and yet no learning at all? Meantime one of eminent learning, as well as unblameable behavior, cannot be ordained "because he was not at the University!" What a mere farce is this! Who would believe that any Christian bishop would stoop to so poor an evasion?[3]

Wesley's use of lay preachers and his connectional system among the People Called Methodists showed his openness to the democratic currents that flowed between England and the American colonies.

The Age of Reason, or the Enlightenment, set the stage for the Wesleyan revival in the last half of the seventeenth century and in the eighteenth century. Wesley, a perennial debater, seemed to be debating many of the "givens" of the reason-oriented culture of his time. For one thing, reason was used increasingly as the chief way of discovering what is true and right. The "unknown" became in large measure the "not yet known" or "still to be discovered." Revelation became less important as the two classical authorities, the Bible and ancient classical literature, seemed to lose some of their traditional attractiveness. Supernatural events became increasingly suspect to rational people, and faith was understood more as rational assent than as dependence on God. Meanwhile, new scientific discoveries in the Scientific Revolution, and especially Newton's cosmology, helped to render God as an impersonal and nearly mechanistic being; the notion of divine intervention seemed distant. In this context it is not surprising that Wesley's notorious belief in the possibility of witchcraft, and his conviction that some of the physical manifestations of a convert's belief were stimulated by the finger of God, set him off from many of the "reasonable" theologians. The Age of Reason also stressed morality, or "duty," as the principal aim and content of Christianity. Wesley's attempt to connect "Christian perfection" with the righteousness of faith, to link love and faith, was his response to this thrust. But for Wesley holiness could be attained only through grace, not mere will power.[4]

The religious revival that was sweeping much of western Europe, the British Isles, and the American colonies during the early part of the eighteenth century was the context within which Wesley's movement received recognition and contemporary reaffirmation. Revival was in the air. It began first among the Pietists in Germany, who borrowed their share from the earlier Puritans. The Moravians spread the revival as a missionary church and had outposts in London and elsewhere. In New England, Jonathan Edwards and others contributed to the Great Awakening, which the English evangelical George Whitefield carried up and down the colonial coastline. The Welsh evangelical movement was followed by revival in the Scottish Highlands in 1739, preceded by a movement in Cornwall. In England the followers of Whitefield and the Countess of Huntingdon eventually left the established church, while a number of other non-Methodist evangelicals remained within the church. Most of the evangelicals in England, including Whitefield, differed from the Wesleys in that they tended to stress Calvinistic predestinarianism and frequently ended up as pastors of independent congregations. Gradually Wesley's followers were distinguished by their Arminian teaching and firm resolve to remain within the Church of England. Wesley's organizing genius was another asset of the People Called Methodists, as we shall see below.[5]

According to most standards, the Church of England stood in need of reform and revival. There was noticeable laxity in the ordering of worship and in pastoral oversight, and in large measure ecclesiastical authority had become an empty show of pomp while political maneuvering consumed energy otherwise channeled into spiritual initiatives. Erastian church polity held the church under tight control, and even the church's convocations had been suspended in 1714 by the government, depriving the church of machinery that could have been used for reform. The Act of Toleration allowed dissenters to organize outside the church, but in the process the Church of England was deprived of the zeal of many reform-minded people. One scholar sums up the situation succinctly: "Over all there hung a stifling miasma of apathy and stale devotion."[6]

The deistic rationalism of the Age of Reason, the stifling apathy of the Church of England, and the appearance of revival and reform movements in many areas of Western Christendom contributed to the development of the Wesleyan revival. John Fletcher of Madeley, a close associate of Wesley, summed up Methodism's mission as "to preach the doctrine of grace against the Socinians—the doctrine of justice against the Calvinists—and the doctrine of holiness against all the world."[7]

The fact that Methodism eventually separated from the Church of England was the result of Wesley's dashed and frustrated hopes for renewal within the church. The breach between Methodism and the Church of England, concretized after Wesley's death, was the result of a chasm that grew deeper and wider in the course of the Wesleyan revival. Some of the important "firsts" that contributed to the widening breach were Wesley's "submitting to be more vile," as he described it, by preaching in the open air in Bristol in the spring of 1739; his convening the first annual conference of preachers in London in 1744; and especially the conference's incorporation as a legal entity in 1784, as well as Wesley's ordination of preachers for America in the same year.[8] Late in his life Wesley distinguished three "rises" or experimental beginnings for his movement which pointed toward his lifelong goal of renewing the Church of England. In his *Short History of the People Called*

Methodists (1781) the seventy-eight year old seer distinguished three groups of people who met for Christian fellowship, in addition to normal worship in the parish church. "The first rise of Methodism," he wrote,

> was in November 1729, when four of us met together at Oxford; the second was at Savannah [Georgia] in April 1735, when twenty or thirty persons met at my house; the last was at London on [1 May 1738] when forty or fifty of us agreed to meet together every Wednesday evening, in order to a free conversation, begun and ended with singing and prayer.[9]

Born in an Anglican manse, Wesley was the child of the Reverend Samuel Wesley and his wife, Susanna. Both parents had been born into staunch Nonconformist families but even before their marriage had converted to the Church of England, becoming equally staunch Tory Anglicans. The couple had nineteen children, eleven of whom survived infancy. In 1709 young "Jackie" was rescued from the flaming rectory in Epworth along with his brother Charles. Wesley and his mother subsequently interpreted this rescue as a sign of providence. Wesley's mother was undoubtedly the greater influence of the two parents, since his father was very much preoccupied with his own scholarly interests and with the business of the unofficial convocations. He was born during his mother's longest period of freedom from pregnancy during her childbearing years. In 1711 she noted a special resolve to "be more particularly careful of the soul of this child." A reading of an account of Danish missionary work in Tranquebar influenced her, and she began to hold family prayers in the parsonage with as many as two hundred people attending, despite the accusation that she had formed a "conventicle." Once a week each child in the family had an hour or so for discussing spiritual and moral problems in the evening; Wesley's turn came on Thursday. His mother's influence was lifelong.[10] From his father he learned dogged commitment of the Church of England and to the church's tradition, available in books. Later in life he edited and republished some of his father's tracts, but refused to serve as his successor in the Epworth parish.

The salient traits of Wesley's character included strong-mindedness, something of a family trait; the absence of caution and faintheartedness; and a constitutional incapacity to do anything halfheartedly. The psychological pattern of his personality has been sketched by the Methodist scholar Albert C. Outler in this word picture:

> hard-driving, yet also sensitive; intense, yet also patient; detached, yet also charming; self-disciplined, yet also intensely emotional; opinionated, yet also curious; open to counsel, yet impervious to pressure; brusque with bad faith, yet also tolerant of contrary opinions.

Wesley's practice of recording his activities in minute detail provides the historian with more autobiographical information on him than most other major figures in the church's history. His published *Journal* is a wide-angle lens for viewing his activity and that of the People Called Methodists. But the *Journal* is not an intimate document since it was material extracted for publication by Wesley, to fill the practical needs of his followers and to further the Methodist revival. It was, says Outler, a "carefully constructed narrative of Wesley's involvement in what he regarded as an unparalleled renewal of essential Christianity."[11]

At Oxford University the tag "Methodist" was first placed on the Wesley brothers and several others in a small group dedicated to holiness of life. The term had been used in the seventeenth century to refer to the Amyraldists or Semi-Arminians, although there is no evidence of direct derivation. Educated at Charterhouse and Christ Church, Oxford, Wesley was elected fellow at Lincoln College there in 1726, after being ordained a deacon in 1725. This position assured him of financial security as long as he remained celibate. He moderated training classes in logic and lectured on Greek, and in 1728 he was ordained a priest. In several intervals between 1726 and 1729 he served as curate in Epworth and Wroot, proving himself to be an authoritarian priest and conscientious pastor, much like his father. His collegiate ordination helped him understand himself as a *minister extraordinarius* with an extraparochial license to preach anywhere, inasmuch as the chancellors and bishops of Oxford traditionally had the right to license preachers to preach throughout the kingdom. He later argued that "being ordained as Fellow of a College, I was not limited to any particular cure, but have an indeterminate commission to preach the Word of God in any part of the Church of England."[12] This argument lay at the foundation of the claim that he was only seeking to revive the Church of England.

In 1729 Wesley returned to Oxford as a full-time tutor. His brother Charles had organized a semi-monastic group for study of the Bible, frequent Communion, and mutual discipline. Wesley joined his brother and three others, and all showed keen interest in ancient liturgies and the piety of the fourth-century desert fathers. Undergraduates had all sorts of nicknames for the group: the Reforming Club, Bible Moths, Supererogation Men, Enthusiasts, and Methodists. Methodists was the name that stuck, and though Wesley disliked it he characteristically used it as a badge of honor, defining a Methodist as one "who lives according to the method laid down in the Bible," who believes and lives "the common principles of Christianity." The Oxford Methodists stressed attendance at Holy Communion (they were also called "Sacramentarians"), visited those who were sick or in prison, served the poor, and strictly observed the fasts of the ancient church on Wednesdays and Fridays. The pursuit of holiness required rules for achieving holiness for self-discipline and, as the acknowledged leader of the group, Wesley provided rules. The intention and general outline of his later *Rules* (1743) originated in the self-examination and rules for conduct composed for the pioneers at Oxford. Wesley later recognized the debt of the Methodist movement to the "fellowship of kindred minds" that functioned under a spiritual director at

Oxford; that was why he called this Holy Club "the first rise of Methodism."[13]

Wesley engaged in deep study of ancient Christian literature with the help of John Clayton, a patristics scholar and fellow "Methodist" at Oxford. In subsequent years he regarded the early church's thought and piety as "the normative pattern of catholic Christianity," according to Outler. Of special interest to him was Ephraem Syrus and the so-called "Macarius the Egyptian," who it has been discovered was actually closely linked to Gregory of Nyssa, the great Eastern Christian whose teaching on the quest for perfection deeply influenced Wesley. The ancients' description of "perfection" (*teleiosis*) as the goal (*skopos*) of the Christian life—and perfection as a process rather than a state—offered Wesley the opportunity to fuse the Eastern tradition of holiness as disciplined love with his own Anglican tradition of holiness as aspiring love, a fusion that later became his most distinctive doctrinal contribution to the Methodist movement.[14]

While his family tried to convince Wesley to assume his father's charge in Epworth, Wesley was reluctant, since the move would deprive him of the support offered by the Holy Club. In the same year that his father died (1735), he was invited by the Society for the Propagation of the Gospel to transfer the Holy Club to the colony of Georgia where its members could serve as missionaries to the Indians and colonists. John, Charles, and Benjamin Ingham, also a member of the club, set sail for Georgia late in 1735. Savannah was the place of Methodism's second "rise," but the experience was in many ways a trial for Wesley.

Soon after landing Wesley spent several hours during which he "revised Common Prayer Book." Bent on reform in a congregation that had all the marks of spiritual lassitude, he warned the pioneers in Georgia that he would follow strict ecclesiastical discipline, admonishing them publicly and privately, requiring prior notification for Holy Communion, dipping in baptism "all the children who were able to endure it," and as a servant of the Chuch of England, not a judge, to "keep to her regulations in all things." He read his principles to the congregation and then began his ministry. Clearly, at this time, the authority of the early fathers ran a close second to the Scriptures for Wesley, with reason a poor third. He engaged in a form of legalistic churchmanship that made him, one Wesley scholar notes, "more harsh and tactless than at any other period in his life." He insisted on rebaptizing dissenters before admitting them to the Lord's Supper and took a condescending attitude toward Lutherans and their pastor in the Salzburger settlement at Ebenezer.[15]

Wesley was widely accused of being too much of a churchman, but also of leaving the Church of England simultaneously by two doors. To some his practices smacked of Roman Catholicism, while others saw him as a Puritan separatist. Official charges were leveled against him when he refused, for what he regarded as canonical irregularities, to administer Communion to a woman who had been his potential bride, but who had chosen to marry another man. The woman's new husband retorted with a suit for slander. The charges examined by the Grand Jury dealt almost exclusively with his excessive zeal and strict adherence to Anglican rubrics. A number of his religious experiments drew fire, including his use of laymen in parish work to catechize and, in emergency, to preach and exercise pastoral care; his use of three women in some of these capacities; extempore prayer and extempore preaching; preaching in the open air; and serving as an itinerant preacher with a number of stations in smaller settlements in Georgia. He also came to know and admire the love feast. He introduced the singing of hymns (rather than metrical psalms) in public worship and sacramental worship, publishing the first American hymn book, *A Collection of Psalms and Hymns,* in Charleston, South Carolina, in 1737. Most important were the societies he organized in Savannah and Frederica for religious fellowship apart from ordered public worship, gatherings he later called the "second rise of Methodism." He subdivided these societies, in the Moravian pattern, into more intimate "bands," an act that led to the charge that he had instituted the Roman Catholic confessional, since mutual confession was part of the band's activity.[16]

A positive development for Wesley was his growing acquaintance with the Moravians both while sailing to Georgia and in the colony. After he returned to England early in 1738 he spent much time with the Moravian missionary in London, Peter Böhler, and for a time joined with him in a pietistic society in Fetter Lane. He felt very uncertain in faith and unclear about his future; the Georgia mission had many of the marks of failure. But one indication of growing spiritual fervor was his adoption of the practice of praying extemporaneously in public after his return.[17] With some remorse Wesley wrote these words in his *Journal* immediately upon returning:

> But what have I learned myself [in the two years and almost four months since I left my native country]? Why, what I the least of all suspected, that I, who went to America to convert others, was never myself converted to God.[18]

The year 1738 was for Wesley the *annus mirabilis*. Firmly convinced of the need for the Christian to live a disciplined life aimed at perfection and holiness, through a series of personal experiences he added the other crucial factor, assurance in the righteousness of faith. Along with many in the Church of England, he had previously been convinced that the "faith of assurance" or inner certitude was merely an intensification of the "faith of adherence" to the means of grace. Doubts persisted, and he kept seeking some inward assurance of faith. In this year, experientially he was able to fuse justifying faith and the sure confidence that by Christ's merit *his own* sins were forgiven. Once and for all he came to know that faith alone is the sole ground of reconciliation. But he was no less insistent that God designed the righteousness of faith to promote the Christian's righteousness in holy living.[19]

The most striking influence may well have been his famous "Aldersgate experience" on May 24, 1738. "In the evening," he recounted in his *Journal,*

> I went very unwillingly to a society in Aldersgate Street [rather heavily domi-
> nated by Moravians], where one was reading Luther's Preface to the Epistle to
> the Romans. About a quarter before nine, while he was describing the change
> which God works in the heart through faith in Christ, I felt my heart strangely
> warmed. I felt I did trust in Christ, Christ alone for salvation; and an assurance
> was given me that he had taken away *my* sins, even *mine,* and saved *me* from
> the law of sin and death.

Despite the fact that this experience has received such widespread attention
in accounts of Wesley's life, he made only one other explicit reference to it
in the course of his writings. One reason may have been that after the Aldersgate experience Wesley's rift with the Moravians, largely caused by his
aversion to their purported antinomianism, became so severe that perhaps he
did not want to give credit to their auspices for such an important event in
his life.[20]

But it is clear that Aldersgate was merely one in a series of turning points
for Wesley in the year 1738 as he made the trek from university don to
missionary to evangelist. His *Journal* for the next six months recorded numerous instances of severe spiritual depression and anxiety; it also mentioned
moments of spiritual exaltation prior to that date. The change from faith in
faith to faith itself, from "aspiration to assurance," was a long journey that
lasted until the spring of 1739. In the previous summer he visited the Moravian
settlements at Herrnhut and Marienborn in Germany, but was disturbed by
the supposed self-righteousness of the Moravians just as he was heartened by
their examples of "the full assurance of Christian faith." In October, while
walking from London to Oxford, he read "the truly surprising narrative of the
conversions lately wrought in and about the town of North Hampton in New
England." This account of Jonathan Edwards's revival made a forceful impact, and Wesley soon published an abridgment of the account and, even
alter, an extract of Edwards's *Treatise Concerning the Religious Affections*
after filtering out the high Calvinism of Edwards.[21]

In 1739 Wesley preached faith with conviction until others received the
assurance of faith, and then his faith was confirmed by theirs. This experience
seemed to solidify and stabilize him, giving him a sense of mission that endured until his death. What is surprising is that Wesley, always concerned with
following the laws and regulations of the church, found himself preaching not
in churches but in the open air! As he carried the revival to the fields and
to "Christ's poor," the People Called Methodists gathered strength as a revival
movement.

On March 20 Wesley wrote in a letter to a former member of the Oxford
Holy Club who had recently taken a parish assignment,

> I look upon *all the world* as *my parish*—thus far I mean, that in whatever part
> of it I am, I judge it meet, right and my bounden duty to declare unto all that
> are willing to hear me the glad tidings of salvation. This is the work which
> I know God has called me to, and sure I am that his blessing attends it.

This claim was the evangelistic teaching that undergirded the Methodist principle that itinerant Methodist preachers were bound only to territorial limits set by God. Eight days later in his *Journal* he spoke of entering upon a "new period" in his life. He was referring to his decision, after much bibliomancy and lot drawing, to share the evangelist Whitefield's extraparochial ministry in Bristol, which involved preaching in the fields. Undoubtedly this decision was one of the great ecclesiastical watersheds in his life.[22]

Wesley had engaged in open-air preaching on several earlier occasions—on board ship, in Georgia, and the previous November. But the deliberate practice of preaching outside parish churches was quite another matter. He studied the Sermon on the Mount and listened carefully as Whitefield, preparing for his second trip to America, sought his leadership for the revival he had stirred in Bristol. Wesley reported that on April 2 "at four in the afternoon I submitted to be more vile, and proclaimed in the [Bristol] highways the glad tidings of salvation, speaking from a little eminence in a ground adjoining to the city, to about three thousand people." The response was overwhelming, and he began to experience the kind of success described by Edwards in New England. In a remarkable way his spiritual life showed an equilibrium that had been missing to this point.[23]

This open-air preaching was the beginning of a life of traveling and preaching. In 1765 Wesley reported that he preached about eight hundred sermons a year. England in three seasons of the year was a green, pleasant land for the itinerant preacher to travel. The open-air preaching bestowed a sense of romantic naturalism and back-to-nature to people who felt somewhat estranged and outcast. "As he preached in Cornwall in the Gwennap pit," writes the English Methodist scholar Gordon Rupp,

> with his back to the last rays of a setting sun, in the quiet of an English summer evening, where not a breath, not a leaf, not one of thousands of human beings stirred, and all melted into one in the growing darkness as they hung on the words of one who commended his Saviour—how right he was, how much more solemn and beautiful and majestic the scene which God had wrought than any Gothic imitation, how much less marvelous the acoustics of the new preaching boxes in Norwich or on City Road, London.

In 1790, when he was nearly ninety years old, Wesley preached his last sermon in the open air under a tree at Winchelsea. His text was an old favorite: "The kingdom of God is at hand; repent and believe the gospel."[24] His final sermon came a week before his death in 1791.

The deliberate decision to engage in open-air preaching, apart from episcopally dedicated sanctuaries, which in most cases were off limits to the Methodist preachers, was part of a larger change in Wesley's view on valid church government that occurred between 1739 and 1745. The refusal to acknowledge the territorial restrictions of parish and diocese was allied with a somewhat cavalier attitude toward the bishop's authority. Wesley continued to insist that the movement remain within the Church of England, but his actions often signaled a different message.[25]

The year 1739 showed increasing Methodist activity in places other than parish churches and society rooms, as well as increasing tension with ecclesiastical authorities in Bristol and London. Wesley remained in Bristol five months, preaching in the open, organizing bands, and beginning to construct the first Methodist chapel, which he prudently called a new "room" or "schoolhouse." Wesley's association with Whitefield, who already was in ecclesiastical trouble, helped sour relations with the Church of England.[26]

Connectionalism and the Church of England

Following a pattern taken largely from the German Pietists, Wesley understood the Methodist societies to be *ecclesiolae in ecclesia,* religious societies within the church working for revival in the Church of England. This working assumption implied a negative judgment against the ordinary polity of the Church of England, which resisted the revival effort in numerous ways. In a positive sense, it was assumed that the church was best defined in terms of its action and function, not as an institution of fixed episcopal polity. The growing strength of the Methodist revival rested largely on the organizational genius of Wesley, who in a masterful way connected all of the Methodist societies. As long as he provided the focus and stood at the center, the societies would continue to function in England as *ecclesiolae in ecclesia,* but his ordination of men to serve in other lands (1784) and his death opened the way for radical changes in polity among the People Called Methodists in England and the United States.

As far as Wesley was concerned, the basic element in the description of the church was the demand for results. It has been said that he evaluated every means by the results it obtained. The church itself was an instrument of God's grace, just as the Lord's Supper was a "converting" ordinance; the episcopacy entailed no theological doctrine in his mind, since basically the bishop was an overseer who was to be judged by the results he obtained.[27] He had settled for himself the question of religious authority, agreeing with the Anglican triad of Scripture, reason, and antiquity as these were reinforced by what one author calls "an intuitive individualist approach deriving in part both from Pietist and mystical influence." However, the appeal to reason had become a form of urgent pragmatism in 1749, and it was for this reason, he argued, that the Methodist connectional polity *worked*, and since it did it must be accepted as part of the divine plan. In sum, "tradition had become of far less importance to him than spiritual success."[28] Working in the period of proto-industrialization in England, Wesley seemed to be mimicking the industrialists in their efforts to order the production process in the most rational way. His connectional polity system and constant interest in results also show the impress of the Age of Reason; thus while Wesley avoided the pervasive rationalism of the culture in his theology, it left indelible marks on his career.

Already by 1746 it was clear that for Wesley the essence of the church and its ministry was functional rather than institutional in nature. In a characteristic and distinctive way he stressed that the church is defined in the action of its witness and mission rather than by its form of polity.[29] A contemporary theologian writes that "the heart of Wesley's ecclesiology . . . is his creative yoking of an emphasis on the *koinonia* of believers with an emphasis on the missionary (evangelistic) character of their calling," an ecclesiastical vision that was given visible expression in the cluster of structures (bands, classes, societies, conferences, itinerancy, lay preachers) which he organized. The church historian Martin Schmidt claims that Wesley "was the first in the whole course of church history who realized that the task of Christendom in the modern world is to be defined as mission."[30]

Wesley's negative feelings toward the bishops of the Church of England derived in part from his understanding of his own mission as a minister extraordinary, called by God to rectify some of the insufficiencies of the ordinary ministry as it functioned under the bishops. He failed to attack any of the bishops in print until 1744. While in 1742 he directly attacked episcopal authority for closing diocesan pulpits to the Methodists, the attack was not published until 1749. But in the first conference of Methodist preachers in 1744 there was a clear answer to the question, "How far is it our duty to obey the bishops?"; "In all things indifferent. And on this ground of obeying them we should observe the canons, so far as we can with a safe conscience." Episcopal authority to silence the preaching of Wesley and his preachers was not conceded.[31]

The question of the value of episcopal succession, as a unique transmission of spiritual grace in ordination, was another area of Wesley's thought that changed as the Methodist revival progressed. Until 1745 he seemed to think that in this respect bishops were of the *esse* rather than the *bene esse* of the church. In that year he gave his last known testimony favoring the argument of apostolic succession, which he threw overboard together with the divine right of the episcopacy in 1747. His earliest published denial of the doctrine that the church's essence was the episcopal succession from the apostles appeared in 1760. For Wesley true apostolic succession, says the eminent scholar Frank Baker, "consisted in having the apostolic spirit, a possibility and a responsibility not only for every preacher, but even for every Christian."[32] In any case, Wesley conceived the continuity of succession as having been maintained by the presbyterial rather than the episcopal office, per se.

By midcentury (1755) Wesley was quite convinced that there were two orders of ministry in the church. Of the two orders, he wrote that the one had "power only to preach and (sometimes) baptise; the other to ordain also and administer the Lord's Supper." The higher order, which alone could administer the sacraments and ordain, was subdivided into bishops and presbyters. His *Explanatory Notes upon the New Testament,* first published that year, repeatedly insisted that his fundamental principles of polity were not inconsistent with the Scripture even though they were not prescribed there.[33] By this point in time he no longer held that ordination necessarily conferred divine grace, imparting an "indelible character" to the priest.

Later in the century Wesley wrote to the bishop of London, who traditionally exercised jurisdiction over the American colonies, begging him to consider the great need for ordained ministers in the area south of the St. Lawrence River, and complaining about the bishop's decision not to ordain a Methodist preacher to serve a little flock in Newfoundland. "In this respect," he wrote in the letter of 1780,

> also I mourn for poor America, for the sheep scattered up and down therein. Part of them have no shepherds at all, particularly in the northern colonies; and the case of the rest is little better, for their own shepherds pity them not.

While Wesley was not openly challenging the bishops to ordain Methodist preachers nor threatening to take that action if they did not, he was probably positioning himself so that later he could say that the bishops offered no help for the problems that Methodists faced in the struggling new country of the United States.[34] Four years later he acted decisively to ordain Methodist preachers, but for some time his ecclesiology had been functional rather than institutional in nature, with corollary opinions about the orders of ministry and their functions.

Wesley's connectionalism, an organizational system that masterfully united leaders and followers in the Methodist revival around his leadership, was constructed in the face of unsympathetic clergymen in the Church of England as well as persecuting mobs that opposed the Enthusiasts. Although not all elements of the system were of equal importance, it included the society (the first organized by Wesley in London in 1739), lay preachers (first used in 1741), the class (first formed in 1742), the rules of society (1743), the Annual Conference (beginning in 1744), and circuits uniting the societies (1746). The whole organization functioned on the basis of itinerant preachers, open-air preaching, and Wesley's final authority as the movement's leader. The connectional system was a halfway house of sorts between a traditional religious society and a new church. The old Anglican societies were clergy-led and exclusively restricted to Anglicans; lay assistants helped Wesley carry out his superintendency of the Methodist societies, which, in contrast with the dissenting churches, were not thought to be self-governing congregations.[35] Wesley relied on an authoritarian system during his lifetime and recommended an aristocratic system under democratic form after his death when he transferred his personal oversight of the whole system to one hundred trusted preachers selected for that task.

The typical Methodist society was organized whenever a self-sustaining group was evangelized. It became the basic unit for administration and worship. Like the older Angelican societies, Methodist societies were dedicated to the cultivation of "holiness of heart and life," and they too had stewards to look after monetary concerns. But Wesley's absolute authority in the society was one of its marked characteristics. Serviced in most cases by lay preachers, the societies assumed all the functions of a church except the sacraments; for many years, in fact, Wesley opposed any effort to conduct services during the hours when the local parish's sacramental services were held. Long before Wesley died it was determined that the only doctrine that could be taught in the Methodist "preaching houses" was that which conformed with Wesley's *Notes upon the New Testament* and his first four volumes of published sermons. The *Rules of the United Societies* (1743) was the standard to which all members had to conform; later the Annual Conference of preachers added other regulations. The societies conducted common worship, which included the reading of Scripture, prayer, hymns, and preaching.[36]

The class soon became the most important working unit for edifying and disciplining the society's members, since each one belonged to a class. The lay leader was used as a lieutenant in the pastoral supervision of the eleven other members in weekly class meetings that could be either perfunctory or inquisitorial. In any case, each person had a sense of "belonging" in these small groups. Soon after class meetings began functioning in 1742, "tickets" were used to admit members; the ticket was renewed each quarter as long as the person lived in conformity with the standards of conduct.[37] The class was Wesley's way of avoiding the evanescent "ropes of sand" that he saw in Whitefield's movement.

Basically the band was another form of the class, although usually its size did not exceed eight persons. Select bands were composed of those who were extraordinarily mature in devotion and life. Penitent bands were made up of those who lapsed momentarily from standards of conduct and were engaged in a trial period before readmission to full participation in the society. Both the band and the class had lay leaders.[38]

The itinerant preachers, who spread the Word of God in open air and in Methodist meetinghouses, were usually not ordained clergymen of the Church of England but lay preachers enlisted in the Wesleyan cause. Wesley's regular travels were made in the triangle that linked London, Bristol, and Newcastle-on-Tyne; most of the Methodist work was concentrated in this area, which included the burgeoning cities of the Midlands. But much of the English countryside was unaffected by the itinerant preachers. Wesley felt so deeply about the lay preachers that he wrote in 1755, "If we cannot stop a separation without stopping lay preachers, the case is clear—we cannot stop it at all." Moving under the iron will and assignment policy of the founder, the preachers regularly traveled the circuits, seven of which serviced all of the societies when the circuit system was created in 1746. Two or three preachers traveled each circuit, changing location monthly; in the next year there were nine circuits, and preachers changed locations every two months. Not all the preachers traveled circuits. Among those who worked in local areas were several women, including Sarah Crosby, who later became an itinerant field preacher.[39]

The itinerant system linked the Methodist societies in a "connection," or living unity, in a way that Wesley's limited travel could not have accomplished. In order to retain his authority and instruct the itinerant lay preachers, in 1744 Wesley called the first conference of preachers in a move that had lasting significance for Methodism. The Welsh Calvinist Methodists had been following the practice for four years, usually meeting monthly or quarterly. The first conference, which soon became the most important element in Methodist polity, was composed of five clergymen and four lay preachers whom Wesley summoned to confer with him. The purpose of the conference was to offer advice and consultation to the leader as he arrived at decisions. It was understood that Wesley would be guided by majority opinion although government by majority vote did not occur during his lifetime. The records of the early conferences show that Wesley was concerned with the lay preachers having sound doctrine as the basis for good preaching. In 1749 he issued two documents that summarized, in the same question-and-answer format used in the conference proceedings, the decisions that had been reached on doctrine and polity. The first reported the basic theological emphases of the preachers in 1744–1746 and 1747; it came to be known as the "Doctrinal Minutes." The second discussed the polity and administrative matters of these conferences as well as the one in 1748; it was called the "Disciplinary Minutes." Theologically the Methodists accepted the historic creeds, their interpretation in the Thirty-Nine Articles, the *Homilies* and Liturgy of the Church of England. Doctrinally the main task of the conference was to explore the theology of salvation and what Wesley called "the Methodist doctrine." Also discussed were proper methods of preaching the doctrines.[40] Wesley considered the lay itinerant ministers to be engaged in an extraordinary form of ministry, like himself.

Wesley's connectional system, especially the classes and societies, was designed for people who felt estranged from church and society. From Wesley and his lay preachers these people heard the good news that God justifies the outcasts, trains his people, and makes them his subjects. Wesley placed them into a network of care structures where they learned to read, grow, and interact as a community. He also developed health dispensaries for primitive health care and published "what to do" pamphlets on such nagging problems as hygiene, drunkenness, and thrift. His societies were more flexible and adaptable, as well as more unified under a common leader, than any other religious societies of his day. But, a noted authority on Wesley adds, "they also came much nearer to offering something like a complete substitute for the parish church and its ordained ministry."[41]

Without question Wesley's views on the nature and authority of church and ministry had changed appreciably by 1755, but as a man of action he was less inclined to formulate a new doctrine of the church than to try to reform the church's ills. That was why any "deliberate separation from the Church of England [that] took place during Wesley's ministry was primarily in the realm of deeds rather than of thought." By 1769 at the latest Wesley knew that it was impossible to link the Methodists societies with the evangelical party in the Church of England, and increasingly during the 1760s and 1770s he turned his attention toward the movement's future after his death, whether in or out of the church.[42]

An early sign of this earnestness was his discussion with the itinerant preachers in the Conference of 1760 of plans to ensure the continuation of Methodism after his death. Three years later he published the most complete summary of Methodist polity to date in the "Large Minutes," a document that showed him leaning toward denominationalism even though the move was clearly disavowed. The minutes carefully described how legally to license Methodist premises for public worship. Wesley also provided an elaborate model deed designed to safeguard Methodist premises for the use of Methodist societies while he lived and after he died. This was an important sign of the increasing sense of denominational self-identity among the Methodists.[43]

A special problem was that few Methodists could receive Communion from their spiritual fathers since very few of the field preachers were ordained as clergy in the Church of England. Among other efforts to deal with this problem, Wesley turned to episcopal ordination from outside the national church. In 1763 he befriended Bishop Erasmus, a Greek who claimed to be bishop of Arcadia. His claims were substantitated to Wesley's satisfaction, and in 1764 Wesley asked him to ordain John Jones, a physician turned preacher. While Wesley was away from London, Erasmus was encouraged to ordain another preacher, and two other times he came from Amsterdam to ordain groups of Methodist preachers without Wesley's knowledge. Wesley acted swiftly to bring the situation under control; he dismissed from the Methodist societies and from their duties those whom he accused of buying ordination, but apparently continued to recognize Jones's ordination.[44]

One other sign of increasing estrangement from the Church of England was the Methodists' burial ground behind the New Chapel, which was built in London in 1777. While not used until 1782, the cemetery showed a degree of ecclesiastical self-sufficiency and was evidence that Wesley's words (he said that episcopal consecration of buildings and grounds was "a thing purely indifferent" and "a mere relic of Romish superstition") were not empty.[45]

The Methodists also took action to provide Holy Communion to their own societies as the revival matured. Up to about 1741, members of the societies were urged to commune frequently at their parish churches. Where this proved impossible, Wesley and other ordained men made extensive use of Communion with the sick to meet the expediency, extending the Communion for a sick individual to a large company of the person's friends. Wesley ensured that no services were held during the hours of public service in local churches, and sometimes led his followers there en masse for worship and

Communion. Persistent interest in conducting Communion under their own auspices led the Methodists to use an episcopally consecrated Huguenot chapel in London temporarily in 1741. A permanent solution was achieved in London in 1743 when they secured a lease on another consecrated Huguenot chapel, in which Wesley and other ordained clergy conducted the Communion service. This was the beginning of congregational Methodist Communion services, but in Bristol and elsewhere the expedient of Communion with the sick was used as late as the 1760s. In 1766 Wesley continued to claim that the Lord's Supper was not being administered in Methodist preaching houses, but the societies pressured for this sacramental mystery in their midst. It is difficult to determine precisely when the first Communion was held in an episcopally unconsecrated Methodist building. In 1741 Charles Wesley held a service in a school in Kingswood, and by 1774 if not earlier the sacrament was distributed at the Foundery where the societies met for worship in London. Wesley firmly refused to permit the nonordained itinerant preachers to administer the sacrament until 1784, when he assumed the power of ordination, and then not in England.[46]

As a strong churchman, Wesley insisted on the need for sacramental worship while recognizing that it could not be adequately supplied through his unordained preachers. While permitting his preachers to bury the dead, he insisted that they should not baptize, threatening that he would "drop all the preachers who will not drop this. Christ has sent them not to baptize, but to preach the Gospel." He strongly supported infant baptism and believed that baptism in some way conferred grace on the child, or at least began the process of regeneration (although he also insisted that another kind of regeneration was possible for adults apart from this sacramental rite). He was a pioneer in urging sprinkling as permissible and desirable (1755), and vacillated on the question of whether or not the use of the sign of the cross on the child was superstitious. In 1756 he prepared an abridged version of his father's longer tract on baptism. Between 1756 and 1758 he dropped the requirement that "an episcopal administrator" was necessary for Christian baptism.[47]

Since Wesley regarded baptism as the proper qualification for admission to the Lord's Supper, he bypassed confirmation as an optional rite of dubious value. In 1745 he published *Hymns on the Lord's Supper*, a collection of more than 150 eucharistic hymns by him and Charles, which included a preface. The work plied the Anglican middle way between an allegorical interpretation of the Supper and extreme eucharistic realism. In 1787 he published a sermon from fifty years earlier (borrowed first from Robert Nelson) on "The Duty of Constant Communion." It stressed practice rather than doctrine, partly to counteract those who denied the need of any means of grace in view of the all-sufficiency of faith, and those who found vital Methodist preaching services preferable to formal liturgy. Wesley described the Lord's Supper as a memorial and a means of grace through which God's grace was made available to the expectant soul. Christ, the one unique sacrifice, made the sacrifice's benefits available to the believer, while the communicant offered himself as a willing sacrifice to God. Wesley viewed the sacrament as a converting and confirming ordinance. The sacrament as a converting ordinance was one of his distinctive contributions. He personally was a frequent communicant, communing more than forty times on Sunday's and fifty-eight times on weekdays in the year between June 1740 and May 1741. Toward the end of his life he received the sacrament on the average every five days.[48]

In 1784 Wesley irrevocably severed himself and Methodism from the Church of England. In that year he legally incorporated Methodism as a distinct denomination, prepared and published drastic revisions of the Anglican Thirty-Nine Articles and Book of Common Prayer, and embraced ordination by presbyters in practice as well as in theory. But still he denied, characteristically, that any irrevocable breach had been made.[49] In many ways these actions were the logical culmination of a long process.

A year earlier the conference had asked Wesley to make legal provisions for Methodism after his death. In February of 1784 he signed, sealed, and delivered to the High Court of the Chancery "The Revd. John Wesley's Declaration and Appointment of the Conference of the People Called Methodists," which listed the names and addresses of preachers who "have been and now are and do on the day of the date hereof constitute the members of the said Conference." Wesley had selected only 100 of the 188 men who were his preachers for inclusion on this list. The document's primary purpose was to define "Conference" in legal terms so as to secure the preaching houses for use by preachers who followed Wesley's ideals. The deed nowhere mentioned the relation of the societies to the Church of England. Clearly after 1784 "his societies were fully incorporated for spiritual purposes never approved of by any ecclesiastical court, purposes to be carried out primarily by laymen not answerable to parish clergy or diocesan officials, in buildings held in trust for a private organization subject to no supervision by the Established Church."[50]

The Reverend Thomas Coke, who played an important role in helping Wesley draw up the deed and who was later a formative figure in American Methodism, was a pivotal person as well in the ordinations that Wesley performed in 1784. Approaching death, Wesley undoubtedly was concerned about the future of the nearly 75,000 People Called Methodists in England; another pressing problem was the new situation that American Methodists faced, both because the colonies were now independent and because the Anglican church in the new nation was in desperate straits. In 1784 Wesley ordained two men, Whatcoat and Vasey, as "elders" for "baptizing and administering the Lord's Supper" in the new nation; he also "appointed," "set apart," and/or "ordained" Coke as superintendent over "the Flock of Christ," indicating as well that the young Francis Asbury, who was already serving in the new nation, should also function in this role.

Wesley took action in view of the end of the Revolutionary War in the fall of 1783, his earlier appeal to the bishop of London to ordain Methodist preachers for the colonies, and the decision of some Methodist preachers in the southern colonies to ordain themselves. His letter to the American Methodists on September 10, 1784, described some of the circumstances that precipitated his decision. He also had before him the recent example of the Countess of Huntingdon's Connection, in which two clergymen seceded from the Church of England in 1783 while six candidates for ministry were ordained.[51]

In 1784 Wesley presented to the Annual Conference of Methodist preachers the needs of America and his plan to send Coke and several volunteers to help, but discussion of the Deed of Declaration overshadowed this concern. Only senior preachers were informed of the plan to ordain, and they unanimously opposed the plan, although they recognized Wesley's determination to act. About a month later the ordinations occurred in Bristol. At five o'clock in the morning on September 1 Wesley, Coke, and Creighton gathered with Whatcoat and Vassey at John Castleman's residence. The public record indicates that these two were "appointed" to "serve the desolate sheep in America," but Wesley's shorthand diary read, "ordained RD Whatcoat and T. Vasey." They were ordained deacons one day and elders (presbyters) the next. Coke, already ordained in the same succession as Wesley, was "set apart," according to the signed certificate, to be a "superintendent," but Wesley's diary read simply, "Ordained Coke." (The unclarity of this action helped stimulate the enduring discussion in American Methodism about the definition of the office of bishop or superintendent.) Since Coke as well as Wesley was already a presbyter, Wesley probably understood the act to mean that Coke was being set apart for a special function as his deputy. Clearly his task would include transmitting ministerial orders to others, as he had already done with Vasey and Whatcoat.[52]

Wesley deliberately conducted the ordinances in private and deliberately tried to restrict the circulation of the letter to his American preachers. His brother Charles was in Bristol at the time, but apparently he did not learn of the happenings until nearly two months later. His poetic pen was capable of expressing deep anger, for he then wrote,

> So easily are Bishops made
> By man's or woman's whim?
> Wesley his hands on Coke hath laid
> But who laid hands on him?

Charles was deeply dismayed by his brother's presumption and was alienated thereafter from the movement.

It is highly doubtful that senility led Wesley to take these steps in 1784, despite his brother's charge that "twas age that made the breach, not he!" Following his conscience, his understanding of God's will, and "the leadings of providence," he acted as he saw fit. Old age did not strike until suddenly in 1789 he reportedly physical changes that showed exhaustion unto death.[53]

Wesley knew that nonseparation from the Church of England would continue to strengthen and protect his own authority within the Methodist societies, but the case in America was a special one.

He had prepared himself much earlier for this step both theoretically and theologically. He was eventually led to assume the powers of ordination by his early reading of seventeenth-century works by Edward Stillingfleet and Lord Peter King; in fact, he mentioned King's work in his letter to the American preachers. In 1785 he wrote to an old friend that "I am now as firmly attached to the Church of England as I ever was since you knew me. But meantime I know myself to be as real a Christian bishop as the archbishop of Canterbury. Yet I always resolved, and am so still, never to act as such except in case of necessity."[54] In 1784 necessity and freedom were one for Wesley.

Other ordinations by Wesley followed in rapid succession. In 1785 he ordained men for Scotland, adding four more in 1786 for a total of twelve by 1789. In 1785 he ordained preachers for Newfoundland, Nova Scotia, and Antigua, and in 1787 he ordained two for Canada and the West Indies. Five more were ordained for overseas in 1788, and at least one (Alexander Mather) for England. This drastic step was part of Wesley's intention to have Mather serve as a "superintendent" (like Coke) in England—as his successor. Clearly he took the step to assure an ordained ministry for English Methodism after his death. In 1789 he ordained two more men for English work. Altogether he had ordained twenty-seven preachers to the rank of presbyter and commissioned one, with Coke, as superintendent. He continued to insist that he was a loyal member and minister of the Church of England. In the midst of his ordaining activities, he wrote in 1787 that "when the Methodists leave the Church of England God will leave them."[55]

After 1786 Wesley increasingly used the phrase "Church of God" both in descriptions of the "catholic or universal church" and the Methodist societies. In 1789 he referred to "any of the Churches of God that are under my care." Sermon treatises also explicated the phrase. Regulations adopted in the Conference of 1786 seemed to open the way for many societies in rural and urban areas to become almost independent of their parish churches, but Wesley watched carefully so that liberty did not become license.[56]

After his death English Methodism survived the strain despite difficulty. Few preachers or societies left the fellowship. The Plan of Pacification of 1795 provided a working compromise in Methodist-Anglican relations; the first major secession occurred two years later.

Wesleyan Theology

Wesley's theological achievements have not usually been given their due. While he was no theologian's theologian, Wesley most certainly was not the theological bumbler some make him out to be in their search for the patron saint of theological indifferentism. He was a folk-theologian who did his theologizing on the run. But seldom has a mass evangelist been so deeply immersed in classical culture, open to "modern" science and social change, and aware of the living resources in Christian tradition.[57] In terms of theology, he was a borrower par excellence. One of his major interpreters asserts that he adapted

> the prime article of justification by faith, from the reformers (Anglican) of the sixteenth century; the emphasis on the assurance of faith, from the Moravian pietists; the ethical notions of divine-human synergism, from the ancient Fathers of the Church; the idea of the Christian life as devotion, from Taylor, a Kempis, Law (and Scougal), the vision and program of "perfection" . . . from Gregory of Nyssa via "Macarius."

His self-consciously Anglican theology had no exact counterpart, partly because it was forged by the events of the revival that he headed. While most of his references to Luther and Calvin were largely negative, he drew some features from the left wing of Protestantism.[58]

The charge that Wesley was theologically indifferent may have originated in part in a misreading of his distinction between truth and opinion. He carefully distinguished between essential doctrine and "opinions," and then regularly condemned the elevation of opinions to too high a level. Underlying this distinction was his understanding of the difference between faith and all conceptualizations of faith. This enabled him to write, "as to all opinions *which do not strike at the root of Christianity,* we think and let think." Similarly, near the end of his life he insisted that "orthodoxy, or right *opinions* is at best a slender part of religion, if it can be allowed any part at all." He continually stressed that religious reality lies deeper than religious conceptuality; the reflection on reality must not be confused with reality itself.[59] The first conference of preachers (1744) showed his deep concern with the doctrinal issues that were agitating the new "societies"; it took up the questions "What to teach?" "How to teach?" and "What to do?" (doctrinal standards, evangelism and nurture, and discipline and ethics).

Wesley apparently felt no compulsion to draw up a single comprehensive summary of his theology, since there seemed to be no practical need for such a document. This did not prevent him from compiling a number of short doctrinal summaries that are scattered throughout his writings, whose purpose it was to edify and guide the societies spiritually and ethically. But the absence of a single comprehensive document does not mean that Wesley lacked organic unity in his thought.[60]

Wesley's concept of theological authority included four primary elements. He spoke of Scripture as "original charter of Christianity. We appeal to this to the written word," he wrote in 1788 and in numerous other places. Historic Christian teaching, for Wesley specifically the witness of the patristic age, was a reliable aid in the process of probing and understanding Scripture. Reason, primarily cogent argumentation and logical statement, was a help in sound theologizing. The fourth element was that the truth of Scripture and tradition had to be experienced in the heart. The theologian is to be grasped by the truth, through the Spirit's charism of personal conviction. This four-fold witness served as the touchstone of authority in doctrine. For Wesley the weight of personal experience was particularly important, moved as he was by his own experience and the experiences of others.[61]

Through study, personal experience and the leadership he exerted in the Methodist revival, Wesley fused two rather distinct and, according to some, divergent interpretations of Christian faith and life. His theology attempted to avoid the two extremes and to balance the two polarities. He developed a theological fusion of "faith and good works, Scripture and tradition, revelation and reason, God's sovereignty and human freedom, universal redemption and conditional election, Christian liberty and ordered polity, the assurance of pardon and the risks of 'falling from grace,' original sin and Christian perfection." In his description of these conjunctions he tediously insisted that God retained the initiative while people responded. As a revivalist he was interested in saving people for Christian living, and at the deepest level of theological inquiry he was engaged in fusing the Eastern Christian emphasis on ontological participation with God (*metousia theou*) and the Western theme of forensic pardon. His alternative was faith alone, working by love, aimed at holy living.[62]

Wesley's constant problematic was soteriology, the nature of the Christian life. His distinctive undertaking, unmatched by any other Anglican theologian, was to create and sustain an authentic dialectic between "faith alone" and "holy living." He became convinced that the polarities described and delineated in the Reformation ("faith" vs. "works") had ceased to be helpful, and he sought to affirm "faith alone" *and* "holy living" in virtual negation of all other polarizations. He broke with Whitefield because of too much emphasis on *sola fide*, and with William Law for the opposite emphasis. He never abandoned *sola fide*, though after 1770 he laid the most stress on "holy living." His several "conversions" (e.g., to "holy living" and to faith alone) reaffirmed in his personal experience the authenticity of this dialectic.[63]

Wesley was prepared to reject the classical Protestant formulations of *sola fide,* since they left no room for his doctrine of perfection and the expectation of being perfected in love in this life. His soteriology linked justification and regeneration, rejected human passivity and self-assertion, evangelized Christian ethics and moralized the evangel. His survey of English Methodism late in life, the sermon "On God's Vineyard" (1788), left little doubt. "Who has wrote more ably than Martin Luther on Justification by faith alone?" he wrote, and then added, "And who was more ignorant of the doctrine of sanctification, or more confused in his conceptions of it?" Turning his attention toward Roman Catholicism, he continued:

> On the other hand, how many writers of the Romish Church . . . have wrote strongly and scripturally on sanctification, who, nevertheless, were entirely unacquainted with the nature of justification! . . . But it has pleased God to

give the Methodists a full and clear knowledge of each, and the wide difference between them.

On two fronts he fought the war for holiness and against antinomianism, his lifelong enemy: against the optimistic "natural" morality of the rationalists, and against Calvinists' pessimism about the Christian's good works. He firmly suported the possibility and necessity of the Christian's unlimited moral progress, depending on God's grace.[64]

Wesley set the course for an authentic theological dialectic between faith and good works early in life. While still reeling from the Aldersgate experience and the unnerving knowledge of Edwards's successes in America, he extracted and printed sections of the Anglican *Homilies* and Articles in a tract entitled *The Doctrine of Salvation, Faith and Good Works According to the Church of England* (1738), his first theological charter. The twelve-page pamphlet went through thirteen editions during his life. It was a theological manifesto that portrayed his position in summary fashion: Scripture was primary in revelation and faith in salvation; the total efficacy of Crrist's atonement, man's dire need, and God's ungrudging, prevenient grace; formal ("dead") faith contrasted with saving ("lively") faith; man's personal agency in receiving the gift of faith and in the "good works done in faith."[65]

The "doctrine of salvation, faith and good works" implied a major problem, namely, sin. As Wesley understood it, sin caused problems both for the Christian holding firmly in faith to the benefits of Christ and to the Christian pursuing the holy life. His longest theological essay was dedicated to "The Doctrine of Original Sin." In stark terms he portrayed the plight of human beings with a perverse will, prone to evil. But while hideous, sin was not perceived by Wesley to have annulled human responsibility; in the *imago dei* that remains the human being has inalienable capacities of reason, freedom, and conscience, while having no merit before God or hope for salvation in himself.[66] This power of "conscience" comes from the personal activity of the Holy Spirit; this is the essence of prevenient grace.

As Wesley described it, the Christian life flows under the power of prevenient, saving, sanctifying, sacramental grace. More than a mere forensic pardon of sin on Christ's behalf, grace is the immanent and active love of God as it is experienced in human life through the agency of the Spirit. It is "preventing," since its prior action makes every human action a reaction; it is universal but spiritual, and thus is not irresistible. Since it is God's grace, it is never at the disposal of man, even though normally mediated through various outward and visible signs. This doctrine of grace as elucidated by Wesley "is hardly to be found, in the form he developed it, anywhere else in the body of Anglican divinity."[67]

For Wesley faith was the foundation of the Christian life. In 1746 he published a popular theological tract that denied any form of human life-sufficiency and showed the radical need for people to appropriate the Gospel's good news by faith alone. Arguing that justification is pardon, Wesley proceeded to insist that the crucial issue is a person's acceptance of this pardon, which is the essence of faith from its human side. Wesley made no mention of Calvin or Luther in this tract, suggesting that he had received sufficient instruction on the doctrine through his own Anglican tradition.[68]

Just as faith was the foundation of the Christian life, love was the fruition of that life. His insistence on Christian morality provoked the antinomians to anger and led to their accusing him of legalism, but he argued that the Gospel's genius was that it had power to generate the faith that impels the believer to a love that works for righteousness. Just as God's grace was God's active love at work in human beings, so love was the active, synergistic cooperation of the Christian with God in the pursuit of his holy will.[69]

As Wesley understood it, it was God's grace, his love-at-work in people, that brought holy living and Christian perfection. The equation "holiness is happiness" had a considerable tradition in British theology, both Anglican and Puritan. In a sense it summarized Wesley's dominant theological motif, which united the doctrines of grace, faith, love, and holy living. Wesley was called to write more precisely about Christian perfection in the sixties, since during this period an increasing number of people in the Methodist societies, especially in the Midlands, professed "entire sanctification." As people came forward, somewhat belatedly, to profess the gift of perfection and "holiness of heart and life," Wesley—himself no "professor"—investigated the claims of others and concluded that many were authentic. He began to stress even more than before the urgency of "fulness of faith," which was implicit in God's gift of faith itself.[70]

In 1759 he published a warning against spiritual pride, to guard against enthusiasm in this matter. He also wrote three sermons rejecting the notion of perfection as static or "sinless," in 1760, 1763, and 1768. He digested his thoughts on the subject in an important tract entitled *A Plain Account of Christian Perfection*, continually revised up to 1787 after it appeared in 1767. Wesley claimed that perfection had been his concern ever since 1725. In the first preachers' conference (1744) one of the questions dealt with whether or not, on the basis of New Testament evidence, a person could expect to be saved from all sin. The answer was Yes. The last petition in the Lord's Prayer ("deliver us from evil") was used as evidence that prayers for entire sanctification are no mockery of God.[71]

As indicated above, Wesley's distinctive emphasis on Christian perfection must be understood in the context of his acquaintance with Eastern theology, especially the stress by Gregory and others on *synelthesis*. An influential commentator on his theology insists that his doctrine of Christian perfection will be consistently misunderstood by those who construe the English word "perfect" as a translation of the Latin word *perfectio* ("faultless"). Rather, Wesley's stress on perfection as the goal of the Christian life derived from the Eastern influence of Gregory and Ephraem, and from the "holiness" of

Jewel, Hall, and Taylor. As Wesley understood it, according to Albert Outler, perfect love

> is the conscious certainty, *in the present moment,* of the fullness of one's love for God and neighbor, as this love has been initiated and fulfilled by God's gifts of faith, hope and love. This is not a state but a dynamic process: saving faith is its beginning; sanctification is its proper climax. . . . It is almost as if Wesley had read *agape* in the place of the Clementine *gnosis,* and then had turned the Eastern notion of a vertical scale of perfection into a genetic scale of development within historical existence.

In this sense people can lapse from perfection just as they may fall from grace at any stage. "Perfection," said Wesley, is the fruition of the desire of faith to love God above everything else insofar as deliberate action and conscious will are concerned. To deny this, according to Wesley, seemed to imply that deliberate sin was both unavoidable and inevitable.[72]

Wesley's theological position led him to a lifelong battle against the Calvinists within the Church of England. His first tract against Whitefield (1739) insisted on the doctrine of universal atonement and the denunciation of predestinarian doctrines as "blasphemy." For the next fifty years he waged war with those who taught that predestination was an essential article of faith, while the other side persisted in attacking his supposed "Arminianism." The real target of Wesley's wrath was antinomianism, which he supposed to be a natural consequence of the doctrine of predestination. His clearest rejection of the predestinarian position was probably an essay published in 1752. Later in life he accepted the badge "Arminian"—much as the Holy Club at Oxford had defiantly accepted the label "Methodists—" and named his house organ *The Arminian Magazine* (1778ff.). But he became an "Arminian" chiefly inasmuch as he did not construe himself to be a Calvinist; Arminius apparently had no influence on him in his formative years and none of his works appears in Wesley's multivolume *A Christian Library.*[73]

Wesley began to be concerned about the doctrinal standards of the Methodist societies before 1746, when he began codifying Methodist doctrine by collecting his own sermons, which were sometimes essays that summarized his preaching on a certain text or topic. In the Model Deed drawn up in 1763 to govern legal arrangements for the preaching houses, the principal doctrinal stipulation was that the majority of the trustees would permit preachers to use the house "provided always, that the said persons preach no other doctrine than is contained in Mr. Wesley's *Notes Upon the New Testament,* and four volumes of Sermons. . . ." These forty-four sermons, which Wesley insisted included those "doctrines . . . which I embrace and teach as the essentials of true religion," continue to serve, together with the *Notes* (1775), as the "Evangelical Doctrines to which the Preachers of the Methodist Church [in Britain] both Ministers and Laymen are pledged."[74] Through this process Wesley placed his written word where his personal presence was impossible, and the Methodist societies were given positive doctrinal guidance.

As part of the effort to give a degree of self-sufficiency to the Methodists in America in 1784, Wesley forwarded not only a pertinent letter in the hands of Coke, Vasey, and Whatcoat, whom he had recently ordained, but a revision of the Book of Common Prayer and the Anglican Articles as well. The Americans proved unwilling to accept his actual leadership, as we shall see below, but they did incorporate his revision of the Articles in their Doctrinal Standards.

Wesley made a number of important editorial changes in the Book of Common Prayer before giving it to Coke for printing (before Coke sailed to America in 1784). He struck words and rubrics and inserted new provisions, producing what one commentator calls "momentous changes" in the work. He reduced the book's size by half and omitted the Calendar, Athanasian Creed, rite for Private Baptism, and a number of other rites. He provided for extempore prayer and retained propers for only three of the thirty-six Holy Days, even omitting All Saints' Day. He greatly shortened the orders for public worship and transformed the Absolution from a priestly declaration to a pastoral prayer. He expunged references to godparents in the baptismal order, deleted the ring and the question "Who giveth this woman . . . ?" from the ceremony of marriage, but included the Ordinal under a new title: "The Form and Manner of Making and Ordaining of Superintendents, Elders, and Deacons."[75]

Wesley clearly indicated his ecclesiastical intentions for Methodists in the new nation by including, in addition to the revised Ordinal, a revision of the Thirty-Nine Articles. The articles were no part of the Book of Common Prayer and were seldom bound with it. His revision reduced the number to twenty-four, omitting six which the Conference of 1744 had listed as scripturally suspect, as well as nine others. Removed from the original version were articles VIII, XIII, XV, XVII, XXI, XXIII, and III, XVIII, XX, XXVI, XXIX, XXXIII, XXXV, XXXVI, XXXVII. The size of the document was cut in half, and Wesley altered some of the articles that were retained. He also appended *A Collection of Psalms and Hymns for the Lord's Day* to the revised Book of Common Prayer, now entitled *Sunday Service of the Methodists in North America.* The volume was taken by the newly ordained clergy to the "Christmas Conference" that met in the United States late in 1784.[76]

The Methodists in America made little use of the *Sunday Service.* In a number of ways they showed their independence from Wesley, willing to accept his preeminence in spiritual but not in actual leadership. They dropped his name from the minutes of the Annual Conference in 1786 (it reappeared in 1789) and refused to follow his advice to elect Whatcoat "superintendent" in 1787. Especially hard for Wesley to bear was the decision of Asbury and Coke to use the title "bishop." "How can you, how dare you, suffer yourself to be called 'bishop': I shudder, I start at the very thought!" he wrote to

Asbury. No less shocking was Asbury's refusal to be set aside as superintendent until both he and Coke were elected by the American preachers.[77]

But Wesley had made his mark in Christian history. The People Called Methodists were on their way to becoming an important denomination in Britain, the third largest denomination in the United States, and a major ecumenical force in Christendom.

World Methodism

In 1790 Wesley wrote to one of the preachers in America, "It is expedient that the Methodists in every part of the globe should be united together as closely as possible." Shortly before his death he wrote to another, "Lose no opportunity of declaring to all men that the Methodists are one people in all the world; and that it is their full determination so to continue."[78] Wesley's vision has sometimes fallen short of reality for Methodists, but the twentieth century has seen a number of reunions among separated Methodist bodies on both sides of the Atlantic. No less significant has been the important role Methodists have played in the century's ecumenical movement.

There are approximately 20 million members of Methodist churches in the world. Autonomous Methodist churches (or union churches formed primarily by Methodists) are found in more than ninety countries on all six continents. Methodist churches entered church unions in North and South India, Canada, Japan, France, Belgium, and Spain. Nearly 4,800 Methodist churches entered the United Church of Canada when the new body was formed in 1925. The United Methodist Church is the third largest denomination in the United States, and the second largest Protestant group. Its larger connection with worldwide Methodism was signaled in 1975 in the "New World Mission" program, which brought international Methodist leaders for one-week missions to 370 communities in the United States.

The World Methodist Council is an association of more than sixty different Methodist denominational groups at work in nearly ninety countries of the world. According to its purpose as stated in its constitution, "It does not seek to legislate for them nor to invade their autonomy. Rather it exists to serve them and to give unity to their witness and enterprise."

Although the name "World Methodist Council" was adopted in 1951, the council dates from 1881 when the first Ecumenical Methodist Conference met in London with some 400 delegates from thirty Methodist bodies throughout the world in attendance, including eighteen American and ten British bodies. As the Ecumenical Methodist Conference, this world organization convened at ensuing ten-year intervals with the exception of the 1941 conference, which because of World War II was not held until 1947.

The 1947 conference, which was the seventh such gathering, changed the interval at which the conferences were held. The eighth conference met in 1951, and since that time the interval between meetings has been five years.

It was at the 1951 conference in Oxford, England, that the name change occurred; organizational changes made the World Methodist Council similar in form to other world conciliar organizations.

With the name change came as well the creation of a permanent Secretariat with headquarters in the United States and Great Britain. Two secretaries were elected, but the administration of the council was unified by the selection of only one set of officers. The first officers of the council were Bishop Ivan Lee Holt, president; Dr. Harold Roberts, vice president; Mr. Edwin L. Jones and Mr. L. A. Ellwood, treasurers; and Dr. Elmer T. Clark and Dr. Benson Perkins, secretaries.

In 1953, by authority of the World Executive Committee and the Executive Committee of Section XIII, representing the Methodist Church, U.S.A., headquarters in North America were established at Lake Junaluska, North Carolina, and a beautiful stone headquarters building was erected. This building, which contains offices, a library, a reading room, and one of the outstanding collections of Wesleyana in the world, was dedicated at the Ninth World Methodist Conference, which was held at Lake Junaluska, North Carolina in 1956. The headquarters building has twice been enlarged to take care of the expanding work and to complete the architectural design.

At the Oslo World Conference in 1961 Dr. Lee F. Tuttle became the first full-time secretary of the council, succeeding Dr. Elmer T. Clark. At this same Conference the Reverend Max W. Woodward was elected to succeed Dr. Benson Perkins, but he remained on a part-time basis until 1964 when he also began giving full-time to the work of the council. The Reverend Joe Hale became general secretary in 1976.

Beginning with the first Ecumenical Methodist Conference in 1881, World Conferences have been held as follows:

1881—London, England
1891—Washington, D.C., U.S.A.
1901—London, England
1911—Toronto, Canada
1921—London, England
1931—Atlanta, Georgia, U.S.A.
1947—Springfield, Massachusetts, U.S.A.
1951—Oxford, England
1956—Lake Junaluska, North Carolina, U.S.A.
1961—Oslo, Norway
1966—London, England
1971—Denver, Colorado, U.S.A.
1976—Dublin, Ireland

While the format of the conferences has changed considerably with an increasingly serious purpose, the conferences continue to hold tremendous appeal to Methodists throughout the world. The 1966 conference in London had 2,900 officially registered delegates and council members from sixty-four countries of the world, as well as hundreds who attended unofficially. At the Dublin meeting in 1976 the conference established the World Methodist Peace Award to be presented annually to an individual somewhere in the world chosen because of an outstanding contribution toward peace. Among the satellite groups presenting reports at this conference were the World Federation of Methodist Women, World Methodist Historical Society, World Methodist Council Youth Committee and Conference, World Methodist Council Evangelism Committee, and World Methodist Family Life Committee. Reports were also given by the Committee on Publishing Interests, Theological Education Committee, Social and International Affairs Consultation, and Worship and Liturgy Committee. Representatives from over sixty churches in ninety countries condemned the slaughter of unarmed blacks in South Africa and decided to allocate at least 20 percent of all committee assignments to women.

In 1951 at Oxford an extensive program of publishing began, which produced a "Who's Who in Methodism," an "Album of Methodist History," an annotated edition of the Journal and Letters of Francis Asbury, and an Encyclopedia of Methodism. Since 1946 the council has sponsored a program of ministerial exchanges between Methodist ministers of different countries for both long and short periods. This Exchange Program has been highly successful and continues to grow rapidly. What started with exchanges between British and American Methodist ministers has now reached out to include Germany, Switzerland, Sweden, India, New Zealand, Canada, and other countries.

Within recent years an important contribution has been made to Methodist theologians through the Oxford Theological Institute, held at four-year intervals at Lincoln College, Oxford. On each occasion one hundred theologians representing all areas of the world participate by invitation in this enterprise.

World Parish is the official periodical of the council, published nine times each year under the editorship of the Secretary Resident in the United States. After a new format was adopted in mid-1962, circulation increased appreciably. News of Methodism in all parts of the world makes up the contents of this periodical.

The council has been actively involved in every phase of the Ecumenical movement through close consultation and cooperation with the World Council of Churches, and national and regional councils. It has also been the agency responsible for Methodist observers at Vatican Council II from 1962 until 1965. At the London World Conference in 1966, for the first time Roman Catholic observers were present by invitation. The council also set up a committee to meet with a committee representing the Roman Catholic Church to conduct conversations at the world level. A number of consultations have been held between representatives of the World Methodist Council and representatives of the Roman Catholic Church, and the joint commission issued a report in 1976 of consultations between 1972 and 1975.[79]

One of the most important and potentially far-reaching decisions of the 1966 council was the creation of a Committee on Structure and Program to review the past work of the World Methodist Council and to make recommendations to later executive and council meetings on expanded structure and procedure. This committee, meeting in Geneva, Switzerland in February 1967, reviewed the entire structure and program of the council, and consulted with the top-level leadership of the World Council of Churches, as well as administrative officers of other world confessional bodies based in Geneva. This committee of twenty, representing ten nations and all six continents of the world, adopted twenty-eight resolutions for strengthening the work of the council. The most important of these resolutions was the recommendation to open and staff a liaison office at the Ecumenical Center in Geneva to replace the London office. This action was taken upon the invitation of the World Council of Churches.

The council's addresses are Lake Junaluska, North Carolina 28745, and 150 Route de Ferney, 1211 Geneva 20, Switzerland.

COSMOS, an agency of the United Methodist Church, was formed by the General Conference of 1948 to study the problems of overseas structure and to make recommendations. Its responsibility was to plan changes in the structure of overseas Methodism, which had originated in missionary work. Its work accelerated after 1964 as regional entities sought autonomy or independence. It recommended that annual conferences "study the form of autonomy best suited to the Church in the area, including the formation of United Churches." COSMOS held a world conference in Wisconsin in 1966, which reaffirmed the intention to decentralize controls over the fruit of Methodist mission work. Another conference met in 1970. In 1972 the General Conference of the United Methodist Church approved a recommendation of COSMOS and the World Methodist Council which gave to the council chief responsibility for maintaining liaison with the many autonomous Methodist and United churches. With this action COSMOS ceased to function.[80]

Methodists have been active in ecumenical relations and church mergers in the twentieth century. In 1932 in Britain the Wesleyan Methodist Church, Primitive Methodist Church, and United Methodist Church adopted a deed of union which formed The Methodist Church. In the United States a series of mergers in 1939 and 1968 brought together the major white Methodist churches, together with the Evangelical United Brethren, in the United Methodist Church. In 1953 the Methodists in Britain opened union conversations with the Church of England, but the elaborate scheme for reuniting the two bodies collapsed in 1972.[81]

The Methodist contribution to ecumenism has been substantial in terms of both the investment of money and the talents of individuals. A leading figure in the history of ecumenism, John Raleigh Mott (1865–1955), was an

American Methodist who decisively influenced the World's Student Christian Federation, International Missionary Council, World Alliance of Young Men's Christian Association, and the World Council of Churches, of which he was co-president. He was a towering figure in the Ecumenical movement as well as a Nobel Peace Prize winner. Other dedicated Methodist ecumenists include Frank Mason North and Harry Ward; Bishop Francis J. McConnell; Bishop Ivan Lee Holt; Bishop G. Bromley Oxnam; Professor Clarence Tucker Craig; Principal J. Newton Flew; Charles Parlin; Philip A. Potter; Albert Outler; and D. T. Niles. Important Methodist biblical scholars have included A. S. Peake, Norman Snaith, and C. Kingsley Barrett; among prominent Reformation scholars are Philip S. Watson and E. Gordon Rupp.

Among the founders of the World Council of Churches in 1948 were a number of American Methodist bodies including The Methodist Church (and the Evangelical United Brethren), the African Methodist Episcopal Church, the A.M.E. Zion Church, and the Christian Methodist Episcopal Church. The three Methodist denominations that later merged to become The Methodist Church were constituent members of the Federal Council of Churches when it was organized in 1908, and The Methodist Church was a constituent member and sizable contributor to the National Council of Churches when it was formed in 1950. Methodists have been able participants in the Consultation on Church Union (COCU) in the United States since its inception.

NOTES

1. Kenneth E. Rowe, ed., *The Place of Wesley in the Christian Tradition* (Metuchen, N.J.: Scarecrow Press, 1976), pp. 4-5. During his lifetime Wesley issued a "collected edition" of 32 volumes (1771–1774); the second edition in 1809–1813 of 17 volumes was more complete but no more critical. The third edition of 14 volumes (1829–1831), published by Thomas Jackson in London, has remained the basic edition of Wesley's "collected works." It lacks a critical apparatus and has never been revised though often reprinted. The first of the new critical volumes is Gerald R. Cragg, ed., *John Wesley, the Appeals of Reason and Religion and Certain Related Letters,* Vol. 11 in *The Works of John Wesley,* ed. Frank Baker (Oxford: Clarendon Press, 1975).

2. See R. R. Palmer, *The Age of the Democratic Revolution: A Political History of Europe and America, 1760–1800* (2 vols.; 1959–1964).

3. Quoted in Frank Baker, *John Wesley and the Church of England* (Nashville: Abingdon Press, 1970), pp. 257-258.

4. For a discussion of several of these themes, see Henry D. Rack, *The Future of John Wesley's Methodism,* Ecumenical Studies in History, No. 2 (Richmond, Va.: John Knox Press, 1965), pp. 10-11.

5. Ibid., p. 7; Baker, p. 81.

6. Albert C. Outler, ed., *John Wesley,* Library of Protestant Thought (New York: Oxford University Press, 1964), p. 20. Hereafter cited as JW.

7. Quoted in Rack, pp. 9-10.

8. Baker, pp. 4-5.

9. Quoted in Baker, p. 74.

10. Baker, p. 9.

11. JW, pp. 5, 38.

12. Baker, p. 22; JW, p. 21.

13. Baker, pp. 26-30; JW, pp. 8-9. Baker indicates that already at Oxford Wesley practiced bibliomancy.

14. JW, p. 10.

15. Baker, pp. 42-43.

16. Ibid., pp. 44, 47, 51-52.

17. JW, p. 13; Baker, p. 52.

18. JW, p. 48. Outler notes that Wesley

later corrected his statement with the words, "I am not sure of this."

19. JW, pp. 30, 52.
20. JW, pp. 51-52, 66. The quotation is from p. 66.
21. JW, pp. 16, 51. Outler adds that "it is not too much to say that one of the effectual causes of the Wesleyan Revival in England was the Great Awakening in New England" (p. 16).
22. JW, p. 72; Baker, p. 140. The quotation is from p. 72.
23. JW, p. 17.
24. JW, p. 77; Gordon Rupp. "Son of Samuel," in Rowe, ed., *Place of Wesley,* p. 59; Baker, p. 316.
25. Baker, pp. 63, 140.
26. Ibid., p. 70.
27. Paul M. Minus, Jr., ed., *Methodism's Destiny in an Ecumenical Age* (Nashville: Abingdon Press, 1969), p. 87.
28. Baker, p. 151.
29. Ibid., p. 149; JW, p. 307.
30. José Miguez-Bonino, "Methodism: A World Movement," in Minus, ed., *Methodism's Destiny,* p. 100; Martin Schmidt, "Wesley's Place in Church History," in Rowe, ed., *Place of Wesley,* p. 88.
31. Baker, pp. 71, 73, 146; JW, p. 306.
32. Baker, pp. 146, 151-152.
33. Ibid., pp. 153-154.
34. Ibid., pp. 259-260.
35. Rack, p. 17.
36. Richard M. Cameron, *Methodism and Society in Historical Perspective* (Nashville: Abingdon Press, 1961), pp. 35-37.
37. Ibid., pp. 38-39.
38. Ibid., p. 38.
39. Baker, p. 114; Frederick A. Norwood, *The Story of American Methodism* (Nashville: Abingdon Press, 1974), pp. 35-36.
40. Baker, pp. 106-108.
41. Ibid., p. 117.
42. Ibid., pp. 2, 197.
43. Ibid., pp. 197-99.
44. Ibid., p. 200.
45. Ibid., p. 214.
46. John C. Bowmer, *The Sacrament of the Lord's Supper in Methodism, 1791-1960* (London: Epworth, 1961), pp. 12-13; Baker, pp. 78, 84-87.
47. Baker, pp. 155-157, 256; JW, 317-318.
48. JW, pp. 332-334; Baker, p. 157; Dow Kirkpatrick, ed., *The Doctrine of the Church* (Nashville: Abingdon Press, 1964), p. 141.
49. Baker, p. 218.
50. Ibid., pp. 218-233. The quotations are found on pp. 225 and 229.
51. Ibid., p. 262.
52. Norwood, pp. 96-97; Baker, pp. 264-270.
53. Baker, pp. 272-273, 324. See *The Journal of John Wesley, as Abridged by Nehemiah Curnock with an Introduction by Bishop Gerald Kennedy* (New York: Capricorn Books, 1963), p. 419 (June 28, 1790).
54. JW, p. 83; Baker, pp. 145, 276. The quotation is from Baker, p. 276.
55. Baker, pp. 315, 255, 279-282, 309.
56. Ibid., pp. 283-285, 293-295.
57. Albert C. Outler, "Wesley in the Christian Tradition," in Rowe, ed., *Place of Wesley,* p. 13.
58. JW, pp. 119-120.
59. JW, pp. 28, 92.
60. JW, p. 27.
61. *The Theological Study Commission on Doctrine and Doctrinal Standards, an Interim Report to the General Conference* (New York: United Methodist Church, n.d.), p. 7; Schmidt, "Wesley's Place in Church History," pp. 78-80.
62. JW, p. viii; Outler, "Wesley in the Christian Tradition," pp. 30-31.
63. Outler, "Wesley in the Christian Tradition," pp. 15-20.
64. Ibid., pp. 21-22; JW, pp. 107-108; Rack, pp. 13-14. The quotation is from pp. 107-108.
65. JW, pp. 121-133.
66. See JW, pp. 128, 324, 441, 495. This was one reason why Wesley argued for the necessity of infant baptism.
67. JW, p. 33.
68. JW, p. 197.
69. JW, p. 221.
70. Schmidt, "Wesley's Place in Church History," p. 73; JW, p. 22.
71. JW, p. 22; see also pp. 283, 299, 251-252, and 169.
72. JW, pp. 30-32. The quotation is from pp. 30-31.
73. JW, 349-350, 425; Outler, "Wesley in the Christian Tradition," p. 26. Wesley's tract *The Question, What is an Arminian? Answered by a Lover of Free Grace* (1770) shows that the nickname was misleading.
74. JW, pp. 87-88; Rupert E. Davies,

Methodism (Baltimore: Penguin, 1963), p. 209. The Doctrinal Standards of the major Methodist bodies in the United States are discussed below. Wesley's *Notes* were based on such previous biblical expositors as Hugo Grotius and the German Pietist Johann Albrecht Bengel (see Schmidt, "Place of Wesley in Church History," p. 87).

75. Baker, pp. 242-249.
76. Ibid., pp. 249-253.
77. JW, pp. 25-26. See the discussion of these subjects in the following chapter.
78. Quoted in Baker pp. 310-311.

79. See Joe Hale, ed., *Proceedings of the Thirteenth World Methodist Conference, Dublin, Ireland, 1976* ([Lake Junaluska, N.C]: World Methodist Council, 1977), pp. 254-270. For one Methodist observer's remarks on Vatican Council II, see Albert C. Outler, *Methodist Observer at Vatican II* (New York: Newman Press, 1967).
80. Norwood, pp. 439-440.
81. Rack, pp. 58-80, discusses this union effort. See also Margaret Deansely and Geoffrey G. Willis. *Anglican-Methodist Unity* (London: Faith Press, 1968).

BIBLIOGRAPHY

WESLEY AND "THE PEOPLE CALLED METHODISTS"

Baker, Frank. "The Oxford Edition of Wesley's Works." *Methodist History* 8, 4 (July 1970): 41-48.

———, ed. *A Union Catalogue of the Publications of John Charles Wesley.* Durham, North Carolina: Duke University, 1966.

Cannon, William R. "John Wesley's Years in Georgia." *Methodist History* N.S., 1, 4 (July 1963): 1-7.

Davies, Rupert E. *Methodism.* Baltimore: Penguin, 1963.

Edwards, Maldwyn. *John Wesley and the Eightenth Century: A Study of His Social and Political Influence.* London: Allen and Unwin, 1933.

Green, V. H. H. *John Wesley.* London: Nelson, 1964.

———. *The Young Mr. Wesley: A Study of John Wesley and Oxford.* London: Arnold, 1961.

Halevy, Elie. *The Birth of Methodism in England.* Trans. with an introduction by Bernard Semmel. Chicago: University of Chicago Press, 1971.

Harrison, G. Elsie. *Son to Susanna: The Private Life of John Wesley.* London: Nicholson and Watson, 1937.

Hildebrandt, Franz. *Christianity according to the Wesleys.* London: Epworth Press. 1955.

Judson, Sandra. *Biographical and Descriptive Works on the Rev. John Wesley.* London: University of London Press, 1963.

McIntosh, Lawrence D. "The Place of John Wesley in the Christian Tradition; A Selected Bibliography." In *The Place of Wesley in the Christian Tradition,* ed. Kenneth E. Rowe. Metuchen, N.J.: Scarecrow Press, 1976. Pp. 134-159.

Melton, J. Gordon. "An Annotated Bibliography of Publications about the Life and Work of John Wesley, 1791–1966." *Methodist History* 7, 4 (July 1969): 29-46.

Norwood, Frederick A. "Wesleyan and Methodist Historical Studies, 1960–1970: A Bibliographical Article." *Church History* XL (1971): 182-199.

Piette, Maximin. *John Wesley in the Evolution of Protestantism.* London: Sheed and Ward, 1937.

Rowe, Kenneth E. *Methodist Union Catalog: Pre-1976 Imprints.* 2 vols. Metuchen, N.J.: Scarecrow Press, 1975–1976.

———, ed. *The Place of Wesley in the Christian Tradition.* Metuchen, N.J.: Scarecrow Press, 1976.

Semmel, Bernard. *The Methodist Revolution.* New York: Basic Books, 1973.

Simon, J. S. *John Wesley.* 5 vols. London: Epworth Press, 1921–1934.

Tyerman, Luke. *The Oxford Methodists.* London: Holder and Stoughton, 1873.

Wearmouth, Robert F. *Methodism and the Common People of the Eighteenth Century.* London: Epworth Press, 1945.

Wesley, John. *The Appeals to Men of Reason and Religion and Certain Related Letters,* ed. Gerald R. Cragg. Vol. XI in *The Works of John Wesley,* ed. Frank Baker. Oxford: Clarendon Press, 1975.

CONNECTIONALISM AND THE CHURCH OF ENGLAND

Armstrong, A. *The Church of England, the Methodists and Society, 1700–1850*. London: University of London Press, 1973.

Baker, Frank. *John Wesley and the Church of England*. Nashville: Abingdon Press, 1970.

Blankenship, Paul F. "The Significance of John Wesley's Abridgment of the Thirty-Nine Articles as Seen from His Deletions." *Methodist History* 2, 3 (April 1964): 35-47.

Bowmer, John C. "The Wesleyan Conception of the Ministry." *Religion in Life* 40, 1 (Spring 1971): 85-96.

Godbold, Albea. "Francis Asbury and His Difficulties with John Wesley and Thomas Rankin." *Methodist History* 3, 3 (April 1965): 3-19.

Lawson, A. B. *John Wesley and the Christian Ministry*. London: S.P.C.K., 1963.

Vickers, John A. *Thomas Coke: Apostle of Methodism*. Nashville: Abingdon, 1970.

WESLEYAN THEOLOGY

Borgen, Ole E. *John Wesley on the Sacraments, a Theological Study*. Nashville: Abingdon Press, 1972.

Bowmer, John C. *The Sacrament of the Lord's Supper in Early Methodism*. London: Dacre, 1951.

Burtner, R. W., and Chiles, R. E. eds. *A Compend of Wesley's Theology*. Nashville: Abingdon, 1954.

Cannon, William R. *The Theology of John Wesley, with Special Reference to the Doctrine of Justification*. Nashville: Abingdon, 1946.

Cell, George Croft. *The Rediscovery of John Wesley*. New York: Henry Holt, 1935.

Cox, Leo G. *John Wesley's Concept of Perfection*. Kansas City, Mo.: Beacon Hill Press, 1964.

Deschner, John. *Wesley's Christology: An Interpretation*. Dallas: Southern Methodist University Press, 1960.

Lindström, Harald. *Wesley and Sanctification*. London: Epworth Press, 1950.

Monk, Robert C. *John Wesley: His Puritan Heritage*. Nashville: Abingdon, 1966.

Outler, Albert C. *Theology in the Wesleyan Spirit*. Nashville: Tidings, 1975.

———, ed. *John Wesley*. Library of Protestant Thought. New York: Oxford University Press, 1964.

Parris, John. *John Wesley's Doctrine of the Sacraments*. London: Epworth Press, 1963.

Rattenbury, John E. *The Eucharistic Hymns of John and Charles Wesley*. London: Epworth Press, 1948.

Schmidt, Martin. *John Wesley: A Theological Biography*. Trans. Norman Goldhawk. 2 vols. in 3 parts. Nashville: Abingdon, 1962–1973.

Todd, John Murray. *John Wesley and the Catholic Church*. London: Hodder and Stoughton, 1958.

Turner, G. A. "John Wesley as an Interpreter of Scripture." In *Inspiration and Interpretation*, ed. John W. Walvoord. Grand Rapids: Wm. B. Eerdmans, 1957. Pp. 156–178.

Williams, Colin W. *John Wesley's Theology Today*. Nashville: Abingdon, 1960.

Wynkoop, Mildred B. *A Theology of Love: The Dynamic of Wesleyanism*. Kansas City, Mo.: Beacon Hill Press, 1972.

Yates, Arthur S. *The Doctrine of Assurance with Special Reference to John Wesley*. London: Epworth Press, 1952.

WORLD METHODISM

Beckwith, R. T. *Priesthood and Sacraments, a Study in the Anglican-Methodist Report*. Appleford: Marcham Manor Press, 1964.

Bowmer, John C. *The Lord's Supper in Methodism, 1791–1960*. London: Epworth Press, 1961.

Cannon, William R. "The Theological

Stance of Methodism in the Ecumenical Movement." *Methodist History* 6, 1 (October 1967): 3-13.

Conversations between the Church of England and the Methodist Church, Interim Statement. Naperville, Ill.: Alec R. Allenson, 1958 and 1963.

Davey, C. J. *The March of Methodism.* London: Epworth Press, 1951.

Davies, Rupert E. *Methodism.* Baltimore: Penguin, 1963.

————. *What Methodists Believe.* London: Mobray, 1976.

Davies, Rupert, and Rupp, Gordon. *A History of the Methodist Church in Great Britain.* London: Epworth Press, 1965.

Deanesly, Margaret, and Willis, Geoffrey G. *Anglican-Methodist Unity; Some Considerations Historical and Liturgical.* London: Faith Press. 1968.

Flew, R. Newton. *The Catholicity of Protestantism.* Philadelphia: Muhlenberg Press, 1950.

Hale, Joe, ed. *Proceedings of the Thirteenth World Methodist Conference, Dublin, Ireland, 1976* [Lake Junaluska, N.C.:] The World Methodist Council, 1977.

Holt, Ivan Lee, and Clark, Elmer T. *The World Methodist* Movement. Nashville: The Upper Room. 1956.

Hunter, Frederick. *John Wesley and the Coming Comprehensive Church.* London:

Epworth Press, 1968.

Minus, Paul M., ed. *Methodism's Destiny in an Ecumenical Age.* Nashville: Abingdon Press, 1969.

Newton, John A. "The Ecumenical Wesley." *The Ecumenical Review* 24, 2 (April 1972): 160-175.

Outler, Albert C. *Methodist Observer at Vatican II.* New York: Newman Press, 1967.

————. *That the World May Believe; A Study of Christian Unity.* New York: Joint Commission on Education and Cultivation, Board of Missions of the Methodist Church, 1966.

Rack. Henry D. *The Future of John Wesley's Methodism.* Ecumenical Studies in History, No. 2. Richmond, Va.: John Knox Press, 1965.

Rupp, Gordon E. "Methodism in Relation to Protestant Tradition." In *Proceedings of the Eighth Ecumenical Methodist Conference, Oxford, 28th August–7th Sepember, 1951.* London: Epworth Press, 1952. Pp. 93-106.

Tuttle, Lee F., ed. *Proceedings of the Twelfth World Methodist Conference, Denver, Colorado. 1971.* Nashville: Abingdon Press, [1972].

World Methodist Council Handbook of Information, 1976–1981. [Lake Junaluska, N.C.: World Methodist Council, 1977.]

16. The United Methodist Church

The United Methodist Church is the result of two major mergers in the twentieth century. The first was the reunion of the Methodist Episcopal Church, the Methodist Episcopal Church, South, and the Methodist Protestant Church in 1939. This merger created The Methodist Church. The second was the merger of this church with the Church of the Evangelical United Brethren in 1968 to form The United Methodist Church. This church's history in the last two centuries forms the backbone of Methodist history in the United States. The United Methodist Church has nearly 10 million members; the largest Methodist body in the world, it includes nearly half of the estimated 20 million Methodist church members in the world.

Formation of American Methodism

Inscribed on the memorial to John and Charles Wesley at Westminster Abbey are these words: "GOD BURIES HIS WORKMEN BUT CARRIES ON HIS WORK." American Methodism is rooted in the Wesleyan revival in England, though indigenous forces have given it a character all its own. Authentic Wesleyan emphases were found in the Methodist message that was preached in the new nation. The message stressed personal religious experience, a legalistic view of Christian behavior, and doctrinal simplicity. It had three primary doctrinal themes: grace is free for all; a person can fully accept or reject grace; and with the Spirit's aid the justified sinner must seek the goal of "perfection," freedom from willful sin.[1]

But Wesley's legacy for Methodists in America was Americanized as Methodists organized their own distinct denomination. While the Wesleyan movement in Britain remained within the Church of England until after Wesley's death, American Methodism was independent from the start. It was first planted in the colonies not by Wesley's emissaries but by lay preachers operating on their own initiative. During the Americanization process, conflict ensued over the relative value of the authoritarian tradition inherited from the Wesleyan movement in England and the voluntary nature of Wesleyan societies in America. Consequently, one major theme in American Methodist history is the oscillation between an authoritarian tendency and democratic self government. The question of the role and power of the superintendent or bishop was a major point of contention.

Nothing is known about the small band of "Methodists" that Wesley gathered in Georgia during his missionary work early in the eighteenth century. The actual beginings of Methodism in America date from the 1760s. Apparently the first plantings occurred in the colony of Maryland, where Anglicanism was strong. A Methodist society began functioning in New York City in 1766, and apparently a class began functioning in Maryland at least six months earlier. Robert Strawbridge (d. 1781) began preaching and organizing societies there, probably before Philip Embury began preaching and organizing a Methodist society in New York City in 1766 (although he arrived there in 1760). Strawbridge had preached as a Methodist in Ireland; in the colony he also administered baptism and the Lord's Supper, which caused difficulty, since he was a layman. He worked in Virginia as well, while Barbara Heck assisted Embury in New York. All the early beginnings of Methodism in America, including those in Pennsylvania, were due to the initiative and efforts of laymen who usually worked under the title "local preacher." They were not ordained or appointed as traveling preachers. Included among them was Captain Thomas Webb, who is associated with the origins of Methodism on Long Island and in Philadelphia. Blacks first entered a Methodist society in New York City.[2]

In 1769 Wesley appointed the first of a number of official missionary preachers who were to guide and assist the struggling societies in the colonies. The first pair was Richard Boardman and Joseph Pilmore, who arrived in Philadelphia in the fall of that year. Pilmore was the more effective minister. Concentrating his efforts in Philadelphia, he told his people early in his career that "the Methodist Society was never designed to make a Separation from the Church of England or be looked upon as a Church." Two more appointees arrived in 1771, Francis Asbury and Richard Wright, followed in 1773 by Thomas Rankin and George Shadford. The last pair, James Dempster and Martin Rodda, arrived in 1774. Undoubtedly the largest mark was left by Francis Asbury (1745–1816), who was less than thirty years old when he arrived. American Methodism is in great measure the shadow of this man.

By 1769 the total number of people in Methodist societies was approximately 600. By 1773 there were nearly 1,200 concentrated in Maryland and Virginia, where the Church of England was strong. The number of Methodists climbed swiftly to 8,675 by 1779 and 15,000 by 1784. In 1781 more than 90 percent lived below the southern boundary of Pennsylvania; until 1784 people placed the movement within the Anglican church. Seventeen itinerant Methodist preachers were traveling through the colonies in 1774, and 24 two years later. By 1784 there were 83 traveling preachers, plus a number of local preachers.[3]

The American Revolution was a difficult time for Methodists, in part because their societies were associated with the enemy's national church, in part because some itinerant preachers showed little patriotism, and in part because Wesley published thirteen royalist tracts and open letters in the course of the Revolution. In 1776 Shadford presented a petition to the General Convention on behalf of the three thousand Methodists in Virginia protesting the disestablishment of the Anglican church, although separation of church and state did occur and the state became a model for the Bill of Rights in this sphere. By 1778 only Shadford and Asbury remained of the original eight English missionaries, and that year Shadford also left. Asbury refused to take the rigid loyalty oath in Maryland and moved to Delaware, where the oath was more liberal. He remained until 1780, but was not able to exercise much influence in his role as acting general assistant. Day-to-day responsibilities for the movement lay with the native preachers, a development that was evident in the Annual Conference of 1777. There are reports of Methodists who were conscientious objectors in the Revolutionary War, but little is known about enthusiastic fighters for independence.[4]

A major crisis arose in 1779. The Methodists had been placed in a difficult situation by Wesley's Tory tracts and the Anglican church's severance from English roots. Now it was difficult to argue that Methodism was a revival movement within the Church of England and that Methodists should receive the ministration of sacraments from that church. As a result two groups began to form. The first recommended that no action be taken until political events settled down and Wesley could act, while the second advised that the Methodists in America should begin dispensing the sacraments on their own authority. In 1779 a decision was made by the Annual Conference, which was attended only by southern preachers because Asbury and the northern preachers were prevented by the war from reaching Virginia. Rejecting Asbury's plea, the majority decided to create a presbytery of four ministers who would ordain one another and others who desired to administer the sacraments. Meanwhile the northern preachers had met with Asbury in an irregular conference, confirmed him as their leader, and then filled their itinerant appointments. In 1780 the northern branch met again, denouncing the southern preachers and refusing to call them Methodists "till they come back." The southerners decided to postpone administration of the sacraments while advice was solicited from Wesley, who strongly supported Asbury. Asbury's peacemaking travels in the southern parts helped ease the crisis by the time the conference met in 1781, although the issues remained alive.[5]

After the Revolutionary War ended, the conference in 1783 appointed two days of public thanksgiving for "temporal and spiritual prosperity, and the glorious revival of the work of God," without mentioning the war victory or independence. In 1784 the conference added an article to Wesley's twenty-four, entitled "Of the Rulers of the United States of America," and the next year Asbury and Thomas Coke (1747–1814) visited General Washington at Mount Vernon. They called on him again in 1789 after he was inaugurated as the first president, although Coke was still an English subject.[6]

Between the Revolutionary War and these visits to Washington, the Methodists organized themselves as a church body. The occasion was the so-called Christmas Conference held in Baltimore, Maryland, on December 24, 1894 and the ten succeeding days. Wesley's preparations for the conference, including his Open Letter, ordinations, and revision of the Book of Common Prayer, have been discussed above.[7] Coke had arrived early in November, together with Vasey and Whatcoat, whom Wesley ordained "to serve the desolate sheep in America." He brought with him the abridged Articles of Religion, a revised *Sunday Service*, ordination certificates for himself, Whatcoat and Vasey, and Wesley's open letter.

Sixty of the eighty-one traveling ministers working in the new nation gathered for the Christmas Conference. Vigorous young men ready to act decisively, they unanimously decided that the Methodist societies "should be erected into an independent church" to be called the Methodist Episcopal Church in America. They agreed to retain Wesley's titles for the superintendent, elder, and deacon, and adopted "the Rev. Mr. Wesley's prayer book," which became "our Liturgy," though the prayer book was quickly laid aside in favor of worship forms that were more useful on the frontier.[8]

While Wesley had appointed Coke as superintendent, planning that he in turn should appoint Asbury to the office as well, Asbury insisted that the conference should confirm their position as general superintendents by election. Their election set a precedent for the way in which American Methodist superintendents or bishops are selected; the conference's action was a major modification of Wesley's plans for the American church. On three successive days Asbury, a layman, was ordained by Coke as deacon, elder, and bishop or superintendent. Twelve or thirteen other men were ordained first as deacons and then as elders. The conference also established Cokesbury College in Maryland in honor of the two superintendents, although the institution had a short life. In addition, the conference adopted most of the disciplinary provisions embodied in the British Conference's Long Minutes. But within six months the *Discipline's* severe antislavery provisions were relinquished because of social pressure. Wesley was not pleased with the superintendents' use of the term "bishop." In the years that followed, the conference clearly showed that it had a mind of its own although it continued to revere him as a spiritual leader.[9]

Frontier and Division

When the United States was formed, the Congregationalists, Presbyterians, and Episcopalians were the largest religious groups (in that order), but by 1820 the Methodists and Baptists occupied the two top places. The Methodists' phenomenal story of success is closely connected with the frontier's rapid movement westward and their ability to evangelize while on horseback. In three or four decades Methodism swept through the frontier territory in a very rapid and vast expansion program that gave it the marks of an unusually successful religious movement.

The 1780s had been an unencouraging decade for Methodists. Cokesbury College burned to the ground in 1795, schism threatened the new church, and there were only about 65,000 members by 1800. But the General Conference in Baltimore that year was the scene of a great revival, which coincided with developments beyond the mountains, and the itinerant preachers returned to their charges with renewed vigor. The early Methodists who worked in the Cane Ridge, Kentucky region did not reject people whose new religious zeal was accompanied by groans and jerks. By 1830 the one conference west of the Alleghenies had grown to eight, and by 1840 the Methodists took a decisive lead over the second-place Baptists. In addition to Asbury and others, William McKendree and Peter Cartwright played important roles in the movement's westward expansion. Methodism reached Mississippi by 1800, Louisiana by 1802, Michigan by 1808, Missouri by 1818, Kansas by 1830, Oregon by 1834, Texas by 1841, Minnesota by 1844, and California by 1849. This rapid process of transcontinental evangelization made the Methodists the first truly national, or continental, denomination. In all but seven cases a Methodist preachers' conference was established before the territory became a state; in most cases the conference was organized in the interim between territorial status and statehood. The formation of the Methodist Missionary Society (1819) for missionary work beyond the nation's borders was a fitting parallel to the denomination's evangelistic zeal at home.[10]

The Methodists used the revival camp meeting to good effect in their spread westward. Linked with the itinerant ministry and the circuit organization of their traveling preachers, it was a powerful instrument of expansion, although the original impulse was slowing appreciably by 1840. Camp meetings offered lonely people on the frontier opportunity to gather in extended meetings that were both social and religious in nature. Two essential ingredients were a strongly emotional personal religious experience and a setting in the woods. At first the camp meeting was an opportunity for cooperation among Baptists, Presbyterians, and Methodists; by 1805 some of the cruder physical expressions of emotion tapered off, and Presbyterians were showing less enthusiasm for the movement.[11]

A number of factors contributed to the Methodists' success on the frontier. The growing attraction of democracy and the rights of the common man during the Jacksonian era strengthened Arminianism and reinforced the preacher's call for the hearer's willful conversion. In addition, the circuit rider showed a zeal for the Lord and his work that often led to worn-out horses and an increasing number of preachers listed in the Annual Conference's "burned out preachers" column. No less important was the work of the local preachers, exhorters and class leaders, who kept the Methodist fires burning between the itinerant preacher's visits. The circuit rider's saddle bags usually contained Wesley's works, a Bible, and various tracts that were left behind for edification. The Methodist connectional system brought to frontier people a sense of a connection with the past, with morals, and with civilization. The circuit rider was a riding newspaper who carried the latest information to news-starved people. He symbolized the frontiersman's connection with the rest of the country and with Europe. The emotional fervor of the preacher and the hearer gave added intensity to the doctrine of free grace; both the doctrine and the emotional response were social levelers that complemented the growing emphasis on the rights of the common man.

One casualty of the massive Methodist success on the frontier was Wesley's skillful collation of Anglican, Roman Catholic, Reformational, Puritan, and Enlightenment theology. The exciting atmosphere of the camp meeting left little room for discussing the theological intricacies of this synthesis. Westward expansion and a number of other factors produced a major transformation in Methodist theology by the end of the nineteenth century, as we will see below. But the conquest of forest, mountain, and plain also contributed much to the development of Methodism. In addition to astronomical growth, it brought, says one commentator, "self-reliance, candor and honesty, simple and direct faith, eager response to human society, stalwart trust in God in the face of great peril and insecurity, heroic devotion."[12]

The Methodist Publishing House (1789) played a strategic role in providing the religious material used by Methodists in their westward expansion. The preachers had an added incentive for selling the material in the fact that all profits went to support retired, disabled, and burned-out preachers and their families. That policy has not changed.

As indicated, general responsibility for deploying the traveling preachers rested with the general superintendent and the district superintendent. The first twelve or thirteen elders ordained in 1784 were "presiding elders," the old term for district superintendents. Each assumed responsibility for guiding a group of circuits; a special assignment was to take the sacraments to the people. A difference of opinion surfaced quickly over the relationship between the district superintendent and the bishop, or general superintendent, but eventually the presiding elder became an arm of the bishop. As the dominant leader in American Methodism, Asbury molded the office of general superintendent, or bishop, in a forceful way. According to the early disciplines, the duties of the general superintendent included the appointment of traveling preachers; presiding at conferences; changing, receiving, and suspending preachers; traveling throughout the connection; giving oversight to spiritual and temporal business; and ordaining bishops, elders, and deacons. The bishop was the focal symbol of Methodism's connectional system.[13]

The itinerant, or traveling, ministry was first practiced in America much as it was in England. This system enabled Methodism to cover the massive expanse of territory in the West in an efficient way. The term "traveling preacher" is both a descriptive and a formal term in Methodism. Descriptively it means the system of itineracy that kept a preacher moving in two ways: first, he was appointed to a charge for a strictly limited period of time, and then appointed to a new area, or charge; second, he kept on the move within the circuit to which he was appointed. Preachers moved around the hoop of their annual conference by being appointed to different circuits, and they also moved in a hoop within the circuit. The fact that Asbury was celibate—and filled with a martyrlike spirit—gave special intensity to the itineracy during his lifetime, although the celibate ministry was beginning to die out in Methodism by about 1816.[14] The traveling preacher was not required to have a large stock of sermons, since he was constantly on the move. The gathering of all the traveling preachers in the annual conference was a festive occasion of camaraderie and good will. At the conclusion of the conference the next appointments were distributed by the bishop.

The time between new appointments gradually increased as the nineteenth century progressed. At first the traveling preacher could expect a change every quarter, but in 1804 a two-year maximum limit was established with the understanding that the normal change was annual; in 1864 the limit became three years in the Methodist Episcopal Church, five years in 1888, and in 1900 the stipulation was removed altogether. In 1866 the limit was changed to four years in the Methodist Episcopal Church, South, although there were numerous exceptions; in 1918 the bishop was authorized to make longer appointments when necessary. District superintendents (called presiding elders in the South) were limited to six-year terms.[15] The stabilizing element in the Methodist itinerant system is the guarantee of pastoral employment. "I have never in my life been listed as an unemployed person, except by my own choice," wrote a Methodist preacher in 1955. "The Methodist Church guaranteed me permanent employment, as it guarantees every other ordained Methodist preacher, the first hour I became a full member of an annual Conference, and through almost a half century it has kept that agreement with absolute fidelity."[16]

As a formal term in Methodism, "traveling preacher" signifies a person who holds membership in an annual conference. It is important to note that historically the admission to membership in an annual conference was not at all related to ordination. "The annual conference and distinctive membership therein," writes the historian Frederick A. Norwood,

> were firmly established eleven years before ordination became an identifying factor in the Methodist ministry. The introduction of ordination provided for the sacraments, but it made almost no difference in the nature of the ministry. From that day to this, the really important factor in definition of the Methodist minister has been membership in an annual conference, not ordination.

It was both belief and practice that the preacher's admission to the annual conference placed him in that select body which possessed the entire power in the church.[17]

In addition to the itineracy, the class meeting was an important factor in Methodism's expansion. In fact, the high-water mark of class meetings and the influence of the class coincided with the heyday of the circuit rider and declined with his dismounting. When the traveling preacher settled down as a stationed minister in a town or village, the class leader (as well as the local preacher or exhorter) became less necessary. Originally a probationary period of two months was required before a seeker was admitted to the Methodist class, but in 1788 the period was extended to six months where it remained until 1908 in the North, but only until 1866 in the South. Usually a small group of no more than twelve people gathered in fellowship to pray, study the Bible, witness to one another, and pursue discipline. Basic training and discipline occurred in this context; minor offenses brought reproof and eventually a trial if the offender persisted. The class meeting was a thriving institution in the first half of the nineteenth century, marking Methodism distinctively, but the meeting began to decline around midcentury. This erosion continued until attendance was made voluntary rather than compulsory, since many failed to attend their class meetings.[18]

As a member of an annual conference, the traveling preacher was distinguished from the local preacher, who was authorized to preach in his place of residence but was not a member of the annual conference, nor was he entitled to a regular appointment. While the local preacher was usually a lay preacher, sometimes he was ordained. The office of lay preacher was first regularized in America in 1796. Often the position was a stepping stone to the position of traveling preacher. While the quality of their work varied widely, local preachers fed the flock between the circuit rider's visits. In 1812 there were 2,000 local preachers compared with 700 itinerants; the number jumped to 8,500 by 1854.[19]

The training of ministers was the responsibility of the General Conference. It suggested books to be read and developed the Conference Course of Study, proposed in 1816 and incorporated in the *Discipline* in 1848. By midcentury the course was designed to last for four years, and twenty-five years later a course was created for the local preacher's use as well. The development of Methodist seminaries owed much to John Dempster, a preacher who pursued the cause of an educated ministry with zeal. What is now Boston University School of Theology had its origin in 1838, while Garrett Seminary in Evanston, Illinois was incorporated in 1857. A third Methodist seminary, Drew, was founded in Madison, New Jersey in 1867. A number of others followed.

Several serious divisions rocked the Methodist Episcopal Church in America during the massive expansion westward. The O'Kelly schism occurred in the 1790s when nearly 3,000 followers of James O'Kelly in Virginia followed their leader out of the church in protest against what they felt was Asbury's increasingly zealous drive for power and highhanded methods. They established what was briefly known as the Republican Methodist Church and later the Christian Church, eventually (1931) participating in the formation of the Congregational Christian Church.[20] Early in the nineteenth century black Methodists showed interest in creating their own ecclesiastical organizations as well. The result was the African Methodist Episcopal Church and the African Methodist Episcopal Zion Church, though later developments at the time of the Civil War were involved in their growth.

The Methodist Protestant Church was formed in 1830 by 5,000 members who shared some of the concerns of O'Kelly about democratic procedures and lay representation in the official body. When the church participated in the major reunion of 1939 it numbered about 200,000 members. In 1820 the reform party succeeded in securing General Conference action to ensure that annual conferences would elect presiding elders rather than having the bishop appoint them. But in 1824 the General Conference narrowly declared the reform resolutions unconstitutional. The reform movement began publishing *Mutual Rights* (1824) while events moved toward schism. In 1828 some reformist local preachers and traveling preachers were expelled. Under the leadership of Alexander McCaine and others, the party sought redress at the General Conference in 1828 but was rebuffed. The schism became a reality as twelve annual conferences were organized and the church formally established in Baltimore late in 1830. The body had no bishops, and laymen were given equal representation in the annual and general conferences. The church did not reject slavery despite its strong insistence on the rights of people in church life.[21]

Another major schism occurred in 1844 when the Methodist Episcopal Church, South, was formed over the question of slavery. Methodists were carefully attuned to the day's social and political currents; the church's division was a precursor of the nation's Civil War over the same issue. The question of slavery was also a major economic factor for the 1,200 Methodist ministers and preachers who owned about 1,500 slaves in 1843, and the 25,000 Methodist members who owned 208,000 slaves. The Wesleyan Methodist Church was formed at the same time by active abolitionists who failed to secure the support of the General Conference in the cause of abolition. This church numbered about 25,000 by the time of the Civil War.[22]

The Methodist Episcopal Church's General Conference of 1844 faced slavery as the fundamental issue, but it preferred to deal with the problem by debating the relative control that the conference exercised over the episcopal office. One of the church's five bishops was James O. Andrews of Georgia, whose first wife had willed him two slaves in her estate; Georgia prohibited their emancipation. The conference voted 110 to 68 that Andrews should "desist from the exercise of this office so long as this impediment remains." A previous vote of 117 to 56 turned down the appeal of a preacher whose annual conference in Maryland suspended him for failing to free the slaves he acquired by marriage, but this case did not involve the constitutional complications of the Andrews case, although it did show the conference's antislavery position. The vote on Andrews indicated that division was certain, and a "Plan of Separation" was prepared for the use of the annual conferences in the South if that decision were reached. One commentator notes that the slavery issue was "a clear theological issue which did not receive very clear theological treatment." Steps were taken to deal with the problem organizationally as the southern delegates met in a constitutional convention in Louisville in 1845. The first General Conference of the Methodist Episcopal Church, South, convened in Petersburg, Virginia in 1846. At first Andrews was the only bishop clearly aligned with the church, but then the senior bishop also aligned himself with the southerners. Major difficulties arose over the question of the boundary between the southern and northern churches and the division of the Publishing House's assets. The United States Supreme Court finally decided the Publishing House case in 1854. The southern church numbered about 500,000 in 1845 and 750,000 in 1860, but then it lost ground because many blacks left. The blacks who remained in the body were invited to form the Colored Methodist Episcopal Church (renamed the Christian Methodist Episcopal Church in 1956) in 1870; they numbered about 100,000.[23]

The General Conference of the northern church gave strong support to the union and President Lincoln when it met in 1864. Bishop Matthew Simpson was a close friend of the president. Four hundred and fifty Methodist ministers volunteered to help the Union soldiers in work that resembled the military chaplaincy. But the war brought havoc to the southern church; by 1866 it had less than 500,000 members, and many of its traveling and local ministers ceased functioning. Thirteen preachers met for the Tennessee Annual Conference in 1864, while two years earlier about two hundred gathered for the meeting. After the war recovery was slow but steady.[24]

After midcentury another major division occurred over the question of "holiness." Two sisters, Sarah A. Langford and Phoebe Palmer, stressed this Wesleyan doctrine in New York City in the 1830s; they enjoyed the patronage of many leading Methodists, including several bishops. The strong emphasis on perfectionism that accompanied midcentury revivals reinforced the movement, and in the late 1860s the National Camp Meeting Association for the Promotion of Holiness was founded, which over the years became the National Holiness Association and the Christian Holiness Association (1971). Methodism was deeply involved in the Holiness movement throughout the early years. In 1860 the Free Methodist Church was formed by founders who were impatient with the northern church's hesitancy on the slavery question and its resistance to their emphasis on holiness; they also opposed what they considered to be abuse of disciplinary authority, and insisted that their church would be free of secret societies, rented pews, outward ornaments, structured worship, and slavery.

While at first the Holiness movement stressed both the regeneration of society and the individual's growth in holiness, by the end of the century this delicate balance disintegrated with the major stress falling on personal holiness. As the movement gained impetus and influence in the 1880s, serious and persistent criticism arose more frequently. While earlier the movement aimed at strengthening faith within the denomination, the trend toward what was called "come-outism" increased; it was countered by a fiery brand of intolerance. As the battle focused on the meaning of entire sanctification, "entire" and "instantaneous" became the battle cry on one side, with "progressive" and "gradual" holiness on the other. The result was the separation of a great number of small groups of people. Among them were the Church of God (Anderson, Indiana), the Church of God (Holiness), the Holiness Church, and groups that eventually clustered in the Church of the Nazarene and the Pilgrim Holiness Church. In the last six years of the century at least ten bodies of predominantly Methodist background were established with entire sanctification as the cardinal doctrine. The movement seemed to find the South and the Midwest as the most fertile for growth.[25] The climax of the long quarrel with the Holiness movement coincided with Methodism's belabored conversion to theological liberalism.

Theological Transition and the Late Nineteenth Century

The beliefs, doctrines, and theology of American Methodists are extremely difficult to summarize for at least two reasons. First, the Doctrinal Standards have been open to varying degrees of acceptance and use, and second, Wesley's theology has exerted varying degrees of influence. That a transition in American Methodist theology occurred at the turn of the twentieth century is certain.

The Christmas Conference in 1784 adopted Wesley's Articles of Religion as well as the other Doctrinal Standards he proposed, and in 1808 the General Conference voted a "Restrictive Rule" (the first) providing that

> the general conference shall not revoke, alter, or change our articles of religion, nor establish any new standards or rules of doctrine contrary to our present existing and and established standards of doctrine.

The Rule was referring to the Twenty-Five Articles, Wesley's *Standard Sermons*, and his *Notes upon the New Testament*. But one informed observer notes that "it would be quite mistaken . . . to conclude that American Methodism generally has conformed to these doctrinal standards, or even that it has felt an obligation to do so." He adds that twentieth-century Methodism has been more concerned with contemporary issues than with preserving a doctrinal heritage that is still legally binding.[26]

In the early years of American Methodism Wesley's influence apparently had greater force than later. Up to about 1840 the Methodist Episcopal Church was characterized by two theological tendencies. Representatives of the first presented and defended Wesley's theology in systematic, reasoned form, relying largely on the second-generation British theologians Richard

Watson, Adam Clarke, and Joseph Benson, in addition to Wesley. Reason played an important role in establishing Christian "evidences" and natural theology. The second development was the beginning of indigenous theological literature which, exerting some independence from original Wesleyan sources, showed the impact of revivalism, the frontier, and American Calvinism. According to Robert E. Chiles, a major historian of Methodist theology, these forces tended to "exaggerate the subjective experience of grace and to accent its emotional accompaniments" and helped "confirm Methodism in an uncritical theological attitude which it seldom escaped for long." The theological challenge of Calvinsim sparked the development of Nathan Bangs (1778–1862) as one of the first indigenous American Methodist theologians. A strong proponent of an educated ministry and theological literature, Bangs stressed the merciful and gracious origin of responsible human participation in salvation as an adequate Methodist answer to Hopkinsian Calvinism.[27]

The encounter with American culture vitally influenced Methodist theology between 1840 and 1890. Evolutionary science and philosophical currents contributed to the centripetal movement of Methodist theological thought around two foci: the philosophical emphasis on free personal agency encouraged the revision of theological categories, while at the same time there were efforts to offer comprehensive statements that would integrate these categories. Around 1890 John Miley (b. 1813), professor of systematic theology at Drew Theological Seminary, synthesized these tendencies in an ethical Arminianism that sought to sustain the Wesleyan-Arminian heritage. He was an excellent representative of Methodist theology in this period; his two-volume *Systematic Theology* appeared in 1892–1894 and was used in the preachers' course of study. His ethical Arminianism stressed free personal agency as the key constructive principle; he severely criticized the theology of native guilt, or original sin, anchored in Augustinian theology and found governmental justice to be the center of the atonement. But his loyalty to the Wesleyan heritage was firm, and he continued to discuss man's helplessness and reliance on grace for every movement toward good. Apparently he was among the last to anchor himself so firmly in Wesley's thought.[28]

Methodist theological literature made only infrequent references to Wesley at the turn of the century. More important according to Chiles were theological responses to cultural forces such as "science and its evolutionary world view, the critical study of the Bible, and philosophy as set forth by Ritschl, Lotze, and Schleiermacher." While some radically embraced the new worldview and rejected traditional theology, most Methodist theologians seemed to mediate the new views and traditional faith. The last fifteen years of the nineteenth century witnessed a major change in leadership in Methodist theology. The "liberal evangelicalism" of Miley and others gave way to the "evangelical liberalism" of Milton Terry (1840–1914) of Garrett, the southern theologian Wilbur F. Tillett (1854–1936) of Vanderbilt, and Albert C. Knudson (1873–1953) of Boston University, among others. In 1916 the General Conference of the northern church removed the 1864 requirement that subscription to the Articles of Religion was a test for membership, despite conservative resistance. That year the course of study showed a radical departure from previous study lists, and the liberal reconstruction of Methodist theology continued to pursue its course.[29]

That Methodist theology had passed through a substantive transition is evident from a brief survey of the treatment of the major doctrine of free grace and redemption. The key to Wesley's theology might well have been his insistence on free grace for all for the accomplishment of full salvation. The first work of Methodist systematic theology, the British Methodist Richard Watson's *Christian Institutes* (1823), faithfully stressed the atonement of Christ as the central doctrine of Wesleyan theology during the period when American Methodist theologians were in part using such British sources as this one. All theologians between 1840 and 1890 continued to treat justification and sanctification as basic identities, but Miley's effort to maintain rapport with the age while faithfully representing the Wesleyan-Arminian heritage showed a decisive commitment to free personal agency that appreciably influenced his doctrines of sin and grace. "With its severe restrictions placed on the role of prevenient grace, and its imposing claims made for the freedom of rational man," Chiles notes, "his theology of salvation represents a reluctant but decided departure from original Wesleyanism." Knudson formulated more precisely the modifications in the doctrine of grace at which Miley hinted. He portrayed salvation not as the rescue of a helpless person but as that person's resolve to improve his condition, a resolve fulfilled with divine assistance. Knudson's personal idealism, says Chiles, was the zenith of "the reconstruction of [Methodist] theology guided by the spirit and principles of liberalism."[30] This sort of major transition in theology was also experienced by many other religious denominations in the United States; in Methodism it coincided with the exodus of many of the small Holiness groups.

The rapid Americanization of Methodists made them probably the most culturally representative Protestant church body in the United States by the end of the nineteenth century. Theodore Roosevelt remarked that he never felt as keenly that he was talking to a typical American audience as when he spoke to a Methodist gathering. Methodists lived up to this billing by seeking to make the American imperialism of this era benevolent in fact as well as in word. In general missionary conferences in New Orleans in 1901 and a year later in Cleveland, both the southern and northern churches declared strong support for the national policy of manifest destiny, especially in the case of the Philippines. A major book by the Methodist preacher James M. King strongly supported divinely ordered expansion and pointed to the menace of "politico-ecclesiastical Romanism" at home and abroad. A recent study of the Methodists' endorsement of national expansion concludes that "through the course of official meetings, their press, and pulpit oratory they provided a means by which imperialism, once undertaken, could be made palatable to a large number of Americans."[31]

The success of the campaign for which Methodists have often been remembered, namely, the prohibition of liquor by constitutional amendment, indicates both the strength of Methodism and its importance as a representative of American culture and values. The campaign culminated in the passage of the Eighteenth Amendment and its ratification by the states immediately after World War I. But this "last hurrah" of American Protestantism—it was in part a campaign against Roman Catholicism as well as a rural-urban battle—was also a portent of growing pluralism in America. Shortly after 1920 the Methodists, for the first time in a century, lost the lead to the Baptists in the total number of church members.[32]

The Methodist concern with temperance and prohibition was an old one. Earlier in the nineteenth century the heavy workload of the circuit rider sometimes brought moral callousness and retreat to the bottle; these preachers knew the devastating effects of the intemperate use of liquor. Early efforts were directed toward instilling a sense of temperance and passing church legislation to promote discipline within the ranks of church members. States began to turn dry in 1851, sometimes under Methodist influence (such as the northern General Conference's recommendation in 1852). Methodists actively promoted the National Prohibition Party (1869), Women's Christian Temperance Union (1874), and the National Anti-Saloon League (1895). In 1880 the northern General Conference amended its *Discipline* with the words, "Temperance is a Christian virtue, Scripturally enjoined." Official Temperance Sunday dated from 1868. The southern General Conference announced in 1890 that "voluntary total abstinence from all intoxicants is the sole and true ground of personal temperance, and complete legal prohibition of the traffic is the duty of the government," and the Methodist Protestant Church took similar action. In the 1870s Frances E. Willard stressed temperance as a way to elevate women's rights. In 1908 the northern General Conference heard a report that "the Methodist Episcopal Church is a temperance society." Methodists actively distributed much of the forty tons of prohibitionist literature published each month in 1912 by the Anti-Saloon League. There is no question that the issue of temperance and prohibition brought the Methodist Episcopal Church, South, into the realm of political social action, just as it appreciably influenced the church in the north. The southern Methodist bishop James Cannon (1864–1944), called the "dry Messiah," worked zealously with others in 1928 to defeat Alfred E. Smith's bid for the presidency both because he was wet and because he was a Roman Catholic.[33]

The question of the traditional use of wine in the Communion caused no problem for Wesley or most American Methodists in the first half of the nineteenth century. Most periodical literature supported this practice until the Civil War, although some insisted that "alcoholic wine was not used on the occasion of the Paschal supper." But in 1864 the northern General Conference recommended in the appendix of the *Discipline* that in all cases "the pure juice of the grape be used in Communion," and the other churches followed suit. In 1968 the General Conference of the United Methodist Church voted by a heavy majority not to permit local congregations the option of using wine in Communion. In 1976 the church's Board of Global Ministries announced that it would sell more than a half-million dollars' worth of Coca-Cola Company stock if the company proceeded with plans to purchase the Taylor Wine Company.[34] In a survey of 5,000 representative members of The Methodist Church in 1959, researchers discovered that 56.8 percent felt they should "totally abstain from alcoholic beverages," while 26.5 percent said that "I, as a Christian, may use alcoholic beverages as long as I do so temperately and within reason." Nearly 9 percent indicated that they should work for prohibition. At that time The Methodist Church's Board of Temperance stressed education, commitment to abstinence, rehabilitation, and legislative efforts.[35]

Campaigning for prohibition along with a number of other Protestant groups, the Methodists had a special advantage because of their great size. By 1920 their various church bodies counted nearly 8 million members. In 1939 the largest of the bodies, The Methodist Church, had a total membership of nearly 8 million members. In the course of nearly a century the 2,700 local Methodist churches of 1820 had grown to nearly 20,000 in 1860 and 53,908 in 1900. By 1950 there were 54,000 Methodist churches; by that year the 5½ million Methodists of 1900 had nearly doubled. But the rate of growth slowed appreciably after 1900 compared with the preceding century. In 1800 the Methodists numbered about 65,000, but in fifty years they increased nearly 2,000 percent to 1¼ million, while the general population increased only 437 percent. In 1800 they made up 1.2 percent of the population; this percentage rose to 5.4 in 1850 and 6 percent in 1900, close to the high point for the movement.[36]

Social Concern and Reunification in the Methodist Church

Like Wesley, the Methodist ministers of the Christmas Conference in 1874 had agreed that God's design in raising up the people called Methodists was "to reform the continent, and to spread scriptural holiness over these lands." During the nineteenth century Methodists fought liquor traffic and opposed public demands for an "open Sunday," but increasingly after the Civil War they were composed of middle-class, fairly well-educated people who were somewhat distant from the laboring people of the land. Most of the Methodist constituency was rural and small town, untouched by the misery of city slums. The approval of a "Social Creed" by the northern General Conference in 1908 was an effort to "spread Scriptural holiness" and "reform the continent" once again.[37]

A year earlier the Methodist Federation for Social Service was organized by five Methodist ministers, including Harry F. Ward, to articulate the social concerns of Methodists. In 1908 a major part of the episcopal address at the northern General Conference was devoted to social themes, including liquor traffic, child labor, international peace, workingmen, immigration, and labor unions. By adopting a committee report, the conference gave semi-official status to a "Methodist Social Creed" written by Ward. Its twelve lines concentrated on the one problem of economics, but pledged the church's support for "equal rights and complete justice for all men in all stations of life," industrial arbitration, abolition of child labor and protection of women workers, factory safety, reduction of hours, guarantee of a living wage, "equitable division of the products of industry," and "for the recognition of the Golden Rule in the mind of Christ as the supreme law of society and the sure remedy for all social ills." In slightly amended form the creed was adopted as the social ideals of the Federal Council of Churches that same year. Among other things, it aimed at reestablishing the close connection of the Wesleyan movement with laboring man and woman.[38]

With no recognized spokesman for the social gospel up to this time, the Methodist Episcopal Church now had a quasi-official statement and a voluntary organization concerned with broad social issues. In 1912 it gave more express approval to the Federation for Social Service and called Ward as executive secretary. In 1914 the southern General Conference adopted the creed, followed in 1916 by the Methodist Protestant Church. In 1939 the Uniting Conference of these three bodies adopted a revised version of the creed. In 1952 The Methodist Church established the Board of Social and Economic Relations in a rebuff of the Federation for Social Service (now Action); the cold-war mentality of the fifties undoubtedly influenced this action, which indicated rather forceful opposition to a progressive left-wing approach to economic life. In 1964 a more encompassing version of the Social Creed was adopted by The Methodist Church; it treated family relationships, economic life, town, country and city, intoxicants and narcotics, crime and rehabilitation, race relations, international affairs and world peace, politics and civil liberties. In 1972 the General Conference of The United Methodist Church adopted another revision of the creed of 1908.[39]

The various branches of Methodism engaged in a variety of social programs during the first half of the twentieth century. Both the northern and southern churches supported the vigorous patriotism that was popular throughout the land in World War I, and liberty bonds were sold in some churches. In 1932 the northern General Conference took a historic position favoring conscientious objection and requesting the government to stop all military training at civilian educational institutions. In 1934 the southern church also supported conscientious objection and asked all of its preachers to preach once a year on world peace.[40]

Common concern for social welfare was one of many signs that the three Methodist bodies that went their separate ways in the nineteenth century were moving toward unity in the twentieth. At a large Uniting Conference in Kansas City, Missouri, in 1939, delegates from the Methodist Episcopal

Church, the Methodist Episcopal Church, South, and the Methodist Protestant Church brought to completion nearly twenty years of negotiations and merged the three bodies to form The Methodist Church, reestablishing a truly national body. A newly edited version of the *Discipline* provided the constitutional basis for union. Fewer than 100 of the 40,000 congregations involved refused to enter the new union; the union's legality was affirmed in a Supreme Court case. The unreconciled minority formed the Southern Methodist Church in Columbia, South Carolina, in 1939, and a few years later another tiny group withdrew to form the Evangelical Methodist Church. The Methodist Episcopal Church brought 4,684,444 members into the new body, the Methodist Episcopal Church, South, 2,847,351, and the Methodist Protestant Church, 197,996.[41]

The most important constitutional modification in the new body was the inauguration of jurisdictions as a level of government functioning between the annual conference and the General Conference. This provision for regionalism led some to fear that provincialism would produce a number of autonomous Methodisms, while others feared that the strong central structure of the General Conference, national administrative agencies, and Council of Bishops would tilt the balance in favor of overcentralization. This basic structure, accepted in 1939, was incorporated in The United Methodist Church when it was formed in 1968; in the new church bishops continue to be elected by jurisdictional conferences to serve in the jurisdiction that elected them. The jurisdictional arrangement was a concession to southern churchmen, and currently it enjoys varying degrees of importance depending on geography.[42]

The issue of race was an integral factor in the formation of the jurisdictional organization in 1939. While the critical issue of negotiation between the Methodist Episcopal Church and the Methodist Protestant Church was the question of equal lay representation at annual conferences, the basic issue with the southern church was the question of black Methodists, nearly 300,000 of whom worshiped in mostly segregated annual conferences.

The Central Jurisdiction was the result of a compromise worked out over a twenty-year period between the Methodist Episcopal Church and the Methodist Episcopal Church, South, to accommodate black churches in the merger. The place of the black churches was one of the principle issues that stood in the way of union. During the period of Reconstruction after the Civil War, northern missionaries and welfare workers had organized blacks into churches in the South that were placed under the control of the Methodist Episcopal Church. While the five other jurisdictions in the merger plan were defined by the geography of states, the new Central Jurisdiction covered all the black churches in the nation. It was a segregated church within the church. This new jurisdiction enabled blacks to elect their own bishops and publish their own church periodical, and allowed fellowship and leadership opportunities on national boards and agencies, whose membership was delegated by the jurisdiction. In establishing the Central Jurisdiction the

Methodist Church gave the appearance of accepting the doctrine of "separate but equal" that characterized social and civil structures.

Black Methodist leaders fought against this segregated structure from the time it was first proposed. While some of them hoped that it would be an interim or transitional measure, little was done to encourage that hope until the 1950s when the courts began to revise the "separate but equal" interpretation of the United States Constitution. In The Methodist Church, strong resistance to integration and civil rights in the South was coupled with opposition to the dissolution of the Central Jurisdiction.

In 1958 an amendment to the church's *Discipline* became effective, which began to dissolve the Central Jurisdiction by allowing churches or annual conferences to identify with a regional annual conference or jurisdiction if these conferences agreed. In 1964 the church's General Conference decided that the Central Jurisdiction should end by 1968, but the process moved slowly, in part because some blacks were uninterested in being absorbed.[43] In 1973 the last two all-black annual conferences in The United Methodist Church were eliminated in the last of a series of mergers to end the all-black jurisdiction; but eight of the five hundred districts in the church remained segregated until all districts based on race were eliminated in 1974. By then thirty-eight of the districts had black superintendents. In 1974 J. Garfield Owens became the first black pastor appointed to an all-white congregation.

Postwar Period and The United Methodist Church

The Methodist Church participated in the national religious revival that followed World War II. Already in 1944 the General Conference approved a program entitled "Crusade for Christ," which solicited funds for refugees and emphasized spirituality, Christian education, and stewardship. The theme between 1948 and 1952 was "Advance for Christ and His Church."

In 1956 the *Discipline* was amended to permit the ordination of women. A number of Methodist women had engaged in preaching, including Maggie Van Cott, who secured a preacher's license in 1866 and pursued a vigorous itinerant ministry for thirty years, as well as the black washerwoman Amanda Smith. But the northern church explicitly refused to permit women to be ordained in 1880. The question remained in constitutional limbo in the Methodist Protestant Church after a woman's ordination in 1880 was declared unlawful. In 1868 the African Methodist Episcopal Zion Church removed the term "male" from its ordination regulations, and in 1896 a female deacon was ordained and two years later an elder.[44]

The social characteristics of people in The Methodist Church in 1959 offer an interesting profile. The information was secured by a representative sample and other data. The study described the typical Methodist parishioner (rather than member, who would have to be about twelve years of age or older) as having a median age of 34.5 years, 15 percent higher than the total

U.S. population median of 30.2 years in 1950. Eleven out of twenty Methodists were female, a higher proportion than in the population. The average family size was 3.6 persons, identical with the average reported in the 1950 census. The number of Methodists forty-five years and older was 40 percent higher than the percentage of the United States population in that age grouping. The educational attainment of Methodists was somewhat higher than the median educational achievement of the total population over twenty-five years of age; a Methodist young person had a chance of graduating from college that was three times higher than a non-Methodist. Three out of four Methodist congregations were located in communities of less than 2,500 population, and 60 percent of Methodists lived in "town and country" or rural areas of less than 10,000 population, a much higher percentage than the national average. Twenty-five percent of the Methodists belonged to churches with less than 250 members, and nearly 50 percent with less than 500 members. One person was added to the church in 1958 for each twenty-six members; the church was growing about half as fast as the total population between 1950 and 1958. Only 5 percent of The Methodist Church was nonwhite, while nearly 25 percent of all Methodist members were black. The Methodist Church had a higher percentage of professional men and women and managers than the general population; the percentage of professional men and women was three times higher than the general population's percentage, and the number of farm operators and managers was 6 percent higher than the population's percentage.[45]

In 1966 The Methodist Church observed the two hundredth anniversary of the organizing of the first preaching societies in the New World. Under the theme "Forever Beginning," more than two thousand people gathered in Mount Olivet Cemetery in Baltimore, Maryland, to bury a time capsule to be opened in 2066.[46]

A merger of considerable importance occurred two years later when The Methodist Church joined with The Evangelical United Brethren Church (EUB) to form The United Methodist Church. Late in the year a census of the new denomination determined that its membership came within 10,000 of reaching 11 million members. In terms of numbers, this was the largest merger in American religious history. Ninety Methodist bishops and nine representing the Evangelical United Brethren processed into the large auditorium in Dallas, Texas, and then two of the bishops clasped hands and joined the 10,000 delegates in declaring, "Lord of the Church, we are united in thee, in thy church, and now in the United Methodist Church. Amen." The two merging bodies passed enabling legislation in simultaneous General Conferences in 1966, ten years after discussions began, the Methodists by a 749 to 40 vote and the Brethren by 325 to 88. More than the required two thirds of their annual conferences ratified these decisions, although the Northwest Annual Conference of the EUB Church voted 4 to 1 in adamant opposition and eventually broke off. Since doctrinal differences between the two groups were minimal, most of the merger negotiations concerned polity questions. Eventually the EUB Church agreed to accept The Methodist Church's practice of electing bishops for life (versus four-year renewable terms) and the appointment of district superintendents by the bishop (versus election by the annual conference in the EUB). The merger plan required that a time limit be set for the dissolution of the Methodists' Central Jurisdiction. The plan incorporated side by side the doctrinal statements of both churches, the EUB's Confession of Faith and the Methodists' Articles of Religion. Both churches' social creeds were left intact.

The Evangelical United Brethren Church came into existence in 1946 when the Church of the United Brethren in Christ merged with the Evangelical Church. These bodies had relatively similar historical, cultural, and doctrinal backgrounds and were closely related to Methodism in theology and piety. At the time of the merger the strength of the Church of the United Brethren in Christ lay chiefly in the Miami Valley of Ohio, as well as in Indiana and Pennsylvania. The Evangelical Church was strong in Ohio, Michigan, Illinois, Wisconsin, and especially Pennsylvania. The new church had a membership of about three quarters of a million; the Brethren were about twice as large as the Evangelical Church. Both merging bodies had participated in the formation of the World Council of Churches, and in fact the Evangelical Church was the first American denomination to join this group. They had also been active in the creation of the Federal and the National Council of Churches.

One of the chief founders of the Church of the United Brethren in Christ was Philip William Otterbein (1726–1813). Trained for the Reformed ministry in Germany, he had come to America in 1752 when Michael Schlatter, a Dutch Reformed pastor in Pennsylvania, invited him to minister to neglected and scattered Germans with Reformed background. Around 1754 Otterbein said that he had a deep religious experience that led him to oppose strenuously "insensible religion," which had no sense of a personal, experienced relationship with the living God and which did not impart to the redeemed a sense of assurance of acceptance. This accent upon convertive, experiential religion aroused the suspicion and opposition of some of his colleagues in the German Reformed Church. About this time he and the Mennonite preacher Martin Boehm (1725–1813), a student of Wesley's books who also preached "experiential religion," started conducting revival meetings among Germans in Virginia, Maryland, and Pennsylvania. In 1774 Otterbein accepted a call to a new German Reformed congregation in Baltimore, which assumed the name German Evangelical Reformed Church. In 1784 he participated in Asbury's consecration during the Methodists' Christmas Conference in that city. In 1789 a number of like-minded men, clergy and laity, met with Otterbein and with 1800 regular annual meetings commenced. In 1800 Otterbein and Boehm were recognized as superintendents (later termed bishops) of the movement.

The first General Conference was held in 1815 at which a *Discipline* was prepared for publication the next year. It showed the direct influence of the Methodists' *Discipline*, but it provided for voting rights for both traveling and local preachers in the annual conference. Although various theological accents from Reformed, Lutheran, Mennonite, and Dunkard traditions were appropriated, Arminian theology and Methodist polity were prominent. The group was greatly influenced by Christian Newcomer, who was elected bishop in 1813 after Otterbein died. The new church's total membership grew from around 10,000 in 1813 to 47,000 in 1850, 61,000 in 1857, 200,00 by 1900, and about a third of a million in 1920. While German continued to be used as a minority language until 1930, by 1837 English was commonly used in general conferences, and the group quite early left the cocoon of German language and culture behind.

Marked and important similarities existed between this church and the Methodists. An early endeavor (1810) to merge the two groups failed. The United Brethren Church experienced few theological controversies and none reached grave significance. But in 1889 the church was shaken by a controversy involving discipline. In 1841 the church had written into its constitution an article forbidding "connection with secret combinations." Following a referendum in the church, this clause was modified in 1889 to apply only to secret societies "which infringe upon the rights of those outside their organization and whose principles and practices are injurious to the Christian character of their members." A protesting minority interpreted this change as permitting membership in fraternal and benevolent orders, and they withdrew to form the Church of the United Brethren in Christ (Old Constitution).

Doctrinally the United Brethren were broadly Arminian, influenced strongly by Wesleyanism and Pietism. After lengthy controversy, the conference defined "depravity" in 1853 as "absence of holiness, which unfits man for heaven, but does not involve guilt." While the nineteenth-century American Holiness movement influenced them mildly, it brought no great controversy. Their pietistic background oriented them toward the simple, personal Christian ethic, which they upheld. The mode of baptism and the practice of foot washing were left to the judgment of the individual. They adopted definite rules and regulations governing the conduct of members and employed the class system, like the Methodists. During the nineteenth century they took strong positions against alcohol and slavery; during the last decades of the nineteenth century and in the twentieth, social reforms, such as the abolition of child labor and passage of the Eighteenth Amendment, played a prominent role in church activities.

The bishops were not a separate order of the ministry but, rather, elders elected by General Conference to superintend the church. Bishops and conference superintendents appointed pastors to churches. The court of highest appeal was the General Conference.[47]

The Evangelical Church had a very similar background, with close affinity for Methodism. Jacob Albright (Albrecht; 1759–1808) was the founder. A Lutheran layman of pietistic background, he experienced a "conversion" in 1791 and began preaching among Germans in eastern Pennsylvania and Maryland. About 1803 the first evidences of an ecclesiastical society began to appear. People called his adherents Albright People or Albright Brethren, or in some communities German Methodists. In 1816 they chose as their name the Evangelical Association (*Evangelische Gemeinschaft*). Regular annual conferences commenced in 1807, when Albright was elected bishop. The first General Conference met in 1816. While most of the early work was done in German, by the end of the century their witness was in English. They adopted the circuit system and itinerant ministry of the Methodists.

In 1891 a painful division occurred. Those who withdrew organized the United Evangelical Church in 1894, but in 1922 the two denominations reunited as the Evangelical Church. This was the first use of the term "church" in the association as such. Objectors to this union organized under the name of the Evangelical Congregational Church. In 1839 the movement had numbered about 8,000; by the end of the century the total strength approximated 170,000. The overshadowing concern of Evangelicals through these years was to call people to salvation and nurture them in the Christian life. While concerned with evangelical faith, they were not doctrinnaire. Only once did a doctrinal controversy disturb the church; it involved the doctrine of Christian perfection.

The Wesleyan influence on Albright's teaching was evident in the Evangelical Articles of Faith (1816), which described the visible church as the communion of true believers. Infant baptism was generally practiced and rebaptism was discouraged. Baptism was considered the sign of entrance into the household of faith and a mark of Christian discipleship. The polity that Evangelicals adopted for their organization paralleled essential features of Methodist church government, including the circuit system, itineracy, and general, annual, and local conferences. The bishop and presiding elders annually appointed pastors. Bishops served four-year terms and were eligible for reelection if they had not reached retirement age.[48]

When these two churches united in 1946 as the Evangelical United Brethren Church (EUB), some alterations in the traditional polity were required. The General Conference, which met every four years, was the highest authority. The General Council of Administration coordinated and promoted the denomination's total program between sessions. The Evangelical Articles (1816) and the United Brethren Confession (1815, 1889) were included in unaltered form in the new *Discipline* because of the Evangelicals' rule against change (1839). In 1958 the General Conference asked the Board of Bishops to provide the church with a new Confession of Faith, a task that was undertaken with wide consultation throughout the church. The General Conference adopted the new confession in 1962, supplanting both former confessions. A striking departure was the inclusion of a long article on "Sanctification and Christian Perfection," a unique Wesleyan doctrinal emphasis. This confession was taken over intact into the *Discipline* of The United Methodist Church when The Methodist Church merged with the Evangelical United Brethren Church in 1968. The confession and the Methodist articles were "deemed congruent if not identical in their doctrinal perspectives, and are not in conflict."[49] In sum, while the vast majority of Evangelical United Brethren united with The Methodist Church in 1968, at different points and for different reasons three small denominations departed from the main Evangelical United Brethren stream: the United Brethren in Christ (Old Constitution), the United Christian Church, and the Evangelical Congregational Church.

The United Methodist Church continued the strong ecumenical thrust of the churches that merged to form it, including membership in the Consultation on Church Union, which The Methodist Church had helped to establish. The new body was also influential in international ecumenical circles, since its membership made up nearly half of world Methodism.[50] In late 1977 the United Methodists provided representatives for the inauguration of bilateral conversations between Lutherans and Methodists around the globe.

Doctrinal Standards, Worship, and Polity

The Doctrinal Standards adopted by the early Methodists, as well as their First Restrictive Rule regarding doctrine, were part of the background against which theological transition occurred in American Methodism. But care must be exercised not to give the Articles of Religion more signficance in the United Methodist Church than they warrant. While early Methodists rejected Wesley's direct control, they retained loyalty to his three-fold *magisterium* (the Conference, *Sermons*, and *Notes*); their First Restrictive Rule (1808) described these as "our present existing and established standard of doctrine." But it was necessary to make explicit reference to the Articles of Religion, which came to America as an appendix of Wesley's hastily abridged Book of Common Prayer, called *Sunday Service*. In the earliest American *Disciplines* the articles were printed as appendices; finally in 1792, without formal authorization, somehow they were moved forward to the position they still occupy in the *Discipline*, immediately following the church's constitution. Remaining in this pivotal location in succeeding editions of the *Discipline*, they gave the appearance of being the Methodists' doctrinal "confession," though they did not serve this purpose for Wesley or for the Church of England in the unabridged version. "They have remained," reported the United Methodists' recent Study Commission on Doctrine and Doctrinal Standards, "unchanged, unchallenged—and largely disregarded."[51]

The rediscovery of Wesley's thought in the decades following George Croft Cell's book in 1935 has stimulated and intensified interest in Methodist belief, doctrine, and theology in the United States. The creation of the Wesley Society in 1955 and the massive project to publish a new critical edition of Wesley's works are signs of this effort to reappropriate his theology.

But the linkage with Wesleyan tradition has not been easy to reestablish, especially since a number of American Methodist theologians in the twentieth century were occupied with theological challenges and currents generated on the European continent.[52]

A sample of the beliefs held by Methodists in the mid-twentieth century was provided when more than five thousand representative members of The Methodist Church gave replies to doctrinal questions in 1959.[53] Regarding the Bible, 49.7 percent of the respondents described it as "the unique historical record of God's revelation to inspired men" which "contains the word of God"; 32 percent said it is "the inspired Word of God, but not all parts are of equal spiritual value." The overwhelming majority (78 percent) chose to describe man as "a rational being capable of knowing God and entering into fellowship with him," while 4 percent said man is "a being who has blurred and distorted the divine image in which God has created him"; the next most popular answer was more optimistic in character. Sin is "voluntary attitudes and actions, partially due to our involvement in society, which are contrary to God's will," according to 50.8 percent; 17 percent described it as "a corruption of man's nature inherited from Adam, and rebellious acts resulting from this condition." Nearly half the respondents (41 percent) agreed that "salvation means peace and joy with God through His forgiveness of our sins," while 50 percent chose to say that "salvation means power to live a new life in fellowship with God and man." Two thirds of the respondents split evenly in describing Jesus Christ as "both divine and human" (37.5 percent) and "a man uniquely endowed and called by God to reveal Him to man" (36.4 percent), while the other respondents split their answers among three other responses. The completion of the sentence "Men are saved" showed a wide variety of difference; 54.3 percent said "by divine grace when they respond in repentance and trustful obedience," 25 percent said "by belief in Jesus Christ and upright living," 11 percent said "by believing that Jesus Christ is the Son of God," and 4 percent said "entirely by divine grace." Under the subject heading "Growth in Grace," 82 percent agreed that "with God's help both individuals and society may progress toward the fulfillment of his purposes." The next most popular response (with 11 percent) was, "Christians should expect through the power of God to attain perfect love in this life." Forty percent said that social change "is a partial responsibility of the church, but secondary to the transformation of individuals," while 25 percent argued that it "is of equal importance with individual transformation." The remaining questions described other areas of belief.

Ten years later the Methodist theologian Albert Outler provided a terse summary of Methodist theology that showed important points of contact with these data on the beliefs of Methodists. In general, he said, Methodist theology

> may best be understood as a peculiar brand of evangelical Christianity, with origins in a catholic environment and with its evolution (especially in America)

within the milieu of modern secularism. Its most distinctive theological characteristic has been its doctrine of God's grace (the active presence of his love in human existence) in which the prime concern is a vital synthesis of the evangelical stress on God's sovereignty and the catholic emphasis on human agency: a dynamic mix of prevenience, justification, regeneration, and holiness. In other words, when Methodists talk about the ancient paradox of God's ways with men, they have their own recognizable way of trying to explain it all.[54]

When the United Methodist Church was formed in 1968, a special Theological Study Commission on Doctrine and Doctrinal Standards was created with Outler as chairman. More than two dozen conferees worked for four years and concluded that the times were unfavorable for a new formal confession, but that guidelines for theological interpretations were extremely important in a period of theological transition. A major statement offered four guidelines firmly rooted in Wesleyan teaching—on Scripture, tradition, experience and reason—within which Methodist theology might properly develop. Theological pluralism was encouraged, and the commission focused on the functional use of doctrine in the first page of an early report: "Doctrine and doctrinal standards," it said,

> are meaningful only as they serve the Christian community in its unending search for authentic mission in the world. . . . Our prime question . . . is not simply, "What do we believe?" or even "What ought we believe?" More deeply, we need to ask, "How and in what ways can our doctrinal heritage illuminate the problems of church and society in the 20th century and beyond?"

The commission minced no words in portraying the apparent absence of such a functioning theology:

> We can scarcely identify ourselves to ourselves; we baffle our separated brethren. Our Wesleyan heritage goes largely unclaimed; the mingling of Methodist and EUB [Evangelical United Brethren] traditions has barely begun. Our doctrinal norms are ill-defined and anomalous. We have a *Discipline* that is generally clear on questions of administrative polity, but blandly vague with respect to doctrine and doctrinal standards. The simplest proof of this is the frequent mention of *"our* doctrines," with no definition of what the phrase refers to. It is as if, once upon a time, an earlier generation understood it all and then forgot to tell their children—who never asked.[55]

The fact that the last heresy trial conducted by the church occurred in 1905, or that a Methodist pastor referred to such an event as a "form of religious entertainment,"[56] seems to reaffirm some of the commission's observations.

In its General Conference in 1972 the United Methodist Church adopted the new statement proposed by the study commission. Rather than replacing or revising traditional creeds, it set up guidelines to assist church members, pastors, and theologians in understanding their beliefs and applying them to life. In describing the core of United Methodism's heritage, the commission suggested that the starting point had always been the insistence that God "is love, but *that* love is not abstract." It is the personal concern and outreach of the Creator. The fathers stressed an "experience" of the God who was active in history and human life, and demanding obedient love. God's love can "never be earned or sought" since it "is and will be there before we are even aware or can begin to respond." Rather than an intellectual understanding or bare assent to doctrine, faith is "active trust and confidence in a loving God who forgives, plus an inward readiness to serve and obey him." Human beings are "God's own special creation," "creatures of incalculable worth to God" and "of significance to each other." But human beings also have "the tragic ease with which our good intentions and high ideals slide into illusion." The grisly paradox is that "we are God's special projects" but "we operate in a world that is fatally flawed by these never fully-intended acts of self-mutilation and ruination in human society." The Christian life of response to God's love is "a reciprocating action (a synergism) in which man's response is integral to God's completed action." The commission added that "the genuine Christian life of faith has its beginning in the miraculous discovery of God's personal love and care, his pardon and forgiveness." Through Christ's suffering love fully extended, his death, "we know that we are genuinely accepted in God's love." Justification and assurance are thus intimately correlated, also with sanctification or "Christian perfection," which means that "you must come to know the full impact of the life of God's spirit in you, so filling your life with love and so motivating your actions that there is less and less room for motivations that spring from other than love."[57]

Many United Methodists seem to agree with Outler that the marks of the church are evangelism, worship, and discipline, all of which imply the validity of Wesley's insistence on the essence of a functional doctrine of the church.[58] Thus in regard to the ministry, many Methodists find it easier and more profitable to agree on the role of the minister than on the theological basis of the ministerial office. Infant baptism is generally administered by sprinkling or pouring, but a wide difference of opinion seems to exist on the exact theological nature of this sacrament. The same appears to be true of the Lord's Supper. The *Discipline* prescribes that at the time of Holy Communion "the elements of bread and wine shall be placed" on the Lord's Table, but adds: "The pure, unfermented juice of the grape shall be used." When the bread is given the minister is instructed to say one or both of the following sentences: "The body of our Lord Jesus Christ, which was given for thee, preserve thy soul and body unto everlasting life." "Take and eat this in remembrance that Christ died for thee, and feed on him in thy heart by faith with thanksgiving." One student of the sacraments in Methodism described the Lord's Supper as "a framework of worship," "physical means through which the spirit of worship may be exercised," adding that "the whole ceremony *sug-*

gests Jesus to the worshiper," produces quietness of mind, offers themes for meditation, and induces a sense of brotherhood.[59]

According to Wesley's plans the worship of early American Methodists was to have been directed by his revision of the Book of Common Prayer, entitled *Sunday Service*. But for a variety of reasons this rich liturgical work found little acceptance and disappeared totally from use at an early date. This was a symbolic loss, one prominent historian suggests, "of the central concept of the church at the very moment the American societies were becoming a church." There was no longer a stated form of worship, and soon the sermon became the center of most services with the other parts considered as adjuncts. The "invitation to Christian discipleship" which concluded Sunday services and camp meetings retains its place of prominence today. The Lord's Supper was celebrated infrequently, usually quarterly, partly because of the scarcity of ordained elders. The various editions of the *Discipline* provided forms of worship, but some ministers devised their own order; special services were created for watch nights and love feasts. Singing was a prominent part of Methodist worship, and at least seventeen hymnbooks for Methodist use appeared between 1805 and 1843 alone. The pattern of worship seemed to become less spontaneous and more formalized as the nineteenth century progressed. Most services included singing, prayer, Old and New Testament Scripture readings, preaching and the benediction, as well as the Lord's Prayer and the doxology in the northern church. Regular orders of Sunday service were used in both the northern and southern churches by the 1880s. A major change from spontaneity toward more ordered worship was signaled by the publication of *The Methodist Hymnal* (1905) for use in both northern and southern churches, but the sermon remained central. In 1935 the three branches that were to unite in 1939 published a joint hymnal. As the first hymn this edition displaced Charles Wesley's "Oh, for a Thousand Tongues to Sing" with the nineteenth-century hymn, "Holy, Holy, Holy."[60] The United Methodist Church's Commission on Worship is charged with making recommendations to the General Conference on forms and orders of worship and with supervising editions of *The Book of Worship for Church and Home* (1964, 1965) and *The Methodist Hymnal* (1964, 1966).

The polity of the United Methodist Church has very clear roots in the Wesleyan revival and in earlier American Methodist history. The episcopacy has often been the storm center of Methodist history and polity in America, but the union of the three churches to form The Methodist Church in 1939 set the broad outline for the church polity that prevails in The United Methodist Church.

In America the early Methodist use of the title "bishop" was part of their movement toward independence from Wesley after the Christmas Conference of 1784. Since Wesley's *Sunday Service* omitted the Order of Confirmation, which in the Church of England required the imposition of the bishop's hands to be valid, it may be inferred that he had no intention of giving the Methodist superintendent any semblance of the power of the English bishop.[61] In any case, the bishop in The United Methodist Church is an elder (ordained, as are all elders) invested with certain executive functions and power. Bishops are not a separate order of the ministry. They are elected by one of the jurisdictions for a certain residence city, and then consecrated by other bishops. The bishop in turn possesses the power to ordain deacons and elders, but only after election by the annual conference, and also consecrates deaconesses.

The bishop determines the boundaries of the *district conference*, which is a subunit of the annual conference of traveling ministers, but the annual conference can determine how many districts it will have. He appoints the district superintendent as well. His most important function is the appointing of traveling ministers to their posts; the appointments are announced at the annual conference. The church provides for a Council of Bishops (there are about a hundred), which meets annually and, as a collective entity, exercises the general superintendency of the whole church. Prior to 1939 each bishop was by rights a general superintendent. Once elected, the bishop serves until retirement.

The *annual conference* is a geographical and organizational entity which maintains the roll of the traveling preachers in the area and also controls admission to this roll (except when a bishop transfers a traveling minister from another conference). It elects delegates to the jurisdictional and general conference, and votes on constitutional actions taken by the General Conference. It includes all the active traveling ministers in the area as well as one lay member for each pastoral charge. In the United States there are about one hundred conferences in the five jurisdictions and about five hundred districts or district conferences.

The *quarterly conference* is the controlling board of the local charge or station. Composed of the traveling preacher and the congregation's leaders, including trustees, as well as any retired preacher, it meets at least twice annually to conduct the local church's business.

The jurisdictional plan was an important factor in securing the successful merger of the three bodies that formed The Methodist Church in 1939. It continues to function in The United Methodist Church. The five geographical jurisdictions are a distinctive alteration in the fundamental pattern of Methodist polity in America. They provide for regional interest and concern, which varies geographically throughout the country. The recent mandated dissolution of the Central Jurisdiction brought to an end the segregation of blacks that was confirmed in the 1939 merger. *Jurisdictional conferences* elect bishops, by a vote of at least 60 percent, who serve in the jurisdiction that elected them. Jurisdiction delegates are selected by the annual conferences. Meetings must occur within a year after the General Conference has met. An equal number of laypersons and ministers make up the jurisdictional conference, which has very limited power beyond electing bishops.

The first *General Conference* met in 1808. In United Methodism the General Conference continues to meet quadrennially, in the spring of the presidential election year. A heavy workload required the conference to meet every two years for nearly a decade after 1964.[62] The General Conference is the highest legislative authority in the church. A number of national boards and agencies administer the church's business between conferences. The *judicial council*, created in the merger of 1939, is the church's highest court; it is charged with interpreting the constitution and in certain cases serving as a court of appeals.

Recent Developments

Strong evangelical forces, which have also at times been conservative, showed increasing strength in the denomination in recent years. In August 1970 more than a thousand members gathered in Dallas, Texas in what was called the Convocation of United Methodists for Evangelical Christianity. Apparently this meeting was the first national convocation of Methodists in this century to meet outside of denominational structures. Dr. Charles W. Keysor, pastor of a Methodist Church in Elgin, Illinois, and one of the convocation leaders, said that the most frequently discussed subjects were teaching in the church's seminaries, diversion of funds, and the Methodist church-school curriculum.[63] Another group, called the Evangelical Missions Council, lamented the decline in the number of overseas missionaries and what its leader David Seamands called the "lack of concern for direct personal evangelism." Keysor subsequently became editor of the unofficial *Good News* magazine.[64] Among developments that apparently disturbed the conservatives was the General Conference's 1970 resolution favoring legalized abortion and sterilization as a partial solution to the population crisis.[65] Reportedly about one half of the denomination's churches participated in the evangelistic effort in 1973 called Key 73. The next year the official Board of Global Ministries (missions) held conversations with the unofficial Evangelical Missions Council, which had accused the board of stressing social, economic, and political action rather than evangelism and missions. At the time 794 missionaries were serving overseas in some 50 countries.

At the 1976 General Conference major programs were adopted to fight world hunger, assist ethnic minorities in local churches, and seek lost souls through evangelization. Nearly $10 million was allocated for the first two programs, and a quarter of a million dollars for the third.[66] The conference's mood was conservative in many respects, reflecting concern over the fact that the church had lost a million members in the last ten years. The conference voted that only United Methodists should serve as board members and executive staff of the church's general agencies. Regarding homosexuals, it clarified phrasing adopted in 1972 ("We do not recommend marriage between two persons of the same sex") by resolving that "We do not recognize a relationship or agreement between two persons of the same sex as constituting marriage." The conference decisively defeated proposals to fund a general church study on human sexuality and agreed to give permanency to the Commission on the Status and Role of Women. The theme for the next quadrennial was designated as "Commitment to Christ—Called to Change."[67]

The 1976 General Conference also adopted a resolution on the Middle East that was a compromise between forces on the staff in the Division of World Peace and the Women's Division, which favored a resolution strongly supporting the Palestinian Liberation Organization, and other staff, clergy, and laypersons who wished to express good will toward Jews and Israel. On November 12, the Council of Bishops adopted a resolution in New Orleans in reaction to the resolution of the United Nations two days earlier that equated Zionism with racism. While intended to be helpful to the cause of Israel, the bishops seemed to emphasize the need for the continued existence of the United Nations, deploring the "one-sidedness of the [U.N.] resolution and its possible impact on delicate negotiations in the Middle East." The bishops also stressed that the United States should take no punitive action against Third World nations that had supported the United Nations resolution; their own resolution made no reference to Israel.

Using the services of Dr. George Gallup's public opinion surveys in 1967–1968 the *Catholic Digest* discovered that in the general population the Methodist church was labeled "the most liked religion" by members of all faith groups when they were asked what denomination they most admired other than their own. A similar poll fifteen years earlier offered the same information.[68] Despite these results, The United Methodist Church suffered a net loss of 518,000 members in the four years between 1968 and 1972, although one new member in 1968 was the famous Pentecostal evangelist Oral Roberts. The massive size of the body still made it the second largest Protestant denomination (after the Southern Baptist Convention) and the third largest in the nation. Only about 1 percent of all white Methodists remained outside The United Methodist Church in 1970 in smaller groups such as the Free Methodist Church, Primitive Methodist Church, and Southern Methodist Church, but an estimated 2,500,000 blacks worshiped in the three leading black Methodist denominations. Taken as a whole, Methodist bodies included about 10 percent of the nearly 130 million church and synagogue members in the United States in 1970.[69]

On a map portraying the geographical spread and reported church membership of denominational families in the United States in the early 1970s, nonblack Methodist denominations (including primarily The United Methodist Church) marked a bold pattern running westward across middle America from Delaware and Maryland to Iowa, Nebraska, Kansas, and eastern Colorado. Despite this geographical spread, Methodists did not dominate any one state. That many important elected officials were Methodists was clear once again after the 1974 elections; neither religious geography nor denominational statistics seemed to explain the fact that there were 17 Methodists in the United States Senate and only 15 Roman Catholic senators. In the House of Representative there were 68 Methodist representatives, a denominational representation surpassed only by the 108 Roman Catholic representatives.[70] The Methodists' continuing concern with higher education is manifested in the approximately 75 colleges and universities that presently maintain organic relationship with The United Methodist Church.

The Conferencia Metodista in Puerto Rico is affiliated with The United Methodist Church. The Canada Conference joined the United Church of Canada in the merger that occurred in 1925.

According to its statistical office in Evanston, Illinois, The United Methodist Church in the United States and Puerto Rico has 9,861,028 members. In addition, about 350,000 United Methodists live in Africa, Asia, and Europe. Also not included are another 1,500,000 preparatory members in the United States.

In 1976 an average of 3,643,138 United Methodists attended worship services each week, while 4,654,211 went to church school. There were 38,-795 organized United Methodist churches. Total expenditures of all churches was $1,081,082,820, an increase of $70 million over 1975. The value of United Methodist property in the United States was $8.37 billion.

Councils and boards have headquarters in Dayton, Ohio; Evanston, Illinois; Washington, D.C.; Nashville, Tennessee; and Philadelphia, Pennsylvania. The Commission on Archives and History is located in Lake Junaluska, North Carolina 28745.

NOTES

1. Sydney E. Ahlstrom, *A Religious History of the American People* (New Haven: Yale University Press, 1972), p. 373.
2. Frederick A. Norwood, *The Story of American Methodism; A History of the United Methodists and Their Relations* (Nashville: Abingdon Press, 1974), pp. 65-69.
3. Ibid., p. 74; Edwin Scott Gaustad, *Historical Atlas of Religion in America* (rev. edn.; New York: Harper & Row, 1976), p. 76.
4. Norwood pp. 82-88; Richard M. Cameron, *Methodism and Society in Historical Perspective*, vol. 1 in Methodism and Society series (Nashville: Abingdon Press, 1961), pp. 89-90.
5. Norwood, pp. 90-93.
6. Ibid., p. 120; Cameron, p. 93.
7. See chap. 15.
8. Frank Baker, *John Wesley and the Church of England* (Nashville: Abingdon Press, 1970), p. 254.
9. Cameron, pp. 110-111; Norwood, pp. 98-101; Gaustad, p. 77.
10. Gaustad, pp. 78-79; Ahlstrom, pp. 436-437; Norwood, p. 145; Cameron, p. 123.
11. Norwood, pp. 158-159; Ahlstrom, p. 437.
12. Cameron, p. 237.
13. Norwood, pp. 141-143.
14. Ibid., pp. 137, 139.
15. Ibid., pp. 137, 364; Cameron. p. 270.
16. Roy L. Smith, *Why I Am a Methodist* (Boston: Beacon Press, 1955), p. 78; Herbert E. Stotts and Paul Deats, Jr., *Methodism and Society: Guidelines for Strategy*, vol. 4 in Methodism and Society series (Nashville: Abingdon Press, 1962), p. 230.
17. Norwood, p. 136.
18. Ibid., pp. 130-132, 157; Cameron, p. 129.
19. Norwood, pp. 133-135.
20. Ibid., pp. 127-128.
21. Ibid., pp. 175-184.

22. Gaustad, p. 80; Ahlstrom, p. 661.
23. Norwood, pp. 197-209; Gaustad, p. 81.
24. Norwood, pp. 242-243, 249.
25. Ibid., pp. 292-301; Cameron, pp. 299-301.
26. Robert E. Chiles, *Theological Transition in American Methodism; 1790–1935* (Nashville: Abingdon Press, 1965), pp. 24-25. In a footnote on pp. 27-28 Chiles quotes a pertinent paragraph from John Deschner's article on "Methodism" in *A Handbook of Christian Theology* (1958): "Methodism in this country has a Wesleyan heart but an American head. Its characteristic emphases remain those of the core of the Wesleyan preaching—'heart religion' and moral renewal. Its theological articulation of this central emphasis has tended to lack stability and continuity, and to be unusually open to stimulus and influence from without. In part this situation roots in a characteristic Methodist attitude toward theology as subordinate to experience. . . . At a deeper level, this Methodist theological eclecticism bears witness to the fact that Methodism was born not as a church but as a movement and emphasis within Anglicanism, and that the Wesleyan heart needs again and again to reach beyond the 'Methodist doctrines' and renew its living contact, first of all, with the scriptural revelation, which Wesley emphasized, but also with the ecumenical theological tradition in which, through the Anglicanism which Wesley presupposed, it originally learned to know its own mind."
27. Chiles, pp. 39, 43-44.
28. Ibid., pp. 49, 58-60.
29. Ibid., pp. 60-62, 65-66, 71.
30. Ibid., pp. 157-158, 165-166, 175-176.
31. Kenneth M. MacKenzie, *The Robe and the Sword; The Methodist Church and the Rise of American Imperialism* (Washington, D.C.: Public Affairs Press, 1961), pp. 113-116.
32. Gaustad, pp. 52-53.
33. Norwood, pp. 236-237, 348-350, 397; Walter G. Muelder, *Methodism and Society in the Twentieth Century*, vol. 2 in Methodism and Society series (Nashville: Abingdon Press, 1961), pp. 65-67; Ahlstrom, pp. 903-904.
34. Norwood, p. 349; Cameron, p. 349; *Lutheran Witness Reporter*, May 19, 1968; *Christian Century*, November 24, 1976, p. 1032.
35. Muelder, pp. 339-343.
36. Gaustad, pp. 43-44, 52-54; Norwood, pp. 154, 259-260. Most of these figures do not include the black Methodist denominations.
37. A. Dudley Ward, *The Social Creed of the Methodist Church, a Living Document* (Nashville: Abingdon Press, 1971), p. 25; Cameron, p. 328.
38. Norwood, pp. 354, 392; Ward, p. 21; Cameron, pp. 13, 323-324.
39. Cameron, p. 325; Ward, pp. 9, 22-25.
40. Muelder, p. 150; Norwood, p. 394.
41. Norwood, pp. 408-410; Smith, p. 91.
42. Muelder, pp. 262-263; Norwood, pp. 409-410.
43. Norwood, pp. 407, 413; Muelder, p. 266.
44. Norwood, pp. 351-352, 416.
45. Muelder, pp. 417-421.
46. *Time,* May 6, 1966.
47. Much of the material on the Church of the United Brethren in Christ was provided in a letter by Paul H. Eller, Ph.D., president, Evangelical Theological Seminary, 329 East School Avenue, Naperville, Illinois 60540. This institution has merged with Garrett Seminary in Evanston, Illinois.
48. Much of the material on the Evangelical Church was provided in a letter by Paul H. Eller, Ph.D., president, Evangelical Theological Seminary, 329 East School Avenue, Naperville, Illinois 60540. See n. 47, above.
49. *The Theological Study Commission on Doctrine and Doctrinal Standards, an Interim Report to the General Conference* (New York: United Methodist Church, n.d.), pp. 13-17.
50. See "World Methodism" section in chap. 15, above.
51. *Theological Study Commission,* pp. 11-12.
52. See Albert C. Outler, *That the World May Believe* (New York: Joint Commission on Education and Cultivation, Board of Missions of the Methodist Church, 1966), p. 72; and the discussion of twentieth-century Methodist theology in Norwood, pp. 382-388.
53. See Stotts and Deats, pp. 321-347, for this information. The following report is based on these data.
54. Albert Outler, "Methodism's Theologi-

cal Heritage: A Study in Perspective," in Paul M. Minus, Jr., ed., *Methodism's Destiny in an Ecumenical Age* (Nashville: Abingdon Press, 1969), p. 49.
55. *Theological Study Commission*, pp. 1, 19.
56. See Smith, p. 88.
57. *Theological Study Commission*, pp. 62-65.
58. See Albert C. Outler, "Do Methodists Have a Doctrine of the Church?" in Dow Kirkpatrick, ed., *The Doctrine of the Church* (Nashville: Abingdon Press, 1964), p. 25.
59. Robert W. Goodloe, *The Sacraments in Methodism* (Nashville: The Methodist Publishing House, 1953), pp. 48-57.
60. Norwood, pp. 229-231, 326-329, 365.
61. See Nolan B. Harmon, *The Organization of the Methodist Church* (Nash-ville: The Methodist Publishing House, 1958), p. 25.
62. An interesting fact is that in 1968 two presidential aspirants with radically different political positions, Senator George McGovern and Governor George Wallace, were both Methodists, members of the same church body.
63. *St. Louis Post Dispatch*, August 30, 1970.
64. *Christian Century*, December 3, 1975, p. 1099.
65. *St. Louis Post Dispatch*, April 24, 1970.
66. *Christian Century*, June 9-16, 1976, pp. 557-558.
67. Ibid., May 26, 1976, pp. 508-509; June 2, 1976, p. 533.
68. *The Miami Herald*, June 1, 1968.
69. Gaustad, pp. 2, 170.
70. Ibid., pp. 165, 169.

BIBLIOGRAPHY

FORMATION OF AMERICAN METHODISM

Asbury, Francis. *The Journal and Letters of Francis Asbury.* ed. E. T. Clark and J. M. Potts. 3 vols. Nashville: Abingdon Press, 1958.

Bucke, Emory Stevens, general ed., et al. *History of American Methodism*. 3 vols. Nashville: Abingdon Press, 1964.

Ferguson, Charles Wright. *Organizing to Beat the Devil; Methodists and the Making of America*. Garden City, N.Y.: Doubleday, 1971.

Fortney, Edward L. "The Literature of the History of Methodism." *Religion in Life* 24 (1955): 443-51.

French, Goldwin. *Parsons and Politics: The Role of the Wesleyan Methodists in Upper Canada and the Maritimes from 1780 to 1855*. Toronto: Ryerson Press, 1962.

Godbold, Albea. "Francis Asbury and His Difficulties with John Wesley and Thomas Rankin." *Methodist History* 3, 3 (April 1965): 3-19.

Lang, Edward M. "The Theology of Francis Asbury." Unpublished dissertation, Northwestern University, 1972.

Maser, Frederick E. *The Dramatic Story of Early American Methodism*. Nashville: Abingdon Press, 1965.

Melton, J. Gordon. *A Bibliography of Black Methodism.* Bibliographic Monograph No. 1. Evanston: Institute for the Study of American Religion, 1970.

Norwood, Frederick A. *The Story of American Methodism; A History of the United Methodists and Their Relations*. Nashville: Abingdon Press, 1974.

Raymond, Allan. " 'I Fear God and Honour the King': John Wesley and the American Revolution." *Church History* 45, 3 (September 1976): 316-328.

Rowe, Kenneth E., ed. *Methodist Union Catalog: Pre-1976 Imprints*. Vols. 1-2. Metuchen, N.J.: Scarecrow Press, 1975-1976.

Rudolph, L. C. *Francis Asbury*. Nashville: Abingdon Press 1966.

Sweet, W. W. *Methodism in American History*. Rev. edn. Nashville: Abingdon Press, 1953.

————, ed. *The Methodists, a Collection of Source Materials*. New York: Cooper Square Publishers, 1964.

Vickers, John. *Thomas Coke: Apostle of Methodism*. Nashville: Abingdon Press, 1969.

FRONTIER AND DIVISION

Dimond, Sydney G. *The Psychology of the Methodist Revival*. London: Oxford University Press, 1926.

Douglass, Paul F. *The Story of German Methodism*. New York: The Methodist Book Concern, 1939.

Drinkhouse, Edward J. *History of Methodist Reform*. 2 vols. Baltimore: The Board of Publication of the Methodist Protestant Church, 1899.

Jones, Charles Edwin. *A Guide to the Study of the Holiness Movement*. ATLA Bibliography Series, No. 1. Metuchen, N.J.: Scarecrow Press, 1974.

Mathews, Donald G. *Slavery and Methodism*. Princeton: Princeton University Press, 1965.

Morrow, Ralph E. *Northern Methodism and Reconstruction*. East Lansing, Mich.: Michigan State University Press, 1956.

Norwood, Frederick A. *Church Membership in the Methodist Tradition*. Nashville: The Methodist Publishing House, 1958.

Peters, John Leland. *Christian Perfection and American Methodism*. Nashville: Abingdon Press, 1956.

Pilkington, James Penn. *The Methodist Publishing House, a History: Beginnings to 1870*. Nashville: Abingdon Press, 1968.

Rowe, Kenneth E. "New Light on Early Methodist Theological Education." *Methodist History* 10 (October 1971): 58-62.

Smith, Timothy L. *Called unto Holiness; the Story of the Nazarenes*. Kansas City, Mo.: Nazarene Publishing House, 1962.

———. *Revivalism and Social Reform in Mid-Nineteenth-Century America*. Nashville: Abingdon Press, 1957.

Sweet, W. W. *The Methodist Episcopal Church and the Civil War*. Cincinnati: Methodist Book Concern Press, 1912.

———. *Religion on the American Frontier, 1783–1840*. Vol. 4, The Methodists. Chicago: University of Chicago Press, 1946.

THEOLOGICAL TRANSITION AND THE LATE NINETEENTH CENTURY

Barclay, Wade Crawford. *History of Methodist Missions*. 3 vols. New York: The Board of Missions and Church Extension of The Methodist Church, 1949–1957.

Bode, Frederick A. *Protestantism and the New South: North Carolina Baptists and Methodists in Political Crisis, 1894–1903*. Charlottesville: University Press of Virginia, 1976.

Chiles, Robert E. *Theological Transition in American Methodism: 1790–1935*. Nashville: Abingdon Press, 1965.

Hogg, W. Richey. "The Missions of American Methodism." In *History of American Methodism*, ed. Emory Stevens Bucke, et al. Nashville: Abingdon Press, 1964. III: 59-128.

MacKenzie, Kenneth M. *The Robe and the Sword; The Methodist Church and the Rise of American Imperialism*. Washington, D.C.: Public Affairs Press, 1961.

Sanders, Paul S. "The Sacraments in Early American Methodism." *Church History* 26 (1957): 355-371.

Scott, Leland H. "Methodist Theology in America in the Ninetenth Century." *Religion in Life* 25 (1955): 87-98.

Shipley, David C. "The Development of Theology in American Methodism in the Nineteenth Century." *London Quarterly and Holborn Review* 28 (1959): 260-264.

———. "Historical Theology—Postscript and Prospect." *The Garrett Tower* 29 (1953): 3-5.

Smith, Harmon L. "Borden Parker Bowne: Heresy at Boston." In *American Religious Heretics: Formal and Informal Trials*, ed. George H. Shriver. Nashville: Abingdon Press, 1966. Pp. 148-187.

SOCIAL CONCERN AND REUNIFICATION IN THE METHODIST CHURCH

Brewer, Earl D. C., and Johnson, Douglas W. *An Inventory of the Harlan Paul Douglass Collection of Religious Research Reports*. New York: Department of Research, National Council of the Churches of Christ, 1970.

Cameron, Richard M. *Methodism and Society in Historical Perspective.* Vol. 1 in Methodism and Society series. Nashville: Abingdon Press, 1961.

Garber, Paul N. *The Methodists Are One People.* Nashville: Cokesbury Press, 1939.

Moore, John M. *The Long Road to Methodist Union.* Nashville: The Methodist Publishing House, 1943.

Muelder, Walter G. *Methodism and Society in the Twentieth Century.* Vol. 2 in Methodism and Society series. Nashville: Abingdon Press, 1961.

Schilling, S. Paul. *Methodism and Society in Theological Perspective.* Vol. 3 in Methodism and Society series. Nashville: Abingdon Press, 1960.

Stotts, Herbert E., and Deats, Paul Jr. *Methodism and Society: Guidelines for Strategy.* Vol. 4 in Methodism and Society series. Nashville: Abingdon Press, 1962.

Straughn, James H. *Inside Methodist Union.* Nashville: Abingdon Press, 1958.

Ward, A. Dudley. *The Social Creed of the Methodist Church, A Living Document.* Nashville: Abingdon Press, 1971.

POSTWAR PERIOD AND THE UNITED METHODIST CHURCH

Albright, R. W. *A History of the Evangelical Church.* Harrisburg: The Evangelical Press, 1942.

Core, Arthur C. *Philip William Otterbein, Pastor, Ecumenist.* Dayton, Ohio: Board of Publication, Evangelical United Brethren Church, 1968.

Drury, A. W. *History of the Church of the United Brethren in Christ.* Dayton, Ohio: U.B. Publishing House, 1924.

Eller, Paul H. *These Evangelical United Brethren.* Dayton, Ohio: Otterbein Press, 1957.

The Methodist Church in Urban America, a Fact Book. Philadelphia: Methodist Church Department of Research and Survey, 1962.

Naumann, William H. "Theology in the Evangelical United Brethren Church." Unpublished dissertation, Yale University, 1966.

Ness, John H. *One Hundred Fifty Years: A History of Publishing in the Evangelical United Church.* Dayton, Ohio: Board of Publication of E.U.B.C., 1966.

O'Malley, John S. *Pilgrimage of Faith: The Legacy of the Otterbeins,* Metuchen, N.J.: Scarecrow Press, 1973.

DOCTRINAL STANDARDS, WORSHIP, AND POLITY

Barton, Jesse Hamby. "The Definition of the Episcopal Office in American Methodism." Unpublished dissertation, Drew University, 1960.

Bishop, John. *Methodist Worship in Relation to Free Church Worship.* London: The Epworth Press, 1950.

Goodloe, Robert W. *The Sacraments in Methodism.* Nashville: The Methodist Publishing House, 1953.

Harmon, Nolan B. *The Organization of the Methodist Church; Historic Development and Present Working Structures.* Rev. edn. Nashville: The Methodist Publishing House, 1958.

———. *The Rites and Ritual of Episcopal Methodism.* Nashville: Publishing House of the M.E. Church, South, 1926.

Kirkpatrick, Dow, ed. *The Doctrine of the Church.* Nashville: Abingdon Press, 1964.

Leiffer, Murray H. *Role of the District Superintendent in the Methodist Church.* Evanston, Ill.: Bureau of Social and Religious Research, 1960.

Moede, Gerald F. "The Office of Bishop in Methodism, Its History and Development." Unpublished dissertation, Yale University, 1964.

Smith, Roy L. *Why I Am a Methodist.* Boston: Beacon Press, 1955.

Spellman, Norman W. "The General Superintendency in American Methodism, 1784–1870." Unpublished dissertation, Yale University, 1962.

The Theological Study Commission on Doctrine and Doctrinal Standards, an Interim Report to the General Conference. New York: United Methodist Church, n.d.

RECENT DEVELOPMENTS

The Book of Discipline of the United Methodist Church, 1972. Nashville: United Methodist Publishing House, [1973].

The Book of Worship for Church and Home. Nashville: The Methodist Publishing House, 1964, 1965.

The Methodist Hymnal. Nashville: The Methodist Publishing House, 1964, 1966.

17. Other Methodist Churches

The African Methodist Episcopal Church

At the beginning of the third quarter of the eighteenth century, every third Methodist in North America was, according to one estimate, black, either slave or free.

In Philadelphia, blacks at first enjoyed full fellowship with the white members at St. George's Church, which the black members had helped to build with contributions of both money and labor. Friction began in 1786. First the blacks were required to take places near the walls or in the rear of the church and to receive Communion only after the white members of the congregation had been communicated. The next step was the erection of a gallery for the blacks, who now were excluded from the main floor. The blacks resisted these pressures, organized the Free African Society, and on occasion some had to be forcibly removed to their own section. On a Sunday morning in November 1787, two white trustees tried to pull Absalom Jones and a companion from their knees while they were at prayer in the white part of the church. At that a group of blacks resigned from the congregation, began building their own church, and secured ordination for Jones from Protestant Episcopal Bishop William White.

Richard Allen (1760–1831), a self-redeemed Methodist slave who had become wealthy, refused to join the Protestant Episcopal Church. In the conviction that the inclusiveness of Methodism was social as well as doctrinal, Allen tried for six years to bring his denomination's practice up to the level of its teaching. When he failed, he finally bought a disused blacksmith shop, hauled it with his own horses to a lot that he owned, and rehabilitated the building as a church. Following his unvarying policy of maintaining contact with those white Methodists who shared his vision, Allen invited Methodist Bishop Francis Asbury to open the new church for divine service. Asbury did so in 1794. This was the beginning of Bethel Church. In 1799 Asbury ordained Allen to the diaconate.

The white ministers exploited Allen's determination to keep his society within the Methodist Conference. After failing in their efforts to take away the black society's property, the Reverend Robert Birch of St. George's Church entered a suit to deny it the Methodist name. The state supreme court found in favor of the black society, and in 1816 the black group received its legal independence from the white conference.

The experience of the black Methodists of Baltimore ran remarkably parallel to that of their co-religionists in Philadelphia. Problems arose about the same issues and at almost the same time. In 1801 Daniel Coker, another black whom Asbury had ordained to the diaconate, associated himself with the Colored Methodist Society. A few weeks before Bethel Church in Philadelphia became independent in 1816, Coker and his supporters organized an independent Bethel Methodist Church in Baltimore.

In that same year Allen invited a number of representatives of black Methodist churches to assemble at Bethel Church in Philadelphia to form an ecclesiastical compact. Delegates came from Philadelphia, Baltimore, Wilmington, Attleborough (Pennsylvania), and Salem (New Jersey); as far away as Charleston, South Carolina, a group of blacks expressed interest in the proposal, even though their delegates could not personally be present for the meeting.

The 1816 assembly voted the African Methodist Episcopal Church into existence.[1] Allen became its first bishop. By 1818 it had grown to 16 congregations in 4 states with a total membership of 6,757. In 1822, in the wake of the Denmark Vesey rebellion in South Carolina, the Charleston congregation, the second largest in the denomination, was to all intents and purposes wiped out.

Five years later the African Methodist Episcopal Church entered Canada. It continued expanding westward and southwestward in the United States; by 1856 it had churches in St. Louis and Sacramento. During the War between the States it returned to the American South, and by 1867 the church had 5 bishops, 10 conferences, and 200,000 members, of whom all but 25,000 lived in the southern states.[2]

In its belief, worship, and organization the African Methodist Episcopal Church follows the conventional Methodist pattern, although from the start it provided for lay representation through local preachers. Its doctrinal affirmations include the twenty-five Articles of Religion, the Catechism on Faith from the 1740s, John Wesley's General Rules for the United Societies (1739), the Rules for Band Societies, and the Rules for Giving. A controversy in the fourth quarter of the nineteenth century led to the inclusion of a "Special Declaration on Apostolic Succession." In this statement the 1884 General Conference affirmed that the doctrine of apostolic succession is erroneous in the Methodist view and that reordination of any bishop, elder, or deacon by another ecclesiastical authority would not be tolerated. In a special section on "ritualism," the declaration went on to discountenance the "use of heavy and prosy ritualistic service in our public congregations" and deprecated efforts to introduce "extreme ritualism."[3] The Holy Communion is celebrated with "unleavened bread and the unfermented juice of the vine."

Children presented for membership are required to learn the Our Father, the Decalogue, and the Apostles' Creed and their meanings. Adults in preparing for membership must acquire an acquaintance with the doctrinal affirmations and the rest of the *Book of Discipline.*

Recent efforts to get information from the church have not been successful. Several years ago, with over 6,000 churches and an inclusive membership of about 1,300,000, the African Methodist Episcopal Church was the second largest Methodist church body in the United States. Of its 18 episcopal districts four are in Africa and one in the Caribbean and South America. There are no central hadquarters. It has an office at 2295 Seventh Avenue, New York, New York 10030.

The bishops of the African Methodist Episcopal Church assert that "African Methodism exists as a protest against segregation in the Christian Church" and welcome into their fellowship all who share their faith without regard to race, nationality, or social distinction.[4] In 1964 the African Methodist Episcopal Church entered into conversations with the African Methodist Episcopal Zion Church and the Christian Methodist Episcopal Church as a preliminary move in the direction of a union of all Methodists, whenever that can be done. The African Methodist Episcopal Church also participates in the Consultation on Church Union.[5]

Reformed Methodist Union Episcopal Church

When the South Carolina Conference of the African Methodist Episcopal Church in 1883 was electing the delegates who were to represent it at the General Conference of the denomination the following year, Bishop William F. Dickerson insisted upon a voice vote rather than a ballot. Dissatisfied with this development, a considerable number of delegates from South Carolina and Georgia met under the leadership of William E. Johnson in 1885, left the African Methodist Episcopal Church, organized the Independent Methodist Church, disavowed episcopacy, and chose Johnson as president. In 1896 the church body reversed the original practice, adopted an episcopal-connexional form of church government, changed its name to Reformed Methodist Union Episcopal Church, and in 1899 secured the consecration of E. Russell Middleton by white Reformed Episcopal Bishop Peter F. Stevens. Later bishops received consecration through the laying on of hands by other elders.[6]

Headquarters are in Charleston, South Carolina. The General Conference meets annually. It reports 18 churches with 2,192 members.

African Methodist Episcopal Zion Church

The African Methodist Episcopal Zion Church takes its name from the mother church of the denomination, "The African Methodist Episcopal Church (Called Zion Church) in the City of New York." This congregation came into being in 1796 in response to a petition of James Varick and other black members of the John Street Methodist Episcopal Church in New York to Bishop Asbury for a congregation of their own, since the number of black members had increased during the three preceding decades to a point where "caste prejudice forbade their taking the Sacrament until the white families were all served."[7] Other complaints were that the white congregations rarely permitted the black preachers to preach to them and the white annual conference would not admit the black preachers as itinerant preachers.

In 1800 the congregation secured its charter and built its first church. Although they owned their own building, they agreed with the Methodist Episcopal Church that the latter should manage their spiritual concerns, name their preachers, and provide them with sacraments. In 1813 a schism took place and the Asbury Church came into being. After a time the two congregations associated themselves with one another under the Zion Church arrangement with the white Methodist Episcopal Church, but in 1820 the pastor of the two united congregations left the Methodist Episcopal Church. The congregations followed suit. In 1821 the first conference of the African Methodist Episcopal Church in America took place. In 1822 they secured ordination for three of their elders-elect from the Methodist Protestant Church. After early losses, the African Methodist Episcopal Church in America began to grow and by 1831 it had nearly 1,700 members in two conferences.[8]

The church moved southward into Maryland and Washington, D.C., and northward into New England and Canada, but its westward penetration was slow. In 1848 it formally added "Zion" to its corporate name. In 1852 three churches were organized in California. In the same year an issue of polity split the church. Out of it came the Wesleyan Methodist Church, which reunited with the parent body in 1860. In 1868 the term "bishop" superseded that of "superintendent." After the War between the States the denomination began to establish itself in the American South, and spread slowly for the rest of the century. In 1898 the first woman received elder's ordination.[9]

In doctrine, worship, and organization, the African Methodist Episcopal Zion Church conforms to the general Methodist pattern. It has the twenty-five Methodist Articles of Religion in its *Discipline*, along with the General Rules and the Special Advices.[10] The 1960 revision of the *Discipline* found it necessary to "admonish unity in following our own form of worship, and in simplest pulpit-wear and expression, avoiding all semblance of high church aspects and formalism," to call for "a more unified interpretation of what makes us Methodists," to urge "more unity, concerting and deference to our Protestant and Methodist origins and beliefs," and to counsel "that evangelism be not smothered by spectacular forms and intonations in order of worship and ritualistic practices."[11]

There are twelve episcopal areas, one of which covers Liberia and Ghana, another Nigeria. Other foreign missions are conducted in Guyana and the

Bahamas. There is a conference in the Virgin Islands. The inclusive membership of the 4,500 churches is 870,421. There are no central headquarters, but a number of agencies are located at Charlotte, North Carolina.

African Union First Colored Methodist Protestant Church of the United States of America or Elsewhere, Incorporated

It was probably Jacob Pindergrass, a Methodist local preacher, who led a group of fellow blacks out of the Asbury Methodist Episcopal Church in Wilmington, Delaware, in 1805, after the white majority restricted their black co-religionists to the balcony of the church at worship services. In addition the white members insisted that the black communicants wait before receiving Holy Communion until the white members had received it, thereby denying to the black membership "the religious privileges guaranteed to [them] by the word of God and his liberal gospel."

The withdrawing group erected its own building, Ezion Methodist Episcopal Church, the same year, but remained under the supervision of the pastor of the Asbury Church. In 1812 a controversy arose about the right of the black congregation to refuse any of the white ministers that the Asbury church sent to preach to them. The white church won the lawsuit that followed. The majority, led by Peter Spencer, a respected mechanic, and William Anderson, withdrew and founded the Union Church of African Members (simplified from the start into the African Union Church) in 1813. The insurgents "set apart William Anderson and Peter Spencer to be their preachers and to perform all the religious services in the said Union Church."[12] The "laconic" history of the denomination describes the Union Church as "the first church in the United States originally organized by and afterward wholly under the care of the Negro race."[13]

Spencer represented the Wilmington church at the Philadelphia meeting that Richard Allen called in 1816 and that resulted in the organization of the African Methodist Episcopal Church, but the Wilmington church, for reasons that are not clear, did not join the new body. Instead it grew into a denomination in its own right, largely by adding congregations, at their own request, into a loose federation.

In 1842 the church adopted an episcopal form of government and chose Spencer as its first bishop and Isaac Barney as its second bishop. (Spencer died in 1843 and was not replaced.) The local congregations chose their own ministers, who at first did not receive any salary.

In 1850–1851 Bishop Barney led thirty churches in Pennsylvania, New Jersey, and Delaware out of the African Union Church.

In the meantime, the First Colored Methodist Protestant Church(es) had withdrawn from the African Methodist Episcopal Church in 1850.

During the next fifteen years the African Union Church recovered from the schism of 1850–1851 to a point where it had thirty churches in Pennsylvania, New Jersey, New York, Connecticut, and Canada. In 1865 representatives of the African Union Church and the First Colored Methodist Protestant Church(es) determined to unite and formally accomplished the union the next year under the name of the African Union First Colored Methodist Protestant Church of the United States or Elsewhere. Its constitution provided for an itinerant ministry, a president acting with the powers of bishop, and a method of compensation of the ministers agreed on by them with the respective congregations.

A decade later, in 1875, the new body divided. One element retained the old name and polity. The other element was desirous of including the office of bishop in its formal structure and took the name Union American Methodist Episcopal Church.

The Articles of Religion of the African Union First Colored Methodist Protestant Church of the United States or Elsewhere consist of the Apostles' Creed and the Methodist Articles of Religion of 1784 (minus the subsequently added twenty-third article, "Of the Rulers of the United States of America").[14]

The church admits women to ordination on a par with men. A deacon must have a high school education, an elder four years of college training. The general president of the General Conference (which meets every four years) bears the style "Right Reverend." There are 40 churches, mostly in the urban centers of the Atlantic seaboard between Washington and New York, with a total inclusive membership of 10,500. A recent letter to the former headquarters at 602 Spruce Street, Wilmington, Delaware 19801 was returned with the notation "Adressee Unknown."

Union American Methodist Episcopal Church

In 1875 a group within the African Union First Colored Methodist Protestant Church of the United States or Elsewhere withdrew in order to form a church body that would include the office of bishop by that name in its formal structure. To accomplish this they organized the Union American Methodist Episcopal Church.

The polity of this church body is typically Methodist, with district superintendents and bishops (who use the style "Right Reverend") and with quarterly, district, and annual conferences. General conferences meet only to consider proposed changes in name, law, and polity.

The headquarters of the church were at 774 Pine Street, Camden, New Jersey but have since moved. The most recent statistics are for 1957, when the church body reported 256 churches and 27,560 members.[15]

Christian Methodist Episcopal Church

In the aftermath of the War between the States black congregations of the Methodist Episcopal Church, South, began an exodus from that body that soon achieved formidable proportions. Sometimes these congregations acted on their own initiative, sometimes their white co-religionists encouraged them to leave. To preserve the unity of the black component of the Methodist Episcopal Church, South, as far as this might still be done, the latter's general conference of 1866 provided for the organization of the black members into separate missions, churches, charges, districts, annual conferences, and a General Conference. The first annual "colored" conference came into being in five southern states in 1870. In December of that year the Colored Methodist Episcopal Church in America was organized and two bishops of the Methodist Episcopal Church, South, consecrated the two bishops-elect of the new denomination. The latter adopted the doctrines and discipline of the mother church as its own, with certain modifications, such as the provision that no white person could be a member of the black body (a requirement that has since been dropped), and a further provision that church buildings were not to be used for political meetings and assemblies. The rivalry between the Colored Methodist Episcopal Church in America and the African Methodist Episcopal and African Methodist Episcopal Zion churches during the early days was extremely bitter, and the feeble efforts at remedying the initial lack of denominational leadership and of an adequately trained ministry in the Colored Methodist Episcopal Church in America by uniting with another branch of black Methodism made little progress. Expansion during the Reconstruction period was modest. Following the Reconstruction, the Methodist Episcopal Church, South, found it possible to be more generous with financial assistance to the daughter denomination, and this obligation was assumed by The Methodist Church in 1939. In spite of this help, however, the Colored Methodist Episcopal Church in America continued to be the smallest of the three major black Methodist groups. In 1956, by way of implementation of a decision of the General Conference of 1954, the church body took the name Christian Methodist Episcopal Church.

The church has no formal headquarters. The secretary's address is 664 Vance Avenue, Memphis, Tennessee 38126. Several years ago there were 2,598 churches throughout the United States, chiefly in the southern, central, and middle-western parts of the country, with a total membership of 466,718. There has been no response to recent efforts to contact the denomination for information.

Reformed Zion Union Apostolic Church

The church "must be holy, united in faith, and apostolic," asserts the *Catechism* of the Reformed Zion Union Apostolic Church. It proceeds to define "holy" as "pure, morally and spiritually, consecrated" and "united in faith" as "joined as one in the belief that Jesus Christ is the true and living God." These qualities can be found, it goes on, in the Reformed Zion Union Apostolic Church, "a living, teaching Christian society, founded upon the teachings of Jesus Christ to spread His Gospel to all people." This episcopally governed church "was revealed to man by God on April 1, 1869, A.D., through

His minister James R. Howell."[16] Howell had been an elder of the African Methodist Episcopal Zion Church in New York. His organization of the new church body, which took place at Boydton, Virginia, under the name of Zion Union Apostolic Church, in 1869, was a protest against both white Methodist discrimination and black Methodist ecclesiasticism. In 1874 controversy about a constitutional change which would have made the president a bishop for life all but destroyed the church. It took until 1882 before the scattered congregations and members were reunited and reorganized under the denomination's present name.

Its theology is trinitarian, its Christology traditionally orthodox. Its *Catechism* affirms original sin; Christ's atonement for our sins by his suffering, bleeding, and death; and the church "as a human institution having a divine purpose, that will last until the end of time" and that is built upon the rock of Peter's faith.[17] There are two sacraments: Baptism by immersion of both children and adults, to be received only once, and the Lord's Supper, of which the *Catechism* says both that "it represents the body and blood of the Lord and is given to us in the form of bread and wine" and that Christ at the Last Supper "changed the bread and wine into the substance of His body and blood by prayer."[18]

While the denomination is in general less liturgical than other bodies in the Methodist tradition, the leadership has encouraged all churches to install altars around which the communicants can kneel to receive the Communion.

The polity of the denomination is that of American Methodism generally. Apart from a struggling mission in New Jersey and another in Michigan, the 50 churches of the denomination are concentrated in North Carolina and Virginia. Membership estimates vary from 10,000 to 16,000.

Primitive Methodist Church, United States of America

The Primitive Methodist Church[19] owes its beginning to the evangelistic preaching of Connecticut-born Lorenzo Dow in 1807 at Mow Cop in Staffordshire, England. In 1810 a class of ten members was organized at Standley. The founders of the Primitive Methodist Church completed its organization in 1812. In 1829 it sent its first missionaries, one woman and three men, to the United States; they began work in New York and Philadelphia the same year. After enjoying indifferent success for a decade, the American mission cut itself off from its English parent in 1840 and organized as the American Primitive Methodist Church. In 1843 John Leekley formed a society at Grant Hill, near Galena, Illinois, out of which grew the Primitive Western Conference of the State of Illinois and Wisconsin Territory. In 1889 the two bodies united as the Primitive Methodist Church. Its strength always has lain in the mill and mining areas of the North; it never penetrated the American South.[20]

The Primitive Methodist Church belongs to the National Association of Evangelicals. It emphasizes such Wesleyan doctrines as redemption, repentance, justification, and sanctification.

Its polity is congregational. Its manner of making pastoral appointments is unique in Methodism. Local churches may invite a first, second, and third choice among the ministers of the conference, but about half the churches prefer to leave the assignments of pastors to the Conference Stationing Committee. The General Conference meets every four years. A proposal to enter the Methodist merger of 1939 failed by only 13 votes.

The Primitive Methodist Church has 85 churches with an inclusive membership of 11,024. Its president resides at 300 Morris Road, Exton, Pennsylvania 19341. It carries on a foreign mission in Guatemala.

New Congregational Methodist Church

In 1881 the decision of a quarterly conference of the Methodist Episcopal Church, South, to consolidate into one a number of rural churches in the southern part of Georgia led to the withdrawal of four churches, which, with a newly organized fifth congregation, founded the New Congregational Methodist Church. The new body rejected episcopacy, but determined to retain its former faith and doctrine. It based its discipline on that of the Methodist Episcopal Church, South, and on the Alabama Congregational Methodist discipline.[21] Its twenty-two Articles of Religion are the twenty-five articles of the rest of Methodism minus the articles on works of supererogation, on purgatory, and on services in the vernacular, with omissions in the articles on the sacraments and the Lord's Supper, and with other minor changes.[22] The order for infant baptism conceives of this sacrament chiefly as an act of dedication of the infant by the parents.[23] The congregations elect their local officers, including the pastor, annually.[24] Without elevating the rite to the level of a sacrament or ordinance, the New Congregational Methodist Church practices foot washing extensively. The General Conference meets every four years. Thirteen churches in Georgia and Florida report an estimated 900 members.[25] There are no specific church headquarters.

Southern Methodist Church

In 1884 the "Plan of Separation" permitted the southern delegates to the General Conference of the Methodist Episcopal Church to organize a separate General Conference in the slave-holding states. The Methodist Episcopal Church, South, was organized the following year. The projected union of the latter body with the Methodist Episcopal Church and the Methodist Protestant Church in 1939 met resistance on the part of some southern Methodists who refused to enter the union because of the "alarming infidelity and apostasy found among Methodists in the north."[26] Organization of a "Layman's Organization for the Preservation of the Methodist Episcopal Church, South," culminated in a convocation at Columbia, South Carolina, on January 14, 1939, at which four hundred representatives set up a provisional plan for a continuing Methodist Episcopal Church, South. Subsequent court decisions gave The Methodist Church control of the name "Methodist Episcopal Church, South," and possession of its properties. For that reason the continuing body adopted the name "Southern Methodist Church." It retains, with the necessary modifications, the 1934 *Discipline* of the Methodist Episcopal Church, South.

In addition to the twenty-five Articles of Religion, a separate section in the *Discipline* sets forth "Other Southern Methodist Beliefs." Thus they affirm that God must take the initiative if man is to be saved. The prevenient grace of God in the blessings of life, the delay of punishment, and the presence and influence of the Bible, the Holy Spirit, and the church are not sufficient for the salvation of fallen man. Yet prevenient grace makes souls susceptible to the saving grace of Christ, and thus God in his grace makes it possible for *all* men to be saved. Salvation comes through faith in Christ as a personal Savior, but this requires a godly sorrow for sin. The Holy Spirit works this grace of repentance and thus leads the sinner to forsake his sins and to seek the justifying mercy of God in Christ. Belief in the Lord Jesus Christ is more than a mere mental assent to any doctrine concerning his person or any of his works. Simultaneously with justification of the soul through the atoning merits of the blood of Christ, the washing of regeneration, resulting in the new creation of the whole spiritual being, takes place through the act of the Holy Spirit. The seed of holiness planted in regeneration or rebirth must be permitted to germinate and spring up with a prayerful cultivation and studying of God's Word. The Holy Spirit must give the penitent sinner the full assurance that he has passed from death to life. Christian perfection is the Holy Spirit's work that follows regeneration. The atonement is universal, and God has given to Adam and all his posterity the ability to choose or reject salvation. God's foreknowledge does not affect the eternal destiny of any soul. The Holy Spirit exercises no absolute compulsion. Man's will, mind, and emotion, aroused and awakened by the Holy Spirit, must cooperate with Him. When the sinner meets the conditions of salvation fully, he is then elected to be saved. Habitual and final failure to meet the basic conditions of repentance and faith will bring eternal loss. There is a visible church, a congregation of faithful men, in which the Word of God is preached and the sacraments duly administered, and an invisible church, all whom Christ knows as belonging to him whether they have joined the visible church or not.[27]

The original manuscripts of the Bible are the inerrant Word of God, verbally inspired. Southern Methodists "recognize the King James Version of the Bible as a trustworthy translation and . . . recommend that it be read from the pulpit." In evangelizing the world emphasis belongs on reaching the individual with the Gospel and its implications; "no humanitarian and philanthropic schemes may be substituted for the preaching of the cross."[28] They believe in the Genesis account of creation, that God by his own fiat instantaneously created every living thing after its kind. The second coming of Christ will be "literal, bodily, personal, imminent, and premillennial."[29] Southern

Methodists "believe in the person of good angels, bad angels, demons and of Satan."[30] They "subscribe heartily to the Scriptural command to give the tithe of all our increase," state that their church "is a segregated church," hold that integration is not the answer to current social problems, and voice the "opinion that integration would produce more problems than it would solve."[31] Believing that "the church should be separated from compromising situations in the world," the Southern Methodist Church belongs to the American and International Council of Christian Churches, "a body of churches that endeavors to preserve the integrity of the Holy Scriptures and combats those who try to destroy the same."[32]

Organization is on Methodist lines, but without bishops or district superintendents. Local congregations own and control local church property and may call their own pastors. The General Conference meets every four years. The four annual conferences of the denomination reported 174 churches with an inclusive membership of 11,000. The president receives mail at Box 132, Orangeburg, South Carolina 29115.

Filipino Community Churches in Hawaii

In the period after World War I the Congregationalist and Methodist Churches in Hawaii recruited a number of Christian workers in the Philippine Islands to come to Hawaii to provide for the religious needs of their fellow countrymen. Among them was the Reverend N. C. Dizon (b. 1891), a Methodist. He later withdrew from the Methodist Church and in 1927 he founded the First Filipino Community Church in Honolulu. As the number of non-Filipinos attending its services increased, it formally dropped the word "Filipino" from its name in 1953. In 1957 the Filipino Community Church in Wahiawa came under the Honolulu church's jurisdiction. The two churches encouraged the Filipino community at Hilo to establish a Sunday school, but the latter was never formally a part of the corporation.

The doctrinal position of the two churches is Methodist. Baptism is administered with the words: "I baptize you in the name of the Father, Son, and Holy Spirit."

The headquarters of the Filipino Community Churches is at 838 Kanoa Street, Honolulu. Population shifts on Oahu and the increasing acculturation of the Filipino community led to a decline in total membership from a high of 175 at the beginning of the 1960s to an estimated 40 in 1970.[33] Recent efforts to contact the community have been unsuccessful.

Bible Protestant Church

In 1939, when the Methodist Protestant Church was about to unite with the Methodist Episcopal Church and the Methodist Episcopal Church, South, to form The Methodist Church, the ministers and delegates of thirty-four churches of the Eastern Conference of the Methodist Protestant Church withdrew. They did so in protest partly against the union, partly against what they saw as a drift from the historic principles of Methodism. Methodist leaders, the withdrawing group felt, were denying the inspiration of the Bible and "practically every fundamental doctrine of the historic Christian faith"; instead they were stressing the social gospel, looking toward union with Roman Catholicism, and playing prominent roles in the Federal Council of the Churches of Christ (subsequently absorbed into the National Council of the Churches of Christ in the United States of America).[34]

Initially the withdrawing ministers and churches regarded themselves as the legitimate continuation of the Eastern Conference of the Methodist Protestant Church, and they still function under the charter issued to that body in 1914. In 1940 they adopted the name Bible Protestant Church, along with a new constitution and by-laws.

The Bible Protestant Church underlines its conservative theological stand by its membership in the American Council of Christian Churches and its demand that each local church "stand firmly and boldly against all ungodliness, apostasy and the teachings of false, fanatical cults." Its Doctrinal Statement affirms the verbal inspiration of the Bible; the Trinity; Christ's deity, virgin birth, blood sacrifice, death, resurrection, ascension, and intercession; salvation through faith in his atonement; the church as the body of Christ begun on Pentecost and having as members everyone who receives Christ as personal Savior; the Lord's Supper and water baptism; Christ's return to rapture the saints, a tribulation period of seven years, Christ's millennial reign on earth, and the judgment of the wicked; the personality and eternal punishment of Satan; the bodily resurrection of all men, and the eternal punishment of the lost and eternal joy of the saved. Its Standards of Practice emphasize Christian education, missions, tithing, evangelism, keeping the Lord's Day, and biblical separation from "organizations that harbor modernism or support the National Council of [the] Churches [of Christ] in [the United States of] America."[35]

The individual congregations are autonomous and own and control their own property. A delegate conference meets annually. A pastoral relations committee formally assigns the pastors to their charges. There are 38 churches in the Eastern Seaboard states from Virginia to New York and in Michigan; their total membership is 2,180. The Bible Protestant Church carries on missions in Japan.[36] Headquarters are at 84 East Clementon Road, Gibbsboro, New Jersey 08026.

The Evangelical Methodist Church

Three groups of Methodists in different parts of the world organized in successive years of the 1930s under the name of the Evangelical Methodist Church. The first was the Evangelical Methodist Church that came into being at Santiago, Chile, in 1936. The second was the Evangelical Methodist

Church in Nigeria, organized in 1937. The third was the Evangelical Methodist Church in France, established in 1938.

In February 1945 the Reverend W. W. Breckbill of Altoona, Pennsylvania, withdrew from The Methodist Church "because of the unbelief and worldly condition that exists within it."[37] Shortly afterward his congregation reorganized under his leadership as The Evangelical Independent Methodist Church.[38] In November 1945 the Reverend John Henry Hamblen of Abilene, Texas, while on a sabbatical leave during which he preached to a congregation that called itself the Independent Methodist Church, likewise withdrew from The Methodist Church because of the "growing tendency toward modernism."[39] In May 1946, at a meeting in Memphis, Tennessee, the two ministers and their supporters joined forces. As a result the Evangelical Methodist Church came into being at an organizational meeting held later that year in Kansas City, Missouri. At this meeting the Mexican Evangelistic Mission (now the Evangelical Methodist Church in Mexico) joined the new fellowship.

By 1950 continuing growth had increased the size of the American body to 59 congregations with 2,654 members. In that year it united with the Evangelical Methodist Churches in Chile, Nigeria, and France to form The Evangelical Methodist Church.

A schism divided the organization in 1952. One faction followed Breckbill, the other Hamblen. The issues involved both doctrinal and administrative matters. In a suit which the followers of Hamblen initiated in California over property rights and jurisdiction in 1953, the court ultimately found in favor of the plaintiffs. To minimize confusion, the Altoona group began to be referred to unofficially as The Evangelical Methodist Church of America, while the Hamblen group continued under the name The Evangelical Methodist Church.

The polity of The Evangelical Methodist Church is congregational in that the local congregation owns its property and calls its pastor. The polity is connectional in that each congregation is governed by the *Discipline* of The Evangelical Methodist Church and participates in district, annual, and general conferences through representation by ministers and lay members. The church body holds membership in the National Association of Evangelicals but disavows any connection with the World Council of Churches or the National Council of Churches.[40]

The Evangelical Methodist Church describes itself as Christ-centered and committed to the Scriptures as God's Word. It encourages evangelism and mission outreach. It seeks to be true to early Methodism and to Methodist concern for "holiness of heart and life."[41]

Since 1962 the church body's headquarters are at 3036 Meridian North, Wichita, Kansas 67204. With churches in 28 of the United States the inclusive membership is 10,675. No membership figures are available for Mexico or Nigeria. *The Voice of Evangelical Methodism* is the official journal.[42]

The Evangelical Methodist Church [of America]

As a result of the division in the Evangelical Methodist Church in 1952 and a subsequent court decision in favor of one party in the division, the other party under the leadership of W. W. Breckbill of Altoona, Pennsylvania, was reluctantly distinguished by adding "of America" to the name "The Evangelical Methodist Church." The group grew both in North America and abroad. At present the church body has congregations and missions in 26 of the United States and in 11 foreign countries, including Argentina, Uruguay, Surinam, Nigeria, and Pakistan. In the United States there are 86 churches and approximately 8,000 members.[43]

Under Breckbill's leadership the Evangelical Methodist Church [of America] adopted Wesley's twenty-five Articles of Religion with a number of changes. Article V declares that Holy Scripture "is the verbally inspired Word of God." Articles XVI and XVIII speak throughout of "ordinances." Article XVIII consistently refers to the Lord's Supper as a "memorial." Article XVII provides for the "dedication" of young children as an alternative to baptism. There is an alternative Article XXIII treating "Of the Duty of Christians to the Civil Authority" for churches outside the United States of America. The *Discipline* also includes Wesley's "General Rules."[44]

Local churches are autonomous, congregational, and connectional. Licensed unordained pastors and local preachers may administer the ordinances. Ministers are not to wear special clerical garb, such as "robes, cutaway coats and ecclesiastical regalia, and tuxedos," when conducting services. The Apostles' Creed in worship substitutes "the blood-bought church" for the "holy catholic church." In the Lord's Supper "pure, unfermented juice of some fruit" is to be used. Parents and guardians of children have a choice of the "dedication of the children with the laying on of hand" or "the laying on of hand with water." Believer's baptism may be by sprinkling, pouring, or immersion.[45]

The General Conference meets every four years. There are three general superintendents, one of whom is also bishop to Latin America. The annual conference is the basic body in the church. Annual meetings are held in local congregations. Following Breckbill's death in 1974, Dr. Donald McKnight of Dublin, Maryland was chosen as presiding superintendent. Headquarters were moved from Altoona, Pennsylvania to Kingsport, Tennessee 37660, where the mailing address is Box 751.

**First Congregational Methodist Church in the
United States of America**

The First Congregational Methodist Church of America shares a common origin with the Congregational Methodist Church in the secession of the founders of both bodies from the Methodist Episcopal Church, South, in 1852, over itinerancy, episcopacy, and inequalities of rank among the ministers. After surviving the secession of about two thirds of its membership to the Congregational Church in 1887–1888, the movement divided into two parts in a controversy about doctrinal issues, chiefly the question of entire sanctification or complete perfection, in 1941, with rival general conferences each claiming to perpetuate the original body.[46] The Congregational Methodist Church in the United States of America prefixed "First" to its name in 1963 to distinguish itself further from the Congregational Methodist Church.

The First Congregational Methodist Church has incorporated the twenty-five Articles of Religion in its constitution and government without alteration.

The congregations of the body are autonomous. There are local church conferences, district conferences, annual conferences, and a General Conference that meets every four years.

The headquarters were at Decatur, Mississippi but a recent letter was returned "Addressee Unknown." There were 100 churches with a total membership of 6,263 several years ago.[47]

The United Wesleyan Methodist Church of America

In 1905 The United Wesleyan Methodist Church of America came into being to meet the needs of West Indian Methodist immigrants who wished to continue the traditions of British Methodism. The president resides at 270 West 126th Street, New York, New York 10027. There are 5 churches with 550 members. The present writer's efforts at securing information about the United Wesleyan Church of America from the officers of the organization were unsuccessful.

Free Christian Zion Church of Christ

Under the leadership of E. D. Brown, a conference missionary of the African Methodist Episcopal Zion Church, a company of black ministers who had withdrawn from the African Methodist Episcopal, African Methodist Episcopal Zion, Colored (now Christian) Methodist Episcopal, Methodist Episcopal, and Baptist churches, formed the Free Christian Zion Church of Christ at Redemption, Arkansas, in 1905. The common objection of all of these ministers was to "taxation" in support of denominational agencies, and this was the reported cause for their withdrawals from their respective parent bodies.[48]

Methodist influence came to predominate in the teaching and structure of the new body. Two chief pastors make all assignments to pastorates and appoint all church officers. Pastors and deacons direct the work of local churches, particularly the relief of the needy. Laymen participate in the direction of the local congregations and in the annual General Assembly.

The headquarters are at Nashville, Arkansas. The constituency of the church is located in Arkansas, Kansas, Texas, and Mississippi. In 1966 the former editor of the church body's monthly, *Zion's Trumpet,* put the number of churches at 5 with a total membership of 100.[49]

Cumberland Methodist Church

In 1950 Carl A. Shadrick, Ed Nunley, and W. H. Caldwell withdrew from the Congregational Methodist Church, Incorporated, and gathered in Caldwell's home in Laager, Grundy County, Tennessee, to organize the Cumberland Methodist Church. The leaders of the new body defended their action by asserting that politics had jeopardized the parent organization and had paralyzed its freedom, with damage to both its growth and its unity. They affirmed the principles of equality in the Christian church; their belief in an old-fashioned mourners' bench (or altar) as "a meeting place between God and man, involving a sacrifice for sin" as well as "heart-felt religion"; the biblical character of the congregational form of church government; and the right of the church to impose and enforce only those regulations and rules that are in accordance with the Bible and that may be necessary for carrying practical Christianity into effect.[50]

The constitution accepts the Bible as the only rule of faith and prohibits the teaching and practice of any other rule of faith or conduct.[51] New members must pass an examination in their doctrinal views and religious experience, and must be found evangelical in both areas before being admitted to baptism.[52]

The twenty-five Methodist Articles of Religion have been reduced to sixteen. Omitted are the articles on the Old Testament (6), works of supererogation (11), purgatory (14), the sacraments (16), both kinds (19), the marriage of ministers (21), rites and ceremonies (22), the rulers of the United States of America (23), Christians' goods (24), and a Christian's oath (25). All but two of the other articles have undergone abbreviation and simplification, sometimes of a radical sort; the article on speaking in tongues that people cannot understand has received an antipentecostal thrust. The articles on the ordinances, baptism and the Lord's Supper, have been expanded, the latter to include foot washing. Baptism is limited to believers; the mode is optional. The Lord's Supper is open to "all Christians who feel worthy"; the bread and wine "are designed to represent the broken body and the blood of Christ." Foot washing—men washing the men's feet, women the women's feet—follows the Lord's Supper. An added article rejects as unbiblical the doctrine of the "second blessing or second work," and sees sanctification as a gradual process.[53]

The General Board meets annually. No information about the number of churches and the total membership is available, but the church has probably declined from the 4 churches, all in Tennessee, with a total membership of 65, that it reported in 1954.

The Church of the United Brethren in Christ

The Church of the United Brethren in Christ traces its history back to 1800. In that year thirteen Pennsylvania and Maryland clergymen, who over more than a decade had withdrawn from their former ministries in the Presbyterian, German Reformed, Mennonite, and Lutheran communities, organized the United Brethren in Christ in Frederick County, Maryland, and elected William Otterbein and Martin Boehm as their bishops. The group adopted its first discipline at the conference of 1815. A minor schism took place when the United Christian Church withdrew in the 1860s and 1870s.

In 1889 the General Conference of the United Brethren in Christ at York, Pennsylvania, adopted an altered constitution. This provoked a controversy chiefly over the issue of membership in secret oath-bound combinations on the part of United Brethren in Christ members. A minority withdrew and declared its adherence to the "Old Constitution" of 1841[54]; this group survives as the Church of the United Brethren in Christ.

The Confession of Faith of the Church of the United Brethren in Christ briefly takes up the Trinity; the deity, manhood, and redemptive activity of Jesus Christ, the Savior and Mediator of the whole human race; the Holy Ghost; the church and the last things; the Holy Bible; the worldwide proclamation of the fall in Adam and redemption in Christ; the obligatory nature of the ordinances, baptism, and the Lord's Supper ("but the manner . . . ought always be left to the judgment and understanding of every individual"); and the strictly optional nature of the practice of "the example of feet-washing."

The Church of the United Brethren in Christ believes in tithing as a minimum standard of giving; permits no connection with "secret combinations" because they "teach that salvation is achieved through human effort alone, apart from faith in Christ, and that such salvation is offered to all men of whatever faith or religion"; and disavows loose views on divorce and intemperance. A lawsuit against another member (except in criminal cases or cases requiring and justifying a process at law) may be punished with expulsion. The Lord's Day is to be kept holy by spending it in exercises of devotion and "such social converse as shall honor God." The church prohibits manufacturing, using, or selling intoxicating beverages or in any way promoting the liquor traffic; admonishes its members to abstain from tobacco; calls upon them to register their disapproval of race prejudice; endorses affirmation as the appropriate mode of legal testimony; positively disapproves participation in voluntary, national, aggressive warfare, but recognizes the responsibility of the government to preserve "our national compact against treason or invasion by any belligerent force"; urges forgiveness and reconciliation even in the case of adultery in perference to divorce, but permits divorce and remarriage in the case of adultery or when the other party has remarried after divorce.

Organizationally the Church of the United Brethren in Christ has the usual Methodist pattern of local and annual conferences and every four years a General Conference, composed of laymen, ministers, general officials of the church, and bishops. Both men and women may be ordained as elders (ministers). The Mission Board of the church operates foreign missions in Sierra Leone, Hong Kong, Jamaica, Honduras, and Nicaragua. The church headquarters are at 48 East Franklin Street, Huntington, Indiana 46750.

There are 276 churches, with an overall membership of 26,335 in 21 states and in Ontario.

United Christian Church (Lebanon County, Pennsylvania)

About the time of the War between the States, George W. Hoffman (1820–1883), Christian Peffley (1802–1885), Ephraim Light, George Landis, John Stamm (1819–1895), Thomas Lesher (1812–1894), and a number of other ministers of the Church of the United Brethren in Christ withdrew from that body. Among the issues were infant baptism, the voluntary bearing of arms, and the admission of members of oath-bound secret societies to church membership.[55] They were reluctant to create a new denomination. But the defection of some of their followers made it clear to the leaders that some kind of organization was necessary. In 1869 the supporters of the new movement adopted a declaration of principles. In these they affirmed their faith in a universal United Christian Church, to which all truly converted persons belong, and repudiated the three practices on account of which they had withdrawn from the parent body, together with human slavery. A conference held in 1877 set forth a more elaborate Confession of Faith. The name United Christian Church was assumed in 1878.[56]

The present Confession of Faith, adopted in 1920 and obviously related to that of the United Brethren in Christ, has articles on the Trinity, creation, Jesus Christ, the Holy Ghost, the church ("a holy Christian church, composed of true believers, in which the word of God is preached by men divinely called, and the ordinances are duly administered"), the resurrection of the dead, the Holy Scriptures, depravity ("[human beings are] not only entirely destitute of holiness, but [are] inclined to evil, and only evil, and that continually"), the redemption and vicarious atonement, justification ("only by faith in our Lord Jesus Christ and not by works, yet that good works in Christ are acceptable to God, and spring out of a true and living faith"), regeneration and adoption, sanctification ("those who have been born again are separated in their acts, words, and thoughts from sin, and are enabled to live unto God"), the church ordinances (baptism, the Lord's Supper, and footwashing, with the mode of baptism left to each individual, "only that it shall be administered in water if possible"), and the Christian Sabbath (that is, Sunday).[57]

The chapter of the *Discipline* on moral reform and temperance describes the manufacture, sale, and use of intoxicating beverages as immoral; advises members to refrain from using tobacco; forbids membership in "oath-bound secret combinations"; places affirmations on a par with oaths; counsels members to abstain on Sunday from everything that does not contribute to their spiritual growth; denies remarriage after divorce; repudiates voluntary participation in war; counsels against introducing musical instruments into Sunday school and church services;[58] forbids membership in clubs that serve alcoholic beverages to members and whose activities center around banqueting and worldly entertainment; and limits song services to congregational singing.[59]

Local churches are called classes; ministers are called elders. The General Conference meets annually. There are 13 churches, all in a fairly small area east of Harrisburg, Pennsylvania; the overall membership is 450. The church body carries on foreign missions in Jamaica and Japan. The presiding elder resides at R.D. 4, Lebanon, Lebanon County, Pennsylvania 17042.

The Evangelical Church in Canada (Northwest Canada Conference of the Evangelical Church)

The Evangelical Church established its first permanent missions in Canada in 1839, after a previous effort in 1816 had proved abortive. The Canada Conference was formed in 1863. After more than two decades of investigation, the Canada Conference began its work in the western provinces in 1899. By 1927 the work had reached such proportions that organization of the Northwest Canada Conference took place.[60] In 1946 the conference became a part of the Evangelical United Brethren Church.

The conference opposed the 1968 union of the Evangelical United Brethren Church with The Methodist Church to form The United Methodist Church. At the uniting conference in Dallas, Texas, the Northwest Canada Conference of the Evangelical United Brethren Church petitioned for autonomous status. This request received favorable action.

The church body chose to continue to be designated as the Northwest Canada Conference of the Evangelical Church, the name by which it had been chartered in 1928, for two reasons. First, the Canadian Methodists had become a part of the United Church in Canada in 1925 and the conference deemed it inappropriate to revive the denominational name for itself. Second, prior to the union of 1946 the churches that constituted the conference had been part of the Evangelical Church. After it achieved autonomy it chose to call itself the Evangelical Church in Canada.

The headquarters of the Evangelical Church in Canada are at 164 Fifth Street Southeast, Medicine Hat, Alberta T1A OM3. There are 44 organized congregations with 3,712 members.

Evangelical Congregational Church

In 1922, when the United Evangelical Church was about to reunite with the Evangelical Church, from which the former body had withdrawn in 1894, the East Pennsylvania Conference of the United Evangelical Church, along with individual churches of four other conferences, elected to continue the denominational name and organization. In 1928 it adopted the name Evangelical Congregational Church. It continues the Arminian tradition in its theology, the Evangelical tradition in its spirit and practice, and the Methodist tradition in its polity. The Articles of Faith have sections on God; Christ; the Holy Spirit; the Bible; human depravity; salvation through Christ; repentance; justification; regeneration; the witness of the Spirit; sanctification ("attainable in this life by faith, both gradually and instantaneously"); good works; apostasy; immortality of the soul; the resurrection of Christ and of the dead; the final judgment; heaven; hell; the holy general church and the individual church; the ministry; baptism; the Lord's Supper ("those who rightly and worthily receive the same partake of the body and blood of Christ by faith, not in a bodily but in a spiritual manner"); church polity ("Christ ordained no particular form of government for His church"); civil government; and the evangelization of the world.[61] Christian perfection is "one of the cherished doctrines of the Evangelical Congregational Church" and is set forth in Wesley's own words.[62]

Local congregations own their church property. There is equal representation of laymen and ministers at the annual and general conferences. The ministry is itinerant; the annual conferences appoint the pastors each year. The General Conference meets every four years. There are 161 churches in the United States, with a total membership of 28,886. The headquarters and residence of the bishop are at 3116 Octagon Avenue, Sinking Springs, Pennsylvania 19608.

NOTES

1. Peter Spencer and his colleagues from Wilmington, where an independent black Methodist church had existed since 1805, participated in the organizing convention but refused to join the new denomination; in 1813 they formed the Union Church of Africans. The New York black Methodists, who also had had friction with their white co-religionists, did not attend the 1816 Philadelphia meeting; ultimately they organized the African Methodist Episcopal Zion Church.

2. Frederick E. Maser and George A. Singleton, "Further Branches of Methodism Are Founded," in Emory Stevens Bucke, ed., *The History of American Methodism* (Nashville: Abingdon Press, 1964), vol. 1, pp. 601-609.

3. *The Book of Discipline of the African Methodist Episcopal Church* (38th edn.; Nashville: The A.M.E. Sunday School Union, 1965), pp. 15-63.

4. Ibid., p. 1.

5. In the 1890s eight clergymen of the African Methodist Episcopal Church in Jacksonville, Florida became involved in disputes with their ecclesiastical superiors. In 1897 they withdrew and founded the Independent African Methodist Episcopal Denomination, with a new Book of Discipline, but with the same Articles of Religion and General Rules as the parent body. Three years later a schism over the authority of presiding elders led to the founding of a second Independent African Methodist Episcopal Church at Coldwater, Mississippi, in 1900. The two factions reunited in 1920.

6. Grant S. Schockley and Leonard L. Haynes, "The A.M.E. and the A.M.E. Zion Churches," in Emery Stevens Bucke, ed., *The History of American Methodism* (Nashville: Abingdon Press, 1964), vol. 2, pp. 579-580; Ralph Stoody, "Other Branches of Methodism, 1960," Bucke, *History,* pp. 3, 595. Repeated efforts to obtain information about this church body from its leaders were unsuccessful.

7. J. P. Thompson and others, "Com-

mittee's Address," in William Jacob Walls and others, eds., *The Doctrines and Discipline of the African Methodist Episcopal Zion Church* (rev. edn.; Charlotte, N.C.: A.M.E. Zion Publishing House, 1961), pp. viii-ix.

8. Frederick E. Master and George A. Singleton, "Further Branches of Methodism Are Founded," in Emory Stevens Bucke, ed., *The History of American Methodism* (Nashville: Abingdon Press, 1964), vol. 1, pp. 609-614.

9. Grant S. Shockley and Leonard L. Haynes, "The A.M.E. and A.M.E. Zion Churches," Bucke, *History*, vol. 2, pp. 555-582.

10. J. P. Thompson and others, in Walls, *The Doctrines and Discipline*, pp. 3-16.

11. "Message from the Bishops," ibid., p. x.

12. Benjamin W. Arnett, *The Budget of 1904* (Philadelphia: The A.M.E. Book Concern, 1904), p. 232, quoted by Frederick E. Maser and George A. Singleton, "Further Branches of Methodism Are Founded," in Emory Stevens Bucke, ed., *The History of American Methodism* (New York: Abingdon Press, 1964), vol. 1, p. 616. There are some aspects of the history of this church body that are not wholly clear. In general, the present writer has followed the account of Maser and Singleton. "Further Branches," pp. 615-617.

13. *The Doctrine and Discipline of the African Union First Colored Methodist Protestant Church and Connection of the United States of America or Elsewhere*, 17th edn. (Wilmington, Del.: n.p., 1958), p. 3.

14. Ibid., pp. 17-27.

15. The present writer's repeated efforts to obtain information about this church body and its present address were unsuccessful.

16. *A Catechism Compiled by the Education Board of the Reformed Zion Union Apostolic Church* (rev. edn.; Lawrenceville, Va.: Johnson's Print Shop, 1958), p. 10.

17. Ibid., p. 9.

18. Ibid., p. 12. See also "Articles of Religion," *General Rules and Discipline of the Reformed Zion Union Apostolic Church* (rev. edn.; Norfolk, Va.: James M. Creecy, 1966), pp. 8-13.

19. To be distinguished from William Hammett's Primitive Methodist Church,

a schism in the Methodist Episcopal Church in the Carolinas that lasted from 1792 to 1804.

20. Frederick E. Maser and George Singleton, "Further Branches of Methodism Are Founded," in Emery Stevens Bucke, ed., *The History of American Methodism* (Nashville: Abingdon Press, 1964), vol 1, pp. 630-635.

21. *Discipline, New Congregational Methodist Church* (undated pamphlet printed after 1956), pp. 1-6.

22. Ibid., pp. 22-27.

23. Ibid., pp. 30-32.

24. Ibid., p. 8.

25. Letters from the Reverend Joseph E. Kelly, Jacksonville, Florida, former president of the General Conference of the New Congregational Methodist Church.

26. *What, Why, How?—History, Organization. and Doctrinal Belief of the Southern Methodist Church* (16-page pamphlet) (Orangeburg, S.C.: Southern Methodism Church, 1966), p. 3.

27. *The Doctrines and Discipline of the Southern Methodist Church* (Orangeburg, S.C.: The Methodist Church, Foundry Press, 1962), pp. 24-32.

28. Ibid., p. 33.

29. Ibid., p. 34.

30. Ibid., pp. 34-35.

31. Ibid., pp. 35-36.

32. Ibid., p. 36.

33. Letter from the Reverend Joseph H. Dizon, pastor, First Community Church Honolulu.

34. Newton C. Conant, *Present Day Methodism and the Bible* (Murfreesboro, Tenn.: Sword of the Lord Publishers, 1949). The author, historian of the Bible Protestant Church, describes the book as "the answer to the question, 'Why did thirty-four churches of the Eastern Conference of the former Methodist Protestant Church (now Bible Protestant Church) refuse to enter the Methodist union?' " p. 9).

35. *The Bible Protestant Church: Doctrinal Statement and Rules of Order* (undated 24-page brochure), pp. 1-10.

36. Communication from the Reverend Newton C. Conant, former conference historian. Bible Protestant Church.

37. W. W. Breckbill, "This Is the Story," *The Methodist (Evangelical)* [cover title: *The Evangelical Methodist*], vol.

22, no. 5 (January 1946), p. 2.

38. Ibid.. pp. 3, 8, 13.

39. W. L. Hankla, "District Superintendent Leaves Methodist Church," *The Methodist,* vol. 22, no. 5 (January 1946), p. 4.

40. *Presenting the Evangelical Methodist Church* (4-page pamphlet published by the church body).

41. Ibid.

42. Communication from Ronald D. Driggers, secretary-treasurer.

43. Communication from the Reverend Mark Rhodes, pastor, Evangelical Independent Methodist Church, Altoona, Pennsylvania.

44. Edwin M. Conn., ed., *The Evangelical Methodist Church Discipline* (rev. edn.; (Altoona, Penn.: The Evangelical Church, 1962), pp. 6-19.

45. Ibid., pp. 53, 118, 120, 126, 130.

46. On the prehistory of this schism, see Wilton R. Fowler, Jr., ed., *Minutes of the General Conference of the Congregational Methodist Church: The The First Through the Twentieth Sessions 1869–1945* (Tehuacana, Texas: Westminster College Print Shop, 1960), pp. 84-130 *passim.*

47. Communication from the Reverend J. J. Mullinax, Decatur, Mississippi.

48. Grant S. Shockley and Leonard L. Haynes, "The A.M.E. and the A.M.E. Zion Churches," in Emory Stevens Bucke, ed., *The History of American Methodism* (Nashville: Abingdon Press, 1964), vol. 2, p. 579.

49. Letter from the Reverend L. A. O. Bryant, Nashville, Arkansas. The Reverend Mr. Bryant was listed as the editor of the church's monthly, *Zion Trumpet,* in the *Yearbook of American Churches for 1967,* although he stated that he had severed his connection with the Free Christian Zion Church of Christ. The present writer's repeated efforts to secure information from Chief Pastor W. M. Benson, Nashville, Arkansas, were unsuccessful.

50. Carl A. Shadrick, Ed Nunley, and W. H. Caldwell, *Constitution and Government of the Cumberland Methodist Church* (Laager, Tenn.: n.p., 1950) (5-page pamphlet), pp. 4-7. The present writer has his copy of this pamphlet from the Reverend Ed Nunley, Tracy City, Tennessee.

51. Ibid., p. 9.

52. Ibid., p. 11, 15-17.

53. Ibid., pp. 37-44.

54. For that reason this group was distinguished from the majority group by the addition of "(Old Constitution)" to its name until the union of the Evangelical Church and the majority group of United Brethren in Christ in 1946.

55. The popular name of the withdrawing group for many years was "Hoffmanites." A minor issue, not mentioned in the official "Historical Sketch." was the "wearing of fashionable clothes."

56. *Origin, Doctrine, Constitution, and Discipline of the United Christian Church* (Myerstown, Penn.: Church Center Press, 1950), pp. 1-6.

57. Ibid., pp. 23-26.

58. This counsel is no longer in force. An effort to have it relaxed failed of the requisite two-thirds affirmative vote at the 1964 Annual Conference (*Minutes of the Eighty-Eighth Annual Conference of the United Christian Church, 1964,* pp. 3-4), but succeeded the following year (*Minutes of the Eighty-Ninth Annual Conference of the United Christian Church,* 1965, p. 7). The 1966 conference ratified the change (*Minutes of the Ninetieth Annual Conference of the United Christian Church, 1966,* p. 2).

59. *Origins, Doctrine, Constitution, and Discipline,* pp. 75-78. The statement at No. 2484 in Johannes Gründler, *Lexikon der christlichen Kirchen und Sekten* (Vienna, Austria: Herder, 1961), vol. 2, 1304, that the Negro Church of God in Christ (Pentecostal), the remnant of a group that had withdrawn from the Church of God in Christ founded by Charles H. Macon, joined the United Christian Church here described in 1930 is not correct. Allegedly there are other church bodies of the same name with reference to which Gründler's statement is true, but the present writer's inquiry has not discovered any information about them.

60. Theodore E. Jesske, *Forty Years and More* (Medicine Hat, Alberta: The Board of Missions, Northwest Canada Conference Evangelical United Brethren Church, 1967) (8-page pamphlet), pp. 2-4.

61. "Articles of Faith," *The Creed, Ritual and Discipline of the Evangelical Congregational Church* 3rd edn.; (Myerstown, Penn.: Church Center Press, 1960). pp. 9-14.

62. "Christian Perfection," *The Creed*, pp. 15-18.

BIBLIOGRAPHY

The Book of Discipline of the African Methodist Episcopal Church. 38th edn. Nashville: The A.M.E. Sunday School Union, 1965.

Burkholder, Walter M., and others, eds. *Origin, Doctrine, Constitution and Discipline of the Church of the United Brethren in Christ 1965–1967.* Huntington, Ind.: United Brethren Publishing Establishment, [1965].

A Catechism Compiled by the Education Board of the Reformed Zion Union Apostolic Church. Rev. edn. Lawrenceville, Va.: Johnson's Print Shop, 1958.

Conant. Newton C. *How God Delivered 34 Churches.* Camden, N.J.: Bible Prottestant Press, 1964. A brief documentary history of the origins of the Bible Protestant Church in the perspective of twenty-five years.

The Creed, Ritual and Discipline of the Evangelical Congregational Church. 3rd edn. Myerstown, Penn.: Church Center Press, 1960.

General Rules and Discipline of the Reformed Zion Union Apostolic Church. Rev. edn. Norfolk, Va.: James M. Creecy, 1966.

Hood, James Walker. *One Hundred Years of the African Methodist Episcopal Zion Church, or, The Centennial of African Methodism.* New York: African Methodist Episcopal Zion Book Concern, 1885.

Mathews, Marcia M. *Richard Allen.* Baltimore: Helicon Press, 1963. A partly fictional biography of "the first American Negro to seek recognition for his people as a minority group."

Melton, John Gordon. *A [First Working] Bibliography of Black Methodism.* Evanston, Ill.: The Institute for the Study of American Religion, 1970. Pp. 5-17:

"African Methodist Episcopal Church" and "African Methodist Episcopal Bishops." Pp. 18-23: "African Methodist Episcopal Zion Church." Pp. 24-27: "Christian (formerly Colored) Methodist Episcopal Church."

Moore, John Jamison. *History of the African Methodist Episcopal Zion Church in America, Founded in the City of New York, Penn.:* Teacher's Journal Office, 1884.

Origin, Doctrine, Constitution, and Discipline of the United Christian Church (Myerstown, Penn.: Church Center Press. 1950).

Payne, Daniel Alexander. *History of the African Methodist Episcopal Church.* Ed. Charles S. Smith. Nashville: The A.M.E. Sunday School Union, 1891.

The Threshold of the Church: A Catechetical Manual of the Evangelical Congregational Church. 2nd edn. Myerstown, Penn.: The Board of Christian Education of the Evangelical Congregational Church, 1965.

Walls, William Jacob. *The Romance of a College.* New York: Vantage Press, 1963. Since 1879, when the present Livingstone College was established at Salisbury, North Carolina, as Zion Wesley Institute, the history of the institution and of the African Methodist Episcopal Zion Church have been closely linked. Bishop Walls traces the story of the school from its founding to 1963.

Wesley, Charles Harris. *Richard Allen, Apostle of Freedom.* Washington, D.C.: Associated Publishers, 1935.

Wilson, Robert Sherer. *A Brief History of the Evangelical Congregational Church for the Enlightenment of Her Pastors and People.* Myerstown, Penn.: Church Center Press, 1953.

PART VI

OTHER PROTESTANT

CHURCHES FORMED

SINCE THE REFORMATION

18. The Christian Restorationist Movement

The Christian Church (Disciples of Christ)

In 1968 at Kansas City, Missouri the International Convention of the Christian Churches (Disciples of Christ) was reconstituted as the Christian Church (Disciples of Christ), and the first representative assembly in the denomination's history was convened. The restructuring was the culmination of more than a century of developments in which a nineteenth-century American frontier movement to achieve Christian unity through the restoration of New Testament Christianity was institutionalized and ultimately found ecclesiastical expression in several denominations.[1]

The Restoration movement arose at the beginning of the nineteenth century among two separate but similar groups on the American frontier in Kentucky and southwest Pennsylvania.[2] In 1801 a camp-meeting revival at Cane Ridge, Kentucky convinced a local Presbyterian pastor, Barton Warren Stone (1772–1844), of the need for denominations to work together in preaching the Gospel and underscored for him the problems in the Calvinist doctrine of election. In 1803 Stone and several other preachers withdrew from the Synod of Kentucky and organized the Springfield Presbytery. Within a year they dissolved the presbytery, publishing *The Last Will and Testament of the Springfield Presbytery*, in which they willed "that this body die, be dissolved, and sink into union with the Body of Christ at large."[3] The Stone-led movement took the name "Christian" as it spread from Kentucky through the Midwest in its evangelization efforts.

Two years after arriving in America from Ireland in 1807 Thomas Campbell (1763–1854) was suspended from his Anti-Burgher Seceder Presbyterian Synod and Presbytery for inviting worshipers from other branches of the Presbyterian church to share in the Lord's Supper. Campbell withdrew from those bodies, forming the Christian Association of Washington (Pennsylvania), and in 1809 published his *Declaration and Address*, in which he affirmed his conviction:

That the church of Christ upon earth is essentially, intentionally, and constitutionally one; consisting of all those in every place that profess their faith in Christ and obedience to him in all things according to the scriptures, and that manifest the same by their tempers and conduct, and of none else, as can be truly and properly called christians.[4]

Campbell's son Alexander (1788–1866) joined him in 1910 and soon became the leader of a reform movement within Baptist associations and, after separation from the Baptists, of evangelistic outreach in association with Walter Scott (1796–1861) of Ohio and "Raccoon" John Smith (1784–1868) of Kentucky. The Campbell-led movement favored "Disciples of Christ" as a description for its followers.

The Christians and the Disciples ultimately discovered each other and were united at a meeting in Lexington, Kentucky, on January 1, 1832, bringing together 12,000 Disciples and 10,000 Christians. The two groups were unable to agree on a single name and bequeathed both names to the movement, a factor which is reflected in the use of both Christian and Disciple to describe the group throughout its history.[5]

Equipped by Walter Scott with a simple method of evangelism[6] and espousing principles and ideas suited to the conditions of frontier life, the Christian-Disciples grew dramatically in numbers. They increased from 22,000 in 1832 to almost 200,000 by 1860, and by the turn of the twentieth century they numbered more than a million. Because of the need for cooperation beyond the local congregation to carry on evangelistic work, they developed working relationships at the county and state levels. In 1849 the first national convention met in Cincinnati and organized the American Christian Missionary Society, though many Disciples regarded the organization as contrary to the principles of the New Testament. Avoiding division over the issue of slavery, a new generation of leaders guided the Disciples in the post-Civil War era, establishing additional agencies, educational institutions, and periodicals, reaching out in mission overseas, and taking on more and more of the characteristics of a denomination.

The Restoration movement, itself a cause of controversy within the church, was not to escape the disruption of internal controversy. A bone of contention was the affirmation: "Where the Scriptures speak, we speak; where the Scriptures are silent, we are silent."[7] Strict restorationists insisted that the New Testament provided a plan for every age to follow. Since New Testament Christians had no mission societies and worshiped without organs, Christians of every age should do the same. A division over this issue became apparent in the 1880s[8] and was recognized officially in 1906 when the United States Religious Census listed the strict restorationists as the churches of Christ (they prefer not to capitalize "churches") separately from the Disciples of Christ.

The separation was not the end of the controversy. Tension continued between the "cooperative" congregations (those in favor of extra-congregational agencies of cooperation) within what was consciously called the Brotherhood, to avoid a denominational stigma. The "independents" resisted the efforts to strengthen and unify the national agencies of the Disciples and in 1927 established the North American Christian Convention as an instrument for mutual support and fellowship without actually withdrawing from the Brotherhood. Objecting to the "liberalism" of Disciples-related colleges and universities, they established institutions of their own; and they gathered funds to support their own missionaries. In 1955 one of their number published a *Directory of the Ministry of the undenominational fellowship of Christian Churches and Churches of Christ*, a listing of preachers and congregations presumed to be sympathetic to the cause of the "independents." As a result of the restructuring decision which produced the Christian Church (Disciples of Christ), many congregations with a membership of about 1 million withdrew and asked to be listed in the 1971 *Yearbook of American Churches* as the "Christian Churches and Churches of Christ" distinct from the "Christian Church (Disciples of Christ)" and from the "churches of Christ."

Without wanting to be one denomination among others, the Christian Church (Disciples of Christ) slowly and reluctantly recognized its denominational status and devised structures for its life and mission. Throughout the decades of the twentieth century Disciples shared the strengths and weaknesses, the successes and failures of mainstream American Protestantism. They were active participants in the Social Gospel movement in the early part of the century and in the civil rights and social movements of the 1950s and 1960s. One of their number, Charles Clayton Morrison (1874–1966), purchased the *Christian Century*, previously a Disciples' publication, and transformed it into "an undenominational journal of religion" and one of the most influential religious journals in the world. Two Disciples have served as presidents of the United States, James A. Garfield in the nineteenth century and Lyndon B. Johnson in the twentieth.

An early twentieth-century effort to provide a representative delegate assembly failed, and the national conventions continued to be strictly advisory in nature with the privilege of vote accorded to all those present. In 1960 a Commission on Brotherhood Restructure was established and its "Provisional Design" produced an organizational structure which gave recognition to national and regional as well as local manifestations of the church. In 1968 the General Assembly of the Christian Church (Disciples of Christ) came into being, comprised of official delegates representing both congregations and regions. Further restructuring has continued at the national and regional level.

The Christian Church (Disciples of Christ) sprang from a movement whose founders understood creeds to be the root cause of sectarian division in the church. "No creed but Christ" became a favorite slogan as Disciples opposed the use of doctrinal standards as tests of fellowship. Strong aversion to theological speculation, which outlawed use of even the word "theology," persisted until midway into the twentieth century. A favorite maxim throughout Disciples' history has been the saying attributed to Rupertus Meldenius of the seventeenth century: "In essentials, unity; in nonessentials, liberty; in all things, charity."[9]

Though the Christian Church (Disciples of Christ) has not adopted a specific formulation of its beliefs, its members do hold specific convictions. Already in 1835 Alexander Campbell published *The Christian System*, a comprehensive statement of biblical doctrine which served as a textbook for generations of Disciples preachers. Against the charge that he had produced a creed for the Disciples, Campbell stated: "We speak for ourselves only; and while we are always willing to give a declaration of our faith and knowledge of the Christian system, we firmly protest against dogmatically propounding our own views, or those of any fallible mortal, as a condition or foundation of church union and cooperation."[10] For a second generation of Disciples Isaac Errett (1820–1888) produced "A Synopsis of the Faith and Practice of the Church of Christ," specifically disclaiming it as a creed, and Robert Milligan (1814–1875) produced *An Exposition and Defense of the Scheme of Redemption as It Is Revealed and Taught in the Holy Scriptures*, a classic in Disciples literature.

In the spirit of their nineteenth-century forebears the Christian Church (Disciples of Christ) adopted a preamble to the "Provisional Design" for restructuring the fellowship. According to A. Dale Fiers (1906–), first general minister and president of the restructured church, the preamble "is not a creed used as a test of fellowship but it is an affirmation of the *common ground of faith, fellowship, and commitment which unites Disciples of Christ in convenantal relationships between themselves, their congregations, and the agencies*."[11] In the preamble, Disciples assert:

As members of the Christian Church (Disciples of Christ), we confess that Jesus is the Christ, the Son of the Living God, and we proclaim him as Lord and Savior of the world; in his name and by his grace we accept our mission of witness and service to mankind. We rejoice in God our Father, maker of heaven and earth, and in the Covenant of love by which he has bound us to himself. In the fellowship and communion of the Holy Spirit we are joined to one another in brotherhood and in our obedience to Christ. In baptism we enter into newness of life and are made one with the Body of Christ. At the table of the Lord we show forth his saving acts in our midst. Within the Church we receive the gift of ministry and the light of scripture. In the bonds of Christian faith we offer ourselves to God, that within the universal Church we may be yielded to him whose kingdom has no end. Blessings, glory, and honor be to him forever. Amen.[12]

Along with "No creed but Christ," the Disciples' slogan has been "No book but the Bible." One of the items in *The Last Will and Testament of the Springfield Presbytery* declared:

We will, that the people henceforth take the Bible as the only sure guide to heaven; and as many as are offended with other books, which stand in competition with it, may cast them into the fire if they choose; for it is better to enter into life having one book, than having many to be cast into hell.[13]

In Thomas Campbell's *Declaration and Address* the New Testament is specifically affirmed as a perfect "constitution for the worship, discipline, and government" of the church and a "rule for the particular duties of its members."[14] Christians and Disciples were united in pursuit of the "restoration of the ancient order of things" as taught in the New Testament.

In time Disciples discovered that the New Testament is not as "simple" as preceding generations had assumed. Disagreements over how to apply the New Testament's silence on the use of organs in worship and of mission societies in evangelism led to division in the Restoration movement and the separate existence of the churches of Christ. Among the Disciples, strict literalism succumbed to historical research.[15] The shift which took place in the Disciples' understanding of scriptural authority is reflected in a three-volume report of a panel of scholars appointed in 1956 to re-examine the doctrine and beliefs of Disciples. As William R. Baird expressed it in volume II, *The Reconstruction of Theology*: "The Bible, particularly the New Testament, gains its authority as witness to the revelation of God in Jesus Christ."[16] Disciples continue to consider themselves as "Bible people," affirming the Scriptures as normative for faith and practice in the church.[17]

The Disciples' rejection of creedal formulations makes it difficult to describe what they believe and teach. Founding father Barton Stone rejected the classical trinitarian formulations to describe God, and Disciples generally substitute functional descriptions for the persons of the Trinity. In Disciples teaching Jesus Christ is seen as preeminent.

Jesus Christ has revealed God's nature, will, and purpose among men. Thus we think of God as personal. He is love. His ways among men are the ways of mercy and kindness as well as righteousness and judgment.[18]

In Disciples teaching, doctrines about Christ, such as the virgin birth, or his preexistence, sinlessness, and deity, are considered important for edifying the church but are not requirements for membership.

The Disciples of Christ believe that the only confession of belief which is required of those who desire to become members of a Disciples of Christ congregation is an affirmative answer to the question, "Do you believe that Jesus is the Christ, the Son of the living God and do you take him as your personal Savior?"[19]

Disciples affirm that the living presence of God is with people always as the Holy Spirit.[20]

Until recently Disciples spoke of baptism and the Lord's Supper as ordinances rather than sacraments, considering them symbolic acts of the church ordained by Christ in which the whole Gospel is recalled and experienced anew. Because their forebears were convinced that the New Testament "ancient order of things" required it, Disciples baptize by immersion and observe the Lord's Supper every Sunday. In contrast to those who baptize infants, Disciples hold to "believer's baptism," viewing it as the action which initiates into membership in the church as the body of Christ. The Christian Church (Disciples of Christ) has both "closed membership" congregations, which admit only those who have been immersed or consent to be, and "open membership" congregations, which do not make immersion a requirement. The issue and the disagreement reach back to the early years of the Restoration movement and to the ambivalence of Alexander Campbell on the subject.[21] Even when there is no sermon at a Disciples Sunday service, the Lord's Supper is observed. "Communion" is the term most frequently used for the sacrament, affirming Disciples' conviction that the Lord's Supper draws them into fellowship with Christ and with one another. Disciples think of the Lord's Supper as an act of remembrance, though they also affirm the "real presence" of Christ.[22]

Church unity has from the beginning been the Disciples' reason for being. The name "Christian Church" bears witness to the founding fathers' intention, not to start another denomination, but to unite Christians on the basis of a restored New Testament Christianity. When it became clear that the Disciples had in fact become another denomination, they determined to make church unity their special mission. Disciples were among the churches represented in the formation of the Federal Council of Churches at the turn of the twentieth century and they participated in the early organizational expressions of the Ecumenical movement. In 1930 American and Canadian Disciples joined with others to form the World Convention of Churches of Christ to serve as an international agency of brotherhood for Disciples. Active as members of the National Council of the Churches of Christ in the United States of America and of the World Council of Churches, the Christian Church (Disciples of Christ) became a member of the Consultation on Church Union (COCU) through which nine churches are seeking to become one.[23] Through their Council on Christian Unity the Disciples have entered into dialogue with representatives of the Roman Catholic Church.[24] In General Assembly action at the 1977 meeting the Disciples resolved to resume union discussions with the United Church of Christ which had been discontinued in favor of the more extensive discussion in COCU.[25]

In the preamble to "A Provisional Design for the Christian Church (Disciples of Christ)" there is the following affirmation concerning the church:

Within the whole family of God on earth, the Church appears wherever believers in Jesus Christ are gathered in his name. Transcending all barriers of race and culture, the Church manifests itself in ordered communities of disciples bound together for worship, for fellowship, and for service, and in varied structures for mission, witness, and mutual discipline, and for the nurture and renewal of its members. The nature of the Church, given by Christ, remains constant through generations; yet in faithfulness to its mission it continues to adapt its structures to the needs and patterns of a changing world. All authority in the Church belongs to Jesus Christ, its Lord and Head.[26]

Concerning the ministry the "Provisional Design" affirms the following:

The fundamental ministry within the Church is that of Jesus Christ. He calls his Church to participate in this ministry.

By virtue of membership in the Church, every Christian enters into the corporate ministry, each Christian fulfills his own calling as a servant of Christ sent into the world to minister. In addition, the Church recognizes an order of the ministry, set apart or ordained, under God, to equip the whole people to fulfill their corporate ministry.[27]

In the "Provisional Design" the Christian Church (Disciples of Christ) recognizes two offices in the order of the ministry, ordained minister and licensed minister, and two local offices, elder and deacon/deaconess, for the performance of certain functions of ministry. Ministers are "called" by congregations and other organizations of the Christian Church (Disciples of Christ).

Disciples' congregations are united in regional multistate organizations, ranging in strength from fewer than a dozen congregations to several hundred. Mission and nurture are the purposes of the regional organization. The General Assembly meets biennially and provides the overarching structure. Though any Disciple has the privilege to speak at meetings of the General Assembly, voting is limited to representatives of congregations, representatives of regions, and ordained ministers with standing in the church. A 225-member General Board meets annually and supervises the general program of the church under policies approved by the General Assembly. A forty-member Administrative Committee meets at least three times a year to carry out decisions of the General Board and to coordinate activities of administrative units.

The Christian Church (Disciples of Christ) has 4,524 congregations with 1,312,326 members. Slightly more than one third of all Disciples in the United States and Canada are in Indiana, Missouri, Ohio, and Texas. Another third are located in the six states of California, Illinois, Iowa, Kansas, Kentucky, and Oklahoma. Headquarters are at 222 South Downey Avenue (Box 1986), Indianapolis, Indiana 46206.

Churches of Christ (Disciples) in Canada

While the Restoration movement was in its first stages in the United States, a parallel development was taking place in Canada. In 1811 three or four persons organized a "little church" (now the Cross Roads Church of Christ) near Charlottestown, Prince Edward Island, whose principles and practices were to be based wholly on the New Testament. Their leader was a "Scottish Baptist" preacher, Alexander Crawford. The next two decades saw an increasing number of these "Scottish Baptist" immigrants arrive in the eastern provinces of Canada. They were the spiritual posterity of John Glas, Robert Sandeman, Archibald McLean, and others who in the eighteenth century had seceded from the Church of Scotland over such matters as the authority of the local congregation, the weekly observance of the Lord's Supper, a human being's free choice to choose or reject salvation, and baptism by immersion. Quite understandably they proved very receptive to the seed that Alexander Campbell and Barton Stone had been sowing in the United States. Indeed, the only Restoration tenet that they did not already hold (and that they had little difficulty in adopting) was the conviction of oneness in some sense with all Christians across denominational lines.

By 1840 almost all the "Scottish Baptist" churches had identified themselves with the Restoration movement. The first annual meeting of the Canadian Disciples met in Ontario in 1843. In 1913 Toronto was host to the International Convention of Disciples. In 1922 the organization of the All-Canada Committee of the Churches of Christ (Disciples) provided an effective Dominion-wide coordinating agency in Toronto.

Like other Canadian church bodies with links to denominations in the United States, Canadian Disciples are plagued by the Dominion's vast distances, by the disproportionately small size of the Canadian body, by the difficulty of developing adequate leadership, and by the rapid changes that are taking place in the social matrix in which they exist. One solution proposes union with the United Church of Canada, and still another a resumption of the union negotiations with the Baptists of Canada which were discontinued after 1925 but the door to which "remains slightly ajar." Disciples were represented on the general commission which produced a Plan of Union as the basis on which to unite the Anglican Church of Canada, the United Church of Canada, and Churches of Christ (Disciples) in Canada. When the Anglican Church of Canada rejected the Plan of Union, the United Church of Canada and the Disciples agreed to pursue bilateral negotiations for union.

There are 40 Disciples churches in Canada with a participating membership of just under 5,000. They support foreign missionaries in India and Mexico. Theologically the Canadian Disciples have generally tended toward conservative positions. The headquarters are at 39 Arkell Road, Route 2, Guelph, Ontario N1H 6H8.

Churches of Christ (Noninstrumental)

When the 1906 Census of Religious Bodies for the first time listed the churches of Christ separately from the Disciples of Christ, the Bureau of the Census was merely recognizing a fact of long standing. How far back this cleavage in the Restoration movement really goes is not easy to determine.

One date that churches of Christ historians give is 1849. In that year the establishment of the American Christian Missionary Society set off a wave of debate among the congregations of the Restoration movement. The process of taking sides was reinforced by a series of historic, geographic, and cultural factors that in combination disposed the wing of the Restoration movement that became the churches of Christ to be more conservative than the wing that became the Disciples of Christ. The debate became a full-fledged controversy. As time passed the controversy finally resulted in a breach that to date has defied healing.

Thomas Campbell had enunciated the principle, "Where the Bible speaks, we speak; where the Bible is silent, we are silent." The churches of Christ segment of the Restoration movement took this principle to mean that if the Bible does not authorize an institution, a practice, or an item of belief, that institution, practice, or item of belief has no place in the church. This line of argument had led Thomas Campbell to abandon infant baptism. In 1849 it seemed to apply with equal force to missionary societies. The churches of Christ saw in such societies a departure from apostolic Christianity and an encouragement of "liberalism." Besides that, missionary societies represented the exaltation of human wisdom over the divine wisdom; they would lead to further centralized organizations that would deprive the local churches of their freedom; they had not been necessary before 1849 and they would not be necessary afterward.

What was true of missionary societies was no less true about another issue in contention, the use of instrumental music in worship. For this, too, there was no New Testament authority.

Other "innovations" of the "digressives" came up for consideration. On each the debate has tended to bring about majority-minority cleavages that still exist and that will be noted below.

To a degree almost without parallel in American Christianity opinion in the churches of Christ has been formed by the religious press. Outside observers find the relative uniformity of conviction on major issues that the churches of Christ publications—all of them unofficial journals—have exhibited as quite extraordinary in view of the lack of a denominational directing organization. At the same time, in the absence of such a denominational organization, the religious press of the churches of Christ has fulfilled many of the functions that denominational organizations supply in other groups.

A leader in the fight against "innovations" and "digressions" has always been the *Gospel Advocate*, still published in Nashville.[28] From the start it had a notable succession of editors, among them Tolbert Fanning and William Lipscomb before the War between the States, and David Lipscomb and E. G. Sewell for many years after 1870. Another influential periodical was *Firm Foundation*, established by Austin McGary and still published in Austin, Texas. The same has been true of *American Christian Review*, which Benjamin Franklin established at Cincinnati, Ohio, in 1856 and that was long published in Indianapolis, and *Christian Leader*, established in Cincinnati in 1886 by John F. Rowe, the second editor of the *Review*. Still others that have appeared over the years are *Christian Chronicle* of Abilene, Texas, *Twentieth Century Christian* of Nashville, *Gospel Broadcast* of Dallas, Texas, and *Gospel Guardian* of Lufkin, Texas.

Despite their common front against the Disciples of Christ,[29] there is a wide spectrum of divergence within the churches of Christ themselves, not all of whom are in fellowship with one another. As many as twenty different types of congregations have been counted within the churches of Christ, "each representing disagreement over proper observance of the 'silences' of Scripture."[30]

The churches of Christ believe unanimously that Jesus is the Christ, the Son of God, Savior and Lord; they believe in Christ's incarnation, virgin birth, and bodily resurrection; and they generally accept the view that the Father, the Son, and the Holy Ghost are united in one Godhead.

They regard the Bible as a true, inspired, and completely adequate revelation of God's will, as the sole rule and norm of faith and practice, and as the "beginning place" from and through which Christian people can arrive at spiritual unity.

They see all human beings as responsible for the sins they commit after the age of accountability and they hold that Christ's vicarious atonement is the only remedy for these sins. The terms of pardon for a non-Christian are faith in Christ as God's only-begotten Son, repentance, confession, and believer's baptism by immersion "into the sublime names of Father, Son, and Holy Spirit."[31]

The churches of Christ believe in the spiritual unity of the church, the body and the bride of Christ. Christ is the final judge of all religious groups and of all individual Christians.[32] They stand committed to the restoration of "the New Testament church" in doctrine, ordinances, and life. Each local church is completely autonomous, and is governed by its own elders and deacons.

They resent the use of "denomination" to describe their fellowship. They have, they point out, no headquarters, no governing boards, and no hierarchy, and cooperation of local churches with one another is a matter of voluntary determination. Indeed, the churches of Christ oppose everything that smacks of what they call "denominationalism," particularly denominational dogmas and written creeds and confessions of faith in addition to the New Testament. To them "denominationalism" destroys what they see as the basic Christian principle of liberation from ecclesiastical loyalties beyond the local congregation. They regard "denominationalism" as intrinsically sinful because in their view it fails to honor Christ as the sole head of the church; it subordinates divine authority to human authority; it contradicts what to them are plain biblical teachings on the nature of Christian unity; and it impedes the fulfillment of Christ's prayer that his disciples may be one. In actual practice this animus against "denominationalism" sometimes results in an exclusivism that keeps the membership of many churches of Christ from any fellowship beyond their own congregations, even with those who have the same basic convictions. To emphasize that they do not consider the churches of Christ a denomination, they generally refuse to capitalize the word "churches."

In withdrawing fellowship because of divergent views, a majority holds that where matters of faith and explicit biblical commands are involved disagreement cannot be tolerated, but that in other matters the "law of love" is in order, unless the "weak brother" forces his "scruples" on others and thereby creates a faction. If he does this, one must "mark, avoid, and refuse" him. A minority accepts these modes of operation in principle, but does not carry them into practice.

Ministers in the churches of Christ are ordained and hold their positions by mutual agreement with the elders of the church in which they officiate. The authority of the ministers is largely moral, and the actual operation of the local church is in the hands of the elders. All the larger churches now build parsonages and have one or more resident ministers to "do the work of an evangelist" under the supervision of the elders. A minority in the churches of Christ holds that a paid, "located" ministry is unbiblical; that the local leadership can and should discharge the duties of such ministers; and that evangelists are to be sent out by local churches and their services requested as needed.

The *Preachers List of the Churches of Christ*, the publication of which has been suspended, was an issue among some churches of Christ. Clearly, they argued, there is no biblical authority for such a list, and an unlisted preacher runs the risk of ostracism. The compilers of the list held that it was merely a roster of men generally regarded as biblical in their beliefs and practices; that unscriptural practice that is not subversive of the faith need not be a barrier to recognition within the fellowship; that the list was intended to be nothing more than a helpful unofficial source of information; that it did not in any way question the supremacy of the local church; and that theoretically the judgment of a local church in discrediting or disfellowshiping a preacher deserved the respect of others.

In the selection of elders and deacons, a majority holds that the congregation must "look out" biblically qualified persons, that the elders must "choose" them, and that the evangelist may "appoint" them. One minority holds that the elders or the "ruling elder" must select the church leadership. Another minority opinion holds that only the evangelist has the right to "appoint elders in the churches."

The increase in missionary interest and activity in recent years has once more created issues among the churches of Christ. A majority holds that, while choosing, sending, supporting, and directing missionaries are responsibilities of the elders of the local church, it is permissible to use a third party or agent to handle missionary funds, as long as this party or agent does not appoint missionaries or take the work of missions into its own hands in other ways. A minority insists that missionary clearing houses are human devices that are in fact as "dangerous as the [missionary] societies of the digressives." This minority also usually takes the position that one local church cannot receive offerings from another local church in support of the former's missionary program, because this "Roman Catholic cathedralism" exalts one church above another, and that if a church cannot support a missionary of its own it may support none and must do all its missionary work through its own members in its own community.

Musical instruments are universally absent from churches of Christ, and congregational singing in the services is unaccompanied. For this reason this part of the Restoration brotherhood is called "noninstrumental." Some churches permit choirs, soloists, and special music, as long as they do not interfere with congregational singing and worship. Other churches see no New Testament precedent for such performances and reject them as "denominational" inventions that are ultimately as dangerous as instrumental music.

Churches of Christ invariably observe the Lord's Supper every Lord's Day. Many churches insist upon the "divine pattern of the order of worship" indicated in Acts 2:42. The elders go into the pulpit to read the Bible and to offer prayer. Then under the supervision of the elders individual brothers provide a few brief teaching lessons on previously assigned subjects, the "fellowship" or offering is taken up, the loaf is broken, and the prayers—in which several persons may take part—are offered. A majority holds that in the Lord's Supper the elders may break the loaf for the congregation, while a minority holds that the elders may break the loaf once, but that each member should break off his own piece. Again, the majority allows the use of individual cups, while a minority holds that multiplicity of cups is unbiblical.

The predominant majority in the churches of Christ is postmillennial or "amillennial" in its doctrine of the last things and is inclined to contend that premillennialism is a heresy that must be eradicated from the fellowship. A minority takes the premillennial view and holds that this is not an issue that should be made a test of fellowship.[33]

No churches of Christ raise money by means of church dinners or similar devices. A majority permits dinners for the purpose of fellowship, while a minority opposes the use of the church building for anything except teaching and worship.

A majority avails itself of educational agencies (Bible, Lord's Day, or Sunday schools), but a majority sees in these "a degenerate of denominationalism without precept, example or necessary inference in the word of God." A majority allows the use of quarterlies and other lesson and study helps, while a minority insists that helps are as vicious as human creeds and dogmas and that each pupil should use the Bible only.

Some churches of Christ in the South have established Christian elementary schools. This reflects in part the opposition of their members to the racial integration of the public schools, in part their view that the pluralistic society of the United States precludes religious and moral indoctrination in tax-supported educational institutions, and in part their strong belief that instruction in the Bible and the inculcation of strict Christian moral principles are an essential part of the total educational process from kindergarten to graduate school.

A majority approves the existence of Bible schools and colleges in the service of the churches as long as they respect the autonomy of the local church and do not try to exercise authority outside their own field. Since the beginning of this century this majority has created an extremely effective church-related system of secondary education. A minority—represented for over a century notably by the *American Christian Review*—holds that all education is a function of the local church and that Bible schools and colleges are merely another attempt to build an institutional hierarchy and to deprive the congregations of their autonomy.

A commendable sensitivity to the demands of Christian social service has increasingly marked the churches of Christ. A majority approves Christian charitable agencies even while conceding that they are unbiblical. But a very large minority insists that to transfer this responsibility of the local church to an extra-congregational agency is wrong and that it threatens the freedom of the local church.

There are no central headquarters or general organization for the non-instrumental churches of Christ. The estimate of 18,000 churches in the United States, with a total membership of 2,400,000 is only an approximation. About 80 percent of the churches are in Texas, Arkansas, Louisiana, Tennessee, Mississippi, Alabama, and Georgia. In Canada there are about 75 congregations, with an estimated membership of 9,000, that follow non-instrumental churches of Christ principles.

Even though the churches of Christ have no missionary societies, their zeal for the establishment of churches after the New Testament pattern has made them increasingly mission-minded. There are over 200 churches-of-Christ foreign missionaries in about 70 countries, including many in Africa and Europe (particularly Italy), as well as Mexico, Japan, Korea, Malaya, Hong Kong, the Republic of China (Taiwan), and the Philippines Republic.

Christian Churches and Churches of Christ ("Centrist")[34]

Quite apart from the very conservative churches of Christ that forbid the use of musical instruments in services of worship, there have always been a great many other churches in the "Restoration brotherhood" that have not supported the educational, missionary, and evangelistic programs of the United Christian Missionary Society and the Christian Church (Disciples of Christ). The infighting between these Christian churches and the more denominationally oriented Disciples of Christ has been marked by bitter court cases, splits in congregations, and battles among the trustees of church-supported colleges. The rift between the two groups, long in development, became manifest in the mid-1920s; it became irremediable with the restructuring of the Disciples wing of the brotherhood in the late 1960s.

The Christian churches here discussed differ theologically from the very conservative churches of Christ chiefly in the willingness of the former freely to admit the use of musical instruments in services of worship. Sociologically, the somewhat greater urbanization of the Christian churches here discussed and their generally somewhat greater sensitivity to the currents of contemporary life also differentiate the two groups. Since the definitive break of the Christian churches with the Christian Church (Disciples of Christ), fellowship between the former and the "noninstrumental" churches of Christ has increased in some areas.

The Christian churches differ from the Christian Church (Disciples of Christ) primarily in the stress of the former upon their polity (that is, the fact that they are congregationally governed bodies with no official organization controlling them) and upon the biblical principles which they see as bequeathed to them in Thomas Campbell's *Declaration and Address* of 1809 and Isaac Errett's pamphlet of 1870, *Our Position*.[35]

The Christian churches reject more consistently and more unanimously than the Christian Church (Disciples of Christ) the liberal theology of the nineteenth and twentieth centuries promoted by the Disciples' Divinity House in Chicago and by the *Christian Century* prior to the time that it became an ecumenical weekly. They also reject the kind of ecumenical activity that they see marking the National Council of the Churches of Christ in the United States of America, in which Disciples have played prominent roles. By admitting Eastern Orthodox church bodies to membership and by acknowledging the Roman Catholic Church as a "sister communion," the National Council of the Churches of Christ in the United States of America, as a prominent leader of the Christian churches sees it, has disqualified itself "as the representative of American Protestantism or of historic Protestant principles and essential Christian doctrine."[36]

A crucial phase in the process of separation between these Christian churches and the Disciples began as early as the first decade of this century. In 1908 the *Christian Century* became an organ of the liberal wing of the Restoration movement when Charles Clayton Morrison bought the journal. Three years later he initiated "the great controversy" with a series of articles in the *Christian Century*'s pages in which he advocated the reception of unimmersed persons into churches of Christ. Another development contributing to the rift was the gradual admission of theologically liberal teachers backed by theologically liberal administrations to the college and seminary faculties of the Restoration movement. This ultimately led the more conservative Christian churches to establish schools like McGarvey Bible College (1923) and the Cincinnati Bible Seminary (1924), since merged. The Memphis convention of 1926 is a kind of watershed in the relations between the Christian churches and the Disciples wing of the Restoration movement. After the Memphis meeting, the Christian churches here described began to organize a large number of independent foreign missions; their refusal to support the Federal Council of the Churches of Christ in America became more deliberate and intransigent; and in 1927 they called into being as their major forum the North American Christian Convention, with its consciously "centrist" aims.[37]

A number of attempts at a reconciliation of the Christian churches here described with the Disciples took place between 1930 and 1944. The Commission on Restudy of the Disciples of Christ (1934–1949) failed to achieve a sufficient basis for internal unity. The National Evangelistic Association and the Christian Action Crusade (1933–1941) sponsored by the Standard Publishing Company, Cincinnati, likewise made only limited progress toward a restoration of mutual confidence.[38] As a result the breach contined to widen.

The Christian churches and churches of Christ profess to stand on historic Restoration ground. They hold the divine inspiration of the Bible, but hold that the New Testament is now authoritative for Christians, as the Old Testament is authoritative for Jews. They affirm the "tripersonality" of Father, Son, and Holy Spirit, but repudiate the "philosophical and theological speculations of Trinitarians and Unitarians." They teach the all-sufficiency of the Bible as a revelation of God's character and will and of the saving gospel, and as a rule of faith and practice; and they repudiate all human authoritative creeds beyond belief in Christ. They affirm the divine excellency and worthiness of Jesus as the Son of God and his complete humanity as the Son of man; his incarnation; his teachings as an end of controversy about salvation, duty, and destiny; his death as a redemptive sin-offering; and his resurrection, ascension, mediatorship, and supreme authority. They assert the personal and perpetual mission of the Holy Spirit; the alienation of all accountable human beings from God and their entire dependence on his truth, mercy, and grace; the necessity of faith and repentance; the perpetual obligation of the two ordinances that Christ commanded, that is, baptism for the remission of sins through the immersion of penitent believers, and the observance of the Lord's Supper on the first day of each week as a simple memorial of Christ's death for the salvation of human beings. They teach that the church of Christ is the company of those who have by faith and baptism confessed his name and that its members should use only biblical names for Christ's followers. They stress the necessity of holiness, in view both of the final salvation of Christians and of their mission to turn the world to God; they lay equal stress on the fullness and freeness of salvation to all who accept it on the terms proposed. They hold the final punishment of the ungodly by an everlasting destruction from the presence of the Lord. They refuse to distinguish between clergymen and laypeople, and admit no ecclesiastical courts outside the individual churches. Their basic principle of church organization is maximum freedom for individual Christians and individual congregations.

The period of negative reaction among the Christian churches here described to the organized ecumenical movement is giving way to a new desire for involvement in the altered ecumenical situation that they see emerging, in which the churches will renounce all human creeds. They feel that the Restoration "plea" will here be able to command a hearing. It must, they hold, stress the centrality of Christ; the need for a return to biblical authority; and the necessity of recognizing the fact that the church is one body in Christ. It must underline the authentic catholicity of the Restoration name for the church, of its creed, of its rule of faith and practice, of its view of the ordinances, and of its polity. Finally, it must accentuate the mission of the church and emphasize the necessity of Christian union in order to accomplish the evangelization of the world.[39]

Among the thirty-five institutions of secondary and graduate education supported by the Christian churches here discussed, two of the most influential are the Cincinnati Bible Seminary and the Lincoln (Illinois) Christian College and Seminary. The major "centrist" periodicals are *The Christian Standard*, *The Lookout*, and *The Restoration Herald*, all published in Cincinnati, and *Horizons*, published in Joliet, Illinois. From 1955 on, an elected "publishing committee" representing Christian churches of the center has been assisting the privately owned Standard Publishing Company of Cincinnati in determining its policies and program.

The Christian churches and churches of Christ have no official headquarters. The largest national assembly continues to be the North American Christian Convention, which meets annually in various cities, with the program planned by a new continuation committee each year; it has had as many as 20,000 persons in actual attendance, but it has neither legislative nor advisory power. There are 5,436 Christian churches and churches of Christ, with 1,034,047 members in the United States, and 76 churches with 5,100 members in Canada. The Christian churches have historically been strongest in the villages and towns of the Midwest, especially in Illinois,[40] Indiana, Ohio, Kentucky, Missouri, and Iowa. In recent years they have branched out strongly into other areas of the United States, notably California, Georgia, and Florida, and they have also made determined efforts to plant congregations in metropolitan centers.

The Christian churches maintain about 650 foreign missionaries in 36 countries, notably in Latin America, the West Indies, Germany, Italy, Africa, the Republic of the Philippines, Japan, Korea, Thailand, Burma, and India. Outside the United States and Canada there are 2,300 congregations with 125,000 members. There is an increasing degree of fellowship with likeminded churches in Australia, New Zealand, Great Britain, Poland, and the Union of Soviet Socialist Republics.[41]

The Christian Congregation, Incorporated

The Christian Congregation traces its history back to the first decade of the nineteenth century and, in part at least, to the evangelistic activity of Barton Stone (1772–1844). From Kentucky, Virginia, West Virginia, and the Carolinas it expanded into Pennsylvania, Ohio, Indiana, and Texas. While most of Stone's followers joined with the supporters of Thomas and Alexander Campbell in 1832 to form what became known as the Christian Church, the Christian Congregation continued as an unincorporated fellowship of clergymen, laymen, and congregations for eighty years after its beginnings. It was finally incorporated in Kokomo, Indiana, in 1887 and reincorporated in 1898. A product of the frontier, its work has been and is largely in neglected mountain and rural areas.

It holds that fellowship is not to be based on doctrinal agreement, creeds, church names, or rites, and it makes its only basis of union and the single motive of its creative ethical activism adherence to Christ's "new commandment" in John 13:34–35 that his disciples love one another. Its objective for its individual members is the development of spiritual maturity along with emotional, intellectual, and mental growth. Since the fellowship is inclusive rather than exclusive, the range of belief within it extends from fundamentalism and Pentecostalism at one end through a variety of orthodox and liberal positions to free thought and humanist outlooks at the other end of the continuum. The fellowship encourages free Bible study and operates a Bible colportage service. Local congregations have a large measure of autonomy. The address of the Christian Congregation's general superintendent is 804 West Hemlock Street, La Follette, Tennessee 37766. There are reported to be 495 churches with 59,600 members.

The Tioga River Christian Conference

The Tioga River Christian Conference was founded in 1844 in Covington, Tioga County, Pennsylvania, as a local fellowship of the association of Christian Churches that had their central headquarters at Dayton, Ohio. When the Christian Churches united with the Congregational Church in 1931, the Tioga River Christian Conference declined as a unit to enter the union on doctrinal grounds. Other Christian churches belonging to neighboring Christian conferences also withdrew from their conferences and joined the Tioga River Conference. To protect its churches from modernism and neo-orthodoxy, the conference adopted fifteen brief Articles of Faith. These affirm the Trinity, "the Bible as the fully inspired Word of God," the special creation of the universe and of man, Christ's deity and substitutionary atonement, the personality and work of the Holy Spirit, the church "in its general aspect as the Body of Christ" and "in its local aspect as a body of believers, whose duty it is to observe the ordinances, edify itself, and evangelize the world"; the bodily resurrection and translation of believers at Christ's return and the bodily resurrection and judgment of unbelievers after his millennial reign; eternal life for the righteous, eternal punishment for the wicked, and the reality and personality of Satan. It rejects baptismal regeneration. Its polity is congregational; the Annual Conference exists for counsel, exchange of ideas, mutual help, the fellowship for the purpose of maintaining a clear and effective home and foreign missionary witness for Christ. The headquarters are at 35 Schiller Street, Binghamton, New York 13905. Several years ago the conference had 14 churches in Pennsylvania and New York, with 1,100 members. It supported (in whole or in cooperation with others) workers in India, Pakistan, the Philippines Republic, Peru, Bolivia, and Mexico. There has been no response to recent efforts to contact the organization.

The Christian Union

In 1864, with the War between the States in progress, the Reverend James F. Given, a Methodist Episcopal minister, as a protest against partisan political preaching, the strong antagonisms that were developing, and the divisions that had taken place, organized members of his own congregation, together with some members of the Church of the United Brethren, Methodist Protestants, New School Presbyterians, Free Will Baptists, Disciples of Christ, and other like-minded persons who had "a desire for more perfect fellowship in Christ" into a new religious body. The place was Columbus, Ohio; the name of the new body was The Christian Union.

It stands broadly in the Restorationist tradition and sees itself committed to a conservative and fundamental interpretation of the Christian faith. It affirms the infallibility of the Bible; the Trinity; Christ's deity, incarnation, vicarious and atoning death, resurrection, ascension, and personal return; salvation by grace alone, conditioned on repentance toward God and faith toward Christ ("regeneration and justification follow the meeting of these conditions"); the indwelling of the Holy Spirit, who carries the sanctification of believers toward perfection; the resurrection of the bodies of believers to immortality at Christ's return; the divine creation of the first human being, his fall, and the condemnation of every unreborn person who has come to the age of accountability; and the church as the company of all Spirit-regenerated believers. It lists seven cardinal principles as essential to the organization: (1) the oneness of the church in Christ; (2) Christ the only head of the Church; (3) the Bible the only rule of faith and practice; (4) good fruits the only condition of fellowship; (5) Christian union without controversy; (6) self-government for each local church; (7) no partisan political preaching. In its evangelistic outreach it tries to persuade people voluntarily to choose Christ and serve him as Savior and Lord.[42]

The ministry is open to both men and women. The form of government is congregational and the individual churches have complete liberty in worship and discipline, and each member has the right of private interpretation of the Bible. The almost universal mode of water baptism is immersion, but the pastor may use another mode when the candidate requests it. Foot washing is no longer a recognized practice in the Christian Union. The Christian Union finances its work through tithes and offerings. The quarterly charge councils, the district councils, the semiannual state councils, and the triennial General

Council have only advisory functions. The headquarters are at Box 38, Excelsior Springs, Missouri 64024. Several years ago there were 130 churches with an estimated total membership of 8,000.[43] The ratio of missionaries to members was 1 to 500. The Christian Union carried on foreign missions in Africa, Japan, and the Dominican Republic in cooperation with a number of interdenominational foreign missionary boards. There has been no response to recent efforts to contact the group.

NOTES

1. Oliver Read Whitley, *Trumpet Call of Reformation* (St. Louis, Mo.: Bethany Press, 1959), tells the history of the Restoration movement in terms of the development of a sect-type organization into a denomination. Winfred Ernest Garrison and Alfred T. DeGroot, *The Disciples of Christ: A History* (St. Louis, Mo.: Bethany Press, 1948), present a fine denominational history. The history has been retold and updated with notes and bibliography by Lester G. McAllister and William E. Tucker, *Journey in Faith: A History of the Christian Church (Disciples of Christ)* (St. Louis, Mo.: Bethany Press, 1975).

2. In separate chapters on American and British backgrounds both Garrison and DeGroot, pp. 38-92, and McAllister and Tucker, pp. 38-60, 89-103, describe the antecedents to the Restoration movement in the revival movements in the American colonies and in the ideas of the English philosopher John Locke and the Scottish churchmen John Glass, Robert Sandeman, and Robert and James Haldane.

3. McAllister and Tucker, pp. 77-79, present the full text of the document. The quotation is on p. 78.

4. Ibid., p. 113. The full text of the *Declaration and Address* are presented in Peter Ainslie, *The Message of the Disciples for the Union of the Church* (New York: Fleming H. Revell, 1913); and *Declaration and Address with The Last Will and Testament of the Springfield Presbytery* (St. Louis: Bethany Press, 1955).

5. Garrison and DeGroot, pp. 16-17, and McAllister and Tucker, pp. 27-29, trace the use of both names throughout the history of the group.

6. Scott arranged the steps of salvation in a precise order: three steps for man to take (faith, repentance, baptism); then three steps that God would take (remission of sins, the gift of the Holy Spirit, the gift of eternal life). See Garrison and DeGroot, p. 13, 180-200.

7. The dictum was originally spoken by Thomas Campbell at the meeting in 1809 when he conceived the idea of forming a Christian Association; see McAllister and Tucker, p. 110.

8. McAllister and Tucker, pp. 189-208, argue that the seeds of division were sown in the controversy over slavery and that the experiences of the Civil War produced an actual if not an official split.

9. For many years *The Christian-Evangelist,* forerunner of the present journal, *The Disciple,* carried the maxim on its masthead.

10. McAllister and Tucker, p. 156.

11. A. Dale Fiers, *Let's think about Characteristic beliefs of the Disciples of Christ* (Indianapolis, Ind.: The United Christian Missionary Society, n.d.), an 8-page pamphlet, p. 2.

12. "A Provisional Design for the Christian Church (Disciples of Christ)," mimeographed document from "A Report from the Commission on Brotherhood Restructure" submitted to the Dallas Assembly of the International Convention of Christian Churches (Disciples of Christ), September 23-28, 1966; the quotation is from p. 1 of the "Provisional Design."

13. McAllister and Tucker, p. 78.

14. The quotation is cited by Kenneth L. Teegarden, *We Call Ourselves Disciples* (St. Louis, Mo.: Bethany Press, 1976), p. 28.

15. In *The Christian System* Alexander

Campbell had laid the groundwork for historical-critical scholarship: "On opening any book in the sacred Scriptures, consider first the historical circumstances of the book. These are the order, the title, the date, the place and the occasion of it." The quotation is

16. Ibid., p. 31.
17. For a contemporary witness to Disciples views on the Bible, see Robert E. Gartman, "The New Testament Is Our Guide," in *This We Believe,* ed. James C. Suggs (St. Louis, Mo.: Bethany Press, 1977), pp. 37-42.
18. Fiers, p. 4.
19. Ibid.
20. For a presentation on the Holy Spirit see David R. Darnell, "God Works through the Holy Spirt," in Suggs, pp. 23-29.
21. In the famous Lunenberg Letter in 1837 Alexander Campbell modified his earlier exclusivist views on believer's baptism by immersion by stating that immersion as a profession of faith was not "absolutely essential to a Christian—though it may be greatly essential to his sanctification and comfort." The quotation is from McAllister and Tucker, p. 158.
22. Teegarden, pp. 83-89, presents a summary of Disciples views on baptism and the Lord's Supper.
23. The Consultation on Church Union is described in chap. 21 of this volume.
24. The course of the dialogues between 1967 and 1973 is summarized in *Confessions in Dialogue,* ed. Nils Ehrenstrom (3rd edn.; Geneva: World Council of Churches, 1975), pp. 74-76.
25. Harold E. Fey, "Disciples Vote to Resume Union Talks with UCC," *Christian Century,* November 9, 1977, pp. 1021-1022.
26. Op. cit., p. 1.
27. Ibid., p. 13.
28. For a representative collection of articles from the pages of the *Gospel Advocate,* see Grover Cleveland Brewer, *Contending for the Faith* (Nashville, Tenn.: Gospel Advocate Company, 1955), first published in 1941. From an earlier period, see David Lipscomb and Elisha Granville Sewell, *Questions Answered . . . Being a Compilation of Queries with Answers . . . Covering a Period of Forty Years*

of Their Joint Editorial Labors on the Gospel Advocate, ed. Marshall Clement Kurfees(Nashville, Tenn.: Gospel Advocate Company, 1963), a reprint of the 1920 edition, and David Lipscomb, *Queries and Answers,* 5th edition by J. W. Shepherd (Nashville, Tennessee: Gospel Advocate Company, 1963), a reprint of the 1910 edition.

29. The churches of Christ refuse fellowship even to the Restorationist center as represented, for example, by the North American Christian Convention on the ground that the centrists cannot worship in a biblical and divinely acceptable manner to the accompaniment of instrumental music in their services and because the centrists do not properly observe the maxim that Christians must be "silent where the Bible is silent."
30. James DeForest Murch, *Christians Only: A History of the Restoration Movement* (Cincinnati, Ohio: Standard Publishing Company, 1962), p. 310. On p. 313 Murch summarizes the difference between the churches of Christ and the Disciples in the matter of human judgment in these terms: "The churches of Christ are harassed by those who fail to understand where human judgment *begins,* the Disciples are troubled by those who do not know where it *ends.*"
31. A classic and perennial churches of Christ formulation of these issues is Thomas W. Brents, *The Gospel Plan of Salvation,* first published in 1874. The 15th edition came from the press of the Gospel Advocate Company, Nashville, Tennessee, in 1966. The quotation is from p. 478.
32. They like to say that they are "Christians only, but not the only Christians."
33. For this premillennial minority *The Word and Work, Set to Declare the Whole Council [sic] of God,* established in Louisville, Kentucky, in 1907, has served as the organ.
34. The churches here described use "Christian Church" and "Church of Christ" almost interchangeably as names for their local congregations. (Occasionally one may call itself "Christ's Church.") As a group they have consistently refused to be labeled "free" or "independent" or "undenomina-

tional." They refer to themselves and prefer that others refer to them simply as "Christian churches" or "churches of Christ" without any qualification. In describing their fellowship they write the word "churches" with a lower-case initial letter; "church" is capitalized only in the name of a specific church, for example, the Ninth Street Church of Christ in Lancaster, Ohio. Their ministers and evangelists reject the adjective "Reverend." The addition of the parenthetic term "Centrist" in the title of this section, in which the present writer follows the usage of James DeForest Murch in both the title and text of chapter 19 of his *Christians Only,* is made only as a convenient way of differentiating these churches of Christ, which freely permit the use of musical instruments in services of worship, from the very conservative "noninstrumental" churches of Christ.

35. Reprinted as a 24-page tract by Standard Publishing Company, Cincinnati, Ohio.
36. James DeForest Murch, *Christians Only: A History of the Restoration Movement* (Cincinnati, Ohio: Standard Publishing Company, 1962), p. 234. See the entire chapter, "The Great Apostasy," pp. 223-235.
37. "To honor the Scriptures as the only ground for the unity of followers of Christ; disclaiming all affiliations with parties, factions, and special interests, to put forward the truth and objects common to the whole brotherhood of believers; to provide opportunity for loyal followers of the cross to show their colors under the banner, 'Where the Scriptures speak, we speak; where the Scriptures are silent, we are silent'; to exalt Christ as the creed that needs no revision; to exhibit a fellowship that springs from absolute freedom in Christ and freedom from ecclesiastical assumptions and machinations" (ibid., p. 257). See the entire chapter, "The Great Controversy," pp. 237-262.
38. See the chapter, "Attempts at Reconciliation," ibid., pp. 263-277.
39. See the chapter, "The Restoration Plea in an Ecumenical Era: An Evaluation," ibid., pp. 359-374 (especially pp. 366-373).
40. Illinois alone has 500 churches, 70 percent of which are in the southern part of the state.
41. Letter from Philip L. Young, professor of church history, St. Louis Christian College, Florissant, Missouri.
42. *The Facts about the Christian Union* (Excelsior Spings, Mo.: Christian Union Headquarters, n.d.) (6-page pamphlet).
43. Letter from the Reverend Wilbur Holman, president, General Council of the Christian Union.

BIBLIOGRAPHY

Adams, Hampton. *Why I Am A Disciple of Christ.* New York: Thomas Nelson & Sons, 1957.

Beazley, George G., Jr., ed. *The Christian Church (Disciples of Christ): An Interpretative Examination in the Cultural Context.* Toronto, Ontario: G. R. Welch Co., 1973.

Blakemore, W. Barnett, ed. *The Renewal of Church.* 3 vols. St. Louis, Mo.: Bethany Press, 1963.

Butchart, Reuben. *The Disciples of Christ in Canada since 1930.* Toronto: Churches of Christ (Disciples) Canadian Headquarters Publications, 1949.

Crain, James A. *The Development of Social Ideas among the Disciples of Christ.* St. Louis, Mo.: Bethany Press, 1969.

DeGroot, Alfred Thomas. *Disciple Thought: A History.* Fort Worth: Texas Christian University Press, 1965.

Fiers, A Dale. *Let's think about Characteristic beliefs of the Disciples of Christ.* Indianapolis, Ind.: The United Christian Missionary Society, n.d. 8-page pamphlet.

Garrison, Winfred E. *Christian Unity and Disciples of Christ.* St. Louis, Mo.: Bethany Press, 1955.

Garrison Winfred E., and Alfred T. DeGroot. *The Disciples of Christ: A History.* St. Louis, Mo.: Bethany Press, 1948.

Gaustad, Edwin S. "Churches of Christ in America." In Donald R. Cutler, ed., *The Religious Situation: 1969.* Boston, Mass.:

Beacon Press, 1969. Chap. 44, pp. 1013-1033.

Harrell, David E., Jr. *Quest for a Christian America: The Disciples of Christ and American Society to 1866.* Nashville, Tenn.: The Disciples of Christ Historical Society, 1966.

———. *The Social Sources of Division in the Disciples of Christ, 1865–1900.* Atlanta: Publishing Systems, 1973.

Hughes, Richard T. "From Primitive Church to Civil Religion: The Millennial Odyssey of Alexander Campbell." *Journal of the American Academy of Religion* 44 (March 1976): pp. 87-103.

Mattox, Fount William. *The Eternal Kingdom: A History of the Church of Christ.* Rev. edn. by John McRay. Delight, Ark.: Gospel Light Publishing Company, 1961.

McAllister, Lester G., and Tucker, William E. *Journey in Faith: A History of the Christian Church (Disciples of Christ).* St. Louis, Mo.: Bethany Press, 1975.

Muir, Shirley L. *Disciples in Canada.* Indianapolis, Ind.: Department of World Outreach of the United Christian Missionary Society, 1966.

Murch, James DeForest. *Christians Only: A History of the Restoration Movement.* Cincinnati, Ohio: The Standard Publishing Company, 1962.

"A Provisional Design for the Christian Church (Disciples of Christ)." Mimeographed document included in *Report of the Commission on Brotherhood Restructure to the International Assembly of Christian Churches, Dallas, Texas, September 23-28, 1966.*

Robinson, William. *What Churches of Christ Stand For.* Birmingham, England: Berean Press, 1959.

Shepherd, James Walton. *The Church, the Falling Away, and the Restoration.* Nashville, Tenn.: Gospel Advocate Company, 1964.

Stevenson, Dwight E. *Disciple Preaching in the First Generation: An Ecological Study.* Nashville, Tenn.: The Disciples of Christ Historical Society, 1969.

Suggs, James C., ed. *This We Believe.* St. Louis, Mo.: Bethany Press, 1977.

Teegarden, Kenneth L. *We Call Ourselves Disciples.* St. Louis, Mo.: Bethany Press, 1976.

Tucker, William E. *J. H. Garrison and the Disciples of Christ.* St. Louis, Mo.: Bethany Press, 1964.

West, Earl Irvin. *The Search for the Ancient Order: A History of the Restoration Movement 1849–1906.* Vol. I: *1849–1865.* Nashville, Tenn.: Gospel Advocate Company, 1964. Vol. II: *1866–1906.* Indianapolis, Ind.: Religious Book Service, 1963 (reprint of the 1950 edn.).

West, William Garrett. *Barton Warren Stone: Early American Advocate of Christian Unity.* Nashville, Tenn.: The Disciples of Christ Historical Society, 1954.

Whitley, Oliver Read. *Trumpet Call of Reformation.* St. Louis, Mo.: Bethany Press, 1959.

19. The General Eldership of the Churches of God in North America

The Churches of God in North America are in one sense a product of the bubbling ferment and the revolt against the traditional denominations that marked American Christianity in the early nineteenth century. In 1816 an independent Church of God came into being in Lancaster, Pennsylvania. Four years later John Winebrenner (1797–1860), newly ordained to the ministry of the German Reformed Church, became a pastor at Harrisburg. His stress on religious experience, generally within a revivalistic context, his close association with the revivalistic Methodists of the community, and his refusal to baptize children of unbelieving parents led to a controversy in his congregation that was complicated by a personality clash between the pastor and the lay leaders.

Winebrenner and his supporters gradually dissociated themselves from the German Reformed Church, and in 1825 they formed a Church of God at Harrisburg that proposed to follow the pattern of the first-century church as Winebrenner understood it. His energetic and eloquent advocacy of his principles resulted in the founding of many other Churches of God in Pennsylvania, in Ohio, and in areas farther west. He became the leading theologian of the movement, but as an administrator his leadership did not always go unquestioned.

In 1830 many of these independent Churches of God (including the churches in Lancaster and Harrisburg) united to form a General Eldership (or presbytery), made up of elders from the local churches. As the denomination expanded it added "in North America" to the name "General Eldership of the Churches of God."

The Churches of God today represent a matured synthesis of German Pietism, the Anabaptist-tinctured revivalism of the early nineteenth-century Eastern Pennsylvania type, a Reformed theology in the Zwinglian tradition, the impact of a century and a half of contact with American denominationalism, and contemporary biblical theology. The theological changes during the last generation, as the Churches of God in North America have moved into a postfundamentalistic phase, have not been inconsiderable. There is a growing appreciation of the continuity of the church from the first century on and a decreased stress on "restorationism." The "leading matters of faith, experience, and practice" that the Twenty-Seven Points of 1849 tried to incorporate (without achieving a real consensus) and the *Doctrinal Statement* of 1925 tend to rate as historical documents rather than as contemporary theological and doctrinal norms. Conversations looking toward the possibility of ultimate union of the Church of the Brethren and the Churches of God in North America are becoming quite serious.

Allowing for the inevitable divergences and variations of opinion in a denomination that has never been strongly creedal, the Churches of God in North America affirm the Trinity; the free moral agency of man along with the universality of sin and of the inherited "disposition to that which when voluntarily performed is sinful"; the deity, humanity, and saviorhood of Christ ("he took man's place on the cross, becoming a substitute for man; he was made a curse for us, offering himself as our sacrifice, and he is now become our intercessor before God"); and Christ's role as the highest revelation of God ("a God of love, rather than only a stern judge") and of God's desire "that all men live the highest life possible." They stress the regenerating work of the Holy Spirit, whose baptism changes man into a new creature, and the inspiration and divine authority of the Bible. They describe the church in its totality as "Christ's body of people called out to live as God's own" and the local church as "the Church of God in that locality."

They oppose war and the sending of "expeditionary forces away from our land," but are ready to share in the defense of the country "which guarantees our religious freedom," and they recognize the individual's right to be a conscientious objector. They oppose the liquor traffic, gambling, racial discrimination, and divorce, and they "disapprove the use of the marriage ceremony" by their ministers when one of the parties is divorced. They are concerned for the preservation of Sunday as the Lord's Day and as a day for worship, rest, and Christian activities.

They generally observe three "symbolic-commemorative" ordinances— adult baptism by immersion, the washing of the saints' feet, and the Lord's Supper. At the same time they receive into membership unbaptized persons as long as they have professed their faith in Christ as Savior in some other way, and they do not require participation in either the foot-washing rite or in the Lord's Supper for the continuance of membership. In place of infant baptism, which they reject, they have a service for dedicating to God infants as well as parents and congregation.

They affirm the immortality of the soul, the resurrection of the dead, the end of the world by transmutation rather than annihilation, and a general judgment followed by everlasting rewards and punishments.

The General Eldership of the Churches of God in North America has 351 churches in 14 states with an inclusive membership of 37,040. Its headquarters are at 611 South 17th Street, Harrisburg, Pennsylvania 17105. The General Eldership meets every three years. It carries on foreign missions in India, Pakistan, and Haiti.[1]

NOTE

1. The present writer gratefully acknowledges the counsel of Professor Richard Kern, president of Winebrenner Theological Seminary. Findlay, Ohio, in the preparation of this section.

BIBLIOGRAPHY

[Kern, Richard.] *Let's Get Better Acquainted.* [Harrisburg, Penn.: Central Publishing House, 1966.] An 8-page pamphlet.

Teachings and Practices of the Churches of God in North America. Rev. edn. Harrisburg, Penn.: Central Publishing House, 1961. The Board of Education of the Churches of God prepared this 41-page brochure for use in adult instruction classes and for individual study in the hope that it might contribute to better churchmanship. The triennial session of the General Eldership approved the presentation in 1959.

20. The New Church (The Church of The New Jerusalem)

Swedenborg and the New Church

Emanuel Swedenborg (1688–1722), as his family called itself after Queen Ulrica Leonora ennobled it in 1719, was the second son of Jesper Svedberg, the Lutheran bishop of Skara, and one of the most learned men that Sweden ever produced. Before he turned to theology at fifty-five he had acquired a solid international reputation as a polymath who had distinguished himself in philosophy, geology, astronomy, physics, mathematics, anatomy, physiology, and other fields.

Swedenborg was neither the spiritualistic medium nor the mystic that he is sometimes made out to have been, and his manner in his researches in religion continued to be that of the scientific and philosophic inquirer. He believed that he had entered upon his theological task in response to a divine vocation; that God had opened his spiritual senses so that he might be in the spiritual world as consciously as he was in the material world; that the twenty volumes of his theological works were both the result and an instrument of the immediate revelation that he had experienced for a new age of truth and reason in religion; and that he had been a witness of Christ's promised second coming in the spiritual world and was himself chosen as an instrument of that event. From 1747 until his death Swedenborg lived in "the world of the spirits." He reports that in 1757 he witnessed a crisis in the spiritual world when the long-awaited Last Judgment took place on all spirits whose real inner character—good or evil—had been concealed by a veneer of Christian piety. In his view the year 1770 marked the beginning of a new age, symbolized by the Jerusalem that St. John the Theologian, in a vision, had seen descending from God out of heaven. Its twelve foundation jewels meant the genuine verities that shine forth from the Old and New Testaments, and its crystal walls meant the doctrinal truths that Swedenborg's theological writings had revealed.

In the year before his death a systematic version of Swedenborg's teaching came out under the title of *Vera christiana religio* (*The True Christian Religion*). Probably the best known of his theological works is *De coelo et ejus mirabilibus et de inferno* (*On Heaven and Its Wonders and on Hell*).

Although Swedenborg regarded himself as the prophet and herald of the world's final religion, the Church of the New Jerusalem, he himself took no formal step to found the new church that he envisioned.

It was not until after his death that a London printer, Robert Hindmarsh, in 1783 gathered together a number of disciples of Swedenborg to discuss his writings. Other societies rapidly came into being elsewhere. James Glen, a planter en route to Guyana, lectured on Swedenborg's ideas in Philadlphia in 1784. A society of disciples of Swedenborg was reported in Halifax, Nova Scotia, in 1791. The first society within the United States came into being at Baltimore in 1792. John Hargrove reorganized it in 1798; ten laymen laid hands on him and on Ralph Mather and to this ordination almost all of the clergy of the New Church in North America trace their ministry. The General Conference of New Church Societies in Great Britain was organized in 1815.

The New Church teaches that God, the infinite power and life within all creation, is absolutely one in both essence and person. The Father, the Son, and the Holy Spirit constitute a Trinity of essential qualities, God's infinite and divine love, wisdom, and activity. A trinity of soul, body, and mind in human beings reproduces the divine Trinity. The essence of the human being is his soul; the body is the covering and representation of the soul during the span of a person's natural life and the mind manifests itself in his various operations. The *esse* or "being" of God is invisible and infinite, and is commonly called the Father.

To redeem and to save man, the divine *esse* or being had to assume tangible and visible form. This incarnation took place in the same way as in human generation, where the soul is from the father and the body is from the mother. The Lord, called the Logos or the Son, had his life or soul from the Father, the divine *esse* or being. Since the divine is indivisible, the Father was the Son's soul or life. In other words, "God sent Himself into the world as the Son of God in the human form received from His mother." Again, when the Bible speaks of the Holy Spirit it is referring to the same divine *esse*, or being.

The redemption of mankind consists in the deliverance of human beings, who are born not in sin but with a tendency toward evil, from the dominion of evil. A vicarious atonement in the traditional sense is unnecessary, because "no first person demands satisfaction from a second." God's very essence is order, and there is always a correct relation between divine attributes and divine words; thus, for example, God uses his almighty power only for the extension of good. This same divine order exists in human beings as well; but human beings can live not only in accordance with, but also contrary to, divine order. The spiritual meaning of Adam's ejection from Eden is that in the course of many generations the human race became completely immersed in selfishness and sin. Wicked human beings took their malignant feelings into the spiritual world and became devils. As they increased in number, they filled the world of the good spirits as well and caused confusion and disorder in the realm of the spirits of departed believers and angels.

Since the union between the world of spirits and the world of men is the same as the union of a human being's soul and his body, the counterpart of mankind in the spirit world must first be redeemed or restored to order. To put heaven in order and to subjugate the evil spirits, God assumed the nature of sinful mankind, and in the tangible and finite form of man he submitted to all the temptations of the devils. The greatest of these was the one he endured on the cross. By victoriously withstanding these temptations, he broke the power of evil over good, and by restoring the laws of order on earth he brought spiritual freedom to human beings. At the same time, he interposed an eternal and infinitely strong barrier between the hells and human beings. By standing between the hells and human beings, the Divine Human (*Divinum Humanum*), possessed of all authority in heaven and on the earth, makes it possible for men once more to know and obey the truth.

Salvation consists in the "unification" or reciprocal conjunction of God and human beings. In the created human world such a unification would result in the divine consuming the human. To avoid this, the Lord himself glorified his humanity and united it with the divine in the God-Man or Man-God. Christ accomplished this when in his redemptive activity he successively laid aside His human qualities, which he had received from his mother and which were only a covering for his divine soul. By submitting to and overcoming all temptations he ceased to be the Son of Mary. Similarly human beings, originally created in God's image, must be recreated in the image of Christ's glorification. Human beings must, like Christ, endure and overcome temptations and bring the external into harmony with the spiritual.

The New Church sees the Bible as concerned throughout with spiritual things; whenever the Bible refers to mundane, historical, or scientific matters, it intends to communicate symbolically realities and truths quite independently of the scientific validity of the text in question. Basic for the understanding of the Bible is the principle of "correspondence." Since the divine love and wisdom has called all creatures into existence, created beings are forms and effects of specific aspects of the divine love and wisdom and "correspond" on the created level with spiritual realities. The New Church holds that the Bible embodies this principle of "correspondence," and Swedenborg produced commentaries on Genesis and Exodus (*Arcana coelestia*), as well as on the book of Revelation (*The Apocalypse Revealed*; *The Apocalypse Explained*), in order to unlock the internal spiritual sense of these books.

The creation account, for example, depicts the rebirth of a human being. Initially our minds are empty and void, but when the Lord says, "Let there be light," we can distinguish between the day of good and the night of evil. At a later stage we realize that there are higher and lower goods that compete for our attention. Thus it is good for a father to remain with his children, but it may be better for him to leave his family in order to protect his country.

Our hearts are at first not really in the good actions in which we engage; they are like the inanimate heavenly bodies or like the trees rooted to one place. But the Lord leads us to take delight in doing good deeds; of this the creation of the animals to which Adam gave names is a symbol. Finally, we become spiritually alive; the creation of man himself signifies this stage. Adam represents the man of the church who has received his loves and his life from the Lord.

The inspiration of the Bible extends to the spiritual sense hidden in the geographical names, the historical data, the lists of animals, and the records of human accomplishments and failures. It is only in the perspective of this spiritual-natural "coreⁿspondence" that one realizes, for instance, that the trees, groves, and orchards that the Bible mentions designate intelligence, wisdom, and knowledge, and that the sheep, the goat, the calf, and the ox signify innocence, charity, and natural affection.

The New Church's doctrine of the last things sees death as the putting off of the material body, never to be resumed. At the same time death does not deprive a human being of his real character, the thoughts and affections that make him the individual that he is. He lives on forever, a man or woman as before, and in his spiritual body he enjoys every faculty of thought, will, memory, and sensation. Human beings have life on earth to choose between good and evil, heaven and hell; but very few people become fitted either for heaven or for hell in this world. After death the spirits are led from one society to another and explored to see if they are willing to receive the truths of heaven. If they are not willing to do so, they go to societies that have conjunction only with hell. Their association with devils will not appear obnoxious to them, just as robbers do not appear to a fellow robber to be morally deformed. Indeed, the wicked spirits enjoy hell as the crow enjoys the rotting carcass or the hog the mire.

The Lord will save Gentiles and people of all religions if they have a simple love of him, avoid sins, and live a life of good will to others because they believe this to be God's will; these will be instructed in the heavenly teaching after death.

Since heaven, like the rest of the spiritual world, lies beyond space and time, it is to be thought of not in spatial or local terms, but as a state in which charity and faith are conjoined. As human beings in the natural world find happiness with those who love similar things, so in heaven people associate with others of like mind. As in this world human beings take pleasure in doing the things they love to do, so each angel performs social duties and useful functions. As the true love of husbands and wives is an indelible part of our life, the denizens of heaven live in blissful marriage with their divinely provided partners. The angels rear those who have died as children. Thus heaven becomes not some far-off, imaginary place, but a state gaining intelligibility from our understanding of life here.

The New Church observes the sacraments of baptism and the Holy

Supper. The former may be administered to infants. The latter is given in unleavened bread and fermented wine, the "correspondential" symbols of the Lord's love and truth. Confirmation is a rite in which young people confess their faith in preparation for joining the church.

The General Convention of the New Jerusalem in the United States of America

The General Convention of the New Jerusalem in the United States of America came into being at Philadelphia in 1817 to unite the societies along the middle eastern seaboard. The movement spread northward to Boston and westward into Pennsylvania,[1] Ohio,[2] Michigan, Canada, and Illinois. Between 1850 and 1890 the membership of the General Convention more than quadrupled. It achieved its peak of about 10,000 in 1899.

In 1890 the former Pennsylvania Association, which had formed itself into the General Church of Pennsylvania, withdrew, chiefly on the issue of the divine authority of Swedenborg's writings. The withdrawing group claimed that the view which the General Convention still champions—namely, that Swedenborg was a divinely illumined seer and that his law of correspondence is the key to the divinely authorized exposition of the spiritual sense of the Bible and a truthful disclosure of the facts, phenomena, and laws of the spiritual world—did not do full justice to Swedenborg's unique vocation.

The liturgy of the General Convention sets forth as its primary doctrines:

> That there is one God, in whom there is a Divine Trinity; and that He is the Lord Jesus Christ;
>
> That saving faith is to believe on Him;
>
> That evils are to be shunned, because they are of the devil and from the devil;
>
> That good actions are to be done, because they are of God and from God;
>
> That these are to be done by a man as from himself; but that it ought to be believed that they are done from the Lord with him and by him.

The General Convention has shown a great measure of hospitality to contemporary theological trends. In 1966 it joined the National Council of the Churches of Christ in the United States of America. Its polity is congregational.

The New Church Theological School at 48 Sargent Street, Newton, Massachusetts 02158, serves in lieu of a headquarters for the General Convention. State conventions and the General Convention meet annually. There are 47 churches in the United States and Canada reporting an inclusive membership of 2,329. The General Convention of the New Jerusalem has affiliated societies in a number of European countries and carries on foreign missions in Korea, Japan, and the Philippines Republic.

The General Church of the New Jerusalem

From an early date in the history of the New Church the followers of Swedenborg disagreed about the authority of Swedenborg's theological writings. One of those who in the mid-nineteenth century ardently championed the divine authority of Swedenborg's works, the distinctiveness of the New Church with a distinctively new way of life, the principle of priestly government, and the need for separate New Church elementary schools for New Church children was the Reverend Richard de Charms, who went so far as to organize a short-lived Central Convention (dissolved in 1852) to underline his position. The same concerns led to the founding of the Academy of the New Church at Philedalphia in 1876. In the wake of the so-called Academy movement, the General Convention permitted the Pennsylvania Association to organize as The General Church of Pennsylvania, in which three degrees of the priesthood—those of minister, pastor, and bishop—were instituted. The Academy movement stressed New Church baptism as the only orderly means of entrance into the New Church and opposed a lay government, which hindered the clergy in their teaching office. The adherents of the movement separated from the General Convention in 1890. In 1897 five ministers of the Academy movement requested the Right Reverend William Frederic Pendleton to lead them in the organization of an episcopally structured New Church body. It soon took the name The General Church of the New Jerusalem. From 1900 on it has grown consistently. It has no constitution. It has a threefold priesthood of ministers, pastors, and bishops, and holds that Swedenborg was not only divinely illumined, but divinely inspired, so that his theological writings have divine authority and must be accepted in their fullness. Regional assemblies meet at the call of the bishop; a General Assembly is held every four years at least. Its international headquarters are at Bryn Athyn, Pennsylvania 19009, the site of its cathedral. In addition to societies in Brazil, South Africa, Australia, Sweden, Holland, France, and England, it has 35 churches in the United States with a membership of 2,028, and 4 churches in Canada with a membership of 366.[3] It conducts a foreign mission in the Republic of South Africa.

The General Church cooperates with the Swedenborg Society in the publication of Swedenborg's works and on a local basis with both the General Convention and the General Conference in occasional joint festival celebrations.

The Lord's New Church Which Is Nova Hierosolyma (Swedenborgian)

The Reverend Theodore Pitcairn (b. 1883) withdrew in 1937 from the General Church of the New Jerusalem and led in the organization of the Lord's New Church Which Is Nova Hierosolyma (Swedenborgian). The Lord's

New Church concurs in the view of the General Church of the New Jerusalem that the writings of Swedenborg along with the Old and the New Testaments are the Word of God and have divine authority. But as a further development beyond this view of the parent body, the Lord's New Church sees that the teaching about the Scriptures contained Swedenborg's writings apply to these writings themselves, that is, the writings also have an internal or spiritual sense as well as a literal sense. This internal sense is the spirit and life of the Word. Human beings come into this spiritual sense as their minds are opened to the Lord through a life of faith and love in accordance with the Word of God.

The Lord's New Church holds that the primary function of the church is to come to the understanding and life of the internal sense of Swedenborg's writings, together with obedience to their literal sense. In contrast to the prevalent view in the General Church of the New Jerusalem that the doctrinal ideas which the people who are in the church form are only human productions, the Lord's New Church regards the ideas drawn from the Word of God according to the rules that the Word of God lays down to be of divine origin and essence. If the church follows the Lord there can be a growth and development of those ideas into eternity. The Lord's New Church describes the genuine doctrine in various ways, as the Word seen from the Lord who is the Light of the world, or as the Word seen in the light of heaven, or as an enlightened seeing of the Word resulting from the influx of the Holy Spirit.

The position taken by the Lord's New Church had antecedents in the views of such Swedenborgian theologians as the Reverend Edward S. Syatt of Toronto and Edward Crach, M.D., of Erie, Pennsylvania. It received its developed form chiefly in the expositions of H. D. G. Groeneveld of The Hague in 1929. The General Council of the New Jerusalem rejected this view in such a way that those who had accepted it felt compelled to withdraw and form The Lord's New Church.

In 1939 The Lord's New Church published a set of "principles" relating principally to the doctrine of faith. These concluded: "The presence of the Lord himself is the understanding of the word, or the doctrine out of the word. This presence is the spirit of the rational form or of the literal sense of the Third Testament, which is the internal sense. The internal sense is then the literal sense, and the literal sense is the internal sense. Then there is the acknowledgment of the second coming of the Lord."[4] In 1949 the Lord's New Church set forth additional "principles" directed principally to the doctrine of life, with a view to charting the way that the church must go for its development. These principles called for stress on both "universals," namely, "the ever more interior advance in the doctrine of the church" and "the ever more interior removal of the proprial [that is, particular] will of man, which opens the way for an ever more interior seeing of the Divine Human."[5]

In 1956 the Lord's New Church formulated as its three essentials: (1) acknowledgment of "the Lord Jesus Christ in His Divine Human as the one only God of heaven and earth, in whom is the divine Trinity"; (2) acknowledgment of the Word of the Lord in the Old Testament, the New Testament, and the Third Testament (the writings of Swedenborg), in the last of which the Lord has fulfilled his second coming and to which everything that it says about the Sacred Scripture applies; (3) the life of faith, charity, and love as the divine essence of eternal life in man and in the church.

The headquarters of the Lord's New Church are Creek Road, Bryn Athyn, Pennsylvania 19009. A single bishop oversees the international church. The Lord's New Church has societies in Holland, Sweden, South Africa, and Japan, and scattered members in Germany and England. Several years ago there were two societies in North America (Bryn Athyn, and Yonkers, New York), with a total of 70 members.[6] Recent efforts to contact the group have been unsuccessful.

NOTES

1. Barefooted Jonathan Chapman ("Johnny Appleseed") from the cider-mill country of Pennsylvania not only planted orchards in the river valleys, but also distributed the works of Swedenborg.
2. The society in Cincinnati dated back to 1811.
3. Communication from the Reverend Norbert F. Rogers, General Church of the New Jerusalem, Bryn Athyn, Pennsylvania.
4. For the complete text, see Theodore Pitcairn, *The Beginning and Development of Doctrine in the New Church* (Bryn Athyn, Penn.: The Lord's New Church, 1968) (61-page brochure), pp. 44-45.
5. For the complete text, see ibid., pp. 45-51. The quotation is from p. 46.
6. Letters from the Reverend Theodore Pitcairn, Bryn Athyn, Pennsylvania.

BIBLIOGRAPHY

Block, Marguerite Beck. *The New Church in the World: A Study of Swedenborgianism in America.* 2nd edn. New York: Octagon Books, 1968.

Book of Worship, Containing Services, Chants, Sacraments, Rites, Prayers, and Hymns, Prepared for the Use of the Church of the New Jerusalem. 2nd printing. Brooklyn N.Y.: New Church Board of Publication, 1960.

The Liturgy of the General Church of the New Jerusalem. Bryn Athyn, Penn.: General Church of the New Jerusalem, 1966.

Odhner, Hugo Ljungberg. *The General Church of the New Jerusalem: A Handbook of Information.* 2nd edn., rev. by Robert S. Junge. Bryn Athyn, Penn.: General Church Publication Committee, 1965. A 48-page pamphlet; both the author and the reviser were secretary of the organization.

Pitcairn, Theodore. *My Lord and My God: Essays on Modern Religion, the Bible and Emanuel Swedenborg.* New York: Exposition Press, 1967.

Sigstedt, Cyriel Sigrid (Ljungberg Odhner). *The Swedenborg Epic: The Life and Works of Emanuel Swedenborg.* New York: Bookman Associates, 1952.

Swedenborg, Emanuel. *The True Christian Religion, Containing the Universal Theology of the New Church, Translated from the Original Latin Edition Printed at Amsterdam in the Year 1771.* 2 vols. New York: Swedenborg Foundation, 1946.

21. Uniting Churches

The United Church of Canada

Shortly after the United Church of Canada was formed on June 10, 1925, Charles Clayton Morrison told the readers of the *Christian Century* to mark the date as monumental in ecclesiastical history. "On that day," he said, "took place the first large scale achievement of organic union of separate denominational families since the Protestant Reformation."[1] Morrison expected the union to be a model for others still to come.[2] After a half century the union stands as one of only several within the twentieth-century Ecumenical movement that have transcended denominational lines.

A number of denominations joined together to form the United Church of Canada: the Presbyterian Church in Canada; the Congregational Churches of Canada; the Methodist Church, Canada; and the General Council of Local Union Churches. These churches were themselves the products of earlier union efforts which had united 40 distinct bodies through 19 specific acts of union.[3] The process which produced the United Church of Canada began as early as 1899 with discussions and consultations between the Presbyterian and Methodist churches. The Congregational Churches of Canada became party to the consultation process in 1902. The Church of England in Canada and the Baptist churches in Canada declined invitations to the discussions which were offered in 1904. From 1921 on the large number of union congregations, established in the more recently settled West, sent representatives to the negotiations.

After the necessary legislation was enacted in 1924 by the Parliament of Canada, the union of the participating churches was consummated in Toronto a year later. The strength of the United Church at the time of union was 8,000 congregations, 600,000 members, and 3,800 ministers. The Joint Union Committee saw the union as "but another step toward the wider union of Evangelical Churches, not only in Canada, but throughout the world."[4]

The formation of the United Church of Canada proved to be divisive for the Presbyterians in Canada. The General Assembly of the Presbyterian Church in Canada ultimately decided for the union, but between one third and one fourth of the Presbyterians did not go along with the union, continuing Presbyterianism as a separate church body.

The doctrinal position of the United Church of Canada was set forth in the Basis of Union approved by the merging bodies. Written between 1904 and 1910, the Basis of Union reflects the confidence of the participating churches that they were already one in the essentials of the faith and needed no lengthy theological statement. A brief preamble affirms the commitment of the United Church of Canada to "the Scriptures of the Old and New Testaments as the primary source and ultimate standard of Christian faith and life," to "the teaching of the great creeds of the ancient Church," and to "the evangelical doctrines of the Reformation, as set forth in common" by the merging churches.[5]

Twenty articles of doctrine constitute the statement of faith set forth in the Basis of Union. Neither the Westminster Confession nor the classic expressions of Methodist doctrine exercised a determining influence on these articles. The formulation of the articles allows for considerable flexibility in interpretation. Article VI, "Of the Grace of God," is a mediating statement between Calvinistic and Arminian views on the doctrine of election:

> We believe that God, out of His great love for the world, has given His only begotten Son to be the Saviour of sinners, and in the Gospel freely offers His all-sufficient salvation to all men. We believe also that God, in His own good pleasure, gave to His Son a people, an innumerable multitude, chosen in Christ unto holiness, service, and salvation.[6]

The main sources for the doctrinal articles were the Brief Statement of the Reformed Faith, prepared by the Presbyterian Church in the U.S.A. in 1905, and the Articles of the Faith of the Presbyterian Church in England, prepared in 1890.

Article II, "Of Revelation" affirms "the Holy Scriptures of the Old and New Testaments" as "given by inspiration of God, . . . a faithful record of God's gracious revelations, and as the sure witness to Christ."[7] Article VII, "Of the Lord Jesus Christ," affirms his virgin birth, sinlessness, sacrificial death, resurrection, ascension, intercession, indwelling presence, and rule over all.[8] Article XII, "Of Sanctification," affirms that "a holy life is the fruit and evidence of saving faith," that "the believer's hope of continuance in such a life is in the persevering grace of God," and that "in this growth in grace Christians may attain that maturity and full assurance of faith whereby the love of God is made perfect in us."[9] Two sacraments, baptism and the Lord's Supper, are acknowledged. Those who receive the Lord's Supper in faith "do, after a spiritual manner, partake of the body and blood of the Lord Jesus Christ."[10] At the time of ordination candidates for ministry are asked if they are "in essential agreement" with the statement of doctrine and if they accept it "as in substance agreeable to the teaching of the Holy Scriptures."[11]

In polity the United Church of Canada is conciliar, with its governing bodies being the Official Board of the local pastoral charge (which may include more than one congregation), the Presbytery, the Conference, and the General Council. In the Presbytery, the Conference, and the General Council representation is half clerical and half lay.

Since 1926 a number of individual congregations of the Christian Church (Disciples of Christ) in Canada have joined with the United Church. In 1968 the Canada Conference of the Evangelical United Brethren entered the union.

Conversations on union between the Anglican Church of Canada and the United Church of Canada were initiated in 1943 and continued for twenty years, resulting in the Principles of Union, which were adopted by the two church bodies in 1965 and 1966. The Principles of Union[12] were envisioned not as final expressions of doctrine or details of organization and liturgy but as a basis in faith and order upon which the two churches could come together.

As union discussions proceeded, the Christian Church (Disciples of Christ) in Canada joined the negotiations. A Plan of Union was adopted by a general commission representing the three church bodies in December 1972 and submitted to the church bodies for action. In June 1975 the Anglican Church of Canada, after a May 1975 survey of its membership, found insufficient support for the visible organic union previously approved by the churches in the Principles of Union, rejected the Plan of Union as a basis of union, and instead recommended a process of stage-by-stage agreements on faith, ministry, and sacraments. When the Anglican church declined to commit itself to "a new embodiment of the One Church of God as envisioned in the Principles of Union," the United Church of Canada proposed a moratorium on negotiations toward organic union, which the Anglican church accepted. The United Church of Canada and the Christian Church (Disciples of Christ) in Canada agreed to pursue bilateral negotiations for union.[13]

Headquarters of the United Church of Canada are at the United Church House, 85 Saint Clair Avenue East, Toronto, Ontario M4T 1M8. There are 4,330 churches with an inclusive membership of 2,140,102.

United Church of Christ

In the emblem of the United Church of Christ, surrounding an ancient symbol known as the Cross of Victory, are the words of Scripture, "THAT THEY MAY ALL BE ONE."[14] The text has been the theme of the twentieth-century Ecumenical movement. Its inclusion in the emblem of the United Church of Christ is evidence of that church body's close relation to the Ecumenical movement both as product and as proponent.

The union which produced the United Church of Christ was effected at Cleveland, Ohio, June 25-27, 1957. It brought together two church bodies, the Evangelical and Reformed Church and the General Council of the Congregational Christian Churches of the United States. The name chosen for the new church body[15] was intended to state the commitment of its members to the prayer in the emblem, "that they may all be one."

Like the United Church of Canada,[16] which was formed a generation earlier, the United Church of Christ brought together church bodies of different denominations and polities. In addition, it united the descendants of different cultures, English and German.[17] Both uniting churches had long and distinguished histories reaching back into the Colonial period of American history. Both were themselves the products of earlier unions.

The Congregational strand in the United Church of Christ began with the establishment of the Plymouth Colony by the Pilgrims in 1620 and of the Massachusetts Bay Colony by English Puritans a decade later. Though the Pilgrims had separated from the Church of England and the Puritans considered themselves nonconforming members of it,[18] they were in agreement on Congregationalism as the only proper form of ecclesiastical government and extended the bond of fellowship to each other. At the Cambridge Synod of 1648 they adopted the Cambridge Platform, the earliest document setting forth American Congregational faith and polity. The platform affirmed the headship of Christ in his church, the independence of the congregation from outside interference with the right to choose its own officials, the necessity of all the churches to preserve church communion with one another because they are all united in Christ, the recognition and office of the civil magistrate, the two orders of deacons and elders, the manner and meaning of ordination, the nature of synods, and the ways to receive, dismiss, and discipline members.[19] The platform provided the charter of the development of what came to be called the Congregational Way in the New World.[20]

Congregational churches grew and proliferated as a result of the evangelical revival of the Great Awakening in the early eighteenth century. Jonathan Edwards (1703–1758) exemplified the essentially Calvinist theological position of the Congregationalism of the colonial period. Because of the privileged position of New England Congregational churches as "established churches"[21] Congregational clergymen exercised major influence in colonial politics.[22] Schools and seminaries were established, and the New England churches reached out in mission to the American Indians and to the westward-expanding frontier.

At the founding of the United States of America the churches of the Congregational Way did not possess a strong sense of denominational identity, seeing themselves more as manifestations of the church in their local area. In 1801 the Congregationalists joined with the Presbyterians in a Plan of Union for the establishment of churches in the West. The plan provided aid for newly formed churches and established reciprocal ministerial relationships among Congregationalists and Presbyterians. Under the "presbygational" plan many churches founded by Congregationalists chose to be associated with the more centralized polity of the Presbyterians. The result was negative for the westward expansion of Congregationalism as a denomination.

During the nineteenth century the Congregational churches slowly developed a denominational consciousness.[23] They created the American Board of Commissioners for Foreign Missions in 1812 and the American Missionary Association in 1846. By midcentury Congregationalists felt the need for a national organization and at a council meeting in Albany, New York, in 1852 ended the Plan of Union with the Presbyterians. In 1865, at a meeting of the council in Boston, the Burial Hill Statement of Faith was adopted, declaring the Westminster Confession and the Savoy Declaration "as being well and freely grounded in Holy Scriptures, the only sufficient and invariable rule of religion."[24] On November 15, 1871 the National Council of Congregational Churches was officially organized at Oberlin, Ohio.

The essentially Calvinist theological orientation of Congregationalists underwent change in the nineteenth and early twentieth centuries, resulting in the development of strong social concern, reflected in the work of Horace Bushnell (1802–1876), Washington Gladden (1836–1918), and William J. Tucker (1839–1926) and exemplified in the establishment of Hull House in Chicago by Jane Addams.

Over the years a number of smaller churches united with the National Council of Congregational Churches. A group of Congregational Methodist Churches in Georgia and Alabama joined in 1892. The Evangelical Protestant Churches, a group of congregations in the Ohio Valley of German and Swiss origin, joined in 1925.

The second major strand in the United Church of Christ was a peculiarly American denomination that emerged from the early nineteenth-century Christian or Restorationist movement, which contrary to its own intentions produced several new denominations designated by the name Christians or Disciples.[25] One of these churches resulted from separate movements among Methodists in North Carolina, Baptists in New England, and Presbyterians in Kentucky to bring about the unity of the church through the restoration of New Testament Christianity. Organized as the United States Convention in 1820, the church was renamed the American Christian Convention and ultimately the General Convention of the Christian Church.

In the nineteenth century the General Convention of the Christian Church pioneered in fostering educational opportunities for women and developed coeducational colleges. Like the Congregationalists, members of Christian churches were strongly congregational in polity. Their greatest numerical strength was in the South, especially in North Carolina and Virginia.[26]

A desire to effect union among the churches of Protestantism led the General Convention of the Christian Church to begin negotiations with the National Council of Congregational Churches in 1924. A Plan of Union was adopted by both churches in 1929 which stated that "the basis of this new relation shall be the recognition by each group that the other is constituted of the followers of Jesus Christ," that each group "shall be free to retain and develop its own form of expression," that "the Bible is the supreme rule of faith and life" but "there is wide room for difference of interpretation among equally good Christians," and that "this union shall be conditioned upon the acceptance of Christianity as primarily a way of life, and not upon uniformity of theological opinion or any uniform practices of ordinances."[27] At Seattle, Washington, on June 27, 1931, The General Council of Congregational and Christian Churches[28] was organized, a church body with 6,670 churches and a membership of 1,050,000.

The third major strand in the United Church of Christ dates back to the immigration of members of the Reformed Church in Germany to Pennsylvania and New York in the early eighteenth century.[29] John Philip Boehm (d. 1749), a devout school teacher who was ordained by New York Dutch pastors under the authority of the Classis of Amsterdam in Holland, was responsible for organizing German Reformed congregations in Pennsylvania. Swiss-born Michael Schlatter (1716–1790) gathered the Reformed congregations together in the Coetus (Latin for "assembly"), which he established in 1747 under the jurisdiction of the Church of Holland. Separated from the Holland ecclesiastical authorities during the Revolutionary War, the German Reformed Church declared its independence in 1793 and constituted itself as the Synod of the Reformed High German Church in the United States of America.

In the nineteenth century the Reformed Church grew in numbers and developed organizationally. It established a college and a seminary, expanded its work with the frontier, and reached out in mission overseas. In 1863 the Reformed Church and an independent Ohio synod, which it had established earlier, united to form the General Synod of the Reformed Church in the United States. By 1934 the church had developed six synods with a membership of 348,189, including other ethnic groups, especially Hungarians who had belonged to the Reformed Church in their homeland.

The fourth major strand of the United Church of Christ was the product of mid-nineteenth-century emigrations from Germany. They came from lands influenced by the formation of the Evangelical Union of Prussia in 1817, the effort of Prussian King Frederick William III (1770–1840) to unite Reformed and Lutherans in his dominion under one form of worship and one church government. Several Evangelical congregations were established in Missouri and Illinois under the auspices of German mission societies. On October 15, 1840 five German evangelical pastors and a Reformed missionary met near St. Louis, Missouri, and formed *Der Kirchenverein des Westens* (The Church Society of the West).

The *Kirchenverein* was primarily a missionary society, assisting in the work of organizing new congregations. Under its auspices a theological seminary and a college were established and a journal was published. Similar organizations were established in other parts of the country. In 1872 these groups were consolidated into one body and in 1877 the name The Evangelical Synod of North America was adopted. The church body reached out in foreign missions and was active in providing for orphans, aged, and invalid members through a variety of benevolent institutions.

In doctrine the Evangelical Synod espoused the Augsburg Confession, Luther's Small Catechism, and the Heidelberg Catechism insofar as they agree, with the provision that "where they disagree, we adhere strictly to the passages of Holy Scripture bearing on the subject, and avail ourselves of the liberty of conscience prevailing in the Evangelical Church."[30] The polity of the Evangelical Synod was a combination of presbyterial and congregational types.

Leaders of the Evangelical Synod and of the Reformed Church, moved by participation in ecumenical meetings in the early twentieth century, began exploring union possibilities in the late 1920s. On June 26, 1934, at Cleveland, Ohio, on the basis of a Plan of Union previously adopted, the two churches became the Evangelical and Reformed Church even though a constitution had not yet been written. Systematically merging its boards and seminaries and publications, the new church adopted a constitution in 1940.

In the early 1940s union explorations were begun by representatives of the Evangelical and Reformed Church and the General Council of the Congregational Christian Churches. By 1944 a Basis of Union had been prepared. The basis was revised five times to meet objections from within the Congregational Christian group. By 1949 both churches had approved the revised basis with a series of interpretations. Legal efforts by a minority of Congregational Christian Churches delayed but ultimately could not prevent the union.[31] At a meeting June 25-27, 1957 in Cleveland, Ohio, the United Church of Christ was formed. The Congregational Christians contributed approximately 1¼ million members to the new church; the Evangelicals and Reformed brought three quarters of a million members to the union. In 1959, at the second General Synod, a Statement of Faith was adopted, and in 1961 at the third General Synod, the constitution and bylaws were approved.

The basic doctrinal position of the United Church of Christ is presented in its constitution and in the Statement of Faith adopted in 1959. The preamble to the constitution of the United Church of Christ states in the second of three paragraphs:

> The United Church of Christ acknowledges as its sole Head, Jesus Christ, Son of God and Saviour. It acknowledges as kindred in Christ all who share in this confession. It looks to the Word of God in the Scriptures, and to the presence and power of the Holy Spirit, to prosper its creative and redemptive work in the world. It claims as its own the faith of the historic Church expressed in the ancient creeds and reclaimed in the basic insights of the Protestant Reformers. It affirms the responsibility of the Church in each generation to make this faith its own in reality of worship, in honesty of thought and expression, and in purity of heart before God. In accordance with the teaching of our Lord and the practice prevailing among evangelical Christians, it recognizes two sacraments: Baptism and the Lord's Supper or Holy Communion.[32]

In the Statement of Faith the United Church of Christ affirms:

We believe in God, the Eternal Spirit, Father of our Lord Jesus Christ and our Father, and to his deeds we testify:

He calls the worlds into being,
   creates man in his own image,
   and sets before him the ways of life and death.
He seeks in holy love to save all people from aimlessness and sin.
He judges men and nations by his righteous will declared through prophets
      and apostles.
In Jesus Christ, the man of Nazareth, our crucified and risen Lord,
   he has come to us
   and shared our common lot,
   conquering sin and death
   and reconciling the world to himself.
He bestows upon us his Holy Spirit,
   creating and renewing the church of Jesus Christ,
   binding in covenant faithful people of all ages, tongues, and races.
He calls us into his church
   to accept the cost and joy of discipleship,
   to be his servants in the service of men,
   to proclaim the gospel to all the world and resist the powers of evil,
   to share in Christ's baptism and eat at his table,
   to join him in his passion and victory.
He promises to all who trust him
   forgiveness of sins and fullness of grace,
   courage in the struggle for justice and peace,
   his presence in trial and rejoicing,
   and eternal life in his kingdom which has no end.
Blessing and honor, glory and power be unto him. Amen.[33]

The doctrinal affirmations in the constitution and in the Statement of Faith must be understood in the light of the place of creeds in the traditions of the churches that formed the United Church of Christ. The Christian Church opposed the use of any creed and united with the Congregational churches only on condition that uniformity of theological opinion would not be required. The Congregational tradition insisted on the right of each congregation to determine its own faith formulations and governance. The Evangelical and Reformed tradition affirmed the historic creeds insofar as they agreed with Scripture. Therefore the Basis of Union, which authorized drafting the Statement of Faith, declared, "This statement shall be regarded as a testimony, and not a test, of faith."[34] It is in that sense that one must understand the affirmation in the constitution concerning "the faith of the historic Church expressed in the ancient creeds and reclaimed in the basic insights of the Protestant Reformers."

The Statement of Faith is very much in use in the United Church of Christ as a "testimony." It is given a prominent place at the beginning of the hymnal of the church body and is included as the first option along with the Apostles' and Nicene creeds in the Affirmation of Faith which follows the sermon in two services of Word and Sacrament included in the hymnal.

Douglas Horton, prominent theologian in the United Church of Christ, explains why the Statement of Faith was produced:

> . . . many in the United Church of Christ [are at home with the congregation and with God] when they stand with the church and recite the Apostles' Creed or the Nicene, but there are those who have desired a statement of common faith that carries not only the truths of the ancient confessions but also the insights that God has given to his church since the early centuries. Though the old creeds imply the fact of God's love, they do not give it the centrality the church has come to feel it deserves. They have nothing to say about the Kingdom of Heaven, though this was our Lord's central theme. And so in our day there has been a felt need for a brief confession in which the complete church can meet the complete contemporary man and invite him to join it in a declaration of common faith. An Apostles' Creed for our own day has been called for, and the United Church of Christ has in humility responded to what it has believed to be the urging of the Holy Spirit by composing a Statement of Faith.[35]

According to the introduction to the hymnal of the United Church of Christ,

> The Statement of Faith has a natural progression which can be stated as follows:
>
>> *Affirmation* of the character of God and his actions.
>> *Proclamation* of what God has done and does for his people.
>> *Our responsibility* for what we are called to be and do as a result of what God has done.
>> *Our assurance,* as set forth in the promises of the gospel.
>> *Doxology,* the climactic affirmation of the Faith.[36]

Hymns in the hymnal have been arranged according to the theological order of the Statement of Faith "to provide the churches with a hymnbook that will serve both as a resource for worship and as an indispensable instrument for teaching the faith."[37]

According to the hymnal, "When the church is at worship the people of God give public expression to the faith that shapes their lives."[38] The worship forms provided in the hymnal for "the chief service of the church for weekly worship"[39] are two variations of the Service of Word and Sacrament. According to the Hymnal Committee, one factor guiding the committee in its work was the concern of contemporary liturgical renewal for "the reunion of the service of the word and the service of the sacrament."[40] The services employ versions of liturgical texts prepared by the International Consultation on English in the Liturgy. The hymnal also recommends that consultation's lectionary.

Baptism and the Lord's Supper are affirmed in the constitution as the two sacraments recognized in the United Church of Christ but nothing more is said about them. In the hymnal's order of service for the baptism of infants,[41] the rubric directs the minister to baptize the child with water and to address the child by name, saying, "You are baptized in the name of the Father and of the Son and of the Holy Spirit. Amen." In the prayer preceding the baptism the minister prays:

> O Lord, giver of life and power, you have promised not only to be our God but also the God and Father of our children. Sanctify with your spirit (this child) whom we baptize according to your word and bless this water, that it may be a sign and seal of new life in Christ our Lord. Amen.

Following the baptism the minister says:

> We praise God for calling this child into the company of Christ's people. We accept (him/her) with joy. Thanks be to God. Amen.

According to Douglas Horton,[42] baptism in the United Church of Christ is the rite of initiation into Christ's church and is normally done by sprinkling.

> The water used is the symbol of washing, and washing means renewal, so that the total rite comes to mean that the person baptized is thereby adopted into the new life which is hid with Christ, and Christ's people, in God.

Infant baptism is proper "because the symbolism is that of Mother Church reaching out to the helpless one and taking him into her care."

Concerning the Lord's Supper Douglas Horton observes:

> In the United Church of Christ are undoubtedly to be found as many interpretations of the Eucharist as there are in Protestant Christendom, since all the major strains of Protestantism are in the United Church, but these are dominated by the one certainty that the Lord's Table is a means of grace to those who partake, and that, because the real presence of Christ is available there . . . the bread and wine are signs of the body and blood of Christ and symbols of his presence, which make the rite a real means of grace, strengthening the union with him.[43]

In the Service of Word and Sacrament I in the *Hymnal of the United Church of Christ*, after speaking Jesus' words of institition, the minister continues the Eucharistic Prayer as follows:

> Obeying the commandment of our Lord Jesus Christ, we, your people, offer you this bread and this cup, recalling his incarnate life, his atoning death, his resurrection and ascension until he come

> Bless and sanctify by your Holy Spirit both us and these your gifts of bread and wine, that in this holy communion of the body and blood of Christ we may be made one with him and he with us, and that we may remain faithful members of his body, until we feast with him in your heavenly kingdom.[44]

The words spoken at the distribution are the following:

> Take and eat; this is the body of Christ, which is broken for you.
> This cup is the new covenant in the blood of Christ. Drink of it, all of you.[45]

In the news media the United Church of Christ is regularly described as a liberal denomination,[46] not just because of its doctrinal orientation but also because of its major involvement in social issues. Its faith commitment can be assessed by the actions of its General Synod and its boards and agencies. In 1977, for example, the General Synod adopted a statement accusing the television industry of "exploiting" sex and violence and calling upon the industry to make voluntary changes in programming. The same convention appealed to American corporations and businesses to withdraw their operations from South Africa because of that nation's apartheid racial policies. It called for universal, accessible, and comprehensive health services; urged its agencies and local churches to provide greater services to the elderly; appealed for special steps to assure full integration of handicapped persons into the life of the churches and society, including changes to remove physical barriers impeding their full participation; and reaffirmed a 1975 resolution deploring the violation of civil rights of homosexual and bisexual persons, calling on its local churches and agencies to continue to work for the enactment of civil rights legislation at federal, state, and local levels.[47]

The 1977 General Synod actions continue a tradition that has been operative in the United Church of Christ since its inception. In 1963 it became the first denomination to threaten broad-scale economic sanction against institutions which lacked a policy of openness without regard for race, national background, or ethnic origin. In 1969 its Office of Communication won a landmark court case that caused Station WLBT-TV of Jackson, Mississippi to lose its license for practicing racial discrimination in television programming. In 1977 the church body's Executive Council authorized expenditures up to $600,000 for the "Wilmington Ten," a group accused and found guilty of violence in Wilmington, North Carolina, in a highly suspect case now being investigated by the United States Justice Department and the North Carolina governor.

In mission policy and program the United Church of Christ has been creative and ready to experiment. Together with other churches the United Church of Christ has been involved in

> . . . the Philadelphia Project, designed to develop a ministry to the structures of a city; the Los Angeles Project, relating a team of theologians and social scientists to the planning department of that great city and set up for the

purpose of theological reflection, while seeking to involve the churches in the goals and objectives of the city; the Detroit Industrial Mission, a crucially important ministry in the work world; the Chicago Urban Training Center; ski ministries; the ministry on the Las Vegas strip; the night ministry in San Francisco; a ministry to drug addicts and homosexuals; coffeehouses and ministries in shopping areas and the ministry in national parks. . . .[48]

The ecumenical concerns which produced the United Church of Christ have involved it in the major ecumenical organizations. It is a member of the World Council of Churches and of the National Council of the Churches of Christ in the United States of America. It belongs to the World Alliance of Reformed Churches (Presbyterian and Congregational). It was engaged in union conversations with the Christian Church (Disciples of Christ) when the Consultation on Church Union was established in 1962 and discontinued its conversations with the Disciples in order to pursue the possibility of even wider union. The General Synod of the United Church of Christ at its 1977 meeting resolved to renew the union discussions with the Christian Church (Disciples of Christ), and the Disciples took similar action at their 1977 convention.

In church polity "the basic unit of the life and organization of the United Church of Christ is the local church," which is defined as "composed of persons who, believing in God as heavenly Father, and accepting Jesus Christ as Lord and Saviour, and depending on the guidance of the Holy Spirit, are organized for Christian worship, for the furtherance of Christian fellowship, and for the ongoing work of Christian witness." Local churches are autonomous, which is defined as including, among other specifics, "the right to retain or adopt its own charter and name; to adopt its own constitution and bylaws; to formulate its own covenants and confessions of faith; . . . and to withdraw by its own decision from the United Church of Christ at any time without forfeiture of ownership or control of any real or personal property owned by it."[49]

Local churches of a geographical area comprise an association, whose primary function is to provide official standing for churches and ministers of the area. Conferences, usually coterminus with the states of the nation, are composed of the churches and the ministers who have standing in the associations within the conference. The purpose of the conference is to assist the local churches in carrying out their mission within the conference boundaries and beyond it. The General Synod is the representative body of the whole church and is composed of delegates chosen by the conferences and of ex-officio delegates. The General Synod meets biennially. Its presiding officer is called the moderator, who must alternately be a lay person and a minister. An Executive Council acts for the General Synod between meetings.

The United Church of Christ carries on its work through two main instruments, the Board for World Ministries and the Board for Homeland

Ministries. It has an Office for Church in Society, an Office of Communication, and a Stewardship Council among several other councils. It is affiliated with thirty-four colleges, two academies, and thirteen theological schools.

According to one observer, the special quality of the United Church of Christ is its creative balance between Christian individuality and Christian communty.[50] Another observer summarizes the special identity of the church body as "a progressive, flexible, creative force in American Protestant Christianity; deeply concerned and willing to take risks in faithful action concerning the problems that confront man in a new age; willing to support experimental ministries in an attempt to peneterate with the gospel the different worlds in which man lives; and ecumenical to the core."[51]

The United Church of Christ has 6,528 congregations and a membership of 1,801,241. Its headquarters are at 297 Park Avenue South, New York, New York 10010.

La Iglesia Evangélica Unida de Puerto Rico
(The United Evangelical Church of Puerto Rico)

In 1931 the American Missionary Association, which represented the General Council of Congregational and Christian Churches in Puerto Rico, and the mission of the Church of the United Brethren in Christ (Hermanos Unidos en Cristo) on the island, joined to form La Iglesia Evangélica Unida de Puerto Rico.[52] They have continued to maintain their ties with both parent bodies even after the latter entered into larger unions, the United Church of Christ and The United Methodist Church.

The headquarters of the church are at Roble 54, Río Piedras. Each congregation has its own assembly and governing committee. The final authority in the church at large is the Annual Assembly. Between sessions the Executive Council carries on the assembly's work. The church draws the funds for its support both from its own local congregations and from the boards of the parent bodies in the continental United States. The interdenominational Evangelical Seminary of Puerto Rico trains its clergymen.

Several years ago 53 churches, organized in 3 districts, had an estimated 5,000 adult members. The church was concentrated in the southern and eastern parts of the island and in the metropolitan area around the capital.[53] Recent efforts to contact the group have been unsuccessful.

Hawaii Conference of the United Church of Christ

The first Hawaiian known to have received Christian Baptism was Henry Opukahaia (d. 1818), whom a New Haven, Connecticut, sailing captain had brought back to North America and whom he had introduced to Samuel Mills. Mills was the leader of the Williams College students whose haystack prayer meeting had sparked the foreign mission movement in the United

States. Opukahaia's death of typhus fever frustrated Mills's plan to return his convert to Hawaii as a Christian leader and missionary to his own people. *The Memoirs of Henry Obookiah,* the first book by a Hawaiian author, served to arouse the interest of thousands of readers and inspired the first penetration of Hawaii by Christian missionaries in 1819, among them the extraordinarily energetic and effective Hiram Bingham. Other missionaries followed. Within thirty years the Hawaiian Christian community was evangelizing other Pacific islands.

When the War between the States reduced both the personnel and the financial resources of the American Board, it cut off its support to the mission in Hawaii. Ultimately the churches of Hawaii developed a strong indigenous and interracial organization, the Hawaiian Evangelical Association of Congregational Christian Churches. In 1963 it voted to become the Hawaii Conference of the United Church of Christ, but at the same time stipulated that Congregational churches which had voted not to join the United Church of Christ or had abstained from voting could still be members of the local associations and of the Hawaii Conference. Four of these Congregational churches affiliated with the National Association of Congregational Christian Churches without severing their connection with the local associations of the Hawaii Conference.[54] Others have become independent.

The headquarters of the Hawaii Conference are at 2103 Nuuanu Avenue, Honolulu Hawaii 96817. The local associations include 112 congregations and missions with a total membership of 18,051. Of these churches and missions, 32, including the four member-congregations of the National Association of Congregational Christian Churches, with a total membership estimated at 1,440, have declined to join the United Church of Christ.[55]

Korean Christian Missions of Hawaii

In 1918 Presbyterian emigrants from Korea found themselves unable to organize a Presbyterian judicatory in Hawaii because of a comity agreement then in force between the Presbyterian Church in the United States of America (now part of the United Presbyterian Church in the United States of America) and the General Council of Congregational Churches (now part of the United Church of Christ). This comity agreement had assigned Alaska to the Presbyterians and Hawaii to the Congregationalists. Accordingly the Korean Presbyterian churches in Hawaii dropped the designation Presbyterian and called themselves simply Korean Christian churches. In spite of their original purpose to remain Presbyterians they assimilated themselves over the next half century to their Congregational environment in polity and confession. Currently they stand in a friendly relation to both the Presbyterian community and the United Church of Christ in Hawaii without being affiliated with either group. Their doctrinal basis is trinitarian; they baptize by sprinkling candidates in the name of the Father and of the Son and of the Holy Spirit; and they accept the Apostles' Creed as their only binding confession. The three churches in the state have a total active membership of about 500. The conference of the Korean Christian Missions of Hawaii meets normally at annual intervals. The Honolulu church is located at 1832 Liliha Street, Honolulu, Hawaii 96817.

Overseas Union Churches

In some island territories of the United States—as in many other areas of the world—the presence of a considerable number of English-speaking Christians of different denominations has resulted in the organization of "union churches." These congregations attempt to serve the spiritual needs of as many of their constitutents as possible without overtly identifying themselves with one particular denomination. Since many of the worshipers are in the area only temporarily and prefer not to transfer their membership to the overseas church, the actual membership is almost always smaller than the number of worshipers would imply in the United States. In general, the preponderant part of both the constituencies and the ministries[56] of these "union churches" comes from the Methodist, Presbyterian, and United Church of Christ communities, although the entire gamut of denominations, "all the way from Quakers to Unitarians or from Southern Baptists to Greek Orthodox,"[57] may be represented in the membership. Both the worship and the statements of faith (where the churches have formulated them) reflect an "ecumenical" orientation. The Overseas Union Churches Committee of the Churchmen Overseas Program, a specialized ministries department of the Division of Overseas Ministries of the National Council of the Churches of Christ in the United States of America, has maintained contact with more than one hundred English-speaking interdenominational churches throughout the world, providing them with advice on administration, nominating pastors to fill vacancies, serving as a channel for religious literature, and in a few instances furnishing minimal financial subsidy.[58] The Churchmen Overseas Program also publishes *A Guide to English Language Congregations in Selected Cities Overseas* that lists not only "union churches," but also English-speaking Episcopal/Anglican, Church of Scotland, Lutheran, Methodist, and Baptist congregations in 117 overseas communities.

The Union Church of the Canal Zone

One of the most successful "union churches" qualifies as a church body in its own right, the Union Church of the Canal Zone. From 1905 on the United States government through the Isthmian Canal Commission provided a chaplaincy service during the period that the Panama Canal was under construction. Christian Leagues came into being among the chaplains' constituencies in each location to provide a voice for the worshiping congregations. With the termination of the chaplaincy in prospect, representatives of the Christian Leagues of eight sites that promised to be relatively permanent organized the Union Church of the Canal Zone in January 1914. The constitution declared: "The object of this organization shall be the advancement of the principles of Christ's Kingdom [in] the Canal Zone, in the carrying on of the various religious activities characteristic of the communities from which our membership shall have come. Its activities shall be nonsectarian and its teaching evangelical."[59] The first sentence was later changed to read: "The object of the church shall be to furnish a basis for the union of Protestant believers, in order to carry on effectively and economically such religious activities as will best promote the interest of Christ's Kingdom."[60] The current form of this article of the constitution is: "The purpose is to maintain and promote cooperation among the constituent churches united in this congregation; to express among His people the spirit of unity for which Christ prayed; to invite and encourage others to make Christian profession; to engage its members in worship both public and private, in Christian education, and in brotherly service; to maintain relations with other bodies of Christians both near and far; and to promote such other activities as shall advance the interests of the Kingdom of God in the community and in the world."[61]

The covenant which members make in affiliating with the church expresses thanks for "God's great gift of salvation through Jesus Christ our Lord" and commits them to accepting "Jesus Christ and His teaching as [the] supreme standard of faith and the Bible as containing God's progressive revelation of Himself to man" and to hearty belief "in the province of private judgment in the interpretation of the Scriptures."[62]

Each pastor is obligated "to make the diversified Christian heritage found among the evangelical churches the common property of the Union Churches." At baptisms, weddings, funerals, Communion services, reception of members, installation of officers, and other ceremonies he may use any order of service of any denomination affiliated with the National Council of the Churches of Christ in the United States of America. He may make selections from these orders or alter them, provided that the result is acceptable to the respective local church council, and to the persons concerned.[63]

In 1921 the Union Church of the Canal Zone became related to the Federal Council of the Churches of Christ in America; the latter and its successor agency, the National Council of the Churches of Christ in the United States of America, have served as trustee for funds contributed to the Union Church's building program by official agencies of the Council of Congregational-Christian Churches, the Methodist Episcopal Church, the Methodist Episcopal Church, South, and the Presbyterian Church of the United States of America.[64]

In the course of its history the Union Church of the Canal Zone has had churches in 11 locations; the maximum at one time was 7. Currently it has

4 churches, all self-supporting, with a reported membership of 1,000.[65] It conducts no missionary enterprises of its own, but channels missionary gifts of its membership to a variety of objectives.

The Union Churches of San Juan, Puerto Rico

The English-speaking Presbyterian and Methodist churches in San Juan, Puerto Rico, merged to form one interdenominational autonomous congregation in 1917. Later it moved from its downtown location to the Santurce district. A second Union Church was begun in the Río Piedras section of the city in 1965.

The churches belong to the Evangelical Council of Puerto Rico and are related to the Churchmen Overseas program of the National Council of the Churches of Christ in the United States of America.

At their reception new members "reaffirm those vows which were taken at the time of [their] baptism and in this light solemnly declare [their] intention to be a disciple of Jesus Christ and to endeavor to do the will of God as revealed through him" and to support and uphold the church "so that in all things and in all ways the Kingdom of God may be a reality."[66]

The churches declare their "faith in Jesus Christ as Lord and Saviour" and recognize and accept Him "as the Author and Source of all authority for the government of His Church."[67]

The two churches have a combined membership of approximately 800.[68]

Other Puerto Rican "Union Churches"

The Union Church of Mayaguez came into being as the English-speaking congregation of the Iglesia Central Presbiteriana in 1952 and subsequently became an interdenominational self-supporting independent church. "It follows the forms and beliefs of an average Methodist or Presbyterian church at home."[69] Its constitution states as the object of the church: "To endeavor to unite all those who believe in Jesus Christ as the Son of God and the Savior of the world . . . especially affiliating itself with the efforts of the Puerto Rican evangelical churches." Like the Union Churches of San Juan it "accepts Jesus Christ as the Author and Source of all authority for the government of His Church."[70] The normal attendance at the Sunday service is about 50.

The United Church of Ponce grew out of the suggestion of a factory owner in 1952 that English services be conducted for the increasing number of North Americans coming to that community. The congregation organized as an autonomous interdenominational church in 1954. It is affiliated with the Churchmen Overseas program of the National Council of the Churches of Christ in the United States of America and is in fellowship with the Evangelical Council of Puerto Rico. Its covenant affirms belief in God the heavenly

Father; in Jesus Christ, "the Son of God, our Divine Lord and personal Savior, whose life and death and resurrection redeem and inspire all who accept Him"; in the Holy Spirit; in the Bible; in the Kingdom of God "as the divine rule in human society"; "in prayer, in the sacraments (or ordinances) of baptism and holy communion, in the church as Christ's body of believers, and in the life everlasting."[71] Its membership is approximately 150 (of whom 100 are resident members).[72]

Consultation on Church Union (COCU)

In December 1960, on the Sunday before the opening of the Tenth Anniversary Biennial Assembly of the National Council of the Churches of Christ in the United States of America, the stated clerk of the United Presbyterian Church in the United States of America, Eugene Carson Blake, delivered a sermon on church union in Grace Protestant Episcopal Cathedral, San Francisco. In it he proposed the union of the United Church of Christ, the United Presbyterian Church in the United States of America, the Protestant Episcopal Church in the United States of America, and The Methodist Church, as well as any other denominations that might wish to associate themselves with those named, into a church body that would be "truly catholic and truly reformed."[73] Out of this proposal grew the Consultation on Church Union, which by 1968 had enlisted the active participation of the African Methodist Episcopal Church, the African Methodist Episcopal Zion Church, the Christian Church (Disciples of Christ), the Christian Methodist Episcopal Church, the Protestant Episcopal Church in the United States of America, the Presbyterian Church in the United States, the United Church of Christ, the United Methodist Church, and the United Presbyterian Church in the United States of America.

On the basis of the consensus reached at a series of annual meetings held at Washington, D.C. (1962), Oberlin, Ohio (1963), Princeton, New Jersey (1964), Lexington, Kentucky (1965), Dallas, Texas (1966), Cambridge, Massachusetts (1967), and Dayton, Ohio (1968), the consultation directed the formulation by 1969 (at the meeting in Atlanta, Georgia), or by 1970 at the latest, of a specific plan of union. In addition to the official negotiations through the consultation, a process of exploration and growing toward union began among various boards, agencies, and congregations of the participating denominations.

In the consultation's Principles of Church Union the members of the consultation affirm their "faith in the one God, Father, Son, and Holy Spirit, who has given us our unity in the one, holy, catholic, and apostolic Church." They voice the resolution of the participants in the consultation to attempt a more inclusive expression of the oneness and of the fullness of the church of Christ than any of the participating churches can suppose itself alone to be. They call for obedience to mission at every level of the church; stress the desirability of mutual enrichment by "the maximum interplay of tradition across traditional lines"; require maintenance and strengthening of existing relationships wherever possible; demand maximum protection of existing diversities and liberties; insist upon maximum openness to continuing renewal and reformation; and emphasize that the church body that finally results must be a uniting as well as a united church.

All members of the uniting bodies will be the initial members of the united church. "This recognition presupposes man's response to God's gracious call, baptism with water in the threefold name of God, and the vows of faith in God as Father, allegiance to Jesus Christ as Lord and Savior, and commitment to the community of God's people in which the Holy Spirit dwells."[74]

The consultation affirms the unique authority and inspiration of the Bible and its role as a witness to God's revelation and of man's response to that revelation. It recognizes the existence of a "historic Christian tradition," and in its duties as guardian of the truth of the Gospel it affirms its intention to use the Apostles' Creed and the Nicene Creed as cardinal embodiments of this tradition.[75] It agrees to the continued use by units of the united church of their corporate covenants and confessions, but will not "permit the use of any single confession as an exclusive requirement for all or as a basis for division within the new community."[76] It undertakes to confess its faith in worship through its liturgies and in exercising its apostolic mission of reconciliation to individuals and to the power-structures of the world.

Normative principles for the worship of the united church will be the sacraments of baptism and the Lord's Supper, reading from the Scriptures, the preaching of the Word of God, public prayer, and congregational participation. Initially the liturgical calendar of any of the uniting churches may be used, although no congregation will be compelled to use any calendar against its will.

Both infant baptism and believer's baptism will be accepted in the united church. The mode may be immersion, pouring, or sprinkling. In any case baptism is to be administered in the name of the Father, the Son, and the Holy Spirit. Christians are to be baptized only once.

The Lord's Supper is seen as an effective sign, whereby God in Christ acts and Christ is present with his people. He is the minister and the high priest of the Eucharist, gives himself to the communicants, and makes effective for his faithful people all that has been accomplished in his incarnation, atoning death, resurrection, and exaltation. The Lord's supper is to be celebrated with the two elements that Christ ordained, with his words of institution, with the visible acts of taking the bread and the cup, with the giving of thanks or blessing over the elements, with a prayer of invocation of the Holy Spirit, and with the reception of the elements by the congregation. Only a bishop or presbyter (ordained elder) may celebrate the Lord's

Supper; all baptized Christians who are eligible to receive Holy Communion in their own churches may receive it in the united church.

Ordination will include the laying on of hands of all offices of ministry in the church, including the general ministry of those unordained. Without setting forth exclusively any single doctrine or theory of the being or authority of bishops, the historic episcopate, constitutionally defined, will be a part of the united church. Bishops will have pastoral oversight, liturgical leadership, and administrative responsibility. Presbyters or elders will also be a part of the united church, without committing the church to any one theory or doctrine about them. The united church also accepts the office of deacon as a distinctive vocation.

The structures of the united church are to be functionally determined and flexible. They are to provide for many different forms of ministry to the world; for the making of policy decisions by democratically chosen representatives; for inclusive representation of all the members of the church; for the total ministry of the church to both its members and the world; for corporate witness and ministry in the communities in which men function, as well as for individual Christian witness and ministry; for the exercise of freedom and order under Christ; for participation in ecumenical action; and for the mutual support of the various parts of the church by one another in witness and service.

COCU envisions six stages or periods of some duration, linked with five steps, as the united church comes into being. Stage 1 was the long ecumenical experience that led to COCU; Step 1 was the establishment of COCU in 1962. Stage 2 is the experience leading to approval of the principles of church union; Step 2 is the approval of the principles, beginning with the Dallas meeting of 1966. Stage 3 is the preparation for a Plan of Union and church renewal; Step 3, initiated with the acceptance of the Plan of Union at the St. Louis meeting in 1970, is the adoption of the plan by the uniting churches. The Plan of Union calls for the creation at the local level of "parishes," normally consisting of several congregations. To ensure racial and economic wholeness these congregations will not necessarily be contiguous. As soon as all of the uniting bodies have had an opportunity to act on the Plan of Union, the united church will be ready to come into being, even if only two of the denominations involved have approved the plan. A central service will inaugurate the united church, to be called the Church of Christ Uniting. Since the uniting churches recognize that the ministers of all the participating churches have been previously ordained, this service will not be regarded as an act of ordination, reordination, or conditional ordination. Stage 4 as envisioned will be preparation for the unification of membership, ministries, and sacraments; Step 4 will be this unification itself and the establishment of a provisional council. Stage 5, which will come after the formation of the united church, will be preparation of a constitution; Step 5 the actual writing and adoption of the constitution. Stage 6 will then begin, and denominations that will not before then have joined COCU will be invited to lose "their separate identities in this wider, visible unity."[77]

The Plan of Union approved by the 1970 plenary of COCU was submitted to the nine participating churches for study and proposed revisions. At its November 1971 meeting the COCU plenary discussed first reactions to the plan. Criticisms concentrated on the structural expression of unity; the statements on the faith, worship, sacraments, and ministry met with general approval.

COCU's efforts at union received a serious setback when, on May 19, 1972, the General Assembly of the United Presbyterian Church in the United States of America, the church body instrumental in establishing COCU, voted to withdraw from further participation in the consultation. When other participating churches renewed their commitment to COCU, the United Presbyterian Church in the United States of America on May 21, 1973, reversed its decision and voted to return to full participation in the consultation.

In April 1973 the eleventh COCU plenary dealt with the churches' responses to the Plan of Union, adopting a statement, "The Way Ahead," which concluded: "The responses show a general agreement among the churches on matters of faith, worship, and the basic nature of the church's ministry, but a general unreadiness to accept the organizational structures proposed for a united church." The plenary decided on a new course: "Viable proposals for organization and structures of the Church of Christ Uniting need to be developed out of the experiences of living and working together. The Consultation, therefore, sees the next stages of its work as actively involving the churches in working together at the various levels of their life. Growing out of this experience, a full plan of union can be developed for a united church—catholic, evangelical, and reformed."[78] The 1973 plenary authorized several commissions to foster the process of living together toward union and initiated a revision of the theological sections of the Plan of Union on which there has been extensive agreement.

The twelfth plenary COCU in November 1974 reviewed the work of the various commissions established by the previous plenary. The commission charged with revising the theological basis proposed that member churches affirm the members of participating churches as being within the body of Christ, based upon recognition of their baptisms. The Worship Commission produced an ecumenical service of baptism and began work on materials for the celebration of the Lord's Supper. Another commission reported on its efforts to bring member churches in a geographical area together for worship and mission. The Commission on Institutional Racism reported on its first steps to overcome racism within the member churches.

In November 1976 the thirteenth plenary of COCU considered the progress of the efforts to assist the participating churches in "living together toward union." The revised theological basis was commended to the member churches for study and response and for guidance in furthering the mutual recognition of members and working toward mutual recognition of ministers. Among the units presently at work are commissions on Generating Communities, on Interim Eucharistic Fellowship, on Worship, on Institutional Rascism, on Task Force of Women, on Middle Judicatories.[79]

In looking to the future Gerald F. Moede, general secretary of COCU since 1974, warns against letting "process serve as an excuse to retreat from hard decisions of union into projects requiring no real risk or commitment." He calls attention to the need for public commitment to grow out of each new agreement and points to the revised theological basis as the foundation on which member churches can "further common life together."[80]

NOTES

1. *Christian Century*, June 25, 1925, p. 819.
2. For an analysis of the significance of the union in relation to both the ecclesiastical and the national history of Canada, see N. K. Clifford, "The Interpreters of the United Church of Canada," *Church History*, vol. 46, no. 2 (June, 1977), pp. 203-214.
3. For the details, see Ruth Rouse and Stephen Charles Neill, eds., *A History of the Ecumenical Movement, 1517–1948* (2nd edn.; Philadelphia: Westminster Press, 1967), pp. 300f., 304f., 454f.
4. Quoted in a brief history of the formation of the United Church of Canada presented in *The Basis of Union* (Toronto: The United Church of Canada, n.d.), p. 37.
5. *The Basis of Union*, op. cit., p. 3.
6. Ibid., p. 5.
7. Ibid., p. 4.
8. Ibid., p. 5.
9. Ibid., p. 6.
10. Ibid., p. 8.
11. Ibid., p. 23.
12. The Principles of Union were published in a printed document as part of a report which the Committee on Christian Unity and the Church Universal of the Anglican Church of Canada and the Committee on Union of the United Church of Canada issued in 1965.
13. For a description of the end to the twenty-five years of negotiations, see "Anglicans Stall Church Union in Canada," *Mid-Stream*, January 1976, pp. 116-118; and John Webster Grant, "A Moratorium on Canadian Union

Talks." *Mid-Stream*, July 1976, p. 256-262.
14. The text is from John 17:21; the emblem is presented and described in the pamphlet *United Church of Christ, History and Program* (New York: Division of Publication, United Church Board for Homeland Ministries, n.d.).
15. Douglas Horton devotes a chapter to the choice of the name in *The United Church of Christ: Its Origins, Organization, and Role in the World Today* (New York: Thomas Nelson & Sons, 1962), pp. 108-111.
16. See the preceding section.
17. Lowell H. Zuck describes the cultural conditioning in *European Roots of the United Church of Christ* (Philadelphia: United Church Press, 1967), a 19-page pamphlet in the 10-pamphlet The Heritage Series, ed. J. Earl Thompson, Jr., and Edward A. Powers.
18. See the presentation on Puritanism in chap. 10, above.
19. *United Church of Christ, History and Program*, p. 8-9.
20. See Arthur A. Rouner, Jr., *The Congregational Way of Life* (Englewood Cliffs, N.J.: Prentice-Hall, 1960).
21. The establishment privilege was terminated as late as 1818 in Connecticut and 1834 in Massachusetts.
22. A specific facet of Congregational political influence in described in J. Earl Thompson, Jr., *Congregational Dissent against the War of 1812* (Philadelphia: United Church Press, 1976), a 14-page pamphlet in The Heritage Series.
23. The development is described in Samuel C. Pearson, Jr., "From Church to

Denomination: American Congregationalism in the Nineteenth Century," *Church History* 38 (March, 1969): 67-87.

24. *United Church of Christ, History and Program*, p. 13.

25. The Christian, or Restorationist, movement and the continuing denominations which resulted from it is described in chap. 18, above.

26. The history of the church is described in Durward T. Stokes and William T. Scott, *A History of the Christian Church in the South* (Elon College, N.C.: Elon College, 1973).

27. Ibid., p. 261.

28. The conjunction was later eliminated from the name.

29. The immigration and its aftermath is described in William T. Parsons, *German Reformed Experience in Colonial America* (Philadelphia: United Church Press, 1976), a 19-page pamphlet in The Heritage Series.

30. The position is quoted in the 31-page pamphlet *Historical Sketches of The Congregational Christian Churches and The Evangelical and Reformed Church* (published jointly by the Executive Committee of the General Council of the Congregational Christian Churches and the General Council of the Evangelical and Reformed Church, 1955), p. 22.

31. The minority congregations that did not go along with the merger formed several new organizations to continue the Congregationalist tradition; those organizations are described in chap. 11, above.

32. *The Constitution and Bylaws, United Church of Christ*, 1976 edn., published by the Executive Council for the United Church of Christ, p. 2.

33. The Statement of Faith is printed in *The Hymnal of the United Church of Christ* (Philadelphia: United Church Press, 1974), p. 11; it is published also in John H. Leith, ed., *Creeds of the Churches* (Richmond, Va.: John Knox Press, 1973), pp. 590-591.

34. The Basis of Union is published as Appendix D in Stokes and Scott; the quotation is on p. 336.

35. Horton, pp. 64-65.

36. *The Hymnal of the United Church of Christ*, p. 8.

37. Ibid., p. 6.

38. Ibid., p. 8.

39. Ibid.

40. Ibid., pp. 6-7.

41. Ibid., pp. 29-31.

42. Horton, pp. 89-90.

43. Ibid., pp. 91-92.

44. *The Hymnal of the United Church of Christ*, p. 21.

45. Ibid., p. 22.

46. The article in the St. Louis *Post-Dispatch*, July 8, 1977, p. 7D, reporting the election of a new moderator of the United Church of Christ, began: "The Rev. Dr. Avery Post of Boston, who was elected president of the United Church of Christ this week, is an outspoken advocate of liberal Protestantism." The July 4, 1977 New York *Times*, described Post as "one of the country's most outspoken voices of liberal Protestantism."

47. Compiled from reports in the New York *Times*, July 5 and 6, 1977.

48. Gerald J. Jud, "Identity and Promise," *Reform and Renewal: Exploring the United Church of Christ* (Philadelphia: United Church Press, 1966), p. 115.

49. From "Article IV. Local Churches," *The Constitution and Bylaws*, 1976 edn., pp. 3-4.

50. Douglas Horton, "Truth in Tension," *Reform and Renewal*, p. 19.

51. Gerald J. Jud, p. 109.

52. On the background of this union, see Donald T. Moore, *Puerto Rico para Cristo: A History of the Progress of the Evangelical Missions on the Island of Puerto Rico* (Cuernavaca, Mexico: Centro Intercultural de Documenacion, 1969), pp. 4/3-4/7. The Disciples of Christ in Puerto Rico (Discípulos de Cristo en Puerto Rico) voted unanimously to join La Iglesia Evangélica Unida de Puerto Rico and the latter's General Assembly of 1934 accepted them, but the participation of the Disciples in the merger never took place.

53. Letter from the Reverend Gilberto Robles, executive secretary, La Iglesia Evangélica Unida de Puerto Rico.

54. John F. Mulholland, *Hawaii's Religions* (Rutland, Vt.: Charles E. Tuttle Company, 1970), pp. 45-88; letters from the Reverend Mr. Mulholland.

55. Letter from the Reverend Chester G. Terpstra, Honolulu, Hawaii.

56. Of the 61 ordained clergymen listed by

Robert H. Rolofson, *Christian Co-operation at the World's Crossroads* (Balboa, Canal Zone: The Union Church of the Canal Zone, 1950), pp. 322-325, as having ministered in the Union Church of the Canal Zone from 1914 to 1950, 22 were Methodist, 11 Presbyterian, 9 Congregational-Christian or Congregational [United Church of Christ], 7 Northern [American] Baptist, 6 Southern Baptist, 2 United Lutheran Church [Lutheran Church in America], and one each Dutch Reformed [Reformed Church in America], Evangelical United Brethren [United Methodist], Salvation Army, and Church of the Foursquare Gospel. This is still a representative distribution.

57. Letter from the Reverend James E. Shapland, The Union Church of San Juan, Puerto Rico.

58. For an appraisal of the "union churches" of the Caribbean area, see Martin H. Marty, "Eye Opener on Latin America" *Christian Century* 84 (1967): 261-263.

59. Quoted in Robert H. Rolofson, *Christian Cooperation at the World's Crossroads* (Balboa: The Union Church of the Canal Zone, 1950), pp. 73.

60. Ibid., p. 91.

61. *The Constitution, the By-Laws, and Other Basic Documents of the Union Church of the Canal Zone* (Balboa: The Union Church of the Zone, 1964), p. 5.

62. Ibid., p. 14. The service for the installation of a pastor declares that the Union Church recognizes the Bible "to be the inspired Word of God and the final authority for all Christian preaching" (ibid., p. 33). The pastor also promises "to exalt the doctrines of the fatherhood of God, the Saviorhood of Christ, the brotherhood of man, and the spiritual fellowship of all God's people" (p. 34).

63. Ibid., p. 18.

64. "Memorandum of Trust Agreement (November 28, 1921)," ibid., pp. 51-61.

65. Letters of the Reverend John A. Toth, minister, Gatun Union Church; the Reverend Daniel B. Merrick, pastor, Margarita Union Church; the Reverend Byron E. Reihart, pastor, Gamboa Union Church; the Reverend

Clarence C. Payne, pastor, The Balboa Union Church.

66. Sunday bulletin, The Union Church of San Juan (Interdenominational), May 21, 1967, p. 3.

67. "Permanent Principles and Rules," The Second Union Church of San Juan, undated 2-page mimeographed document.

68. Letters from the Reverend James E. Shapland, minister. The Union Church of San Juan, and the Reverend Roger O. Colvin, minister, Second Union Church, San Juan.

69. Letter from the Reverend Palmer W. Manson, minister, The Union Church of Mayaguez.

70. "The Constitution and By-Laws of the Union Church of Mayaguez," undated 3-page mimeographed document.

71. "Constitution of the United Church, Ponce, Puerto Rico," undated 1-page mimeographed document.

72. Letters from the Reverend Harry E. Zech, D.D., pastor, The United Church, Ponce.

73. Subsequently the formula was expanded to "truly evangelical, truly catholic, and truly reformed." The sermon, as well as the statement of the then Protestant Episcopal Bishop of California, James A. Pike, is reprinted in the *Christian Century* 77 (1960): 1508-1511.

74. *Consultation on Church Union 1967: Principles of Church Union, Guidelines for Structure, and a Study Guide* (Cincinnati, Ohio: The Forward Movement, 1967), p. 27.

75. The Dayton meeting of 1968 resolved that "the creeds are for the guidance of the members and are to be used persuasively and not coercively" (Religious News Service dispatch quoted in the *Lutheran Witness Reporter* for April 7, 1968).

76. *Consultation on Church Union 1967*, p. 32.

77. Ibid., p. 88.

78. Cf. 'Survey of Church Union Negotiations 1971–73," the *Ecumenical Review* 26 (1974): 323.

79. The reports of the commissions to the thirteenth COCU plenary, together with addresses presented there, are published in *Mid-Stream*, vol. XVI, no. 1 (January 1977).

80. Ibid., p. 115.

BIBLIOGRAPHY

THE UNITED CHURCH OF CANADA

The Basis of Union. Toronto: The United Church of Canada, n.d. The statement of doctrine and polity on which the United Church of Canada was founded, together with a brief history of the events prior to 1925 which led to the union.

Chown, S. D. *The Story of Church Union in Canada.* Toronto: Ryerson Press, 1930. The story as told by a major participant.

Clifford, N. K. "The Interpreters of the United Church of Canada." *Church History,* vol. 46, no. 2 (June 1977), pp. 203-214. An analysis of the variety of interpretations as to the reasons for the 1925 union.

Cragg, Gerald R. "The European Wellsprings of Canadian Christianity." *Theological Bulletin of McMaster Divinity College,* January 1968, pp. 4-14.

Elgee, William Harris. *The Social Teachings of the Canadian Churches—Protestant: The Early Period, Before 1850.* Toronto: Ryerson Press, 1964. This expanded doctoral dissertation describes, on the basis of careful research, the patterns that became fixed in the formative period of the older Canadian Christian traditions on such issues as church and state, education, social relations, tolerance, temperance, welfare, and religious expression.

French, Goldwin S. "The Impact of Christianity on Canadian Culture and Society to 1867." *Theological Bulletin of McMaster Divinity College,* January, 1968, pp. 16-38.

Grant, John W. *The Canadian Experience of Church Union.* Richmond, Va.: John Knox Press, 1967. A major interpretation of the union effort in terms of consensus.

———. *The Church in the Canadian Era.* Toronto: McGraw-Hill Ryerson Ltd., 1972. The story of the United Church is told within the context of the national development of all the churches in Canada.

———. "The Impact of Christianity on Canadian Culture and Society, 1867 to the Present." *Theological Bulletin of McMaster Divinity College,* January, 1968, pp. 40-50.

Mann, W. E. "The Canadian Church Union 1925." In *Institutionalism and Church Unity,* ed. Nils Ehrenstrom and Walter S. Muelder. New York: Association Press, 1963. A study of the nontheological factors in the church union movement in Canada.

Moir, John S. "American Influences on Canadian Protestant Churches before Confederation." *Church History* 36 (1967): 440-455.

———. *Enduring Witness: A History of the Presbyterian Church in Canada.* Toronto: Presbyterian Publications, 1975. Provides new insights into reasons why some Presbyterians refused to enter the 1925 union.

Pidgeon, George C. *The United Church of Canada: The Story of the Union.* Toronto: Ryerson Press, 1950. The first moderator of the United Church of Canada describes the steps that led to the 1925 merger with the perspective that twenty-five years provide.

Silcox, Claris Edwin. *Church Union in Canada: Its Causes and Consequences.* New York: Institute of Social and Religious Research, 1933. A presentation of the formation of the United Church in Canada which traces its interconnection with Canadian history and consciousness.

UNITED CHURCH OF CHRIST

Arndt, Elmer J. F. *The Faith We Proclaim: The Doctrinal Viewpoint Generally Prevailing in the Evangelical and Reformed Church.* Philadelphia: The Christian Education Press, 1960.

Atkins, Gaius Glenn. *An Adventure in Liberty.* Boston: Pilgrim Press, 1961. A brief history of the Congregational Christian Churches.

"The Church in Our World: A Study of

the Nature and Mission of the United Church of Christ." 156 manuscript pages. New York: Division of Publication, United Church Board for Homeland Ministries, 1965.

The Constitution and Bylaws, United Church of Christ, 1976 edn. Published by the Executive Council for the United Church of Christ.

Dunn, David, ed. *History of the Evangelical and Reformed Church.* Philadelphia: Christian Education Press, 1961.

Historical Sketches of The Congregational Christian Churches and The Evangelical and Reformed Church. Published jointly by the Executive Committee of the General Council of the Congregational Christian Church and the General Council of the Evangelical and Reformed Church, 1955.

Horstmann, Julius H, and Wernecke, Herbert H. *Through Four Centuries: The Story of the Beginnings of the Evangelical and Reformed Church, in the Old World and the New, from the Sixteenth to the Twentieth Century.* St. Louis: Eden Publishing House, 1938.

Horton, Douglas. *The United Church of Christ: Origins, Organization, and Role in the World Today.* New York: Thomas Nelson & Sons, 1962.

The Hymnal of the United Church of Christ. Philadelphia: United Church Press, 1974.

Jones, Lawrence Neale. *From Consciousness to Conscience: Blacks and the United Church of Christ.* Philadelphia: United Church Press, 1976.

Keiling, Hanns Peter, compiler. *The Formation of the United Church of Christ (USA): A Bibliography.* Pittsburgh: Pittsburgh Theological Seminary, 1970.

Long, Stuart. *Two Spirits Meet.* Philadelphia: United Church Press, 1976.

Lovejoy, David S. *Samuel Hopkins: Religion, Slavery, and the Revolution.* Philadelphia: United Church Press, 1976.

The Manual on the Ministry in the United Church of Christ, rev. 1968. New York: Council for Church and Ministry, United Church of Christ, 1968.

Parsons, William T. *German Reformed Experience in Colonial America.* Philadelphia: United Church Press, 1976.

Pearson, Samuel C., Jr. "From Church to Denomination: American Congregationalism in the Nineteenth Century." *Church History* 38 (March 1969): 67-87.

Reform and Renewal: Exploring the United Church of Christ. Philadelphia: United Church of Christ, 1966. Nine essays by six authors.

Rouner, Arthur A., Jr. *The Congregational Way of Life.* Englewood Cliffs, N.J.: Prentice-Hall, 1960.

Stokes, Durward T., and Scott, William T. *A History of the Christian Church in the South.* Elon College, N.C.: Elon College, 1973.

Thompson, J. Earl, Jr. *Congregational Dissent against the War of 1812.* Philadelphia: United Church Press, 1976.

United Church of Christ, History and Program. New York: Division of Publication, United Church Board for Homeland Ministries, n.d.

Walker, Williston. *The Creeds and Platform of Congregationalism.* Boston: Pilgrim Press, 1960.

Wilson, John F. *Puritanism and the Public Realm.* Philadelphia: United Church Press, 1967.

Withers, Barbara A. *Women of Faith and Our History.* Philadelphia: United Church Press, 1976.

Zuck, Lowell H. *European Roots of the United Church of Christ.* Philadelphia: United Church Press, 1967.

CONSULTATION ON CHURCH UNION

An Order of Worship for the Proclamation of the Word of God and the Celebration of the Lord's Supper. Cincinnati, Ohio: Forward Movement Publications, 1968.

Brown, Robert McAfee, and Scott, David H., eds. *The Challenge to Reunion.* New York: McGraw-Hill Book Company, 1963.

"Cambridge Teach-In on COCU." *The*

Ecumenist: A Journal for Promoting Christian Unity 6 (1967–1968): 113-125. A defense of COCU by James McCord, with reactions by Harvey Cox, Charles Spivey, and Gregory Baum.

COCU: The Official Reports of the Four Meetings of the Consultation. Cincinnati, Ohio: Forward Movement Publications, 1966.

Consultation on Church Union 1967: Principles of Church Union, Guidelines for Strucutre, and a Study Guide. Cincinnati, Ohio: Forward Movement Publications, 1967.

Crow, Paul A., Jr. *A Bibliography of the Consultation on Church Union.* Lexington, Ky.: Consultation on Church Union, 1967.

————. "Ecumenism and the Consultation on Church Union," *Journal of Ecumenical Studies* 4 (1967): 58-602.

Crow, Paul A., Jr., and others. "COCU 1970: A Symposium." *Christian Century* 87 (1970): 231-243.

Day, Peter. *Tomorrow's Church: Catholic —Evangelical—Reformed.* New York: Seabury Press, 1969.

Digest of the Proceedings of the Consultation on Church Union. Princeton, N.J.: Consultation on Church Union, 1963–. Published annually.

Nelson, J. Robert. *Church Union in Focus.* Philadelphia: United Church Press, 1967.

Index

Gladden, Washington, 666
Glas, John, 636
Glen, James, 655
Gnesio-Lutherans, 16
Gnosticism and creation, 51
"God-is-dead" movement, 400
Golden Gate Baptist Theological Seminary, 410
Goodchild, Frank M., 423
Goodchild Confession (1921), 423, 424
Gospel centrality, 44
Gospel Advocate, 637
Gospel Broadcast, 638
Gospel Guardian, 638
"Gospel Missionism," 405
Gossner Evangelical Lutheran Church, 32–33
Gossner Mission Society, 33
Gottskalkson, Oddur, 21
"Grace Brethren," 484
Graham, Billy, 415, 420
Grammatical-historical method. *See* Biblical studies
Graves, J. R., 403
Gray, James M., 249
Great Awakening, 192, 200, 288, 289, 296, 401, 535. 665
"Great Disruption," 333
Great Ejection, 144
Grebel, Conrad, 361, 362
Green Book. *See Services for Trial Use*
Greetings of Peace, 128
Gregory, Brother, 344
Gregory of Nyssa, 538, 555
Greybill, Joseph, 497
Grice, Homer L., 403
Griswold, Alexander Victor, 201
Groeneveld, H. D. G., 660
Grosse Gemeinde, 383
Gruber, Eberhard Louis, 499
Grundtvig, Nicolai F. S., 112

Haas, William Clarence, 430
Habaner, 385
Haden, Clarence J. Jr., Bp., 222
Halbstadt Confession, 387
Haldane, James Alexander, 503, 506
Haldane, Robert, 503, 506
Hale, Joe, 559
Hall, William, 251, 556
Hamblen, John Henry, 615
Hamilton, Patrick, 272
Hamilton, William, 400
Hampton Court Conference (1604), 143
Hanson, R. D. C., 151
Hapsburg-Valais rivalry, 18

Hargrove, John, 655
Harkness, Georgia, 282
Harless, Adolf von, 28
Harmony of the Confessions of Faith of the Orthodox and Reformed Churches (1581), 141
Harms, Claus, 28; *Ninety-Five Theses*, 28
Hauge, Hans Nielsen, 111
Hauge's Norwegian Evangelical Lutheran Synod in America, 121
Hauge's Synod, 111
Hawaii Conference of the United Church of Christ, 674–675
Hawaiian Evangelical Association of Congregational Christian Churches, 675
Heard, Herbert James Monzani, 251
Hebert, A. G., 169
Heck, Barbara, 568
Heidelberg Catechism (1563), 23–24, 276, 277, 308, 328, 334, 335, 337, 338, 339, 341, 342, 668
Heideman, Arthur Leopold, 127, 128
Heinemann, Barbara. *See* Landmann, Barbara Heinemann
Helwys, Thomas, 367, 432
Henderlite, Rachel, 317
Henderson, Ebenezer, 503
Hengstenberg, Ernst Wilhelm, 28
Henry II, 271
Henry IV, 272
Henry VII, 135–136
Henry VIII, 136, 137, 139, 271
Henry, Carl F. H., 400
Henry of Lausanne, 441
Hermanos Unidos en Cristo. *See* Church of the United Brethren in Christ
Hermeneutics. *See* Biblical studies
Herr, Francis, 375, 376
Hess, John, 375, 376, 377
"Herrites," 377
Heyer, Johann Christian Friedrich, 122
Heyer, J. F. C., 32
High Church. *See* Anglo-Catholics
Hilary of Poitiers, Saint, 80
Hilsheimer, George von, 487
Hindmarsh, Robert, 655
Hinduism, 32
Hines, John E., Bp., 212, 222
Hippo, Synod of (397), 97
"Historic Articles of Faith of the Evangelical Mennonite Church of North America, 1954," 384
Historical Magazine of the Protestant Episcopal Church, 214
Hobart, John Henry, 201
Hobbs, Herschel, H., 414
Hock, Daniel, 375, 378